Collins

Collins Italian Dictionary

HarperCollins Publishers
Westerhill Road
Bishopbriggs
Glasgow
G64 2QT
Great Britain

Second Edition 2007

Previously published as Collins Pocket Italian Dictionary

Reprint 10 9 8 7 6 5 4 3 2 1 0

ISBN-13 978-0-00-725345-6
ISBN-10 0-00-725345-1

www.collins.co.uk

A catalogue record for this book is available from the British Library

HarperCollins Publishers, 10 East 53rd Street, New York, NY 10022

COLLINS POCKET ITALIAN DICTIONARY.
Third US Edition 2007

ISBN-13 978-0-06-114187-4
ISBN-10 0-06-114187-9

Library of Congress Cataloging-in-Publication Data has been applied for

www.harpercollins.com

HarperCollins books may be purchased for educational, business, or sales promotional use. For information, please write to: Special Markets Department, HarperCollins Publishers, 10 East 53rd Street, New York, NY 10022

Dictionary text typeset by Thomas Callan

Supplement text typeset by Davidson's Prepress, Glasgow

Printed in Italy by Rotolito Lombarda S.p.A.

Acknowledgements
We would like to thank those authors and publishers who kindly gave permission for copyright material to be used in the Collins Word Web. We would also like to thank Times Newspapers Ltd for providing valuable data.

GENERAL EDITOR
Maree Airlie

CONTRIBUTORS
Gabriella Bacchelli
Daphne Day

EDITORIAL COORDINATION
Susie Beattie

SERIES EDITOR
Lorna Knight

This book is set in Collins Fedra, a typeface specially created for Collins Dictionaries by Peter Bil'ak

William Collins' dream of knowledge for all began with the publication of his first book in 1819. A self-educated mill worker, he not only enriched millions of lives, but also founded a flourising publishing house. Today, staying true to this spirit, Collins books are packed with inspiration, innovation, and practical expertise. They place you at the centre of a world of possibility and give you exactly what you need to explore it.

Language is the key to this exploration, and at the heart of Collins Dictionaries is language as it is really used. New words, phrases, and meanings spring up every day, and all of them are captured and analysed by the Collins Word Web. Constantly updated, and with over 2.5 billion entries, this living language resource is unique to our dictionaries.

Words are tools for life. And a Collins Dictionary makes them work for you.

Collins. Do more.

INDICE — CONTENTS

INTRODUZIONE

Vi ringraziamo di aver scelto questo dizionario inglese e ci auguriamo che esso si riveli uno strumento utile e piacevole da usare nello studio, in vacanza e sul lavoro.

In questa introduzione troverete alcuni suggerimenti per aiutarvi a trarre il massimo beneficio dal vostro nuovo dizionario, ricco non solo per il suo ampio lemmario ma anche per il gran numero di informazioni contenute in ciascuna voce.

All'inizio del dizionario troverete l'elenco delle abbreviazioni usate nel testo e una guida alla pronuncia. Troverete inoltre un utile elenco delle forme dei verbi irregolari inglesi e italiani, seguito da una sezione finale con i numeri, l'ora e la data.

Come usare il dizionario

Per imparare ad usare in modo efficace il dizionario è importante comprendere la funzione delle differenziazioni tipografiche, dei simboli e delle abbreviazioni usati nel testo. Vi forniamo pertanto qui di seguito alcuni chiarimenti in merito a tali convenzioni.

I lemmi

Sono le parole in **neretto** elencate in ordine alfabetico. Il primo e l'ultimo lemma di ciascuna pagina appaiono al margine superiore.

Dove opportuno, informazioni sull'ambito d'uso o il livello di formalità di certe parole vengono fornite tra parentesi in corsivo e spesso in forma abbreviata dopo l'indicazione della categoria grammaticale (es. (*Comm*), (*inf*)).

In certi casi più parole con radice comune sono raggruppate sotto lo stesso lemma. Tali parole appaiono in neretto ma in un carattere leggermente ridotto (es. **acceptance**).

Esempi d'uso del lemma sono a loro volta in neretto ma in un carattere diverso dal lemma (es. **to be cold**).

La trascrizione fonetica

La trascrizione fonetica che illustra la corretta pronuncia del lemma è tra parentesi quadre e segue immediatamente il lemma (es. **knee** [ni:]). L'elenco dei simboli fonetici è alle pagine xii-xiii.

Le traduzioni

Le traduzioni sono in carattere tondo e, quando il lemma ha più di un significato, le traduzioni sono separate da un punto e virgola. Spesso diverse traduzioni di un lemma sono introdotte da una o più parole in corsivo tra parentesi tonde: la loro funzione è di chiarire a quale significato del lemma si riferisce la traduzione. Possono essere sinonimi, indicazioni di ambito d'uso o di registro del lemma (es. **party** *(Pol)*, *(team)*, *(celebration)*; **laid back** *(inf)* ecc.).

Le 'parole chiave' O

Un trattamento particolare è stato riservato a quelle parole che, per frequenza d'uso o complessità, necessitano una strutturazione più chiara ed esauriente (es. **da, di, avere** in italiano, **at, to, be, this** in inglese). Frecce e numeri vi guidano attraverso le varie distinzioni grammaticali e di significato; ulteriori informazioni sono fornite in corsivo tra parentesi.

Informazioni grammaticali

Le parti del discorso (noun, adjective ecc.) sono espresse da abbreviazioni convenzionali in corsivo (*n*, *adj* ecc.) e seguono la trascrizione fonetica del lemma.

Eventuali ulteriori informazioni grammaticali, come ad esempio le forme di un verbo irregolare o il plurale irregolare di un sostantivo, precedono tra parentesi la parte del discorso (es. **give** (*pt* **gave**, *pp* **given**) *vt*; **man** [...] (*pl* **men**) *n*).

INTRODUCTION

We are delighted that you have decided to buy this Italian Dictionary and hope you will enjoy and benefit from using it at school, at home, on holiday or at work.

This introduction gives you a few tips on how to get the most out of your dictionary – not simply from its comprehensive wordlist but also from the information provided in each entry. This will help you to read and understand modern Italian, as well as communicate and express yourself in the language.

The dictionary begins by listing the abbreviations used in the text and illustrating the sounds shown by the phonetic symbols. You will also find Italian and English verb tables, followed by a section on numbers and time expressions.

Using your dictionary

A wealth of information is presented in the dictionary, using various typefaces, sizes of type, symbols, abbreviations and brackets. The various conventions and symbols used are explained in the following sections.

Headwords

The words you look up in a dictionary – "headwords" – are listed alphabetically. They are printed in **bold type** for rapid identification. The two headwords appearing at the top of each page indicate the first and last word dealt with on the page in question.

Information about the usage or form of certain headwords is given in brackets after the part of speech. This usually appears in abbreviated form and in italics (e.g. (*fam*), (*Comm*)).

Where appropriate, words related to headwords are grouped in the same entry (e.g. **illustrare, illustrazione**) in a slightly smaller bold type than the headword.

Common expressions in which the headword appears are shown in a different bold roman type (e.g. **aver freddo**).

Phonetic spellings

Where the phonetic spelling of headwords (indicating their pronunciation) is given, it will appear in square brackets immediately after the headword (e.g. calza ['kaltsa]). A list of these symbols is given on pages xii-xiii.

Translations

Headword translations are given in ordinary type and, where more than one meaning or usage exists, these are separated by a semi-colon. You will often find other words in italics in brackets before the translations. These offer suggested contexts in which the headword might appear (e.g. duro (*pietra*) or (*lavoro*)) or provide synonyms (e.g. duro (*ostinato*)).

"Key" words

Special status is given to certain Italian and English words which are considered as "key" words in each language. They may, for example, occur very frequently or have several types of usage (e.g. da, di, avere in Italian, at, to, be, this in English). A combination of arrows and numbers helps you to distinguish different parts of speech and different meanings. Further helpful information is provided in brackets and italics.

Grammatical information

Parts of speech are given in abbreviated form in italics after the phonetic spellings of headwords (e.g. *vt*, *av*, *cong*).

Genders of Italian nouns are indicated as follows: *sm* for a masculine and *sf* for a feminine noun. Feminine and irregular plural forms of nouns are also shown (e.g. uovo, (*pl(f)* **uova**); dottore, essa).

Feminine adjective endings are given, as are plural forms (e.g. opaco, a, chi, che).

ABBREVIAZIONI		ABBREVIATIONS
abbreviazione	*abbr*	abbreviation
aggettivo	*adj*	adjective
amministrazione	*Admin*	administration
avverbio	*adv*	adverb
aeronautica, viaggi aerei	*Aer*	flying, air travel
aggettivo	*ag*	adjective
agricoltura	*Agr*	agriculture
amministrazione	*Amm*	administration
anatomia	*Anat*	anatomy
architettura	*Archit*	architecture
articolo determinativo	*art def*	definite article
articolo indeterminativo	*art indef*	indefinite article
attributivo	*attrib*	attributive
ausiliare	*aus, aux*	auxiliary
automobile	*Aut*	motor car and motoring
avverbio	*av*	adverb
aeronautica, viaggi aerei	*Aviat*	flying, air travel
biologia	*Biol*	biology
botanica	*Bot*	botany
inglese britannico	*BRIT*	British English
consonante	*C*	consonant
chimica	*Chim, Chem*	chemistry
commercio, finanza	*Comm*	commerce, finance
comparativo	*compar*	comparative
informatica	*Comput*	computing
congiunzione	*cong, conj*	conjunction
edilizia	*Constr*	building
sostantivo usato come aggettivo, ma mai con funzione predicativa	*cpd*	compound element: noun used as adjective and which cannot follow the noun it qualifies
cucina	*Cuc, Culin*	cookery
davanti a	*dav*	before

ABBREVIAZIONI		ABBREVIATIONS
articolo determinativo	*def art*	definite article
determinativo; articolo, aggettivo dimostrativo o indefinito ecc	*det*	determiner: article, demonstrative etc
diminutivo	*dimin*	diminutive
diritto	*Dir*	law
economia	*Econ*	economics
edilizia	*Edil*	building
elettricità, elettronica	*Elettr, Elec*	electricity, electronics
esclamazione	*escl, excl*	exclamation
femminile	*f*	feminine
familiare (! da evitare)	*fam(!)*	colloquial usage (! particularly offensive)
ferrovia	*Ferr*	railways
senso figurato	*fig*	figurative use
fisiologia	*Fisiol*	physiology
fotografia	*Fot*	photography
verbo inglese la cui particella è inseparabile dal verbo	*fus*	(phrasal verb) where the particle cannot be separated from the main verb
nella maggior parte dei sensi; generalmente	*gen*	in most or all senses; generally
geografia, geologia	*Geo*	geography, geology
geometria	*Geom*	geometry
storia, storico	*Hist*	history, historical
impersonale	*impers*	impersonal
articolo indeterminativo	*indef art*	indefinite article
familiare (! da evitare)	*inf(!)*	colloquial usage (! particularly offensive)
infinito	*infin*	infinitive
informatica	*Inform*	computing

ABBREVIAZIONI		ABBREVIATIONS
insegnamento, sistema scolastico e universitario	*Ins*	schooling, schools and universities
invariabile	*inv*	invariable
irregolare	*irreg*	irregular
grammatica, linguistica	*Ling*	grammar, linguistics
maschile	*m*	masculine
matematica	*Mat(h)*	mathematics
termine medico, medicina	*Med*	medical term, medicine
il tempo, meteorologia	*Meteor*	the weather, meteorology
maschile o femminile	*m/f*	masculine or feminine
esercito, linguaggio militare	*Mil*	military matters
musica	*Mus*	music
sostantivo	*n*	noun
nautica	*Naut*	sailing, navigation
numerale (aggettivo, sostantivo)	*num*	numeral adjective or noun
	o.s.	oneself
peggiorativo	*peg, pej*	derogatory, pejorative
fotografia	*Phot*	photography
fisiologia	*Physiol*	physiology
plurale	*pl*	plural
politica	*Pol*	politics
participio passato	*pp*	past participle
preposizione	*prep*	preposition
pronome	*pron*	pronoun
psicologia, psichiatria	*Psic, Psych*	psychology, psychiatry
tempo passato	*pt*	past tense
qualcosa	*qc*	
qualcuno	*qn*	
religione, liturgia	*Rel*	religions, church service
sostantivo	*s*	noun
	sb	somebody

ABBREVIAZIONI		ABBREVIATIONS
insegnamento, sistema scolastico e universitario	*Scol*	schooling, schools and universities
singolare	*sg*	singular
soggetto (grammaticale)	*sog*	(grammatical) subject
	sth	something
congiuntivo	*sub*	subjunctive
soggetto (grammaticale)	*subj*	(grammatical) subject
superlativo	*superl*	superlative
termine tecnico, tecnologia	*Tecn, Tech*	technical term, technology
telecomunicazioni	*Tel*	telecommunications
tipografia	*Tip*	typography, printing
televisione	*TV*	television
tipografia	*Typ*	typography, printing
università	*Univ*	university
inglese americano	*US*	American English
vocale	*V*	vowel
verbo	*vb*	verb
verbo o gruppo verbale con funzione intransitiva	*vi*	verb or phrasal verb used intransitively
verbo pronominale o riflessivo	*vpr*	pronominal or reflexive verb
verbo o gruppo verbale con funzione transitiva	*vt*	verb or phrasal verb used transitively
zoologia	*Zool*	zoology
marchio registrato	®	registered trademark
introduce un'equivalenza culturale	≈	introduces a cultural equivalent

TRASCRIZIONE FONETICA

Consonanti		Consonants
NB **p, b, t, d, k, g** sono seguite da un'aspirazione in inglese.		NB **p, b, t, d, k, g** are not aspirated in Italian.
padre	p	**p**u**pp**y
bam**b**ino	b	**b**a**b**y
tu**tt**o	t	**t**en**t**
da**d**o	d	**d**a**dd**y
cane **ch**e	k	**c**or**k** **k**iss **ch**ord
gola **gh**iro	g	**g**a**g** **gu**ess
sano	s	**s**o ri**c**e ki**ss**
svago e**s**ame	z	cou**s**in bu**zz**
scena	ʃ	**sh**eep **s**ugar
	ʒ	plea**s**ure bei**ge**
pe**c**e lan**ci**are	tʃ	**ch**ur**ch**
giro **gi**oco	dʒ	**j**u**dge** **g**eneral
a**f**a **f**aro	f	**f**arm ra**ff**le
vero bra**v**o	v	**v**ery re**v**
	θ	**th**in ma**th**s
	ð	**th**at o**th**er
letto a**l**a	l	**l**itt**l**e ba**ll**
gli	ʎ	mi**lli**on
rete a**r**co	r	**r**at **r**a**r**e
ra**m**o **m**adre	m	**m**u**mm**y co**mb**
no fuma**n**te	n	**n**o ra**n**
gnomo	ɲ	ca**ny**on
	ŋ	si**ng**i**ng** ba**n**k
	h	**h**at re**h**eat
bu**i**o p**i**acere	j	**y**et
uomo g**u**aio	w	**w**all be**w**ail
	x	lo**ch**

Varie		Miscellaneous
per l'inglese: la "r" finale viene pronunciata se seguita da una vocale	r	
precede la sillaba accentata	ˈ	precedes the stressed syllable

PHONETIC TRANSCRIPTION

Vocali		Vowels
NB La messa in equivalenza di certi suoni indica solo una rassomiglianza approssimativa.		NB The pairing of some vowel sounds only indicates approximate equivalence.
vino idea	i iː	heel bead
	ɪ	hit pity
stella edera	e	
epoca eccetto	ɛ	set tent
mamma amore	a æ	bat apple
	ɑː	after car calm
	ɑ̃	fiancé
	ʌ	fun cousin
müsli	y	
	ə	over above
	əː	urn fern work
rosa occhio	ɔ	wash pot
	ɔː	born cork
ponte ognuno	o	
föhn	ø	
utile zucca	u	full soot
	uː	boon lewd

Dittonghi		Diphthongs
	ɪə	beer tier
	ɛə	tear fair there
	eɪ	date plaice day
	aɪ	life buy cry
	au	owl foul now
	əu	low no
	ɔɪ	boil boy oily
	uə	poor tour

ITALIAN PRONUNCIATION

Vowels

Where the vowel **e** or the vowel **o** appears in a stressed syllable it can be either open [ɛ], [ɔ] or closed [e], [o]. As the open or closed pronunciation of these vowels is subject to regional variation, the distinction is of little importance to the user of this dictionary. Phonetic transcription for headwords containing these vowels will therefore only appear where other pronunciation difficulties are present.

Consonants

c before "e" or "i" is pronounced like the *"tch"* in match.
ch is pronounced like the "*k*" in "kit".
g before "e" or "i" is pronounced like the "*j*" in "jet".
gh is pronounced like the "*g*" in "get".
gl before "e" or "i" is normally pronounced like the "*lli*" in "million", and in a few cases only like the "*gl*" in "glove".
gn is pronounced like the "*ny*" in "canyon"
sc before "e" or "i" is pronounced "*sh*".
z is pronounced like the "*ts*" in "stetson", or like the "*d's*" in "bird's-eye".

Headwords containing the above consonants and consonantal groups have been given full phonetic transcription in this dictionary.

NB All double written consonants in Italian are fully sounded: e.g. the *tt* in "tutto" is pronounced as in "hat trick".

ITALIAN VERB FORMS

1 Gerundio **2** Participio passato **3** Presente **4** Imperfetto **5** Passato remoto **6** Futuro **7** Condizionale **8** Congiuntivo presente **9** Congiuntivo passato **10** Imperativo

andare 3 vado, vai, va, andiamo, andate, vanno **6** andrò *ecc.* **8** vada **10** va'!, vada!, andate!, vadano!

apparire 2 apparso **3** appaio, appari *o* apparisci, appare *o* apparisce, appaiono *o* appariscono **5** apparvi *o* apparsi, apparisti, apparve *o* apparì *o* apparse, apparvero *o* apparirono *o* apparsero **8** appaia *o* apparisca

aprire 2 aperto **3** apro **5** aprii, apristi **8** apra

AVERE 3 ho, hai, ha, abbiamo, avete, hanno **5** ebbi, avesti, ebbe, avemmo, aveste, ebbero **6** avrò *ecc.* **8** abbia *ecc.* **10** abbi!, abbia!, abbiate!, abbiano!

bere 1 bevendo **2** bevuto **3** bevo *ecc.* **4** bevevo *ecc.* **5** bevvi *o* bevetti, bevesti **6** berrò *ecc.* **8** beva *ecc.* **9** bevessi *ecc.*

cadere 5 caddi, cadesti **6** cadrò *ecc.*

cogliere 2 colto **3** colgo, colgono **5** colsi, cogliesti **8** colga

correre 2 corso **5** corsi, corresti

cuocere 2 cotto **3** cuocio, cociamo, cuociono **5** cossi, cocesti

dare 3 do, dai, dà, diamo, date, danno **5** diedi *o* detti, desti **6** darò *ecc.* **8** dia *ecc.* **9** dessi *ecc.* **10** da'!, dai!, date!, diano!

dire 1 dicendo **2** detto **3** dico, dici, dice, diciamo, dite, dicono **4** dicevo *ecc.* **5** dissi, dicesti **6** dirò *ecc.* **8** dica, diciamo, diciate, dicano **9** dicessi *ecc.* **10** di'!, dica!, dite!, dicano!

dolere 3 dolgo, duoli, duole, dolgono **5** dolsi, dolesti **6** dorrò *ecc.* **8** dolga

dovere 3 devo *o* debbo, devi, deve, dobbiamo, dovete, devono *o* debbono **6** dovrò *ecc.* **8** debba, dobbiamo, dobbiate, devano *o* debbano

ESSERE 2 stato **3** sono, sei, è, siamo, siete, sono **4** ero, eri, era, eravamo, eravate, erano **5** fui, fosti, fu, fummo, foste, furono **6** sarò *ecc.* **8** sia *ecc.* **9** fossi, fossi, fosse, fossimo, foste, fossero **10** sii!, sia!, siate!, siano!

fare 1 facendo **2** fatto **3** faccio, fai, fa, facciamo, fate, fanno **4** facevo *ecc.* **5** feci, facesti **6** farò *ecc.* **8** faccia *ecc.* **9** facessi *ecc.* **10** fa'!, faccia!, fate!, facciano!

FINIRE 1 finendo **2** finito **3** finisco, finisci, finisce, finiamo, finite, finiscono **4** finivo, finivi, finiva, finivamo, finivate, finivano **5** finii, finisti, finì, finimmo, fineste, finirono **6** finirò, finirai, finirà, finiremo, finirete, finiranno **7** finirei, finiresti, finirebbe, finiremmo, finireste, finirebbero **8** finisca, finisca, finisca, finiamo, finiate, finiscano **9** finissi, finissi, finisse, finissimo, finiste, finissero **10** finisci!, finisca!, finite!, finiscano!

giungere 2 giunto **5** giunsi, giungesti

leggere 2 letto **5** lessi, leggesti

mettere 2 messo **5** misi, mettesti

morire 2 morto **3** muoio, muori, muore, moriamo, morite, muoiono **6** morirò *o* morrò *ecc.* **8** muoia

muovere 2 mosso **5** mossi, movesti

nascere 2 nato **5** nacqui, nascesti

nuocere 2 nuociuto **3** nuoccio, nuoci, nuoce, nociamo *o* nuociamo, nuocete, nuocciono **4** nuocevo *ecc.* **5** nocqui, nuocesti **6** nuocerò *ecc.* **7** nuoccia

offrire 2 offerto **3** offro **5** offersi *o* offrii, offristi **8** offra

parere 2 parso **3** paio, paiamo, paiono **5** parvi *o* parsi, paresti **6** parrò *ecc.* **8** paia, paiamo, paiate, paiano

PARLARE **1** parlando **2** parlato **3** parlo, parli, parla, parliamo, parlate, parlano **4** parlavo, parlavi, parlava, parlavamo, parlavate, parlavano **5** parlai, parlasti, parlò, parlammo, parlaste, parlarono **6** parlerò, parlerai, parlerà, parleremo, parlerete, parleranno **7** parlerei, parleresti, parlerebbe, parleremmo, parlereste, parlerebbero **8** parli, parli, parli, parliamo, parliate, parlino **9** parlassi, parlassi, parlasse, parlassimo, parlaste, parlassero **10** parla!, parli!, parlate!, parlino!

piacere **2** piaciuto **3** piaccio, piacciamo, piacciono **5** piacqui, piacesti **8** piacci *ecc.*

porre **1** ponendo **2** posto **3** pongo, poni, pone, poniamo, ponete, pongono **4** ponevo *ecc.* **5** posi, ponesti **6** porrò *ecc.* **8** ponga, poniamo, poniate, pongano **9** ponessi *ecc.*

potere **3** posso, puoi, può, possiamo, potete, possono **6** potrò *ecc.* **8** possa, possiamo, possiate, possano

prendere **2** preso **5** presi, prendesti

ridurre **1** riducendo **2** ridotto **3** riduco *ecc.* **4** riducevo *ecc.* **5** ridussi, riducesti **6** ridurrò *ecc.* **8** riduca *ecc.* **9** riducessi *ecc.*

riempire **1** riempiendo **3** riempio, riempi, riempie, riempiono

rimanere **2** rimasto **3** rimango, rimangono **5** rimasi, rimanesti **6** rimarrò *ecc.* **8** rimanga

rispondere **2** risposto **5** risposi, rispondesti

salire **3** salgo, sali, salgono **8** salga

sapere **3** so, sai, sa, sappiamo, sapete, sanno **5** seppi, sapesti **6** saprò *ecc.* **8** sappia *ecc.* **10** sappi!, sappia!, sappiate!, sappiano!

scrivere **2** scritto **5** scrissi, scrivesti

sedere **3** siedo, siedi, siede, siedono **8** sieda

spegnere **2** spento **3** spengo, spengono **5** spensi, spegnesti **8** spenga

stare **2** stato **3** sto, stai, sta, stiamo, state, stanno **5** stetti, stesti **6** starò *ecc.* **8** stia *ecc.* **9** stessi *ecc.* **10** sta'!, stia!, state!, stiano!

tacere **2** taciuto **3** taccio, tacciono **5** tacqui, tacesti **8** taccia

tenere **3** tengo, tieni, tiene, tengono **5** tenni, tenesti **6** terrò *ecc.* **8** tenga

trarre **1** traendo **2** tratto **3** traggo, trai, trae, traiamo, traete, traggono **4** traevo *ecc.* **5** trassi, traesti **6** trarrò *ecc.* **8** tragga **9** traessi *ecc.*

udire **3** odo, odi, ode, odono **8** oda

uscire **3** esco, esci, esce, escono **8** esca

valere **2** valso **3** valgo, valgono **5** valsi, valesti **6** varrò *ecc.* **8** valga

vedere **2** visto *o* veduto **5** vidi, vedesti **6** vedrò *ecc.*

VENDERE **1** vendendo **2** venduto **3** vendo, vendi, vende, vendiamo, vendete, vendono **4** vendevo, vendevi, vendeva, vendevamo, vendevate, vendevano **5** vendei *o* vendetti, vendesti, vendé *o* vendette, vendemmo, vendeste, venderono *o* vendettero **6** venderò, venderai, venderà, venderemo, venderete, venderanno **7** venderei, venderesti, venderebbe, venderemmo, vendereste, venderebbero **8** venda, venda, venda, vendiamo, vendiate, vendano **9** vendessi, vendessi, vendesse, vendessimo, vendeste, vendessero **10** vendi!, venda!, vendete!, vendano!

venire **2** venuto **3** vengo, vieni, viene, vengono **5** venni, venisti **6** verrò *ecc.* **8** venga

vivere **2** vissuto **5** vissi, vivesti

volere **3** voglio, vuoi, vuole, vogliamo, volete, vogliono **5** volli, volesti **6** vorrò *ecc.* **8** voglia *ecc.* **10** vogli!, voglia!, vogliate!, vogliano!

ENGLISH VERB FORMS

present	*pt*	*pp*
arise	arose	arisen
awake	awoke	awoken
be (am, is, are; being)	was, were	been
bear	bore	born(e)
beat	beat	beaten
become	became	become
begin	began	begun
bend	bent	bent
bet	bet, betted	bet, betted
bid *(at auction, cards)*	bid	bid
bid *(say)*	bade	bidden
bind	bound	bound
bite	bit	bitten
bleed	bled	bled
blow	blew	blown
break	broke	broken
breed	bred	bred
bring	brought	brought
build	built	built
burn	burnt, burned	burnt, burned
burst	burst	burst
buy	bought	bought
can	could	(been able)
cast	cast	cast
catch	caught	caught
choose	chose	chosen
cling	clung	clung
come	came	come
cost	cost	cost
cost *(work out price of)*	costed	costed
creep	crept	crept
cut	cut	cut
deal	dealt	dealt
dig	dug	dug
do (does)	did	done
draw	drew	drawn
dream	dreamed, dreamt	dreamed, dreamt
drink	drank	drunk
drive	drove	driven
dwell	dwelt	dwelt
eat	ate	eaten
fall	fell	fallen
feed	fed	fed
feel	felt	felt
fight	fought	fought
find	found	found
flee	fled	fled
fling	flung	flung
fly	flew	flown
forbid	forbade	forbidden
forecast	forecast	forecast
forget	forgot	forgotten
forgive	forgave	forgiven
forsake	forsook	forsaken
freeze	froze	frozen
get	got	got, (US) gotten
give	gave	given
go (goes)	went	gone
grind	ground	ground
grow	grew	grown
hang	hung	hung
hang *(execute)*	hanged	hanged
have (has; having)	had	had
hear	heard	heard
hide	hid	hidden
hit	hit	hit
hold	held	held
hurt	hurt	hurt
keep	kept	kept
kneel	knelt, kneeled	knelt, kneeled
know	knew	known
lay	laid	laid
lead	led	led
lean	leant, leaned	leant, leaned
leap	leapt, leaped	leapt, leaped
learn	learnt, learned	learnt, learned
leave	left	left
lend	lent	lent
let	let	let
lie (lying)	lay	lain
light	lit, lighted	lit, lighted
lose	lost	lost
make	made	made

present	pt	pp	present	pt	pp
may	might	—	**spell**	spelt, spelled	spelt, spelled
mean	meant	meant	**spend**	spent	spent
meet	met	met	**spill**	spilt, spilled	spilt, spilled
mistake	mistook	mistaken	**spin**	spun	spun
mow	mowed	mown, mowed	**spit**	spat	spat
must	(had to)	(had to)	**split**	split	split
pay	paid	paid	**spoil**	spoiled, spoilt	spoiled, spoilt
put	put	put	**spread**	spread	spread
quit	quit, quitted	quit, quitted	**spring**	sprang	sprung
read	read	read	**stand**	stood	stood
rid	rid	rid	**steal**	stole	stolen
ride	rode	ridden	**stick**	stuck	stuck
ring	rang	rung	**sting**	stung	stung
rise	rose	risen	**stink**	stank	stunk
run	ran	run	**stride**	strode	stridden
saw	sawed	sawed, sawn	**strike**	struck	struck, stricken
say	said	said	**strive**	strove	striven
see	saw	seen	**swear**	swore	sworn
seek	sought	sought	**sweep**	swept	swept
sell	sold	sold	**swell**	swelled	swollen, swelled
send	sent	sent	**swim**	swam	swum
set	set	set	**swing**	swung	swung
sew	sewed	sewn	**take**	took	taken
shake	shook	shaken	**teach**	taught	taught
shear	sheared	shorn, sheared	**tear**	tore	torn
shed	shed	shed	**tell**	told	told
shine	shone	shone	**think**	thought	thought
shoot	shot	shot	**throw**	threw	thrown
show	showed	shown	**thrust**	thrust	thrust
shrink	shrank	shrunk	**tread**	trod	trodden
shut	shut	shut	**wake**	woke, waked	woken, waked
sing	sang	sung	**wear**	wore	worn
sink	sank	sunk	**weave**	wove, weaved	woven, weaved
sit	sat	sat	**wed**	wedded, wed	wedded, wed
slay	slew	slain	**weep**	wept	wept
sleep	slept	slept	**win**	won	won
slide	slid	slid	**wind**	wound	wound
sling	slung	slung	**wring**	wrung	wrung
slit	slit	slit	**write**	wrote	written
smell	smelt, smelled	smelt, smelled			
sow	sowed	sown, sowed			
speak	spoke	spoken			
speed	sped, speeded	sped, speeded			

I NUMERI		NUMBERS
uno(a)	1	one
due	2	two
tre	3	three
quattro	4	four
cinque	5	five
sei	6	six
sette	7	seven
otto	8	eight
nove	9	nine
dieci	10	ten
undici	11	eleven
dodici	12	twelve
tredici	13	thirteen
quattordici	14	fourteen
quindici	15	fifteen
sedici	16	sixteen
diciassette	17	seventeen
diciotto	18	eighteen
diciannove	19	nineteen
venti	20	twenty
ventuno	21	twenty-one
ventidue	22	twenty-two
ventitré	23	twenty-three
ventotto	28	twenty-eight
trenta	30	thirty
quaranta	40	forty
cinquanta	50	fifty
sessanta	60	sixty
settanta	70	seventy
ottanta	80	eighty
novanta	90	ninety
cento	100	a hundred
cento uno	101	a hundred and one
duecento	200	two hundred
mille	1000	a thousand
milleduecentodue	1202	one thousand two hundred and two
cinquemila	5000	five thousand
un milione	1000000	a million

I NUMERI	NUMBERS
primo(a)	first, 1st
secondo(a)	second, 2nd
terzo(a)	third, 3rd
quarto(a)	fourth, 4th
quinto(a)	fifth, 5th
sesto(a)	sixth, 6th
settimo(a)	seventh
ottavo(a)	eighth
nono(a)	ninth
decimo(a)	tenth
undicesimo(a)	eleventh
dodicesimo(a)	twelfth
tredicesimo(a)	thirteenth
quattordicesimo(a)	fourteenth
quindicesimo(a)	fifteenth
sedicesimo(a)	sixteenth
diciassettesimo(a)	seventeenth
diciottesimo(a)	eighteenth
diciannovesimo(a)	nineteenth
ventesimo(a)	twentieth
ventunesimo(a)	twenty-first
ventiduesimo(a)	twenty-second
ventitreesimo(a)	twenty-third
ventottesimo(a)	twenty-eighth
trentesimo(a)	thirtieth
centesimo(a)	hundredth
centunesimo(a)	hundred-and-first
millesimo(a)	thousandth
milionesimo(a)	millionth

Frazioni	Fractions
mezzo	half
terzo	third
due terzi	two thirds
quarto	quarter
quinto	fifth
zero virgola cinque, 0,5	(nought) point five, 0.5
tre virgola quattro, 3,4	three point four, 3.4
dieci per cento	ten per cent
cento per cento	a hundred per cent

Esempi	Examples
abita al numero dieci	he lives at number 10
si trova nel capitolo sette, a pagina sette	it's in chapter 7, on page 7
abita al terzo piano	he lives on the 3rd floor
arrivò quarto	he came in 4th
scala uno a venticinquemila	scale 1:25,000

L'ORA	THE TIME
che ora è?, che ore sono?	*what time is it?*
è …, sono …	*it's …*
mezzanotte	midnight
l'una (di notte)	one o'clock (in the morning), one (a.m.)
le tre del mattino	three o'clock (in the morning), three (a.m.)
l'una e cinque	five past one
l'una e dieci	ten past one
l'una e un quarto, l'una e quindici	a quarter past one, one fifteen
l'una e venticinque	twenty-five past one, one twenty-five
l'una e mezzo *or* mezza, l'una e trenta	half past one, one thirty
le due meno venticinque, l'una e trentacinque	twenty-five to two, one thirty-five
le due meno venti, l'una e quaranta	twenty to two, one forty
le due meno un quarto, l'una e tre quarti	a quarter to two, one forty-five
le due meno dieci, l'una e cinquanta	ten to two, one fifty
le dodici, mezzogiorno	twelve o'clock, midday, noon
l'una, le tredici	one o'clock (in the afternoon), one (p.m.)
le sette (di sera), le diciannove	seven o'clock (in the evening), seven (p.m.)
a che ora?	*at what time?*
a mezzanotte	at midnight
all'una, alle tredici	at one o'clock
fra venti minuti	in twenty minutes
venti minuti fa	twenty minutes ago

LA DATA	DATES
oggi	today
ogni giorno, tutti i giorni	every day
ieri	yesterday
stamattina	this morning
domani notte; domani sera	tomorrow night
l'altroieri notte; l'altroieri sera	the night before last
l'altroieri	the day before yesterday
ieri notte; ieri sera	last night
due giorni/sei anni fa	two days/six years ago
domani pomeriggio	tomorrow afternoon
dopodomani	the day after tomorrow
tutti i giovedì, di *or* il giovedì	every Thursday, on Thursdays
ci va di *or* il venerdì	he goes on Fridays
"chiuso il mercoledì"	"closed on Wednesdays"
dal lunedì al venerdì	from Monday to Friday
per giovedì, entro giovedì	by Thursday
un sabato di marzo	one Saturday in March
tra una settimana	in a week's time
martedì a otto	a week next *or* on Tuesday
questa/la prossima/la scorsa settimana	this/next/last week
tra due settimane, tra quindici giorni	in two weeks *or* a fortnight
lunedì a quindici	two weeks on Monday
il primo/l'ultimo venerdì del mese	the first/last Friday of the month
il mese prossimo	next month
l'anno scorso	last year
il primo giugno	the 1st of June, June first
il due ottobre	the 2nd of October *or* October 2nd
sono nato nel 1987	I was born in 1987
il suo compleano è il 5 giugno	his birthday is on June 5th (*BRIT*) *or* 5th June (*US*)
il 18 agosto	on 18th August (*BRIT*) *or* August 18 (*US*)
nel '96	in '96
nella primavera del '94	in the Spring of '94
dal 19 al 3	from the 19th to the 3rd
quanti ne abbiamo oggi?	what's the date? *or* what date is it today?

oggi è il 15	today's date is the 15th *or* today is the 15th
1988 - millenovecentottantotto	1988 - nineteen eighty-eight
2005 - duemilacinque	2005 - two thousand and five
10 anni esatti	10 years to the day
alla fine del mese	at the end of the month
la settimana del 30/7	week ending 30/7
giornalmente *or* al giorno	daily
settimanalmente *or* alla settimana	weekly
mensilmente, al mese	monthly
annualmente *or* all'anno	annually
due volte alla settimana/al mese/all'anno	twice a week/month/year
bimestralmente	bi-monthly
nel 4 a.C.	in 4 B.C. *or* B.C. 4
nel 79 d.C.	in 79 A.D *or* A.D. 79
nel tredicesimo secolo	in the 13th century
negli anni '80	in *or* during the 80s
nel 1990 e rotti	in 1990 something

La data nelle lettere	**Headings of letters**
9 ottobre 2004	9th October 2004 *or* 9 October 2004

a

A *abbr* (= *autostrada*) ≈ M (*motorway*)

PAROLA CHIAVE

a (*a* + *il* = **al**, *a* + *lo* = **allo**, *a* + *l'* = **all'**, *a* + *la* = **alla**, *a* + *i* = **ai**, *a* + *gli* = **agli**, *a* + *le* = **alle**) *prep* **1** (*stato in luogo*) at; (: *in*) in; **essere alla stazione** to be at the station; **essere a casa/a scuola/a Roma** to be at home/at school/in Rome; **è a 10 km da qui** it's 10 km from here, it's 10 km away
2 (*moto a luogo*) to; **andare a casa/a scuola** to go home/to school
3 (*tempo*) at; (*epoca, stagione*) in; **alle cinque** at five (o'clock); **a mezzanotte/Natale** at midnight/Christmas; **al mattino** in the morning; **a maggio/primavera** in May/spring; **a cinquant'anni** at fifty (years of age); **a domani!** see you tomorrow!
4 (*complemento di termine*) to; **dare qc a qn** to give sth to sb
5 (*mezzo, modo*) with, by; **a piedi/cavallo** on foot/horseback; **fatto a mano** made by hand, handmade; **una barca a motore** a motorboat; **a uno a uno** one by one; **all'italiana** the Italian way, in the Italian fashion
6 (*rapporto*) a, per; (: *con prezzi*) at; **prendo 850 euro al mese** I get 850 euros a *o* per month; **pagato a ore** paid by the hour; **vendere qc a 2 euro il chilo** to sell sth at 2 euros a *o* per kilo

abbagli'ante [abbaʎ'ʎante] *ag* dazzling; **abbaglianti** *smpl* (*Aut*): **accendere gli abbaglianti** to put one's headlights on full (BRIT) *o* high (US) beam
abbagli'are [abbaʎ'ʎare] *vt* to dazzle; (*illudere*) to delude
abbai'are *vi* to bark
abbando'nare *vt* to leave, abandon, desert; (*trascurare*) to neglect; (*rinunciare a*) to abandon, give up; **abbandonarsi** *vpr* to let o.s. go; **abbandonarsi a** (*ricordi, vizio*) to give o.s. up to
abbas'sare *vt* to lower; (*radio*) to turn down; **abbassarsi** *vpr* (*chinarsi*) to stoop; (*livello, sole*) to go down; (*fig*: *umiliarsi*) to demean o.s.; **~ i fari** (*Aut*) to dip *o* dim (US) one's lights
ab'basso *escl*: **~ il re!** down with the king!
abbas'tanza [abbas'tantsa] *av* (*a sufficienza*) enough; (*alquanto*) quite, rather, fairly; **non è ~ furbo** he's not shrewd enough; **un vino ~ dolce** quite a sweet wine; **averne ~ di qn/qc** to have had enough of sb/sth
ab'battere *vt* (*muro, casa*) to pull down; (*ostacolo*) to knock down; (*albero*) to fell; (: *vento*) to bring down; (*bestie da macello*) to slaughter; (*cane, cavallo*) to destroy, put down; (*selvaggina, aereo*) to shoot down; (*fig*: *malattia, disgrazia*) to lay low; **abbattersi** *vpr* (*avvilirsi*) to lose heart;

abbat'tuto, -a *ag* (*fig*) depressed
abba'zia [abbat'tsia] *sf* abbey
'abbia *vb vedi* **avere**
abbi'ente *ag* well-to-do, well-off; **abbienti** *smpl* **gli abbienti** the well-to-do
abbiglia'mento [abbiʎʎa'mento] *sm* dress *no pl*; (*indumenti*) clothes *pl*; (*industria*) clothing industry
abbi'nare *vt*: **~ (a)** to combine (with)
abboc'care *vi* (*pesce*) to bite; (*tubi*) to join; **~ (all'amo)** (*fig*) to swallow the bait
abbona'mento *sm* subscription; (*alle ferrovie ecc*) season ticket; **fare l'~** to take out a subscription (*o* season ticket)
abbo'narsi *vpr*: **~ a un giornale** to take out a subscription to a newspaper; **~ al teatro/alle ferrovie** to take out a season ticket for the theatre/the train
abbon'dante *ag* abundant, plentiful; (*giacca*) roomy
abbon'danza [abbon'dantsa] *sf* abundance; plenty
abbor'dabile *ag* (*persona*) approachable; (*prezzo*) reasonable
abbotto'nare *vt* to button up, do up
abbracci'are [abbrat'tʃare] *vt* to embrace; (*persona*) to hug, embrace; (*professione*) to take up; (*contenere*) to include; **abbracciarsi** *vpr* to hug *o* embrace (one another); **ab'braccio** *sm* hug, embrace
abbrevi'are *vt* to shorten; (*parola*) to abbreviate
abbreviazi'one [abbrevjat'tsjone] *sf* abbreviation
abbron'zante [abbron'dzante] *ag* tanning, sun *cpd*
abbronzarsi *vpr* to tan, get a tan
abbron'zato, -a [abbron'dzato] *ag* (sun)tanned
abbrusto'lire *vt* (*pane*) to toast; (*caffè*) to roast; **abbrustolirsi** *vpr* to toast; (*fig*: *al sole*) to soak up the sun
abbuf'farsi *vpr* (*fam*): **~ (di qc)** to stuff o.s. (with sth)
abdi'care *vi* to abdicate; **~ a** to give up, renounce
a'bete *sm* fir (tree); **abete rosso** spruce
'abile *ag* (*idoneo*): **~ (a qc/a fare qc)** fit (for sth/to do sth); (*capace*) able; (*astuto*) clever; (*accorto*) skilful; **~ al servizio militare** fit for military service; **abilità** *sf inv* ability; cleverness; skill
a'bisso *sm* abyss, gulf
abi'tante *sm/f* inhabitant
abi'tare *vt* to live in, dwell in ▷ *vi* **~ in campagna/a Roma** to live in the country/in Rome; **dove abita?** where do you live?; **abitazi'one** *sf* residence; house
'abito *sm* dress *no pl*; (*da uomo*) suit; (*da donna*) dress; (*abitudine, disposizione, Rel*) habit; **abiti** *smpl* (*vestiti*) clothes; **in ~ da sera** in evening dress
abitu'ale *ag* usual, habitual; (*cliente*) regular
abitual'mente *av* usually, normally
abitu'are *vt*: **~ qn a** to get sb used *o* accustomed to; **abituarsi a** to get used to, accustom o.s. to
abitudi'nario, -a *ag* of fixed habits ▷ *sm/f* regular customer
abi'tudine *sf* habit; **aver l'~ di fare qc** to be in the habit of doing sth; **d'~** usually; **per ~** from *o* out of habit
abo'lire *vt* to abolish; (*Dir*) to repeal
abor'tire *vi* (*Med*) to miscarry, have a miscarriage; (: *deliberatamente*) to have an abortion; (*fig*) to miscarry, fail; **a'borto** *sm* miscarriage; abortion
ABS [abiɛse] *sigla m* (= *Anti-Blockier System*) ABS
'abside *sf* apse
abu'sare *vi*: **~ di** to abuse, misuse; (*alcool*) to take to excess; (*approfittare, violare*) to take advantage of
abu'sivo, -a *ag* unauthorized,

unlawful; **(occupante) ~** (*di una casa*) squatter

> Attenzione! In inglese esiste la parola *abusive* che però vuol dire *ingiurioso*.

a.C. *av abbr* (= *avanti Cristo*) B.C.
a'cacia, -cie [a'katʃa] *sf* (*Bot*) acacia
ac'cadde *vb vedi* **accadere**
acca'demia *sf* (*società*) learned society; (*scuola: d'arte, militare*) academy
acca'dere *vb impers* to happen, occur
accal'dato *ag* hot
accalo'rarsi *vpr* (*fig*) to get excited
accampa'mento *sm* camp
accamparsi *vpr* to camp
acca'nirsi *vpr* (*infierire*) to rage; (*ostinarsi*) to persist; **acca'nito, -a** *ag* (*odio, gelosia*) fierce, bitter; (*lavoratore*) assiduous, dogged; (*fumatore*) inveterate
ac'canto *av* near, nearby; **~ a** *prep* near, beside, close to
accanto'nare *vt* (*problema*) to shelve; (*somma*) to set aside
accappa'toio *sm* bathrobe
accarez'zare [akkaret'tsare] *vt* to caress, stroke, fondle; (*fig*) to toy with
acca'sarsi *vpr* to set up house; to get married
accasci'arsi [akkaʃʃarsi] *vpr* to collapse; (*fig*) to lose heart
accat'tone, -a *sm/f* beggar
accaval'lare *vt* (*gambe*) to cross
acce'care [attʃe'kare] *vt* to blind ▷ *vi* to go blind
ac'cedere [at'tʃedere] *vi*: **~ a** to enter; (*richiesta*) to grant, accede to
accele'rare [attʃele'rare] *vt* to speed up ▷ *vi* (*Aut*) to accelerate; **~ il passo** to quicken one's pace; **accelera'tore** *sm* (*Aut*) accelerator
ac'cendere [at'tʃɛndere] *vt* (*fuoco, sigaretta*) to light; (*luce, televisione*) to put on, switch on, turn on; (*Aut: motore*) to switch on; (*Comm: conto*) to open; (*fig: suscitare*) to inflame, stir up; **ha da ~?** have you got a light?; **non riesco ad ~ il riscaldamento** I can't turn the heating on; **accen'dino, accendi'sigaro** *sm* (cigarette) lighter
accen'nare [attʃen'nare] *vt* (*Mus*) to pick out the notes of; to hum ▷ *vi* **~ a** (*fig: alludere a*) to hint at; (*: far atto di*) to make as if; **~ un saluto** (*con la mano*) to make as if to wave; (*col capo*) to half nod; **accenna a piovere** it looks as if it's going to rain
ac'cenno [at'tʃenno] *sm* (*cenno*) sign; nod; (*allusione*) hint
accensi'one [attʃen'sjone] *sf* (*vedi verbo*) lighting; switching on; opening; (*Aut*) ignition
ac'cento [at'tʃɛnto] *sm* accent; (*Fonetica, fig*) stress; (*inflessione*) tone (of voice)
accentu'are [attʃentu'are] *vt* to stress, emphasize; **accentuarsi** *vpr* to become more noticeable
accerchi'are [attʃer'kjare] *vt* to surround, encircle
accerta'mento [attʃerta'mento] *sm* check; assessment
accer'tare [attʃer'tare] *vt* to ascertain; (*verificare*) to check; (*reddito*) to assess; **accertarsi** *vpr* **accertarsi (di)** to make sure (of)
ac'ceso, -a [at'tʃeso] *pp di* **accendere** ▷ *ag* lit; on; open; (*colore*) bright
acces'sibile [attʃes'sibile] *ag* (*luogo*) accessible; (*persona*) approachable; (*prezzo*) reasonable
ac'cesso [at'tʃɛsso] *sm* (*anche Inform*) access; (*Med*) attack, fit; (*impulso violento*) fit, outburst
accessori *smpl* accessories
ac'cetta [at'tʃetta] *sf* hatchet
accet'tabile [attʃet'tabile] *ag* acceptable
accet'tare [attʃet'tare] *vt* to accept; **accettate carte di credito?** do you accept credit cards?; **~ di fare qc** to agree to do sth; **accettazi'one** *sf* acceptance; (*locale di servizio pubblico*)

reception; **accettazione bagagli** (*Aer*) check-in (desk)
acchiap'pare [akkjap'pare] *vt* to catch
acciaie'ria [attʃaje'ria] *sf* steelworks *sg*
acci'aio [at'tʃajo] *sm* steel
acciden'tato, -a [attʃiden'tato] *ag* (*terreno ecc*) uneven
accigli'ato, -a [attʃiʎ'ʎato] *ag* frowning
ac'cingersi [at'tʃindʒersi] *vpr*: **~ a fare qc** to be about to do sth
acciuf'fare [attʃuf'fare] *vt* to seize, catch
acci'uga, -ghe [at'tʃuga] *sf* anchovy
ac'cludere *vt* to enclose
accocco'larsi *vpr* to crouch
accogli'ente [akkoʎ'ʎɛnte] *ag* welcoming, friendly
ac'cogliere [ak'koʎʎere] *vt* (*ricevere*) to receive; (*dare il benvenuto*) to welcome; (*approvare*) to agree to, accept; (*contenere*) to hold, accommodate
ac'colgo *ecc vb vedi* **accogliere**
ac'colsi *ecc vb vedi* **accogliere**
accoltel'lare *vt* to knife, stab
accomoda'mento *sm* agreement, settlement
accomo'dante *ag* accommodating
accomodarsi *vpr* (*sedersi*) to sit down; (*entrare*) to come in; **s'accomodi!** (*venga avanti*) come in!; (*si sieda*) take a seat!
accompagna'mento [akkompaɲɲa'mento] *sm* (*Mus*) accompaniment
accompa'gnare [akkompaɲ'ɲare] *vt* to accompany, come *o* go with; (*Mus*) to accompany; (*unire*) to couple; **~ la porta** to close the door gently
accompagna'tore, -trice *sm/f* companion; **~ turistico** courier
acconcia'tura [akkontʃa'tura] *sf* hairstyle
accondiscen'dente [akkondiʃʃen'dɛnte] *ag* affable
acconsen'tire *vi*: **~ (a)** to agree *o* consent (to)
acconten'tare *vt* to satisfy; **accontentarsi** *vpr* **accontentarsi di** to be satisfied with, content o.s. with
ac'conto *sm* part payment; **pagare una somma in ~** to pay a sum of money as a deposit
acco'rato, -a *ag* heartfelt
accorci'are [akkor'tʃare] *vt* to shorten; **accorciarsi** *vpr* to become shorter
accor'dare *vt* to reconcile; (*colori*) to match; (*Mus*) to tune; (*Ling*): **~ qc con qc** to make sth agree with sth; (*Dir*) to grant; **accordarsi** *vpr* to agree, come to an agreement; (*colori*) to match
ac'cordo *sm* agreement; (*armonia*) harmony; (*Mus*) chord; **essere d'~** to agree; **andare d'~** to get on well together; **d'~!** all right!, agreed!; **accordo commerciale** trade agreement
ac'corgersi [ak'kordʒersi] *vpr*: **~ di** to notice; (*fig*) to realize
ac'correre *vi* to run up
ac'corto, -a *pp di* **accorgersi** ▷ *ag* shrewd; **stare ~** to be on one's guard
accos'tare *vt* (*avvicinare*): **~ qc a** to bring sth near to, put sth near to; (*avvicinarsi a*) to approach; (*socchiudere*: *imposte*) to half-close; (: *porta*) to leave ajar ▷ *vi* (*Naut*) to come alongside; **accostarsi** *vpr* **accostarsi a** to draw near, approach; (*fig*) to support
accredi'tare *vt* (*notizia*) to confirm the truth of; (*Comm*) to credit; (*diplomatico*) to accredit
ac'credito *sm* (*Comm*: *atto*) crediting; (: *effetto*) credit
accucci'arsi [akkut'tʃarsi] *vpr* (*cane*) to lie down
accu'dire *vt* (*anche*: *vi* **~ a**) to attend to
accumu'lare *vt* to accumulate; **accumularsi** *vpr* to accumulate;

(*Finanza*) to accrue
accu'rato, -a *ag* (*diligente*) careful; (*preciso*) accurate
ac'cusa *sf* accusation; (*Dir*) charge; **la pubblica ~** the prosecution
accu'sare *vt*: **~ qn di qc** to accuse sb of sth; (*Dir*) to charge sb with sth; **~ ricevuta di** (*Comm*) to acknowledge receipt of
accusa'tore, -'trice *sm/f* accuser ▷ *sm* (*Dir*) prosecutor
a'cerbo, -a [a'tʃɛrbo] *ag* bitter; (*frutta*) sour, unripe; (*persona*) immature
'acero ['atʃero] *sm* maple
a'cerrimo, -a [a'tʃɛrrimo] *ag* very fierce
a'ceto [a'tʃeto] *sm* vinegar
ace'tone [atʃe'tone] *sm* nail varnish remover
A.C.I. ['atʃi] *sigla m* = **Automobile Club d'Italia**
'acido, -a ['atʃido] *ag* (*sapore*) acid, sour; (*Chim*) acid ▷ *sm* (*Chim*) acid
'acino ['atʃino] *sm* berry; **acino d'uva** grape
'acne *sf* acne
'acqua *sf* water; (*pioggia*) rain; **acque** *sfpl* (*di mare, fiume ecc*) waters; **fare ~** (*Naut*) to leak, take in water; **~ in bocca!** mum's the word!; **acqua corrente** running water; **acqua dolce/salata** fresh/salt water; **acqua minerale/potabile/tonica** mineral/drinking/tonic water; **acque termali** thermal waters
a'cquaio *sm* sink
acqua'ragia [akkwa'radʒa] *sf* turpentine
a'cquario *sm* aquarium; (*dello zodiaco*): **A~** Aquarius
acquascooter [akkwas'kuter] *sm inv* Jet Ski®
ac'quatico, -a, -ci, -che *ag* aquatic; (*Sport, Scienza*) water *cpd*
acqua'vite *sf* brandy
acquaz'zone [akkwat'tsone] *sm* cloudburst, heavy shower
acque'dotto *sm* aqueduct; waterworks *pl*, water system
acque'rello *sm* watercolour
acqui'rente *sm/f* purchaser, buyer
acquis'tare *vt* to purchase, buy; (*fig*) to gain; **a'cquisto** *sm* purchase; **fare acquisti** to go shopping
acquo'lina *sf*: **far venire l'~ in bocca a qn** to make sb's mouth water
a'crobata, -i, -e *sm/f* acrobat
a'culeo *sm* (*Zool*) sting; (*Bot*) prickle
a'cume *sm* acumen, perspicacity
a'custico, -a, ci, che *ag* acoustic ▷ *sf* (*scienza*) acoustics *sg*; (*di una sala*) acoustics *pl*; **cornetto ~** ear trumpet; **apparecchio ~** hearing aid
a'cuto, -a *ag* (*appuntito*) sharp, pointed; (*suono, voce*) shrill, piercing; (*Mat, Ling, Med*) acute; (*Mus*) high-pitched; (*fig*: *dolore, desiderio*) intense; (: *perspicace*) acute, keen
a'dagio [a'dadʒo] *av* slowly ▷ *sm* (*Mus*) adagio; (*proverbio*) adage, saying
adatta'mento *sm* adaptation
adat'tare *vt* to adapt; (*sistemare*) to fit; **adattarsi** *vpr* **adattarsi (a)** (*ambiente, tempi*) to adapt (to); (*essere adatto*) to be suitable (for)
a'datto, -a *ag* **~ (a)** suitable (for), right (for)
addebi'tare *vt*: **~ qc a qn** to debit sb with sth
ad'debito *sm* (*Comm*) debit
adden'tare *vt* to bite into
adden'trarsi *vpr* **~ in** to penetrate, go into
addestra'mento *sm* training
addes'trare *vt* to train
ad'detto, -a *ag* **~ a** (*persona*) assigned to; (*oggetto*) intended for ▷ *sm* employee; (*funzionario*) attaché; **gli addetti ai lavori** authorized personnel; (*fig*) those in the know; **addetto commerciale** commercial attaché; **addetto stampa** press attaché
ad'dio *sm, escl* goodbye, farewell

addirit'tura *av* (*veramente*) really, absolutely; (*perfino*) even; (*direttamente*) directly, right away
addi'tare *vt* to point out; (*fig*) to expose
addi'tivo *sm* additive
addizi'one *sf* addition
addob'bare *vt* to decorate; **ad'dobbo** *sm* decoration
addolo'rare *vt* to pain, grieve; **addolorarsi (per)** to be distressed (by)
addolo'rato, -a *ag* distressed, upset; **l'Addolorata** (*Rel*) Our Lady of Sorrows
ad'dome *sm* abdomen
addomesti'care *vt* to tame
addomi'nale *ag* abdominal; **(muscoli** *mpl***) addominali** stomach muscles
addormen'tare *vt* to put to sleep; **addormentarsi** *vpr* to fall asleep, go to sleep
ad'dosso *av* on; **mettersi ~ il cappotto** to put one's coat on; **~ a** (*sopra*) on; (*molto vicino*) right next to; **stare ~ a qn** (*fig*) to breathe down sb's neck; **dare ~ a qn** (*fig*) to attack sb
adeguarsi *vpr* to adapt
adegu'ato, -a *ag* adequate; (*conveniente*) suitable; (*equo*) fair
a'dempiere *vt* to fulfil, carry out
ade'rente *ag* adhesive; (*vestito*) close-fitting ▹ *sm/f* follower
ade'rire *vi* (*stare attaccato*) to adhere, stick; **~ a** to adhere to, stick to; (*fig: società, partito*) to join; (*: opinione*) to support; (*richiesta*) to agree to
adesi'one *sf* adhesion; (*fig*) agreement, acceptance; **ade'sivo, -a** *ag, sm* adhesive
a'desso *av* (*ora*) now; (*or ora, poco fa*) just now; (*tra poco*) any moment now
adia'cente [adja'tʃɛnte] *ag* adjacent
adi'bire *vt* (*usare*): **~ qc a** to turn sth into
adole'scente [adoleʃʃɛnte] *ag, sm/f* adolescent
adope'rare *vt* to use
ado'rare *vt* to adore; (*Rel*) to adore, worship
adot'tare *vt* to adopt; (*decisione, provvedimenti*) to pass; **adot'tivo, -a** *ag* (*genitori*) adoptive; (*figlio, patria*) adopted; **adozi'one** *sf* adoption; **adozione a distanza** child sponsorship
adri'atico, -a, -ci, -che *ag* Adriatic ▹ *sm* **l'A~, il mare A~** the Adriatic, the Adriatic Sea
adu'lare *vt* to adulate, flatter
a'dultero, -a *ag* adulterous ▹ *sm/f* adulterer (adulteress)
a'dulto, -a *ag* adult; (*fig*) mature ▹ *sm* adult, grown-up
a'ereo, -a *ag* air *cpd*; (*radice*) aerial ▹ *sm* aerial; (*aeroplano*) plane; **aereo da caccia** fighter (plane); **aereo di linea** airliner; **aereo a reazione** jet (plane); **ae'robica** *sf* aerobics *sg*; **aero'nautica** *sf* (*scienza*) aeronautics *sg*; **aeronautica militare** air force
aero'porto *sm* airport; **all'~ per favore** to the airport, please
aero'sol *sm inv* aerosol
'afa *sf* sultriness
af'fabile *ag* affable
affaccen'dato, -a [affattʃen'dato] *ag* (*persona*) busy
affacci'arsi [affat'tʃarsi] *vpr* **~ (a)** to appear (at)
affa'mato, -a *ag* starving; (*fig*): **~ (di)** eager (for)
affan'noso, -a *ag* (*respiro*) difficult; (*fig*) troubled, anxious
af'fare *sm* (*faccenda*) matter, affair; (*Comm*) piece of business, (business) deal; (*occasione*) bargain; (*Dir*) case; (*fam: cosa*) thing; **affari** *smpl* (*Comm*) business *sg*; **Ministro degli Affari esteri** Foreign Secretary (BRIT), Secretary of State (US)
affasci'nante [affaʃʃi'nante] *ag* fascinating

affasci'nare [affaʃʃi'nare] *vt* to bewitch; (*fig*) to charm, fascinate
affati'care *vt* to tire; **affaticarsi** *vpr* (*durar fatica*) to tire o.s. out; **affati'cato, -a** *ag* tired
af'fatto *av* completely; **non ... ~** not ... at all; **niente ~** not at all
affer'mare *vt* (*dichiarare*) to maintain, affirm; **affermarsi** *vpr* to assert o.s., make one's name known; **affer'mato, -a** *ag* established, well-known; **affermazi'one** *sf* affirmation, assertion; (*successo*) achievement
affer'rare *vt* to seize, grasp; (*fig: idea*) to grasp; **afferrarsi** *vpr* **afferrarsi a** to cling to
affet'tare *vt* (*tagliare a fette*) to slice; (*ostentare*) to affect
affetta'trice [affetta'tritʃe] *sf* meat slicer
affet'tivo, -a *ag* emotional, affective
af'fetto *sm* affection; **affettu'oso, -a** *ag* affectionate
affezio'narsi [affettsjo'narsi] *vpr* **~ a** to grow fond of
affezio'nato, -a [affettsjo'nato] *ag* **~ a qn/qc** fond of sb/sth; (*attaccato*) attached to sb/sth
affia'tato, -a *ag* **essere molto affiatati** to get on very well
affibbi'are *vt* (*fig: dare*) to give
affi'dabile *ag* reliable
affida'mento *sm* (*Dir: di bambino*) custody; (*fiducia*): **fare ~ su qn** to rely on sb; **non dà nessun ~** he's not to be trusted
affi'dare *vt*: **~ qc** *o* **qn a qn** to entrust sth *o* sb to sb; **affidarsi** *vpr* **affidarsi a** to place one's trust in
affi'lare *vt* to sharpen
affi'lato, -a *ag* (*gen*) sharp; (*volto, naso*) thin
affinché [affin'ke] *cong* in order that, so that
affit'tare *vt* (*dare in affitto*) to let, rent (out); (*prendere in affitto*) to rent; **af'fitto** *sm* rent; (*contratto*) lease
af'fliggere [af'fliddʒere] *vt* to torment; **affliggersi** *vpr* to grieve
af'flissi *ecc vb vedi* **affliggere**
afflosci'arsi [affloʃ'ʃarsi] *vpr* to go limp
afflu'ente *sm* tributary
affo'gare *vt, vi* to drown
affol'lare *vt* to crowd; **affollarsi** *vpr* to crowd; **affol'lato, -a** *ag* crowded
affon'dare *vt* to sink
affran'care *vt* to free, liberate; (*Amm*) to redeem; (*lettera*) to stamp; (: *meccanicamente*) to frank (BRIT), meter (US)
af'fresco, -schi *sm* fresco
affrettarsi *vpr* to hurry; **~ a fare qc** to hurry *o* hasten to do sth
affret'tato, -a *ag* (*veloce: passo, ritmo*) quick, fast; (*frettoloso: decisione*) hurried, hasty; (: *lavoro*) rushed
affron'tare *vt* (*pericolo ecc*) to face; (*nemico*) to confront; **affrontarsi** *vpr* (*reciproco*) to come to blows
affumi'cato, -a *ag* (*prosciutto, aringa ecc*) smoked
affuso'lato, -a *ag* tapering
Af'ganistan *sm* **l'~** Afghanistan
a'foso, -a *ag* sultry, close
'Africa *sf* **l'~** Africa; **afri'cano, -a** *ag, sm/f* African
a'genda [a'dʒɛnda] *sf* diary

> Attenzione! In inglese esiste la parola *agenda* che però vuol dire *ordine del giorno*.

a'gente [a'dʒɛnte] *sm* agent; **agente di cambio** stockbroker; **agente di polizia** police officer; **agente segreto** secret agent; **agen'zia** *sf* agency; (*succursale*) branch; **agenzia immobiliare** estate agent's (office) (BRIT), real estate office (US); **agenzia di collocamento/stampa** employment/press agency; **agenzia viaggi** travel agency

agevo'lare [adʒevo'lare] *vt* to facilitate, make easy
agevolazi'one [adʒevolat'tsjone] *sf* (*facilitazione economica*) facility; **agevolazione di pagamento** payment on easy terms; **agevolazioni creditizie** credit facilities; **agevolazioni fiscali** tax concessions
a'gevole [a'dʒevole] *ag* easy; (*strada*) smooth
agganci'are [aggan'tʃare] *vt* to hook up; (*Ferr*) to couple
ag'geggio [ad'dʒeddʒo] *sm* gadget, contraption
agget'tivo [addʒet'tivo] *sm* adjective
agghiacci'ante [aggjat'tʃante] *ag* chilling
aggior'nare [addʒor'nare] *vt* (*opera, manuale*) to bring up-to-date; (*seduta ecc*) to postpone; **aggiornarsi** *vpr* to bring (*o* keep) o.s. up-to-date; **aggior'nato, -a** *ag* up-to-date
aggi'rare [addʒi'rare] *vt* to go round; (*fig*: *ingannare*) to trick; **aggirarsi** *vpr* to wander about; **il prezzo s'aggira sul milione** the price is around the million mark
aggi'ungere [ad'dʒundʒere] *vt* to add
aggi'unsi *ecc* [ad'dʒunsi] *vb vedi* **aggiungere**
aggius'tare [addʒus'tare] *vt* (*accomodare*) to mend, repair; (*riassettare*) to adjust; (*fig*: *lite*) to settle
aggrap'parsi *vpr* **~ a** to cling to
aggra'vare *vt* (*aumentare*) to increase; (*appesantire*: *anche fig*) to weigh down, make heavy; (*pena*) to make worse; **aggravarsi** *vpr* to worsen, become worse
aggre'dire *vt* to attack, assault
aggressi'one *sf* aggression; (*atto*) attack, assault
aggres'sivo, -a *ag* aggressive
aggres'sore *sm* aggressor, attacker
aggrot'tare *vt*: **~ le sopracciglia** to frown
aggrovigliarsi *vpr* (*fig*) to become complicated
aggu'ato *sm* trap; (*imboscata*) ambush; **tendere un ~ a qn** to set a trap for sb
agguer'rito, -a *ag* fierce
agi'ato, -a [a'dʒato] *ag* (*vita*) easy; (*persona*) well-off, well-to-do
'agile ['adʒile] *ag* agile, nimble
'agio ['adʒo] *sm* ease, comfort; **mettersi a proprio ~** to make o.s. at home *o* comfortable; **agi** *smpl* comforts; **mettersi a proprio ~** to make o.s. at home *o* comfortable; **dare ~ a qn di fare qc** to give sb the chance of doing sth
a'gire [a'dʒire] *vi* to act; (*esercitare un'azione*) to take effect; (*Tecn*) to work, function; **~ contro qn** (*Dir*) to take action against sb
agi'tare [adʒi'tare] *vt* (*bottiglia*) to shake; (*mano, fazzoletto*) to wave; (*fig*: *turbare*) to disturb; (: *incitare*) to stir (up); (: *dibattere*) to discuss; **agitarsi** *vpr* (*mare*) to be rough; (*malato, dormitore*) to toss and turn; (*bambino*) to fidget; (*emozionarsi*) to get upset; (*Pol*) to agitate; **agi'tato, -a** *ag* rough; restless; fidgety; upset, perturbed
'aglio ['aʎʎo] *sm* garlic
a'gnello [aɲ'ɲɛllo] *sm* lamb
'ago (*pl* **'aghi**) *sm* needle
ago'nistico, -a, -ci, -che *ag* athletic; (*fig*) competitive
agopun'tura *sf* acupuncture
a'gosto *sm* August
a'grario, -a *ag* agrarian, agricultural; (*riforma*) land *cpd*
a'gricolo, -a *ag* agricultural, farm *cpd*; **agricol'tore** *sm* farmer; **agricol'tura** *sf* agriculture, farming
agri'foglio [agri'fɔʎʎo] *sm* holly
agritu'rismo *sm* farm holidays *pl*
agrodolce *ag* bittersweet; (*salsa*) sweet and sour

a'grume *sm* (*spesso al pl: pianta*) citrus; (*: frutto*) citrus fruit
a'guzzo, -a [a'guttso] *ag* sharp
'ahi *escl* (*dolore*) ouch!
'Aia *sf* **l'~** the Hague
'aids *abbr m o f* Aids
airbag *sm inv* air bag
ai'rone *sm* heron
aiu'ola *sf* flower bed
aiu'tante *sm/f* assistant ▷ *sm* (*Mil*) adjutant; (*Naut*) master-at-arms; **aiutante di campo** aide-de-camp
aiu'tare *vt* to help; **~ qn (a fare)** to help sb (to do); **aiutarsi** *vpr* to help each other; **~ qn in qc/a fare qc** to help sb with sth/to do sth; **può aiutarmi?** can you help me?
ai'uto *sm* help, assistance, aid; (*aiutante*) assistant; **venire in ~ di qn** to come to sb's aid; **aiuto chirurgo** assistant surgeon
'ala (*pl* **'ali**) *sf* wing; **fare ~** to fall back, make way; **ala destra/sinistra** (*Sport*) right/left wing
ala'bastro *sm* alabaster
a'lano *sm* Great Dane
'alba *sf* dawn
alba'nese *ag, sm/f, sm* Albanian
Alba'nia *sf* **l'~** Albania
albe'rato, -a *ag* (*viale, piazza*) lined with trees, tree-lined
al'bergo, -ghi *sm* hotel; **albergo della gioventù** youth hostel
'albero *sm* tree; (*Naut*) mast; (*Tecn*) shaft; **albero genealogico** family tree; **albero a gomiti** crankshaft; **albero maestro** mainmast; **albero di Natale** Christmas tree; **albero di trasmissione** transmission shaft
albi'cocca, -che *sf* apricot
'album *sm* album; **album da disegno** sketch book
al'bume *sm* albumen
'alce ['altʃe] *sm* elk
'alcol *sm inv* = **alcool**
al'colico, -a, -ci, -che *ag* alcoholic ▷ *sm* alcoholic drink
alcoliz'zato, -a [alcolid'dzato] *sm/f* alcoholic
'alcool *sm inv* alcohol
al'cuno, -a (*det: dav sm:* **alcun** + *C, V,* **alcuno** + *s impura, gn, pn, ps, x, z; dav sf:* **alcuna** + *C,* **alcun'** + *V*) *det* (*nessuno*): **non ... ~** no, not any; **alcuni, e** *det pl* some, a few; **non c'è alcuna fretta** there's no hurry, there isn't any hurry; **senza alcun riguardo** without any consideration ▷ *pron pl* **alcuni, e** some, a few
alfa'betico, -a, ci, che *ag* alphabetical
alfa'beto *sm* alphabet
'alga, -ghe *sf* seaweed *no pl*, alga
'algebra ['aldʒebra] *sf* algebra
Alge'ria [aldʒe'ria] *sf* **l'~** Algeria
alge'rino, -a [aldʒe'rino] *ag, sm/f* Algerian
ali'ante *sm* (*Aer*) glider
'alibi *sm inv* alibi
a'lice [a'litʃe] *sf* anchovy
ali'eno, -a *ag* (*avverso*): **~ (da)** opposed (to), averse (to) ▷ *sm/f* alien
alimen'tare *vt* to feed; (*Tecn*) to feed; to supply; (*fig*) to sustain ▷ *ag* food *cpd*; **alimentari** *smpl* foodstuffs; (*anche:* **negozio di alimentari**) grocer's shop; **alimentazi'one** *sf* feeding; supplying; sustaining; (*gli alimenti*) diet
a'liquota *sf* share; (*d'imposta*) rate; **aliquota d'imposta** tax rate
alis'cafo *sm* hydrofoil
'alito *sm* breath
all. *abbr* (*= allegato*) encl.
allaccia'mento [allattʃa'mento] *sm* (*Tecn*) connection
allacci'are [allat'tʃare] *vt* (*scarpe*) to tie, lace (up); (*cintura*) to do up, fasten; (*luce, gas*) to connect; (*amicizia*) to form
allaccia'tura [allattʃa'tura] *sf* fastening
alla'gare *vt* to flood; **allagarsi** *vpr* to flood

allar'gare *vt* to widen; (*vestito*) to let out; (*aprire*) to open; (*fig*: *dilatare*) to extend; **allargarsi** *vpr* (*gen*) to widen; (*scarpe, pantaloni*) to stretch; (*fig*: *problema, fenomeno*) to spread
allar'mare *vt* to alarm
al'larme *sm* alarm; **allarme aereo** air-raid warning
allat'tare *vt* to feed
alle'anza [alle'antsa] *sf* alliance
alle'arsi *vpr* to form an alliance; **alle'ato, -a** *ag* allied ▷ *sm/f* ally
alle'gare *vt* (*accludere*) to enclose; (*Dir*: *citare*) to cite, adduce; (*denti*) to set on edge; **alle'gato, -a** *ag* enclosed ▷ *sm* enclosure; (*di e-mail*) attachment; **in allegato** enclosed
allegge'rire [alleddʒe'rire] *vt* to lighten, make lighter; (*fig*: *lavoro, tasse*) to reduce
alle'gria *sf* gaiety, cheerfulness
al'legro, -a *ag* cheerful, merry; (*un po' brillo*) merry, tipsy; (*vivace*: *colore*) bright ▷ *sm* (*Mus*) allegro
allena'mento *sm* training
alle'nare *vt* to train; **allenarsi** *vpr* to train; **allena'tore** *sm* (*Sport*) trainer, coach
allen'tare *vt* to slacken; (*disciplina*) to relax; **allentarsi** *vpr* to become slack; (*ingranaggio*) to work loose
aller'gia, -'gie [aller'dʒia] *sf* allergy; **al'lergico, -a, -ci, -che** *ag* allergic; **sono allergico alla penicillina** I'm allergic to penicillin
alles'tire *vt* (*cena*) to prepare; (*esercito, nave*) to equip, fit out; (*spettacolo*) to stage
allet'tante *ag* attractive, alluring
alle'vare *vt* (*animale*) to breed, rear; (*bambino*) to bring up
allevi'are *vt* to alleviate
alli'bito, -a *ag* astounded
alli'evo *sm* pupil; (*apprendista*) apprentice; (*Mil*) cadet
alliga'tore *sm* alligator
alline'are *vt* (*persone, cose*) to line up; (*Tip*) to align; (*fig*: *economia, salari*) to adjust, align; **allinearsi** *vpr* to line up; (*fig*: *a idee*): **allinearsi a** to come into line with
al'lodola *sf* (sky)lark
alloggi'are [allod'dʒare] *vt* to accommodate ▷ *vi* to live; **al'loggio** *sm* lodging, accommodation (BRIT), accommodations (US)
allonta'nare *vt* to send away, send off; (*impiegato*) to dismiss; (*pericolo*) to avert, remove; (*estraniare*) to alienate; **allontanarsi** *vpr* **allontanarsi (da)** to go away (from); (*estraniarsi*) to become estranged (from)
al'lora *av* (*in quel momento*) then ▷ *cong* (*in questo caso*) well then; (*dunque*) well then, so; **la gente d'~** people then *o* in those days; **da ~ in poi** from then on
al'loro *sm* laurel
'alluce ['allutʃe] *sm* big toe
alluci'nante [allutʃi'nante] *ag* awful; (*fam*) amazing
allucinazi'one [allutʃinat'tsjone] *sf* hallucination
al'ludere *vi*: **~ a** to allude to, hint at
allu'minio *sm* aluminium (BRIT), aluminum (US)
allun'gare *vt* to lengthen; (*distendere*) to prolong, extend; (*diluire*) to water down; **allungarsi** *vpr* to lengthen; (*ragazzo*) to stretch, grow taller; (*sdraiarsi*) to lie down, stretch out
al'lusi *ecc vb vedi* **alludere**
allusi'one *sf* hint, allusion
alluvi'one *sf* flood
al'meno *av* at least ▷ *cong* **(se) ~** if only; **(se) ~ piovesse!** if only it would rain!
a'logeno, -a [a'lɔdʒeno] *ag* **lampada alogena** halogen lamp
a'lone *sm* halo
'Alpi *sfpl* **le ~** the Alps
alpi'nismo *sm* mountaineering, climbing; **alpi'nista, -i, -e** *sm/f*

mountaineer, climber
al'pino, -a *ag* Alpine; mountain *cpd*; **alpini** *smpl* (*Mil*) Italian Alpine troops
alt *escl* halt!, stop!
alta'lena *sf* (*a funi*) swing; (*in bilico*) seesaw
al'tare *sm* altar
alter'nare *vt* to alternate; **alternarsi** *vpr* to alternate; **alterna'tiva** *sf* alternative; **alterna'tivo, -a** *ag* alternative
al'terno, -a *ag* alternate; **a giorni alterni** on alternate days, every other day
al'tero, -a *ag* proud
al'tezza [al'tettsa] *sf* height; width, breadth; depth; pitch; (*Geo*) latitude; (*titolo*) highness; (*fig: nobiltà*) greatness; **essere all'~ di** to be on a level with; (*fig*) to be up to *o* equal to
al'ticcio, -a, -ci, -ce [al'tittʃo] *ag* tipsy
alti'tudine *sf* altitude
'alto, -a *ag* high; (*persona*) tall; (*tessuto*) wide, broad; (*sonno, acque*) deep; (*suono*) high(-pitched); (*Geo*) upper; (*settentrionale*) northern ▷ *sm* top (part) ▷ *av* high; (*parlare*) aloud, loudly; **il palazzo è ~ 20 metri** the building is 20 metres high; **ad alta voce** aloud; **a notte alta** in the dead of night; **in ~** up, upwards; at the top; **dall'~ in** *o* **al basso** up and down; **degli alti e bassi** (*fig*) ups and downs; **alta definizione** (*TV*) high definition; **alta fedeltà** high fidelity, hi-fi; **alta finanza/società** high finance/ society; **alta moda** haute couture; **alta velocità** (*Ferr*) high speed rail system
altopar'lante *sm* loudspeaker
altopi'ano (*pl* **altipi'ani**) *sm* plateau, upland plain
altret'tanto, -a *ag, pron* as much; (*pl*) as many ▷ *av* equally; **tanti auguri! — grazie, ~** all the best! — thank you, the same to you
altri'menti *av* otherwise

PAROLA CHIAVE

'altro, -a *det* **1** (*diverso*) other, different; **questa è un'altra cosa** that's another *o* a different thing
2 (*supplementare*) other; **prendi un altro cioccolatino** have another chocolate; **hai avuto altre notizie?** have you had any more *o* any other news?
3 (*nel tempo*): **l'altro giorno** the other day; **l'altr'anno** last year; **l'altro ieri** the day before yesterday; **domani l'altro** the day after tomorrow; **quest'altro mese** next month
4: **d'altra parte** on the other hand
▷ *pron* **1** (*persona, cosa diversa o supplementare*): **un altro, un'altra** another (one); **lo farà un altro** someone else will do it; **altri, e** others; **gli altri** (*la gente*) others, other people; **l'uno e l'altro** both (of them); **aiutarsi l'un l'altro** to help one another; **da un giorno all'altro** from day to day; (*nel giro di 24 ore*) from one day to the next; (*da un momento all'altro*) any day now
2 (*sostantivato: solo maschile*) something else; (: *in espressioni interrogative*) anything else; **non ho altro da dire** I have nothing else *o* I don't have anything else to say; **più che altro** above all; **se non altro** at least; **tra l'altro** among other things; **ci mancherebbe altro!** that's all we need!; **non faccio altro che lavorare** I do nothing but work; **contento? — altro che!** are you pleased? — and how!; *vedi* **senza**; **noialtri**; **voialtri**; **tutto**

al'trove *av* elsewhere, somewhere else
altru'ista, -i, -e *ag* altruistic
a'lunno, -a *sm/f* pupil

alve'are *sm* hive
al'zare [al'tsare] *vt* to raise, lift; (*issare*) to hoist; (*costruire*) to build, erect; **alzarsi** *vpr* to rise; (*dal letto*) to get up; (*crescere*) to grow tall (*o* taller); **~ le spalle** to shrug one's shoulders; **alzarsi in piedi** to stand up, get to one's feet
a'maca, -che *sf* hammock
amalga'mare *vt* to amalgamate; **amalgamarsi** *vpr* to amalgamate
a'mante *ag*: **~ di** (*musica ecc*) fond of ▷ *sm/f* lover/mistress
a'mare *vt* to love; (*amico, musica, sport*) to like; **amarsi** *vpr* to love each other
amareggi'ato, -a [amared'dʒato] *ag* upset, saddened
ama'rena *sf* sour black cherry
ama'rezza [ama'rettsa] *sf* bitterness
a'maro, -a *ag* bitter ▷ *sm* bitterness; (*liquore*) bitters *pl*
amaz'zonico, -a, ci, che [amad'dzɔniko] *ag* Amazonian; Amazon *cpd*
ambasci'ata [ambaʃ'ʃata] *sf* embassy; (*messaggio*) message; **ambascia'tore, -'trice** *sm/f* ambassador/ambassadress
ambe'due *ag inv*: **~ i ragazzi** both boys ▷ *pron inv* both
ambienta'lista, -i, e *ag* environmental ▷ *sm/f* environmentalist
ambien'tare *vt* to acclimatize; (*romanzo, film*) to set; **ambientarsi** *vpr* to get used to one's surroundings
ambi'ente *sm* environment; (*fig: insieme di persone*) milieu; (*stanza*) room
am'biguo, -a *ag* ambiguous
ambizi'one [ambit'tsjone] *sf* ambition; **ambizi'oso, -a** *ag* ambitious
'ambo *ag inv* both ▷ *sm* (*al gioco*) double
'ambra *sf* amber; **ambra grigia** ambergris
ambu'lante *ag* itinerant ▷ *sm* peddler
ambu'lanza [ambu'lantsa] *sf* ambulance; **chiamate un ~** call an ambulance
ambula'torio *sm* (*studio medico*) surgery
A'merica *sf* **l'~** America; **l'~ latina** Latin America; **ameri'cano, -a** *ag, sm/f* American
ami'anto *sm* asbestos
ami'chevole [ami'kevole] *ag* friendly
ami'cizia [ami'tʃittsja] *sf* friendship; **amicizie** *sfpl* (*amici*) friends
a'mico, -a, -ci, -che *sm/f* friend; (*fidanzato*) boyfriend/girlfriend; **amico del cuore** bosom friend
'amido *sm* starch
ammac'care *vt* (*pentola*) to dent; (*persona*) to bruise
ammacca'tura *sf* dent; bruise
ammaes'trare *vt* (*animale*) to train
ammai'nare *vt* to lower, haul down
amma'larsi *vpr* to fall ill; **amma'lato, -a** *ag* ill, sick ▷ *sm/f* sick person; (*paziente*) patient
ammanet'tare *vt* to handcuff
ammas'sare *vt* (*ammucchiare*) to amass; (*raccogliere*) to gather together; **ammassarsi** *vpr* to pile up; to gather
ammat'tire *vi* to go mad
ammaz'zare [ammat'tsare] *vt* to kill; **ammazzarsi** *vpr* (*uccidersi*) to kill o.s.; (*rimanere ucciso*) to be killed; **ammazzarsi di lavoro** to work o.s. to death
am'mettere *vt* to admit; (*riconoscere: fatto*) to acknowledge, admit; (*permettere*) to allow, accept; (*supporre*) to suppose
amminis'trare *vt* to run, manage; (*Rel, Dir*) to administer; **amministra'tore** *sm* administrator; (*di condominio*) flats manager; **amministratore**

delegato managing director; **amministrazi'one** *sf* management; administration
ammi'raglio [ammi'raʎʎo] *sm* admiral
ammi'rare *vt* to admire; **ammirazi'one** *sf* admiration
am'misi *ecc vb vedi* **ammettere**
ammobili'ato, -a *ag* furnished
am'mollo *sm*: **lasciare in ~** to leave to soak
ammo'niaca *sf* ammonia
ammo'nire *vt* (*avvertire*) to warn; (*rimproverare*) to admonish; (*Dir*) to caution
ammonizi'one [ammonit'tsjone] *sf* (*monito: anche Sport*) warning; (*rimprovero*) reprimand; (*Dir*) caution
ammon'tare *vi*: **~ a** to amount to ▷ *sm* (total) amount
ammorbi'dente *sm* fabric conditioner
ammorbi'dire *vt* to soften
ammortizza'tore *sm* (*Aut, Tecn*) shock-absorber
ammucchi'are [ammuk'kjare] *vt* to pile up, accumulate
ammuf'fire *vi* to go mouldy (BRIT) *o* moldy (US)
ammuto'lire *vi* to be struck dumb
amne'sia *sf* amnesia
amnis'tia *sf* amnesty
'amo *sm* (*Pesca*) hook; (*fig*) bait
a'more *sm* love; **amori** *smpl* love affairs; **il tuo bambino è un ~** your baby's a darling; **fare l'~** *o* **all'~** to make love; **per ~ o per forza** by hook or by crook; **amor proprio** self-esteem, pride
amo'roso, -a *ag* (*affettuoso*) loving, affectionate; (*d'amore: sguardo*) amorous; (*: poesia, relazione*) love *cpd*
'ampio, -a *ag* wide, broad; (*spazioso*) spacious; (*abbondante: vestito*) loose; (*: gonna*) full; (*: spiegazione*) ample, full
am'plesso *sm* intercourse
ampli'are *vt* (*ingrandire*) to enlarge; (*allargare*) to widen; **ampliarsi** *vpr* to grow, increase
amplifica'tore *sm* (*Tecn, Mus*) amplifier
ampu'tare *vt* (*Med*) to amputate
A.N. *sigla f* (= *Alleanza Nazionale*) *Italian right-wing party*
anabbaglianti *smpl* dipped (BRIT) *o* dimmed (US) headlights
anaboliz'zante *ag* anabolic ▷ *sm* anabolic steroid
anal'colico, -a, -ci, -che *ag* non-alcoholic ▷ *sm* soft drink
analfa'beta, -i, -e *ag, sm/f* illiterate
anal'gesico, -a, -ci, -che [anal'dʒɛziko] *ag, sm* analgesic
a'nalisi *sf inv* analysis; (*Med: esame*) test; **analisi del sangue** blood test *sg*
analiz'zare [analid'dzare] *vt* to analyse; (*Med*) to test
a'nalogo, -a, -ghi, -ghe *ag* analogous
'ananas *sm inv* pineapple
anar'chia [anar'kia] *sf* anarchy; **a'narchico, -a, -ci, -che** *ag* anarchic(al) ▷ *sm/f* anarchist
anarco-insurreziona'lista *ag* anarcho-revolutionary
'A.N.A.S. *sigla f* (= *Azienda Nazionale Autonoma delle Strade*) national roads department
anato'mia *sf* anatomy
'anatra *sf* duck
'anca, -che *sf* (*Anat*) hip
'anche ['anke] *cong* (*inoltre, pure*) also, too; (*perfino*) even; **vengo anch'io** I'm coming too; **~ se** even if
an'cora *av* still; (*di nuovo*) again; (*di più*) some more; (*persino*): **~ più forte** even stronger; **non ~** not yet; **~ una volta** once more, once again; **~ un po'** a little more; (*di tempo*) a little longer
an'dare *sm*: **a lungo ~** in the long run ▷ *vi* to go; (*essere adatto*): **~ a** to suit; (*piacere*): **il suo comportamento non mi va** I don't like the way he behaves; **ti va di ~ al cinema?** do you feel like

going to the cinema?; **andarsene** to go away; **questa camicia va lavata** this shirt needs a wash *o* should be washed; **~ a cavallo** to ride; **~ in macchina/aereo** to go by car/plane; **~ a fare qc** to go and do sth; **~ a pescare/sciare** to go fishing/skiing; **~ a male** to go bad; **come va?** (*lavoro, progetto*) how are things?; **come va? — bene, grazie!** how are you? — fine, thanks!; **va fatto entro oggi** it's got to be done today; **ne va della nostra vita** our lives are at stake; **an'data** *sf* going; (*viaggio*) outward journey; **biglietto di sola andata** single (BRIT) *o* one-way ticket; **biglietto di andata e ritorno** return (BRIT) *o* round-trip (US) ticket

andrò *ecc vb vedi* **andare**

a'neddoto *sm* anecdote

a'nello *sm* ring; (*di catena*) link; **anelli** *smpl* (*Ginnastica*) rings

a'nemico, -a, -ci, -che *ag* anaemic

aneste'sia *sf* anaesthesia

'angelo ['andʒelo] *sm* angel; **angelo custode** guardian angel

anghe'ria [ange'ria] *sf* vexation

angli'cano, -a *ag* Anglican

anglo'sassone *ag* Anglo-Saxon

'angolo *sm* corner; (*Mat*) angle; **angolo cottura** (*di appartamento ecc*) cooking area

an'goscia, -sce [an'gɔʃʃa] *sf* deep anxiety, anguish *no pl*

angu'illa *sf* eel

an'guria *sf* watermelon

'anice ['anitʃe] *sm* (*Cuc*) aniseed; (*Bot*) anise

'anima *sf* soul; (*abitante*) inhabitant; **non c'era ~ viva** there wasn't a living soul; **anima gemella** soul mate

ani'male *sm, ag* animal; **animale domestico** pet

anna'cquare *vt* to water down, dilute

annaffi'are *vt* to water; **annaffia'toio** *sm* watering can

an'nata *sf* year; (*importo annuo*) annual amount; **vino d'~** vintage wine

anne'gare *vt, vi* to drown

anne'rire *vt* to blacken ▷ *vi* to become black

annien'tare *vt* to annihilate, destroy

anniver'sario *sm* anniversary; **anniversario di matrimonio** wedding anniversary

'anno *sm* year; **ha 8 anni** he's 8 (years old)

anno'dare *vt* to knot, tie; (*fig: rapporto*) to form

annoi'are *vt* to bore; **annoiarsi** *vpr* to be bored

> Attenzione! In inglese esiste il verbo *to annoy* che però vuol dire *dare fastidio a*.

anno'tare *vt* (*registrare*) to note, note down; (*commentare*) to annotate

annu'ale *ag* annual

annu'ire *vi* to nod; (*acconsentire*) to agree

annul'lare *vt* to annihilate, destroy; (*contratto, francobollo*) to cancel; (*matrimonio*) to annul; (*sentenza*) to quash; (*risultati*) to declare void

annunci'are [annun'tʃare] *vt* to announce; (*dar segni rivelatori*) to herald

an'nuncio [an'nuntʃo] *sm* announcement; (*fig*) sign; **annunci economici** classified advertisements, small ads; **annunci mortuari** (*colonna*) obituary column; **annuncio pubblicitario** advertisement

'annuo, -a *ag* annual, yearly

annu'sare *vt* to sniff, smell; **~ tabacco** to take snuff

a'nomalo, -a *ag* anomalous

a'nonimo, -a *ag* anonymous ▷ *sm* (*autore*) anonymous writer (*o* painter *ecc*); **società anonima** (*Comm*) joint stock company

anores'sia *sf* anorexia

ano'ressico, -a, ci, che *ag* anorexic

anor'male *ag* abnormal ▷ *sm/f* subnormal person
ANSA *sigla f* (= *Agenzia Nazionale Stampa Associata*) *press agency*
'ansia *sf* anxiety
ansi'mare *vi* to pant
ansi'oso, -a *ag* anxious
'anta *sf* (*di finestra*) shutter; (*di armadio*) door
An'tartide *sf*: **l'~** Antarctica
an'tenna *sf* (*Radio, TV*) aerial; (*Zool*) antenna, feeler; (*Naut*) yard; **antenna parabolica** satellite dish
ante'prima *sf* preview; **anteprima di stampa** (*Inform*) print preview
anteri'ore *ag* (*ruota, zampa*) front; (*fatti*) previous, preceding
antiade'rente *ag* non-stick
antibi'otico, -a, -ci, -che *ag, sm* antibiotic
anti'camera *sf* anteroom; **fare ~** to wait (for an audience)
antici'pare [antitʃi'pare] *vt* (*consegna, visita*) to bring forward, anticipate; (*somma di denaro*) to pay in advance; (*notizia*) to disclose ▷ *vi* to be ahead of time; **an'ticipo** *sm* anticipation; (*di denaro*) advance; **in anticipo** early, in advance; **occorre che prenoti in anticipo?** do I need to book in advance?
an'tico, -a, -chi, -che *ag* (*quadro, mobili*) antique; (*dell'antichità*) ancient; **all'antica** old-fashioned
anticoncezio'nale [antikontʃettsjo'nale] *sm* contraceptive
anticonfor'mista, -i, -e *ag, sm/f* nonconformist
anti'corpo *sm* antibody
antidolo'rifico, -ci *sm* painkiller
anti'doping *sm* drug testing ▷ *ag inv* **test ~** drugs (BRIT) *o* drug (US) test
an'tifona *sf* (*Mus, Rel*) antiphon; **capire l'~** (*fig*) to take the hint
anti'forfora *ag inv* anti-dandruff
anti'furto *sm* anti-theft device
anti'gelo [anti'dʒɛlo] *ag inv* **(liquido) ~** (*per motore*) antifreeze; (*per cristalli*) de-icer
antiglobalizzazione [antiglobaliddzat'tsjone] *ag inv* **movimento ~** anti-globalization movement
An'tille *sfpl*: **le ~** the West Indies
antin'cendio [antin'tʃɛndjo] *ag inv* fire *cpd*
anti'nebbia *sm inv* (*anche*: **faro ~**: *Aut*) fog lamp
antinfiamma'torio, -a *ag, sm* anti-inflammatory
antio'rario [antio'rarjo] *ag*: **in senso ~** anticlockwise
anti'pasto *sm* hors d'œuvre
antipa'tia *sf* antipathy, dislike; **anti'patico, -a, -ci, -che** *ag* unpleasant, disagreeable
antiproi'ettile *ag inv* bulletproof
antiquari'ato *sm* antique trade; **un oggetto d'~** an antique
anti'quario *sm* antique dealer
anti'quato, -a *ag* antiquated, old-fashioned
anti'rughe *ag inv* (*crema, prodotto*) anti-wrinkle
antitraspi'rante *ag* antiperspirant
anti'vipera *ag inv*: **siero ~** remedy for snake bites
antivirus [anti'virus] *sm inv* antivirus software *no pl* ▷ *ag inv* antivirus
antolo'gia, -'gie [antolo'dʒia] *sf* anthology
anu'lare *ag* ring *cpd* ▷ *sm* third finger
'anzi ['antsi] *av* (*invece*) on the contrary; (*o meglio*) or rather, or better still
anzi'ano, -a [an'tsjano] *ag* old; (*Amm*) senior ▷ *sm/f* old person; senior member
anziché [antsi'ke] *cong* rather than
a'patico, -a, -ci, -che *ag* apathetic
'ape *sf* bee
aperi'tivo *sm* apéritif
aperta'mente *av* openly
a'perto, -a *pp di* **aprire** ▷ *ag* open;

all'~ in the open (air); **è ~ al pubblico?** is it open to the public?; **quando è ~ il museo?** when is the museum open?
aper'tura *sf* opening; (*ampiezza*) width; (*Fot*) aperture; **apertura alare** wing span; **apertura mentale** open-mindedness
ap'nea *sf*: **immergersi in ~** to dive without breathing apparatus
a'postrofo *sm* apostrophe
ap'paio *ecc vb vedi* **apparire**
ap'palto *sm* (*Comm*) contract; **dare/prendere in ~ un lavoro** to let out/undertake a job on contract
appannarsi *vpr* to mist over; to grow dim
apparecchi'are [apparek'kjare] *vt* to prepare; (*tavola*) to set ▷ *vi* to set the table
appa'recchio [appa'rekkjo] *sm* piece of apparatus, device; (*aeroplano*) aircraft *inv*; **apparecchio acustico** hearing aid; **apparecchio telefonico** telephone; **apparecchio televisivo** television set
appa'rente *ag* apparent
appa'rire *vi* to appear; (*sembrare*) to seem, appear
apparta'mento *sm* flat (BRIT), apartment (US)
appar'tarsi *vpr* to withdraw
apparte'nere *vi* **~ a** to belong to
ap'parvi *ecc vb vedi* **apparire**
appassio'nare *vt* to thrill; (*commuovere*) to move; **appassionarsi** *vpr* **appassionarsi a qc** to take a great interest in sth; **appassio'nato, -a** *ag* passionate; (*entusiasta*): **appassionato (di)** keen (on)
appas'sire *vi* to wither
appas'sito, -a *ag* dead
ap'pello *sm* roll-call; (*implorazione, Dir*) appeal; **fare ~ a** to appeal to
ap'pena *av* (*a stento*) hardly, scarcely; (*solamente, da poco*) just ▷ *cong* as soon as; **(non) ~ furono arrivati ...** as soon as they had arrived ...; **~ ... che** *o* **quando** no sooner ... than
ap'pendere *vt* to hang (up)
appen'dice [appen'ditʃe] *sf* appendix; **romanzo d'~** popular serial
appendi'cite [appendi'tʃite] *sf* appendicitis
Appen'nini *smpl*: **gli ~** the Apennines
appesan'tire *vt* to make heavy; **appesantirsi** *vpr* to grow stout
appe'tito *sm* appetite
appic'care *vt*: **~ il fuoco a** to set fire to, set on fire
appicci'care [appittʃi'kare] *vt* to stick; **appiccicarsi** *vpr* to stick; (*fig*: *persona*) to cling
appiso'larsi *vpr* to doze off
applau'dire *vt, vi* to applaud; **ap'plauso** *sm* applause
appli'care *vt* to apply; (*regolamento*) to enforce; **applicarsi** *vpr* to apply o.s.
appoggi'are [appod'dʒare] *vt* (*mettere contro*): **~ qc a qc** to lean *o* rest sth against sth; (*fig*: *sostenere*) to support; **appoggiarsi** *vpr* **appoggiarsi a** to lean against; (*fig*) to rely upon; **ap'poggio** *sm* support
apposita'mente *av* specially; (*apposta*) on purpose
ap'posito, -a *ag* appropriate
ap'posta *av* on purpose, deliberately
appos'tarsi *vpr* to lie in wait
ap'prendere *vt* (*imparare*) to learn
appren'dista, -i, -e *sm/f* apprentice
apprensi'one *sf* apprehension
apprez'zare [appret'tsare] *vt* to appreciate
appro'dare *vi* (*Naut*) to land; (*fig*): **non ~ a nulla** to come to nothing
approfit'tare *vi* **~ di** to make the most of; (*peg*) to take advantage of
approfon'dire *vt* to deepen; (*fig*) to study in depth
appropri'ato, -a *ag* appropriate
approssima'tivo, -a *ag* approximate, rough; (*impreciso*) inexact, imprecise

appro'vare *vt* (*condotta, azione*) to approve of; (*candidato*) to pass; (*progetto di legge*) to approve
appunta'mento *sm* appointment; (*amoroso*) date; **darsi ~** to arrange to meet (one another); **ho un ~ con...** I have an appointment with ...; **vorrei prendere un ~** I'd like to make an appointment
ap'punto *sm* note; (*rimprovero*) reproach ▷ *av* (*proprio*) exactly, just; **per l'~!, ~!** exactly!
apribot'tiglie [apribot'tiʎʎe] *sm inv* bottle opener
a'prile *sm* April
a'prire *vt* to open; (*via, cadavere*) to open up; (*gas, luce, acqua*) to turn on ▷ *vi* to open; **aprirsi** *vpr* to open; **aprirsi a qn** to confide in sb, open one's heart to sb; **a che ora aprite?** what time do you open?
apris'catole *sm inv* tin (BRIT) *o* can opener
APT *sigla f* (= *Azienda di Promozione*) ≈ tourist board
aquagym [akkwa'dʒim] *sf* aquaerobics
'aquila *sf* (*Zool*) eagle; (*fig*) genius
aqui'lone *sm* (*giocattolo*) kite; (*vento*) North wind
A/R *abbr* = **andata e ritorno** (*biglietto*) return ticket (BRIT), round-trip ticket (US)
A'rabia Sau'dita *sf* **l'~** Saudi Arabia
'arabo, -a *ag, sm/f* Arab ▷ *sm* (*Ling*) Arabic
a'rachide [a'rakide] *sf* peanut
ara'gosta *sf* crayfish; lobster
a'rancia, -ce [a'rantʃa] *sf* orange; **aranci'ata** *sf* orangeade; **aranci'one** *ag inv* **(color) arancione** bright orange
a'rare *vt* to plough (BRIT), plow (US)
a'ratro *sm* plough (BRIT), plow (US)
a'razzo [a'rattso] *sm* tapestry
arbi'trare *vt* (*Sport*) to referee; to umpire; (*Dir*) to arbitrate
arbi'trario, -a *ag* arbitrary
'arbitro *sm* arbiter, judge; (*Dir*) arbitrator; (*Sport*) referee; (: *Tennis, Cricket*) umpire
ar'busto *sm* shrub
archeolo'gia [arkeolo'dʒia] *sf* arch(a)eology; **arche'ologo, -a, -gi, -ghe** *sm/f* arch(a)eologist
architet'tare [arkitet'tare] *vt* (*fig*: *ideare*) to devise; (: *macchinare*) to plan, concoct
archi'tetto [arki'tetto] *sm* architect; **architet'tura** *sf* architecture
ar'chivio [ar'kivjo] *sm* archives *pl*; (*Inform*) file
'arco *sm* (*arma, Mus*) bow; (*Archit*) arch; (*Mat*) arc
arcoba'leno *sm* rainbow
arcu'ato, -a *ag* curved, bent
'ardere *vt, vi* to burn
ar'desia *sf* slate
'area *sf* area; (*Edil*) land, ground; **area di rigore** (*Sport*) penalty area; **area di servizio** (*Aut*) service area
a'rena *sf* arena; (*per corride*) bullring; (*sabbia*) sand
are'narsi *vpr* to run aground
argente'ria [ardʒente'ria] *sf* silverware, silver
Argen'tina [ardʒen'tina] *sf*: **l'~** Argentina; **argen'tino, -a** *ag, sm/f* Argentinian
ar'gento [ar'dʒɛnto] *sm* silver; **argento vivo** quicksilver
ar'gilla [ar'dʒilla] *sf* clay
'argine ['ardʒine] *sm* embankment, bank; (*diga*) dyke, dike
argo'mento *sm* argument; (*motivo*) motive; (*materia, tema*) subject
'aria *sf* air; (*espressione, aspetto*) air, look; (*Mus*: *melodia*) tune; (*di opera*) aria; **mandare all'~ qc** to ruin *o* upset sth; **all'~ aperta** in the open (air)
'arido, -a *ag* arid
arieggi'are [arjed'dʒare] *vt* (*cambiare aria*) to air; (*imitare*) to imitate
ari'ete *sm* ram; (*Mil*) battering ram;

(*dello zodiaco*): **A~** Aries
a'ringa, -ghe *sf* herring *inv*
arit'metica *sf* arithmetic
'arma, -i *sf* weapon, arm; (*parte dell'esercito*) arm; **chiamare alle armi** to call up (BRIT), draft (US); **sotto le armi** in the army (*o* forces); **alle armi!** to arms!; **arma atomica/nucleare** atomic/nuclear weapon; **arma da fuoco** firearm; **armi di distruzione di massa** weapons of mass destruction
arma'dietto *sm* (*di medicinali*) medicine cabinet; (*in palestra ecc*) locker; (*in cucina*) (kitchen) cupboard
ar'madio *sm* cupboard; (*per abiti*) wardrobe; **armadio a muro** built-in cupboard
ar'mato, -a *ag*: **~ (di)** (*anche fig*) armed (with) ▷ *sf* (*Mil*) army; (*Naut*) fleet; **rapina a mano armata** armed robbery
arma'tura *sf* (*struttura di sostegno*) framework; (*impalcatura*) scaffolding; (*Storia*) armour *no pl*, suit of armour
armis'tizio [armis'tittsjo] *sm* armistice
armo'nia *sf* harmony
ar'nese *sm* tool, implement; (*oggetto indeterminato*) thing, contraption; **male in ~** (*malvestito*) badly dressed; (*di salute malferma*) in poor health; (*povero*) down-at-heel
'arnia *sf* hive
a'roma, -i *sm* aroma; fragrance; **aromi** *smpl* (*Cuc*) herbs and spices; **aromatera'pia** *sf* aromatherapy
'arpa *sf* (*Mus*) harp
arrabbi'are *vi* (*cane*) to be affected with rabies; **arrabbiarsi** *vpr* (*essere preso dall'ira*) to get angry, fly into a rage; **arrabbi'ato, -a** *ag* rabid, with rabies; furious, angry
arrampi'carsi *vpr* to climb (up)
arrangiarsi *vpr* to manage, do the best one can
arreda'mento *sm* (*studio*) interior design; (*mobili ecc*) furnishings *pl*
arre'dare *vt* to furnish
ar'rendersi *vpr* to surrender
arres'tare *vt* (*fermare*) to stop, halt; (*catturare*) to arrest; **arrestarsi** *vpr* (*fermarsi*) to stop; **ar'resto** *sm* (*cessazione*) stopping; (*fermata*) stop; (*cattura, Med*) arrest; **subire un arresto** to come to a stop *o* standstill; **mettere agli arresti** to place under arrest; **arresti domiciliari** house arrest *sg*
arre'trare *vt, vi* to withdraw; **arre'trato, -a** *ag* (*lavoro*) behind schedule; (*paese, bambino*) backward; (*numero di giornale*) back *cpd*; **arretrati** *smpl* arrears
arric'chire [arrik'kire] *vt* to enrich; **arricchirsi** *vpr* to become rich
arri'vare *vi* to arrive; (*accadere*) to happen, occur; **~ a** (*livello, grado ecc*) to reach; **a che ora arriva il treno da Londra?** what time does the train from London arrive?; **non ci arrivo** I can't reach it; (*fig*: *non capisco*) I can't understand it
arrive'derci [arrive'dertʃi] *escl* goodbye!
arri'vista, -i, -e *sm/f* go-getter
ar'rivo *sm* arrival; (*Sport*) finish, finishing line
arro'gante *ag* arrogant
arros'sire *vi* (*per vergogna, timidezza*) to blush, flush; (*per gioia, rabbia*) to flush
arros'tire *vt* to roast; (*pane*) to toast; (*ai ferri*) to grill
ar'rosto *sm, ag inv* roast
arroto'lare *vt* to roll up
arroton'dare *vt* (*forma, oggetto*) to round; (*stipendio*) to add to; (*somma*) to round off
arrugginito, -a [arruddʒin'nito] *ag* rusty
'arsi *vb vedi* **ardere**
'arte *sf* art; (*abilità*) skill
ar'teria *sf* artery; **arteria stradale** main road

'artico, -a, -ci, -che *ag* Arctic
articolazi'one *sf* articulation; (*Anat, Tecn*) joint
ar'ticolo *sm* article; **articolo di fondo** (*Stampa*) leader, leading article
artifici'ale [artifi'tʃale] *ag* artificial
artigia'nato [artidʒa'nato] *sm* craftsmanship; craftsmen *pl*
artigi'ano, -a [arti'dʒano] *sm/f* craftsman/woman
ar'tista, -i, -e *sm/f* artist; **ar'tistico, -a, -ci, -che** *ag* artistic
ar'trite *sf* (*Med*) arthritis
a'scella [aʃ'ʃɛlla] *sf* (*Anat*) armpit
ascen'dente [aʃʃen'dɛnte] *sm* ancestor; (*fig*) ascendancy; (*Astr*) ascendant
ascen'sore [aʃʃen'sore] *sm* lift
a'scesso [aʃ'ʃɛsso] *sm* (*Med*) abscess
asciugaca'pelli [aʃʃugaka'pelli] *sm* hair-drier
asciuga'mano [aʃʃuga'mano] *sm* towel
asciu'gare [aʃʃu'gare] *vt* to dry; **asciugarsi** *vpr* to dry o.s.; (*diventare asciutto*) to dry
asci'utto, -a [aʃ'ʃutto] *ag* dry; (*fig: magro*) lean; (*: burbero*) curt; **restare a bocca asciutta** (*fig*) to be disappointed
ascol'tare *vt* to listen to
as'falto *sm* asphalt
'Asia *sf* **l'~** Asia; **asi'atico, -a, -ci, -che** *ag, sm/f* Asiatic, Asian
a'silo *sm* refuge, sanctuary; **~ (d'infanzia)** nursery(-school); **asilo nido** crèche; **asilo politico** political asylum
'asino *sm* donkey, ass
ASL *sigla f* (*= Azienda Sanitaria Locale*) *local health centre*
'asma *sf* asthma
as'parago, -gi *sm* asparagus *no pl*
aspet'tare *vt* to wait for; (*anche Comm*) to await; (*aspettarsi*) to expect ▷ *vi* to wait; **aspettami, per favore** wait for me, please
as'petto *sm* (*apparenza*) aspect, appearance, look; (*punto di vista*) point of view; **di bell'~** good-looking
aspira'polvere *sm inv* vacuum cleaner
aspi'rare *vt* (*respirare*) to breathe in, inhale; (*apparecchi*) to suck (up) ▷ *vi* **~ a** to aspire to
aspi'rina *sf* aspirin
'aspro, -a *ag* (*sapore*) sour, tart; (*odore*) acrid, pungent; (*voce, clima, fig*) harsh; (*superficie*) rough; (*paesaggio*) rugged
assaggi'are [assad'dʒare] *vt* to taste; **posso assaggiarlo?** can I have a taste?; **assaggino** [assad'dʒino] *sm* **assaggini** (*Cuc*) *selection of first courses*; **solo un assaggino** just a little
as'sai *av* (*molto*) a lot, much; (*: con ag*) very; (*a sufficienza*) enough ▷ *ag inv* (*quantità*) a lot of, much; (*numero*) a lot of, many; **~ contento** very pleased
as'salgo *ecc vb vedi* **assalire**
assa'lire *vt* to attack, assail
assal'tare *vt* (*Mil*) to storm; (*banca*) to raid; (*treno, diligenza*) to hold up
as'salto *sm* attack, assault
assassi'nare *vt* to murder; to assassinate; (*fig*) to ruin; **assas'sino, -a** *ag* murderous ▷ *sm/f* murderer; assassin
'asse *sm* (*Tecn*) axle; (*Mat*) axis ▷ *sf* board; **asse** *sf* **da stiro** ironing board
assedi'are *vt* to besiege
asse'gnare [asseɲ'ɲare] *vt* to assign, allot; (*premio*) to award
as'segno [as'seɲɲo] *sm* allowance; (*anche:* **~ bancario**) cheque (BRIT), check (US); **contro ~** cash on delivery; **posso pagare con un ~?** can I pay by cheque?; **assegno circolare** bank draft; **assegni familiari** ≈ child benefit *no pl*; **assegno sbarrato** crossed cheque; **assegno di viaggio** traveller's cheque; **assegno a vuoto** dud cheque; **assegno di malattia/di invalidità** sick pay/disability benefit
assem'blea *sf* assembly

assen'tarsi *vpr* to go out
as'sente *ag* absent; (*fig*) faraway, vacant; **as'senza** *sf* absence
asse'tato, -a *ag* thirsty, parched
assicu'rare *vt* (*accertare*) to ensure; (*infondere certezza*) to assure; (*fermare, legare*) to make fast, secure; (*fare un contratto di assicurazione*) to insure; **assicurarsi** *vpr* (*accertarsi*): **assicurarsi (di)** to make sure (of); (*contro il furto ecc*): **assicurarsi (contro)** to insure o.s. (against); **assicurazi'one** *sf* assurance; insurance
assi'eme *av* (*insieme*) together; **~ a** (together) with
assil'lare *vt* to pester, torment
assis'tente *sm/f* assistant; **assistente sociale** social worker; **assistente di volo** (*Aer*) steward/stewardess
assis'tenza [assis'tɛntsa] *sf* assistance; **~ ospedaliera** free hospital treatment; **~ sociale** welfare services *pl*; **assistenza sanitaria** health service
as'sistere *vt* (*aiutare*) to assist, help; (*curare*) to treat ▷ *vi* **~ (a qc)** (*essere presente*) to be present (at sth), to attend (sth)
'asso *sm* ace; **piantare qn in ~** to leave sb in the lurch
associ'are [asso'tʃare] *vt* to associate; **associarsi** *vpr* to enter into partnership; **associarsi a** to become a member of, join; (*dolori, gioie*) to share in; **~ qn alle carceri** to take sb to prison
associazi'one [assotʃat'tsjone] *sf* association; (*Comm*) association, society; **~ a delinquere** (*Dir*) criminal association
as'solsi *ecc vb vedi* **assolvere**
assoluta'mente *av* absolutely
asso'luto, -a *ag* absolute
assoluzi'one [assolut'tsjone] *sf* (*Dir*) acquittal; (*Rel*) absolution
as'solvere *vt* (*Dir*) to acquit; (*Rel*) to absolve; (*adempiere*) to carry out, perform
assomigli'are [assomiʎ'ʎare] *vi* **~ a** to resemble, look like; **assomigliarsi** *vpr* to look alike; (*nel carattere*) to be alike
asson'nato, -a *ag* sleepy
asso'pirsi *vpr* to doze off
assor'bente *ag* absorbent ▷ *sm*: **assorbente interno** tampon; **assorbente esterno/igienico** sanitary towel
assor'bire *vt* to absorb
assor'dare *vt* to deafen
assorti'mento *sm* assortment
assor'tito, -a *ag* assorted; matched, matching
assuefazi'one [assuefat'tsjone] *sf* (*Med*) addiction
as'sumere *vt* (*impiegato*) to take on, engage; (*responsabilità*) to assume, take upon o.s.; (*contegno, espressione*) to assume, put on; (*droga*) to consume
as'sunsi *ecc vb vedi* **assumere**
assurdità *sf inv* absurdity; **dire delle ~** to talk nonsense
as'surdo, -a *ag* absurd
'asta *sf* pole; (*vendita*) auction
as'temio, -a *ag* teetotal ▷ *sm/f* teetotaller

> Attenzione! In inglese esiste la parola *abstemious* che però vuol dire *moderato*.

aste'nersi *vpr*: **~ (da)** to abstain (from), refrain (from); (*Pol*) to abstain (from)
aste'risco, -schi *sm* asterisk
'astice ['astitʃe] *sm* lobster
astig'matico, -a, ci, che *ag* astigmatic
asti'nenza [asti'nɛntsa] *sf* abstinence; **essere in crisi di ~** to suffer from withdrawal symptoms
as'tratto, -a *ag* abstract
'astro... *prefisso*; **astrolo'gia** [astrolo'dʒia] *sf* astrology;

astro'nauta, -i, -e *sm/f* astronaut; **astro'nave** *sf* space ship; **astrono'mia** *sf* astronomy; **astro'nomico, -a, -ci, -che** *ag* astronomic(al)
as'tuccio [as'tuttʃo] *sm* case, box, holder
as'tuto, -a *ag* astute, cunning, shrewd
A'tene *sf* Athens
'ateo, -a *ag, sm/f* atheist
at'lante *sm* atlas
at'lantico, -a, -ci, -che *ag* Atlantic ▷ *sm* **l'A~, l'Oceano A~** the Atlantic, the Atlantic Ocean
at'leta, -i, -e *sm/f* athlete; **at'letica** *sf* athletics *sg*; **atletica leggera** track and field events *pl*; **atletica pesante** weightlifting and wrestling
atmos'fera *sf* atmosphere
a'tomico, -a, -ci, -che *ag* atomic; (*nucleare*) atomic, atom *cpd*, nuclear
'atomo *sm* atom
'atrio *sm* entrance hall, lobby
a'troce [a'trotʃe] *ag* (*che provoca orrore*) dreadful; (*terribile*) atrocious
attac'cante *sm/f* (*Sport*) forward
attacca'panni *sm* hook, peg; (*mobile*) hall stand
attac'care *vt* (*unire*) to attach; (*cucendo*) to sew on; (*far aderire*) to stick (on); (*appendere*) to hang (up); (*assalire: anche fig*) to attack; (*iniziare*) to begin, start; (*fig: contagiare*) to pass on ▷ *vi* to stick, adhere; **attaccarsi** *vpr* to stick, adhere; (*trasmettersi per contagio*) to be contagious; (*afferrarsi*): **attaccarsi (a)** to cling (to); (*fig: affezionarsi*): **attaccarsi (a)** to become attached (to); **~ discorso** to start a conversation; **at'tacco, -chi** *sm* (*azione offensiva: anche fig*) attack; (*Med*) attack, fit; (*Sci*) binding; (*Elettr*) socket
atteggia'mento [atteddʒa'mento] *sm* attitude
at'tendere *vt* to wait for, await ▷ *vi* **~ a** to attend to
atten'dibile *ag* (*storia*) credible; (*testimone*) reliable
atten'tato *sm* attack; **~ alla vita di qn** attempt on sb's life
attenta'tore, -trice *sm/f* bomber; **attentatore suicida** suicide bomber
at'tento, -a *ag* attentive; (*accurato*) careful, thorough; **stare ~ a qc** to pay attention to sth; **~!** be careful!
attenzi'one [atten'tsjone] *sf* attention; **~!** watch out!, be careful!; **attenzioni** *sfpl* (*premure*) attentions; **fare ~ a** to watch out for; **coprire qn di attenzioni** to lavish attentions on sb
atter'raggio [atter'raddʒo] *sm* landing
atter'rare *vt* to bring down ▷ *vi* to land
at'tesa *sf* waiting; (*tempo trascorso aspettando*) wait; **essere in ~ di qc** to be waiting for sth
at'tesi *ecc vb vedi* **attendere**
at'teso, -a *pp di* **attendere**
'attico, -ci *sm* attic
attil'lato, -a *ag* (*vestito*) close-fitting
'attimo *sm* moment; **in un ~** in a moment
atti'rare *vt* to attract
atti'tudine *sf* (*disposizione*) aptitude; (*atteggiamento*) attitude
attività *sf inv* activity; (*Comm*) assets *pl*
at'tivo, -a *ag* active; (*Comm*) profit-making, credit *cpd* ▷ *sm* (*Comm*) assets *pl*; **in ~** in credit
'atto *sm* act; (*azione, gesto*) action, act, deed; (*Dir: documento*) deed, document; **atti** *smpl* (*di congressi ecc*) proceedings; **mettere in ~** to put into action; **fare ~ di fare qc** to make as if to do sth; **atto di morte/di nascita** death/birth certificate
at'tore, -'trice *sm/f* actor/actress
at'torno *av* round, around, about; **~ a** round, around, about

attrac'care *vt, vi* (*Naut*) to dock, berth
at'tracco, -chi *sm* (*Naut*) docking *no pl*; berth
at'trae *ecc vb vedi* **attrarre**
attra'ente *ag* attractive
at'traggo *ecc vb vedi* **attrarre**
at'trarre *vt* to attract
at'trassi *ecc vb vedi* **attrarre**
attraver'sare *vt* to cross; (*città, bosco, fig: periodo*) to go through; (*fiume*) to run through
attra'verso *prep* through; (*da una parte all'altra*) across
attrazi'one [attrat'tsjone] *sf* attraction
at'trezzo *sm* tool, instrument; (*Sport*) piece of equipment
at'trice [at'tritʃe] *sf vedi* **attore**
attu'ale *ag* (*presente*) present; (*di attualità*) topical

> Attenzione! In inglese esiste la parola *actual* che però vuol dire *effettivo*.

attualità *sf inv* topicality; (*avvenimento*) current event
attual'mente *av* at the moment, at present

> Attenzione! In inglese esiste la parola *actually* che però vuol dire *effettivamente* oppure *veramente*.

attu'are *vt* to carry out
attu'tire *vt* to deaden, reduce
'audio *sm* (*TV, Radio, Cine*) sound
audiovi'sivo, -a *ag* audiovisual
audizi'one [audit'tsjone] *sf* hearing; (*Mus*) audition
augu'rare *vt* to wish; **augurarsi qc** to hope for sth
au'guri *smpl* best wishes; **fare gli ~ a qn** to give sb one's best wishes; **tanti ~!** best wishes!; (*per compleanno*) happy birthday!
'aula *sf* (*scolastica*) classroom; (*universitaria*) lecture theatre; (*di edificio pubblico*) hall
aumen'tare *vt, vi* to increase; **au'mento** *sm* increase
au'rora *sf* dawn
ausili'are *ag, sm, sm/f* auxiliary
Aus'tralia *sf* **l'~** Australia; **australi'ano, -a** *ag, sm/f* Australian
'Austria *sf* **l'~** Austria; **aus'triaco, -a, -ci, -che** *ag, sm/f* Austrian
au'tentico, -a, -ci, -che *ag* authentic, genuine
au'tista, -i *sm* driver
'auto *sf inv* car
autoabbron'zante *sm, ag* self-tan
autoade'sivo, -a *ag* self-adhesive ▷ *sm* sticker
autobio'grafico, -a, ci, che *ag* autobiographic(al)
'autobus *sm inv* bus
auto'carro *sm* lorry (BRIT), truck
autocertificazi'one [autotʃertifi-kat'tsjone] *sf* self-declaration
autodistrut'tivo, -a *ag* self-destructive
auto'gol *sm inv* own goal
au'tografo, -a *ag, sm* autograph
auto'grill® *sm inv* motorway restaurant
auto'matico, -a, -ci, -che *ag* automatic ▷ *sm* (*bottone*) snap fastener; (*fucile*) automatic
auto'mobile *sf* (motor) car
automobi'lista, -i, -e *sm/f* motorist
autono'leggio *sm* car hire
autono'mia *sf* autonomy; (*di volo*) range
au'tonomo, -a *ag* autonomous, independent
autop'sia *sf* post-mortem, autopsy
auto'radio *sf inv* (*apparecchio*) car radio; (*autoveicolo*) radio car
au'tore, -'trice *sm/f* author
autoreggente [autored'dʒɛnte] *ag* **calze autoreggenti** hold ups
auto'revole *ag* authoritative; (*persona*) influential
autoricari'cabile *ag* **scheda ~** top-up card
autori'messa *sf* garage
autorità *sf inv* authority

autoriz'zare [autorid'dzare] *vt* (*permettere*) to authorize; (*giustificare*) to allow, sanction
autos'contro *sm* dodgem car (BRIT), bumper car (US)
autoscu'ola *sf* driving school
autos'tima *sf* self-esteem
autos'top *sm* hitchhiking; **autostop'pista, -i, -e** *sm/f* hitchhiker
autos'trada *sf* motorway (BRIT), highway (US); **autostrada informatica** information superhighway

AUTOSTRADE

You have to pay to use Italian motorways. They are indicated by an "A" followed by a number on a green sign. The speed limit on Italian motorways is 130 kph.

auto'velox® *sm inv* (police) speed camera
autovet'tura *sf* (motor) car
au'tunno *sm* autumn
avam'braccio [avam'brattʃo] (*pl* (*f*) **-cia**) *sm* forearm
avangu'ardia *sf* vanguard
a'vanti *av* (*stato in luogo*) in front; (*moto: andare, venire*) forward; (*tempo: prima*) before ▷ *prep* (*luogo*): **~ a** before, in front of; (*tempo*): **~ Cristo** before Christ ▷ *escl* (*entrate*) come (*o* go) in!; (*Mil*) forward!; (*coraggio*) come on! ▷ *sm inv* (*Sport*) forward; **~ e indietro** backwards and forwards; **andare ~** to go forward; (*continuare*) to go on; (*precedere*) to go (on) ahead; (*orologio*) to be fast; **essere ~ negli studi** to be well advanced with one's studies
avan'zare [avan'tsare] *vt* (*spostare in avanti*) to move forward, advance; (*domanda*) to put forward; (*promuovere*) to promote; (*essere creditore*): **~ qc da qn** to be owed sth by sb ▷ *vi* (*andare avanti*) to move forward, advance; (*progredire*) to make progress; (*essere d'avanzo*) to be left, remain
ava'ria *sf* (*guasto*) damage; (: *meccanico*) breakdown
a'varo, -a *ag* avaricious, miserly ▷ *sm* miser

PAROLA CHIAVE

a'vere *sm* (*Comm*) credit; **gli averi** (*ricchezze*) wealth *sg*
▷ *vt* 1 (*possedere*) to have; **ha due bambini/una bella casa** she has (got) two children/a lovely house; **ha i capelli lunghi** he has (got) long hair; **non ho da mangiare/bere** I've (got) nothing to eat/drink, I don't have anything to eat/drink
2 (*indossare*) to wear, have on; **aveva una maglietta rossa** he was wearing *o* he had on a red tee-shirt; **ha gli occhiali** he wears *o* has glasses
3 (*ricevere*) to get; **hai avuto l'assegno?** did you get *o* have you had the cheque?
4 (*età, dimensione*) to be; **ha 9 anni** he is 9 (years old); **la stanza ha 3 metri di lunghezza** the room is 3 metres in length; *vedi* **fame**; **paura** *ecc*
5 (*tempo*): **quanti ne abbiamo oggi?** what's the date today?; **ne hai per molto?** will you be long?
6 (*fraseologia*): **avercela con qn** to be angry with sb; **cos'hai?** what's wrong *o* what's the matter (with you)?; **non ha niente a che vedere** *o* **fare con me** it's got nothing to do with me
▷ *vb aus* 1 to have; **aver bevuto/mangiato** to have drunk/eaten
2 (*+ da + infinito*): **avere da fare qc** to have to do sth; **non hai che da chiederlo** you only have to ask him

avi'ario, -a *agg*: **influenza aviaria** bird flu
aviazi'one [avjat'tsjone] *sf* aviation;

(*Mil*) air force
'avido, -a *ag* eager; (*peg*) greedy
avo'cado *sm* avocado
a'vorio *sm* ivory
Avv. *abbr* = **avvocato**
avvantaggi'are [avvantad'dʒare] *vt* to favour; **avvantaggiarsi** *vpr* **avvantaggiarsi negli affari/sui concorrenti** to get ahead in business/ of one's competitors
avvele'nare *vt* to poison
av'vengo *ecc vb vedi* **avvenire**
avveni'mento *sm* event
avve'nire *vi, vb impers* to happen, occur ▷ *sm* future
av'venni *ecc vb vedi* **avvenire**
avven'tato, -a *ag* rash, reckless
avven'tura *sf* adventure; (*amorosa*) affair
avventu'rarsi *vpr* to venture
avventu'roso, -a *ag* adventurous
avve'rarsi *vpr* to come true
av'verbio *sm* adverb
avverrò *ecc vb vedi* **avvenire**
avver'sario, -a *ag* opposing ▷ *sm* opponent, adversary
avver'tenza [avver'tɛntsa] *sf* (*ammonimento*) warning; (*cautela*) care; (*premessa*) foreword; **avvertenze** *sfpl* (*istruzioni per l'uso*) instructions
avverti'mento *sm* warning
avver'tire *vt* (*avvisare*) to warn; (*rendere consapevole*) to inform, notify; (*percepire*) to feel
avvi'are *vt* (*mettere sul cammino*) to direct; (*impresa, trattative*) to begin, start; (*motore*) to start; **avviarsi** *vpr* to set off, set out
avvici'nare [avvitʃi'nare] *vt* to bring near; (*trattare con: persona*) to approach; **avvicinarsi** *vpr* **avvicinarsi (a qn/qc)** to approach (sb/sth), draw near (to sb/sth)
avvi'lito, -a *ag* discouraged
avvin'cente *ag* captivating
avvi'sare *vt* (*far sapere*) to inform; (*mettere in guardia*) to warn;
av'viso *sm* warning; (*annuncio*) announcement; (: *affisso*) notice; (*inserzione pubblicitaria*) advertisement; **a mio avviso** in my opinion; **avviso di chiamata** (*servizio*) call waiting; (*segnale*) call waiting signal; **avviso di garanzia** (*Dir*) notification (*of impending investigation and of the right to name a defence lawyer*)

> Attenzione! In inglese esiste la parola *advice* che però vuol dire *consiglio*.

avvis'tare *vt* to sight
avvi'tare *vt* to screw down (*o* in)
avvo'cato, -'essa *sm/f* (*Dir*) barrister (BRIT), lawyer; (*fig*) defender, advocate
av'volgere [av'voldʒere] *vt* to roll up; (*avviluppare*) to wrap up; **avvolgersi** *vpr* (*avvilupparsi*) to wrap o.s. up;
avvol'gibile *sm* roller blind (BRIT), blind
av'volsi *ecc vb vedi* **avvolgere**
avvol'toio *sm* vulture
aza'lea [addza'lɛa] *sf* azalea
azi'enda [ad'dzjɛnda] *sf* business, firm, concern; **azienda agricola** farm
azi'one [at'tsjone] *sf* action; (*Comm*) share
a'zoto [ad'dzɔto] *sm* nitrogen
azzar'dare [addzar'dare] *vt* (*soldi, vita*) to risk, hazard; (*domanda, ipotesi*) to hazard, venture; **azzardarsi** *vpr* **azzardarsi a fare** to dare (to) do
az'zardo [ad'dzardo] *sm* risk
azzec'care [attsek'kare] *vt* (*risposta ecc*) to get right
azzuf'farsi [attsuf'farsi] *vpr* to come to blows
az'zurro, -a [ad'dzurro] *ag* blue ▷ *sm* (*colore*) blue; **gli azzurri** (*Sport*) the Italian national team

b

'babbo *sm* (*fam*) dad, daddy; **Babbo Natale** Father Christmas

baby'sitter ['beɪbɪsitəʳ] *sm/f inv* baby-sitter

'bacca, -che *sf* berry

baccalà *sm* dried salted cod; (*fig: peg*) dummy

bac'chetta [bak'ketta] *sf* (*verga*) stick, rod; (*di direttore d'orchestra*) baton; (*di tamburo*) drumstick; **~ magica** magic wand

ba'checa, -che [ba'kɛka] *sf* (*mobile*) showcase, display case; (*Univ, in ufficio*) notice board (BRIT), bulletin board (US)

baci'are [ba'tʃare] *vt* to kiss; **baciarsi** *vpr* to kiss (one another)

baci'nella [batʃi'nɛlla] *sf* basin

ba'cino [ba'tʃino] *sm* basin; (*Mineralogia*) field, bed; (*Anat*) pelvis; (*Naut*) dock

'bacio ['batʃo] *sm* kiss

'baco, -chi *sm* worm; **baco da seta** silkworm

ba'dante *sm/f* care worker

ba'dare *vi* (*fare attenzione*) to take care, be careful; (*occuparsi di*): **~ a** to look after, take care of; (*dar ascolto*): **~ a** to pay attention to; **bada ai fatti tuoi!** mind your own business!

'baffi *smpl* moustache *sg*; (*di animale*) whiskers; **ridere sotto i ~** to laugh up one's sleeve; **leccarsi i ~** to lick one's lips

bagagli'aio [bagaʎ'ʎajo] *sm* luggage van (BRIT) *o* car (US); (*Aut*) boot (BRIT), trunk (US)

ba'gaglio [ba'gaʎʎo] *sm* luggage *no pl*, baggage *no pl*; **fare/disfare i bagagli** to pack/unpack; **i nostri bagagli non sono arrivati** our luggage has not arrived; **può mandare qualcuno a prendere i nostri bagagli?** could you send someone to collect our luggage?; **bagaglio a mano** hand luggage

bagli'ore [baʎ'ʎore] *sm* flash, dazzling light; **un ~ di speranza** a ray of hope

ba'gnante [baɲ'ɲante] *sm/f* bather

ba'gnare [baɲ'ɲare] *vt* to wet; (*inzuppare*) to soak; (*innaffiare*) to water; (*fiume*) to flow through; (*: mare*) to wash, bathe; **bagnarsi** *vpr* to get wet; (*al mare*) to go swimming *o* bathing; (*in vasca*) to have a bath

ba'gnato, -a [baɲ'ɲato] *ag* wet

ba'gnino [baɲ'ɲino] *sm* lifeguard

'bagno ['baɲɲo] *sm* bath; (*stanza*) bathroom; (*toilette*) toilet; **bagni** *smpl* (*stabilimento*) baths; **fare il ~** to have a bath; (*nel mare*) to go swimming *o* bathing; **dov'è il ~?** where's the toilet?; **fare il ~ a qn** to give sb a bath; **mettere a ~** to soak; **~ schiuma** bubble bath

bagnoma'ria [baɲɲoma'ria] *sm* **cuocere a ~** to cook in a double saucepan

bagnoschi'uma [baɲɲoskj'uma] *sm inv* bubble bath

'baia *sf* bay

balbet'tare *vi* to stutter, stammer; (*bimbo*) to babble ▷ *vt* to stammer out
bal'canico, -a, ci, che *ag* Balkan
bal'cone *sm* balcony; **avete una camera con ~?** do you have a room with a balcony?
bal'doria *sf* **fare ~** to have a riotous time
ba'lena *sf* whale
ba'leno *sm* flash of lightning; **in un ~** in a flash
bal'lare *vt, vi* to dance
balle'rina *sf* dancer; ballet dancer; (*scarpa*) ballet shoe
balle'rino *sm* dancer; ballet dancer
bal'letto *sm* ballet
'ballo *sm* dance; (*azione*) dancing *no pl*; **essere in ~** (*fig*: *persona*) to be involved; (: *cosa*) to be at stake
balne'are *ag* seaside *cpd*; (*stagione*) bathing
'balsamo *sm* (*aroma*) balsam; (*lenimento, fig*) balm
bal'zare [bal'tsare] *vi* to bounce; (*lanciarsi*) to jump, leap; **'balzo** *sm* bounce; jump, leap; (*del terreno*) crag
bam'bina *ag, sf vedi* **bambino**
bam'bino, -a *sm/f* child
'bambola *sf* doll
bambù *sm* bamboo
ba'nale *ag* banal, commonplace
ba'nana *sf* banana
'banca, -che *sf* bank; **banca dati** data bank
banca'rella *sf* stall
banca'rotta *sf* bankruptcy; **fare ~** to go bankrupt
ban'chetto [ban'ketto] *sm* banquet
banchi'ere [ban'kjɛre] *sm* banker
ban'china [ban'kina] *sf* (*di porto*) quay; (*per pedoni, ciclisti*) path; (*di stazione*) platform; **~ cedevole** (*Aut*) soft verge (BRIT) *o* shoulder (US)
'banco, -chi *sm* bench; (*di negozio*) counter; (*di mercato*) stall; (*di officina*) (work-)bench; (*Geo, banca*) bank; **banco di corallo** coral reef; **banco degli imputati** dock; **banco di prova** (*fig*) testing ground; **banco dei testimoni** witness box; **banco dei pegni** pawnshop; **banco di nebbia** bank of fog
'Bancomat® *sm inv* automated banking; (*tessera*) cash card
banco'nota *sf* banknote
'banda *sf* band; (*di stoffa*) band, stripe; (*lato, parte*) side; **~ perforata** punch tape
bandi'era *sf* flag, banner
ban'dito *sm* outlaw, bandit
'bando *sm* proclamation; (*esilio*) exile, banishment; **~ alle chiacchiere!** that's enough talk!; **bando di concorso** announcement of a competition
bar *sm inv* bar
'bara *sf* coffin
ba'racca, -che *sf* shed, hut; (*peg*) hovel; **mandare avanti la ~** to keep things going
ba'rare *vi* to cheat
'baratro *sm* abyss
ba'ratto *sm* barter
ba'rattolo *sm* (*di latta*) tin; (*di vetro*) jar; (*di coccio*) pot
'barba *sf* beard; **farsi la ~** to shave; **farla in ~ a qn** (*fig*) to do sth to sb's face; **che ~!** what a bore!
barbabi'etola *sf* beetroot (BRIT), beet (US); **barbabietola da zucchero** sugar beet
barbi'ere *sm* barber
bar'bone *sm* (*cane*) poodle; (*vagabondo*) tramp
'barca, -che *sf* boat; **barca a motore** motorboat; **barca a remi** rowing boat; **barca a vela** sail(ing) boat
barcol'lare *vi* to stagger
ba'rella *sf* (*lettiga*) stretcher
ba'rile *sm* barrel, cask
ba'rista, -i, -e *sm/f* barman/maid; (*proprietario*) bar owner
ba'rocco, -a, -chi, -che *ag, sm* baroque

ba'rometro *sm* barometer
ba'rone *sm* baron; **baro'nessa** *sf* baroness
'barra *sf* bar; (*Naut*) helm; (*linea grafica*) line, stroke
bar'rare *vt* to bar
barri'carsi *vpr* to barricade o.s.
barri'era *sf* barrier; (*Geo*) reef
ba'ruffa *sf* scuffle
barzel'letta [bardzel'letta] *sf* joke, funny story
ba'sare *vt* to base, found; **basarsi** *vpr* **basarsi su** (*fatti, prove*) to be based *o* founded on; (: *persona*) to base one's arguments on
'basco, -a, -schi, -sche *ag* Basque ▷ *sm* (*copricapo*) beret
'base *sf* base; (*fig: fondamento*) basis; (*Pol*) rank and file; **di ~** basic; **in ~ a** on the basis of, according to; **a ~ di caffè** coffee-based
'baseball ['beisbɔ:l] *sm* baseball
ba'sette *sfpl* sideburns
ba'silica, -che *sf* basilica
ba'silico *sm* basil
basket ['basket] *sm* basketball
bas'sista, -i, -e *sm/f* bass player
'basso, -a *ag* low; (*di statura*) short; (*meridionale*) southern ▷ *sm* bottom, lower part; (*Mus*) bass; **la bassa Italia** southern Italy
bassorili'evo *sm* bas-relief
bas'sotto, -a *ag* squat ▷ *sm* (*cane*) dachshund
'basta *escl* (that's) enough!, that will do!
bas'tardo, -a *ag* (*animale, pianta*) hybrid, crossbreed; (*persona*) illegitimate, bastard; (*peg*) ▷ *sm/f* illegitimate child, bastard (*peg*)
bas'tare *vi, vb impers* to be enough, be sufficient; **~ a qn** to be enough for sb; **basta chiedere** *o* **che chieda a un vigile** you have only to *o* need only ask a policeman; **basta così, grazie** that's enough, thanks
basto'nare *vt* to beat, thrash
baston'cino [baston'tʃino] *sm* (*Sci*) ski pole; **bastoncini di pesce** fish fingers
bas'tone *sm* stick; **~ da passeggio** walking stick
bat'taglia [bat'taʎʎa] *sf* battle; fight
bat'tello *sm* boat
bat'tente *sm* (*imposta: di porta*) wing, flap; (: *di finestra*) shutter; (*batacchio: di porta*) knocker; (: *di orologio*) hammer; **chiudere i battenti** (*fig*) to shut up shop
'battere *vt* to beat; (*grano*) to thresh; (*percorrere*) to scour ▷ *vi* (*bussare*) to knock; (*urtare*): **~ contro** to hit *o* strike against; (*pioggia, sole*) to beat down; (*cuore*) to beat; (*Tennis*) to serve; **battersi** *vpr* to fight; **~ le mani** to clap; **~ i piedi** to stamp one's feet; **~ a macchina** to type; **~ bandiera italiana** to fly the Italian flag; **~ in testa** (*Aut*) to knock; **in un batter d'occhio** in the twinkling of an eye
batte'ria *sf* battery; (*Mus*) drums *pl*
bat'terio *sm* bacterium
batte'rista, -i, -e *sm/f* drummer
bat'tesimo *sm* (*rito*) baptism; christening
battez'zare [batted'dzare] *vt* to baptize; to christen
batti'panni *sm inv* carpet-beater
battis'trada *sm inv* (*di pneumatico*) tread; (*di gara*) pacemaker
'battito *sm* beat, throb; **battito cardiaco** heartbeat
bat'tuta *sf* blow; (*di macchina da scrivere*) stroke; (*Mus*) bar; beat; (*Teatro*) cue; (*frase spiritosa*) witty remark; (*di caccia*) beating; (*Polizia*) combing, scouring; (*Tennis*) service
ba'tuffolo *sm* wad
ba'ule *sm* trunk; (*Aut*) boot (BRIT), trunk (US)
'bava *sf* (*di animale*) slaver, slobber; (*di lumaca*) slime; (*di vento*) breath
bava'glino [bavaʎ'ʎino] *sm* bib
ba'vaglio [ba'vaʎʎo] *sm* gag

'bavero *sm* collar
ba'zar [bad'dzar] *sm inv* bazaar
BCE *sigla f* (= *Banca centrale europea*) ECB
be'ato, -a *ag* blessed; (*fig*) happy; **~te!** lucky you!
bec'care *vt* to peck; (*fig*: *raffreddore*) to catch; **beccarsi** *vpr* (*fig*) to squabble; **beccarsi qc** to catch sth
beccherò *ecc* [bekke'rɔ] *vb vedi* **beccare**
'becco, -chi *sm* beak, bill; (*di caffettiera ecc*) spout; lip
be'fana *sf* hag, witch; **la B~** *old woman who, according to legend, brings children their presents at the Epiphany*; (*Epifania*) Epiphany

Befana

The **Befana** is a national holiday on the feast of the Epiphany. It takes its name from **la Befana**, the old woman who, according to Italian legend comes down the chimney during the night leaving gifts for children who have been good, and coal for those who have not.

bef'fardo, -a *ag* scornful, mocking
'begli ['bɛʎʎi] *ag vedi* **bello**
'bei *ag vedi* **bello**
beige [bɛʒ] *ag inv* beige
bel *ag vedi* **bello**
be'lare *vi* to bleat
'belga, -gi, -ghe *ag, sm/f* Belgian
'Belgio ['bɛldʒo] *sm* **il ~** Belgium
'bella *sf* (*Sport*) decider; *vedi anche* **bello**
bel'lezza [bel'lettsa] *sf* beauty

PAROLA CHIAVE

'bello, -a (*ag*: *dav sm* **bel** + *C*, **bell'** + *V*, **bello** + *s impura, gn, pn, ps, x, z, pl* **bei** + *C*, **begli** + *s impura ecc o V*) *ag* **1** (*oggetto, donna, paesaggio*) beautiful, lovely; (*uomo*) handsome; (*tempo*) beautiful, fine, lovely; **le belle arti** fine arts
2 (*quantità*): **una bella cifra** a considerable sum of money; **un bel niente** absolutely nothing
3 (*rafforzativo*): **è una truffa bella e buona!** it's a real fraud!; **è bell'e finito** it's already finished
▷ *sm* **1** (*bellezza*) beauty; (*tempo*) fine weather
2: **adesso viene il bello** now comes the best bit; **sul più bello** at the crucial point; **cosa fai di bello?** are you doing anything interesting?
▷ *av* **fa bello** the weather is fine, it's fine

'belva *sf* wild animal
belve'dere *sm inv* panoramic viewpoint
benché [ben'ke] *cong* although
'benda *sf* bandage; (*per gli occhi*) blindfold; **ben'dare** *vt* to bandage; to blindfold
'bene *av* well; (*completamente, affatto*): **è ben difficile** it's very difficult ▷ *ag inv* **gente ~** well-to-do people ▷ *sm* good; **beni** *smpl* (*averi*) property *sg*, estate *sg*; **io sto ~/poco ~** I'm well/not very well; **va ~** all right; **volere un ~ dell'anima a qn** to love sb very much; **un uomo per ~** a respectable man; **fare ~** to do the right thing; **fare ~ a** (*salute*) to be good for; **fare del ~ a qn** to do sb a good turn; **beni di consumo** consumer goods
bene'detto, -a *pp di* **benedire** ▷ *ag* blessed, holy
bene'dire *vt* to bless; to consecrate
benedu'cato, -a *ag* well-mannered
benefi'cenza [benefi'tʃɛntsa] *sf* charity
bene'ficio [bene'fitʃo] *sm* benefit; **con ~ d'inventario** (*fig*) with reservations
be'nessere *sm* well-being
benes'tante *ag* well-to-do

be'nigno, -a [be'niɲɲo] *ag* kind, kindly; (*critica ecc*) favourable; (*Med*) benign
benve'nuto, -a *ag, sm* welcome; **dare il ~ a qn** to welcome sb
ben'zina [ben'dzina] *sf* petrol (BRIT), gas (US); **fare ~** to get petrol (BRIT) *o* gas (US); **sono rimasto senza ~** I have run out of petrol (BRIT) *o* gas (US); **benzina verde** unleaded (petrol); **benzi'naio** *sm* petrol (BRIT) *o* gas (US) pump attendant
'bere *vt* to drink; **darla a ~ a qn** (*fig*) to fool sb; **vuoi qualcosa da ~?** would you like a drink?
ber'lina *sf* (*Aut*) saloon (car) (BRIT), sedan (US)
Ber'lino *sf* Berlin
ber'muda *smpl* (*calzoncini*) Bermuda shorts
ber'noccolo *sm* bump; (*inclinazione*) flair
ber'retto *sm* cap
berrò *ecc vb vedi* **bere**
ber'saglio [ber'saʎʎo] *sm* target
besciamella [beʃʃa'mɛlla] *sf* béchamel sauce
bes'temmia *sf* curse; (*Rel*) blasphemy
bestemmi'are *vi* to curse, swear; to blaspheme ▷ *vt* to curse, swear at; to blaspheme
'bestia *sf* animal; **andare in ~** (*fig*) to fly into a rage; **besti'ale** *ag* beastly; animal *cpd*; (*fam*): **fa un freddo bestiale** it's bitterly cold; **besti'ame** *sm* livestock; (*bovino*) cattle *pl*
be'tulla *sf* birch
be'vanda *sf* drink, beverage
'bevo *ecc vb vedi* **bere**
be'vuto, -a *pp di* **bere**
'bevvi *ecc vb vedi* **bere**
bianche'ria [bjanke'ria] *sf* linen; **~ da donna** ladies' underwear, lingerie; **biancheria femminile** lingerie; **biancheria intima** underwear
bi'anco, -a, -chi, -che *ag* white; (*non scritto*) blank ▷ *sm* white; (*intonaco*) whitewash ▷ *sm/f* white, white man/woman; **in ~** (*foglio, assegno*) blank; (*notte*) sleepless; **in ~ e nero** (*TV, Fot*) black and white; **mangiare in ~** to follow a bland diet; **pesce in ~** boiled fish; **andare in ~** (*non riuscire*) to fail; **bianco dell'uovo** egg-white
biasi'mare *vt* to disapprove of, censure
'Bibbia *sf* (*anche fig*) bible
bibe'ron *sm inv* feeding bottle
'bibita *sf* (soft) drink
biblio'teca, -che *sf* library; (*mobile*) bookcase
bicarbo'nato *sm*: **~ (di sodio)** bicarbonate (of soda)
bicchi'ere [bik'kjɛre] *sm* glass
bici'cletta [bitʃi'kletta] *sf* bicycle; **andare in ~** to cycle
bidè *sm inv* bidet
bi'dello, -a *sm/f* (*Ins*) janitor
bi'done *sm* drum, can; (*anche*: **~ dell'immondizia**) (dust)bin; (*fam*: *truffa*) swindle; **fare un ~ a qn** (*fam*) to let sb down; to cheat sb
bien'nale *ag* biennial

BIENNALE DI VENEZIA

The **Biennale di Venezia** is an international contemporary art festival, which takes place every two years at Giardini in Venice. In its current form, it includes exhibits by artists from the many countries taking part, a thematic exhibition and a section for young artists.

bifamili'are *sf* ≈ semi-detached house
bifor'carsi *vpr* to fork
bigiotte'ria [bidʒotte'ria] *sf* costume jewellery; (*negozio*) jeweller's (*selling only costume jewellery*)
bigliet'taio, -a *sm/f* (*in treno*) ticket inspector; (*in autobus*) conductor

bigliette'ria [biʎʎette'ria] *sf* (*di stazione*) ticket office; booking office; (*di teatro*) box office

bigli'etto [biʎ'ʎetto] *sm* (*per viaggi, spettacoli ecc*) ticket; (*cartoncino*) card; (*anche:* **~ di banca**) (bank)note; **biglietto d'auguri** greetings card; **biglietto da visita** visiting card; **biglietto d'andata e ritorno** return (ticket), round-trip ticket (*US*); **biglietto di sola andata** single (ticket); **biglietto elettronico** e-ticket

bignè [biɲ'ɲe] *sm inv* cream puff

bigo'dino *sm* roller, curler

bi'gotto, -a *ag* over-pious ▷ *sm/f* church fiend

bi'kini *sm inv* bikini

bi'lancia, -ce [bi'lantʃa] *sf* (*pesa*) scales *pl*; (: *di precisione*) balance; (*dello zodiaco*): **B~** Libra; **bilancia commerciale** balance of trade; **bilancia dei pagamenti** balance of payments

bi'lancio [bi'lantʃo] *sm* (*Comm*) balance(-sheet); (*statale*) budget; **fare il ~ di** (*fig*) to assess; **bilancio consuntivo** (final) balance; **bilancio preventivo** budget

bili'ardo *sm* billiards *sg*; billiard table

bi'lingue *ag* bilingual

bilo'cale *sm* two-room flat (*Brit*) *o* apartment (*US*)

bi'nario, -a *ag* (*sistema*) binary ▷ *sm* (railway) track *o* line; (*piattaforma*) platform; **da che ~ parte il treno per Londra?** which platform does the train for London go from?; **binario morto** dead-end track

bi'nocolo *sm* binoculars *pl*

bio... *prefisso*; **biodegra'dabile** *ag* biodegradable; **biodi'namico, -a, -ci, -che** *ag* biodynamic; **biogra'fia** *sf* biography; **biolo'gia** *sf* biology

bio'logico, -a, -ci, -che *ag* (*scienze, fenomeni ecc*}) biological; (*agricoltura, prodotti*) organic; **guerra biologica** biological warfare

bi'ondo, -a *ag* blond, fair

biotecnologia [bioteknolo'dʒia] *sf* biotechnology

biri'chino, -a [biri'kino] *ag* mischievous ▷ *sm/f* scamp, little rascal

bi'rillo *sm* skittle (*BRIT*), pin (*US*)

'biro® *sf inv* biro®

'birra *sf* beer; **a tutta ~** (*fig*) at top speed; **birra chiara/scura** ≈ lager/stout; **birre'ria** *sf* ≈ bierkeller

bis *escl, sm inv* encore

bis'betico, -a, -ci, -che *ag* ill-tempered, crabby

bisbigli'are [bisbiʎ'ʎare] *vt, vi* to whisper

'bisca, -sche *sf* gambling-house

'biscia, -sce ['biʃʃa] *sf* snake; **biscia d'acqua** grass snake

biscot'tato, -a *ag* crisp; **fette biscottate** rusks

bis'cotto *sm* biscuit

bisessu'ale *ag, sm/f* bisexual

bises'tile *ag* **anno ~** leap year

bis'nonno, -a *sm/f* great grandfather/grandmother

biso'gnare [bizoɲ'ɲare] *vb impers*: **bisogna che tu parta/lo faccia** you'll have to go/do it; **bisogna parlargli** we'll (*o* I'll) have to talk to him

bi'sogno [bi'zoɲɲo] *sm* need; **ha ~ di qualcosa?** do you need anything?

bis'tecca, -che *sf* steak, beefsteak

bisticci'are [bistit'tʃare] *vi* to quarrel, bicker; **bisticciarsi** *vpr* to quarrel, bicker

'bisturi *sm* scalpel

'bivio *sm* fork; (*fig*) dilemma

biz'zarro, -a [bid'dzarro] *ag* bizarre, strange

blate'rare *vi* to chatter

blin'dato, -a *ag* armoured

bloc'care *vt* to block; (*isolare*) to isolate, cut off; (*porto*) to blockade; (*prezzi, beni*) to freeze; (*meccanismo*) to jam; **bloccarsi** *vpr* (*motore*) to stall;

(*freni, porta*) to jam, stick; (*ascensore*) to stop, get stuck
bloccherò *ecc* [blokke'rɔ] *vb vedi* **bloccare**
bloc'chetto [blok'ketto] *sm* notebook; (*di biglietti*) book
'blocco, -chi *sm* block; (*Mil*) blockade; (*dei fitti*) restriction; (*quadernetto*) pad; (*fig: unione*) coalition; (*il bloccare*) blocking; isolating, cutting-off; blockading; freezing; jamming; **in ~** (*nell'insieme*) as a whole; (*Comm*) in bulk; **blocco cardiaco** cardiac arrest; **blocco stradale** road block
blu *ag inv, sm* dark blue
'blusa *sf* (*camiciotto*) smock; (*camicetta*) blouse
'boa *sm inv* (*Zool*) boa constrictor; (*sciarpa*) feather boa ▷ *sf* buoy
bo'ato *sm* rumble, roar
bob [bɔb] *sm inv* bobsleigh
'bocca, -che *sf* mouth; **in ~ al lupo!** good luck!
boc'caccia, -ce [bok'kattʃa] *sf* (*malalingua*) gossip; **fare le boccacce** to pull faces
boc'cale *sm* jug; **boccale da birra** tankard
boc'cetta [bot'tʃetta] *sf* small bottle
'boccia, -ce ['bottʃa] *sf* bottle; (*da vino*) decanter, carafe; (*palla*) bowl; **gioco delle bocce** bowls *sg*
bocci'are [bot'tʃare] *vt* (*proposta, progetto*) to reject; (*Ins*) to fail; (*Bocce*) to hit
bocci'olo [bot'tʃɔlo] *sm* bud
boc'cone *sm* mouthful, morsel
boicot'tare *vt* to boycott
'bolla *sf* bubble; (*Med*) blister; **bolla di consegna** (*Comm*) delivery note; **bolla papale** papal bull
bol'lente *ag* boiling; boiling hot
bol'letta *sf* bill; (*ricevuta*) receipt; **essere in ~** to be hard up
bollet'tino *sm* bulletin; (*Comm*) note; **bollettino meteorologico** weather report; **bollettino di spedizione** consignment note
bollicina [bolli'tʃina] *sf* bubble
bol'lire *vt, vi* to boil
bolli'tore *sm* (*Cuc*) kettle; (*per riscaldamento*) boiler
'bollo *sm* stamp; **bollo per patente** *driving licence tax*; **bollo postale** postmark
'bomba *sf* bomb; **bomba atomica** atom bomb; **bomba a mano** hand grenade; **bomba ad orologeria** time bomb
bombarda'mento *sm* bombardment; bombing
bombar'dare *vt* to bombard; (*da aereo*) to bomb
'bombola *sf* cylinder
bombo'letta *sf* aerosol
bomboni'era *sf* box of sweets (*as souvenir at weddings, first communions etc*)
bo'nifico, -ci *sm* (*riduzione, abbuono*) discount; (*versamento a terzi*) credit transfer
bontà *sf* goodness; (*cortesia*) kindness; **aver la ~ di fare qc** to be good *o* kind enough to do sth
borbot'tare *vi* to mumble
'borchia ['borkja] *sf* stud
bor'deaux [bor'dɔ] *ag inv, sm inv* maroon
'bordo *sm* (*Naut*) ship's side; (*orlo*) edge; (*striscia di guarnizione*) border, trim; **a ~ di** (*nave, aereo*) aboard, on board; (*macchina*) in
bor'ghese [bor'geze] *ag* (*spesso peg*) middle-class; bourgeois; **abito ~** civilian dress
'borgo, -ghi *sm* (*paesino*) village; (*quartiere*) district; (*sobborgo*) suburb
boro'talco *sm* talcum powder
bor'raccia, -ce [bor'rattʃa] *sf* canteen, water-bottle
'borsa *sf* bag; (*anche:* **~ da signora**) handbag; (*Econ*): **la B~ (valori)** the Stock Exchange; **borsa dell'acqua calda** hot-water bottle; **borsa nera**

black market; **borsa della spesa** shopping bag; **borsa di studio** grant; **borsel'lino** *sm* purse; **bor'setta** *sf* handbag
'bosco, -schi *sm* wood
bos'niaco, -a, ci, che *ag, sm/f* Bosnian
'Bosnia Erze'govina ['bɔsnja erdze'govina] *sf* **la ~** Bosnia Herzegovina
Bot, bot *sigla m inv* (= *buono ordinario del Tesoro*) short-term Treasury bond
bo'tanica *sf* botany
bo'tanico, -a, -ci, -che *ag* botanical ▷ *sm* botanist
'botola *sf* trap door
'botta *sf* blow; (*rumore*) bang
'botte *sf* barrel, cask
bot'tega, -ghe *sf* shop; (*officina*) workshop
bot'tiglia [bot'tiʎʎa] *sf* bottle; **bottiglie'ria** *sf* wine shop
bot'tino *sm* (*di guerra*) booty; (*di rapina, furto*) loot
'botto *sm* bang; crash; **di ~** suddenly
bot'tone *sm* button; **attaccare ~ a qn** (*fig*) to buttonhole sb
bo'vino, -a *ag* bovine; **bovini** *smpl* cattle
box [bɔks] *sm inv* (*per cavalli*) horsebox; (*per macchina*) lock-up; (*per macchina da corsa*) pit; (*per bambini*) playpen
boxe [bɔks] *sf* boxing
'boxer ['bɔkser] *sm inv* (*cane*) boxer ▷ *smpl* (*mutande*): **un paio di ~** a pair of boxer shorts
BR *sigla fpl* = **Brigate Rosse**
brac'cetto [brat'tʃetto] *sm*: **a ~** arm in arm
braccia'letto *sm* bracelet, bangle
bracci'ata [brat'tʃata] *sf* (*nel nuoto*) stroke
'braccio ['brattʃo] (*pl(f)* **braccia**) *sm* (*Anat*) arm; (*pl(m) bracci*: *di gru, fiume*) arm; (: *di edificio*) wing; **braccio di mare** sound; **bracci'olo** *sm* (*appoggio*) arm
'bracco, -chi *sm* hound
'brace ['bratʃe] *sf* embers *pl*
braci'ola [bra'tʃɔla] *sf* (*Cuc*) chop
'branca, -che *sf* branch
'branchia ['brankja] *sf* (*Zool*) gill
'branco, -chi *sm* (*di cani, lupi*) pack; (*di pecore*) flock; (*peg: di persone*) gang, pack
bran'dina *sf* camp bed (BRIT), cot (US)
'brano *sm* piece; (*di libro*) passage
Bra'sile *sm* **il ~** Brazil; **brasili'ano, -a** *ag, sm/f* Brazilian
'bravo, -a *ag* (*abile*) clever, capable, skilful; (*buono*) good, honest; (: *bambino*) good; (*coraggioso*) brave; **~!** well done!; (*a teatro*) bravo!
bra'vura *sf* cleverness, skill
Bre'tagna [bre'taɲɲa] *sf*: **la ~** Brittany
bre'tella *sf* (*Aut*) link; **bretelle** *sfpl* (*di calzoni*) braces
'bretone *ag, sm/f* Breton
'breve *ag* brief, short; **in ~** in short
brevet'tare *vt* to patent
bre'vetto *sm* patent; **brevetto di pilotaggio** pilot's licence (BRIT) *o* license (US)
'bricco, -chi *sm* jug; **bricco del caffè** coffeepot
'briciola ['britʃola] *sf* crumb
'briciolo ['britʃolo] *sm* (*specie fig*) bit
'briga, -ghe *sf* (*fastidio*) trouble, bother; **pigliarsi la ~ di fare qc** to take the trouble to do sth
bri'gata *sf* (*Mil*) brigade; (*gruppo*) group, party; **Brigate Rosse** (*Pol*) Red Brigades
'briglia ['briʎʎa] *sf* rein; **a ~ sciolta** at full gallop; (*fig*) at full speed
bril'lante *ag* bright; (*anche fig*) brilliant; (*che luccica*) shining ▷ *sm* diamond
bril'lare *vi* to shine; (*mina*) to blow up ▷ *vt* (*mina*) to set off
'brillo, -a *ag* merry, tipsy
'brina *sf* hoarfrost
brin'dare *vi*: **~ a qn/qc** to drink to *o* toast sb/sth

'brindisi *sm inv* toast
bri'oche [bri'ɔʃ] *sf inv* brioche
bri'tannico, -a, -ci, -che *ag* British
'brivido *sm* shiver; (*di ribrezzo*) shudder; (*fig*) thrill
brizzo'lato, -a [brittso'lato] *ag* (*persona*) going grey; (*barba, capelli*) greying
'brocca, -che *sf* jug
'broccoli *smpl* broccoli *sg*
'brodo *sm* broth; (*per cucinare*) stock; **brodo ristretto** consommé
bron'chite [bron'kite] *sf* (*Med*) bronchitis
bronto'lare *vi* to grumble; (*tuono, stomaco*) to rumble
'bronzo ['brondzo] *sm* bronze
'browser ['brauzer] *sm inv* (*Inform*) browser
brucia'pelo [brutʃa'pelo]: **a ~** *av* point-blank
bruci'are [bru'tʃare] *vt* to burn; (*scottare*) to scald ▷ *vi* to burn; **bruciarsi** *vpr* to burn o.s.; (*fallire*) to ruin one's chances; **~ le tappe** (*fig*) to shoot ahead; **bruciarsi la carriera** to ruin one's career
'bruco, -chi *sm* caterpillar; grub
'brufolo *sm* pimple, spot
'brullo, -a *ag* bare, bleak
'bruno, -a *ag* brown, dark; (*persona*) dark(-haired)
'brusco, -a, -schi, -sche *ag* (*sapore*) sharp; (*modi, persona*) brusque, abrupt; (*movimento*) abrupt, sudden
bru'sio *sm* buzz, buzzing
bru'tale *ag* brutal
'brutto, -a *ag* ugly; (*cattivo*) bad; (*malattia, strada, affare*) nasty, bad; **~ tempo** bad weather
Bru'xelles [bry'sɛl] *sf* Brussels
BSE [biɛssɛ'e] *sigla f* (= *encefalopatia spongiforme bovina*) BSE
'buca, -che *sf* hole; (*avvallamento*) hollow; **buca delle lettere** letterbox
buca'neve *sm inv* snowdrop
bu'care *vt* (*forare*) to make a hole (*o* holes) in; (*pungere*) to pierce; (*biglietto*) to punch; **bucarsi** *vpr* (*di eroina*) to mainline; **~ una gomma** to have a puncture
bu'cato *sm* (*operazione*) washing; (*panni*) wash, washing
'buccia, -ce ['buttʃa] *sf* skin, peel
bucherò *ecc* [buke'rɔ] *vb vedi* **bucare**
'buco, -chi *sm* hole
bud'dismo *sm* Buddhism
bu'dino *sm* pudding
'bue *sm* ox; **carne di ~** beef
bu'fera *sf* storm
'buffo, -a *ag* funny; (*Teatro*) comic
bu'gia, -'gie [bu'dʒia] *sf* lie; **dire una ~** to tell a lie; **bugi'ardo, -a** *ag* lying, deceitful ▷ *sm/f* liar
'buio, -a *ag* dark ▷ *sm* dark, darkness
'bulbo *sm* (*Bot*) bulb; **bulbo oculare** eyeball
Bulga'ria *sf* **la ~** Bulgaria
'bulgaro, -a *ag, sm/f, sm* Bulgarian
buli'mia *sf* bulimia; **bu'limico, -a, -ci, -che** *ag* bulimic
bul'lone *sm* bolt
buona'notte *escl* good night! ▷ *sf* **dare la ~ a** to say good night to
buona'sera *escl* good evening!
buongi'orno [bwon'dʒorno] *escl* good morning (*o* afternoon)!
buongus'taio, -a *sm/f* gourmet

PAROLA CHIAVE

bu'ono, -a (*ag: dav sm* **buon** + *C o V*, **buono** + *s impura, gn, pn, ps, x, z; dav sf* **buon'** + *V*) *ag* **1** (*gen*) good; **un buon pranzo/ristorante** a good lunch/ restaurant; **(stai) buono!** behave!
2 (*benevolo*): **buono (con)** good (to), kind (to)
3 (*giusto, valido*) right; **al momento buono** at the right moment
4 (*adatto*): **buono a/da** fit for/to; **essere buono a nulla** to be no good *o* use at anything
5 (*auguri*): **buon anno!** happy New

Year!; **buon appetito!** enjoy your meal!; **buon compleanno!** happy birthday!; **buon divertimento!** have a nice time!; **buona fortuna!** good luck!; **buon riposo!** sleep well!; **buon viaggio!** bon voyage!, have a good trip!
6: **a buon mercato** cheap; **di buon'ora** early; **buon senso** common sense; **alla buona** *ag* simple
▷ *av* in a simple way, without any fuss
▷ *sm* **1** (*bontà*) goodness, good
2 (*Comm*) voucher, coupon; **buono di cassa** cash voucher; **buono di consegna** delivery note; **buono del Tesoro** Treasury bill

buon'senso *sm* = **buon senso**
burat'tino *sm* puppet
'burbero, -a *ag* surly, gruff
buro'cratico, -a, ci, che *ag* bureaucratic
burocra'zia [burokrat'tsia] *sf* bureaucracy
bur'rasca, -sche *sf* storm
'burro *sm* butter
bur'rone *sm* ravine
bus'sare *vi* to knock
'bussola *sf* compass
'busta *sf* (*da lettera*) envelope; (*astuccio*) case; **in ~ aperta/chiusa** in an unsealed/sealed envelope; **busta paga** pay packet
busta'rella *sf* bribe, backhander
bus'tina *sf* (*piccola busta*) envelope; (*di cibi, farmaci*) sachet; (*Mil*) forage cap; **bustina di tè** tea bag
'busto *sm* bust; (*indumento*) corset, girdle; **a mezzo ~** (*foto*) half-length
but'tare *vt* to throw; (*anche*: **~ via**) to throw away; **~ giù** (*scritto*) to scribble down; (*cibo*) to gulp down; (*edificio*) to pull down, demolish; (*pasta, verdura*) to put into boiling water; **buttarsi** *vpr* (*saltare*) to jump; **buttarsi dalla finestra** to jump out of the window
byte ['bait] *sm inv* byte

C

ca'bina *sf* (*di nave*) cabin; (*da spiaggia*) beach hut; (*di autocarro, treno*) cab; (*di aereo*) cockpit; (*di ascensore*) cage; **cabi'nato** *sm* cabin cruiser; **cabina di pilotaggio** cockpit; **cabina telefonica** call *o* (tele)phone box
ca'cao *sm* cocoa
'caccia ['kattʃa] *sf* hunting; (*con fucile*) shooting; (*inseguimento*) chase; (*cacciagione*) game ▷ *sm inv* (*aereo*) fighter; (*nave*) destroyer; **caccia grossa** big-game hunting; **caccia all'uomo** manhunt
cacci'are [kat'tʃare] *vt* to hunt; (*mandar via*) to chase away; (*ficcare*) to shove, stick ▷ *vi* to hunt; **cacciarsi** *vpr* **dove s'è cacciata la mia borsa?** where has my bag got to?; **cacciarsi nei guai** to get into trouble; **~ fuori qc** to whip *o* pull sth out; **~ un urlo** to let out a yell; **caccia'tore** *sm* hunter; **cacciatore di frodo** poacher
caccia'vite [kattʃa'vite] *sm inv* screwdriver

'cactus *sm inv* cactus
ca'davere *sm* (dead) body, corpse
'caddi *ecc vb vedi* **cadere**
ca'denza [ka'dɛntsa] *sf* cadence; (*ritmo*) rhythm; (*Mus*) cadenza
ca'dere *vi* to fall; (*denti, capelli*) to fall out; (*tetto*) to fall in; **questa gonna cade bene** this skirt hangs well; **lasciar ~** (*anche fig*) to drop; (*anche:* **~ dal sonno**) to be falling asleep on one's feet; **~ dalle nuvole** (*fig*) to be taken aback
cadrò *ecc vb vedi* **cadere**
ca'duta *sf* fall; **la ~ dei capelli** hair loss
caffè *sm inv* coffee; (*locale*) café; **caffè corretto** *espresso coffee with a shot of spirits*; **caffè macchiato** coffee with a dash of milk; **caffè macinato** ground coffee
caffel'latte *sm inv* white coffee
caffetti'era *sf* coffeepot
'cagna ['kaɲɲa] *sf* (*Zool, peg*) bitch
CAI *sigla m* = **Club Alpino Italiano**
cala'brone *sm* hornet
cala'maro *sm* squid
cala'mita *sf* magnet
calamità *sf inv* calamity, disaster
ca'lare *vt* (*far discendere*) to lower; (*Maglia*) to decrease ▷ *vi* (*discendere*) to go (*o* come) down; (*tramontare*) to set, go down; **~ di peso** to lose weight
cal'cagno [kal'kaɲɲo] *sm* heel
cal'care *sm* (*incrostazione*) (lime)scale
'calce ['kaltʃe] *sm* **in ~** at the foot of the page ▷ *sf* lime; **calce viva** quicklime
calci'are [kal'tʃare] *vt, vi* to kick; **calcia'tore** *sm* footballer
'calcio ['kaltʃo] *sm* (*pedata*) kick; (*sport*) football, soccer; (*di pistola, fucile*) butt; (*Chim*) calcium; **calcio d'angolo** (*Sport*) corner (kick); **calcio di punizione** (*Sport*) free kick; **calcio di rigore** penalty
calco'lare *vt* to calculate, work out, reckon; (*ponderare*) to weigh (up);
calcola'tore, -'trice *ag* calculating ▷ *sm* calculator; (*fig*) calculating person; **calcolatore elettronico** computer; **calcola'trice** *sf* calculator
'calcolo *sm* (*anche Mat*) calculation; (*infinitesimale ecc*) calculus; (*Med*) stone; **fare i propri calcoli** (*fig*) to weigh the pros and cons; **per ~** out of self-interest
cal'daia *sf* boiler
'caldo, -a *ag* warm; (*molto caldo*) hot; (*fig*: *appassionato*) keen; hearty ▷ *sm* heat; **ho ~** I'm warm; I'm hot; **fa ~** it's warm; it's hot
caleidos'copio *sm* kaleidoscope
calen'dario *sm* calendar
'calibro *sm* (*di arma*) calibre, bore; (*Tecn*) callipers *pl*; (*fig*) calibre; **di grosso ~** (*fig*) prominent
'calice ['kalitʃe] *sm* goblet; (*Rel*) chalice
Cali'fornia *sf* California
californi'ano, -a *ag* Californian
calligra'fia *sf* (*scrittura*) handwriting; (*arte*) calligraphy
'callo *sm* callus; (*ai piedi*) corn
'calma *sf* calm
cal'mante *sm* tranquillizer
cal'mare *vt* to calm; (*lenire*) to soothe; **calmarsi** *vpr* to grow calm, calm down; (*vento*) to abate; (*dolori*) to ease
'calmo, -a *ag* calm, quiet
'calo *sm* (*Comm*: *di prezzi*) fall; (: *di volume*) shrinkage; (: *di peso*) loss
ca'lore *sm* warmth; heat; **in ~** (*Zool*) on heat
calo'ria *sf* calorie
calo'rifero *sm* radiator
calo'roso, -a *ag* warm
calpes'tare *vt* to tread on, trample on; **"è vietato ~ l'erba"** "keep off the grass"
ca'lunnia *sf* slander; (*scritta*) libel
cal'vizie [kal'vittsje] *sf* baldness
'calvo, -a *ag* bald
'calza ['kaltsa] *sf* (*da donna*) stocking; (*da uomo*) sock; **fare la ~** to knit; **calze**

di nailon nylons, (nylon) stockings

calza'maglia [kaltsa'maʎʎa] *sf* tights *pl*; (*per danza, ginnastica*) leotard

calzet'tone [kaltset'tone] *sm* heavy knee-length sock

cal'zino [kal'tsino] *sm* sock

calzo'laio [kaltso'lajo] *sm* shoemaker; (*che ripara scarpe*) cobbler

calzon'cini [kaltson'tʃini] *smpl* shorts; **calzoncini da bagno** (swimming) trunks

cal'zone [kal'tsone] *sm* trouser leg; (*Cuc*) *savoury turnover made with pizza dough*; **calzoni** *smpl* (*pantaloni*) trousers (BRIT), pants (US)

camale'onte *sm* chameleon

cambia'mento *sm* change; **cambiamenti climatici** climate change *sg*

cambi'are *vt* to change; (*modificare*) to alter, change; (*barattare*): **~ (qc con qn/qc)** to exchange (sth with sb/for sth) ▷ *vi* to change, alter; **cambiarsi** *vpr* (*d'abito*) to change; **~ casa** to move (house); **~ idea** to change one's mind; **~ treno** to change trains; **dove posso ~ dei soldi?** where can I change some money?; **ha da ~?** have you got any change?; **posso cambiarlo, per favore?** could I exchange this, please?

cambiava'lute *sm inv* exchange office

'cambio *sm* change; (*modifica*) alteration, change; (*scambio, Comm*) exchange; (*corso dei cambi*) rate (of exchange); (*Tecn, Aut*) gears *pl*; **in ~ di** in exchange for; **dare il ~ a qn** to take over from sb

'camera *sf* room; (*anche:* **~ da letto**) bedroom; (*Pol*) chamber, house; **camera ardente** mortuary chapel; **camera d'aria** inner tube; (*di pallone*) bladder; **camera di commercio** Chamber of Commerce; **Camera dei Deputati** Chamber of Deputies, ≈ House of Commons (BRIT), ≈ House of Representatives (US); **camera a gas** gas chamber; **camera a un letto/due letti** single/twin-bedded room; **camera matrimoniale** double room; **camera oscura** (*Fot*) dark room

> Attenzione! In inglese esiste la parola *camera*, che però significa *macchina fotografica*.

came'rata, -i, -e *sm/f* companion, mate ▷ *sf* dormitory

cameri'era *sf* (*domestica*) maid; (*che serve a tavola*) waitress; (*che fa le camere*) chambermaid

cameri'ere *sm* (man)servant; (*di ristorante*) waiter

came'rino *sm* (*Teatro*) dressing room

'camice ['kamitʃe] *sm* (*Rel*) alb; (*per medici ecc*) white coat

cami'cetta [kami'tʃetta] *sf* blouse

ca'micia, -cie [ka'mitʃa] *sf* (*da uomo*) shirt; (*da donna*) blouse; **camicia di forza** straitjacket; **camicia da notte** (*da donna*) nightdress; (*da uomo*) nightshirt

cami'netto *sm* hearth, fireplace

ca'mino *sm* chimney; (*focolare*) fireplace, hearth

'camion *sm inv* lorry (BRIT), truck (US)

camio'nista, -i *sm* lorry driver (BRIT), truck driver (US)

cam'mello *sm* (*Zool*) camel; (*tessuto*) camel hair

cammi'nare *vi* to walk; (*funzionare*) to work, go

cam'mino *sm* walk; (*sentiero*) path; (*itinerario, direzione, tragitto*) way; **mettersi in ~** to set *o* start off

camo'milla *sf* camomile; (*infuso*) camomile tea

ca'moscio [ka'moʃʃo] *sm* chamois; **di ~** (*scarpe, borsa*) suede *cpd*

cam'pagna [kam'paɲɲa] *sf* country, countryside; (*Pol, Comm, Mil*) campaign; **in ~** in the country; **andare in ~** to go to the country; **fare una ~** to campaign; **campagna pubblicitaria** advertising campaign

cam'pana *sf* bell; (*anche:* **~ di vetro**)

bell jar; **campana (per la raccolta del vetro)** bottle bank; **campa'nello** *sm* (*all'uscio, da tavola*) bell

campa'nile *sm* bell tower, belfry

cam'peggio *sm* camping; (*terreno*) camp site; **fare (del) ~** to go camping

camper ['kamper] *sm inv* motor caravan (BRIT), motor home (US)

campio'nario, -a *ag* **fiera campionaria** trade fair ▷ *sm* collection of samples

campio'nato *sm* championship

campi'one, -'essa *sm/f* (*Sport*) champion ▷ *sm* (*Comm*) sample

'campo *sm* field; (*Mil*) field; (*accampamento*) camp; (*spazio delimitato: sportivo ecc*) ground; field; (*di quadro*) background; **i campi** (*campagna*) the countryside; **campo da aviazione** airfield; **campo di battaglia** (*Mil, fig*) battlefield; **campo di concentramento** concentration camp; **campo da golf** golf course; **campo profughi** refugee camp; **campo sportivo** sports ground; **campo da tennis** tennis court; **campo visivo** field of vision

'Canada *sm*: **il ~** Canada; **cana'dese** *ag, sm/f* Canadian ▷ *sf* (*anche:* **tenda canadese**) ridge tent

ca'naglia [ka'naʎʎa] *sf* rabble, mob; (*persona*) scoundrel, rogue

ca'nale *sm* (*anche fig*) channel; (*artificiale*) canal

'canapa *sf* hemp; **canapa indiana** (*droga*) cannabis

cana'rino *sm* canary

cancel'lare [kantʃel'lare] *vt* (*con la gomma*) to rub out, erase; (*con la penna*) to strike out; (*annullare*) to annul, cancel; (*disdire*) to cancel

cancelle'ria [kantʃelle'ria] *sf* chancery; (*materiale per scrivere*) stationery

can'cello [kan'tʃɛllo] *sm* gate

'cancro *sm* (*Med*) cancer; (*dello zodiaco*): **C~** Cancer

candeg'gina [kanded'dʒina] *sf* bleach

can'dela *sf* candle; **candela (di accensione)** (*Aut*) spark(ing) plug

cande'labro *sm* candelabra

candeli'ere *sm* candlestick

candi'dare *vt* to present as candidate; **candidarsi** *vpr* to present o.s. as candidate

candi'dato, -a *sm/f* candidate; (*aspirante a una carica*) applicant

'candido, -a *ag* white as snow; (*puro*) pure; (*sincero*) sincere, candid

can'dito, -a *ag* candied

'cane *sm* dog; (*di pistola, fucile*) cock; **fa un freddo ~** it's bitterly cold; **non c'era un ~** there wasn't a soul; **cane da caccia/da guardia** hunting/guard dog; **cane lupo** Alsatian; **cane pastore** sheepdog

ca'nestro *sm* basket

can'guro *sm* kangaroo

ca'nile *sm* kennel; (*di allevamento*) kennels *pl*; **canile municipale** dog pound

'canna *sf* (*pianta*) reed; (*: indica, da zucchero*) cane; (*bastone*) stick, cane; (*di fucile*) barrel; (*di organo*) pipe; (*fam: droga*) joint; **canna fumaria** chimney flue; **canna da pesca** (fishing) rod; **canna da zucchero** sugar cane

cannel'loni *smpl pasta tubes stuffed with sauce and baked*

cannocchi'ale [kannok'kjale] *sm* telescope

can'none *sm* (*Mil*) gun; (*Storia*) cannon; (*tubo*) pipe, tube; (*piega*) box pleat; (*fig*) ace

can'nuccia, -ce [kan'nuttʃa] *sf* (drinking) straw

ca'noa *sf* canoe

'canone *sm* canon, criterion; (*mensile, annuo*) rent; fee

canot'taggio [kanot'taddʒo] *sm* rowing

canotti'era *sf* vest

ca'notto *sm* small boat, dinghy;

canoe
can'tante *sm/f* singer
can'tare *vt, vi* to sing; **cantau'tore, -'trice** *sm/f* singer-composer
canti'ere *sm* (*Edil*) (building) site; (*cantiere navale*) shipyard
can'tina *sf* cellar; (*bottega*) wine shop; **cantina sociale** cooperative winegrowers' association

Attenzione! In inglese esiste la parola *canteen*, che però significa *mensa*.

'canto *sm* song; (*arte*) singing; (*Rel*) chant; chanting; (*poesia*) poem, lyric; (*parte di una poesia*) canto; (*parte, lato*): **da un ~** on the one hand; **d'altro ~** on the other hand
canzo'nare [kantso'nare] *vt* to tease
can'zone [kan'tsone] *sf* song; (*Poesia*) canzone
'caos *sm inv* chaos; **ca'otico, -a, -ci, -che** *ag* chaotic
CAP *sigla m* = **codice di avviamento postale**
ca'pace [ka'patʃe] *ag* able, capable; (*ampio, vasto*) large, capacious; **sei ~ di farlo?** can you *o* are you able to do it?; **capacità** *sf inv* ability; (*Dir, di recipiente*) capacity
ca'panna *sf* hut
capan'none *sm* (*Agr*) barn; (*fabbricato industriale*) (factory) shed
ca'parbio, -a *ag* stubborn
ca'parra *sf* deposit, down payment
ca'pello *sm* hair; **capelli** *smpl* (*capigliatura*) hair *sg*
ca'pezzolo [ka'pettsolo] *sm* nipple
ca'pire *vt* to understand; **non capisco** I don't understand
capi'tale *ag* (*mortale*) capital; (*fondamentale*) main, chief ▷ *sf* (*città*) capital ▷ *sm* (*Econ*) capital
capi'tano *sm* captain
capi'tare *vi* (*giungere casualmente*) to happen to go, find o.s.; (*accadere*) to happen; (*presentarsi*: *cosa*) to turn up, present itself ▷ *vb impers* to happen; **mi è capitato un guaio** I've had a spot of trouble
capi'tello *sm* (*Archit*) capital
ca'pitolo *sm* chapter
capi'tombolo *sm* headlong fall, tumble
'capo *sm* head; (*persona*) head, leader; (*: in ufficio*) head, boss; (*: in tribù*) chief; (*di oggetti*) head; top; end; (*Geo*) cape; **andare a ~** to start a new paragraph; **da ~** over again; **capo di bestiame** head *inv* of cattle; **capo di vestiario** item of clothing; **Capo'danno** *sm* New Year; **capo'giro** *sm* dizziness *no pl*; **capola'voro, -i** *sm* masterpiece; **capo'linea** (*pl* **capi'linea**) *sm* terminus; **capostazi'one** (*pl* **capistazi'one**) *sm* station master
capo'tavola (*pl(m)* **capi'tavola**) *pl(f) inv sm/f* (*persona*) head of the table; **sedere a ~** to sit at the head of the table
capo'volgere [kapo'voldʒere] *vt* to overturn; (*fig*) to reverse; **capovolgersi** *vpr* to overturn; (*barca*) to capsize; (*fig*) to be reversed
'cappa *sf* (*mantello*) cape, cloak; (*del camino*) hood
cap'pella *sf* (*Rel*) chapel
cap'pello *sm* hat
'cappero *sm* caper
cap'pone *sm* capon
cap'potto *sm* (over)coat
cappuc'cino [kapput'tʃino] *sm* (*frate*) Capuchin monk; (*bevanda*) cappuccino, *frothy white coffee*
cap'puccio [kap'puttʃo] *sm* (*copricapo*) hood; (*della biro*) cap
'capra *sf* (she-)goat
ca'priccio [ka'prittʃo] *sm* caprice, whim; (*bizza*) tantrum; **fare i capricci** to be very naughty; **capricci'oso, -a** *ag* capricious, whimsical; naughty
Capri'corno *sm* Capricorn
capri'ola *sf* somersault
capri'olo *sm* roe deer
'capro *sm*: **~ espiatorio** scapegoat

ca'prone *sm* billy-goat
'capsula *sf* capsule; (*di arma, per bottiglie*) cap
cap'tare *vt* (*Radio, TV*) to pick up; (*cattivarsi*) to gain, win
carabini'ere *sm* *member of Italian military police force*

CARABINIERI

Originally part of the armed forces, the **carabinieri** are police who perform both military and civil duties. They include paratroopers and mounted divisions.

ca'raffa *sf* carafe
Ca'raibi *smpl*: **il mar dei ~** the Caribbean (Sea)
cara'mella *sf* sweet
ca'rattere *sm* character; (*caratteristica*) characteristic, trait; **avere un buon ~** to be good-natured; **carattere jolly** wild card; **caratte'ristica, -che** *sf* characteristic, trait, peculiarity; **caratte'ristico, -a, -ci, -che** *ag* characteristic
car'bone *sm* coal
carbu'rante *sm* (motor) fuel
carbura'tore *sm* carburettor
carce'rato, -a [kartʃe'rato] *sm/f* prisoner
'carcere ['kartʃere] *sm* prison; (*pena*) imprisonment
carci'ofo [kar'tʃɔfo] *sm* artichoke
cardel'lino *sm* goldfinch
car'diaco, -a, -ci, -che *ag* cardiac, heart *cpd*
cardi'nale *ag, sm* cardinal
'cardine *sm* hinge
'cardo *sm* thistle
ca'rente *ag* **~ di** lacking in
cares'tia *sf* famine; (*penuria*) scarcity, dearth
ca'rezza [ka'rettsa] *sf* caress
'carica, -che *sf* (*mansione ufficiale*) office, position; (*Mil, Tecn, Elettr*) charge; **ha una forte ~ di simpatia** he's very likeable; *vedi anche* **carico**
caricabatte'ria *sm inv* battery charger
cari'care *vt* (*merce, Inform*) to load; (*orologio*) to wind up; (*batteria, Mil*) to charge
'carico, -a, -chi, -che *ag* (*che porta un peso*): **~ di** loaded *o* laden with; (*fucile*) loaded; (*orologio*) wound up; (*batteria*) charged; (*colore*) deep; (*caffè, tè*) strong ▷ *sm* (*il caricare*) loading; (*ciò che si carica*) load; (*fig: peso*) burden, weight; **persona a ~** dependent; **essere a ~ di qn** (*spese ecc*) to be charged to sb
'carie *sf* (*dentaria*) decay
ca'rino, -a *ag* (*grazioso*) lovely, pretty, nice; (*riferito a uomo, anche simpatico*) nice
carità *sf* charity; **per ~!** (*escl di rifiuto*) good heavens, no!
carnagi'one [karna'dʒone] *sf* complexion
'carne *sf* flesh; (*bovina, ovina ecc*) meat; **non mangio ~** I don't eat meat; **carne di maiale/manzo/pecora** pork/beef/mutton; **carne in scatola** tinned *o* canned meat; **carne tritata** *o* **macinata** mince (BRIT), hamburger meat (US), minced (BRIT) *o* ground (US) meat
carne'vale *sm* carnival

CARNEVALE

Carnevale is the period between Epiphany (Jan. 6th) and the beginning of Lent. People wear fancy dress, and there are parties, processions of floats and bonfires. It culminates immediately before Lent in the festivities of **martedì grasso** (Shrove Tuesday).

'caro, -a *ag* (*amato*) dear; (*costoso*)

dear, expensive; **è troppo ~** it's too expensive

ca'rogna [ka'roɲɲa] *sf* carrion; (*anche:* **fig**: *fam*) swine

ca'rota *sf* carrot

caro'vana *sf* caravan

car'poni *av* on all fours

car'rabile *ag* suitable for vehicles; **"passo ~"** "keep clear"

carreggi'ata [karred'dʒata] *sf* carriageway (BRIT), (road)way

car'rello *sm* trolley; (*Aer*) undercarriage; (*Cinema*) dolly; (*di macchina da scrivere*) carriage

carri'era *sf* career; **fare ~** to get on; **a gran ~** at full speed

carri'ola *sf* wheelbarrow

'carro *sm* cart, wagon; **carro armato** tank; **carro attrezzi** breakdown van

car'rozza [kar'rɔttsa] *sf* carriage, coach

carrozze'ria [karrottse'ria] *sf* body, coachwork (BRIT); (*officina*) coachbuilder's workshop (BRIT), body shop

carroz'zina [karrot'tsina] *sf* pram (BRIT), baby carriage (US)

'carta *sf* paper; (*al ristorante*) menu; (*Geo*) map; plan; (*documento*) card; (*costituzione*) charter; **carte** *sfpl* (*documenti*) papers, documents; **alla ~** (*al ristorante*) à la carte; **carta assegni** bank card; **carta assorbente** blotting paper; **carta bollata** *o* **da bollo** official stamped paper; **carta (da gioco)** playing card; **carta di credito** credit card; **carta fedeltà** loyalty card; **carta (geografica)** map; **carta d'identità** identity card; **carta igienica** toilet paper; **carta d'imbarco** (*Aer, Naut*) boarding card; **carta da lettere** writing paper; **carta da pacchi** wrapping paper; **carta da parati** wallpaper; **carta libera** (*Amm*) unstamped paper; **carta stradale** road map; **carta verde** (*Aut*) green card; **carta vetrata** sandpaper; **carta da visita** visiting card

car'taccia, -ce [kar'tattʃa] *sf* waste paper

carta'pesta *sf* papier-mâché

car'tella *sf* (*scheda*) card; (*Inform, custodia: di cartone*) folder; (*: di uomo d'affari ecc*) briefcase; (*: di scolaro*) schoolbag, satchel; **cartella clinica** (*Med*) case sheet

cartel'lino *sm* (*etichetta*) label; (*su porta*) notice; (*scheda*) card; **timbrare il ~** (*all'entrata*) to clock in; (*all'uscita*) to clock out; **cartellino di presenza** clock card, timecard

car'tello *sm* sign; (*pubblicitario*) poster; (*stradale*) sign, signpost; (*Econ*) cartel; (*in dimostrazioni*) placard; **cartello stradale** sign; **cartel'lone** *sm* (*della tombola*) scoring frame; (*Teatro*) playbill; **tenere il cartellone** (*spettacolo*) to have a long run; **cartellone pubblicitario** advertising poster

car'tina *sf* (*Aut, Geo*) map; **può indicarmelo sulla ~?** can you show it to me on the map?

car'toccio [kar'tɔttʃo] *sm* paper bag

cartole'ria *sf* stationer's (shop)

carto'lina *sf* postcard; **cartolina postale** ready-stamped postcard

car'tone *sm* cardboard; (*Arte*) cartoon; **cartoni animati** (*Cinema*) cartoons

car'tuccia, -ce [kar'tuttʃa] *sf* cartridge

'casa *sf* house; (*in senso astratto*) home; (*Comm*) firm, house; **essere a ~** to be at home; **vado a ~ mia/tua** I'm going home/to your house; **vino della ~** house wine; **casa di cura** nursing home; **casa editrice** publishing house; **Casa delle Libertà** *centre-right coalition*; **casa di riposo** (old people's) home, care home; **case popolari** ≈ council houses (*o* flats) (BRIT), ≈ public housing units (US); **casa dello studente** student hostel

ca'sacca, -che *sf* military coat; (*di fantino*) blouse
casa'linga, -ghe *sf* housewife
casa'lingo, -a, -ghi, -ghe *ag* household, domestic; (*fatto a casa*) home-made; (*semplice*) homely; (*amante della casa*) home-loving
cas'care *vi* to fall; **cas'cata** *sf* fall; (*d'acqua*) cascade, waterfall
cascherò *ecc* [kaske'rɔ] *vb vedi* **cascare**
'casco, -schi *sm* helmet; (*del parrucchiere*) hair-drier; (*di banane*) bunch; **casco blu** (*Mil*) blue helmet (*UN soldier*)
casei'ficio [kazei'fitʃo] *sm* creamery
ca'sella *sf* pigeon-hole; **casella di posta elettronica** mailbox; **casella postale** post office box
ca'sello *sm* (*di autostrada*) toll-house
ca'serma *sf* barracks *pl*
ca'sino (*fam*) *sm* brothel; (*confusione*) row, racket
casinò *sm inv* casino
'caso *sm* chance; (*fatto, vicenda*) event, incident; (*possibilità*) possibility; (*Med, Ling*) case; **a ~** at random; **per ~** by chance, by accident; **in ogni ~, in tutti i casi** in any case, at any rate; **al ~** should the opportunity arise; **nel ~ che** in case; **~ mai** if by chance; **caso limite** borderline case
caso'lare *sm* cottage
'caspita *escl* (*di sorpresa*) good heavens!; (*di impazienza*) for goodness' sake!
'cassa *sf* case, crate, box; (*bara*) coffin; (*mobile*) chest; (*involucro: di orologio ecc*) case; (*macchina*) cash register, till; (*luogo di pagamento*) checkout (counter); (*fondo*) fund; (*istituto bancario*) bank; **cassa automatica prelievi** cash dispenser; **cassa continua** night safe; **cassa mutua** *o* **malattia** health insurance scheme; **cassa integrazione: mettere in cassa integrazione** ≈ to lay off; **cassa di risparmio** savings bank; **cassa toracica** (*Anat*) chest
cassa'forte (*pl* **casse'forti**) *sf* safe; **lo potrebbe mettere nella ~?** could you put this in the safe, please?
cassa'panca (*pl* **cassa'panche** *o* **casse'panche**) *sf* settle
casseru'ola *sf* saucepan
cas'setta *sf* box; (*per registratore*) cassette; (*Cinema, Teatro*) box-office takings *pl*; **film di ~** box-office draw; **cassetta di sicurezza** strongbox; **cassetta delle lettere** letterbox
cas'setto *sm* drawer
cassi'ere, -a *sm/f* cashier; (*di banca*) teller
casso'netto *sm* wheelie-bin
cas'tagna [kas'taɲɲa] *sf* chestnut
cas'tagno [kas'taɲɲo] *sm* chestnut (tree)
cas'tano, -a *ag* chestnut (brown)
cas'tello *sm* castle; (*Tecn*) scaffolding
casti'gare *vt* to punish; **cas'tigo, -ghi** *sm* punishment
cas'toro *sm* beaver
casu'ale *ag* chance *cpd*; (*Inform*) random *cpd*
catalizza'tore [kataliddza'tore] *sm* (*anche fig*) catalyst; (*Aut*) catalytic converter
ca'talogo, -ghi *sm* catalogue
catarifran'gente [katarifran'dʒɛnte] *sm* (*Aut*) reflector
ca'tarro *sm* catarrh
ca'tastrofe *sf* catastrophe, disaster; **catastro'fista, -i, -e** *agg, sm/f* doom-monger
catego'ria *sf* category
ca'tena *sf* chain; **catena di montaggio** assembly line; **catene da neve** (*Aut*) snow chains; **cate'nina** *sf* (*gioiello*) (thin) chain
cate'ratta *sf* cataract; (*chiusa*) sluice-gate
ca'tino *sm* basin
ca'trame *sm* tar
'cattedra *sf* teacher's desk; (*di*

docente) chair
catte'drale *sf* cathedral
catti'veria *sf* malice, spite; naughtiness; (*atto*) spiteful act; (*parole*) malicious *o* spiteful remark
cat'tivo, -a *ag* bad; (*malvagio*) bad, wicked; (*turbolento*: *bambino*) bad, naughty; (: *mare*) rough; (*odore, sapore*) nasty, bad
cat'tolico, -a, -ci, -che *ag, sm/f* (Roman) Catholic
cattu'rare *vt* to capture
'causa *sf* cause; (*Dir*) lawsuit, case, action; **a ~ di, per ~ di** because of; **fare** *o* **muovere ~ a qn** to take legal action against sb
cau'sare *vt* to cause
cau'tela *sf* caution, prudence
'cauto, -a *ag* cautious, prudent
cauzi'one [kaut'tsjone] *sf* security; (*Dir*) bail
'cava *sf* quarry
caval'care *vt* (*cavallo*) to ride; (*muro*) to sit astride; (*ponte*) to span; **caval'cata** *sf* ride; (*gruppo di persone*) riding party
cavalca'via *sm inv* flyover
cavalci'oni [kaval'tʃoni]: **a ~ di** *prep* astride
cavali'ere *sm* rider; (*feudale, titolo*) knight; (*soldato*) cavalryman; (*al ballo*) partner
caval'letta *sf* grasshopper
caval'letto *sm* (*Fot*) tripod; (*da pittore*) easel
ca'vallo *sm* horse; (*Scacchi*) knight; (*Aut*: *anche*: **~ vapore**) horsepower; (*dei pantaloni*) crotch; **a ~** on horseback; **a ~ di** astride, straddling; **cavallo di battaglia** (*fig*) hobby-horse; **cavallo da corsa** racehorse; **cavallo a dondolo** rocking horse
ca'vare *vt* (*togliere*) to draw out, extract, take out; (: *giacca, scarpe*) to take off; (: *fame, sete, voglia*) to satisfy; **cavarsela** to manage, get on all right; (*scamparla*) to get away with it
cava'tappi *sm inv* corkscrew
ca'verna *sf* cave
'cavia *sf* guinea pig
cavi'ale *sm* caviar
ca'viglia [ka'viʎʎa] *sf* ankle
'cavo, -a *ag* hollow ▷ *sm* (*Anat*) cavity; (*corda, Elettr, Tel*) cable
cavo'letto *sm*: **~ di Bruxelles** Brussels sprout
cavolfi'ore *sm* cauliflower
'cavolo *sm* cabbage; (*fam*): **non m'importa un ~** I don't give a damn
'cazzo ['kattso] *sm* (*fam!*: *pene*) prick (!); **non gliene importa un ~** (*fig fam!*) he doesn't give a damn about it; **fatti i cazzi tuoi** (*fig fam!*) mind your own damn business
C.C.D. *sigla m* (= *Centro Cristiano Democratico*) *Italian political party of the centre*
CD *sm inv* CD; (*lettore*) CD player
CD-Rom [tʃidi'rom] *sm inv* CD-ROM
C.D.U. *sigla m* (= *Cristiano Democratici Uniti*) *Italian centre-right political party*
ce [tʃe] *pron, av vedi* **ci**
Ce'cenia [tʃe'tʃenia] *sf* **la ~** Chechnya
ce'ceno, -a [tʃe'tʃeno] *sm/f, ag* Chechen
'ceco, -a, -chi, -che ['tʃɛko] *ag, sm/f* Czech; **la Repubblica Ceca** the Czech Republic
'cedere ['tʃɛdere] *vt* (*concedere posto*) to give up; (*Dir*) to transfer, make over ▷ *vi* (*cadere*) to give way, subside; **~ (a)** to surrender (to), yield (to), give in (to)
'cedola ['tʃɛdola] *sf* (*Comm*) coupon; voucher
'ceffo ['tʃɛffo] (*peg*) *sm* ugly mug
cef'fone [tʃef'fone] *sm* slap, smack
cele'brare [tʃele'brare] *vt* to celebrate
'celebre ['tʃɛlebre] *ag* famous, celebrated
ce'leste [tʃe'lɛste] *ag* celestial; heavenly; (*colore*) sky-blue
'celibe ['tʃɛlibe] *ag* single, unmarried
'cella ['tʃɛlla] *sf* cell; **cella frigorifera** cold store

'cellula ['tʃɛllula] *sf (Biol, Elettr, Pol)* cell; **cellu'lare** *sm* cellphone
cellu'lite [tʃellu'lite] *sf* cellulite
cemen'tare [tʃemen'tare] *vt (anche fig)* to cement
ce'mento [tʃe'mento] *sm* cement; **cemento armato** reinforced concrete
'cena ['tʃena] *sf* dinner; *(leggera)* supper
ce'nare [tʃe'nare] *vi* to dine, have dinner
'cenere ['tʃenere] *sf* ash
'cenno ['tʃenno] *sm (segno)* sign, signal; *(gesto)* gesture; *(col capo)* nod; *(con la mano)* wave; *(allusione)* hint, mention; *(breve esposizione)* short account; **far ~ di sì/no** to nod (one's head)/shake one's head
censi'mento [tʃensi'mento] *sm* census
cen'sura [tʃen'sura] *sf* censorship; censor's office; *(fig)* censure
cente'nario, -a [tʃente'narjo] *ag (che ha cento anni)* hundred-year-old; *(che ricorre ogni cento anni)* centennial, centenary *cpd* ▷ *sm/f* centenarian ▷ *sm* centenary
cen'tesimo, -a [tʃen'tezimo] *ag, sm* hundredth; *(di euro, dollaro)* cent
cen'tigrado, -a [tʃen'tigrado] *ag* centigrade; **20 gradi centigradi** 20 degrees centigrade
cen'timetro [tʃen'timetro] *sm* centimetre
centi'naio [tʃenti'najo] *(pl(f)* **-aia**) *sm* **un ~ (di)** a hundred; about a hundred
'cento ['tʃɛnto] *num* a hundred, one hundred
cento'mila [tʃento'mila] *num* a *o* one hundred thousand; **te l'ho detto ~ volte** *(fig)* I've told you a thousand times
cen'trale [tʃen'trale] *ag* central ▷ *sf*: **centrale telefonica** (telephone) exchange; **centrale elettrica** electric power station; **centrali'nista** *sm/f* operator; **centra'lino** *sm* (telephone) exchange; *(di albergo ecc)* switchboard; **centralizzato, -a** [tʃentralid'dzato] *ag* central
cen'trare [tʃen'trare] *vt* to hit the centre of; *(Tecn)* to centre
cen'trifuga [tʃen'trifuga] *sf* spin-drier
'centro ['tʃɛntro] *sm* centre; **centro civico** civic centre; **centro commerciale** shopping centre; *(città)* commercial centre; **centro di permanenza temporanea** reception centre
centro'destra [tʃentro'dɛstra] *sm (Pol)* centre right
centrosi'nistra [tʃentrosi'nistra] *sm (Pol)* centre left
'ceppo ['tʃeppo] *sm (di albero)* stump; *(pezzo di legno)* log
'cera ['tʃera] *sf* wax; *(aspetto)* appearance
ce'ramica, -che [tʃe'ramika] *sf* ceramic; *(Arte)* ceramics *sg*
cerbi'atto [tʃer'bjatto] *sm (Zool)* fawn
cer'care [tʃer'kare] *vt* to look for, search for ▷ *vi* **~ di fare qc** to try to do sth; **stiamo cercando un albergo/ristorante** we're looking for a hotel/restaurant
cercherò *ecc* [tʃerke'rɔ] *vb vedi* **cercare**
'cerchia ['tʃerkja] *sf* circle
cerchietto [tʃer'kjetto] *sm (per capelli)* hairband
'cerchio ['tʃerkjo] *sm* circle; *(giocattolo, di botte)* hoop
cereali [tʃere'ali] *smpl* cereal *sg*
ceri'monia [tʃeri'mɔnja] *sf* ceremony
ce'rino [tʃe'rino] *sm* wax match
'cernia ['tʃɛrnja] *sf (Zool)* stone bass
cerni'era [tʃer'njɛra] *sf* hinge; **cerniera lampo** zip (fastener) (BRIT), zipper (US)
'cero ['tʃero] *sm* (church) candle

ce'rotto [tʃe'rɔtto] *sm* sticking plaster
certa'mente [tʃerta'mente] *av* certainly
certifi'cato *sm* certificate; **certificato medico** medical certificate; **certificato di nascita/di morte** birth/death certificate

PAROLA CHIAVE

'certo, -a ['tʃɛrto] *ag* (*sicuro*): **certo (di/che)** certain *o* sure (of/that)
▷ *det* **1** (*tale*) certain; **un certo signor Smith** a (certain) Mr Smith
2 (*qualche*: *con valore intensivo*) some; **dopo un certo tempo** after some time; **un fatto di una certa importanza** a matter of some importance; **di una certa età** past one's prime, not so young
▷ *pron* **certi, e** *pl* some ▷ *av* (*certamente*) certainly; (*senz'altro*) of course; **di certo** certainly; **no (di) certo!, certo che no!** certainly not!; **sì certo** yes indeed, certainly

cer'vello, -i [tʃer'vɛllo] (*Anat*) (*pl(f)* **-a**) *sm* brain; **cervello elettronico** computer
'cervo, -a ['tʃɛrvo] *sm/f* stag/doe ▷ *sm* deer; **cervo volante** stag beetle
ces'puglio [tʃes'puʎʎo] *sm* bush
ces'sare [tʃes'sare] *vi, vt* to stop, cease; **~ di fare qc** to stop doing sth
ces'tino [tʃes'tino] *sm* basket; (*per la carta straccia*) wastepaper basket; **cestino da viaggio** (*Ferr*) packed lunch (*o* dinner)
'cesto ['tʃesto] *sm* basket
'ceto ['tʃɛto] *sm* (social) class
cetrio'lino [tʃetrio'lino] *sm* gherkin
cetri'olo [tʃetri'ɔlo] *sm* cucumber
Cfr. *abbr* (= *confronta*) cf.
CGIL *sigla f* (= *Confederazione Generale Italiana del Lavoro*) *trades union organization*
chat line [tʃæt'laen] *sf inv* chat room
chattare [tʃat'tare] *vi* (*Inform*) to chat online; **chat'tata** [tʃat'tata] *sf* chat

PAROLA CHIAVE

che [ke] *pron* **1** (*relativo*: *persona*: *soggetto*) who; (: *oggetto*) whom, that; (: *cosa, animale*) which, that; **il ragazzo che è venuto** the boy who came; **l'uomo che io vedo** the man (whom) I see; **il libro che è sul tavolo** the book which *o* that is on the table; **il libro che vedi** the book (which *o* that) you see; **la sera che ti ho visto** the evening I saw you
2 (*interrogativo, esclamativo*) what; **che (cosa) fai?** what are you doing?; **a che (cosa) pensi?** what are you thinking about?; **non sa che (cosa) fare** he doesn't know what to do; **ma che dici!** what are you saying!
3 (*indefinito*): **quell'uomo ha un che di losco** there's something suspicious about that man; **un certo non so che** an indefinable something
▷ *det* **1** (*interrogativo*: *tra tanti*) what; (: *tra pochi*) which; **che tipo di film preferisci?** what sort of film do you prefer?; **che vestito ti vuoi mettere?** what (*o* which) dress do you want to put on?
2 (*esclamativo*: *seguito da aggettivo*) how; (: *seguito da sostantivo*) what; **che buono!** how delicious!; **che bel vestito!** what a lovely dress!
▷ *cong* **1** (*con proposizioni subordinate*) that; **credo che verrà** I think he'll come; **voglio che tu studi** I want you to study; **so che tu c'eri** I know (that) you were there; **non che, non che sia sbagliato, ma ...** not that it's wrong, but ...
2 (*finale*) so that; **vieni qua, che ti veda** come here, so (that) I can see you
3 (*temporale*): **arrivai che eri già partito** you had already left when I

arrived; **sono anni che non lo vedo** I haven't seen him for years
4 (*in frasi imperative, concessive*): **che venga pure!** let him come by all means!; **che tu sia benedetto!** may God bless you!
5 (*comparativo*: *con più, meno*) than; *vedi anche* **più**; **meno**; **così** *ecc*

chemiotera'pia [kemjotera'pia] *sf* chemotherapy
chero'sene [kero'zɛne] *sm* kerosene

PAROLA CHIAVE

chi [ki] *pron* **1** (*interrogativo*: *soggetto*) who; (: *oggetto*) who, whom; **chi è?** who is it?; **di chi è questo libro?** whose book is this?, whose is this book?; **con chi parli?** who are you talking to?; **a chi pensi?** who are you thinking about?; **chi di voi?** which of you?; **non so a chi rivolgermi** I don't know who to ask
2 (*relativo*) whoever, anyone who; **dillo a chi vuoi** tell whoever you like
3 (*indefinito*): **chi ... chi ...** some ... others ...; **chi dice una cosa, chi dice un'altra** some say one thing, others say another

chiacchie'rare [kjakkje'rare] *vi* to chat; (*discorrere futilmente*) to chatter; (*far pettegolezzi*) to gossip; **chi'acchiere** *sfpl* **fare due** *o* **quattro chiacchiere** to have a chat
chia'mare [kja'mare] *vt* to call; (*rivolgersi a qn*) to call (in), send for; **chiamarsi** *vpr* (*aver nome*) to be called; **come ti chiami?** what's your name?; **mi chiamo Paolo** my name is Paolo, I'm called Paolo; **~ alle armi** to call up; **~ in giudizio** to summon; **chia'mata** *sf* (*Tel*) call; (*Mil*) call-up
chia'rezza [kja'rettsa] *sf* clearness; clarity
chia'rire [kja'rire] *vt* to make clear; (*fig*: *spiegare*) to clear up, explain
chi'aro, -a ['kjaro] *ag* clear; (*luminoso*) clear, bright; (*colore*) pale, light
chi'asso ['kjasso] *sm* uproar, row
chi'ave ['kjave] *sf* key ▷ *ag inv* key *cpd*; **posso avere la mia ~?** can I have my key?; **chiave d'accensione** (*Aut*) ignition key; **chiave di volta** keystone; **chiave inglese** monkey wrench; **chiave USB** (*Inform*) USB key
chi'azza ['kjattsa] *sf* stain; splash
'chicco, -chi ['kikko] *sm* grain; (*di caffè*) bean; **chicco d'uva** grape
chi'edere ['kjɛdere] *vt* (*per sapere*) to ask; (*per avere*) to ask for ▷ *vi* **~ di qn** to ask after sb; (*al telefono*) to ask for *o* want sb; **~ qc a qn** to ask sb sth; to ask sb for sth; **chiedersi** *vpr* **chiedersi (se)** to wonder (whether)
chi'esa ['kjɛza] *sf* church
chi'esi *ecc* ['kjɛzi] *vb vedi* **chiedere**
'chiglia ['kiʎʎa] *sf* keel
'chilo ['kilo] *sm* kilo; **chi'lometro** *sm* kilometre
'chimica ['kimika] *sf* chemistry
'chimico, -a, -ci, -che ['kimiko] *ag* chemical ▷ *sm/f* chemist
chi'nare [ki'nare] *vt* to lower, bend; **chinarsi** *vpr* to stoop, bend
chi'occiola ['kjɔttʃola] *sf* snail; (*di indirizzo e-mail*) at sign, @; **scala a ~** spiral staircase
chi'odo ['kjɔdo] *sm* nail; (*fig*) obsession; **chiodo di garofano** (*Cuc*) clove
chi'osco, -schi ['kjɔsko] *sm* kiosk, stall
chi'ostro ['kjɔstro] *sm* cloister
chiro'mante [kiro'mante] *sm/f* palmist
chirur'gia [kirur'dʒia] *sf* surgery; **chirurgia estetica** cosmetic surgery; **chi'rurgo, -ghi** *o* **gi** *sm* surgeon
chissà [kis'sa] *av* who knows, I wonder
chi'tarra [ki'tarra] *sf* guitar
chitar'rista, -i, e [kitar'rista] *sm/f*

guitarist, guitar player

chi'udere ['kjudere] *vt* to close, shut; (*luce, acqua*) to put off, turn off; (*definitivamente: fabbrica*) to close down, shut down; (*strada*) to close; (*recingere*) to enclose; (*porre termine a*) to end ▷ *vi* to close, shut; to close down, shut down; to end; **chiudersi** *vpr* to shut, close; (*ritirarsi: anche fig*) to shut o.s. away; (*ferita*) to close up; **a che ora chiudete?** what time do you close?

chi'unque [ki'unkwe] *pron* (*relativo*) whoever; (*indefinito*) anyone, anybody; **~ sia** whoever it is

'chiusi *ecc* ['kjusi] *vb vedi* **chiudere**

chi'uso, -a ['kjuso] *pp di* **chiudere** ▷ *sf* (*di corso d'acqua*) sluice, lock; (*recinto*) enclosure; (*di discorso ecc*) conclusion, ending; **chiu'sura** *sf* (*vedi* **chiudere**) closing; shutting; closing *o* shutting down; enclosing; putting *o* turning off; ending; (*dispositivo*) catch; fastening; fastener; **chiusura lampo®** zip (fastener) (BRIT), zipper (US)

C.I. *abbr* = **carta d'identità**

PAROLA CHIAVE

ci [tʃi] (*dav lo, la, li, le, ne diventa* **ce**) *pron*
1 (*personale: complemento oggetto*) us; (: *a noi: complemento di termine*) (to) us; (: *riflessivo*) ourselves; (: *reciproco*) each other, one another; (*impersonale*): **ci si veste** we get dressed; **ci ha visti** he's seen us; **non ci ha dato niente** he gave us nothing; **ci vestiamo** we get dressed; **ci amiamo** we love one another *o* each other
2 (*dimostrativo: di ciò, su ciò, in ciò ecc*) about (*o* on *o* of) it; **non so cosa farci** I don't know what to do about it; **che c'entro io?** what have I got to do with it?
▷ *av* (*qui*) here; (*lì*) there; (*moto attraverso luogo*): **ci passa sopra un ponte** a bridge passes over it; **non ci passa più nessuno** nobody comes this way any more; **esserci** *vedi* **essere**

cia'batta [tʃa'batta] *sf* slipper; (*pane*) ciabatta

ciam'bella [tʃam'bɛlla] *sf* (*Cuc*) ring-shaped cake; (*salvagente*) rubber ring

ci'ao ['tʃao] *escl* (*all'arrivo*) hello!; (*alla partenza*) cheerio! (BRIT), bye!

cias'cuno, -a [tʃas'kuno] (*det: dav sm:* **ciascun** +C, V, **ciascuno** +*s impura, gn, pn, ps, x, z; dav sf:* **ciascuna** +C, **ciascun'** +V) *det* every, each; (*ogni*) every ▷ *pron* each (one); (*tutti*) everyone, everybody

ci'barie [tʃi'barje] *sfpl* foodstuffs

cibernauta, -i, -e [tʃiber'nauta] *sm/f* Internet surfer

ciberspazio [tʃiber'spattsjo] *sm* cyberspace

'cibo ['tʃibo] *sm* food

ci'cala [tʃi'kala] *sf* cicada

cica'trice [tʃika'tritʃe] *sf* scar

'cicca ['tʃikka] *sf* cigarette end

'ciccia ['tʃittʃa] (*fam*) *sf* fat

cicci'one, -a [tʃit'tʃone] *sm/f* (*fam*) fatty

cicla'mino [tʃikla'mino] *sm* cyclamen

ci'clismo [tʃi'klizmo] *sm* cycling; **ci'clista, -i, -e** *sm/f* cyclist

'ciclo ['tʃiklo] *sm* cycle; (*di malattia*) course

ciclomo'tore [tʃiklomo'tore] *sm* moped

ci'clone [tʃi'klone] *sm* cyclone

ci'cogna [tʃi'koɲɲa] *sf* stork

ci'eco, -a, -chi, -che ['tʃɛko] *ag* blind ▷ *sm/f* blind man/woman

ci'elo ['tʃɛlo] *sm* sky; (*Rel*) heaven

'cifra ['tʃifra] *sf* (*numero*) figure; numeral; (*somma di denaro*) sum, figure; (*monogramma*) monogram, initials *pl*; (*codice*) code, cipher

'ciglio, -i ['tʃiʎʎo] (*delle palpebre*) (*pl(f)* **ciglia**) *sm* (*margine*) edge, verge;

(eye)lash; (eye)lid; (*sopracciglio*) eyebrow
'cigno ['tʃiɲɲo] *sm* swan
cigo'lare [tʃigo'lare] *vi* to squeak, creak
'Cile ['tʃile] *sm*: **il ~** Chile
ci'leno, -a [tʃi'lɛno] *ag, sm/f* Chilean
cili'egia, -gie *o* **ge** [tʃi'ljɛdʒa] *sf* cherry
ciliegina [tʃilje'dʒina] *sf* glacé cherry
cilin'drata [tʃilin'drata] *sf* (*Aut*) (cubic) capacity; **una macchina di grossa ~** a big-engined car
ci'lindro [tʃi'lindro] *sm* cylinder; (*cappello*) top hat
'cima ['tʃima] *sf* (*sommità*) top; (*di monte*) top, summit; (*estremità*) end; **in ~ a** at the top of; **da ~ a fondo** from top to bottom; (*fig*) from beginning to end
'cimice ['tʃimitʃe] *sf* (*Zool*) bug; (*puntina*) drawing pin (BRIT), thumbtack (US)
cimini'era [tʃimi'njɛra] *sf* chimney; (*di nave*) funnel
cimi'tero [tʃimi'tɛro] *sm* cemetery
'Cina ['tʃina] *sf*: **la ~** China
cin'cin [tʃin'tʃin] *escl* cheers!
'cinema ['tʃinema] *sm inv* cinema
ci'nese [tʃi'nese] *ag, sm/f, sm* Chinese *inv*
'cinghia ['tʃingja] *sf* strap; (*cintura, Tecn*) belt
cinghi'ale [tʃin'gjale] *sm* wild boar
cinguet'tare [tʃingwet'tare] *vi* to twitter
'cinico, -a, -ci, -che ['tʃiniko] *ag* cynical ▷ *sm/f* cynic
cin'quanta [tʃin'kwanta] *num* fifty; **cinquan'tesimo, -a** *num* fiftieth
cinquan'tina [tʃinkwan'tina] *sf* (*serie*): **una ~ (di)** about fifty; (*età*): **essere sulla ~** to be about fifty
'cinque ['tʃinkwe] *num* five; **avere ~ anni** to be five (years old); **il ~ dicembre 1998** the fifth of December 1998; **alle ~** (*ora*) at five (o'clock)
cinque'cento [tʃinkwe'tʃɛnto] *num* five hundred ▷ *sm* **il C~** the sixteenth century
cin'tura [tʃin'tura] *sf* belt; **cintura di salvataggio** lifebelt (BRIT), life preserver (US); **cintura di sicurezza** (*Aut, Aer*) safety *o* seat belt
cintu'rino [tʃintu'rino] *sm* strap; **~ dell'orologio** watch strap
ciò [tʃɔ] *pron* this; that; **~ che** what; **~ nonostante** *o* **nondimeno** nevertheless, in spite of that
ci'occa, -che ['tʃɔkka] *sf* (*di capelli*) lock
ciocco'lata [tʃokko'lata] *sf* chocolate; (*bevanda*) (hot) chocolate; **cioccola'tino** *sm* chocolate
cioè [tʃo'ɛ] *av* that is (to say)
ci'otola ['tʃɔtola] *sf* bowl
ci'ottolo ['tʃɔttolo] *sm* pebble; (*di strada*) cobble(stone)
ci'polla [tʃi'polla] *sf* onion; (*di tulipano ecc*) bulb
cipol'lina [tʃipol'lina] *sf* **cipolline sottaceto** pickled onions
ci'presso [tʃi'prɛsso] *sm* cypress (tree)
'cipria ['tʃiprja] *sf* (face) powder
'Cipro ['tʃipro] *sm* Cyprus
'circa ['tʃirka] *av* about, roughly ▷ *prep* about, concerning; **a mezzogiorno ~** about midday
'circo, -chi ['tʃirko] *sm* circus
circo'lare [tʃirko'lare] *vi* to circulate; (*Aut*) to drive (along), move (along) ▷ *ag* circular ▷ *sf* (*Amm*) circular; (*di autobus*) circle (line)
'circolo ['tʃirkolo] *sm* circle
circon'dare [tʃirkon'dare] *vt* to surround; **circondarsi** *vpr* **circondarsi di** to surround o.s. with
circonvallazi'one [tʃirkonvallat'tsjone] *sf* ring road (BRIT), beltway (US); (*per evitare una città*) by-pass
circos'petto, -a [tʃirkos'pɛtto] *ag* circumspect, cautious
circos'tante [tʃirkos'tante] *ag*

surrounding, neighbouring
circos'tanza [tʃirkos'tantsa] *sf* circumstance; (*occasione*) occasion
cir'cuito [tʃir'kuito] *sm* circuit
CISL *sigla f* (= *Confederazione Italiana Sindacati Lavoratori*) *trades union organization*
cis'terna [tʃis'tɛrna] *sf* tank, cistern
'cisti ['tʃisti] *sf* cyst
cis'tite [tʃis'tite] *sf* cystitis
ci'tare [tʃi'tare] *vt* (*Dir*) to summon; (*autore*) to quote; (*a esempio, modello*) to cite
ci'tofono [tʃi'tɔfono] *sm* entry phone; (*in uffici*) intercom
città [tʃit'ta] *sf inv* town; (*importante*) city; **città universitaria** university campus
cittadi'nanza [tʃittadi'nantsa] *sf* citizens *pl*; (*Dir*) citizenship
citta'dino, -a [tʃitta'dino] *ag* town *cpd*; city *cpd* ▷ *sm/f* (*di uno Stato*) citizen; (*abitante di città*) townsman, city dweller
ci'uccio ['tʃuttʃo] *sm* (*fam*) comforter, dummy (BRIT), pacifier (US)
ci'uffo ['tʃuffo] *sm* tuft
ci'vetta [tʃi'vetta] *sf* (*Zool*) owl; (*fig: donna*) coquette, flirt ▷ *ag inv* **auto/ nave ~** decoy car/ship
'civico, -a, -ci, -che ['tʃivico] *ag* civic; (*museo*) municipal, town *cpd*; city *cpd*
ci'vile [tʃi'vile] *ag* civil; (*non militare*) civilian; (*nazione*) civilized ▷ *sm* civilian
civiltà [tʃivil'ta] *sf* civilization; (*cortesia*) civility
'clacson *sm inv* (*Aut*) horn
clandes'tino, -a *ag* clandestine; (*Pol*) underground, clandestine; (*immigrato*) illegal ▷ *sm/f* stowaway; (*anche: **immigrato ~***) illegal immigrant
'classe *sf* class; **di ~** (*fig*) with class; of excellent quality; **classe operaia** working class; **classe turistica** (*Aer*) economy class
'classico, -a, -ci, -che *ag* classical; (*tradizionale: moda*) classic(al) ▷ *sm* classic; classical author
clas'sifica *sf* classification; (*Sport*) placings *pl*
classifi'care *vt* to classify; (*candidato, compito*) to grade; **classificarsi** *vpr* to be placed
'clausola *sf* (*Dir*) clause
clavi'cembalo [klavi'tʃembalo] *sm* harpsichord
cla'vicola *sf* (*Anat*) collar bone
clic'care *vi* (*Inform*): **~ su** to click on
cli'ente *sm/f* customer, client
'clima, -i *sm* climate; **climatizzatore** *sm* air conditioning system
'clinica, -che *sf* (*scienza*) clinical medicine; (*casa di cura*) clinic, nursing home; (*settore d'ospedale*) clinic
clo'nare *vt* to clone; **clonazione** [klona'tsjone] *sf* cloning
'cloro *sm* chlorine
club *sm inv* club
c.m. *abbr* = **corrente mese**
cm *abbr* (= *centimetro*) cm
coalizi'one [koalit'tsjone] *sf* coalition
'COBAS *sigla mpl* (= *Comitati di base*) *independent trades unions*
'coca *sf* (*bibita*) Coke®; (*droga*) cocaine
coca'ina *sf* cocaine
cocci'nella [kottʃi'nɛlla] *sf* ladybird (BRIT), ladybug (US)
cocci'uto, -a [kot'tʃuto] *ag* stubborn, pigheaded
'cocco, -chi *sm* (*pianta*) coconut palm; (*frutto*): **noce di ~** coconut ▷ *sm/f* (*fam*) darling
cocco'drillo *sm* crocodile
cocco'lare *vt* to cuddle, fondle
cocerò *ecc* [kotʃe'rɔ] *vb vedi* **cuocere**
co'comero *sm* watermelon
'coda *sf* tail; (*fila di persone, auto*) queue (BRIT), line (US); (*di abiti*) train; **con la ~ dell'occhio** out of the corner of one's eye; **mettersi in ~** to queue (up) (BRIT), line up (US); to join the queue (BRIT) *o* line (US); **coda di cavallo** (*acconciatura*) ponytail

co'dardo, -a *ag* cowardly ▷ *sm/f* coward

'codice ['kodit∫e] *sm* code; **codice di avviamento postale** postcode (BRIT), zip code (US); **codice a barre** bar code; **codice civile** civil code; **codice fiscale** tax code; **codice penale** penal code; **codice segreto** (*di tessera magnetica*) PIN (number); **codice della strada** highway code

coe'rente *ag* coherent

coe'taneo, -a *ag, sm/f* contemporary

'cofano *sm* (*Aut*) bonnet (BRIT), hood (US); (*forziere*) chest

'cogliere ['kɔʎʎere] *vt* (*fiore: frutto*) to pick, gather; (*sorprendere*) to catch, surprise; (*bersaglio*) to hit; (*fig: momento opportuno ecc*) to grasp, seize, take; (: *capire*) to grasp; **~ qn in flagrante** *o* **in fallo** to catch sb red-handed

co'gnato, -a [koɲ'ɲato] *sm/f* brother-/sister-in-law

co'gnome [koɲ'ɲome] *sm* surname

coinci'denza [kointʃi'dɛntsa] *sf* coincidence; (*Ferr, Aer, di autobus*) connection

coin'cidere [koin'tʃidere] *vi* to coincide

coin'volgere [koin'vɔldʒere] *vt*: **~ in** to involve in

cola'pasta *sm inv* colander

co'lare *vt* (*liquido*) to strain; (*pasta*) to drain; (*oro fuso*) to pour ▷ *vi* (*sudore*) to drip; (*botte*) to leak; (*cera*) to melt; **~ a picco** *vt, vi* (*nave*) to sink

colazi'one [kolat'tsjone] *sf* breakfast; **fare ~** to have breakfast; **a che ora è servita la ~?** what time is breakfast?

co'lera *sm* (*Med*) cholera

'colgo *ecc vb vedi* **cogliere**

'colica *sf* (*Med*) colic

co'lino *sm* strainer

'colla *sf* glue; (*di farina*) paste

collabo'rare *vi* to collaborate; **~ a** to collaborate on; (*giornale*) to contribute to; **collabora'tore, -'trice** *sm/f* collaborator; contributor; **collaboratore esterno** freelance; **collaboratrice familiare** home help

col'lana *sf* necklace; (*collezione*) collection, series

col'lant [kɔ'lɑ̃] *sm inv* tights *pl*

col'lare *sm* collar

col'lasso *sm* (*Med*) collapse

collau'dare *vt* to test, try out

col'lega, -ghi, -ghe *sm/f* colleague

collega'mento *sm* connection; (*Mil*) liaison

colle'gare *vt* to connect, join, link; **collegarsi** *vpr* (*Radio, TV*) to link up; **collegarsi con** (*Tel*) to get through to

col'legio [kol'lɛdʒo] *sm* college; (*convitto*) boarding school; **collegio elettorale** (*Pol*) constituency

'collera *sf* anger

col'lerico, -a, -ci, -che *ag* quick-tempered, irascible

col'letta *sf* collection

col'letto *sm* collar

collezio'nare [kollettsjo'nare] *vt* to collect

collezi'one [kollet'tsjone] *sf* collection

col'lina *sf* hill

col'lirio *sm* eyewash

'collo *sm* neck; (*di abito*) neck, collar; (*pacco*) parcel; **collo del piede** instep

colloca'mento *sm* (*impiego*) employment; (*disposizione*) placing, arrangement

collo'care *vt* (*libri, mobili*) to place; (*Comm: merce*) to find a market for

collocazi'one [kollokat'tsjone] *sf* placing; (*di libro*) classification

col'loquio *sm* conversation, talk; (*ufficiale, per un lavoro*) interview; (*Ins*) preliminary oral exam

col'mare *vt* **~ di** (*anche fig*) to fill with; (*dare in abbondanza*) to load *o* overwhelm with

co'lombo, -a *sm/f* dove; pigeon

co'lonia *sf* colony; (*per bambini*)

holiday camp; **(acqua di) ~** (eau de) cologne
co'lonna *sf* column; **colonna sonora** (*Cinema*) sound track; **colonna vertebrale** spine, spinal column
colon'nello *sm* colonel
colo'rante *sm* colouring
colo'rare *vt* to colour; (*disegno*) to colour in
co'lore *sm* colour; **a colori** in colour, colour *cpd*; **farne di tutti i colori** to get up to all sorts of mischief; **vorrei un ~ diverso** I'd like a different colour
colo'rito, -a *ag* coloured; (*viso*) rosy, pink; (*linguaggio*) colourful ▷ *sm* (*tinta*) colour; (*carnagione*) complexion
'colpa *sf* fault; (*biasimo*) blame; (*colpevolezza*) guilt; (*azione colpevole*) offence; (*peccato*) sin; **di chi è la ~?** whose fault is it?; **è ~ sua** it's his fault; **per ~ di** through, owing to; **col'pevole** *ag* guilty
col'pire *vt* to hit, strike; (*fig*) to strike; **rimanere colpito da qc** to be amazed *o* struck by sth
'colpo *sm* (*urto*) knock; (*: affettivo*) blow, shock; (*: aggressivo*) blow; (*di pistola*) shot; (*Med*) stroke; (*rapina*) raid; **di ~** suddenly; **fare ~** to make a strong impression; **colpo d'aria** chill; **colpo in banca** bank job *o* raid; **colpo basso** (*Pugilato, fig*) punch below the belt; **colpo di fulmine** love at first sight; **colpo di grazia** coup de grâce; **colpo di scena** (*Teatro*) coup de théâtre; (*fig*) dramatic turn of events; **colpo di sole** sunstroke; **colpo di Stato** coup d'état; **colpo di telefono** phone call; **colpo di testa** (sudden) impulse *o* whim; **colpo di vento** gust (of wind); **colpi di sole** (*nei capelli*) highlights
'colsi *ecc vb vedi* **cogliere**
coltel'lata *sf* stab
col'tello *sm* knife; **coltello a serramanico** clasp knife
colti'vare *vt* to cultivate; (*verdura*) to grow, cultivate
'colto, -a *pp di* **cogliere** ▷ *ag* (*istruito*) cultured, educated
'coma *sm inv* coma
comanda'mento *sm* (*Rel*) commandment
coman'dante *sm* (*Mil*) commander, commandant; (*di reggimento*) commanding officer; (*Naut, Aer*) captain
coman'dare *vi* to be in command ▷ *vt* to command; (*imporre*) to order, command; **~ a qn di fare** to order sb to do
combaci'are [komba'tʃare] *vi* to meet; (*fig: coincidere*) to coincide
com'battere *vt, vi* to fight
combi'nare *vt* to combine; (*organizzare*) to arrange; (*fam: fare*) to make, cause; **combinazi'one** *sf* combination; (*caso fortuito*) coincidence; **per combinazione** by chance
combus'tibile *ag* combustible ▷ *sm* fuel

PAROLA CHIAVE

'come *av* 1 (*alla maniera di*) like; **ti comporti come lui** you behave like him *o* like he does; **bianco come la neve** (as) white as snow; **come se** as if, as though
2 (*in qualità di*) as a; **lavora come autista** he works as a driver
3 (*interrogativo*) how; **come ti chiami?** what's your name?; **come sta?** how are you?; **com'è il tuo amico?** what is your friend like?; **come?** (*prego?*) pardon?, sorry?; **come mai?** how come?; **come mai non ci hai avvertiti?** why on earth didn't you warn us?
4 (*esclamativo*): **come sei bravo!** how clever you are!; **come mi dispiace!** I'm terribly sorry!
▷ *cong* 1 (*in che modo*) how; **mi ha**

spiegato come l'ha conosciuto he told me how he met him
2 (*correlativo*) as; (*con comparativi di maggioranza*) than; **non è bravo come pensavo** he isn't as clever as I thought; **è meglio di come pensassi** it's better than I thought
3 (*appena che, quando*) as soon as; **come arrivò, iniziò a lavorare** as soon as he arrived, he set to work; *vedi* **così**; **tanto**

'comico, -a, -ci, -che *ag* (*Teatro*) comic; (*buffo*) comical ▷ *sm* (*attore*) comedian, comic actor
cominci'are [komin'tʃare] *vt, vi* to begin, start; **~ a fare/col fare** to begin to do/by doing; **a che ora comincia il film?** when does the film start?
comi'tato *sm* committee
comi'tiva *sf* party, group
co'mizio [ko'mittsjo] *sm* (*Pol*) meeting, assembly
com'media *sf* comedy; (*opera teatrale*) play; (*: che fa ridere*) comedy; (*fig*) playacting *no pl*
commemo'rare *vt* to commemorate
commen'tare *vt* to comment on; (*testo*) to annotate; (*Radio, TV*) to give a commentary on
commerci'ale [kommer'tʃale] *ag* commercial, trading; (*peg*) commercial
commercia'lista, -i, e [kommertʃa'lista] *sm/f* (*laureato*) graduate in economics and commerce; (*consulente*) business consultant
commerci'ante [kommer'tʃante] *sm/f* trader, dealer; (*negoziante*) shopkeeper
commerci'are [kommer'tʃare] *vt, vi* **~ in** to deal *o* trade in
com'mercio [kom'mɛrtʃo] *sm* trade, commerce; **essere in ~** (*prodotto*) to be on the market *o* on sale; **essere nel ~** (*persona*) to be in business; **commercio al dettaglio/all'ingrosso** retail/wholesale trade; **commercio elettronico** e-commerce
com'messo, -a *pp di* **commettere** ▷ *sm/f* shop assistant (BRIT), sales clerk (US) ▷ *sm* (*impiegato*) clerk; **commesso viaggiatore** commercial traveller
commes'tibile *ag* edible
com'mettere *vt* to commit
com'misi *ecc vb vedi* **commettere**
commissari'ato *sm* (*Amm*) commissionership; (*: sede*) commissioner's office; **commissariato di polizia** police station
commis'sario *sm* commissioner; (*di pubblica sicurezza*) ≈ (police) superintendent (BRIT), ≈ (police) captain (US); (*Sport*) steward; (*membro di commissione*) member of a committee *o* board
commissi'one *sf* (*incarico*) errand; (*comitato, percentuale*) commission; (*Comm: ordinazione*) order; **commissioni** *sfpl* (*acquisti*) shopping *sg*; **commissioni bancarie** bank charges; **commissione d'esame** examining board
com'mosso, -a *pp di* **commuovere**
commo'vente *ag* moving
commozi'one [kommot'tsjone] *sf* emotion, deep feeling; **commozione cerebrale** (*Med*) concussion
commu'overe *vt* to move, affect; **commuoversi** *vpr* to be moved
como'dino *sm* bedside table
comodità *sf inv* comfort; convenience
'comodo, -a *ag* comfortable; (*facile*) easy; (*conveniente*) convenient; (*utile*) useful, handy ▷ *sm* comfort; convenience; **con ~** at one's convenience *o* leisure; **fare il proprio ~** to do as one pleases; **far ~** to be

useful *o* handy
compa'gnia [kompaɲ'ɲia] *sf* company; (*gruppo*) gathering
com'pagno, -a [kom'paɲɲo] *sm/f* (*di classe, gioco*) companion; (*Pol*) comrade
com'paio *ecc vb vedi* **comparire**
compa'rare *vt* to compare
compara'tivo, -a *ag, sm* comparative
compa'rire *vi* to appear
com'parvi *ecc vb vedi* **comparire**
compassi'one *sf* compassion, pity; **avere ~ di qn** to feel sorry for sb, to pity sb
com'passo *sm* (pair of) compasses *pl*; callipers *pl*
compa'tibile *ag* (*scusabile*) excusable; (*conciliabile, Inform*) compatible
compa'tire *vt* (*aver compassione di*) to sympathize with, feel sorry for; (*scusare*) to make allowances for
com'patto, -a *ag* compact; (*roccia*) solid; (*folla*) dense; (*fig: gruppo, partito*) united
compen'sare *vt* (*equilibrare*) to compensate for, make up for; **~ qn di** (*rimunerare*) to pay *o* remunerate sb for; (*risarcire*) to pay compensation to sb for; (*fig: fatiche, dolori*) to reward sb for; **com'penso** *sm* compensation payment, remuneration; reward; **in compenso** (*d'altra parte*) on the other hand
compe'rare *vt* = **comprare**
'compere *sfpl*: **fare ~** to do the shopping
compe'tente *ag* competent; (*mancia*) apt, suitable
com'petere *vi* to compete, vie; (*Dir: spettare*): **~ a** to lie within the competence of; **competizi'one** *sf* competition
compi'angere [kom'pjandʒere] *vt* to sympathize with, feel sorry for
'compiere *vt* (*concludere*) to finish, complete; (*adempiere*) to carry out, fulfil; **compiersi** *vpr* (*avverarsi*) to be fulfilled, come true; **~ gli anni** to have one's birthday
compi'lare *vt* (*modulo*) to fill in; (*dizionario, elenco*) to compile
'compito *sm* (*incarico*) task, duty; (*dovere*) duty; (*Ins*) exercise; (*: a casa*) piece of homework; **fare i compiti** to do one's homework
comple'anno *sm* birthday
complessità *sf* complexity
comples'sivo, -a *ag* (*globale*) comprehensive, overall; (*totale: cifra*) total
com'plesso, -a *ag* complex ▷ *sm* (*Psic, Edil*) complex; (*Mus: corale*) ensemble; (*: orchestrina*) band; (*: di musica pop*) group; **in** *o* **nel ~** on the whole; **complesso alberghiero** hotel complex; **complesso edilizio** building complex; **complesso vitaminico** vitamin complex
completa'mente *av* completely
comple'tare *vt* to complete
com'pleto, -a *ag* complete; (*teatro, autobus*) full ▷ *sm* suit; **al ~** full; (*tutti presenti*) all present; **completo da sci** ski suit
compli'care *vt* to complicate; **complicarsi** *vpr* to become complicated
'complice ['kɔmplitʃe] *sm/f* accomplice
complicità [komplitʃi'ta] *sf inv* complicity; **un sorriso/uno sguardo di ~** a knowing smile/look
complimen'tarsi *vpr*: **~ con** to congratulate
compli'mento *sm* compliment; **complimenti** *smpl* (*cortesia eccessiva*) ceremony *sg*; (*ossequi*) regards, compliments; **complimenti!** congratulations!; **senza complimenti!** don't stand on ceremony!; make yourself at home!; help yourself!

complot'tare *vi* to plot, conspire
com'plotto *sm* plot, conspiracy
com'pone *ecc vb vedi* **comporre**
compo'nente *sm/f* member ▷ *sm* component
com'pongo *ecc vb vedi* **comporre**
componi'mento *sm* (*Dir*) settlement; (*Ins*) composition; (*poetico, teatrale*) work
com'porre *vt* (*musica, testo*) to compose; (*mettere in ordine*) to arrange; (*Dir: lite*) to settle; (*Tip*) to set; (*Tel*) to dial; **comporsi** *vpr* **comporsi di** to consist of, be composed of
comporta'mento *sm* behaviour
compor'tare *vt* (*implicare*) to involve; **comportarsi** *vpr* to behave
com'posi *ecc vb vedi* **comporre**
composi'tore, -'trice *sm/f* composer; (*Tip*) compositor, typesetter
com'posto, -a *pp di* **comporre** ▷ *ag* (*persona*) composed, self-possessed; (: *decoroso*) dignified; (*formato da più elementi*) compound *cpd* ▷ *sm* compound
com'prare *vt* to buy; **dove posso ~ delle cartoline?** where can I buy some postcards?
com'prendere *vt* (*contenere*) to comprise, consist of; (*capire*) to understand
compren'sibile *ag* understandable
comprensi'one *sf* understanding
compren'sivo, -a *ag* (*prezzo*): **~ di** inclusive of; (*indulgente*) understanding

> Attenzione! In inglese esiste la parola *comprehensive*, che però in genere significa *completo*.

com'preso, -a *pp di* **comprendere** ▷ *ag* (*incluso*) included; **il servizio è ~?** is service included?
com'pressa *sf* (*Med: garza*) compress; (: *pastiglia*) tablet; *vedi anche* **compresso**
com'primere *vt* (*premere*) to press; (*Fisica*) to compress; (*fig*) to repress
compro'messo, -a *pp di* **compromettere** ▷ *sm* compromise
compro'mettere *vt* to compromise; **compromettersi** *vpr* to compromise o.s.
com'puter *sm inv* computer
comu'nale *ag* municipal, town *cpd*, ≈ borough *cpd*
co'mune *ag* common; (*consueto*) common, everyday; (*di livello medio*) average; (*ordinario*) ordinary ▷ *sm* (*Amm*) town council; (: *sede*) town hall ▷ *sf* (*di persone*) commune; **fuori del ~** out of the ordinary; **avere in ~** to have in common, share; **mettere in ~** to share
comuni'care *vt* (*notizia*) to pass on, convey; (*malattia*) to pass on; (*ansia ecc*) to communicate; (*trasmettere: calore ecc*) to transmit, communicate; (*Rel*) to administer communion to ▷ *vi* to communicate
comuni'cato *sm* communiqué; **comunicato stampa** press release
comunicazi'one [komunikat'tsjone] *sf* communication; (*annuncio*) announcement; (*Tel*): **dare la ~ a qn** to put sb through; **ottenere la ~** to get through; **comunicazione (telefonica)** (telephone) call
comuni'one *sf* communion; **comunione di beni** (*Dir*) joint ownership of property
comu'nismo *sm* communism
comunità *sf inv* community; **Comunità Europea** European Community
co'munque *cong* however, no matter how ▷ *av* (*in ogni modo*) in any case; (*tuttavia*) however, nevertheless
con *prep* with; **partire col treno** to leave by train; **~ mio grande stupore** to my great astonishment; **~ tutto ciò** for all that
con'cedere [kon'tʃɛdere] *vt*

(*accordare*) to grant; (*ammettere*) to admit, concede; **concedersi qc** to treat o.s. to sth, to allow o.s. sth

concentrarsi *vpr* to concentrate

concentrazi'one *sf* concentration

conce'pire [kontʃe'pire] *vt* (*bambino*) to conceive; (*progetto, idea*) to conceive (of); (*metodo, piano*) to devise

con'certo [kon'tʃɛrto] *sm* (*Mus*) concert; (: *componimento*) concerto

con'cessi *ecc* [kon'tʃɛssi] *vb vedi* **concedere**

con'cetto [kon'tʃɛtto] *sm* (*pensiero, idea*) concept; (*opinione*) opinion

concezi'one [kontʃet'tsjone] *sf* conception

con'chiglia [kon'kiʎʎa] *sf* shell

conci'are [kon'tʃare] *vt* (*pelli*) to tan; (*tabacco*) to cure; (*fig*: *ridurre in cattivo stato*) to beat up; **conciarsi** *vpr* (*sporcarsi*) to get in a mess; (*vestirsi male*) to dress badly

concili'are [kontʃi'ljare] *vt* to reconcile; (*contravvenzione*) to pay on the spot; (*sonno*) to be conducive to, induce; **conciliarsi qc** to gain *o* win sth (for o.s.); **conciliarsi qn** to win sb over; **conciliarsi con** to be reconciled with

con'cime [kon'tʃime] *sm* manure; (*chimico*) fertilizer

con'ciso, -a [kon'tʃizo] *ag* concise, succinct

concitta'dino, -a [kontʃitta'dino] *sm/f* fellow citizen

con'cludere *vt* to conclude; (*portare a compimento*) to conclude, finish, bring to an end; (*operare positivamente*) to achieve ▷ *vi* (*essere convincente*) to be conclusive; **concludersi** *vpr* to come to an end, close

concor'dare *vt* (*tregua, prezzo*) to agree on; (*Ling*) to make agree ▷ *vi* to agree

con'corde *ag* (*d'accordo*) in agreement; (*simultaneo*) simultaneous

concor'rente *sm/f* competitor; (*Ins*) candidate; **concor'renza** *sf* competition

concorrenzi'ale [konkorren'tsjale] *ag* competitive

con'correre *vi*: **~ (in)** (*Mat*) to converge *o* meet (in); **~ (a)** (*competere*) to compete (for); (: *Ins*: *a una cattedra*) to apply (for); (*partecipare*: *a un'impresa*) to take part (in), contribute (to); **con'corso, -a** *pp di* **concorrere** ▷ *sm* competition; (*Ins*) competitive examination; **concorso di colpa** (*Dir*) contributory negligence

con'creto, -a *ag* concrete

con'danna *sf* sentence; conviction; condemnation

condan'nare *vt* (*Dir*): **~ a** to sentence to; **~ per** to convict of; (*disapprovare*) to condemn

conden'sare *vt* to condense

condi'mento *sm* seasoning; dressing

con'dire *vt* to season; (*insalata*) to dress

condi'videre *vt* to share

condizio'nale [kondittsjo'nale] *ag* conditional ▷ *sm* (*Ling*) conditional ▷ *sf* (*Dir*) suspended sentence

condizio'nare [kondittsjo'nare] *vt* to condition; **ad aria condizionata** air-conditioned; **condiziona'tore** *sm* air conditioner

condizi'one [kondit'tsjone] *sf* condition

condogli'anze [kondoʎ'ʎantse] *sfpl* condolences

condo'minio *sm* joint ownership; (*edificio*) jointly-owned building

con'dotta *sf* (*modo di comportarsi*) conduct, behaviour; (*di un affare ecc*) handling; (*di acqua*) piping; (*incarico sanitario*) *country medical practice controlled by a local authority*

condu'cente [kondu'tʃɛnte] *sm* driver

con'duco *ecc vb vedi* **condurre**

con'durre *vt* to conduct; (*azienda*) to manage; (*accompagnare*: *bambino*) to

take; (*automobile*) to drive; (*trasportare*: *acqua, gas*) to convey, conduct; (*fig*) to lead ▷ *vi* to lead
con'dussi *ecc vb vedi* **condurre**
confe'renza [konfe'rɛntsa] *sf* (*discorso*) lecture; (*riunione*) conference; **conferenza stampa** press conference
con'ferma *sf* confirmation
confer'mare *vt* to confirm
confes'sare *vt* to confess; **confessarsi** *vpr* to confess; **andare a confessarsi** (*Rel*) to go to confession
con'fetto *sm* sugared almond; (*Med*) pill

> Attenzione! In inglese esiste la parola *confetti*, che però significa *coriandoli*.

confet'tura *sf* (*gen*) jam; (*di arance*) marmalade
confezio'nare [konfettsjo'nare] *vt* (*vestito*) to make (up); (*merci, pacchi*) to package
confezi'one [konfet'tsjone] *sf* (*di abiti*: *da uomo*) tailoring; (: *da donna*) dressmaking; (*imballaggio*) packaging; **confezioni per signora** ladies' wear; **confezioni da uomo** menswear; **confezione regalo** gift pack
confic'care *vt* **~ qc in** to hammer *o* drive sth into; **conficcarsi** *vpr* to stick
confi'dare *vi*: **~ in** to confide in, rely on ▷ *vt* to confide; **confidarsi con qn** to confide in sb
configu'rare *vt* (*Inform*) to set
configurazi'one [konfigurat'tsjone] *sf* configuration; (*Inform*) setting
confi'nare *vi* **~ con** to border on ▷ *vt* (*Pol*) to intern; (*fig*) to confine
Confin'dustria *sigla f* (= *Confederazione Generale dell'Industria Italiana*) *employers' association*, ≈ CBI (BRIT)
con'fine *sm* boundary; (*di paese*) border, frontier
confis'care *vt* to confiscate
con'flitto *sm* conflict; **conflitto d'interessi** conflict of interests
conflu'enza [konflu'ɛntsa] *sf* (*di fiumi*) confluence; (*di strade*) junction
con'fondere *vt* to mix up, confuse; (*imbarazzare*) to embarrass; **confondersi** *vpr* (*mescolarsi*) to mingle; (*turbarsi*) to be confused; (*sbagliare*) to get mixed up
confor'tare *vt* to comfort, console
confron'tare *vt* to compare
con'fronto *sm* comparison; **in** *o* **a ~ di** in comparison with, compared to; **nei miei (*o* tuoi *ecc*) confronti** towards me (*o* you *ecc*)
con'fusi *ecc vb vedi* **confondere**
confusi'one *sf* confusion; (*chiasso*) racket, noise; (*imbarazzo*) embarrassment
con'fuso, -a *pp di* **confondere** ▷ *ag* (*vedi confondere*) confused; embarrassed
conge'dare [kondʒe'dare] *vt* to dismiss; (*Mil*) to demobilize; **congedarsi** *vpr* to take one's leave
con'gegno *sm* device, mechanism
conge'lare [kondʒe'lare] *vt* to freeze; **congelarsi** *vpr* to freeze;
congela'tore *sm* freezer
congesti'one [kondʒes'tjone] *sf* congestion
conget'tura [kondʒet'tura] *sf* conjecture
con'giungere [kon'dʒundʒere] *vt* to join (together); **congiungersi** *vpr* to join (together)
congiunti'vite [kondʒunti'vite] *sf* conjunctivitis
congiun'tivo [kondʒun'tivo] *sm* (*Ling*) subjunctive
congi'unto, -a [kon'dʒunto] *pp di* **congiungere** ▷ *ag* (*unito*) joined ▷ *sm/f* relative
congiunzi'one [kondʒun'tsjone] *sf* (*Ling*) conjunction
congi'ura [kon'dʒura] *sf* conspiracy
congratu'larsi *vpr*: **~ con qn per qc** to congratulate sb on sth

congratulazi'oni [kongratulat'tsjoni] *sfpl* congratulations
con'gresso *sm* congress
C.O.N.I. *sigla m* (= *Comitato Olimpico Nazionale Italiano*) Italian Olympic Games Committee
coni'are *vt* to mint, coin; (*fig*) to coin
co'niglio [ko'niʎʎo] *sm* rabbit
coniu'gare *vt* (*Ling*) to conjugate; **coniugarsi** *vpr* to get married
'coniuge ['kɔnjudʒe] *sm/f* spouse
connazio'nale [konnattsjo'nale] *sm/f* fellow-countryman/woman
connessi'one *sf* connection
con'nettere *vt* to connect, join ▷ *vi* (*fig*) to think straight
'cono *sm* cone; **cono gelato** ice-cream cone
co'nobbi *ecc vb vedi* **conoscere**
cono'scente [konoʃ'ʃɛnte] *sm/f* acquaintance
cono'scenza [konoʃ'ʃɛntsa] *sf* (*il sapere*) knowledge *no pl*; (*persona*) acquaintance; (*facoltà sensoriale*) consciousness *no pl*; **perdere ~** to lose consciousness
co'noscere [ko'noʃʃere] *vt* to know; **ci siamo conosciuti a Firenze** we (first) met in Florence; **conoscersi** *vpr* to know o.s.; (*reciproco*) to know each other; (*incontrarsi*) to meet; **~ qn di vista** to know sb by sight; **farsi ~** (*fig*) to make a name for o.s.; **conosci'uto, -a** *pp di* **conoscere** ▷ *ag* well-known
con'quista *sf* conquest
conquis'tare *vt* to conquer; (*fig*) to gain, win
consa'pevole *ag*: **~ di** aware *o* conscious of
'conscio, -a, -sci, -sce ['kɔnʃo] *ag*: **~ di** aware *o* conscious of
consecu'tivo, -a *ag* consecutive; (*successivo*: *giorno*) following, next
con'segna [kon'seɲɲa] *sf* delivery; (*merce consegnata*) consignment; (*custodia*) care, custody; (*Mil*: *ordine*) orders *pl*; (: *punizione*) confinement to barracks; **pagamento alla ~** cash on delivery; **dare qc in ~ a qn** to entrust sth to sb
conse'gnare [konseɲ'ɲare] *vt* to deliver; (*affidare*) to entrust, hand over; (*Mil*) to confine to barracks
consegu'enza [konse'gwɛntsa] *sf* consequence; **per** *o* **di ~** consequently
con'senso *sm* approval, consent; **consenso informato** informed consent
consen'tire *vi*: **~ a** to consent *o* agree to ▷ *vt* to allow, permit
con'serva *sf* (*Cuc*) preserve; **conserva di frutta** jam; **conserva di pomodoro** tomato purée
conser'vante *sm* (*per alimenti*) preservative
conser'vare *vt* (*Cuc*) to preserve; (*custodire*) to keep; (: *dalla distruzione ecc*) to preserve, conserve
conserva'tore, -'trice *sm/f* (*Pol*) conservative
conserva'torio *sm* (*di musica*) conservatory
conservazi'one [konservat'tsjone] *sf* preservation; conservation
conside'rare *vt* to consider; (*reputare*) to consider, regard; **considerarsi** *vpr* to consider o.s.
consigli'are [konsiʎ'ʎare] *vt* (*persona*) to advise; (*metodo, azione*) to recommend, advise, suggest; **mi può ~ un buon ristorante?** can you recommend a good restaurant?; **con'siglio** *sm* (*suggerimento*) advice *no pl*, piece of advice; (*assemblea*) council; **consiglio d'amministrazione** board; **Consiglio d'Europa** Council of Europe; **Consiglio dei Ministri** (*Pol*): **il Consiglio dei Ministri** ≈ the Cabinet
consis'tente *ag* thick; solid; (*fig*) sound, valid
con'sistere *vi*: **~ in** to consist of
conso'lare *ag* consular ▷ *vt* (*confortare*) to console, comfort;

(*rallegrare*) to cheer up; **consolarsi** *vpr* to be comforted; to cheer up
conso'lato *sm* consulate
consolazi'one [konsolat'tsjone] *sf* consolation, comfort
'console *sm* consul
conso'nante *sf* consonant
'consono, -a *ag* **~ a** consistent with, consonant with
con'sorte *sm/f* consort
consta'tare *vt* to establish, verify
consu'eto, -a *ag* habitual, usual
consu'lente *sm/f* consultant
consul'tare *vt* to consult; **consultarsi** *vpr* **consultarsi con qn** to seek the advice of sb
consul'torio *sm*: **~ familiare** family planning clinic
consu'mare *vt* (*logorare*: *abiti, scarpe*) to wear out; (*usare*) to consume, use up; (*mangiare, bere*) to consume; (*Dir*) to consummate; **consumarsi** *vpr* to wear out; to be used up; (*anche fig*) to be consumed; (*combustibile*) to burn out
con'tabile *ag* accounts *cpd*, accounting ▷ *sm/f* accountant
contachi'lometri [kontaki'lɔmetri] *sm inv* ≈ mileometer
conta'dino, -a *sm/f* countryman/woman, farm worker; (*peg*) peasant
contagi'are [konta'dʒare] *vt* to infect
contagi'oso, -a *ag* infectious; contagious
conta'gocce [konta'gottʃe] *sm inv* (*Med*) dropper
contami'nare *vt* to contaminate
con'tante *sm* cash; **pagare in contanti** to pay cash; **non ho contanti** I haven't got any cash
con'tare *vt* to count; (*considerare*) to consider ▷ *vi* to count, be of importance; **~ su qn** to count *o* rely on sb; **~ di fare qc** to intend to do sth; **conta'tore** *sm* meter
contat'tare *vt* to contact
con'tatto *sm* contact
'conte *sm* count
conteggi'are [konted'dʒare] *vt* to charge, put on the bill
con'tegno [kon'teɲɲo] *sm* (*comportamento*) behaviour; (*atteggiamento*) attitude; **darsi un ~** to act nonchalant; to pull o.s. together
contemporanea'mente *av* simultaneously; at the same time
contempo'raneo, -a *ag, sm/f* contemporary
conten'dente *sm/f* opponent, adversary
conte'nere *vt* to contain; **conteni'tore** *sm* container
conten'tezza [konten'tettsa] *sf* contentment
con'tento, -a *ag* pleased, glad; **~ di** pleased with
conte'nuto *sm* contents *pl*; (*argomento*) content
con'tessa *sf* countess
contes'tare *vt* (*Dir*) to notify; (*fig*) to dispute
con'testo *sm* context
continen'tale *ag, sm/f* continental
conti'nente *ag* continent ▷ *sm* (*Geo*) continent; (: *terra ferma*) mainland
contin'gente [kontin'dʒɛnte] *ag* contingent ▷ *sm* (*Comm*) quota; (*Mil*) contingent
continua'mente *av* (*senza interruzione*) continuously, nonstop; (*ripetutamente*) continually
continu'are *vt* to continue (with), go on with ▷ *vi* to continue, go on; **~ a fare qc** to go on *o* continue doing sth
continuità *sf* continuity
con'tinuo, -a *ag* (*numerazione*) continuous; (*pioggia*) continual, constant; (*Elettr*): **corrente continua** direct current; **di ~** continually
'conto *sm* (*calcolo*) calculation; (*Comm, Econ*) account; (*di ristorante, albergo*) bill; (*fig*: *stima*) consideration, esteem; **il ~, per favore** can I have the

bill, please?; **lo metta sul mio ~** put it on my bill; **fare i conti con qn** to settle one's account with sb; **fare ~ su qn/qc** to count *o* rely on sb; **rendere ~ a qn di qc** to be accountable to sb for sth; **tener ~ di qn/qc** to take sb/sth into account; **per ~ di** on behalf of; **per ~ mio** as far as I'm concerned; **a conti fatti, in fin dei conti** all things considered; **conto corrente** current account; **conto alla rovescia** countdown

con'torno *sm* (*linea*) outline, contour; (*ornamento*) border; (*Cuc*) vegetables *pl*

con'torto, -a *pp di* **contorcere**

contrabbandi'ere, -a *sm/f* smuggler

contrab'bando *sm* smuggling, contraband; **merce di ~** contraband, smuggled goods *pl*

contrab'basso *sm* (*Mus*) (double) bass

contraccambi'are *vt* (*favore ecc*) to return

contraccet'tivo, -a [kontrattʃet'tivo] *ag, sm* contraceptive

contrac'colpo *sm* rebound; (*di arma da fuoco*) recoil; (*fig*) repercussion

contrad'dire *vt* to contradict; **contraddirsi** *vpr* to contradict o.s.; (*uso reciproco: persone*) to contradict each other *o* one another; (*: testimonianze ecc*) to be contradictory

contraf'fare *vt* (*persona*) to mimic; (*alterare: voce*) to disguise; (*firma*) to forge, counterfeit

contraria'mente *av*: **~ a** contrary to

contrari'are *vt* (*contrastare*) to thwart, oppose; (*irritare*) to annoy, bother

con'trario, -a *ag* opposite; (*sfavorevole*) unfavourable ▷ *sm* opposite; **essere ~ a qc** (*persona*) to be against sth; **in caso ~** otherwise; **avere qc in ~** to have some objection; **al ~** on the contrary

contrasse'gnare [kontrassen'ɲare] *vt* to mark

contras'tare *vt* (*avversare*) to oppose; (*impedire*) to bar; (*negare: diritto*) to contest, dispute ▷ *vi* **~ (con)** (*essere in disaccordo*) to contrast (with); (*lottare*) to struggle (with)

contrat'tacco *sm* counterattack

contrat'tare *vt, vi* to negotiate

contrat'tempo *sm* hitch

con'tratto, -a *pp di* **contrarre** ▷ *sm* contract

contravvenzi'one [contravven'tsjone] *sf* contravention; (*ammenda*) fine

contrazi'one [kontrat'tsjone] *sf* contraction; (*di prezzi ecc*) reduction

contribu'ente *sm/f* taxpayer; ratepayer (BRIT), property tax payer (US)

contribu'ire *vi* to contribute

'contro *prep* against; **~ di me/lui** against me/him; **pastiglie ~ la tosse** throat lozenges; **~ pagamento** (*Comm*) on payment ▷ *prefisso*: **controfi'gura** *sf* (*Cinema*) double

control'lare *vt* (*accertare*) to check; (*sorvegliare*) to watch, control; (*tenere nel proprio potere, fig: dominare*) to control; **controllarsi** *vpr* to control o.s.; **con'trollo** *sm* check; watch; control; **controllo delle nascite** birth control; **control'lore** *sm* (*Ferr, Autobus*) (ticket) inspector

contro'luce [kontro'lutʃe] *sf inv* (*Fot*) backlit shot ▷ *av* **(in) ~** against the light; (*fotografare*) into the light

contro'mano *av*: **guidare ~** to drive on the wrong side of the road; (*in un senso unico*) to drive the wrong way up a one-way street

controprodu'cente [kontroprodu'tʃɛnte] *ag* counterproductive

contro'senso *sm* (*contraddizione*) contradiction in terms; (*assurdità*)

nonsense
controspio'naggio [kontrospio'naddʒo] *sm* counterespionage
contro'versia *sf* controversy; (*Dir*) dispute
contro'verso, -a *ag* controversial
contro'voglia [kontro'vɔʎʎa] *av* unwillingly
contusi'one *sf* (*Med*) bruise
convale'scente [konvaleʃ'ʃɛnte] *ag, sm/f* convalescent
convali'dare *vt* (*Amm*) to validate; (*fig*: *sospetto, dubbio*) to confirm
con'vegno [kon'veɲɲo] *sm* (*incontro*) meeting; (*congresso*) convention, congress; (*luogo*) meeting place
conve'nevoli *smpl* civilities
conveni'ente *ag* suitable; (*vantaggioso*) profitable; (: *prezzo*) cheap

> Attenzione! In inglese esiste la parola *convenient*, che però significa *comodo*.

conve'nire *vi* (*riunirsi*) to gather, assemble; (*concordare*) to agree; (*tornare utile*) to be worthwhile ▷ *vb impers* **conviene fare questo** it is advisable to do this; **conviene andarsene** we should go; **ne convengo** I agree
con'vento *sm* (*di frati*) monastery; (*di suore*) convent
convenzio'nale [konventsjo'nale] *ag* conventional
convenzi'one [konven'tsjone] *sf* (*Dir*) agreement; (*nella società*) convention
conver'sare *vi* to have a conversation, converse
conversazi'one [konversat'tsjone] *sf* conversation; **fare ~** to chat, have a chat
conversi'one *sf* conversion; **conversione ad U** (*Aut*) U-turn
conver'tire *vt* (*trasformare*) to change; (*Pol, Rel*) to convert; **convertirsi** *vpr* **convertirsi (a)** to be converted (to)
con'vesso, -a *ag* convex
convin'cente [konvin'tʃɛnte] *ag* convincing
con'vincere [kon'vintʃere] *vt* to convince; **~ qn di qc** to convince sb of sth; **~ qn a fare qc** to persuade sb to do sth; **convincersi** *vpr* **convincersi (di qc)** to convince o.s. (of sth); **~ qn di qc** to convince sb of sth; **~ qn a fare qc** to convince sb to do sth
convi'vente *sm/f* common-law husband/wife
con'vivere *vi* to live together
convo'care *vt* to call, convene; (*Dir*) to summon
convulsi'one *sf* convulsion
coope'rare *vi* **~ (a)** to cooperate (in); **coopera'tiva** *sf* cooperative
coordi'nare *vt* to coordinate
co'perchio [ko'pɛrkjo] *sm* cover; (*di pentola*) lid
co'perta *sf* cover; (*di lana*) blanket; (*da viaggio*) rug; (*Naut*) deck
coper'tina *sf* (*Stampa*) cover, jacket
co'perto, -a *pp di* **coprire** ▷ *ag* covered; (*cielo*) overcast ▷ *sm* place setting; (*posto a tavola*) place; (*al ristorante*) cover charge; **~ di** covered in *o* with
coper'tone *sm* (*Aut*) rubber tyre
coper'tura *sf* (*anche Econ, Mil*) cover; (*di edificio*) roofing
'copia *sf* copy; **brutta/bella ~** rough/final copy
copi'are *vt* to copy
copi'one *sm* (*Cinema, Teatro*) script
'coppa *sf* (*bicchiere*) goblet; (*per frutta, gelato*) dish; (*trofeo*) cup, trophy; **coppa dell'olio** oil sump (BRIT) *o* pan (US)
'coppia *sf* (*di persone*) couple; (*di animali, Sport*) pair
coprifu'oco, -chi *sm* curfew
copri'letto *sm* bedspread
copripiu'mino *sm* duvet cover

co'prire *vt* to cover; (*occupare*: *carica, posto*) to hold; **coprirsi** *vpr* (*cielo*) to cloud over; (*vestirsi*) to wrap up, cover up; (*Econ*) to cover o.s.; **coprirsi di** (*macchie, muffa*) to become covered in
coque [kɔk] *sf*: **uovo alla ~** boiled egg
co'raggio [ko'raddʒo] *sm* courage, bravery; **~!** (*forza!*) come on!; (*animo!*) cheer up!
co'rallo *sm* coral
Co'rano *sm* (*Rel*) Koran
co'razza [ko'rattsa] *sf* armour; (*di animali*) carapace, shell; (*Mil*) armour(-plating)
'corda *sf* cord; (*fune*) rope; (*spago, Mus*) string; **dare ~ a qn** to let sb have his (*o* her) way; **tenere sulla ~ qn** to keep sb on tenterhooks; **tagliare la ~** to slip away, sneak off; **corda vocale** vocal cords
cordi'ale *ag* cordial, warm ▷ *sm* (*bevanda*) cordial
'cordless ['kɔːdlɪs] *sm inv* cordless phone
cor'done *sm* cord, string; (*linea*: *di polizia*) cordon; **cordone ombelicale** umbilical cord
Co'rea *sf* **la ~** Korea
coreogra'fia *sf* choreography
cori'andolo *sm* (*Bot*) coriander; **coriandoli** *smpl* confetti *sg*
cor'nacchia [kor'nakkja] *sf* crow
corna'musa *sf* bagpipes *pl*
cor'netta *sf* (*Mus*) cornet; (*Tel*) receiver
cor'netto *sm* (*Cuc*) croissant; (*gelato*) cone
cor'nice [kor'nitʃe] *sf* frame; (*fig*) setting, background
cornici'one [korni'tʃone] *sm* (*di edificio*) ledge; (*Archit*) cornice
'corno (*pl(f)* **-a**) *sm* (*Zool*) horn; (*pl(m)* *-i*: *Mus*) horn; **fare le corna a qn** to be unfaithful to sb
Corno'vaglia [korno'vaʎʎa] *sf*: **la ~** Cornwall
cor'nuto, -a *ag* (*con corna*) horned; (*fam!*: *marito*) cuckolded ▷ *sm* (*fam!*) cuckold; (: *insulto*) bastard (!)
'coro *sm* chorus; (*Rel*) choir
co'rona *sf* crown; (*di fiori*) wreath
'corpo *sm* body; (*militare, diplomatico*) corps *inv*; **prendere ~** to take shape; **a ~ a ~** hand-to-hand; **corpo di ballo** corps de ballet; **corpo insegnante** teaching staff
corpora'tura *sf* build, physique
cor'reggere [kor'rɛddʒere] *vt* to correct; (*compiti*) to correct, mark
cor'rente *ag* (*acqua*: *di fiume*) flowing; (: *di rubinetto*) running; (*moneta, prezzo*) current; (*comune*) everyday ▷ *sm* **essere al ~ (di)** to be well-informed (about); **mettere al ~ (di)** to inform (of) ▷ *sf* (*d'acqua*) current, stream; (*spiffero*) draught; (*Elettr, Meteor*) current; (*fig*) trend, tendency; **la vostra lettera del 5 ~ mese** (*Comm*) your letter of the 5th of this month; **corrente alternata/continua** alternate/direct current; **corrente'mente** *av* commonly; **parlare una lingua correntemente** to speak a language fluently
'correre *vi* to run; (*precipitarsi*) to rush; (*partecipare a una gara*) to race, run; (*fig*: *diffondersi*) to go round ▷ *vt* (*Sport*: *gara*) to compete in; (*rischio*) to run; (*pericolo*) to face; **~ dietro a qn** to run after sb; **corre voce che ...** it is rumoured that ...
cor'ressi *ecc vb vedi* **correggere**
correzi'one [korret'tsjone] *sf* correction; marking; **correzione di bozze** proofreading
corri'doio *sm* corridor; (*in aereo, al cinema*) aisle; **vorrei un posto sul ~** I'd like an aisle seat
corri'dore *sm* (*Sport*) runner; (: *su veicolo*) racer
corri'era *sf* coach (BRIT), bus
corri'ere *sm* (*diplomatico, di guerra, postale*) courier; (*Comm*) carrier
corri'mano *sm* handrail

corrispon'dente *ag* corresponding ▷ *sm/f* correspondent
corrispon'denza [korrispon'dɛntsa] *sf* correspondence
corris'pondere *vi* (*equivalere*): **~ (a)** to correspond (to) ▷ *vt* (*stipendio*) to pay; (*fig*: *amore*) to return
cor'rodere *vt* to corrode
cor'rompere *vt* to corrupt; (*comprare*) to bribe
cor'roso, -a *pp di* **corrodere**
cor'rotto, -a *pp di* **corrompere** ▷ *ag* corrupt
corru'gare *vt* to wrinkle; **~ la fronte** to knit one's brows
cor'ruppi *ecc vb vedi* **corrompere**
corruzi'one [korrut'tsjone] *sf* corruption; bribery
'corsa *sf* running *no pl*; (*gara*) race; (*di autobus, taxi*) journey, trip; **fare una ~** to run, dash; (*Sport*) to run a race; **corsa campestre** cross-country race
'corsi *ecc vb vedi* **correre**
cor'sia *sf* (*Aut, Sport*) lane; (*di ospedale*) ward
'Corsica *sf* **la ~** Corsica
cor'sivo *sm* cursive (writing); (*Tip*) italics *pl*
'corso, -a *pp di* **correre** ▷ *sm* course; (*strada cittadina*) main street; (*di unità monetaria*) circulation; (*di titoli, valori*) rate, price; **in ~** in progress, under way; (*annata*) current; **corso d'acqua** river, stream; (*artificiale*) waterway; **corso d'aggiornamento** refresher course; **corso serale** evening class
'corte *sf* (court)yard; (*Dir, regale*) court; **fare la ~ a qn** to court sb; **corte marziale** court-martial
cor'teccia, -ce [kor'tettʃa] *sf* bark
corteggi'are [korted'dʒare] *vt* to court
cor'teo *sm* procession
cor'tese *ag* courteous; **corte'sia** *sf* courtesy; **per cortesia ...** excuse me, please ...
cor'tile *sm* (court)yard
cor'tina *sf* curtain; (*anche fig*) screen
'corto, -a *ag* short; **essere a ~ di qc** to be short of sth; **corto circuito** short-circuit
'corvo *sm* raven
'cosa *sf* thing; (*faccenda*) affair, matter, business *no pl*; **(che) ~?** what?; **(che) cos'è?** what is it?; **a ~ pensi?** what are you thinking about?
'coscia, -sce ['kɔʃʃa] *sf* thigh; **coscia di pollo** (*Cuc*) chicken leg
cosci'ente [koʃ'ʃɛnte] *ag* conscious; **~ di** conscious *o* aware of

PAROLA CHIAVE

così *av* **1** (*in questo modo*) like this, (in) this way; (*in tal modo*) so; **le cose stanno così** this is the way things stand; **non ho detto così!** I didn't say that!; **come stai? — (e) così** how are you? — so-so; **e così via** and so on; **per così dire** so to speak
2 (*tanto*) so; **così lontano** so far away; **un ragazzo così intelligente** such an intelligent boy
▷ *ag inv* (*tale*): **non ho mai visto un film così** I've never seen such a film ▷ *cong* **1** (*perciò*) so, therefore
2: **così ... come** as ... as; **non è così bravo come te** he's not as good as you; **così ... che** so ... that

cosid'detto, -a *ag* so-called
cos'metico, -a, -ci, -che *ag, sm* cosmetic
cos'pargere [kos'pardʒere] *vt* **~ di** to sprinkle with
cos'picuo, -a *ag* considerable, large
cospi'rare *vi* to conspire
'cossi *ecc vb vedi* **cuocere**
'costa *sf* (*tra terra e mare*) coast(line); (*litorale*) shore; (*Anat*) rib; **la C~ Azzurra** the French Riviera
cos'tante *ag* constant; (*persona*) steadfast ▷ *sf* constant
cos'tare *vi, vt* to cost; **quanto costa?**

how much does it cost?; **~ caro** to be expensive, cost a lot
cos'tata *sf* (*Cuc*) large chop
costeggi'are [kosted'dʒare] *vt* to be close to; to run alongside
costi'ero, -a *ag* coastal, coast *cpd*
costitu'ire *vt* (*comitato, gruppo*) to set up, form; (*elementi, parti: comporre*) to make up, constitute; (*rappresentare*) to constitute; (*Dir*) to appoint; **costituirsi** *vpr* **costituirsi alla polizia** to give o.s. up to the police
costituzi'one [kostitut'tsjone] *sf* setting up; building up; constitution
'costo *sm* cost; **a ogni** *o* **qualunque ~, a tutti i costi** at all costs
'costola *sf* (*Anat*) rib
cos'toso, -a *ag* expensive, costly
cos'tringere [kos'trindʒere] *vt* **~ qn a fare qc** to force sb to do sth
costru'ire *vt* to construct, build; **costruzi'one** *sf* construction, building
cos'tume *sm* (*uso*) custom; (*foggia di vestire, indumento*) costume; **costume da bagno** bathing *o* swimming costume (BRIT), swimsuit; (*da uomo*) bathing *o* swimming trunks *pl*
co'tenna *sf* bacon rind
coto'letta *sf* (*di maiale, montone*) chop; (*di vitello, agnello*) cutlet
co'tone *sm* cotton; **cotone idrofilo** cotton wool (BRIT), absorbent cotton (US)
'cotta *sf* (*fam: innamoramento*) crush
'cottimo *sm*: **lavorare a ~** to do piecework
'cotto, -a *pp di* **cuocere** ▷ *ag* cooked; (*fam: innamorato*) head-over-heels in love; **ben ~** (*carne*) well done
cot'tura *sf* cooking; (*in forno*) baking; (*in umido*) stewing
co'vare *vt* to hatch; (*fig: malattia*) to be sickening for; (*: odio, rancore*) to nurse ▷ *vi* (*fuoco, fig*) to smoulder
'covo *sm* den
co'vone *sm* sheaf
'cozza ['kɔttsa] *sf* mussel
coz'zare [kot'tsare] *vi*: **~ contro** to bang into, collide with
CPT *sigla m inv* = **Centro di Permanenza Temporanea**
crac'care *vt* (*Inform*) to crack
'crampo *sm* cramp; **ho un ~ alla gamba** I've got cramp in my leg
'cranio *sm* skull
cra'tere *sm* crater
cra'vatta *sf* tie
cre'are *vt* to create
'crebbi *ecc vb vedi* **crescere**
cre'dente *sm/f* (*Rel*) believer
cre'denza [kre'dɛntsa] *sf* belief; (*armadio*) sideboard
'credere *vt* to believe ▷ *vi* **~ in, ~ a** to believe in; **~ qn onesto** to believe sb (to be) honest; **~ che** to believe *o* think that; **credersi furbo** to think one is clever
'credito *sm* (*anche Comm*) credit; (*reputazione*) esteem, repute; **comprare a ~** to buy on credit
'crema *sf* cream; (*con uova, zucchero ecc*) custard; **crema pasticciera** confectioner's custard; **crema solare** sun cream
cre'mare *vt* to cremate
'crepa *sf* crack
cre'paccio [kre'pattʃo] *sm* large crack, fissure; (*di ghiacciaio*) crevasse
crepacu'ore *sm* broken heart
cre'pare *vi* (*fam: morire*) to snuff it, kick the bucket; **~ dalle risa** to split one's sides laughing
crêpe [krɛp] *sf inv* pancake
cre'puscolo *sm* twilight, dusk
'crescere ['krɛʃʃere] *vi* to grow ▷ *vt* (*figli*) to raise
'cresima *sf* (*Rel*) confirmation
'crespo, -a *ag* (*capelli*) frizzy; (*tessuto*) puckered ▷ *sm* crêpe
'cresta *sf* crest; (*di polli, uccelli*) crest, comb
'creta *sf* chalk; clay
creti'nata *sf* (*fam*): **dire/fare una ~**

to say/do a stupid thing
cre'tino, -a *ag* stupid ▷ *sm/f* idiot, fool
CRI *sigla f* = **Croce Rossa Italiana**
cric *sm inv* (*Tecn*) jack
cri'ceto [kri'tʃɛto] *sm* hamster
crimi'nale *ag, sm/f* criminal
criminalità *sf* crime; **criminalità organizzata** organized crime
'crimine *sm* (*Dir*) crime
crip'tare *vt* (*TV: programma*) to encrypt
crisan'temo *sm* chrysanthemum
'crisi *sf inv* crisis; (*Med*) attack, fit; **crisi di nervi** attack *o* fit of nerves
cris'tallo *sm* crystal; **cristalli liquidi** liquid crystals
cristia'nesimo *sm* Christianity
cristi'ano, -a *ag, sm/f* Christian
'Cristo *sm* Christ
cri'terio *sm* criterion; (*buon senso*) (common) sense
'critica, -che *sf* criticism; **la ~** (*attività*) criticism; (*persone*) the critics *pl*; *vedi anche* **critico**
criti'care *vt* to criticize
'critico, -a, -ci, -che *ag* critical ▷ *sm* critic
cro'ato, -a *ag, sm/f* Croatian, Croat
Croa'zia [kroa'ttsja] *sf* Croatia
croc'cante *ag* crisp, crunchy
'croce ['krotʃe] *sf* cross; **in ~** (*di traverso*) crosswise; (*fig*) on tenterhooks; **Croce Rossa** Red Cross
croci'ata [kro'tʃata] *sf* crusade
croci'era [kro'tʃɛra] *sf* (*viaggio*) cruise; (*Archit*) transept
croci'fisso, -a *pp di* **crocifiggere**
crol'lare *vi* to collapse; **'crollo** *sm* collapse; (*di prezzi*) slump, sudden fall; **crollo in Borsa** *slump in prices on the Stock Exchange*
cro'mato, -a *ag* chromium-plated
'cromo *sm* chrome, chromium
'cronaca, -che *sf* (*Stampa*) news *sg*; (*: rubrica*) column; (*TV, Radio*) commentary; **fatto** *o* **episodio di ~** news item; **cronaca nera** crime news *sg*; crime column
'cronico, -a, -ci, -che *ag* chronic
cro'nista, -i *sm* (*Stampa*) reporter
cro'nometro *sm* chronometer; (*a scatto*) stopwatch
'crosta *sf* crust
cros'tacei [kros'tatʃei] *smpl* shellfish
cros'tata *sf* (*Cuc*) tart
cros'tino *sm* (*Cuc*) crouton; (*: da antipasto*) canapé
cruci'ale [kru'tʃale] *ag* crucial
cruci'verba *sm inv* crossword (puzzle)
cru'dele *ag* cruel
'crudo, -a *ag* (*non cotto*) raw; (*aspro*) harsh, severe
cru'miro (*peg*) *sm* blackleg (BRIT), scab
'crusca *sf* bran
crus'cotto *sm* (*Aut*) dashboard
CSI *sigla f inv* (= *Comunità Stati Indipendenti*) CIS
CSM [tʃiɛsse'ɛmme] *sigla m* (= *consiglio superiore della magistratura*) Magistrates' Board of Supervisors
'Cuba *sf* Cuba
cu'bano, -a *ag, sm/f* Cuban
cu'betto *sm*; **cubetto di ghiaccio** ice cube
'cubico, -a, -ci, -che *ag* cubic
cu'bista, -i, -e *ag* (*Arte*) Cubist ▷ *sf* (*in discoteca*) podium dancer
'cubo, -a *ag* cubic ▷ *sm* cube; **elevare al ~** (*Mat*) to cube
cuc'cagna [kuk'kaɲɲa] *sf* **paese della ~** land of plenty; **albero della ~** greasy pole (*fig*)
cuc'cetta [kut'tʃetta] *sf* (*Ferr*) couchette; (*Naut*) berth
cucchiai'ata [kukja'jata] *sf* spoonful
cucchia'ino [kukkja'ino] *sm* teaspoon; coffee spoon
cucchi'aio [kuk'kjajo] *sm* spoon
'cuccia, -ce ['kuttʃa] *sf* dog's bed; **a ~!** down!
'cucciolo ['kuttʃolo] *sm* cub; (*di cane*) puppy

cu'cina [ku'tʃina] *sf* (*locale*) kitchen; (*arte culinaria*) cooking, cookery; (*le vivande*) food, cooking; (*apparecchio*) cooker; **cucina componibile** fitted kitchen; **cuci'nare** *vt* to cook
cu'cire [ku'tʃire] *vt* to sew, stitch; **cuci'trice** *sf* stapler
cucù *sm inv* cuckoo
'cuffia *sf* bonnet, cap; (*da infermiera*) cap; (*da bagno*) (bathing) cap; (*per ascoltare*) headphones *pl*, headset
cu'gino, -a [ku'dʒino] *sm/f* cousin

PAROLA CHIAVE

'cui *pron* **1** (*nei complementi indiretti: persona*) whom; (*: oggetto, animale*) which; **la persona/le persone a cui accennavi** the person/people you were referring to *o* to whom you were referring; **i libri di cui parlavo** the books I was talking about *o* about which I was talking; **il quartiere in cui abito** the district where I live; **la ragione per cui** the reason why
2 (*inserito tra articolo e sostantivo*) whose; **la donna i cui figli sono scomparsi** the woman whose children have disappeared; **il signore, dal cui figlio ho avuto il libro** the man from whose son I got the book

culi'naria *sf* cookery
'culla *sf* cradle
cul'lare *vt* to rock
'culmine *sm* top, summit
'culo (*fam!*) *sm* arse (BRIT!), ass (US!); (*fig: fortuna*): **aver ~** to have the luck of the devil
'culto *sm* (*religione*) religion; (*adorazione*) worship, adoration; (*venerazione: anche fig*) cult
cul'tura *sf* culture; education, learning; **cultu'rale** *ag* cultural
cultu'rismo *sm* body-building
cumula'tivo, -a *ag* cumulative; (*prezzo*) inclusive; (*biglietto*) group *cpd*
'cumulo *sm* (*mucchio*) pile, heap; (*Meteor*) cumulus
cu'netta *sf* (*avvallamento*) dip; (*di scolo*) gutter
cu'ocere ['kwɔtʃere] *vt* (*alimenti*) to cook; (*mattoni ecc*) to fire ▷ *vi* to cook; **~ al forno** (*pane*) to bake; (*arrosto*) to roast; **cu'oco, -a, -chi, -che** *sm/f* cook; (*di ristorante*) chef
cu'oio *sm* leather; **cuoio capelluto** scalp
cu'ore *sm* heart; **cuori** *smpl* (*Carte*) hearts; **avere buon ~** to be kind-hearted; **stare a ~ a qn** to be important to sb
'cupo, -a *ag* dark; (*suono*) dull; (*fig*) gloomy, dismal
'cupola *sf* dome; cupola
'cura *sf* care; (*Med: trattamento*) (course of) treatment; **aver ~ di** (*occuparsi di*) to look after; **a ~ di** (*libro*) edited by; **cura dimagrante** diet
cu'rare *vt* (*malato, malattia*) to treat; (*: guarire*) to cure; (*aver cura di*) to take care of; (*testo*) to edit; **curarsi** *vpr* to take care of o.s.; (*Med*) to follow a course of treatment; **curarsi di** to pay attention to
curio'sare *vi* to look round, wander round; (*tra libri*) to browse; **~ nei negozi** to look *o* wander round the shops
curiosità *sf inv* curiosity; (*cosa rara*) curio, curiosity
curi'oso, -a *ag* curious; **essere ~ di** to be curious about
cur'sore *sm* (*Inform*) cursor
'curva *sf* curve; (*stradale*) bend, curve
cur'vare *vt* to bend ▷ *vi* (*veicolo*) to take a bend; (*strada*) to bend, curve; **curvarsi** *vpr* to bend; (*legno*) to warp
'curvo, -a *ag* curved; (*piegato*) bent
cusci'netto [kuʃʃi'netto] *sm* pad; (*Tecn*) bearing ▷ *ag inv* **stato ~** buffer state; **cuscinetto a sfere** ball bearing
cu'scino [kuʃ'ʃino] *sm* cushion; (*guanciale*) pillow

cus'tode *sm/f* keeper, custodian
cus'todia *sf* care; (*Dir*) custody; (*astuccio*) case, holder
custo'dire *vt* (*conservare*) to keep; (*assistere*) to look after, take care of; (*fare la guardia*) to guard
CV *abbr* (= *cavallo vapore*) h.p.
cybercaffè [tʃiberka'fe] *sm inv* cybercafé
cybernauta, -i, -e *sm/f* Internet surfer
cyberspazio *sm* cyberspace

d

PAROLA CHIAVE

da (*da+il* = **dal**, *da+lo* = **dallo**, *da+l'* = **dall'**, *da+la* = **dalla**, *da+i* = **dai**, *da+gli* = **dagli, da+le = dalle**) *prep* **1** (*agente*) by; **dipinto da un grande artista** painted by a great artist
2 (*causa*) with; **tremare dalla paura** to tremble with fear
3 (*stato in luogo*) at; **abito da lui** I'm living at his house *o* with him; **sono dal giornalaio/da Francesco** I'm at the newsagent's/Francesco's (house)
4 (*moto a luogo*) to; (*moto per luogo*) through; **vado da Pietro/dal giornalaio** I'm going to Pietro's (house)/to the newsagent's; **sono passati dalla finestra** they came in through the window
5 (*provenienza, allontanamento*) from; **arrivare/partire da Milano** to arrive/depart from Milan; **scendere dal treno/dalla macchina** to get off the train/out of the car; **si trova a 5**

km da qui it's 5 km from here
6 (*tempo*: *durata*) for; (: *a partire da*: *nel passato*) since; (: *nel futuro*) from; **vivo qui da un anno** I've been living here for a year; **è dalle 3 che ti aspetto** I've been waiting for you since 3 (o'clock); **da oggi in poi** from today onwards; **da bambino** as a child, when I (*o* he *ecc*) was a child
7 (*modo*, *maniera*) like; **comportarsi da uomo** to behave like a man; **l'ho fatto da me** I did it (by) myself
8 (*descrittivo*): **una macchina da corsa** a racing car; **una ragazza dai capelli biondi** a girl with blonde hair; **un vestito da 60 euro** a 60 euros dress

dà *vb vedi* **dare**
dac'capo *av* (*di nuovo*) (once) again; (*dal principio*) all over again, from the beginning
'dado *sm* (*da gioco*) dice *o* die; (*Cuc*) stock (BRIT) *o* bouillon (US) cube; (*Tecn*) (screw)nut; **dadi** *smpl* (game of) dice; **giocare a dadi** to play dice
'daino *sm* (fallow) deer *inv*; (*pelle*) buckskin
dal'tonico, -a, -ci, -che *ag* colour-blind
'dama *sf* lady; (*nei balli*) partner; (*gioco*) draughts *sg* (BRIT), checkers *sg* (US)
damigi'ana [dami'dʒana] *sf* demijohn
da'nese *ag* Danish ▷ *sm/f* Dane ▷ *sm* (*Ling*) Danish
Dani'marca *sf* **la ~** Denmark
dannazi'one *sf* damnation
danneggi'are [danned'dʒare] *vt* to damage; (*rovinare*) to spoil; (*nuocere*) to harm
'danno *sm* damage; (*a persona*) harm, injury; **danni** *smpl* (*Dir*) damages; **dan'noso, -a** *ag* **dannoso (a, per)** harmful (to), bad (for)
Da'nubio *sm* **il ~** the Danube
'danza ['dantsa] *sf* **la ~** dancing; **una ~** a dance
dan'zare [dan'tsare] *vt*, *vi* to dance
dapper'tutto *av* everywhere
dap'prima *av* at first
'dare *sm* (*Comm*) debit ▷ *vt* to give; (*produrre*: *frutti*, *suono*) to produce ▷ *vi* (*guardare*): **~ su** to look (out) onto; **darsi** *vpr* **darsi a** to dedicate o.s. to; **darsi al commercio** to go into business; **darsi al bere** to take to drink; **~ da mangiare a qn** to give sb sth to eat; **~ per certo qc** to consider sth certain; **~ per morto qn** to give sb up for dead; **darsi per vinto** to give in
'data *sf* date; **~ limite d'utilizzo** *or* **di consumo** best-before date; **data di nascita** date of birth; **data di scadenza** expiry date
'dato, -a *ag* (*stabilito*) given ▷ *sm* datum; **dati** *smpl* data *pl*; **~ che** given that; **un ~ di fatto** a fact; **dati sensibili** personal information
da'tore, -'trice *sm/f*; **datore di lavoro** employer
'dattero *sm* date
dattilogra'fia *sf* typing
datti'lografo, -a *sm/f* typist
da'vanti *av* in front; (*dirimpetto*) opposite ▷ *ag inv* front ▷ *sm* front; **~ a** in front of; facing, opposite; (*in presenza di*) before, in front of
davan'zale [davan'tsale] *sm* windowsill
dav'vero *av* really, indeed
d.C. *adv abbr* (= *dopo Cristo*) A.D.
'dea *sf* goddess
'debbo *ecc vb vedi* **dovere**
'debito, -a *ag* due, proper ▷ *sm* debt; (*Comm*: *dare*) debit; **a tempo ~** at the right time
'debole *ag* weak, feeble; (*suono*) faint; (*luce*) dim ▷ *sm* weakness; **debo'lezza** *sf* weakness
debut'tare *vi* to make one's debut
deca'denza [deka'dɛntsa] *sf* decline; (*Dir*) loss, forfeiture

decaffei'nato, -a *ag* decaffeinated
decapi'tare *vt* to decapitate, behead
decappot'tabile *ag, sf* convertible
de'cennio [de'tʃɛnnjo] *sm* decade
de'cente [de'tʃɛnte] *ag* decent, respectable, proper; (*accettabile*) satisfactory, decent
de'cesso [de'tʃɛsso] *sm* death
de'cidere [de'tʃidere] *vt*: **~ qc** to decide on sth; (*questione, lite*) to settle sth; **~ di fare/che** to decide to do/that; **~ di qc** (*cosa*) to determine sth; **decidersi (a fare)** to decide (to do), make up one's mind (to do)
deci'frare [detʃi'frare] *vt* to decode; (*fig*) to decipher, make out
deci'male [detʃi'male] *ag* decimal
'decimo, -a ['dɛtʃimo] *num* tenth
de'cina [de'tʃina] *sf* ten; (*circa dieci*): **una ~ (di)** about ten
de'cisi *ecc* [de'tʃizi] *vb vedi* **decidere**
decisi'one [detʃi'zjone] *sf* decision; **prendere una ~** to make a decision
deci'sivo, -a [detʃi'zivo] *ag* (*gen*) decisive; (*fattore*) deciding
de'ciso, -a [de'tʃizo] *pp di* **decidere**
decli'nare *vi* (*pendio*) to slope down; (*fig: diminuire*) to decline ▷ *vt* to decline
declinazi'one *sf* (*Ling*) declension
de'clino *sm* decline
decodifica'tore *sm* (*Tel*) decoder
decol'lare *vi* (*Aer*) to take off; **de'collo** *sm* take-off
deco'rare *vt* to decorate; **decorazi'one** *sf* decoration
de'creto *sm* decree; **decreto legge** *decree with the force of law*
'dedica, -che *sf* dedication
dedi'care *vt* to dedicate; **dedicarsi** *vpr* **dedicarsi a** to devote o.s. to
dedicherò *ecc* [dedike'rɔ] *vb vedi* **dedicare**
'dedito, -a *ag*: **~ a** (*studio ecc*) dedicated *o* devoted to; (*vizio*) addicted to
de'duco *ecc vb vedi* **dedurre**
de'durre *vt* (*concludere*) to deduce; (*defalcare*) to deduct
de'dussi *ecc vb vedi* **dedurre**
defici'ente [defi'tʃɛnte] *ag* (*mancante*): **~ di** deficient in; (*insufficiente*) insufficient ▷ *sm/f* mental defective; (*peg: cretino*) idiot
'deficit ['dɛfitʃit] *sm inv* (*Econ*) deficit
defi'nire *vt* to define; (*risolvere*) to settle; **defini'tiva** *sf* **in ~** (*dopotutto*) in the end; (*dunque*) hence; **defini'tivo, -a** *ag* definitive, final; **definizi'one** *sf* definition; settlement
defor'mare *vt* (*alterare*) to put out of shape; (*corpo*) to deform; (*pensiero, fatto*) to distort; **deformarsi** *vpr* to lose its shape
de'forme *ag* deformed; disfigured
de'funto, -a *ag* late *cpd* ▷ *sm/f* deceased
degene'rare [dedʒene'rare] *vi* to degenerate
de'gente [de'dʒɛnte] *sm/f* (*in ospedale*) in-patient
deglu'tire *vt* to swallow
de'gnare [deɲ'ɲare] *vt*: **~ qn della propria presenza** to honour sb with one's presence; **degnarsi** *vpr* **degnarsi di fare qc** to deign *o* condescend to do sth
'degno, -a *ag* dignified; **~ di** worthy of; **~ di lode** praiseworthy
de'grado *sm*; **degrado urbano** urban decline
'delega, -ghe *sf* (*procura*) proxy
dele'terio, -a *ag* damaging; (*per salute ecc*) harmful
del'fino *sm* (*Zool*) dolphin; (*Storia*) dauphin; (*fig*) probable successor
deli'cato, -a *ag* delicate; (*salute*) delicate, frail; (*fig: gentile*) thoughtful, considerate; (*: che dimostra tatto*) tactful
delin'quente *sm/f* criminal, delinquent; **delinquente abituale** regular offender, habitual offender;

delin'quenza *sf* criminality, delinquency; **delinquenza minorile** juvenile delinquency
deli'rare *vi* to be delirious, rave; (*fig*) to rave
de'lirio *sm* delirium; (*ragionamento insensato*) raving; (*fig*): **andare/mandare in ~** to go/send into a frenzy
de'litto *sm* crime
delizi'oso, -a *ag* delightful; (*cibi*) delicious
delta'plano *sm* hang-glider; **volo col ~** hang-gliding
delu'dente *ag* disappointing
de'ludere *vt* to disappoint; **delusi'one** *sf* disappointment; **de'luso, -a** *pp di* **deludere**
'demmo *vb vedi* **dare**
demo'cratico, -a, -ci, -che *ag* democratic
democra'zia [demokrat'tsia] *sf* democracy
demo'lire *vt* to demolish
de'monio *sm* demon, devil; **il D~** the Devil
de'naro *sm* money
densità *sf inv* density
'denso, -a *ag* thick, dense
den'tale *ag* dental
'dente *sm* tooth; (*di forchetta*) prong; **al ~** (*Cuc*: *pasta*) al dente; **denti del giudizio** wisdom teeth; **denti da latte** milk teeth; **denti'era** *sf* (set of) false teeth *pl*
denti'fricio [denti'fritʃo] *sm* toothpaste
den'tista, -i, -e *sm/f* dentist
'dentro *av* inside; (*in casa*) indoors; (*fig*: *nell'intimo*) inwardly ▷ *prep* **~ (a)** in; **piegato in ~** folded over; **qui/là ~** in here/there; **~ di sé** (*pensare, brontolare*) to oneself
de'nuncia, -ce *o* **cie** [de'nuntʃa] *sf* denunciation; declaration; **denuncia dei redditi** (income) tax return
denunci'are [denun'tʃare] *vt* to denounce; (*dichiarare*) to declare; (*persona, smarrimento ecc*) report; **vorrei ~ un furto** I'd like to report a theft
denu'trito, -a *ag* undernourished
denutrizi'one [denutrit'tsjone] *sf* malnutrition
deodo'rante *sm* deodorant
depe'rire *vi* to waste away
depi'larsi *vpr*: **~ (le gambe)** (*con rasoio*) to shave (one's legs); (*con ceretta*) to wax (one's legs)
depila'torio, -a *ag* hair-removing *cpd*, depilatory
dépli'ant [depli'ã] *sm inv* leaflet; (*opuscolo*) brochure
deplo'revole *ag* deplorable
de'pone, de'pongo *ecc vb vedi* **deporre**
de'porre *vt* (*depositare*) to put down; (*rimuovere*: *da una carica*) to remove; (: *re*) to depose; (*Dir*) to testify
depor'tare *vt* to deport
de'posi *ecc vb vedi* **deporre**
deposi'tare *vt* (*gen, Geo, Econ*) to deposit; (*lasciare*) to leave; (*merci*) to store; **depositarsi** *vpr* (*sabbia, polvere*) to settle
de'posito *sm* deposit; (*luogo*) warehouse; depot; (: *Mil*) depot; **deposito bagagli** left-luggage office
deposizi'one [depozit'tsjone] *sf* deposition; (*da una carica*) removal
depra'vato, -a *ag* depraved ▷ *sm/f* degenerate
depre'dare *vt* to rob, plunder
depressi'one *sf* depression
de'presso, -a *pp di* **deprimere** ▷ *ag* depressed
deprez'zare [depret'tsare] *vt* (*Econ*) to depreciate
depri'mente *ag* depressing
de'primere *vt* to depress
depu'rare *vt* to purify
depu'tato *sm* (*Pol*) deputy, ≈ Member of Parliament (BRIT), ≈ Member of Congress (US)
deragli'are [deraʎ'ʎare] *vi* to be

derailed; **far ~** to derail

de'ridere *vt* to mock, deride

de'risi *ecc vb vedi* **deridere**

de'riva *sf* (*Naut, Aer*) drift; **andare alla ~** (*anche fig*) to drift

deri'vare *vi* **~ da** to derive from ▷ *vt* to derive; (*corso d'acqua*) to divert

derma'tologo, -a, -gi, -ghe *sm/f* dermatologist

deru'bare *vt* to rob

des'crivere *vt* to describe; **descrizi'one** *sf* description

de'serto, -a *ag* deserted ▷ *sm* (*Geo*) desert; **isola deserta** desert island

deside'rare *vt* to want, wish for; (*sessualmente*) to desire; **~ fare/che qn faccia** to want *o* wish to do/sb to do; **desidera fare una passeggiata?** would you like to go for a walk?

desi'derio *sm* wish; (*più intenso, carnale*) desire

deside'roso, -a *ag* **~ di** longing *o* eager for

desi'nenza [dezi'nɛntsa] *sf* (*Ling*) ending, inflexion

de'sistere *vi* **~ da** to give up, desist from

deso'lato, -a *ag* (*paesaggio*) desolate; (*persona*: *spiacente*) sorry

'dessi *ecc vb vedi* **dare**

'deste *ecc vb vedi* **dare**

desti'nare *vt* to destine; (*assegnare*) to appoint, assign; (*indirizzare*) to address; **~ qc a qn** to intend to give sth to sb, intend sb to have sth; **destina'tario, -a** *sm/f* (*di lettera*) addressee

destinazi'one [destinat'tsjone] *sf* destination; (*uso*) purpose

des'tino *sm* destiny, fate

destitu'ire *vt* to dismiss, remove

'destra *sf* (*mano*) right hand; (*parte*) right (side); (*Pol*): **la ~** the Right; **a ~** (*essere*) on the right; (*andare*) to the right

destreggi'arsi [destred'dʒarsi] *vpr* to manoeuvre (BRIT), maneuver (US)

des'trezza [des'trettsa] *sf* skill, dexterity

'destro, -a *ag* right, right-hand

dete'nuto, -a *sm/f* prisoner

deter'gente [deter'dʒɛnte] *ag* (*crema, latte*) cleansing ▷ *sm* cleanser

> Attenzione! In inglese esiste la parola *detergent* che però significa *detersivo*.

determi'nare *vt* to determine

determina'tivo, -a *ag* determining; **articolo ~** (*Ling*) definite article

determi'nato, -a *ag* (*gen*) certain; (*particolare*) specific; (*risoluto*) determined, resolute

deter'sivo *sm* detergent

detes'tare *vt* to detest, hate

de'trae, de'traggo *ecc vb vedi* **detrarre**

de'trarre *vt*: **~ (da)** to deduct (from), take away (from)

de'trassi *ecc vb vedi* **detrarre**

'detta *sf* **a ~ di** according to

det'taglio [det'taʎʎo] *sm* detail; (*Comm*): **il ~** retail; **al ~** (*Comm*) retail; separately

det'tare *vt* to dictate; **~ legge** (*fig*) to lay down the law; **det'tato** *sm* dictation

'detto, -a *pp di* **dire** ▷ *ag* (*soprannominato*) called, known as; (*già nominato*) above-mentioned ▷ *sm* saying; **~ fatto** no sooner said than done

devas'tare *vt* to devastate; (*fig*) to ravage

devi'are *vi* **~ (da)** to turn off (from) ▷ *vt* to divert; **deviazi'one** *sf* (*anche Aut*) diversion

'devo *ecc vb vedi* **dovere**

devoluzi'one [devolut'tsjone] *sf* (*Dir*) devolution, transfer

de'volvere *vt* (*Dir*) to transfer, devolve

de'voto, -a *ag* (*Rel*) devout, pious; (*affezionato*) devoted

devozi'one [devot'tsjone] *sf*

devoutness; (*anche Rel*) devotion

PAROLA CHIAVE

di (*di+il* = **del**, *di+lo* = **dello**, *di+l'* = **dell'**, *di+la* = **della**, *di+i* = **dei**, *di+gli* = **degli**, *di+le* = **delle**) *prep* 1 (*possesso, specificazione*) of; (*composto da, scritto da*) by; **la macchina di Paolo/mio fratello** Paolo's/my brother's car; **un amico di mio fratello** a friend of my brother's, one of my brother's friends; **un quadro di Botticelli** a painting by Botticelli
2 (*caratterizzazione, misura*) of; **una casa di mattoni** a brick house, a house made of bricks; **un orologio d'oro** a gold watch; **un bimbo di 3 anni** a child of 3, a 3-year-old child
3 (*causa, mezzo, modo*) with; **tremare di paura** to tremble with fear; **morire di cancro** to die of cancer; **spalmare di burro** to spread with butter
4 (*argomento*) about, of; **discutere di sport** to talk about sport
5 (*luogo: provenienza*) from; out of; **essere di Roma** to be from Rome; **uscire di casa** to come out of *o* leave the house
6 (*tempo*) in; **d'estate/d'inverno** in (the) summer/winter; **di notte** by night, at night; **di mattina/sera** in the morning/evening; **di lunedì** on Mondays
▷ *det* (*una certa quantità di*) some; (*: negativo*) any; (*interrogativo*) any; some; **del pane** (some) bread; **delle caramelle** (some) sweets; **degli amici miei** some friends of mine; **vuoi del vino?** do you want some *o* any wine?

dia'bete *sm* diabetes *sg*
dia'betico, -a, ci, che *ag, sm/f* diabetic
dia'framma, -i *sm* (*divisione*) screen; (*Anat, Fot, contraccettivo*) diaphragm
di'agnosi [di'aɲɲozi] *sf* diagnosis *sg*
diago'nale *ag, sf* diagonal
dia'gramma, -i *sm* diagram
dia'letto *sm* dialect
di'alisi *sf* dialysis *sg*
di'alogo, -ghi *sm* dialogue
dia'mante *sm* diamond
di'ametro *sm* diameter
diaposi'tiva *sf* transparency, slide
di'ario *sm* diary
diar'rea *sf* diarrhoea
di'avolo *sm* devil
di'battito *sm* debate, discussion
'dice ['ditʃe] *vb vedi* **dire**
di'cembre [di'tʃɛmbre] *sm* December
dice'ria [ditʃe'ria] *sf* rumour, piece of gossip
dichia'rare [dikja'rare] *vt* to declare; **dichiararsi** *vpr* to declare o.s.; (*innamorato*) to declare one's love; **dichiararsi vinto** to acknowledge defeat; **dichiarazi'one** *sf* declaration; **dichiarazione dei redditi** statement of income; (*modulo*) tax return
dician'nove [ditʃan'nɔve] *num* nineteen
dicias'sette [ditʃas'sɛtte] *num* seventeen
dici'otto [di'tʃɔtto] *num* eighteen
dici'tura [ditʃi'tura] *sf* words *pl*, wording
'dico *ecc vb vedi* **dire**
didasca'lia *sf* (*di illustrazione*) caption; (*Cine*) subtitle; (*Teatro*) stage directions *pl*
di'eci ['djɛtʃi] *num* ten
di'edi *ecc vb vedi* **dare**
'diesel ['dizəl] *sm inv* diesel engine
dies'sino, -a *sm/f member of the DS political party*
di'eta *sf* diet; **essere a ~** to be on a diet
di'etro *av* behind; (*in fondo*) at the back ▷ *prep* behind; (*tempo: dopo*) after ▷ *sm* back, rear ▷ *ag inv* back *cpd*; **le zampe di ~** the hind legs; **~ richiesta** on demand; (*scritta*) on application

di'fendere *vt* to defend; **difendersi** *vpr* (*cavarsela*) to get by; **difendersi da/contro** to defend o.s. from/ against; **difendersi dal freddo** to protect o.s. from the cold; **difen'sore, -a** *sm/f* defender; **avvocato difensore** counsel for the defence; **di'fesa** *sf* defence
di'fesi *ecc vb vedi* **difendere**
di'fetto *sm* (*mancanza*): **~ di** lack of; shortage of; (*di fabbricazione*) fault, flaw, defect; (*morale*) fault, failing, defect; (*fisico*) defect; **far ~** to be lacking; **in ~** at fault; in the wrong; **difet'toso, -a** *ag* defective, faulty
diffe'rente *ag* different
diffe'renza [diffe'rɛntsa] *sf* difference; **a ~ di** unlike
diffe'rire *vt* to postpone, defer ▷ *vi* to be different
diffe'rita *sf*: **in ~** (*trasmettere*) prerecorded
dif'ficile [dif'fitʃile] *ag* difficult; (*persona*) hard to please, difficult (to please); (*poco probabile*): **è ~ che sia libero** it is unlikely that he'll be free ▷ *sm* difficult part; difficulty; **difficoltà** *sf inv* difficulty
diffi'dente *ag* suspicious, distrustful
diffi'denza *sf* suspicion, distrust
dif'fondere *vt* (*luce, calore*) to diffuse; (*notizie*) to spread, circulate; **diffondersi** *vpr* to spread
dif'fusi *ecc vb vedi* **diffondere**
dif'fuso, -a *pp di* **diffondere** ▷ *ag* (*malattia, fenomeno*) widespread
'diga, -ghe *sf* dam; (*portuale*) breakwater
dige'rente [didʒe'rɛnte] *ag* (*apparato*) digestive
dige'rire [didʒe'rire] *vt* to digest; **digesti'one** *sf* digestion; **diges'tivo, -a** *ag* digestive ▷ *sm* (after-dinner) liqueur
digi'tale [didʒi'tale] *ag* digital; (*delle dita*) finger *cpd*, digital ▷ *sf* (*Bot*) foxglove
digi'tare [didʒi'tare] *vt, vi* (*Inform*) to key (in)
digiu'nare [didʒu'nare] *vi* to starve o.s.; (*Rel*) to fast; **digi'uno, -a** *ag* **essere digiuno** not to have eaten ▷ *sm* fast; **a digiuno** on an empty stomach
dignità [diɲɲi'ta] *sf inv* dignity
'DIGOS ['digɔs] *sigla f* (= *Divisione Investigazioni Generali e Operazioni Speciali*) *police department dealing with political security*
digri'gnare [digriɲ'ɲare] *vt*: **~ i denti** to grind one's teeth
dilapi'dare *vt* to squander, waste
dila'tare *vt* to dilate; (*gas*) to cause to expand; (*passaggio, cavità*) to open (up); **dilatarsi** *vpr* to dilate; (*Fisica*) to expand
dilazio'nare [dilattsjo'nare] *vt* to delay, defer
di'lemma, -i *sm* dilemma
dilet'tante *sm/f* dilettante; (*anche Sport*) amateur
dili'gente [dili'dʒɛnte] *ag* (*scrupoloso*) diligent; (*accurato*) careful, accurate
dilu'ire *vt* to dilute
dilun'garsi *vpr* (*fig*): **~ su** to talk at length on *o* about
diluvi'are *vb impers* to pour (down)
di'luvio *sm* downpour; (*inondazione, fig*) flood
dima'grante *ag* slimming *cpd*
dima'grire *vi* to get thinner, lose weight
dime'nare *vt* to wave, shake; **dimenarsi** *vpr* to toss and turn; (*fig*) to struggle; **~ la coda** (*cane*) to wag its tail
dimensi'one *sf* dimension; (*grandezza*) size
dimenti'canza [dimenti'kantsa] *sf* forgetfulness; (*errore*) oversight, slip; **per ~** inadvertently
dimenti'care *vt* to forget; **ho dimenticato la chiave/il passaporto** I forgot the key/my

passport; **dimenticarsi** *vpr* **dimenticarsi di qc** to forget sth

dimesti'chezza [dimesti'kettsa] *sf* familiarity

di'mettere *vt*: **~ qn da** to dismiss sb from; (*dall'ospedale*) to discharge sb from; **dimettersi** *vpr* **dimettersi (da)** to resign (from)

dimez'zare [dimed'dzare] *vt* to halve

diminu'ire *vt* to reduce, diminish; (*prezzi*) to bring down, reduce ▷ *vi* to decrease, diminish; (*rumore*) to die down, die away; (*prezzi*) to fall, go down

diminu'tivo, -a *ag, sm* diminutive

diminuzi'one *sf* decreasing, diminishing

di'misi *ecc vb vedi* **dimettere**

dimissi'oni *sfpl* resignation *sg*; **dare** *o* **presentare le ~** to resign, hand in one's resignation

dimos'trare *vt* to demonstrate, show; (*provare*) to prove, demonstrate; **dimostrarsi** *vpr* **dimostrarsi molto abile** to show o.s. *o* prove to be very clever; **dimostra 30 anni** he looks about 30 (years old); **dimostrazi'one** *sf* demonstration; proof

di'namica *sf* dynamics *sg*

di'namico, -a, -ci, -che *ag* dynamic

dina'mite *sf* dynamite

'dinamo *sf inv* dynamo

dino'sauro *sm* dinosaur

dintorni *smpl* outskirts; **nei ~ di** in the vicinity *o* neighbourhood of

'dio (*pl* **'dei**) *sm* god; **D~** God; **gli dei** the gods; **D~ mio!** my goodness!, my God!

diparti'mento *sm* department

dipen'dente *ag* dependent ▷ *sm/f* employee; **dipendente statale** state employee

di'pendere *vi*: **~ da** to depend on; (*finanziariamente*) to be dependent on; (*derivare*) to come from, be due to

di'pesi *ecc vb vedi* **dipendere**

di'pingere [di'pindʒere] *vt* to paint

di'pinsi *ecc vb vedi* **dipingere**

di'pinto, -a *pp di* **dipingere** ▷ *sm* painting

di'ploma, -i *sm* diploma

diplo'matico, -a, -ci, -che *ag* diplomatic ▷ *sm* diplomat

diploma'zia [diplomat'tsia] *sf* diplomacy

di'porto: **imbarcazione da ~** *sf* pleasure craft

dira'dare *vt* to thin (out); (*visite*) to reduce, make less frequent; **diradarsi** *vpr* to disperse; (*nebbia*) to clear (up)

'dire *vt* to say; (*segreto, fatto*) to tell; **~ qc a qn** to tell sb sth; **~ a qn di fare qc** to tell sb to do sth; **~ di sì/no** to say yes/no; **si dice che ...** they say that ...; **si ~bbe che ...** it looks (*o* sounds) as though ...; **dica, signora?** (*in un negozio*) yes, Madam, can I help you?; **come si dice in inglese...?** what's the English (word) for ...?

di'ressi *ecc vb vedi* **dirigere**

di'retta *sf vedi* **diretto**

di'retto, -a *pp di* **dirigere** ▷ *ag* direct ▷ *sm* (*Ferr*) through train

diret'tore, -'trice *sm/f* (*di azienda*) director; manager/ess; (*di scuola elementare*) head (teacher) (BRIT), principal (US); **direttore d'orchestra** conductor; **direttore vendite** sales director *o* manager

direzi'one [diret'tsjone] *sf* board of directors; management; (*senso di movimento*) direction; **in ~ di** in the direction of, towards

diri'gente [diri'dʒɛnte] *sm/f* executive; (*Pol*) leader ▷ *ag* **classe ~** ruling class

di'rigere [di'ridʒere] *vt* to direct; (*impresa*) to run, manage; (*Mus*) to conduct; **dirigersi** *vpr* **dirigersi verso** *o* **a** to make *o* head for

dirim'petto *av* opposite; **~ a** opposite, facing

di'ritto, -a *ag* straight; (*onesto*)

straight, upright ▷ *av* straight, directly; **andare ~** to go straight on ▷ *sm* right side; (*Tennis*) forehand; (*Maglia*) plain stitch; (*prerogativa*) right; (*leggi, scienza*): **il ~** law; **diritti** *smpl* (*tasse*) duty *sg*; **stare ~** to stand up straight; **aver ~ a qc** to be entitled to sth; **diritti d'autore** royalties

dirotta'mento *sm*; **dirottamento (aereo)** hijack

dirot'tare *vt* (*nave, aereo*) to change the course of; (*aereo sotto minaccia*) to hijack; (*traffico*) to divert ▷ *vi* (*nave, aereo*) to change course; **dirotta'tore, -'trice** *sm/f* hijacker

di'rotto, -a *ag* (*pioggia*) torrential; (*pianto*) unrestrained; **piovere a ~** to pour; **piangere a ~** to cry one's heart out

di'rupo *sm* crag, precipice

di'sabile *sm/f* disabled person ▷ *ag* disabled; **i disabili** the disabled

disabi'tato, -a *ag* uninhabited

disabitu'arsi *vpr*: **~ a** to get out of the habit of

disac'cordo *sm* disagreement

disadat'tato, -a *ag* (*Psic*) maladjusted

disa'dorno, -a *ag* plain, unadorned

disagi'ato, -a [diza'dʒato] *ag* poor, needy; (*vita*) hard

di'sagio [di'zadʒo] *sm* discomfort; (*disturbo*) inconvenience; (*fig*: *imbarazzo*) embarrassment; **essere a ~** to be ill at ease

disappro'vare *vt* to disapprove of; **disapprovazi'one** *sf* disapproval

disap'punto *sm* disappointment

disar'mare *vt, vi* to disarm; **di'sarmo** *sm* (*Mil*) disarmament

di'sastro *sm* disaster

disas'troso, -a *ag* disastrous

disat'tento, -a *ag* inattentive; **disattenzi'one** *sf* carelessness, lack of attention

disavven'tura *sf* misadventure, mishap

dis'capito *sm*: **a ~ di** to the detriment of

dis'carica, -che *sf* (*di rifiuti*) rubbish tip *o* dump

di'scendere [diʃ'ʃendere] *vt* to go (*o* come) down ▷ *vi* to go (*o* come) down; (*strada*) to go down; (*smontare*) to get off; **~ da** (*famiglia*) to be descended from; **~ dalla macchina/dal treno** to get out of the car/out of *o* off the train; **~ da cavallo** to dismount, get off one's horse

di'scesa [diʃ'ʃesa] *sf* descent; (*pendio*) slope; **in ~** (*strada*) downhill *cpd*, sloping; **discesa libera** (*Sci*) downhill (race)

disci'plina [diʃʃi'plina] *sf* discipline

'disco, -schi *sm* disc; (*Sport*) discus; (*fonografico*) record; (*Inform*) disk; **disco orario** (*Aut*) parking disc; **disco rigido** (*Inform*) hard disk; **disco volante** flying saucer

disco'grafico, -a, ci, che *ag* record *cpd*, recording *cpd* ▷ *sm* record producer; **casa discografica** record(ing) company

dis'correre *vi*: **~ (di)** to talk (about)

dis'corso, -a *pp di* **discorrere** ▷ *sm* speech; (*conversazione*) conversation, talk

disco'teca, -che *sf* (*raccolta*) record library; (*locale*) disco

discount [dis'kaunt] *sm inv* (*supermercato*) *cut-price supermarket*

discre'panza [diskre'pantsa] *sf* disagreement

dis'creto, -a *ag* discreet; (*abbastanza buono*) reasonable, fair

discriminazi'one [diskriminat'tsjone] *sf* discrimination

dis'cussi *ecc vb vedi* **discutere**

discussi'one *sf* discussion; (*litigio*) argument; **fuori ~** out of the question

dis'cutere *vt* to discuss, debate; (*contestare*) to question ▷ *vi* (*conversare*): **~ (di)** to discuss; (*litigare*)

to argue
dis'detta *sf* (*di prenotazione ecc*) cancellation; (*sfortuna*) bad luck
dis'dire *vt* (*prenotazione*) to cancel; (*Dir*): **~ un contratto d'affitto** to give notice (to quit); **vorrei ~ la mia prenotazione** I want to cancel my booking
dise'gnare [disen'nare] *vt* to draw; (*progettare*) to design; (*fig*) to outline
disegna'tore, -'trice *sm/f* designer
di'segno [di'senno] *sm* drawing; design; outline; **disegno di legge** (*Dir*) bill
diser'bante *sm* weed-killer
diser'tare *vt, vi* to desert
dis'fare *vt* to undo; (*valigie*) to unpack; (*meccanismo*) to take to pieces; (*neve*) to melt; **disfarsi** *vpr* to come undone; (*neve*) to melt; **~ il letto** to strip the bed; **disfarsi di qn** (*liberarsi*) to get rid of sb; **dis'fatto, -a** *pp di* **disfare**
dis'gelo [diz'dʒɛlo] *sm* thaw
dis'grazia [diz'grattsja] *sf* (*sventura*) misfortune; (*incidente*) accident, mishap
disgu'ido *sm* hitch; **disguido postale** error in postal delivery
disgus'tare *vt* to disgust
dis'gusto *sm* disgust; **disgus'toso, -a** *ag* disgusting
disidra'tare *vt* to dehydrate
disimpa'rare *vt* to forget
disinfet'tante *ag, sm* disinfectant
disinfet'tare *vt* to disinfect
disini'bito, -a *ag* uninhibited
disinstal'lare *vt* (*software*) to uninstall
disinte'grare *vt, vi* to disintegrate; **disintegrarsi** *vpr* to disintegrate
disinteres'sarsi *vpr* **~ di** to take no interest in
disinte'resse *sm* indifference; (*generosità*) unselfishness
disintossicarsi *vpr* to clear out one's system; (*alcolizzato, drogato*) to be treated for alcoholism (*o* drug addiction)
disin'volto, -a *ag* casual, free and easy
dismi'sura *sf* excess; **a ~** to excess, excessively
disoccu'pato, -a *ag* unemployed ▷ *sm/f* unemployed person; **disoccupazi'one** *sf* unemployment
diso'nesto, -a *ag* dishonest
disordi'nato, -a *ag* untidy; (*privo di misura*) irregular, wild
di'sordine *sm* (*confusione*) disorder, confusion; (*sregolatezza*) debauchery; **disordini** *smpl* (*Pol ecc*) disorder *sg*; (*tumulti*) riots
disorien'tare *vt* to disorientate
disorien'tato, -a *ag* disorientated
'dispari *ag inv* odd, uneven
dis'parte: **in ~** *av* (*da lato*) aside, apart; **tenersi** *o* **starsene in ~** to keep to o.s., hold o.s. aloof
dispendi'oso, -a *ag* expensive
dis'pensa *sf* pantry, larder; (*mobile*) sideboard; (*Dir*) exemption; (*Rel*) dispensation; (*fascicolo*) number, issue
dispe'rato, -a *ag* (*persona*) in despair; (*caso, tentativo*) desperate
disperazi'one *sf* despair
dis'perdere *vt* (*disseminare*) to disperse; (*Mil*) to scatter, rout; (*fig: consumare*) to waste, squander; **disperdersi** *vpr* to disperse; to scatter; **dis'perso, -a** *pp di* **disperdere** ▷ *sm/f* missing person
dis'petto *sm* spite *no pl*, spitefulness *no pl*; **fare un ~ a qn** to play a (nasty) trick on sb; **a ~ di** in spite of; **dispet'toso, -a** *ag* spiteful
dispia'cere [dispja'tʃere] *sm* (*rammarico*) regret, sorrow; (*dolore*) grief; **dispiaceri** *smpl* (*preoccupazioni*) troubles, worries *vi* **~ a** to displease *vb impers* **mi dispiace (che)** I am sorry (that); **le dispiace se...?** do you mind if...?
dis'pone, dis'pongo *ecc vb vedi*

disporre
dispo'nibile *ag* available
dis'porre *vt* (*sistemare*) to arrange; (*preparare*) to prepare; (*Dir*) to order; (*persuadere*): **~ qn a** to incline *o* dispose sb towards ▷ *vi* (*decidere*) to decide; (*usufruire*): **~ di** to use, have at one's disposal; (*essere dotato*): **~ di** to have
dis'posi *ecc vb vedi* **disporre**
disposi'tivo *sm* (*meccanismo*) device
disposizi'one [dispozit'tsjone] *sf* arrangement, layout; (*stato d'animo*) mood; (*tendenza*) bent, inclination; (*comando*) order; (*Dir*) provision, regulation; **a ~ di qn** at sb's disposal
dis'posto, -a *pp di* **disporre**
disprez'zare [dispret'tsare] *vt* to despise
dis'prezzo [dis'prɛttso] *sm* contempt
'disputa *sf* dispute, quarrel
dispu'tare *vt* (*contendere*) to dispute, contest; (*gara*) to take part in ▷ *vi* to quarrel; **~ di** to discuss; **disputarsi qc** to fight for sth
'disse *vb vedi* **dire**
dissente'ria *sf* dysentery
dissen'tire *vi*: **~ (da)** to disagree (with)
disse'tante *ag* refreshing
'dissi *vb vedi* **dire**
dissimu'lare *vt* (*fingere*) to dissemble; (*nascondere*) to conceal
dissi'pare *vt* to dissipate; (*scialacquare*) to squander, waste
dissu'adere *vt*: **~ qn da** to dissuade sb from
dissua'sore *sm*: **~ di velocità** (*Auto*) speed bump
distac'care *vt* to detach, separate; (*Sport*) to leave behind; **distaccarsi** *vpr* to be detached; (*fig*) to stand out; **distaccarsi da** (*fig*: *allontanarsi*) to grow away from
dis'tacco, -chi *sm* (*separazione*) separation; (*fig*: *indifferenza*) detachment; (*Sport*): **vincere con un ~ di ...** to win by a distance of ...
dis'tante *av* far away ▷ *ag*: **~ (da)** distant (from), far away (from)
dis'tanza [dis'tantsa] *sf* distance
distanzi'are [distan'tsjare] *vt* to space out, place at intervals; (*Sport*) to outdistance; (*fig*: *superare*) to outstrip, surpass
dis'tare *vi* **distiamo pochi chilometri da Roma** we are only a few kilometres (away) from Rome; **quanto dista il centro da qui?** how far is the town centre?
dis'tendere *vt* (*coperta*) to spread out; (*gambe*) to stretch (out); (*mettere a giacere*) to lay; (*rilassare*: *muscoli, nervi*) to relax; **distendersi** *vpr* (*rilassarsi*) to relax; (*sdraiarsi*) to lie down
dis'tesa *sf* expanse, stretch
dis'teso, -a *pp di* **distendere**
distil'lare *vt* to distil
distille'ria *sf* distillery
dis'tinguere *vt* to distinguish; **distinguersi** *vpr* (*essere riconoscibile*) to be distinguished; (*emergere*) to stand out, be conspicuous, distinguish o.s.
dis'tinta *sf* (*nota*) note; (*elenco*) list; **distinta di versamento** pay-in slip
distin'tivo, -a *ag* distinctive; distinguishing ▷ *sm* badge
dis'tinto, -a *pp di* **distinguere** ▷ *ag* (*dignitoso ed elegante*) distinguished; **"distinti saluti"** (*in lettera*) yours faithfully
distinzi'one [distin'tsjone] *sf* distinction
dis'togliere [dis'tɔʎʎere] *vt* **~ da** to take away from; (*fig*) to dissuade from
distorsi'one *sf* (*Med*) sprain; (*Fisica, Ottica*) distortion
dis'trarre *vt* to distract; (*divertire*) to entertain, amuse; **distrarsi** *vpr* (*non fare attenzione*) to be distracted, let one's mind wander; (*svagarsi*) to amuse *o* enjoy o.s.; **dis'tratto, -a** *pp di* **distrarre** ▷ *ag* absent-minded; (*disattento*) inattentive; **distrazi'one**

sf absent-mindedness; inattention; (*svago*) distraction, entertainment
dis'tretto *sm* district
distribu'ire *vt* to distribute; (*Carte*) to deal (out); (*posta*) to deliver; (*lavoro*) to allocate, assign; (*ripartire*) to share out; **distribu'tore** *sm* (*di benzina*) petrol (BRIT) *o* gas (US) pump; (*Aut, Elettr*) distributor; **distributore automatico** vending machine
distri'care *vt* to disentangle, unravel; **districarsi** *vpr* (*tirarsi fuori*): **districarsi da** to get out of, disentangle o.s. from
dis'truggere [dis'truddʒere] *vt* to destroy; **distruzi'one** *sf* destruction
distur'bare *vt* to disturb, trouble; (*sonno, lezioni*) to disturb, interrupt; **disturbarsi** *vpr* to put o.s. out
dis'turbo *sm* trouble, bother, inconvenience; (*indisposizione*) (slight) disorder, ailment; **scusi il ~** I'm sorry to trouble you
disubbidi'ente *ag* disobedient
disubbi'dire *vi*: **~ (a qn)** to disobey (sb)
disu'mano, -a *ag* inhuman
di'tale *sm* thimble
'dito (*pl(f)* **'dita**) *sm* finger; (*misura*) finger, finger's breadth; **dito (del piede)** toe
'ditta *sf* firm, business
ditta'tore *sm* dictator
ditta'tura *sf* dictatorship
dit'tongo, -ghi *sm* diphthong
di'urno, -a *ag* day *cpd*, daytime *cpd*
'diva *sf vedi* **divo**
di'vano *sm* sofa; divan; **divano letto** bed settee, sofa bed
divari'care *vt* to open wide
di'vario *sm* difference
diven'tare *vi* to become; **~ famoso/professore** to become famous/a teacher
diversifi'care *vt* to diversify, vary; to differentiate; **diversificarsi** *vpr* **diversificarsi (per)** to differ (in)
diversità *sf inv* difference, diversity; (*varietà*) variety
diver'sivo *sm* diversion, distraction
di'verso, -a *ag* (*differente*): **~ (da)** different (from); **diversi, -e** *det pl* several, various; (*Comm*) sundry *pron pl* several (people), many (people)
diver'tente *ag* amusing
diverti'mento *sm* amusement, pleasure; (*passatempo*) pastime, recreation
diver'tire *vt* to amuse, entertain; **divertirsi** *vpr* to amuse *o* enjoy o.s.
di'videre *vt* (*anche Mat*) to divide; (*distribuire, ripartire*) to divide (up), split (up); **dividersi** *vpr* (*separarsi*) to separate; (*strade*) to fork
divi'eto *sm* prohibition; **"~ di sosta"** (*Aut*) "no parking"
divinco'larsi *vpr* to wriggle, writhe
di'vino, -a *ag* divine
di'visa *sf* (*Mil ecc*) uniform; (*Comm*) foreign currency
di'visi *ecc vb vedi* **dividere**
divisi'one *sf* division
'divo, -a *sm/f* star
divo'rare *vt* to devour
divorzi'are [divor'tsjare] *vi*: **~ (da qn)** to divorce (sb)
di'vorzio [di'vɔrtsjo] *sm* divorce
divul'gare *vt* to divulge, disclose; (*rendere comprensibile*) to popularize
dizio'nario [ditsjo'narjo] *sm* dictionary
DJ [di'dʒei] *sigla m/f* (= *Disc Jockey*) DJ
do *sm* (*Mus*) C; (: *solfeggiando*) do(h)
dobbi'amo *vb vedi* **dovere**
D.O.C. [dɔk] *abbr* (= *denominazione di origine controllata*) *label guaranteeing the quality of wine*
'doccia, -ce ['dottʃa] *sf* (*bagno*) shower; **fare la ~** to have a shower
docciaschi'uma [dottʃas'kjuma] *sm inv* shower gel
do'cente [do'tʃɛnte] *ag* teaching ▷ *sm/f* teacher; (*di università*) lecturer
'docile ['dɔtʃile] *ag* docile

documen'tario *sm* documentary
documentarsi *vpr*: **~ (su)** to gather information *o* material (about)
docu'mento *sm* document; **documenti** *smpl* (*d'identità ecc*) papers
dodi'cesimo, -a [dodi'tʃɛzimo] *num* twelfth
'dodici ['doditʃi] *num* twelve
do'gana *sf* (*ufficio*) customs *pl*; (*tassa*) (customs) duty; **passare la ~** to go through customs; **dogani'ere** *sm* customs officer
'doglie ['dɔʎʎe] *sfpl* (*Med*) labour *sg*, labour pains
'dolce ['doltʃe] *ag* sweet; (*carattere, persona*) gentle, mild; (*fig*: *mite*: *clima*) mild; (*non ripido*: *pendio*) gentle ▷ *sm* (*sapore dolce*) sweetness, sweet taste; (*Cuc*: *portata*) sweet, dessert; (: *torta*) cake; **dolcifi'cante** *sm* sweetener
'dollaro *sm* dollar
Dolo'miti *sfpl*: **le ~** the Dolomites
do'lore *sm* (*fisico*) pain; (*morale*) sorrow, grief; **dolo'roso, -a** *ag* painful; sorrowful, sad
do'manda *sf* (*interrogazione*) question; (*richiesta*) demand; (: *cortese*) request; (*Dir*: *richiesta scritta*) application; (*Econ*): **la ~** demand; **fare una ~ a qn** to ask sb a question; **fare ~ (per un lavoro)** to apply (for a job)
doman'dare *vt* (*per avere*) to ask for; (*per sapere*) to ask; (*esigere*) to demand; **domandarsi** *vpr* to wonder; to ask o.s.; **~ qc a qn** to ask sb for sth; to ask sb sth
do'mani *av* tomorrow ▷ *sm*: **il ~** (*il futuro*) the future; (*il giorno successivo*) the next day; **~ l'altro** the day after tomorrow
do'mare *vt* to tame
doma'tore, -'trice *sm/f* (*gen*) tamer; **domatore di cavalli** horsebreaker; **domatore di leoni** lion tamer
domat'tina *av* tomorrow morning
do'menica, -che *sf* Sunday; **di** *o* **la ~** on Sundays
do'mestico, -a, -ci, -che *ag* domestic ▷ *sm/f* servant, domestic
domi'cilio [domi'tʃiljo] *sm* (*Dir*) domicile, place of residence
domi'nare *vt* to dominate; (*fig*: *sentimenti*) to control, master ▷ *vi* to be in the dominant position
do'nare *vt* to give, present; (*per beneficenza ecc*) to donate ▷ *vi* (*fig*): **~ a** to suit, become; **~ sangue** to give blood; **dona'tore, -'trice** *sm/f* donor; **donatore di sangue/di organi** blood/organ donor
dondo'lare *vt* (*cullare*) to rock; **dondolarsi** *vpr* to swing, sway; **'dondolo** *sm* **sedia/cavallo a dondolo** rocking chair/horse
'donna *sf* woman; **donna di casa** housewife; home-loving woman; **donna di servizio** maid
donnai'olo *sm* ladykiller
'donnola *sf* weasel
'dono *sm* gift
doping ['dɔpiŋ] *sm* doping
'dopo *av* (*tempo*) afterwards; (*più tardi*) later; (*luogo*) after, next ▷ *prep* after ▷ *cong* (*temporale*): **~ aver studiato** after having studied; **~ mangiato va a dormire** after having eaten *o* after a meal he goes for a sleep ▷ *ag inv* **il giorno ~** the following day; **un anno ~** a year later; **~ di me/lui** after me/him; **~, a ~!** see you later!
dopo'barba *sm inv* after-shave
dopodo'mani *av* the day after tomorrow
doposcì [dopoʃʃi] *sm inv* après-ski outfit
dopo'sole *sm inv* aftersun (lotion)
dopo'tutto *av* (*tutto considerato*) after all
doppi'aggio [dop'pjaddʒo] *sm* (*Cinema*) dubbing
doppi'are *vt* (*Naut*) to round; (*Sport*) to lap; (*Cinema*) to dub
'doppio, -a *ag* double; (*fig*: *falso*)

double-dealing, deceitful ▷ *sm* (*quantità*): **il ~ (di)** twice as much (*o* many), double the amount (*o* number) of; (*Sport*) doubles *pl* ▷ *av* double
doppi'one *sm* duplicate (copy)
doppio'petto *sm* double-breasted jacket
dormicchi'are [dormik'kjare] *vi* to doze
dormigli'one, -a [dormiʎ'ʎone] *sm/f* sleepyhead
dor'mire *vt, vi* to sleep; **andare a ~** to go to bed; **dor'mita** *sf* **farsi una dormita** to have a good sleep
dormi'torio *sm* dormitory
dormi'veglia [dormi'veʎʎa] *sm* drowsiness
'dorso *sm* back; (*di montagna*) ridge, crest; (*di libro*) spine; **a ~ di cavallo** on horseback
do'sare *vt* to measure out; (*Med*) to dose
'dose *sf* quantity, amount; (*Med*) dose
do'tato, -a *ag* **~ di** (*attrezzature*) equipped with; (*bellezza, intelligenza*) endowed with; **un uomo ~** a gifted man
'dote *sf* (*di sposa*) dowry; (*assegnata a un ente*) endowment; (*fig*) gift, talent
Dott. *abbr* (= *dottore*) Dr.
dotto'rato *sm* degree; **dottorato di ricerca** doctorate, doctor's degree
dot'tore, -essa *sm/f* doctor; **chiamate un ~** call a doctor

DOTTORE

In Italy, anyone who has a degree in any subject can use the title **dottore**. Thus a person who is addressed as **dottore** is not necessarily a doctor of medicine.

dot'trina *sf* doctrine
Dott.ssa *abbr* (= *dottoressa*) Dr.
'dove *av* (*gen*) where; (*in cui*) where, in which; (*dovunque*) wherever ▷ *cong* (*mentre, laddove*) whereas; **~ sei?/vai?** where are you?/are you going?; **dimmi dov'è** tell me where it is; **di ~ sei?** where are you from?; **per ~ si passa?** which way should we go?; **la città ~ abito** the town where *o* in which I live; **siediti ~ vuoi** sit wherever you like
do'vere *sm* (*obbligo*) duty ▷ *vt* (*essere debitore*): **~ qc (a qn)** to owe (sb) sth ▷ *vi* (*seguito dall'infinito: obbligo*) to have to; **rivolgersi a chi di ~** to apply to the appropriate authority *o* person; **lui deve farlo** he has to do it, he must do it; **quanto le devo?** how much do I owe you?; **è dovuto partire** he had to leave; **ha dovuto pagare** he had to pay; (: *intenzione*): **devo partire domani** I'm (due) to leave tomorrow; (: *probabilità*): **dev'essere tardi** it must be late; **come si deve** (*lavorare, comportarsi*) properly; **una persona come si deve** a respectable person
dove'roso, -a *ag* (right and) proper
dovrò *ecc vb vedi* **dovere**
do'vunque *av* (*in qualunque luogo*) wherever; (*dappertutto*) everywhere; **~ io vada** wherever I go
do'vuto, -a *ag* (*causato*): **~ a** due to
doz'zina [dod'dzina] *sf* dozen; **una ~ di uova** a dozen eggs
dozzi'nale [doddzi'nale] *ag* cheap, second-rate
'drago, -ghi *sm* dragon
'dramma, -i *sm* drama; **dram'matico, -a, -ci, -che** *ag* dramatic
'drastico, -a, -ci, -che *ag* drastic
'dritto, -a *ag, av* = **diritto**
'droga, -ghe *sf* (*sostanza aromatica*) spice; (*stupefacente*) drug; **droghe leggere/pesanti** soft/hard drugs
drogarsi *vpr* to take drugs
dro'gato, -a *sm/f* drug addict
droghe'ria [droge'ria] *sf* grocer's shop (BRIT), grocery (store) (US)
drome'dario *sm* dromedary

DS [di'ɛsse] *sigla mpl* (*= Democratici di Sinistra*) *Italian left-wing party*

'dubbio, -a *ag* (*incerto*) doubtful, dubious; (*ambiguo*) dubious ▷ *sm* (*incertezza*) doubt; **avere il ~ che** to be afraid that, suspect that; **mettere in ~ qc** to question sth

dubi'tare *vi* **~ di** to doubt; (*risultato*) to be doubtful of

Dub'lino *sf* Dublin

'duca, -chi *sm* duke

du'chessa [du'kessa] *sf* duchess

'due *num* two

due'cento [due'tʃɛnto] *num* two hundred ▷ *sm* **il D~** the thirteenth century

due'pezzi [due'pɛttsi] *sm* (*costume da bagno*) two-piece swimsuit; (*abito femminile*) two-piece suit

'dunque *cong* (*perciò*) so, therefore; (*riprendendo il discorso*) well (then) ▷ *sm inv* **venire al ~** to come to the point

du'omo *sm* cathedral

> Attenzione! In inglese esiste la parola *dome*, che però significa *cupola*.

dupli'cato *sm* duplicate

'duplice ['duplitʃe] *ag* double, twofold; **in ~ copia** in duplicate

du'rante *prep* during

du'rare *vi* to last; **~ fatica a** to have difficulty in

du'rezza [du'rettsa] *sf* hardness; stubbornness; harshness; toughness

'duro, -a *ag* (*pietra, lavoro, materasso, problema*) hard; (*persona: ostinato*) stubborn, obstinate; (*severo*) harsh, hard; (*voce*) harsh; (*carne*) tough ▷ *sm* hardness; (*difficoltà*) hard part; (*persona*) tough guy; **tener ~** to stand firm, hold out; **~ d'orecchi** hard of hearing

DVD [divu'di] *sigla m* (*= digital versatile (or) video disc*) DVD; (*lettore*) DVD player

e

e (*dav V spesso* **ed**) *cong* and; **e lui?** what about him?; **e compralo!** well buy it then!

E *abbr* (*= est*) E

è *vb vedi* **essere**

eb'bene *cong* well (then)

'ebbi *ecc vb vedi* **avere**

e'braico, -a, -ci, -che *ag* Hebrew, Hebraic ▷ *sm* (*Ling*) Hebrew

e'breo, -a *ag* Jewish ▷ *sm/f* Jew/ess

EC *abbr* (*= Eurocity*) *fast train connecting Western European cities*

ecc. *av abbr* (*= eccetera*) etc

eccel'lente [ettʃel'lɛnte] *ag* excellent

ec'centrico, -a, -ci, -che [et'tʃɛntriko] *ag* eccentric

ecces'sivo, -a [ettʃes'sivo] *ag* excessive

ec'cesso [et'tʃɛsso] *sm* excess; **all'~** (*gentile, generoso*) to excess, excessively; **eccesso di velocità** (*Aut*) speeding

ec'cetera [et'tʃɛtera] *av* et cetera, and so on

ec'cetto [et'tʃɛtto] *prep* except, with the exception of; **~ che** except, other than; **~ che (non)** unless
eccezio'nale [ettʃetsjo'nale] *ag* exceptional
eccezi'one [ettʃet'tsjone] *sf* exception; (*Dir*) objection; **a ~ di** with the exception of, except for; **d'~** exceptional
ecci'tare [ettʃi'tare] *vt* (*curiosità, interesse*) to excite, arouse; (*folla*) to incite; **eccitarsi** *vpr* to get excited; (*sessualmente*) to become aroused
'ecco *av* (*per dimostrare*): **~ il treno!** here's *o* here comes the train!; (*dav pron*): **~mi!** here I am!; **~ne uno!** here's one (of them)!; (*dav pp*): **~ fatto!** there, that's it done!
ec'come *av* rather; **ti piace? — ~!** do you like it? — I'll say! *o* and how! *o* rather! (BRIT)
e'clisse *sf* eclipse
'eco (*pl(m)* **'echi**) *sm o f* echo
ecogra'fia *sf* (*Med*) scan
ecolo'gia [ekolo'dʒia] *sf* ecology
eco'logico, -a, ci, che [eko'lɔdʒiko] *ag* ecological
econo'mia *sf* economy; (*scienza*) economics *sg*; (*risparmio: azione*) saving; **fare ~** to economize, make economies; **eco'nomico, -a, -ci, -che** *ag* economic; (*poco costoso*) economical
ecstasy ['ekstazi] *sf* Ecstasy
'edera *sf* ivy
e'dicola *sf* newspaper kiosk *o* stand (US)
edi'ficio [edi'fitʃo] *sm* building
e'dile *ag* building *cpd*
Edim'burgo *sf* Edinburgh
edi'tore, -'trice *ag* publishing *cpd* ▷ *sm/f* publisher

> Attenzione! In inglese esiste la parola *editor*, che però significa *redattore*.

edizi'one [edit'tsjone] *sf* edition; (*tiratura*) printing; **edizione straordinaria** special edition
edu'care *vt* to educate; (*gusto, mente*) to train; **~ qn a fare** to train sb to do; **edu'cato, -a** *ag* polite, well-mannered; **educazi'one** *sf* education; (*familiare*) upbringing; (*comportamento*) (good) manners *pl*; **educazione fisica** (*Ins*) physical training *o* education

> Attenzione! In inglese esiste la parola *educated*, che però significa *istruito*.

educherò *ecc* [eduke'rɔ] *vb vedi* **educare**
effemi'nato, -a *ag* effeminate
efferve'scente [effervеʃ'ʃɛnte] *ag* effervescent
effet'tivo, -a *ag* (*reale*) real, actual; (*impiegato, professore*) permanent; (*Mil*) regular ▷ *sm* (*Mil*) strength; (*di patrimonio ecc*) sum total
ef'fetto *sm* effect; (*Comm: cambiale*) bill; (*fig: impressione*) impression; **in effetti** in fact, actually; **effetto serra** greenhouse effect; **effetti personali** personal effects, personal belongings
effi'cace [effi'katʃe] *ag* effective
effici'ente [effi'tʃɛnte] *ag* efficient
E'geo [e'dʒɛo] *sm* **l'~, il mare ~** the Aegean (Sea)
E'gitto [e'dʒitto] *sm* **l'~** Egypt
egizi'ano, -a [edʒit'tsjano] *ag, sm/f* Egyptian
'egli ['eʎʎi] *pron* he; **~ stesso** he himself
ego'ismo *sm* selfishness, egoism; **ego'ista, -i, -e** *ag* selfish, egoistic ▷ *sm/f* egoist
Egr. *abbr* = **egregio**
e'gregio, -a, -gi, -gie [e'grɛdʒo] *ag* (*nelle lettere*): **E~ Signore** Dear Sir
E.I. *abbr* = **Esercito Italiano**
elabo'rare *vt* (*progetto*) to work out, elaborate; (*dati*) to process
elasticiz'zato, -a [elastit[illegible]to] *ag* stretch *cpd*
e'lastico, -a, -ci, -che *ag* elastic; (*fig:*

andatura) springy; (: *decisione, vedute*) flexible ▷ *sm* (*di gomma*) rubber band; (*per il cucito*) elastic *no pl*
ele'fante *sm* elephant
ele'gante *ag* elegant
e'leggere [e'lɛddʒere] *vt* to elect
elemen'tare *ag* elementary; **le (scuole) elementari** *sfpl* primary (BRIT) *o* grade (US) school
ele'mento *sm* element; (*parte componente*) element, component, part; **elementi** *smpl* (*della scienza ecc*) elements, rudiments
ele'mosina *sf* charity, alms *pl*; **chiedere l'~** to beg
elen'care *vt* to list
elencherò *ecc* [elenke'rɔ] *vb vedi* **elencare**
e'lenco, -chi *sm* list; **elenco telefonico** telephone directory
e'lessi *ecc vb vedi* **eleggere**
eletto'rale *ag* electoral, election *cpd*
elet'tore, -'trice *sm/f* voter, elector
elet'trauto *sm inv* workshop for car electrical repairs; (*tecnico*) car electrician
elettri'cista, -i [elettri'tʃista] *sm* electrician
elettricità [elettritʃi'ta] *sf* electricity
e'lettrico, -a, -ci, -che *ag* electric(al)
elettriz'zante [elettrid'dzante] *ag* (*fig*) electrifying, thrilling
elettriz'zare [elettrid'dzare] *vt* to electrify; **elettrizzarsi** *vpr* to become charged with electricity
e'lettro... *prefisso*; **elettrodo'mestico, -a, -ci, -che** *ag* **apparecchi elettrodomestici** domestic (electrical) appliances; **elet'tronico, -a, -ci, -che** *ag* electronic
elezi'one [elet'tsjone] *sf* election; **elezioni** *sfpl* (*Pol*) election(s)
'elica, -che *sf* propeller
eli'cottero *sm* helicopter
elimi'nare *vt* to eliminate
elisoc'corso *sm* helicopter ambulance
el'metto *sm* helmet
elogi'are [elo'dʒare] *vt* to praise
elo'quente *ag* eloquent
e'ludere *vt* to evade
e'lusi *ecc vb vedi* **eludere**
e-mail [i'mɛil] *sf inv* (*messaggio, sistema*) e-mail ▷ *ag inv* (*indirizzo*) e-mail
emargi'nato, -a [emardʒi'nato] *sm/f* outcast; **emarginazione** [emardʒinat'tsjone] *sf* marginalization
embri'one *sm* embryo
emenda'mento *sm* amendment
emer'genza [emer'dʒɛntsa] *sf* emergency; **in caso di ~** in an emergency
e'mergere [e'mɛrdʒere] *vi* to emerge; (*sommergibile*) to surface; (*fig: distinguersi*) to stand out
e'mersi *ecc vb vedi* **emergere**
e'mettere *vt* (*suono, luce*) to give out, emit; (*onde radio*) to send out; (*assegno, francobollo, ordine*) to issue
emi'crania *sf* migraine
emi'grare *vi* to emigrate
emis'fero *sm* hemisphere; **emisfero australe** southern hemisphere; **emisfero boreale** northern hemisphere
e'misi *ecc vb vedi* **emettere**
emit'tente *ag* (*banca*) issuing; (*Radio*) broadcasting, transmitting ▷ *sf* (*Radio*) transmitter
emorra'gia, -'gie [emorra'dʒia] *sf* haemorrhage
emor'roidi *sfpl* haemorrhoids *pl* (BRIT), hemorrhoids *pl* (US)
emo'tivo, -a *ag* emotional
emozio'nante [emottsjo'nante] *ag* exciting, thrilling
emozionare [emottsjo'nare] *vt* (*commuovere*) to move; (*agitare*) to make nervous; (*elettrizzare*) to excite; **emozionarsi** *vpr* to be moved; to be

nervous; to be excited; **emozionato, -a** [emottsjo'nato] *ag* (*commosso*) moved; (*agitato*) nervous; (*elettrizzato*) excited

emozi'one [emot'tsjone] *sf* emotion; (*agitazione*) excitement

enciclope'dia [entʃiklope'dia] *sf* encyclopaedia

endove'noso, -a *ag* (*Med*) intravenous

'E.N.E.L. ['enel] *sigla m* (= *Ente Nazionale per l'Energia Elettrica*) *national electricity company*

ener'getico, -a, ci, che [ener'dʒɛtiko] *ag* (*risorse, crisi*) energy *cpd*; (*sostanza, alimento*) energy-giving

ener'gia, -'gie [ener'dʒia] *sf* (*Fisica*) energy; (*fig*) energy, strength, vigour; **energia eolica** wind power; **energia solare** solar energy, solar power; **e'nergico, -a, -ci, -che** *ag* energetic, vigorous

'enfasi *sf* emphasis; (*peg*) bombast, pomposity

en'nesimo, -a *ag* (*Mat, fig*) nth; **per l'ennesima volta** for the umpteenth time

e'norme *ag* enormous, huge

'ente *sm* (*istituzione*) body, board, corporation; (*Filosofia*) being; **enti pubblici** public bodies; **ente di ricerca** research organization

en'trambi, -e *pron pl* both (of them) ▷ *ag pl* **~ i ragazzi** both boys, both of the boys

en'trare *vi* to go (*o* come) in; **~ in** (*luogo*) to enter, go (*o* come) into; (*trovar posto, poter stare*) to fit into; (*essere ammesso a: club ecc*) to join, become a member of; **~ in automobile** to get into the car; **far ~ qn** (*visitatore ecc*) to show sb in; **questo non c'entra** (*fig*) that's got nothing to do with it; **en'trata** *sf* entrance, entry; **dov'è l'entrata?** where's the entrance?; **entrate** *sfpl* (*Comm*) receipts, takings; (*Econ*) income *sg*

'entro *prep* (*temporale*) within

entusias'mare *vt* to excite, fill with enthusiasm; **entusiasmarsi** *vpr* **entusiasmarsi (per qc/qn)** to become enthusiastic (about sth/sb); **entusi'asmo** *sm* enthusiasm; **entusi'asta, -i, -e** *ag* enthusiastic ▷ *sm/f* enthusiast

epa'tite *sf* hepatitis

epide'mia *sf* epidemic

epiles'sia *sf* epilepsy

epi'lettico, -a, ci, che *ag, sm/f* epileptic

epi'sodio *sm* episode

'epoca, -che *sf* (*periodo storico*) age, era; (*tempo*) time; (*Geo*) age

ep'pure *cong* and yet, nevertheless

EPT *sigla m* (= *Ente Provinciale per il Turismo*) *district tourist bureau*

equa'tore *sm* equator

equazi'one [ekwat'tsjone] *sf* (*Mat*) equation

e'questre *ag* equestrian

equi'librio *sm* balance, equilibrium; **perdere l'equilibrare** to lose one's balance

e'quino, -a *ag* horse *cpd*, equine

equipaggia'mento [ekwipaddʒa'mento] *sm* (*operazione: di nave*) equipping, fitting out; (*: di spedizione, esercito*) equipping, kitting out; (*attrezzatura*) equipment

equipaggi'are [ekwipad'dʒare] *vt* (*di persone*) to man; (*di mezzi*) to equip; **equipaggiarsi** *vpr* to equip o.s; **equi'paggio** *sm* crew

equitazi'one [ekwitat'tsjone] *sf* (horse-)riding

equiva'lente *ag, sm* equivalent

e'quivoco, -a, -ci, -che *ag* equivocal, ambiguous; (*sospetto*) dubious ▷ *sm* misunderstanding; **a scanso di equivoci** to avoid any misunderstanding; **giocare sull'~** to equivocate

'equo, -a *ag* fair, just

'era *sf* era
'era *ecc vb vedi* **essere**
'erba *sf* grass; **in ~** (*fig*) budding; **erbe aromatiche** herbs; **erba medica** lucerne; **er'baccia, -ce** *sf* weed
erboriste'ria *sf* (*scienza*) study of medicinal herbs; (*negozio*) herbalist's (shop)
e'rede *sm/f* heir; **eredità** *sf* (*Dir*) inheritance; (*Biol*) heredity; **lasciare qc in eredità a qn** to leave *o* bequeath sth to sb; **eredi'tare** *vt* to inherit; **eredi'tario, -a** *ag* hereditary
ere'mita, -i *sm* hermit
er'gastolo *sm* (*Dir: pena*) life imprisonment
'erica *sf* heather
er'metico, -a, -ci, -che *ag* hermetic
'ernia *sf* (*Med*) hernia
'ero *vb vedi* **essere**
e'roe *sm* hero
ero'gare *vt* (*somme*) to distribute; (*gas, servizi*) to supply
e'roico, -a, -ci, -che *ag* heroic
ero'ina *sf* heroine; (*droga*) heroin
erosi'one *sf* erosion
e'rotico, -a, -ci, -che *ag* erotic
er'rato, -a *ag* wrong
er'rore *sm* error, mistake; (*morale*) error; **per ~** by mistake; **ci dev'essere un ~** there must be some mistake; **errore giudiziario** miscarriage of justice
eruzi'one [erut'tsjone] *sf* eruption
esacer'bare [ezatʃer'bare] *vt* to exacerbate
esage'rare [ezadʒe'rare] *vt* to exaggerate ▷ *vi* to exaggerate; (*eccedere*) to go too far
esal'tare *vt* to exalt; (*entusiasmare*) to excite, stir
e'same *sm* examination; (*Ins*) exam, examination; **fare** *o* **dare un ~** to sit *o* take an exam; **esame di guida** driving test; **esame del sangue** blood test
esami'nare *vt* to examine
esaspe'rare *vt* to exasperate; to exacerbate
esatta'mente *av* exactly; accurately, precisely
esat'tezza [ezat'tettsa] *sf* exactitude, accuracy, precision
e'satto, -a *pp di* **esigere** ▷ *ag* (*calcolo, ora*) correct, right, exact; (*preciso*) accurate, precise; (*puntuale*) punctual
esau'dire *vt* to grant, fulfil
esauri'ente *ag* exhaustive
esauri'mento *sm* exhaustion; **esaurimento nervoso** nervous breakdown
esau'rire *vt* (*stancare*) to exhaust, wear out; (*provviste, miniera*) to exhaust; **esaurirsi** *vpr* to exhaust o.s., wear o.s. out; (*provviste*) to run out; **esau'rito, -a** *ag* exhausted; (*merci*) sold out; **registrare il tutto esaurito** (*Teatro*) to have a full house; **e'sausto, -a** *ag* exhausted
'esca (*pl* **'esche**) *sf* bait
'esce ['ɛʃʃe] *vb vedi* **uscire**
eschi'mese [eski'mese] *ag, sm/f* Eskimo
'esci ['ɛʃʃi] *vb vedi* **uscire**
escla'mare *vi* to exclaim, cry out
esclama'tivo, -a *ag*: **punto ~** exclamation mark
esclamazi'one *sf* exclamation
es'cludere *vt* to exclude
es'clusi *ecc vb vedi* **escludere**
esclusi'one *sf* exclusion; **a ~ di, fatta ~ per** except (for), apart from; **senza ~ (alcuna)** without exception; **procedere per ~** to follow a process of elimination; **senza ~ di colpi** (*fig*) with no holds barred; **esclusione sociale** social exclusion
esclu'siva *sf* (*Dir, Comm*) exclusive *o* sole rights *pl*
esclusiva'mente *av* exclusively, solely
esclu'sivo, -a *ag* exclusive
es'cluso, -a *pp di* **escludere**
'esco *vb vedi* **uscire**
escogi'tare [eskodʒi'tare] *vt* to

devise, think up
'escono *vb vedi* **uscire**
escursi'one *sf* (*gita*) excursion, trip; (: *a piedi*) hike, walk; (*Meteor*) range; **escursione termica** temperature range
esecuzi'one [ezekut'tsjone] *sf* execution, carrying out; (*Mus*) performance; **esecuzione capitale** execution
esegu'ire *vt* to carry out, execute; (*Mus*) to perform, execute
e'sempio *sm* example; **per ~** for example, for instance; **fare un ~** to give an example; **esem'plare** *ag* exemplary ▷ *sm* example; (*copia*) copy
eserci'tare [ezertʃi'tare] *vt* (*professione*) to practise (BRIT), practice (US); (*allenare: corpo, mente*) to exercise, train; (*diritto*) to exercise; (*influenza, pressione*) to exert; **esercitarsi** *vpr* to practise; **esercitarsi alla lotta** to practise fighting
e'sercito [e'zɛrtʃito] *sm* army
eser'cizio [ezer'tʃittsjo] *sm* practice; exercising; (*fisico: di matematica*) exercise; (*Econ*) financial year; (*azienda*) business, concern; **in ~** (*medico ecc*) practising; **esercizio pubblico** (*Comm*) commercial concern
esi'bire *vt* to exhibit, display; (*documenti*) to produce, present; **esibirsi** *vpr* (*attore*) to perform; (*fig*) to show off; **esibizi'one** *sf* exhibition; (*di documento*) presentation; (*spettacolo*) show, performance
esi'gente [ezi'dʒɛnte] *ag* demanding
e'sigere [e'zidʒere] *vt* (*pretendere*) to demand; (*richiedere*) to demand, require; (*imposte*) to collect
'esile *ag* (*persona*) slender, slim; (*stelo*) thin; (*voce*) faint
esili'are *vt* to exile; **e'silio** *sm* exile
esis'tenza [ezis'tɛntsa] *sf* existence
e'sistere *vi* to exist
esi'tare *vi* to hesitate
'esito *sm* result, outcome
'esodo *sm* exodus
esone'rare *vt* to exempt
e'sordio *sm* debut
esor'tare *vt*: **~ qn a fare** to urge sb to do
e'sotico, -a, -ci, -che *ag* exotic
es'pandere *vt* to expand; (*confini*) to extend; (*influenza*) to extend, spread; **espandersi** *vpr* to expand; **espansi'one** *sf* expansion; **espansione di memoria** (*Inform*) memory upgrade; **espan'sivo, -a** *ag* expansive, communicative
espatri'are *vi* to leave one's country
espedi'ente *sm* expedient
es'pellere *vt* to expel
esperi'enza [espe'rjɛntsa] *sf* experience
esperi'mento *sm* experiment
es'perto, -a *ag, sm* expert
espi'rare *vt, vi* to breathe out
es'plicito, -a [es'plitʃito] *ag* explicit
es'plodere *vi* (*anche fig*) to explode ▷ *vt* to fire
esplo'rare *vt* to explore
esplosi'one *sf* explosion
es'pone *ecc vb vedi* **esporre**
es'pongo, es'poni *ecc vb vedi* **esporre**
es'porre *vt* (*merci*) to display; (*quadro*) to exhibit, show; (*fatti, idee*) to explain, set out; (*porre in pericolo, Fot*) to expose; **esporsi** *vpr* **esporsi a** (*sole, pericolo*) to expose o.s. to; (*critiche*) to lay o.s. open to
espor'tare *vt* to export
es'pose *ecc vb vedi* **esporre**
esposizi'one [espozit'tsjone] *sf* displaying; exhibiting; setting out; (*anche Fot*) exposure; (*mostra*) exhibition; (*narrazione*) explanation, exposition
es'posto, -a *pp di* **esporre** ▷ *ag* **~ a nord** facing north ▷ *sm* (*Amm*) statement, account; (: *petizione*) petition
espressi'one *sf* expression

espres'sivo, -a *ag* expressive
es'presso, -a *pp di* **esprimere** ▷ *ag* express ▷ *sm* (*lettera*) express letter; (*anche:* **treno ~**) express train; (*anche:* **caffè ~**) espresso
es'primere *vt* to express; **esprimersi** *vpr* to express o.s.
es'pulsi *ecc vb vedi* **espellere**
espulsi'one *sf* expulsion
es'senza [es'sɛntsa] *sf* essence; **essenzi'ale** *ag* essential; **l'essenziale** the main *o* most important thing

PAROLA CHIAVE

'essere *sm* being; **essere umano** human being
▷ *vb copulativo* 1 (*con attributo, sostantivo*) to be; **sei giovane/simpatico** you are *o* you're young/nice; **è medico** he is *o* he's a doctor
2 (+ *di: appartenere*) to be; **di chi è la penna?** whose pen is it?; **è di Carla** it is *o* it's Carla's, it belongs to Carla
3 (+ *di: provenire*) to be; **è di Venezia** he is *o* he's from Venice
4 (*data, ora*): **è il 15 agosto/lunedì** it is *o* it's the 15th of August/Monday; **che ora è?, che ore sono?** what time is it?; **è l'una** it is *o* it's one o'clock; **sono le due** it is *o* it's two o'clock
5 (*costare*): **quant'è?** how much is it?; **sono 10 euro** it's 10 euros
▷ *vb aus* 1 (*attivo*): **essere arrivato/venuto** to have arrived/come; **è gia partita** she has already left
2 (*passivo*) to be; **essere fatto da** to be made by; **è stata uccisa** she has been killed
3 (*riflessivo*): **si sono lavati** they washed, they got washed
4 (+ *da* + *infinito*): **è da farsi subito** it must be *o* is to be done immediately
▷ *vi* 1 (*esistere, trovarsi*) to be; **sono a casa** I'm at home; **essere in piedi/seduto** to be standing/sitting
2: **esserci: c'è** there is; **ci sono** there are; **che c'è?** what's the matter?, what is it?; **ci sono!** (*fig: ho capito*) I get it!; *vedi anche* **ci**
▷ *vb impers* **è tardi/Pasqua** it's late/Easter; **è possibile che venga** he may come; **è così** that's the way it is

'essi *pron mpl vedi* **esso**
'esso, -a *pron* it; (*riferito a persona: soggetto*) he/she; (*: complemento*) him/her
est *sm* east
es'tate *sf* summer
esteri'ore *ag* outward, external
es'terno, -a *ag* (*porta, muro*) outer, outside; (*scala*) outside; (*alunno, impressione*) external ▷ *sm* outside, exterior ▷ *sm/f* (*allievo*) day pupil; **all'~** outside; **per uso ~** for external use only; **esterni** *smpl* (*Cinema*) location shots
'estero, -a *ag* foreign ▷ *sm* **all'~** abroad
es'teso, -a *pp di* **estendere** ▷ *ag* extensive, large; **scrivere per ~** to write in full
es'tetico, -a, -ci, -che *ag* aesthetic ▷ *sf* (*disciplina*) aesthetics *sg*; (*bellezza*) attractiveness; **este'tista, -i, -e** *sm/f* beautician
es'tinguere *vt* to extinguish, put out; (*debito*) to pay off; **estinguersi** *vpr* to go out; (*specie*) to become extinct
es'tinsi *ecc vb vedi* **estinguere**
estin'tore *sm* (fire) extinguisher
estinzi'one *sf* putting out; (*di specie*) extinction
estir'pare *vt* (*pianta*) to uproot, pull up; (*fig: vizio*) to eradicate
es'tivo, -a *ag* summer *cpd*
es'torcere [es'tɔrtʃere] *vt*: **~ qc (a qn)** to extort sth (from sb)
estradizi'one [estradit'tsjone] *sf* extradition
es'trae, es'traggo *ecc vb vedi* **estrarre**
es'traneo, -a *ag* foreign ▷ *sm/f*

stranger; **rimanere ~ a qc** to take no part in sth
es'trarre *vt* to extract; (*minerali*) to mine; (*sorteggiare*) to draw
es'trassi *ecc vb vedi* **estrarre**
estrema'mente *av* extremely
estre'mista, -i, e *sm/f* extremist
estremità *sf inv* extremity, end ▷ *sfpl* (*Anat*) extremities
es'tremo, -a *ag* extreme; (*ultimo*: *ora, tentativo*) final, last ▷ *sm* extreme; (*di pazienza, forze*) limit, end; **estremi** *smpl* (*Amm*: *dati essenziali*) details, particulars; **l'~ Oriente** the Far East
estro'verso, -a *ag, sm* extrovert
età *sf inv* age; **all'~ di 8 anni** at the age of 8, at 8 years of age; **ha la mia ~** he (*o* she) is the same age as me *o* as I am; **raggiungere la maggiore ~** to come of age; **essere in ~ minore** to be under age
'etere *sm* ether
eternità *sf* eternity
e'terno, -a *ag* eternal
etero'geneo, -a [etero'dʒɛneo] *ag* heterogeneous
eterosessu'ale *ag, sm/f* heterosexual
'etica *sf* ethics *sg*; *vedi anche* **etico**
eti'chetta [eti'ketta] *sf* label; (*cerimoniale*): **l'~** etiquette
'etico, -a, -ci, -che *ag* ethical
eti'lometro *sm* Breathalyzer®
etimolo'gia, -'gie [etimolo'dʒia] *sf* etymology
Eti'opia *sf* **l'~** Ethiopia
'etnico, -a, -ci, -che *ag* ethnic
e'trusco, -a, -schi, -sche *ag, sm/f* Etruscan
'ettaro *sm* hectare (= 10,000 m^2)
'etto *sm abbr* (= *ettogrammo*) 100 grams
'euro *sm inv* (*divisa*) euro
Eu'ropa *sf* **l'~** Europe
europarlamen'tare *sm/f* Member of the European Parliament, MEP
euro'peo, -a *ag, sm/f* European
eutana'sia *sf* euthanasia
evacu'are *vt* to evacuate
e'vadere *vi* (*fuggire*): **~ da** to escape from ▷ *vt* (*sbrigare*) to deal with, dispatch; (*tasse*) to evade
evapo'rare *vi* to evaporate
e'vasi *ecc vb vedi* **evadere**
evasi'one *sf* (*vedi evadere*) escape; dispatch; **evasione fiscale** tax evasion
eva'sivo, -a *ag* evasive
e'vaso, -a *pp di* **evadere** ▷ *sm* escapee
e'vento *sm* event
eventu'ale *ag* possible

> Attenzione! In inglese esiste la parola *eventual*, che però significa *finale*.

eventual'mente *av* if necessary

> Attenzione! In inglese esiste la parola *eventually*, che però significa *alla fine*.

evi'dente *ag* evident, obvious
evidente'mente *av* evidently; (*palesemente*) obviously, evidently
evi'tare *vt* to avoid; **~ di fare** to avoid doing; **~ qc a qn** to spare sb sth
evoluzi'one [evolut'tsjone] *sf* evolution
e'volversi *vpr* to evolve
ev'viva *escl* hurrah!; **~ il re!** long live the king!, hurrah for the king!
ex *prefisso* ex, former
'extra *ag inv* first-rate; top-quality ▷ *sm inv* extra; **extracomuni'tario, -a** *ag* from outside the EC ▷ *sm/f* non-EC citizen
extrater'restre *ag, sm/f* extraterrestrial

f

fa *vb vedi* **fare** ▷ *sm inv* (*Mus*) F; (: *solfeggiando la scala*) fa ▷ *av* **10 anni fa** 10 years ago

'fabbrica *sf* factory; **fabbri'care** *vt* to build; (*produrre*) to manufacture, make; (*fig*) to fabricate, invent

> Attenzione! In inglese esiste la parola *fabric*, che però significa *stoffa*.

fac'cenda [fat'tʃɛnda] *sf* matter, affair; (*cosa da fare*) task, chore

fac'chino [fak'kino] *sm* porter

'faccia, -ce ['fattʃa] *sf* face; (*di moneta, medaglia*) side; **faccia a faccia** face to face

facci'ata [fat'tʃata] *sf* façade; (*di pagina*) side

'faccio ['fattʃo] *vb vedi* **fare**

fa'cessi *ecc* [fa'tʃessi] *vb vedi* **fare**

fa'cevo *ecc* [fa'tʃevo] *vb vedi* **fare**

'facile ['fatʃile] *ag* easy; (*disposto*): **~ a** inclined to, prone to; (*probabile*): **è ~ che piova** it's likely to rain

facoltà *sf inv* faculty; (*autorità*) power

facolta'tivo, -a *ag* optional; (*fermata d'autobus*) request *cpd*

'faggio ['faddʒo] *sm* beech

fagi'ano [fa'dʒano] *sm* pheasant

fagio'lino [fadʒo'lino] *sm* French (BRIT) *o* string bean

fagi'olo [fa'dʒɔlo] *sm* bean

'fai *vb vedi* **fare**

'fai-da-'te *sm inv* DIY, do-it-yourself

'falce ['faltʃe] *sf* scythe; **falci'are** *vt* to cut; (*fig*) to mow down

falcia'trice [faltʃa'tritʃe] *sf* (*per fieno*) reaping machine; (*per erba*) mowing machine

'falco, -chi *sm* hawk

'falda *sf* layer, stratum; (*di cappello*) brim; (*di cappotto*) tails *pl*; (*di monte*) lower slope; (*di tetto*) pitch

fale'gname [faleɲ'ɲame] *sm* joiner

falli'mento *sm* failure; bankruptcy

fal'lire *vi* (*non riuscire*): **~ (in)** to fail (in); (*Dir*) to go bankrupt ▷ *vt* (*colpo, bersaglio*) to miss

'fallo *sm* error, mistake; (*imperfezione*) defect, flaw; (*Sport*) foul; fault; **senza ~** without fail

falò *sm inv* bonfire

falsifi'care *vt* to forge; (*monete*) to forge, counterfeit

'falso, -a *ag* false; (*errato*) wrong; (*falsificato*) forged; fake; (: *oro, gioielli*) imitation *cpd* ▷ *sm* forgery; **giurare il ~** to commit perjury

'fama *sf* fame; (*reputazione*) reputation, name

'fame *sf* hunger; **aver ~** to be hungry

fa'miglia [fa'miʎʎa] *sf* family

famili'are *ag* (*della famiglia*) family *cpd*; (*ben noto*) familiar; (*rapporti, atmosfera*) friendly; (*Ling*) informal, colloquial ▷ *sm/f* relative, relation

fa'moso, -a *ag* famous, well-known

fa'nale *sm* (*Aut*) light, lamp (BRIT); (*luce stradale, Naut*) light; (*di faro*) beacon

fa'natico, -a, -ci, -che *ag* fanatical; (*del teatro, calcio ecc*): **~ di** *o* **per** mad *o* crazy about ▷ *sm/f* fanatic; (*tifoso*) fan

'fango, -ghi *sm* mud

'fanno *vb vedi* **fare**

fannul'lone, -a *sm/f* idler, loafer

fantasci'enza [fantaʃʃɛntsa] *sf* science fiction

fanta'sia *sf* fantasy, imagination; (*capriccio*) whim, caprice ▷ *ag inv* **vestito ~** patterned dress

fan'tasma, -i *sm* ghost, phantom

fan'tastico, -a, -ci, -che *ag* fantastic; (*potenza, ingegno*) imaginative

fan'tino *sm* jockey

fara'butto *sm* crook

fard *sm inv* blusher

PAROLA CHIAVE

'fare *sm* **1** (*modo di fare*): **con fare distratto** absent-mindedly; **ha un fare simpatico** he has a pleasant manner

2: **sul far del giorno/della notte** at daybreak/nightfall

▷ *vt* **1** (*fabbricare, creare*) to make; (: *casa*) to build; (: *assegno*) to make out; **fare un pasto/una promessa/un film** to make a meal/a promise/a film; **fare rumore** to make a noise

2 (*effettuare*: *lavoro, attività, studi*) to do; (: *sport*) to play; **cosa fa?** (*adesso*) what are you doing?; (*di professione*) what do you do?; **fare psicologia/italiano** (*Ins*) to do psychology/Italian; **fare un viaggio** to go on a trip *o* journey; **fare una passeggiata** to go for a walk; **fare la spesa** to do the shopping

3 (*funzione*) to be; (*Teatro*) to play, be; **fare il medico** to be a doctor; **fare il malato** (*fingere*) to act the invalid

4 (*suscitare*: *sentimenti*): **fare paura a qn** to frighten sb; **(non) fa niente** (*non importa*) it doesn't matter

5 (*ammontare*): **3 più 3 fa 6** 3 and 3 are *o* make 6; **fanno 3 euro** that's 3 euros; **Roma fa 2.000.000 di abitanti** Rome has 2,000,000 inhabitants; **che ora fai?** what time do you make it?

6 (*+ infinito*): **far fare qc a qn** (*obbligare*) to make sb do sth; (*permettere*) to let sb do sth; **fammi vedere** let me see; **far partire il motore** to start (up) the engine; **far riparare la macchina/costruire una casa** to get *o* have the car repaired/a house built

7: **farsi: farsi una gonna** to make o.s. a skirt; **farsi un nome** to make a name for o.s.; **farsi la permanente** to get a perm; **farsi tagliare i capelli** to get one's hair cut; **farsi operare** to have an operation

8 (*fraseologia*): **farcela** to succeed, manage; **non ce la faccio più** I can't go on; **ce la faremo** we'll make it; **me l'hanno fatta!** (*imbrogliare*) I've been done!; **lo facevo più giovane** I thought he was younger; **fare sì/no con la testa** to nod/shake one's head

▷ *vi* **1** (*agire*) to act, do; **fate come volete** do as you like; **fare presto** to be quick; **fare da** to act as; **non c'è niente da fare** it's no use; **saperci fare con qn/qc** to know how to deal with sb/sth; **faccia pure!** go ahead!

2 (*dire*) to say; **"davvero?" fece** "really?" he said

3: **fare per** (*essere adatto*) to be suitable for; **fare per fare qc** to be about to do sth; **fece per andarsene** he made as if to leave

4: **farsi: si fa così** you do it like this, this is the way it's done; **non si fa così!** (*rimprovero*) that's no way to behave!; **la festa non si fa** the party is off

5: **fare a gara con qn** to compete *o* vie with sb; **fare a pugni** to come to blows; **fare in tempo a fare** to be in time to do

▷ *vb impers* **fa bel tempo** the weather is fine; **fa caldo/freddo** it's hot/cold;

fa notte it's getting dark ▷ *vpr* **farsi** 1 (*diventare*) to become; **farsi prete** to become a priest; **farsi grande/vecchio** to grow tall/old
2 (*spostarsi*): **farsi avanti/indietro** to move forward/back
3 (*fam*: *drogarsi*) to be a junkie

far'falla *sf* butterfly
fa'rina *sf* flour
farma'cia, -'cie [farma'tʃia] *sf* pharmacy; (*negozio*) chemist's (shop) (BRIT), pharmacy; **farma'cista, -i, -e** *sm/f* chemist (BRIT), pharmacist
'farmaco, -ci *o* **chi** *sm* drug, medicine
'faro *sm* (*Naut*) lighthouse; (*Aer*) beacon; (*Aut*) headlight
'fascia, -sce ['faʃʃa] *sf* band, strip; (*Med*) bandage; (*di sindaco, ufficiale*) sash; (*parte di territorio*) strip, belt; (*di contribuenti ecc*) group, band; **essere in fasce** (*anche fig*) to be in one's infancy; **fascia oraria** time band
fasci'are [faʃ'ʃare] *vt* to bind; (*Med*) to bandage
fa'scicolo [faʃ'ʃikolo] *sm* (*di documenti*) file, dossier; (*di rivista*) issue, number; (*opuscolo*) booklet, pamphlet
'fascino ['faʃʃino] *sm* charm, fascination
fa'scismo [faʃ'ʃizmo] *sm* fascism
'fase *sf* phase; (*Tecn*) stroke; **fuori ~** (*motore*) rough
fas'tidio *sm* bother, trouble; **dare ~ a qn** to bother *o* annoy sb; **sento ~ allo stomaco** my stomach's upset; **avere fastidi con la polizia** to have trouble *o* bother with the police; **fastidi'oso, -a** *ag* annoying, tiresome

> Attenzione! In inglese esiste la parola *fastidious*, che però significa *pignolo*.

'fata *sf* fairy
fa'tale *ag* fatal; (*inevitabile*) inevitable; (*fig*) irresistible
fa'tica, -che *sf* hard work, toil; (*sforzo*) effort; (*di metalli*) fatigue; **a ~** with difficulty; **fare ~ a fare qc** to have a job doing sth; **fati'coso, -a** *ag* tiring, exhausting; (*lavoro*) laborious
'fatto, -a *pp di* **fare** ▷ *ag*: **un uomo ~** a grown man; **~ a mano/in casa** hand-/home-made ▷ *sm* fact; (*azione*) deed; (*avvenimento*) event, occurrence; (*di romanzo, film*) action, story; **cogliere qn sul ~** to catch sb red-handed; **il ~ sta** *o* **è che** the fact remains *o* is that; **in ~ di** as for, as far as ... is concerned; **coppia/unione di ~** long-standing relationship
fat'tore *sm* (*Agr*) farm manager; (*Mat, elemento costitutivo*) factor; **fattore di protezione** (*di lozione solare*) factor; **vorrei una crema solare con ~ di protezione 15** I'd like a factor 15 suntan cream
fatto'ria *sf* farm; farmhouse

> Attenzione! In inglese esiste la parola *factory*, che però significa *fabbrica*.

fatto'rino *sm* errand-boy; (*di ufficio*) office-boy; (*d'albergo*) porter
fat'tura *sf* (*Comm*) invoice; (*di abito*) tailoring; (*malia*) spell
fattu'rato *sm* (*Comm*) turnover
'fauna *sf* fauna
'fava *sf* broad bean
'favola *sf* (*fiaba*) fairy tale; (*d'intento morale*) fable; (*fandonia*) yarn; **favo'loso, -a** *ag* fabulous; (*incredibile*) incredible
fa'vore *sm* favour; **per ~** please; **fare un ~ a qn** to do sb a favour
favo'rire *vt* to favour; (*il commercio, l'industria, le arti*) to promote, encourage; **vuole ~?** won't you help yourself?; **favorisca in salotto** please come into the sitting room
fax *sm inv* fax; **mandare qc via ~** to fax sth
fazzo'letto [fattso'letto] *sm* handkerchief; (*per la testa*) (head)scarf; **fazzoletto di carta** tissue

feb'braio *sm* February
'febbre *sf* fever; **aver la ~** to have a high temperature; **febbre da fieno** hay fever
'feci *ecc* ['fɛtʃi] *vb vedi* **fare**
fecondazi'one [fekondat'tsjone] *sf* fertilization; **fecondazione artificiale** artificial insemination
fe'condo, -a *ag* fertile
'fede *sf* (*credenza*) belief, faith; (*Rel*) faith; (*fiducia*) faith, trust; (*fedeltà*) loyalty; (*anello*) wedding ring; (*attestato*) certificate; **aver ~ in qn** to have faith in sb; **in buona/cattiva ~** in good/bad faith; **"in ~"** (*Dir*) "in witness whereof"; **fe'dele** *ag* **fedele (a)** faithful (to) ▷ *sm/f* follower; **i fedeli** (*Rel*) the faithful
'federa *sf* pillowslip, pillowcase
fede'rale *ag* federal
'fegato *sm* liver; (*fig*) guts *pl*, nerve
'felce ['feltʃe] *sf* fern
fe'lice [fe'litʃe] *ag* happy; (*fortunato*) lucky; **felicità** *sf* happiness
felici'tarsi [felitʃi'tarsi] *vpr* (*congratularsi*): **~ con qn per qc** to congratulate sb on sth
fe'lino, -a *ag, sm* feline
'felpa *sf* sweatshirt
'femmina *sf* (*Zool, Tecn*) female; (*figlia*) girl, daughter; (*spesso peg*) woman; **femmi'nile** *ag* feminine; (*sesso*) female; (*lavoro, giornale, moda*) woman's ▷ *sm* (*Ling*) feminine
'femore *sm* thighbone, femur
fe'nomeno *sm* phenomenon
feri'ale *ag*: **giorno ~** weekday
'ferie *sfpl* holidays (BRIT), vacation *sg* (US); **andare in ~** to go on holiday *o* vacation
fe'rire *vt* to injure; (*deliberatamente: Mil ecc*) to wound; (*colpire*) to hurt; **ferirsi** *vpr* to hurt o.s., injure o.s; **fe'rita** *sf* injury, wound; **fe'rito, -a** *sm/f* wounded *o* injured man/woman
fer'maglio [fer'maʎʎo] *sm* clasp; (*per documenti*) clip
fer'mare *vt* to stop, halt; (*Polizia*) to detain, hold ▷ *vi* to stop; **fermarsi** *vpr* to stop, halt; **fermarsi a fare qc** to stop to do sth; **può fermarsi qui/all'angolo?** could you stop here/at the corner?
fer'mata *sf* stop; **fermata dell'autobus** bus stop
fer'menti *smpl*: **~ lattici** probiotic bacteria
fer'mezza [fer'mettsa] *sf* (*fig*) firmness, steadfastness
'fermo, -a *ag* still, motionless; (*veicolo*) stationary; (*orologio*) not working; (*saldo: anche fig*) firm; (*voce, mano*) steady ▷ *escl* stop!; keep still! ▷ *sm* (*chiusura*) catch, lock; (*Dir*): **fermo di polizia** police detention
fe'roce [fe'rɔtʃe] *ag* (*animale*) fierce, ferocious; (*persona*) cruel, fierce; (*fame, dolore*) raging; **le bestie feroci** wild animals
ferra'gosto *sm* (*festa*) feast of the Assumption; (*periodo*) August holidays *pl*

FERRAGOSTO

Ferragosto, August 15th, is a national holiday. Marking the Feast of the Assumption, its origins are religious but in recent years it has simply become the most important public holiday of the summer season. Most people take some extra time off work and head out of town to the holiday resorts.

ferra'menta *sfpl*: **negozio di ~** ironmonger's (BRIT), hardware shop *o* store (US)
'ferro *sm* iron; **una bistecca ai ferri** a grilled steak; **ferro battuto** wrought iron; **ferro da calza** knitting needle; **ferro di cavallo** horseshoe; **ferro da stiro** iron
ferro'via *sf* railway (BRIT), railroad

(US); **ferrovi'ario, -a** *ag* railway *cpd* (BRIT), railroad *cpd* (US); **ferrovi'ere** *sm* railwayman (BRIT), railroad man (US)
'fertile *ag* fertile
'fesso, -a *pp di* **fendere** ▷ *ag* (*fam: sciocco*) crazy, cracked
fes'sura *sf* crack, split; (*per gettone, moneta*) slot
'festa *sf* (*religiosa*) feast; (*pubblica*) holiday; (*compleanno*) birthday; (*onomastico*) name day; (*ricevimento*) celebration, party; **far ~** to have a holiday; to live it up; **far ~ a qn** to give sb a warm welcome
festeggi'are [fested'dʒare] *vt* to celebrate; (*persona*) to have a celebration for
fes'tivo, -a *ag* (*atmosfera*) festive; **giorno ~** holiday
'feto *sm* foetus (BRIT), fetus (US)
'fetta *sf* slice
fettuc'cine [fettut'tʃine] *sfpl* (*Cuc*) ribbon-shaped pasta
FF.SS. *abbr* = **Ferrovie dello Stato**
FI *sigla* = **Firenze** ▷ *abbr* (= *Forza Italia*) *Italian centre-right political party*
fi'aba *sf* fairy tale
fi'acca *sf* weariness; (*svogliatezza*) listlessness
fi'acco, -a, -chi, -che *ag* (*stanco*) tired, weary; (*svogliato*) listless; (*debole*) weak; (*mercato*) slack
fi'accola *sf* torch
fi'ala *sf* phial
fi'amma *sf* flame
fiam'mante *ag* (*colore*) flaming; **nuovo ~** brand new
fiam'mifero *sm* match
fiam'mingo, -a, -ghi, -ghe *ag* Flemish ▷ *sm/f* Fleming ▷ *sm* (*Ling*) Flemish; **i Fiamminghi** the Flemish
fi'anco, -chi *sm* side; (*Mil*) flank; **di ~** sideways, from the side; **a ~ a ~** side by side
fi'asco, -schi *sm* flask; (*fig*) fiasco; **fare ~** to fail
fia'tare *vi* (*fig: parlare*): **senza ~** without saying a word
fi'ato *sm* breath; (*resistenza*) stamina; **avere il ~ grosso** to be out of breath; **prendere ~** to catch one's breath
'fibbia *sf* buckle
'fibra *sf* fibre; (*fig*) constitution
fic'care *vt* to push, thrust, drive; **ficcarsi** *vpr* (*andare a finire*) to get to
ficcherò *ecc* [fikke'rɔ] *vb vedi* **ficcare**
'fico, -chi *sm* (*pianta*) fig tree; (*frutto*) fig; **fico d'India** prickly pear; **fico secco** dried fig
fiction ['fikʃon] *sf inv* TV drama

> Attenzione! In inglese esiste la parola *fiction* che però significa narrativa oppure *finzione*.

fidanza'mento [fidantsa'mento] *sm* engagement
fidan'zarsi [fidan'tsarsi] *vpr* to get engaged; **fidan'zato, -a** *sm/f* fiancé/fiancée
fi'darsi *vpr* **~ di** to trust; **fi'dato, -a** *ag* reliable, trustworthy
fi'ducia [fi'dutʃa] *sf* confidence, trust; **incarico di ~** position of trust, responsible position; **persona di ~** reliable person
fie'nile *sm* barn; hayloft
fi'eno *sm* hay
fi'era *sf* fair
fi'ero, -a *ag* proud; (*audace*) bold
'fifa (*fam*) *sf* **aver ~** to have the jitters
fig. *abbr* (= *figura*) fig.
'figlia ['fiʎʎa] *sf* daughter
figli'astro, -a [fiʎ'ʎastro] *sm/f* stepson/daughter
'figlio ['fiʎʎo] *sm* son; (*senza distinzione di sesso*) child; **figlio di papà** spoilt, wealthy young man; **figlio unico** only child
fi'gura *sf* figure; (*forma, aspetto esterno*) form, shape; (*illustrazione*) picture, illustration; **far ~** to look smart; **fare una brutta ~** to make a bad impression
figu'rina *sf* figurine; (*cartoncino*)

picture card

'fila *sf* row, line; (*coda*) queue; (*serie*) series, string; **di ~** in succession; **fare la ~** to queue; **in ~ indiana** in single file

fi'lare *vt* to spin ▷ *vi* (*baco, ragno*) to spin; (*formaggio fuso*) to go stringy; (*discorso*) to hang together; (*fam*: *amoreggiare*) to go steady; (*muoversi a forte velocità*) to go at full speed; **~ diritto** (*fig*) to toe the line; **~ via** to dash off

filas'trocca, -che *sf* nursery rhyme

filate'lia *sf* philately, stamp collecting

fi'letto *sm* (*di vite*) thread; (*di carne*) fillet

fili'ale *ag* filial ▷ *sf* (*di impresa*) branch

film *sm inv* film

'filo *sm* (*anche fig*) thread; (*filato*) yarn; (*metallico*) wire; (*di lama, rasoio*) edge; **per ~ e per segno** in detail; **con un ~ di voce** in a whisper; **filo d'erba** blade of grass; **filo interdentale** dental floss; **filo di perle** string of pearls; **filo spinato** barbed wire

fi'lone *sm* (*di minerali*) seam, vein; (*pane*) ≈ Vienna loaf; (*fig*) trend

filoso'fia *sf* philosophy; **fi'losofo, -a** *sm/f* philosopher

fil'trare *vt, vi* to filter

'filtro *sm* filter; **filtro dell'olio** (*Aut*) oil filter

fi'nale *ag* final ▷ *sm* (*di opera*) end, ending; (: *Mus*) finale ▷ *sf* (*Sport*) final; **final'mente** *av* finally, at last

fi'nanza [fi'nantsa] *sf* finance; **finanze** *sfpl* (*di individuo, Stato*) finances

finché [fin'ke] *cong* (*per tutto il tempo che*) as long as; (*fino al momento in cui*) until; **aspetta ~ io (non) sia ritornato** wait until I get back

'fine *ag* (*lamina, carta*) thin; (*capelli, polvere*) fine; (*vista, udito*) keen, sharp; (*persona*: *raffinata*) refined, distinguished; (*osservazione*) subtle ▷ *sf* end ▷ *sm* aim, purpose; (*esito*) result, outcome; **secondo ~** ulterior motive; **in** *o* **alla ~** in the end, finally

fi'nestra *sf* window; **fines'trino** *sm* window; **vorrei un posto vicino al finestrino** I'd like a window seat

'fingere ['findʒere] *vt* to feign; (*supporre*) to imagine, suppose; **fingersi** *vpr* **fingersi ubriaco/pazzo** to pretend to be drunk/mad; **~ di fare** to pretend to do

fi'nire *vt* to finish ▷ *vi* to finish, end; **quando finisce lo spettacolo?** when does the show finish?; **~ di fare** (*compiere*) to finish doing; (*smettere*) to stop doing; **~ in galera** to end up *o* finish up in prison

finlan'dese *ag, sm* (*Ling*) Finnish ▷ *sm/f* Finn

Fin'landia *sf* **la ~** Finland

'fino, -a *ag* (*capelli, seta*) fine; (*oro*) pure; (*fig*: *acuto*) shrewd ▷ *av* (*spesso troncato in* **fin**: *pure, anche*) even ▷ *prep* (*spesso troncato in* **fin**: *tempo*): **fin quando?** till when?; (: *luogo*): **fin qui** as far as here; **~ a** (*tempo*) until, till; (*luogo*) as far as, (up) to; **fin da domani** from tomorrow onwards; **fin da ieri** since yesterday; **fin dalla nascita** from *o* since birth

fi'nocchio [fi'nɔkkjo] *sm* fennel; (*fam*: *peg*: *omosessuale*) queer

fi'nora *av* up till now

'finsi *ecc vb vedi* **fingere**

'finta *sf* pretence, sham; (*Sport*) feint; **far ~ (di fare)** to pretend (to do)

'finto, -a *pp di* **fingere** ▷ *ag* false; artificial

finzi'one [fin'tsjone] *sf* pretence, sham

fi'occo, -chi *sm* (*di nastro*) bow; (*di stoffa, lana*) flock; (*di neve*) flake; (*Naut*) jib; **coi fiocchi** (*fig*) first-rate; **fiocchi di avena** oatflakes; **fiocchi di granturco** cornflakes

fi'ocina ['fjɔtʃina] *sf* harpoon

fi'oco, -a, -chi, -che *ag* faint, dim

fi'onda *sf* catapult

fio'raio, -a *sm/f* florist
fi'ore *sm* flower; **fiori** *smpl* (*Carte*) clubs; **a fior d'acqua** on the surface of the water; **avere i nervi a fior di pelle** to be on edge; **fior di latte** cream; **fiori di campo** wild flowers
fioren'tino, -a *ag* Florentine
fio'retto *sm* (*Scherma*) foil
fio'rire *vi* (*rosa*) to flower; (*albero*) to blossom; (*fig*) to flourish
Fi'renze [fi'rɛntse] *sf* Florence
'firma *sf* signature

> Attenzione! In inglese esiste la parola *firm*, che però significa *ditta*.

fir'mare *vt* to sign; **un abito firmato** a designer suit; **dove devo ~?** where do I sign?
fisar'monica, -che *sf* accordion
fis'cale *ag* fiscal, tax *cpd*; **medico ~** *doctor employed by Social Security to verify cases of sick leave*
fischi'are [fis'kjare] *vi* to whistle ▷ *vt* to whistle; (*attore*) to boo, hiss
fischi'etto [fis'kjetto] *sm* (*strumento*) whistle
'fischio ['fiskjo] *sm* whistle
'fisco *sm* tax authorities *pl*, ≈ Inland Revenue (BRIT), ≈ Internal Revenue Service (US)
'fisica *sf* physics *sg*
'fisico, -a, -ci, -che *ag* physical ▷ *sm/f* physicist ▷ *sm* physique
fisiotera'pia *sf* physiotherapy
fisiotera'pista *sm/f* physiotherapist
fis'sare *vt* to fix, fasten; (*guardare intensamente*) to stare at; (*data, condizioni*) to fix, establish, set; (*prenotare*) to book; **fissarsi** *vpr* **fissarsi su** (*sguardo, attenzione*) to focus on; (*fig*: *idea*) to become obsessed with
'fisso, -a *ag* fixed; (*stipendio, impiego*) regular ▷ *av* **guardare ~ qc/qn** to stare at sth/sb; **telefono ~** landline
'fitta *sf* sharp pain; *vedi anche* **fitto**
fit'tizio, -a *ag* fictitious, imaginary
'fitto, -a *ag* thick, dense; (*pioggia*) heavy ▷ *sm* depths *pl*, middle; (*affitto, pigione*) rent
fi'ume *sm* river
fiu'tare *vt* to smell, sniff; (*animale*) to scent; (*fig*: *inganno*) to get wind of, smell; **~ tabacco/cocaina** to take snuff/cocaine
fla'grante *ag*: **cogliere qn in ~** to catch sb red-handed
fla'nella *sf* flannel
flash [flaʃ] *sm inv* (*Fot*) flash; (*giornalistico*) newsflash
'flauto *sm* flute
fles'sibile *ag* pliable; (*fig*: *che si adatta*) flexible
flessibili'tà *sf* (*anche fig*) flexibility
flessi'one *sf* (*gen*) bending; (*Ginnastica*: *a terra*) sit-up; (: *in piedi*) forward bend; (: *sulle gambe*) knee-bend; (*diminuzione*) slight drop, slight fall; (*Ling*) inflection; **fare una ~** to bend; **una ~ economica** a downward trend in the economy
'flettere *vt* to bend
'flipper *sm inv* pinball machine
F.lli *abbr* (= *fratelli*) Bros.
'flora *sf* flora
'florido, -a *ag* flourishing; (*fig*) glowing with health
'floscio, -a, -sci, -sce ['flɔʃʃo] *ag* (*cappello*) floppy, soft; (*muscoli*) flabby
'flotta *sf* fleet
'fluido, -a *ag, sm* fluid
flu'oro *sm* fluorine
'flusso *sm* flow; (*Fisica, Med*) flux; **~ e ri~** ebb and flow
fluvi'ale *ag* river *cpd*, fluvial
FMI *sigla m* (= *Fondo Monetario Internazionale*) IMF
'foca, -che *sf* (*Zool*) seal
fo'caccia, -ce [fo'kattʃa] *sf kind of pizza*; (*dolce*) bun
'foce ['fotʃe] *sf* (*Geo*) mouth
foco'laio *sm* (*Med*) centre of infection; (*fig*) hotbed
foco'lare *sm* hearth, fireside; (*Tecn*)

furnace
'fodera *sf* (*di vestito*) lining; (*di libro, poltrona*) cover
'fodero *sm* (*di spada*) scabbard; (*di pugnale*) sheath; (*di pistola*) holster
'foga *sf* enthusiasm, ardour
'foglia ['fɔʎʎa] *sf* leaf; **foglia d'argento/d'oro** silver/gold leaf
'foglio ['fɔʎʎo] *sm* (*di carta*) sheet (of paper); (*di metallo*) sheet; **foglio di calcolo** (*Inform*) spreadsheet; **foglio rosa** (*Aut*) provisional licence; **foglio di via** (*Dir*) expulsion order; **foglio volante** pamphlet
'fogna ['foɲɲa] *sf* drain, sewer
föhn [fø:n] *sm inv* hair dryer
'folla *sf* crowd, throng
'folle *ag* mad, insane; (*Tecn*) idle; **in ~** (*Aut*) in neutral
fol'lia *sf* folly, foolishness; foolish act; (*pazzia*) madness, lunacy
'folto, -a *ag* thick
fon *sm inv* hair dryer
fondamen'tale *ag* fundamental, basic
fonda'mento *sm* foundation; **fondamenta** *sfpl* (*Edil*) foundations
fon'dare *vt* to found; (*fig*: *dar base*): **~ qc su** to base sth on
fon'dente *ag*: **cioccolato ~** plain *o* dark chocolate
'fondere *vt* (*neve*) to melt; (*metallo*) to fuse, melt; (*fig*: *colori*) to merge, blend; (: *imprese, gruppi*) to merge ▷ *vi* to melt; **fondersi** *vpr* to melt; (*fig*: *partiti, correnti*) to unite, merge
'fondo, -a *ag* deep ▷ *sm* (*di recipiente, pozzo*) bottom; (*di stanza*) back; (*quantità di liquido che resta, deposito*) dregs *pl*; (*sfondo*) background; (*unità immobiliare*) property, estate; (*somma di denaro*) fund; (*Sport*) long-distance race; **fondi** *smpl* (*denaro*) funds; **a notte fonda** at dead of night; **in ~ a** at the bottom of; at the back of; (*strada*) at the end of; **andare a ~** (*nave*) to sink; **conoscere a ~** to know inside out; **dar ~ a** (*fig*: *provviste, soldi*) to use up; **in ~** (*fig*) after all, all things considered; **andare fino in ~ a** (*fig*) to examine thoroughly; **a ~ perduto** (*Comm*) without security; **fondi di magazzino** old *o* unsold stock *sg*; **fondi di caffè** coffee grounds; **fondo comune di investimento** investment trust
fondo'tinta *sm inv* (*cosmetico*) foundation
fo'netica *sf* phonetics *sg*
fon'tana *sf* fountain
'fonte *sf* spring, source; (*fig*) source ▷ *sm*: **fonte battesimale** (*Rel*) font; **fonte energetica** source of energy
fo'raggio [fo'raddʒo] *sm* fodder, forage
fo'rare *vt* to pierce, make a hole in; (*pallone*) to burst; (*biglietto*) to punch; **~ una gomma** to burst a tyre (BRIT) *o* tire (US)
'forbici ['fɔrbitʃi] *sfpl* scissors
'forca, -che *sf* (*Agr*) fork, pitchfork; (*patibolo*) gallows *sg*
for'chetta [for'ketta] *sf* fork
for'cina [for'tʃina] *sf* hairpin
fo'resta *sf* forest
foresti'ero, -a *ag* foreign ▷ *sm/f* foreigner
'forfora *sf* dandruff
'forma *sf* form; (*aspetto esteriore*) form, shape; (*Dir*: *procedura*) procedure; (*per calzature*) last; (*stampo da cucina*) mould
formag'gino [formad'dʒino] *sm* processed cheese
for'maggio [for'maddʒo] *sm* cheese
for'male *ag* formal
for'mare *vt* to form, shape, make; (*numero di telefono*) to dial; (*fig*: *carattere*) to form, mould; **formarsi** *vpr* to form, take shape; **for'mato** *sm* format, size; **formazi'one** *sf* formation; (*fig*: *educazione*) training; **formazione continua** continuing education; **formazione permanente**

lifelong learning; **formazione professionale** vocational training
for'mica¹, -che *sf* ant
formica®² ['fɔrmika] *sf* (*materiale*) Formica®
formi'dabile *ag* powerful, formidable; (*straordinario*) remarkable
'formula *sf* formula; **formula di cortesia** courtesy form
formu'lare *vt* to formulate; to express
for'naio *sm* baker
for'nello *sm* (*elettrico, a gas*) ring; (*di pipa*) bowl
for'nire *vt*: **~ qn di qc, ~ qc a qn** to provide *o* supply sb with sth, supply sth to sb
'forno *sm* (*di cucina*) oven; (*panetteria*) bakery; (*Tecn*: *per calce ecc*) kiln; (: *per metalli*) furnace; **forno a microonde** microwave oven
'foro *sm* (*buco*) hole; (*Storia*) forum; (*tribunale*) (law) court
'forse *av* perhaps, maybe; (*circa*) about; **essere in ~** to be in doubt
'forte *ag* strong; (*suono*) loud; (*spesa*) considerable, great; (*passione, dolore*) great, deep ▷ *av* strongly; (*velocemente*) fast; (*a voce alta*) loud(ly); (*violentemente*) hard ▷ *sm* (*edificio*) fort; (*specialità*) forte, strong point; **essere ~ in qc** to be good at sth
for'tezza [for'tettsa] *sf* (*morale*) strength; (*luogo fortificato*) fortress
for'tuito, -a *ag* fortuitous, chance
for'tuna *sf* (*destino*) fortune, luck; (*buona sorte*) success, fortune; (*eredità, averi*) fortune; **per ~** luckily, fortunately; **di ~** makeshift, improvised; **atterraggio di ~** emergency landing; **fortu'nato, -a** *ag* lucky, fortunate; (*coronato da successo*) successful
'forza ['fɔrtsa] *sf* strength; (*potere*) power; (*Fisica*) force; **forze** *sfpl* (*fisiche*) strength *sg*; (*Mil*) forces *escl* come on!; **per ~** against one's will; (*naturalmente*) of course; **a viva ~** by force; **a ~ di** by dint of; **~ maggiore** circumstances beyond one's control; **la ~ pubblica** the police *pl*; **forze armate** armed forces; **forze dell'ordine** the forces of law and order; **Forza Italia** *Italian centre-right political party*; **forza di pace** peacekeeping force
for'zare [for'tsare] *vt* to force; **~ qn a fare** to force sb to do
for'zista, -i, e [for'tsista] *ag* of Forza Italia ▷ *sm/f* member (*o* supporter) of Forza Italia
fos'chia [fos'kia] *sf* mist, haze
'fosco, -a, -schi, -sche *ag* dark, gloomy
'fosforo *sm* phosphorous
'fossa *sf* pit; (*di cimitero*) grave; **fossa biologica** septic tank
fos'sato *sm* ditch; (*di fortezza*) moat
fos'setta *sf* dimple
'fossi *ecc vb vedi* **essere**
'fossile *ag, sm* fossil
'fosso *sm* ditch; (*Mil*) trench
'foste *ecc vb vedi* **essere**
'foto *sf* photo; **può farci una ~, per favore?** would you take a picture of us, please? ▷ *prefisso*: **foto ricordo** souvenir photo; **foto tessera** passport(-type) photo; **foto'camera** *sf* **fotocamera digitale** digital camera; **foto'copia** *sf* photocopy; **fotocopi'are** *vt* to photocopy; **fotocopia'trice** [fotokopja'tritʃe] *sf* photocopier; **fotofo'nino** *sm* camera phone; **fotogra'fare** *vt* to photograph; **fotogra'fia** *sf* (*procedimento*) photography; (*immagine*) photograph; **fare una fotografia** to take a photograph; **una fotografia a colori/in bianco e nero** a colour/black and white photograph; **foto'grafico, -a, ci, che** *ag* photographic; **macchina fotografica** camera; **fo'tografo, -a** *sm/f* photographer; **fotoro'manzo**

sm romantic picture story
fou'lard [fu'lar] *sm inv* scarf
fra *prep* = **tra**
'fradicio, -a, -ci, -ce ['fraditʃo] *ag* (*molto bagnato*) soaking (wet); **ubriaco ~** blind drunk
'fragile ['fradʒile] *ag* fragile; (*fig*: *salute*) delicate
'fragola *sf* strawberry
fra'grante *ag* fragrant
frain'tendere *vt* to misunderstand
fram'mento *sm* fragment
'frana *sf* landslide; (*fig*: *persona*): **essere una ~** to be useless
fran'cese [fran'tʃeze] *ag* French ▷ *sm/f* Frenchman/woman ▷ *sm* (*Ling*) French; **i Francesi** the French
'Francia ['frantʃa] *sf*: **la ~** France
'franco, -a, -chi, -che *ag* (*Comm*) free; (*sincero*) frank, open, sincere ▷ *sm* (*moneta*) franc; **farla franca** (*fig*) to get off scot-free; **prezzo ~ fabbrica** ex-works price; **franco di dogana** duty-free
franco'bollo *sm* (postage) stamp
'frangia, -ge ['frandʒa] *sf* fringe
frap'pé *sm* milk shake
'frase *sf* (*Ling*) sentence; (*locuzione, espressione, Mus*) phrase; **frase fatta** set phrase
'frassino *sm* ash (tree)
frastagli'ato, -a [frastaʎ'ʎato] *ag* (*costa*) indented, jagged
frastor'nare *vt* to daze; to befuddle
frastu'ono *sm* hubbub, din
'frate *sm* friar, monk
fratel'lastro *sm* stepbrother; (*con genitore in comune*) half-brother
fra'tello *sm* brother; **fratelli** *smpl* brothers; (*nel senso di fratelli e sorelle*) brothers and sisters
fra'terno, -a *ag* fraternal, brotherly
frat'tempo *sm* **nel ~** in the meantime, meanwhile
frat'tura *sf* fracture; (*fig*) split, break
frazi'one [frat'tsjone] *sf* fraction; (*di comune*) small town
'freccia, -ce ['frettʃa] *sf* arrow; **freccia di direzione** (*Aut*) indicator
fred'dezza [fred'dettsa] *sf* coldness
'freddo, -a *ag, sm* cold; **fa ~** it's cold; **aver ~** to be cold; **a ~** (*fig*) deliberately; **freddo'loso, -a** *ag* sensitive to the cold
fre'gare *vt* to rub; (*fam*: *truffare*) to take in, cheat; (: *rubare*) to swipe, pinch; **fregarsene** (*fam!*): **chi se ne frega?** who gives a damn (about it)?
fregherò *ecc* [frege'rɔ] *vb vedi* **fregare**
fre'nare *vt* (*veicolo*) to slow down; (*cavallo*) to rein in; (*lacrime*) to restrain, hold back ▷ *vi* to brake; **frenarsi** *vpr* (*fig*) to restrain o.s., control o.s.
'freno *sm* brake; (*morso*) bit; **tenere a ~** to restrain; **freno a disco** disc brake; **freno a mano** handbrake
frequen'tare *vt* (*scuola, corso*) to attend; (*locale, bar*) to go to, frequent; (*persone*) to see (often)
frequen'tato, -a *ag* (*locale*) busy
fre'quente *ag* frequent; **di ~** frequently
fres'chezza [fres'kettsa] *sf* freshness
'fresco, -a, -schi, -sche *ag* fresh; (*temperatura*) cool; (*notizia*) recent, fresh ▷ *sm* **godere il ~** to enjoy the cool air; **stare ~** (*fig*) to be in for it; **mettere al ~** to put in a cool place
'fretta *sf* hurry, haste; **in ~** in a hurry; **in ~ e furia** in a mad rush; **aver ~** to be in a hurry
'friggere ['friddʒere] *vt* to fry ▷ *vi* (*olio ecc*) to sizzle
'frigido, -a ['fridʒido] *ag* (*Med*) frigid
'frigo *sm* fridge
frigo'bar *sm inv* minibar
frigo'rifero, -a *ag* refrigerating ▷ *sm* refrigerator
fringu'ello *sm* chaffinch
'frissi *ecc vb vedi* **friggere**
frit'tata *sf* omelette; **fare una ~** (*fig*) to make a mess of things
frit'tella *sf* (*Cuc*) fritter
'fritto, -a *pp di* **friggere** ▷ *ag* fried

▷ *sm* fried food; **fritto misto** mixed fry
frit'tura *sf* (*Cuc*): **frittura di pesce** mixed fried fish
'frivolo, -a *ag* frivolous
frizi'one [frit'tsjone] *sf* friction; (*sulla pelle*) rub, rub-down; (*Aut*) clutch
friz'zante [frid'dzante] *ag* (*anche fig*) sparkling
fro'dare *vt* to defraud, cheat
'frode *sf* fraud; **frode fiscale** tax evasion
'fronda *sf* (leafy) branch; (*di partito politico*) internal opposition; **fronde** *sfpl* (*di albero*) foliage *sg*
fron'tale *ag* frontal; (*scontro*) head-on
'fronte *sf* (*Anat*) forehead; (*di edificio*) front, façade ▷ *sm* (*Mil, Pol, Meteor*) front; **a ~, di ~** facing, opposite; **di ~ a** (*posizione*) opposite, facing, in front of; (*a paragone di*) compared with
fronti'era *sf* border, frontier
'frottola *sf* fib
fru'gare *vi* to rummage ▷ *vt* to search
frugherò *ecc* [fruge'rɔ] *vb vedi* **frugare**
frul'lare *vt* (*Cuc*) to whisk ▷ *vi* (*uccelli*) to flutter; **frul'lato** *sm* milk shake; fruit drink; **frulla'tore** *sm* electric mixer
fru'mento *sm* wheat
fru'scio [fruʃʃio] *sm* rustle; rustling; (*di acque*) murmur
'frusta *sf* whip; (*Cuc*) whisk
frus'tare *vt* to whip
frus'trato, -a *ag* frustrated
'frutta *sf* fruit; (*portata*) dessert; **frutta candita** candied fruit; **frutta secca** dried fruit
frut'tare *vi* to bear dividends, give a return
frut'teto *sm* orchard
frutti'vendolo, -a *sm/f* greengrocer (BRIT), produce dealer (US)
'frutto *sm* fruit; (*fig: risultato*) result(s); (*Econ: interesse*) interest; (*: reddito*) income; **frutti di bosco** berries; **frutti di mare** seafood *sg*
FS *abbr* = **Ferrovie dello Stato**
fu *vb vedi* **essere** ▷ *ag inv* **il fu Paolo Bianchi** the late Paolo Bianchi
fuci'lare [futʃi'lare] *vt* to shoot
fu'cile [fu'tʃile] *sm* rifle, gun; (*da caccia*) shotgun, gun
'fucsia *sf* fuchsia
'fuga *sf* escape, flight; (*di gas, liquidi*) leak; (*Mus*) fugue; **fuga di cervelli** brain drain
fug'gire [fud'dʒire] *vi* to flee, run away; (*fig: passar veloce*) to fly ▷ *vt* to avoid
'fui *vb vedi* **essere**
fu'liggine [fu'liddʒine] *sf* soot
'fulmine *sm* thunderbolt; lightning *no pl*
fu'mare *vi* to smoke; (*emettere vapore*) to steam ▷ *vt* to smoke; **le dà fastidio se fumo?** do you mind if I smoke?; **fuma'tore, -'trice** *sm/f* smoker
fu'metto *sm* comic strip; **giornale** *sm*, **a fumetti** comic
'fummo *vb vedi* **essere**
'fumo *sm* smoke; (*vapore*) steam; (*il fumare tabacco*) smoking; **fumi** *smpl* (*industriali ecc*) fumes; **i fumi dell'alcool** the after-effects of drink; **vendere ~** to deceive, cheat; **fumo passivo** passive smoking
'fune *sf* rope, cord; (*più grossa*) cable
'funebre *ag* (*rito*) funeral; (*aspetto*) gloomy, funereal
fune'rale *sm* funeral
'fungere ['fundʒere] *vi* **~ da** to act as
'fungo, -ghi *sm* fungus; (*commestibile*) mushroom; **fungo velenoso** toadstool
funico'lare *sf* funicular railway
funi'via *sf* cable railway
'funsi *ecc vb vedi* **fungere**
funzio'nare [funtsjo'nare] *vi* to work, function; (*fungere*): **~ da** to act as; **come funziona?** how does this work?; **la TV non funziona** the TV isn't working
funzio'nario [funtsjo'narjo] *sm*

official; **funzionario statale** civil servant

funzi'one [fun'tsjone] *sf* function; (*carica*) post, position; (*Rel*) service; **in ~** (*meccanismo*) in operation; **in ~ di** (*come*) as; **fare la ~ di qn** (*farne le veci*) to take sb's place

fu'oco, -chi *sm* fire; (*fornello*) ring; (*Fot, Fisica*) focus; **dare ~ a qc** to set fire to sth; **far ~** (*sparare*) to fire; **al ~!** fire!; **fuoco d'artificio** firework

fuorché [fwor'ke] *cong, prep* except

fu'ori *av* outside; (*all'aperto*) outdoors, outside; (*fuori di casa, Sport*) out; (*esclamativo*) get out! ▷ *prep* **~ (di)** out of, outside ▷ *sm* outside; **lasciar ~ qc/qn** to leave sth/sb out; **far ~ qn** (*fam*) to kill sb, do sb in; **essere ~ di sé** to be beside o.s.; **~ luogo** (*inopportuno*) out of place, uncalled for; **~ mano** out of the way, remote; **~ pericolo** out of danger; **~ uso** old-fashioned; obsolete; **fuorigi'oco** *sm* offside; **fuori'strada** *sm* (*Aut*) cross-country vehicle

'furbo, -a *ag* clever, smart; (*peg*) cunning

fu'rente *ag* **~ (contro)** furious (with)

fur'fante *sm* rascal, scoundrel

fur'gone *sm* van

'furia *sf* (*ira*) fury, rage; (*fig: impeto*) fury, violence; (*fretta*) rush; **a ~ di** by dint of; **andare su tutte le furie** to get into a towering rage; **furi'bondo, -a** *ag* furious

furi'oso, -a *ag* furious

'furono *vb vedi* **essere**

fur'tivo, -a *ag* furtive

'furto *sm* theft; **vorrei denunciare un ~** I'd like to report a theft; **furto con scasso** burglary

'fusa *sfpl* **fare le ~** to purr

fu'seaux [fy'zo] *smpl inv* leggings

'fusi *ecc vb vedi* **fondere**

fu'sibile *sm* (*Elettr*) fuse

fusi'one *sf* (*di metalli*) fusion, melting; (*colata*) casting; (*Comm*) merger; (*fig*) merging

'fuso, -a *pp di* **fondere** ▷ *sm* (*Filatura*) spindle; **fuso orario** time zone

fus'tino *sm* (*di detersivo*) tub

'fusto *sm* stem; (*Anat, di albero*) trunk; (*recipiente*) drum, can

fu'turo, -a *ag, sm* future

g

'gabbia *sf* cage; (*da imballaggio*) crate; **gabbia dell'ascensore** lift (BRIT) *o* elevator (US) shaft; **gabbia toracica** (*Anat*) rib cage
gabbi'ano *sm* (sea)gull
gabi'netto *sm* (*Med ecc*) consulting room; (*Pol*) ministry; (*WC*) toilet, lavatory; (*Ins*: *di fisica ecc*) laboratory
'gaffe [gaf] *sf inv* blunder
ga'lante *ag* gallant, courteous; (*avventura*) amorous
ga'lassia *sf* galaxy
ga'lera *sf* (*Naut*) galley; (*prigione*) prison
'galla *sf* **a ~** afloat; **venire a ~** to surface, come to the surface; (*fig*: *verità*) to come out
galleggi'are [galled'dʒare] *vi* to float
galle'ria *sf* (*traforo*) tunnel; (*Archit*, *d'arte*) gallery; (*Teatro*) circle; (*strada coperta con negozi*) arcade
'Galles *sm* **il ~** Wales
gal'lina *sf* hen
'gallo *sm* cock
galop'pare *vi* to gallop
ga'loppo *sm* gallop; **al** *o* **di ~** at a gallop
'gamba *sf* leg; (*asta*: *di lettera*) stem; **in ~** (*in buona salute*) well; (*bravo, sveglio*) bright, smart; **prendere qc sotto ~** (*fig*) to treat sth too lightly
gambe'retto *sm* shrimp
'gambero *sm* (*di acqua dolce*) crayfish; (*di mare*) prawn
'gambo *sm* stem; (*di frutta*) stalk
'gamma *sf* (*Mus*) scale; (*di colori, fig*) range
'gancio ['gantʃo] *sm* hook
'gara *sf* competition; (*Sport*) competition; contest; match; (: *corsa*) race; **fare a ~** to compete, vie
ga'rage [ga'raʒ] *sm inv* garage
garan'tire *vt* to guarantee; (*debito*) to stand surety for; (*dare per certo*) to assure
garan'zia [garan'tsia] *sf* guarantee; (*pegno*) security
gar'bato, -a *ag* courteous, polite
gareggi'are [gared'dʒare] *vi* to compete
garga'rismo *sm* gargle; **fare i gargarismi** to gargle
ga'rofano *sm* carnation; **chiodo di ~** clove
'garza ['gardza] *sf* (*per bende*) gauze
gar'zone [gar'dzone] *sm* (*di negozio*) boy
gas *sm inv* gas; **sento odore di ~** I can smell gas; **a tutto ~** at full speed; **dare ~** (*Aut*) to accelerate
ga'solio *sm* diesel (oil)
gas'sato, -a *ag* fizzy
gast'rite *sf* gastritis
gastrono'mia *sf* gastronomy
gat'tino *sm* kitten
'gatto, -a *sm/f* cat, tomcat/she-cat; **gatto delle nevi** (*Aut, Sci*) snowcat; **gatto selvatico** wildcat
'gazza ['gaddza] *sf* magpie
gel [dʒɛl] *sm inv* gel
ge'lare [dʒe'lare] *vt, vi, vb impers* to

freeze
gelate'ria [dʒelate'ria] *sf* ice-cream shop
gela'tina [dʒela'tina] *sf* gelatine; **gelatina esplosiva** dynamite; **gelatina di frutta** fruit jelly
ge'lato, -a [dʒe'lato] *ag* frozen ▷ *sm* ice cream
'gelido, -a ['dʒɛlido] *ag* icy, ice-cold
'gelo ['dʒɛlo] *sm* (*temperatura*) intense cold; (*brina*) frost; (*fig*) chill
gelo'sia [dʒelo'sia] *sf* jealousy
ge'loso, -a [dʒe'loso] *ag* jealous
'gelso ['dʒɛlso] *sm* mulberry (tree)
gelso'mino [dʒelso'mino] *sm* jasmine
ge'mello, -a [dʒe'mɛllo] *ag, sm/f* twin; **gemelli** *smpl* (*di camicia*) cufflinks; (*dello zodiaco*): **Gemelli** Gemini *sg*
'gemere ['dʒɛmere] *vi* to moan, groan; (*cigolare*) to creak
'gemma ['dʒɛmma] *sf* (*Bot*) bud; (*pietra preziosa*) gem
gene'rale [dʒene'rale] *ag, sm* general; **in ~** (*per sommi capi*) in general terms; (*di solito*) usually, in general
gene'rare [dʒene'rare] *vt* (*dar vita*) to give birth to; (*produrre*) to produce; (*causare*) to arouse; (*Tecn*) to produce, generate; **generazi'one** *sf* generation
'genere ['dʒɛnere] *sm* kind, type, sort; (*Biol*) genus; (*merce*) article, product; (*Ling*) gender; (*Arte, Letteratura*) genre; **in ~** generally, as a rule; **genere umano** mankind; **generi alimentari** foodstuffs
ge'nerico, -a, -ci, -che [dʒe'nɛriko] *ag* generic; (*vago*) vague, imprecise
'genero ['dʒɛnero] *sm* son-in-law
gene'roso, -a [dʒene'roso] *ag* generous
ge'netica [dʒe'nɛtika] *sf* genetics *sg*
ge'netico, -a, -ci, -che [dʒe'nɛtiko] *ag* genetic
gen'giva [dʒen'dʒiva] *sf* (*Anat*) gum
geni'ale [dʒen'jale] *ag* (*persona*) of genius; (*idea*) ingenious, brilliant
'genio ['dʒɛnjo] *sm* genius; **andare a ~ a qn** to be to sb's liking, appeal to sb
geni'tore [dʒeni'tore] *sm* parent, father *o* mother; **i miei genitori** my parents, my father and mother
gen'naio [dʒen'najo] *sm* January
'Genova ['dʒɛnova] *sf* Genoa
'gente ['dʒɛnte] *sf* people *pl*
gen'tile [dʒen'tile] *ag* (*persona, atto*) kind; (: *garbato*) courteous, polite; (*nelle lettere*): **G~ Signore** Dear Sir; (: *sulla busta*): **G~ Signor Fernando Villa** Mr Fernando Villa
genu'ino, -a [dʒenu'ino] *ag* (*prodotto*) natural; (*persona, sentimento*) genuine, sincere
geogra'fia [dʒeogra'fia] *sf* geography
geolo'gia [dʒeolo'dʒia] *sf* geology
ge'ometra, -i, -e [dʒe'ɔmetra] *sm/f* (*professionista*) surveyor
geome'tria [dʒeome'tria] *sf* geometry
ge'ranio [dʒe'ranjo] *sm* geranium
gerar'chia [dʒerar'kia] *sf* hierarchy
'gergo, -ghi ['dʒɛrgo] *sm* jargon; slang
geria'tria [dʒerja'tria] *sf* geriatrics *sg*
Ger'mania [dʒer'manja] *sf*: **la ~** Germany; **la ~ occidentale/orientale** West/East Germany
'germe ['dʒɛrme] *sm* germ; (*fig*) seed
germogli'are [dʒermoʎ'ʎare] *vi* to sprout; to germinate
gero'glifico, -ci [dʒero'glifiko] *sm* hieroglyphic
ge'rundio [dʒe'rundjo] *sm* gerund
'gesso ['dʒɛsso] *sm* chalk; (*Scultura, Med, Edil*) plaster; (*statua*) plaster figure; (*minerale*) gypsum
gesti'one [dʒes'tjone] *sf* management
ges'tire [dʒes'tire] *vt* to run, manage
'gesto ['dʒɛsto] *sm* gesture
Gesù [dʒe'zu] *sm* Jesus
gesu'ita, -i [dʒezu'ita] *sm* Jesuit

get'tare [dʒet'tare] *vt* to throw; (*anche*: **~ via**) to throw away *o* out; (*Scultura*) to cast; (*Edil*) to lay; (*acqua*) to spout; (*grido*) to utter; **gettarsi** *vpr* **gettarsi in** (*fiume*) to flow into; **~ uno sguardo su** to take a quick look at
'getto ['dʒɛtto] *sm* (*di gas, liquido, Aer*) jet; **a ~ continuo** uninterruptedly; **di ~** (*fig*) straight off, in one go
get'tone [dʒet'tone] *sm* token; (*per giochi*) counter; (*: roulette ecc*) chip; **gettone telefonico** telephone token
ghiacci'aio [gjat'tʃajo] *sm* glacier
ghiacci'ato, -a *ag* frozen; (*bevanda*) ice-cold
ghi'accio ['gjattʃo] *sm* ice
ghiacci'olo [gjat'tʃɔlo] *sm* icicle; (*tipo di gelato*) ice lolly (BRIT), Popsicle® (US)
ghi'aia ['gjaja] *sf* gravel
ghi'anda ['gjanda] *sf* (*Bot*) acorn
ghi'andola ['gjandola] *sf* gland
ghi'otto, -a ['gjotto] *ag* greedy; (*cibo*) delicious, appetizing
ghir'landa [gir'landa] *sf* garland, wreath
'ghiro ['giro] *sm* dormouse
'ghisa ['giza] *sf* cast iron
già [dʒa] *av* already; (*ex, in precedenza*) formerly ▷ *escl* of course!, yes indeed!
gi'acca, -che ['dʒakka] *sf* jacket; **giacca a vento** windcheater (BRIT), windbreaker (US)
giacché [dʒak'ke] *cong* since, as
giac'cone [dʒak'kone] *sm* heavy jacket
gi'ada ['dʒada] *sf* jade
giagu'aro [dʒa'gwaro] *sm* jaguar
gi'allo ['dʒallo] *ag* yellow; (*carnagione*) sallow ▷ *sm* yellow; (*anche*: **romanzo ~**) detective novel; (*anche*: **film ~**) detective film; **giallo dell'uovo** yolk
Giamaica [dʒa'maika] *sf* **la ~** Jamaica
Giap'pone [dʒap'pone] *sm* Japan; **giappo'nese** *ag, sm/f, sm* Japanese *inv*
giardi'naggio [dʒardi'naddʒo] *sm* gardening
giardini'ere, -a [dʒardi'njɛre] *sm/f* gardener
giar'dino [dʒar'dino] *sm* garden; **giardino d'infanzia** nursery school; **giardino pubblico** public gardens *pl*, (public) park; **giardino zoologico** zoo
giavel'lotto [dʒavel'lɔtto] *sm* javelin
gigabyte [dʒiga'bait] *sm inv* gigabyte
gi'gante, -'essa [dʒi'gante] *sm/f* giant ▷ *ag* giant, gigantic; (*Comm*) giant-size
'giglio ['dʒiʎʎo] *sm* lily
gilè [dʒi'lɛ] *sm inv* waistcoat
gin [dʒin] *sm inv* gin
gine'cologo, -a, -gi, -ghe [dʒine'kɔlogo] *sm/f* gynaecologist
gi'nepro [dʒi'nepro] *sm* juniper
gi'nestra [dʒi'nɛstra] *sf* (*Bot*) broom
Gi'nevra [dʒi'nevra] *sf* Geneva
gin'nastica *sf* gymnastics *sg*; (*esercizio fisico*) keep-fit exercises; (*Ins*) physical education
gi'nocchio [dʒi'nɔkkjo] (*pl(m)* **gi'nocchi**, *o pl(f)* **gi'nocchia**) *sm* knee; **stare in ~** to kneel, be on one's knees; **mettersi in ~** to kneel (down)
gio'care [dʒo'kare] *vt* to play; (*scommettere*) to stake, wager, bet; (*ingannare*) to take in ▷ *vi* to play; (*a roulette ecc*) to gamble; (*fig*) to play a part, be important; **~ a** (*gioco, sport*) to play; (*cavalli*) to bet on; **giocarsi la carriera** to put one's career at risk; **gioca'tore, -'trice** *sm/f* player; gambler
gio'cattolo [dʒo'kattolo] *sm* toy
giocherò *ecc* [dʒoke'rɔ] *vb vedi* **giocare**
gi'oco, -chi ['dʒɔko] *sm* game; (*divertimento, Tecn*) play; (*al casinò*) gambling; (*Carte*) hand; (*insieme di pezzi ecc necessari per un gioco*) set; **per ~** for fun; **fare il doppio ~ con qn** to double-cross sb; **i Giochi Olimpici** the Olympic Games; **gioco d'azzardo** game of chance; **gioco degli scacchi** chess set
giocoli'ere [dʒoko'ljɛre] *sm* juggler

gi'oia ['dʒɔja] *sf* joy, delight; (*pietra preziosa*) jewel, precious stone
gioielle'ria [dʒojelle'ria] *sf* jeweller's craft; jeweller's (shop)
gioielli'ere, -a [dʒojel'ljɛre] *sm/f* jeweller
gioi'ello [dʒo'jɛllo] *sm* jewel, piece of jewellery; **i miei gioielli** my jewels *o* jewellery; **gioielli** *smpl* (*anelli, collane ecc*) jewellery; **i gioielli della Corona** the crown jewels
Gior'dania [dʒor'danja] *sf*: **la ~** Jordan
giorna'laio, -a [dʒorna'lajo] *sm/f* newsagent (BRIT), newsdealer (US)
gior'nale [dʒor'nale] *sm* (news) paper; (*diario*) journal, diary; (*Comm*) journal; **giornale di bordo** log; **giornale radio** radio news *sg*
giornali'ero, -a [dʒorna'ljɛro] *ag* daily; (*che varia: umore*) changeable ▷ *sm* day labourer
giorna'lismo [dʒorna'lizmo] *sm* journalism
giorna'lista, -i, -e [dʒorna'lista] *sm/f* journalist
gior'nata [dʒor'nata] *sf* day; **giornata lavorativa** working day
gi'orno ['dʒorno] *sm* day; (*opposto alla notte*) day, daytime; (*anche*: **luce del ~**) daylight; **al ~** per day; **di ~** by day; **al ~ d'oggi** nowadays
gi'ostra ['dʒɔstra] *sf* (*per bimbi*) merry-go-round; (*torneo storico*) joust
gi'ovane ['dʒovane] *ag* young; (*aspetto*) youthful ▷ *sm/f* youth/girl, young man/woman; **i giovani** young people
gio'vare [dʒo'vare] *vi*: **~ a** (*essere utile*) to be useful to; (*far bene*) to be good for ▷ *vb impers* (*essere bene, utile*) to be useful; **giovarsi di qc** to make use of sth
giovedì [dʒove'di] *sm inv* Thursday; **di** *o* **il ~** on Thursdays
gioventù [dʒoven'tu] *sf* (*periodo*) youth; (*i giovani*) young people *pl*, youth
G.I.P. [dʒip] *sigla m inv* (= *Giudice per le Indagini Preliminari*) judge for preliminary enquiries
gira'dischi [dʒira'diski] *sm inv* record player
gi'raffa [dʒi'raffa] *sf* giraffe
gi'rare [dʒi'rare] *vt* (*far ruotare*) to turn; (*percorrere, visitare*) to go round; (*Cinema*) to shoot; to make; (*Comm*) to endorse ▷ *vi* to turn; (*più veloce*) to spin; (*andare in giro*) to wander, go around; **girarsi** *vpr* to turn; **~ attorno a** to go round; to revolve round; **al prossimo incrocio giri a destra/sinistra** turn right/left at the next junction; **far ~ la testa a qn** to make sb dizzy; (*fig*) to turn sb's head
girar'rosto [dʒirar'rɔsto] *sm* (*Cuc*) spit
gira'sole [dʒira'sole] *sm* sunflower
gi'revole [dʒi'revole] *ag* revolving, turning
gi'rino [dʒi'rino] *sm* tadpole
'giro ['dʒiro] *sm* (*circuito, cerchio*) circle; (*di chiave, manovella*) turn; (*viaggio*) tour, excursion; (*passeggiata*) stroll, walk; (*in macchina*) drive; (*in bicicletta*) ride; (*Sport: della pista*) lap; (*di denaro*) circulation; (*Carte*) hand; (*Tecn*) revolution; **prendere in ~ qn** (*fig*) to pull sb's leg; **fare un ~** to go for a walk (*o* a drive *o* a ride); **andare in ~** to go about, walk around; **a stretto ~ di posta** by return of post; **nel ~ di un mese** in a month's time; **essere nel ~** (*fig*) to belong to a circle (of friends); **giro d'affari** (*Comm*) turnover; **giro di parole** circumlocution; **giro di prova** (*Aut*) test drive; **giro turistico** sightseeing tour; **giro'collo** *sm* **a girocollo** crew-neck *cpd*
gironzo'lare [dʒirondzo'lare] *vi* to stroll about
'gita ['dʒita] *sf* excursion, trip; **fare una ~** to go for a trip, go on an outing
gi'tano, -a [dʒi'tano] *sm/f* gipsy
giù [dʒu] *av* down; (*dabbasso*)

downstairs; **in ~** downwards, down; **~ di lì** (*pressappoco*) thereabouts; **bambini dai 6 anni in ~** children aged 6 and under; **~ per**: **cadere ~ per le scale** to fall down the stairs; **essere ~** (*fig*: *di salute*) to be run down; (: *di spirito*) to be depressed

giub'botto [dʒub'bɔtto] *sm* jerkin; **giubbotto antiproiettile** bulletproof vest; **giubbotto salvagente** life jacket

giudi'care [dʒudi'kare] *vt* to judge; (*accusato*) to try; (*lite*) to arbitrate in; **~ qn/qc bello** to consider sb/sth (to be) beautiful

gi'udice ['dʒuditʃe] *sm* judge; **giudice conciliatore** justice of the peace; **giudice istruttore** examining (BRIT) *o* committing (US) magistrate; **giudice popolare** member of a jury

giu'dizio [dʒu'dittsjo] *sm* judgment; (*opinione*) opinion; (*Dir*) judgment, sentence; (: *processo*) trial; (: *verdetto*) verdict; **aver ~** to be wise *o* prudent; **citare in ~** to summons

gi'ugno ['dʒuɲɲo] *sm* June

gi'ungere ['dʒundʒere] *vi* to arrive ▷ *vt* (*mani ecc*) to join; **~ a** to arrive at, reach

gi'ungla ['dʒungla] *sf* jungle

gi'unsi *ecc* ['dʒunsi] *vb vedi* **giungere**

giura'mento [dʒura'mento] *sm* oath; **giuramento falso** perjury

giu'rare [dʒu'rare] *vt* to swear ▷ *vi* to swear, take an oath

giu'ria [dʒu'ria] *sf* jury

giu'ridico, -a, -ci, -che [dʒu'ridiko] *ag* legal

giustifi'care [dʒustifi'kare] *vt* to justify; **giustificazi'one** *sf* justification; (*Ins*) (note of) excuse

gius'tizia [dʒus'tittsja] *sf* justice; **giustizi'are** *vt* to execute, put to death

gi'usto, -a ['dʒusto] *ag* (*equo*) fair, just; (*vero*) true, correct; (*adatto*) right, suitable; (*preciso*) exact, correct ▷ *av* (*esattamente*) exactly, precisely; (*per l'appunto, appena*) just; **arrivare ~** to arrive just in time; **ho ~ bisogno di te** you're just the person I need

glaci'ale [gla'tʃale] *ag* glacial

gli [ʎi] (*davV, s impura, gn, pn, ps, x, z*) *det mpl* the ▷ *pron* (*a lui*) to him; (*a esso*) to it; (*in coppia con lo, la, li, le, ne*: *a lui, a lei, a loro ecc*): **gliele do** I'm giving them to him (*o* her *o* them); *vedi anche* **il**

glo'bale *ag* overall

'globo *sm* globe

'globulo *sm* (*Anat*): **globulo rosso/bianco** red/white corpuscle

'gloria *sf* glory

'gnocchi ['ɲɔkki] *smpl* (*Cuc*) *small dumplings made of semolina pasta or potato*

'gobba *sf* (*Anat*) hump; (*protuberanza*) bump

'gobbo, -a *ag* hunchbacked; (*ricurvo*) round-shouldered ▷ *sm/f* hunchback

'goccia, -ce ['gottʃa] *sf* drop; **goccio'lare** *vi, vt* to drip

go'dere *vi* (*compiacersi*): **~ (di)** to be delighted (at), rejoice (at); (*trarre vantaggio*): **~ di** benefit from ▷ *vt* to enjoy; **godersi la vita** to enjoy life; **godersela** to have a good time, enjoy o.s.

godrò *ecc vb vedi* **godere**

'goffo, -a *ag* clumsy, awkward

'gola *sf* (*Anat*) throat; (*golosità*) gluttony, greed; (*di camino*) flue; (*di monte*) gorge; **fare ~** (*anche fig*) to tempt

golf *sm inv* (*Sport*) golf; (*maglia*) cardigan

'golfo *sm* gulf

go'loso, -a *ag* greedy

gomi'tata *sf*: **dare una ~ a qn** to elbow sb; **farsi avanti a (forza** *o* **furia di) gomitate** to elbow one's way through; **fare a gomitate per qc** to fight to get sth

'gomito *sm* elbow; (*di strada ecc*) sharp bend

go'mitolo *sm* ball
'gomma *sf* rubber; (*per cancellare*) rubber, eraser; (*di veicolo*) tyre (BRIT), tire (US); **gomma americana** *o* **da masticare** chewing gum; **gomma a terra** flat tyre (BRIT) *o* tire (US); **ho una ~ a terra** I've got a flat tyre; **gom'mone** *sm* rubber dinghy
gonfi'are *vt* (*pallone*) to blow up, inflate; (*dilatare, ingrossare*) to swell; (*fig: notizia*) to exaggerate; **gonfiarsi** *vpr* to swell; (*fiume*) to rise; **'gonfio, -a** *ag* swollen; (*stomaco*) bloated; (*vela*) full; **gonfi'ore** *sm* swelling
'gonna *sf* skirt; **gonna pantalone** culottes *pl*
'gorgo, -ghi *sm* whirlpool
gorgogli'are [gorgoʎ'ʎare] *vi* to gurgle
go'rilla *sm inv* gorilla; (*guardia del corpo*) bodyguard
'gotico, -a, ci, che *ag, sm* Gothic
'gotta *sf* gout
gover'nare *vt* (*stato*) to govern, rule; (*pilotare, guidare*) to steer; (*bestiame*) to tend, look after
go'verno *sm* government
GPL *sigla m* (= *Gas di Petrolio Liquefatto*) LPG
GPS *sigla m* (= *Global Positioning System*) GPS
graci'dare [gratʃi'dare] *vi* to croak
'gracile ['gratʃile] *ag* frail, delicate
gradazi'one [gradat'tsjone] *sf* (*sfumatura*) gradation; **gradazione alcolica** alcoholic content, strength
gra'devole *ag* pleasant, agreeable
gradi'nata *sf* flight of steps; (*in teatro, stadio*) tiers *pl*
gra'dino *sm* step; (*Alpinismo*) foothold
gra'dire *vt* (*accettare con piacere*) to accept; (*desiderare*) to wish, like; **gradisce una tazza di tè?** would you like a cup of tea?
'grado *sm* (*Mat, Fisica ecc*) degree; (*stadio*) degree, level; (*Mil, sociale*) rank; **essere in ~ di fare** to be in a position to do
gradu'ale *ag* gradual
graf'fetta *sf* paper clip
graffi'are *vt* to scratch; **graffiarsi** *vpr* to get scratched; (*con unghie*) to scratch o.s.
'graffio *sm* scratch
gra'fia *sf* spelling; (*scrittura*) handwriting
'grafico, -a, -ci, -che *ag* graphic ▷ *sm* graph; (*persona*) graphic designer
gram'matica, -che *sf* grammar
'grammo *sm* gram(me)
'grana *sf* (*granello, di minerali, corpi spezzati*) grain; (*fam: seccatura*) trouble; (*: soldi*) cash ▷ *sm inv* Parmesan (cheese)
gra'naio *sm* granary, barn
gra'nata *sf* (*proiettile*) grenade
Gran Bre'tagna [-bre'taɲɲa] *sf*: **la ~** Great Britain
'granchio ['grankjo] *sm* crab; (*fig*) blunder; **prendere un ~** (*fig*) to blunder
'grande (*qualche volta* **gran** + C, **grand'** + V) *ag* (*grosso, largo, vasto*) big, large; (*alto*) tall; (*lungo*) long; (*in sensi astratti*) great ▷ *sm/f* (*persona adulta*) adult, grown-up; (*chi ha ingegno e potenza*) great man/woman; **fare le cose in ~** to do things in style; **una gran bella donna** a very beautiful woman; **non è una gran cosa** *o* **un gran che** it's nothing special; **non ne so gran che** I don't know very much about it
gran'dezza [gran'dettsa] *sf* (*dimensione*) size; magnitude; (*fig*) greatness; **in ~ naturale** life-size(d)
grandi'nare *vb impers* to hail
'grandine *sf* hail
gra'nello *sm* (*di cereali, uva*) seed; (*di frutta*) pip; (*di sabbia, sale ecc*) grain
gra'nito *sm* granite
'grano *sm* (*in quasi tutti i sensi*) grain; (*frumento*) wheat; (*di rosario, collana*) bead; **grano di pepe** peppercorn
gran'turco *sm* maize

'grappa *sf rough, strong brandy*
'grappolo *sm* bunch, cluster
gras'setto *sm* (*Tip*) bold (type)
'grasso, -a *ag* fat; (*cibo*) fatty; (*pelle*) greasy; (*terreno*) rich; (*fig: guadagno, annata*) plentiful ▷ *sm* (*di persona, animale*) fat; (*sostanza che unge*) grease
'grata *sf* grating
gra'ticola *sf* grill
'gratis *av* free, for nothing
grati'tudine *sf* gratitude
'grato, -a *ag* grateful; (*gradito*) pleasant, agreeable
gratta'capo *sm* worry, headache
grattaci'elo [gratta'tʃɛlo] *sm* skyscraper
gratta e 'sosta *sm inv scratch card used to pay for parking*
gratta e vinci ['gratta e 'vintʃi] *sm inv* (*biglietto*) scratchcard; (*lotteria*) scratchcard lottery
grat'tare *vt* (*pelle*) to scratch; (*raschiare*) to scrape; (*pane, formaggio, carote*) to grate; (*fam: rubare*) to pinch ▷ *vi* (*stridere*) to grate; (*Aut*) to grind; **grattarsi** *vpr* to scratch o.s.; **grattarsi la pancia** (*fig*) to twiddle one's thumbs
grat'tugia, -gie [grat'tudʒa] *sf* grater; **grattugi'are** *vt* to grate; **pane grattugiato** breadcrumbs *pl*
gra'tuito, -a *ag* free; (*fig*) gratuitous
'grave *ag* (*danno, pericolo, peccato ecc*) grave, serious; (*responsabilità*) heavy, grave; (*contegno*) grave, solemn; (*voce, suono*) deep, low-pitched; (*Ling*): **accento ~** grave accent; **un malato ~** a person who is seriously ill
grave'mente *av* (*ammalato, ferito*) seriously
gravi'danza [gravi'dantsa] *sf* pregnancy
gravità *sf* seriousness; (*anche Fisica*) gravity
gra'voso, -a *ag* heavy, onerous
'grazia ['grattsja] *sf* grace; (*favore*) favour; (*Dir*) pardon
'grazie ['grattsje] *escl* thank you!; **~ mille!** *o* **tante!** *o* **infinite!** thank you very much!; **~ a** thanks to
grazi'oso, -a [grat'tsjoso] *ag* charming, delightful; (*gentile*) gracious
'Grecia ['grɛtʃa] *sf* **la ~** Greece; **'greco, -a, -ci, -che** *ag, sm/f, sm* Greek
'gregge ['greddʒe] (*pl(f)* **-i**) *sm* flock
grembi'ule *sm* apron; (*sopravveste*) overall
'grembo *sm* lap; (*ventre della madre*) womb
'grezzo, -a ['greddzo] *ag* raw, unrefined; (*diamante*) rough, uncut; (*tessuto*) unbleached
gri'dare *vi* (*per chiamare*) to shout, cry (out); (*strillare*) to scream, yell ▷ *vt* to shout (out), yell (out); **~ aiuto** to cry *o* shout for help
'grido (*pl(m)* **-i**, *o pl(f)* **-a**) *sm* shout, cry; scream, yell; (*di animale*) cry; **di ~** famous
'grigio, -a, -gi, -gie ['gridʒo] *ag, sm* grey
'griglia ['griʎʎa] *sf* (*per arrostire*) grill; (*Elettr*) grid; (*inferriata*) grating; **alla ~** (*Cuc*) grilled
gril'letto *sm* trigger
'grillo *sm* (*Zool*) cricket; (*fig*) whim
'grinta *sf* grim expression; (*Sport*) fighting spirit
gris'sino *sm* bread-stick
Groen'landia *sf* **la ~** Greenland
gron'daia *sf* gutter
gron'dare *vi* to pour; (*essere bagnato*): **~ di** to be dripping with ▷ *vt* to drip with
'groppa *sf* (*di animale*) back, rump; (*fam: dell'uomo*) back, shoulders *pl*
gros'sezza [gros'settsa] *sf* size; thickness
gros'sista, -i, -e *sm/f* (*Comm*) wholesaler
'grosso, -a *ag* big, large; (*di spessore*) thick; (*grossolano: anche fig*) coarse; (*grave, insopportabile*) serious, great;

(*tempo, mare*) rough ▷ *sm*: **il ~ di** the bulk of; **un pezzo ~** (*fig*) a VIP, a bigwig; **farla grossa** to do something very stupid; **dirle grosse** to tell tall stories; **sbagliarsi di ~** to be completely wrong

'grotta *sf* cave; grotto

grot'tesco, -a, -schi, -sche *ag* grotesque

gro'viglio [gro'viʎʎo] *sm* tangle; (*fig*) muddle

gru *sf inv* crane

'gruccia, -ce ['gruttʃa] *sf* (*per camminare*) crutch; (*per abiti*) coat-hanger

'grumo *sm* (*di sangue*) clot; (*di farina ecc*) lump

'gruppo *sm* group; **gruppo sanguigno** blood group

GSM *sigla m* (= *Global System for Mobile Communication*) GSM

guada'gnare [gwadaɲ'ɲare] *vt* (*ottenere*) to gain; (*soldi, stipendio*) to earn; (*vincere*) to win; (*raggiungere*) to reach

gua'dagno [gwa'daɲɲo] *sm* earnings *pl*; (*Comm*) profit; (*vantaggio, utile*) advantage, gain; **guadagno lordo/netto** gross/net earnings *pl*

gu'ado *sm* ford; **passare a ~** to ford

gu'ai *escl* **~ a te (*o* lui *ecc*)!** woe betide you (*o* him *ecc*)!

gu'aio *sm* trouble, mishap; (*inconveniente*) trouble, snag

gua'ire *vi* to whine, yelp

gu'ancia, -ce ['gwantʃa] *sf* cheek

guanci'ale [gwan'tʃale] *sm* pillow

gu'anto *sm* glove

guarda'linee *sm inv* (*Sport*) linesman

guar'dare *vt* (*con lo sguardo: osservare*) to look at; (*film, televisione*) to watch; (*custodire*) to look after, take care of ▷ *vi* to look; (*badare*): **~ a** to pay attention to; (*luoghi: esser orientato*): **~ a** to face; **guardarsi** *vpr* to look at o.s.; **guardarsi da** (*astenersi*) to refrain from; (*stare in guardia*) to beware of; **guardarsi dal fare** to take care not to do; **guarda di non sbagliare** try not to make a mistake; **~ a vista qn** to keep a close watch on sb

guarda'roba *sm inv* wardrobe; (*locale*) cloakroom

gu'ardia *sf* (*individuo, corpo*) guard; (*sorveglianza*) watch; **fare la ~ a qc/qn** to guard sth/sb; **stare in ~** (*fig*) to be on one's guard; **di ~** (*medico*) on call; **guardia carceraria** (prison) warder; **guardia del corpo** bodyguard; **Guardia di finanza** (*corpo*) customs *pl*; (*persona*) customs officer; **guardia medica** emergency doctor service

GUARDIA DI FINANZA

The **Guardia di Finanza** is a military body which deals with infringements of the laws governing income tax and monopolies. It reports to the Ministers of Finance, Justice or Agriculture, depending on the function it is performing.

guardi'ano, -a *sm/f* (*di carcere*) warder; (*di villa ecc*) caretaker; (*di museo*) custodian; (*di zoo*) keeper; **guardiano notturno** night watchman

guarigi'one [gwari'dʒone] *sf* recovery

gua'rire *vt* (*persona, malattia*) to cure; (*ferita*) to heal ▷ *vi* to recover, be cured; to heal (up)

guar'nire *vt* (*ornare: abiti*) to trim; (*Cuc*) to garnish

guasta'feste *sm/f inv* spoilsport

guastarsi *vpr* (*cibo*) to go bad; (*meccanismo*) to break down; (*tempo*) to change for the worse

gu'asto, -a *ag* (*non funzionante*) broken; (*: telefono ecc*) out of order; (*andato a male*) bad, rotten; (*: dente*) decayed, bad; (*fig: corrotto*) depraved

▷ *sm* breakdown; (*avaria*) failure; **guasto al motore** engine failure
gu'erra *sf* war; (*tecnica: atomica, chimica ecc*) warfare; **fare la ~ (a)** to wage war (against); **guerra mondiale** world war; **guerra preventiva** preventive war
'gufo *sm* owl
gu'ida *sf* (*libro*) guidebook; (*persona*) guide; (*comando, direzione*) guidance, direction; (*Aut*) driving; (*tappeto: di tenda, cassetto*) runner; **avete una ~ in italiano?** do you have a guidebook in Italian?; **c'è una ~ che parla italiano?** is there an Italian-speaking guide?; **guida a destra/a sinistra** (*Aut*) right-/left-hand drive; **guida telefonica** telephone directory; **guida turistica** tourist guide
gui'dare *vt* to guide; (*squadra, rivolta*) to lead; (*auto*) to drive; (*aereo, nave*) to pilot; **sai ~?** can you drive?; **guida'tore, -trice** *sm/f* (*conducente*) driver
guin'zaglio [gwin'tsaʎʎo] *sm* leash, lead
'guscio ['guʃʃo] *sm* shell
gus'tare *vt* (*cibi*) to taste; (*: assaporare con piacere*) to enjoy, savour; (*fig*) to enjoy, appreciate ▷ *vi* **~ a** to please; **non mi gusta affatto** I don't like it at all
'gusto *sm* taste; (*sapore*) flavour; (*godimento*) enjoyment; **che gusti avete?** which flavours do you have?; **al ~ di fragola** strawberry-flavoured; **mangiare di ~** to eat heartily; **prenderci ~: ci ha preso ~** he's acquired a taste for it, he's got to like it; **gus'toso, -a** *ag* tasty; (*fig*) agreeable

h

H, h ['akka] *sf o m inv* (*lettera*) H, h ▷ *abbr* (= *ora*) hr; (= *etto, altezza*) h; **H come hotel** ≈ H for Harry (BRIT), H for How (US)
ha, 'hai [a, ai] *vb vedi* **avere**
ha'cker ['hakər] *sm inv* hacker
hall [hɔl] *sf inv* hall, foyer
hamburger [am'burger] *sm inv* (*carne*) hamburger; (*panino*) burger
'handicap ['handikap] *sm inv* handicap; **handicap'pato, -a** *ag* handicapped ▷ *sm/f* handicapped person, disabled person
'hanno ['anno] *vb vedi* **avere**
hard discount [ardis'kaunt] *sm inv* discount supermarket
hard disk [ar'disk] *sm inv* hard disk
hardware ['ardwer] *sm inv* hardware
hascisch [aʃʃiʃ] *sm* hashish
Hawaii [a'vai] *sfpl* **le ~** Hawaii *sg*
help [ɛlp] *sm inv* (*Inform*) help
'herpes ['ɛrpes] *sm* (*Med*) herpes *sg*; **herpes zoster** shingles *sg*
'hi-fi ['haifai] *sm inv, ag inv* hi-fi

ho [ɔ] *vb vedi* **avere**
'hobby ['hɔbi] *sm inv* hobby
'hockey ['hɔki] *sm* hockey; **hockey su ghiaccio** ice hockey
home page ['houm'pɛidʒ] *sf inv* home page
Hong Kong ['ɔŋ'kɔŋg] *sf* Hong Kong
'hostess ['houstis] *sf inv* air hostess (BRIT) *o* stewardess
hot dog ['hɔtdɔg] *sm inv* hot dog
ho'tel *sm inv* hotel
humour ['jumor] *sm inv* (sense of) humour
'humus *sm* humus
husky ['aski] *sm inv* (*cane*) husky *m inv*

i

i *det mpl* the
IC *abbr* (= *Intercity*) Intercity
ICI ['itʃi] *sigla f* (= *Imposta Comunale sugli Immobili*) ≈ Council Tax
i'cona *sf* (*Rel, Inform, fig*) icon
i'dea *sf* idea; (*opinione*) opinion, view; (*ideale*) ideal; **dare l'~ di** to seem, look like; **neanche** *o* **neppure per ~!** certainly not!; **idea fissa** obsession
ide'ale *ag, sm* ideal
ide'are *vt* (*immaginare*) to think up, conceive; (*progettare*) to plan
i'dentico, -a, -ci, -che *ag* identical
identifi'care *vt* to identify; **identificarsi** *vpr* **identificarsi (con)** to identify o.s. (with)
identità *sf inv* identity
ideolo'gia, -'gie [ideolo'dʒia] *sf* ideology
idio'matico, -a, -ci, -che *ag* idiomatic; **frase idiomatica** idiom
idi'ota, -i, -e *ag* idiotic ▷ *sm/f* idiot
'idolo *sm* idol
idoneità *sf* suitability

i'doneo, -a *ag*: **~ a** suitable for, fit for; (*Mil*) fit for; (*qualificato*) qualified for
i'drante *sm* hydrant
idra'tante *ag* moisturizing ▷ *sm* moisturizer
i'draulico, -a, -ci, -che *ag* hydraulic ▷ *sm* plumber
idroe'lettrico, -a, -ci, -che *ag* hydroelectric
i'drofilo, -a *ag vedi* **cotone**
i'drogeno [i'drɔdʒeno] *sm* hydrogen
idrovo'lante *sm* seaplane
i'ena *sf* hyena
i'eri *av, sm* yesterday; **il giornale di ~** yesterday's paper; **~ l'altro** the day before yesterday; **~ sera** yesterday evening
igi'ene [i'dʒɛne] *sf* hygiene; **igiene pubblica** public health; **igi'enico, -a, -ci, -he** *ag* hygienic; (*salubre*) healthy
i'gnaro, -a [iɲ'ɲaro] *ag* **~ di** unaware of, ignorant of
i'gnobile [iɲ'ɲɔbile] *ag* despicable, vile
igno'rante [iɲɲo'rante] *ag* ignorant
igno'rare [iɲɲo'rare] *vt* (*non sapere, conoscere*) to be ignorant *o* unaware of, not to know; (*fingere di non vedere, sentire*) to ignore
i'gnoto, -a [iɲ'ɲɔto] *ag* unknown

PAROLA CHIAVE

il (*pl(m)* **i**; *diventa* **lo** (*pl* **gli**) *davanti a s impura, gn, pn, ps, x, z; f* **la** (*pl* **le**)) *det m*
1 the; **il libro/lo studente/l'acqua** the book/the student/the water; **gli scolari** the pupils
2 (*astrazione*): **il coraggio/l'amore/la giovinezza** courage/love/youth
3 (*tempo*): **il mattino/la sera** in the morning/evening; **il venerdì** *ecc* (*abitualmente*) on Fridays *ecc*; (*quel giorno*) on (the) Friday *ecc*; **la settimana prossima** next week
4 (*distributivo*) a, an; **2 euro il chilo/paio** 2 euros a *o* per kilo/pair
5 (*partitivo*) some, any; **hai messo lo zucchero?** have you added sugar?; **hai comprato il latte?** did you buy (some *o* any) milk?
6 (*possesso*): **aprire gli occhi** to open one's eyes; **rompersi la gamba** to break one's leg; **avere i capelli neri/il naso rosso** to have dark hair/a red nose
7 (*con nomi propri*): **il Petrarca** Petrarch; **il Presidente Bush** President Bush; **dov'è la Francesca?** where's Francesca?
8 (*con nomi geografici*): **il Tevere** the Tiber; **l'Italia** Italy; **il Regno Unito** the United Kingdom; **l'Everest** Everest

ille'gale *ag* illegal
illeg'gibile [illed'dʒibile] *ag* illegible
ille'gittimo, -a [ille'dʒittimo] *ag* illegitimate
il'leso, -a *ag* unhurt, unharmed
illimi'tato, -a *ag* boundless; unlimited
ill.mo *abbr* = **illustrissimo**
il'ludere *vt* to deceive, delude; **illudersi** *vpr* to deceive o.s., delude o.s.
illumi'nare *vt* to light up, illuminate; (*fig*) to enlighten; **illuminarsi** *vpr* to light up; **~ a giorno** to floodlight; **illuminazi'one** *sf* lighting; illumination; floodlighting; (*fig*) flash of inspiration
il'lusi *ecc vb vedi* **illudere**
illusi'one *sf* illusion; **farsi delle illusioni** to delude o.s.; **illusione ottica** optical illusion
il'luso, -a *pp di* **illudere**
illus'trare *vt* to illustrate; **illustrazi'one** *sf* illustration
il'lustre *ag* eminent, renowned; **illus'trissimo, -a** *ag* (*negli indirizzi*) very revered
imbal'laggio [imbal'laddʒo] *sm* packing *no pl*
imbal'lare *vt* to pack; (*Aut*) to race

imbalsa'mare *vt* to embalm
imbambo'lato, -a *ag* (*sguardo*) vacant, blank
imbaraz'zante [imbarat'tsante] *ag* embarrassing, awkward
imbaraz'zare [imbarat'tsare] *vt* (*mettere a disagio*) to embarrass; (*ostacolare movimenti*) to hamper
imbaraz'zato, -a [imbarat'tsato] *ag* embarrassed; **avere lo stomaco ~** to have an upset stomach
imba'razzo [imba'rattso] *sm* (*disagio*) embarrassment; (*perplessità*) puzzlement, bewilderment; **imbarazzo di stomaco** indigestion
imbar'care *vt* (*passeggeri*) to embark; (*merci*) to load; **imbarcarsi** *vpr* **imbarcarsi su** to board; **imbarcarsi per l'America** to sail for America; **imbarcarsi in** (*fig*: *affare ecc*) to embark on
imbarcazi'one [imbarkat'tsjone] *sf* (small) boat, (small) craft *inv*; **imbarcazione di salvataggio** lifeboat
im'barco, -chi *sm* embarkation; loading; boarding; (*banchina*) landing stage
imbas'tire *vt* (*cucire*) to tack; (*fig*: *abbozzare*) to sketch, outline
im'battersi *vpr*: **~ in** (*incontrare*) to bump *o* run into
imbat'tibile *ag* unbeatable, invincible
imbavagli'are [imbavaʎ'ʎare] *vt* to gag
imbe'cille [imbe'tʃille] *ag* idiotic ▷ *sm/f* idiot; (*Med*) imbecile
imbian'care *vt* to whiten; (*muro*) to whitewash ▷ *vi* to become *o* turn white
imbian'chino [imbjan'kino] *sm* (house) painter, painter and decorator
imboc'care *vt* (*bambino*) to feed; (*entrare*: *strada*) to enter, turn into
imbocca'tura *sf* mouth; (*di strada, porto*) entrance; (*Mus, del morso*) mouthpiece
imbos'cata *sf* ambush
imbottigli'are [imbottiʎ'ʎare] *vt* to bottle; (*Naut*) to blockade; (*Mil*) to hem in; **imbottigliarsi** *vpr* to be stuck in a traffic jam
imbot'tire *vt* to stuff; (*giacca*) to pad; **imbottirsi** *vpr* **imbottirsi di** (*rimpinzarsi*) to stuff o.s. with;
imbot'tito, -a *ag* stuffed; (*giacca*) padded; **panino imbottito** filled roll
imbra'nato, -a *ag* clumsy, awkward ▷ *sm/f* clumsy person
imbrogli'are [imbroʎ'ʎare] *vt* to mix up; (*fig*: *raggirare*) to deceive, cheat; (: *confondere*) to confuse, mix up; **imbrogli'one, -a** *sm/f* cheat, swindler
imbronci'ato, -a *ag* sulky
imbu'care *vt* to post; **dove posso ~ queste cartoline?** where can I post these cards?
imbur'rare *vt* to butter
im'buto *sm* funnel
imi'tare *vt* to imitate; (*riprodurre*) to copy; (*assomigliare*) to look like
immagazzi'nare [immagaddzi'nare] *vt* to store
immagi'nare [immadʒi'nare] *vt* to imagine; (*supporre*) to suppose; (*inventare*) to invent; **s'immagini!** don't mention it!, not at all!; **immaginazi'one** *sf* imagination; (*cosa immaginata*) fancy
im'magine [im'madʒine] *sf* image; (*rappresentazione grafica, mentale*) picture
imman'cabile *ag* certain; unfailing
im'mane *ag* (*smisurato*) enormous; (*spaventoso*) terrible
immangi'abile [imman'dʒabile] *ag* inedible
immatrico'lare *vt* to register; **immatricolarsi** *vpr* (*Ins*) to matriculate, enrol
imma'turo, -a *ag* (*frutto*) unripe; (*persona*) immature; (*prematuro*)

premature
immedesi'marsi *vpr*: **~ in** to identify with
immediata'mente *av* immediately, at once
immedi'ato, -a *ag* immediate
im'menso, -a *ag* immense
im'mergere [im'mɛrdʒere] *vt* to immerse, plunge; **immergersi** *vpr* to plunge; (*sommergibile*) to dive, submerge; (*dedicarsi a*): **immergersi in** to immerse o.s. in
immeri'tato, -a *ag* undeserved
immersi'one *sf* immersion; (*di sommergibile*) submersion, dive; (*di palombaro*) dive
im'mettere *vt*: **~ (in)** to introduce (into); **~ dati in un computer** to enter data on a computer
immi'grato, -a *sm/f* immigrant
immi'nente *ag* imminent
immischiarsi *vpr*: **~ in** to interfere *o* meddle in
im'mobile *ag* motionless, still; **immobili'are** *ag* (*Dir*) property *cpd*
immon'dizia [immon'dittsja] *sf* dirt, filth; (*spesso al pl*: *spazzatura, rifiuti*) rubbish *no pl*, refuse *no pl*
immo'rale *ag* immoral
immor'tale *ag* immortal
im'mune *ag* (*esente*) exempt; (*Med, Dir*) immune
immu'tabile *ag* immutable; unchanging
impacchet'tare [impakket'tare] *vt* to pack up
impacci'ato, -a *ag* awkward, clumsy; (*imbarazzato*) embarrassed
im'pacco, -chi *sm* (*Med*) compress
impadro'nirsi *vpr*: **~ di** to seize, take possession of; (*fig*: *apprendere a fondo*) to master
impa'gabile *ag* priceless
impa'lato, -a *ag* (*fig*) stiff as a board
impalca'tura *sf* scaffolding
impalli'dire *vi* to turn pale; (*fig*) to fade
impa'nato, -a *ag* (*Cuc*) coated in breadcrumbs
impanta'narsi *vpr* to sink (in the mud); (*fig*) to get bogged down
impappi'narsi *vpr* to stammer, falter
impa'rare *vt* to learn
impar'tire *vt* to bestow, give
imparzi'ale [impar'tsjale] *ag* impartial, unbiased
impas'sibile *ag* impassive
impas'tare *vt* (*pasta*) to knead
impastic'carsi *vpr* to pop pills
im'pasto *sm* (*l'impastare*: *di pane*) kneading; (: *di cemento*) mixing; (*pasta*) dough; (*anche fig*) mixture
im'patto *sm* impact
impau'rire *vt* to scare, frighten ▷ *vi* (*anche*: **impaurirsi**) to become scared *o* frightened
impazi'ente [impat'tsjɛnte] *ag* impatient
impaz'zata [impat'tsata] *sf*: **all'~** (*precipitosamente*) at breakneck speed
impaz'zire [impat'tsire] *vi* to go mad; **~ per qn/qc** to be crazy about sb/sth
impec'cabile *ag* impeccable
impedi'mento *sm* obstacle, hindrance
impe'dire *vt* (*vietare*): **~ a qn di fare** to prevent sb from doing; (*ostruire*) to obstruct; (*impacciare*) to hamper, hinder
impegnarsi *vpr* (*vincolarsi*): **~ a fare** to undertake to do; (*mettersi risolutamente*): **~ in qc** to devote o.s. to sth; **~ con qn** (*accordarsi*) to come to an agreement with sb
impegna'tivo, -a *ag* binding; (*lavoro*) demanding, exacting
impe'gnato, -a *ag* (*occupato*) busy; (*fig*: *romanzo, autore*) committed, engagé
im'pegno [im'peɲɲo] *sm* (*obbligo*) obligation; (*promessa*) promise, pledge; (*zelo*) diligence, zeal; (*compito, d'autore*) commitment

impel'lente *ag* pressing, urgent
impen'narsi *vpr* (*cavallo*) to rear up; (*Aer*) to nose up; (*fig*) to bridle
impensie'rire *vt* to worry; **impensierirsi** *vpr* to worry
impera'tivo, -a *ag, sm* imperative
impera'tore, -'trice *sm/f* emperor/empress
imperdo'nabile *ag* unforgivable, unpardonable
imper'fetto, -a *ag* imperfect ▷ *sm* (*Ling*) imperfect (tense)
imperi'ale *ag* imperial
imperi'oso, -a *ag* (*persona*) imperious; (*motivo, esigenza*) urgent, pressing
imperme'abile *ag* waterproof ▷ *sm* raincoat
im'pero *sm* empire; (*forza, autorità*) rule, control
imperso'nale *ag* impersonal
imperso'nare *vt* to personify; (*Teatro*) to play, act (the part of)
imperter'rito, -a *ag* fearless, undaunted; impassive
imperti'nente *ag* impertinent
'impeto *sm* (*moto, forza*) force, impetus; (*assalto*) onslaught; (*fig*: *impulso*) impulse; (: *slancio*) transport; **con ~** energetically; vehemently
impet'tito, -a *ag* stiff, erect
impetu'oso, -a *ag* (*vento*) strong, raging; (*persona*) impetuous
impi'anto *sm* (*installazione*) installation; (*apparecchiature*) plant; (*sistema*) system; **impianto elettrico** wiring; **impianto di risalita** (*Sci*) ski lift; **impianto di riscaldamento** heating system; **impianto sportivo** sports complex
impic'care *vt* to hang; **impiccarsi** *vpr* to hang o.s.
impicciarsi [impit'tʃarsi] *vpr* (*immischiarsi*): **~ (in)** to meddle (in); **impicciati degli affari tuoi!** mind your own business!
impicci'one, -a [impit'tʃone] *sm/f* busybody
impie'gare *vt* (*usare*) to use, employ; (*spendere*: *denaro, tempo*) to spend; (*investire*) to invest; **impie'gato, -a** *sm/f* employee
impi'ego, -ghi *sm* (*uso*) use; (*occupazione*) employment; (*posto di lavoro*) (regular) job, post; (*Econ*) investment
impieto'sire *vt* to move to pity; **impietosirsi** *vpr* to be moved to pity
impigli'arsi *vpr* to get caught up *o* entangled
impi'grirsi *vpr* to grow lazy
impli'care *vt* to imply; (*coinvolgere*) to involve
im'plicito, -a [im'plitʃito] *ag* implicit
implo'rare *vt* to implore; (*pietà ecc*) to beg for
impolve'rarsi *vpr* to get dusty
im'pone *ecc vb vedi* **imporre**
impo'nente *ag* imposing, impressive
im'pongo *ecc vb vedi* **imporre**
impo'nibile *ag* taxable ▷ *sm* taxable income
impopo'lare *ag* unpopular
im'porre *vt* to impose; (*costringere*) to force, make; (*far valere*) to impose, enforce; **imporsi** *vpr* (*persona*) to assert o.s.; (*cosa*: *rendersi necessario*) to become necessary; (*aver successo*: *moda, attore*) to become popular; **~ a qn di fare** to force sb to do, make sb do
impor'tante *ag* important; **impor'tanza** *sf* importance; **dare importanza a qc** to attach importance to sth; **darsi importanza** to give o.s. airs
impor'tare *vt* (*introdurre dall'estero*) to import ▷ *vi* to matter, be important ▷ *vb impers* (*essere necessario*) to be necessary; (*interessare*) to matter; **non importa!** it doesn't matter!; **non me ne importa!** I don't care!
im'porto *sm* (total) amount
importu'nare *vt* to bother

im'posi *ecc vb vedi* **imporre**
imposizi'one [impozit'tsjone] *sf* imposition; order, command; (*onere, imposta*) tax
imposses'sarsi *vpr*: **~ di** to seize, take possession of
impos'sibile *ag* impossible; **fare l'~** to do one's utmost, do all one can
im'posta *sf* (*di finestra*) shutter; (*tassa*) tax; **imposta sul reddito** income tax; **imposta sul valore aggiunto** value added tax (BRIT), sales tax (US)
impos'tare *vt* (*imbucare*) to post; (*preparare*) to plan, set out; (*avviare*) to begin, start off; (*voce*) to pitch
impostazi'one [impostat'tsjone] *sf* (*di lettera*) posting (BRIT), mailing (US); (*di problema, questione*) formulation, statement; (*di lavoro*) organization, planning; (*di attività*) setting up; (*Mus: di voce*) pitch; **impostazioni** *sfpl* (*di computer*) settings
impo'tente *ag* weak, powerless; (*anche Med*) impotent
imprati'cabile *ag* (*strada*) impassable; (*campo da gioco*) unplayable
impre'care *vi* to curse, swear; **~ contro** to hurl abuse at
imprecazi'one [imprekat'tsjone] *sf* abuse, curse
impre'gnare [impreɲ'ɲare] *vt*: **~ (di)** (*imbevere*) to soak *o* impregnate (with); (*riempire*) to fill (with)
imprendi'tore *sm* (*industriale*) entrepreneur; (*appaltatore*) contractor; **piccolo ~** small businessman
im'presa *sf* (*iniziativa*) enterprise; (*azione*) exploit; (*azienda*) firm, concern
impressio'nante *ag* impressive; upsetting
impressio'nare *vt* to impress; (*turbare*) to upset; (*Fot*) to expose; **impressionarsi** *vpr* to be easily upset
impressi'one *sf* impression; (*fig: sensazione*) sensation, feeling; (*stampa*) printing; **fare ~** (*colpire*) to impress; (*turbare*) to frighten, upset; **fare buona/cattiva ~ a** to make a good/bad impression on
impreve'dibile *ag* unforeseeable; (*persona*) unpredictable
impre'visto, -a *ag* unexpected, unforeseen ▷ *sm* unforeseen event; **salvo imprevisti** unless anything unexpected happens
imprigio'nare [impridʒo'nare] *vt* to imprison
impro'babile *ag* improbable, unlikely
im'pronta *sf* imprint, impression, sign; (*di piede, mano*) print; (*fig*) mark, stamp; **impronta digitale** fingerprint
improvvisa'mente *av* suddenly; unexpectedly
improvvi'sare *vt* to improvise
improv'viso, -a *ag* (*imprevisto*) unexpected; (*subitaneo*) sudden; **all'~** unexpectedly; suddenly
impru'dente *ag* unwise, rash
impu'gnare [impuɲ'ɲare] *vt* to grasp, grip; (*Dir*) to contest
impul'sivo, -a *ag* impulsive
im'pulso *sm* impulse
impun'tarsi *vpr* to stop dead, refuse to budge; (*fig*) to be obstinate
impu'tato, -a *sm/f* (*Dir*) accused, defendant

PAROLA CHIAVE

in (*in + il =* **nel**, *in + lo =* **nello**, *in + l' =* **nell'**, *in + la =* **nella**, *in + i =* **nei**, *in + gli =* **negli**, *in + le =* **nelle**) *prep* **1** (*stato in luogo*) in; **vivere in Italia/città** to live in Italy/town; **essere in casa/ufficio** to be at home/the office; **se fossi in te** if I were you
2 (*moto a luogo*) to; (*: dentro*) into; **andare in Germania/città** to go to Germany/town; **andare in ufficio** to go to the office; **entrare in macchina/casa** to get into the

car/go into the house
3 (*tempo*) in; **nel 1989** in 1989; **in giugno/estate** in June/summer
4 (*modo, maniera*) in; **in silenzio** in silence; **in abito da sera** in evening dress; **in guerra** at war; **in vacanza** on holiday; **Maria Bianchi in Rossi** Maria Rossi née Bianchi
5 (*mezzo*) by; **viaggiare in autobus/treno** to travel by bus/train
6 (*materia*) made of; **in marmo** made of marble, marble *cpd*; **una collana in oro** a gold necklace
7 (*misura*) in; **siamo in quattro** there are four of us; **in tutto** in all
8 (*fine*): **dare in dono** to give as a gift; **spende tutto in alcool** he spends all his money on drink; **in onore di** in honour of

inabi'tabile *ag* uninhabitable
inacces'sibile [inattʃes'sibile] *ag* (*luogo*) inaccessible; (*persona*) unapproachable
inaccet'tabile [inattʃet'tabile] *ag* unacceptable
ina'datto, -a *ag*: **~ (a)** unsuitable *o* unfit (for)
inadegu'ato, -a *ag* inadequate
inaffi'dabile *ag* unreliable
inami'dato, -a *ag* starched
inar'care *vt* (*schiena*) to arch; (*sopracciglia*) to raise
inaspet'tato, -a *ag* unexpected
inas'prire *vt* (*disciplina*) to tighten up, make harsher; (*carattere*) to embitter; **inasprirsi** *vpr* to become harsher; to become bitter; to become worse
inattac'cabile *ag* (*anche fig*) unassailable; (*alibi*) cast-iron
inatten'dibile *ag* unreliable
inat'teso, -a *ag* unexpected
inattu'abile *ag* impracticable
inau'dito, -a *ag* unheard of
inaugu'rare *vt* to inaugurate, open; (*monumento*) to unveil
inaugurazi'one [inaugurat'tsjone] *sf* inauguration; unveiling
incal'lito, -a *ag* calloused; (*fig*) hardened, inveterate; (: *insensibile*) hard
incande'scente [inkandeʃʃɛnte] *ag* incandescent, white-hot
incan'tare *vt* to enchant, bewitch; **incantarsi** *vpr* (*rimanere intontito*) to be spellbound; to be in a daze; (*meccanismo: bloccarsi*) to jam; **incan'tevole** *ag* charming, enchanting
in'canto *sm* spell, charm, enchantment; (*asta*) auction; **come per ~** as if by magic; **mettere all'~** to put up for auction
inca'pace [inka'patʃe] *ag* incapable
incarce'rare [inkartʃe'rare] *vt* to imprison
incari'care *vt*: **~ qn di fare** to give sb the responsibility of doing; **incaricarsi di** to take care *o* charge of
in'carico, -chi *sm* task, job
incarta'mento *sm* dossier, file
incar'tare *vt* to wrap (in paper)
incas'sare *vt* (*merce*) to pack (in cases); (*gemma: incastonare*) to set; (*Econ: riscuotere*) to collect; (*Pugilato: colpi*) to take, stand up to; **in'casso** *sm* cashing, encashment; (*introito*) takings *pl*
incas'trare *vt* to fit in, insert; (*fig: intrappolare*) to catch; **incastrarsi** *vpr* (*combaciare*) to fit together; (*restare bloccato*) to become stuck
incate'nare *vt* to chain up
in'cauto, -a *ag* imprudent, rash
inca'vato, -a *ag* hollow; (*occhi*) sunken
incendi'are [intʃen'djare] *vt* to set fire to; **incendiarsi** *vpr* to catch fire, burst into flames
in'cendio [in'tʃɛndjo] *sm* fire
inceneri'tore [intʃeneri'tore] *sm* incinerator
in'censo [in'tʃɛnso] *sm* incense
incensu'rato, -a [intʃensu'rato] *ag*

(*Dir*): **essere ~** to have a clean record
incenti'vare [intʃenti'vare] *vt* (*produzione, vendite*) to boost; (*persona*) to motivate
incen'tivo [intʃen'tivo] *sm* incentive
incepparsi *vpr* to jam
incer'tezza [intʃer'tettsa] *sf* uncertainty
in'certo, -a [in'tʃɛrto] *ag* uncertain; (*irresoluto*) undecided, hesitating ▷ *sm* uncertainty
in'cetta [in'tʃetta] *sf* buying up; **fare ~ di qc** to buy up sth
inchi'esta [in'kjɛsta] *sf* investigation, inquiry
inchinarsi *vpr* to bend down; (*per riverenza*) to bow; (: *donna*) to curtsy
inchio'dare [inkjo'dare] *vt* to nail (down); **~ la macchina** (*Aut*) to jam on the brakes
inchi'ostro [in'kjɔstro] *sm* ink; **inchiostro simpatico** invisible ink
inciam'pare [intʃam'pare] *vi* to trip, stumble
inci'dente [intʃi'dɛnte] *sm* accident; **ho avuto un ~** I've had an accident; **incidente automobilistico** *o* **d'auto** car accident; **incidente diplomatico** diplomatic incident
in'cidere [in'tʃidere] *vi*: **~ su** to bear upon, affect ▷ *vt* (*tagliare incavando*) to cut into; (*Arte*) to engrave; to etch; (*canzone*) to record
in'cinta [in'tʃinta] *ag f* pregnant
incipri'are [intʃi'prjare] *vt* to powder; **incipriarsi** ▷ *vpr* to powder one's face
in'circa [in'tʃirka] *av*: **all'~** more or less, very nearly
in'cisi *ecc* [in'tʃizi] *vb vedi* **incidere**
incisi'one [intʃi'zjone] *sf* cut; (*disegno*) engraving; etching; (*registrazione*) recording; (*Med*) incision
in'ciso, -a [in'tʃizo] *pp di* **incidere** ▷ *sm* **per ~** incidentally, by the way
inci'tare [intʃi'tare] *vt* to incite
inci'vile [intʃi'vile] *ag* uncivilized; (*villano*) impolite
incl. *abbr* (= *incluso*) encl.
incli'nare *vt* to tilt; **inclinarsi** *vpr* (*barca*) to list; (*aereo*) to bank
in'cludere *vt* to include; (*accludere*) to enclose; **in'cluso, -a** *pp di* **includere** ▷ *ag* included; enclosed
incoe'rente *ag* incoherent; (*contraddittorio*) inconsistent
in'cognita [in'kɔɲɲita] *sf* (*Mat, fig*) unknown quantity
in'cognito, -a [in'kɔɲɲito] *ag* unknown ▷ *sm* **in ~** incognito
incol'lare *vt* to glue, gum; (*unire con colla*) to stick together
inco'lore *ag* colourless
incol'pare *vt*: **~ qn di** to charge sb with
in'colto, -a *ag* (*terreno*) uncultivated; (*trascurato: capelli*) neglected; (*persona*) uneducated
in'colume *ag* safe and sound, unhurt
incom'benza [inkom'bɛntsa] *sf* duty, task
in'combere *vi* (*sovrastare minacciando*): **~ su** to threaten, hang over
incominci'are [inkomin'tʃare] *vi, vt* to begin, start
incompe'tente *ag* incompetent
incompi'uto, -a *ag* unfinished, incomplete
incom'pleto, -a *ag* incomplete
incompren'sibile *ag* incomprehensible
inconce'pibile [inkontʃe'pibile] *ag* inconceivable
inconcili'abile [inkontʃi'ljabile] *ag* irreconcilable
inconclu'dente *ag* inconclusive; (*persona*) ineffectual
incondizio'nato, -a [inkondittsjo'nato] *ag* unconditional
inconfon'dibile *ag* unmistakable
inconsa'pevole *ag*: **~ di** unaware of,

ignorant of
in'conscio, -a, -sci, -sce [in'kɔnʃo] *ag* unconscious ▷ *sm* (*Psic*): **l'~** the unconscious
inconsis'tente *ag* insubstantial; unfounded
inconsu'eto, -a *ag* unusual
incon'trare *vt* to meet; (*difficoltà*) to meet with; **incontrarsi** *vpr* to meet
in'contro *av* **~ a** (*verso*) towards ▷ *sm* meeting; (*Sport*) match; meeting; **incontro di calcio** football match
inconveni'ente *sm* drawback, snag
incoraggia'mento [inkoraddʒa'mento] *sm* encouragement
incoraggi'are [inkorad'dʒare] *vt* to encourage
incornici'are [inkorni'tʃare] *vt* to frame
incoro'nare *vt* to crown
in'correre *vi*: **~ in** to meet with, run into
incosci'ente [inkoʃʃɛnte] *ag* (*inconscio*) unconscious; (*irresponsabile*) reckless, thoughtless
incre'dibile *ag* incredible, unbelievable
in'credulo, -a *ag* incredulous, disbelieving
incremen'tare *vt* to increase; (*dar sviluppo a*) to promote
incre'mento *sm* (*sviluppo*) development; (*aumento numerico*) increase, growth
incresci'oso, -a [inkreʃʃoso] *ag* (*incidente ecc*) regrettable
incrimi'nare *vt* (*Dir*) to charge
incri'nare *vt* to crack; (*fig*: *rapporti, amicizia*) to cause to deteriorate; **incrinarsi** *vpr* to crack; to deteriorate
incroci'are [inkro'tʃare] *vt* to cross; (*incontrare*) to meet ▷ *vi* (*Naut, Aer*) to cruise; **incrociarsi** *vpr* (*strade*) to cross, intersect; (*persone, veicoli*) to pass each other; **~ le braccia/le gambe** to fold one's arms/cross one's legs
in'crocio [in'krotʃo] *sm* (*anche Ferr*) crossing; (*di strade*) crossroads
incuba'trice [inkuba'tritʃe] *sf* incubator
'incubo *sm* nightmare
incu'rabile *ag* incurable
incu'rante *ag*: **~ (di)** heedless (of), careless (of)
incurio'sire *vt* to make curious; **incuriosirsi** *vpr* to become curious
incursi'one *sf* raid
incur'vare *vt* to bend, curve; **incurvarsi** *vpr* to bend, curve
incusto'dito, -a *ag* unguarded, unattended
in'cutere *vt*: **~ timore/rispetto a qn** to strike fear into sb/command sb's respect
'indaco *sm* indigo
indaffa'rato, -a *ag* busy
inda'gare *vt* to investigate
in'dagine [in'dadʒine] *sf* investigation, inquiry; (*ricerca*) research, study; **indagine di mercato** market survey
indebi'tarsi *vpr* to run *o* get into debt
indebo'lire *vt, vi* (*anche*: **indebolirsi**) to weaken
inde'cente [inde'tʃɛnte] *ag* indecent
inde'ciso, -a [inde'tʃizo] *ag* indecisive; (*irresoluto*) undecided
indefi'nito, -a *ag* (*anche Ling*) indefinite; (*impreciso, non determinato*) undefined
in'degno, -a [in'deɲɲo] *ag* (*atto*) shameful; (*persona*) unworthy
indemoni'ato, -a *ag* possessed (by the devil)
in'denne *ag* unhurt, uninjured
indenniz'zare [indennid'dzare] *vt* to compensate
indetermina'tivo, -a *ag* (*Ling*) indefinite
'India *sf* **l'~** India; **indi'ano, -a** *ag* Indian ▷ *sm/f* (*d'India*) Indian; (*d'America*) Native American,

(American) Indian

indi'care *vt* (*mostrare*) to show, indicate; (: *col dito*) to point to, point out; (*consigliare*) to suggest, recommend; **indica'tivo, -a** *ag* indicative ▷ *sm* (*Ling*) indicative (mood); **indicazi'one** *sf* indication; (*informazione*) piece of information

'indice ['inditʃe] *sm* index; (*fig*) sign; (*dito*) index finger, forefinger; **indice di gradimento** (*Radio, TV*) popularity rating

indicherò *ecc* [indike'rɔ] *vb vedi* **indicare**

indi'cibile [indi'tʃibile] *ag* inexpressible

indietreggi'are [indietred'dʒare] *vi* to draw back, retreat

indi'etro *av* back; (*guardare*) behind, back; (*andare, cadere*: *anche*: **all'~**) backwards; **rimanere ~** to be left behind; **essere ~** (*col lavoro*) to be behind; (*orologio*) to be slow; **rimandare qc ~** to send sth back

indi'feso, -a *ag* (*città ecc*) undefended; (*persona*) defenceless

indiffe'rente *ag* indifferent

in'digeno, -a [in'didʒeno] *ag* indigenous, native ▷ *sm/f* native

indigesti'one [indidʒes'tjone] *sf* indigestion

indi'gesto, -a [indi'dʒɛsto] *ag* indigestible

indi'gnare [indiɲ'ɲare] *vt* to fill with indignation; **indignarsi** *vpr* to get indignant

indimenti'cabile *ag* unforgettable

indipen'dente *ag* independent

in'dire *vt* (*concorso*) to announce; (*elezioni*) to call

indi'retto, -a *ag* indirect

indiriz'zare [indirit'tsare] *vt* (*dirigere*) to direct; (*mandare*) to send; (*lettera*) to address

indi'rizzo [indi'rittso] *sm* address; (*direzione*) direction; (*avvio*) trend, course; **il mio ~ è...** my address is ...

indis'creto, -a *ag* indiscreet

indis'cusso, -a *ag* unquestioned

indispen'sabile *ag* indispensable, essential

indispet'tire *vt* to irritate, annoy ▷ *vi* (*anche*: **indispettirsi**) to get irritated *o* annoyed

individu'ale *ag* individual

individu'are *vt* (*dar forma distinta a*) to characterize; (*determinare*) to locate; (*riconoscere*) to single out

indi'viduo *sm* individual

indizi'ato, -a *ag* suspected ▷ *sm/f* suspect

in'dizio [in'dittsjo] *sm* (*segno*) sign, indication; (*Polizia*) clue; (*Dir*) piece of evidence

'indole *sf* nature, character

indolen'zito, -a [indolen'tsito] *ag* stiff, aching; (*intorpidito*) numb

indo'lore *ag* painless

indo'mani *sm* **l'~** the next day, the following day

Indo'nesia *sf* **l'~** Indonesia

indos'sare *vt* (*mettere indosso*) to put on; (*avere indosso*) to have on; **indossa'tore, -'trice** *sm/f* model

indottri'nare *vt* to indoctrinate

indovi'nare *vt* (*scoprire*) to guess; (*immaginare*) to imagine, guess; (*il futuro*) to foretell; **indovi'nello** *sm* riddle

indubbia'mente *av* undoubtedly

in'dubbio, -a *ag* certain, undoubted

in'duco *ecc vb vedi* **indurre**

indugi'are [indu'dʒare] *vi* to take one's time, delay

in'dugio [in'dudʒo] *sm* (*ritardo*) delay; **senza ~** without delay

indul'gente [indul'dʒɛnte] *ag* indulgent; (*giudice*) lenient

indu'mento *sm* article of clothing, garment

indu'rire *vt* to harden ▷ *vi* (*anche*: **indurirsi**) to harden, become hard

in'durre *vt* **~ qn a fare qc** to induce *o* persuade sb to do sth; **~ qn in errore**

to mislead sb
in'dussi *ecc vb vedi* **indurre**
in'dustria *sf* industry; **industri'ale** *ag* industrial ▷ *sm* industrialist
inecce'pibile [inettʃe'pibile] *ag* unexceptionable
i'nedito, -a *ag* unpublished
ine'rente *ag* **~ a** concerning, regarding
i'nerme *ag* unarmed; defenceless
inerpi'carsi *vpr* **~ (su)** to clamber (up)
i'nerte *ag* inert; (*inattivo*) indolent, sluggish
ine'satto, -a *ag* (*impreciso*) inexact; (*erroneo*) incorrect; (*Amm*: *non riscosso*) uncollected
inesis'tente *ag* non-existent
inesperi'enza [inespe'rjɛntsa] *sf* inexperience
ines'perto, -a *ag* inexperienced
inevi'tabile *ag* inevitable
i'nezia [i'nɛttsja] *sf* trifle, thing of no importance
infagot'tare *vt* to bundle up, wrap up; **infagottarsi** *vpr* to wrap up
infal'libile *ag* infallible
infa'mante *ag* defamatory
in'fame *ag* infamous; (*fig*: *cosa, compito*) awful, dreadful
infan'gare *vt* to cover with mud; (*fig*: *reputazione*) to sully; **infangarsi** *vpr* to get covered in mud; to be sullied
infan'tile *ag* child *cpd*; childlike; (*adulto, azione*) childish; **letteratura ~** children's books *pl*
in'fanzia [in'fantsja] *sf* childhood; (*bambini*) children *pl*; **prima ~** babyhood, infancy
infari'nare *vt* to cover with (*o* sprinkle with *o* dip in) flour; **infarina'tura** *sf* (*fig*) smattering
in'farto *sm* (*Med*) heart attack
infasti'dire *vt* to annoy, irritate; **infastidirsi** *vpr* to get annoyed *o* irritated
infati'cabile *ag* tireless, untiring
in'fatti *cong* actually, as a matter of fact

> Attenzione! In inglese esiste l'espressione *in fact* che però vuol dire *in effetti*.

infatu'arsi *vpr*: **~ di** to become infatuated with, fall for
infe'dele *ag* unfaithful
infe'lice [infe'litʃe] *ag* unhappy; (*sfortunato*) unlucky, unfortunate; (*inopportuno*) inopportune, ill-timed; (*mal riuscito*: *lavoro*) bad, poor
inferi'ore *ag* lower; (*per intelligenza, qualità*) inferior ▷ *sm/f* inferior; **~ a** (*numero, quantità*) less *o* smaller than; (*meno buono*) inferior to; **~ alla media** below average; **inferiorità** *sf* inferiority
inferme'ria *sf* infirmary; (*di scuola, nave*) sick bay
infermi'ere, -a *sm/f* nurse
infermità *sf inv* illness; infirmity; **infermità mentale** mental illness; (*Dir*) insanity
in'fermo, -a *ag* (*ammalato*) ill; (*debole*) infirm
infer'nale *ag* infernal; (*proposito, complotto*) diabolical
in'ferno *sm* hell
inferri'ata *sf* grating
infes'tare *vt* to infest
infet'tare *vt* to infect; **infettarsi** *vpr* to become infected; **infezi'one** *sf* infection
infiam'mabile *ag* inflammable
infiam'mare *vt* to set alight; (*fig, Med*) to inflame; **infiammarsi** *vpr* to catch fire; (*Med*) to become inflamed; **infiammazi'one** *sf* (*Med*) inflammation
infie'rire *vi*: **~ su** (*fisicamente*) to attack furiously; (*verbalmente*) to rage at
infi'lare *vt* (*ago*) to thread; (*mettere*: *chiave*) to insert; (: *anello, vestito*) to slip *o* put on; (*strada*) to turn into, take; **infilarsi** *vpr* **infilarsi in** to slip into; (*indossare*) to slip on; **~ l'uscio** to slip

in; to slip out
infil'trarsi *vpr* to penetrate, seep through; (*Mil*) to infiltrate
infil'zare [infil'tsare] *vt* (*infilare*) to string together; (*trafiggere*) to pierce
'infimo, -a *ag* lowest
in'fine *av* finally; (*insomma*) in short
infinità *sf* infinity; (*in quantità*): **un'~ di** an infinite number of
infi'nito, -a *ag* infinite; (*Ling*) infinitive ▷ *sm* infinity; (*Ling*) infinitive; **all'~** (*senza fine*) endlessly
infinocchi'are [infinok'kjare] (*fam*) *vt* to hoodwink
infischi'arsi [infis'kjarsi] *vpr*: **~ di** not to care about
in'fisso, -a *pp di* **infiggere** ▷ *sm* fixture; (*di porta, finestra*) frame
inflazi'one [inflat'tsjone] *sf* inflation
in'fliggere [in'fliddʒere] *vt* to inflict
in'flissi *ecc vb vedi* **infliggere**
influ'ente *ag* influential; **influ'enza** *sf* influence; (*Med*) influenza, flu
influen'zare [influen'tsare] *vt* to influence, have an influence on
influ'ire *vi*: **~ su** to influence
in'flusso *sm* influence
infon'dato, -a *ag* unfounded, groundless
in'fondere *vt*: **~ qc in qn** to instill sth in sb
infor'mare *vt* to inform, tell; **informarsi** *vpr* **informarsi (di** *o* **su)** to inquire (about)
infor'matica *sf* computer science
informa'tivo, -a *ag* informative
infor'mato, -a *ag* informed; **tenersi ~** to keep o.s. (well-)informed
informa'tore *sm* informer
informazi'one [informat'tsjone] *sf* piece of information; **prendere informazioni sul conto di qn** to get information about sb; **chiedere un'~** to ask for (some) information
in'forme *ag* shapeless
informico'larsi *vpr* to have pins and needles
infortu'nato, -a *ag* injured, hurt ▷ *sm/f* injured person
infor'tunio *sm* accident; **infortunio sul lavoro** industrial accident, accident at work
infra'dito *sm inv* (*calzatura*) flip flop (BRIT), thong (US)
infrazi'one [infrat'tsjone] *sf*: **~ a** breaking of, violation of
infredda'tura *sf* slight cold
infreddo'lito, -a *ag* cold, chilled
infu'ori *av* out; **all'~** outwards; **all'~ di** (*eccetto*) except, with the exception of
infuri'arsi *vpr* to fly into a rage
infusi'one *sf* infusion
in'fuso, -a *pp di* **infondere** ▷ *sm* infusion
Ing. *abbr* = **ingegnere**
ingaggi'are [ingad'dʒare] *vt* (*assumere con compenso*) to take on, hire; (*Sport*) to sign on; (*Mil*) to engage
ingan'nare *vt* to deceive; (*fisco*) to cheat; (*eludere*) to dodge, elude; (*fig*: *tempo*) to while away ▷ *vi* (*apparenza*) to be deceptive; **ingannarsi** *vpr* to be mistaken, be wrong
in'ganno *sm* deceit, deception; (*azione*) trick; (*menzogna, frode*) cheat, swindle; (*illusione*) illusion
inge'gnarsi [indʒeɲ'ɲarsi] *vpr* to do one's best, try hard; **~ per vivere** to live by one's wits
inge'gnere [indʒeɲ'ɲɛre] *sm* engineer; **~ civile/navale** civil/naval engineer; **ingegne'ria** *sf* engineering; **ingegnere genetica** genetic engineering
in'gegno [in'dʒeɲɲo] *sm* (*intelligenza*) intelligence, brains *pl*; (*capacità creativa*) ingenuity; (*disposizione*) talent; **inge'gnoso, -a** *ag* ingenious, clever
ingelo'sire [indʒelo'zire] *vt* to make jealous ▷ *vi* (*anche*: **ingelosirsi**) to become jealous
in'gente [in'dʒɛnte] *ag* huge,

enormous

ingenuità [indʒenui'ta] *sf* ingenuousness

in'genuo, -a [in'dʒɛnuo] *ag* naïve

> Attenzione! In inglese esiste la parola *ingenious*, che però significa *ingegnoso*.

inge'rire [indʒe'rire] *vt* to ingest

inges'sare [indʒes'sare] *vt* (*Med*) to put in plaster; **ingessa'tura** *sf* plaster

Inghil'terra [ingil'tɛrra] *sf*: **l'~** England

inghiot'tire [ingjot'tire] *vt* to swallow

ingial'lire [indʒal'lire] *vi* to go yellow

inginocchi'arsi [indʒinok'kjarsi] *vpr* to kneel (down)

ingiù [in'dʒu] *av* down, downwards

ingi'uria [in'dʒurja] *sf* insult; (*fig: danno*) damage

ingius'tizia [indʒus'tittsja] *sf* injustice

ingi'usto, -a [in'dʒusto] *ag* unjust, unfair

in'glese *ag* English ▷ *sm/f* Englishman/woman ▷ *sm* (*Ling*) English; **gli Inglesi** the English; **andarsene** *o* **filare all'~** to take French leave

ingoi'are *vt* to gulp (down); (*fig*) to swallow (up)

ingol'farsi *vpr* to flood

ingom'brante *ag* cumbersome

ingom'brare *vt* (*strada*) to block; (*stanza*) to clutter up

in'gordo, -a *ag*: **~ di** greedy for; (*fig*) greedy *o* avid for

in'gorgo, -ghi *sm* blockage, obstruction; (*anche:* **~ stradale**) traffic jam

ingoz'zarsi *vpr*: **~ (di)** to stuff o.s. (with)

ingra'naggio [ingra'naddʒo] *sm* (*Tecn*) gear; (*di orologio*) mechanism; **gli ingranaggi della burocrazia** the bureaucratic machinery

ingra'nare *vi* to mesh, engage ▷ *vt* to engage; **~ la marcia** to get into gear

ingrandi'mento *sm* enlargement; extension

ingran'dire *vt* (*anche Fot*) to enlarge; (*estendere*) to extend; (*Ottica, fig*) to magnify ▷ *vi* (*anche:* **ingrandirsi**) to become larger *o* bigger; (*aumentare*) to grow, increase; (*espandersi*) to expand

ingras'sare *vt* to make fat; (*animali*) to fatten; (*lubrificare*) to oil, lubricate ▷ *vi* (*anche:* **ingrassarsi**) to get fat, put on weight

in'grato, -a *ag* ungrateful; (*lavoro*) thankless, unrewarding

ingredi'ente *sm* ingredient

in'gresso *sm* (*porta*) entrance; (*atrio*) hall; (*l'entrare*) entrance, entry; (*facoltà di entrare*) admission; **ingresso libero** admission free

ingros'sare *vt* to increase; (*folla, livello*) to swell ▷ *vi* (*anche:* **ingrossarsi**) to increase; to swell

in'grosso *av*: **all'~** (*Comm*) wholesale; (*all'incirca*) roughly, about

ingua'ribile *ag* incurable

'inguine *sm* (*Anat*) groin

ini'bire *vt* to forbid, prohibit; (*Psic*) to inhibit; **inibirsi** *vpr* to restrain o.s.

ini'bito, -a *ag* inhibited ▷ *sm/f* inhibited person

iniet'tare *vt* to inject; **iniezi'one** *sf* injection

ininterrotta'mente *av* non-stop, continuously

ininter'rotto, -a *ag* unbroken; uninterrupted

inizi'ale [init'tsjale] *ag, sf* initial

inizi'are [init'tsjare] *vi, vt* to begin, start; **a che ora inizia il film?** when does the film start?; **~ qn a** to initiate sb into; (*pittura ecc*) to introduce sb to; **~ a fare qc** to start doing sth

inizia'tiva [inittsja'tiva] *sf* initiative; **iniziativa privata** private enterprise

i'nizio [i'nittsjo] *sm* beginning; **all'~** at the beginning, at the start; **dare ~ a qc** to start sth, get sth going

innaffi'are *ecc* = **annaffiare** *ecc*
innamo'rarsi *vpr*: **~ (di qn)** to fall in love (with sb); **innamo'rato, -a** *ag* (*che nutre amore*): **innamorato (di)** in love (with); (*appassionato*): **innamorato di** very fond of ▷ *sm/f* lover; sweetheart
innanzi'tutto *av* first of all
in'nato, -a *ag* innate
innatu'rale *ag* unnatural
inne'gabile *ag* undeniable
innervo'sire *vt*: **~ qn** to get on sb's nerves; **innervosirsi** *vpr* to get irritated *o* upset
innes'care *vt* to prime
'inno *sm* hymn; **inno nazionale** national anthem
inno'cente [inno'tʃɛnte] *ag* innocent
in'nocuo, -a *ag* innocuous, harmless
innova'tivo, -a *ag* innovative
innume'revole *ag* innumerable
inol'trare *vt* (*Amm*) to pass on, forward
i'noltre *av* besides, moreover
inon'dare *vt* to flood
inoppor'tuno, -a *ag* untimely, ill-timed; inappropriate; (*momento*) inopportune
inorri'dire *vt* to horrify ▷ *vi* to be horrified
inosser'vato, -a *ag* (*non notato*) unobserved; (*non rispettato*) not observed, not kept
inossi'dabile *ag* stainless
INPS *sigla m* (= *Istituto Nazionale Previdenza Sociale*) *social security service*
inqua'drare *vt* (*foto, immagine*) to frame; (*fig*) to situate, set
inqui'eto, -a *ag* restless; (*preoccupato*) worried, anxious
inqui'lino, -a *sm/f* tenant
inquina'mento *sm* pollution
inqui'nare *vt* to pollute
insabbi'are *vt* (*fig*: *pratica*) to shelve; **insabbiarsi** *vpr* (*arenarsi*: *barca*) to run aground; (*fig*: *pratica*) to be shelved
insac'cati *smpl* (*Cuc*) sausages
insa'lata *sf* salad; **insalata mista** mixed salad; **insalata russa** (*Cuc*) Russian salad (*comprised of cold diced cooked vegetables in mayonnaise*); **insalati'era** *sf* salad bowl
insa'nabile *ag* (*piaga*) which cannot be healed; (*situazione*) irremediable; (*odio*) implacable
insa'puta *sf*: **all'~ di qn** without sb knowing
inse'diarsi *vpr* to take up office; (*popolo, colonia*) to settle
in'segna [in'seɲɲa] *sf* sign; (*emblema*) sign, emblem; (*bandiera*) flag, banner
insegna'mento [inseɲɲa'mento] *sm* teaching
inse'gnante [inseɲ'ɲante] *ag* teaching ▷ *sm/f* teacher
inse'gnare [inseɲ'ɲare] *vt, vi* to teach; **~ a qn qc** to teach sb sth; **~ a qn a fare qc** to teach sb (how) to do sth
insegui'mento *sm* pursuit, chase
insegu'ire *vt* to pursue, chase
insena'tura *sf* inlet, creek
insen'sato, -a *ag* senseless, stupid
insen'sibile *ag* (*nervo*) insensible; (*persona*) indifferent
inse'rire *vt* to insert; (*Elettr*) to connect; (*allegare*) to enclose; (*annuncio*) to put in, place; **inserirsi** *vpr* (*fig*): **inserirsi in** to become part of
inservi'ente *sm/f* attendant
inserzi'one [inser'tsjone] *sf* insertion; (*avviso*) advertisement; **fare un'~ sul giornale** to put an advertisement in the paper
insetti'cida, -i [insetti'tʃida] *sm* insecticide
in'setto *sm* insect
insi'curo, -a *ag* insecure
insi'eme *av* together ▷ *prep* **~ a** *o* **con** together with ▷ *sm* whole; (*Mat, servizio, assortimento*) set; (*Moda*) ensemble, outfit; **tutti ~** all together; **tutto ~** all together; (*in una volta*) at one go; **nell'~** on the whole; **d'~** (*veduta ecc*) overall

in'signe [in'siɲɲe] *ag* (*persona*) famous, distinguished; (*città, monumento*) notable
insignifi'cante [insiɲɲifi'kante] *ag* insignificant
insinu'are *vt* (*introdurre*): **~ qc in** to slip *o* slide sth into; (*fig*) to insinuate, imply; **insinuarsi** *vpr* **insinuarsi in** to seep into; (*fig*) to creep into; to worm one's way into
in'sipido, -a *ag* insipid
insis'tente *ag* insistent; persistent
in'sistere *vi*: **~ su qc** to insist on sth; **~ in qc/a fare** (*perseverare*) to persist in sth/in doing
insoddis'fatto, -a *ag* dissatisfied
insoffe'rente *ag* intolerant
insolazi'one [insolat'tsjone] *sf* (*Med*) sunstroke
inso'lente *ag* insolent
in'solito, -a *ag* unusual, out of the ordinary
inso'luto, -a *ag* (*non risolto*) unsolved
in'somma *av* (*in conclusione*) in short; (*dunque*) well ▷ *escl* for heaven's sake!
in'sonne *ag* sleepless; **in'sonnia** *sf* insomnia, sleeplessness
insonno'lito, -a *ag* sleepy, drowsy
insoppor'tabile *ag* unbearable
in'sorgere [in'sordʒere] *vi* (*ribellarsi*) to rise up, rebel; (*apparire*) to come up, arise
in'sorsi *ecc vb vedi* **insorgere**
insospet'tire *vt* to make suspicious ▷ *vi* (*anche*: **insospettirsi**) to become suspicious
inspi'rare *vt* to breathe in, inhale
in'stabile *ag* (*carico, indole*) unstable; (*tempo*) unsettled; (*equilibrio*) unsteady
instal'lare *vt* to install
instan'cabile *ag* untiring, indefatigable
instau'rare *vt* to introduce, institute
insuc'cesso [insut'tʃɛsso] *sm* failure, flop
insuffici'ente [insuffi'tʃɛnte] *ag* insufficient; (*compito, allievo*) inadequate; **insuffici'enza** *sf* insufficiency; inadequacy; (*Ins*) fail; **insufficienza di prove** (*Dir*) lack of evidence; **insufficienza renale** renal insufficiency
insu'lina *sf* insulin
in'sulso, -a *ag* (*sciocco*) inane, silly; (*persona*) dull, insipid
insul'tare *vt* to insult, affront
in'sulto *sm* insult, affront
intac'care *vt* (*fare tacche*) to cut into; (*corrodere*) to corrode; (*fig*: *cominciare ad usare*: *risparmi*) to break into; (: *ledere*) to damage
intagli'are [intaʎ'ʎare] *vt* to carve
in'tanto *av* (*nel frattempo*) meanwhile, in the meantime; (*per cominciare*) just to begin with; **~ che** while
inta'sare *vt* to choke (up), block (up); (*Aut*) to obstruct, block; **intasarsi** *vpr* to become choked *o* blocked
intas'care *vt* to pocket
in'tatto, -a *ag* intact; (*puro*) unsullied
intavo'lare *vt* to start, enter into
inte'grale *ag* complete; (*pane, farina*) wholemeal (BRIT), whole-wheat (US); (*Mat*): **calcolo ~** integral calculus
inte'grante *ag*: **parte ~** integral part
inte'grare *vt* to complete; (*Mat*) to integrate; **integrarsi** *vpr* (*persona*) to become integrated
integra'tore *sm*: **integratori alimentari** nutritional supplements
integrità *sf* integrity
'integro, -a *ag* (*intatto, intero*) complete, whole; (*retto*) upright
intelaia'tura *sf* frame; (*fig*) structure, framework
intel'letto *sm* intellect; **intellettu'ale** *ag, sm/f* intellectual
intelli'gente [intelli'dʒɛnte] *ag* intelligent
intem'perie *sfpl* bad weather *sg*
in'tendere *vt* (*avere intenzione*): **~ fare qc** to intend *o* mean to do sth; (*comprendere*) to understand; (*udire*) to

hear; (*significare*) to mean; **intendersi** *vpr* (*conoscere*): **intendersi di** to know a lot about, be a connoisseur of; (*accordarsi*) to get on (well); **intendersela con qn** (*avere una relazione amorosa*) to have an affair with sb; **intendi'tore, -'trice** *sm/f* connoisseur, expert

inten'sivo, -a *ag* intensive

in'tenso, -a *ag* intense

in'tento, -a *ag* (*teso, assorto*): **~ (a)** intent (on), absorbed (in) ▷ *sm* aim, purpose

intenzio'nale [intentsjo'nale] *ag* intentional

intenzi'one [inten'tsjone] *sf* intention; (*Dir*) intent; **avere ~ di fare qc** to intend to do sth, have the intention of doing sth

interat'tivo, -a *ag* interactive

intercet'tare [intertʃet'tare] *vt* to intercept

intercity [inter'siti] *sm inv* (*Ferr*) ≈ intercity (train)

inter'detto, -a *pp di* **interdire** ▷ *ag* forbidden, prohibited; (*sconcertato*) dumbfounded ▷ *sm* (*Rel*) interdict

interes'sante *ag* interesting; **essere in stato ~** to be expecting (a baby)

interes'sare *vt* to interest; (*concernere*) to concern, be of interest to; (*far intervenire*): **~ qn a** to draw sb's attention to ▷ *vi* **~ a** to interest, matter to; **interessarsi** *vpr* (*mostrare interesse*): **interessarsi a** to take an interest in, be interested in; (*occuparsi*): **interessarsi di** to take care of

inte'resse *sm* (*anche Comm*) interest

inter'faccia, -ce [inter'fattʃa] *sf* (*Inform*) interface

interfe'renza [interfe'rɛntsa] *sf* interference

interfe'rire *vi* to interfere

interiezi'one [interjet'tsjone] *sf* exclamation, interjection

interi'nale *agg*: **lavoro ~** temporary work (*gained through an agency*)

interi'ora *sfpl* entrails

interi'ore *ag* interior, inner, inside, internal; (*fig*) inner

inter'medio, -a *ag* intermediate

inter'nare *vt* (*arrestare*) to intern; (*Med*) to commit (to a mental institution)

inter'nauta *sm/f* Internet user

internazio'nale [internattsjo'nale] *ag* international

'Internet ['internet] *sf* Internet; **in ~** on the Internet

in'terno, -a *ag* (*di dentro*) internal, interior, inner; (*: mare*) inland; (*nazionale*) domestic; (*allievo*) boarding ▷ *sm* inside, interior; (*di paese*) interior; (*fodera*) lining; (*di appartamento*) flat (number); (*Tel*) extension ▷ *sm/f* (*Ins*) boarder; **interni** *smpl* (*Cinema*) interior shots; **all'~** inside; **Ministero degli Interni** Ministry of the Interior, ≈ Home Office (BRIT), Department of the Interior (US)

in'tero, -a *ag* (*integro, intatto*) whole, entire; (*completo, totale*) complete; (*numero*) whole; (*non ridotto*: *biglietto*) full; (*latte*) full-cream

interpel'lare *vt* to consult

interpre'tare *vt* to interpret; **in'terprete** *sm/f* interpreter; (*Teatro*) actor/actress, performer; (*Mus*) performer; **ci potrebbe fare da interprete?** could you act as an interpreter for us?

interregio'nale [interredʒo'nale] *sm train that travels between two or more regions of Italy, stopping frequently*

interro'gare *vt* to question; (*Ins*) to test; **interrogazi'one** *sf* questioning *no pl*; (*Ins*) oral test

inter'rompere *vt* to interrupt; (*studi, trattative*) to break off, interrupt; **interrompersi** *vpr* to break off, stop

interrut'tore *sm* switch

interruzi'one [interrut'tsjone] *sf* interruption; break

interur'bana *sf* trunk *o* long-distance call
inter'vallo *sm* interval; (*spazio*) space, gap
interve'nire *vi* (*partecipare*): **~ a** to take part in; (*intromettersi*: *anche Pol*) to intervene; (*Med*: *operare*) to operate; **inter'vento** *sm* participation; (*intromissione*) intervention; (*Med*) operation; **fare un intervento nel corso di** (*dibattito, programma*) to take part in
inter'vista *sf* interview; **intervis'tare** *vt* to interview
intes'tare *vt* (*lettera*) to address; (*proprietà*): **~ a** to register in the name of; **~ un assegno a qn** to make out a cheque to sb
intestato, -a *ag* (*proprietà, casa, conto*) in the name of; (*assegno*) made out to; **carta intestata** headed paper
intes'tino *sm* (*Anat*) intestine
intimidazi'one [intimidat'tsjone] *sf* intimidation
intimi'dire *vt* to intimidate ▷ *vi* (*intimidirsi*) to grow shy
intimità *sf* intimacy; privacy; (*familiarità*) familiarity
'intimo, -a *ag* intimate; (*affetti, vita*) private; (*fig*: *profondo*) inmost ▷ *sm* (*persona*) intimate *o* close friend; (*dell'animo*) bottom, depths *pl*; **parti intime** (*Anat*) private parts
in'tingolo *sm* sauce; (*pietanza*) stew
intito'lare *vt* to give a title to; (*dedicare*) to dedicate; **intitolarsi** *vpr* (*libro, film*) to be called
intolle'rabile *ag* intolerable
intolle'rante *ag* intolerant
in'tonaco, -ci *o* **chi** *sm* plaster
into'nare *vt* (*canto*) to start to sing; (*armonizzare*) to match; **intonarsi** *vpr* (*colori*) to go together; **intonarsi a** (*carnagione*) to suit; (*abito*) to go with, match
inton'tito, -a *ag* stunned, dazed; **~ dal sonno** stupid with sleep
in'toppo *sm* stumbling block, obstacle
in'torno *av* around; **~ a** (*attorno a*) around; (*riguardo, circa*) about
intossi'care *vt* to poison; **intossicazi'one** *sf* poisoning
intralci'are [intral'tʃare] *vt* to hamper, hold up
intransi'tivo, -a *ag, sm* intransitive
intrapren'dente *ag* enterprising, go-ahead
intra'prendere *vt* to undertake
intrat'tabile *ag* intractable
intratte'nere *vt* to entertain; to engage in conversation; **intrattenersi** *vpr* to linger; **intrattenersi su qc** to dwell on sth
intrave'dere *vt* to catch a glimpse of; (*fig*) to foresee
intrecci'are [intret'tʃare] *vt* (*capelli*) to plait, braid; (*intessere*: *anche fig*) to weave, interweave, intertwine
intri'gante *ag* scheming ▷ *sm/f* schemer, intriguer
in'trinseco, -a, -ci, -che *ag* intrinsic
in'triso, -a *ag*: **~ (di)** soaked (in)
intro'durre *vt* to introduce; (*chiave ecc*): **~ qc in** to insert sth into; (*persone*: *far entrare*) to show in; **introdursi** *vpr* (*moda, tecniche*) to be introduced; **introdursi in** (*persona*: *penetrare*) to enter; (: *entrare furtivamente*) to steal *o* slip into; **introduzi'one** *sf* introduction
in'troito *sm* income, revenue
intro'mettersi *vpr* to interfere, meddle; (*interporsi*) to intervene
in'truglio [in'truʎʎo] *sm* concoction
intrusi'one *sf* intrusion; interference
in'truso, -a *sm/f* intruder
intu'ire *vt* to perceive by intuition; (*rendersi conto*) to realize; **in'tuito** *sm* intuition; (*perspicacia*) perspicacity
inu'mano, -a *ag* inhuman
inumi'dire *vt* to dampen, moisten; **inumidirsi** *vpr* to become damp *o* wet
i'nutile *ag* useless; (*superfluo*)

pointless, unnecessary
inutil'mente *av* unnecessarily; (*senza risultato*) in vain
inva'dente *ag* (*fig*) interfering, nosey
in'vadere *vt* to invade; (*affollare*) to swarm into, overrun; (*acque*) to flood
inva'ghirsi [inva'girsi] *vpr*: **~ di** to take a fancy to
invalidità *sf* infirmity; disability; (*Dir*) invalidity
in'valido, -a *ag* (*infermo*) infirm, invalid; (*al lavoro*) disabled; (*Dir: nullo*) invalid ▷ *sm/f* invalid; disabled person
in'vano *av* in vain
invasi'one *sf* invasion
inva'sore, invadi'trice [invadi'tritʃe] *ag* invading ▷ *sm* invader
invecchi'are [invek'kjare] *vi* (*persona*) to grow old; (*vino, popolazione*) to age; (*moda*) to become dated ▷ *vt* to age; (*far apparire più vecchio*) to make look older
in'vece [in'vetʃe] *av* instead; (*al contrario*) on the contrary; **~ di** instead of
inve'ire *vi* **~ contro** to rail against
inven'tare *vt* to invent; (*pericoli, pettegolezzi*) to make up, invent
inven'tario *sm* inventory; (*Comm*) stocktaking *no pl*
inven'tore *sm* inventor
invenzi'one [inven'tsjone] *sf* invention; (*bugia*) lie, story
inver'nale *ag* winter *cpd*; (*simile all'inverno*) wintry
in'verno *sm* winter
invero'simile *ag* unlikely
inversi'one *sf* inversion; reversal; **"divieto d'~"** (*Aut*) "no U-turns"
in'verso, -a *ag* opposite; (*Mat*) inverse ▷ *sm* contrary, opposite; **in senso ~** in the opposite direction; **in ordine ~** in reverse order
inver'tire *vt* to invert, reverse; **~ la marcia** (*Aut*) to do a U-turn
investi'gare *vt, vi* to investigate;
investiga'tore, -'trice *sm/f* investigator, detective; **investigatore privato** private investigator
investi'mento *sm* (*Econ*) investment
inves'tire *vt* (*denaro*) to invest; (*veicolo: pedone*) to knock down; (*: altro veicolo*) to crash into; (*apostrofare*) to assail; (*incaricare*): **~ qn di** to invest sb with
invi'are *vt* to send; **invi'ato, -a** *sm/f* envoy; (*Stampa*) correspondent; **inviato speciale** (*Pol*) special envoy; (*di giornale*) special correspondent
in'vidia *sf* envy; **invidi'are** *vt* **invidiare qn (per qc)** to envy sb for sth; **invidiare qc a qn** to envy sb sth; **invidi'oso, -a** *ag* envious
in'vio, -'vii *sm* sending; (*insieme di merci*) consignment; (*tasto*) return (key), enter (key)
invipe'rito, -a *ag* furious
invi'sibile *ag* invisible
invi'tare *vt* to invite; **~ qn a fare** to invite sb to do; **invi'tato, -a** *sm/f* guest; **in'vito** *sm* invitation
invo'care *vt* (*chiedere: aiuto, pace*) to cry out for; (*appellarsi: la legge, Dio*) to appeal to, invoke
invogli'are [invoʎ'ʎare] *vt*: **~ qn a fare** to tempt sb to do, induce sb to do
involon'tario, -a *ag* (*errore*) unintentional; (*gesto*) involuntary
invol'tino *sm* (*Cuc*) roulade
in'volto *sm* (*pacco*) parcel; (*fagotto*) bundle
in'volucro *sm* cover, wrapping
inzup'pare [intsup'pare] *vt* to soak; **inzupparsi** *vpr* to get soaked
'io *pron* I ▷ *sm inv* **l'~** the ego, the self; **~ stesso(a)** I myself
i'odio *sm* iodine
I'onio *sm*: **lo ~, il mar ~** the Ionian (Sea)
ipermer'cato *sm* hypermarket
ipertensi'one *sf* high blood pressure, hypertension
iper'testo *sm* hypertext;

ipertestu'ale *agg* (*Inform*) hypertext *cpd*
ip'nosi *sf* hypnosis; **ipnotiz'zare** *vt* to hypnotize
ipocri'sia *sf* hypocrisy
i'pocrita, -i, -e *ag* hypocritical ▷ *sm/f* hypocrite
ipo'teca, -che *sf* mortgage
i'potesi *sf inv* hypothesis
'ippica *sf* horseracing
'ippico, -a, -ci, -che *ag* horse *cpd*
ippocas'tano *sm* horse chestnut
ip'podromo *sm* racecourse
ippo'potamo *sm* hippopotamus
'ipsilon *sf o m inv* (*lettera*) Y, y; (: *dell'alfabeto greco*) epsilon
IR *abbr* (= *Interregionale*) *long distance train which stops frequently*
ira'cheno, -a [ira'kɛno] *ag, sm/f* Iraqi
I'ran *sm* **l'~** Iran
irani'ano, -a *ag, sm/f* Iranian
I'raq *sm* **l'~** Iraq
'iride *sf* (*arcobaleno*) rainbow; (*Anat, Bot*) iris
'iris *sm inv* iris
Ir'landa *sf*: **l'~** Ireland; **l'~ del Nord** Northern Ireland, Ulster; **la Repubblica d'~** Eire, the Republic of Ireland; **irlan'dese** *ag* Irish ▷ *sm/f* Irishman/woman; **gli Irlandesi** the Irish
iro'nia *sf* irony; **i'ronico, -a, -ci, -che** *ag* ironic(al)
irragio'nevole [irradʒo'nevole] *ag* irrational; unreasonable
irrazio'nale [irrattsjo'nale] *ag* irrational
irre'ale *ag* unreal
irrego'lare *ag* irregular; (*terreno*) uneven
irremo'vibile *ag* (*fig*) unshakeable, unyielding
irrequi'eto, -a *ag* restless
irresis'tibile *ag* irresistible
irrespon'sabile *ag* irresponsible
irri'gare *vt* (*annaffiare*) to irrigate; (*fiume ecc*) to flow through
irrigi'dire [irridʒi'dire] *vt* to stiffen; **irrigidirsi** *vpr* to stiffen
irri'sorio, -a *ag* derisory
irri'tare *vt* (*mettere di malumore*) to irritate, annoy; (*Med*) to irritate; **irritarsi** *vpr* (*stizzirsi*) to become irritated *o* annoyed; (*Med*) to become irritated
ir'rompere *vi*: **~ in** to burst into
irru'ente *ag* (*fig*) impetuous, violent
ir'ruppi *ecc vb vedi* **irrompere**
irruzi'one [irrut'tsjone] *sf* **fare ~ in** to burst into; (*polizia*) to raid
is'crissi *ecc vb vedi* **iscrivere**
is'critto, -a *pp di* **iscrivere** ▷ *sm/f* member; **per *o* in ~** in writing
is'crivere *vt* to register, enter; (*persona*): **~ (a)** to register (in), enrol (in); **iscriversi** *vpr* **iscriversi (a)** (*club, partito*) to join; (*università*) to register *o* enrol (at); (*esame, concorso*) to register *o* enter (for); **iscrizi'one** *sf* (*epigrafe ecc*) inscription; (*a scuola, società*) enrolment, registration; (*registrazione*) registration
Is'lam *sm*: **l'~** Islam
Is'landa *sf*: **l'~** Iceland
islan'dese *ag* Icelandic ▷ *sm/f* Icelander ▷ *sm* (*Ling*) Icelandic
'isola *sf* island; **isola pedonale** (*Aut*) pedestrian precinct
isola'mento *sm* isolation; (*Tecn*) insulation
iso'lante *ag* insulating ▷ *sm* insulator
iso'lare *vt* to isolate; (*Tecn*) to insulate; (: *acusticamente*) to soundproof; **isolarsi** *vpr* to isolate o.s.; **iso'lato, -a** *ag* isolated; insulated ▷ *sm* (*gruppo di edifici*) block
ispet'tore *sm* inspector
ispezio'nare [ispettsjo'nare] *vt* to inspect
'ispido, -a *ag* bristly, shaggy
ispi'rare *vt* to inspire
Isra'ele *sm* **l'~** Israel; **israeli'ano, -a** *ag, sm/f* Israeli
is'sare *vt* to hoist

istan'taneo, -a *ag* instantaneous ▷ *sf* (*Fot*) snapshot
is'tante *sm* instant, moment; **all'~, sull'~** instantly, immediately
is'terico, -a, -ci, -che *ag* hysterical
isti'gare *vt* to incite
is'tinto *sm* instinct
istitu'ire *vt* (*fondare*) to institute, found; (*porre: confronto*) to establish; (*intraprendere: inchiesta*) to set up
isti'tuto *sm* institute; (*di università*) department; (*ente, Dir*) institution; **istituto di bellezza** beauty salon; **istituto di credito** bank, banking institution; **istituto di ricerca** research institute
istituzi'one [istitut'tsjone] *sf* institution
'istmo *sm* (*Geo*) isthmus
'istrice ['istritʃe] *sm* porcupine
istru'ito, -a *ag* educated
istrut'tore, -'trice *sm/f* instructor ▷ *ag* **giudice ~** *vedi* **giudice**
istruzi'one *sf* education; training; (*direttiva*) instruction; **istruzioni** *sfpl* (*norme*) instructions; **istruzioni per l'uso** instructions for use; **~ obbligatoria** (*Scol*) compulsory education
I'talia *sf*: **l'~** Italy
itali'ano, -a *ag* Italian ▷ *sm/f* Italian ▷ *sm* (*Ling*) Italian; **gli Italiani** the Italians
itine'rario *sm* itinerary
'ittico, -a, -ci, -che *ag* fish *cpd*; fishing *cpd*
Iugos'lavia = **Jugoslavia**
IVA ['iva] *sigla f* (= *imposta sul valore aggiunto*) VAT

◆ j

jazz [dʒaz] *sm* jazz
jeans [dʒinz] *smpl* jeans
jeep® [dʒip] *sm inv* jeep
'jogging ['dʒɔgiŋ] *sm* jogging; **fare ~** to go jogging
'jolly ['dʒɔli] *sm inv* joker
joystick [dʒois'tik] *sm inv* joystick
ju'do [dʒu'dɔ] *sm* judo
Jugos'lavia [jugoz'lavja] *sf* (*Storia*): **la ~** Yugoslavia; **la ex-~** former Yugoslavia; **jugos'lavo, -a** *ag, sm/f* (*Storia*) Yugoslav(ian)

k

l

k *abbr* (= *kilo-, chilo-*) k; (*Inform*) K
kamikaze [kami'kaddze] *sm inv* kamikaze
karaoke [ka'raokɛ] *sm inv* karaoke
karatè *sm* karate
ka'yak [ka'jak] *sm inv* kayak
Kenia ['kenja] *sm*: **il ~** Kenya
kg *abbr* (= *chilogrammo*) kg
'killer *sm inv* gunman, hired gun
kitsch [kitʃ] *sm* kitsch
'kiwi ['kiwi] *sm inv* kiwi fruit
km *abbr* (= *chilometro*) km
K.O. [kappa'o] *sm inv* knockout
ko'ala [ko'ala] *sm inv* koala (bear)
koso'varo, -a [koso'varo] *ag, sm/f* Kosovan
Ko'sovo *sm* Kosovo
'krapfen *sm inv* (*Cuc*) doughnut
Kuwait [ku'vait] *sm*: **il ~** Kuwait

l' *det vedi* **la**; **lo**; **il**
la (*dav V* **l'**) *det f* the ▷ *pron* (*oggetto: persona*) her; (: *cosa*) it; (: *forma di cortesia*) you; *vedi anche* **il**
là *av* there; **di là** (*da quel luogo*) from there; (*in quel luogo*) in there; (*dall'altra parte*) over there; **di là di** beyond; **per di là** that way; **più in là** further on; (*tempo*) later on; **fatti in là** move up; **là dentro/sopra/sotto** in/up (*o* on)/under there; *vedi anche* **quello**
'labbro (*pl(f)* **labbra**) (*solo nel senso Anat*) *sm* lip
labi'rinto *sm* labyrinth, maze
labora'torio *sm* (*di ricerca*) laboratory; (*di arti, mestieri*) workshop; **laboratorio linguistico** language laboratory
labori'oso, -a *ag* (*faticoso*) laborious; (*attivo*) hard-working
'lacca, -che *sf* lacquer
'laccio ['lattʃo] *sm* noose; (*legaccio, tirante*) lasso; (*di scarpa*) lace; **laccio emostatico** tourniquet

lace'rare [latʃe'rare] *vt* to tear to shreds, lacerate; **lacerarsi** *vpr* to tear
'lacrima *sf* tear; **in lacrime** in tears; **lacri'mogeno, -a** *ag* **gas lacrimogeno** tear gas
la'cuna *sf* (*fig*) gap
'ladro *sm* thief
laggiù [lad'dʒu] *av* down there; (*di là*) over there
la'gnarsi [laɲ'ɲarsi] *vpr*: **~ (di)** to complain (about)
'lago, -ghi *sm* lake
la'guna *sf* lagoon
'laico, -a, -ci, -che *ag* (*apostolato*) lay; (*vita*) secular; (*scuola*) non-denominational ▷ *sm/f* layman/woman
'lama *sm inv* (*Zool*) llama; (*Rel*) lama ▷ *sf* blade
lamentarsi *vpr* (*emettere lamenti*) to moan, groan; (*rammaricarsi*): **~ (di)** to complain (about)
lamen'tela *sf* complaining *no pl*
la'metta *sf* razor blade
'lamina *sf* (*lastra sottile*) thin sheet (*o* layer *o* plate); **lamina d'oro** gold leaf; gold foil
'lampada *sf* lamp; **lampada a gas** gas lamp; **lampada da tavolo** table lamp
lampa'dario *sm* chandelier
lampa'dina *sf* light bulb; **lampadina tascabile** pocket torch (BRIT) *o* flashlight (US)
lam'pante *ag* (*fig*: *evidente*) crystal clear, evident
lampeggi'are [lamped'dʒare] *vi* (*luce, fari*) to flash ▷ *vb impers* **lampeggia** there's lightning; **lampeggia'tore** *sm* (*Aut*) indicator
lampi'one *sm* street light *o* lamp (BRIT)
'lampo *sm* (*Meteor*) flash of lightning; (*di luce*: *fig*) flash
lam'pone *sm* raspberry
'lana *sf* wool; **pura ~ vergine** pure new wool; **lana d'acciaio** steel wool; **lana di vetro** glass wool
lan'cetta [lan'tʃetta] *sf* (*indice*) pointer, needle; (*di orologio*) hand
'lancia ['lantʃa] *sf* (*arma*) lance; (*: picca*) spear; (*di pompa antincendio*) nozzle; (*imbarcazione*) launch; **lancia di salvataggio** lifeboat
lanciafi'amme [lantʃa'fjamme] *sm inv* flamethrower
lanci'are [lan'tʃare] *vt* to throw, hurl, fling; (*Sport*) to throw; (*far partire*: *automobile*) to get up to full speed; (*bombe*) to drop; (*razzo, prodotto, moda*) to launch; **lanciarsi** *vpr* **lanciarsi contro/su** to throw *o* hurl *o* fling o.s. against/on; **lanciarsi in** (*fig*) to embark on
lanci'nante [lantʃi'nante] *ag* (*dolore*) shooting, throbbing; (*grido*) piercing
'lancio ['lantʃo] *sm* throwing *no pl*; throw; dropping *no pl*; drop; launching *no pl*; launch; **lancio del disco** (*Sport*) throwing the discus; **lancio del peso** putting the shot
'languido, -a *ag* (*fiacco*) languid, weak; (*tenero, malinconico*) languishing
lan'terna *sf* lantern; (*faro*) lighthouse
'lapide *sf* (*di sepolcro*) tombstone; (*commemorativa*) plaque
'lapsus *sm inv* slip
'lardo *sm* bacon fat, lard
lar'ghezza [lar'gettsa] *sf* width; breadth; looseness; generosity; **larghezza di vedute** broad-mindedness
'largo, -a, -ghi, -ghe *ag* wide; broad; (*maniche*) wide; (*abito*: *troppo ampio*) loose; (*fig*) generous ▷ *sm* width; breadth; (*mare aperto*): **il ~** the open sea ▷ *sf* **stare** *o* **tenersi alla larga (da qn/qc)** to keep one's distance (from sb/sth), keep away (from sb/sth); **~ due metri** two metres wide; **~ di spalle** broad-shouldered; **di larghe**

vedute broad-minded; **su larga scala** on a large scale; **di manica larga** generous, open-handed; **al ~ di Genova** off (the coast of) Genoa; **farsi ~ tra la folla** to push one's way through the crowd

'larice ['laritʃe] *sm* (*Bot*) larch

larin'gite [larin'dʒite] *sf* laryngitis

'larva *sf* larva; (*fig*) shadow

la'sagne [la'zaɲɲe] *sfpl* lasagna *sg*

lasci'are [laʃ'ʃare] *vt* to leave; (*abbandonare*) to leave, abandon, give up; (*cessare di tenere*) to let go of ▷ *vb aus* **~ fare qn** to let sb do; **~ andare** *o* **correre** *o* **perdere** to let things go their own way; **~ stare qc/qn** to leave sth/sb alone; **lasciarsi** *vpr* (*persone*) to part; (*coppia*) to split up; **lasciarsi andare** to let o.s. go

'laser ['lazer] *ag, sm inv*: **(raggio) ~** laser (beam)

lassa'tivo, -a *ag, sm* laxative

'lasso *sm*; **lasso di tempo** interval, lapse of time

lassù *av* up there

'lastra *sf* (*di pietra*) slab; (*di metallo, Fot*) plate; (*di ghiaccio, vetro*) sheet; (*radiografica*) X-ray (plate)

lastri'cato *sm* paving

late'rale *ag* lateral, side *cpd*; (*uscita, ingresso ecc*) side *cpd* ▷ *sm* (*Calcio*) half-back

la'tino, -a *ag, sm* Latin

lati'tante *sm/f* fugitive (from justice)

lati'tudine *sf* latitude

'lato, -a *ag* (*fig*) wide, broad ▷ *sm* side; (*fig*) aspect, point of view; **in senso ~** broadly speaking

'latta *sf* tin (plate); (*recipiente*) tin, can

lat'tante *ag* unweaned

'latte *sm* milk; **latte detergente** cleansing milk *o* lotion; **latte intero** full-cream milk; **latte a lunga conservazione** UHT milk, long-life milk; **latte magro** *o* **scremato** skimmed milk; **latte in polvere** dried *o* powdered milk; **latte solare** suntan lotion; **latti'cini** *smpl* dairy products

lat'tina *sf* (*di birra ecc*) can

lat'tuga, -ghe *sf* lettuce

'laurea *sf* degree; **laurea in ingegneria** engineering degree; **laurea in lettere** ≈ arts degree

LAUREA

The **laurea** is awarded to students who successfully complete their degree courses. Traditionally, this takes between four and six years; a major element of the final examinations is the presentation and discussion of a dissertation. A shorter, more vocational course of study, taking from two to three years, is also available; at the end of this time students receive a diploma called the **laurea breve**.

laure'arsi *vpr* to graduate

laure'ato, -a *ag, sm/f* graduate

'lauro *sm* laurel

'lauto, -a *ag* (*pranzo, mancia*) lavish

'lava *sf* lava

la'vabo *sm* washbasin

la'vaggio [la'vaddʒo] *sm* washing *no pl*; **lavaggio del cervello** brainwashing *no pl*; **lavaggio a secco** dry-cleaning

la'vagna [la'vaɲɲa] *sf* (*Geo*) slate; (*di scuola*) blackboard

la'vanda *sf* (*anche Med*) wash; (*Bot*) lavender; **lavande'ria** *sf* laundry; **lavanderia automatica** launderette; **lavanderia a secco** dry-cleaner's; **lavan'dino** *sm* sink

lavapi'atti *sm/f* dishwasher

la'vare *vt* to wash; **lavarsi** *vpr* to wash, have a wash; **~ a secco** to dry-clean; **lavarsi le mani/i denti** to wash one's hands/clean one's teeth

lava'secco *sm o f inv* dry cleaner's

lavasto'viglie [lavasto'viʎʎe] *sm o f inv* (*macchina*) dishwasher
lava'trice [lava'tritʃe] *sf* washing machine
lavo'rare *vi* to work; (*fig*: *bar, studio ecc*) to do good business ▷ *vt* to work; **lavorarsi qn** (*persuaderlo*) to work on sb; **~ a** to work on; **~ a maglia** to knit; **lavora'tivo, -a** *ag* working; **lavora'tore, -'trice** *sm/f* worker ▷ *ag* working
la'voro *sm* work; (*occupazione*) job, work *no pl*; (*opera*) piece of work, job; (*Econ*) labour; **che ~ fa?** what do you do?; **lavori forzati** hard labour *sg*; **lavoro interinale** *o* **in affitto** temporary work
le *det fpl* the ▷ *pron* (*oggetto*) them; (: *a lei, a essa*) (to) her; (: *forma di cortesia*) (to) you; *vedi anche* **il**
le'ale *ag* loyal; (*sincero*) sincere; (*onesto*) fair
'lecca 'lecca *sm inv* lollipop
leccapi'edi (*peg*) *sm/f inv* toady, bootlicker
lec'care *vt* to lick; (*gatto*: *latte ecc*) to lick *o* lap up; (*fig*) to flatter; **leccarsi i baffi** to lick one's lips
leccherò *ecc* [lekke'rɔ] *vb vedi* **leccare**
'leccio ['lettʃo] *sm* holm oak, ilex
leccor'nia *sf* titbit, delicacy
'lecito, -a ['lɛtʃito] *ag* permitted, allowed
'lega, -ghe *sf* league; (*di metalli*) alloy
le'gaccio [le'gattʃo] *sm* string, lace
le'gale *ag* legal ▷ *sm* lawyer; **legaliz'zare** *vt* to authenticate; (*regolarizzare*) to legalize
le'game *sm* (*corda, fig*: *affettivo*) tie, bond; (*nesso logico*) link, connection
le'gare *vt* (*prigioniero, capelli, cane*) to tie (up); (*libro*) to bind; (*Chim*) to alloy; (*fig*: *collegare*) to bind, join ▷ *vi* (*far lega*) to unite; (*fig*) to get on well
le'genda [le'dʒɛnda] *sf* (*di carta geografica ecc*) = **leggenda**
'legge ['leddʒe] *sf* law
leg'genda [led'dʒɛnda] *sf* (*narrazione*) legend; (*di carta geografica ecc*) key, legend
'leggere ['lɛddʒere] *vt, vi* to read
legge'rezza [leddʒe'rettsa] *sf* lightness; thoughtlessness; fickleness
leg'gero, -a [led'dʒɛro] *ag* light; (*agile, snello*) nimble, agile, light; (*tè, caffè*) weak; (*fig*: *non grave, piccolo*) slight; (: *spensierato*) thoughtless; (: *incostante*) fickle; free and easy; **alla leggera** thoughtlessly
leg'gio, -'gii [led'dʒio] *sm* lectern; (*Mus*) music stand
legherò *ecc* [lege'rɔ] *vb vedi* **legare**
legisla'tivo, -a [ledʒizla'tivo] *ag* legislative
legisla'tura [ledʒizla'tura] *sf* legislature
le'gittimo, -a [le'dʒittimo] *ag* legitimate; (*fig*: *giustificato, lecito*) justified, legitimate; **legittima difesa** (*Dir*) self-defence
'legna ['leɲɲa] *sf* firewood
'legno ['leɲɲo] *sm* wood; (*pezzo di legno*) piece of wood; **di ~** wooden; **legno compensato** plywood
'lei *pron* (*soggetto*) she; (*oggetto*: *per dare rilievo, con preposizione*) her; (*forma di cortesia*: *anche*: **L~**) you ▷ *sm* **dare del ~ a qn** to address sb as "lei"; **~ stessa** she herself; you yourself

LEI

lei is the third person singular pronoun. It is used in Italian to address an adult whom you do not know or with whom you are on formal terms.

lenta'mente *av* slowly
'lente *sf* (*Ottica*) lens *sg*; **lenti a contatto** *o* **corneali** contact lenses; **lenti (a contatto) morbide/rigide**

soft/hard contact lenses; **lente d'ingrandimento** magnifying glass; **lenti** *sfpl* (*occhiali*) lenses
len'tezza [len'tettsa] *sf* slowness
len'ticchia [len'tikkja] *sf* (*Bot*) lentil
len'tiggine [len'tiddʒine] *sf* freckle
'lento, -a *ag* slow; (*molle*: *fune*) slack; (*non stretto*: *vite, abito*) loose ▷ *sm* (*ballo*) slow dance
'lenza ['lɛntsa] *sf* fishing-line
lenzu'olo [len'tswɔlo] *sm* sheet
le'one *sm* lion; (*dello zodiaco*): **L~** Leo
lepo'rino, -a *ag* **labbro ~** harelip
'lepre *sf* hare
'lercio, -a, -ci, -cie ['lɛrtʃo] *ag* filthy
lesi'one *sf* (*Med*) lesion; (*Dir*) injury, damage; (*Edil*) crack
les'sare *vt* (*Cuc*) to boil
'lessi *ecc vb vedi* **leggere**
'lessico, -ci *sm* vocabulary; lexicon
'lesso, -a *ag* boiled ▷ *sm* boiled meat
le'tale *ag* lethal; fatal
leta'maio *sm* dunghill
le'tame *sm* manure, dung
le'targo, -ghi *sm* lethargy; (*Zool*) hibernation
'lettera *sf* letter; **lettere** *sfpl* (*letteratura*) literature *sg*; (*studi umanistici*) arts (subjects); **alla ~** literally; **in lettere** in words, in full
letteral'mente *av* literally
lette'rario, -a *ag* literary
lette'rato, -a *ag* well-read, scholarly
lettera'tura *sf* literature
let'tiga, -ghe *sf* (*barella*) stretcher
let'tino *sm* cot (BRIT), crib (US); **lettino solare** sunbed
'letto, -a *pp di* **leggere** ▷ *sm* bed; **andare a ~** to go to bed; **letto a castello** bunk beds *pl*; **letto a una piazza** single; **letto a due piazze** *o* **matrimoniale** double bed
let'tore, -'trice *sm/f* reader; (*Ins*) (foreign language) assistant (BRIT), (foreign) teaching assistant (US) ▷ *sm* (*Tecn*): **~ ottico** optical character reader; **lettore CD** CD player; **lettore DVD** DVD player
let'tura *sf* reading

> Attenzione! In inglese esiste la parola *lecture*, che però significa *lezione* oppure *conferenza*.

leuce'mia [leutʃe'mia] *sf* leukaemia
'leva *sf* lever; (*Mil*) conscription; **far ~ su qn** to work on sb; **leva del cambio** (*Aut*) gear lever
le'vante *sm* east; (*vento*) East wind; **il L~** the Levant
le'vare *vt* (*occhi, braccio*) to raise; (*sollevare, togliere*: *tassa, divieto*) to lift; (*indumenti*) to take off, remove; (*rimuovere*) to take away; (: *dal di sopra*) to take off; (: *dal di dentro*) to take out
leva'toio, -a *ag*: **ponte ~** drawbridge
lezi'one [let'tsjone] *sf* lesson; (*Univ*) lecture; **fare ~** to teach; to lecture; **dare una ~ a qn** to teach sb a lesson; **lezioni private** private lessons
li *pron pl* (*oggetto*) them
lì *av* there; **di** *o* **da lì** from there; **per di lì** that way; **di lì a pochi giorni** a few days later; **lì per lì** there and then; at first; **essere lì (lì) per fare** to be on the point of doing, be about to do; **lì dentro** in there; **lì sotto** under there; **lì sopra** on there; up there; *vedi anche* **quello**
liba'nese *ag, sm/f* Lebanese *inv*
Li'bano *sm*: **il ~** the Lebanon
'libbra *sf* (*peso*) pound
li'beccio [li'bettʃo] *sm* south-west wind
li'bellula *sf* dragonfly
libe'rale *ag, sm/f* liberal
liberaliz'zare [liberalid'dzare] *vt* to liberalize
libe'rare *vt* (*rendere libero*: *prigioniero*) to release; (: *popolo*) to free, liberate; (*sgombrare*: *passaggio*) to clear; (: *stanza*) to vacate; (*produrre*: *energia*) to release; **liberarsi** *vpr* **liberarsi di qc/qn** to get rid of sth/sb;

liberazi'one *sf* liberation, freeing; release; rescuing

> **LIBERAZIONE**
>
> The **Liberazione** is a national holiday which falls on April 25th. It commemorates the liberation of Italy at the end of the Second World War.

'libero, -a *ag* free; (*strada*) clear; (*non occupato*: *posto ecc*) vacant; free; not taken; empty; not engaged; **~ di fare qc** free to do sth; **~ da** free from; **è ~ questo posto?** is this seat free?; **~ arbitrio** free will; **~ professionista** self-employed professional person; **~ scambio** free trade; **libertà** *sf inv* freedom; (*tempo disponibile*) free time ▷ *sfpl* (*licenza*) liberties; **in libertà provvisoria/vigilata** released without bail/on probation

'Libia *sf* **la ~** Libya; **'libico, -a, -ci, -che** *ag, sm/f* Libyan

li'bidine *sf* lust

li'braio *sm* bookseller

li'brarsi *vpr* to hover

libre'ria *sf* (*bottega*) bookshop; (*mobile*) bookcase

> Attenzione! In inglese esiste la parola *library*, che però significa *biblioteca*.

li'bretto *sm* booklet; (*taccuino*) notebook; (*Mus*) libretto; **libretto degli assegni** cheque book; **libretto di circolazione** (*Aut*) logbook; **libretto di risparmio** (savings) bank-book, passbook; **libretto universitario** student's report book

'libro *sm* book; **libro di cassa** cash book; **libro mastro** ledger; **libro paga** payroll; **libro di testo** textbook

li'cenza [li'tʃɛntsa] *sf* (*permesso*) permission, leave; (*di pesca, caccia, circolazione*) permit, licence; (*Mil*) leave; (*Ins*) school leaving certificate; (*libertà*) liberty; licence; licentiousness; **andare in ~** (*Mil*) to go on leave

licenzia'mento [litʃentsja'mento] *sm* dismissal

licenzi'are [litʃen'tsjare] *vt* (*impiegato*) to dismiss; (*Comm*: *per eccesso di personale*) to make redundant; (*Ins*) to award a certificate to; **licenziarsi** *vpr* (*impiegato*) to resign, hand in one's notice; (*Ins*) to obtain one's school-leaving certificate

li'ceo [li'tʃɛo] *sm* (*Ins*) secondary (BRIT) *o* high (US) school (*for 14- to 19-year-olds*)

'lido *sm* beach, shore

Liechtenstein ['liktənstain] *sm*: **il ~** Liechtenstein

li'eto, -a *ag* happy, glad; **"molto ~"** (*nelle presentazioni*) "pleased to meet you"

li'eve *ag* light; (*di poco conto*) slight; (*sommesso*: *voce*) faint, soft

lievi'tare *vi* (*anche fig*) to rise ▷ *vt* to leaven

li'evito *sm* yeast; **lievito di birra** brewer's yeast

'ligio, -a, -gi, -gie ['lidʒo] *ag* faithful, loyal

'lilla *sm inv* lilac

'lillà *sm inv* lilac

'lima *sf* file; **lima da unghie** nail file

limacci'oso, -a [limat'tʃoso] *ag* slimy; muddy

li'mare *vt* to file (down); (*fig*) to polish

limi'tare *vt* to limit, restrict; (*circoscrivere*) to bound, surround; **limitarsi** *vpr* **limitarsi nel mangiare** to limit one's eating; **limitarsi a qc/a fare qc** to limit o.s. to sth/to doing sth

'limite *sm* limit; (*confine*) border, boundary; **limite di velocità** speed limit

limo'nata *sf* lemonade (BRIT), (lemon) soda (US); lemon squash (BRIT), lemonade (US)

li'mone *sm* (*pianta*) lemon tree; (*frutto*) lemon

'limpido, -a *ag* clear; (*acqua*) limpid, clear
'lince ['lintʃe] *sf* lynx
linci'are *vt* to lynch
'linea *sf* line; (*di mezzi pubblici di trasporto: itinerario*) route; (*: servizio*) service; **a grandi linee** in outline; **mantenere la ~** to look after one's figure; **aereo di ~** airliner; **nave di ~** liner; **volo di ~** scheduled flight; **linea aerea** airline; **linea di partenza/d'arrivo** (*Sport*) starting/finishing line; **linea di tiro** line of fire
linea'menti *smpl* features; (*fig*) outlines
line'are *ag* linear; (*fig*) coherent, logical
line'etta *sf* (*trattino*) dash; (*d'unione*) hyphen
lin'gotto *sm* ingot, bar
'lingua *sf* (*Anat, Cuc*) tongue; (*idioma*) language; **mostrare la ~** to stick out one's tongue; **di ~ italiana** Italian-speaking; **che lingue parla?** what languages do you speak?; **una ~ di terra** a spit of land; **lingua madre** mother tongue
lingu'aggio [lin'gwaddʒo] *sm* language
lingu'etta *sf* (*di strumento*) reed; (*di scarpa, Tecn*) tongue; (*di busta*) flap
'lino *sm* (*pianta*) flax; (*tessuto*) linen
li'noleum *sm inv* linoleum, lino
liposuzi'one [liposut'tsjone] *sf* liposuction
lique'fatto, -a *pp di* **liquefare**
liqui'dare *vt* (*società, beni: persona: uccidere*) to liquidate; (*persona: sbarazzarsene*) to get rid of; (*conto, problema*) to settle; (*Comm: merce*) to sell off, clear; **liquidazi'one** *sf* liquidation; settlement; clearance sale
liquidità *sf* liquidity
'liquido, -a *ag, sm* liquid; **liquido per freni** brake fluid
liqui'rizia [likwi'rittsja] *sf* liquorice
li'quore *sm* liqueur
'lira *sf* (*Storia: unità monetaria*) lira; (*Mus*) lyre; **lira sterlina** pound sterling
'lirico, -a, -ci, -che *ag* lyric(al); (*Mus*) lyric; **cantante/teatro ~** opera singer/house
Lis'bona *sf* Lisbon
'lisca, -sche *sf* (*di pesce*) fishbone
lisci'are [liʃ'ʃare] *vt* to smooth; (*fig*) to flatter
'liscio, -a, -sci, -sce ['liʃʃo] *ag* smooth; (*capelli*) straight; (*mobile*) plain; (*bevanda alcolica*) neat; (*fig*) straightforward, simple ▷ *av* **andare ~** to go smoothly; **passarla liscia** to get away with it
'liso, -a *ag* worn out, threadbare
'lista *sf* (*elenco*) list; **lista elettorale** electoral roll; **lista delle spese** shopping list; **lista dei vini** wine list; **lista delle vivande** menu
lis'tino *sm* list; **listino dei cambi** (foreign) exchange rate; **listino dei prezzi** price list
'lite *sf* quarrel, argument; (*Dir*) lawsuit
liti'gare *vi* to quarrel; (*Dir*) to litigate
li'tigio [li'tidʒo] *sm* quarrel
lito'rale *ag* coastal, coast *cpd* ▷ *sm* coast
'litro *sm* litre
livel'lare *vt* to level, make level
li'vello *sm* level; (*fig*) level, standard; **ad alto ~** (*fig*) high-level; **livello del mare** sea level
'livido, -a *ag* livid; (*per percosse*) bruised, black and blue; (*cielo*) leaden ▷ *sm* bruise
Li'vorno *sf* Livorno, Leghorn
'lizza ['littsa] *sf* lists *pl*; **scendere in ~** to enter the lists
lo (*dav s impura, gn, pn, ps, x, z; dav V* **l'**) *det m* the ▷ *pron* (*oggetto: persona*) him; (*: cosa*) it; **lo sapevo** I knew it; **lo so** I know; **sii buono, anche se lui non lo è** be good, even if he isn't; *vedi anche* **il**
lo'cale *ag* local ▷ *sm* room; (*luogo*

pubblico) premises *pl*; **locale notturno** nightclub; **località** *sf inv* locality
lo'canda *sf* inn
locomo'tiva *sf* locomotive
locuzi'one [lokut'tsjone] *sf* phrase, expression
lo'dare *vt* to praise
'lode *sf* praise; (*Ins*): **laurearsi con 110 e ~** ≈ to graduate with a first-class honours degree (BRIT), graduate summa cum laude (US)
'loden *sm inv* (*stoffa*) loden; (*cappotto*) loden overcoat
lo'devole *ag* praiseworthy
loga'ritmo *sm* logarithm
'loggia, -ge ['lɔddʒa] *sf* (*Archit*) loggia; (*circolo massonico*) lodge; **loggi'one** *sm* (*di teatro*): **il loggione** the Gods *sg*
'logico, -a, -ci, -che ['lɔdʒiko] *ag* logical
logo'rare *vt* to wear out; (*sciupare*) to waste; **logorarsi** *vpr* to wear out; (*fig*) to wear o.s. out
'logoro, -a *ag* (*stoffa*) worn out, threadbare; (*persona*) worn out
Lombar'dia *sf* **la ~** Lombardy
lom'bata *sf* (*taglio di carne*) loin
lom'brico, -chi *sm* earthworm
londi'nese *ag* London *cpd* ▷ *sm/f* Londoner
'Londra *sf* London
lon'gevo, -a [lon'dʒevo] *ag* long-lived
longi'tudine [londʒi'tudine] *sf* longitude
lonta'nanza [lonta'nantsa] *sf* distance; absence
lon'tano, -a *ag* (*distante*) distant, faraway; (*assente*) absent; (*vago*: *sospetto*) slight, remote; (*tempo*: *remoto*) far-off, distant; (*parente*) distant, remote ▷ *av* far; **è lontana la casa?** is it far to the house?, is the house far from here?; **è ~ un chilometro** it's a kilometre away *o* a kilometre from here; **più ~** farther; **da** *o* **di ~** from a distance; **~ da** a long way from; **è molto ~ da qui?** is it far from here?; **alla lontana** slightly, vaguely
lo'quace [lo'kwatʃe] *ag* talkative, loquacious; (*fig*: *gesto ecc*) eloquent
'lordo, -a *ag* dirty, filthy; (*peso, stipendio*) gross
'loro *pron pl* (*oggetto, con preposizione*) them; (*complemento di termine*) to them; (*soggetto*) they; (*forma di cortesia*: *anche*: **L~**) you; to you; **il (la) ~, i (le) ~** *det* their; (*forma di cortesia*: *anche*: **L~**) your ▷ *pron* theirs; (*forma di cortesia*: *anche*: **L~**) yours; **~ stessi(e)** they themselves; you yourselves
'losco, -a, -schi, -sche *ag* (*fig*) shady, suspicious
'lotta *sf* struggle, fight; (*Sport*) wrestling; **lotta libera** all-in wrestling; **lot'tare** *vi* to fight, struggle; to wrestle
lotte'ria *sf* lottery; (*di gara ippica*) sweepstake
'lotto *sm* (*gioco*) (state) lottery; (*parte*) lot; (*Edil*) site

LOTTO

The **Lotto** is an official lottery run by the Italian Finance Ministry. It consists of a weekly draw of numbers and is very popular.

lozi'one [lot'tsjone] *sf* lotion
lubrifi'cante *sm* lubricant
lubrifi'care *vt* to lubricate
luc'chetto [luk'ketto] *sm* padlock
lucci'care [luttʃi'kare] *vi* to sparkle, glitter, twinkle
'luccio ['luttʃo] *sm* (*Zool*) pike
'lucciola ['luttʃola] *sf* (*Zool*) firefly; glowworm
'luce ['lutʃe] *sf* light; (*finestra*) window; **alla ~ di** by the light of; **fare ~ su qc** (*fig*) to shed *o* throw light on sth; **~ del sole/della luna** sun/moonlight
lucer'nario [lutʃer'narjo] *sm* skylight
lu'certola [lu'tʃɛrtola] *sf* lizard

luci'dare [lutʃi'dare] *vt* to polish
lucida'trice [lutʃida'tritʃe] *sf* floor polisher
'lucido, -a ['lutʃido] *ag* shining, bright; (*lucidato*) polished; (*fig*) lucid ▷ *sm* shine, lustre; (*disegno*) tracing; **lucido per scarpe** shoe polish
'lucro *sm* profit, gain
'luglio ['luʎʎo] *sm* July
'lugubre *ag* gloomy
'lui *pron* (*soggetto*) he; (*oggetto: per dare rilievo, con preposizione*) him; **~ stesso** he himself
lu'maca, -che *sf* slug; (*chiocciola*) snail
lumi'noso, -a *ag* (*che emette luce*) luminous; (*cielo, colore, stanza*) bright; (*sorgente*) of light, light *cpd*; (*fig: sorriso*) bright, radiant
'luna *sf* moon; **luna nuova/piena** new/full moon; **luna di miele** honeymoon; **siamo in ~ di miele** we're on honeymoon
'luna park *sm inv* amusement park, funfair
lu'nare *ag* lunar, moon *cpd*
lu'nario *sm* almanac; **sbarcare il ~** to make ends meet
lu'natico, -a, -ci, -che *ag* whimsical, temperamental
lunedì *sm inv* Monday; **di** *o* **il ~** on Mondays
lun'ghezza [lun'gettsa] *sf* length; **lunghezza d'onda** (*Fisica*) wavelength
'lungo, -a, -ghi, -ghe *ag* long; (*lento: persona*) slow; (*diluito: caffè, brodo*) weak, watery, thin ▷ *sm* length ▷ *prep* along; **~ 3 metri** 3 metres long; **a ~** for a long time; **a ~ andare** in the long run; **di gran lunga** (*molto*) by far; **andare in ~** *o* **per le lunghe** to drag on; **saperla lunga** to know what's what; **in ~ e in largo** far and wide, all over; **~ il corso dei secoli** throughout the centuries
lungo'mare *sm* promenade
lu'notto *sm* (*Aut*) rear *o* back window; **lunotto termico** heated rear window
lu'ogo, -ghi *sm* place; (*posto: di incidente ecc*) scene, site; (*punto, passo di libro*) passage; **in ~ di** instead of; **in primo ~** in the first place; **aver ~** to take place; **dar ~ a** to give rise to; **luogo di nascita** birthplace; (*Amm*) place of birth; **luogo di provenienza** place of origin; **luogo comune** commonplace
'lupo, -a *sm/f* wolf
'luppolo *sm* (*Bot*) hop
'lurido, -a *ag* filthy
lusin'gare *vt* to flatter
Lussem'burgo *sm* (*stato*): **il ~** Luxembourg ▷ *sf* (*città*) Luxembourg
'lusso *sm* luxury; **di ~** luxury *cpd*; **lussu'oso, -a** *ag* luxurious
lus'suria *sf* lust
lus'trino *sm* sequin
'lutto *sm* mourning; **essere in/portare il ~** to be in/wear mourning

m

m. *abbr* = **mese**; **metro**; **miglia**; **monte**
ma *cong* but; **ma insomma!** for goodness sake!; **ma no!** of course not!
'macabro, -a *ag* gruesome, macabre
macché [mak'ke] *escl* not at all!, certainly not!
macche'roni [makke'roni] *smpl* macaroni *sg*
'macchia ['makkja] *sf* stain, spot; (*chiazza di diverso colore*) spot, splash, patch; (*tipo di boscaglia*) scrub; **alla ~** (*fig*) in hiding; **macchi'are** *vt* (*sporcare*) to stain, mark; **macchiarsi** *vpr* (*persona*) to get o.s. dirty; (*stoffa*) to stain; to get stained *o* marked
macchi'ato, -a [mak'kjato] *ag* (*pelle, pelo*) spotted; **~ di** stained with; **caffè ~** coffee with a dash of milk
'macchina ['makkina] *sf* machine; (*motore, locomotiva*) engine; (*automobile*) car; (*fig: meccanismo*) machinery; **andare in ~** (*Aut*) to go by car; (*Stampa*) to go to press; **macchina da cucire** sewing machine; **macchina fotografica** camera; **macchina da presa** cine *o* movie camera; **macchina da scrivere** typewriter; **macchina a vapore** steam engine
macchi'nario [makki'narjo] *sm* machinery
macchi'nista, -i [makki'nista] *sm* (*di treno*) engine-driver; (*di nave*) engineer
Macedonia [matʃe'donja] *sf*: **la ~** Macedonia
mace'donia [matʃe'dɔnja] *sf* fruit salad
macel'laio [matʃel'lajo] *sm* butcher
macelle'ria *sf* butcher's (shop)
ma'cerie [ma'tʃɛrje] *sfpl* rubble *sg*, debris *sg*
ma'cigno [ma'tʃiɲɲo] *sm* (*masso*) rock, boulder
maci'nare [matʃi'nare] *vt* to grind; (*carne*) to mince (BRIT), grind (US)
macrobi'otico, -a *ag* macrobiotic ▷ *sf* macrobiotics *sg*
Ma'donna *sf* (*Rel*) Our Lady
mador'nale *ag* enormous, huge
'madre *sf* mother; (*matrice di bolletta*) counterfoil ▷ *ag inv* mother *cpd*; **ragazza ~** unmarried mother; **scena ~** (*Teatro*) principal scene; (*fig*) terrible scene
madre'lingua *sf* mother tongue, native language
madre'perla *sf* mother-of-pearl
ma'drina *sf* godmother
maestà *sf inv* majesty
ma'estra *sf vedi* **maestro**
maes'trale *sm* north-west wind, mistral
ma'estro, -a *sm/f* (*Ins: anche:* **~ di scuola o elementare**) primary (BRIT) *o* grade school (US) teacher; (*esperto*) expert ▷ *sm* (*artigiano, fig: guida*) master; (*Mus*) maestro ▷ *ag* (*principale*) main; (*di grande abilità*) masterly, skilful; **maestra d'asilo**

nursery teacher; **~ di cerimonie** master of ceremonies
'mafia *sf* Mafia
'maga *sf* sorceress
ma'gari *escl* (*esprime desiderio*): **~ fosse vero!** if only it were true!; **ti piacerebbe andare in Scozia? — ~!** would you like to go to Scotland? — and how! ▷ *av* (*anche*) even; (*forse*) perhaps
magaz'zino [magad'dzino] *sm* warehouse; **grande ~** department store

Attenzione! In inglese esiste la parola *magazine* che però significa *rivista*.

'maggio ['maddʒo] *sm* May
maggio'rana [maddʒo'rana] *sf* (*Bot*) (sweet) marjoram
maggio'ranza [maddʒo'rantsa] *sf* majority
maggior'domo [maddʒor'dɔmo] *sm* butler
maggi'ore [mad'dʒore] *ag* (*comparativo*: *più grande*) bigger, larger; taller; greater; (: *più vecchio*: *sorella, fratello*) older, elder; (: *di grado superiore*) senior; (: *più importante*: *Mil, Mus*) major; (*superlativo*) biggest, largest; tallest; greatest; oldest, eldest ▷ *sm/f* (*di grado*) superior; (*di età*) elder; (*Mil*) major; (: *Aer*) squadron leader; **la maggior parte** the majority; **andare per la ~** (*cantante ecc*) to be very popular; **maggio'renne** *ag* of age ▷ *sm/f* person who has come of age
ma'gia [ma'dʒia] *sf* magic; **'magico, -a, -ci, -che** *ag* magic; (*fig*) fascinating, charming, magical
magis'trato [madʒis'trato] *sm* magistrate
'maglia ['maʎʎa] *sf* stitch; (*lavoro ai ferri*) knitting *no pl*; (*tessuto, Sport*) jersey; (*maglione*) jersey, sweater; (*di catena*) link; (*di rete*) mesh; **maglia diritta/rovescia** plain/purl;
magli'etta *sf* (*canottiera*) vest; (*tipo camicia*) T-shirt
magli'one *sm* sweater, jumper
ma'gnetico, -a, -ci, -che *ag* magnetic
ma'gnifico, -a, -ci, -che [maɲ'ɲifiko] *ag* magnificent, splendid; (*ospite*) generous
ma'gnolia [maɲ'ɲɔlja] *sf* magnolia
'mago, -ghi *sm* (*stregone*) magician, wizard; (*illusionista*) magician
ma'grezza [ma'grettsa] *sf* thinness
'magro, -a *ag* (very) thin, skinny; (*carne*) lean; (*formaggio*) low-fat; (*fig*: *scarso, misero*) meagre, poor; (: *meschino*: *scusa*) poor, lame; **mangiare di ~** not to eat meat
'mai *av* (*nessuna volta*) never; (*talvolta*) ever; **non ... ~** never; **~ più** never again; **non sono ~ stato in Spagna** I've never been to Spain; **come ~?** why (*o* how) on earth?; **chi/dove/quando ~?** whoever/wherever/whenever?
mai'ale *sm* (*Zool*) pig; (*carne*) pork
maio'nese *sf* mayonnaise
'mais *sm inv* maize
mai'uscolo, -a *ag* (*lettera*) capital; (*fig*) enormous, huge
mala'fede *sf* bad faith
malan'dato, -a *ag* (*persona*: *di salute*) in poor health; (: *di condizioni finanziarie*) badly off; (*trascurato*) shabby
ma'lanno *sm* (*disgrazia*) misfortune; (*malattia*) ailment
mala'pena *sf*: **a ~** hardly, scarcely
ma'laria *sf* (*Med*) malaria
ma'lato, -a *ag* ill, sick; (*gamba*) bad; (*pianta*) diseased ▷ *sm/f* sick person; (*in ospedale*) patient; **malat'tia** *sf* (*infettiva ecc*) illness, disease; (*cattiva salute*) illness, sickness; (*di pianta*) disease
mala'vita *sf* underworld
mala'voglia [mala'vɔʎʎa] *sf*: **di ~** unwillingly, reluctantly
Ma'laysia *sf* Malaysia

mal'concio, -a, -ci, -ce [mal'kontʃo] *ag* in a sorry state
malcon'tento *sm* discontent
malcos'tume *sm* immorality
mal'destro, -a *ag* (*inabile*) inexpert, inexperienced; (*goffo*) awkward
'male *av* badly ▷ *sm* (*ciò che è ingiusto, disonesto*) evil; (*danno, svantaggio*) harm; (*sventura*) misfortune; (*dolore fisico, morale*) pain, ache; **di ~ in peggio** from bad to worse; **sentirsi ~** to feel ill; **far ~** (*dolere*) to hurt; **far ~ alla salute** to be bad for one's health; **far del ~ a qn** to hurt *o* harm sb; **restare** *o* **rimanere ~** to be sorry; to be disappointed; to be hurt; **andare a ~** to go bad; **come va? — non c'è ~** how are you? — not bad; **avere mal di gola/testa** to have a sore throat/a headache; **aver ~ ai piedi** to have sore feet; **mal d'auto** carsickness; **mal di cuore** heart trouble; **male di dente** toothache; **mal di mare** seasickness
male'detto, -a *pp di* **maledire** ▷ *ag* cursed, damned; (*fig: fam*) damned, blasted
male'dire *vt* to curse; **maledizi'one** *sf* curse; **maledizione!** damn it!
maledu'cato, -a *ag* rude, ill-mannered
maleducazi'one [maledukat'tsjone] *sf* rudeness
ma'lefico, -a, -ci, -che *ag* (*influsso, azione*) evil
ma'lessere *sm* indisposition, slight illness; (*fig*) uneasiness
malfa'mato, -a *ag* notorious
malfat'tore, -'trice *sm/f* wrongdoer
mal'fermo, -a *ag* unsteady, shaky; (*salute*) poor, delicate
mal'grado *prep* in spite of, despite ▷ *cong* although; **mio (***o* **tuo** *ecc***) ~** against my (*o* your *ecc*) will
ma'ligno, -a [ma'liɲɲo] *ag* (*malvagio*) malicious, malignant; (*Med*) malignant
malinco'nia *sf* melancholy, gloom; **malin'conico, -a, -ci, -che** *ag* melancholy
malincu'ore: **a ~** *av* reluctantly, unwillingly
malin'teso, -a *ag* misunderstood; (*riguardo, senso del dovere*) mistaken, wrong ▷ *sm* misunderstanding; **c'è stato un ~** there's been a misunderstanding
ma'lizia [ma'littsja] *sf* (*malignità*) malice; (*furbizia*) cunning; (*espediente*) trick; **malizi'oso, -a** *ag* malicious; cunning; (*vivace, birichino*) mischievous
malme'nare *vt* to beat up
ma'locchio [ma'lɔkkjo] *sm* evil eye
ma'lora *sf*: **andare in ~** to go to the dogs
ma'lore *sm* (sudden) illness
mal'sano, -a *ag* unhealthy
'malta *sf* (*Edil*) mortar
mal'tempo *sm* bad weather
'malto *sm* malt
maltrat'tare *vt* to ill-treat
malu'more *sm* bad mood; (*irritabilità*) bad temper; (*discordia*) ill feeling; **di ~** in a bad mood
'malva *sf* (*Bot*) mallow ▷ *ag, sm inv* mauve
mal'vagio, -a, -gi, -gie [mal'vadʒo] *ag* wicked, evil
malvi'vente *sm* criminal
malvolenti'eri *av* unwillingly, reluctantly
'mamma *sf* mummy, mum; **~ mia!** my goodness!
mam'mella *sf* (*Anat*) breast; (*di vacca, capra ecc*) udder
mam'mifero *sm* mammal
ma'nata *sf* (*colpo*) slap; (*quantità*) handful
man'canza [man'kantsa] *sf* lack; (*carenza*) shortage, scarcity; (*fallo*) fault; (*imperfezione*) failing, shortcoming; **per ~ di tempo** through lack of time; **in ~ di meglio** for lack of anything better

man'care *vi* (*essere insufficiente*) to be lacking; (*venir meno*) to fail; (*sbagliare*) to be wrong, make a mistake; (*non esserci*) to be missing, not to be there; (*essere lontano*): **~ (da)** to be away (from) ▷ *vt* to miss; **~ di** to lack; **~ a** (*promessa*) to fail to keep; **tu mi manchi** I miss you; **mancò poco che morisse** he very nearly died; **mancano ancora 10 sterline** we're still £10 short; **manca un quarto alle 6** it's a quarter to 6

mancherò *ecc* [manke'rɔ] *vb vedi* **mancare**

'mancia, -ce ['mantʃa] *sf* tip; **quanto devo lasciare di ~?** how much should I tip?; **~ competente** reward

manci'ata [man'tʃata] *sf* handful

man'cino, -a [man'tʃino] *ag* (*braccio*) left; (*persona*) left-handed; (*fig*) underhand

manda'rancio [manda'rantʃo] *sm* clementine

man'dare *vt* to send; (*far funzionare*: *macchina*) to drive; (*emettere*) to send out; (: *grido*) to give, utter, let out; **~ a chiamare qn** to send for sb; **~ avanti** (*fig*: *famiglia*) to provide for; (: *fabbrica*) to run, look after; **~ giù** to send down; (*anche fig*) to swallow; **~ via** to send away; (*licenziare*) to fire

manda'rino *sm* mandarin (orange); (*cinese*) mandarin

man'data *sf* (*quantità*) lot, batch; (*di chiave*) turn; **chiudere a doppia ~** to double-lock

man'dato *sm* (*incarico*) commission; (*Dir*: *provvedimento*) warrant; (*di deputato ecc*) mandate; (*ordine di pagamento*) postal *o* money order; **mandato d'arresto** warrant for arrest

man'dibola *sf* mandible, jaw

'mandorla *sf* almond; **'mandorlo** *sm* almond tree

'mandria *sf* herd

maneggi'are [maned'dʒare] *vt* (*creta, cera*) to mould, work, fashion; (*arnesi, utensili*) to handle; (: *adoperare*) to use; (*fig*: *persone, denaro*) to handle, deal with; **ma'neggio** *sm* moulding; handling; use; (*intrigo*) plot, scheme; (*per cavalli*) riding school

ma'nesco, -a, -schi, -sche *ag* free with one's fists

ma'nette *sfpl* handcuffs

manga'nello *sm* club

mangi'are [man'dʒare] *vt* to eat; (*intaccare*) to eat into *o* away; (*Carte, Scacchi ecc*) to take ▷ *vi* to eat ▷ *sm* eating; (*cibo*) food; (*cucina*) cooking; **possiamo ~ qualcosa?** can we have something to eat?; **mangiarsi le parole** to mumble; **mangiarsi le unghie** to bite one's nails

man'gime [man'dʒime] *sm* fodder

'mango, -ghi *sm* mango

ma'nia *sf* (*Psic*) mania; (*fig*) obsession, craze; **ma'niaco, -a, -ci, -che** *ag* suffering from a mania; **maniaco (di)** obsessed (by), crazy (about)

'manica *sf* sleeve; (*fig*: *gruppo*) gang, bunch; (*Geo*): **la M~, il Canale della M~** the (English) Channel; **essere di ~ larga/stretta** to be easy-going/strict; **manica a vento** (*Aer*) wind sock

mani'chino [mani'kino] *sm* (*di sarto, vetrina*) dummy

'manico, -ci *sm* handle; (*Mus*) neck

mani'comio *sm* mental hospital; (*fig*) madhouse

mani'cure *sm o f inv* manicure ▷ *sf inv* manicurist

mani'era *sf* way, manner; (*stile*) style, manner; **maniere** *sfpl* (*comportamento*) manners; **in ~ che** so that; **in ~ da** so as to; **in tutte le maniere** at all costs

manifes'tare *vt* to show, display; (*esprimere*) to express; (*rivelare*) to reveal, disclose ▷ *vi* to demonstrate; **manifestazi'one** *sf* show, display; expression; (*sintomo*) sign,

symptom; (*dimostrazione pubblica*) demonstration; (*cerimonia*) event
mani'festo, -a *ag* obvious, evident ▷ *sm* poster, bill; (*scritto ideologico*) manifesto
ma'niglia [ma'niʎʎa] *sf* handle; (*sostegno: negli autobus ecc*) strap
manipo'lare *vt* to manipulate; (*alterare: vino*) to adulterate
man'naro: **lupo ~** *sm* werewolf
'mano, -i *sf* hand; (*strato: di vernice ecc*) coat; **di prima ~** (*notizia*) first-hand; **di seconda ~** second-hand; **man ~** little by little, gradually; **man ~ che** as; **darsi** *o* **stringersi la ~** to shake hands; **mettere le mani avanti** (*fig*) to safeguard o.s.; **restare a mani vuote** to be left empty-handed; **venire alle mani** to come to blows; **a ~** by hand; **mani in alto!** hands up!
mano'dopera *sf* labour
ma'nometro *sm* gauge, manometer
mano'mettere *vt* (*alterare*) to tamper with; (*aprire indebitamente*) to break open illegally
ma'nopola *sf* (*dell'armatura*) gauntlet; (*guanto*) mitt; (*di impugnatura*) hand-grip; (*pomello*) knob
manos'critto, -a *ag* handwritten ▷ *sm* manuscript
mano'vale *sm* labourer
mano'vella *sf* handle; (*Tecn*) crank
ma'novra *sf* manoeuvre (BRIT), maneuver (US); (*Ferr*) shunting
man'sarda *sf* attic
mansi'one *sf* task, duty, job
mansu'eto, -a *ag* gentle, docile
man'tello *sm* cloak; (*fig: di neve ecc*) blanket, mantle; (*Zool*) coat
mante'nere *vt* to maintain; (*adempiere: promesse*) to keep, abide by; (*provvedere a*) to support, maintain; **mantenersi** *vpr* **mantenersi calmo/giovane** to stay calm/young
'Mantova *sf* Mantua
manu'ale *ag* manual ▷ *sm* (*testo*) manual, handbook
ma'nubrio *sm* handle; (*di bicicletta ecc*) handlebars *pl*; (*Sport*) dumbbell
manutenzi'one [manuten'tsjone] *sf* maintenance, upkeep; (*d'impianti*) maintenance, servicing
'manzo ['mandzo] *sm* (*Zool*) steer; (*carne*) beef
'mappa *sf* (*Geo*) map; **mappa'mondo** *sm* map of the world; (*globo girevole*) globe
mara'tona *sf* marathon
'marca, -che *sf* (*Comm: di prodotti*) brand; (*contrassegno, scontrino*) ticket, check; **prodotto di ~** (*di buona qualità*) high-class product; **marca da bollo** official stamp
mar'care *vt* (*munire di contrassegno*) to mark; (*a fuoco*) to brand; (*Sport: gol*) to score; (*: avversario*) to mark; (*accentuare*) to stress; **~ visita** (*Mil*) to report sick
marcherò *ecc* [marke'rɔ] *vb vedi* **marcare**
mar'chese, -a [mar'keze] *sm/f* marquis *o* marquess/marchioness
marchi'are [mar'kjare] *vt* to brand
'marcia, -ce ['martʃa] *sf* (*anche Mus, Mil*) march; (*funzionamento*) running; (*il camminare*) walking; (*Aut*) gear; **mettere in ~** to start; **mettersi in ~** to get moving; **far ~ indietro** (*Aut*) to reverse; (*fig*) to back-pedal
marciapi'ede [martʃa'pjɛde] *sm* (*di strada*) pavement (BRIT), sidewalk (US); (*Ferr*) platform
marci'are [mar'tʃare] *vi* to march; (*andare: treno, macchina*) to go; (*funzionare*) to run, work
'marcio, -a, -ci, -ce ['martʃo] *ag* (*frutta, legno*) rotten, bad; (*Med*) festering; (*fig*) corrupt, rotten
mar'cire [mar'tʃire] *vi* (*andare a male*) to go bad, rot; (*suppurare*) to fester; (*fig*) to rot, waste away
'marco, -chi *sm* (*unità monetaria*) mark
'mare *sm* sea; **in ~** at sea; **andare al ~**

(*in vacanza ecc*) to go to the seaside; **il M~ del Nord** the North Sea
ma'rea *sf* tide; **alta/bassa ~** high/low tide
mareggi'ata [mared'dʒata] *sf* heavy sea
mare'moto *sm* seaquake
maresci'allo [mareʃʃallo] *sm* (*Mil*) marshal; (: *sottufficiale*) warrant officer
marga'rina *sf* margarine
marghe'rita [marge'rita] *sf* (ox-eye) daisy, marguerite; (*di stampante*) daisy wheel
'margine ['mardʒine] *sm* margin; (*di bosco, via*) edge, border
mariju'ana [mæri'wa:nə] *sf* marijuana
ma'rina *sf* navy; (*costa*) coast; (*quadro*) seascape; **marina mercantile/militare** navy/merchant navy (BRIT) *o* marine (US)
mari'naio *sm* sailor
mari'nare *vt* (*Cuc*) to marinate; **~ la scuola** to play truant
ma'rino, -a *ag* sea *cpd*, marine
mario'netta *sf* puppet
ma'rito *sm* husband
ma'rittimo, -a *ag* maritime, sea *cpd*
marmel'lata *sf* jam; (*di agrumi*) marmalade
mar'mitta *sf* (*recipiente*) pot; (*Aut*) silencer; **marmitta catalitica** catalytic converter
'marmo *sm* marble
mar'motta *sf* (*Zool*) marmot
maroc'chino, -a [marok'kino] *ag, sm/f* Moroccan
Ma'rocco *sm* **il ~** Morocco
mar'rone *ag inv* brown ▷ *sm* (*Bot*) chestnut

> Attenzione! In inglese esiste la parola *maroon*, che però indica un altro colore, il rosso bordeaux.

mar'supio *sm* pouch; (*per denaro*) bum bag; (*per neonato*) sling
martedì *sm inv* Tuesday; **di** *o* **il ~** on Tuesdays; **martedì grasso** Shrove Tuesday
martel'lare *vt* to hammer ▷ *vi* (*pulsare*) to throb; (: *cuore*) to thump
mar'tello *sm* hammer; (: *di uscio*) knocker; **martello pneumatico** pneumatic drill
'martire *sm/f* martyr
mar'xista, -i, -e *ag, sm/f* Marxist
marza'pane [martsa'pane] *sm* marzipan
'marzo ['martso] *sm* March
mascal'zone [maskal'tsone] *sm* rascal, scoundrel
mas'cara *sm inv* mascara
ma'scella [maʃʃɛlla] *sf* (*Anat*) jaw
'maschera ['maskera] *sf* mask; (*travestimento*) disguise; (: *per un ballo ecc*) fancy dress; (*Teatro, Cinema*) usher/usherette; (*personaggio del teatro*) stock character; **masche'rare** *vt* to mask; (*travestire*) to disguise; to dress up; (*fig*: *celare*) to hide, conceal; (*Mil*) to camouflage; **mascherarsi da** to disguise o.s. as; to dress up as; (*fig*) to masquerade as
mas'chile [mas'kile] *ag* masculine; (*sesso, popolazione*) male; (*abiti*) men's; (*per ragazzi*: *scuola*) boys'
mas'chilista, -i, -e *ag, sm/f* (*uomo*) (male) chauvinist, sexist; (*donna*) sexist
'maschio, -a ['maskjo] *ag* (*Biol*) male; (*virile*) manly ▷ *sm* (*anche Zool, Tecn*) male; (*uomo*) man; (*ragazzo*) boy; (*figlio*) son
masco'lino, -a *ag* masculine
'massa *sf* mass; (*di errori ecc*): **una ~ di** heaps of, masses of; (*di gente*) mass, multitude; (*Elettr*) earth; **in ~** (*Comm*) in bulk; (*tutti insieme*) en masse; **adunata in ~** mass meeting; **di ~** (*cultura, manifestazione*) mass *cpd*
mas'sacro *sm* massacre, slaughter; (*fig*) mess, disaster
massaggi'are [massad'dʒare] *vt* to massage

mas'saggio [mas'saddʒo] *sm* massage; **massaggio cardiaco** cardiac massage
mas'saia *sf* housewife
masse'rizie [masse'rittsje] *sfpl* (household) furnishings
mas'siccio, -a, -ci, -ce [mas'sittʃo] *ag* (*oro, legno*) solid; (*palazzo*) massive; (*corporatura*) stout ▷ *sm* (*Geo*) massif
'massima *sf* (*sentenza, regola*) maxim; (*Meteor*) maximum temperature; **in linea di ~** generally speaking; *vedi* **massimo**
massi'male *sm* maximum
'massimo, -a *ag, sm* maximum; **al ~** at (the) most
'masso *sm* rock, boulder
masteriz'zare [masterid'dzare] *vt* (*CD, DVD*) to burn
masterizza'tore [masteriddza'tore] *sm* CD burner *o* writer
masti'care *vt* to chew
'mastice ['mastitʃe] *sm* mastic; (*per vetri*) putty
mas'tino *sm* mastiff
ma'tassa *sf* skein
mate'matica *sf* mathematics *sg*
mate'matico, -a, -ci, -che *ag* mathematical ▷ *sm/f* mathematician
materas'sino *sm* mat; **materassino gonfiabile** air bed
mate'rasso *sm* mattress; **materasso a molle** spring *o* interior-sprung mattress
ma'teria *sf* (*Fisica*) matter; (*Tecn, Comm*) material, matter *no pl*; (*disciplina*) subject; (*argomento*) subject matter, material; **in ~ di** (*per quanto concerne*) on the subject of; **materie prime** raw materials
materi'ale *ag* material; (*fig: grossolano*) rough, rude ▷ *sm* material; (*insieme di strumenti ecc*) equipment *no pl*, materials *pl*
maternità *sf* motherhood, maternity; (*reparto*) maternity ward
ma'terno, -a *ag* (*amore, cura ecc*) maternal, motherly; (*nonno*) maternal; (*lingua, terra*) mother *cpd*
ma'tita *sf* pencil; **matite colorate** coloured pencils; **matita per gli occhi** eyeliner (pencil)
ma'tricola *sf* (*registro*) register; (*numero*) registration number; (*nell'università*) freshman, fresher
ma'trigna [ma'triɲɲa] *sf* stepmother
matrimoni'ale *ag* matrimonial, marriage *cpd*
matri'monio *sm* marriage, matrimony; (*durata*) marriage, married life; (*cerimonia*) wedding
mat'tina *sf* morning
'matto, -a *ag* mad, crazy; (*fig: falso*) false, imitation ▷ *sm/f* madman/woman; **avere una voglia matta di qc** to be dying for sth
mat'tone *sm* brick; (*fig*): **questo libro/film è un ~** this book/film is heavy going
matto'nella *sf* tile
matu'rare *vi* (*anche*: **maturarsi**: *frutta, grano*) to ripen; (*ascesso*) to come to a head; (*fig: persona, idea, Econ*) to mature ▷ *vt* to ripen, to (make) mature
maturità *sf* maturity; (*di frutta*) ripeness, maturity; (*Ins*) school-leaving examination, ≈ GCE A-levels (BRIT)
ma'turo, -a *ag* mature; (*frutto*) ripe, mature
max. *abbr* (= *massimo*) max
maxischermo [maxis'kermo] *sm* giant screen
'mazza ['mattsa] *sf* (*bastone*) club; (*martello*) sledge-hammer; (*Sport: da golf*) club; (*: da baseball, cricket*) bat
maz'zata [mat'tsata] *sf* (*anche fig*) heavy blow
'mazzo ['mattso] *sm* (*di fiori, chiavi ecc*) bunch; (*di carte da gioco*) pack
me *pron* me; **me stesso(-a)** myself; **sei bravo quanto me** you are as clever as

I (am) *o* as me

mec'canico, -a, -ci, -che *ag* mechanical ▷ *sm* mechanic; **può mandare un ~?** can you send a mechanic?

mecca'nismo *sm* mechanism

me'daglia [me'daʎʎa] *sf* medal

me'desimo, -a *ag* same; (*in persona*): **io ~** I myself

'media *sf* average; (*Mat*) mean; (*Ins: voto*) end-of-term average; **le medie** *sfpl* = **scuola media**; **in ~** on average; *vedi anche* **medio**

medi'ante *prep* by means of

media'tore, -'trice *sm/f* mediator; (*Comm*) middle man, agent

medi'care *vt* to treat; (*ferita*) to dress

medi'cina [medi'tʃina] *sf* medicine; **medicina legale** forensic medicine

'medico, -a, -ci, -che *ag* medical ▷ *sm* doctor; **chiamate un ~** call a doctor; **medico generico** general practitioner, GP

medie'vale *ag* medieval

'medio, -a *ag* average; (*punto, ceto*) middle; (*altezza, statura*) medium ▷ *sm* (*dito*) middle finger; **licenza media** *leaving certificate awarded at the end of 3 years of secondary education*; **scuola media** *first 3 years of secondary school*

medi'ocre *ag* mediocre, poor

medi'tare *vt* to ponder over, meditate on; (*progettare*) to plan, think out ▷ *vi* to meditate

mediter'raneo, -a *ag* Mediterranean; **il (mare) M~** the Mediterranean (Sea)

me'dusa *sf* (*Zool*) jellyfish

mega'byte *sm inv* (*Comput*) megabyte

me'gafono *sm* megaphone

'meglio ['mɛʎʎo] *av, ag inv* better; (*con senso superlativo*) best ▷ *sm* (*la cosa migliore*): **il ~** the best (thing); **faresti ~ ad andartene** you had better leave; **alla ~** as best one can; **andar di bene in ~** to get better and better; **fare del proprio ~** to do one's best; **per il ~** for the best; **aver la ~ su qn** to get the better of sb

'mela *sf* apple; **mela cotogna** quince

mela'grana *sf* pomegranate

melan'zana [melan'dzana] *sf* aubergine (BRIT), eggplant (US)

melato'nina *sf* melatonin

'melma *sf* mud, mire

'melo *sm* apple tree

melo'dia *sf* melody

me'lone *sm* (musk)melon

'membro *sm* member; (*pl(f)* **membra**) (*arto*) limb

memo'randum *sm inv* memorandum

me'moria *sf* memory; **memorie** *sfpl* (*opera autobiografica*) memoirs; **a ~** (*imparare, sapere*) by heart; **a ~ d'uomo** within living memory

mendi'cante *sm/f* beggar

PAROLA CHIAVE

'meno *av* **1** (*in minore misura*) less; **dovresti mangiare meno** you should eat less, you shouldn't eat so much

2 (*comparativo*): **meno ... di** not as ... as, less ... than; **sono meno alto di te** I'm not as tall as you (are), I'm less tall than you (are); **meno ... che** not as ... as, less ... than; **meno che mai** less than ever; **è meno intelligente che ricco** he's more rich than intelligent; **meno fumo più mangio** the less I smoke the more I eat

3 (*superlativo*) least; **il meno dotato degli studenti** the least gifted of the students; **è quello che compro meno spesso** it's the one I buy least often

4 (*Mat*) minus; **8 meno 5** 8 minus 5, 8 take away 5; **sono le 8 meno un quarto** it's a quarter to 8; **meno 5 gradi** 5 degrees below zero [illegible] 5 degrees; **1 euro in meno** 1 euro less

5 (*fraseologia*): **quanto meno poteva**

telefonare he could at least have phoned; **non so se accettare o meno** I don't know whether to accept or not; **fare a meno di qc/qn** to do without sth/sb; **non potevo fare a meno di ridere** I couldn't help laughing; **meno male!** thank goodness!; **meno male che sei arrivato** it's a good job that you've come
▷ *ag inv* (*tempo, denaro*) less; (*errori, persone*) fewer; **ha fatto meno errori di tutti** he made fewer mistakes than anyone, he made the fewest mistakes of all
▷ *sm inv* **1**: **il meno** (*il minimo*) the least; **parlare del più e del meno** to talk about this and that
2 (*Mat*) minus
▷ *prep* (*eccetto*) except (for), apart from; **a meno che, a meno di** unless; **a meno che non piova** unless it rains; **non posso, a meno di prendere ferie** I can't, unless I take some leave

meno'pausa *sf* menopause
'mensa *sf* (*locale*) canteen; (: *Mil*) mess; (: *nelle università*) refectory
men'sile *ag* monthly ▷ *sm* (*periodico*) monthly (magazine); (*stipendio*) monthly salary
'mensola *sf* bracket; (*ripiano*) shelf; (*Archit*) corbel
'menta *sf* mint; (*anche*: **~ piperita**) peppermint; (*bibita*) peppermint cordial; (*caramella*) mint, peppermint
men'tale *ag* mental; **mentalità** *sf inv* mentality
'mente *sf* mind; **imparare/sapere qc a ~** to learn/know sth by heart; **avere in ~ qc** to have sth in mind; **passare di ~ a qn** to slip sb's mind
men'tire *vi* to lie
'mento *sm* chin
'mentre *cong* (*temporale*) while; (*avversativo*) whereas
menù *sm inv* menu; **ci può portare il ~?** could we see the menu?; **menù turistico** set menu
menzio'nare [mentsjo'nare] *vt* to mention
men'zogna [men'tsɔɲɲa] *sf* lie
mera'viglia [mera'viʎʎa] *sf* amazement, wonder; (*persona, cosa*) marvel, wonder; **a ~** perfectly, wonderfully; **meravigli'are** *vt* to amaze, astonish; **meravigliarsi (di)** to marvel (at); (*stupirsi*) to be amazed (at), be astonished (at); **meravigli'oso, -a** *ag* wonderful, marvellous
mer'cante *sm* merchant; **mercante d'arte** art dealer
merca'tino *sm* (*rionale*) local street market; (*Econ*) unofficial stock market
mer'cato *sm* market; **mercato dei cambi** exchange market; **mercato nero** black market
'merce ['mɛrtʃe] *sf* goods *pl*, merchandise
mercé [mer'tʃe] *sf* mercy
merce'ria [mertʃe'ria] *sf* (*articoli*) haberdashery (BRIT), notions *pl* (US); (*bottega*) haberdasher's shop (BRIT), notions store (US)
mercoledì *sm inv* Wednesday; **di** *o* **il ~** on Wednesdays; **mercoledì delle Ceneri** Ash Wednesday
mer'curio *sm* mercury
'merda (*fam!*) *sf* shit (*!*)
me'renda *sf* afternoon snack
meren'dina *sf* snack
meridi'ana *sf* (*orologio*) sundial
meridi'ano, -a *ag* meridian; midday *cpd*, noonday ▷ *sm* meridian
meridio'nale *ag* southern ▷ *sm/f* southerner
meridi'one *sm* south
me'ringa, -ghe *sf* (*Cuc*) meringue
meri'tare *vt* to deserve, merit ▷ *vb impers* **merita andare** it's worth going
meri'tevole *ag* worthy
'merito *sm* merit; (*valore*) worth; **in ~ a** as regards, with regard to; **dare ~ a qn di** to give sb credit for; **finire**

a pari ~ to finish joint first (*o* second *ecc*); to tie
mer'letto *sm* lace
'merlo *sm* (*Zool*) blackbird; (*Archit*) battlement
mer'luzzo [mer'luttso] *sm* (*Zool*) cod
mes'chino, -a [mes'kino] *ag* wretched; (*scarso*) scanty, poor; (*persona*: *gretta*) mean; (: *limitata*) narrow-minded, petty
mesco'lare *vt* to mix; (*vini, colori*) to blend; (*mettere in disordine*) to mix up, muddle up; (*carte*) to shuffle
'mese *sm* month
'messa *sf* (*Rel*) mass; (*il mettere*): **messa in moto** starting; **messa in piega** set; **messa a punto** (*Tecn*) adjustment; (*Aut*) tuning; (*fig*) clarification; **messa in scena** = **messinscena**
messag'gero [messad'dʒɛro] *sm* messenger
messaggi'arsi [messad'dʒarsi] *vip*: **messaggiamoci** let's text each other
messaggino [messad'dʒino] *sm* (*di telefonino*) text (message)
mes'saggio [mes'saddʒo] *sm* message; **posso lasciare un ~?** can I leave a message?; **ci sono messaggi per me?** are there any messages for me?; **messaggio di posta elettronica** e-mail message
messag'gistica [messad'dʒistica] *sf* **~ immediata** (*Inform*) instant messaging; **programma di ~ immediata** instant messenger
mes'sale *sm* (*Rel*) missal
messi'cano, -a *ag, sm/f* Mexican
'Messico *sm* **il ~** Mexico
messin'scena [messin'ʃɛna] *sf* (*Teatro*) production
'messo, -a *pp di* **mettere** ▷ *sm* messenger
mesti'ere *sm* (*professione*) job; (: *manuale*) trade; (: *artigianale*) craft; (*fig*: *abilità nel lavoro*) skill, technique; **essere del ~** to know the tricks of the trade
'mestolo *sm* (*Cuc*) ladle
mestruazi'one [mestruat'tsjone] *sf* menstruation
'meta *sf* destination; (*fig*) aim, goal
metà *sf inv* half; (*punto di mezzo*) middle; **dividere qc a** *o* **per ~** to divide sth in half, halve sth; **fare a ~ (di qc con qn)** to go halves (with sb in sth); **a ~ prezzo** at half price; **a ~ strada** halfway
meta'done *sm* methadone
me'tafora *sf* metaphor
me'tallico, -a, -ci, -che *ag* (*di metallo*) metal *cpd*; (*splendore, rumore ecc*) metallic
me'tallo *sm* metal
metalmec'canico, -a, -ci, -che *ag* engineering *cpd* ▷ *sm* engineering worker
me'tano *sm* methane
me'ticcio, -a, -ci, -ce [me'tittʃo] *sm/f* half-caste, half-breed
me'todico, -a, -ci, -che *ag* methodical
'metodo *sm* method
'metro *sm* metre; (*nastro*) tape measure; (*asta*) (metre) rule
metropoli'tana *sf* underground, subway
metrosessu'ale *agg* metrosexual
'mettere *vt* to put; (*abito*) to put on; (: *portare*) to wear; (*installare*: *telefono*) to put in; (*fig*: *provocare*): **~ fame/allegria a qn** to make sb hungry/happy; (*supporre*): **mettiamo che ...** let's suppose *o* say that ...; **mettersi** *vpr* (*persona*) to put o.s.; (*oggetto*) to go; (*disporsi*: *faccenda*) to turn out; **mettersi a sedere** to sit down; **mettersi a letto** to get into bed; (*per malattia*) to take to one's bed; **mettersi il cappello** to put on one's hat; **mettersi a** (*cominciare*) to begin to, start to; **mettersi al lavoro** to set to work; **mettersi con qn** (*in società*) to team up with sb; (*in coppia*)

to start going out with sb; **metterci: metterci molta cura/molto tempo** to take a lot of care/a lot of time; **ci ho messo 3 ore per venire** it's taken me 3 hours to get here; **mettercela tutta** to do one's best; **~ a tacere qn/qc** to keep sb/sth quiet; **~ su casa** to set up house; **~ su un negozio** to start a shop; **~ via** to put away

mezza'notte [meddza'nɔtte] *sf* midnight

'mezzo, -a ['mɛddzo] *ag* half; **un ~ litro/panino** half a litre/roll ▷ *av* half-; **~ morto** half-dead ▷ *sm* (*metà*) half; (*parte centrale: di strada ecc*) middle; (*per raggiungere un fine*) means *sg*; (*veicolo*) vehicle; (*nell'indicare l'ora*): **le nove e ~** half past nine; **~giorno e ~** half past twelve; **mezzi** *smpl* (*possibilità economiche*) means; **di mezza età** middle-aged; **un soprabito di mezza stagione** a spring (*o* autumn) coat; **di ~** middle, in the middle; **andarci di ~** (*patir danno*) to suffer; **levarsi** *o* **togliersi di ~** to get out of the way; **in ~ a** in the middle of; **per** *o* **a ~ di** by means of; **mezzi di comunicazione di massa** mass media *pl*; **mezzi pubblici** public transport *sg*; **mezzi di trasporto** means of transport

mezzogi'orno [meddzo'dʒorno] *sm* midday, noon; **a ~** at 12 (o'clock) *o* midday *o* noon; **il ~ d'Italia** southern Italy

mi (*dav lo, la, li, le, ne diventa* **me**) *pron* (*oggetto*) me; (*complemento di termine*) to me; (*riflessivo*) myself ▷ *sm* (*Mus*) E; (: *solfeggiando la scala*) mi

miago'lare *vi* to miaow, mew

'mica *av* (*fam*): **non ... ~** not ... at all; **non sono ~ stanco** I'm not a bit tired; **non sarà ~ partito?** he wouldn't have left, would he?; **~ male** not bad

'miccia, -ce ['mittʃa] *sf* fuse

micidi'ale [mitʃi'djale] *ag* fatal; (*dannosissimo*) deadly

micro'fibra *sf* microfibre

mi'crofono *sm* microphone

micros'copio *sm* microscope

mi'dollo (*pl(f)* **midolla**) *sm* (*Anat*) marrow; **midollo osseo** bone marrow

mi'ele *sm* honey

'miglia ['miʎʎa] *sfpl di* **miglio**

migli'aio [miʎ'ʎajo] ((*pl*)*f* **migliaia**) *sm* thousand; **un ~ (di)** about a thousand; **a migliaia** by the thousand, in thousands

'miglio ['miʎʎo] *sm* (*Bot*) millet; (*pl(f)* **miglia**) (*unità di misura*) mile; **~ marino** *o* **nautico** nautical mile

migliora'mento [miʎʎora'mento] *sm* improvement

miglio'rare [miʎʎo'rare] *vt, vi* to improve

migli'ore [miʎ'ʎore] *ag* (*comparativo*) better; (*superlativo*) best ▷ *sm* **il ~** the best (thing) ▷ *sm/f* **il(la) ~** the best (person); **il miglior vino di questa regione** the best wine in this area

'mignolo ['miɲɲolo] *sm* (*Anat*) little finger, pinkie; (: *dito del piede*) little toe

Mi'lano *sf* Milan

miliar'dario, -a *sm/f* millionaire

mili'ardo *sm* thousand million, billion (US)

mili'one *sm* million

mili'tante *ag, sm/f* militant

mili'tare *vi* (*Mil*) to be a soldier, serve; (*fig: in un partito*) to be a militant ▷ *ag* military ▷ *sm* serviceman; **fare il ~** to do one's military service

'mille (*pl* **mila**) *num* a *o* one thousand; **dieci mila** ten thousand; **mille euro** one thousand euros

mil'lennio *sm* millennium

millepi'edi *sm inv* centipede

mil'lesimo, -a *ag, sm* thousandth

milli'grammo *sm* milligram(me)

mil'limetro *sm* millimetre

'milza ['miltsa] *sf* (*Anat*) spleen

mimetiz'zare [mimetid'dzare] *vt* to camouflage; **mimetizzarsi** *vpr* to camouflage o.s.

'mimo *sm* (*attore, componimento*) mime
mi'mosa *sf* mimosa
min. *abbr* (= *minuto, minimo*) min.
'mina *sf* (*esplosiva*) mine; (*di matita*) lead
mi'naccia, -ce [mi'nattʃa] *sf* threat; **minacci'are** *vt* to threaten; **minacciare qn di morte** to threaten to kill sb; **minacciare di fare qc** to threaten to do sth
mi'nare *vt* (*Mil*) to mine; (*fig*) to undermine
mina'tore *sm* miner
mine'rale *ag, sm* mineral
mine'rario, -a *ag* (*delle miniere*) mining; (*dei minerali*) ore *cpd*
mi'nestra *sf* soup; **minestra in brodo** noodle soup; **minestra di verdure** vegetable soup
minia'tura *sf* miniature
mini'bar *sm inv* minibar
mini'era *sf* mine
mini'gonna *sf* miniskirt
'minimo, -a *ag* minimum, least, slightest; (*piccolissimo*) very small, slight; (*il più basso*) lowest, minimum ▷ *sm* minimum; **al ~** at least; **girare al ~** (*Aut*) to idle
minis'tero *sm* (*Pol, Rel*) ministry; (*governo*) government; **M~ delle Finanze** Ministry of Finance, ≈ Treasury
mi'nistro *sm* (*Pol, Rel*) minister
mino'ranza [mino'rantsa] *sf* minority
mi'nore *ag* (*comparativo*) less; (*più piccolo*) smaller; (*numero*) lower; (*inferiore*) lower, inferior; (*meno importante*) minor; (*più giovane*) younger; (*superlativo*) least; smallest; lowest; youngest ▷ *sm/f* = **minorenne**
mino'renne *ag* under age ▷ *sm/f* minor, person under age
mi'nuscolo, -a *ag* (*scrittura, carattere*) small; (*piccolissimo*) tiny ▷ *sf* small letter
mi'nuto, -a *ag* tiny, minute; (*pioggia*) fine; (*corporatura*) delicate, fine ▷ *sm* (*unità di misura*) minute; **al ~** (*Comm*) retail
'mio (*f* **'mia**, *pl* **mi'ei** *or* **'mie**) *det* **il ~, la mia** *ecc* my ▷ *pron* **il ~, la mia** *ecc* mine; **i miei** my family; **un ~ amico** a friend of mine
'miope *ag* short-sighted
'mira *sf* (*anche fig*) aim; **prendere la ~** to take aim; **prendere di ~ qn** (*fig*) to pick on sb
mi'racolo *sm* miracle
mi'raggio [mi'raddʒo] *sm* mirage
mi'rare *vi* **~ a** to aim at; **mi'rato, -a** *agg* (*targetted*)
mi'rino *sm* (*Tecn*) sight; (*Fot*) viewer, viewfinder
mir'tillo *sm* bilberry (BRIT), blueberry (US), whortleberry
mi'scela [miʃʃela] *sf* mixture; (*di caffè*) blend
'mischia ['miskja] *sf* scuffle; (*Rugby*) scrum, scrummage
mis'cuglio [mis'kuʎʎo] *sm* mixture, hotchpotch, jumble
'mise *vb vedi* **mettere**
mise'rabile *ag* (*infelice*) miserable, wretched; (*povero*) poverty-stricken; (*di scarso valore*) miserable
mi'seria *sf* extreme poverty; (*infelicità*) misery
miseri'cordia *sf* mercy, pity
'misero, -a *ag* miserable, wretched; (*povero*) poverty-stricken; (*insufficiente*) miserable
'misi *vb vedi* **mettere**
mi'sogino [mi'zɔdʒino] *sm* misogynist
'missile *sm* missile
missio'nario, -a *ag, sm/f* missionary
missi'one *sf* mission
misteri'oso, -a *ag* mysterious
mis'tero *sm* mystery
'misto, -a *ag* mixed; (*scuola*) mixed, coeducational ▷ *sm* mixture

mis'tura *sf* mixture
mi'sura *sf* measure; (*misurazione, dimensione*) measurement; (*taglia*) size; (*provvedimento*) measure, step; (*moderazione*) moderation; (*Mus*) time; (: *divisione*) bar; (*fig*: *limite*) bounds *pl*, limit; **nella ~ in cui** inasmuch as, insofar as; **(fatto) su ~** made to measure
misu'rare *vt* (*ambiente, stoffa*) to measure; (*terreno*) to survey; (*abito*) to try on; (*pesare*) to weigh; (*fig*: *parole ecc*) to weigh up; (: *spese, cibo*) to limit ▷ *vi* to measure; **misurarsi** *vpr* **misurarsi con qn** to have a confrontation with sb; to compete with sb
'mite *ag* mild
'mitico, -a, ci, che *ag* mythical
'mito *sm* myth; **mitolo'gia, -'gie** *sf* mythology
'mitra *sf* (*Rel*) mitre ▷ *sm inv* (*arma*) sub-machine gun
mit'tente *sm/f* sender
mm *abbr* (= *millimetro*) mm
'mobile *ag* mobile; (*parte di macchina*) moving; (*Dir*: *bene*) movable, personal ▷ *sm* (*arredamento*) piece of furniture; **mobili** *smpl* (*mobilia*) furniture *sg*
mocas'sino *sm* moccasin
'moda *sf* fashion; **alla ~, di ~** fashionable, in fashion
modalità *sf inv* formality
mo'della *sf* model
mo'dello *sm* model; (*stampo*) mould ▷ *ag inv* model *cpd*
'modem *sm inv* modem
modera'tore, -'trice *sm/f* moderator
mo'derno, -a *ag* modern
mo'desto, -a *ag* modest
'modico, -a, -ci, -che *ag* reasonable, moderate
mo'difica, -che *sf* modification
modifi'care *vt* to modify, alter
'modo *sm* way, manner; (*mezzo*) means, way; (*occasione*) opportunity; (*Ling*) mood; (*Mus*) mode; **modi** *smpl* (*comportamento*) manners; **a suo ~, a ~ suo** in his own way; **ad** *o* **in ogni ~** anyway; **di** *o* **in ~ che** so that; **in ~ da** so as to; **in tutti i modi** at all costs; (*comunque sia*) anyway; (*in ogni caso*) in any case; **in qualche ~** somehow or other; **per ~ di dire** so to speak; **modo di dire** turn of phrase
'modulo *sm* (*modello*) form; (*Archit, lunare, di comando*) module
'mogano *sm* mahogany
'mogio, -a, -gi, -gie ['mɔdʒo] *ag* down in the dumps, dejected
'moglie ['moʎʎe] *sf* wife
mo'ine *sfpl* cajolery *sg*; (*leziosità*) affectation *sg*
mo'lare *sm* (*dente*) molar
'mole *sf* mass; (*dimensioni*) size; (*edificio grandioso*) massive structure
moles'tare *vt* to bother, annoy; **mo'lestia** *sf* annoyance, bother; **recar molestia a qn** to bother sb; **molestie sessuali** sexual harassment *sg*
'molla *sf* spring; **molle** *sfpl* (*per camino*) tongs
mol'lare *vt* to release, let go; (*Naut*) to ease; (*fig*: *ceffone*) to give ▷ *vi* (*cedere*) to give in
'molle *ag* soft; (*muscoli*) flabby
mol'letta *sf* (*per capelli*) hairgrip; (*per panni stesi*) clothes peg
'mollica, -che *sf* crumb, soft part
mol'lusco, -schi *sm* mollusc
'molo *sm* mole, breakwater; jetty
moltipli'care *vt* to multiply; **moltiplicarsi** *vpr* to multiply; to increase in number; **moltiplicazi'one** *sf* multiplication

PAROLA CHIAVE

'molto, -a *det* (*quantità*) a lot of, much; (*numero*) a lot of, many; **molto pane/carbone** a lot of bread/coal; **molta gente** a lot of people, many people; **molti libri** a lot of books, many books;

non ho molto tempo I haven't got much time; **per molto (tempo)** for a long time
▷ *av* **1** a lot, (very) much; **viaggia molto** he travels a lot; **non viaggia molto** he doesn't travel much *o* a lot **2** (*intensivo: con aggettivi, avverbi*) very; (*: con participio passato*) (very) much; **molto buono** very good; **molto migliore, molto meglio** much *o* a lot better
▷ *pron* much, a lot

momentanea'mente *av* at the moment, at present
momen'taneo, -a *ag* momentary, fleeting
mo'mento *sm* moment; **da un ~ all'altro** at any moment; (*all'improvviso*) suddenly; **al ~ di fare** just as I was (*o* you were *o* he was *ecc*) doing; **per il ~** for the time being; **dal ~ che** ever since; (*dato che*) since; **a momenti** (*da un momento all'altro*) any time *o* moment now; (*quasi*) nearly
'monaca, -che *sf* nun
'Monaco *sf* Monaco; **Monaco (di Baviera)** Munich
'monaco, -ci *sm* monk
monar'chia *sf* monarchy
monas'tero *sm* (*di monaci*) monastery; (*di monache*) convent
mon'dano, -a *ag* (*anche fig*) worldly; (*anche:* **dell'alta società**) society *cpd*; fashionable
mondi'ale *ag* (*campionato, popolazione*) world *cpd*; (*influenza*) world-wide
'mondo *sm* world; (*grande quantità*): **un ~ di** lots of, a host of; **il bel ~** high society
mo'nello, -a *sm/f* street urchin; (*ragazzo vivace*) scamp, imp
mo'neta *sf* coin; (*Econ: valuta*) currency; (*denaro spicciolo*) (small) change; **moneta estera** foreign currency; **moneta legale** legal tender
mongol'fiera *sf* hot-air balloon
'monitor *sm inv* (*Tecn, TV*) monitor
monolo'cale *sm* studio flat
mono'polio *sm* monopoly
mo'notono, -a *ag* monotonous
monovo'lume *ag inv, sf inv* **(automobile) ~** people carrier, MPV
mon'sone *sm* monsoon
monta'carichi [monta'kariki] *sm inv* hoist, goods lift
mon'taggio [mon'taddʒo] *sm* (*Tecn*) assembly; (*Cinema*) editing
mon'tagna [mon'taɲɲa] *sf* mountain; (*zona montuosa*): **la ~** the mountains *pl*; **andare in ~** to go to the mountains; **montagne russe** roller coaster *sg*, big dipper *sg* (BRIT)
monta'naro, -a *ag* mountain *cpd*
▷ *sm/f* mountain dweller
mon'tano, -a *ag* mountain *cpd*; alpine
mon'tare *vt* to go (*o* come) up; (*cavallo*) to ride; (*apparecchiatura*) to set up, assemble; (*Cuc*) to whip; (*Zool*) to cover; (*incastonare*) to mount, set; (*Cinema*) to edit; (*Fot*) to mount ▷ *vi* to go (*o* come) up; (*a cavallo*): **~ bene/male** to ride well/badly; (*aumentare di livello, volume*) to rise
monta'tura *sf* assembling *no pl*; (*di occhiali*) frames *pl*; (*di gioiello*) mounting, setting; (*fig*): **montatura pubblicitaria** publicity stunt
'monte *sm* mountain; **a ~** upstream; **mandare a ~ qc** to upset sth, cause sth to fail; **il M~ Bianco** Mont Blanc; **monte di pietà** pawnshop; **monte premi** prize
mon'tone *sm* (*Zool*) ram; **carne di ~** mutton
montu'oso, -a *ag* mountainous
monu'mento *sm* monument
mo'quette [mɔ'kɛt] *sf inv* fitted carpet
'mora *sf* (*del rovo*) blackberry; (*del gelso*) mulberry; (*Dir*) delay; (*: somma*) arrears *pl*

mo'rale *ag* moral ▷ *sf* (*scienza*) ethics *sg*, moral philosophy; (*complesso di norme*) moral standards *pl*, morality; (*condotta*) morals *pl*; (*insegnamento morale*) moral ▷ *sm* morale; **essere giù di ~** to be feeling down

'morbido, -a *ag* soft; (*pelle*) soft, smooth

> Attenzione! In inglese esiste la parola *morbid*, che però significa *morboso*.

mor'billo *sm* (*Med*) measles *sg*

'morbo *sm* disease

mor'boso, -a *ag* (*fig*) morbid

'mordere *vt* to bite; (*addentare*) to bite into

mori'bondo, -a *ag* dying, moribund

mo'rire *vi* to die; (*abitudine, civiltà*) to die out; **~ di fame** to die of hunger; (*fig*) to be starving; **~ di noia/paura** to be bored/scared to death; **fa un caldo da ~** it's terribly hot

mormo'rare *vi* to murmur; (*brontolare*) to grumble

'moro, -a *ag* dark(-haired), dark(-complexioned)

'morsa *sf* (*Tecn*) vice; (*fig: stretta*) grip

morsi'care *vt* to nibble (at), gnaw (at); (*insetto*) to bite

'morso, -a *pp di* **mordere** ▷ *sm* bite; (*di insetto*) sting; (*parte della briglia*) bit; **morsi della fame** pangs of hunger

morta'della *sf* (*Cuc*) mortadella (*type of salted pork meat*)

mor'taio *sm* mortar

mor'tale *ag, sm* mortal

'morte *sf* death

'morto, -a *pp di* **morire** ▷ *ag* dead ▷ *sm/f* dead man/woman; **i morti** the dead; **fare il ~** (*nell'acqua*) to float on one's back; **il Mar M~** the Dead Sea

mo'saico, -ci *sm* mosaic

'Mosca *sf* Moscow

'mosca, -sche *sf* fly; **mosca cieca** blind-man's-buff

mosce'rino [moʃʃe'rino] *sm* midge, gnat

mos'chea [mos'kɛa] *sf* mosque

'moscio, -a, -sci, -sce ['mɔʃʃo] *ag* (*fig*) lifeless

mos'cone *sm* (*Zool*) bluebottle; (*barca*) pedalo; (*: a remi*) *kind of pedalo with oars*

'mossa *sf* movement; (*nel gioco*) move

'mossi *ecc vb vedi* **muovere**

'mosso, -a *pp di* **muovere** ▷ *ag* (*mare*) rough; (*capelli*) wavy; (*Fot*) blurred

mos'tarda *sf* mustard; **mostarda di Cremona** *pickled fruit with mustard*

'mostra *sf* exhibition, show; (*ostentazione*) show; **in ~** on show; **far ~ di** (*fingere*) to pretend; **far ~ di sé** to show off

mos'trare *vt* to show; **può mostrarmi dov'è, per favore?** can you show me where it is, please?

'mostro *sm* monster; **mostru'oso, -a** *ag* monstrous

mo'tel *sm inv* motel

moti'vare *vt* (*causare*) to cause; (*giustificare*) to justify, account for

mo'tivo *sm* (*causa*) reason, cause; (*movente*) motive; (*letterario*) (central) theme; (*disegno*) motif, design, pattern; (*Mus*) motif; **per quale ~?** why?, for what reason?

'moto *sm* (*anche Fisica*) motion; (*movimento, gesto*) movement; (*esercizio fisico*) exercise; (*sommossa*) rising, revolt; (*commozione*) feeling, impulse ▷ *sf inv* (*motocicletta*) motorbike; **mettere in ~** to set in motion; (*Aut*) to start up

motoci'clista, -i, -e *sm/f* motorcyclist

mo'tore, -'trice *ag* motor; (*Tecn*) driving ▷ *sm* engine, motor; **a ~** motor *cpd*, power-driven; **~ a combustione interna/a reazione** internal combustion/jet engine; **motore di ricerca** (*Inform*) search engine; **moto'rino** *sm* moped; **motorino di avviamento** (*Aut*) starter

motos'cafo *sm* motorboat

'motto *sm* (*battuta scherzosa*) witty remark; (*frase emblematica*) motto, maxim
'mouse ['maus] *sm inv* (*Inform*) mouse
mo'vente *sm* motive
movi'mento *sm* movement; (*fig*) activity, hustle and bustle; (*Mus*) tempo, movement
mozi'one [mot'tsjone] *sf* (*Pol*) motion
mozza'rella [mottsa'rɛlla] *sf* mozzarella, *a moist Neapolitan curd cheese*
mozzi'cone [mottsi'kone] *sm* stub, butt, end; (*anche*: **~ di sigaretta**) cigarette end
'mucca, -che *sf* cow; **mucca pazza** mad cow disease
'mucchio ['mukkjo] *sm* pile, heap; (*fig*): **un ~ di** lots of, heaps of
'muco, -chi *sm* mucus
'muffa *sf* mould, mildew
mug'gire [mud'dʒire] *vi* (*vacca*) to low, moo; (*toro*) to bellow; (*fig*) to roar
mu'ghetto [mu'getto] *sm* lily of the valley
mu'lino *sm* mill; **mulino a vento** windmill
'mulo *sm* mule
'multa *sf* fine
multi'etnico, -a, -ci, -che *ag* multiethnic
multirazziale [multirat'tsjale] *ag* multiracial
multi'sala *ag inv* multiscreen
multivitami'nico, -a, -ci, -che *ag* **complesso ~** multivitamin
'mummia *sf* mummy
'mungere ['mundʒere] *vt* (*anche fig*) to milk
munici'pale [munitʃi'pale] *ag* municipal; town *cpd*
muni'cipio [muni'tʃipjo] *sm* town council, corporation; (*edificio*) town hall
munizi'oni [munit'tsjoni] *sfpl* (*Mil*) ammunition *sg*
'munsi *ecc vb vedi* **mungere**
mu'oio *ecc vb vedi* **morire**
mu'overe *vt* to move; (*ruota, macchina*) to drive; (*sollevare*: *questione, obiezione*) to raise, bring up; (: *accusa*) to make, bring forward; **muoversi** *vpr* to move; **muoviti!** hurry up!, get a move on!
'mura *sfpl vedi* **muro**
mu'rale *ag* wall *cpd*; mural
mura'tore *sm* mason; bricklayer
'muro *sm* wall
'muschio ['muskjo] *sm* (*Zool*) musk; (*Bot*) moss
musco'lare *ag* muscular, muscle *cpd*
'muscolo *sm* (*Anat*) muscle
mu'seo *sm* museum
museru'ola *sf* muzzle
'musica *sf* music; **musica da ballo/camera** dance/chamber music; **musi'cale** *ag* musical; **musi'cista, -i, -e** *sm/f* musician
'müsli ['mysli] *sm* muesli
'muso *sm* muzzle; (*di auto, aereo*) nose; **tenere il ~** to sulk
mussul'mano, -a *ag, sm/f* Muslim, Moslem
'muta *sf* (*di animali*) moulting; (*di serpenti*) sloughing; (*per immersioni subacquee*) diving suit; (*gruppo di cani*) pack
mu'tande *sfpl* (*da uomo*) (under)pants
'muto, -a *ag* (*Med*) dumb; (*emozione, dolore, Cinema*) silent; (*Ling*) silent, mute; (*carta geografica*) blank; **~ per lo stupore** *ecc* speechless with amazement *ecc*
'mutuo, -a *ag* (*reciproco*) mutual ▷ *sm* (*Econ*) (long-term) loan

n

N *abbr* (*= nord*) N
n. *abbr* (*= numero*) no.
'nafta *sf* naphtha; (*per motori diesel*) diesel oil
nafta'lina *sf* (*Chim*) naphthalene; (*tarmicida*) mothballs *pl*
'naia *sf* (*Mil*) *slang term for national service*
na'ïf [na'if] *ag inv* naïve
'nanna *sf* (*linguaggio infantile*): **andare a ~** to go to beddy-byes
'nano, -a *ag, sm/f* dwarf
napole'tano, -a *ag, sm/f* Neapolitan
'Napoli *sf* Naples
nar'ciso [nar'tʃizo] *sm* narcissus
nar'cotico, -ci *sm* narcotic
na'rice [na'ritʃe] *sf* nostril
nar'rare *vt* to tell the story of, recount; **narra'tiva** *sf* (*branca letteraria*) fiction
na'sale *ag* nasal
'nascere ['naʃʃere] *vi* (*bambino*) to be born; (*pianta*) to come *o* spring up; (*fiume*) to rise, have its source; (*sole*) to rise; (*dente*) to come through; (*fig: derivare, conseguire*): **~ da** to arise from, be born out of; **è nata nel 1952** she was born in 1952; **'nascita** *sf* birth
nas'condere *vt* to hide, conceal; **nascondersi** *vpr* to hide; **nascon'diglio** *sm* hiding place; **nascon'dino** *sm* (*gioco*) hide-and-seek; **nas'cosi** *ecc vb vedi* **nascondere**; **nas'costo, -a** *pp di* **nascondere** ▷ *ag* hidden; **di nascosto** secretly
na'sello *sm* (*Zool*) hake
'naso *sm* nose
'nastro *sm* ribbon; (*magnetico, isolante, Sport*) tape; **nastro adesivo** adhesive tape; **nastro trasportatore** conveyor belt
nas'turzio [nas'turtsjo] *sm* nasturtium
na'tale *ag* of one's birth ▷ *sm* (*Rel*): **N~** Christmas; (*giorno della nascita*) birthday; **nata'lizio, -a** *ag* (*del Natale*) Christmas *cpd*
'natica, -che *sf* (*Anat*) buttock
'nato, -a *pp di* **nascere** ▷ *ag* **un attore ~** a born actor; **nata Pieri** née Pieri
na'tura *sf* nature; **pagare in ~** to pay in kind; **natura morta** still life
natu'rale *ag* natural
natural'mente *av* naturally; (*certamente, sì*) of course
natu'rista, -i, e *ag, sm/f* naturist, nudist
naufra'gare *vi* (*nave*) to be wrecked; (*persona*) to be shipwrecked; (*fig*) to fall through; **'naufrago, -ghi** *sm* castaway, shipwreck victim
'nausea *sf* nausea; **nause'ante** *ag* (*odore*) nauseating; (*sapore*) disgusting; (*fig*) sickening
'nautico, -a, -ci, -che *ag* nautical
na'vale *ag* naval
na'vata *sf* (*anche:* **~ centrale**) nave; (*anche:* **~ laterale**) aisle
'nave *sf* ship, vessel; **nave cisterna**

tanker; **nave da guerra** warship; **nave passeggeri** passenger ship
na'vetta *sf* shuttle; (*servizio di collegamento*) shuttle (service)
navi'cella [navi'tʃɛlla] *sf* (*di aerostato*) gondola; **navicella spaziale** spaceship
navi'gare *vi* to sail; **~ in Internet** to surf the Net; **navigazi'one** *sf* navigation
nazio'nale [nattsjo'nale] *ag* national ▷ *sf* (*Sport*) national team; **nazionalità** *sf inv* nationality
nazi'one [nat'tsjone] *sf* nation
naziskin ['na:tsiskin] *sm inv* Nazi skinhead
NB *abbr* (= *nota bene*) NB

PAROLA CHIAVE

ne *pron* **1** (*di lui, lei, loro*) of him/her/them; about him/her/them; **ne riconosco la voce** I recognize his (*o* her) voice
2 (*di questa, quella cosa*) of it; about it; **ne voglio ancora** I want some more (of it *o* them); **non parliamone più!** let's not talk about it any more!
3 (*con valore partitivo*): **hai dei libri? — sì, ne ho** have you any books? — yes, I have (some); **hai del pane? — no, non ne ho** have you any bread? — no, I haven't any; **quanti anni hai? — ne ho 17** how old are you? — I'm 17
▷ *av* (*moto da luogo: da lì*) from there; **ne vengo ora** I've just come from there

né *cong*: **né ... né** neither ... nor; **né l'uno né l'altro lo vuole** neither of them wants it; **non parla né l'italiano né il tedesco** he speaks neither Italian nor German, he doesn't speak either Italian or German; **non piove né nevica** it isn't raining or snowing
ne'anche [ne'anke] *av, cong* not even; **non ... ~** not even; **~ se volesse potrebbe venire** he couldn't come even if he wanted to; **non l'ho visto — ~ io** I didn't see him — neither did I *o* I didn't either; **~ per idea** *o* **sogno!** not on your life!
'nebbia *sf* fog; (*foschia*) mist
necessaria'mente [netʃessarjamɛnte] *av* necessarily
neces'sario, -a [netʃes'sarjo] *ag* necessary
necessità [netʃessi'ta] *sf inv* necessity; (*povertà*) need, poverty
necro'logio [nekro'lɔdʒo] *sm* obituary notice
ne'gare *vt* to deny; (*rifiutare*) to deny, refuse; **~ di aver fatto/che** to deny having done/that; **nega'tivo, -a** *ag, sf, sm* negative
negherò *ecc* [nege'rɔ] *vb vedi* **negare**
negli'gente [negli'dʒɛnte] *ag* negligent, careless
negozi'ante [negot'tsjante] *sm/f* trader, dealer; (*bottegaio*) shopkeeper (BRIT), storekeeper (US)
negozi'are [negot'tsjare] *vt* to negotiate ▷ *vi*: **~ in** to trade *o* deal in; **negozi'ato** *sm* negotiation
ne'gozio [ne'gɔttsjo] *sm* (*locale*) shop (BRIT), store (US)
'negro, -a *ag, sm/f* Negro
ne'mico, -a, -ci, -che *ag* hostile; (*Mil*) enemy *cpd* ▷ *sm/f* enemy; **essere ~ di** to be strongly averse *o* opposed to
nem'meno *av, cong* = **neanche**
'neo *sm* mole; (*fig*) (slight) flaw
'neon *sm* (*Chim*) neon
neo'nato, -a *ag* newborn ▷ *sm/f* newborn baby
neozelan'dese [neoddzelan'dese] *ag* New Zealand *cpd* ▷ *sm/f* New Zealander
'Nepal *sm* **il ~** Nepal
nep'pure *av, cong* = **neanche**
'nero, -a *ag* black; (*scuro*) dark ▷ *sm* black; **il Mar N~** the Black Sea
'nervo *sm* (*Anat*) nerve; (*Bot*) vein;

avere i nervi to be on edge; **dare sui nervi a qn** to get on sb's nerves;
ner'voso, -a *ag* nervous; (*irritabile*) irritable ▷ *sm* (*fam*): **far venire il nervoso a qn** to get on sb's nerves
'nespola *sf* (*Bot*) medlar; (*fig*) blow, punch
'nesso *sm* connection, link

PAROLA CHIAVE

nes'suno, -a (*det: dav sm* **nessun** +C, V, **nessuno** +*s impura, gn, pn, ps, x, z; dav sf* **nessuna** +C, **nessun'** +V) *det* **1** (*non uno*) no; (, *espressione negativa* +) any; **non c'è nessun libro** there isn't any book, there is no book; **nessun altro** no one else, nobody else; **nessun'altra cosa** nothing else; **in nessun luogo** nowhere
2 (*qualche*) any; **hai nessuna obiezione?** do you have any objections?
▷ *pron* **1** (*non uno*) no one, nobody, *espressione negativa* + any(one); (: *cosa*) none, *espressione negativa* + any; **nessuno è venuto, non è venuto nessuno** nobody came
2 (*qualcuno*) anyone, anybody; **ha telefonato nessuno?** did anyone phone?

net'tare *vt* to clean
net'tezza [net'tettsa] *sf* cleanness, cleanliness; **nettezza urbana** cleansing department
'netto, -a *ag* (*pulito*) clean; (*chiaro*) clear, clear-cut; (*deciso*) definite; (*Econ*) net
nettur'bino *sm* dustman (BRIT), garbage collector (US)
neu'trale *ag* neutral
'neutro, -a *ag* neutral; (*Ling*) neuter ▷ *sm* (*Ling*) neuter
'neve *sf* snow; **nevi'care** *vb impers* to snow; **nevi'cata** *sf* snowfall
ne'vischio [ne'viskjo] *sm* sleet
ne'voso, -a *ag* snowy; snow-covered
nevral'gia [nevral'dʒia] *sf* neuralgia
nevras'tenico, -a, -ci, -che *ag* (*Med*) neurasthenic; (*fig*) hot-tempered
ne'vrosi *sf* neurosis
ne'vrotico, -a, ci, che *ag, sm/f* (*anche fig*) neurotic
'nicchia ['nikkja] *sf* niche; (*naturale*) cavity, hollow; **nicchia di mercato** (*Comm*) niche market
nicchi'are [nik'kjare] *vi* to shilly-shally, hesitate
'nichel ['nikel] *sm* nickel
nico'tina *sf* nicotine
'nido *sm* nest; **a ~ d'ape** (*tessuto ecc*) honeycomb *cpd*

PAROLA CHIAVE

ni'ente *pron* **1** (*nessuna cosa*) nothing; **niente può fermarlo** nothing can stop him; **niente di niente** absolutely nothing; **nient'altro** nothing else; **nient'altro che** nothing but, just, only; **niente affatto** not at all, not in the least; **come se niente fosse** as if nothing had happened; **cose da niente** trivial matters; **per niente** (*gratis, invano*) for nothing
2 (*qualcosa*): **hai bisogno di niente?** do you need anything?
3: **non ... niente** nothing; (*espressione negativa* +) anything; **non ho visto niente** I saw nothing, I didn't see anything; **non ho niente da dire** I have nothing *o* haven't anything to say
▷ *sm* nothing; **un bel niente** absolutely nothing; **basta un niente per farla piangere** the slightest thing is enough to make her cry
▷ *av* (*in nessuna misura*): **non ... niente** not ... at all; **non è (per) niente buono** it isn't good at all

Ni'geria [ni'dʒɛrja] *sf* **la ~** Nigeria
'ninfa *sf* nymph

nin'fea *sf* water lily
ninna-'nanna *sf* lullaby
'ninnolo *sm* (*gingillo*) knick-knack
ni'pote *sm/f* (*di zii*) nephew/niece; (*di nonni*) grandson/daughter, grandchild
'nitido, -a *ag* clear; (*specchio*) bright
ni'trire *vi* to neigh
ni'trito *sm* (*di cavallo*) neighing *no pl*; neigh; (*Chim*) nitrite
nitroglice'rina [nitroglitʃe'rina] *sf* nitroglycerine
no *av* (*risposta*) no; **vieni o no?** are you coming or not?; **perché no?** why not?; **lo conosciamo? — tu no ma io sì** do we know him? — you don't but I do; **verrai, no?** you'll come, won't you?
'nobile *ag* noble ▷ *sm/f* noble, nobleman/woman
'nocca, -che *sf* (*Anat*) knuckle
'noccio *ecc* ['nɔttʃo] *vb vedi* **nuocere**
nocci'ola [not'tʃɔla] *ag inv* (*colore*) hazel, light brown ▷ *sf* hazelnut
noccio'lina [nottʃo'lina] *sf*; **nocciolina americana** peanut
'nocciolo ['nɔttʃolo] *sm* (*di frutto*) stone; (*fig*) heart, core
'noce ['notʃe] *sm* (*albero*) walnut tree ▷ *sf* (*frutto*) walnut; **noce di cocco** coconut; **noce moscata** nutmeg
no'cevo *ecc* [no'tʃevo] *vb vedi* **nuocere**
no'civo, -a [no'tʃivo] *ag* harmful, noxious
'nocqui *ecc vb vedi* **nuocere**
'nodo *sm* (*di cravatta, legname, Naut*) knot; (*Aut, Ferr*) junction; (*Med, Astr, Bot*) node; (*fig*: *legame*) bond, tie; (: *punto centrale*) heart, crux; **avere un ~ alla gola** to have a lump in one's throat
no-'global *sm/f* anti-globalization protester ▷ *ag* (*movimento, manifestante*) anti-globalization
'noi *pron* (*soggetto*) we; (*oggetto*: *per dare rilievo, con preposizione*) us; **~ stessi(e)** we ourselves; (*oggetto*) ourselves
'noia *sf* boredom; (*disturbo, impaccio*) bother *no pl*, trouble *no pl*; **avere qn/qc a ~** not to like sb/sth; **mi è venuto a ~** I'm tired of it; **dare ~ a** to annoy; **avere delle noie con qn** to have trouble with sb
noi'oso, -a *ag* boring; (*fastidioso*) annoying, troublesome

> Attenzione! In inglese esiste la parola *noisy*, che però significa *rumoroso*.

noleggi'are [noled'dʒare] *vt* (*prendere a noleggio*) to hire (BRIT), rent; (*dare a noleggio*) to hire out (BRIT), rent (out); (*aereo, nave*) to charter; **vorrei ~ una macchina** I'd like to hire a car;
no'leggio *sm* hire (BRIT), rental; charter
'nomade *ag* nomadic ▷ *sm/f* nomad
'nome *sm* name; (*Ling*) noun; **in/a ~ di** in the name of; **di** *o* **per ~** (*chiamato*) called, named; **conoscere qn di ~** to know sb by name; **nome d'arte** stage name; **nome di battesimo** Christian name; **nome di famiglia** surname
no'mignolo [no'miɲɲolo] *sm* nickname
'nomina *sf* appointment
nomi'nale *ag* nominal; (*Ling*) noun *cpd*
nomi'nare *vt* to name; (*eleggere*) to appoint; (*citare*) to mention
nomina'tivo, -a *ag* (*Ling*) nominative; (*Econ*) registered ▷ *sm* (*Ling*: *anche*: **caso ~**) nominative (case); (*Amm*) name
non *av* not ▷ *prefisso* non-; *vedi* **affatto**; **appena** *ecc*
nonché [non'ke] *cong* (*tanto più, tanto meno*) let alone; (*e inoltre*) as well as
noncu'rante *ag*: **~ (di)** careless (of), indifferent (to)
'nonno, -a *sm/f* grandfather/ mother; (*in senso più familiare*) grandma/grandpa; **i nonni** *smpl* the grandparents
non'nulla *sm inv*: **un ~** nothing, a trifle
'nono, -a *ag, sm* ninth

nonos'tante *prep* in spite of, notwithstanding ▷ *cong* although, even though
nontiscordardimé *sm inv* (*Bot*) forget-me-not
nord *sm* North ▷ *ag inv* north; northern; **il Mare del N~** the North Sea; **nor'dest** *sm* north-east; **nor'dovest** *sm* north-west
'norma *sf* (*principio*) norm; (*regola*) regulation, rule; (*consuetudine*) custom, rule; **a ~ di legge** according to law, as laid down by law; **norme per l'uso** instructions for use; **norme di sicurezza** safety regulations
nor'male *ag* normal; standard *cpd*
normal'mente *av* normally
norve'gese [norve'dʒese] *ag, sm/f, sm* Norwegian
Nor'vegia [nor'vedʒa] *sf*: **la ~** Norway
nostal'gia [nostal'dʒia] *sf* (*di casa, paese*) homesickness; (*del passato*) nostalgia
nos'trano, -a *ag* local; national; home-produced
'nostro, -a *det* **il (la) ~(-a)** *ecc* our ▷ *pron* **il (la) ~(-a)** *ecc* ours ▷ *sm* **il ~** our money; our belongings; **i nostri** our family; our own people; **è dei nostri** he's one of us
'nota *sf* (*segno*) mark; (*comunicazione scritta, Mus*) note; (*fattura*) bill; (*elenco*) list; **degno di ~** noteworthy, worthy of note
no'taio *sm* notary
no'tare *vt* (*segnare: errori*) to mark; (*registrare*) to note (down), write down; (*rilevare, osservare*) to note, notice; **farsi ~** to get o.s. noticed
no'tevole *ag* (*talento*) notable, remarkable; (*peso*) considerable
no'tifica, -che *sf* notification
no'tizia [no'tittsja] *sf* (piece of) news *sg*; (*informazione*) piece of information; **notizi'ario** *sm* (*Radio, TV, Stampa*) news *sg*
'noto, -a *ag* (well-)known
notorietà *sf* fame; notoriety
no'torio, -a *ag* well-known; (*peg*) notorious
not'tambulo, -a *sm/f* night-bird; (*fig*)
not'tata *sf* night
'notte *sf* night; **di ~** at night; (*durante la notte*) in the night, during the night; **notte bianca** sleepless night
not'turno, -a *ag* nocturnal; (*servizio, guardiano*) night *cpd*
no'vanta *num* ninety; **novan'tesimo, -a** *num* ninetieth
'nove *num* nine
nove'cento [nove'tʃɛnto] *num* nine hundred ▷ *sm*: **il N~** the twentieth century
no'vella *sf* (*Letteratura*) short story
no'vello, -a *ag* (*piante, patate*) new; (*insalata, verdura*) early; (*sposo*) newly-married
no'vembre *sm* November
novità *sf inv* novelty; (*innovazione*) innovation; (*cosa originale, insolita*) something new; (*notizia*) (piece of) news *sg*; **le ~ della moda** the latest fashions
nozi'one [not'tsjone] *sf* notion, idea
'nozze ['nɔttse] *sfpl* wedding *sg*, marriage *sg*; **nozze d'argento/d'oro** silver/golden wedding *sg*
'nubile *ag* (*donna*) unmarried, single
'nuca *sf* nape of the neck
nucle'are *ag* nuclear
'nucleo *sm* nucleus; (*gruppo*) team, unit, group; (*Mil, Polizia*) squad; **nucleo familiare** family unit
nu'dista, -i, -e *sm/f* nudist
'nudo, -a *ag* (*persona*) bare, naked, nude; (*membra*) bare, naked; (*montagna*) bare ▷ *sm* (*Arte*) nude
'nulla *pron, av* = **niente** ▷ *sm* **il nulla** nothing
nullità *sf inv* nullity; (*persona*) nonentity
'nullo, -a *ag* useless, worthless; (*Dir*) null (and void); (*Sport*): **incontro ~**

draw
nume'rale *ag, sm* numeral
nume'rare *vt* to number
nu'merico, -a, -ci, -che *ag* numerical
'numero *sm* number; (*romano, arabo*) numeral; (*di spettacolo*) act, turn; **numero civico** house number; **numero di scarpe** shoe size; **numero di telefono** telephone number; **nume'roso, -a** *ag* numerous, many; (*con sostantivo sg*) large
nu'occio *ecc* ['nwɔttʃo] *vb vedi* **nuocere**
nu'ocere ['nwɔtʃere] *vi*: **~ a** to harm, damage
nu'ora *sf* daughter-in-law
nuo'tare *vi* to swim; (*galleggiare: oggetti*) to float; **nuota'tore, -'trice** *sm/f* swimmer; **nu'oto** *sm* swimming
nu'ova *sf* (*notizia*) (piece of) news *sg*; *vedi anche* **nuovo**
nuova'mente *av* again
Nu'ova Ze'landa [-dze'landa] *sf*: **la ~** New Zealand
nu'ovo, -a *ag* new; **di ~** again; **~ fiammante** *o* **di zecca** brand-new
nutri'ente *ag* nutritious, nourishing
nutri'mento *sm* food, nourishment
nu'trire *vt* to feed; (*fig: sentimenti*) to harbour, nurse; **nutrirsi** *vpr* **nutrirsi di** to feed on, to eat
'nuvola *sf* cloud; **nuvo'loso, -a** *ag* cloudy
nuzi'ale [nut'tsjale] *ag* nuptial; wedding *cpd*
'nylon ['nailən] *sm* nylon

O

o (*dav V spesso* **od**) *cong* or; **o ... o** either ... or; **o l'uno o l'altro** either (of them)
O *abbr* (= *ovest*) W
'oasi *sf inv* oasis
obbedi'ente *ecc* = **ubbidiente** *ecc*
obbli'gare *vt* (*costringere*): **~ qn a fare** to force *o* oblige sb to do; (*Dir*) to bind; **obbliga'torio, -a** *ag* compulsory, obligatory; **'obbligo, -ghi** *sm* obligation; (*dovere*) duty; **avere l'obbligo di fare** to be obliged to do; **essere d'obbligo** (*discorso, applauso*) to be called for
o'beso, -a *ag* obese
obiet'tare *vt* **~ che** to object that; **~ su qc** to object to sth, raise objections concerning sth
obiet'tivo, -a *ag* objective ▷ *sm* (*Ottica, Fot*) lens *sg*, objective; (*Mil, fig*) objective
obiet'tore *sm* objector; **obiettore di coscienza** conscientious objector
obiezi'one [objet'tsjone] *sf* objection

obi'torio *sm* morgue, mortuary
o'bliquo, -a *ag* oblique; (*inclinato*) slanting; (*fig*) devious, underhand
oblite'rare *vt* (*biglietto*) to stamp; (*francobollo*) to cancel
oblò *sm inv* porthole
'oboe *sm* (*Mus*) oboe
'oca (*pl* **'oche**) *sf* goose
occasi'one *sf* (*caso favorevole*) opportunity; (*causa, motivo, circostanza*) occasion; (*Comm*) bargain; **d'~** (*a buon prezzo*) bargain *cpd*; (*usato*) secondhand
occhi'aia [ok'kjaja] *sf*: **avere le occhiaie** to have shadows under one's eyes
occhi'ali [ok'kjali] *smpl* glasses, spectacles; **occhiali da sole/da vista** sunglasses/(prescription) glasses
occhi'ata [ok'kjata] *sf* look, glance; **dare un'~ a** to have a look at
occhi'ello [ok'kjɛllo] *sm* buttonhole; (*asola*) eyelet
'occhio ['ɔkkjo] *sm* eye; **~!** careful!, watch out!; **a ~ nudo** with the naked eye; **a quattr'occhi** privately, tête-à-tête; **dare all'~** *o* **nell'~ a qn** to catch sb's eye; **fare l'~ a qc** to get used to sth; **tenere d'~ qn** to keep an eye on sb; **vedere di buon/mal ~ qc** to look favourably/unfavourably on sth
occhio'lino [okkjo'lino] *sm*: **fare l'~ a qn** to wink at sb
occiden'tale [ottʃiden'tale] *ag* western ▷ *sm/f* Westerner
occi'dente [ottʃi'dɛnte] *sm* west; (*Pol*): **l'O~** the West; **a ~** in the west
occor'rente *ag* necessary ▷ *sm* all that is necessary
occor'renza [okkor'rɛntsa] *sf* necessity, need; **all'~** in case of need
oc'correre *vi* to be needed, be required ▷ *vb impers* **occorre farlo** it must be done; **occorre che tu parta** you must leave, you'll have to leave; **mi occorrono i soldi** I need the money

> Attenzione! In inglese esiste il verbo *to occur*, che però significa *succedere*.

oc'culto, -a *ag* hidden, concealed; (*scienze, forze*) occult
occu'pare *vt* to occupy; (*manodopera*) to employ; (*ingombrare*) to occupy, take up; **occuparsi** *vpr* to occupy o.s., keep o.s. busy; (*impiegarsi*) to get a job; **occuparsi di** (*interessarsi*) to take an interest in; (*prendersi cura di*) to look after, take care of; **occu'pato, -a** *ag* (*Mil, Pol*) occupied; (*persona: affaccendato*) busy; (*posto, sedia*) taken; (*toilette, Tel*) engaged; **la linea è occupata** the line's engaged; **è occupato questo posto?** is this seat taken?; **occupazi'one** *sf* occupation; (*impiego, lavoro*) job; (*Econ*) employment
o'ceano [o'tʃeano] *sm* ocean
'ocra *sf* ochre
'OCSE *sigla f* (= *Organizzazione per la Cooperazione e lo Sviluppo Economico*) OECD (*Organization for Economic Cooperation and Development*)
ocu'lare *ag* ocular, eye *cpd*; **testimone ~** eye witness
ocu'lato, -a *ag* (*attento*) cautious, prudent; (*accorto*) shrewd
ocu'lista, -i, -e *sm/f* eye specialist, oculist
odi'are *vt* to hate, detest
odi'erno, -a *ag* today's, of today; (*attuale*) present
'odio *sm* hatred; **avere in ~ qc/qn** to hate *o* detest sth/sb; **odi'oso, -a** *ag* hateful, odious
odo'rare *vt* (*annusare*) to smell; (*profumare*) to perfume, scent ▷ *vi* **~ (di)** to smell (of)
o'dore *sm* smell; **odori** *smpl* (*Cuc*) (aromatic) herbs
of'fendere *vt* to offend; (*violare*) to break, violate; (*insultare*) to insult;

(*ferire*) to hurt; **offendersi** *vpr* (*con senso reciproco*) to insult one another; (*risentirsi*): **offendersi (di)** to take offence (at), be offended (by)
offe'rente *sm* (*in aste*): **al maggior ~** to the highest bidder
of'ferta *sf* offer; (*donazione, anche Rel*) offering; (*in gara d'appalto*) tender; (*in aste*) bid; (*Econ*) supply; **fare un'~** to make an offer; to tender; to bid; **"offerte d'impiego"** "situations vacant"; **offerta speciale** special offer
of'fesa *sf* insult, affront; (*Mil*) attack; (*Dir*) offence; *vedi anche* **offeso**
of'feso, -a *pp di* **offendere** ▷ *ag* offended; (*fisicamente*) hurt, injured ▷ *sm/f* offended party; **essere ~ con qn** to be annoyed with sb; **parte offesa** (*Dir*) plaintiff
offi'cina [offi'tʃina] *sf* workshop
of'frire *vt* to offer; **offrirsi** *vpr* (*proporsi*) to offer (o.s.), volunteer; (*occasione*) to present itself; (*esporsi*): **offrirsi a** to expose o.s. to; **ti offro da bere** I'll buy you a drink
offus'care *vt* to obscure, darken; (*fig: intelletto*) to dim, cloud; (*: fama*) to obscure, overshadow; **offuscarsi** *vpr* to grow dark; to cloud, grow dim; to be obscured
ogget'tivo, -a [oddʒet'tivo] *ag* objective
og'getto [od'dʒɛtto] *sm* object; (*materia, argomento*) subject (matter); **oggetti smarriti** lost property *sg*
'oggi ['ɔddʒi] *av, sm* today; **~ a otto** a week today; **oggigi'orno** *av* nowadays
OGM *sigla m* (= *organismo geneticamente modificato*) GMO
'ogni ['oɲɲi] *det* every, each; (*tutti*) all; (*con valore distributivo*) every; **~ uomo è mortale** all men are mortal; **viene ~ due giorni** he comes every two days; **~ cosa** everything; **ad ~ costo** at all costs, at any price; **in ~ luogo** everywhere; **~ tanto** every so often; **~ volta che** every time that
Ognis'santi [oɲɲis'santi] *sm* All Saints' Day
o'gnuno [oɲ'ɲuno] *pron* everyone, everybody
O'landa *sf* **l'~** Holland; **olan'dese** *ag* Dutch ▷ *sm* (*Ling*) Dutch ▷ *sm/f* Dutchman/woman; **gli Olandesi** the Dutch
ole'andro *sm* oleander
oleo'dotto *sm* oil pipeline
ole'oso, -a *ag* oily; (*che contiene olio*) oil-yielding
ol'fatto *sm* sense of smell
oli'are *vt* to oil
oli'era *sf* oil cruet
Olim'piadi *sfpl* Olympic games; **o'limpico, -a, -ci, -che** *ag* Olympic
'olio *sm* oil; **sott'~** (*Cuc*) in oil; **~ di fegato di merluzzo** cod liver oil; **oli essenziali** essential oils; **olio d'oliva** olive oil; **olio di semi** vegetable oil
o'liva *sf* olive; **o'livo** *sm* olive tree
'olmo *sm* elm
OLP *sigla f* (= *Organizzazione per la Liberazione della Palestina*) PLO
ol'traggio [ol'traddʒo] *sm* outrage; offence, insult; **~ a pubblico ufficiale** (*Dir*) insulting a public official; **oltraggio al pudore** (*Dir*) indecent behaviour
ol'tranza [ol'trantsa] *sf* **a ~** to the last, to the bitter end
'oltre *av* (*più in là*) further; (*di più: aspettare*) longer, more ▷ *prep* (*di là da*) beyond, over, on the other side of; (*più di*) more than, over; (*in aggiunta a*) besides; (*eccetto*): **~ a** except, apart from; **oltrepas'sare** *vt* to go beyond, exceed
o'maggio [o'maddʒo] *sm* (*dono*) gift; (*segno di rispetto*) homage, tribute; **omaggi** *smpl* (*complimenti*) respects; **rendere ~ a** to pay homage *o* tribute to; **in ~** (*copia, biglietto*) complimentary
ombe'lico, -chi *sm* navel

'ombra *sf* (*zona non assolata, fantasma*) shade; (*sagoma scura*) shadow; **sedere all'~** to sit in the shade; **restare nell'~** (*fig*) to remain in obscurity
om'brello *sm* umbrella; **ombrel'lone** *sm* beach umbrella
om'bretto *sm* eye shadow
O.M.C. *sigla f* (= *Organizzazione Mondiale del Commercio*) WTO
ome'lette [ɔmə'lɛt] *sf inv* omelet(te)
ome'lia *sf* (*Rel*) homily, sermon
omeopa'tia *sf* homoeopathy
omertà *sf* conspiracy of silence
o'mettere *vt* to omit, leave out; **~ di fare** to omit *o* fail to do
omi'cida, -i, -e [omi'tʃida] *ag* homicidal, murderous ▷ *sm/f* murderer/eress
omi'cidio [omi'tʃidjo] *sm* murder; **omicidio colposo** culpable homicide
o'misi *ecc vb vedi* **omettere**
omissi'one *sf* omission; **omissione di soccorso** (*Dir*) failure to stop and give assistance
omogeneiz'zato [omodʒeneid'dzato] *sm* baby food
omo'geneo, -a [omo'dʒɛneo] *ag* homogeneous
o'monimo, -a *sm/f* namesake ▷ *sm* (*Ling*) homonym
omosessu'ale *ag, sm/f* homosexual
O.M.S. *sigla f* (= *Organizzazione Mondiale della Sanità*) WHO
On. *abbr* (*Pol*) = **onorevole**
'onda *sf* wave; **mettere** *o* **mandare in ~** (*Radio, TV*) to broadcast; **andare in ~** (*Radio, TV*) to go on the air; **onde corte/lunghe/medie** short/long/medium wave
'onere *sm* burden; **oneri fiscali** taxes
onestà *sf* honesty
o'nesto, -a *ag* (*probo, retto*) honest; (*giusto*) fair; (*casto*) chaste, virtuous
ONG *sigla f inv* (= *Organizzazione Non Governativa*) NGO
onnipo'tente *ag* omnipotent
ono'mastico, -ci *sm* name-day
ono'rare *vt* to honour; (*far onore a*) to do credit to
ono'rario, -a *ag* honorary ▷ *sm* fee
o'nore *sm* honour; **in ~ di** in honour of; **fare gli onori di casa** to play host (*o* hostess); **fare ~ a** to honour; (*pranzo*) to do justice to; (*famiglia*) to be a credit to; **farsi ~** to distinguish o.s.; **ono'revole** *ag* honourable ▷ *sm/f* (*Pol*) ≈ Member of Parliament (BRIT), ≈ Congressman/woman (US)
on'tano *sm* (*Bot*) alder
'O.N.U. ['ɔnu] *sigla f* (= *Organizzazione delle Nazioni Unite*) UN, UNO
o'paco, -a, -chi, -che *ag* (*vetro*) opaque; (*metallo*) dull, matt
o'pale *sm o f* opal
'opera *sf* work; (*azione rilevante*) action, deed, work; (*Mus*) work; opus; (: *melodramma*) opera; (: *teatro*) opera house; (*ente*) institution, organization; **opere pubbliche** public works; **opera d'arte** work of art; **opera lirica** (grand) opera
ope'raio, -a *ag* working-class; workers' ▷ *sm/f* worker; **classe operaia** working class
ope'rare *vt* to carry out, make; (*Med*) to operate on ▷ *vi* to operate, work; (*rimedio*) to act, work; (*Med*) to operate; **operarsi** *vpr* (*Med*) to have an operation; **operarsi d'appendicite** to have one's appendix out; **operazi'one** *sf* operation
ope'retta *sf* (*Mus*) operetta, light opera
opini'one *sf* opinion; **opinione pubblica** public opinion
'oppio *sm* opium
op'pongo *ecc vb vedi* **opporre**
op'porre *vt* to oppose; **opporsi** *vpr* **opporsi (a qc)** to oppose (sth); to object (to sth); **~ resistenza/un rifiuto** to offer resistance/refuse
opportu'nista, -i, -e *sm/f* opportunist
opportunità *sf inv* opportunity;

(*convenienza*) opportuneness, timeliness
oppor'tuno, -a *ag* timely, opportune
op'posi *ecc vb vedi* **opporre**
opposizi'one [oppozit'tsjone] *sf* opposition; (*Dir*) objection
op'posto, -a *pp di* **opporre** ▷ *ag* opposite; (*opinioni*) conflicting ▷ *sm* opposite, contrary; **all'~** on the contrary
oppressi'one *sf* oppression
oppri'mente *ag* (*caldo, noia*) oppressive; (*persona*) tiresome; (*deprimente*) depressing
op'primere *vt* (*premere, gravare*) to weigh down; (*estenuare*: *caldo*) to suffocate, oppress; (*tiranneggiare*: *popolo*) to oppress
op'pure *cong* or (else)
op'tare *vi*: **~ per** to opt for
o'puscolo *sm* booklet, pamphlet
opzi'one [op'tsjone] *sf* option
'ora *sf* (60 *minuti*) hour; (*momento*) time; **che ~ è?, che ore sono?** what time is it?; **a che ~ apre il museo/negozio?** what time does the museum/shop open?; **non veder l'~ di fare** to long to do, look forward to doing; **di buon'~** early; **alla buon'~!** at last!; **~ legale** *o* **estiva** summer time (BRIT), daylight saving time (US); **ora di cena** dinner time; **ora locale** local time; **ora di pranzo** lunchtime; **ora di punta** (*Aut*) rush hour
o'racolo *sm* oracle
o'rale *ag, sm* oral
o'rario, -a *ag* hourly; (*fuso, segnale*) time *cpd*; (*velocità*) per hour ▷ *sm* timetable, schedule; (*di ufficio, visite ecc*) hours *pl*, time(s *pl*); **in ~** on time
o'rata *sf* (*Zool*) sea bream
ora'tore, -'trice *sm/f* speaker; orator
'orbita *sf* (*Astr, Fisica*) orbit; (*Anat*) (eye-)socket
or'chestra [or'kɛstra] *sf* orchestra
orchi'dea [orki'dɛa] *sf* orchid
or'digno [or'diɲɲo] *sm* (*esplosivo*) explosive device
ordi'nale *ag, sm* ordinal
ordi'nare *vt* (*mettere in ordine*) to arrange, organize; (*Comm*) to order; (*prescrivere*: *medicina*) to prescribe; (*comandare*): **posso ~ per favore?** can I order now please?; **~ a qn di fare qc** to order *o* command sb to do sth; (*Rel*) to ordain
ordi'nario, -a *ag* (*comune*) ordinary; everyday; standard; (*grossolano*) coarse, common ▷ *sm* ordinary; (*Ins*: *di università*) full professor
ordi'nato, -a *ag* tidy, orderly
ordinazi'one [ordinat'tsjone] *sf* (*Comm*) order; (*Rel*) ordination; **eseguire qc su ~** to make sth to order
'ordine *sm* order; (*carattere*): **d'~ pratico** of a practical nature; **all'~** (*Comm*: *assegno*) to order; **di prim'~** first-class; **fino a nuovo ~** until further notice; **essere in ~** (*documenti*) to be in order; (*stanza, persona*) to be tidy; **mettere in ~** to put in order, tidy (up); **l'~ pubblico** law and order; **ordini (sacri)** (*Rel*) holy orders; **ordine del giorno** (*di seduta*) agenda; (*Mil*) order of the day; **ordine di pagamento** (*Comm*) order for payment
orec'chino [orek'kino] *sm* earring
o'recchio [o'rekkjo] (*pl(f)* **o'recchie**) *sm* (*Anat*) ear
orecchi'oni [orek'kjoni] *smpl* (*Med*) mumps *sg*
o'refice [o'rɛfitʃe] *sm* goldsmith; jeweller; **orefice'ria** *sf* (*arte*) goldsmith's art; (*negozio*) jeweller's (shop)
'orfano, -a *ag* orphan(ed) ▷ *sm/f* orphan; **~ di padre/madre** fatherless/motherless
orga'netto *sm* barrel organ; (*fam*: *armonica a bocca*) mouth organ; (: *fisarmonica*) accordion
or'ganico, -a, -ci, -che *ag* organic ▷ *sm* personnel, staff

organi'gramma, -i *sm* organization chart
orga'nismo *sm* (*Biol*) organism; (*corpo umano*) body; (*Amm*) body, organism
organiz'zare [organid'dzare] *vt* to organize; **organizzarsi** *vpr* to get organized; **organizzazi'one** *sf* organization
'organo *sm* organ; (*di congegno*) part; (*portavoce*) spokesman, mouthpiece
'orgia, -ge ['ɔrdʒa] *sf* orgy
or'goglio [or'goʎʎo] *sm* pride; **orgogli'oso, -a** *ag* proud
orien'tale *ag* oriental; eastern; east
orienta'mento *sm* positioning; orientation; direction; **senso di ~** sense of direction; **perdere l'~** to lose one's bearings; **orientamento professionale** careers guidance
orientarsi *vpr* to find one's bearings; (*fig*: *tendere*) to tend, lean; (: *indirizzarsi*): **~ verso** to take up, go in for
ori'ente *sm* east; **l'O~** the East, the Orient; **a ~** in the east
o'rigano *sm* oregano
origi'nale [oridʒi'nale] *ag* original; (*bizzarro*) eccentric ▷ *sm* original
origi'nario, -a [oridʒi'narjo] *ag* original; **essere ~ di** to be a native of; (*provenire da*) to originate from; to be native to
o'rigine [o'ridʒine] *sf* origin; **all'~** originally; **d'~ inglese** of English origin; **dare ~ a** to give rise to
origli'are [oriʎ'ʎare] *vi* **~ (a)** to eavesdrop (on)
o'rina *sf* urine
ori'nare *vi* to urinate ▷ *vt* to pass
orizzon'tale [oriddzon'tale] *ag* horizontal
oriz'zonte [orid'dzonte] *sm* horizon
'orlo *sm* edge, border; (*di recipiente*) rim, brim; (*di vestito ecc*) hem
'orma *sf* (*di persona*) footprint; (*di animale*) track; (*impronta, traccia*) mark, trace
or'mai *av* by now, by this time; (*adesso*) now; (*quasi*) almost, nearly
ormeggi'are [ormed'dʒare] *vt* (*Naut*) to moor
or'mone *sm* hormone
ornamen'tale *ag* ornamental, decorative
or'nare *vt* to adorn, decorate; **ornarsi** *vpr* **ornarsi (di)** to deck o.s. (out) (with)
ornitolo'gia [ornitolo'dʒia] *sf* ornithology
'oro *sm* gold; **d'~, in ~** gold *cpd*; **d'~** (*colore, occasione*) golden; (*persona*) marvellous
oro'logio [oro'lɔdʒo] *sm* clock; (*da tasca, da polso*) watch; **orologio al quarzo** quartz watch; **orologio da polso** wristwatch
o'roscopo *sm* horoscope
or'rendo, -a *ag* (*spaventoso*) horrible, awful; (*bruttissimo*) hideous
or'ribile *ag* horrible
or'rore *sm* horror; **avere in ~ qn/qc** to loathe *o* detest sb/sth; **mi fanno ~** I loathe *o* detest them
orsacchi'otto [orsak'kjɔtto] *sm* teddy bear
'orso *sm* bear; **orso bruno/bianco** brown/polar bear
or'taggio [or'taddʒo] *sm* vegetable
or'tensia *sf* hydrangea
or'tica, -che *sf* (stinging) nettle
orti'caria *sf* nettle rash
'orto *sm* vegetable garden, kitchen garden; (*Agr*) market garden (BRIT), truck farm (US); **orto botanico** botanical garden(s) (*pl*)
orto'dosso, -a *ag* orthodox
ortogra'fia *sf* spelling
orto'pedico, -a, -ci, -che *ag* orthopaedic ▷ *sm* orthopaedic specialist
orzai'olo [ordza'jɔlo] *sm* (*Med*) stye
'orzo ['ɔrdzo] *sm* barley
o'sare *vt, vi* to dare; **~ fare** to dare

(to) do
oscenità [oʃʃeni'ta] *sf inv* obscenity
o'sceno, -a [oʃ'ʃeno] *ag* obscene; (*ripugnante*) ghastly
oscil'lare [oʃʃil'lare] *vi* (*pendolo*) to swing; (*dondolare: al vento ecc*) to rock; (*variare*) to fluctuate; (*Tecn*) to oscillate; (*fig*): **~ fra** to waver *o* hesitate between
oscu'rare *vt* to darken, obscure; (*fig*) to obscure; **oscurarsi** *vpr* (*cielo*) to darken, cloud over; (*persona*): **si oscurò in volto** his face clouded over
oscurità *sf* (*vedi ag*) darkness; obscurity
os'curo, -a *ag* dark; (*fig*) obscure; humble, lowly ▷ *sm* **all'~** in the dark; **tenere qn all'~ di qc** to keep sb in the dark about sth
ospe'dale *sm* hospital; **dov'è l'~ più vicino?** where's the nearest hospital?
ospi'tale *ag* hospitable
ospi'tare *vt* to give hospitality to; (*albergo*) to accommodate
'ospite *sm/f* (*persona che ospita*) host/hostess; (*persona ospitata*) guest
os'pizio [os'pittsjo] *sm* (*per vecchi ecc*) home
osser'vare *vt* to observe, watch; (*esaminare*) to examine; (*notare, rilevare*) to notice, observe; (*Dir: la legge*) to observe, respect; (*mantenere: silenzio*) to keep, observe; **far ~ qc a qn** to point sth out to sb; **osservazi'one** *sf* observation; (*di legge ecc*) observance; (*considerazione critica*) observation, remark; (*rimprovero*) reproof; **in osservazione** under observation
ossessio'nare *vt* to obsess, haunt; (*tormentare*) to torment, harass
ossessi'one *sf* obsession
os'sia *cong* that is, to be precise
'ossido *sm* oxide; **ossido di carbonio** carbon monoxide
ossige'nare [ossidʒe'nare] *vt* to oxygenate; (*decolorare*) to bleach; **acqua ossigenata** hydrogen peroxide
os'sigeno *sm* oxygen
'osso (*pl(f)* **ossa**) *sm* bone; **d'~** (*bottone ecc*) of bone, bone *cpd*; **osso di seppia** cuttlebone
ostaco'lare *vt* to block, obstruct
os'tacolo *sm* obstacle; (*Equitazione*) hurdle, jump
os'taggio [os'taddʒo] *sm* hostage
os'tello *sm*: **~ della gioventù** youth hostel
osten'tare *vt* to make a show of, flaunt
oste'ria *sf* inn
os'tetrico, -a, -ci, -che *ag* obstetric ▷ *sm* obstetrician
'ostia *sf* (*Rel*) host; (*per medicinali*) wafer
'ostico, -a, -ci, -che *ag* (*fig*) harsh; hard, difficult; unpleasant
os'tile *ag* hostile
osti'narsi *vpr* to insist, dig one's heels in; **~ a fare** to persist (obstinately) in doing; **osti'nato, -a** *ag* (*caparbio*) obstinate; (*tenace*) persistent, determined
'ostrica, -che *sf* oyster

> Attenzione! In inglese esiste la parola *ostrich*, che però significa *struzzo*.

ostru'ire *vt* to obstruct, block
o'tite *sf* ear infection
ot'tanta *num* eighty
ot'tavo, -a *num* eighth
otte'nere *vt* to obtain, get; (*risultato*) to achieve, obtain
'ottica *sf* (*scienza*) optics *sg*; (*Fot: lenti, prismi ecc*) optics *pl*
'ottico, -a, -ci, -che *ag* (*della vista: nervo*) optic; (*dell'ottica*) optical ▷ *sm* optician
ottima'mente *av* excellently, very well
otti'mismo *sm* optimism; **otti'mista, -i, -e** *sm/f* optimist
'ottimo, -a *ag* excellent, very good
'otto *num* eight

ot'tobre *sm* October
otto'cento [otto'tʃɛnto] *num* eight hundred ▷ *sm* **l'O~** the nineteenth century
ot'tone *sm* brass; **gli ottoni** (*Mus*) the brass
ottu'rare *vt* to close (up); (*dente*) to fill; **il lavandino è otturato** the sink is blocked; **otturarsi** *vpr* to become *o* get blocked up; **otturazi'one** *sf* closing (up); (*dentaria*) filling
ot'tuso, -a *ag* (*Mat, fig*) obtuse; (*suono*) dull
o'vaia *sf* (*Anat*) ovary
o'vale *ag, sm* oval
o'vatta *sf* cotton wool; (*per imbottire*) padding, wadding
'ovest *sm* west
o'vile *sm* pen, enclosure
ovulazi'one [ovulat'tsjone] *sf* ovulation
'ovulo *sm* (*Fisiol*) ovum
o'vunque *av* = **dovunque**
ovvi'are *vi* **~ a** to obviate
'ovvio, -a *ag* obvious
ozi'are [ot'tsjare] *vi* to laze, idle
'ozio ['ɔttsjo] *sm* idleness; (*tempo libero*) leisure; **ore d'~** leisure time; **stare in ~** to be idle
o'zono [o'dzɔno] *sm* ozone

p

P *abbr* (= *parcheggio*) P; (*Aut*: = *principiante*) L
p. *abbr* (= *pagina*) p.
pac'chetto [pak'ketto] *sm* packet; **pacchetto azionario** (*Comm*) shareholding
'pacco, -chi *sm* parcel; (*involto*) bundle; **pacco postale** parcel
'pace ['patʃe] *sf* peace; **darsi ~** to resign o.s.; **fare la ~ con** to make it up with
pa'cifico, -a, -ci, -che [pa'tʃi:fiko] *ag* (*persona*) peaceable; (*vita*) peaceful; (*fig*: *indiscusso*) indisputable; (: *ovvio*) obvious, clear ▷ *sm* **il P~, l'Oceano P~** the Pacific (Ocean)
paci'fista, -i, -e [patʃi'fista] *sm/f* pacifist
PACS *sigla mpl* civil partnership
pa'della *sf* frying pan; (*per infermi*) bedpan
padigli'one [padiʎ'ʎone] *sm* pavilion
'Padova *sf* Padua
'padre *sm* father

pa'drino *sm* godfather
padro'nanza [padro'nantsa] *sf* command, mastery
pa'drone, -a *sm/f* master/mistress; (*proprietario*) owner; (*datore di lavoro*) employer; **essere ~ di sé** to be in control of o.s.; **padrone(a) di casa** master/mistress of the house; (*per gli inquilini*) landlord/lady
pae'saggio [pae'zaddʒo] *sm* landscape
pa'ese *sm* (*nazione*) country, nation; (*terra*) country, land; (*villaggio*) village, (small) town; **i Paesi Bassi** the Netherlands; **paese di provenienza** country of origin
'paga, -ghe *sf* pay, wages *pl*
paga'mento *sm* payment
pa'gare *vt* to pay; (*acquisto, fig*: *colpa*) to pay for; (*contraccambiare*) to repay, pay back ▷ *vi* to pay; **quanto l'hai pagato?** how much did you pay for it?; **posso ~ con la carta di credito?** can I pay by credit card?; **~ in contanti** to pay cash
pa'gella [pa'dʒɛlla] *sf* (*Ins*) report card
pagherò [page'rɔ] *sm inv* acknowledgement of a debt, IOU
'pagina ['padʒina] *sf* page; **pagine bianche** phone book, telephone directory; **pagine gialle** Yellow Pages
'paglia ['paʎʎa] *sf* straw
pagli'accio [paʎ'ʎattʃo] *sm* clown
pagli'etta [paʎ'ʎetta] *sf* (*cappello per uomo*) (straw) boater; (*per tegami ecc*) steel wool
pa'gnotta [paɲ'ɲɔtta] *sf* round loaf
'paio (*pl(f)* **'paia**) *sm* pair; **un ~ di** (*alcuni*) a couple of
'Pakistan *sm* **il ~** Pakistan
'pala *sf* shovel; (*di remo, ventilatore, elica*) blade; (*di ruota*) paddle
pa'lato *sm* palate
pa'lazzo [pa'lattso] *sm* (*reggia*) palace; (*edificio*) building; **palazzo di giustizia** courthouse; **palazzo dello sport** sports stadium
'palco, -chi *sm* (*Teatro*) box; (*tavolato*) platform, stand; (*ripiano*) layer
palco'scenico, -ci [palkoʃ'ʃɛniko] *sm* (*Teatro*) stage
pa'lese *ag* clear, evident
Pales'tina *sf* **la ~** Palestine
palesti'nese *ag, sm/f* Palestinian
pa'lestra *sf* gymnasium; (*esercizio atletico*) exercise, training; (*fig*) training ground, school
pa'letta *sf* spade; (*per il focolare*) shovel; (*del capostazione*) signalling disc
pa'letto *sm* stake, peg; (*spranga*) bolt
'palio *sm* (*gara*): **il P~** *horse race run at Siena*; **mettere qc in ~** to offer sth as a prize

PALIO

The **palio** is a horse race which takes place in a number of Italian towns, the most famous being the one in Siena. This is usually held twice a year on July 2nd and August 16th in the Piazza del Campo in Siena. 10 of the 17 **contrade** or districts take part, each represented by a horse and rider. The winner is the first horse to complete the course, whether it has a rider or not.

'palla *sf* ball; (*pallottola*) bullet; **palla di neve** snowball; **palla ovale** rugby ball; **pallaca'nestro** *sf* basketball; **palla'mano** *sf* handball; **pallanu'oto** *sf* water polo; **palla'volo** *sf* volleyball
palleggi'are [palled'dʒare] *vi* (*Calcio*) to practise with the ball; (*Tennis*) to knock up
pallia'tivo *sm* palliative; (*fig*) stopgap measure
'pallido, -a *ag* pale
pal'lina *sf* (*bilia*) marble
pallon'cino [pallon'tʃino] *sm*

balloon; (*lampioncino*) Chinese lantern
pal'lone *sm* (*palla*) ball; (*Calcio*) football; (*aerostato*) balloon; **gioco del ~** football
pal'lottola *sf* pellet; (*proiettile*) bullet
'palma *sf* (*Anat*) = **palmo**; (*Bot, simbolo*) palm; **palma da datteri** date palm
'palmo *sm* (*Anat*) palm; **restare con un ~ di naso** to be badly disappointed
'palo *sm* (*legno appuntito*) stake; (*sostegno*) pole; **fare da** *o* **il ~** (*fig*) to act as look-out
palom'baro *sm* diver
pal'pare *vt* to feel, finger
'palpebra *sf* eyelid
pa'lude *sf* marsh, swamp
pan'cetta [pan'tʃetta] *sf* (*Cuc*) bacon
pan'china [pan'kina] *sf* garden seat; (*di giardino pubblico*) (park) bench
'pancia, -ce ['pantʃa] *sf* belly, stomach; **mettere** *o* **fare ~** to be getting a paunch; **avere mal di ~** to have stomachache *o* a sore stomach
panci'otto [pan'tʃɔtto] *sm* waistcoat
'pancreas *sm inv* pancreas
'panda *sm inv* panda
pande'mia *sf* pandemic
'pane *sm* bread; (*pagnotta*) loaf (of bread); (*forma*): **un ~ di burro** a pat of butter; **guadagnarsi il ~** to earn one's living; **pane a cassetta** sliced bread; **pane di Spagna** sponge cake; **pane integrale** wholemeal bread; **pane tostato** toast
panette'ria *sf* (*forno*) bakery; (*negozio*) baker's (shop), bakery
panetti'ere, -a *sm/f* baker
panet'tone *sm a kind of spiced brioche with sultanas, eaten at Christmas*
pangrat'tato *sm* breadcrumbs *pl*
'panico, -a, -ci, -che *ag, sm* panic
pani'ere *sm* basket
pani'ficio [pani'fitʃo] *sm* (*forno*) bakery; (*negozio*) baker's (shop), bakery
pa'nino *sm* roll; **panino caldo** toasted sandwich; **panino imbottito** filled roll; sandwich
'panna *sf* (*Cuc*) cream; (*Tecn*) = **panne**; **panna da cucina** cooking cream; **panna montata** whipped cream
'panne *sf inv*: **essere in ~** (*Aut*) to have broken down
pan'nello *sm* panel; **pannello solare** solar panel
'panno *sm* cloth; **panni** *smpl* (*abiti*) clothes; **mettiti nei miei panni** (*fig*) put yourself in my shoes
pan'nocchia [pan'nɔkkja] *sf* (*di mais ecc*) ear
panno'lino *sm* (*per bambini*) nappy (BRIT), diaper (US)
panno'lone *sm* incontinence pad
pano'rama, -i *sm* panorama
panta'loni *smpl* trousers (BRIT), pants (US), pair *sg*, of trousers *o* pants
pan'tano *sm* bog
pan'tera *sf* panther
pan'tofola *sf* slipper
'Papa, -i *sm* pope
papà *sm inv* dad(dy)
pa'pavero *sm* poppy
'pappa *sf* baby cereal; **pappa reale** royal jelly
pappa'gallo *sm* parrot; (*fig: uomo*) Romeo, wolf
pa'rabola *sf* (*Mat*) parabola; (*Rel*) parable
para'bolico, -a, ci, che *ag* (*Mat*) parabolic; *vedi anche* **antenna**
para'brezza [para'breddza] *sm inv* (*Aut*) windscreen (BRIT), windshield (US)
paraca'dute *sm inv* parachute
para'diso *sm* paradise
parados'sale *ag* paradoxical
para'fulmine *sm* lightning conductor
pa'raggi [pa'raddʒi] *smpl*: **nei ~** in the vicinity, in the neighbourhood
parago'nare *vt*: **~ con/a** to compare

with/to
para'gone *sm* comparison; (*esempio analogo*) analogy, parallel; **reggere al ~** to stand comparison
pa'ragrafo *sm* paragraph
pa'ralisi *sf* paralysis
paral'lelo, -a *ag* parallel ▷ *sm* (*Geo*) parallel; (*comparazione*): **fare un ~ tra** to draw a parallel between
para'lume *sm* lampshade
pa'rametro *sm* parameter
para'noia *sf* paranoia; **para'noico, -a, -ci, -che** *ag, sm/f* paranoid
para'occhi [para'ɔkki] *smpl* blinkers
paraolim'piadi *sfpl* paralympics
para'petto *sm* balustrade
pa'rare *vt* (*addobbare*) to adorn, deck; (*proteggere*) to shield, protect; (*scansare*: *colpo*) to parry; (*Calcio*) to save ▷ *vi* **dove vuole andare a ~?** what are you driving at?
pa'rata *sf* (*Sport*) save; (*Mil*) review, parade
para'urti *sm inv* (*Aut*) bumper
para'vento *sm* folding screen; **fare da ~ a qn** (*fig*) to shield sb
par'cella [par'tʃɛlla] *sf* account, fee (*of lawyer etc*)
parcheggi'are [parked'dʒare] *vt* to park; **posso ~ qui?** can I park here?; **parcheggiatore, -trice** [parkeddʒa'tore] *sm/f* (*Aut*) parking attendant
par'cheggio *sm* parking *no pl*; (*luogo*) car park; (*singolo posto*) parking space
par'chimetro [par'kimetro] *sm* parking meter
'parco, -chi *sm* park; (*spazio per deposito*) depot; (*complesso di veicoli*) fleet
par'cometro *sm* (pay-and-display) ticket machine
pa'recchio, -a [pa'rekkjo] *det* quite a lot of; (*tempo*) quite a lot of, a long
pareggi'are [pared'dʒare] *vt* to make equal; (*terreno*) to level, make level; (*bilancio, conti*) to balance ▷ *vi* (*Sport*) to draw; **pa'reggio** *sm* (*Econ*) balance; (*Sport*) draw
pa'rente *sm/f* relative, relation

> Attenzione! In inglese esiste la parola *parent*, che però significa *genitore*.

paren'tela *sf* (*vincolo di sangue, fig*) relationship
pa'rentesi *sf* (*segno grafico*) bracket, parenthesis; (*frase incisa*) parenthesis; (*digressione*) parenthesis, digression
pa'rere *sm* (*opinione*) opinion; (*consiglio*) advice, opinion; **a mio ~** in my opinion ▷ *vi* to seem, appear ▷ *vb impers* **pare che** it seems *o* appears that, they say that; **mi pare che** it seems to me that; **mi pare di sì** I think so; **fai come ti pare** do as you like; **che ti pare del mio libro?** what do you think of my book?
pa'rete *sf* wall
'pari *ag inv* (*uguale*) equal, same; (*in giochi*) equal; drawn, tied; (*Mat*) even ▷ *sm inv* (*Pol*: *di Gran Bretagna*) peer ▷ *sm/f inv* peer, equal; **copiato ~ ~** copied word for word; **alla ~** on the same level; **ragazza alla ~** au pair girl; **mettersi alla ~ con** to place o.s. on the same level as; **mettersi in ~ con** to catch up with; **andare di ~ passo con qn** to keep pace with sb
Pa'rigi [pa'ridʒi] *sf* Paris
pari'gino, -a [pari'dʒino] *ag, sm/f* Parisian
parità *sf* parity, equality; (*Sport*) draw, tie
parlamen'tare *ag* parliamentary ▷ *sm/f* ≈ Member of Parliament (BRIT), ≈ Congressman/woman (US) ▷ *vi* to negotiate, parley
parla'mento *sm* parliament

PARLAMENTO

The Italian **Parlamento** is made up of two chambers, the **Camera** dei deputati and the **Senato**. Parliamentary elections are held every 5 years.

parlan'tina (*fam*) *sf* talkativeness; **avere ~** to have the gift of the gab

par'lare *vi* to speak, talk; (*confidare cose segrete*) to talk ▷ *vt* to speak; **~ (a qn) di** to speak *o* talk (to sb) about; **posso ~ con...?** can I speak to ...?; **parla italiano?** do you speak Italian?; **non parlo inglese** I don't speak English

parmigi'ano [parmi'dʒano] *sm* (*grana*) Parmesan (cheese)

pa'rola *sf* word; (*facoltà*) speech; **parole** *sfpl* (*chiacchiere*) talk *sg*; **chiedere la ~** to ask permission to speak; **prendere la ~** to take the floor; **parola d'onore** word of honour; **parola d'ordine** (*Mil*) password; **parole incrociate** crossword (puzzle) *sg*; **paro'laccia, -ce** *sf* bad word, swearword

parrò *ecc vb vedi* **parere**

par'rocchia [par'rɔkkja] *sf* parish; parish church

par'rucca, -che *sf* wig

parrucchi'ere, -a [parruk'kjɛre] *sm/f* hairdresser ▷ *sm* barber

'parte *sf* part; (*lato*) side; (*quota spettante a ciascuno*) share; (*direzione*) direction; (*Pol*) party; faction; (*Dir*) party; **a ~** *ag* separate ▷ *av* separately; **scherzi a ~** joking aside; **a ~ ciò** apart from that; **da ~** (*in disparte*) to one side, aside; **d'altra ~** on the other hand; **da ~ di** (*per conto di*) on behalf of; **da ~ mia** as far as I'm concerned, as for me; **da ~ a ~** right through; **da ogni ~** on all sides, everywhere; (*moto da luogo*) from all sides; **da nessuna ~** nowhere; **da questa ~** (*in questa direzione*) this way; **prendere ~ a qc** to take part in sth; **mettere da ~** to put aside; **mettere qn a ~ di** to inform sb of

parteci'pare [partetʃi'pare] *vi* **~ a** to take part in, participate in; (*utili ecc*) to share in; (*spese ecc*) to contribute to; (*dolore, successo di qn*) to share (in)

parteggi'are [parted'dʒare] *vi*: **~ per** to side with, be on the side of

par'tenza [par'tɛntsa] *sf* departure; (*Sport*) start; **essere in ~** to be about to leave, be leaving

parti'cipio [parti'tʃipjo] *sm* participle

partico'lare *ag* (*specifico*) particular; (*proprio*) personal, private; (*speciale*) special, particular; (*caratteristico*) distinctive, characteristic; (*fuori dal comune*) peculiar ▷ *sm* detail, particular; **in ~** in particular, particularly

par'tire *vi* to go, leave; (*allontanarsi*) to go (*o* drive ecc) away *o* off; (*petardo, colpo*) to go off; (*fig*: *avere inizio, Sport*) to start; **sono partita da Roma alle 7** I left Rome at 7; **a che ora parte il treno/l'autobus?** what time does the train/bus leave?; **il volo parte da Ciampino** the flight leaves from Ciampino; **a ~ da** from

par'tita *sf* (*Comm*) lot, consignment; (*Econ*: *registrazione*) entry, item; (*Carte, Sport*: *gioco*) game; (: *competizione*) match, game; **partita di caccia** hunting party; **partita IVA** VAT registration number

par'tito *sm* (*Pol*) party; (*decisione*) decision, resolution; (*persona da maritare*) match

'parto *sm* (*Med*) delivery, (child)birth; labour

'parvi *ecc vb vedi* **parere**

parzi'ale [par'tsjale] *ag* (*limitato*) partial; (*non obiettivo*) biased, partial

pasco'lare *vt, vi* to graze

'pascolo *sm* pasture

'Pasqua *sf* Easter; **Pas'quetta** *sf* Easter Monday

pas'sabile *ag* fairly good, passable

pas'saggio [pas'saddʒo] *sm* passing *no pl*, passage; (*traversata*) crossing *no pl*, passage; (*luogo, prezzo della traversata, brano di libro ecc*) passage; (*su veicolo altrui*) lift (BRIT), ride; (*Sport*) pass; **di ~** (*persona*) passing through; **può darmi un ~ fino alla stazione?** can you give me a lift to the station?; **passaggio a livello** level (BRIT) *o* grade (US) crossing; **passaggio pedonale** pedestrian crossing

passamon'tagna [passamon'taɲɲa] *sm inv* balaclava

pas'sante *sm/f* passer-by ▷ *sm* loop

passa'porto *sm* passport

pas'sare *vi* (*andare*) to go; (*veicolo, pedone*) to pass (by), go by; (*fare una breve sosta*: *postino ecc*) to come, call; (: *amico*: *per fare una visita*) to call *o* drop in; (*sole, aria, luce*) to get through; (*trascorrere*: *giorni, tempo*) to pass, go by; (*fig*: *proposta di legge*) to be passed; (: *dolore*) to pass, go away; (*Carte*) to pass ▷ *vt* (*attraversare*) to cross; (*trasmettere*: *messaggio*): **~ qc a qn** to pass sth on to sb; (*dare*): **~ qc a qn** to pass sth to sb, give sb sth; (*trascorrere*: *tempo*) to spend; (*superare*: *esame*) to pass; (*triturare*: *verdura*) to strain; (*approvare*) to pass, approve; (*oltrepassare, sorpassare*: *anche fig*) to go beyond, pass; (*fig*: *subire*) to go through; **mi passa il sale/l'olio per favore?** could you pass the salt/oil please?; **~ da ... a** to pass from ... to; **~ di padre in figlio** to be handed down *o* to pass from father to son; **~ per** (*anche fig*) to go through; **~ per stupido/un genio** to be taken for a fool/a genius; **~ sopra** (*anche fig*) to pass over; **~ attraverso** (*anche fig*) to go through; **~ alla storia** to pass into history; **~ a un esame** to go up (to the next class) after an exam; **~ inosservato** to go unnoticed; **~ di moda** to go out of fashion; **le passo il Signor X** (*al telefono*) here is Mr X; I'm putting you through to Mr X; **lasciar ~ qn/qc** to let sb/sth through; **come te la passi?** how are you getting on *o* along?

passa'tempo *sm* pastime, hobby

pas'sato, -a *ag* past; (*sfiorito*) faded ▷ *sm* past; (*Ling*) past (tense); **passato prossimo/remoto** (*Ling*) present perfect/past historic; **passato di verdura** (*Cuc*) vegetable purée

passeg'gero, -a [passed'dʒɛro] *ag* passing ▷ *sm/f* passenger

passeggi'are [passed'dʒare] *vi* to go for a walk; (*in veicolo*) to go for a drive; **passeggi'ata** *sf* walk; drive; (*luogo*) promenade; **fare una passeggiata** to go for a walk (*o* drive); **passeg'gino** *sm* pushchair (BRIT), stroller (US)

passe'rella *sf* footbridge; (*di nave, aereo*) gangway; (*pedana*) catwalk

'passero *sm* sparrow

passi'one *sf* passion

pas'sivo, -a *ag* passive ▷ *sm* (*Ling*) passive; (*Econ*) debit; (: *complesso dei debiti*) liabilities *pl*

'passo *sm* step; (*andatura*) pace; (*rumore*) (foot)step; (*orma*) footprint; (*passaggio, fig*: *brano*) passage; (*valico*) pass; **a ~ d'uomo** at walking pace; **~ (a) ~** step by step; **fare due** *o* **quattro passi** to go for a walk *o* a stroll; **di questo ~** at this rate; **"passo carraio"** "vehicle entrance — keep clear"

'pasta *sf* (*Cuc*) dough; (: *impasto per dolce*) pastry; (: *anche*: **~ alimentare**) pasta; (*massa molle di materia*) paste; (*fig*: *indole*) nature; **paste** *sfpl* (*pasticcini*) pastries; **pasta in brodo** noodle soup; **pasta sfoglia** puff pastry *o* paste (US)

pastasci'utta [pastaʃˈʃutta] *sf* pasta

pas'tella *sf* batter

pas'tello *sm* pastel

pasticce'ria [pastittʃe'ria] *sf* (*pasticcini*) pastries *pl*, cakes *pl*; (*negozio*) cake shop; (*arte*) confectionery

pasticci'ere, -a [pastit'tʃɛre] *sm/f* pastrycook; confectioner

pastic'cino [pastit'tʃino] *sm* petit four

pas'ticcio [pas'tittʃo] *sm* (*Cuc*) pie; (*lavoro disordinato, imbroglio*) mess; **trovarsi nei pasticci** to get into trouble

pas'tiglia [pas'tiʎʎa] *sf* pastille, lozenge

pas'tina *sf small pasta shapes used in soup*

'pasto *sm* meal

pas'tore *sm* shepherd; (*Rel*) pastor, minister; (*anche:* **cane ~**) sheepdog; **pastore tedesco** (*Zool*) Alsatian, German shepherd

pa'tata *sf* potato; **patate fritte** chips (BRIT), French fries; **pata'tine** *sfpl* (potato) crisps; **patatine fritte** chips

pa'tente *sf* licence; **patente di guida** driving licence (BRIT), driver's license (US); **patente a punti** *driving licence with penalty points*

> Attenzione! In inglese esiste la parola *patent*, che però significa *brevetto*.

paternità *sf* paternity, fatherhood

pa'tetico, -a, -ci, -che *ag* pathetic; (*commovente*) moving, touching

pa'tibolo *sm* gallows *sg*, scaffold

'patina *sf* (*su rame ecc*) patina; (*sulla lingua*) fur, coating

pa'tire *vt, vi* to suffer

pa'tito, -a *sm/f* enthusiast, fan, lover

patolo'gia [patolo'dʒia] *sf* pathology

'patria *sf* homeland

pa'trigno [pa'triɲɲo] *sm* stepfather

patri'monio *sm* estate, property; (*fig*) heritage

pa'trono *sm* (*Rel*) patron saint; (*socio di patronato*) patron; (*Dir*) counsel

patteggi'are [patted'dʒare] *vt, vi* to negotiate; (*Dir*) to plea-bargain

patti'naggio [patti'naddʒo] *sm* skating; **pattinaggio a rotelle/sul ghiaccio** roller-/ice-skating

patti'nare *vi* to skate; **~ sul ghiaccio** to ice-skate; **pattina'tore, -'trice** *sm/f* skater; **'pattino** *sm* skate; (*di slitta*) runner; (*Aer*) skid; (*Tecn*) sliding block; **pattini in linea** Rollerblades®; **pattini da ghiaccio/a rotelle** ice/roller skates

'patto *sm* (*accordo*) pact, agreement; (*condizione*) term, condition; **a ~ che** on condition that

pat'tuglia [pat'tuʎʎa] *sf* (*Mil*) patrol

pattu'ire *vt* to reach an agreement on

pattumi'era *sf* (dust)bin (BRIT), ashcan (US)

pa'ura *sf* fear; **aver ~ di/di fare/che** to be frightened *o* afraid of/of doing/that; **far ~ a** to frighten; **per ~ di/che** for fear of/that; **pau'roso, -a** *ag* (*che fa paura*) frightening; (*che ha paura*) fearful, timorous

'pausa *sf* (*sosta*) break; (*nel parlare, Mus*) pause

pavi'mento *sm* floor

> Attenzione! In inglese esiste la parola *pavement*, che però significa *marciapiede*.

pa'vone *sm* peacock

pazien'tare [pattsjen'tare] *vi* to be patient

pazi'ente [pat'tsjɛnte] *ag, sm/f* patient; **pazi'enza** *sf* patience

paz'zesco, -a, -schi, -sche [pat'tsesko] *ag* mad, crazy

paz'zia [pat'tsia] *sf* (*Med*) madness, insanity; (*azione*) folly; (*di azione, decisione*) madness, folly

'pazzo, -a ['pattso] *ag* (*Med*) mad, insane; (*strano*) wild, mad ▷ *sm/f* madman/woman; **~ di** (*gioia, amore ecc*) mad *o* crazy with; **~ per qc/qn** mad *o* crazy about sth/sb

PC [pit'tʃi] *sigla m inv* (*= personal computer*) PC; **PC portatile** laptop

pec'care *vi* to sin; (*fig*) to err

pec'cato *sm* sin; **è un ~ che** it's a pity that; **che ~!** what a shame *o* pity!

peccherò *ecc* [pekke'rɔ] *vb vedi* **peccare**

'pece ['petʃe] *sf* pitch

Pe'chino [pe'kino] *sf* Beijing
'pecora *sf* sheep; **peco'rino** *sm* sheep's milk cheese
pe'daggio [pe'daddʒo] *sm* toll
pedago'gia [pedago'dʒia] *sf* pedagogy, educational methods *pl*
peda'lare *vi* to pedal; (*andare in bicicletta*) to cycle
pe'dale *sm* pedal
pe'dana *sf* footboard; (*Sport: nel salto*) springboard; (*: nella scherma*) piste
pe'dante *ag* pedantic ▷ *sm/f* pedant
pe'data *sf* (*impronta*) footprint; (*colpo*) kick; **prendere a pedate qn/qc** to kick sb/sth
pedi'atra, -i, -e *sm/f* paediatrician
pedi'cure *sm/f inv* chiropodist
pe'dina *sf* (*della dama*) draughtsman (BRIT), draftsman (US); (*fig*) pawn
pedi'nare *vt* to shadow, tail
pe'dofilo, -a *ag, sm/f* paedophile
pedo'nale *ag* pedestrian
pe'done, -a *sm/f* pedestrian ▷ *sm* (*Scacchi*) pawn
'peggio ['pɛddʒo] *av, ag inv* worse ▷ *sm o f*: **il** *o* **la ~** the worst; **alla ~** at worst, if the worst comes to the worst; **peggio'rare** *vt* to make worse, worsen ▷ *vi* to grow worse, worsen; **peggi'ore** *ag* (*comparativo*) worse; (*superlativo*) worst ▷ *sm/f*: **il(la) peggiore** the worst (person)
'pegno ['peɲɲo] *sm* (*Dir*) security, pledge; (*nei giochi di società*) forfeit; (*fig*) pledge, token; **dare in ~ qc** to pawn sth
pe'lare *vt* (*spennare*) to pluck; (*spellare*) to skin; (*sbucciare*) to peel; (*fig*) to make pay through the nose
pe'lato, -a *ag*: **pomodori pelati** tinned tomatoes
'pelle *sf* skin; (*di animale*) skin, hide; (*cuoio*) leather; **avere la ~ d'oca** to have goose pimples *o* goose flesh
pellegri'naggio [pellegri'naddʒo] *sm* pilgrimage
pelle'rossa (*pl* **pelli'rosse**) *sm/f* Red Indian
pelli'cano *sm* pelican
pel'liccia, -ce [pel'littʃa] *sf* (*mantello di animale*) coat, fur; (*indumento*) fur coat; **pelliccia ecologica** fake fur
pel'licola *sf* (*membrana sottile*) film, layer; (*Fot, Cinema*) film
'pelo *sm* hair; (*pelame*) coat, hair; (*pelliccia*) fur; (*di tappeto*) pile; (*di liquido*) surface; **per un ~: per un ~ non ho perduto il treno** I very nearly missed the train; **c'è mancato un ~ che affogasse** he escaped drowning by the skin of his teeth; **pe'loso, -a** *ag* hairy
'peltro *sm* pewter
pe'luche [pə'lyʃ] *sm* plush; **giocattoli di ~** soft toys
pe'luria *sf* down
'pena *sf* (*Dir*) sentence; (*punizione*) punishment; (*sofferenza*) sadness *no pl*, sorrow; (*fatica*) trouble *no pl*, effort; (*difficoltà*) difficulty; **far ~** to be pitiful; **mi fai ~** I feel sorry for you; **prendersi** *o* **darsi la ~ di fare** to go to the trouble of doing; **pena di morte** death sentence; **pena pecuniaria** fine; **pe'nale** *ag* penal
pen'dente *ag* hanging; leaning ▷ *sm* (*ciondolo*) pendant; (*orecchino*) drop earring
'pendere *vi* (*essere appeso*): **~ da** to hang from; (*essere inclinato*) to lean; (*fig: incombere*): **~ su** to hang over
pen'dio, -'dii *sm* slope, slant; (*luogo in pendenza*) slope
'pendola *sf* pendulum clock
pendo'lare *sm/f* commuter
pendo'lino *sm* *high-speed train*
pene'trante *ag* piercing, penetrating
pene'trare *vi* to come *o* get in ▷ *vt* to penetrate; **~ in** to enter; (*proiettile*) to penetrate; (*: acqua, aria*) to go *o* come into
penicil'lina [penitʃil'lina] *sf*

penicillin
pe'nisola *sf* peninsula
penitenzi'ario [peniten'tsjarjo] *sm* prison
'penna *sf* (*di uccello*) feather; (*per scrivere*) pen; **penne** *sfpl* (*Cuc*) quills (*type of pasta*); **penna a sfera** ballpoint pen; **penna stilografica** fountain pen
penna'rello *sm* felt(-tip) pen
pen'nello *sm* brush; (*per dipingere*) (paint)brush; **a ~** (*perfettamente*) to perfection, perfectly; **pennello per la barba** shaving brush
pe'nombra *sf* half-light, dim light
pen'sare *vi* to think ▷ *vt* to think; (*inventare, escogitare*) to think out; **~ a** to think of; (*amico, vacanze*) to think of *o* about; (*problema*) to think about; **~ di fare qc** to think of doing sth; **ci penso io** I'll see to *o* take care of it
pensi'ero *sm* thought; (*modo di pensare, dottrina*) thinking *no pl*; (*preoccupazione*) worry, care, trouble; **stare in ~ per qn** to be worried about sb; **pensie'roso, -a** *ag* thoughtful
'pensile *ag* hanging
pensio'nato, -a *sm/f* pensioner
pensi'one *sf* (*al prestatore di lavoro*) pension; (*vitto e alloggio*) board and lodging; (*albergo*) boarding house; **andare in ~** to retire; **mezza ~** half board; **pensione completa** full board
pen'tirsi *vpr* **~ di** to repent of; (*rammaricarsi*) to regret, be sorry for
'pentola *sf* pot; **pentola a pressione** pressure cooker
pe'nultimo, -a *ag* last but one (BRIT), next to last, penultimate
penzo'lare [pendzo'lare] *vi* to dangle, hang loosely
'pepe *sm* pepper; **pepe in grani/macinato** whole/ground pepper
peperon'cino [peperon'tʃino] *sm* chilli pepper
pepe'rone *sm* pepper, capsicum; (*piccante*) chili
pe'pita *sf* nugget

PAROLA CHIAVE

per *prep* **1** (*moto attraverso luogo*) through; **i ladri sono passati per la finestra** the thieves got in (*o* out) through the window; **l'ho cercato per tutta la casa** I've searched the whole house *o* all over the house for it
2 (*moto a luogo*) for, to; **partire per la Germania/il mare** to leave for Germany/the sea; **il treno per Roma** the Rome train, the train for *o* to Rome
3 (*stato in luogo*): **seduto/sdraiato per terra** sitting/lying on the ground
4 (*tempo*) for; **per anni/lungo tempo** for years/a long time; **per tutta l'estate** throughout the summer, all summer long; **lo rividi per Natale** I saw him again at Christmas; **lo faccio per lunedì** I'll do it for Monday
5 (*mezzo, maniera*) by; **per lettera/via aerea/ferrovia** by letter/airmail/rail; **prendere qn per un braccio** to take sb by the arm
6 (*causa, scopo*) for; **assente per malattia** absent because of *o* through *o* owing to illness; **ottimo per il mal di gola** excellent for sore throats
7 (*limitazione*) for; **è troppo difficile per lui** it's too difficult for him; **per quel che mi riguarda** as far as I'm concerned; **per poco che sia** however little it may be; **per questa volta ti perdono** I'll forgive you this time
8 (*prezzo, misura*) for; (*distributivo*) a, per; **venduto per 3 milioni** sold for 3 million; **1 euro per persona** 1 euro a *o* per person; **uno per volta** one at a time; **uno per uno** one by one; **5 per cento** 5 per cent; **3 per 4 fa 12** 3 times 4 equals 12; **dividere/moltiplicare 12 per 4** to divide/multiply 12 by 4
9 (*in qualità di*) as; (*al posto di*) for; **avere qn per professore** to have sb

as a teacher; **ti ho preso per Mario** I mistook you for Mario, I thought you were Mario; **dare per morto qn** to give sb up for dead
10 (*seguito da vb: finale*): **per fare qc** so as to do sth, in order to do sth; (*: causale*): **per aver fatto qc** for having done sth; (*: consecutivo*): **è abbastanza grande per andarci da solo** he's big enough to go on his own

'pera *sf* pear
per'bene *ag inv* respectable, decent ▷ *av* (*con cura*) properly, well
percentu'ale [pertʃentu'ale] *sf* percentage
perce'pire [pertʃe'pire] *vt* (*sentire*) to perceive; (*ricevere*) to receive

PAROLA CHIAVE

perché [per'ke] *av* why; **perché no?** why not?; **perché non vuoi andarci?** why don't you want to go?; **spiegami perché l'hai fatto** tell me why you did it
▷ *cong* 1 (*causale*) because; **non posso uscire perché ho da fare** I can't go out because *o* as I've a lot to do
2 (*finale*) in order that, so that; **te lo do perché tu lo legga** I'm giving it to you so (that) you can read it
3 (*consecutivo*): **è troppo forte perché si possa batterlo** he's too strong to be beaten
▷ *sm inv* reason; **il perché di** the reason for

perciò [per'tʃɔ] *cong* so, for this (*o* that) reason
per'correre *vt* (*luogo*) to go all over; (*: paese*) to travel up and down, go all over; (*distanza*) to cover
per'corso, -a *pp di* **percorrere** ▷ *sm* (*tragitto*) journey; (*tratto*) route
percu'otere *vt* to hit, strike
percussi'one *sf* percussion; **strumenti a ~** (*Mus*) percussion instruments
'perdere *vt* to lose; (*lasciarsi sfuggire*) to miss; (*sprecare: tempo, denaro*) to waste ▷ *vi* to lose; (*serbatoio ecc*) to leak; **perdersi** *vpr* (*smarrirsi*) to get lost; (*svanire*) to disappear, vanish; **mi sono perso** I'm lost; **ho perso il portafoglio/passaporto** I've lost my wallet/passport; **abbiamo perso il treno** we missed our train; **saper ~** to be a good loser; **lascia ~!** forget it!, never mind!
perdigi'orno [perdi'dʒorno] *sm/f inv* idler, waster
'perdita *sf* loss; (*spreco*) waste; (*fuoriuscita*) leak; **siamo in ~** (*Comm*) we are running at a loss; **a ~ d'occhio** as far as the eye can see
perdo'nare *vt* to pardon, forgive; (*scusare*) to excuse, pardon
per'dono *sm* forgiveness; (*Dir*) pardon
perduta'mente *av* desperately, passionately
pe'renne *ag* eternal, perpetual, perennial; (*Bot*) perennial
perfetta'mente *av* perfectly; **sai ~ che ...** you know perfectly well that ...
per'fetto, -a *ag* perfect ▷ *sm* (*Ling*) perfect (tense)
perfeziona'mento [perfettsjona'mento] *sm* **~ (di)** improvement (in), perfection (of); **corso di ~** proficiency course
perfezio'nare [perfettsjo'nare] *vt* to improve, perfect; **perfezionarsi** *vpr* to improve
perfezi'one [perfet'tsjone] *sf* perfection
per'fino *av* even
perfo'rare *vt* to perforate, to punch a hole (*o* holes) in; (*banda, schede*) to punch; (*trivellare*) to drill
perga'mena *sf* parchment
perico'lante *ag* precarious
pe'ricolo *sm* danger; **mettere in ~** to endanger, put in danger;

perico'loso, -a *ag* dangerous
perife'ria *sf* (*di città*) outskirts *pl*
pe'rifrasi *sf* circumlocution
pe'rimetro *sm* perimeter
peri'odico, -a, -ci, -che *ag* periodic(al); (*Mat*) recurring ▷ *sm* periodical
pe'riodo *sm* period
peripe'zie [peripet'tsie] *sfpl* ups and downs, vicissitudes
pe'rito, -a *ag* expert, skilled ▷ *sm/f* expert; (*agronomo, navale*) surveyor; **perito chimico** qualified chemist
peri'zoma, -i [peri'dzoma] *sm* G-string
'perla *sf* pearl; **per'lina** *sf* bead
perlus'trare *vt* to patrol
perma'loso, -a *ag* touchy
perma'nente *ag* permanent ▷ *sf* permanent wave, perm; **perma'nenza** *sf* permanence; (*soggiorno*) stay
perme'are *vt* to permeate
per'messo, -a *pp di* **permettere** ▷ *sm* (*autorizzazione*) permission, leave; (*dato a militare, impiegato*) leave; (*licenza*) licence, permit; (*Mil: foglio*) pass; **~?, è ~?** (*posso entrare?*) may I come in?; (*posso passare?*) excuse me; **permesso di lavoro/pesca** work/fishing permit; **permesso di soggiorno** residence permit
per'mettere *vt* to allow, permit; **~ a qn qc/di fare qc** to allow sb sth/to do sth; **permettersi qc/di fare qc** to allow o.s. sth/to do sth; (*avere la possibilità*) to afford sth/to do sth
per'misi *ecc vb vedi* **permettere**
per'nacchia [per'nakkja] (*fam*) *sf* **fare una ~** to blow a raspberry
per'nice [per'nitʃe] *sf* partridge
'perno *sm* pivot
pernot'tare *vi* to spend the night, stay overnight
'pero *sm* pear tree
però *cong* (*ma*) but; (*tuttavia*) however, nevertheless
perpendico'lare *ag, sf* perpendicular
per'plesso, -a *ag* perplexed; uncertain, undecided
perqui'sire *vt* to search; **perquisizi'one** *sf* (police) search
'perse *ecc vb vedi* **perdere**
persecuzi'one [persekut'tsjone] *sf* persecution
persegui'tare *vt* to persecute
perseve'rante *ag* persevering
'persi *ecc vb vedi* **perdere**
persi'ana *sf* shutter; **persiana avvolgibile** roller shutter
per'sino *av* = **perfino**
persis'tente *ag* persistent
'perso, -a *pp di* **perdere**
per'sona *sf* person; (*qualcuno*): **una ~** someone, somebody; (*espressione interrogativa*) anyone *o* anybody
perso'naggio [perso'naddʒo] *sm* (*persona ragguardevole*) personality, figure; (*tipo*) character, individual; (*Letteratura*) character
perso'nale *ag* personal ▷ *sm* staff; personnel; (*figura fisica*) build
personalità *sf inv* personality
perspi'cace [perspi'katʃe] *ag* shrewd, discerning
persu'adere *vt*: **~ qn (di qc/a fare)** to persuade sb (of sth/to do)
per'tanto *cong* (*quindi*) so, therefore
'pertica, -che *sf* pole
perti'nente *ag* **~ (a)** relevant (to), pertinent (to)
per'tosse *sf* whooping cough
perturbazi'one [perturbat'tsjone] *sf* disruption; perturbation; **perturbazione atmosferica** atmospheric disturbance
per'vadere *vt* to pervade
per'verso, -a *ag* depraved; perverse
perver'tito, -a *sm/f* pervert
p.es. *abbr* (= *per esempio*) e.g.
pe'sante *ag* heavy; **è troppo ~** it's too heavy
pe'sare *vt* to weigh ▷ *vi* (*avere un peso*) to weigh; (*essere pesante*) to

be heavy; (*fig*) to carry weight; **~ su** (*fig*) to lie heavy on; to influence; to hang over; **pesarsi** *vpr* to weigh o.s.; **~ le parole** to weigh one's words; **~ sulla coscienza** to weigh on sb's conscience; **mi pesa ammetterlo** I don't like admitting it; **tutta la responsabilità pesa su di lui** all the responsibility rests on him; **è una situazione che mi pesa** I find the situation difficult; **il suo parere pesa molto** his opinion counts for a lot

'pesca (*pl* **pesche**: *frutto*) *sf* peach; (*il pescare*) fishing; **andare a ~** to go fishing; **~ con la lenza** angling; **pesca di beneficenza** (*lotteria*) lucky dip

pes'care *vt* (*pesce*) to fish for; to catch; (*qc nell'acqua*) to fish out; (*fig*: *trovare*) to get hold of, find; **andare a ~** to go fishing

pesca'tore *sm* fisherman; angler

'pesce ['peʃʃe] *sm* fish *gen inv*; **Pesci** (*dello zodiaco*) Pisces; **pesce d'aprile!** April Fool!; **pesce rosso** goldfish; **pesce spada** swordfish; **pesce'cane** *sm* shark

pesche'reccio [peske'rettʃo] *sm* fishing boat

pesche'ria [peske'ria] *sf* fishmonger's (shop) (BRIT), fish store (US)

pescherò *ecc* [peske'rɔ] *vb vedi* **pescare**

'peso *sm* weight; (*Sport*) shot; **rubare sul ~** to give short weight; **essere di ~ a qn** (*fig*) to be a burden to sb; **peso lordo/netto** gross/net weight; **peso massimo/medio** (*Pugilato*) heavy/ middleweight

pessi'mismo *sm* pessimism; **pessi'mista, -i, -e** *ag* pessimistic ▷ *sm/f* pessimist

'pessimo, -a *ag* very bad, awful

pes'tare *vt* to tread on, trample on; (*sale, pepe*) to grind; (*uva, aglio*) to crush; (*fig*: *picchiare*): **~ qn** to beat sb up

'peste *sf* plague; (*persona*) nuisance, pest

pes'tello *sm* pestle

'petalo *sm* (*Bot*) petal

pe'tardo *sm* firecracker, banger (BRIT)

petizi'one [petit'tsjone] *sf* petition

petroli'era *sf* (*nave*) oil tanker

pe'trolio *sm* oil, petroleum; (*per lampada, fornello*) paraffin

> Attenzione! In inglese esiste la parola *petrol* che però significa *benzina*.

pettego'lare *vi* to gossip

pettego'lezzo [pettego'leddzo] *sm* gossip *no pl*; **fare pettegolezzi** to gossip

pet'tegolo, -a *ag* gossipy ▷ *sm/f* gossip

petti'nare *vt* to comb (the hair of); **pettinarsi** *vpr* to comb one's hair; **pettina'tura** *sf* (*acconciatura*) hairstyle

'pettine *sm* comb; (*Zool*) scallop

petti'rosso *sm* robin

'petto *sm* chest; (*seno*) breast, bust; (*Cuc*: *di carne bovina*) brisket; (: *di pollo ecc*) breast; **a doppio ~** (*abito*) double-breasted

petu'lante *ag* insolent

'pezza ['pɛttsa] *sf* piece of cloth; (*toppa*) patch; (*cencio*) rag, cloth

pez'zente [pet'tsɛnte] *sm/f* beggar

'pezzo ['pɛttso] *sm* (*gen*) piece; (*brandello, frammento*) piece, bit; (*di macchina, arnese ecc*) part; (*Stampa*) article; (*di tempo*): **aspettare un ~** to wait quite a while *o* some time; **in** *o* **a pezzi** in pieces; **andare in pezzi** to break into pieces; **un bel ~ d'uomo** a fine figure of a man; **abito a due pezzi** two-piece suit; **pezzo di cronaca** (*Stampa*) report; **pezzo grosso** (*fig*) bigwig; **pezzo di ricambio** spare part

pi'accio *ecc* ['pjattʃo] *vb vedi* **piacere**

pia'cente [pja'tʃɛnte] *ag* attractive

pia'cere [pja'tʃere] *vi* to please; **una ragazza che piace** a likeable girl;

an attractive girl; **~ a: mi piace** I like it; **quei ragazzi non mi piacciono** I don't like those boys; **gli piacerebbe andare al cinema** he would like to go to the cinema ▷ *sm* pleasure; (*favore*) favour; **"~!"** (*nelle presentazioni*) "pleased to meet you!"; **~ (di conoscerla)** nice to meet you; **con ~** certainly, with pleasure; **per ~!** please; **fare un ~ a qn** to do sb a favour; **pia'cevole** *ag* pleasant, agreeable

pi'acqui *ecc vb vedi* **piacere**

pi'aga, -ghe *sf* (*lesione*) sore; (*ferita*: *anche fig*) wound; (*fig*: *flagello*) scourge, curse; (: *persona*) pest, nuisance

piagnuco'lare [pjaɲɲuko'lare] *vi* to whimper

pianeggi'ante [pjaned'dʒante] *ag* flat, level

piane'rottolo *sm* landing

pia'neta *sm* (*Astr*) planet

pi'angere ['pjandʒere] *vi* to cry, weep; (*occhi*) to water ▷ *vt* to cry, weep; (*lamentare*) to bewail, lament; **~ la morte di qn** to mourn sb's death

pianifi'care *vt* to plan

pia'nista, -i, -e *sm/f* pianist

pi'ano, -a *ag* (*piatto*) flat, level; (*Mat*) plane; (*chiaro*) clear, plain ▷ *av* (*adagio*) slowly; (*a bassa voce*) softly; (*con cautela*) slowly, carefully ▷ *sm* (*Mat*) plane; (*Geo*) plain; (*livello*) level, plane; (*di edificio*) floor; (*programma*) plan; (*Mus*) piano; **a che ~ si trova?** what floor is it on?; **pian ~** very slowly; (*poco a poco*) little by little; **in primo/secondo ~** in the foreground/background; **di primo ~** (*fig*) prominent, high-ranking

piano'forte *sm* piano, pianoforte

piano'terra *sm inv* ground floor

pi'ansi *ecc vb vedi* **piangere**

pi'anta *sf* (*Bot*) plant; (*Anat*: *anche*: **~ del piede**) sole (of the foot); (*grafico*) plan; (*topografica*) map; **in ~ stabile** on the permanent staff; **pian'tare** *vt* to plant; (*conficcare*) to drive *o* hammer in; (*tenda*) to put up, pitch; (*fig*: *lasciare*) to leave, desert; **piantarsi** *vpr* **piantarsi davanti a qn** to plant o.s. in front of sb; **piantala!** (*fam*) cut it out!

pianter'reno *sm* = **pianoterra**

pia'nura *sf* plain

pi'astra *sf* plate; (*di pietra*) slab; (*di fornello*) hotplate; **panino alla ~** ≈ toasted sandwich; **piastra di registrazione** tape deck

pias'trella *sf* tile

pias'trina *sf* (*Mil*) identity disc

piatta'forma *sf* (*anche fig*) platform

piat'tino *sm* saucer

pi'atto, -a *ag* flat; (*fig*: *scialbo*) dull ▷ *sm* (*recipiente, vivanda*) dish; (*portata*) course; (*parte piana*) flat (part); **piatti** *smpl* (*Mus*) cymbals; **piatto fondo** soup dish; **piatto forte** main course; **piatto del giorno** dish of the day, plat du jour; **piatto del giradischi** turntable; **piatto piano** dinner plate

pi'azza ['pjattsa] *sf* square; (*Comm*) market; **far ~ pulita** to make a clean sweep; **piazza d'armi** (*Mil*) parade ground; **piaz'zale** *sm* (large) square

piaz'zola [pjat'tsɔla] *sf* (*Aut*) lay-by; (*di tenda*) pitch

pic'cante *ag* hot, pungent; (*fig*) racy; biting

pic'chetto [pik'ketto] *sm* (*Mil, di scioperanti*) picket; (*di tenda*) peg

picchi'are [pik'kjare] *vt* (*persona*: *colpire*) to hit, strike; (: *prendere a botte*) to beat (up); (*battere*) to beat; (*sbattere*) to bang ▷ *vi* (*bussare*) to knock; (: *con forza*) to bang; (*colpire*) to hit, strike; (*sole*) to beat down; **picchi'ata** *sf* (*Aer*) dive

'picchio ['pikkjo] *sm* woodpecker

pic'cino, -a [pit'tʃino] *ag* tiny, very small

picci'one [pit'tʃone] *sm* pigeon

'picco, -chi *sm* peak; **a ~** vertically

'piccolo, -a *ag* small; (*oggetto, mano, di età*: *bambino*) small, little; (*dav* *sostantivo*: *di breve durata*: *viaggio*) short; (*fig*) mean, petty ▷ *sm/f* child, little one

pic'cone *sm* pick(-axe)

pic'cozza [pik'kɔttsa] *sf* ice-axe

pic'nic *sm inv* picnic

pi'docchio [pi'dɔkkjo] *sm* louse

pi'ede *sm* foot; (*di mobile*) leg; **in piedi** standing; **a piedi** on foot; **a piedi nudi** barefoot; **su due piedi** (*fig*) at once; **prendere ~** (*fig*) to gain ground, catch on; **sul ~ di guerra** (*Mil*) ready for action; **piede di porco** crowbar

pi'ega, -ghe *sf* (*piegatura, Geo*) fold; (*di gonna*) pleat; (*di pantaloni*) crease; (*grinza*) wrinkle, crease; **prendere una brutta ~** (*fig*) to take a turn for the worse

pie'gare *vt* to fold; (*braccia, gambe, testa*) to bend ▷ *vi* to bend; **piegarsi** *vpr* to bend; (*fig*): **piegarsi (a)** to yield (to), submit (to)

piegherò *ecc* [pjege'rɔ] *vb vedi* **piegare**

pie'ghevole *ag* pliable, flexible; (*porta*) folding

Pie'monte *sm*: **il ~** Piedmont

pi'ena *sf* (*di fiume*) flood, spate

pi'eno, -a *ag* full; (*muro, mattone*) solid ▷ *sm* (*colmo*) height, peak; (*carico*) full load; **~ di** full of; **in ~ giorno** in broad daylight; **il ~, per favore** (*Aut*) fill it up, please

piercing ['pirsing] *sm* piercing; **farsi il ~ all'ombelico** to have one's navel pierced

pietà *sf* pity; (*Rel*) piety; **senza ~** pitiless, merciless; **avere ~ di** (*compassione*) to pity, feel sorry for; (*misericordia*) to have pity *o* mercy on

pie'tanza [pje'tantsa] *sf* dish, course

pie'toso, -a *ag* (*compassionevole*) pitying, compassionate; (*che desta pietà*) pitiful

pi'etra *sf* stone; **pietra preziosa** precious stone, gem

'piffero *sm* (*Mus*) pipe

pigi'ama, -i [pi'dʒama] *sm* pyjamas *pl*

pigli'are [piʎ'ʎare] *vt* to take, grab; (*afferrare*) to catch

'pigna ['piɲɲa] *sf* pine cone

pi'gnolo, -a [piɲ'ɲɔlo] *ag* pernickety

pi'grizia [pi'grittsja] *sf* laziness

'pigro, -a *ag* lazy

PIL *sigla m* (= *prodotto interno lordo*) GDP

'pila *sf* (*catasta, di ponte*) pile; (*Elettr*) battery; (*torcia*) torch (BRIT), flashlight

pi'lastro *sm* pillar

'pile ['pail] *sm inv* fleece

'pillola *sf* pill; **prendere la ~** to be on the pill

pi'lone *sm* (*di ponte*) pier; (*di linea elettrica*) pylon

pi'lota, -i, -e *sm/f* pilot; (*Aut*) driver ▷ *ag inv* pilot *cpd*; **pilota automatico** automatic pilot

pinaco'teca, -che *sf* art gallery

pi'neta *sf* pinewood

ping-'pong [pɪŋ'pɔŋ] *sm* table tennis

pingu'ino *sm* (*Zool*) penguin

'pinna *sf* (*di pesce*) fin; (*di cetaceo, per nuotare*) flipper

'pino *sm* pine (tree); **pi'nolo** *sm* pine kernel

'pinza ['pintsa] *sf* pliers *pl*; (*Med*) forceps *pl*; (*Zool*) pincer

pinzette [pin'tsette] *sfpl* tweezers

pi'oggia, -ge ['pjɔddʒa] *sf* rain; **pioggia acida** acid rain

pi'olo *sm* peg; (*di scala*) rung

piom'bare *vi* to fall heavily; (*gettarsi con impeto*): **~ su** to fall upon, assail ▷ *vt* (*dente*) to fill; **piomba'tura** *sf* (*di dente*) filling

piom'bino *sm* (*sigillo*) (lead) seal; (*del filo a piombo*) plummet; (*Pesca*) sinker

pi'ombo *sm* (*Chim*) lead; **a ~** (*cadere*) straight down; **senza ~** (*benzina*) unleaded

pioni'ere, -a *sm/f* pioneer

pi'oppo *sm* poplar

pi'overe *vb impers* to rain ▷ *vi* (*fig*: *scendere dall'alto*) to rain down; (*lettere, regali*) to pour into; **pioviggi'nare**

vb impers to drizzle; **pio'voso, -a** *ag* rainy
pi'ovra *sf* octopus
pi'ovve *ecc vb vedi* **piovere**
'pipa *sf* pipe
pipì (*fam*) *sf*: **fare ~** to have a wee (wee)
pipis'trello *sm* (*Zool*) bat
pi'ramide *sf* pyramid
pi'rata, -i *sm* pirate; **pirata della strada** hit-and-run driver; **pirata informatica** hacker
Pire'nei *smpl* **i ~** the Pyrenees
pi'romane *sm/f* pyromaniac; arsonist
pi'roscafo *sm* steamer, steamship
pisci'are [piʃʃare] (*fam!*) *vi* to piss (*!*), pee (*!*)
pi'scina [piʃʃina] *sf* (swimming) pool; (*stabilimento*) (swimming) baths *pl*
pi'sello *sm* pea
piso'lino *sm* nap
'pista *sf* (*traccia*) track, trail; (*di stadio*) track; (*di pattinaggio*) rink; (*da sci*) run; (*Aer*) runway; (*di circo*) ring; **pista da ballo** dance floor
pis'tacchio [pis'takkjo] *sm* pistachio (tree); pistachio (nut)
pis'tola *sf* pistol, gun
pis'tone *sm* piston
pi'tone *sm* python
pit'tore, -'trice *sm/f* painter; **pitto'resco, -a, -schi, -sche** *ag* picturesque
pit'tura *sf* painting; **pittu'rare** *vt* to paint

PAROLA CHIAVE

più *av* **1** (*in maggiore quantità*) more; **più del solito** more than usual; **in più, di più** more; **ne voglio di più** I want some more; **ci sono 3 persone in** *o* **di più** there are 3 more *o* extra people; **più o meno** more or less; **per di più** (*inoltre*) what's more, moreover
2 (*comparativo*) more; (*se monosillabo, spesso*): + ...er; **più ... di/che** more ... than; **lavoro più di te/Paola** I work harder than you/Paola; **è più intelligente che ricco** he's more intelligent than rich
3 (*superlativo*) most; (*se monosillabo, spesso*): + ...est; **il più grande/ intelligente** the biggest/most intelligent; **è quello che compro più spesso** that's the one I buy most often; **al più presto** as soon as possible; **al più tardi** at the latest
4 (*negazione*): **non ... più** no more, no longer; **non ho più soldi** I've got no more money, I don't have any more money; **non lavoro più** I'm no longer working, I don't work any more; **a più non posso** (*gridare*) at the top of one's voice; (*correre*) as fast as one can
5 (*Mat*) plus; **4 più 5 fa 9** 4 plus 5 equals 9; **più 5 gradi** 5 degrees above freezing, plus 5
▷ *prep* plus ▷ *ag inv* **1**: **più ... (di)** more ... (than); **più denaro/tempo** more money/time; **più persone di quante ci aspettassimo** more people than we expected
2 (*numerosi, diversi*) several; **l'aspettai per più giorni** I waited for it for several days
▷ *sm* **1** (*la maggior parte*): **il più è fatto** most of it is done
2 (*Mat*) plus (sign)
3: **i più** the majority

pi'uma *sf* feather; **piu'mino** *sm* (eider)down; (*per letto*) eiderdown; (: *tipo danese*) duvet, continental quilt; (*giacca*) quilted jacket (*with goose-feather padding*); (*per cipria*) powder puff; (*per spolverare*) feather duster
piut'tosto *av* rather; **~ che** (*anziché*) rather than
'pizza ['pittsa] *sf* pizza; **pizze'ria** *sf* *place where pizzas are made, sold or eaten*
pizzi'care [pittsi'kare] *vt* (*stringere*) to nip, pinch; (*pungere*) to sting; to bite; (*Mus*) to pluck ▷ *vi* (*prudere*) to itch, be itchy; (*cibo*) to be hot *o* spicy

'pizzico, -chi ['pittsiko] *sm* (*pizzicotto*) pinch, nip; (*piccola quantità*) pinch, dash; (*d'insetto*) sting; bite

pizzi'cotto [pittsi'kɔtto] *sm* pinch, nip

'pizzo ['pittso] *sm* (*merletto*) lace; (*barbetta*) goatee beard

plagi'are [pla'dʒare] *vt* (*copiare*) to plagiarize

plaid [plɛd] *sm inv* (travelling) rug (BRIT), lap robe (US)

pla'nare *vi* (*Aer*) to glide

'plasma *sm* plasma

plas'mare *vt* to mould, shape

'plastica, -che *sf* (*arte*) plastic arts *pl*; (*Med*) plastic surgery; (*sostanza*) plastic; **plastica facciale** face lift

'platano *sm* plane tree

pla'tea *sf* (*Teatro*) stalls *pl*

'platino *sm* platinum

plau'sibile *ag* plausible

pleni'lunio *sm* full moon

'plettro *sm* plectrum

pleu'rite *sf* pleurisy

'plico, -chi *sm* (*pacco*) parcel; **in ~ a parte** (*Comm*) under separate cover

plo'tone *sm* (*Mil*) platoon; **plotone d'esecuzione** firing squad

plu'rale *ag, sm* plural

PM *abbr* (*Pol*) = **Pubblico Ministero**; (= *Polizia Militare*) MP (*Military Police*)

PMI *sigla fpl*: **Piccole e Medie Imprese** SME (*Small and Medium-sized Enterprises*)

pneu'matico, -a, -ci, -che *ag* inflatable; pneumatic ▷ *sm* (*Aut*) tyre (BRIT), tire (US)

po' *av, sm vedi* **poco**

PAROLA CHIAVE

'poco, -a, -chi, -che *ag* (*quantità*) little, not much; (*numero*) few, not many; **poco pane/denaro/spazio** little *o* not much bread/money/space; **poche persone/idee** few *o* not many people/ideas; **ci vediamo tra poco** (*sottinteso: tempo*) see you soon

▷ *av* **1** (*in piccola quantità*) little, not much; (*numero limitato*) few, not many; **guadagna poco** he doesn't earn much, he earns little

2 (*con ag, av*) (a) little, not very; **sta poco bene** he isn't very well; **è poco più vecchia di lui** she's a little *o* slightly older than him

3 (*tempo*): **poco dopo/prima** shortly afterwards/before; **il film dura poco** the film doesn't last very long; **ci vediamo molto poco** we don't see each other very often, we hardly ever see each other

4: **un po'** a little, a bit; **è un po' corto** it's a little *o* a bit short; **arriverà fra un po'** he'll arrive shortly *o* in a little while

5: **a dir poco** to say the least; **a poco a poco** little by little; **per poco non cadevo** I nearly fell; **è una cosa da poco** it's nothing, it's of no importance; **una persona da poco** a worthless person

▷ *pron* (a) little

po'dere *sm* (*Agr*) farm

'podio *sm* dais, platform; (*Mus*) podium

po'dismo *sm* (*Sport*) track events *pl*

poe'sia *sf* (*arte*) poetry; (*componimento*) poem

po'eta, -'essa *sm/f* poet/poetess

poggi'are [pod'dʒare] *vt* to lean, rest; (*posare*) to lay, place; **poggia'testa** *sm inv* (*Aut*) headrest

'poggio ['pɔddʒo] *sm* hillock, knoll

'poi *av* then; (*alla fine*) finally, at last; **e ~** (*inoltre*) and besides; **questa ~ (è bella)!** (*ironico*) that's a good one!

poiché [poi'ke] *cong* since, as

'poker *sm* poker

po'lacco, -a, -chi, -che *ag* Polish ▷ *sm/f* Pole

po'lare *ag* polar

po'lemica, -che *sf* controversy

po'lemico, -a, -ci, -che *ag*

polemic(al), controversial
po'lenta *sf* (*Cuc*) *sort of thick porridge made with maize flour*
'polio(mie'lite) *sf* polio(myelitis)
'polipo *sm* polyp
polisti'rolo *sm* polystyrene
po'litica, -che *sf* politics *sg*; (*linea di condotta*) policy; **politica'mente** *av* politically; **politicamente corretto** politically correct
po'litico, -a, -ci, -che *ag* political ▷ *sm/f* politician
poli'zia [polit'tsia] *sf* police; **polizia giudiziaria** ≈ Criminal Investigation Department (BRIT), ≈ Federal Bureau of Investigation (US); **polizia stradale** traffic police; **polizi'esco, -a, -schi, -sche** *ag* police *cpd*; (*film, romanzo*) detective *cpd*; **polizi'otto** *sm* policeman; **cane poliziotto** police dog; **donna poliziotto** policewoman; **poliziotto di quartiere** local police officer

POLIZIA DI STATO

The function of the **polizia di stato** is to maintain public order, to uphold the law and prevent and investigate crime. It is a civil body, reporting to the Minister of the Interior.

'polizza ['pɔlittsa] *sf* (*Comm*) bill; **~ di assicurazione** insurance policy; **polizza di carico** bill of lading
pol'laio *sm* henhouse
'pollice ['pɔllitʃe] *sm* thumb
'polline *sm* pollen
'pollo *sm* chicken
pol'mone *sm* lung; **polmone d'acciaio** (*Med*) iron lung; **polmo'nite** *sf* pneumonia; **polmonite atipica** SARS
'polo *sm* (*Geo, Fisica*) pole; (*gioco*) polo; **polo nord/sud** North/South Pole
Po'lonia *sf* **la ~** Poland
'polpa *sf* flesh, pulp; (*carne*) lean meat
pol'paccio [pol'pattʃo] *sm* (*Anat*) calf
polpas'trello *sm* fingertip
pol'petta *sf* (*Cuc*) meatball
'polpo *sm* octopus
pol'sino *sm* cuff
'polso *sm* (*Anat*) wrist; (*pulsazione*) pulse; (*fig: forza*) drive, vigour
pol'trire *vi* to laze about
pol'trona *sf* armchair; (*Teatro: posto*) seat in the front stalls (BRIT) *o* orchestra (US)
'polvere *sf* dust; (*sostanza ridotta minutissima*) powder, dust; **latte in ~** dried *o* powdered milk; **caffè in ~** instant coffee; **sapone in ~** soap powder; **polvere da sparo/pirica** gunpowder
po'mata *sf* ointment, cream
po'mello *sm* knob
pome'riggio [pome'riddʒo] *sm* afternoon
'pomice ['pɔmitʃe] *sf* pumice
'pomo *sm* (*mela*) apple; (*ornamentale*) knob; (*di sella*) pommel; **pomo d'Adamo** (*Anat*) Adam's apple
pomo'doro *sm* tomato; **pomodori pelati** skinned tomatoes
'pompa *sf* pump; (*sfarzo*) pomp (and ceremony); **pompe funebri** funeral parlour *sg* (BRIT), undertaker's *sg*; **pompa di benzina** petrol (BRIT) *o* gas (US) pump; (*distributore*) filling *o* gas (US) station; **pom'pare** *vt* to pump; (*trarre*) to pump out; (*gonfiare d'aria*) to pump up
pom'pelmo *sm* grapefruit
pompi'ere *sm* fireman
po'nente *sm* west
pongo, poni *ecc vb vedi* **porre**
'ponte *sm* bridge; (*di nave*) deck; (*: anche:* **~ di comando**) bridge; (*impalcatura*) scaffold; **fare il ~** (*fig*) to take the extra day off (*between 2 public holidays*); **governo ~** interim government; **ponte aereo** airlift;

ponte levatoio drawbridge; **ponte sospeso** suspension bridge
pon'tefice [pon'tɛfitʃe] *sm* (*Rel*) pontiff
'popcorn ['pɔpkɔːn] *sm inv* popcorn
popo'lare *ag* popular; (*quartiere, clientela*) working-class ▷ *vt* (*rendere abitato*) to populate; **popolarsi** *vpr* to fill with people, get crowded; **popolazi'one** *sf* population
'popolo *sm* people
'poppa *sf* (*di nave*) stern; (*seno*) breast
porcel'lana [portʃel'lana] *sf* porcelain, china; piece of china
porcel'lino, -a [portʃel'lino] *sm/f* piglet; **porcellino d'India** guinea pig
porche'ria [porke'ria] *sf* filth, muck; (*fig: oscenità*) obscenity; (*: azione disonesta*) dirty trick; (*: cosa mal fatta*) rubbish
por'cile [por'tʃile] *sm* pigsty
por'cino, -a [por'tʃino] *ag* of pigs, pork *cpd* ▷ *sm* (*fungo*) *type of edible mushroom*
'porco, -ci *sm* pig; (*carne*) pork
porcos'pino *sm* porcupine
'porgere ['pɔrdʒere] *vt* to hand, give; (*tendere*) to hold out
pornogra'fia *sf* pornography; **porno'grafico, -a, -ci, -che** *ag* pornographic
'poro *sm* pore
'porpora *sf* purple
'porre *vt* (*mettere*) to put; (*collocare*) to place; (*posare*) to lay (down), put (down); (*fig: supporre*): **poniamo (il caso) che ...** let's suppose that ...
'porro *sm* (*Bot*) leek; (*Med*) wart
'porsi *ecc vb vedi* **porgere**
'porta *sf* door; (*Sport*) goal; **portaba'gagli** *sm inv* (*facchino*) porter; (*Aut, Ferr*) luggage rack; **porta-CD** [portatʃi'di] *sm inv* (*mobile*) CD rack; (*astuccio*) CD holder; **porta'cenere** *sm inv* ashtray; **portachi'avi** *sm inv* keyring; **porta'erei** *sf inv* (*nave*) aircraft carrier; **portafi'nestra** (*pl* **portefi'nestre**) *sf* French window; **porta'foglio** *sm* wallet; (*Pol, Borsa*) portfolio; **non trovo il portafoglio** I can't find my wallet; **portafor'tuna** *sm inv* lucky charm; mascot
por'tale *sm* (*di chiesa, Inform*) portal
porta'mento *sm* carriage, bearing
portamo'nete *sm inv* purse
por'tante *ag* (*muro ecc*) supporting, load-bearing
portan'tina *sf* sedan chair; (*per ammalati*) stretcher
portaom'brelli *sm inv* umbrella stand
porta'pacchi [porta'pakki] *sm inv* (*di moto, bicicletta*) luggage rack
por'tare *vt* (*sostenere, sorreggere: peso, bambino, pacco*) to carry; (*indossare: abito, occhiali*) to wear; (*: capelli lunghi*) to have; (*avere: nome, titolo*) to have, bear; (*recare*): **~ qc a qn** to take (*o* bring) sth to sb; (*fig: sentimenti*) to bear
portasiga'rette *sm inv* cigarette case
por'tata *sf* (*vivanda*) course; (*Aut*) carrying (*o* loading) capacity; (*di arma*) range; (*volume d'acqua*) (rate of) flow; (*fig: limite*) scope, capability; (*: importanza*) impact, import; **alla ~ di tutti** (*conoscenza*) within everybody's capabilities; (*prezzo*) within everybody's means; **a/fuori ~ (di)** within/out of reach (of); **a ~ di mano** within (arm's) reach
por'tatile *ag* portable
por'tato, -a *ag* (*incline*): **~ a** inclined *o* apt to
portau'ovo *sm inv* eggcup
porta'voce [porta'votʃe] *sm/f inv* spokesman/woman
por'tento *sm* wonder, marvel
porti'era *sf* (*Aut*) door
porti'ere *sm* (*portinaio*) concierge, caretaker; (*di hotel*) porter; (*nel calcio*) goalkeeper
porti'naio, -a *sm/f* concierge,

caretaker

portine'ria *sf* caretaker's lodge

'porto, -a *pp di* **porgere** ▷ *sm* (*Naut*) harbour, port ▷ *sm inv* port (wine); **porto d'armi** (*documento*) gun licence

Porto'gallo *sm*: **il ~** Portugal; **porto'ghese** *ag, sm/f, sm* Portuguese *inv*

por'tone *sm* main entrance, main door

portu'ale *ag* harbour *cpd*, port *cpd* ▷ *sm* dock worker

porzi'one [por'tsjone] *sf* portion, share; (*di cibo*) portion, helping

'posa *sf* (*Fot*) exposure; (*atteggiamento, di modello*) pose

po'sare *vt* to put (down), lay (down) ▷ *vi* (*ponte, edificio, teoria*): **~ su** to rest on; (*Fot: atteggiarsi*) to pose; **posarsi** *vpr* (*aereo*) to land; (*uccello*) to alight; (*sguardo*) to settle

po'sata *sf* piece of cutlery

pos'critto *sm* postscript

'posi *ecc vb vedi* **porre**

posi'tivo, -a *ag* positive

posizi'one [pozit'tsjone] *sf* position; **prendere ~** (*fig*) to take a stand; **luci di ~** (*Aut*) sidelights

pos'porre *vt* to place after; (*differire*) to postpone, defer

posse'dere *vt* to own, possess; (*qualità, virtù*) to have, possess

posses'sivo, -a *ag* possessive

pos'sesso *sm* ownership *no pl*; possession

posses'sore *sm* owner

pos'sibile *ag* possible ▷ *sm* **fare tutto il ~** to do everything possible; **nei limiti del ~** as far as possible; **al più tardi ~** as late as possible; **possibilità** *sf inv* possibility ▷ *sfpl* (*mezzi*) means; **aver la possibilità di fare** to be in a position to do; to have the opportunity to do

possi'dente *sm/f* landowner

possi'edo *ecc vb vedi* **possedere**

'posso *ecc vb vedi* **potere**

'posta *sf* (*servizio*) post, postal service; (*corrispondenza*) post, mail; (*ufficio postale*) post office; (*nei giochi d'azzardo*) stake; **Poste** *sfpl* (*amministrazione*) post office; **c'è ~ per me?** are there any letters for me?; **ministro delle Poste e Telecomunicazioni** Postmaster General; **posta aerea** airmail; **posta elettronica** E-mail, e-mail, electronic mail; **posta ordinaria** ≈ second-class mail; **posta prioritaria** ≈ first-class post; **pos'tale** *ag* postal, post office *cpd*

posteggi'are [posted'dʒare] *vt, vi* to park; **pos'teggio** *sm* car park (BRIT), parking lot (US); (*di taxi*) rank (BRIT), stand (US)

'poster *sm inv* poster

posteri'ore *ag* (*dietro*) back; (*dopo*) later ▷ *sm* (*fam: sedere*) behind

postici'pare [postitʃi'pare] *vt* to defer, postpone

pos'tino *sm* postman (BRIT), mailman (US)

'posto, -a *pp di* **porre** ▷ *sm* (*sito, posizione*) place; (*impiego*) job; (*spazio libero*) room, space; (*di parcheggio*) space; (*sedile: al teatro, in treno ecc*) seat; (*Mil*) post; **a ~** (*in ordine*) in place, tidy; (*fig*) settled; (*: persona*) reliable; **vorrei prenotare due posti** I'd like to book two seats; **al ~ di** in place of; **sul ~** on the spot; **mettere a ~** to tidy (up), put in order; (*faccende*) to straighten out; **posto di blocco** roadblock; **posto di lavoro** job; **posti in piedi** (*in teatro, in autobus*) standing room; **posto di polizia** police station

po'tabile *ag* drinkable; **acqua ~** drinking water

po'tare *vt* to prune

po'tassio *sm* potassium

po'tente *ag* (*nazione*) strong, powerful; (*veleno, farmaco*) potent, strong; **po'tenza** *sf* power; (*forza*) strength

potenzi'ale [poten'tsjale] *ag, sm* potential

PAROLA CHIAVE

po'tere *sm* power; **al potere** (*partito ecc*) in power; **potere d'acquisto** purchasing power
▷ *vb aus* **1** (*essere in grado di*) can, be able to; **non ha potuto ripararlo** he couldn't *o* he wasn't able to repair it; **non è potuto venire** he couldn't *o* he wasn't able to come; **spiacente di non poter aiutare** sorry not to be able to help
2 (*avere il permesso*) can, may, be allowed to; **posso entrare?** can *o* may I come in?; **si può sapere dove sei stato?** where on earth have you been?
3 (*eventualità*) may, might, could; **potrebbe essere vero** it might *o* could be true; **può aver avuto un incidente** he may *o* might *o* could have had an accident; **può darsi** perhaps; **può darsi** *o* **essere che non venga** he may *o* might not come
4 (*augurio*): **potessi almeno parlargli!** if only I could speak to him!
5 (*suggerimento*): **potresti almeno scusarti!** you could at least apologize!
▷ *vt* can, be able to; **può molto per noi** he can do a lot for us; **non ne posso più** (*per stanchezza*) I'm exhausted; (*per rabbia*) I can't take any more

potrò *ecc vb vedi* **potere**
'povero, -a *ag* poor; (*disadorno*) plain, bare ▷ *sm/f* poor man/woman; **i poveri** the poor; **~ di** lacking in, having little; **povertà** *sf* poverty
poz'zanghera [pot'tsangera] *sf* puddle
'pozzo ['pottso] *sm* well; (*cava: di carbone*) pit; (*di miniera*) shaft; **pozzo petrolifero** oil well
P.R.A. [pra] *sigla m* (= *Pubblico Registro Automobilistico*) ≈ DVLA
pran'zare [pran'dzare] *vi* to dine, have dinner; to lunch, have lunch
'pranzo ['prandzo] *sm* dinner; (*a mezzogiorno*) lunch
'prassi *sf* usual procedure
'pratica, -che *sf* practice; (*esperienza*) experience; (*conoscenza*) knowledge, familiarity; (*tirocinio*) training, practice; (*Amm: affare*) matter, case; (*: incartamento*) file, dossier; **in ~** (*praticamente*) in practice; **mettere in ~** to put into practice
prati'cabile *ag* (*progetto*) practicable, feasible; (*luogo*) passable, practicable
pratica'mente *av* (*in modo pratico*) in a practical way, practically; (*quasi*) practically, almost
prati'care *vt* to practise; (*Sport: tennis ecc*) to play; (*: nuoto, scherma ecc*) to go in for; (*eseguire: apertura, buco*) to make; **~ uno sconto** to give a discount
'pratico, -a, -ci, -che *ag* practical; **~ di** (*esperto*) experienced *o* skilled in; (*familiare*) familiar with
'prato *sm* meadow; (*di giardino*) lawn
preav'viso *sm* notice; **telefonata con ~** personal *o* person to person call
pre'cario, -a *ag* precarious; (*Ins*) temporary
precauzi'one [prekaut'tsjone] *sf* caution, care; (*misura*) precaution
prece'dente [pretʃe'dɛnte] *ag* previous ▷ *sm* precedent; **il discorso/film ~** the previous *o* preceding speech/film; **senza precedenti** unprecedented; **precedenti penali** criminal record *sg*; **prece'denza** *sf* priority, precedence; (*Aut*) right of way
pre'cedere [pre'tʃɛdere] *vt* to precede, go (*o* come) before
precipi'tare [pretʃipi'tare] *vi* (*cadere*) to fall headlong; (*fig: situazione*) to get out of control ▷ *vt* (*gettare dall'alto in basso*) to hurl, fling; (*fig: affrettare*) to rush; **precipitarsi** *vpr* (*gettarsi*)

to hurl *o* fling o.s.; (*affrettarsi*) to rush; **precipi'toso, -a** *ag* (*caduta, fuga*) headlong; (*fig: avventato*) rash, reckless; (: *affrettato*) hasty, rushed
preci'pizio [pretʃi'pittsjo] *sm* precipice; **a ~** (*fig: correre*) headlong
precisa'mente [pretʃiza'mente] *av* (*gen*) precisely; (*con esattezza*) exactly
preci'sare [pretʃi'zare] *vt* to state, specify; (*spiegare*) to explain (in detail)
precisi'one [pretʃi'zjone] *sf* precision; accuracy
pre'ciso, -a [pre'tʃizo] *ag* (*esatto*) precise; (*accurato*) accurate, precise; (*deciso: idee*) precise, definite; (*uguale*): **2 vestiti precisi** 2 dresses exactly the same; **sono le 9 precise** it's exactly 9 o'clock
pre'cludere *vt* to block, obstruct
pre'coce [pre'kɔtʃe] *ag* early; (*bambino*) precocious; (*vecchiaia*) premature
precon'cetto [prekon'tʃɛtto] *sm* preconceived idea, prejudice
precur'sore *sm* forerunner, precursor
'preda *sf* (*bottino*) booty; (*animale, fig*) prey; **essere ~ di** to fall prey to; **essere in ~ a** to be prey to
'predica, -che *sf* sermon; (*fig*) lecture, talking-to
predi'care *vt, vi* to preach
predi'cato *sm* (*Ling*) predicate
predi'letto, -a *pp di* **prediligere** ▷ *ag, sm/f* favourite
predi'ligere [predi'lidʒere] *vt* to prefer, have a preference for
pre'dire *vt* to foretell, predict
predis'porre *vt* to get ready, prepare; **~ qn a qc** to predispose sb to sth
predizi'one [predit'tsjone] *sf* prediction
prefazi'one [prefat'tsjone] *sf* preface, foreword
prefe'renza [prefe'rɛntsa] *sf* preference
prefe'rire *vt* to prefer, like better; **~ il caffè al tè** to prefer coffee to tea, like coffee better than tea
pre'figgersi [pre'fiddʒersi] *vpr*: **~ uno scopo** to set o.s. a goal
pre'fisso, -a *pp di* **prefiggere** ▷ *sm* (*Ling*) prefix; (*Tel*) dialling (BRIT) *o* dial (US) code; **qual è il ~ telefonico di Londra?** what is the dialling code for London?
pre'gare *vi* to pray ▷ *vt* (*Rel*) to pray to; (*implorare*) to beg; (*chiedere*): **~ qn di fare** to ask sb to do; **farsi ~** to need coaxing *o* persuading
pre'gevole [pre'dʒevole] *ag* valuable
pregherò *ecc* [prege'rɔ] *vb vedi* **pregare**
preghi'era [pre'gjɛra] *sf* (*Rel*) prayer; (*domanda*) request
pregi'ato, -a [pre'dʒato] *ag* (*di valore*) valuable; **vino ~** vintage wine
'pregio ['prɛdʒo] *sm* (*stima*) esteem, regard; (*qualità*) (good) quality, merit; (*valore*) value, worth
pregiudi'care [predʒudi'kare] *vt* to prejudice, harm, be detrimental to
pregiu'dizio [predʒu'dittsjo] *sm* (*idea errata*) prejudice; (*danno*) harm *no pl*
'prego *escl* (*a chi ringrazia*) don't mention it!; (*invitando qn ad accomodarsi*) please sit down!; (*invitando qn ad andare prima*) after you!
pregus'tare *vt* to look forward to
prele'vare *vt* (*denaro*) to withdraw; (*campione*) to take; (*polizia*) to take, capture
preli'evo *sm* (*di denaro*) withdrawal; (*Med*): **fare un ~ (di)** to take a sample (of); **prelievo di sangue**; **fare un ~ di sangue** to take a blood sample
prelimi'nare *ag* preliminary
'premere *vt* to press ▷ *vi* **~ su** to press down on; (*fig*) to put pressure on; **~ a** (*fig: importare*) to matter to
pre'mettere *vt* to put before; (*dire prima*) to start by saying, state first
premi'are *vt* to give a prize to; (*fig: merito, onestà*) to reward
premiazi'one [premjat'tsjone] *sf*

prize giving
'premio *sm* prize; (*ricompensa*) reward; (*Comm*) premium; (*Amm: indennità*) bonus
pre'misi *ecc vb vedi* **premettere**
premu'nirsi *vpr*: **~ di** to provide o.s. with; **~ contro** to protect o.s. from, guard o.s. against
pre'mura *sf* (*fretta*) haste, hurry; (*riguardo*) attention, care; **premure** *sfpl* (*attenzioni, cure*) care *sg*; **aver ~** to be in a hurry; **far ~ a qn** to hurry sb; **usare ogni ~ nei riguardi di qn** to be very attentive to sb; **premu'roso, -a** *ag* thoughtful, considerate
'prendere *vt* to take; (*andare a prendere*) to get, fetch; (*ottenere*) to get; (*guadagnare*) to get, earn; (*catturare: ladro, pesce*) to catch; (*collaboratore, dipendente*) to take on; (*passeggero*) to pick up; (*chiedere: somma, prezzo*) to charge, ask; (*trattare: persona*) to handle ▷ *vi* (*colla, cemento*) to set; (*pianta*) to take; (*fuoco: nel camino*) to catch; (*voltare*): **~ a destra** to turn (to the) right; **prendersi** *vpr* (*azzuffarsi*): **prendersi a pugni** to come to blows; **dove si prende il traghetto per...** where do we get the ferry to ...; **prendi qualcosa?** (*da bere, da mangiare*) would you like something to eat (*o* drink)?; **prendo un caffè** I'll have a coffee; **~ qn/qc per** (*scambiare*) to take sb/sth for; **~ fuoco** to catch fire; **~ parte a** to take part in; **prendersi cura di qn/qc** to look after sb/sth; **prendersela** (*adirarsi*) to get annoyed; (*preoccuparsi*) to get upset, worry
preno'tare *vt* to book, reserve; **vorrei ~ una camera doppia** I'd like to book a double room; **ho prenotato un tavolo al nome di ...** I booked a table in the name of ...; **prenotazi'one** *sf* booking, reservation; **ho confermato la prenotazione per fax/e-mail** I confirmed my booking by fax/e-mail
preoccu'pare *vt* to worry; to preoccupy; **preoccuparsi** *vpr* **preoccuparsi di qn/qc** to worry about sb/sth; **preoccuparsi per qn** to be anxious for sb; **preoccupazi'one** *sf* worry, anxiety
prepa'rare *vt* to prepare; (*esame, concorso*) to prepare for; **prepararsi** *vpr* (*vestirsi*) to get ready; **prepararsi a qc/a fare** to get ready *o* prepare (o.s.) for sth/to do; **~ da mangiare** to prepare a meal; **prepara'tivi** *smpl* preparations
preposizi'one [prepozit'tsjone] *sf* (*Ling*) preposition
prepo'tente *ag* (*persona*) domineering, arrogant; (*bisogno, desiderio*) overwhelming, pressing ▷ *sm/f* bully
'presa *sf* taking *no pl*; catching *no pl*; (*di città*) capture; (*indurimento: di cemento*) setting; (*appiglio, Sport*) hold; (*di acqua, gas*) (supply) point; (*piccola quantità: di sale ecc*) pinch; (*Carte*) trick; **far ~** (*colla*) to set; **far ~ sul pubblico** to catch the public's imagination; **essere alle prese con** (*fig*) to be struggling with; **presa d'aria** air inlet; **presa (di corrente)** (*Elettr*) socket; (*: al muro*) point
pre'sagio [pre'zadʒo] *sm* omen
'presbite *ag* long-sighted
pres'crivere *vt* to prescribe
'prese *ecc vb vedi* **prendere**
presen'tare *vt* to present; (*far conoscere*): **~ qn (a)** to introduce sb (to); (*Amm: inoltrare*) to submit; **presentarsi** *vpr* (*recarsi, farsi vedere*) to present o.s., appear; (*farsi conoscere*) to introduce o.s.; (*occasione*) to arise; **presentarsi come candidato** (*Pol*) to stand as a candidate; **presentarsi bene/male** to have a good/poor appearance
pre'sente *ag* present; (*questo*) this ▷ *sm* present; **i presenti** those present; **aver ~ qc/qn** to remember

sth/sb; **presenti** (*persone*) people present; **aver ~ qc/qn** to remember sth/sb; **tenere ~ qn/qc** to keep sth/sb in mind

presenti'mento *sm* premonition

pre'senza [pre'zɛntsa] *sf* presence; (*aspetto esteriore*) appearance; **presenza di spirito** presence of mind

pre'sepio, pre'sepe *sm* crib

preser'vare *vt* to protect; to save; **preserva'tivo** *sm* sheath, condom

'presi *ecc vb vedi* **prendere**

'preside *sm/f* (*Ins*) head (teacher) (BRIT), principal (US); (*di facoltà universitaria*) dean; **preside di facoltà** (*Univ*) dean of faculty

presi'dente *sm* (*Pol*) president; (*di assemblea, Comm*) chairman; **presidente del consiglio** prime minister

presi'edere *vt* to preside over ▷ *vi* **~ a** to direct, be in charge of

pressap'poco *av* about, roughly

pres'sare *vt* to press

pressi'one *sf* pressure; **far ~ su qn** to put pressure on sb; **pressione sanguigna** blood pressure; **pressione atmosferica** atmospheric pressure

'presso *av* (*vicino*) nearby, close at hand ▷ *prep* (*vicino a*) near; (*accanto a*) beside, next to; (*in casa di*): **~ qn** at sb's home; (*nelle lettere*) care of, c/o; (*alle dipendenze di*): **lavora ~ di noi** he works for *o* with us ▷ *smpl* **nei pressi di** near, in the vicinity of

pres'tante *ag* good-looking

pres'tare *vt*: **~ (qc a qn)** to lend (sb sth *o* sth to sb); **prestarsi** *vpr* (*offrirsi*): **prestarsi a fare** to offer to do; (*essere adatto*): **prestarsi a** to lend itself to, be suitable for; **mi può ~ dei soldi?** can you lend me some money?; **~ aiuto** to lend a hand; **~ attenzione** to pay attention; **~ fede a qc/qn** to give credence to sth/sb; **~ orecchio** to listen; **prestazi'one** *sf* (*Tecn, Sport*) performance

prestigia'tore, -'trice [prestidʒa'tore] *sm/f* conjurer

pres'tigio [pres'tidʒo] *sm* (*fama*) prestige; (*illusione*): **gioco di ~** conjuring trick

'prestito *sm* lending *no pl*; loan; **dar in ~** to lend; **prendere in ~** to borrow

'presto *av* (*tra poco*) soon; (*in fretta*) quickly; (*di buon'ora*) early; **a ~** see you soon; **fare ~ a fare qc** to hurry up and do sth; (*non costare fatica*) to have no trouble doing sth; **si fa ~ a criticare** it's easy to criticize

pre'sumere *vt* to presume, assume

pre'sunsi *ecc vb vedi* **presumere**

presuntu'oso, -a *ag* presumptuous

presunzi'one [prezun'tsjone] *sf* presumption

'prete *sm* priest

preten'dente *sm/f* pretender ▷ *sm* (*corteggiatore*) suitor

pre'tendere *vt* (*esigere*) to demand, require; (*sostenere*): **~ che** to claim that; **pretende di aver sempre ragione** he thinks he's always right

> Attenzione! In inglese esiste il verbo *to pretend*, che però significa *far finta*.

pre'tesa *sf* (*esigenza*) claim, demand; (*presunzione, sfarzo*) pretentiousness; **senza pretese** unpretentious

pre'testo *sm* pretext, excuse

preva'lere *vi* to prevail

preve'dere *vt* (*indovinare*) to foresee; (*presagire*) to foretell; (*considerare*) to make provision for

preve'nire *vt* (*anticipare*) to forestall; to anticipate; (*evitare*) to avoid, prevent

preven'tivo, -a *ag* preventive ▷ *sm* (*Comm*) estimate

prevenzi'one [preven'tsjone] *sf* prevention; (*preconcetto*) prejudice

previ'dente *ag* showing foresight; prudent; **previ'denza** *sf* foresight; **istituto di previdenza** provident

institution; **previdenza sociale** social security (BRIT), welfare (US)
pre'vidi *ecc vb vedi* **prevedere**
previsi'one *sf* forecast, prediction; **previsioni meteorologiche** weather forecast *sg*; **previsioni del tempo** weather forecast *sg*
pre'visto, -a *pp di* **prevedere** ▷ *sm* **più/meno del ~** more/less than expected
prezi'oso, -a [pret'tsjoso] *ag* precious; invaluable ▷ *sm* jewel; valuable
prez'zemolo [pret'tsemolo] *sm* parsley
'prezzo ['prɛttso] *sm* price; **prezzo d'acquisto/di vendita** buying/selling price
prigi'one [pri'dʒone] *sf* prison; **prigioni'ero, -a** *ag* captive ▷ *sm/f* prisoner
'prima *sf* (*Teatro*) first night; (*Cinema*) première; (*Aut*) first gear; *vedi anche* **primo** ▷ *av* before; (*in anticipo*) in advance, beforehand; (*per l'addietro*) at one time, formerly; (*più presto*) sooner, earlier; (*in primo luogo*) first ▷ *cong* **~ di fare/che parta** before doing/he leaves; **~ di** before; **~ o poi** sooner or later
pri'mario, -a *ag* primary; (*principale*) chief, leading, primary ▷ *sm* (*Med*) chief physician
prima'tista, -i, e *sm/f* (*Sport*) record holder
pri'mato *sm* supremacy; (*Sport*) record
prima'vera *sf* spring
primi'tivo, -a *ag* primitive; original
pri'mizie [pri'mittsje] *sfpl* early produce *sg*
'primo, -a *ag* first; (*fig*) initial; basic; prime ▷ *sm/f* first (one) ▷ *sm* (*Cuc*) first course; (*in date*): **il ~ luglio** the first of July; **le prime ore del mattino** the early hours of the morning; **ai primi di maggio** at the beginning of May; **viaggiare in prima** to travel first-class; **in ~ luogo** first of all, in the first place; **di prim'ordine** *o* **prima qualità** first-class, first-rate; **in un ~ tempo** at first; **prima donna** leading lady; (*di opera lirica*) prima donna
primordi'ale *ag* primordial
'primula *sf* primrose
princi'pale [printʃi'pale] *ag* main, principal ▷ *sm* manager, boss
principal'mente [printʃipal'mente] *av* mainly, principally
'principe ['printʃipe] *sm* prince; **principe ereditario** crown prince; **princi'pessa** *sf* princess
principi'ante [printʃi'pjante] *sm/f* beginner
prin'cipio [prin'tʃipjo] *sm* (*inizio*) beginning, start; (*origine*) origin, cause; (*concetto, norma*) principle; **al** *o* **in ~** at first; **per ~** on principle; **principi** *smpl* (*concetti fondamentali*) principles; **una questione di ~** a matter of principle
priorità *sf* priority
priori'tario, -a *ag* having priority, of utmost importance
pri'vare *vt* **~ qn di** to deprive sb of; **privarsi di** to go *o* do without
pri'vato, -a *ag* private ▷ *sm/f* private citizen; **in ~** in private
privilegi'are [privile'dʒare] *vt* to grant a privilege to
privilegi'ato, -a [privile'dʒato] *ag* (*individuo, classe*) privileged; (*trattamento, Comm: credito*) preferential; **azioni ~e** preference shares (BRIT), preferred stock (US)
privi'legio [privi'lɛdʒo] *sm* privilege
'privo, -a *ag* **~ di** without, lacking
pro *prep* for, on behalf of ▷ *sm inv* (*utilità*) advantage, benefit; **a che ~?** what's the use?; **il ~ e il contro** the pros and cons
pro'babile *ag* probable, likely; **probabilità** *sf inv* probability
probabil'mente *av* probably

pro'blema, -i *sm* problem
pro'boscide [pro'bɔʃʃide] *sf* (*di elefante*) trunk
pro'cedere [pro'tʃɛdere] *vi* to proceed; (*comportarsi*) to behave; (*iniziare*): **~ a** to start; **~ contro** (*Dir*) to start legal proceedings against; **proce'dura** *sf* (*Dir*) procedure
proces'sare [protʃes'sare] *vt* (*Dir*) to try
processi'one [protʃes'sjone] *sf* procession
pro'cesso [pro'tʃɛsso] *sm* (*Dir*) trial; proceedings *pl*; (*metodo*) process
pro'cinto [pro'tʃinto] *sm*: **in ~ di fare** about to do, on the point of doing
procla'mare *vt* to proclaim
procre'are *vt* to procreate
procu'rare *vt*: **~ qc a qn** (*fornire*) to get *o* obtain sth for sb; (*causare*: *noie ecc*) to bring *o* give sb sth
pro'digio [pro'didʒo] *sm* marvel, wonder; (*persona*) prodigy
pro'dotto, -a *pp di* **produrre** ▷ *sm* product; **prodotti agricoli** farm produce *sg*
pro'duco *ecc vb vedi* **produrre**
pro'durre *vt* to produce
pro'dussi *ecc vb vedi* **produrre**
produzi'one *sf* production; (*rendimento*) output
Prof. *abbr* (= *professore*) Prof.
profa'nare *vt* to desecrate
profes'sare *vt* to profess; (*medicina ecc*) to practise
professio'nale *ag* professional
professi'one *sf* profession; **professio'nista, -i, -e** *sm/f* professional
profes'sore, -'essa *sm/f* (*Ins*) teacher; (: *di università*) lecturer; (: *titolare di cattedra*) professor
pro'filo *sm* profile; (*breve descrizione*) sketch, outline; **di ~** in profile
pro'fitto *sm* advantage, profit, benefit; (*fig*: *progresso*) progress; (*Comm*) profit
profondità *sf inv* depth
pro'fondo, -a *ag* deep; (*rancore, meditazione*) profound ▷ *sm* depth(s *pl*), bottom; **quanto è profonda l'acqua?** how deep is the water?; **~ 8 metri** 8 metres deep
'profugo, -a, -ghi, -ghe *sm/f* refugee
profu'mare *vt* to perfume ▷ *vi* to be fragrant; **profumarsi** *vpr* to put on perfume *o* scent
profu'mato, -a *ag* (*fiore, aria*) fragrant; (*fazzoletto, saponetta*) scented; (*pelle*) sweet-smelling; (*persona*) with perfume on
profume'ria *sf* perfumery; (*negozio*) perfume shop
pro'fumo *sm* (*prodotto*) perfume, scent; (*fragranza*) scent, fragrance
proget'tare [prodʒet'tare] *vt* to plan; (*edificio*) to plan, design; **pro'getto** *sm* plan; (*idea*) plan, project; **progetto di legge** bill
pro'gramma, -i *sm* programme; (*TV, Radio*) programmes *pl*; (*Ins*) syllabus, curriculum; (*Inform*) program; **program'mare** *vt* (*TV, Radio*) to put on; (*Inform*) to program; (*Econ*) to plan; **programma'tore, -'trice** *sm/f* (*Inform*) computer programmer
progre'dire *vi* to progress, make progress
pro'gresso *sm* progress *no pl*; **fare progressi** to make progress
proi'bire *vt* to forbid, prohibit
proiet'tare *vt* (*gen, Geom, Cinema*) to project; (: *presentare*) to show, screen; (*luce, ombra*) to throw, cast, project; **proi'ettile** *sm* projectile, bullet (*o* shell *ecc*); **proiet'tore** *sm* (*Cinema*) projector; (*Aut*) headlamp; (*Mil*) searchlight; **proiezi'one** *sf* (*Cinema*) projection; showing
prolife'rare *vi* (*fig*) to proliferate
pro'lunga, -ghe *sf* (*di cavo ecc*) extension
prolun'gare *vt* (*discorso, attesa*) to

prolong; (*linea, termine*) to extend
prome'moria *sm inv* memorandum
pro'messa *sf* promise
pro'mettere *vt* to promise ▷ *vi* to be *o* look promising; **~ a qn di fare** to promise sb that one will do
promi'nente *ag* prominent
pro'misi *ecc vb vedi* **promettere**
promon'torio *sm* promontory, headland
promozi'one [promot'tsjone] *sf* promotion
promu'overe *vt* to promote
proni'pote *sm/f* (*di nonni*) great-grandchild, great-grandson/granddaughter; (*di zii*) great-nephew/niece
pro'nome *sm* (*Ling*) pronoun
pron'tezza [pron'tettsa] *sf* readiness; quickness, promptness
'pronto, -a *ag* ready; (*rapido*) fast, quick, prompt; **quando saranno pronte le mie foto?** when will my photos be ready?; **~!** (*Tel*) hello!; **~ all'ira** quick-tempered; **pronto soccorso** (*cure*) first aid; (*reparto*) A&E (BRIT), ER (US)
prontu'ario *sm* manual, handbook
pro'nuncia [pro'nuntʃa] *sf* pronunciation
pronunci'are [pronun'tʃare] *vt* (*parola, sentenza*) to pronounce; (*dire*) to utter; (*discorso*) to deliver; **come si pronuncia?** how do you pronounce it?
propa'ganda *sf* propaganda
pro'pendere *vi* **~ per** to favour, lean towards
propi'nare *vt* to administer
pro'porre *vt* (*suggerire*): **~ qc (a qn)** to suggest sth (to sb); (*candidato*) to put forward; (*legge, brindisi*) to propose; **~ di fare** to suggest *o* propose doing; **proporsi di fare** to propose *o* intend to do; **proporsi una meta** to set o.s. a goal
proporzio'nale [proportsjo'nale] *ag* proportional
proporzi'one [propor'tsjone] *sf* proportion; **in ~ a** in proportion to; **proporzioni** *sfpl* (*dimensioni*) proportions; **di vaste proporzioni** huge
pro'posito *sm* (*intenzione*) intention, aim; (*argomento*) subject, matter; **a ~ di** regarding, with regard to; **di ~** (*apposta*) deliberately, on purpose; **a ~** by the way; **capitare a ~** (*cosa, persona*) to turn up at the right time
proposizi'one [propozit'tsjone] *sf* (*Ling*) clause; (: *periodo*) sentence
pro'posta *sf* proposal; (*suggerimento*) suggestion; **proposta di legge** bill
proprietà *sf inv* (*ciò che si possiede*) property *gen no pl*, estate; (*caratteristica*) property; (*correttezza*) correctness; **proprietà privata** private property; **proprie'tario, -a** *sm/f* owner; (*di albergo ecc*) proprietor, owner; (*per l'inquilino*) landlord/lady
'proprio, -a *ag* (*possessivo*) own; (: *impersonale*) one's; (*esatto*) exact, correct, proper; (*senso, significato*) literal; (*Ling*: *nome*) proper; (*particolare*): **~ di** characteristic of, peculiar to ▷ *av* (*precisamente*) just, exactly; (*davvero*) really; (*affatto*): **non ... ~** not ... at all; **l'ha visto con i (suoi) propri occhi** he saw it with his own eyes
proro'gare *vt* to extend; (*differire*) to postpone, defer
'prosa *sf* prose
pro'sciogliere [proʃ'ʃɔʎʎere] *vt* to release; (*Dir*) to acquit
prosciu'gare [proʃʃu'gare] *vt* (*terreni*) to drain, reclaim; **prosciugarsi** *vpr* to dry up
prosci'utto [proʃ'ʃutto] *sm* ham; **prosciutto cotto/crudo** cooked/cured ham
prosegui'mento *sm* continuation; **buon ~!** all the best!; (*a chi viaggia*) enjoy the rest of your journey!
prosegu'ire *vt* to carry on with,

continue ▷ *vi* to carry on, go on
prospe'rare *vi* to thrive
prospet'tare *vt* (*esporre*) to point out, show; **prospettarsi** *vpr* to look, appear
prospet'tiva *sf* (*Arte*) perspective; (*veduta*) view; (*fig: previsione, possibilità*) prospect
pros'petto *sm* (*Disegno*) elevation; (*veduta*) view, prospect; (*facciata*) façade, front; (*tabella*) table; (*sommario*) summary; **prospetto informativo** prospectus
prossimità *sf* nearness, proximity; **in ~ di** near (to), close to
'prossimo, -a *ag* (*vicino*): **~ a** near (to), close to; (*che viene subito dopo*) next; (*parente*) close ▷ *sm* neighbour, fellow man
prostitu'irsi *vpr* to prostitute o.s.
prosti'tuta *sf* prostitute
protago'nista, -i, -e *sm/f* protagonist
pro'teggere [pro'tɛddʒere] *vt* to protect
prote'ina *sf* protein
pro'tendere *vt* to stretch out
pro'testa *sf* protest
protes'tante *ag, sm/f* Protestant
protes'tare *vt, vi* to protest
pro'tetto, -a *pp di* **proteggere**
protezi'one [protet'tsjone] *sf* protection; (*patrocinio*) patronage
pro'totipo *sm* prototype
pro'trarre *vt* (*prolungare*) to prolong; **protrarsi** *vpr* to go on, continue
protube'ranza [protube'rantsa] *sf* protuberance, bulge
'prova *sf* (*esperimento, cimento*) test, trial; (*tentativo*) attempt, try; (*Mat, testimonianza, documento ecc*) proof; (*Dir*) evidence *no pl*, proof; (*Ins*) exam, test; (*Teatro*) rehearsal; (*di abito*) fitting; **a ~ di** (*in testimonianza di*) as proof of; **a ~ di fuoco** fireproof; **fino a ~ contraria** until it is proved otherwise; **mettere alla ~** to put to the test; **giro di ~** test *o* trial run; **prova generale** (*Teatro*) dress rehearsal
pro'vare *vt* (*sperimentare*) to test; (*tentare*) to try, attempt; (*assaggiare*) to try, taste; (*sperimentare in sé*) to experience; (*sentire*) to feel; (*cimentare*) to put to the test; (*dimostrare*) to prove; (*abito*) to try on; **~ a fare** to try *o* attempt to do
proveni'enza [prove'njɛntsa] *sf* origin, source
prove'nire *vi* **~ da** to come from
pro'venti *smpl* revenue *sg*
pro'verbio *sm* proverb
pro'vetta *sf* test tube; **bambino in ~** test-tube baby
pro'vider [pro'vaider] *sm inv* (*Inform*) service provider
pro'vincia, -ce *o* **cie** [pro'vintʃa] *sf* province
pro'vino *sm* (*Cinema*) screen test; (*campione*) specimen
provo'cante *ag* (*attraente*) provocative
provo'care *vt* (*causare*) to cause, bring about; (*eccitare: riso, pietà*) to arouse; (*irritare, sfidare*) to provoke; **provocazi'one** *sf* provocation
provve'dere *vi* (*disporre*): **~ (a)** to provide (for); (*prendere un provvedimento*) to take steps, act; **provvedi'mento** *sm* measure; (*di previdenza*) precaution
provvi'denza [provvi'dɛntsa] *sf*: **la ~** providence
provvigi'one [provvi'dʒone] *sf* (*Comm*) commission
provvi'sorio, -a *ag* temporary
prov'viste *sfpl* supplies
'prua *sf* (*Naut*) bow(s) (*pl*), prow
pru'dente *ag* cautious, prudent; (*assennato*) sensible, wise; **pru'denza** *sf* prudence, caution; wisdom
'prudere *vi* to itch, be itchy
'prugna ['pruɲɲa] *sf* plum; **prugna secca** prune

pru'rito *sm* itchiness *no pl*; itch
P.S. *abbr* (= *postscriptum*) P.S.; (*Polizia*) = **Pubblica Sicurezza**
pseu'donimo *sm* pseudonym
psica'nalisi *sf* psychoanalysis
psicana'lista, -i, -e *sm/f* psychoanalyst
'psiche ['psike] *sf* (*Psic*) psyche
psichi'atra, -i, -e [psi'kjatra] *sm/f* psychiatrist; **psichi'atrico, -a, -ci, -che** *ag* psychiatric
psicolo'gia [psikolo'dʒia] *sf* psychology; **psico'logico, -a, -ci, -che** *ag* psychological; **psi'cologo, -a, -gi, -ghe** *sm/f* psychologist
psico'patico, -a, -ci, -che *ag* psychopathic ▷ *sm/f* psychopath
pubbli'care *vt* to publish
pubblicazi'one [pubblikat'tsjone] *sf* publication
pubblicità [pubblitʃi'ta] *sf* (*diffusione*) publicity; (*attività*) advertising; (*annunci nei giornali*) advertisements *pl*
'pubblico, -a, -ci, -che *ag* public; (*statale: scuola ecc*) state *cpd* ▷ *sm* public; (*spettatori*) audience; **in ~** in public; **P~ Ministero** Public Prosecutor's Office; **la Pubblica Sicurezza** the police; **pubblico funzionario** civil servant
'pube *sm* (*Anat*) pubis
pubertà *sf* puberty
'pudico, -a, -ci, -che *ag* modest
pu'dore *sm* modesty
pue'rile *ag* childish
pugi'lato [pudʒi'lato] *sm* boxing
'pugile ['pudʒile] *sm* boxer
pugna'lare [puɲɲa'lare] *vt* to stab
pu'gnale [puɲ'ɲale] *sm* dagger
'pugno ['puɲɲo] *sm* fist; (*colpo*) punch; (*quantità*) fistful
'pulce ['pultʃe] *sf* flea
pul'cino [pul'tʃino] *sm* chick
pu'lire *vt* to clean; (*lucidare*) to polish; **pu'lito, -a** *ag* (*anche fig*) clean; (*ordinato*) neat, tidy; **puli'tura** *sf* cleaning; **pulitura a secco** dry cleaning; **puli'zia** *sf* cleaning; cleanness; **fare le pulizie** to do the cleaning *o* the housework; **pulizia etnica** ethnic cleansing
'pullman *sm inv* coach
pul'lover *sm inv* pullover, jumper
pullu'lare *vi* to swarm, teem
pul'mino *sm* minibus
'pulpito *sm* pulpit
pul'sante *sm* (push-)button
pul'sare *vi* to pulsate, beat
pul'viscolo *sm* fine dust; **pulviscolo atmosferico** specks *pl* of dust
'puma *sm inv* puma
pun'gente [pun'dʒɛnte] *ag* prickly; stinging; (*anche fig*) biting
'pungere ['pundʒere] *vt* to prick; (*insetto, ortica*) to sting; (*freddo*) to bite
pungigli'one [pundʒiʎ'ʎone] *sm* sting
pu'nire *vt* to punish; **punizi'one** *sf* punishment; (*Sport*) penalty
'punsi *ecc vb vedi* **pungere**
'punta *sf* point; (*parte terminale*) tip, end; (*di monte*) peak; (*di costa*) promontory; (*minima parte*) touch, trace; **in ~ di piedi** on tip-toe; **ore di ~** peak hours; **uomo di ~** front-rank *o* leading man
pun'tare *vt* (*piedi a terra, gomiti sul tavolo*) to plant; (*dirigere: pistola*) to point; (*scommettere*) to bet ▷ *vi* (*mirare*): **~ a** to aim at; **~ su** (*dirigersi*) to head *o* make for; (*fig: contare*) to count *o* rely on
pun'tata *sf* (*gita*) short trip; (*scommessa*) bet; (*parte di opera*) instalment; **romanzo a puntate** serial
punteggia'tura [punteddʒa'tura] *sf* (*Ling*) punctuation
pun'teggio [pun'teddʒo] *sm* score
puntel'lare *vt* to support
pun'tello *sm* prop, support
pun'tina *sf*: **puntina da disegno** drawing pin

pun'tino *sm* dot; **fare qc a ~** to do sth properly

'punto, -a *pp di* **pungere** ▷ *sm* (*segno, macchiolina*) dot; (*Ling*) full stop; (*di indirizzo e-mail*) dot; (*Mat, momento, di punteggio: fig: argomento*) point; (*posto*) spot; (*a scuola*) mark; (*nel cucire, nella maglia, Med*) stitch ▷ *av* **non ... ~** not at all; **punto cardinale** point of the compass, cardinal point; **punto debole** weak point; **punto esclamativo** exclamation mark; **punto interrogativo** question mark; **punto nero** (*comedone*) blackhead; **punto di partenza** (*anche fig*) starting point; **punto di riferimento** landmark; (*fig*) point of reference; **punto (di) vendita** retail outlet; **punto e virgola** semicolon; **punto di vista** (*fig*) point of view

puntu'ale *ag* punctual

pun'tura *sf* (*di ago*) prick; (*Med*) puncture; (: *iniezione*) injection; (*dolore*) sharp pain; **puntura d'insetto** sting, bite

> Attenzione! In inglese esiste la parola *puncture*, che si usa per indicare la foratura di una gomma.

punzecchi'are [puntsek'kjare] *vt* to prick; (*fig*) to tease

può *ecc*, **-pu'oi** *vb vedi* **potere**

pu'pazzo [pu'pattso] *sm* puppet

pu'pilla *sf* (*Anat*) pupil

purché [pur'ke] *cong* provided that, on condition that

'pure *cong* (*tuttavia*) and yet, nevertheless; (*anche se*) even if ▷ *av* (*anche*) too, also; **pur di** (*al fine di*) just to; **faccia ~!** go ahead!, please do!

purè *sm* (*Cuc*) purée; (: *di patate*) mashed potatoes

pu'rezza [pu'rettsa] *sf* purity

pur'gante *sm* (*Med*) purgative, purge

purga'torio *sm* purgatory

purifi'care *vt* to purify; (*metallo*) to refine

'puro, -a *ag* pure; (*acqua*) clear, limpid; (*vino*) undiluted; **puro'sangue** *sm/f inv* thoroughbred

pur'troppo *av* unfortunately

pus *sm* pus

'pustola *sf* pimple

puti'ferio *sm* rumpus, row

putre'fatto, -a *pp di* **putrefare**

put'tana (*fam!*) *sf* whore (*!*)

puz'zare [put'tsare] *vi* to stink

'puzzo ['puttso] *sm* stink, foul smell

'puzzola ['puttsola] *sf* polecat

puzzo'lente [puttso'lɛnte] *ag* stinking

pvc [pivi'tʃi] *sigla m* (*= polyvinyl chloride*) PVC

q

q *abbr* (= *quintale*) q.
qua *av* here; **in ~** (*verso questa parte*) this way; **da un anno in ~** for a year now; **da ~ndo in ~?** since when?; **per di ~** (*passare*) this way; **al di ~ di** (*fiume, strada*) on this side of; **~ dentro/fuori** *ecc* in/out here *ecc*; *vedi anche* **questo**
qua'derno *sm* notebook; (*per scuola*) exercise book
qua'drante *sm* quadrant; (*di orologio*) face
qua'drare *vi* (*bilancio*) to balance, tally; (*descrizione*) to correspond ▷ *vt* (*Mat*) to square; **non mi quadra** I don't like it; **qua'drato, -a** *ag* square; (*fig*: *equilibrato*) level-headed, sensible; (: *peg*) square ▷ *sm* (*Mat*) square; (*Pugilato*) ring; **5 al quadrato** 5 squared
quadri'foglio [kwadri'fɔʎʎo] *sm* four-leaf clover
quadri'mestre *sm* (*periodo*) four-month period; (*Ins*) term
'quadro *sm* (*pittura*) painting, picture; (*quadrato*) square; (*tabella*) table, chart; (*Tecn*) board, panel; (*Teatro*) scene; (*fig*: *scena, spettacolo*) sight; (: *descrizione*) outline, description; **quadri** *smpl* (*Pol*) party organizers; (*Mil*) cadres; (*Comm*) managerial staff; (*Carte*) diamonds
'quadruplo, -a *ag, sm* quadruple
quaggiù [kwad'dʒu] *av* down here
'quaglia ['kwaʎʎa] *sf* quail

PAROLA CHIAVE

'qualche ['kwalke] *det* **1** some, a few; (*in interrogative*) any; **ho comprato qualche libro** I've bought some *o* a few books; **qualche volta** sometimes; **hai qualche sigaretta?** have you any cigarettes?
2 (*uno*): **c'è qualche medico?** is there a doctor?; **in qualche modo** somehow
3 (*un certo, parecchio*) some; **un personaggio di qualche rilievo** a figure of some importance
4: **qualche cosa = qualcosa**

qual'cosa *pron* something; (*in espressioni interrogative*) anything; **qualcos'altro** something else; anything else; **~ di nuovo** something new; anything new; **~ da mangiare** something to eat; anything to eat; **c'è ~ che non va?** is there something *o* anything wrong?
qual'cuno *pron* (*persona*) someone, somebody; (: *in espressioni interrogative*) anyone, anybody; (*alcuni*) some; **~ è favorevole a noi** some are on our side; **qualcun altro** someone *o* somebody else; anyone *o* anybody else

PAROLA CHIAVE

'quale (*spesso troncato in* **qual**) *det* **1** (*interrogativo*) what; (: *scegliendo tra*

due o più cose o persone) which; **quale uomo/denaro?** what man/money?, which man/money?; **quali sono i tuoi programmi?** what are your plans?; **quale stanza preferisci?** which room do you prefer?
2 (*relativo*: *come*): **il risultato fu quale ci si aspettava** the result was as expected
3 (*esclamativo*) what; **quale disgrazia!** what bad luck!
▷ *pron* **1** (*interrogativo*) which; **quale dei due scegli?** which of the two do you want?
2 (*relativo*): **il (la) quale** (*persona*: *soggetto*) who; (: *oggetto, con preposizione*) whom; (*cosa*) which; (*possessivo*) whose; **suo padre, il quale è avvocato, ...** his father, who is a lawyer, ...; **il signore con il quale parlavo** the gentleman to whom I was speaking; **l'albergo al quale ci siamo fermati** the hotel where we stayed *o* which we stayed at; **la signora della quale ammiriamo la bellezza** the lady whose beauty we admire
3 (*relativo*: *in elenchi*) such as, like; **piante quali l'edera** plants like *o* such as ivy; **quale sindaco di questa città** as mayor of this town

qua'lifica, -che *sf* qualification; (*titolo*) title
qualifi'cato, -a *ag* (*dotato di qualifica*) qualified; (*esperto, abile*) skilled; **non mi ritengo ~ per questo lavoro** I don't think I'm qualified for this job; **è un medico molto ~** he is a very distinguished doctor
qualificazi'one *sf*: **gara di ~** (*Sport*) qualifying event
qualità *sf inv* quality; **in ~ di** in one's capacity as
qua'lora *cong* in case, if
qual'siasi *det inv* = **qualunque**
qua'lunque *det inv* any; (*quale che sia*) whatever; (*discriminativo*) whichever; (*posposto*: *mediocre*) poor, indifferent; ordinary; **mettiti un vestito ~** put on any old dress; **~ cosa** anything; **~ cosa accada** whatever happens; **a ~ costo** at any cost, whatever the cost; **l'uomo ~** the man in the street; **~ persona** anyone, anybody
'quando *cong, av* when; **~ sarò ricco** when I'm rich; **da ~** (*dacché*) since; (*interrogativo*): **da ~ sei qui?** how long have you been here?; **quand'anche** even if
quantità *sf inv* quantity; (*gran numero*): **una ~ di** a great deal of; a lot of; **in grande ~** in large quantities

PAROLA CHIAVE

'quanto, -a *det* **1** (*interrogativo*: *quantità*) how much; (: *numero*) how many; **quanto pane/denaro?** how much bread/money?; **quanti libri/ragazzi?** how many books/boys?; **quanto tempo?** how long?; **quanti anni hai?** how old are you?
2 (*esclamativo*): **quante storie!** what a lot of nonsense!; **quanto tempo sprecato!** what a waste of time!
3 (*relativo*: *quantità*) as much ... as; (: *numero*) as many ... as; **ho quanto denaro mi occorre** I have as much money as I need; **prendi quanti libri vuoi** take as many books as you like
▷ *pron* **1** (*interrogativo*: *quantità*) how much; (: *numero*) how many; (: *tempo*) how long; **quanto mi dai?** how much will you give me?; **quanti me ne hai portati?** how many did you bring me?; **da quanto sei qui?** how long have you been here?; **quanti ne abbiamo oggi?** what's the date today?
2 (*relativo*: *quantità*) as much as; (: *numero*) as many as; **farò quanto posso** I'll do as much as I can; **possono venire quanti sono stati**

invitati all those who have been invited can come
▷ *av* 1 (*interrogativo: con ag, av*) how; (: *con vb*) how much; **quanto stanco ti sembrava?** how tired did he seem to you?; **quanto corre la tua moto?** how fast can your motorbike go?; **quanto costa?** how much does it cost?; **quant'è?** how much is it?
2 (*esclamativo: con ag, av*) how; (: *con vb*) how much; **quanto sono felice!** how happy I am!; **sapessi quanto abbiamo camminato!** if you knew how far we've walked!; **studierò quanto posso** I'll study as much as *o* all I can; **quanto prima** as soon as possible
3: **in quanto** (*in qualità di*) as; (*perché, per il fatto che*) as, since; **(in) quanto a** (*per ciò che riguarda*) as for, as regards
4: **per quanto** (*nonostante, anche se*) however; **per quanto si sforzi, non ce la farà** try as he may, he won't manage it; **per quanto sia brava, fa degli errori** however good she may be, she makes mistakes; **per quanto io sappia** as far as I know

qua'ranta *num* forty
quaran'tena *sf* quarantine
quaran'tesimo, -a *num* fortieth
quaran'tina *sf* **una ~ (di)** about forty
'quarta *sf* (*Aut*) fourth (gear); *vedi anche* **quarto**
quar'tetto *sm* quartet(te)
quarti'ere *sm* district, area; (*Mil*) quarters *pl*; **quartier generale** headquarters *pl*
'quarto, -a *ag* fourth ▷ *sm* fourth; (*quarta parte*) quarter; **le 6 e un ~** a quarter past six; **quarti di finale** quarter final; **quarto d'ora** quarter of an hour
'quarzo ['kwartso] *sm* quartz
'quasi *av* almost, nearly ▷ *cong* (*anche:* **~ che**) as if; **(non) ... ~ mai** hardly ever; **~ ~ me ne andrei** I've half a mind to leave
quassù *av* up here
quat'tordici [kwat'torditʃi] *num* fourteen
quat'trini *smpl* money *sg*, cash *sg*
'quattro *num* four; **in ~ e quattr'otto** in less than no time;
quattro'cento *num* four hundred ▷ *sm* **il Quattrocento** the fifteenth century

PAROLA CHIAVE

'quello, -a (*dav sm* **quel** + C, **quell'** + V, **quello** + *s impura, gn, pn, ps, x, z; pl* **quei** + C, **quegli** + V *o s impura, gn, pn, ps, x, z; dav sf* **quella** + C, **quell'** + V; *pl* **quelle**) *det* that; those *pl*; **quella casa** that house; **quegli uomini** those men; **voglio quella camicia (lì** *o* **là)** I want that shirt
▷ *pron* 1 (*dimostrativo*) that (one), those (ones) *pl*; (*ciò*) that; **conosci quella?** do you know that woman?; **prendo quello bianco** I'll take the white one; **chi è quello?** who's that?; **prendi quello (lì** *o* **là)** take that one (there)
2 (*relativo*): **quello(a) che** (*persona*) the one (who); (*cosa*) the one (which), the one (that); **quelli(e) che** (*persone*) those who; (*cose*) those which; **è lui quello che non voleva venire** he's the one who didn't want to come; **ho fatto quello che potevo** I did what I could

'quercia, -ce ['kwɛrtʃa] *sf* oak (tree); (*legno*) oak
que'rela *sf* (*Dir*) (legal) action
que'sito *sm* question, query; problem
questio'nario *sm* questionnaire
questi'one *sf* problem, question; (*controversia*) issue; (*litigio*) quarrel;

in ~ in question; **è ~ di tempo** it's a matter *o* question of time

PAROLA CHIAVE

'questo, -a *det* **1** (*dimostrativo*) this; these *pl*; **questo libro (qui** *o* **qua)** this book; **io prendo questo cappotto, tu quello** I'll take this coat, you take that one; **quest'oggi** today; **questa sera** this evening
2 (*enfatico*): **non fatemi più prendere di queste paure** don't frighten me like that again
▷ *pron* (*dimostrativo*) this (one); these (ones) *pl*; (*ciò*) this; **prendo questo (qui** *o* **qua)** I'll take this one; **preferisci questi o quelli?** do you prefer these (ones) or those (ones)?; **questo intendevo io** this is what I meant; **vengono Paolo e Luca: questo da Roma, quello da Palermo** Paolo and Luca are coming: the former from Palermo, the latter from Rome

ques'tura *sf* police headquarters
qui *av* here; **da** *o* **di ~** from here; **di ~ in avanti** from now on; **di ~ a poco/una settimana** in a little while/a week's time; **~ dentro/sopra/vicino** in/up/near here; *vedi anche* **questo**
quie'tanza [kwje'tantsa] *sf* receipt
qui'ete *sf* quiet, quietness; calmness; stillness; peace
qui'eto, -a *ag* quiet; (*notte*) calm, still; (*mare*) calm
'quindi *av* then ▷ *cong* therefore, so
'quindici ['kwinditʃi] *num* fifteen; **~ giorni** a fortnight (BRIT), two weeks
quindi'cina [kwindi'tʃina] *sf* (*serie*): **una ~ (di)** about fifteen; **fra una ~ di giorni** in a fortnight
quinta *sf vedi* **quinto**
quin'tale *sm* quintal (100 kg)
'quinto, -a *num* fifth
quiz [kwidz] *sm inv* (*domanda*) question; (*anche*): **gioco a ~** quiz game
'quota *sf* (*parte*) quota, share; (*Aer*) height, altitude; (*Ippica*) odds *pl*; **prendere/perdere ~** (*Aer*) to gain/lose height *o* altitude; **quota d'iscrizione** enrolment fee; (*a club*) membership fee
quotidi'ano, -a *ag* daily; (*banale*) everyday ▷ *sm* (*giornale*) daily (paper)
quozi'ente [kwot'tsjɛnte] *sm* (*Mat*) quotient; **quoziente d'intelligenza** intelligence quotient, IQ

r

R, r ['ɛrre] *sf o m* (*lettera*) R, r; **R come Roma** ≈ R for Robert (BRIT), R for Roger (US)

'rabbia *sf* (*ira*) anger, rage; (*accanimento, furia*) fury; (*Med*: *idrofobia*) rabies *sg*

rab'bino *sm* rabbi

rabbi'oso, -a *ag* angry, furious; (*facile all'ira*) quick-tempered; (*forze, acqua ecc*) furious, raging; (*Med*) rabid, mad

rabbo'nire *vt* to calm down

rabbrivi'dire *vi* to shudder, shiver

raccapez'zarsi [rakkapet'tsarsi] *vpr* **non ~** to be at a loss

raccapricci'ante [rakkaprit'tʃante] *ag* horrifying

raccatta'palle *sm inv* (*Sport*) ballboy

raccat'tare *vt* to pick up

rac'chetta [rak'ketta] *sf* (*per tennis*) racket; (*per ping-pong*) bat; **racchetta da neve** snowshoe; **racchetta da sci** ski stick

racchi'udere [rak'kjudere] *vt* to contain

rac'cogliere [rak'kɔʎʎere] *vt* to collect; (*raccattare*) to pick up; (*frutti, fiori*) to pick, pluck; (*Agr*) to harvest; (*approvazione, voti*) to win

rac'colta *sf* collecting *no pl*; collection; (*Agr*) harvesting *no pl*, gathering *no pl*; harvest, crop; (*adunata*) gathering; **raccolta differenziata** (*dei rifiuti*) *separate collection of different kinds of household waste*

rac'colto, -a *pp di* **raccogliere** ▷ *ag* (*persona*: *pensoso*) thoughtful; (*luogo*: *appartato*) secluded, quiet ▷ *sm* (*Agr*) crop, harvest

raccoman'dabile *ag* (highly) commendable; **è un tipo poco ~** he is not to be trusted

raccoman'dare *vt* to recommend; (*affidare*) to entrust; (*esortare*): **~ a qn di non fare** to tell *o* warn sb not to do; **raccoman'data** *sf* (*anche*: **lettera raccomandata**) recorded-delivery letter

raccon'tare *vt* **~ (a qn)** (*dire*) to tell (sb); (*narrare*) to relate (to sb), tell (sb) about; **rac'conto** *sm* telling *no pl*, relating *no pl*; (*fatto raccontato*) story, tale; **racconti per bambini** children's stories

rac'cordo *sm* (*Tecn*: *giunto*) connection, joint; (*Aut*): **raccordo anulare** (*Aut*) ring road (BRIT), beltway (US); **raccordo autostradale** slip road (BRIT), entrance (*o* exit) ramp (US); **raccordo ferroviario** siding; **raccordo stradale** link road

racimo'lare [ratʃimo'lare] *vt* (*fig*) to scrape together, glean

'rada *sf* (natural) harbour

'radar *sm* radar

raddoppi'are *vt, vi* to double

raddriz'zare [raddrit'tsare] *vt* to straighten; (*fig*: *correggere*) to put straight, correct

'radere *vt* (*barba*) to shave off; (*mento*) to shave; (*fig*: *rasentare*) to graze; to

skim; **radersi** *vpr* to shave (o.s.); **~ al suolo** to raze to the ground
radi'are *vt* to strike off
radia'tore *sm* radiator
radiazi'one [radjat'tsjone] *sf* (*Fisica*) radiation; (*cancellazione*) striking off
radi'cale *ag* radical ▷ *sm* (*Ling*) root; **radicali liberi** free radicals
ra'dicchio [ra'dikkjo] *sm* chicory
ra'dice [ra'ditʃe] *sf* root
'radio *sf inv* radio ▷ *sm* (*Chim*) radium; **radioat'tivo, -a** *ag* radioactive; **radio'cronaca, -che** *sf* radio commentary; **radiogra'fia** *sf* radiography; (*foto*) X-ray photograph
radi'oso, -a *ag* radiant
radios'veglia [radjoz'veʎʎa] *sf* radio alarm
'rado, -a *ag* (*capelli*) sparse, thin; (*visite*) infrequent; **di ~** rarely
radu'nare *vt* to gather, assemble; **radunarsi** *vpr* to gather, assemble
ra'dura *sf* clearing
raf'fermo, -a *ag* stale
'raffica, -che *sf* (*Meteor*) gust (of wind); (*di colpi*: *scarica*) burst of gunfire
raffigu'rare *vt* to represent
raffi'nato, -a *ag* refined
raffor'zare [raffor'tsare] *vt* to reinforce
raffredda'mento *sm* cooling
raffred'dare *vt* to cool; (*fig*) to dampen, have a cooling effect on; **raffreddarsi** *vpr* to grow cool *o* cold; (*prendere un raffreddore*) to catch a cold; (*fig*) to cool (off)
raffred'dato, -a *ag* (*Med*): **essere ~** to have a cold
raffred'dore *sm* (*Med*) cold
raf'fronto *sm* comparison
'rafia *sf* (*fibra*) raffia
rafting ['rafting] *sm* white-water rafting
ra'gazza [ra'gattsa] *sf* girl; (*fam*: *fidanzato*) girlfriend; **nome da ~** maiden name; **ragazza madre** unmarried mother
ra'gazzo [ra'gattso] *sm* boy; (*fam*: *fidanzato*) boyfriend; **ragazzi** *smpl* (*figli*) kids; **ciao ragazzi!** (*gruppo*) hi guys!
raggi'ante [rad'dʒante] *ag* radiant, shining
'raggio ['raddʒo] *sm* (*di sole ecc*) ray; (*Mat, distanza*) radius; (*di ruota ecc*) spoke; **raggio d'azione** range; **raggi X** X-rays
raggi'rare [raddʒi'rare] *vt* to take in, trick
raggi'ungere [rad'dʒundʒere] *vt* to reach; (*persona*: *riprendere*) to catch up (with); (*bersaglio*) to hit; (*fig*: *meta*) to achieve
raggomito'larsi *vpr* to curl up
raggranel'lare *vt* to scrape together
raggrup'pare *vt* to group (together)
ragiona'mento [radʒona'mento] *sm* reasoning *no pl*; arguing *no pl*; argument
ragio'nare [radʒo'nare] *vi* to reason; **~ di** (*discorrere*) to talk about
ragi'one [ra'dʒone] *sf* reason; (*dimostrazione, prova*) argument, reason; (*diritto*) right; **aver ~** to be right; **aver ~ di qn** to get the better of sb; **dare ~ a qn** to agree with sb; to prove sb right; **perdere la ~** to become insane; (*fig*) to take leave of one's senses; **in ~ di** at the rate of; to the amount of; according to; **a** *o* **con ~** rightly, justly; **a ragion veduta** after due consideration; **ragione sociale** (*Comm*) corporate name
ragione'ria [radʒone'ria] *sf* accountancy; accounts department
ragio'nevole [radʒo'nevole] *ag* reasonable
ragioni'ere, -a [radʒo'njɛre] *sm/f* accountant
ragli'are [raʎ'ʎare] *vi* to bray
ragna'tela [raɲɲa'tela] *sf* cobweb, spider's web
'ragno ['raɲɲo] *sm* spider
ragù *sm inv* (*Cuc*) meat sauce; stew

RAI-TV [raiti'vu] *sigla f* = **Radio televisione italiana**
ralle'grare *vt* to cheer up; **rallegrarsi** *vpr* to cheer up; (*provare allegrezza*) to rejoice; **rallegrarsi con qn** to congratulate sb
rallen'tare *vt* to slow down; (*fig*) to lessen, slacken ▷ *vi* to slow down
rallenta'tore *sm* (*Cinema*) slow-motion camera; **al ~** (*anche fig*) in slow motion
raman'zina [raman'dzina] *sf* lecture, telling-off
'rame *sm* (*Chim*) copper
rammari'carsi *vpr*: **~ (di)** (*rincrescersi*) to be sorry (about), regret; (*lamentarsi*) to complain (about)
rammen'dare *vt* to mend; (*calza*) to darn
'ramo *sm* branch
ramo'scello [ramoʃ'ʃɛllo] *sm* twig
'rampa *sf* flight (of stairs); **rampa di lancio** launching pad
rampi'cante *ag* (*Bot*) climbing
'rana *sf* frog
'rancido, -a ['rantʃido] *ag* rancid
ran'core *sm* rancour, resentment
ran'dagio, -a, -gi, -gie *o* **ge** [ran'dadʒo] *ag* (*gatto, cane*) stray
ran'dello *sm* club, cudgel
'rango, -ghi *sm* (*condizione sociale, Mil, riga*) rank
rannicchi'arsi [rannik'kjarsi] *vpr* to crouch, huddle
rannuvo'larsi *vpr* to cloud over, become overcast
'rapa *sf* (*Bot*) turnip
ra'pace [ra'patʃe] *ag* (*animale*) predatory; (*fig*) rapacious, grasping ▷ *sm* bird of prey
ra'pare *vt* (*capelli*) to crop, cut very short
rapida'mente *av* quickly, rapidly
rapidità *sf* speed
'rapido, -a *ag* fast; (*esame, occhiata*) quick, rapid ▷ *sm* (*Ferr*) express (train)
rapi'mento *sm* kidnapping; (*fig*) rapture
ra'pina *sf* robbery; **rapina in banca** bank robbery; **rapina a mano armata** armed robbery; **rapi'nare** *vt* to rob; **rapina'tore, -'trice** *sm/f* robber
ra'pire *vt* (*cose*) to steal; (*persone*) to kidnap; (*fig*) to enrapture, delight; **rapi'tore, -'trice** *sm/f* kidnapper
rap'porto *sm* (*resoconto*) report; (*legame*) relationship; (*Mat, Tecn*) ratio; **rapporti sessuali** sexual intercourse *sg*
rappre'saglia [rappre'saʎʎa] *sf* reprisal, retaliation
rappresen'tante *sm/f* representative
rappresen'tare *vt* to represent; (*Teatro*) to perform; **rappresentazi'one** *sf* representation; performing *no pl*; (*spettacolo*) performance
rara'mente *av* seldom, rarely
rare'fatto, -a *ag* rarefied
'raro, -a *ag* rare
ra'sare *vt* (*barba ecc*) to shave off; (*siepi, erba*) to trim, cut; **rasarsi** *vpr* to shave (o.s.)
raschi'are [ras'kjare] *vt* to scrape; (*macchia, fango*) to scrape off ▷ *vi* to clear one's throat
ra'sente *prep*: **~ (a)** close to, very near
'raso, -a *pp di* **radere** ▷ *ag* (*barba*) shaved; (*capelli*) cropped; (*con misure di capacità*) level; (*pieno: bicchiere*) full to the brim ▷ *sm* (*tessuto*) satin; **un cucchiaio ~** a level spoonful; **raso terra** close to the ground
ra'soio *sm* razor; **rasoio elettrico** electric shaver *o* razor
ras'segna [ras'seɲɲa] *sf* (*Mil*) inspection, review; (*esame*) inspection; (*resoconto*) review, survey; (*pubblicazione letteraria ecc*) review; (*mostra*) exhibition, show; **passare in ~** (*Mil, fig*) to review
rassegnarsi *vpr* (*accettare*): **~ (a qc/a**

fare) to resign o.s. (to sth/to doing)
rassicu'rare *vt* to reassure
rasso'dare *vt* to harden, stiffen; **rassodarsi** *vpr* to harden, to strengthen
rassomigli'anza [rassomiʎ'ʎantsa] *sf* resemblance
rassomigli'are [rassomiʎ'ʎare] *vi*: **~ a** to resemble, look like
rastrel'lare *vt* to rake; (*fig*: *perlustrare*) to comb
ras'trello *sm* rake
'rata *sf* (*quota*) instalment; **pagare a rate** to pay by instalments *o* on hire purchase (BRIT)
ratifi'care *vt* (*Dir*) to ratify
'ratto *sm* (*Dir*) abduction; (*Zool*) rat
rattop'pare *vt* to patch
rattris'tare *vt* to sadden; **rattristarsi** *vpr* to become sad
'rauco, -a, -chi, -che *ag* hoarse
rava'nello *sm* radish
ravi'oli *smpl* ravioli *sg*
ravvi'vare *vt* to revive; (*fig*) to brighten up, enliven
razio'nale [rattsjo'nale] *ag* rational
razio'nare [rattsjo'nare] *vt* to ration
razi'one [rat'tsjone] *sf* ration; (*porzione*) portion, share
'razza ['rattsa] *sf* race; (*Zool*) breed; (*discendenza, stirpe*) stock, race; (*sorta*) sort, kind
razzi'ale [rat'tsjale] *ag* racial
raz'zismo [rat'tsizmo] *sm* racism, racialism
raz'zista, -i, -e [rat'tsista] *ag, sm/f* racist, racialist
'razzo ['raddzo] *sm* rocket
R.C. *sigla m* (= *partito della Rifondazione Comunista*) *left-wing Italian political party*
re *sm inv* king; (*Mus*) D; (: *solfeggiando*) re
rea'gire [rea'dʒire] *vi* to react
re'ale *ag* real; (*di, da re*) royal ▷ *sm* **il ~** reality
reality [ri'aliti] *sm inv* reality show
realiz'zare [realid'dzare] *vt* (*progetto ecc*) to realize, carry out; (*sogno, desiderio*) to realize, fulfil; (*scopo*) to achieve; (*Comm*: *titoli ecc*) to realize; (*Calcio ecc*) to score; **realizzarsi** *vpr* to be realized
real'mente *av* really, actually
realtà *sf inv* reality
re'ato *sm* offence
reat'tore *sm* (*Fisica*) reactor; (*Aer*: *aereo*) jet; (: *motore*) jet engine
reazio'nario, -a [reattsjo'narjo] *ag* (*Pol*) reactionary
reazi'one [reat'tsjone] *sf* reaction
'rebus *sm inv* rebus; (*fig*) puzzle; enigma
recapi'tare *vt* to deliver
re'capito *sm* (*indirizzo*) address; (*consegna*) delivery; **recapito a domicilio** home delivery (service); **recapito telefonico** phone number
re'cedere [re'tʃɛdere] *vi* to withdraw
recensi'one [retʃen'sjone] *sf* review
re'cente [re'tʃɛnte] *ag* recent; **di ~** recently; **recente'mente** *av* recently
re'cidere [re'tʃidere] *vt* to cut off, chop off
recin'tare [retʃin'tare] *vt* to enclose, fence off
re'cinto [re'tʃinto] *sm* enclosure; (*ciò che recinge*) fence; surrounding wall
recipi'ente [retʃi'pjɛnte] *sm* container
re'ciproco, -a, -ci, -che [re'tʃiproko] *ag* reciprocal
'recita ['rɛtʃita] *sf* performance
reci'tare [retʃi'tare] *vt* (*poesia, lezione*) to recite; (*dramma*) to perform; (*ruolo*) to play *o* act (the part of)
recla'mare *vi* to complain ▷ *vt* (*richiedere*) to demand
re'clamo *sm* complaint
recli'nabile *ag* (*sedile*) reclining
reclusi'one *sf* (*Dir*) imprisonment
'recluta *sf* recruit
re'condito, -a *ag* secluded; (*fig*) secret, hidden

'record *ag inv* record *cpd* ▷ *sm inv* record; **in tempo ~, a tempo di ~** in record time; **detenere il ~ di** to hold the record for; **record mondiale** world record

recriminazi'one [rekriminat'tsjone] *sf* recrimination

recupe'rare *vt* (*rientrare in possesso di*) to recover, get back; (*tempo perduto*) to make up for; (*Naut*) to salvage; (: *naufraghi*) to rescue; (*delinquente*) to rehabilitate; **~ lo svantaggio** (*Sport*) to close the gap

redargu'ire *vt* to rebuke

re'dassi *ecc vb vedi* **redigere**

reddi'tizio, -a [reddi'tittsjo] *ag* profitable

'reddito *sm* income; (*dello Stato*) revenue; (*di un capitale*) yield

re'digere [re'didʒere] *vt* to write; (*contratto*) to draw up

'redini *sfpl* reins

'reduce ['rɛdutʃe] *ag*: **~ da** returning from, back from ▷ *sm/f* survivor

refe'rendum *sm inv* referendum

referenze [refe'rɛntse] *sfpl* references

re'ferto *sm* medical report

rega'lare *vt* to give (as a present), make a present of

re'galo *sm* gift, present

re'gata *sf* regatta

'reggere ['rɛddʒere] *vt* (*tenere*) to hold; (*sostenere*) to support, bear, hold up; (*portare*) to carry, bear; (*resistere*) to withstand; (*dirigere*: *impresa*) to manage, run; (*governare*) to rule, govern; (*Ling*) to take, be followed by ▷ *vi* (*resistere*): **~ a** to stand up to, hold out against; (*sopportare*): **~ a** to stand; (*durare*) to last; (*fig*: *teoria ecc*) to hold water; **reggersi** *vpr* (*stare ritto*) to stand

'reggia, -ge ['rɛddʒa] *sf* royal palace

reggi'calze [reddʒi'kaltse] *sm inv* suspender belt

reggi'mento [reddʒi'mento] *sm* (*Mil*) regiment

reggi'seno [reddʒi'seno] *sm* bra

re'gia, -'gie [re'dʒia] *sf* (*TV, Cinema ecc*) direction

re'gime [re'dʒime] *sm* (*Pol*) regime; (*Dir*: *aureo, patrimoniale ecc*) system; (*Med*) diet; (*Tecn*) (engine) speed

re'gina [re'dʒina] *sf* queen

regio'nale [redʒo'nale] *ag* regional ▷ *sm* local train (*stopping frequently*)

regi'one [re'dʒone] *sf* region; (*territorio*) region, district, area

re'gista, -i, -e [re'dʒista] *sm/f* (*TV, Cinema ecc*) director

regis'trare [redʒis'trare] *vt* (*Amm*) to register; (*Comm*) to enter; (*notare*) to note, take note of; (*canzone, conversazione*: *strumento di misura*) to record; (*mettere a punto*) to adjust, regulate; (*bagagli*) to check in; **registra'tore** *sm* (*strumento*) recorder, register; (*magnetofono*) tape recorder; **registratore di cassa** cash register; **registratore a cassette** cassette recorder

re'gistro [re'dʒistro] *sm* (*libro, Mus, Tech*) register; ledger; logbook; (*Dir*) registry

re'gnare [reɲ'ɲare] *vi* to reign, rule

'regno ['reɲɲo] *sm* kingdom; (*periodo*) reign; (*fig*) realm; **il R~ Unito** the United Kingdom; **regno animale/vegetale** animal/vegetable kingdom

'regola *sf* rule; **a ~ d'arte** duly; perfectly; **in ~** in order

rego'labile *ag* adjustable

regola'mento *sm* (*complesso di norme*) regulations *pl*; (*di debito*) settlement; **regolamento di conti** (*fig*) settling of scores

rego'lare *ag* regular; (*in regola*: *domanda*) in order, lawful ▷ *vt* to regulate, control; (*apparecchio*) to adjust, regulate; (*questione, conto, debito*) to settle; **regolarsi** *vpr* (*moderarsi*): **regolarsi nel bere/nello spendere** to control one's drinking/

spending; (*comportarsi*) to behave, act
rela'tivo, -a *ag* relative
relazi'one [relat'tsjone] *sf* (*fra cose, persone*) relation(ship); (*resoconto*) report, account
rele'gare *vt* to banish; (*fig*) to relegate
religi'one [reli'dʒone] *sf* religion
re'liquia *sf* relic
re'litto *sm* wreck; (*fig*) down-and-out
re'mare *vi* to row
remini'scenze [reminiʃʃɛntse] *sfpl* reminiscences
remis'sivo, -a *ag* submissive, compliant
'remo *sm* oar
re'moto, -a *ag* remote
'rendere *vt* (*ridare*) to return, give back; (*: saluto ecc*) to return; (*produrre*) to yield, bring in; (*esprimere, tradurre*) to render; **~ qc possibile** to make sth possible; **rendersi** *vpr* **rendersi utile** to make o.s. useful; **rendersi conto di qc** to realize sth; **~ qc possibile** to make sth possible; **~ grazie a qn** give thanks to sb; **~ omaggio a qn** to pay homage to sb; **~ un servizio a qn** to do sb a service; **~ una testimonianza** to give evidence; **non so se rendo l'idea** I don't know if I'm making myself clear
rendi'mento *sm* (*reddito*) yield; (*di manodopera, Tecn*) efficiency; (*capacità di produrre*) output; (*di studenti*) performance
'rendita *sf* (*di individuo*) private *o* unearned income; (*Comm*) revenue; **rendita annua** annuity
'rene *sm* kidney
'renna *sf* reindeer *inv*
re'parto *sm* department, section; (*Mil*) detachment
repel'lente *ag* repulsive
repen'taglio [repen'taʎʎo] *sm* **mettere a ~** to jeopardize, risk
repen'tino, -a *ag* sudden, unexpected
reper'torio *sm* (*Teatro*) repertory; (*elenco*) index, (alphabetical) list
'replica, -che *sf* repetition; reply, answer; (*obiezione*) objection; (*Teatro, Cinema*) repeat performance; (*copia*) replica
repli'care *vt* (*ripetere*) to repeat; (*rispondere*) to answer, reply
repressi'one *sf* repression
re'presso, -a *pp di* **reprimere**
re'primere *vt* to suppress, repress
re'pubblica, -che *sf* republic
reputazi'one [reputat'tsjone] *sf* reputation
requi'sire *vt* to requisition
requi'sito *sm* requirement
'resa *sf* (*l'arrendersi*) surrender; (*restituzione, rendimento*) return; **resa dei conti** rendering of accounts; (*fig*) day of reckoning
'resi *ecc vb vedi* **rendere**
resi'dente *ag* resident; **residenzi'ale** *ag* residential
re'siduo, -a *ag* residual, remaining ▷ *sm* remainder; (*Chim*) residue
'resina *sf* resin
resis'tente *ag* (*che resiste*): **~ a** resistant to; (*forte*) strong; (*duraturo*) long-lasting, durable; **~ al caldo** heat-resistant; **resis'tenza** *sf* resistance; (*di persona: fisica*) stamina, endurance; (*: mentale*) endurance, resistance

RESISTENZA

The **Resistenza** in Italy fought against the Nazis and the Fascists during the Second World War. Members of the **Resistenza** spanned a wide political spectrum and played a vital role in the Liberation and in the formation of the new democratic government at the end of the war.

re'sistere *vi* to resist; **~ a** (*assalto, tentazioni*) to resist; (*dolore*) to withstand; (*non patir danno*) to be resistant to

reso'conto *sm* report, account

res'pingere [res'pindʒere] *vt* to drive back, repel; (*rifiutare*) to reject; (*Ins: bocciare*) to fail

respi'rare *vi* to breathe; (*fig*) to get one's breath; to breathe again ▷ *vt* to breathe (in), inhale; **respirazi'one** *sf* breathing; **respirazione artificiale** artificial respiration; **res'piro** *sm* breathing *no pl*; (*singolo atto*) breath; (*fig*) respite, rest; **mandare un respiro di sollievo** to give a sigh of relief

respon'sabile *ag* responsible ▷ *sm/f* person responsible; (*capo*) person in charge; **~ di** responsible for; (*Dir*) liable for; **responsabilità** *sf inv* responsibility; (*legale*) liability

res'ponso *sm* answer

'ressa *sf* crowd, throng

'ressi *ecc vb vedi* **reggere**

res'tare *vi* (*rimanere*) to remain, stay; (*avanzare*) to be left, remain; **~ orfano/cieco** to become *o* be left an orphan/become blind; **~ d'accordo** to agree; **non resta più niente** there's nothing left; **restano pochi giorni** there are only a few days left

restau'rare *vt* to restore

res'tio, -a, -'tii, -'tie *ag*: **~ a** reluctant to

restitu'ire *vt* to return, give back; (*energie, forze*) to restore

'resto *sm* remainder, rest; (*denaro*) change; (*Mat*) remainder; **resti** *smpl* (*di cibo*) leftovers; (*di città*) remains; **del ~** moreover, besides; **tenga pure il ~** keep the change; **resti mortali** (mortal) remains

res'tringere [res'trindʒere] *vt* to reduce; (*vestito*) to take in; (*stoffa*) to shrink; (*fig*) to restrict, limit; **restringersi** *vpr* (*strada*) to narrow; (*stoffa*) to shrink

'rete *sf* net; (*fig*) trap, snare; (*di recinzione*) wire netting; (*Aut, Ferr, di spionaggio ecc*) network; **segnare una ~** (*Calcio*) to score a goal; **la R~** the Web; **rete ferroviaria** railway network; **rete del letto** (sprung) bed base; **rete stradale** road network; **rete (televisiva)** (*sistema*) network; (*canale*) channel

reti'cente [reti'tʃɛnte] *ag* reticent

retico'lato *sm* grid; (*rete*) wire netting; (*di filo spinato*) barbed wire (fence)

'retina *sf* (*Anat*) retina

re'torico, -a, -ci, -che *ag* rhetorical

retribu'ire *vt* to pay

'retro *sm inv* back ▷ *av* (*dietro*): **vedi ~** see over(leaf)

retro'cedere [retro'tʃɛdere] *vi* to withdraw ▷ *vt* (*Calcio*) to relegate; (*Mil*) to degrade

re'trogrado, -a *ag* (*fig*) reactionary, backward-looking

retro'marcia [retro'martʃa] *sf* (*Aut*) reverse; (: *dispositivo*) reverse gear

retro'scena [retroʃ'ʃɛna] *sm inv* (*Teatro*) backstage; **i ~** (*fig*) the behind-the-scenes activities

retrovi'sore *sm* (*Aut*) (rear-view) mirror

'retta *sf* (*Mat*) straight line; (*di convitto*) charge for bed and board; (*fig: ascolto*): **dar ~ a** to listen to, pay attention to

rettango'lare *ag* rectangular

ret'tangolo, -a *ag* right-angled ▷ *sm* rectangle

ret'tifica, -che *sf* rectification, correction

'rettile *sm* reptile

retti'lineo, -a *ag* rectilinear

'retto, -a *pp di* **reggere** ▷ *ag* straight; (*Mat*): **angolo ~** right angle; (*onesto*) honest, upright; (*giusto, esatto*) correct, proper, right

ret'tore *sm* (*Rel*) rector; (*di università*) ≈ chancellor

reuma'tismo *sm* rheumatism

revisi'one *sf* auditing *no pl*; audit;

servicing *no pl*; overhaul; review; revision; **revisione di bozze** proofreading
revi'sore *sm*; **revisore di bozze** proofreader; **revisore di conti** auditor
revival [ri'vaivəl] *sm inv* revival
'revoca *sf* revocation
revo'care *vt* to revoke
re'volver *sm inv* revolver
ri'abbia *ecc vb vedi* **riavere**
riabili'tare *vt* to rehabilitate
rianimazi'one [rianimat'tsjone] *sf* (*Med*) resuscitation; **centro di ~** intensive care unit
ria'prire *vt* to reopen, open again; **riaprirsi** *vpr* to reopen, open again
ri'armo *sm* (*Mil*) rearmament
rias'sumere *vt* (*riprendere*) to resume; (*impiegare di nuovo*) to re-employ; (*sintetizzare*) to summarize; **rias'sunto, -a** *pp di* **riassumere** ▷ *sm* summary
riattac'care *vt* (*attaccare di nuovo*): **~ (a)** (*manifesto, francobollo*) to stick back (on); (*bottone*) to sew back (on); (*quadro, chiavi*) to hang back up (on); **~ (il telefono** *o* **il ricevitore)** to hang up (the receiver)
ria'vere *vt* to have again; (*avere indietro*) to get back; (*riacquistare*) to recover; **riaversi** *vpr* to recover
riba'dire *vt* (*fig*) to confirm
ri'balta *sf* flap; (*Teatro*: *proscenio*) front of the stage; (*fig*) limelight; **luci della ~** footlights *pl*
ribal'tabile *ag* (*sedile*) tip-up
ribal'tare *vt, vi* (*anche*: **ribaltarsi**) to turn over, tip over
ribas'sare *vt* to lower, bring down ▷ *vi* to come down, fall
ri'battere *vt* to return, hit back; (*confutare*) to refute; **~ che** to retort that
ribel'larsi *vpr* **~ (a)** to rebel (against); **ri'belle** *ag* (*soldati*) rebel; (*ragazzo*) rebellious ▷ *sm/f* rebel
'ribes *sm inv* currant; **ribes nero** blackcurrant; **ribes rosso** redcurrant
ri'brezzo [ri'breddzo] *sm* disgust, loathing; **far ~ a** to disgust
ribut'tante *ag* disgusting, revolting
rica'dere *vi* to fall again; (*scendere a terra*: *fig*: *nel peccato ecc*) to fall back; (*vestiti, capelli ecc*) to hang (down); (*riversarsi*: *fatiche, colpe*): **~ su** to fall on; **rica'duta** *sf* (*Med*) relapse
rica'mare *vt* to embroider
ricambi'are *vt* to change again; (*contraccambiare*) to repay, return; **ri'cambio** *sm* exchange, return; (*Fisiol*) metabolism
ri'camo *sm* embroidery
ricapito'lare *vt* to recapitulate, sum up
ricari'care *vt* (*arma, macchina fotografica*) to reload; (*pipa*) to refill; (*orologio*) to rewind; (*batteria*) to recharge
ricat'tare *vt* to blackmail; **ri'catto** *sm* blackmail
rica'vare *vt* (*estrarre*) to draw out, extract; (*ottenere*) to obtain, gain
ric'chezza [rik'kettsa] *sf* wealth; (*fig*) richness
'riccio, -a ['rittʃo] *ag* curly ▷ *sm* (*Zool*) hedgehog; **riccio di mare** sea urchin; **'ricciolo** *sm* curl
'ricco, -a, -chi, -che *ag* rich; (*persona, paese*) rich, wealthy ▷ *sm/f* rich man/woman; **i ricchi** the rich; **~ di** full of; rich in
ri'cerca, -che [ri'tʃerka] *sf* search; (*indagine*) investigation, inquiry; (*studio*): **la ~** research; **una ~** piece of research; **ricerca di mercato** market research
ricer'care [ritʃer'kare] *vt* (*motivi, cause*) to look for, try to determine; (*successo, piacere*) to pursue; (*onore, gloria*) to seek; **ricer'cato, -a** *ag* (*apprezzato*) much sought-after; (*affettato*) studied, affected ▷ *sm/f* (*Polizia*) wanted man/woman

ricerca'tore, -'trice [ritʃerka'tore] *sm/f* (*Ins*) researcher
ri'cetta [ri'tʃɛtta] *sf* (*Med*) prescription; (*Cuc*) recipe; **mi può fare una ~ medica?** could you write me a prescription?
ricettazi'one [ritʃettat'tsjone] *sf* (*Dir*) receiving (stolen goods)
ri'cevere [ri'tʃevere] *vt* to receive; (*stipendio, lettera*) to get, receive; (*accogliere*: *ospite*) to welcome; (*vedere*: *cliente, rappresentante ecc*) to see; **ricevi'mento** *sm* receiving *no pl*; (*festa*) reception; **ricevi'tore** *sm* (*Tecn*) receiver; **rice'vuta** *sf* receipt; **posso avere una ricevuta, per favore?** can I have a receipt, please?; **ricevuta fiscale** receipt for tax purposes; **ricevuta di ritorno** (*Posta*) advice of receipt
richia'mare [rikja'mare] *vt* (*chiamare indietro, ritelefonare*) to call back; (*ambasciatore, truppe*) to recall; (*rimproverare*) to reprimand; (*attirare*) to attract, draw; **può ~ più tardi?** can you call back later?; **richiamarsi a** (*riferirsi a*) to refer to
richi'edere [ri'kjɛdere] *vt* to ask again for; (*chiedere indietro*): **~ qc** to ask for sth back; (*chiedere*: *per sapere*) to ask; (: *per avere*) to ask for; (*Amm*: *documenti*) to apply for; (*esigere*) to need, require; **richi'esta** *sf* (*domanda*) request; (*Amm*) application, request; (*esigenza*) demand, request; **a richiesta** on request
rici'clare [ritʃi'klare] *vt* to recycle
'ricino ['ritʃino] *sm*: **olio di ~** castor oil
ricognizi'one [rikoɲɲit'tsjone] *sf* (*Mil*) reconnaissance; (*Dir*) recognition, acknowledgement
ricominci'are [rikomin'tʃare] *vt, vi* to start again, begin again
ricom'pensa *sf* reward
ricompen'sare *vt* to reward
riconciliarsi *vpr* to be reconciled
ricono'scente [rikonoʃ'ʃɛnte] *ag* grateful
rico'noscere [riko'noʃʃere] *vt* to recognize; (*Dir*: *figlio, debito*) to acknowledge; (*ammettere*: *errore*) to admit, acknowledge
rico'perto, -a *pp di* **ricoprire**
ricopi'are *vt* to copy
rico'prire *vt* (*coprire*) to cover; (*occupare*: *carica*) to hold
ricor'dare *vt* to remember, recall; (*richiamare alla memoria*): **~ qc a qn** to remind sb of sth; **ricordarsi** *vpr* **ricordarsi (di)** to remember; **ricordarsi di qc/di aver fatto** to remember sth/having done
ri'cordo *sm* memory; (*regalo*) keepsake, souvenir; (*di viaggio*) souvenir
ricor'rente *ag* recurrent, recurring; **ricor'renza** *sf* recurrence; (*festività*) anniversary
ri'correre *vi* (*ripetersi*) to recur; **~ a** (*rivolgersi*) to turn to; (: *Dir*) to appeal to; (*servirsi di*) to have recourse to
ricostitu'ente *ag* (*Med*): **cura ~** tonic
ricostru'ire *vt* (*casa*) to rebuild; (*fatti*) to reconstruct
ri'cotta *sf* *soft white unsalted cheese made from sheep's milk*
ricove'rare *vt* to give shelter to; **~ qn in ospedale** to admit sb to hospital
ri'covero *sm* shelter, refuge; (*Mil*) shelter; (*Med*) admission (to hospital)
ricreazi'one [rikreat'tsjone] *sf* recreation, entertainment; (*Ins*) break
ri'credersi *vpr* to change one's mind
ridacchi'are [ridak'kjare] *vi* to snigger
ri'dare *vt* to return, give back
'ridere *vi* to laugh; (*deridere, beffare*): **~ di** to laugh at, make fun of
ri'dicolo, -a *ag* ridiculous, absurd
ridimensio'nare *vt* to reorganize; (*fig*) to see in the right perspective
ri'dire *vt* to repeat; (*criticare*) to find fault with; to object to; **trova sempre qualcosa da ~** he always manages to

find fault
ridon'dante *ag* redundant
ri'dotto, -a *pp di* **ridurre** ▷ *ag* (*biglietto*) reduced; (*formato*) small
ri'duco *ecc vb vedi* **ridurre**
ri'durre *vt* (*anche Chim, Mat*) to reduce; (*prezzo, spese*) to cut, reduce; (*accorciare: opera letteraria*) to abridge; (: *Radio, TV*) to adapt; **ridursi** *vpr* (*diminuirsi*) to be reduced, shrink; **ridursi a** to be reduced to; **ridursi pelle e ossa** to be reduced to skin and bone; **ri'dussi** *ecc vb vedi* **ridurre**; **ridut'tore** *sm* (*Elec*) adaptor; **riduzi'one** *sf* reduction; abridgement; adaptation; **ci sono riduzioni per i bambini/gli studenti?** is there a reduction for children/students?
ri'ebbi *ecc vb vedi* **riavere**
riem'pire *vt* to fill (up); (*modulo*) to fill in *o* out; **riempirsi** *vpr* to fill (up); **~ qc di** to fill sth (up) with
rien'tranza [rien'trantsa] *sf* recess; indentation
rien'trare *vi* (*entrare di nuovo*) to go (*o* come) back in; (*tornare*) to return; (*fare una rientranza*) to go in, curve inwards; to be indented; (*riguardare*): **~ in** to be included among, form part of
riepilo'gare *vt* to summarize ▷ *vi* to recapitulate
ri'esco *ecc vb vedi* **riuscire**
ri'fare *vt* to do again; (*ricostruire*) to make again; (*nodo*) to tie again, do up again; (*imitare*) to imitate, copy; **rifarsi** *vpr* (*risarcirsi*): **rifarsi di** to make up for; (*vendicarsi*): **rifarsi di qc su qn** to get one's own back on sb for sth; (*riferirsi*): **rifarsi a** to go back to; to follow; **~ il letto** to make the bed; **rifarsi una vita** to make a new life for o.s.
riferi'mento *sm* reference; **in** *o* **con ~ a** with reference to
rife'rire *vt* (*riportare*) to report ▷ *vi* to do a report; **riferirsi** *vpr* **riferirsi a** to refer to
rifi'nire *vt* to finish off, put the finishing touches to
rifiu'tare *vt* to refuse; **~ di fare** to refuse to do; **rifi'uto** *sm* refusal; **rifiuti** *smpl* (*spazzatura*) rubbish *sg*, refuse *sg*
riflessi'one *sf* (*Fisica, meditazione*) reflection; (*il pensare*) thought, reflection; (*osservazione*) remark
rifles'sivo, -a *ag* (*persona*) thoughtful, reflective; (*Ling*) reflexive
ri'flesso, -a *pp di* **riflettere** ▷ *sm* (*di luce, allo specchio*) reflection; (*Fisiol*) reflex; **di** *o* **per ~** indirectly
riflessologia [riflessolo'dʒia] *sf* reflexology
ri'flettere *vt* to reflect ▷ *vi* to think; **riflettersi** *vpr* to be reflected; **~ su** to think over
riflet'tore *sm* reflector; (*proiettore*) floodlight; searchlight
ri'flusso *sm* flowing back; (*della marea*) ebb; **un'epoca di ~** an era of nostalgia
ri'forma *sf* reform; **la R~** (*Rel*) the Reformation
riforma'torio *sm* (*Dir*) community home (BRIT), reformatory (US)
riforni'mento *sm* supplying, providing; restocking; **rifornimenti** *smpl* (*provviste*) supplies, provisions
rifor'nire *vt* (*provvedere*): **~ di** to supply *o* provide with; (*fornire di nuovo: casa ecc*) to restock; **rifornirsi** *vpr* **rifornirsi di qc** to stock up on sth
rifugi'arsi [rifu'dʒarsi] *vpr* to take refuge; **rifugi'ato, -a** *sm/f* refugee
ri'fugio [ri'fudʒo] *sm* refuge, shelter; (*in montagna*) shelter; **rifugio antiaereo** air-raid shelter
'riga, -ghe *sf* line; (*striscia*) stripe; (*di persone, cose*) line, row; (*regolo*) ruler; (*scriminatura*) parting; **mettersi in ~** to line up; **a righe** (*foglio*) lined; (*vestito*) striped
ri'gare *vt* (*foglio*) to rule ▷ *vi* **~ diritto**

(*fig*) to toe the line
rigatti'ere *sm* junk dealer
righerò *ecc* [rige'rɔ] *vb vedi* **rigare**
'rigido, -a ['ridʒido] *ag* rigid, stiff; (*membra ecc: indurite*) stiff; (*Meteor*) harsh, severe; (*fig*) strict
rigogli'oso, -a [rigoʎ'ʎoso] *ag* (*pianta*) luxuriant; (*fig: commercio, sviluppo*) thriving
ri'gore *sm* (*Meteor*) harshness, rigours *pl*; (*fig*) severity, strictness; (*anche:* **calcio di ~**) penalty; **di ~** compulsory; **a rigor di termini** strictly speaking
riguar'dare *vt* to look at again; (*considerare*) to regard, consider; (*concernere*) to regard, concern; **riguardarsi** *vpr* (*aver cura di sé*) to look after o.s.
rigu'ardo *sm* (*attenzione*) care; (*considerazione*) regard, respect; **~ a** concerning, with regard to; **non aver riguardi nell'agire/nel parlare** to act/speak freely
rilasci'are [rilaʃ'ʃare] *vt* (*rimettere in libertà*) to release; (*Amm: documenti*) to issue
rilassarsi *vpr* to relax; (*fig: disciplina*) to become slack
rile'gare *vt* (*libro*) to bind
ri'leggere [ri'lɛddʒere] *vt* to reread, read again; (*rivedere*) to read over
ri'lento: **a ~** *av* slowly
rile'vante *ag* considerable; important
rile'vare *vt* (*ricavare*) to find; (*notare*) to notice; (*mettere in evidenza*) to point out; (*venire a conoscere: notizia*) to learn; (*raccogliere: dati*) to gather, collect; (*Topografia*) to survey; (*Mil*) to relieve; (*Comm*) to take over
rili'evo *sm* (*Arte, Geo*) relief; (*fig: rilevanza*) importance; (*Topografia*) survey; **dar ~ a** *o* **mettere in ~ qc** (*fig*) to bring sth out, highlight sth
rilut'tante *ag* reluctant
'rima *sf* rhyme; (*verso*) verse
riman'dare *vt* to send again; (*restituire, rinviare*) to send back, return; (*differire*): **~ qc (a)** to postpone sth *o* put sth off (till); (*fare riferimento*): **~ qn a** to refer sb to; **essere rimandato** (*Ins*) to have to repeat one's exams
ri'mando *sm* (*rinvio*) return; (*dilazione*) postponement; (*riferimento*) cross-reference
rima'nente *ag* remaining ▷ *sm* rest, remainder; **i rimanenti** (*persone*) the rest of them, the others
rima'nere *vi* (*restare*) to remain, stay; (*avanzare*) to be left, remain; (*restare stupito*) to be amazed; (*restare, mancare*): **rimangono poche settimane a Pasqua** there are only a few weeks left till Easter; **rimane da vedere se** it remains to be seen whether; (*diventare*): **~ vedovo** to be left a widower; (*trovarsi*): **~ sorpreso** to be surprised
rimangi'are [riman'dʒare] *vt* to eat again; **~rsi la parola/una promessa** (*fig*) to go back on one's word/one's promise
ri'mango *ecc* *vb vedi* **rimanere**
rimargi'narsi *vpr* to heal
rimbal'zare [rimbal'tsare] *vi* to bounce back, rebound; (*proiettile*) to ricochet
rimbam'bito, -a *ag* senile, in one's dotage
rimboc'care *vt* (*coperta*) to tuck in; (*maniche, pantaloni*) to turn *o* roll up
rimbom'bare *vi* to resound
rimbor'sare *vt* to pay back, repay
rimedi'are *vi* **~ a** to remedy ▷ *vt* (*fam: procurarsi*) to get *o* scrape together
ri'medio *sm* (*medicina*) medicine; (*cura, fig*) remedy, cure
ri'mettere *vt* (*mettere di nuovo*) to put back; (*indossare di nuovo*): **~ qc** to put sth back on, put sth on again; (*affidare*) to entrust; (*: decisione*) to r[illegible] (*condonare*) to remit; (*Comm: merci*) to deliver; (*: denaro*) to remit; (*vomitare*) to

bring up; (*perdere*: *anche*: **rimetterci**) to lose; **rimettersi al bello** (*tempo*) to clear up; **rimettersi in salute** to get better, recover one's health
ri'misi *ecc vb vedi* **rimettere**
'rimmel® *sm inv* mascara
rimoder'nare *vt* to modernize
rimorchi'are [rimor'kjare] *vt* to tow; (*fig*: *ragazza*) to pick up
ri'morchio [ri'mɔrkjo] *sm* tow; (*veicolo*) trailer
ri'morso *sm* remorse
rimozi'one [rimot'tsjone] *sf* removal; (*da un impiego*) dismissal; (*Psic*) repression
rimpatri'are *vi* to return home ▷ *vt* to repatriate
rimpi'angere [rim'pjandʒere] *vt* to regret; (*persona*) to miss; **rimpi'anto, -a** *pp di* **rimpiangere** ▷ *sm* regret
rimpiaz'zare [rimpjat'tsare] *vt* to replace
rimpiccio'lire [rimpittʃo'lire] *vt* to make smaller ▷ *vi* (*anche*: **rimpicciolirsi**) to become smaller
rimpinzarsi [rimpin'tsarsi] *vpr* **~ (di qc)** to stuff o.s. (with sth)
rimprove'rare *vt* to rebuke, reprimand
rimu'overe *vt* to remove; (*destituire*) to dismiss
Rinasci'mento [rinaʃʃi'mento] *sm* **il ~** the Renaissance
ri'nascita [ri'naʃʃita] *sf* rebirth, revival
rinca'rare *vt* to increase the price of ▷ *vi* to go up, become more expensive
rinca'sare *vi* to go home
rinchi'udere [rin'kjudere] *vt* to shut (*o* lock) up; **rinchiudersi** *vpr* **rinchiudersi in** to shut o.s. up in; **rinchiudersi in se stesso** to withdraw into o.s.
rin'correre *vt* to chase, run after; **rin'corsa** *sf* short run
rin'crescere [rin'kreʃʃere] *vb impers* **mi rincresce che/di non poter fare** I'm sorry that/I can't do, I regret that/being unable to do
rinfacci'are [rinfat'tʃare] *vt* (*fig*): **~ qc a qn** to throw sth in sb's face
rinfor'zare [rinfor'tsare] *vt* to reinforce, strengthen ▷ *vi* (*anche*: **rinforzarsi**) to grow stronger
rinfres'care *vt* (*atmosfera, temperatura*) to cool (down); (*abito, pareti*) to freshen up ▷ *vi* (*tempo*) to grow cooler; **rinfrescarsi** *vpr* (*ristorarsi*) to refresh o.s.; (*lavarsi*) to freshen up; **rin'fresco, -schi** *sm* (*festa*) party; **rinfreschi** *smpl* refreshments
rin'fusa *sf* **alla ~** in confusion, higgledy-piggledy
ringhi'are [rin'gjare] *vi* to growl, snarl
ringhi'era [rin'gjɛra] *sf* railing; (*delle scale*) banister(s) (*pl*)
ringiova'nire [rindʒova'nire] *vt* (*vestito, acconciatura ecc*): **~ qn** to make sb look younger; (: *vacanze ecc*) to rejuvenate ▷ *vi* (*anche*: **ringiovanirsi**) to become (*o* look) younger
ringrazia'mento [ringrattsja'mento] *sm* thanks *pl*
ringrazi'are [ringrat'tsjare] *vt* to thank; **~ qn di qc** to thank sb for sth
rinne'gare *vt* (*fede*) to renounce; (*figlio*) to disown, repudiate
rinnova'mento *sm* renewal; (*economico*) revival
rinno'vare *vt* to renew; (*ripetere*) to repeat, renew
rinoce'ronte [rinotʃe'ronte] *sm* rhinoceros
rino'mato, -a *ag* renowned, celebrated
rintracci'are [rintrat'tʃare] *vt* to track down
rintro'nare *vi* to boom, roar ▷ *vt* (*assordare*) to deafen; (*stordire*) to stun
rinunci'are [rinun'tʃare] *vi* **~ a** to give up, renounce; **~ a fare qc** to give up doing sth

rinvi'are *vt* (*rimandare indietro*) to send back, return; (*differire*): **~ qc (a)** to postpone sth *o* put sth off (till); to adjourn sth (till); (*fare un rimando*): **~ qn a** to refer sb to

rin'vio, -'vii *sm* (*rimando*) return; (*differimento*) postponement; (: *di seduta*) adjournment; (*in un testo*) cross-reference; **rinvio a giudizio** (*Dir*) indictment

riò *ecc vb vedi* **riavere**

ri'one *sm* district, quarter

riordi'nare *vt* (*rimettere in ordine*) to tidy; (*riorganizzare*) to reorganize

riorganiz'zare [riorganid'dzare] *vt* to reorganize

ripa'gare *vt* to repay

ripa'rare *vt* (*proteggere*) to protect, defend; (*correggere*: *male, torto*) to make up for; (: *errore*) to put right; (*aggiustare*) to repair ▷ *vi* (*mettere rimedio*): **~ a** to make up for; **ripararsi** *vpr* (*rifugiarsi*) to take refuge *o* shelter; **dove lo posso far ~?** where can I get this repaired?; **riparazi'one** *sf* (*di un torto*) reparation; (*di guasto, scarpe*) repairing *no pl*; repair; (*risarcimento*) compensation

ri'paro *sm* (*protezione*) shelter, protection; (*rimedio*) remedy

ripar'tire *vt* (*dividere*) to divide up; (*distribuire*) to share out ▷ *vi* to set off again; to leave again

ripas'sare *vi* to come (*o* go) back ▷ *vt* (*scritto, lezione*) to go over (again)

ripen'sare *vi* to think; (*cambiare pensiero*) to change one's mind; (*tornare col pensiero*): **~ a** to recall

ripercu'otersi *vpr* **~ su** (*fig*) to have repercussions on

ripercussi'one *sf* (*fig*): **avere una ~** *o* **delle ripercussioni su** to have repercussions on

ripes'care *vt* (*pesce*) to catch again; (*persona, cosa*) to fish out; (*fig*: *ritrovare*) to dig out

ri'petere *vt* to repeat; (*ripassare*) to go over; **può ~ per favore?** can you repeat that please?; **ripetizi'one** *sf* repetition; (*di lezione*) revision; **ripetizioni** *sfpl* (*Ins*) private tutoring *o* coaching *sg*

ripi'ano *sm* (*di mobile*) shelf

ri'picca *sf* **per ~** out of spite

'ripido, -a *ag* steep

ripie'gare *vt* to refold; (*piegare più volte*) to fold (up) ▷ *vi* (*Mil*) to retreat, fall back; (*fig*: *accontentarsi*): **~ su** to make do with

ripi'eno, -a *ag* full; (*Cuc*) stuffed; (: *panino*) filled ▷ *sm* (*Cuc*) stuffing

ri'pone, ri'pongo *ecc vb vedi* **riporre**

ri'porre *vt* (*porre al suo posto*) to put back, replace; (*mettere via*) to put away; (*fiducia, speranza*): **~ qc in qn** to place *o* put sth in sb

ripor'tare *vt* (*portare indietro*) to bring (*o* take) back; (*riferire*) to report; (*citare*) to quote; (*vittoria*) to gain; (*successo*) to have; (*Mat*) to carry; **riportarsi a** (*anche fig*) to go back to; (*riferirsi a*) to refer to; **~ danni** to suffer damage

ripo'sare *vt, vi* to rest; **riposarsi** *vpr* to rest

ri'posi *ecc vb vedi* **riporre**

ri'poso *sm* rest; (*Mil*): **~!** at ease!; **a ~** (*in pensione*) retired; **giorno di ~** day off

ripos'tiglio [ripos'tiʎʎo] *sm* lumber-room

ri'prendere *vt* (*prigioniero, fortezza*) to recapture; (*prendere indietro*) to take back; (*ricominciare*: *lavoro*) to resume; (*andare a prendere*) to fetch, come back for; (*riassumere*: *impiegati*) to take on again, re-employ; (*rimproverare*) to tell off; (*restringere*: *abito*) to take in; (*Cinema*) to shoot; **riprendersi** *vpr* to recover; (*correggersi*) to correct o.s.; **ri'presa** *sf* recapture; resumption; (*economica, da malattia, emozione*) recovery; (*Aut*) acceleration *no pl*; (*Teatro, Cinema*) rerun; (*Cinema*: *presa*) shooting *no pl*; shot; (*Sport*) second

half; (: *Pugilato*) round; **a più riprese** on several occasions, several times; **ripresa cinematografica** shot
ripristi'nare *vt* to restore
ripro'durre *vt* to reproduce; **riprodursi** *vpr* (*Biol*) to reproduce; (*riformarsi*) to form again
ripro'vare *vt* (*provare di nuovo*: *gen*) to try again; (*vestito*) to try on again; (: *sensazione*) to experience again ▷ *vi* (*tentare*): **~ (a fare qc)** to try (to do sth) again; **riproverò più tardi** I'll try again later
ripudi'are *vt* to repudiate, disown
ripu'gnante [ripuɲ'ɲante] *ag* disgusting, repulsive
ri'quadro *sm* square; (*Archit*) panel
ri'saia *sf* paddy field
risa'lire *vi* (*ritornare in su*) to go back up; **~ a** (*ritornare con la mente*) to go back to; (*datare da*) to date back to, go back to
risal'tare *vi* (*fig*: *distinguersi*) to stand out; (*Archit*) to project, jut out
risa'puto, -a *ag* **è ~ che ...** everyone knows that ..., it is common knowledge that ...
risarci'mento [risartʃi'mento] *sm* **~ (di)** compensation (for); **risarcimento danni** damages
risar'cire [risar'tʃire] *vt* (*cose*) to pay compensation for; (*persona*): **~ qn di qc** to compensate sb for sth
ri'sata *sf* laugh
riscalda'mento *sm* heating; **riscaldamento centrale** central heating
riscal'dare *vt* (*scaldare*) to heat; (: *mani, persona*) to warm; (*minestra*) to reheat; **riscaldarsi** *vpr* to warm up
ris'catto *sm* ransom; redemption
rischia'rare [riskja'rare] *vt* (*illuminare*) to light up; (*colore*) to make lighter; **rischiararsi** *vpr* (*tempo*) to clear up; (*cielo*) to clear; (*fig*: *volto*) to brighten up; **rischiararsi la voce** to clear one's throat
rischi'are [ris'kjare] *vt* to risk ▷ *vi* **~ di fare qc** to risk *o* run the risk of doing sth
'rischio ['riskjo] *sm* risk; **rischi'oso, -a** *ag* risky, dangerous
riscia'cquare [riʃʃa'kware] *vt* to rinse
riscon'trare *vt* (*rilevare*) to find
ris'cuotere *vt* (*ritirare*: *somma*) to collect; (: *stipendio*) to draw, collect; (*assegno*) to cash; (*fig*: *successo ecc*) to win, earn
'rise *ecc vb vedi* **ridere**
risenti'mento *sm* resentment
risen'tire *vt* to hear again; (*provare*) to feel ▷ *vi* **~ di** to feel (*o* show) the effects of; **risentirsi** *vpr* **risentirsi di** *o* **per** to take offence at, resent; **risen'tito, -a** *ag* resentful
ri'serbo *sm* reserve
ri'serva *sf* reserve; (*di caccia, pesca*) preserve; (*restrizione, di indigeni*) reservation; **di ~** (*provviste ecc*) in reserve
riser'vare *vt* (*tenere in serbo*) to keep, put aside; (*prenotare*) to book, reserve; **ho riservato un tavolo a nome...** I booked a table in the name of ...; **riser'vato, -a** *ag* (*prenotato*: *fig*: *persona*) reserved; (*confidenziale*) confidential
'risi *ecc vb vedi* **ridere**
risi'edere *vi* **~ a** *o* **in** to reside in
'risma *sf* (*di carta*) ream; (*fig*) kind, sort
'riso (*pl(f)* **risa**) (: *il ridere*) *sm* **il ~** laughter; (*pianta*) rice ▷ *pp di* **ridere**
riso'lino *sm* snigger
ri'solsi *ecc vb vedi* **risolvere**
ri'solto, -a *pp di* **risolvere**
riso'luto, -a *ag* determined, resolute
risoluzi'one [risolut'tsjone] *sf* solving *no pl*; (*Mat*) solution; (*decisione, di schermo, immagine*) resolution
ri'solvere *vt* (*difficoltà, controversia*) to resolve; (*problema*) to solve; (*decidere*): **~ di fare** to resolve to do; **risolversi** *vpr* (*decidersi*): **risolversi a fare** to make up one's mind to do; (*andare a*

finire): **risolversi in** to end up, turn out; **risolversi in nulla** to come to nothing

riso'nanza [riso'nantsa] *sf* resonance; **aver vasta ~** (*fig*: *fatto ecc*) to be known far and wide

ri'sorgere [ri'sordʒere] *vi* to rise again; **risorgi'mento** *sm* revival; **il Risorgimento** (*Storia*) the Risorgimento

RISORGIMENTO

The **Risorgimento** was the political movement which led to the proclamation of the Kingdom of Italy in 1861, and eventually to unification in 1871.

ri'sorsa *sf* expedient, resort; **risorse umane** human resources

ri'sorsi *ecc vb vedi* **risorgere**

ri'sotto *sm* (*Cuc*) risotto

risparmi'are *vt* to save; (*non uccidere*) to spare ▷ *vi* to save; **~ qc a qn** to spare sb sth

ris'parmio *sm* saving *no pl*; (*denaro*) savings *pl*; **risparmi** *smpl* (*denaro*) savings

rispec'chiare [rispek'kjare] *vt* to reflect

rispet'tabile *ag* respectable

rispet'tare *vt* to respect; **farsi ~** to command respect

rispet'tivo, -a *ag* respective

ris'petto *sm* respect; **rispetti** *smpl* (*saluti*) respects, regards; **~ a** (*in paragone a*) compared to; (*in relazione a*) as regards, as for

ris'pondere *vi* to answer, reply; (*freni*) to respond; **~ a** (*domanda*) to answer, reply to; (*persona*) to answer; (*invito*) to reply to; (*provocazione*: *veicolo, apparecchio*) to respond to; (*corrispondere a*) to correspond to; (: *speranze, bisogno*) to answer; **~ di** to answer for; **ris'posta** *sf* answer, reply; **in risposta a** in reply to

'rissa *sf* brawl

ris'tampa *sf* reprinting *no pl*; reprint

risto'rante *sm* restaurant; **mi può consigliare un buon ~?** can you recommend a good restaurant?

ris'tretto, -a *pp di* **restringere** ▷ *ag* (*racchiuso*) enclosed, hemmed in; (*angusto*) narrow; (*limitato*): **~ (a)** restricted *o* limited (to); (*Cuc*: *brodo*) thick; (: *caffè*) extra strong

ristruttu'rare *vt* (*azienda*) to reorganize; (*edificio*) to restore; (*appartamento*) to alter; (*crema, balsamo*) to repair

risucchi'are [risuk'kjare] *vt* to suck in

risul'tare *vi* (*dimostrarsi*) to prove (to be), turn out (to be); (*riuscire*): **~ vincitore** to emerge as the winner; **~ da** (*provenire*) to result from, be the result of; **mi risulta che ...** I understand that ...; **non mi risulta** not as far as I know; **risul'tato** *sm* result

risuo'nare *vi* (*rimbombare*) to resound

risurrezi'one [risurret'tsjone] *sf* (*Rel*) resurrection

risusci'tare [risuʃʃi'tare] *vt* to resuscitate, restore to life; (*fig*) to revive, bring back ▷ *vi* to rise (from the dead)

ris'veglio [riz'veʎʎo] *sm* waking up; (*fig*) revival

ris'volto *sm* (*di giacca*) lapel; (*di pantaloni*) turn-up; (*di manica*) cuff; (*di tasca*) flap; (*di libro*) inside flap; (*fig*) implication

ritagli'are [ritaʎ'ʎare] *vt* (*tagliar via*) to cut out

ritar'dare *vi* (*persona, treno*) to be late; (*orologio*) to be slow ▷ *vt* (*rallentare*) to slow down; (*impedire*) to delay, hold up; (*differire*) to postpone, delay

ri'tardo *sm* delay; (*di persona aspettata*) lateness *no pl*; (*fig*: *mentale*) backwardness; **in ~** late; **il volo ha**

due ore di ~ the flight is two hours late; **scusi il ~** sorry I'm late
ri'tegno [ri'teɲɲo] *sm* restraint
rite'nere *vt* (*trattenere*) to hold back; (: *somma*) to deduct; (*giudicare*) to consider, believe
ri'tengo, ri'tenni *ecc vb vedi* **ritenere**
riterrò, ritiene *ecc vb vedi* **ritenere**
riti'rare *vt* to withdraw; (*Pol*: *richiamare*) to recall; (*andare a prendere*: *pacco ecc*) to collect, pick up; **ritirarsi** *vpr* to withdraw; (*da un'attività*) to retire; (*stoffa*) to shrink; (*marea*) to recede
'ritmo *sm* rhythm; (*fig*) rate; (: *della vita*) pace, tempo
'rito *sm* rite; **di ~** usual, customary
ritoc'care *vt* (*disegno, fotografia*) to touch up; (*testo*) to alter
ritor'nare *vi* to return, go (*o* come) back, to get back; (*ripresentarsi*) to recur; (*ridiventare*): **~ ricco** to become rich again ▷ *vt* (*restituire*) to return, give back; **quando ritorniamo?** when do we get back?
ritor'nello *sm* refrain
ri'torno *sm* return; **essere di ~** to be back; **avere un ~ di fiamma** (*Aut*) to backfire; (*fig*: *persona*) to be back in love again
ri'trarre *vt* (*trarre indietro, via*) to withdraw; (*distogliere*: *sguardo*) to turn away; (*rappresentare*) to portray, depict; (*ricavare*) to get, obtain
ritrat'tare *vt* (*disdire*) to retract, take back; (*trattare nuovamente*) to deal with again
ri'tratto, -a *pp di* **ritrarre** ▷ *sm* portrait
ritro'vare *vt* to find; (*salute*) to regain; (*persona*) to find; to meet again; **ritrovarsi** *vpr* (*essere, capitare*) to find o.s.; (*raccapezzarsi*) to find one's way; (*con senso reciproco*) to meet (again)
'ritto, -a *ag* (*in piedi*) standing, on one's feet; (*levato in alto*) erect, raised; (: *capelli*) standing on end; (*posto verticalmente*) upright
ritu'ale *ag, sm* ritual
riuni'one *sf* (*adunanza*) meeting; (*riconciliazione*) reunion
riu'nire *vt* (*ricongiungere*) to join (together); (*riconciliare*) to reunite, bring together (again); **riunirsi** *vpr* (*adunarsi*) to meet; (*tornare insieme*) to be reunited
riu'scire [riuʃʃire] *vi* (*uscire di nuovo*) to go out again, go back out; (*aver esito*: *fatti, azioni*) to go, turn out; (*aver successo*) to succeed, be successful; (*essere, apparire*) to be, prove; (*raggiungere il fine*) to manage, succeed; **~ a fare qc** to manage to do *o* succeed in doing *o* be able to do sth
'riva *sf* (*di fiume*) bank; (*di lago, mare*) shore
ri'vale *sm/f* rival; **rivalità** *sf* rivalry
rivalu'tare *vt* (*Econ*) to revalue
rive'dere *vt* to see again; (*ripassare*) to revise; (*verificare*) to check
rivedrò *ecc vb vedi* **rivedere**
rive'lare *vt* to reveal; (*divulgare*) to reveal, disclose; (*dare indizio*) to reveal, show; **rivelarsi** *vpr* (*manifestarsi*) to be revealed; **rivelarsi onesto** *ecc* to prove to be honest *ecc*; **rivelazi'one** *sf* revelation
rivendi'care *vt* to claim, demand
rivendi'tore, -'trice *sm/f* retailer; **rivenditore autorizzato** (*Comm*) authorized dealer
ri'verbero *sm* (*di luce, calore*) reflection; (*di suono*) reverberation
rivesti'mento *sm* covering; coating
rives'tire *vt* to dress again; (*ricoprire*) to cover; to coat; (*fig*: *carica*) to hold
ri'vidi *ecc vb vedi* **rivedere**
ri'vincita [ri'vintʃita] *sf* (*Sport*) return match; (*fig*) revenge
ri'vista *sf* review; (*periodico*) magazine, review; (*Teatro*) revue; variety show
ri'volgere [ri'vɔldʒere] *vt* (*attenzione,*

sguardo) to turn, direct; (*parole*) to address; **rivolgersi** *vpr* to turn round; (*fig*: *dirigersi per informazioni*): **rivolgersi a** to go and see, go and speak to; (: *ufficio*) to enquire at

ri'volsi *ecc vb vedi* **rivolgere**

ri'volta *sf* revolt, rebellion

rivol'tella *sf* revolver

rivoluzio'nare [rivoluttsjo'nare] *vt* to revolutionize

rivoluzio'nario, -a [rivoluttsjo'narjo] *ag, sm/f* revolutionary

rivoluzi'one [rivolut'tsjone] *sf* revolution

riz'zare [rit'tsare] *vt* to raise, erect; **rizzarsi** *vpr* to stand up; (*capelli*) to stand on end

'roba *sf* stuff, things *pl*; (*possessi, beni*) belongings *pl*, things *pl*, possessions *pl*; **~ da mangiare** things *pl* to eat, food; **~ da matti** sheer madness *o* lunacy

'robot *sm inv* robot

ro'busto, -a *ag* robust, sturdy; (*solido*: *catena*) strong

roc'chetto [rok'ketto] *sm* reel, spool

'roccia, -ce ['rɔttʃa] *sf* rock; **fare ~** (*Sport*) to go rock climbing

'roco, -a, chi, che *ag* hoarse

ro'daggio [ro'daddʒo] *sm* running (BRIT) *o* breaking (US) in; **in ~** running (BRIT) *o* breaking (US) in

rodi'tore *sm* (*Zool*) rodent

rodo'dendro *sm* rhododendron

ro'gnone [roɲ'ɲone] *sm* (*Cuc*) kidney

'rogo, -ghi *sm* (*per cadaveri*) (funeral) pyre; (*supplizio*): **il ~** the stake

rol'lio *sm* roll(ing)

'Roma *sf* Rome

Roma'nia *sf*: **la ~** Romania

ro'manico, -a, -ci, -che *ag* Romanesque

ro'mano, -a *ag, sm/f* Roman

ro'mantico, -a, -ci, -che *ag* romantic

romanzi'ere [roman'dzjɛre] *sm* novelist

ro'manzo, -a [ro'mandzo] *ag* (*Ling*) romance *cpd* ▷ *sm* novel; **romanzo d'appendice** serial (story); **romanzo giallo/poliziesco** detective story; **romanzo rosa** romantic novel

'rombo *sm* rumble, thunder, roar; (*Mat*) rhombus; (*Zool*) turbot; brill

'rompere *vt* to break; (*fidanzamento*) to break off ▷ *vi* to break; **rompersi** *vpr* to break; **mi rompe le scatole** (*fam*) he (*o* she) is a pain in the neck; **rompersi un braccio** to break an arm; **mi si è rotta la macchina** my car has broken down; **rompis'catole** (*fam*) *sm/f inv* pest, pain in the neck

'rondine *sf* (*Zool*) swallow

ron'zare [ron'dzare] *vi* to buzz, hum

ron'zio [ron'dzio] *sm* buzzing

'rosa *sf* rose ▷ *ag inv, sm* pink; **ro'sato, -a** *ag* pink, rosy ▷ *sm* (*vino*) rosé (wine)

rosicchi'are [rosik'kjare] *vt* to gnaw (at); (*mangiucchiare*) to nibble (at)

rosma'rino *sm* rosemary

roso'lare *vt* (*Cuc*) to brown

roso'lia *sf* (*Med*) German measles *sg*, rubella

ro'sone *sm* rosette; (*vetrata*) rose window

'rospo *sm* (*Zool*) toad

ros'setto *sm* (*per labbra*) lipstick

'rosso, -a *ag, sm, sm/f* red; **il mar R~** the Red Sea; **rosso d'uovo** egg yolk

rosticce'ria [rostittʃe'ria] *sf shop selling roast meat and other cooked food*

ro'taia *sf* rut, track; (*Ferr*) rail

ro'tella *sf* small wheel; (*di mobile*) castor

roto'lare *vt, vi* to roll; **rotolarsi** *vpr* to roll (about)

'rotolo *sm* roll; **andare a rotoli** (*fig*) to go to rack and ruin

ro'tondo, -a *ag* round

'rotta *sf* (*Aer, Naut*) course, route; (*Mil*) rout; **a ~ di collo** at breakneck speed; **essere in ~ con qn** to be on bad terms

with sb
rotta'mare *vt* to scrap
rottamazione [rottama'tsjone] *sf (come incentivo) the scrapping of old vehicles in return for incentives*
rot'tame *sm* fragment, scrap, broken bit; **rottami** *smpl (di nave, aereo ecc)* wreckage *sg*
'rotto, -a *pp di* **rompere** ▷ *ag* broken; (*calzoni*) torn, split; **per il ~ della cuffia** by the skin of one's teeth
rot'tura *sf* breaking *no pl*; break; breaking off; (*Med*) fracture, break
rou'lotte [ru'lɔt] *sf* caravan
ro'vente *ag* red-hot
'rovere *sm* oak
ro'vescia [ro'vɛʃʃa] *sf* **alla ~** upside-down; inside-out; **oggi mi va tutto alla ~** everything is going wrong (for me) today
rovesci'are [roveʃʃare] *vt* (*versare in giù*) to pour; (*: accidentalmente*) to spill; (*capovolgere*) to turn upside down; (*gettare a terra*) to knock down; (*: fig: governo*) to overthrow; (*piegare all'indietro: testa*) to throw back; **rovesciarsi** *vpr* (*sedia, macchina*) to overturn; (*barca*) to capsize; (*liquido*) to spill; (*fig: situazione*) to be reversed
ro'vescio, -sci [ro'vɛʃʃo] *sm* other side, wrong side; (*della mano*) back; (*di moneta*) reverse; (*pioggia*) sudden downpour; (*fig*) setback; (*Maglia: anche:* **punto ~**) purl (stitch); (*Tennis*) backhand (stroke); **a ~** upside-down; inside-out; **capire qc a ~** to misunderstand sth
ro'vina *sf* ruin; **andare in ~** (*andare a pezzi*) to collapse; (*fig*) to go to rack and ruin; **rovine** *sfpl* (*ruderi*) ruins; **mandare in ~** to ruin
rovi'nare *vi* to collapse, fall down ▷ *vt* (*danneggiare: fig*) to ruin; **rovinarsi** *vpr* (*persona*) to ruin o.s.; (*oggetto, vestito*) to be ruined
rovis'tare *vt* (*casa*) to ransack; (*tasche*) to rummage in (*o* through)
'rovo *sm* (*Bot*) blackberry bush, bramble bush
'rozzo, -a ['roddzo] *ag* rough, coarse
ru'bare *vt* to steal; **~ qc a qn** to steal sth from sb; **mi hanno rubato il portafoglio** my wallet has been stolen
rubi'netto *sm* tap, faucet (*US*)
ru'bino *sm* ruby
ru'brica, -che *sf* (*Stampa*) column; (*quadernetto*) index book; address book; **rubrica d'indirizzi** address book; **rubrica telefonica** list of telephone numbers
'rudere *sm* (*rovina*) ruins *pl*
rudimen'tale *ag* rudimentary, basic
rudi'menti *smpl* rudiments; basic principles; basic knowledge *sg*
ruffi'ano *sm* pimp
'ruga, -ghe *sf* wrinkle
'ruggine ['ruddʒine] *sf* rust
rug'gire [rud'dʒire] *vi* to roar
rugi'ada [ru'dʒada] *sf* dew
ru'goso, -a *ag* wrinkled
rul'lino *sm* (*Fot*) spool; (*: pellicola*) film; **vorrei un ~ da 36 pose** I'd like a 36-exposure film
'rullo *sm* (*di tamburi*) roll; (*arnese cilindrico, Tip*) roller; **rullo compressore** steam roller; **rullo di pellicola** roll of film
rum *sm* rum
ru'meno, -a *ag, sm/f, sm* Romanian
rumi'nare *vt* (*Zool*) to ruminate
ru'more *sm* **un ~** a noise, a sound; **il ~** noise; **non riesco a dormire a causa del ~** I can't sleep for the noise;
rumo'roso, -a *ag* noisy

> Attenzione! In inglese esiste la parola *rumour*, che però significa *voce* nel senso *diceria*.

ru'olo *sm* (*Teatro: fig*) role, part; (*elenco*) roll, register, list; **di ~** permanent, on the permanent staff
ru'ota *sf* wheel; **ruota anteriore/posteriore** front/back wheel; **ruota di scorta** spare wheel

ruo'tare *vt, vi* to rotate
'rupe *sf* cliff
'ruppi *ecc vb vedi* **rompere**
ru'rale *ag* rural, country *cpd*
ru'scello [ruʃ'ʃɛllo] *sm* stream
'ruspa *sf* excavator
rus'sare *vi* to snore
'Russia *sf* **la ~** Russia; **'russo, -a** *ag, sm/f, sm* Russian
'rustico, -a, -ci, -che *ag* rustic; (*fig*) rough, unrefined
rut'tare *vi* to belch; **'rutto** *sm* belch
'ruvido, -a *ag* rough, coarse

S

S. *abbr* (= *sud*) S; (= *santo*) St
sa *vb vedi* **sapere**
'sabato *sm* Saturday; **di** *o* **il ~** on Saturdays
'sabbia *sf* sand; **sabbie mobili** quicksand(s); **sabbi'oso, -a** *ag* sandy
'sacca, -che *sf* bag; (*bisaccia*) haversack; **sacca da viaggio** travelling bag
sacca'rina *sf* saccharin(e)
saccheggi'are [sakked'dʒare] *vt* to sack, plunder
sac'chetto [sak'ketto] *sm* (small) bag, (small) sack; **sacchetto di carta/di plastica** paper/plastic bag
'sacco, -chi *sm* bag; (*per carbone ecc*) sack; (*Anat, Biol*) sac; (*tela*) sacking; (*saccheggio*) sack(ing); (*fig: grande quantità*): **un ~ di** lots of, heaps of; **sacco a pelo** sleeping bag; **sacco per i rifiuti** bin bag
sacer'dote [satʃer'dɔte] *sm* priest
sacrifi'care *vt* to sacrifice; **sacrificarsi** *vpr* to sacrifice o.s.;

(*privarsi di qc*) to make sacrifices
sacri'ficio [sakri'fitʃo] *sm* sacrifice
'sacro, -a *ag* sacred
'sadico, -a, -ci, -che *ag* sadistic ▷ *sm/f* sadist
sa'etta *sf* arrow; (*fulmine*) thunderbolt; flash of lightning
sa'fari *sm inv* safari
sag'gezza [sad'dʒettsa] *sf* wisdom
'saggio, -a, -gi, -ge ['saddʒo] *ag* wise ▷ *sm* (*persona*) sage; (*esperimento*) test; (*fig*: *prova*) proof; (*campione*) sample; (*scritto*) essay
Sagit'tario [sadʒit'tarjo] *sm* Sagittarius
'sagoma *sf* (*profilo*) outline, profile; (*forma*) form, shape; (*Tecn*) template; (*bersaglio*) target; (*fig*: *persona*) character
'sagra *sf* festival
sagres'tano *sm* sacristan; sexton
sagres'tia *sf* sacristy
Sa'hara [sa'ara] *sm*: **il (deserto del) ~** the Sahara (Desert)
'sai *vb vedi* **sapere**
'sala *sf* hall; (*stanza*) room; (*Cinema*: *di proiezione*) cinema; **sala d'aspetto** waiting room; **sala da ballo** ballroom; **sala giochi** amusement arcade; **sala operatoria** operating theatre; **sala da pranzo** dining room; **sala per concerti** concert hall
sa'lame *sm* salami *no pl*, salami sausage
sala'moia *sf* (*Cuc*) brine
sa'lato, -a *ag* (*sapore*) salty; (*Cuc*) salted, salt *cpd*; (*fig*: *prezzo*) steep, stiff
sal'dare *vt* (*congiungere*) to join, bind; (*parti metalliche*) to solder; (: *con saldatura autogena*) to weld; (*conto*) to settle, pay
'saldo, -a *ag* (*resistente, forte*) strong, firm; (*fermo*) firm, steady, stable; (*fig*) firm, steadfast ▷ *sm* (*svendita*) sale; (*di conto*) settlement; (*Econ*) balance; **saldi** *smpl* (*Comm*) sales; **essere ~ nella propria fede** (*fig*) to stick to one's guns
'sale *sm* salt; (*fig*): **ha poco ~ in zucca** he doesn't have much sense; **sale fino** table salt; **sale grosso** cooking salt
'salgo *ecc vb vedi* **salire**
'salice ['salitʃe] *sm* willow; **salice piangente** weeping willow
sali'ente *ag* (*fig*) salient, main
sali'era *sf* salt cellar
sa'lire *vi* to go (*o* come) up; (*aereo ecc*) to climb, go up; (*passeggero*) to get on; (*sentiero, prezzi, livello*) to go up, rise ▷ *vt* (*scale, gradini*) to go (*o* come) up; **~ su** to climb (up); **~ sul treno/sull'autobus** to board the train/the bus; **~ in macchina** to get into the car; **sa'lita** *sf* climb, ascent; (*erta*) hill, slope; **in salita** *ag, av* uphill
sa'liva *sf* saliva
'salma *sf* corpse
'salmo *sm* psalm
sal'mone *sm* salmon
sa'lone *sm* (*stanza*) sitting room, lounge; (*in albergo*) lounge; (*su nave*) lounge, saloon; (*mostra*) show, exhibition; **salone di bellezza** beauty salon
sa'lotto *sm* lounge, sitting room; (*mobilio*) lounge suite
sal'pare *vi* (*Naut*) to set sail; (*anche*: **~ l'ancora**) to weigh anchor
'salsa *sf* (*Cuc*) sauce; **salsa di pomodoro** tomato sauce
sal'siccia, -ce [sal'sittʃa] *sf* pork sausage
sal'tare *vi* to jump, leap; (*esplodere*) to blow up, explode; (: *valvola*) to blow; (*venir via*) to pop off; (*non aver luogo*: *corso ecc*) to be cancelled ▷ *vt* to jump (over), leap (over); (*fig*: *pranzo, capitolo*) to skip, miss (out); (*Cuc*) to sauté; **far ~** to blow up; to burst open; **~ fuori** (*fig*: *apparire all'improvviso*) to turn up
saltel'lare *vi* to skip; to hop
'salto *sm* jump; (*Sport*) jumping; **fare un ~** to jump, leap; **fare un ~ da qn** to

pop over to sb's (place); **salto in alto/ lungo** high/long jump; **salto con l'asta** pole vaulting; **salto mortale** somersault

saltu'ario, -a *ag* occasional, irregular

sa'lubre *ag* healthy, salubrious

salume'ria *sf* delicatessen

sa'lumi *smpl* salted pork meats

salu'tare *ag* healthy; (*fig*) salutary, beneficial ▷ *vt* (*incontrandosi*) to greet; (*congedandosi*) to say goodbye to; (*Mil*) to salute

sa'lute *sf* health; **~!** (*a chi starnutisce*) bless you!; (*nei brindisi*) cheers!; **bere alla ~ di qn** to drink (to) sb's health

sa'luto *sm* (*gesto*) wave; (*parola*) greeting; (*Mil*) salute

salvada'naio *sm* money box, piggy bank

salva'gente [salva'dʒɛnte] *sm* (*Naut*) lifebuoy; (*ciambella*) life belt; (*giubbotto*) life jacket; (*stradale*) traffic island

salvaguar'dare *vt* to safeguard

sal'vare *vt* to save; (*trarre da un pericolo*) to rescue; (*proteggere*) to protect; **salvarsi** *vpr* to save o.s.; to escape; **salvaschermo** [salvas'kermo] *sm* (*Inform*) screen saver; **salvaslip** [salva'zlip] *sm inv* panty liner; **salva'taggio** *sm* rescue

'salve (*fam*) *escl* hi!

'salvia *sf* (*Bot*) sage

salvi'etta *sf* napkin; **salvietta umidificata** baby wipe

'salvo, -a *ag* safe, unhurt, unharmed; (*fuori pericolo*) safe, out of danger ▷ *sm* **in ~** safe ▷ *prep* (*eccetto*) except; **mettere qc in ~** to put sth in a safe place; **~ che** (*a meno che*) unless; (*eccetto che*) except (that); **~ imprevisti** barring accidents

sam'buco *sm* elder (tree)

'sandalo *sm* (*Bot*) sandalwood; (*calzatura*) sandal

'sangue *sm* blood; **farsi cattivo ~** to fret, get in a state; **sangue freddo** (*fig*) sang-froid, calm; **a ~ freddo** in cold blood; **sangui'nare** *vi* to bleed

sanità *sf* health; (*salubrità*) healthiness; **Ministero della S~** Department of Health; **sanità mentale** sanity

sani'tario, -a *ag* health *cpd*; (*condizioni*) sanitary ▷ *sm* (*Amm*) doctor; **sanitari** *smpl* (*impianti*) bathroom *o* sanitary fittings

'sanno *vb vedi* **sapere**

'sano, -a *ag* healthy; (*denti, costituzione*) healthy, sound; (*integro*) whole, unbroken; (*fig: politica, consigli*) sound; **~ di mente** sane; **di sana pianta** completely, entirely; **~ e salvo** safe and sound

'santo, -a *ag* holy; (*fig*) saintly; (*seguito da nome proprio*) saint ▷ *sm/f* saint; **la Santa Sede** the Holy See

santu'ario *sm* sanctuary

sanzi'one [san'tsjone] *sf* sanction; (*penale, civile*) sanction, penalty

sa'pere *vt* to know; (*essere capace di*): **so nuotare** I know how to swim, I can swim ▷ *vi* **~ di** (*aver sapore*) to taste of; (*aver odore*) to smell of ▷ *sm* knowledge; **far ~ qc a qn** to inform sb about sth, let sb know sth; **mi sa che non sia vero** I don't think that's true; **non lo so** I don't know; **non so l'inglese** I don't speak English; **sa dove posso...?** do you know where I can ...?

sa'pone *sm* soap; **sapone da bucato** washing soap

sa'pore *sm* taste, flavour; **sapo'rito, -a** *ag* tasty

sappi'amo *vb vedi* **sapere**

saprò *ecc vb vedi* **sapere**

sarà *ecc vb vedi* **essere**

saraci'nesca [saratʃi'neska] *sf* (*serranda*) rolling shutter

sar'castico, -a, ci, che *ag* sarcastic

Sar'degna [sar'deɲɲa] *sf*: **la ~** Sardinia

sar'dina *sf* sardine

sa'rei *ecc vb vedi* **essere**
SARS *sigla f (Med: = severe acute respiratory syndrome)* SARS
'sarta *sf vedi* **sarto**
'sarto, -a *sm/f* tailor/dressmaker
'sasso *sm* stone; (*ciottolo*) pebble; (*masso*) rock
sas'sofono *sm* saxophone
sas'soso, -a *ag* stony; pebbly
'Satana *sm* Satan
satelli'tare *agg* satellite *cpd*
sa'tellite *sm, ag* satellite
'satira *sf* satire
'sauna *sf* sauna
sazi'are [sat'tsjare] *vt* to satisfy, satiate; **saziarsi** *vpr* **saziarsi (di)** to eat one's fill (of); (*fig*): **saziarsi di** to grow tired *o* weary of
'sazio, -a ['sattsjo] *ag*: **~ (di)** sated (with), full (of); (*fig: stufo*) fed up (with), sick (of); **sono ~** I'm full (up)
sba'dato, -a *ag* careless, inattentive
sbadigli'are [zbadiʎ'ʎare] *vi* to yawn; **sba'diglio** *sm* yawn
sbagli'are [zbaʎ'ʎare] *vt* to make a mistake in, get wrong ▷ *vi* to make a mistake, be mistaken, be wrong; (*operare in modo non giusto*) to err; **sbagliarsi** *vpr* to make a mistake, be mistaken, be wrong; **~ strada/la mira** to take the wrong road/miss one's aim
sbagli'ato, -a [zbaʎ'ʎato] *ag* (*gen*) wrong; (*compito*) full of mistakes; (*conclusione*) erroneous
'sbaglio *sm* mistake, error; (*morale*) error; **fare uno ~** to make a mistake
sbalor'dire *vt* to stun, amaze ▷ *vi* to be stunned, be amazed
sbal'zare [zbal'tsare] *vt* to throw, hurl ▷ *vi* (*balzare*) to bounce; (*saltare*) to leap, bound
sban'dare *vi* (*Naut*) to list; (*Aer*) to bank; (*Aut*) to skid
sba'raglio [zba'raʎʎo] *sm* rout; defeat; **gettarsi allo ~** to risk everything
sbaraz'zarsi [zbarat'tsarsi] *vpr*: **~ di** to get rid of, rid o.s. of
sbar'care *vt* (*passeggeri*) to disembark; (*merci*) to unload ▷ *vi* to disembark
'sbarra *sf* bar; (*di passaggio a livello*) barrier; (*Dir*): **presentarsi alla ~** to appear before the court
sbar'rare *vt* (*strada ecc*) to block, bar; (*assegno*) to cross; **~ il passo** to bar the way; **~ gli occhi** to open one's eyes wide
'sbattere *vt* (*porta*) to slam, bang; (*tappeti, ali, Cuc*) to beat; (*urtare*) to knock, hit ▷ *vi* (*porta, finestra*) to bang; (*agitarsi: ali, vele ecc*) to flap; **me ne sbatto!** (*fam*) I don't give a damn!
sba'vare *vi* to dribble; (*colore*) to smear, smudge
'sberla *sf* slap
sbia'dire *vi, vt* to fade; **sbia'dito, -a** *ag* faded; (*fig*) colourless, dull
sbian'care *vt* to whiten; (*tessuto*) to bleach ▷ *vi* (*impallidire*) to grow pale *o* white
sbirci'ata [zbir'tʃata] *sf*: **dare una ~ a qc** to glance at sth, have a look at sth
sbloc'care *vt* to unblock, free; (*freno*) to release; (*prezzi, affitti*) to decontrol; **sbloccarsi** *vpr* (*gen*) to become unblocked; (*passaggio, strada*) to clear, become unblocked
sboc'care *vi*: **~ in** (*fiume*) to flow into; (*strada*) to lead into; (*persona*) to come (out) into; (*fig: concludersi*) to end (up) in
sboc'cato, -a *ag* (*persona*) foul-mouthed; (*linguaggio*) foul
sbocci'are [zbot'tʃare] *vi* (*fiore*) to bloom, open (out)
sbol'lire *vi* (*fig*) to cool down, calm down
'sbornia (*fam*) *sf*: **prendersi una ~** to get plastered
sbor'sare *vt* (*denaro*) to pay out
sbot'tare *vi*: **~ in una risata/per la collera** to burst out laughing/explode

with anger
sbotto'nare *vt* to unbutton, undo
sbrai'tare *vi* to yell, bawl
sbra'nare *vt* to tear to pieces
sbricio'lare [zbritʃo'lare] *vt* to crumble; **sbriciolarsi** *vpr* to crumble
sbri'gare *vt* to deal with; **sbrigarsi** *vpr* to hurry (up)
'sbronza ['zbrontsa] (*fam*) *sf* (*ubriaco*): **prendersi una ~** to get plastered
sbron'zarsi [zbron'tsarsi] *vpr* (*fam*) to get sozzled
'sbronzo, -a ['zbrontso] (*fam*) *ag* plastered
sbruf'fone, -a *sm/f* boaster
sbu'care *vi* to come out, emerge; (*improvvisamente*) to pop out (*o* up)
sbucci'are [zbut'tʃare] *vt* (*arancia, patata*) to peel; (*piselli*) to shell; **sbucciarsi un ginocchio** to graze one's knee
sbucherò *ecc* [zbuke'rɔ] *vb vedi* **sbucare**
sbuf'fare *vi* (*persona, cavallo*) to snort; (*ansimare*) to puff, pant; (*treno*) to puff
sca'broso, -a *ag* (*fig: difficile*) difficult, thorny; (: *imbarazzante*) embarrassing; (: *sconcio*) indecent
scacchi *smpl* (*gioco*) chess *sg*; **a ~** (*tessuto*) check(ed)
scacchi'era [skak'kjɛra] *sf* chessboard
scacci'are [skat'tʃare] *vt* to chase away *o* out, drive away *o* out
'scaddi *ecc vb vedi* **scadere**
sca'dente *ag* shoddy, of poor quality
sca'denza [ska'dɛntsa] *sf* (*di cambiale, contratto*) maturity; (*di passaporto*) expiry date; **a breve/lunga ~** short-/long-term; **data di ~** expiry date
sca'dere *vi* (*contratto ecc*) to expire; (*debito*) to fall due; (*valore, forze, peso*) to decline, go down
sca'fandro *sm* (*di palombaro*) diving suit; (*di astronauta*) space-suit
scaf'fale *sm* shelf; (*mobile*) set of shelves
'scafo *sm* (*Naut, Aer*) hull
scagio'nare [skadʒo'nare] *vt* to exonerate, free from blame
'scaglia ['skaʎʎa] *sf* (*Zool*) scale; (*scheggia*) chip, flake
scagli'are [skaʎ'ʎare] *vt* (*lanciare: anche fig*) to hurl, fling; **scagliarsi** (*anche:* **vr**): **scagliarsi su** *o* **contro** to hurl *o* fling o.s. at; (*fig*) to rail at
'scala *sf* (*a gradini ecc*) staircase, stairs *pl*; (*a pioli, di corda*) ladder; (*Mus, Geo, di colori, valori, fig*) scale; **scale** *sfpl* (*scalinata*) stairs; **su vasta ~/~ ridotta** on a large/small scale; **~ mobile (dei salari)** index-linked pay scale; **scala a libretto** stepladder; **scala mobile** escalator; (*Econ*) sliding scale

SCALA

Milan's world-famous **la Scala** theatre first opened its doors in 1778 with a performance of Salieri's opera, "L'Europa riconosciuta". It suffered serious damage in the bombing of Milan in 1943 and reopened in 1946 with a concert conducted by Toscanini. It also has a famous classical dance school.

sca'lare *vt* (*Alpinismo, muro*) to climb, scale; (*debito*) to scale down, reduce
scalda'bagno [skalda'baɲɲo] *sm* water-heater
scal'dare *vt* to heat; **scaldarsi** *vpr* to warm up, heat up; (*al fuoco, al sole*) to warm o.s.; (*fig*) to get excited
scal'fire *vt* to scratch
scali'nata *sf* staircase
sca'lino *sm* (*anche fig*) step; (*di scala a pioli*) rung
'scalo *sm* (*Naut*) slipway; (: *porto d'approdo*) port of call; (*Aer*) stopover; **fare ~ (a)** (*Naut*) to call (at), put in (at); (*Aer*) to land (at), make a stop (at); **scalo merci** (*Ferr*) goods (BRIT) *o*

freight yard
scalop'pina *sf* (*Cuc*) escalope
scal'pello *sm* chisel
scal'pore *sm* noise, row; **far ~** (*notizia*) to cause a sensation *o* a stir
'scaltro, -a *ag* cunning, shrewd
'scalzo, -a ['skaltso] *ag* barefoot
scambi'are *vt* to exchange; (*confondere*): **~ qn/qc per** to take *o* mistake sb/sth for; **mi hanno scambiato il cappello** they've given me the wrong hat; **scambiarsi** *vpr* (*auguri, confidenze, visite*) to exchange; **~ qn/qc per** (*confondere*) to mistake sth/sb for
'scambio *sm* exchange; (*Ferr*) points *pl*; **fare (uno) ~** to make a swap
scampa'gnata [skampaɲ'ɲata] *sf* trip to the country
scam'pare *vt* (*salvare*) to rescue, save; (*evitare*: *morte, prigione*) to escape ▷ *vi* **~ (a qc)** to survive (sth), escape (sth); **scamparla bella** to have a narrow escape
'scampo *sm* (*salvezza*) escape; (*Zool*) prawn; **cercare ~ nella fuga** to seek safety in flight
'scampolo *sm* remnant
scanala'tura *sf* (*incavo*) channel, groove
scandagli'are [skandaʎ'ʎare] *vt* (*Naut*) to sound; (*fig*) to sound out; to probe
scandaliz'zare [skandalid'dzare] *vt* to shock, scandalize; **scandalizzarsi** *vpr* to be shocked
'scandalo *sm* scandal
Scandi'navia *sf*: **la ~** Scandinavia; **scandi'navo, -a** *ag, sm/f* Scandinavian
scanner ['skanner] *sm inv* (*Inform*) scanner
scansafa'tiche [skansafa'tike] *sm/f inv* idler, loafer
scan'sare *vt* (*rimuovere*) to move (aside), shift; (*schivare*: *schiaffo*) to dodge; (*sfuggire*) to avoid; **scansarsi** *vpr* to move aside
scan'sia *sf* shelves *pl*; (*per libri*) bookcase
'scanso *sm*: **a ~ di** in order to avoid, as a precaution against
scanti'nato *sm* basement
scapacci'one [skapat'tʃone] *sm* clout
scapes'trato, -a *ag* dissolute
'scapola *sf* shoulder blade
'scapolo *sm* bachelor
scappa'mento *sm* (*Aut*) exhaust
scap'pare *vi* (*fuggire*) to escape; (*andare via in fretta*) to rush off; **lasciarsi ~ un'occasione** to let an opportunity go by; **~ di prigione** to escape from prison; **~ di mano** (*oggetto*) to slip out of one's hands; **~ di mente a qn** to slip sb's mind; **mi scappò detto** I let it slip; **scappa'toia** *sf* way out
scara'beo *sm* beetle
scarabocchi'are [skarabok'kjare] *vt* to scribble, scrawl; **scara'bocchio** *sm* scribble, scrawl
scara'faggio [skara'faddʒo] *sm* cockroach
scaraman'zia [skaraman'tsia] *sf* **per ~** for luck
scaraven'tare *vt* to fling, hurl; **scaraventarsi** *vpr* to fling o.s.
scarce'rare [skartʃe'rare] *vt* to release (from prison)
scardi'nare *vt*: **~ una porta** to take a door off its hinges
scari'care *vt* (*merci, camion ecc*) to unload; (*passeggeri*) to set down, put off; (*arma*) to unload; (: *sparare, Elettr*) to discharge; (*corso d'acqua*) to empty, pour; (*fig*: *liberare da un peso*) to unburden, relieve; (*da Internet*) to download; **scaricarsi** *vpr* (*orologio*) to run *o* wind down; (*batteria, accumulatore*) to go flat *o* dead; (*fig*: *rilassarsi*) to unwind; (: *sfogarsi*) to let off steam
'scarico, -a, -chi, -che *ag* unloaded;

(*orologio*) run down; (*accumulatore*) dead, flat ▷ *sm* (*di merci, materiali*) unloading; (*di immondizie*) dumping, tipping (BRIT); (*Tecn*: *deflusso*) draining; (: *dispositivo*) drain; (*Aut*) exhaust

scarlat'tina *sf* scarlet fever

scar'latto, -a *ag* scarlet

'scarpa *sf* shoe; **scarpe da ginnastica/tennis** gym/tennis shoes

scar'pata *sf* escarpment

scarpi'era *sf* shoe rack

scar'pone *sm* boot; **scarponi da montagna** climbing boots; **scarponi da sci** ski-boots

scarseggi'are [skarsed'dʒare] *vi* to be scarce; **~ di** to be short of, lack

'scarso, -a *ag* (*insufficiente*) insufficient, meagre; (*povero*: *annata*) poor, lean; (*Ins*: *voto*) poor; **~ di** lacking in; **3 chili scarsi** just under 3 kilos, barely 3 kilos

scar'tare *vt* (*pacco*) to unwrap; (*idea*) to reject; (*Mil*) to declare unfit for military service; (*carte da gioco*) to discard; (*Calcio*) to dodge (past) ▷ *vi* to swerve

'scarto *sm* (*cosa scartata*: *anche Comm*) reject; (*di veicolo*) swerve; (*differenza*) gap, difference

scassi'nare *vt* to break, force

scate'nare *vt* (*fig*) to incite, stir up; **scatenarsi** *vpr* (*temporale*) to break; (*rivolta*) to break out; (*persona*: *infuriarsi*) to rage

'scatola *sf* box; (*di latta*) tin (BRIT), can; **cibi in ~** tinned (BRIT) *o* canned foods; **scatola cranica** cranium; **scato'lone** *sm* (big) box

scat'tare *vt* (*fotografia*) to take ▷ *vi* (*congegno, molla ecc*) to be released; (*balzare*) to spring up; (*Sport*) to put on a spurt; (*fig*: *per l'ira*) to fly into a rage; **~ in piedi** to spring to one's feet

'scatto *sm* (*dispositivo*) release; (: *di arma da fuoco*) trigger mechanism; (*rumore*) click; (*balzo*) jump, start; (*Sport*) spurt; (*fig*: *di ira ecc*) fit; (: *di stipendio*) increment; **di ~** suddenly

scaval'care *vt* (*ostacolo*) to pass (*o* climb) over; (*fig*) to get ahead of, overtake

sca'vare *vt* (*terreno*) to dig; (*legno*) to hollow out; (*pozzo, galleria*) to bore; (*città sepolta ecc*) to excavate

'scavo *sm* excavating *no pl*; excavation

'scegliere ['ʃeʎʎere] *vt* to choose, select

sce'icco, -chi [ʃe'ikko] *sm* sheik

'scelgo *ecc* ['ʃelgo] *vb vedi* **scegliere**

scel'lino [ʃel'lino] *sm* shilling

'scelta ['ʃelta] *sf* choice; selection; **di prima ~** top grade *o* quality; **frutta o formaggi a ~** choice of fruit or cheese

'scelto, -a ['ʃelto] *pp di* **scegliere** ▷ *ag* (*gruppo*) carefully selected; (*frutta, verdura*) choice, top quality; (*Mil*: *specializzato*) crack *cpd*, highly skilled

'scemo, -a ['ʃemo] *ag* stupid, silly

'scena ['ʃɛna] *sf* (*gen*) scene; (*palcoscenico*) stage; **le scene** (*fig*: *teatro*) the stage; **fare una ~** to make a scene; **andare in ~** to be staged *o* put on *o* performed; **mettere in ~** to stage

sce'nario [ʃe'narjo] *sm* scenery; (*di film*) scenario

sce'nata [ʃe'nata] *sf* row, scene

'scendere ['ʃendere] *vi* to go (*o* come) down; (*strada, sole*) to go down; (*notte*) to fall; (*passeggero*: *fermarsi*) to get out, alight; (*fig*: *temperatura, prezzi*) to go *o* come down, fall, drop ▷ *vt* (*scale, pendio*) to go (*o* come) down; **~ dalle scale** to go (*o* come) down the stairs; **~ dal treno** to get off *o* out of the train; **dove devo ~?** where do I get off?; **~ dalla macchina** to get out of the car; **~ da cavallo** to dismount, get off one's horse

sceneggi'ato [ʃened'dʒato] *sm* television drama

'scettico, -a, -ci, -che ['ʃɛttiko] *ag* sceptical

'scettro ['ʃɛttro] *sm* sceptre

'scheda ['skɛda] *sf* (index) card; **scheda elettorale** ballot paper; **scheda ricaricabile** (*Tel*) top-up card; **scheda telefonica** phone card; **sche'dario** *sm* file; (*mobile*) filing cabinet
sche'dina [ske'dina] *sf* ≈ pools coupon (BRIT)
'scheggia, -ge ['skeddʒa] *sf* splinter, sliver
'scheletro ['skɛletro] *sm* skeleton
'schema, -i ['skɛma] *sm* (*diagramma*) diagram, sketch; (*progetto, abbozzo*) outline, plan
'scherma ['skerma] *sf* fencing
scher'maglia [sker'maʎʎa] *sf* (*fig*) skirmish
'schermo ['skermo] *sm* shield, screen; (*Cinema, TV*) screen; **a ~ panoramico** (*TV*) widescreen
scher'nire [sker'nire] *vt* to mock, sneer at
scher'zare [sker'tsare] *vi* to joke
'scherzo ['skertso] *sm* joke; (*tiro*) trick; (*Mus*) scherzo; **è uno ~!** (*una cosa facile*) it's child's play!, it's easy!; **per ~** in jest; for a joke *o* a laugh; **fare un brutto ~ a qn** to play a nasty trick on sb
schiaccia'noci [skjattʃa'notʃi] *sm inv* nutcracker
schiacci'are [skjat'tʃare] *vt* (*dito*) to crush; (*noci*) to crack; **~ un pisolino** to have a nap; **schiacciarsi** *vpr* (*appiattirsi*) to get squashed; (*frantumarsi*) to get crushed
schiaffeggi'are [skjaffed'dʒare] *vt* to slap
schi'affo ['skjaffo] *sm* slap
schiantarsi *vpr* to break (up), shatter
schia'rire [skja'rire] *vt* to lighten, make lighter; **schiarirsi** *vpr* to grow lighter; (*tornar sereno*) to clear, brighten up; **schiarirsi la voce** to clear one's throat
schiavitù [skjavi'tu] *sf* slavery
schi'avo, -a ['skjavo] *sm/f* slave
schi'ena ['skjɛna] *sf* (*Anat*) back; **schie'nale** *sm* (*di sedia*) back
schi'era ['skjɛra] *sf* (*Mil*) rank; (*gruppo*) group, band
schiera'mento [skjera'mento] *sm* (*Mil, Sport*) formation; (*fig*) alliance
schie'rare [skje'rare] *vt* (*esercito*) to line up, draw up, marshal; **schierarsi** *vpr* to line up; (*fig*): **schierarsi con** *o* **dalla parte di/contro qn** to side with/oppose sb
'schifo ['skifo] *sm* disgust; **fare ~** (*essere fatto male, dare pessimi risultati*) to be awful; **mi fa ~** it makes me sick, it's disgusting; **quel libro è uno ~** that book's rotten; **schi'foso, -a** *ag* disgusting, revolting; (*molto scadente*) rotten, lousy
schioc'care [skjɔk'kare] *vt* (*frusta*) to crack; (*dita*) to snap; (*lingua*) to click; **~ le labbra** to smack one's lips
schiudersi *vpr* to open
schi'uma ['skjuma] *sf* foam; (*di sapone*) lather; (*di latte*) froth; (*fig: feccia*) scum
schi'vare [ski'vare] *vt* to dodge, avoid
'schivo, -a ['skivo] *ag* (*ritroso*) stand-offish, reserved; (*timido*) shy
schiz'zare [skit'tsare] *vt* (*spruzzare*) to spurt, squirt; (*sporcare*) to splash, spatter; (*fig: abbozzare*) to sketch ▷ *vi* to spurt, squirt; (*saltar fuori*) to dart up (*o* off *ecc*)
schizzi'noso, -a [skittsi'noso] *ag* fussy, finicky
'schizzo ['skittso] *sm* (*di liquido*) spurt; splash, spatter; (*abbozzo*) sketch
sci [ʃi] *sm* (*attrezzo*) ski; (*attività*) skiing; **sci d'acqua** water-skiing; **sci di fondo** cross-country skiing, ski touring (US); **sci nautico** water-skiing
'scia ['ʃia] (*pl* **scie**) *sf* (*di imbarcazione*) wake; (*di profumo*) trail
scià [ʃa] *sm inv* shah
sci'abola ['ʃabola] *sf* sabre
scia'callo [ʃa'kallo] *sm* jackal
sciac'quare [ʃak'kware] *vt* to rinse

scia'gura [ʃa'gura] *sf* disaster, calamity; misfortune
scialac'quare [ʃalak'kware] *vt* to squander
sci'albo, -a ['ʃalbo] *ag* pale, dull; (*fig*) dull, colourless
sci'alle ['ʃalle] *sm* shawl
scia'luppa [ʃa'luppa] *sf*; **scialuppa di salvataggio** lifeboat
sci'ame ['ʃame] *sm* swarm
sci'are [ʃi'are] *vi* to ski
sci'arpa ['ʃarpa] *sf* scarf; (*fascia*) sash
scia'tore, -'trice [ʃia'tore] *sm/f* skier
sci'atto, -a ['ʃatto] *ag* (*persona*) slovenly, unkempt
scien'tifico, -a, -ci, -che [ʃen'tifiko] *ag* scientific
sci'enza ['ʃɛntsa] *sf* science; (*sapere*) knowledge; **scienze** *sfpl* (*Ins*) science *sg*; **scienze naturali** natural sciences; **scienzi'ato, -a** *sm/f* scientist
'scimmia ['ʃimmja] *sf* monkey
scimpanzé [ʃimpan'tse] *sm inv* chimpanzee
scin'tilla [ʃin'tilla] *sf* spark; **scintil'lare** *vi* to spark; (*acqua, occhi*) to sparkle
scioc'chezza [ʃok'kettsa] *sf* stupidity *no pl*; stupid *o* foolish thing; **dire sciocchezze** to talk nonsense
sci'occo, -a, -chi, -che ['ʃɔkko] *ag* stupid, foolish
sci'ogliere ['ʃɔʎʎere] *vt* (*nodo*) to untie; (*capelli*) to loosen; (*persona, animale*) to untie, release; (*fig*: *persona*): **~ da** to release from; (*neve*) to melt; (*nell'acqua*: *zucchero ecc*) to dissolve; (*fig*: *mistero*) to solve; (*porre fine a*: *contratto*) to cancel; (: *società, matrimonio*) to dissolve; (: *riunione*) to bring to an end; **sciogliersi** *vpr* to loosen, come untied; to melt; to dissolve; (*assemblea ecc*) to break up; **~ i muscoli** to limber up; **scioglilingua** [ʃoʎʎi'lingwa] *sm inv* tongue-twister
sci'olgo *ecc* ['ʃɔlgo] *vb vedi* **sciogliere**
sci'olto, -a ['ʃɔlto] *pp di* **sciogliere** ▷ *ag* loose; (*agile*) agile, nimble; supple; (*disinvolto*) free and easy; **versi sciolti** (*Poesia*) blank verse
sciope'rare [ʃope'rare] *vi* to strike, go on strike
sci'opero ['ʃɔpero] *sm* strike; **fare ~** to strike; **sciopero bianco** work-to-rule (BRIT), slowdown (US); **sciopero selvaggio** wildcat strike; **sciopero a singhiozzo** on-off strike
scio'via [ʃio'via] *sf* ski lift
scip'pare [ʃip'pare] *vt*: **~ qn** to snatch sb's bag; **mi hanno scippato** they snatched my bag
sci'rocco [ʃi'rɔkko] *sm* sirocco
sci'roppo [ʃi'rɔppo] *sm* syrup
'scisma, -i ['ʃizma] *sm* (*Rel*) schism
scissi'one [ʃis'sjone] *sf* (*anche fig*) split, division; (*Fisica*) fission
sciu'pare [ʃu'pare] *vt* (*abito, libro, appetito*) to spoil, ruin; (*tempo, denaro*) to waste
scivo'lare [ʃivo'lare] *vi* to slide *o* glide along; (*involontariamente*) to slip, slide; **'scivolo** *sm* slide; (*Tecn*) chute; **scivo'loso, -a** *ag* slippery
scle'rosi *sf* sclerosis
scoc'care *vt* (*freccia*) to shoot ▷ *vi* (*guizzare*) to shoot up; (*battere*: *ora*) to strike
scoccherò *ecc* [skokke'rɔ] *vb vedi* **scoccare**
scocci'are [skot'tʃare] (*fam*) *vt* to bother, annoy; **scocciarsi** *vpr* to be bothered *o* annoyed
sco'della *sf* bowl
scodinzo'lare [skodintso'lare] *vi* to wag its tail
scogli'era [skoʎ'ʎɛra] *sf* reef; cliff
'scoglio ['skɔʎʎo] *sm* (*al mare*) rock
scoi'attolo *sm* squirrel
scola'pasta *sm inv* colander
scolapi'atti *sm inv* drainer (*for plates*)
sco'lare *ag* **età scolare** school age ▷ *vt* to drain ▷ *vi* to drip
scola'resca *sf* schoolchildren *pl*, pupils *pl*

sco'laro, -a *sm/f* pupil, schoolboy/ girl

> Attenzione! In inglese esiste la parola *scholar*, che però significa *studioso*.

sco'lastico, -a, -ci, -che *ag* school *cpd*; scholastic
scol'lato, -a *ag* (*vestito*) low-cut, low-necked; (*donna*) wearing a low-cut dress (*o* blouse *ecc*)
scolla'tura *sf* neckline
scolle'gare *vt* (*fili, apparecchi*) to disconnect
'scolo *sm* drainage
scolo'rire *vt* to fade; to discolour; **scolorirsi** *vpr* to fade; to become discoloured; (*impallidire*) to turn pale
scol'pire *vt* to carve, sculpt
scombusso'lare *vt* to upset
scom'messa *sf* bet, wager
scom'mettere *vt, vi* to bet
scomo'dare *vt* to trouble, bother; to disturb; **scomodarsi** *vpr* to put o.s. out; **scomodarsi a fare** to go to the bother *o* trouble of doing
'scomodo, -a *ag* uncomfortable; (*sistemazione, posto*) awkward, inconvenient
scompa'rire *vi* (*sparire*) to disappear, vanish; (*fig*) to be insignificant
scomparti'mento *sm* compartment; **uno ~ per non-fumatori** a non-smoking compartment
scompigli'are [skompiʎ'ʎare] *vt* (*cassetto, capelli*) to mess up, disarrange; (*fig: piani*) to upset
scomuni'care *vt* to excommunicate
'sconcio, -a, -ci, -ce ['skontʃo] *ag* (*osceno*) indecent, obscene ▷ *sm* disgrace
scon'figgere [skon'fiddʒere] *vt* to defeat, overcome
sconfi'nare *vi* to cross the border; (*in proprietà privata*) to trespass; (*fig*): **~ da** to stray *o* digress from
scon'fitta *sf* defeat
scon'forto *sm* despondency
sconge'lare [skondʒe'lare] *vt* to defrost
scongiu'rare [skondʒu'rare] *vt* (*implorare*) to entreat, beseech, implore; (*eludere: pericolo*) to ward off, avert; **scongi'uro** *sm* entreaty; (*esorcismo*) exorcism; **fare gli scongiuri** to touch wood (BRIT), knock on wood (US)
scon'nesso, -a *ag* incoherent
sconosci'uto, -a [skonoʃ'ʃuto] *ag* unknown; new, strange ▷ *sm/f* stranger; unknown person
sconsigli'are [skonsiʎ'ʎare] *vt*: **~ qc a qn** to advise sb against sth; **~ qn dal fare qc** to advise sb not to do *o* against doing sth
sconso'lato, -a *ag* inconsolable; desolate
scon'tare *vt* (*Comm: detrarre*) to deduct; (*: debito*) to pay off; (*: cambiale*) to discount; (*pena*) to serve; (*colpa, errori*) to pay for, suffer for
scon'tato, -a *ag* (*previsto*) foreseen, taken for granted; **dare per ~ che** to take it for granted that
scon'tento, -a *ag*: **~ (di)** dissatisfied (with) ▷ *sm* dissatisfaction
'sconto *sm* discount; **fare uno ~** to give a discount; **ci sono sconti per studenti?** are there discounts for students?
scon'trarsi *vpr* (*treni ecc*) to crash, collide; (*venire ad uno scontro, fig*) to clash; **~ con** to crash into, collide with
scon'trino *sm* ticket; (*di cassa*) receipt; **potrei avere lo ~ per favore?** can I have a receipt, please?
'scontro *sm* clash, encounter; crash, collision
scon'troso, -a *ag* sullen, surly; (*permaloso*) touchy
sconveni'ente *ag* unseemly, improper
scon'volgere [skon'vɔldʒere] *vt* to throw into confusion, upset; (*turbare*)

to shake, disturb, upset; **scon'volto, -a** *pp di* **sconvolgere**
scooter ['skuter] *sm inv* scooter
'scopa *sf* broom; (*Carte*) *Italian card game*; **sco'pare** *vt* to sweep
sco'perta *sf* discovery
sco'perto, -a *pp di* **scoprire** ▷ *ag* uncovered; (*capo*) uncovered, bare; (*macchina*) open; (*Mil*) exposed, without cover; (*conto*) overdrawn
'scopo *sm* aim, purpose; **a che ~?** what for?
scoppi'are *vi* (*spaccarsi*) to burst; (*esplodere*) to explode; (*fig*) to break out; **~ in pianto** *o* **a piangere** to burst out crying; **~ dalle risa** *o* **dal ridere** to split one's sides laughing
scoppiet'tare *vi* to crackle
'scoppio *sm* explosion; (*di tuono, arma ecc*) crash, bang; (*fig: di risa, ira*) fit, outburst; (*: di guerra*) outbreak; **a ~ ritardato** delayed-action
sco'prire *vt* to discover; (*liberare da ciò che copre*) to uncover; (*: monumento*) to unveil; **scoprirsi** *vpr* to put on lighter clothes; (*fig*) to give o.s. away
scoraggi'are [skorad'dʒare] *vt* to discourage; **scoraggiarsi** *vpr* to become discouraged, lose heart
scorcia'toia [skortʃa'toja] *sf* short cut
'scorcio ['skortʃo] *sm* (*Arte*) foreshortening; (*di secolo, periodo*) end, close; **scorcio panoramico** vista
scor'dare *vt* to forget; **scordarsi** *vpr* **scordarsi di qc/di fare** to forget sth/to do
'scorgere ['skɔrdʒere] *vt* to make out, distinguish, see
scorpacci'ata [skorpat'tʃata] *sf*: **fare una ~ (di)** to stuff o.s. (with), eat one's fill (of)
scorpi'one *sm* scorpion; (*dello zodiaco*): **S~** Scorpio
'scorrere *vt* (*giornale, lettera*) to run *o* skim through ▷ *vi* (*liquido, fiume*) to run, flow; (*fune*) to run; (*cassetto, porta*) to slide easily; (*tempo*) to pass (by)
scor'retto, -a *ag* incorrect; (*sgarbato*) impolite; (*sconveniente*) improper
scor'revole *ag* (*porta*) sliding; (*fig: stile*) fluent, flowing
'scorsi *ecc vb vedi* **scorgere**
'scorso, -a *pp di* **scorrere** ▷ *ag* last
scor'soio, -a *ag*: **nodo ~** noose
'scorta *sf* (*di personalità, convoglio*) escort; (*provvista*) supply, stock
scor'tese *ag* discourteous, rude
'scorza ['skɔrdza] *sf* (*di albero*) bark; (*di agrumi*) peel, skin
sco'sceso, -a [skoʃ'ʃeso] *ag* steep
'scossa *sf* jerk, jolt, shake; (*Elettr: fig*) shock; **scossa di terremoto** earth tremor
'scosso, -a *pp di* **scuotere** ▷ *ag* (*turbato*) shaken, upset
scos'tante *ag* (*fig*) off-putting (BRIT), unpleasant
scotch [skɔtʃ] *sm inv* (*whisky*) Scotch; (*nastro adesivo*) Scotch tape®, Sellotape®
scot'tare *vt* (*ustionare*) to burn; (*: con liquido bollente*) to scald ▷ *vi* to burn; (*caffè*) to be too hot; **scottarsi** *vpr* to burn/scald o.s.; (*fig*) to have one's fingers burnt; **scotta'tura** *sf* burn; scald
'scotto, -a *ag* overcooked ▷ *sm* (*fig*): **pagare lo ~ (di)** to pay the penalty (for)
sco'vare *vt* to drive out, flush out; (*fig*) to discover
'Scozia ['skɔttsia] *sf*: **la ~** Scotland; **scoz'zese** *ag* Scottish ▷ *sm/f* Scot
scredi'tare *vt* to discredit
screen saver ['skriin'sɛivər] *sm inv* (*Inform*) screen saver
scre'mato, -a *ag* skimmed; **parzialmente ~** semi-skimmed
screpo'lato, -a *ag* (*labbra*) chapped; (*muro*) cracked
'screzio ['skrɛttsjo] *sm* disagreement
scricchio'lare [skrikkjo'lare] *vi* to creak, squeak

'scrigno ['skriɲɲo] *sm* casket
scrimina'tura *sf* parting
'scrissi *ecc vb vedi* **scrivere**
'scritta *sf* inscription
'scritto, -a *pp di* **scrivere** ▷ *ag* written ▷ *sm* writing; (*lettera*) letter, note
scrit'toio *sm* writing desk
scrit'tore, -'trice *sm/f* writer
scrit'tura *sf* writing; (*Comm*) entry; (*contratto*) contract; (*Rel*): **la Sacra S~** the Scriptures *pl*
scrittu'rare *vt* (*Teatro, Cinema*) to sign up, engage; (*Comm*) to enter
scriva'nia *sf* desk
'scrivere *vt* to write; **come si scrive?** how is it spelt?, how do you write it?
scroc'cone, -a *sm/f* scrounger
'scrofa *sf* (*Zool*) sow
scrol'lare *vt* to shake; **scrollarsi** *vpr* (*anche fig*) to give o.s. a shake; (*anche:* **~ le spalle/il capo**) to shrug one's shoulders/shake one's head
'scrupolo *sm* scruple; (*meticolosità*) care, conscientiousness
scrupo'loso, -a *ag* scrupulous; conscientious
scru'tare *vt* to scrutinize; (*intenzioni, causa*) to examine, scrutinize
scu'cire [sku'tʃire] *vt* (*orlo ecc*) to unpick, undo; **scucirsi** *vpr* to come unstitched
scude'ria *sf* stable
scu'detto *sm* (*Sport*) (championship) shield; (*distintivo*) badge
'scudo *sm* shield
sculacci'are [skulat'tʃare] *vt* to spank
scul'tore, -'trice *sm/f* sculptor
scul'tura *sf* sculpture
scu'ola *sf* school; **scuola elementare/materna** primary (BRIT) *o* grade (US) /nursery school; **scuola guida** driving school; **scuola media** secondary (BRIT) *o* high (US) school; **scuola dell'obbligo** compulsory education; **scuola tecnica** technical college; **scuole serali** evening classes, night school *sg*
scu'otere *vt* to shake
'scure *sf* axe
'scuro, -a *ag* dark; (*fig: espressione*) grim ▷ *sm* darkness; dark colour; (*imposta*) (window) shutter; **verde/rosso** *ecc* **~** dark green/red *ecc*
'scusa *sf* apology; (*pretesto*) excuse; **chiedere ~ a qn (per)** to apologize to sb (for); **chiedo ~** I'm sorry; (*disturbando ecc*) excuse me
scu'sare *vt* to excuse; **scusarsi** *vpr* **scusarsi (di)** to apologize (for); **(mi) scusi** I'm sorry; (*per richiamare l'attenzione*) excuse me
sde'gnato, -a [zdeɲ'ɲato] *ag* indignant, angry
'sdegno ['zdeɲɲo] *sm* scorn, disdain
sdolci'nato, -a [zdoltʃi'nato] *ag* mawkish, oversentimental
sdrai'arsi *vpr* to stretch out, lie down
'sdraio *sm* **sedia a ~** deck chair
sdruccio'levole [zdruttʃo'levole] *ag* slippery

PAROLA CHIAVE

se *pron vedi* **si**
▷ *cong* **1** (*condizionale, ipotetica*) if; **se nevica non vengo** I won't come if it snows; **sarei rimasto se me l'avessero chiesto** I would have stayed if they'd asked me; **non puoi fare altro se non telefonare** all you can do is phone; **se mai** if, if ever; **siamo noi se mai che le siamo grati** it is we who should be grateful to you; **se no** (*altrimenti*) or (else), otherwise
2 (*in frasi dubitative, interrogative indirette*) if, whether; **non so se scrivere o telefonare** I don't know whether *o* if I should write or phone

sé *pron* (*gen*) oneself; (*esso, essa, lui, lei, loro*) itself; himself; herself; themselves; **sé stesso(a)** *pron*

oneself; itself; himself; herself
seb'bene *cong* although, though
sec. *abbr* (= *secolo*) c.
'secca *sf* (*del mare*) shallows *pl*; *vedi anche* **secco**
sec'care *vt* to dry; (*prosciugare*) to dry up; (*fig*: *importunare*) to annoy, bother ▷ *vi* to dry; to dry up; **seccarsi** *vpr* to dry; to dry up; (*fig*) to grow annoyed
sec'cato, -a *ag* (*fig*: *infastidito*) bothered, annoyed; (: *stufo*) fed up
secca'tura *sf* (*fig*) bother *no pl*, trouble *no pl*
seccherò *ecc* [sekke'rɔ] *vb vedi* **seccare**
secchi'ello *sm* bucket; **secchiello del ghiaccio** ice bucket
'secchio ['sekkjo] *sm* bucket, pail
'secco, -a, -chi, -che *ag* dry; (*fichi, pesce*) dried; (*foglie, ramo*) withered; (*magro*: *persona*) thin, skinny; (*fig*: *risposta, modo di fare*) curt, abrupt; (: *colpo*) clean, sharp ▷ *sm* (*siccità*) drought; **restarci ~** (*fig*: *morire sul colpo*) to drop dead; **mettere in ~** (*barca*) to beach; **rimanere a ~** (*fig*) to be left in the lurch
seco'lare *ag* age-old, centuries-old; (*laico, mondano*) secular
'secolo *sm* century; (*epoca*) age
se'conda *sf* (*Aut*) second (gear); **viaggiare in ~** to travel second-class; *vedi anche* **secondo**; **seconda colazione** lunch
secon'dario, -a *ag* secondary
se'condo, -a *ag* second ▷ *sm* second; (*di pranzo*) main course ▷ *prep* according to; (*nel modo prescritto*) in accordance with; **~ me** in my opinion, to my mind; **di seconda mano** second-hand; **a seconda di** according to; in accordance with; **seconda classe** second-class
'sedano *sm* celery
seda'tivo, -a *ag, sm* sedative
'sede *sf* seat; (*di ditta*) head office; (*di organizzazione*) headquarters *pl*; **sede centrale** head office; **sede sociale** registered office
seden'tario, -a *ag* sedentary
se'dere *vi* to sit, be seated
'sedia *sf* chair; **sedia elettrica** electric chair; **sedia a rotelle** wheelchair
'sedici ['seditʃi] *num* sixteen
se'dile *sm* seat; (*panchina*) bench
sedu'cente [sedu'tʃɛnte] *ag* seductive; (*proposta*) very attractive
se'durre *vt* to seduce
se'duta *sf* session, sitting; (*riunione*) meeting; **seduta spiritica** séance; **seduta stante** (*fig*) immediately
seduzi'one [sedut'tsjone] *sf* seduction; (*fascino*) charm, appeal
SEeO *abbr* (= *salvo errori e omissioni*) E and OE
'sega, -ghe *sf* saw
'segale *sf* rye
se'gare *vt* to saw; (*recidere*) to saw off
'seggio ['sɛddʒo] *sm* seat; **seggio elettorale** polling station
'seggiola ['sɛddʒola] *sf* chair; **seggio'lone** *sm* (*per bambini*) highchair
seggio'via [seddʒo'via] *sf* chairlift
segherò *ecc* [sege'rɔ] *vb vedi* **segare**
segna'lare [seɲɲa'lare] *vt* (*manovra ecc*) to signal; to indicate; (*annunciare*) to announce; to report; (*fig*: *far conoscere*) to point out; (: *persona*) to single out
se'gnale [seɲ'ɲale] *sm* signal; (*cartello*): **segnale acustico** acoustic *o* sound signal; **segnale d'allarme** alarm; (*Ferr*) communication cord; **segnale orario** (*Radio*) time signal; **segnale stradale** road sign
segna'libro [seɲɲa'libro] *sm* (*anche Inform*) bookmark
se'gnare [seɲ'ɲare] *vt* to mark; (*prendere nota*) to note; (*indicare*) to indicate, mark; (*Sport*: *goal*) to score
'segno ['seɲɲo] *sm* sign; (*impronta,*

contrassegno) mark; (*limite*) limit, bounds *pl*; (*bersaglio*) target; **fare ~ di sì/no** to nod (one's head)/shake one's head; **fare ~ a qn di fermarsi** to motion (to) sb to stop; **cogliere** *o* **colpire nel ~** (*fig*) to hit the mark; **segno zodiacale** star sign

segre'tario, -a *sm/f* secretary; **segretario comunale** town clerk; **Segretario di Stato** Secretary of State

segrete'ria *sf* (*di ditta, scuola*) (secretary's) office; (*d'organizzazione internazionale*) secretariat; (*Pol ecc*: *carica*) office of Secretary; **segreteria telefonica** answering service

se'greto, -a *ag* secret ▷ *sm* secret; secrecy *no pl*; **in ~** in secret, secretly

segu'ace [se'gwatʃe] *sm/f* follower, disciple

segu'ente *ag* following, next

segu'ire *vt* to follow; (*frequentare*: *corso*) to attend ▷ *vi* to follow; (*continuare*: *testo*) to continue

segui'tare *vt* to continue, carry on with ▷ *vi* to continue, carry on

'seguito *sm* (*scorta*) suite, retinue; (*discepoli*) followers *pl*; (*favore*) following; (*continuazione*) continuation; (*conseguenza*) result; **di ~** at a stretch, on end; **in ~** later on; **in ~ a, a ~ di** following; (*a causa di*) as a result of, owing to

'sei *vb vedi* **essere** ▷ *num* six

sei'cento [sei'tʃɛnto] *num* six hundred ▷ *sm* **il S~** the seventeenth century

selci'ato [sel'tʃato] *sm* cobbled surface

selezio'nare [selettsjo'nare] *vt* to select

selezi'one [selet'tsjone] *sf* selection

'sella *sf* saddle

sel'lino *sm* saddle

selvag'gina [selvad'dʒina] *sf* (*animali*) game

sel'vaggio, -a, -gi, -ge [sel'vaddʒo] *ag* wild; (*tribù*) savage, uncivilized; (*fig*) savage, brutal ▷ *sm/f* savage

sel'vatico, -a, -ci, -che *ag* wild

se'maforo *sm* (*Aut*) traffic lights *pl*

sem'brare *vi* to seem ▷ *vb impers* **sembra che** it seems that; **mi sembra che** it seems to me that, I think (that); **~ di essere** to seem to be

'seme *sm* seed; (*sperma*) semen; (*Carte*) suit

se'mestre *sm* half-year, six-month period

semifi'nale *sf* semifinal

semi'freddo *sm* ice-cream cake

semi'nare *vt* to sow

semi'nario *sm* seminar; (*Rel*) seminary

seminter'rato *sm* basement; (*appartamento*) basement flat

'semola *sf*; **semola di grano duro** durum wheat

semo'lino *sm* semolina

'semplice ['semplitʃe] *ag* simple; (*di un solo elemento*) single

'sempre *av* always; (*ancora*) still; **posso ~ tentare** I can always *o* still try; **da ~** always; **per ~** forever; **una volta per ~** once and for all; **~ che** provided (that); **~ più** more and more; **~ meno** less and less

sempre'verde *ag, sm o f* (*Bot*) evergreen

'senape *sf* (*Cuc*) mustard

se'nato *sm* senate; **sena'tore, -'trice** *sm/f* senator

'senno *sm* judgment, (common) sense; **col ~ di poi** with hindsight

'seno *sm* (*Anat*: *petto, mammella*) breast; (*: grembo, fig*) womb; (*: cavità*) sinus

sen'sato, -a *ag* sensible

sensazio'nale [sensattsjo'nale] *ag* sensational

sensazi'one [sensat'tsjone] *sf* feeling, sensation; **avere la ~ che** to have a feeling that; **fare ~** to cause a sensation, create a stir

sen'sibile *ag* sensitive; (*ai sensi*) perceptible; (*rilevante, notevole*) appreciable, noticeable; **~ a** sensitive to

> Attenzione! In inglese esiste la parola *sensible*, che però significa *ragionevole*.

'senso *sm* (*Fisiol, istinto*) sense; (*impressione, sensazione*) feeling, sensation; (*significato*) meaning, sense; (*direzione*) direction; **sensi** *smpl* (*coscienza*) consciousness *sg*; (*sensualità*) senses; **ciò non ha ~** that doesn't make sense; **fare ~ a** (*ripugnare*) to disgust, repel; **in ~ orario/antiorario** clockwise/ anticlockwise; **senso di colpa** sense of guilt; **senso comune** common sense; **senso unico** (*strada*) one-way; **senso vietato** (*Aut*) no entry

sensu'ale *ag* sensual; sensuous

sen'tenza [sen'tɛntsa] *sf* (*Dir*) sentence; (*massima*) maxim

senti'ero *sm* path

sentimen'tale *ag* sentimental; (*vita, avventura*) love *cpd*

senti'mento *sm* feeling

senti'nella *sf* sentry

sen'tire *vt* (*percepire al tatto, fig*) to feel; (*udire*) to hear; (*ascoltare*) to listen to; (*odore*) to smell; (*avvertire con il gusto, assaggiare*) to taste ▷ *vi* **~ di** (*avere sapore*) to taste of; (*avere odore*) to smell of; **sentirsi** *vpr* (*uso reciproco*) to be in touch; **sentirsi bene/male** to feel well/unwell *o* ill; **non mi sento bene** I don't feel well; **sentirsi di fare qc** (*essere disposto*) to feel like doing sth

sen'tito, -a *ag* (*sincero*) sincere, warm; **per ~ dire** by hearsay

'senza ['sɛntsa] *prep, cong* without; **~ dir nulla** without saying a word; **fare ~ qc** to do without sth; **~ di me** without me; **~ che io lo sapessi** without me *o* my knowing; **senz'altro** of course, certainly; **~ dubbio** no doubt; **~ scrupoli** unscrupulous; **~ amici** friendless

sepa'rare *vt* to separate; (*dividere*) to divide; (*tenere distinto*) to distinguish; **separarsi** *vpr* (*coniugi*) to separate, part; (*amici*) to part, leave each other; **separarsi da** (*coniuge*) to separate *o* part from; (*amico, socio*) to part company with; (*oggetto*) to part with; **sepa'rato, -a** *ag* (*letti, conto ecc*) separate; (*coniugi*) separated

seppel'lire *vt* to bury

'seppi *ecc vb vedi* **sapere**

'seppia *sf* cuttlefish ▷ *ag inv* sepia

se'quenza [se'kwentsa] *sf* sequence

seques'trare *vt* (*Dir*) to impound; (*rapire*) to kidnap; **se'questro** *sm* (*Dir*) impoundment; **sequestro di persona** kidnapping

'sera *sf* evening; **di ~** in the evening; **domani ~** tomorrow evening, tomorrow night; **se'rale** *ag* evening *cpd*; **se'rata** *sf* evening; (*ricevimento*) party

ser'bare *vt* to keep; (*mettere da parte*) to put aside; **~ rancore/odio verso qn** to bear sb a grudge/hate sb

serba'toio *sm* tank; (*cisterna*) cistern

'Serbia *sf* **la ~** Serbia

'serbo *ag* Serbian ▷ *sm/f* Serbian, Serb ▷ *sm* (*Ling*) Serbian; (*il serbare*): **mettere/tenere** *o* **avere in ~ qc** to put/keep sth aside

se'reno, -a *ag* (*tempo, cielo*) clear; (*fig*) serene, calm

ser'gente [ser'dʒɛnte] *sm* (*Mil*) sergeant

'serie *sf inv* (*successione*) series *inv*; (*gruppo, collezione*) set; (*Sport*) division; league; (*Comm*): **modello di ~/fuori ~** standard/custom-built model; **in ~** in quick succession; (*Comm*) mass *cpd*

serietà *sf* seriousness; reliability

'serio, -a *ag* serious; (*impiegato*) responsible, reliable; (*ditta, cliente*) reliable, dependable; **sul ~** (*davvero*) really, truly; (*seriamente*) seriously, in earnest

ser'pente *sm* snake; **serpente a sonagli** rattlesnake
'serra *sf* greenhouse; hothouse
ser'randa *sf* roller shutter
serra'tura *sf* lock
server ['sɛrver] *sm inv* (*Inform*) server
ser'vire *vt* to serve; (*clienti: al ristorante*) to wait on; (*: al negozio*) to serve, attend to; (*fig: giovare*) to aid, help; (*Carte*) to deal ▷ *vi* (*Tennis*) to serve; (*essere utile*): **~ a qn** to be of use to sb; **~ a qc/a fare** (*utensile ecc*) to be used for sth/for doing; **~ (a qn) da** to serve as (for sb); **servirsi** *vpr* (*usare*): **servirsi di** to use; (*prendere: cibo*): **servirsi (di)** to help o.s. (to); **serviti pure!** help yourself!; (*essere cliente abituale*): **servirsi da** to be a regular customer at, go to
servizi'evole [servit'tsjevole] *ag* obliging, willing to help
ser'vizio [ser'vittsjo] *sm* service; (*al ristorante: sul conto*) service (charge); (*Stampa, TV, Radio*) report; (*da tè, caffè ecc*) set, service; **servizi** *smpl* (*di casa*) kitchen and bathroom; (*Econ*) services; **essere di ~** to be on duty; **fuori ~** (*telefono ecc*) out of order; **~ compreso** service included; **servizio militare** military service; **servizio di posate** set of cutlery; **servizi segreti** secret service *sg*; **servizio da tè** tea set
ses'santa *num* sixty; **sessan'tesimo, -a** *num* sixtieth
sessi'one *sf* session
'sesso *sm* sex; **sessu'ale** *ag* sexual, sex *cpd*
ses'tante *sm* sextant
'sesto, -a *ag, sm* sixth
'seta *sf* silk
'sete *sf* thirst; **avere ~** to be thirsty
'setola *sf* bristle
'setta *sf* sect
set'tanta *num* seventy; **settan'tesimo, -a** *num* seventieth
set'tare *vt* (*Inform*) to set up
'sette *num* seven
sette'cento [sette'tʃɛnto] *num* seven hundred ▷ *sm* **il S~** the eighteenth century
set'tembre *sm* September
settentrio'nale *ag* northern
settentri'one *sm* north
setti'mana *sf* week; **settima'nale** *ag, sm* weekly

SETTIMANA BIANCA

Settimana bianca is the name given to a week-long winter-sports holiday taken by many Italians some time in the skiing season.

'settimo, -a *ag, sm* seventh
set'tore *sm* sector
severità *sf* severity
se'vero, -a *ag* severe
sevizi'are [sevit'tsjare] *vt* to torture
sezio'nare [settsjo'nare] *vt* to divide into sections; (*Med*) to dissect
sezi'one [set'tsjone] *sf* section
sfacchi'nata [sfakki'nata] *sf* (*fam*) chore, drudgery *no pl*
sfacci'ato, -a [sfat'tʃato] *ag* (*maleducato*) cheeky, impudent; (*vistoso*) gaudy
sfa'mare *vt* to feed; (*cibo*) to fill; **sfamarsi** *vpr* to satisfy one's hunger, fill o.s. up
sfasci'are [sfaʃ'ʃare] *vt* (*ferita*) to unbandage; (*distruggere*) to smash, shatter; **sfasciarsi** *vpr* (*rompersi*) to smash, shatter
sfavo'revole *ag* unfavourable
'sfera *sf* sphere
sfer'rare *vt* (*fig: colpo*) to land, deal; (*: attacco*) to launch
'sfida *sf* challenge
sfi'dare *vt* to challenge; (*fig*) to defy, brave
sfi'ducia [sfi'dutʃa] *sf* distrust, mistrust
sfi'gato, -a (*fam*) *ag* (*sfortunato*)

unlucky

sfigu'rare *vt* (*persona*) to disfigure; (*quadro, statua*) to deface ▷ *vi* (*far cattiva figura*) to make a bad impression

sfi'lare *vt* (*ago*) to unthread; (*abito, scarpe*) to slip off ▷ *vi* (*truppe*) to march past; (*atleti*) to parade; **sfilarsi** *vpr* (*perle ecc*) to come unstrung; (*orlo, tessuto*) to fray; (*calza*) to run, ladder; **sfi'lata** *sf* march past; parade; **sfilata di moda** fashion show

'sfinge ['sfindʒe] *sf* sphinx

sfi'nito, -a *ag* exhausted

sfio'rare *vt* to brush (against); (*argomento*) to touch upon

sfio'rire *vi* to wither, fade

sfo'cato, -a *ag* (*Fot*) out of focus

sfoci'are [sfo'tʃare] *vi*: **~ in** to flow into; (*fig*: *malcontento*) to develop into

sfode'rato, -a *ag* (*vestito*) unlined

sfogarsi *vpr* (*sfogare la propria rabbia*) to give vent to one's anger; (*confidarsi*): **~ (con)** to pour out one's feelings (to); **non sfogarti su di me!** don't take your bad temper out on me!

sfoggi'are [sfod'dʒare] *vt, vi* to show off

'sfoglia ['sfoʎʎa] *sf* sheet of pasta dough; **pasta ~** (*Cuc*) puff pastry

sfogli'are [sfɔʎ'ʎare] *vt* (*libro*) to leaf through

'sfogo, -ghi *sm* (*eruzione cutanea*) rash; (*fig*) outburst; **dare ~ a** (*fig*) to give vent to

sfon'dare *vt* (*porta*) to break down; (*scarpe*) to wear a hole in; (*cesto, scatola*) to burst, knock the bottom out of; (*Mil*) to break through ▷ *vi* (*riuscire*) to make a name for o.s.

'sfondo *sm* background

sfor'mato *sm* (*Cuc*) *type of soufflé*

sfor'tuna *sf* misfortune, ill luck *no pl*; **avere ~** to be unlucky; **sfortu'nato, -a** *ag* unlucky; (*impresa, film*) unsuccessful

sforzarsi *vpr*: **~ di** *o* **a** *o* **per fare** to try hard to do

'sforzo ['sfɔrtso] *sm* effort; (*tensione eccessiva, Tecn*) strain; **fare uno ~** to make an effort

sfrat'tare *vt* to evict; **'sfratto** *sm* eviction

sfrecci'are [sfret'tʃare] *vi* to shoot *o* flash past

sfre'gare *vt* (*strofinare*) to rub; (*graffiare*) to scratch; **sfregarsi le mani** to rub one's hands; **~ un fiammifero** to strike a match

sfregi'are [sfre'dʒare] *vt* to slash, gash; (*persona*) to disfigure; (*quadro*) to deface

sfre'nato, -a *ag* (*fig*) unrestrained, unbridled

sfron'tato, -a *ag* shameless

sfrutta'mento *sm* exploitation

sfrut'tare *vt* (*terreno*) to overwork, exhaust; (*miniera*) to exploit, work; (*fig*: *operai, occasione, potere*) to exploit

sfug'gire [sfud'dʒire] *vi* to escape; **~ a** (*custode*) to escape (from); (*morte*) to escape; **~ a qn** (*dettaglio, nome*) to escape sb; **~ di mano a qn** to slip out of sb's hand (*o* hands)

sfu'mare *vt* (*colori, contorni*) to soften, shade off ▷ *vi* to shade (off), fade; (*fig*: *svanire*) to vanish, disappear; (: *speranze*) to come to nothing

sfuma'tura *sf* shading off *no pl*; (*tonalità*) shade, tone; (*fig*) touch, hint

sfuri'ata *sf* (*scatto di collera*) fit of anger; (*rimprovero*) sharp rebuke

sga'bello *sm* stool

sgabuz'zino [sgabud'dzino] *sm* lumber room

sgambet'tare *vi* to kick one's legs about

sgam'betto *sm* **far lo ~ a qn** to trip sb up; (*fig*) to oust sb

sganci'are [zgan'tʃare] *vt* to unhook; (*Ferr*) to uncouple; (*bombe*: *da aereo*) to release, drop; (*fig*: *fam*: *soldi*) to fork out; **sganciarsi** *vpr* (*fig*): **sganciarsi (da)** to get away (from)

sganghe'rato, -a [zgange'rato] *ag* (*porta*) off its hinges; (*auto*) ramshackle; (*risata*) wild, boisterous
sgar'bato, -a *ag* rude, impolite
'sgarbo *sm* **fare uno ~ a qn** to be rude to sb
sgargi'ante [zgar'dʒante] *ag* gaudy, showy
sgattaio'lare *vi* to sneak away *o* off
sge'lare [zdʒe'lare] *vi, vt* to thaw
sghignaz'zare [zgiɲɲat'tsare] *vi* to laugh scornfully
sgob'bare (*fam*) *vi* (*scolaro*) to swot; (*operaio*) to slog
sgombe'rare *vt* (*tavolo, stanza*) to clear; (*piazza, città*) to evacuate ▷ *vi* to move
'sgombro, -a *ag*: **~ (di)** clear (of), free (from) ▷ *sm* (*Zool*) mackerel; (*anche*: **sgombero**) clearing; vacating; evacuation; (: *trasloco*) removal
sgonfi'are *vt* to let down, deflate; **sgonfiarsi** *vpr* to go down
'sgonfio, -a *ag* (*pneumatico, pallone*) flat
'sgorbio *sm* blot; scribble
sgra'devole *ag* unpleasant, disagreeable
sgra'dito, -a *ag* unpleasant, unwelcome
sgra'nare *vt* (*piselli*) to shell; **~ gli occhi** to open one's eyes wide
sgranchire [zgran'kire] *vt* (*anche*: **sgranchirsi**) to stretch; **~ le gambe** to stretch one's legs
sgranocchi'are [zgranok'kjare] *vt* to munch
'sgravio *sm* **~ fiscale** tax relief
sgrazi'ato, -a [zgrat'tsjato] *ag* clumsy, ungainly
sgri'dare *vt* to scold
sgual'cire [zgwal'tʃire] *vt* to crumple (up), crease
sgual'drina (*peg*) *sf* slut
sgu'ardo *sm* (*occhiata*) look, glance; (*espressione*) look (in one's eye)
sguaz'zare [zgwat'tsare] *vi* (*nell'acqua*) to splash about; (*nella melma*) to wallow; **~ nell'oro** to be rolling in money
sguinzagli'are [zgwintsaʎ'ʎare] *vt* to let off the leash; (*fig*: *persona*): **~ qn dietro a qn** to set sb on sb
sgusci'are [zguʃ'ʃare] *vt* to shell ▷ *vi* (*sfuggire di mano*) to slip; **~ via** to slip *o* slink away
'shampoo ['ʃampo] *sm inv* shampoo
shiatzu [ʃi'atstsu] *sm inv* shiatsu
shock [ʃɔk] *sm inv* shock

PAROLA CHIAVE

si (*dav lo, la, li, le, ne diventa* **se**) *pron*
1 (*riflessivo*: *maschile*) himself; (: *femminile*) herself; (: *neutro*) itself; (: *impersonale*) oneself; (: *pl*) themselves; **lavarsi** to wash (oneself); **si è tagliato** he has cut himself; **si credono importanti** they think a lot of themselves
2 (*riflessivo*: *con complemento oggetto*): **lavarsi le mani** to wash one's hands; **si sta lavando i capelli** he (*o* she) is washing his (*o* her) hair
3 (*reciproco*) one another, each other; **si amano** they love one another *o* each other
4 (*passivo*): **si ripara facilmente** it is easily repaired
5 (*impersonale*): **si dice che ...** they *o* people say that ...; **si vede che è vecchio** one *o* you can see that it's old
6 (*noi*) we; **tra poco si parte** we're leaving soon

sì *av* yes; **un giorno sì e uno no** every other day
'sia *cong* **~ ... ~** (*o ... o*): **~ che lavori, ~ che non lavori** whether he works or not; (*tanto ... quanto*): **verranno ~ Luigi ~ suo fratello** both Luigi and his brother will be coming
si'amo *vb vedi* **essere**
si'cario *sm* hired killer

sicché [sik'ke] *cong* (*perciò*) so (that), therefore; (*e quindi*) (and) so
siccità [sittʃi'ta] *sf* drought
sic'come *cong* since, as
Si'cilia [si'tʃilja] *sf* **la ~** Sicily
si'cura *sf* safety catch; (*Aut*) safety lock
sicu'rezza [siku'rettsa] *sf* safety; security; (*fiducia*) confidence; (*certezza*) certainty; **di ~** safety *cpd*; **la ~ stradale** road safety
si'curo, -a *ag* safe; (*ben difeso*) secure; (*fiducioso*) confident; (*certo*) sure, certain; (*notizia, amico*) reliable; (*esperto*) skilled ▷ *av* (*anche:* **di ~**) certainly; **essere/mettere al ~** to be safe/put in a safe place; **~ di sé** self-confident, sure of o.s.; **sentirsi ~** to feel safe *o* secure
si'edo *ecc vb vedi* **sedere**
si'epe *sf* hedge
si'ero *sm* (*Med*) serum;
sieronega'tivo, -a *ag* HIV-negative;
sieroposi'tivo, -a *ag* HIV-positive
si'ete *vb vedi* **essere**
si'filide *sf* syphilis
Sig. *abbr* (= *signore*) Mr
siga'retta *sf* cigarette
'sigaro *sm* cigar
Sigg. *abbr* (= *signori*) Messrs
sigil'lare [sidʒil'lare] *vt* to seal
si'gillo [si'dʒillo] *sm* seal
'sigla *sf* initials *pl*; acronym, abbreviation; **sigla automobilistica** *abbreviation of province on vehicle number plate*; **sigla musicale** signature tune
Sig.na *abbr* (= *signorina*) Miss
signifi'care [siɲɲifi'kare] *vt* to mean; **signifi'cato** *sm* meaning
si'gnora [siɲ'ɲora] *sf* lady; **la ~ X** Mrs X; **buon giorno S~/Signore/Signorina** good morning; (*deferente*) good morning Madam/Sir/Madam; (*quando si conosce il nome*) good morning Mrs/Mr/Miss X; **Gentile S~/Signore/Signorina** (*in una lettera*) Dear Madam/Sir/Madam; **il signor Rossi e ~** Mr Rossi and his wife; **signore e signori** ladies and gentlemen
si'gnore [siɲ'ɲore] *sm* gentleman; (*padrone*) lord, master; (*Rel*): **il S~** the Lord; **il signor X** Mr X; **i signori Bianchi** (*coniugi*) Mr and Mrs Bianchi; *vedi anche* **signora**
signo'rile [siɲɲo'rile] *ag* refined
signo'rina [siɲɲo'rina] *sf* young lady; **la ~ X** Miss X; *vedi anche* **signora**
Sig.ra *abbr* (= *signora*) Mrs
silenzia'tore [silentsja'tore] *sm* silencer
si'lenzio [si'lɛntsjo] *sm* silence; **fare ~** to be quiet, stop talking;
silenzi'oso, -a *ag* silent, quiet
si'licio [si'litʃo] *sm* silicon
sili'cone *sm* silicone
'sillaba *sf* syllable
si'luro *sm* torpedo
simboleggi'are [simboled'dʒare] *vt* to symbolize
'simbolo *sm* symbol
'simile *ag* (*analogo*) similar; (*di questo tipo*): **un uomo ~** such a man, a man like this; **libri simili** such books; **~ a** similar to; **i suoi simili** one's fellow men; one's peers
simme'tria *sf* symmetry
simpa'tia *sf* (*qualità*) pleasantness; (*inclinazione*) liking; **avere ~ per qn** to like sb, have a liking for sb;
sim'patico, -a, -ci, -che *ag* (*persona*) nice, pleasant, likeable; (*casa, albergo ecc*) nice, pleasant

> Attenzione! In inglese esiste la parola *sympathetic*, che però significa *comprensivo*.

simpatiz'zare [simpatid'dzare] *vi* **~ con** to take a liking to
simu'lare *vt* to sham, simulate; (*Tecn*) to simulate
simul'taneo, -a *ag* simultaneous
sina'goga, -ghe *sf* synagogue
sincerità [sintʃeri'ta] *sf* sincerity

sin'cero, -a [sin'tʃero] *ag* sincere; genuine; heartfelt
sinda'cale *ag* (trade-)union *cpd*
sinda'cato *sm* (*di lavoratori*) (trade) union; (*Amm, Econ, Dir*) syndicate, trust, pool
'sindaco, -ci *sm* mayor
sinfo'nia *sf* (*Mus*) symphony
singhioz'zare [singjot'tsare] *vi* to sob; to hiccup
singhi'ozzo [sin'gjottso] *sm* sob; (*Med*) hiccup; **avere il ~** to have the hiccups; **a ~** (*fig*) by fits and starts
single ['siŋgol] *ag inv, sm/f inv* single
singo'lare *ag* (*insolito*) remarkable, singular; (*Ling*) singular ▷ *sm* (*Ling*) singular; (*Tennis*): **~ maschile/femminile** men's/women's singles
'singolo, -a *ag* single, individual ▷ *sm* (*persona*) individual; (*Tennis*) = **singolare**
si'nistra *sf* (*Pol*) left (wing); **a ~** on the left; (*direzione*) to the left
si'nistro, -a *ag* left, left-hand; (*fig*) sinister ▷ *sm* (*incidente*) accident
si'nonimo *sm* synonym; **~ di** synonymous with
sin'tassi *sf* syntax
'sintesi *sf* synthesis; (*riassunto*) summary, résumé
sin'tetico, -a, -ci, -che *ag* synthetic
sintetiz'zare [sintetid'dzare] *vt* to synthesize; (*riassumere*) to summarize
sinto'matico, -a, -ci, -che *ag* symptomatic
'sintomo *sm* symptom
sintonizzarsi *vpr* **~ su** to tune in to
si'pario *sm* (*Teatro*) curtain
si'rena *sf* (*apparecchio*) siren; (*nella mitologia, fig*) siren, mermaid
'Siria *sf* **la ~** Syria
si'ringa, -ghe *sf* syringe
'sismico, -a, -ci, -che *ag* seismic
sis'tema, -i *sm* system; method, way; **sistema nervoso** nervous system; **sistema operativo** (*Inform*) operating system; **sistema solare** solar system
siste'mare *vt* (*mettere a posto*) to tidy, put in order; (*risolvere: questione*) to sort out, settle; (*procurare un lavoro a*) to find a job for; (*dare un alloggio a*) to settle, find accommodation for; **sistemarsi** *vpr* (*problema*) to be settled; (*persona: trovare alloggio*) to find accommodation (BRIT) *o* accommodations (US); (*: trovarsi un lavoro*) to get fixed up with a job; **ti sistemo io!** I'll soon sort you out!
siste'matico, -a, -ci, -che *ag* systematic
sistemazi'one [sistemat'tsjone] *sf* arrangement, order; settlement; employment; accommodation (BRIT), accommodations (US)
'sito *sm* **~ Internet** website
situazi'one [situat'tsjone] *sf* situation
ski-lift ['ski:lift] *sm inv* ski tow
slacci'are [zlat'tʃare] *vt* to undo, unfasten
slanci'ato, -a [zlan'tʃato] *ag* slender
'slancio *sm* dash, leap; (*fig*) surge; **di ~** impetuously
'slavo, -a *ag* Slav(onic), Slavic
sle'ale *ag* disloyal; (*concorrenza ecc*) unfair
sle'gare *vt* to untie
slip [zlip] *sm inv* briefs *pl*
'slitta *sf* sledge; (*trainata*) sleigh
slit'tare *vi* to slip, slide; (*Aut*) to skid
s.l.m. *abbr* (= *sul livello del mare*) a.s.l.
slo'gare *vt* (*Med*) to dislocate
sloggi'are [zlod'dʒare] *vt* (*inquilino*) to turn out ▷ *vi* to move out
Slo'vacchia [zlo'vakkja] *sf* Slovakia
slo'vacco, -a, -chi, -che *ag, sm/f* Slovak
Slovenia [zlo'vɛnja] *sf* Slovenia
slo'veno, -a *ag, sm/f* Slovene, Slovenian ▷ *sm* (*Ling*) Slovene
smacchi'are [zmak'kjare] *vt* to remove stains from; **smacchia'tore** *sm* stain remover

'smacco, -chi *sm* humiliating defeat
smagli'ante [zmaʎ'ʎante] *ag* brilliant, dazzling
smaglia'tura [zmaʎʎa'tura] *sf* (*su maglia, calza*) ladder; (*della pelle*) stretch mark
smalizi'ato, -a [smalit'tsjato] *ag* shrewd, cunning
smalti'mento *sm* (*di rifiuti*) disposal
smal'tire *vt* (*merce*) to sell off; (*rifiuti*) to dispose of; (*cibo*) to digest; (*peso*) to lose; (*rabbia*) to get over; **~ la sbornia** to sober up
'smalto *sm* (*anche*: **di denti**) enamel; (*per ceramica*) glaze; **smalto per unghie** nail varnish
smantel'lare *vt* to dismantle
smarri'mento *sm* loss; (*fig*) bewilderment; dismay
smar'rire *vt* to lose; (*non riuscire a trovare*) to mislay; **smarrirsi** *vpr* (*perdersi*) to lose one's way, get lost; (: *oggetto*) to go astray
smasche'rare [zmaske'rare] *vt* to unmask
SME *sigla m* (= *Sistema Monetario Europeo*) EMS (*European Monetary System*)
smen'tire *vt* (*negare*) to deny; (*testimonianza*) to refute; **smentirsi** *vpr* to be inconsistent
sme'raldo *sm* emerald
'smesso, -a *pp di* **smettere**
'smettere *vt* to stop; (*vestiti*) to stop wearing ▷ *vi* to stop, cease; **~ di fare** to stop doing
'smilzo, -a ['zmiltso] *ag* thin, lean
sminu'ire *vt* to diminish, lessen; (*fig*) to belittle
sminuz'zare [zminut'tsare] *vt* to break into small pieces; to crumble
'smisi *ecc vb vedi* **smettere**
smis'tare *vt* (*pacchi ecc*) to sort; (*Ferr*) to shunt
smisu'rato, -a *ag* boundless, immeasurable; (*grandissimo*) immense, enormous
smoking ['sməukɪŋ] *sm inv* dinner jacket
smon'tare *vt* (*mobile, macchina ecc*) to take to pieces, dismantle; (*fig*: *scoraggiare*) to dishearten ▷ *vi* (*scendere*: *da cavallo*) to dismount; (: *da treno*) to get off; (*terminare il lavoro*) to stop (work); **smontarsi** *vpr* to lose heart; to lose one's enthusiasm
'smorfia *sf* grimace; (*atteggiamento lezioso*) simpering; **fare smorfie** to make faces; to simper
'smorto, -a *ag* (*viso*) pale, wan; (*colore*) dull
smor'zare [zmor'tsare] *vt* (*suoni*) to deaden; (*colori*) to tone down; (*luce*) to dim; (*sete*) to quench; (*entusiasmo*) to dampen; **smorzarsi** *vpr* (*suono, luce*) to fade; (*entusiasmo*) to dampen
SMS *sigla m inv* (= *short message service*) text (message)
smu'overe *vt* to move, shift; (*fig*: *commuovere*) to move; (: *dall'inerzia*) to rouse, stir
snatu'rato, -a *ag* inhuman, heartless
'snello, -a *ag* (*agile*) agile; (*svelto*) slender, slim
sner'vante *ag* (*attesa, lavoro*) exasperating
snob'bare *vt* to snub
sno'dare *vt* (*rendere agile, mobile*) to loosen; **snodarsi** *vpr* to come loose; (*articolarsi*) to bend; (*strada, fiume*) to wind
sno'dato, -a *ag* (*articolazione, persona*) flexible; (*fune ecc*) undone
so *vb vedi* **sapere**
sobbar'carsi *vpr*: **~ a** to take on, undertake
'sobrio, -a *ag* sober
socchi'udere [sok'kjudere] *vt* (*porta*) to leave ajar; (*occhi*) to half-close; **socchi'uso, -a** *pp di* **socchiudere**
soc'correre *vt* to help, assist
soccorri'tore, -'trice *sm/f* rescuer

soc'corso, -a *pp di* **soccorrere** ▷ *sm* help, aid, assistance; **soccorso stradale** breakdown service
soci'ale [so'tʃale] *ag* social; (*di associazione*) club *cpd*, association *cpd*
socia'lismo [sotʃa'lizmo] *sm* socialism; **socia'lista, -i, -e** *ag, sm/f* socialist
società [sotʃe'ta] *sf inv* society; (*sportiva*) club; (*Comm*) company; **~ a responsabilità limitata** *type of limited liability company*; **società per azioni** limited (BRIT) *o* incorporated (US) company
soci'evole [so'tʃevole] *ag* sociable
'socio ['sɔtʃo] *sm* (*Dir, Comm*) partner; (*membro di associazione*) member
'soda *sf* (*Chim*) soda; (*bibita*) soda (water)
soddisfa'cente [soddisfa'tʃɛnte] *ag* satisfactory
soddis'fare *vt, vi*: **~ a** to satisfy; (*impegno*) to fulfil; (*debito*) to pay off; (*richiesta*) to meet, comply with; **soddis'fatto, -a** *pp di* **soddisfare** ▷ *ag* satisfied; **soddisfatto di** happy *o* satisfied with; pleased with; **soddisfazi'one** *sf* satisfaction
'sodo, -a *ag* firm, hard; (*uovo*) hard-boiled ▷ *av* (*picchiare, lavorare*) hard; (*dormire*) soundly
sofà *sm inv* sofa
soffe'renza [soffe'rɛntsa] *sf* suffering
sof'ferto, -a *pp di* **soffrire**
soffi'are *vt* to blow; (*notizia, segreto*) to whisper ▷ *vi* to blow; (*sbuffare*) to puff (and blow); **soffiarsi il naso** to blow one's nose; **~ qc/qn a qn** (*fig*) to pinch *o* steal sth/sb from sb; **~ via qc** to blow sth away
soffi'ata *sf* (*fam*) tip-off; **fare una ~ alla polizia** to tip off the police
'soffice ['sɔffitʃe] *ag* soft
'soffio *sm* (*di vento*) breath; **soffio al cuore** heart murmur
sof'fitta *sf* attic
sof'fitto *sm* ceiling
soffo'cante *ag* suffocating, stifling
soffo'care *vi* (*anche*: **soffocarsi**) to suffocate, choke ▷ *vt* to suffocate, choke; (*fig*) to stifle, suppress
sof'frire *vt* to suffer, endure; (*sopportare*) to bear, stand ▷ *vi* to suffer; to be in pain; **~ (di) qc** (*Med*) to suffer from sth
sof'fritto, -a *pp di* **soffriggere** ▷ *sm* (*Cuc*) *fried mixture of herbs, bacon and onions*
sofisti'cato, -a *ag* sophisticated; (*vino*) adulterated
'software ['sɔftwɛə] *sm* **~ applicativo** applications package
sogget'tivo, -a [soddʒet'tivo] *ag* subjective
sog'getto, -a [sod'dʒɛtto] *ag*: **~ a** (*sottomesso*) subject to; (*esposto*: *a variazioni, danni ecc*) subject *o* liable to ▷ *sm* subject
soggezi'one [soddʒet'tsjone] *sf* subjection; (*timidezza*) awe; **avere ~ di qn** to stand in awe of sb; to be ill at ease in sb's presence
soggi'orno *sm* (*invernale, marino*) stay; (*stanza*) living room
'soglia ['sɔʎʎa] *sf* doorstep; (*anche fig*) threshold
'sogliola ['sɔʎʎola] *sf* (*Zool*) sole
so'gnare [soɲ'ɲare] *vt, vi* to dream; **~ a occhi aperti** to daydream
'sogno ['soɲɲo] *sm* dream
'soia *sf* (*Bot*) soya
sol *sm* (*Mus*) G; (: *solfeggiando*) so(h)
so'laio *sm* (*soffitta*) attic
sola'mente *av* only, just
so'lare *ag* solar, sun *cpd*
'solco, -chi *sm* (*scavo, fig*: *ruga*) furrow; (*incavo*) rut, track; (*di disco*) groove
sol'dato *sm* soldier; **soldato semplice** private
soldi *smpl* (*denaro*) money *sg*; **non ho ~** I haven't got any money
'sole *sm* sun; (*luce*) sun(light); (*tempo*

assolato) sun(shine); **prendere il ~** to sunbathe
soleggi'ato, -a [soled'dʒato] *ag* sunny
so'lenne *ag* solemn
soli'dale *ag*: **essere ~ (con)** to be in agreement (with)
solidarietà *sf* solidarity
'solido, -a *ag* solid; (*forte, robusto*) sturdy, solid; (*fig: ditta*) sound, solid ▷ *sm* (*Mat*) solid
so'lista, -i, -e *ag* solo ▷ *sm/f* soloist
solita'mente *av* usually, as a rule
soli'tario, -a *ag* (*senza compagnia*) solitary, lonely; (*solo, isolato*) solitary, lone; (*deserto*) lonely ▷ *sm* (*gioiello, gioco*) solitaire
'solito, -a *ag* usual; **essere ~ fare** to be in the habit of doing; **di ~** usually; **più tardi del ~** later than usual; **come al ~** as usual
soli'tudine *sf* solitude
sol'letico *sm* tickling; **soffrire il ~** to be ticklish
solleva'mento *sm* raising; lifting; revolt; **sollevamento pesi** (*Sport*) weight-lifting
solle'vare *vt* to lift, raise; (*fig: persona: alleggerire*): **~ (da)** to relieve (of); (*: dar conforto*) to comfort, relieve; (*: questione*) to raise; (*: far insorgere*) to stir (to revolt); **sollevarsi** *vpr* to rise; (*fig: riprendersi*) to recover; (*: ribellarsi*) to rise up
solli'evo *sm* relief; (*conforto*) comfort
'solo, -a *ag* alone; (*in senso spirituale: isolato*) lonely; (*unico*): **un ~ libro** only one book, a single book; (*con ag numerale*): **veniamo noi tre soli** just *o* only the three of us are coming ▷ *av* (*soltanto*) only, just; **non ~ ... ma anche** not only ... but also; **fare qc da ~** to do sth (all) by oneself
sol'tanto *av* only
so'lubile *ag* (*sostanza*) soluble
soluzi'one [solut'tsjone] *sf* solution
sol'vente *ag, sm* solvent
so'maro *sm* ass, donkey
somigli'anza [somiʎ'ʎantsa] *sf* resemblance
somigli'are [somiʎ'ʎare] *vi*: **~ a** to be like, resemble; (*nell'aspetto fisico*) to look like; **somigliarsi** *vpr* to be (*o* look) alike
'somma *sf* (*Mat*) sum; (*di denaro*) sum (of money)
som'mare *vt* to add up; (*aggiungere*) to add; **tutto sommato** all things considered
som'mario, -a *ag* (*racconto, indagine*) brief; (*giustizia*) summary ▷ *sm* summary
sommer'gibile [sommer'dʒibile] *sm* submarine
som'merso, -a *pp di* **sommergere**
sommità *sf inv* summit, top; (*fig*) height
som'mossa *sf* uprising
'sonda *sf* (*Med, Meteor, Aer*) probe; (*Mineralogia*) drill ▷ *ag inv* **pallone** *m* **~** weather balloon
son'daggio [son'daddʒo] *sm* sounding; probe; boring, drilling; (*indagine*) survey; **sondaggio d'opinioni** opinion poll
son'dare *vt* (*Naut*) to sound; (*atmosfera, piaga*) to probe; (*Mineralogia*) to bore, drill; (*fig: opinione ecc*) to survey, poll
so'netto *sm* sonnet
son'nambulo, -a *sm/f* sleepwalker
sonnel'lino *sm* nap
son'nifero *sm* sleeping drug (*o* pill)
'sonno *sm* sleep; **prendere ~** to fall asleep; **aver ~** to be sleepy
'sono *vb vedi* **essere**
so'noro, -a *ag* (*ambiente*) resonant; (*voce*) sonorous, ringing; (*onde, film*) sound *cpd*
sontu'oso, -a *ag* sumptuous; lavish
sop'palco, -chi *sm* mezzanine
soppor'tare *vt* (*subire: perdita, spese*) to bear, sustain; (*soffrire: dolore*) to bear, endure; (*cosa: freddo*) to

withstand; (*persona*: *freddo, vino*) to take; (*tollerare*) to put up with, tolerate

Attenzione! In inglese esiste il verbo *to support*, che però non significa *sopportare*.

sop'primere *vt* (*carica, privilegi, testimone*) to do away with; (*pubblicazione*) to suppress; (*parola, frase*) to delete

'sopra *prep* (*gen*) on; (*al di sopra di, più in alto di*) above; over; (*riguardo a*) on, about ▷ *av* on top; (*attaccato, scritto*) on it; (*al di sopra*) above; (*al piano superiore*) upstairs; **donne ~ i 30 anni** women over 30 (years of age); **abito di ~** I live upstairs; **dormirci ~** (*fig*) to sleep on it

so'prabito *sm* overcoat

soprac'ciglio [soprat'tʃiʎʎo] (*pl*(*f*) **soprac'ciglia**) *sm* eyebrow

sopraf'fare *vt* to overcome, overwhelm

sopral'luogo, -ghi *sm* (*di esperti*) inspection; (*di polizia*) on-the-spot investigation

sopram'mobile *sm* ornament

soprannatu'rale *ag* supernatural

sopran'nome *sm* nickname

so'prano, -a *sm/f* (*persona*) soprano ▷ *sm* (*voce*) soprano

soprappensi'ero *av* lost in thought

sopras'salto *sm*: **di ~** with a start; suddenly

soprasse'dere *vi*: **~ a** to delay, put off

soprat'tutto *av* (*anzitutto*) above all; (*specialmente*) especially

sopravvalu'tare *vt* to overestimate

soprav'vento *sm* **avere/prendere il ~ su** to have/get the upper hand over

sopravvis'suto, -a *pp di* **sopravvivere**

soprav'vivere *vi* to survive; (*continuare a vivere*): **~ (in)** to live on (in); **~ a** (*incidente ecc*) to survive; (*persona*) to outlive

so'pruso *sm* abuse of power; **subire un ~** to be abused

soq'quadro *sm*: **mettere a ~** to turn upside-down

sor'betto *sm* sorbet, water ice

sor'dina *sf* **in ~** softly; (*fig*) on the sly

'sordo, -a *ag* deaf; (*rumore*) muffled; (*dolore*) dull; (*odio, rancore*) veiled ▷ *sm/f* deaf person; **sordo'muto, -a** *ag* deaf-and-dumb ▷ *sm/f* deaf-mute

so'rella *sf* sister; **sorel'lastra** *sf* stepsister; (*con genitore in comune*) half-sister

sor'gente [sor'dʒɛnte] *sf* (*d'acqua*) spring; (*di fiume, Fisica, fig*) source

'sorgere ['sordʒere] *vi* to rise; (*scaturire*) to spring, rise; (*fig*: *difficoltà*) to arise

sorni'one, -a *ag* sly

sorpas'sare *vt* (*Aut*) to overtake; (*fig*) to surpass; (: *eccedere*) to exceed, go beyond; **~ in altezza** to be higher than; (*persona*) to be taller than

sorpren'dente *ag* surprising

sor'prendere *vt* (*cogliere*: *in flagrante ecc*) to catch; (*stupire*) to surprise; **sorprendersi** *vpr*: **sorprendersi (di)** to be surprised (at); **sor'presa** *sf* surprise; **fare una sorpresa a qn** to give sb a surprise; **sor'preso, -a** *pp di* **sorprendere**

sor'reggere [sor'rɛddʒere] *vt* to support, hold up; (*fig*) to sustain; **sorreggersi** *vpr* (*tenersi ritto*) to stay upright

sor'ridere *vi* to smile; **sor'riso, -a** *pp di* **sorridere** ▷ *sm* smile

'sorsi *ecc vb vedi* **sorgere**

'sorso *sm* sip

'sorta *sf* sort, kind; **di ~** whatever, of any kind, at all

'sorte *sf* (*fato*) fate, destiny; (*evento fortuito*) chance; **tirare a ~** to draw lots

sor'teggio [sor'teddʒo] *sm* draw

sorvegli'ante [sorveʎ'ʎante] *sm/f* (*di carcere*) guard, warder (BRIT); (*di fabbrica ecc*) supervisor

sorvegli'anza [sorveʎ'ʎantsa] *sf*

watch; supervision; (*Polizia, Mil*) surveillance

sorvegli'are [sorveʎ'ʎare] *vt* (*bambino, bagagli, prigioniero*) to watch, keep an eye on; (*malato*) to watch over; (*territorio, casa*) to watch *o* keep watch over; (*lavori*) to supervise

sorvo'lare *vt* (*territorio*) to fly over ▷ *vi* **~ su** (*fig*) to skim over

S.O.S. *sigla m* mayday, SOS

'sosia *sm inv* double

sos'pendere *vt* (*appendere*) to hang (up); (*interrompere, privare di una carica*) to suspend; (*rimandare*) to defer; (*appendere*) to hang

sospet'tare *vt* to suspect ▷ *vi*: **~ di** to suspect; (*diffidare*) to be suspicious of

sos'petto, -a *ag* suspicious ▷ *sm* suspicion; **sospet'toso, -a** *ag* suspicious

sospi'rare *vi* to sigh ▷ *vt* to long for, yearn for; **sos'piro** *sm* sigh

'sosta *sf* (*fermata*) stop, halt; (*pausa*) pause, break; **senza ~** non-stop, without a break

sostan'tivo *sm* noun, substantive

sos'tanza [sos'tantsa] *sf* substance; **sostanze** *sfpl* (*ricchezze*) wealth *sg*, possessions; **in ~** in short, to sum up

sos'tare *vi* (*fermarsi*) to stop (for a while), stay; (*fare una pausa*) to take a break

sos'tegno [sos'teɲɲo] *sm* support

soste'nere *vt* to support; (*prendere su di sé*) to take on, bear; (*resistere*) to withstand, stand up to; (*affermare*): **~ che** to maintain that; **sostenersi** *vpr* to hold o.s. up, support o.s.; (*fig*) to keep up one's strength; **~ gli esami** to sit exams

sostenta'mento *sm* maintenance, support

sostitu'ire *vt* (*mettere al posto di*): **~ qn/qc a** to substitute sb/sth for; (*prendere il posto di*: *persona*) to substitute for; (: *cosa*) to take the place of

sosti'tuto, -a *sm/f* substitute

sostituzi'one [sostitut'tsjone] *sf* substitution; **in ~ di** as a substitute for, in place of

sotta'ceti [sotta'tʃeti] *smpl* pickles

sot'tana *sf* (*sottoveste*) underskirt; (*gonna*) skirt; (*Rel*) soutane, cassock

sotter'fugio [sotter'fudʒo] *sm* subterfuge

sotter'raneo, -a *ag* underground ▷ *sm* cellar

sotter'rare *vt* to bury

sot'tile *ag* thin; (*figura, caviglia*) thin, slim, slender; (*fine*: *polvere, capelli*) fine; (*fig*: *leggero*) light; (: *vista*) sharp, keen; (: *olfatto*) fine, discriminating; (: *mente*) subtle; shrewd ▷ *sm* **non andare per il ~** not to mince matters

sottin'teso, -a *pp di* **sottintendere** ▷ *sm* allusion; **parlare senza sottintesi** to speak plainly

'sotto *prep* (*gen*) under; (*più in basso di*) below ▷ *av* underneath, beneath; below; **(al piano) di ~** downstairs; **~ forma di** in the form of; **~ il monte** at the foot of the mountain; **siamo ~ Natale** it's nearly Christmas; **~ la pioggia/il sole** in the rain/sun(shine); **~ terra** underground; **chiuso ~ vuoto** vacuum-packed

sotto'fondo *sm* background; **sottofondo musicale** background music

sottoline'are *vt* to underline; (*fig*) to emphasize, stress

sottoma'rino, -a *ag* (*flora*) submarine; (*cavo, navigazione*) underwater ▷ *sm* (*Naut*) submarine

sottopas'saggio [sottopas'saddʒo] *sm* (*Aut*) underpass; (*pedonale*) subway, underpass

sotto'porre *vt* (*costringere*) to subject; (*fig*: *presentare*) to submit; **sottoporsi** *vpr* to submit; **sottoporsi a** (*subire*) to undergo

sottos'critto, -a *pp di* **sottoscrivere**

sotto'sopra *av* upside-down

sotto'terra *av* underground
sotto'titolo *sm* subtitle
sottovalu'tare *vt* to underestimate
sotto'veste *sf* underskirt
sotto'voce [sotto'votʃe] *av* in a low voice
sottovu'oto *av*: **confezionare ~** to vacuum-pack ▷ *ag* **confezione** *f* **~** vacuum packed
sot'trarre *vt* (*Mat*) to subtract, take away; **~ qn/qc a** (*togliere*) to remove sb/sth from; (*salvare*) to save *o* rescue sb/sth from; **~ qc a qn** (*rubare*) to steal sth from sb; **sottrarsi** *vpr* **sottrarsi a** (*sfuggire*) to escape; (*evitare*) to avoid; **sottrazi'one** *sf* subtraction; removal
souve'nir [suv(ə)'nir] *sm inv* souvenir
sovi'etico, -a, -ci, -che *ag* Soviet ▷ *sm/f* Soviet citizen
sovrac'carico, -a, chi, che *ag*: **~ (di)** overloaded (with) ▷ *sm* excess load; **~ di lavoro** extra work
sovraffol'lato, -a *ag* overcrowded
sovrannatu'rale *ag* = **soprannatu'rale**
so'vrano, -a *ag* sovereign; (*fig*: *sommo*) supreme ▷ *sm/f* sovereign, monarch
sovrap'porre *vt* to place on top of, put on top of
sovvenzi'one [sovven'tsjone] *sf* subsidy, grant
'sozzo, -a ['sottso] *ag* filthy, dirty
S.P.A. *abbr* = **società per azioni**
spac'care *vt* to split, break; (*legna*) to chop; **spaccarsi** *vpr* to split, break; **spacca'tura** *sf* split
spaccherò *ecc* [spakke'rɔ] *vb vedi* **spaccare**
spacci'are [spat'tʃare] *vt* (*vendere*) to sell (off); (*mettere in circolazione*) to circulate; (*droga*) to peddle, push; **spacciarsi** *vpr* **spacciarsi per** (*farsi credere*) to pass o.s. off as, pretend to be; **spaccia'tore, -'trice** *sm/f* (*di droga*) pusher; (*di denaro falso*) dealer; **'spaccio** *sm* (*di merce rubata, droga*): **spaccio (di)** trafficking (in); **spaccio (di)** passing (of); (*vendita*) sale; (*bottega*) shop
'spacco, -chi *sm* (*fenditura*) split, crack; (*strappo*) tear; (*di gonna*) slit
spac'cone *sm/f* boaster, braggart
'spada *sf* sword
spae'sato, -a *ag* disorientated, lost
spa'ghetti [spa'getti] *smpl* (*Cuc*) spaghetti *sg*
'Spagna ['spaɲɲa] *sf*: **la ~** Spain; **spa'gnolo, -a** *ag* Spanish ▷ *sm/f* Spaniard ▷ *sm* (*Ling*) Spanish; **gli Spagnoli** the Spanish
'spago, -ghi *sm* string, twine
spai'ato, -a *ag* (*calza, guanto*) odd
spalan'care *vt* to open wide; **spalancarsi** *vpr* to open wide
spa'lare *vt* to shovel
'spalla *sf* shoulder; (*fig*: *Teatro*) stooge; **spalle** *sfpl* (*dorso*) back
spalli'era *sf* (*di sedia ecc*) back; (*di letto*: *da capo*) head(board); (: *da piedi*) foot(board); (*Ginnastica*) wall bars *pl*
spal'lina *sf* (*bretella*) strap; (*imbottitura*) shoulder pad
spal'mare *vt* to spread
'spalti *smpl* (*di stadio*) terracing
'spandere *vt* to spread; (*versare*) to pour (out)
spa'rare *vt* to fire ▷ *vi* (*far fuoco*) to fire; (*tirare*) to shoot; **spara'toria** *sf* exchange of shots
sparecchi'are [sparek'kjare] *vt*: **~ (la tavola)** to clear the table
spa'reggio [spa'reddʒo] *sm* (*Sport*) play-off
'spargere ['spardʒere] *vt* (*sparpagliare*) to scatter; (*versare*: *vino*) to spill; (: *lacrime, sangue*) to shed; (*diffondere*) to spread; (*emanare*) to give off (*o* out); **spargersi** *vpr* to spread
spa'rire *vi* to disappear, vanish
spar'lare *vi* **~ di** to run down, speak ill of
'sparo *sm* shot
spar'tire *vt* (*eredità, bottino*) to share

out; (*avversari*) to separate
spar'tito *sm* (*Mus*) score
sparti'traffico *sm inv* (*Aut*) central reservation (BRIT), median (strip) (US)
sparvi'ero *sm* (*Zool*) sparrowhawk
spasi'mante *sm* suitor
spassio'nato, -a *ag* dispassionate, impartial
'spasso *sm* (*divertimento*) amusement, enjoyment; **andare a ~** to go out for a walk; **essere a ~** (*fig*) to be out of work; **mandare qn a ~** (*fig*) to give sb the sack
'spatola *sf* spatula; (*di muratore*) trowel
spa'valdo, -a *ag* arrogant, bold
spaventa'passeri *sm inv* scarecrow
spaven'tare *vt* to frighten, scare; **spaventarsi** *vpr* to be frightened, be scared; to get a fright; **spa'vento** *sm* fear, fright; **far spavento a qn** to give sb a fright; **spaven'toso, -a** *ag* frightening, terrible; (*fig: fam*) tremendous, fantastic
spazientirsi [spattsjen'tirsi] *vpr* to lose one's patience
'spazio ['spattsjo] *sm* space; **spazio aereo** airspace; **spazi'oso, -a** *ag* spacious
spazzaca'mino [spattsaka'mino] *sm* chimney sweep
spazza'neve [spattsa'neve] *sm inv* snowplough
spaz'zare [spat'tsare] *vt* to sweep; (*foglie ecc*) to sweep up; (*cacciare*) to sweep away; **spazza'tura** *sf* sweepings *pl*; (*immondizia*) rubbish; **spaz'zino** *sm* street sweeper
'spazzola ['spattsola] *sf* brush; **spazzola da capelli** hairbrush; **spazzola per abiti** clothesbrush; **spazzo'lare** *vt* to brush; **spazzo'lino** *sm* (small) brush; **spazzolino da denti** toothbrush
specchi'arsi [spek'kjarsi] *vpr* to look at o.s. in a mirror; (*riflettersi*) to be mirrored, be reflected
specchi'etto [spek'kjetto] *sm* (*tabella*) table, chart; **specchietto da borsetta** pocket mirror; **specchietto retrovisore** (*Aut*) rear-view mirror
'specchio ['spɛkkjo] *sm* mirror
speci'ale [spe'tʃale] *ag* special; **specia'lista, -i, -e** *sm/f* specialist; **specialità** *sf inv* speciality; (*branca di studio*) special field, speciality; **vorrei assaggiare una specialità del posto** I'd like to try a local speciality; **special'mente** *av* especially, particularly
'specie ['spɛtʃe] *sf inv* (*Biol, Bot, Zool*) species *inv*; (*tipo*) kind, sort ▷ *av* especially, particularly; **una ~ di** a kind of; **fare ~ a qn** to surprise sb; **la ~ umana** mankind
specifi'care [spetʃifi'kare] *vt* to specify, state
spe'cifico, -a, -ci, -che [spe'tʃifiko] *ag* specific
specu'lare *vi*: **~ su** (*Comm*) to speculate in; (*sfruttare*) to exploit; (*meditare*) to speculate on; **speculazi'one** *sf* speculation
spe'dire *vt* to send
'spegnere ['spɛɲɲere] *vt* (*fuoco, sigaretta*) to put out, extinguish; (*apparecchio elettrico*) to turn *o* switch off; (*gas*) to turn off; (*fig: suoni, passioni*) to stifle; (*debito*) to extinguish; **spegnersi** *vpr* to go out; to go off; (*morire*) to pass away; **puoi ~ la luce?** could you switch off the light?; **non riesco a ~ il riscaldamento** I can't turn the heating off
spellarsi *vpr* to peel
'spendere *vt* to spend
'spengo *ecc vb vedi* **spegnere**
'spensi *ecc vb vedi* **spegnere**
spensie'rato, -a *ag* carefree
'spento, -a *pp di* **spegnere** ▷ *ag* (*suono*) muffled; (*colore*) dull; (*sigaretta*) out; (*civiltà, vulcano*) extinct
spe'ranza [spe'rantsa] *sf* hope

spe'rare *vt* to hope for ▷ *vi* **~ in** to trust in; **~ che/di fare** to hope that/to do; **lo spero, spero di sì** I hope so
sper'duto, -a *ag* (*isolato*) out-of-the-way; (*persona*: *smarrita, a disagio*) lost
sperimen'tale *ag* experimental
sperimen'tare *vt* to experiment with, test; (*fig*) to test, put to the test
'sperma, -i *sm* sperm
spe'rone *sm* spur
sperpe'rare *vt* to squander
'spesa *sf* (*somma di denaro*) expense; (*costo*) cost; (*acquisto*) purchase; (*fam*: *acquisto del cibo quotidiano*) shopping; **spese postali** postage *sg*; **spese di viaggio** travelling expenses
'spesso, -a *ag* (*fitto*) thick; (*frequente*) frequent ▷ *av* often; **spesse volte** frequently, often
spes'sore *sm* thickness
Spett. *abbr vedi* **spettabile**
spet'tabile (*abbr*: **Spett.**: *in lettere*) *ag* **~ Ditta X** Messrs X and Co.
spet'tacolo *sm* (*rappresentazione*) performance, show; (*vista, scena*) sight; **dare ~ di sé** to make an exhibition *o* a spectacle of o.s.
spet'tare *vi*: **~ a** (*decisione*) to be up to; (*stipendio*) to be due to; **spetta a te decidere** it's up to you to decide
spetta'tore, -'trice *sm/f* (*Cinema, Teatro*) member of the audience; (*di avvenimento*) onlooker, witness
spettego'lare *vi* to gossip
spetti'nato, -a *ag* dishevelled
'spettro *sm* (*fantasma*) spectre; (*Fisica*) spectrum
'spezie ['spɛttsje] *sfpl* (*Cuc*) spices
spez'zare [spet'tsare] *vt* (*rompere*) to break; (*fig*: *interrompere*) to break up; **spezzarsi** *vpr* to break
spezza'tino [spettsa'tino] *sm* (*Cuc*) stew
spezzet'tare [spettset'tare] *vt* to break up (*o* chop) into small pieces
'spia *sf* spy; (*confidente della polizia*) informer; (*Elettr*) indicating light; warning light; (*fessura*) peep-hole; (*fig*: *sintomo*) sign, indication
spia'cente [spja'tʃɛnte] *ag* sorry; **essere ~ di qc/di fare qc** to be sorry about sth/for doing sth
spia'cevole [spja'tʃevole] *ag* unpleasant
spi'aggia, -ge ['spjaddʒa] *sf* beach; **spiaggia libera** public beach
spia'nare *vt* (*terreno*) to level, make level; (*edificio*) to raze to the ground; (*pasta*) to roll out; (*rendere liscio*) to smooth (out)
spi'are *vt* to spy on
spi'azzo ['spjattso] *sm* open space; (*radura*) clearing
'spicchio ['spikkjo] *sm* (*di agrumi*) segment; (*di aglio*) clove; (*parte*) piece, slice
spicciarsi *vpr* to hurry up
spiccioli *smpl* (small) change; **mi dispiace, non ho ~** sorry, I don't have any change
'spicco, -chi *sm*: **di ~** outstanding; (*tema*) main, principal; **fare ~** to stand out
spie'dino *sm* (*utensile*) skewer; (*pietanza*) kebab
spi'edo *sm* (*Cuc*) spit
spie'gare *vt* (*far capire*) to explain; (*tovaglia*) to unfold; (*vele*) to unfurl; **spiegarsi** *vpr* to explain o.s., make o.s. clear; **~ qc a qn** to explain sth to sb; **spiegazi'one** *sf* explanation
spiegherò *ecc* [spjege'rɔ] *vb vedi* **spiegare**
spie'tato, -a *ag* ruthless, pitiless
spiffe'rare (*fam*) *vt* to blurt out, blab
'spiffero *sm* draught (BRIT), draft (US)
'spiga, -ghe *sf* (*Bot*) ear
spigli'ato, -a [spiʎ'ʎato] *ag* self-possessed, self-confident
'spigolo *sm* corner; (*Mat*) edge
'spilla *sf* brooch; (*da cravatta, cappello*) pin; **~ di sicurezza** *o* **da balia** safety pin
'spillo *sm* pin; **spillo da balia** *o* **di**

sicurezza safety pin
spi'lorcio, -a, -ci, -ce [spi'lortʃo] *ag* mean, stingy
'spina *sf* (*Bot*) thorn; (*Zool*) spine, prickle; (*di pesce*) bone; (*Elettr*) plug; (*di botte*) bunghole; **birra alla ~** draught beer; **spina dorsale** (*Anat*) backbone
spinaci [spi'natʃi] *smpl* spinach *sg*
spi'nello *sm* (*Droga*: *gergo*) joint
'spingere ['spindʒere] *vt* to push; (*condurre*: *anche fig*) to drive; (*stimolare*): **~ qn a fare** to urge *o* press sb to do
spi'noso, -a *ag* thorny, prickly
'spinsi *ecc vb vedi* **spingere**
'spinta *sf* (*urto*) push; (*Fisica*) thrust; (*fig*: *stimolo*) incentive, spur; (: *appoggio*) string-pulling *no pl*; **dare una ~ a qn** (*fig*) to pull strings for sb
'spinto, -a *pp di* **spingere**
spio'naggio [spio'naddʒo] *sm* espionage, spying
spion'cino [spion'tʃino] *sm* peephole
spi'raglio [spi'raʎʎo] *sm* (*fessura*) chink, narrow opening; (*raggio di luce, fig*) glimmer, gleam
spi'rale *sf* spiral; (*contraccettivo*) coil; **a ~** spiral(-shaped)
spiri'tato, -a *ag* possessed; (*fig*: *persona, espressione*) wild
spiri'tismo *sm* spiritualism
'spirito *sm* (*Rel, Chim, disposizione d'animo, di legge ecc, fantasma*) spirit; (*pensieri, intelletto*) mind; (*arguzia*) wit; (*umorismo*) humour, wit; **lo S~ Santo** the Holy Spirit *o* Ghost
spirito'saggine [spirito'saddʒine] *sf* witticism; (*peg*) wisecrack
spiri'toso, -a *ag* witty
spiritu'ale *ag* spiritual
'splendere *vi* to shine
'splendido, -a *ag* splendid; (*splendente*) shining; (*sfarzoso*) magnificent, splendid
splen'dore *sm* splendour; (*luce intensa*) brilliance, brightness
spogli'are [spoʎ'ʎare] *vt* (*svestire*) to undress; (*privare, fig*: *depredare*): **~ qn di qc** to deprive sb of sth; (*togliere ornamenti*: *anche fig*): **~ qn/qc di** to strip sb/sth of; **spogliarsi** *vpr* to undress, strip; **spogliarsi di** (*ricchezze ecc*) to deprive o.s. of, give up; (*pregiudizi*) to rid o.s. of; **spoglia'rello** [spoʎʎa'rɛllo] *sm* striptease; **spoglia'toio** *sm* dressing room; (*di scuola ecc*) cloakroom; (*Sport*) changing room
'spola *sf* (*bobina di filo*) spool; **fare la ~ (fra)** to go to and fro *o* shuttle (between)
spolve'rare *vt* (*anche Cuc*) to dust; (*con spazzola*) to brush; (*con battipanni*) to beat; (*fig*) to polish off ▷ *vi* to dust
spon'taneo, -a *ag* spontaneous; (*persona*) unaffected, natural
spor'care *vt* to dirty, make dirty; (*fig*) to sully, soil; **sporcarsi** *vpr* to get dirty
spor'cizia [spor'tʃittsja] *sf* (*stato*) dirtiness; (*sudiciume*) dirt, filth; (*cosa sporca*) dirt *no pl*, something dirty
'sporco, -a, -chi, -che *ag* dirty, filthy
spor'genza [spor'dʒɛntsa] *sf* projection
'sporgere ['spɔrdʒere] *vt* to put out, stretch out ▷ *vi* (*venire in fuori*) to stick out; **sporgersi** *vpr* to lean out; **~ querela contro qn** (*Dir*) to take legal action against sb
'sporsi *ecc vb vedi* **sporgere**
sport *sm inv* sport
spor'tello *sm* (*di treno, auto ecc*) door; (*di banca, ufficio*) window, counter; **sportello automatico** (*Banca*) cash dispenser, automated telling machine
spor'tivo, -a *ag* (*gara, giornale, centro*) sports *cpd*; (*persona*) sporty; (*abito*) casual; (*spirito, atteggiamento*) sporting
'sposa *sf* bride; (*moglie*) wife
sposa'lizio [spoza'littsjo] *sm* wedding
spo'sare *vt* to marry; (*fig*: *idea, fede*) to espouse; **sposarsi** *vpr* to get married,

marry; **sposarsi con qn** to marry sb, get married to sb; **spo'sato, -a** *ag* married
'sposo *sm* (bride)groom; (*marito*) husband
spos'sato, -a *ag* exhausted, weary
spos'tare *vt* to move, shift; (*cambiare: orario*) to change; **spostarsi** *vpr* to move; **può ~ la macchina, per favore?** can you move your car please?
'spranga, -ghe *sf* (*sbarra*) bar
spre'care *vt* to waste
spre'gevole [spre'dʒevole] *ag* contemptible, despicable
'spremere *vt* to squeeze
spremia'grumi *sm inv* lemon squeezer
spre'muta *sf* fresh juice; **spremuta d'arancia** fresh orange juice
sprez'zante [spret'tsante] *ag* scornful, contemptuous
sprofon'dare *vi* to sink; (*casa*) to collapse; (*suolo*) to give way, subside
spro'nare *vt* to spur (on)
sproporzio'nato, -a [sproportsjo'nato] *ag* disproportionate, out of all proportion
sproporzi'one [spropor'tsjone] *sf* disproportion
spro'posito *sm* blunder; **a ~** at the wrong time; (*rispondere, parlare*) irrelevantly
sprovve'duto, -a *ag* inexperienced, naïve
sprov'visto, -a *ag* (*mancante*): **~ di** lacking in, without; **alla sprovvista** unawares
spruz'zare [sprut'tsare] *vt* (*a nebulizzazione*) to spray; (*aspergere*) to sprinkle; (*inzaccherare*) to splash
'spugna ['spuɲɲa] *sf* (*Zool*) sponge; (*tessuto*) towelling
'spuma *sf* (*schiuma*) foam; (*bibita*) fizzy drink
spu'mante *sm* sparkling wine
spun'tare *vt* (*coltello*) to break the point of; (*capelli*) to trim ▷ *vi* (*uscire: germogli*) to sprout; (*: capelli*) to begin to grow; (*: denti*) to come through; (*apparire*) to appear (suddenly)
spun'tino *sm* snack
'spunto *sm* (*Teatro, Mus*) cue; (*fig*) starting point; **dare lo ~ a** (*fig*) to give rise to
spu'tare *vt* to spit out; (*fig*) to belch (out) ▷ *vi* to spit
'squadra *sf* (*strumento*) (set) square; (*gruppo*) team, squad; (*di operai*) gang, squad; (*Mil*) squad; (*: Aer, Naut*) squadron; (*Sport*) team; **lavoro a squadre** teamwork
squagli'arsi [skwaʎ'ʎarsi] *vpr* to melt; (*fig*) to sneak off
squa'lifica *sf* disqualification
squalifi'care *vt* to disqualify
'squallido, -a *ag* wretched, bleak
'squalo *sm* shark
'squama *sf* scale
squarcia'gola [skwartʃa'gola]: **a ~** *av* at the top of one's voice
squattri'nato, -a *ag* penniless
squili'brato, -a *ag* (*Psic*) unbalanced
squil'lante *ag* shrill, sharp
squil'lare *vi* (*campanello, telefono*) to ring (out); (*tromba*) to blare; **'squillo** *sm* ring, ringing *no pl*; blare; **ragazza** *f* **squillo** *inv* call girl
squi'sito, -a *ag* exquisite; (*cibo*) delicious; (*persona*) delightful
squit'tire *vi* (*uccello*) to squawk; (*topo*) to squeak
sradi'care *vt* to uproot; (*fig*) to eradicate
srego'lato, -a *ag* (*senza ordine: vita*) disorderly; (*smodato*) immoderate; (*dissoluto*) dissolute
S.r.l. *abbr* = **società a responsabilità limitata**
sroto'lare *vt*, **sroto'larsi** ▷ *vpr* to unroll
SS *sigla* = **strada statale**
S.S.N. *abbr* (= *Servizio Sanitario Nazionale*) ≈ NHS

sta *ecc vb vedi* **stare**
'stabile *ag* stable, steady; (*tempo: non variabile*) settled; (*Teatro: compagnia*) resident ▷ *sm* (*edificio*) building
stabili'mento *sm* (*edificio*) establishment; (*fabbrica*) plant, factory
stabi'lire *vt* to establish; (*fissare: prezzi, data*) to fix; (*decidere*) to decide; **stabilirsi** *vpr* (*prendere dimora*) to settle
stac'care *vt* (*levare*) to detach, remove; (*separare: anche fig*) to separate, divide; (*strappare*) to tear off (*o* out); (*scandire: parole*) to pronounce clearly; (*Sport*) to leave behind; **staccarsi** *vpr* (*bottone ecc*) to come off; (*scostarsi*): **staccarsi (da)** to move away (from); (*fig: separarsi*): **staccarsi da** to leave; **non ~ gli occhi da qn** not to take one's eyes off sb
'stadio *sm* (*Sport*) stadium; (*periodo, fase*) phase, stage
'staffa *sf* (*di sella, Tecn*) stirrup; **perdere le staffe** (*fig*) to fly off the handle
staf'fetta *sf* (*messo*) dispatch rider; (*Sport*) relay race
stagio'nale [stadʒo'nale] *ag* seasonal
stagio'nato, -a [stadʒo'nato] *ag* (*vedi vb*) seasoned; matured; (*scherzoso: attempato*) getting on in years
stagi'one [sta'dʒone] *sf* season; **alta/bassa ~** high/low season
stagista, -i, -e [sta'd[gh]ista] *sm/f* trainee, intern (*US*)
'stagno, -a ['staɲɲo] *ag* watertight; (*a tenuta d'aria*) airtight ▷ *sm* (*acquitrino*) pond; (*Chim*) tin
sta'gnola [staɲ'ɲɔla] *sf* tinfoil
'stalla *sf* (*per bovini*) cowshed; (*per cavalli*) stable
stal'lone *sm* stallion
stamat'tina *av* this morning
stam'becco, -chi *sm* ibex
stami'nale *agg*: **cellula ~** stem cell
'stampa *sf* (*Tip, Fot: tecnica*) printing; (*impressione, copia fotografica*) print; (*insieme di quotidiani, giornalisti ecc*) press
stam'pante *sf* (*Inform*) printer
stam'pare *vt* to print; (*pubblicare*) to publish; (*coniare*) to strike, coin; (*imprimere: anche fig*) to impress
stampa'tello *sm* block letters *pl*
stam'pella *sf* crutch
'stampo *sm* mould; (*fig: indole*) type, kind, sort
sta'nare *vt* to drive out
stan'care *vt* to tire, make tired; (*annoiare*) to bore; (*infastidire*) to annoy; **stancarsi** *vpr* to get tired, tire o.s. out; **stancarsi (di)** to grow weary (of), grow tired (of)
stan'chezza [stan'kettsa] *sf* tiredness, fatigue
'stanco, -a, -chi, -che *ag* tired; **~ di** tired of, fed up with
stan'ghetta [stan'getta] *sf* (*di occhiali*) leg; (*Mus, di scrittura*) bar
'stanno *vb vedi* **stare**
sta'notte *av* tonight; (*notte passata*) last night
'stante *prep* **a sé ~** (*appartamento, casa*) independent, separate
stan'tio, -a, -'tii, -'tie *ag* stale; (*burro*) rancid; (*fig*) old
stan'tuffo *sm* piston
'stanza ['stantsa] *sf* room; (*Poesia*) stanza; **stanza da bagno** bathroom; **stanza da letto** bedroom
stap'pare *vt* to uncork; to uncap
'stare *vi* (*restare in un luogo*) to stay, remain; (*abitare*) to stay, live; (*essere situato*) to be, be situated; (*anche:* **~ in piedi**) to be, stand; (*essere, trovarsi*) to be; (*dipendere*): **se stesse in me** if it were up to me, if it depended on me; (*seguito da gerundio*): **sta studiando** he's studying; **starci** (*esserci spazio*): **nel baule non ci sta più niente** there's no more room in the boot;

(*accettare*) to accept; **ci stai?** is that okay with you?; **~ a** (*attenersi a*) to follow, stick to; (*seguito dall'infinito*): **stiamo a discutere** we're talking; (*toccare a*): **sta a te giocare** it's your turn to play; **~ per fare qc** to be about to do sth; **come sta?** how are you?; **io sto bene/male** I'm very well/not very well; **~ a qn** (*abiti ecc*) to fit sb; **queste scarpe mi stanno strette** these shoes are tight on me; **il rosso ti sta bene** red suits you

starnu'tire *vi* to sneeze; **star'nuto** *sm* sneeze

sta'sera *av* this evening, tonight

sta'tale *ag* state *cpd*; government *cpd* ▷ *sm/f* state employee, local authority employee; (*nell'amministrazione*) ≈ civil servant; **strada statale** ≈ trunk (*Brit*) *o* main road

sta'tista, -i *sm* statesman

sta'tistica *sf* statistics *sg*

'stato, -a *pp di* **essere; stare** ▷ *sm* (*condizione*) state, condition; (*Pol*) state; (*Dir*) status; **essere in ~ d'accusa** (*Dir*) to be committed for trial; **~ d'assedio/d'emergenza** state of siege/emergency; **~ civile** (*Amm*) marital status; **gli Stati Uniti (d'America)** the United States (of America); **stato d'animo** mood; **stato maggiore** (*Mil*) staff

'statua *sf* statue

statuni'tense *ag* United States *cpd*, of the United States

sta'tura *sf* (*Anat*) height, stature; (*fig*) stature

sta'tuto *sm* (*Dir*) statute; constitution

sta'volta *av* this time

stazio'nario, -a [stattsjo'narjo] *ag* stationary; (*fig*) unchanged

stazi'one [stat'tsjone] *sf* station; (*balneare, termale*) resort; **stazione degli autobus** bus station; **stazione balneare** seaside resort; **stazione ferroviaria** railway (BRIT) *o* railroad (US) station; **stazione invernale** winter sports resort; **stazione di polizia** police station (*in small town*); **stazione di servizio** service *o* petrol (BRIT) *o* filling station

'stecca, -che *sf* stick; (*di ombrello*) rib; (*di sigarette*) carton; (*Med*) splint; (*stonatura*): **fare una ~** to sing (*o* play) a wrong note

stec'cato *sm* fence

'stella *sf* star; **stella alpina** (*Bot*) edelweiss; **stella cadente** shooting star; **stella di mare** (*Zool*) starfish

'stelo *sm* stem; (*asta*) rod; **lampada a ~** standard lamp

'stemma, -i *sm* coat of arms

'stemmo *vb vedi* **stare**

stempi'ato, -a *ag* with a receding hairline

'stendere *vt* (*braccia, gambe*) to stretch (out); (*tovaglia*) to spread (out); (*bucato*) to hang out; (*mettere a giacere*) to lay (down); (*spalmare: colore*) to spread; (*mettere per iscritto*) to draw up; **stendersi** *vpr* (*coricarsi*) to stretch out, lie down; (*estendersi*) to extend, stretch

stenogra'fia *sf* shorthand

sten'tare *vi* **~ a fare** to find it hard to do, have difficulty doing

'stento *sm* (*fatica*) difficulty; **stenti** *smpl* (*privazioni*) hardship *sg*, privation *sg*; **a ~** with difficulty, barely

'sterco *sm* dung

stereo ['stɛreo] *ag inv* stereo ▷ *sm inv* (*impianto*) stereo

'sterile *ag* sterile; (*terra*) barren; (*fig*) futile, fruitless

steriliz'zare [sterilid'dzare] *vt* to sterilize

ster'lina *sf* pound (sterling)

stermi'nare *vt* to exterminate, wipe out

stermi'nato, -a *ag* immense; endless

ster'minio *sm* extermination, destruction

'sterno *sm* (*Anat*) breastbone
ste'roide *sm* steroid
ster'zare [ster'tsare] *vt, vi* (*Aut*) to steer; **'sterzo** *sm* steering; (*volante*) steering wheel
'stessi *ecc vb vedi* **stare**
'stesso, -a *ag* same; (*rafforzativo*: *in persona, proprio*): **il re ~** the king himself *o* in person ▷ *pron* **lo(la) ~(a)** the same (one); **i suoi stessi avversari lo ammirano** even his enemies admire him; **fa lo ~** it doesn't matter; **per me è lo ~** it's all the same to me, it doesn't matter to me; *vedi* **io**; **tu** *ecc*
ste'sura *sf* drafting *no pl*, drawing up *no pl*; draft
'stetti *ecc vb vedi* **stare**
'stia *ecc vb vedi* **stare**
sti'lare *vt* to draw up, draft
'stile *sm* style; **stile libero** freestyle; **sti'lista, -i** *sm* designer
stilo'grafica, -che *sf* (*anche*: **penna ~**) fountain pen
'stima *sf* esteem; valuation; assessment, estimate
sti'mare *vt* (*persona*) to esteem, hold in high regard; (*terreno, casa ecc*) to value; (*stabilire in misura approssimativa*) to estimate, assess; (*ritenere*): **~ che** to consider that; **stimarsi fortunato** to consider o.s. (to be) lucky
stimo'lare *vt* to stimulate; (*incitare*): **~ qn (a fare)** to spur sb on (to do)
'stimolo *sm* (*anche fig*) stimulus
'stingere ['stindʒere] *vt, vi* (*anche*: **stingersi**) to fade; **'stinto, -a** *pp di* **stingere**
sti'pare *vt* to cram, pack; **stiparsi** *vpr* (*accalcarsi*) to crowd, throng
sti'pendio *sm* salary
'stipite *sm* (*di porta, finestra*) jamb
stipu'lare *vt* (*redigere*) to draw up
sti'rare *vt* (*abito*) to iron; (*distendere*) to stretch; (*strappare*: *muscolo*) to strain; **stirarsi** *vpr* to stretch (o.s.)
stiti'chezza [stiti'kettsa] *sf* constipation
'stitico, -a, -ci, -che *ag* constipated
'stiva *sf* (*di nave*) hold
sti'vale *sm* boot
'stizza ['stittsa] *sf* anger, vexation
'stoffa *sf* material, fabric; (*fig*): **aver la ~ di** to have the makings of
'stomaco, -chi *sm* stomach; **dare di ~** to vomit, be sick
sto'nato, -a *ag* (*persona*) off-key; (*strumento*) off-key, out of tune
stop *sm inv* (*Tel*) stop; (*Aut*: *cartello*) stop sign; (: *fanalino d'arresto*) brake-light
'storcere ['stɔrtʃere] *vt* to twist; **storcersi** *vpr* to writhe, twist; **~ il naso** (*fig*) to turn up one's nose; **storcersi la caviglia** to twist one's ankle
stor'dire *vt* (*intontire*) to stun, daze; **stor'dito, -a** *ag* stunned
'storia *sf* (*scienza, avvenimenti*) history; (*racconto, bugia*) story; (*faccenda, questione*) business *no pl*; (*pretesto*) excuse, pretext; **storie** *sfpl* (*smancerie*) fuss *sg*; **'storico, -a, -ci, -che** *ag* historic(al) ▷ *sm* historian
stori'one *sm* (*Zool*) sturgeon
'stormo *sm* (*di uccelli*) flock
'storpio, -a *ag* crippled, maimed
'storsi *ecc vb vedi* **storcere**
'storta *sf* (*distorsione*) sprain, twist
'storto, -a *pp di* **storcere** ▷ *ag* (*chiodo*) twisted, bent; (*gamba, quadro*) crooked
sto'viglie [sto'viʎʎe] *sfpl* dishes, crockery *sg*
'strabico, -a, -ci, -che *ag* squint-eyed; (*occhi*) squint
strac'chino [strak'kino] *sm type of soft cheese*
stracci'are [strat'tʃare] *vt* to tear; **stracciarsi** *vpr* to tear
'straccio, -a, -ci, -ce ['strattʃo] *ag* **carta straccia** waste paper ▷ *sm* rag; (*per pulire*) cloth, duster; **stracci** *smpl*

(*peg*: *indumenti*) rags; **si è ridotto a uno ~** he's worn himself out; **non ha uno ~ di lavoro** he's not got a job of any sort
'strada *sf* road; (*di città*) street; (*cammino, via, fig*) way; **che ~ devo prendere per andare a ...?** which road do I take for ...?; **farsi ~** (*fig*) to do well for o.s.; **essere fuori ~** (*fig*) to be on the wrong track; **~ facendo** on the way; **strada senza uscita** dead end; **stra'dale** *ag* road *cpd*
strafalci'one [strafal'tʃone] *sm* blunder, howler
stra'fare *vi* to overdo it
strafot'tente *ag*: **è ~** he doesn't give a damn, he couldn't care less
'strage ['stradʒe] *sf* massacre, slaughter
stralu'nato, -a *ag* (*occhi*) rolling; (*persona*) beside o.s., very upset
'strambo, -a *ag* strange, queer
strampa'lato, -a *ag* odd, eccentric
stra'nezza [stra'nettsa] *sf* strangeness
strango'lare *vt* to strangle
strani'ero, -a *ag* foreign ▷ *sm/f* foreigner

> Attenzione! In inglese esiste la parola *stranger*, che però significa *sconosciuto* oppure *estraneo*.

'strano, -a *ag* strange, odd
straordi'nario, -a *ag* extraordinary; (*treno ecc*) special ▷ *sm* (*lavoro*) overtime
strapi'ombo *sm* overhanging rock; **a ~** overhanging
strap'pare *vt* (*gen*) to tear, rip; (*pagina ecc*) to tear off, tear out; (*sradicare*) to pull up; (*togliere*): **~ qc a qn** to snatch sth from sb; (*fig*) to wrest sth from sb; **strapparsi** *vpr* (*lacerarsi*) to rip, tear; (*rompersi*) to break; **strapparsi un muscolo** to tear a muscle; **'strappo** *sm* pull, tug; tear, rip; **fare uno strappo alla regola** to make an exception to the rule; **strappo muscolare** torn muscle
strari'pare *vi* to overflow
'strascico, -chi ['straʃʃiko] *sm* (*di abito*) train; (*conseguenza*) after-effect
strata'gemma, -i [strata'dʒɛmma] *sm* stratagem
strate'gia, -'gie [strate'dʒia] *sf* strategy; **stra'tegico, -a, -ci, -che** *ag* strategic
'strato *sm* layer; (*rivestimento*) coat, coating; (*Geo, fig*) stratum; (*Meteor*) stratus; **strato d'ozono** ozone layer
strat'tone *sm* tug, jerk; **dare uno ~ a qc** to tug *o* jerk sth, give sth a tug *o* jerk
strava'gante *ag* odd, eccentric
stra'volto, -a *pp di* **stravolgere**
'strazio *sm* torture; (*fig*: *cosa fatta male*): **essere uno ~** to be appalling
'strega, -ghe *sf* witch
stre'gare *vt* to bewitch
stre'gone *sm* (*mago*) wizard; (*di tribù*) witch doctor
strepi'toso, -a *ag* clamorous, deafening; (*fig*: *successo*) resounding
stres'sante *ag* stressful
stres'sato, -a *ag* under stress
stretch [stretʃ] *ag inv* stretch
'stretta *sf* (*di mano*) grasp; (*finanziaria*) squeeze; (*fig*: *dolore, turbamento*) pang; **una ~ di mano** a handshake; **essere alle strette** to have one's back to the wall; *vedi anche* **stretto**
stretta'mente *av* tightly; (*rigorosamente*) strictly
'stretto, -a *pp di* **stringere** ▷ *ag* (*corridoio, limiti*) narrow; (*gonna, scarpe, nodo, curva*) tight; (*intimo*: *parente, amico*) close; (*rigoroso*: *osservanza*) strict; (*preciso*: *significato*) precise, exact ▷ *sm* (*braccio di mare*) strait; **a denti stretti** with clenched teeth; **lo ~ necessario** the bare minimum; **stret'toia** *sf* bottleneck; (*fig*) tricky situation
stri'ato, -a *ag* streaked
'stridulo, -a *ag* shrill

stril'lare *vt, vi* to scream, shriek; **'strillo** *sm* scream, shriek
strimin'zito, -a [strimin'tsito] *ag* (*misero*) shabby; (*molto magro*) skinny
strimpel'lare *vt* (*Mus*) to strum
'stringa, -ghe *sf* lace
strin'gato, -a *ag* (*fig*) concise
'stringere ['strindʒere] *vt* (*avvicinare due cose*) to press (together), squeeze (together); (*tenere stretto*) to hold tight, clasp, clutch; (*pugno, mascella, denti*) to clench; (*labbra*) to compress; (*avvitare*) to tighten; (*abito*) to take in; (*scarpe*) to pinch, be tight for; (*fig*: *concludere*: *patto*) to make; (: *accelerare*: *passo, tempo*) to quicken ▷ *vi* (*essere stretto*) to be tight; (*tempo*: *incalzare*) to be pressing
'strinsi *ecc vb vedi* **stringere**
'striscia, -sce ['striʃʃa] *sf* (*di carta, tessuto ecc*) strip; (*riga*) stripe; **strisce (pedonali)** zebra crossing *sg*
strisci'are [striʃ'ʃare] *vt* (*piedi*) to drag; (*muro, macchina*) to graze ▷ *vi* to crawl, creep
'striscio ['striʃʃo] *sm* graze; (*Med*) smear; **colpire di ~** to graze
strisci'one [striʃ'ʃone] *sm* banner
strito'lare *vt* to grind
striz'zare [strit'tsare] *vt* (*panni*) to wring (out); **~ l'occhio** to wink
'strofa *sf* strophe
strofi'naccio [strofi'nattʃo] *sm* duster, cloth; (*per piatti*) dishcloth; (*per pavimenti*) floorcloth
strofi'nare *vt* to rub
stron'care *vt* to break off; (*fig*: *ribellione*) to suppress, put down; (: *film, libro*) to tear to pieces
'stronzo ['strontso] *sm* (*sterco*) turd; (*fig fam!*: *persona*) shit (*!*)
stroz'zare [strot'tsare] *vt* (*soffocare*) to choke, strangle
struccarsi *vpr* to remove one's make-up
strumen'tale *ag* (*Mus*) instrumental
strumentaliz'zare [strumentalid'dzare] *vt* to exploit, use to one's own ends
stru'mento *sm* (*arnese, fig*) instrument, tool; (*Mus*) instrument; **~ a corda** *o* **ad arco/a fiato** stringed/ wind instrument
'strutto *sm* lard
strut'tura *sf* structure
'struzzo ['struttso] *sm* ostrich
stuc'care *vt* (*muro*) to plaster; (*vetro*) to putty; (*decorare con stucchi*) to stucco
'stucco, -chi *sm* plaster; (*da vetri*) putty; (*ornamentale*) stucco; **rimanere di ~** (*fig*) to be dumbfounded
stu'dente, -'essa *sm/f* student; (*scolaro*) pupil, schoolboy/girl
studi'are *vt* to study
'studio *sm* studying; (*ricerca, saggio, stanza*) study; (*di professionista*) office; (*di artista, Cinema, TV, Radio*) studio; **studi** *smpl* (*Ins*) studies; **studio medico** doctor's surgery (BRIT) *o* office (US)
studi'oso, -a *ag* studious, hard-working ▷ *sm/f* scholar
'stufa *sf* stove; **stufa elettrica** electric fire *o* heater
stu'fare *vt* (*Cuc*) to stew; (*fig*: *fam*) to bore; **stufarsi** *vpr* (*fam*): **stufarsi (di)** (*fig*) to get fed up (with); **'stufo, -a** (*fam*) *ag* **essere stufo di** to be fed up with, be sick and tired of
stu'oia *sf* mat
stupefa'cente [stupefa'tʃɛnte] *ag* stunning, astounding ▷ *sm* drug, narcotic
stupe'fatto, -a *pp di* **stupefare**
stu'pendo, -a *ag* marvellous, wonderful
stupi'daggine [stupi'daddʒine] *sf* stupid thing (to do *o* say)
stupidità *sf* stupidity
'stupido, -a *ag* stupid
stu'pire *vt* to amaze, stun ▷ *vi* **stupirsi**; **~ (di)** to be amazed (at), be stunned (by)

stu'pore *sm* amazement, astonishment
stu'prare *vt* to rape
'stupro *sm* rape
stu'rare *vt* (*lavandino*) to clear
stuzzica'denti [stuttsika'dɛnti] *sm* toothpick
stuzzi'care [stuttsi'kare] *vt* (*ferita ecc*) to poke (at), prod (at); (*fig*) to tease; (: *appetito*) to whet; (: *curiosità*) to stimulate; **~ i denti** to pick one's teeth

PAROLA CHIAVE

su (*su + il* = **sul**, *su + lo* = **sullo**, *su + l'* = **sull'**, *su + la* = **sulla**, *su + i* = **sui**, *su + gli* = **sugli**, *su + le* = **sulle**) *prep* **1** (*gen*) on; (*moto*) on(to); (*in cima a*) on (top of); **mettilo sul tavolo** put it on the table; **un paesino sul mare** a village by the sea
2 (*argomento*) about, on; **un libro su Cesare** a book on *o* about Caesar
3 (*circa*) about; **costerà sui 3 milioni** it will cost about 3 million; **una ragazza sui 17 anni** a girl of about 17 (years of age)
4: **su misura** made to measure; **su richiesta** on request; **3 casi su dieci** 3 cases out of 10
▷ *av* **1** (*in alto, verso l'alto*) up; **vieni su** come on up; **guarda su** look up; **su le mani!** hands up!; **in su** (*verso l'alto*) up(wards); (*in poi*) onwards; **dai 20 anni in su** from the age of 20 onwards
2 (*addosso*) on; **cos'hai su?** what have you got on?
▷ *escl* come on!; **su coraggio!** come on, cheer up!

su'bacqueo, -a *ag* underwater ▷ *sm* skin-diver
sub'buglio [sub'buʎʎo] *sm* confusion, turmoil
'subdolo, -a *ag* underhand, sneaky
suben'trare *vi*: **~ a qn in qc** to take over sth from sb
su'bire *vt* to suffer, endure
'subito *av* immediately, at once, straight away
subodo'rare *vt* (*insidia ecc*) to smell, suspect
subordi'nato, -a *ag* subordinate; (*dipendente*): **~ a** dependent on, subject to
suc'cedere [sut'tʃɛdere] *vi* (*prendere il posto di qn*): **~ a** to succeed; (*venire dopo*): **~ a** to follow; (*accadere*) to happen; **cos'è successo?** what happened?; **succes'sivo, -a** *ag* successive; **suc'cesso, -a** *pp di* **succedere** ▷ *sm* (*esito*) outcome; (*buona riuscita*) success; **di successo** (*libro, personaggio*) successful
succhi'are [suk'kjare] *vt* to suck (up)
succhi'otto [suk'kjɔtto] *sm* dummy (BRIT), pacifier (US), comforter (US)
suc'cinto, -a [sut'tʃinto] *ag* (*discorso*) succinct; (*abito*) brief
'succo, -chi *sm* juice; (*fig*) essence, gist; **succo di frutta/pomodoro** fruit/tomato juice
succur'sale *sf* branch (office)
sud *sm* south ▷ *ag inv* south; (*lato*) south, southern
Su'dafrica *sm* **il ~** South Africa; **sudafri'cano, -a** *ag, sm/f* South African
Suda'merica *sm*: **il ~** South America
su'dare *vi* to perspire, sweat; **~ freddo** to come out in a cold sweat
su'dato, -a *ag* (*persona, mani*) sweaty; (*fig*: *denaro*) hard-earned ▷ *sf* (*anche fig*) sweat; **una vittoria sudata** a hard-won victory; **ho fatto una bella sudata per finirlo in tempo** it was a real sweat to get it finished in time
suddi'videre *vt* to subdivide
su'dest *sm* south-east
'sudicio, -a, -ci, -ce ['suditʃo] *ag* dirty, filthy
sudoku *sm inv* sudoku

su'dore *sm* perspiration, sweat
su'dovest *sm* south-west
suffici'ente [suffi'tʃɛnte] *ag* enough, sufficient; (*borioso*) self-important; (*Ins*) satisfactory; **suffici'enza** *sf* self-importance; pass mark; **a sufficienza** enough; **ne ho avuto a sufficienza!** I've had enough of this!
suf'fisso *sm* (*Ling*) suffix
suggeri'mento [suddʒeri'mento] *sm* suggestion; (*consiglio*) piece of advice, advice *no pl*
sugge'rire [suddʒe'rire] *vt* (*risposta*) to tell; (*consigliare*) to advise; (*proporre*) to suggest; (*Teatro*) to prompt
suggestio'nare [suddʒestjo'nare] *vt* to influence
sugges'tivo, -a [suddʒes'tivo] *ag* (*paesaggio*) evocative; (*teoria*) interesting, attractive
'sughero ['sugero] *sm* cork
'sugo, -ghi *sm* (*succo*) juice; (*di carne*) gravy; (*condimento*) sauce; (*fig*) gist, essence
sui'cida, -i, -e [sui'tʃida] *ag* suicidal ▷ *sm/f* suicide
suici'darsi [suitʃi'darsi] *vpr* to commit suicide
sui'cidio [sui'tʃidjo] *sm* suicide
su'ino, -a *ag*: **carne suina** pork ▷ *sm* pig
sul'tano, -a *sm/f* sultan/sultana
'suo (*f* **'sua**, *pl* **'sue, su'oi**) *det* **il ~, la sua** *ecc* (*di lui*) his; (*di lei*) her; (*di esso*) its; (*con valore indefinito*) one's, his/her; (*anche*: **S~**: *forma di cortesia*) your ▷ *pron* **il ~, la sua** *ecc* his; hers; yours; **i ~i** his (*o* her *o* one's *o* your) family
su'ocero, -a ['swɔtʃero] *sm/f* father/mother-in-law
su'ola *sf* (*di scarpa*) sole
su'olo *sm* (*terreno*) ground; (*terra*) soil
suo'nare *vt* (*Mus*) to play; (*campana*) to ring; (*ore*) to strike; (*clacson, allarme*) to sound ▷ *vi* to play; (*telefono, campana*) to ring; (*ore*) to strike; (*clacson, fig*: *parole*) to sound
suone'ria *sf* alarm
su'ono *sm* sound
su'ora *sf* (*Rel*) sister
'super *sf* (*anche*: **benzina ~**) ≈ four-star (petrol) (BRIT), premium (US)
supe'rare *vt* (*oltrepassare*: *limite*) to exceed, surpass; (*percorrere*) to cover; (*attraversare*: *fiume*) to cross; (*sorpassare*: *veicolo*) to overtake; (*fig*: *essere più bravo di*) to surpass, outdo; (: *difficoltà*) to overcome; (: *esame*) to get through; **~ qn in altezza/peso** to be taller/heavier than sb; **ha superato la cinquantina** he's over fifty (years of age)
su'perbia *sf* pride; **su'perbo, -a** *ag* proud; (*fig*) magnificent, superb
superfici'ale [superfi'tʃale] *ag* superficial
super'ficie, -ci [super'fitʃe] *sf* surface
su'perfluo, -a *ag* superfluous
superi'ore *ag* (*piano, arto, classi*) upper; (*più elevato*: *temperatura, livello*): **~ (a)** higher (than); (*migliore*): **~ (a)** superior (to)
superla'tivo, -a *ag, sm* superlative
supermer'cato *sm* supermarket
su'perstite *ag* surviving ▷ *sm/f* survivor
superstizi'one [superstit'tsjone] *sf* superstition; **superstizi'oso, -a** *ag* superstitious
super'strada *sf* ≈ (toll-free) motorway
su'pino, -a *ag* supine
supplemen'tare *ag* extra; (*treno*) relief *cpd*; (*entrate*) additional
supple'mento *sm* supplement
sup'plente *sm/f* temporary member of staff, supply (*o* substitute) teacher
'supplica, -che *sf* (*preghiera*) plea; (*domanda scritta*) petition, request
suppli'care *vt* to implore, beseech
sup'plizio [sup'plittsjo] *sm* torture
sup'pongo, sup'poni *ecc vb vedi*

suppore
sup'porre *vt* to suppose
sup'porto *sm* (*sostegno*) support
sup'posta *sf* (*Med*) suppository
su'premo, -a *ag* supreme
surge'lare [surdʒe'lare] *vt* to (deep-) freeze
surge'lato, -a [surdʒe'lato] *ag* (deep-)frozen ▷ *smpl* **i surgelati** frozen food *sg*
sur'plus *sm inv* (*Econ*) surplus
surriscal'dare *vt* to overheat
suscet'tibile [suʃʃet'tibile] *ag* (*sensibile*) touchy, sensitive
susci'tare [suʃʃi'tare] *vt* to provoke, arouse
su'sina *sf* plum
susseguirsi *vpr* to follow one another
sus'sidio *sm* subsidy; **sussidi didattici** teaching aids
sussul'tare *vi* to shudder
sussur'rare *vt, vi* to whisper, murmur; **sus'surro** *sm* whisper, murmur
svagarsi *vpr* to amuse o.s.; to enjoy o.s.
'svago, -ghi *sm* (*riposo*) relaxation; (*ricreazione*) amusement; (*passatempo*) pastime
svaligi'are [zvali'dʒare] *vt* to rob, burgle (BRIT), burglarize (US)
svalutarsi *vpr* (*Econ*) to be devalued
svalutazi'one *sf* devaluation
sva'nire *vi* to disappear, vanish
svantaggi'ato, -a [zvantad'dʒato] *ag* at a disadvantage
svan'taggio [zvan'taddʒo] *sm* disadvantage; (*inconveniente*) drawback, disadvantage
svari'ato, -a *ag* varied; various
'svastica *sf* swastika
sve'dese *ag* Swedish ▷ *sm/f* Swede ▷ *sm* (*Ling*) Swedish
'sveglia ['zveʎʎa] *sf* waking up; (*orologio*) alarm (clock); **sveglia telefonica** alarm call
svegli'are [zveʎ'ʎare] *vt* to wake up; (*fig*) to awaken, arouse; **svegliarsi** *vpr* to wake up; (*fig*) to be revived, reawaken; **vorrei essere svegliato alle 7, per favore** could I have an alarm call at 7 am, please?
'sveglio, -a ['zveʎʎo] *ag* awake; (*fig*) quick-witted
sve'lare *vt* to reveal
'svelto, -a *ag* (*passo*) quick; (*mente*) quick, alert; **alla svelta** quickly
'svendere *vt* to sell off, clear
'svendita *sf* (*Comm*) (clearance) sale
'svengo *ecc vb vedi* **svenire**
sveni'mento *sm* fainting fit, faint
sve'nire *vi* to faint
sven'tare *vt* to foil, thwart
sven'tato, -a *ag* (*distratto*) scatterbrained; (*imprudente*) rash
svento'lare *vt, vi* to wave, flutter
sven'tura *sf* misfortune
sverrò *ecc vb vedi* **svenire**
sves'tire *vt* to undress; **svestirsi** *vpr* to get undressed
'Svezia ['zvɛttsja] *sf*: **la ~** Sweden
svi'are *vt* to divert; (*fig*) to lead astray
svi'gnarsela [zviɲ'ɲarsela] *vpr* to slip away, sneak off
svilup'pare *vt* to develop; **svilupparsi** *vpr* to develop; **può ~ questo rullino?** can you develop this film?
svi'luppo *sm* development
'svincolo *sm* (*stradale*) motorway (BRIT) *o* expressway (US) intersection
'svista *sf* oversight
svi'tare *vt* to unscrew
'Svizzera ['zvittsera] *sf*: **la ~** Switzerland
'svizzero, -a ['zvittsero] *ag, sm/f* Swiss
svogli'ato, -a [zvoʎ'ʎato] *ag* listless; (*pigro*) lazy
'svolgere ['zvɔldʒere] *vt* to unwind; (*srotolare*) to unroll; (*fig*: *argomento*) to develop; (*: piano, programma*) to carry out; **svolgersi** *vpr* to unwind; to unroll; (*fig*: *aver luogo*) to take place; (*: procedere*) to go on

'svolsi *ecc vb vedi* **svolgere**
'svolta *sf* (*atto*) turning *no pl*; (*curva*) turn, bend; (*fig*) turning-point
svol'tare *vi* to turn
svuo'tare *vt* to empty (out)

t

T, t [ti] *sf o m inv* (*lettera*) T, t; **T come Taranto** ≈ T for Tommy
t *abbr* = **tonnellata**
tabacche'ria [tabakke'ria] *sf* tobacconist's (shop)

TABACCHERIA

Tabaccherie sell cigarettes and tobacco and can easily be identified by their sign, a large white "T" on a black background. You can buy postage stamps and bus tickets at a **tabaccheria** and some also sell newspapers.

ta'bacco, -chi *sm* tobacco
ta'bella *sf* (*tavola*) table; (*elenco*) list
tabel'lone *sm* (*pubblicitario*) billboard; (*con orario*) timetable board
tabu'lato *sm* (*Inform*) printout
TAC *sigla f* (*Med*: = *Tomografia Assiale Computerizzata*) CAT

tac'chino [tak'kino] *sm* turkey
'tacco, -chi *sm* heel; **tacchi a spillo** stiletto heels
taccu'ino *sm* notebook
ta'cere [ta'tʃere] *vi* to be silent *o* quiet; (*smettere di parlare*) to fall silent ▷ *vt* to keep to oneself, say nothing about; **far ~ qn** to make sb be quiet; (*fig*) to silence sb
ta'chimetro [ta'kimetro] *sm* speedometer
'tacqui *ecc vb vedi* **tacere**
ta'fano *sm* horsefly
'taglia ['taʎʎa] *sf* (*statura*) height; (*misura*) size; (*riscatto*) ransom; (*ricompensa*) reward; **taglia forte** (*di abito*) large size
taglia'carte [taʎʎa'karte] *sm inv* paperknife
tagli'ando [taʎ'ʎando] *sm* coupon
tagli'are [taʎ'ʎare] *vt* to cut; (*recidere, interrompere*) to cut off; (*intersecare*) to cut across, intersect; (*carne*) to carve; (*vini*) to blend ▷ *vi* to cut; (*prendere una scorciatoia*) to take a short-cut; **tagliarsi** *vpr* to cut o.s.; **mi sono tagliato** I've cut myself; **~ corto** (*fig*) to cut short; **~ la corda** (*fig*) to sneak off; **~ i ponti (con)** (*fig*) to break off relations (with); **~ la strada a qn** to cut across sb
taglia'telle [taʎʎa'tɛlle] *sfpl* tagliatelle *pl*
taglia'unghie [taʎʎa'ungje] *sm inv* nail clippers *pl*
tagli'ente [taʎ'ʎɛnte] *ag* sharp
'taglio ['taʎʎo] *sm* cutting *no pl*; cut; (*parte tagliente*) cutting edge; (*di abito*) cut, style; (*di stoffa*: *lunghezza*) length; (*di vini*) blending; **di ~** on edge, edgeways; **banconote di piccolo/grosso ~** notes of small/large denomination; **taglio cesareo** Caesarean section
tailan'dese *ag, sm/f, sm* Thai
Tai'landia *sf*: **la ~** Thailand

'talco *sm* talcum powder

PAROLA CHIAVE

'tale *det* 1 (*simile, così grande*) such; **un(a) tale ...** such (a) ...; **non accetto tali discorsi** I won't allow such talk; **è di una tale arroganza** he is so arrogant; **fa una tale confusione!** he makes such a mess!
2 (*persona o cosa indeterminata*) such-and-such; **il giorno tale all'ora tale** on such-and-such a day at such-and-such a time; **la tal persona** that person; **ha telefonato una tale Giovanna** somebody called Giovanna phoned
3 (*nelle similitudini*): **tale ... tale** like ... like; **tale padre tale figlio** like father, like son; **hai il vestito tale quale il mio** your dress is just *o* exactly like mine
▷ *pron* (*indefinito*: *persona*): **un(a) tale** someone; **quel (*o* quella) tale** that person, that man (*o* woman); **il tal dei tali** what's-his-name

tale'bano *sm* Taliban
ta'lento *sm* talent
talis'mano *sm* talisman
tallon'cino [tallon'tʃino] *sm* counterfoil
tal'lone *sm* heel
tal'mente *av* so
'talpa *sf* (*Zool*) mole
tal'volta *av* sometimes, at times
tambu'rello *sm* tambourine
tam'buro *sm* drum
Ta'migi [ta'midʒi] *sm* **il ~** the Thames
tampo'nare *vt* (*otturare*) to plug; (*urtare*: *macchina*) to crash *o* ram into
tam'pone *sm* (*Med*) wad, pad; (*per timbri*) ink-pad; (*respingente*) buffer; **tampone assorbente** tampon
'tana *sf* lair, den
'tanga *sm inv* G-string
tan'gente [tan'dʒɛnte] *ag* (*Mat*): **~**

a tangential to ▷ *sf* tangent; (*quota*) share

tangenzi'ale [tandʒen'tsjale] *sf* (*Aut*) bypass

'tanica *sf* (*contenitore*) jerry can

PAROLA CHIAVE

'tanto, -a *det* **1** (*molto*: *quantità*) a lot of, much; (: *numero*) a lot of, many; (*così tanto*: *quantità*) so much, such a lot of; (: *numero*) so many, such a lot of; **tante volte** so many times, so often; **tanti auguri!** all the best!; **tante grazie** many thanks; **tanto tempo** so long, such a long time; **ogni tanti chilometri** every so many kilometres
2: **tanto ... quanto** (*quantità*) as much ... as; (*numero*) as many ... as; **ho tanta pazienza quanta ne hai tu** I have as much patience as you have *o* as you; **ha tanti amici quanti nemici** he has as many friends as he has enemies
3 (*rafforzativo*) such; **ho aspettato per tanto tempo** I waited so long *o* for such a long time
▷ *pron* **1** (*molto*) much, a lot; (*così tanto*) so much, such a lot; **tanti, e** many, a lot; so many, such a lot; **credevo ce ne fosse tanto** I thought there was (such) a lot, I thought there was plenty
2: **tanto quanto** (*denaro*) as much as; (*cioccolatini*) as many as; **ne ho tanto quanto basta** I have as much as I need; **due volte tanto** twice as much
3 (*indeterminato*) so much; **tanto per l'affitto, tanto per il gas** so much for the rent, so much for the gas; **costa un tanto al metro** it costs so much per metre; **di tanto in tanto, ogni tanto** every so often; **tanto vale che ...** I (*o* we *ecc*) may as well ...; **tanto meglio!** so much the better!; **tanto peggio per lui!** so much the worse for him!
▷ *av* **1** (*molto*) very; **vengo tanto volentieri** I'd be very glad to come; **non ci vuole tanto a capirlo** it doesn't take much to understand it
2 (*così tanto*: *con ag, av*) so; (: *con vb*) so much, such a lot; **è tanto bella!** she's so beautiful!; **non urlare tanto** don't shout so much; **sto tanto meglio adesso** I'm so much better now; **tanto ... che** so ... (that); **tanto ... da** so ... as
3: **tanto ... quanto** as ... as; **conosco tanto Carlo quanto suo padre** I know both Carlo and his father; **non è poi tanto complicato quanto sembri** it's not as difficult as it seems; **tanto più insisti, tanto più non mollerà** the more you insist, the more stubborn he'll be; **quanto più ... tanto meno** the more ... the less
4 (*solamente*) just; **tanto per cambiare/scherzare** just for a change/a joke; **una volta tanto** for once
5 (*a lungo*) (for) long
▷ *cong* after all

'tappa *sf* (*luogo di sosta, fermata*) stop, halt; (*parte di un percorso*) stage, leg; (*Sport*) lap; **a tappe** in stages

tap'pare *vt* to plug, stop up; (*bottiglia*) to cork; **tapparsi** *vpr* **tapparsi in casa** to shut o.s. up at home; **tapparsi la bocca** to shut up; **tapparsi le orecchie** to turn a deaf ear

tappa'rella *sf* rolling shutter

tappe'tino *sm* (*per auto*) car mat; **tappetino antiscivolo** (*da bagno*) non-slip mat

tap'peto *sm* carpet; (*anche*: **tappetino**) rug; (*Sport*): **andare al ~** to go down for the count; **mettere sul ~** (*fig*) to bring up for discussion

tappez'zare [tappet'tsare] *vt* (*con carta*) to paper; (*rivestire*): **~ qc (di)** to cover sth (with); **tappezze'ria** *sf* (*tessuto*) tapestry; (*carta da parati*)

wallpaper; (*arte*) upholstery; **far da tappezzeria** (*fig*) to be a wallflower
'tappo *sm* stopper; (*in sughero*) cork
tar'dare *vi* to be late ▷ *vt* to delay; **~ a fare** to delay doing
'tardi *av* late; **più ~** later (on); **al più ~** at the latest; **sul ~** (*verso sera*) late in the day; **far ~** to be late; (*restare alzato*) to stay up late; **è troppo ~** it's too late
'targa, -ghe *sf* plate; (*Aut*) number (BRIT) *o* license (US) plate; **tar'ghetta** *sf* (*su bagaglio*) name tag; (*su porta*) nameplate
ta'riffa *sf* (*gen*) rate, tariff; (*di trasporti*) fare; (*elenco*) price list; tariff
'tarlo *sm* woodworm
'tarma *sf* moth
tarocchi *smpl* (*gioco*) tarot *sg*
tarta'ruga, -ghe *sf* tortoise; (*di mare*) turtle; (*materiale*) tortoiseshell
tar'tina *sf* canapé
tar'tufo *sm* (*Bot*) truffle
'tasca, -sche *sf* pocket; **tas'cabile** *ag* (*libro*) pocket *cpd*
'tassa *sf* (*imposta*) tax; (*doganale*) duty; (*per iscrizione: a scuola ecc*) fee; **tassa di circolazione** road tax; **tassa di soggiorno** tourist tax
tas'sare *vt* to tax; to levy a duty on
tas'sello *sm* plug; wedge
tassì *sm inv* = **taxi**; **tas'sista, -i, -e** *sm/f* taxi driver
'tasso *sm* (*di natalità, d'interesse ecc*) rate; (*Bot*) yew; (*Zool*) badger; **tasso di cambio/d'interesse** rate of exchange/interest
tas'tare *vt* to feel; **~ il terreno** (*fig*) to see how the land lies
tasti'era *sf* keyboard
'tasto *sm* key; (*tatto*) touch, feel
tas'toni *av*: **procedere (a) ~** to grope one's way forward
'tatto *sm* (*senso*) touch; (*fig*) tact; **duro al ~** hard to the touch; **aver ~** to be tactful, have tact
tatu'aggio [tatu'addʒo] *sm* tattooing; (*disegno*) tattoo
tatu'are *vt* to tattoo
TAV *sigla fsg* = **Treni Alta Velocità**; (*treno*) high-speed train; (*sistema*) high-speed rail system
'tavola *sf* table; (*asse*) plank, board; (*lastra*) tablet; (*quadro*) panel (painting); (*illustrazione*) plate; **tavola calda** snack bar; **tavola rotonda** (*fig*) round table; **tavola a vela** windsurfer
tavo'letta *sf* tablet, bar; **a ~** (*Aut*) flat out
tavo'lino *sm* small table; (*scrivania*) desk
'tavolo *sm* table; **un ~ per 4 per favore** a table for 4, please
'taxi *sm inv* taxi; **può chiamarmi un ~ per favore?** can you call me a taxi, please?
'tazza ['tattsa] *sf* cup; **una ~ di caffè/tè** a cup of coffee/tea; **tazza da tè/caffè** tea/coffee cup
TBC *abbr f* (= *tubercolosi*) TB
te *pron* (*soggetto: in forme comparative, oggetto*) you
tè *sm inv* tea; (*trattenimento*) tea party
tea'trale *ag* theatrical
te'atro *sm* theatre
techno ['tɛkno] *ag inv* (*musica*) techno
'tecnica, -che *sf* technique; (*tecnologia*) technology
'tecnico, -a, -ci, -che *ag* technical ▷ *sm/f* technician
tecnolo'gia [teknolo'dʒia] *sf* technology
te'desco, -a, -schi, -sche *ag, sm/f, sm* German
te'game *sm* (*Cuc*) pan
'tegola *sf* tile
tei'era *sf* teapot
tel. *abbr* (= *telefono*) tel.
'tela *sf* (*tessuto*) cloth; (*per vele, quadri*) canvas; (*dipinto*) canvas, painting; **di ~** (*calzoni*) (heavy) cotton *cpd*; (*scarpe, borsa*) canvas *cpd*; **tela cerata** oilcloth
te'laio *sm* (*apparecchio*) loom; (*struttura*) frame
tele'camera *sf* television camera

teleco'mando *sm* remote control
tele'cronaca *sf* television report
telefo'nare *vi* to telephone, ring; to make a phone call ▷ *vt* to telephone; **~ a** to phone up, ring up, call up
telefo'nata *sf* (telephone) call; **~ a carico del destinatario** reverse charge (BRIT) *o* collect (US) call
tele'fonico, -a, -ci, -che *ag* (tele)phone *cpd*
telefon'ino *sm* mobile phone
te'lefono *sm* telephone; **telefono a gettoni** ≈ pay phone
telegior'nale [teledʒor'nale] *sm* television news (programme)
tele'gramma, -i *sm* telegram
telela'voro *sm* teleworking
Tele'pass® *sm inv automatic payment card for use on Italian motorways*
telepa'tia *sf* telepathy
teles'copio *sm* telescope
teleselezi'one [teleselet'tsjone] *sf* direct dialling
telespetta'tore, -'trice *sm/f* (television) viewer
tele'vendita *sf* teleshopping
televisi'one *sf* television
televi'sore *sm* television set
'tema, -i *sm* theme; (*Ins*) essay, composition
te'mere *vt* to fear, be afraid of; (*essere sensibile a*: *freddo, calore*) to be sensitive to ▷ *vi* to be afraid; (*essere preoccupato*): **~ per** to worry about, fear for; **~ di/che** to be afraid of/that
temperama'tite *sm inv* pencil sharpener
tempera'mento *sm* temperament
tempera'tura *sf* temperature
tempe'rino *sm* penknife
tem'pesta *sf* storm; **tempesta di sabbia/neve** sand/snowstorm
'tempia *sf* (*Anat*) temple
'tempio *sm* (*edificio*) temple
'tempo *sm* (*Meteor*) weather; (*cronologico*) time; (*epoca*) time, times *pl*; (*di film, gioco*: *parte*) part; (*Mus*) time; (: *battuta*) beat; (*Ling*) tense; **che ~ fa?** what's the weather like?; **un ~** once; **~ fa** some time ago; **al ~ stesso** *o* **a un ~** at the same time; **per ~** early; **ha fatto il suo ~** it has had its day; **primo/secondo ~** (*Teatro*) first/second part; (*Sport*) first/second half; **in ~ utile** in due time *o* course; **a ~ pieno** full-time; **tempo libero** free time
tempo'rale *ag* temporal ▷ *sm* (*Meteor*) (thunder)storm
tempo'raneo, -a *ag* temporary
te'nace [te'natʃe] *ag* strong, tough; (*fig*) tenacious
te'naglie [te'naʎʎe] *sfpl* pincers *pl*
'tenda *sf* (*riparo*) awning; (*di finestra*) curtain; (*per campeggio ecc*) tent
ten'denza [ten'dɛntsa] *sf* tendency; (*orientamento*) trend; **avere ~ a** *o* **per qc** to have a bent for sth
'tendere *vt* (*allungare al massimo*) to stretch, draw tight; (*porgere*: *mano*) to hold out; (*fig*: *trappola*) to lay, set ▷ *vi* **~ a qc/a fare** to tend towards sth/to do; **~ l'orecchio** to prick up one's ears; **il tempo tende al caldo** the weather is getting hot; **un blu che tende al verde** a greenish blue
'tendine *sm* tendon, sinew
ten'done *sm* (*da circo*) tent
'tenebre *sfpl* darkness *sg*
te'nente *sm* lieutenant
te'nere *vt* to hold; (*conservare, mantenere*) to keep; (*ritenere, considerare*) to consider; (*spazio*: *occupare*) to take up, occupy; (*seguire*: *strada*) to keep to ▷ *vi* to hold; (*colori*) to be fast; (*dare importanza*): **~ a** to care about; **~ a fare** to want to do, be keen to do; **tenersi** *vpr* (*stare in una determinata posizione*) to stand; (*stimarsi*) to consider o.s.; (*aggrapparsi*): **tenersi a** to hold on to; (*attenersi*): **tenersi a** to stick to; **~ una conferenza** to give a lecture; **~ conto di qc** to take sth into consideration; **~**

presente qc to bear sth in mind
'tenero, -a *ag* tender; (*pietra, cera, colore*) soft; (*fig*) tender, loving
'tengo *ecc vb vedi* **tenere**
'tenni *ecc vb vedi* **tenere**
'tennis *sm* tennis
ten'nista, -i, e *sm/f* tennis player
te'nore *sm* (*tono*) tone; (*Mus*) tenor; **tenore di vita** (*livello*) standard of living
tensi'one *sf* tension
ten'tare *vt* (*indurre*) to tempt; (*provare*): **~ qc/di fare** to attempt *o* try sth/to do; **tenta'tivo** *sm* attempt; **tentazi'one** *sf* temptation
tenten'nare *vi* to shake, be unsteady; (*fig*) to hesitate, waver
ten'toni *av* **andare a ~** (*anche fig*) to grope one's way
'tenue *ag* (*sottile*) fine; (*colore*) soft; (*fig*) slender, slight
te'nuta *sf* (*capacità*) capacity; (*divisa*) uniform; (*abito*) dress; (*Agr*) estate; **a ~ d'aria** airtight; **tenuta di strada** roadholding power
teolo'gia [teolo'dʒia] *sf* theology
teo'ria *sf* theory
te'pore *sm* warmth
tep'pista, -i *sm* hooligan
tera'pia *sf* therapy; **terapia intensiva** intensive care
tergicris'tallo [terdʒikris'tallo] *sm* windscreen (BRIT) *o* windshield (US) wiper
tergiver'sare [terdʒiver'sare] *vi* to shilly-shally
ter'male *ag* thermal; **stazione** *sf* **~** spa
'terme *sfpl* thermal baths
termi'nale *ag, sm* terminal
termi'nare *vt* to end; (*lavoro*) to finish ▷ *vi* to end
'termine *sm* term; (*fine, estremità*) end; (*di territorio*) boundary, limit; **contratto a ~** (*Comm*) forward contract; **a breve/lungo ~** short-/long-term; **parlare senza mezzi termini** to talk frankly, not to mince one's words
ter'mometro *sm* thermometer
'termos *sm inv* = **thermos®**
termosi'fone *sm* radiator
ter'mostato *sm* thermostat
'terra *sf* (*gen, Elettr*) earth; (*sostanza*) soil, earth; (*opposto al mare*) land *no pl*; (*regione, paese*) land; (*argilla*) clay; **terre** *sfpl* (*possedimento*) lands, land *sg*; **a** *o* **per ~** (*stato*) on the ground (*o* floor); (*moto*) to the ground, down; **mettere a ~** (*Elettr*) to earth
terra'cotta *sf* terracotta; **vasellame** *sm* **di ~** earthenware
terra'ferma *sf* dry land, terra firma; (*continente*) mainland
ter'razza [ter'rattsa] *sf* terrace
ter'razzo [ter'rattso] *sm* = **terrazza**
terre'moto *sm* earthquake
ter'reno, -a *ag* (*vita, beni*) earthly ▷ *sm* (*suolo, fig*) ground; (*Comm*) land *no pl*, plot (of land); site; (*Sport, Mil*) field
ter'restre *ag* (*superficie*) of the earth, earth's; (*di terra: battaglia, animale*) land *cpd*; (*Rel*) earthly, worldly
ter'ribile *ag* terrible, dreadful
terrifi'cante *ag* terrifying
ter'rina *sf* tureen
territori'ale *ag* territorial
terri'torio *sm* territory
ter'rore *sm* terror; **terro'rismo** *sm* terrorism; **terro'rista, -i, -e** *sm/f* terrorist
terroriz'zare [terrorid'dzare] *vt* to terrorize
terza ['tɛrtsa] *sf* (*Scol: elementare*) third year at primary school; (*: media*) third year at secondary school; (*: superiore*) sixth year at secondary school; (*Aut*) third gear
ter'zino [ter'tsino] *sm* (*Calcio*) fullback, back
'terzo, -a ['tɛrtso] *ag* third ▷ *sm* (*frazione*) third; (*Dir*) third party; **terza pagina** (*Stampa*) Arts page; **terzi** *smpl*

(*altri*) others, other people

'teschio ['tɛskjo] *sm* skull

'tesi[1] *sf* thesis; **tesi di laurea** degree thesis

'tesi *ecc*[2] *vb vedi* **tendere**

'teso, -a *pp di* **tendere** ▷ *ag* (*tirato*) taut, tight; (*fig*) tense

te'soro *sm* treasure; **il Ministero del T~** the Treasury

'tessera *sf* (*documento*) card

tes'suto *sm* fabric, material; (*Biol*) tissue

test ['tɛst] *sm inv* test

'testa *sf* head; (*di cose: estremità, parte anteriore*) head, front; **di ~** (*vettura ecc*) front; **tenere ~ a qn** (*nemico ecc*) to stand up to sb; **fare di ~ propria** to go one's own way; **in ~** (*Sport*) in the lead; **~ o croce?** heads or tails?; **avere la ~ dura** to be stubborn; **testa d'aglio** bulb of garlic; **testa di serie** (*Tennis*) seed, seeded player

testa'mento *sm* (*atto*) will; **l'Antico/il Nuovo T~** (*Rel*) the Old/New Testament

tes'tardo, -a *ag* stubborn, pig-headed

tes'tata *sf* (*parte anteriore*) head; (*intestazione*) heading

tes'ticolo *sm* testicle

testi'mone *sm/f* (*Dir*) witness; **testimone oculare** eye witness

testimoni'are *vt* to testify; (*fig*) to bear witness to, testify to ▷ *vi* to give evidence, testify

'testo *sm* text; **fare ~** (*opera, autore*) to be authoritative; **questo libro non fa ~** this book is not essential reading

tes'tuggine [tes'tuddʒine] *sf* tortoise; (*di mare*) turtle

'tetano *sm* (*Med*) tetanus

'tetto *sm* roof; **tet'toia** *sf* roofing; canopy

tettuccio [tet'tuttʃo] *sm* **~ apribile** (*Aut*) sunroof

'Tevere *sm* **il ~** the Tiber

TG, Tg *abbr* = **telegiornale**

'thermos® ['tɛrmos] *sm inv* vacuum *o* Thermos® flask

ti *pron* (*dav lo, la, li, le, ne diventa* **te**) ▷ *pron* (*oggetto*) you; (*complemento di termine*) (to) you; (*riflessivo*) yourself

'Tibet *sm*: **il ~** Tibet

'tibia *sf* tibia, shinbone

tic *sm inv* tic, (nervous) twitch; (*fig*) mannerism

ticchet'tio [tikket'tio] *sm* (*di macchina da scrivere*) clatter; (*di orologio*) ticking; (*della pioggia*) patter

'ticket *sm inv* (*su farmaci*) prescription charge

ti'ene *ecc vb vedi* **tenere**

ti'epido, -a *ag* lukewarm, tepid

'tifo *sm* (*Med*) typhus; (*fig*): **fare il ~ per** to be a fan of

ti'fone *sm* typhoon

ti'foso, -a *sm/f* (*Sport ecc*) fan

tigì [ti'dʒi] *sm inv* TV news

'tiglio ['tiʎʎo] *sm* lime (tree), linden (tree)

'tigre *sf* tiger

tim'brare *vt* to stamp; (*annullare: francobolli*) to postmark; **~ il cartellino** to clock in

'timbro *sm* stamp; (*Mus*) timbre, tone

'timido, -a *ag* shy; timid

'timo *sm* thyme

ti'mone *sm* (*Naut*) rudder

ti'more *sm* (*paura*) fear; (*rispetto*) awe

'timpano *sm* (*Anat*) eardrum

'tingere ['tindʒere] *vt* to dye

'tinsi *ecc vb vedi* **tingere**

'tinta *sf* (*materia colorante*) dye; (*colore*) colour, shade

tintin'nare *vi* to tinkle

tinto'ria *sf* (*lavasecco*) dry cleaner's (shop)

tin'tura *sf* (*operazione*) dyeing; (*colorante*) dye; **tintura di iodio** tincture of iodine

'tipico, -a, -ci, -che *ag* typical

'tipo *sm* type; (*genere*) kind, type; (*fam*) chap, fellow; **che ~ di...?** what kind of ...?

tipogra'fia *sf* typography; (*procedimento*) letterpress (printing); (*officina*) printing house
TIR *sigla m* (= *Transports Internationaux Routiers*) *International Heavy Goods Vehicle*
ti'rare *vt* (*gen*) to pull; (*estrarre*): **~ qc da** to take *o* pull sth out of; to get sth out of; to extract sth from; (*chiudere*: *tenda ecc*) to draw, pull; (*tracciare, disegnare*) to draw, trace; (*lanciare*: *sasso, palla*) to throw; (*stampare*) to print; (*pistola, freccia*) to fire ▷ *vi* (*pipa, camino*) to draw; (*vento*) to blow; (*abito*) to be tight; (*fare fuoco*) to fire; (*fare del tiro, Calcio*) to shoot; **~ avanti** *vi* to struggle on ▷ *vt* to keep going; **~ fuori** (*estrarre*) to take out, pull out; **~ giù** (*abbassare*) to bring down, to lower; (*da scaffale ecc.*) to take down; **~ su** to pull up; (*capelli*) to put up; (*fig*: *bambino*) to bring up; **tirarsi** *vpr* **tirarsi indietro** to draw back; (*fig*) to back out; **~ a indovinare** to take a guess; **~ sul prezzo** to bargain; **tirar dritto** to keep right on going; **tirati su!** (*fig*) cheer up!; **~ via** (*togliere*) to take off
tira'tura *sf* (*azione*) printing; (*di libro*) (print) run; (*di giornale*) circulation
'tirchio, -a ['tirkjo] *ag* mean, stingy
'tiro *sm* shooting *no pl*, firing *no pl*; (*colpo, sparo*) shot; (*di palla*: *lancio*) throwing *no pl*; throw; (*fig*) trick; **cavallo da ~** draught (BRIT) *o* draft (US) horse; **tiro a segno** target shooting; (*luogo*) shooting range; **tiro con l'arco** archery
tiro'cinio [tiro'tʃinjo] *sm* apprenticeship; (*professionale*) training
ti'roide *sf* thyroid (gland)
Tir'reno *sm*: **il (mar) ~** the Tyrrhenian Sea
ti'sana *sf* herb tea
tito'lare *sm/f* incumbent; (*proprietario*) owner; (*Calcio*) regular player
'titolo *sm* title; (*di giornale*) headline; (*diploma*) qualification; (*Comm*) security; (: *azione*) share; **a che ~?** for what reason?; **a ~ di amicizia** out of friendship; **a ~ di premio** as a prize; **titolo di credito** share; **titoli di stato** government securities; **titoli di testa** (*Cinema*) credits
titu'bante *ag* hesitant, irresolute
toast [toust] *sm inv* toasted sandwich (*generally with ham and cheese*)
toc'cante *ag* touching
toc'care *vt* to touch; (*tastare*) to feel; (*fig*: *riguardare*) to concern; (: *commuovere*) to touch, move; (: *pungere*) to hurt, wound; (: *far cenno a*: *argomento*) to touch on, mention ▷ *vi* **~ a** (*accadere*) to happen to; (*spettare*) to be up to; **~ (il fondo)** (*in acqua*) to touch the bottom; **tocca a te difenderci** it's up to you to defend us; **a chi tocca?** whose turn is it?; **mi toccò pagare** I had to pay
toccherò *ecc* [tokke'rɔ] *vb vedi* **toccare**
'togliere ['tɔʎʎere] *vt* (*rimuovere*) to take away (*o* off), remove; (*riprendere, non concedere più*) to take away, remove; (*Mat*) to take away, subtract; **~ qc a qn** to take sth (away) from sb; **ciò non toglie che** nevertheless, be that as it may; **togliersi il cappello** to take off one's hat
toi'lette [twa'lɛt] *sf inv* toilet; (*mobile*) dressing table; **dov'è la ~?** where's the toilet?
'Tokyo *sf* Tokyo
'tolgo *ecc vb vedi* **togliere**
tolle'rare *vt* to tolerate
'tolsi *ecc vb vedi* **togliere**
'tomba *sf* tomb
tom'bino *sm* manhole cover
'tombola *sf* (*gioco*) tombola; (*ruzzolone*) tumble
'tondo, -a *ag* round
'tonfo *sm* splash; (*rumore sordo*) thud; (*caduta*): **fare un ~** to take a tumble

tonifi'care *vt* (*muscoli, pelle*) to tone up; (*irrobustire*) to invigorate, brace
tonnel'lata *sf* ton
'tonno *sm* tuna (fish)
'tono *sm* (*gen*) tone; (*Mus: di pezzo*) key; (*di colore*) shade, tone
ton'silla *sf* tonsil
'tonto, -a *ag* dull, stupid
to'pazio [to'pattsjo] *sm* topaz
'topo *sm* mouse
'toppa *sf* (*serratura*) keyhole; (*pezza*) patch
to'race [to'ratʃe] *sm* chest
'torba *sf* peat
'torcere ['tɔrtʃere] *vt* to twist; **torcersi** *vpr* to twist, writhe
'torcia, -ce ['tɔrtʃa] *sf* torch; **torcia elettrica** torch (BRIT), flashlight (US)
torci'collo [tortʃi'kɔllo] *sm* stiff neck
'tordo *sm* thrush
To'rino *sf* Turin
tor'menta *sf* snowstorm
tormen'tare *vt* to torment; **tormentarsi** *vpr* to fret, worry o.s.
tor'nado *sm* tornado
tor'nante *sm* hairpin bend
tor'nare *vi* to return, go (*o* come) back; (*ridiventare: anche fig*) to become (again); (*riuscire giusto, esatto: conto*) to work out; (*risultare*) to turn out (to be), prove (to be); **~ utile** to prove *o* turn out (to be) useful; **~ a casa** to go (*o* come) home; **torno a casa martedì** I'm going home on Tuesday
tor'neo *sm* tournament
'tornio *sm* lathe
'toro *sm* bull; (*dello zodiaco*): **T~** Taurus
'torre *sf* tower; (*Scacchi*) rook, castle; **torre di controllo** (*Aer*) control tower
tor'rente *sm* torrent
torri'one *sm* keep
tor'rone *sm* nougat
'torsi *ecc vb vedi* **torcere**
torsi'one *sf* twisting; torsion
'torso *sm* torso, trunk; (*Arte*) torso
'torsolo *sm* (*di cavolo ecc*) stump; (*di frutta*) core
'torta *sf* cake
tortel'lini *smpl* (*Cuc*) tortellini
'torto, -a *pp di* **torcere** ▷ *ag* (*ritorto*) twisted; (*storto*) twisted, crooked ▷ *sm* (*ingiustizia*) wrong; (*colpa*) fault; **a ~** wrongly; **aver ~** to be wrong
'tortora *sf* turtle dove
tor'tura *sf* torture; **tortu'rare** *vt* to torture
to'sare *vt* (*pecora*) to shear; (*siepe*) to clip
Tos'cana *sf*: **la ~** Tuscany
'tosse *sf* cough; **ho la ~** I've got a cough
'tossico, -a, -ci, -che *ag* toxic
tossicodipen'dente *sm/f* drug addict
tos'sire *vi* to cough
tosta'pane *sm inv* toaster
to'tale *ag, sm* total
toto'calcio [toto'kaltʃo] *sm gambling pool betting on football results*, ≈ (football) pools *pl* (BRIT)
to'vaglia [to'vaʎʎa] *sf* tablecloth; **tovagli'olo** *sm* napkin
tra *prep* (*di due persone, cose*) between; (*di più persone, cose*) among(st); (*tempo: entro*) within, in; **~ 5 giorni** in 5 days' time; **sia detto ~ noi ...** between you and me ...; **litigano ~ (di) loro** they're fighting amongst themselves; **~ breve** soon; **~ sé e sé** (*parlare ecc*) to oneself
traboc'care *vi* to overflow
traboc'chetto [trabok'ketto] *sm* (*fig*) trap
'traccia, -ce ['trattʃa] *sf* (*segno, striscia*) trail, track; (*orma*) tracks *pl*; (*residuo, testimonianza*) trace, sign; (*abbozzo*) outline
tracci'are [trat'tʃare] *vt* to trace, mark (out); (*disegnare*) to draw; (*fig: abbozzare*) to outline
tra'chea [tra'kεa] *sf* windpipe, trachea
tra'colla *sf* shoulder strap; **borsa a ~** shoulder bag

tradi'mento *sm* betrayal; (*Dir, Mil*) treason
tra'dire *vt* to betray; (*coniuge*) to be unfaithful to; (*doveri: mancare*) to fail in; (*rivelare*) to give away, reveal; **tradirsi** *vpr* to give o.s. away
tradizio'nale [tradittsjo'nale] *ag* traditional
tradizi'one [tradit'tsjone] *sf* tradition
tra'durre *vt* to translate; (*spiegare*) to render, convey; **me lo può ~?** can you translate this for me?; **traduzi'one** *sf* translation
'trae *vb vedi* **trarre**
traffi'cante *sm/f* dealer; (*peg*) trafficker
traffi'care *vi* (*commerciare*): **~ (in)** to trade (in), deal (in); (*affaccendarsi*) to busy o.s. ▷ *vt* (*peg*) to traffic in
'traffico, -ci *sm* traffic; (*commercio*) trade, traffic; **traffico di armi/droga** arms/drug trafficking
tra'gedia [tra'dʒɛdja] *sf* tragedy
'traggo *ecc vb vedi* **trarre**
tra'ghetto [tra'getto] *sm* ferry(boat)
'tragico, -a, -ci, -che ['tradʒiko] *ag* tragic
tra'gitto [tra'dʒitto] *sm* (*passaggio*) crossing; (*viaggio*) journey
tragu'ardo *sm* (*Sport*) finishing line; (*fig*) goal, aim
'trai *ecc vb vedi* **trarre**
traiet'toria *sf* trajectory
trai'nare *vt* to drag, haul; (*rimorchiare*) to tow
tralasci'are [tralaʃ'ʃare] *vt* (*studi*) to neglect; (*dettagli*) to leave out, omit
tra'liccio [tra'littʃo] *sm* (*Elettr*) pylon
tram *sm inv* tram
'trama *sf* (*filo*) weft, woof; (*fig: argomento, maneggio*) plot
traman'dare *vt* to pass on, hand down
tram'busto *sm* turmoil
tramez'zino [tramed'dzino] *sm* sandwich
'tramite *prep* through
tramon'tare *vi* to set, go down; **tra'monto** *sm* setting; (*del sole*) sunset
trampo'lino *sm* (*per tuffi*) springboard, diving board; (*per lo sci*) ski-jump
tra'nello *sm* trap
'tranne *prep* except (for), but (for); **~ che** unless
tranquil'lante *sm* (*Med*) tranquillizer
tranquillità *sf* calm, stillness; quietness; peace of mind
tranquilliz'zare [trankwillid'dzare] *vt* to reassure

> Attenzione! In inglese esiste il verbo *to tranquillize*, che però significa "calmare con un tranquillante".

tran'quillo, -a *ag* calm, quiet; (*bambino, scolaro*) quiet; (*sereno*) with one's mind at rest; **sta' ~** don't worry
transazi'one [transat'tsjone] *sf* compromise; (*Dir*) settlement; (*Comm*) transaction, deal
tran'senna *sf* barrier
transgenico, -a, -ci, -che [trans'dʒɛniko] *ag* genetically modified
tran'sigere [tran'sidʒere] *vi* (*venire a patti*) to compromise, come to an agreement
transi'tabile *ag* passable
transi'tare *vi* to pass
transi'tivo, -a *ag* transitive
'transito *sm* transit; **di ~** (*merci*) in transit; (*stazione*) transit *cpd*; **"divieto di ~"** "no entry"
'trapano *sm* (*utensile*) drill; (*Med*) trepan
trape'lare *vi* to leak, drip; (*fig*) to leak out
tra'pezio [tra'pɛttsjo] *sm* (*Mat*) trapezium; (*attrezzo ginnico*) trapeze
trapian'tare *vt* to transplant; **trapi'anto** *sm* transplanting; (*Med*) transplant; **trapianto cardiaco** heart

transplant
'trappola *sf* trap
tra'punta *sf* quilt
'trarre *vt* to draw, pull; (*portare*) to take; (*prendere, tirare fuori*) to take (out), draw; (*derivare*) to obtain; **~ origine da qc** to have its origins *o* originate in sth
trasa'lire *vi* to start, jump
trasan'dato, -a *ag* shabby
trasci'nare [traʃʃi'nare] *vt* to drag; **trascinarsi** *vpr* to drag o.s. along; (*fig*) to drag on
tras'correre *vt* (*tempo*) to spend, pass ▷ *vi* to pass
tras'crivere *vt* to transcribe
trascu'rare *vt* to neglect; (*non considerare*) to disregard
trasferi'mento *sm* transfer; (*trasloco*) removal, move; **trasferimento di chiamata** (*Tel*) call forwarding
trasfe'rire *vt* to transfer; **trasferirsi** *vpr* to move; **tras'ferta** *sf* transfer; (*indennità*) travelling expenses *pl*; (*Sport*) away game
trasfor'mare *vt* to transform, change; **trasformarsi** *vpr* to be transformed; **trasformarsi in qc** to turn into sth; **trasforma'tore** *sm* (*Elec*) transformer
trasfusi'one *sf* (*Med*) transfusion
trasgre'dire *vt* to disobey, contravene
traslo'care *vt* to move, transfer; **tras'loco, -chi** *sm* removal
tras'mettere *vt* (*passare*): **~ qc a qn** to pass sth on to sb; (*mandare*) to send; (*Tecn, Tel, Med*) to transmit; (*TV, Radio*) to broadcast; **trasmissi'one** *sf* (*gen, Fisica, Tecn*) transmission; (*passaggio*) transmission, passing on; (*TV, Radio*) broadcast
traspa'rente *ag* transparent
traspor'tare *vt* to carry, move; (*merce*) to transport, convey; **lasciarsi ~ (da qc)** (*fig*) to let o.s. be carried away (by sth); **tras'porto** *sm* transport
'trassi *ecc vb vedi* **trarre**
trasver'sale *ag* transverse, cross(-); running at right angles
'tratta *sf* (*Econ*) draft; (*di persone*): **la ~ delle bianche** the white slave trade
tratta'mento *sm* treatment; (*servizio*) service
trat'tare *vt* (*gen*) to treat; (*commerciare*) to deal in; (*svolgere: argomento*) to discuss, deal with; (*negoziare*) to negotiate ▷ *vi* **~ di** to deal with; **~ con** (*persona*) to deal with; **si tratta di ...** it's about ...
tratte'nere *vt* (*far rimanere: persona*) to detain; (*intrattenere: ospiti*) to entertain; (*tenere, frenare, reprimere*) to hold back, keep back; (*astenersi dal consegnare*) to hold, keep; (*detrarre: somma*) to deduct; **trattenersi** *vpr* (*astenersi*) to restrain o.s., stop o.s.; (*soffermarsi*) to stay, remain
trat'tino *sm* dash; (*in parole composte*) hyphen
'tratto, -a *pp di* **trarre** ▷ *sm* (*di penna, matita*) stroke; (*parte*) part, piece; (*di strada*) stretch; (*di mare, cielo*) expanse; (*di tempo*) period (of time)
trat'tore *sm* tractor
tratto'ria *sf* restaurant
'trauma, -i *sm* trauma
tra'vaglio [tra'vaʎʎo] *sm* (*angoscia*) pain, suffering; (*Med*) pains *pl*
trava'sare *vt* to decant
tra'versa *sf* (*trave*) crosspiece; (*via*) side street; (*Ferr*) sleeper (BRIT), (railroad) tie (US); (*Calcio*) crossbar
traver'sata *sf* crossing; (*Aer*) flight, trip; **quanto dura la ~?** how long does the crossing take?
traver'sie *sfpl* mishaps, misfortunes
tra'verso, -a *ag* oblique; **di ~** *ag* askew ▷ *av* sideways; **andare di ~** (*cibo*) to go down the wrong way; **guardare di ~** to look askance at
travesti'mento *sm* disguise

travestirsi *vpr* to disguise o.s.
tra'volgere [tra'vɔldʒere] *vt* to sweep away, carry away; (*fig*) to overwhelm
tre *num* three
'treccia, -ce ['trettʃa] *sf* plait, braid
tre'cento [tre'tʃɛnto] *num* three hundred ▷ *sm*: **il T~** the fourteenth century
'tredici ['treditʃi] *num* thirteen
'tregua *sf* truce; (*fig*) respite
tre'mare *vi*: **~ di** (*freddo ecc*) to shiver *o* tremble with; (*paura, rabbia*) to shake *o* tremble with
tre'mendo, -a *ag* terrible, awful

> Attenzione! In inglese esiste la parola *tremendous*, che però significa *enorme* oppure *fantastico, strepitoso*.

'tremito *sm* trembling *no pl*; shaking *no pl*; shivering *no pl*
'treno *sm* train; **è questo il ~ per...?** is this the train for ...?; **treno di gomme** set of tyres (BRIT) *o* tires (US); **treno merci** goods (BRIT) *o* freight train; **treno viaggiatori** passenger train

TRENI

There are various types of train in Italy. For short journeys there are the "Regionali" (R), which generally operate within a particular region, and the "Interregionali" (IR), which operate beyond regional boundaries. Medium- and long-distance passenger journeys are carried out by "Intercity" (I) and "Eurocity" (EC) trains. The "Eurostar" service (ES) offers fast connections between the major Italian cities. Night services are operated by "Intercity Notte" (ICN), "Euronight" (EN) and "Espressi" (EXP).

'trenta *num* thirty; **tren'tesimo, -a** *num* thirtieth; **tren'tina** *sf* **una trentina (di)** thirty or so, about thirty
'trepidante *ag* anxious
tri'angolo *sm* triangle
tribù *sf inv* tribe
tri'buna *sf* (*podio*) platform; (*in aule ecc*) gallery; (*di stadio*) stand
tribu'nale *sm* court
tri'ciclo [tri'tʃiklo] *sm* tricycle
tri'foglio [tri'fɔʎʎo] *sm* clover
'triglia ['triʎʎa] *sf* red mullet
tri'mestre *sm* period of three months; (*Ins*) term, quarter (*US*); (*Comm*) quarter
trin'cea [trin'tʃɛa] *sf* trench
trion'fare *vi* to triumph, win; **~ su** to triumph over, overcome; **tri'onfo** *sm* triumph
tripli'care *vt* to triple
'triplo, -a *ag* triple; treble ▷ *sm*: **il ~ (di)** three times as much (as); **la spesa è tripla** it costs three times as much
'trippa *sf* (*Cuc*) tripe
'triste *ag* sad; (*luogo*) dreary, gloomy
tri'tare *vt* to mince, grind (*US*)
trivi'ale *ag* vulgar, low
tro'feo *sm* trophy
'tromba *sf* (*Mus*) trumpet; (*Aut*) horn; **tromba d'aria** whirlwind; **tromba delle scale** stairwell
trom'bone *sm* trombone
trom'bosi *sf* thrombosis
tron'care *vt* to cut off; (*spezzare*) to break off
'tronco, -a, -chi, -che *ag* cut off; broken off; (*Ling*) truncated; (*fig*) cut short ▷ *sm* (*Bot, Anat*) trunk; (*fig: tratto*) section; **licenziare qn in ~** to fire sb on the spot
'trono *sm* throne
tropi'cale *ag* tropical

PAROLA CHIAVE

'troppo, -a *det* (*in eccesso: quantità*) too much; (*: numero*) too many; **c'era troppa gente** there were too many people; **fa troppo caldo** it's too hot

▷ *pron* (*in eccesso*: *quantità*) too much; (: *numero*) too many; **ne hai messo troppo** you've put in too much; **meglio troppi che pochi** better too many than too few ▷ *av* (*eccessivamente*: *con ag, av*) too; (: *con vb*) too much; **troppo amaro/tardi** too bitter/late; **lavora troppo** he works too much; **costa troppo** it costs too much; **di troppo** too much; too many; **qualche tazza di troppo** a few cups too many; **2 euro di troppo** 2 euros too much; **essere di troppo** to be in the way

'trota *sf* trout
'trottola *sf* spinning top
tro'vare *vt* to find; (*giudicare*): **trovo che** I find *o* think that; **trovarsi** *vpr* (*reciproco*: *incontrarsi*) to meet; (*essere, stare*) to be; (*arrivare, capitare*) to find o.s.; **non trovo più il portafoglio** I can't find my wallet; **andare a ~ qn** to go and see sb; **~ qn colpevole** to find sb guilty; **trovarsi bene** (*in un luogo, con qn*) to get on well
truc'care *vt* (*falsare*) to fake; (*attore ecc*) to make up; (*travestire*) to disguise; (*Sport*) to fix; (*Aut*) to soup up; **truccarsi** *vpr* to make up (one's face)
'trucco, -chi *sm* trick; (*cosmesi*) make-up
'truffa *sf* fraud, swindle; **truf'fare** *vt* to swindle, cheat
truffa'tore, -'trice *sm/f* swindler, cheat
'truppa *sf* troop
tu *pron* you; **tu stesso(a)** you yourself; **dare del tu a qn** to address sb as "tu"
'tubo *sm* tube; pipe; **tubo digerente** (*Anat*) alimentary canal, digestive tract; **tubo di scappamento** (*Aut*) exhaust pipe
tuffarsi *vpr* to plunge, dive
'tuffo *sm* dive; (*breve bagno*) dip
tuli'pano *sm* tulip
tu'more *sm* (*Med*) tumour
Tuni'sia *sf*: **la ~** Tunisia
'tuo (*f* **'tua**, *pl* **tu'oi, 'tue**) *det* **il ~, la tua** *ecc* your ▷ *pron* **il ~, la tua** *ecc* yours
tuo'nare *vi* to thunder; **tuona** it is thundering, there's some thunder
tu'ono *sm* thunder
tu'orlo *sm* yolk
tur'bante *sm* turban
tur'bare *vt* to disturb, trouble
tur'bato, -a *ag* upset; (*preoccupato, ansioso*) anxious
turbo'lenza [turbo'lɛntsa] *sf* turbulence
tur'chese [tur'kese] *sf* turquoise
Tur'chia [tur'kia] *sf*: **la ~** Turkey
'turco, -a, -chi, -che *ag* Turkish ▷ *sm/f* Turk/Turkish woman ▷ *sm* (*Ling*) Turkish; **parlare ~** (*fig*) to talk double-dutch
tu'rismo *sm* tourism; tourist industry; **tu'rista, -i, -e** *sm/f* tourist; **turismo sessuale** sex tourism; **tu'ristico, -a, -ci, -che** *ag* tourist *cpd*
'turno *sm* turn; (*di lavoro*) shift; **di ~** (*soldato, medico, custode*) on duty; **a ~** (*rispondere*) in turn; (*lavorare*) in shifts; **fare a ~ a fare qc** to take turns to do sth; **è il suo ~** it's your (*o* his *ecc* turn)
'turpe *ag* filthy, vile
'tuta *sf* overalls *pl*; (*Sport*) tracksuit
tu'tela *sf* (*Dir*: *di minore*) guardianship; (: *protezione*) protection; (*difesa*) defence
tutta'via *cong* nevertheless, yet

PAROLA CHIAVE

'tutto, -a *det* 1 (*intero*) all; **tutto il latte** all the milk; **tutta la notte** all night, the whole night; **tutto il libro** the whole book; **tutta una bottiglia** a whole bottle
2 (*pl, collettivo*) all; every; **tutti i libri** all the books; **tutte le notti** every night; **tutti i venerdì** every

Friday; **tutti gli uomini** all the men; (*collettivo*) all men; **tutto l'anno** all year long; **tutti e due** both *o* each of us (*o* them *o* you); **tutti e cinque** all five of us (*o* them *o* you)
3 (*completamente*): **era tutta sporca** she was all dirty; **tremava tutto** he was trembling all over; **è tutta sua madre** she's just *o* exactly like her mother
4: **a tutt'oggi** so far, up till now; **a tutta velocità** at full *o* top speed
▷ *pron* 1 (*ogni cosa*) everything, all; (*qualsiasi cosa*) anything; **ha mangiato tutto** he's eaten everything; **tutto considerato** all things considered; **in tutto: 5 euro in tutto** 5 euros in all; **in tutto eravamo 50** there were 50 of us in all
2: **tutti, e** (*ognuno*) all, everybody; **vengono tutti** they are all coming, everybody's coming; **tutti quanti** all and sundry
▷ *av* (*completamente*) entirely, quite; **è tutto il contrario** it's quite *o* exactly the opposite; **tutt'al più: saranno stati tutt'al più una cinquantina** there were about fifty of them at (the very) most; **tutt'al più possiamo prendere un treno** if the worst comes to the worst we can take a train; **tutt'altro** on the contrary; **è tutt'altro che felice** he's anything but happy; **tutt'a un tratto** suddenly
▷ *sm* **il tutto** the whole lot, all of it

tut'tora *av* still
TV [ti'vu] *sf inv* (= *televisione*) TV ▷ *sigla* = **Treviso**

U

ubbidi'ente *ag* obedient
ubbi'dire *vi* to obey; **~ a** to obey; (*veicolo, macchina*) to respond to
ubria'care *vt* **~ qn** to get sb drunk; (*alcool*) to make sb drunk; (*fig*) to make sb's head spin *o* reel; **ubriacarsi** *vpr* to get drunk; **ubriacarsi di** (*fig*) to become intoxicated with
ubri'aco, -a, -chi, -che *ag, sm/f* drunk
uc'cello [ut'tʃɛllo] *sm* bird
uc'cidere [ut'tʃidere] *vt* to kill; **uccidersi** *vpr* (*suicidarsi*) to kill o.s.; (*perdere la vita*) to be killed
u'dito *sm* (sense of) hearing
UE *sigla f* (= *Unione Europea*) EU
UEM *sigla f* (= *Unione economica e monetaria*) EMU
'uffa *escl* tut!
uffici'ale [uffi'tʃale] *ag* official ▷ *sm* (*Amm*) official, officer; (*Mil*) officer; **~ di stato civile** registrar
uf'ficio [uf'fitʃo] *sm* (*gen*) office; (*dovere*) duty; (*mansione*) task,

function, job; (*agenzia*) agency, bureau; (*Rel*) service; **d'~** *ag* office *cpd*; official ▷ *av* officially; **ufficio di collocamento** employment office; **ufficio informazioni** information bureau; **ufficio oggetti smarriti** lost property office (BRIT), lost and found (US); **ufficio (del) personale** personnel department; **ufficio postale** post office

uffici'oso, -a [uffi'tʃoso] *ag* unofficial

uguagli'anza [ugwaʎ'ʎantsa] *sf* equality

uguagli'are [ugwaʎ'ʎare] *vt* to make equal; (*essere uguale*) to equal, be equal to; (*livellare*) to level; **uguagliarsi a** *o* **con qn** (*paragonarsi*) to compare o.s. to sb

ugu'ale *ag* equal; (*identico*) identical, the same; (*uniforme*) level, even ▷ *av* **costano ~** they cost the same; **sono bravi ~** they're equally good

UIL *sigla f* (= *Unione Italiana del Lavoro*) *trade union federation*

'ulcera ['ultʃera] *sf* ulcer

U'livo *sm*: **l'~** *centre-left Italian political grouping*

u'livo = **olivo**

ulteri'ore *ag* further

ultima'mente *av* lately, of late

ulti'mare *vt* to finish, complete

'ultimo, -a *ag* (*finale*) last; (*estremo*) farthest, utmost; (*recente*: *notizia, moda*) latest; (*fig*: *sommo, fondamentale*) ultimate ▷ *sm/f* last (one); **fino all'~** to the last, until the end; **da ~, in ~** in the end; **abitare all'~ piano** to live on the top floor; **per ~** (*entrare, arrivare*) last

ulu'lare *vi* to howl

umanità *sf* humanity

u'mano, -a *ag* human; (*comprensivo*) humane

umidità *sf* dampness; humidity

'umido, -a *ag* damp; (*mano, occhi*) moist; (*clima*) humid ▷ *sm* dampness, damp; **carne in ~** stew

'umile *ag* humble

umili'are *vt* to humiliate; **umiliarsi** *vpr* to humble o.s.

u'more *sm* (*disposizione d'animo*) mood; (*carattere*) temper; **di buon/cattivo ~** in a good/bad mood

umo'rismo *sm* humour; **avere il senso dell'~** to have a sense of humour; **umo'ristico, -a, -ci, -che** *ag* humorous, funny

u'nanime *ag* unanimous

unci'netto [untʃi'netto] *sm* crochet hook

un'cino [un'tʃino] *sm* hook

undi'cenne [undi'tʃɛnne] *ag, sm/f* eleven-year-old

undi'cesimo, -a [undi'tʃɛzimo] *num* eleventh

'undici ['unditʃi] *num* eleven

'ungere ['undʒere] *vt* to grease, oil; (*Rel*) to anoint; (*fig*) to flatter, butter up

unghe'rese [unge'rese] *ag, sm/f, sm* Hungarian

Unghe'ria [unge'ria] *sf* **l'~** Hungary

'unghia ['ungja] *sf* (*Anat*) nail; (*di animale*) claw; (*di rapace*) talon; (*di cavallo*) hoof

ungu'ento *sm* ointment

'unico, -a, -ci, -che *ag* (*solo*) only; (*ineguagliabile*) unique; (*singolo*: *binario*) single; **figlio(a) ~(a)** only son/daughter, only child

unifi'care *vt* to unite, unify; (*sistemi*) to standardize; **unificazi'one** *sf* uniting; unification; standardization

uni'forme *ag* uniform; (*superficie*) even ▷ *sf* (*divisa*) uniform

uni'one *sf* union; (*fig*: *concordia*) unity, harmony; **Unione europea** European Union; **ex Unione Sovietica** former Soviet Union

u'nire *vt* to unite; (*congiungere*) to join, connect; (: *ingredienti, colori*) to combine; (*in matrimonio*) to unite, join together; **unirsi** *vpr* to unite; (*in matrimonio*) to be joined together; **~ qc**

a to unite sth with; to join *o* connect sth with; to combine sth with; **unirsi a** (*gruppo, società*) to join
unità *sf inv* (*unione, concordia*) unity; (*Mat, Mil, Comm, di misura*) unit; **unità di misura** unit of measurement
u'nito, -a *ag* (*paese*) united; (*amici, famiglia*) close; **in tinta unita** plain, self-coloured
univer'sale *ag* universal; general
università *sf inv* university
uni'verso *sm* universe

PAROLA CHIAVE

'uno, -a (*dav sm* **un** + *C, V,* **uno** + *s impura, gn, pn, ps, x, z; dav sf* **un'** + *V,* **una** + *C*) *art indef* **1** a; (*dav vocale*) an; **un bambino** a child; **una strada** a street; **uno zingaro** a gypsy
2 (*intensivo*): **ho avuto una paura!** I got such a fright!
▷ *pron* **1** one; **prendine uno** take one (of them); **l'uno o l'altro** either (of them); **l'uno e l'altro** both (of them); **aiutarsi l'un l'altro** to help one another *o* each other; **sono entrati l'uno dopo l'altro** they came in one after the other
2 (*un tale*) someone, somebody
3 (*con valore impersonale*) one, you; **se uno vuole** if one wants, if you want
▷ *num* one; **una mela e due pere** one apple and two pears; **uno più uno fa due** one plus one equals two, one and one are two ▷ *sf* **è l'una** it's one (o'clock)

'unsi *ecc vb vedi* **ungere**
'unto, -a *pp di* **ungere** ▷ *ag* greasy, oily ▷ *sm* grease
u'omo (*pl* **u'omini**) *sm* man; **da ~** (*abito, scarpe*) men's, for men; **uomo d'affari** businessman; **uomo di paglia** stooge; **uomo politico** politician; **uomo rana** frogman
u'ovo (*pl(f)* **u'ova**) *sm* egg; **uovo affogato/alla coque** poached/boiled egg; **uovo bazzotto/sodo** soft-/hard-boiled egg; **uovo di Pasqua** Easter egg; **uovo in camicia** poached egg; **uova strapazzate/al tegame** scrambled/fried eggs
ura'gano *sm* hurricane
urba'nistica *sf* town planning
ur'bano, -a *ag* urban, city *cpd*, town *cpd*; (*Tel: chiamata*) local; (*fig*) urbane
ur'gente [ur'dʒɛnte] *ag* urgent; **ur'genza** *sf* urgency; **in caso d'urgenza** in (case of) an emergency; **d'urgenza** *ag* emergency ▷ *av* urgently, as a matter of urgency
ur'lare *vi* (*persona*) to scream, yell; (*animale, vento*) to howl ▷ *vt* to scream, yell
'urlo (*pl(m)* **'urli**, *pl(f)* **'urla**) *sm* scream, yell; howl
URP *sigla m* (= *Ufficio Relazioni con il Pubblico*) PR Office
urrà *escl* hurrah!
U.R.S.S. *abbr f* **l'U.R.S.S.** the USSR
ur'tare *vt* to bump into, knock against; (*fig: irritare*) to annoy ▷ *vi* **~ contro** *o* **in** to bump into, knock against, crash into; (*fig: imbattersi*) to come up against; **urtarsi** *vpr* (*reciproco: scontrarsi*) to collide; (*: fig*) to clash; (*irritarsi*) to get annoyed
'U.S.A. ['uza] *smpl* **gli U.S.A.** the USA
u'sanza [u'zantsa] *sf* custom; (*moda*) fashion
u'sare *vt* to use, employ ▷ *vi* (*servirsi*): **~ di** to use; (*: diritto*) to exercise; (*essere di moda*) to be fashionable; (*essere solito*): **~ fare** to be in the habit of doing, be accustomed to doing ▷ *vb impers* **qui usa così** it's the custom round here; **u'sato, -a** *ag* used; (*consumato*) worn; (*di seconda mano*) used, second-hand ▷ *sm* second-hand goods *pl*
u'scire [uʃ'ʃire] *vi* (*gen*) to come out; (*partire, andare a passeggio, a uno spettacolo ecc*) to go out; (*essere

sorteggiato: *numero*) to come up; **~ da** (*gen*) to leave; (*posto*) to go (*o* come) out of, leave; (*solco, vasca ecc*) to come out of; (*muro*) to stick out of; (*competenza ecc*) to be outside; (*infanzia, adolescenza*) to leave behind; (*famiglia nobile ecc*) to come from; **~ da** *o* **di casa** to go out; (*fig*) to leave home; **~ in automobile** to go out in the car, go for a drive; **~ di strada** (*Aut*) to go off *o* leave the road

u'scita [uʃ'ʃita] *sf* (*passaggio, varco*) exit, way out; (*per divertimento*) outing; (*Econ*: *somma*) expenditure; (*Teatro*) entrance; (*fig*: *battuta*) witty remark; **dov'è l'~?** where's the exit?; **uscita di sicurezza** emergency exit

usi'gnolo [uziɲ'ɲɔlo] *sm* nightingale

'uso *sm* (*utilizzazione*) use; (*esercizio*) practice; (*abitudine*) custom; **a ~ di** for (the use of); **d'~** (*corrente*) in use; **fuori ~** out of use; **uso esterno**; **per ~ esterno** for external use only

usti'one *sf* burn

usu'ale *ag* common, everyday

u'sura *sf* usury; (*logoramento*) wear (and tear)

uten'sile *sm* tool, implement; **utensili da cucina** kitchen utensils

u'tente *sm/f* user

'utero *sm* uterus

'utile *ag* useful ▷ *sm* (*vantaggio*) advantage, benefit; (*Econ*: *profitto*) profit

utiliz'zare [utilid'dzare] *vt* to use, make use of, utilize

'uva *sf* grapes *pl*; **uva passa** raisins *pl*; **uva spina** gooseberry

UVA *abbr* (= *ultravioletto prossimo*) UVA

UVB *abbr* (= *ultravioletto remoto*) UVB

V

v. *abbr* (= *vedi*) v

va, va' *vb vedi* **andare**

va'cante *ag* vacant

va'canza [va'kantsa] *sf* (*riposo, ferie*) holiday(s) *pl* (BRIT), vacation (US); (*giorno di permesso*) day off, holiday; **vacanze** *sfpl* (*periodo di ferie*) holidays (BRIT), vacation *sg* (US); **essere/andare in ~** to be/go on holiday *o* vacation; **sono qui in ~** I'm on holiday here; **vacanze estive** summer holiday(s) *o* vacation; **vacanze natalizie** Christmas holidays *o* vacation

> Attenzione! In inglese esiste la parola *vacancy* che però indica un posto vacante o una camera disponibile.

'vacca, -che *sf* cow

vacci'nare [vattʃi'nare] *vt* to vaccinate

vac'cino [vat'tʃino] *sm* (*Med*) vaccine

vacil'lare [vatʃil'lare] *vi* to sway, wobble; (*luce*) to flicker; (*fig*: *memoria*,

coraggio) to be failing, falter
'vacuo, -a *ag* (*fig*) empty, vacuous
'vado *ecc vb vedi* **andare**
vaga'bondo, -a *sm/f* tramp, vagrant
va'gare *vi* to wander
vagherò *ecc* [vage'rɔ] *vb vedi* **vagare**
va'gina [va'dʒina] *sf* vagina
'vaglia ['vaʎʎa] *sm inv* money order; **vaglia postale** postal order
vagli'are [vaʎ'ʎare] *vt* to sift; (*fig*) to weigh up
'vago, -a, -ghi, -ghe *ag* vague
va'gone *sm* (*Ferr: per passeggeri*) coach; (*: per merci*) truck, wagon; **vagone letto** sleeper, sleeping car; **vagone ristorante** dining *o* restaurant car
'vai *vb vedi* **andare**
vai'olo *sm* smallpox
va'langa, -ghe *sf* avalanche
va'lere *vi* (*avere forza, potenza*) to have influence; (*essere valido*) to be valid; (*avere vigore, autorità*) to hold, apply; (*essere capace: poeta, studente*) to be good, be able ▷ *vt* (*prezzo, sforzo*) to be worth; (*corrispondere*) to correspond to; (*procurare*): **~ qc a qn** to earn sb sth; **valersi di** to make use of, take advantage of; **far ~** (*autorità ecc*) to assert; **vale a dire** that is to say; **~ la pena** to be worth the effort *o* worth it
'valgo *ecc vb vedi* **valere**
vali'care *vt* to cross
'valico, -chi *sm* (*passo*) pass
'valido, -a *ag* valid; (*rimedio*) effective; (*aiuto*) real; (*persona*) worthwhile
vali'getta [vali'dʒetta] *sf* briefcase; **valigetta ventiquattrore** overnight bag *o* case
va'ligia, -gie *o* **ge** [va'lidʒa] *sf* (suit)case; **fare le valigie** to pack (up)
'valle *sf* valley; **a ~** (*di fiume*) downstream; **scendere a ~** to go downhill
va'lore *sm* (*gen*) value; (*merito*) merit, worth; (*coraggio*) valour, courage; (*Comm: titolo*) security; **valori** *smpl* (*oggetti preziosi*) valuables
valoriz'zare [valorid'dzare] *vt* (*terreno*) to develop; (*fig*) to make the most of
va'luta *sf* currency, money; (*Banca*): **~ 15 gennaio** interest to run from January 15th
valu'tare *vt* (*casa, gioiello, fig*) to value; (*stabilire: peso, entrate, fig*) to estimate
'valvola *sf* (*Tecn, Anat*) valve; (*Elettr*) fuse
'valzer ['valtser] *sm inv* waltz
vam'pata *sf* (*di fiamma*) blaze; (*di calore*) blast; (*: al viso*) flush
vam'piro *sm* vampire
vanda'lismo *sm* vandalism
'vandalo *sm* vandal
vaneggi'are [vaned'dʒare] *vi* to rave
'vanga, -ghe *sf* spade
van'gelo [van'dʒɛlo] *sm* gospel
va'niglia [va'niʎʎa] *sf* vanilla
vanità *sf* vanity; (*di promessa*) emptiness; (*di sforzo*) futility; **vani'toso, -a** *ag* vain, conceited
'vanno *vb vedi* **andare**
'vano, -a *ag* vain ▷ *sm* (*spazio*) space; (*apertura*) opening; (*stanza*) room
van'taggio [van'taddʒo] *sm* advantage; **essere/portarsi in ~** (*Sport*) to be in/take the lead; **vantaggi'oso, -a** *ag* advantageous; favourable
vantarsi *vpr*: **~ (di/di aver fatto)** to boast *o* brag (about/about having done)
'vanvera *sf* **a ~** haphazardly; **parlare a ~** to talk nonsense
va'pore *sm* vapour; (*anche:* **~ acqueo**) steam; (*nave*) steamer; **a ~** (*turbina ecc*) steam *cpd*; **al ~** (*Cuc*) steamed
va'rare *vt* (*Naut, fig*) to launch; (*Dir*) to pass
var'care *vt* to cross
'varco, -chi *sm* passage; **aprirsi un ~ tra la folla** to push one's way through the crowd

vare'china [vare'kina] *sf* bleach
vari'abile *ag* variable; (*tempo, umore*) changeable, variable ▷ *sf* (*Mat*) variable
vari'cella [vari'tʃɛlla] *sf* chickenpox
vari'coso, -a *ag* varicose
varietà *sf inv* variety ▷ *sm inv* variety show
'vario, -a *ag* varied; (*parecchi: col sostantivo al pl*) various; (*mutevole: umore*) changeable
'varo *sm* (*Naut: fig*) launch; (*di leggi*) passing
varrò *ecc vb vedi* **valere**
Var'savia *sf* Warsaw
va'saio *sm* potter
'vasca, -sche *sf* basin; **vasca da bagno** bathtub, bath
vas'chetta [vas'ketta] *sf* (*per gelato*) tub; (*per sviluppare fotografie*) dish
vase'lina *sf* Vaseline®
'vaso *sm* (*recipiente*) pot; (*: barattolo*) jar; (*: decorativo*) vase; (*Anat*) vessel; **vaso da fiori** vase; (*per piante*) flowerpot
vas'soio *sm* tray
'vasto, -a *ag* vast, immense
Vati'cano *sm*: **il ~** the Vatican
ve *pron, av vedi* **vi**
vecchi'aia [vek'kjaja] *sf* old age
'vecchio, -a ['vɛkkjo] *ag* old ▷ *sm/f* old man/woman; **i vecchii** the old
ve'dere *vt, vi* to see; **vedersi** *vpr* to meet, see one another; **avere a che ~ con** to have something to do with; **far ~ qc a qn** to show sb sth; **farsi ~** to show o.s.; (*farsi vivo*) to show one's face; **vedi di non farlo** make sure *o* see you don't do it; **non (ci) si vede** (*è buio ecc*) you can't see a thing; **non lo posso ~** (*fig*) I can't stand him
ve'detta *sf* (*sentinella, posto*) look-out; (*Naut*) patrol boat
'vedovo, -a *sm/f* widower/widow
vedrò *ecc vb vedi* **vedere**
ve'duta *sf* view; **vedute** *sfpl* (*fig: opinioni*) views; **di larghe** *o* **ampie vedute** broad-minded; **di vedute limitate** narrow-minded
vege'tale [vedʒe'tale] *ag, sm* vegetable
vegetari'ano, -a [vedʒeta'rjano] *ag, sm/f* vegetarian; **avete piatti vegetariani?** do you have any vegetarian dishes?
vegetazi'one [vedʒetat'tsjone] *sf* vegetation
'vegeto, -a ['vɛdʒeto] *ag* (*pianta*) thriving; (*persona*) strong, vigorous
'veglia ['veʎʎa] *sf* wakefulness; (*sorveglianza*) watch; (*trattenimento*) evening gathering; **fare la ~ a un malato** to watch over a sick person
vegli'one [veʎ'ʎone] *sm* ball, dance; **veglione di Capodanno** New Year's Eve party
ve'icolo *sm* vehicle
'vela *sf* (*Naut: tela*) sail; (*Sport*) sailing
ve'leno *sm* poison; **vele'noso, -a** *ag* poisonous
veli'ero *sm* sailing ship
vel'luto *sm* velvet; **velluto a coste** cord
'velo *sm* veil; (*tessuto*) voile
ve'loce [ve'lotʃe] *ag* fast, quick ▷ *av* fast, quickly; **velocità** *sf* speed; **a forte velocità** at high speed; **velocità di crociera** cruising speed
'vena *sf* (*gen*) vein; (*filone*) vein, seam; (*fig: ispirazione*) inspiration; (*: umore*) mood; **essere in ~ di qc** to be in the mood for sth
ve'nale *ag* (*prezzo, valore*) market *cpd*; (*fig*) venal; mercenary
ven'demmia *sf* (*raccolta*) grape harvest; (*quantità d'uva*) grape crop, grapes *pl*; (*vino ottenuto*) vintage
'vendere *vt* to sell; **"vendesi"** "for sale"
ven'detta *sf* revenge
vendicarsi *vpr*: **~ (di)** to avenge o.s. (for); (*per rancore*) to ta[illegible]'s revenge (for); **~ su qn** to revenge o.s. on sb

'vendita *sf* sale; **la ~** (*attività*) selling; (*smercio*) sales *pl*; **in ~** on sale; **vendita all'asta** sale by auction; **vendita per telefono** telesales *sg*
vene'rare *vt* to venerate
venerdì *sm inv* Friday; **di** *o* **il ~** on Fridays; **V~ Santo** Good Friday
ve'nereo, -a *ag* venereal
Ve'nezia [ve'nεttsja] *sf* Venice
'vengo *ecc vb vedi* **venire**
veni'ale *ag* venial
ve'nire *vi* to come; (*riuscire: dolce, fotografia*) to turn out; (*come ausiliare: essere*): **viene ammirato da tutti** he is admired by everyone; **~ da** to come from; **quanto viene?** how much does it cost?; **far ~** (*mandare a chiamare*) to send for; **~ giù** to come down; **~ meno** (*svenire*) to faint; **~ meno a qc** not to fulfil sth; **~ su** to come up; **~ a trovare qn** to come and see sb; **~ via** to come away
'venni *ecc vb vedi* **venire**
ven'taglio [ven'taʎʎo] *sm* fan
ven'tata *sf* gust (of wind)
ven'tenne *ag*: **una ragazza ~** a twenty-year-old girl, a girl of twenty
ven'tesimo, -a *num* twentieth
'venti *num* twenty
venti'lare *vt* (*stanza*) to air, ventilate; (*fig: idea, proposta*) to air; **ventila'tore** *sm* ventilator, fan
ven'tina *sf*: **una ~ (di)** around twenty, twenty or so
'vento *sm* wind
'ventola *sf* (*Aut, Tecn*) fan
ven'tosa *sf* (*Zool*) sucker; (*di gomma*) suction pad
ven'toso, -a *ag* windy
'ventre *sm* stomach
'vera *sf* wedding ring
vera'mente *av* really
ve'randa *sf* veranda(h)
ver'bale *ag* verbal ▷ *sm* (*di riunione*) minutes *pl*
'verbo *sm* (*Ling*) verb; (*parola*) word; (*Rel*): **il V~** the Word
'verde *ag, sm* green; **essere al ~** to be broke; **verde bottiglia/oliva** bottle/olive green
ver'detto *sm* verdict
ver'dura *sf* vegetables *pl*
'vergine ['verdʒine] *sf* virgin; (*dello zodiaco*): **V~** Virgo ▷ *ag* virgin; (*ragazza*): **essere ~** to be a virgin
ver'gogna [ver'goɲɲa] *sf* shame; (*timidezza*) shyness, embarrassment; **vergo'gnarsi** *vpr* **vergognarsi (di)** to be *o* feel ashamed (of); to be shy (about), be embarrassed (about); **vergo'gnoso, -a** *ag* ashamed; (*timido*) shy, embarrassed; (*causa di vergogna: azione*) shameful
ve'rifica, -che *sf* checking *no pl*, check
verifi'care *vt* (*controllare*) to check; (*confermare*) to confirm, bear out
verità *sf inv* truth
'verme *sm* worm
ver'miglio [ver'miʎʎo] *sm* vermilion, scarlet
ver'nice [ver'nitʃe] *sf* (*colorazione*) paint; (*trasparente*) varnish; (*pelle*) patent leather; **"~ fresca"** "wet paint"; **vernici'are** *vt* to paint; to varnish
'vero, -a *ag* (*veridico: fatti, testimonianza*) true; (*autentico*) real ▷ *sm* (*verità*) truth; (*realtà*) (real) life; **un ~ e proprio delinquente** a real criminal, an out-and-out criminal
vero'simile *ag* likely, probable
verrò *ecc vb vedi* **venire**
ver'ruca, -che *sf* wart
versa'mento *sm* (*pagamento*) payment; (*deposito di denaro*) deposit
ver'sante *sm* slopes *pl*, side
ver'sare *vt* (*fare uscire: vino, farina*) to pour (out); (*spargere: lacrime, sangue*) to shed; (*rovesciare*) to spill; (*Econ*) to pay; (*: depositare*) to deposit, pay in
versa'tile *ag* versatile
versi'one *sf* version; (*traduzione*) translation
'verso *sm* (*di poesia*) verse, line; (*di animale, uccello*) cry; (*direzione*)

direction; (*modo*) way; (*di foglio di carta*) verso; (*di moneta*) reverse; **versi** *smpl* (*poesia*) verse *sg*; **non c'è ~ di persuaderlo** there's no way of persuading him, he can't be persuaded *prep* (*in direzione di*) toward(s); (*nei pressi di*) near, around (about); (*in senso temporale*) about, around; (*nei confronti di*) for; **~ di me** towards me; **~ sera** towards evening

'vertebra *sf* vertebra

verte'brale *ag* vertebral; **colonna ~** spinal column, spine

verti'cale *ag, sf* vertical

'vertice ['vɛrtitʃe] *sm* summit, top; (*Mat*) vertex; **conferenza al ~** (*Pol*) summit conference

ver'tigine [ver'tidʒine] *sf* dizziness *no pl*; dizzy spell; (*Med*) vertigo; **avere le vertigini** to feel dizzy

ve'scica, -che [veʃʃika] *sf* (*Anat*) bladder; (*Med*) blister

'vescovo *sm* bishop

'vespa *sf* wasp

ves'taglia [ves'taʎʎa] *sf* dressing gown

ves'tire *vt* (*bambino, malato*) to dress; (*avere indosso*) to have on, wear; **vestirsi** *vpr* to dress, get dressed; **ves'tito, -a** *ag* dressed ▷ *sm* garment; (*da donna*) dress; (*da uomo*) suit; **vestiti** *smpl* (*indumenti*) clothes; **vestito di bianco** dressed in white

veteri'nario, -a *ag* veterinary ▷ *sm* veterinary surgeon (BRIT), veterinarian (US), vet

'veto *sm inv* veto

ve'traio *sm* glassmaker; glazier

ve'trata *sf* glass door (*o* window); (*di chiesa*) stained glass window

ve'trato, -a *ag* (*porta, finestra*) glazed; (*che contiene vetro*) glass *cpd* ▷ *sf* glass door (*o* window); (*di chiesa*) stained glass window; **carta vetrata** sandpaper

ve'trina *sf* (*di negozio*) (shop) window; (*armadio*) display cabinet; **vetri'nista, -i, -e** *sm/f* window dresser

'vetro *sm* glass; (*per finestra, porta*) pane (of glass)

'vetta *sf* peak, summit, top

vet'tura *sf* (*carrozza*) carriage; (*Ferr*) carriage (BRIT), car (US); (*auto*) car (BRIT), automobile (US)

vezzeggia'tivo [vettseddʒa'tivo] *sm* (*Ling*) term of endearment

vi (*dav lo, la, li, le, ne diventa* **ve**) *pron* (*oggetto*) you; (*complemento di termine*) (to) you; (*riflessivo*) yourselves; (*reciproco*) each other ▷ *av* (*lì*) there; (*qui*) here; (*per questo/quel luogo*) through here/there; **vi è/sono** there is/are

'via *sf* (*gen*) way; (*strada*) street; (*sentiero, pista*) path, track; (*Amm*: *procedimento*) channels *pl* ▷ *prep* (*passando per*) via, by way of ▷ *av* away ▷ *escl* go away!; (*suvvia*) come on!; (*Sport*) go! ▷ *sm* (*Sport*) starting signal; **in ~ di guarigione** on the road to recovery; **per ~ di** (*a causa di*) because of, on account of; **in** *o* **per ~** on the way; **per ~ aerea** by air; (*lettere*) by airmail; **andare/essere ~** to go/be away; **~ ~ che** (*a mano a mano*) as; **dare il ~** (*Sport*) to give the starting signal; **dare il ~ a** (*fig*) to start; **in ~ provvisoria** provisionally; **Via lattea** (*Astr*) Milky Way; **via di mezzo** middle course; **via d'uscita** (*fig*) way out

via'dotto *sm* viaduct

viaggi'are [viad'dʒare] *vi* to travel; **viaggia'tore, -'trice** *ag* travelling ▷ *sm* traveller; (*passeggero*) passenger

vi'aggio ['vjaddʒo] *sm* travel(ling); (*tragitto*) journey, trip; **buon ~!** have a good trip!; **com'è andato il ~?** how was your journey?; **il ~ dura due ore** the journey takes two hours; **viaggio di nozze** honeymoon; **siamo in ~ di nozze** we're on honeymoon

vi'ale *sm* avenue

via'vai *sm* coming and going, bustle
vi'brare *vi* to vibrate
'vice ['vitʃe] *sm/f* deputy
vi'cenda [vi'tʃɛnda] *sf* event; **a ~** in turn
vice'versa [vitʃe'vɛrsa] *av* vice versa; **da Roma a Pisa e ~** from Rome to Pisa and back
vici'nanza [vitʃi'nantsa] *sf* nearness, closeness
vi'cino, -a [vi'tʃino] *ag* (*gen*) near; (*nello spazio*) near, nearby; (*accanto*) next; (*nel tempo*) near, close at hand ▷ *sm/f* neighbour ▷ *av* near, close; **da ~** (*guardare*) close up; (*esaminare, seguire*) closely; (*conoscere*) well, intimately; **~ a** near (to), close to; (*accanto a*) beside; **c'è una banca qui ~?** is there a bank nearby?; **~ di casa** neighbour
'vicolo *sm* alley; **vicolo cieco** blind alley
'video *sm inv* (*TV*: *schermo*) screen; **video'camera** *sf* camcorder; **videocas'setta** *sf* videocassette; **videochia'mare** [videokja'mare] *vt* to video call; **videoclip** [video'klip] *sm inv* videoclip; **videogi'oco, -chi** [video'dʒɔko] *sm* video game; **videoregistra'tore** *sm* video (recorder); **videote'lefono** *sm* videophone
'vidi *ecc vb vedi* **vedere**
vie'tare *vt* to forbid; (*Amm*) to prohibit; **~ a qn di fare** to forbid sb to do; to prohibit sb from doing
vie'tato, -a *ag* (*vedi vb*) forbidden; prohibited; banned; **"~ fumare/l'ingresso"** "no smoking/admittance"; **~ ai minori di 14/18 anni** prohibited to children under 14/18; **"senso ~"** (*Aut*) "no entry"; **"sosta vietata"** (*Aut*) "no parking"
Viet'nam *sm*: **il ~** Vietnam; **vietna'mita, -i, -e** *ag, sm/f, sm* Vietnamese *inv*
vi'gente [vi'dʒɛnte] *ag* in force
'vigile ['vidʒile] *ag* watchful ▷ *sm* (*anche*: **~ urbano**) policeman (*in towns*); **vigile del fuoco** fireman
vi'gilia [vi'dʒilja] *sf* (*giorno antecedente*) eve; **la ~ di Natale** Christmas Eve
vigli'acco, -a, -chi, -che [viʎ'ʎakko] *ag* cowardly ▷ *sm/f* coward
vi'gneto [viɲ'ɲeto] *sm* vineyard
vi'gnetta [viɲ'ɲetta] *sf* cartoon
vi'gore *sm* vigour; (*Dir*): **essere/entrare in ~** to be in/come into force
'vile *ag* (*spregevole*) low, mean, base; (*codardo*) cowardly
'villa *sf* villa
vil'laggio [vil'laddʒo] *sm* village; **villaggio turistico** holiday village
vil'lano, -a *ag* rude, ill-mannered
villeggia'tura [villeddʒa'tura] *sf* holiday(s) *pl* (BRIT), vacation (*US*)
vil'letta *sf*, **vil'lino** ▷ *sm* small house (with a garden), cottage
'vimini *smpl*: **di ~** wicker
'vincere ['vintʃere] *vt* (*in guerra, al gioco, a una gara*) to defeat, beat; (*premio, guerra, partita*) to win; (*fig*) to overcome, conquer ▷ *vi* to win; **~ qn in bellezza** to be better-looking than sb; **vinci'tore** *sm* winner; (*Mil*) victor
vi'nicolo, -a *ag* wine *cpd*
'vino *sm* wine; **vino bianco/rosato/rosso** white/rosé/red wine; **vino da pasto** table wine
'vinsi *ecc vb vedi* **vincere**
vi'ola *sf* (*Bot*) violet; (*Mus*) viola ▷ *ag, sm inv* (*colore*) purple
vio'lare *vt* (*chiesa*) to desecrate, violate; (*giuramento, legge*) to violate
violen'tare *vt* to use violence on; (*donna*) to rape
vio'lento, -a *ag* violent; **vio'lenza** *sf* violence; **violenza carnale** rape
vio'letta *sf* (*Bot*) violet
vio'letto, -a *ag, sm* (*colore*) violet
violi'nista, -i, -e *sm/f* violinist
vio'lino *sm* violin
violon'cello [violon'tʃɛllo] *sm* cello

vi'ottolo *sm* path, track
vip [vip] *sigla m* (*= very important person*) VIP
'vipera *sf* viper, adder
vi'rare *vi* (*Naut, Aer*) to turn; (*Fot*) to tone; **~ di bordo** (*Naut*) to tack
'virgola *sf* (*Ling*) comma; (*Mat*) point; **virgo'lette** *sfpl* inverted commas, quotation marks
vi'rile *ag* (*proprio dell'uomo*) masculine; (*non puerile, da uomo*) manly, virile
virtù *sf inv* virtue; **in** *o* **per ~ di** by virtue of, by
virtu'ale *ag* virtual
'virus *sm inv* (*anche Inform*) virus
'viscere ['viʃʃere] *sfpl* (*di animale*) entrails *pl*; (*fig*) bowels *pl*
'vischio ['viskjo] *sm* (*Bot*) mistletoe; (*pania*) birdlime
'viscido, -a ['viʃʃido] *ag* slimy
vi'sibile *ag* visible
visibilità *sf* visibility
visi'era *sf* (*di elmo*) visor; (*di berretto*) peak
visi'one *sf* vision; **prendere ~ di qc** to examine sth, look sth over; **prima/seconda ~** (*Cinema*) first/second showing
'visita *sf* visit; (*Med*) visit, call; (*: esame*) examination; **visita guidata** guided tour; **a che ora comincia la ~ guidata?** what time does the guided tour start?; **visita medica** medical examination; **visi'tare** *vt* to visit; (*Med*) to visit, call on; (*: esaminare*) to examine; **visita'tore, -'trice** *sm/f* visitor
vi'sivo, -a *ag* visual
'viso *sm* face
vi'sone *sm* mink
'vispo, -a *ag* quick, lively
'vissi *ecc vb vedi* **vivere**
'vista *sf* (*facoltà*) (eye)sight; (*fatto di vedere*): **la ~ di** the sight of; (*veduta*) view; **sparare a ~** to shoot on sight; **in ~** in sight; **perdere qn di ~** to lose sight of sb; (*fig*) to lose touch with sb; **a ~ d'occhio** as far as the eye can see; (*fig*) before one's very eyes; **far ~ di fare** to pretend to do
'visto, -a *pp di* **vedere** ▷ *sm* visa; **~ che** seeing (that)
vis'toso, -a *ag* gaudy, garish; (*ingente*) considerable
visu'ale *ag* visual
'vita *sf* life; (*Anat*) waist; **a ~** for life
vi'tale *ag* vital
vita'mina *sf* vitamin
'vite *sf* (*Bot*) vine; (*Tecn*) screw
vi'tello *sm* (*Zool*) calf; (*carne*) veal; (*pelle*) calfskin
'vittima *sf* victim
'vitto *sm* food; (*in un albergo ecc*) board; **vitto e alloggio** board and lodging
vit'toria *sf* victory
'viva *escl*: **~ il re!** long live the king!
vi'vace [vi'vatʃe] *ag* (*vivo, animato*) lively; (*: mente*) lively, sharp; (*colore*) bright
vi'vaio *sm* (*di pesci*) hatchery; (*Agr*) nursery
vivavoce [viva'votʃe] *sm inv* (*dispositivo*) loudspeaker; **mettere il ~** to switch on the loudspeaker
vi'vente *ag* living, alive; **i viventi** the living
'vivere *vi* to live ▷ *vt* to live; (*passare: brutto momento*) to live through, go through; (*sentire: gioie, pene di qn*) to share ▷ *sm* life; (*anche:* **modo di ~**) way of life; **viveri** *smpl* (*cibo*) food *sg*, provisions; **~ di** to live on
'vivido, -a *ag* (*colore*) vivid, bright
vivisezi'one [viviset'tsjone] *sf* vivisection
'vivo, -a *ag* (*vivente*) alive, living; (*: animale*) live; (*fig*) lively; (*: colore*) bright, brilliant; **i vivi** the living; **~ e vegeto** hale and hearty; **farsi ~** to show one's face; to be heard from; **ritrarre dal ~** to paint from life; **pungere qn nel ~** (*fig*) to cut sb to the quick

vivrò *ecc vb vedi* **vivere**
vizi'are [vit'tsjare] *vt* (*bambino*) to spoil; (*corrompere moralmente*) to corrupt; **vizi'ato, -a** *ag* spoilt; (*aria, acqua*) polluted
'vizio ['vittsjo] *sm* (*morale*) vice; (*cattiva abitudine*) bad habit; (*imperfezione*) flaw, defect; (*errore*) fault, mistake
V.le *abbr* = **viale**
vocabo'lario *sm* (*dizionario*) dictionary; (*lessico*) vocabulary
vo'cabolo *sm* word
vo'cale *ag* vocal ▷ *sf* vowel
vocazi'one [vokat'tsjone] *sf* vocation; (*fig*) natural bent
'voce ['votʃe] *sf* voice; (*diceria*) rumour; (*di un elenco, in bilancio*) item; **aver ~ in capitolo** (*fig*) to have a say in the matter
'voga *sf* (*Naut*) rowing; (*usanza*): **essere in ~** to be in fashion *o* in vogue
vo'gare *vi* to row
vogherò *ecc* [voge'rɔ] *vb vedi* **vogare**
'voglia ['vɔʎʎa] *sf* desire, wish; (*macchia*) birthmark; **aver ~ di qc/di fare** to feel like sth/like doing; (*più forte*) to want sth/to do
'voglio *ecc* ['vɔʎʎo] *vb vedi* **volere**
'voi *pron* you; **voi'altri** *pron* you
vo'lante *ag* flying ▷ *sm* (steering) wheel
volan'tino *sm* leaflet
vo'lare *vi* (*uccello, aereo, fig*) to fly; (*cappello*) to blow away *o* off, fly away *o* off; **~ via** to fly away *o* off
vo'latile *ag* (*Chim*) volatile ▷ *sm* (*Zool*) bird
volente'roso, -a *ag* willing
volenti'eri *av* willingly; **"~"** "with pleasure", "I'd be glad to"

PAROLA CHIAVE

vo'lere *sm* will, wish(es); **contro il volere di** against the wishes of; **per volere di qn** in obedience to sb's will *o* wishes
▷ *vt* 1 (*esigere, desiderare*) to want; **voler fare/che qn faccia** to want to do/sb to do; **volete del caffè?** would you like *o* do you want some coffee?; **vorrei questo/fare** I would *o* I'd like this/to do; **come vuoi** as you like; **senza volere** (*inavvertitamente*) without meaning to, unintentionally
2 (*consentire*): **vogliate attendere, per piacere** please wait; **vogliamo andare?** shall we go?; **vuole essere così gentile da ...?** would you be so kind as to ...?; **non ha voluto ricevermi** he wouldn't see me
3: **volerci** (*essere necessario: materiale, attenzione*) to need; (*: tempo*) to take; **quanta farina ci vuole per questa torta?** how much flour do you need for this cake?; **ci vuole un'ora per arrivare a Venezia** it takes an hour to get to Venice
4: **voler bene a qn** (*amore*) to love sb; (*affetto*) to be fond of sb, like sb very much; **voler male a qn** to dislike sb; **volerne a qn** to bear sb a grudge; **voler dire** to mean

vol'gare *ag* vulgar
voli'era *sf* aviary
voli'tivo, -a *ag* strong-willed
'volli *ecc vb vedi* **volere**
'volo *sm* flight; **al ~: colpire qc al ~** to hit sth as it flies past; **capire al ~** to understand straight away; **volo charter** charter flight; **volo di linea** scheduled flight
volontà *sf* will; **a ~** (*mangiare, bere*) as much as one likes; **buona/cattiva ~** goodwill/lack of goodwill
volon'tario, -a *ag* voluntary ▷ *sm* (*Mil*) volunteer
'volpe *sf* fox
'volta *sf* (*momento, circostanza*) time; (*turno, giro*) turn; (*curva*) turn, bend; (*Archit*) vault; (*direzione*): **partire alla ~ di** to set off for; **a mia (*o* tua *ecc*) ~**

in turn; **una ~** once; **una ~ sola** only once; **due volte** twice; **una cosa per ~** one thing at a time; **una ~ per tutte** once and for all; **a volte** at times, sometimes; **una ~ che** (*temporale*) once; (*causale*) since; **3 volte 4** 3 times 4

volta'faccia [volta'fattʃa] *sm inv* (*fig*) volte-face

vol'taggio [vol'taddʒo] *sm* (*Elettr*) voltage

vol'tare *vt* to turn; (*girare*: *moneta*) to turn over; (*rigirare*) to turn round ▷ *vi* to turn; **voltarsi** *vpr* to turn; to turn over; to turn round

voltas'tomaco *sm* nausea; (*fig*) disgust

'volto, -a *pp di* **volgere** ▷ *sm* face

vo'lubile *ag* changeable, fickle

vo'lume *sm* volume

vomi'tare *vt, vi* to vomit; **'vomito** *sm* vomiting *no pl*; vomit

'vongola *sf* clam

vo'race [vo'ratʃe] *ag* voracious, greedy

vo'ragine [vo'radʒine] *sf* abyss, chasm

vorrò *ecc vb vedi* **volere**

'vortice ['vɔrtitʃe] *sm* whirlwind; whirlpool; (*fig*) whirl

'vostro, -a *det*: **il(la) ~(a)** *ecc* your ▷ *pron* **il(la) ~(a)** *ecc* yours

vo'tante *sm/f* voter

vo'tare *vi* to vote ▷ *vt* (*sottoporre a votazione*) to take a vote on; (*approvare*) to vote for; (*Rel*): **~ qc a** to dedicate sth to

'voto *sm* (*Pol*) vote; (*Ins*) mark; (*Rel*) vow; (: *offerta*) votive offering; **aver voti belli/brutti** (*Ins*) to get good/bad marks

vs. *abbr* (*Comm*) = **vostro**

vul'cano *sm* volcano

vulne'rabile *ag* vulnerable

vu'oi, vu'ole *vb vedi* **volere**

vuo'tare *vt* to empty; **vuotarsi** *vpr* to empty

vu'oto, -a *ag* empty; (*fig*: *privo*): **~ di** (*senso ecc*) devoid of ▷ *sm* empty space, gap; (*spazio in bianco*) blank; (*Fisica*) vacuum; (*fig*: *mancanza*) gap, void; **a mani vuote** empty-handed; **vuoto d'aria** air pocket; **vuoto a rendere** returnable bottle

W X

'wafer ['vafer] *sm inv* (*Cuc, Elettr*) wafer
'water ['wɔ:təʳ] *sm inv* toilet
watt [vat] *sm inv* watt
W.C. *sm inv* WC
web [ueb] *sm*: **il ~** the Web; **cercare nel ~** to search the Web ▷ *ag inv* **pagina ~** web page
'weekend ['wi:kend] *sm inv* weekend
'western ['wɛstern] *ag* (*Cinema*) cowboy *cpd* ▷ *sm inv* western, cowboy film; **western all'italiana** spaghetti western
'whisky ['wiski] *sm inv* whisky
'windsurf ['windsə:f] *sm inv* (*tavola*) windsurfer; (*sport*) windsurfing
'würstel ['vyrstəl] *sm inv* frankfurter
xe'nofobo, -a [kse'nɔfobo] *ag* xenophobic ▷ *sm/f* xenophobe
xi'lofono [ksi'lɔfono] *sm* xylophone

Y

yacht [jɔt] *sm inv* yacht
'yoga ['jɔga] *ag inv, sm* yoga (*cpd*)
yogurt ['jɔgurt] *sm inv* yog(h)urt

Z

zabai'one [dzaba'jone] *sm dessert made of egg yolks, sugar and marsala*
zaf'fata [tsaf'fata] *sf* (*tanfo*) stench
zaffe'rano [dzaffe'rano] *sm* saffron
zaf'firo [dzaf'firo] *sm* sapphire
'zaino ['dzaino] *sm* rucksack
'zampa ['tsampa] *sf* (*di animale*: *gamba*) leg; (: *piede*) paw; **a quattro zampe** on all fours
zampil'lare [tsampil'lare] *vi* to gush, spurt
zan'zara [dzan'dzara] *sf* mosquito; **zanzari'era** *sf* mosquito net
'zappa ['tsappa] *sf* hoe
'zapping ['tsapiŋ] *sm* (*TV*) channel-hopping
zar, za'rina [tsar, tsa'rina] *sm/f* tsar/tsarina
'zattera ['dzattera] *sf* raft
'zebra ['dzɛbra] *sf* zebra; **zebre** *sfpl* (*Aut*) zebra crossing *sg* (BRIT), crosswalk *sg* (US)
'zecca, -che ['tsekka] *sf* (*Zool*) tick; (*officina di monete*) mint

'zelo ['dzɛlo] *sm* zeal
'zenzero ['dzendzero] *sm* ginger
'zeppa ['tseppa] *sf* wedge
'zeppo, -a ['tseppo] *ag*: **~ di** crammed *o* packed with
zer'bino [dzer'bino] *sm* doormat
'zero ['dzɛro] *sm* zero, nought; **vincere per tre a ~** (*Sport*) to win three-nil
'zia ['tsia] *sf* aunt
zibel'lino [dzibel'lino] *sm* sable
'zigomo ['dzigomo] *sm* cheekbone
zig'zag [dzig'dzag] *sm inv* zigzag; **andare a ~** to zigzag
Zimbabwe [tsim'babwe] *sm*: **lo ~** Zimbabwe
'zinco ['dzinko] *sm* zinc
'zingaro, -a ['dzingaro] *sm/f* gipsy
'zio ['tsio] (*pl* **'zii**) *sm* uncle
zip'pare *vt* (*Inform*: *file*) to zip
zi'tella [dzi'tɛlla] *sf* spinster; (*peg*) old maid
'zitto, -a ['tsitto] *ag* quiet, silent; **sta' ~!** be quiet!
'zoccolo ['tsɔkkolo] *sm* (*calzatura*) clog; (*di cavallo ecc*) hoof; (*basamento*) base; plinth
zodia'cale [dzodia'kale] *ag* zodiac *cpd*; **segno ~** sign of the zodiac
zo'diaco [dzo'diako] *sm* zodiac
'zolfo ['tsolfo] *sm* sulphur
'zolla ['dzɔlla] *sf* clod (of earth)
zol'letta [dzol'letta] *sf* sugar lump
'zona ['dzɔna] *sf* zone, area; **zona di depressione** (*Meteor*) trough of low pressure; **zona disco** (*Aut*) ≈ meter zone; **zona industriale** industrial estate; **zona pedonale** pedestrian precinct; **zona verde** (*di abitato*) green area
'zonzo ['dzondzo]: **a ~** *av*, **andare a ~** to wander about, stroll about
zoo ['dzɔo] *sm inv* zoo
zoolo'gia [dzoolo'dʒia] *sf* zoology
zoppi'care [tsoppi'kare] *vi* to limp; to be shaky, rickety
'zoppo, -a ['tsɔppo] *ag* lame; (*fig*: *mobile*) shaky, rickety
Z.T.L. *sigla f* (= *Zona a Traffico Limitato*) *controlled traffic zone*
'zucca, -che ['tsukka] *sf* (*Bot*) marrow; pumpkin
zucche'rare [tsukke'rare] *vt* to put sugar in; **zucche'rato, -a** *ag* sweet, sweetened
zuccheri'era [tsukke'rjɛra] *sf* sugar bowl
'zucchero ['tsukkero] *sm* sugar; **zucchero di canna** cane sugar; **zucchero filato** candy floss, cotton candy (US)
zuc'china [tsuk'kina] *sf* courgette (BRIT), zucchini (US)
'zuffa ['tsuffa] *sf* brawl
'zuppa ['tsuppa] *sf* soup; (*fig*) mixture, muddle; **zuppa inglese** (*Cuc*) *dessert made with sponge cake, custard and chocolate*, ≈ trifle (BRIT)
'zuppo, -a ['tsuppo] *ag*: **~ (di)** drenched (with), soaked (with)

Italian in focus

Introduction

Italian in focus gives you an introduction to various aspects of Italy and the Italian language. The following pages help you get to know the country where the language is spoken and the people who speak it.

Practical language tips and helpful notes on common translation difficulties will enable you to become a more confident Italian speaker. A useful correspondence section gives you all the information you need to be able to communicate effectively.

We've also included a number of links to useful websites, which will give you the opportunity to read more about Italy and the Italian language.

We hope you will enjoy using your *Italian in focus* supplement. We are sure it will help you find out more about Italy and Italians and become more confident in writing and speaking Italian.

Cominciamo!

Italy and its regions

Italy's neighbours

Italian is an official language in two Swiss cantons – Ticino and Grigioni, in the republic of San Marino and in Vatican City. Italian is also spoken in Malta, part of Croatia, and part of Slovenia.

Italy and its regions

The six biggest Italian cities

City	*Name of inhabitants*	*Population*
Roma	i romani	2,542,003
Milano	i milanesi	1,272,898
Napoli	i napoletani	1,000,449
Torino	i torinesi	867,857
Palermo	i palermitani	679,430
Genova	i genovesi	601,338

Italy consists of the mainland and two large islands, Sardegna and Sicilia, together with smaller islands such as Elba and Capri.

There are 20 administrative regions, five of which are *regioni autonome*, which have more decision-making powers than the others. Three of the 'autonomous regions' are in the north – Valle d'Aosta, Friuli-Venezia Giulia and Trentino-Alto Adige. The other two are the islands of Sardegna and Sicilia. Central government retains jurisdiction for matters such as defence, foreign affairs and the legal system, which affect the country as a whole.

Italy has only been a unified country since 1870. Before then parts of the peninsula were under the control of various countries, such as Spain, Austria and France. There was, and still is, a strong regional identity, with many people speaking one of the diverse local dialects. Nowadays everyone learns standard Italian at school; however many people speak *dialetto* with neighbours, friends and family.

As is often the case in areas bordering other countries, there are some bilingual communities. For example, in the Trentino-Alto Adige area in the far north of Italy, the majority language is German.

A snapshot of Italy

- In area, Italy (301, 323 km^2) is somewhat bigger than the UK (244,110 km^2).
- The Po (652 km) is Italy's longest river. It rises in the Alps and flows into the Adriatic near Venice.
- The population of Italy is about 58.4 million, which is slightly less than that of the UK. The birth rate is very low (1.2 children per woman). Deaths outnumber births.
- The Italian economy is the fourth biggest in the EU and seventh biggest in the world.
- Italy is the world's biggest wine-producing country.
- Gran Paradiso (4061) is Italy's highest peak.
- About 37 million tourists visit Italy every year, making it the 5th most popular tourist destination in the world.
- Italy has four active volcanoes: Etna, Vesuvius, Stromboli and Vulcano. Etna erupts frequently and is Europe's most active volcano.

Some useful links are:

www. governo.it
Website of the Italian government.
www.istat.it
The Italian statistics office.
www.enit.it
Italian state tourist board.

The Italian-speaking world

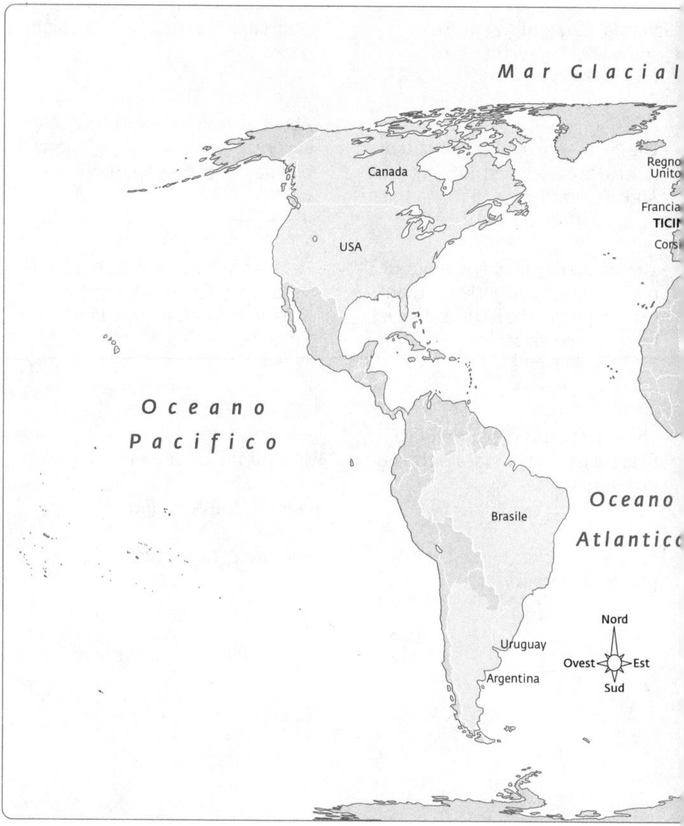

COUNTRIES OR REGIONS WHERE ITALIAN IS THE MOTHER TONGUE OR AN OFFICIAL LANGUAGE

Countries with large numbers of Italian speakers

Many Italians went to the Americas – particularly to the US and Argentina – and to Australia. There are 1 ½ million Italian speakers in Argentina and nearly a milion in the US. Italian has had a major influence on the way Spanish is spoken in Argentina

The Italian State

- Italy has dozens of political parties. The two main political groupings are the centre-right and the centre-left. The government tends to be formed by a coalition consisting of several parties.

- Italy has two houses of parliament: the Senate (*il Senato*) and the Chamber of Deputies (*la Camera dei Deputati*). The President of the Republic (*il Presidente della Repubblica*), who is the head of state, has a tenure of seven years.

- The Prime Minister (*il Presidente del Consiglio*) is the head of government.

- Inside Italy there are two tiny independent states: San Marino and Vatican City.

- San Marino is the smallest republic in Europe.

- Vatican City is the spiritual and administrative centre of the Roman Catholic Church. It has two official languages, Italian and Latin.

Italian words that have travelled the world

An important part of the language Italians took to foreign countries was to do with food – many immigrants opened cafés and restaurants. These days people all over the world drink cappuccinos and espressos, and eat ciabatta, spaghetti, minestrone and pizza.

While everyone is familiar with these food items, they may not realize that the Italian words themselves have interesting, highly descriptive meanings. Here are just a few:

- cappuccino
  This comes from the word capuchin. Capuchins are friars whose habits are brown – the colour of cappuccino coffee.

- ciabatta
  This means 'slipper'. The bread has this name because of its shape.

- macchiato
  macchiato means 'stained' and describes the look of a dark coffee with a little spot of milk on it .

- spaghetti
  spago means 'string' – so *spaghetti* are 'little strings'. There's another pasta called *orecchiette*. If you bear in mind that *un orecchio* is an ear, you can probably guess what this pasta looks like.

- tiramisù
  This word doesn't describe the appearance of the dessert, but the effect it has, as it means 'pick-me-up' (a reference to the stimulating effect of the coffee it contains).

- vermicelli
  This kind of pasta is very, very thin, and its name means 'little worms'.

Italian words used in English

Apart from lots of words to do with food, there are other Italian words that are very often used in English. Here are a few interesting examples:

• solo
This means 'alone' in Italian and was originally borrowed as a musical term – but it's now used in all kinds of contexts.

• fiasco
English has borrowed only one of this word's two senses: the other one is 'wine bottle'!

• piano
This is the Italian for 'soft'. When the pianoforte was invented it was so called because it could be played either soft (*piano*), or loud (*forte*), unlike its predecessor, the harpsichord.

• prima donna
This word for leading lady means 'first woman'. This is another musical term which has come to be used more generally.

• bimbo
Unlike in English, in Italian this is not a derogatory word for a woman – it just means 'little boy'. *Una bimba* is a little girl.

• al fresco
In Italian this doesn't mean 'outside' but 'in the cool', and in a figurative sense, 'in jail'.

English words used in Italian

Italians have as great an appetite for English words as other people have for Italian food. Words from every conceivable field are borrowed; daily life, popular culture, science, computing, sport, business and so on.

- Countless words are borrowed in their original form:

lo stress	*la privacy*
lo shopping	*il gay*
il fast food	*il blues*
il jazz	*lo show*
il talk show	*il computer*
il mouse	*il golf*
lo sport	*il supporter,*
il record	*il training*
il manager	*il target.*

In the plural, these words get a plural article (*i*, *gli* or *le*) but no final 's':

Singular	Plural
il talk show	*i talk show*
lo sport	*gli sport*
la star	*le star*

- Other words are Italianized, but still recognizably English:

chattare	to chat
craccare	to crack
dribblare	to dribble
sprintare	to sprint
scrollare	to scroll
standardizzare	to standardize
interfaccia	interface
reality	reality show

- Some words look English, but have taken on a different meaning:

un box	a garage
un golf	a cardigan (it also means the sport)
un ticket	a prescription charge
uno smoking	a dinner jacket
uno spot	a tv *or* radio advert

Improving your pronunciation

Italian sounds

Vowels

Each English vowel can be pronounced in several quite different ways – think of the sound the letter **i** has, for example, in the words m**i**lk, k**i**nd and c**i**rcus. Italian vowels vary much less in their pronunciation:

a – is like the ***a*** in father
e – is like the ***e*** in set
i – is like the ***ee*** in sheep OR is pronounced like ***y*** in yard
o – is like the ***o*** in orange
u – is like the ***oo*** in soon

Avoid saying Italian words like their English lookalikes: the *i* in *Milano* and in *aprile*, for example is the long ee sound, not the short I used in Milan and April.

Unlike English, Italian is pronounced exactly as it is written, so *interessante*, for example, has five syllables, with a clearly pronounced vowel in each one: *in-te-res-san-te*.

- Italian vowels never disappear as they do in English words like interesting (int-res-ting) and camera (cam-ra). Always pronounce them fully.

- Italian vowels never have the indistinct 'uh' sound to be heard at the end of many English words, for example, hos<u>tel</u>, hospi<u>tal</u> and cir<u>cus</u>. Always pronounce Italian vowels clearly.

- When ***i*** is pronounced ***y***, make sure that it's ***y*** as in yard, not ***y*** as in very:

andiamo	an-dya-mo (not an-dy-a-mo)
ravioli	rav-yo-lee (not ra-vee-o-lee)
stazione	sta-zyo-ne (not sta-zee-o-ne)

Improving your pronunciation

Consonants

- The presence of a double consonant in Italian makes the consonant sound longer: *cat-ti-vo, inte-res-san-te, An-na*.

- ***c*** followed by ***e*** or ***i***, is pronounced **tch** as in *centro* and *facile*.

- ***ch*** is pronounced **k**, as in *fuochi* and *chiuso*.

- ***g*** followed by ***e*** and ***i*** is pronounced ***j*** as in *leggero* and *giardino*.

- ***gh*** is pronounced like ***g*** in get, as in *lunghi* and *spaghetti*.

- ***gl*** followed by ***e*** and ***i*** is normally pronounced like the ***lli*** in million, for example *luglio, bagagli*.

- ***gn*** is pronounced **ny**, for example *gnocchi, giugno*.

- ***sc*** followed by ***e*** and ***i*** is pronounced **sh**, as in *lasciare* and *sciare*.

Stress

- Italian words are usually stressed on the next to the last syllable, for example *cucina, studente, straniero, diciassette, parlare, avere*.

- If a word is spelled with an accent on the last vowel, for example, *fedeltà, università, però, così, caffè*, put the stress on this vowel.

- Some words are stressed on other syllables; the 'they' form of verbs, for example, usually stresses the second to last syllable: *capiscono* (= they understand); *parlano* (= they speak).

- Other words, such as *subito, macchina, vendere* and *camera* stress the first syllable. Be aware that words aren't always stressed as you'd expect and when in doubt look in the dictionary: you'll see that in each headword there's a mark that looks like an apostrophe. The syllable immediately following this apostrophe is the one you stress.

A useful link is:
www.accademiadellacrusca.it
National language academy of Italy.

Improving your fluency

Conversational words and phrases

In English we insert lots of words and phrases, such as *so*, *then*, *by the way*, into our conversation, to give our thoughts a structure and often to show our attitude. The Italian words below do the same thing. If you use them you'll sound more fluent and natural.

- ***allora***
  Allora, *che facciamo stasera?* (= so)

- ***va bene***
  Va bene, *ho capito.* (= okay)

- ***ecco***
  Ecco *perché non sono venuti.* (= that's)
  Ecco *Mario!* (= here's)
  Eccolo! (= there ... is)

- ***forse***
  Sì, ma **forse** *hanno ragione.* (= maybe)

- ***certo***
  Certo *che puoi.* (= of course)

- ***dunque***
  Dunque, *come dicevo ...* (= well)
  Dunque *ha ragione lui.* (= so)

- ***può darsi***
  Sì, lo so, ma **può darsi** *che ...* (= perhaps)

- ***purtroppo***
  Sì, **purtroppo**. (= unfortunately)

- ***sinceramente***
  Sinceramente, *non m'importa niente.* (= really)

- ***comunque***
  Comunque, *non è sempre così.* (= however)

- ***senz'altro***
  Mi scriverai? – **Senz'altro**! (= of course)
  È **senz'altro** *meglio lui.* (= definitely)

- ***davvero***
  Ha pagato lui. – **Davvero**? (= really)

Improving your fluency

Varying the words you use to get your message across will also make you sound more fluent in Italian. For example, instead of *Mi piace molto il calcio*, you could say *Il calcio è la mia passione*. Here are some other suggestions.

Saying what you like or dislike

Adoro le ciliege.	I love ...
Mi è piaciuto molto il tuo regalo.	I (really) liked ...
Non mi piace il tennis.	I don't like ...
Il suo ultimo film *non mi piace per niente.*	I don't like ... (at all).
Detesto mentire.	I hate ...

Expressing your opinion

Credo che sia giusto.	I think ...
Penso che costino di più.	I think ...
Sono sicuro/sicura che ti piacerà.	I'm sure ...
Secondo me è stato un errore.	In my opinion ...
A mio parere vincerà lui.	In my opinion ...
A me sembra che qualche volta ...	It seems to me ...

Agreeing or disagreeing

Ha ragione.	You're right.
Giusto!	Quite right!
(Non) sono d'accordo.	I (don't) agree.
Non direi.	I wouldn't say so.
Certo!	Of course!

Correspondence

The following section on correspondence has been designed to help you communicate confidently in written as well as spoken Italian. Sample letters, e-mails and sections on text messaging and making telephone calls will ensure that you have all the vocabulary you need to correspond successfully.

Text messaging

un sms *(esse emme esse)* = text message
mandare un sms a qualcuno = to text somebody

Abbreviation	Italian	English
+ tardi	*più tardi*	later
+o-	*più o meno*	more or less
ba	*bacio*	kiss
bn	*bene*	well
C6?	*ci sei?*	are you there?
cs	*cosa*	what
c ved	*ci vediamo*	see you soon
dv	*dove*	where
k6?	*chi sei?*	who are you?
ke cs?	*che cosa?*	what?
tu6	*tu sei*	you are
k	*che*	that, what
qd	*quando*	when
nn	*non*	not
k fai?	*che fai?*	what are you doing?
qnd	*quando*	when
TVB	*ti voglio bene*	I love you
TVTB	*ti voglio tanto bene*	I love you so much
x	*per*	for
xke	*perché*	because
xke?	*perché?*	why?
TAT	*ti amo tanto*	love you loads

Writing an e-mail

| File | Modifica | Visualizza | Inserisci | Formato | Strumenti | Messaggio |

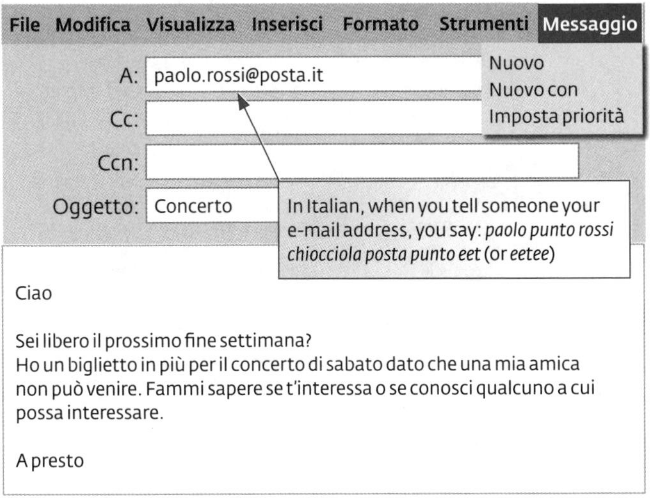

Nuovo
Nuovo con
Imposta priorità

A: paolo.rossi@posta.it

Cc:

Ccn:

Oggetto: Concerto

In Italian, when you tell someone your e-mail address, you say: *paolo punto rossi chiocciola posta punto eet* (or *eetee*)

Ciao

Sei libero il prossimo fine settimana?
Ho un biglietto in più per il concerto di sabato dato che una mia amica non può venire. Fammi sapere se t'interessa o se conosci qualcuno a cui possa interessare.

A presto

file	file		*rispondi al mittente*	reply to sender
modifica	edit		*rispondi a tutti*	reply to all
visualizza	view		*inoltrare*	to forward
formato	format		*allega*	attachment
inserisci	insert		*A*	to
?	help		*Cc (copia carbone)*	cc (carbon copy)
strumenti	tools		*Ccn (copia carbone nascosta)*	bcc (blind carbon copy)
scrivere	to compose			
help	help		*oggetto*	subject
invia	send		*da*	from
crea messaggio	new message		*dat*	sent

Here is some additional useful Internet vocabulary:

ADSL	broadband	*Internet*	the Internet
avanti	forward	*la Rete*	the (World-Wide) Web
cartella	folder	*motore di recerca*	search engine
cercare	to search	*navigare in Internet*	to surf the Net
cliccare	to click	*pagina iniziale*	home page
collegamenti	links	*pagina web*	web page
collegarsi	to log on	*prefereti*	favorites
copiare	to copy	*programma*	program
cronologia	history	*provider*	Internet Service Provider
domande frequenti	FAQs	*salvare*	to save
fare doppio click	to double-click	*scaricare*	to download
finestra	window	*scollegarsi*	to log off
foglio di calcolo	spreadsheet	*sito Internet*	website
icona	icon	*stampare*	print
impostazioni	settings	*tagliare*	to cut
incollare	to paste	*tartiera*	keyboard
indietro	back	*visualizzare*	to view

Writing a personal letter

Town/city you are writing from, and the date → *Siena, 5 giugno 2006*

Cara Maria,

No capital for start of letter

ti ringrazio moltissimo del biglietto che mi hai mandato per il mio compleanno, che è arrivato proprio il giorno della mia festa!

Mi dispiace che tu non sia potuta venire a Milano per il mio compleanno e spero che ti sia ripresa dopo l'influenza. Mi piacerebbe poterti incontrare presto perché ho molte novità da raccontarti. Forse tra due settimane verrò a Torino con degli amici. Pensi di essere libera il giorno 12? Ti telefono la prossima settimana, così ci mettiamo d'accordo.

Baci,

Anna

Writing a personal letter

Other ways of starting a personal letter	Other ways of ending a personal letter
Carissima Maria *Mia cara Maria* *Cari Luigi e Silvia*	*Un abbraccio* *Bacioni* *Con affetto* *A presto*

Some useful phrases

Ti ringrazio per la tua lettera.	Thank you for your letter.
Mi ha fatto piacere ricevere tue notizie.	It was lovely to hear from you.
Scusami se non ti ho scritto prima.	I'm sorry I didn't reply sooner.
Salutami tanto Lucia.	Give my love to Lucia.
Tanti saluti anche da Paolo.	Paolo sends his best wishes.
Scrivi presto!	Write soon!

Writing a formal letter

Your own name and address →

Paola Rossotti
Via San Francesco, 28
10100 Torino

19 settembre 2006 ← Date

Agenzia immobiliare
Il giardino
Via Roma, 18
47900 Rimini

← Name and address of the person or company you are writing to

OGGETTO: Richiesta di rimborso

Egr. signori,
vi scrivo per presentare reclamo in merito all'appartamento che ho affittato nel condominio Le Torri per il periodo 5-12 agosto. Avevo espressamente richiesto un appartamento con due camere e invece mi è stato assegnato un appartamento con una camera sola; mancava inoltre il condizionatore d'aria di cui il contratto di locazione fa specifica menzione.
Chiedo quindi un rimborso di 1000 euro comprensivo della differenza tra la tariffa che ho pagato per un appartamento con due camere e aria condizionata e quella per un appartamento con una camera sola senza aria condizionata, e di un risarcimento per i disagi subiti.

Allego fotocopia del contratto di locazione.

Distinti saluti

Paola Rossotti

Writing a formal letter

Other ways of starting a formal letter	Other ways of ending a formal letter
Egregio signore, *Gentile signora,* *Egregio Signor Paolozzo,* *Gentile Signora Paolozzo,* *Spett. Ditta,* (when writing to a firm)	*Distinti saluti* *La prego di accettare i miei più distinti saluti* *Cordiali saluti*

Some useful phrases

La ringrazio della sua lettera del ...	Thank you for your letter of ...
In riferimento a ...	With reference to ...
Vi prego di inviarmi ...	Please send me ...
In attesa di una sua risposta la ringrazio per l'attenzione.	I look forward to hearing from you.
La ringrazio in anticipo per ...	Thank you in advance for ...

Agenzia immobiliare
Il giardino
Via Roma, 18
47900 Rimini

The house number comes after the street name, and the postcode comes before the name of the town.

Making a call

Asking for information

Qual è il prefisso di Livorno?	What's the code for Livorno?
Cosa devo fare per ottenere la linea esterna?	How do I get an outside line?
Può darmi il numero dell'interno della Signora Busi?	Could you give me Ms Busi's extension number?

When your number answers

Buongiorno, c'è Andrea?	Hello! Is Andrea there?
Potrei parlare con Lucia, per favore?	Could I speak to Lucia, please?
Parla la signora de Maggio?	Is that Mrs de Maggio?
Può chiedergli/chiederle di richiamarmi?	Could you ask him/her to call me back?
Richiamo fra mezz'ora.	I'll call back in half an hour.
Posso lasciare un messaggio, per favore?	Could I leave a message, please?

When you answer the telephone

Pronto!	Hello!
Chi parla?	Who's speaking?
Sono Marco.	It's Marco speaking.
Sì, sono io.	Speaking.
Vuole lasciare un messaggio?	Would you like to leave a message?

What you may hear

Chi devo dire?	Who shall I say is calling?
Le passo la comunicazione.	I'm putting you through now.
Attenda in linea.	Please hold.
Non risponde nessuno.	There's no reply.
La linea è occupata.	The line is engaged (*Brit*)/busy (*US*).
Vuole lasciare un messaggio?	Would you like to leave a message?

If you have a problem

Scusi, ho sbagliato numero.	Sorry, I dialled the wrong number.
La linea è molto disturbata.	This is a very bad line.
Qui non c'è campo.	There's no signal here.
Ho la batteria quasi scarica.	My battery's low.
Non ti sento.	I can't hear you.

Italian phrases and sayings

In Italian, as in many languages, people use vivid expressions based on images from their experience of real life. We've grouped the common expressions below according to the type of image they use. For fun, we have given you the word-for-word translation as well as the English equivalent.

Food and drink

dire pane al pane e vino al vino → to call a spade a spade
word for word: *to call bread bread and wine wine*

Se non è zuppa è pan bagnato. → It's much of a muchness.
word for word: *if it's not soup it's wet bread*

rendere pan per focaccia → to give as good as you get
word for word: *to give bread for focaccia*

avere le mani in pasta → to have a finger in the pie
word for word: *to have your hands in the dough*

lavorare per la pagnotta → to earn your living
word for word: *to work for your loaf*

Ormai la frittata è fatta. → The damage is done.
word for word: *the omelette is made now*

Weather

fare il bello e il cattivo tempo → to do as one pleases
word for word: *to make the good and bad weather*

una tempesta in un bicchier d'acqua → a storm in a teacup
word for word: *a storm in a glass of water*

sposa bagnata sposa fortunata → rain on your wedding day is lucky
word for word: *wet bride, lucky bride*

Italian phrases and sayings

Animals

prendere due piccioni con una fava → to kill two birds with one stone
word for word: *to get two pigeons with one broad bean*

Quando il gatto non c'è i topi ballano. → When the cat's away the mice will play.
word for word: *when the cat's not there the mice dance*

Chi dorme non piglia pesci. → The early bird catches the worm.
word for word: *if you're asleep you don't catch any fish*

In bocca al lupo! → Break a leg!
word for word: *into the wolf's mouth!*

Meglio un uovo oggi che una gallina domani. → A bird in the hand is worth two in the bush.
word for word: *better an egg today than a hen tomorrow*

L'ospite è come il pesce, dopo tre giorni puzza. → It's nice when they come and it's nice when they go.
word for word: *guests are like fish – after three days they start to smell*

Parts of the body

essere un pugno in un occhio → to be an eyesore
word for word: *to be a punch in the eye*

Chi non ha testa ha gambe. → Use your head to save your legs.
word for word: *people who have no head have legs*

rimanere a bocca aperta → to be amazed
word for word: *to be left open-mouthed*

avere le mani bucate → to spend money like water
word for word: *to have holes in your hands*

Italian phrases and sayings

Clothes

nascere con la camicia → to be born with a silver spoon in your mouth
word for word: *to be born with with a shirt on*

sudare sette camicie → to work like a dog
word for word: *to sweat seven shirts*

tirare qualcuno per la giacca → to twist someone's arm
word for word: *to pull someone by the coat*

Plants

Se sono rose fioriranno. → The proof of the pudding is in the eating.
word for word: *if they're roses they'll bloom*

fare di ogni erba un fascio → to lump everything together
word for word: *to put all the grasses into one bundle*

Non sono tutte rose e fiori. → It's not all a bed of roses.
word for word: *it's not all roses and flowers*

Colours

Rosso di sera, bel tempo si spera. → Red sky at night, shepherd's delight.
word for word: *(if the sky's) red at night you can hope for good weather*

vedere tutto nero → to look on the black side
word for word: *to see everything as black*

Al buio tutti i gatti sono neri. → At night all cats are grey.
word for word: *in the dark all cats are black*

Some common translation difficulties

On the following pages we have shown some of the translation difficulties you are most likely to come across. We hope that the tips we have given will help you to avoid these common pitfalls when writing or speaking Italian.

How to say 'you' in Italian

There are three ways of saying *you* in Italian: ***tu*** and ***lei*** are used to speak to one person, and ***voi*** is used to speak to more than one person.

- Use ***tu*** when you are speaking to a person you know well, or to a child. If you are a student you can call another student ***tu***.

  And how old are you, Roberto? → *E **tu**, Roberto, quanti anni hai?*

- Use ***lei*** when speaking to strangers, or anyone you're not on familiar terms with. As you get to know someone better they may suggest that you call each other ***tu*** instead of ***lei***. In shops, hotels and restaurants customers are always addressed as ***lei***.

  Would you like a coffee too, madam? → *Vuole un caffè anche **lei**, signora?*

It may seem potentially confusing that ***lei*** also means 'she', but in practice it's quite obvious that if someone speaks directly to you using ***lei***, the meaning is ***you***.

- Use ***voi*** when you are speaking to more than one person.

  Where are you boys from? → ***Voi** ragazzi, di dove siete?*

'You' has to go with the verb in English, but in Italian you often use the verb alone:

How old are you? → *Quanti anni hai?*
You speak good Italian, madam. → *Parla bene l'italiano, signora.*
You're young. → *Siete giovani.*

Some common translation difficulties

You use the words ***tu***, ***lei*** and ***voi*** to attract someone's attention, or for the sake of emphasis.

Tu cosa pensi?	→ What do you think?
Lei quale preferisce?	→ Which one do you prefer?

Showing possession

In English -*'s* is a common way of showing who or what something belongs to. In Italian you have to use ***di***:

my brother**'s** car	→ *la macchina* ***di*** *mio fratello*
Maria**'s** house	→ *la casa* ***di*** *Maria*

Translating 'to like'

There are two ways of saying you like something, depending whether it is singular or plural:

I like Italy. → ***Mi piace*** *l'Italia.*
word-for-word meaning of Italian: ***to me is pleasing Italy***

I like dogs. → ***Mi piacciono*** *i cani.*
word-for-word meaning of Italian: ***to me are pleasing dogs***

If you bear in mind the word-for-word meaning of the Italian you'll have no trouble deciding whether to use ***piace*** or ***piacciono***.

To say 'we like', change ***mi*** to ***ci***.

We like the sea.	→ ***Ci piace*** *il mare.*
We like his films.	→ ***Ci piacciono*** *i suoi film.*

Some common translation difficulties

If you want to ask someone if they like something:

• Use ***ti*** when asking someone you know well.

Do you like my shoes? → ***Ti piacciono*** *le mie scarpe?*

• Use ***le*** when speaking politely

Do you like Italian food, madam? → ***Le piace*** *la cucina italiana, signora?*

• Use ***vi*** when talking to more than one person.

Do you like football, boys? → ***Vi piace*** *il calcio, ragazzi?*

Translating *-ing*

The English *-ing* form is used to talk about something you are doing or were doing. This can be translated into Italian by using the Italian present continuous tense (the verb form that ends ***-ando*** or ***-endo***).

They were gett**ing** bored. → *Si stavano annoi**ando**.*
He's read**ing** the paper. → *Sta legg**endo** il giornale.*
She's talk**ing** to Mum. → *Sta parl**ando** con la mamma.*

It is, however, just as common to translate the *-ing* form in English with the present simple tense in Italian.

He's read**ing** the paper. → ***Legge*** *il giornale.*
She's talk**ing** to Mum. → ***Parla*** *con la mamma.*

In other cases the Italian infinitive (the verb form that ends in ***-are***, ***-ere***, or ***-ire***) is often used where the *-ing* form is used in English.

• Use the infinitive when talking about activities:

I love **reading**. → *Mi piace moltissimo **leggere**.*
We don't like **walking**. → *Non ci piace **camminare**.*
Smoking is bad for you. → ***Fumare*** *fa male.*

Some common translation difficulties

Use the infinitive to translate prepositions such as without + *-ing* (***senza*** + infinitive), before + *-ing* (***prima di*** + infinitive), after + *-ing* (***dopo aver*** + past participle).

He went away **without saying** anything. → *È andato via **senza dire** niente.*
Before opening the packet, read the instructions. → ***Prima di aprire** il pacchetto, leggi le istruzioni.*
After making a phone call she went out. → ***Dopo aver** telefonato è uscita.*

More on prepositions

Sentences that have no preposition in English may contain a preposition in Italian. The dictionary can help you with these. For example:

They started **laughing**. → *Hanno cominciato **a ridere**.*
Have you finished **eating**? → *Hai finito **di mangiare**?*
When did you stop **smoking**? → *Quando hai smesso **di fumare**?*

Saying Sorry

- To apologize about something, use ***scusi*** to someone you're on formal terms with, and ***scusa*** to a friend. Use ***scusate*** to more than one person.

Sorry. → ***Scusi.***
Sorry I'm late. → ***Scusi** il ritardo.*
Sorry, Paola, I've got to go. → ***Scusa**, Paola, devo andare.*
Sorry to disturb you. → ***Scusate** il disturbo.*

- **Scusi** is also used to mean '*excuse me*' when you stop somebody to ask something.

Excuse me, where is the station? → ***Scusi**, dov'è la stazione?*

Some common translation difficulties

When you haven't heard what someone said, say ***come, scusi***?

- To express regret use ***mi dispiace***:

My grandfather has died. – Oh, **I'm sorry**.	→ *È morto mio nonno. – Oh, **mi dispiace**.*
I haven't got time, **sorry**.	→ *Non ho tempo, **mi dispiace**.*
I'm sorry but I can't come.	→ ***Mi dispiace** ma non posso venire.*
I'm sorry for them.	→ ***Mi dispiace** per loro.*

Translating 'to be'

'To be' usually corresponds to ***essere***, but remember:

- In phrases describing how you feel, use ***avere***:

I **am** hot/cold	→ ***ho** caldo/freddo*
they **are** hungry/thirsty	→ ***hanno** fame/sete*
he **is** scared	→ ***ha** paura*

- To describe the weather, use ***fare***:

It**'s** nice weather today.	→ ***Fa** bel tempo oggi.*

- To say your age, use ***avere***:

I'**m** fifteen.	→ ***Ho** quindici anni.*

- To talk about your health, use ***stare***:

I'**m** fine, thanks.	→ ***Sto** bene, grazie*

Some common translation difficulties

Translating 'have'

'Have' or 'have got' usually correspond to ***avere***:

I've **got** two brothers.	→ ***Ho*** *due fratelli.*
Have you **got** a bike?	→ ***Hai*** *una bici?*
I**'ve** spent a lot of money.	→ ***Ho*** *speso molti soldi.*
What **have** you done?	→ *Cos'* ***hai*** *fatto?*

Remember, though that 'have' and 'has' are translated by ***essere***.

- In the perfect tense of some common verbs such as to go (*andare*), to come (*venire*) and to arrive (*arrivare*):

Where **have** they gone?	→ *Dove* ***sono*** *andati?*
She **has** come too.	→ ***È*** *venuta anche lei.*
We**'ve** arrived.	→ ***Siamo*** *arrivati.*

- In the perfect tense of all reflexive verbs:

I**'ve** hurt myself.	→ *Mi* ***sono*** *fatto male.*
Has she had a good time?	→ *Si* ***è*** *divertita?*

a

A [eɪ] *n (Mus)* la *m*
A2 *n abbr* (BRIT: *Scol*) *seconda parte del diploma di studi superiori chiamato "A level"*

KEYWORD

a [ə] (*before vowel or silent h* **an**) *indef art* **1** un (uno + *s impure, gn, pn, ps, x, z*), una *f* (un' + *vowel*); **a book** un libro; **a mirror** uno specchio; **an apple** una mela; **she's a doctor** è medico
2 (*instead of the number "one"*) un(o), *f* una; **a year ago** un anno fa; **a hundred/thousand** *etc* **pounds** cento/mille *etc* sterline
3 (*in expressing ratios, prices etc*) a, per; **3 a day/week** 3 al giorno/alla settimana; **10 km an hour** 10 km all'ora; **£5 a person** 5 sterline a persona *or* per persona

A.A. *n abbr* (= *Alcoholics Anonymous*) AA; (BRIT: = *Automobile Association*) ≈ A.C.I. *m*
A.A.A. (US) *n abbr* (= *American Automobile Association*) ≈ A.C.I. *m*
aback [ə'bæk] *adv* **to be taken ~** essere sbalordito(-a)
abandon [ə'bændən] *vt* abbandonare ▷ *n* **with ~** sfrenatamente, spensieratamente
abattoir ['æbətwɑːʳ] (BRIT) *n* mattatoio
abbey ['æbɪ] *n* abbazia, badia
abbreviation [əbriːvɪ'eɪʃən] *n* abbreviazione *f*
abdomen ['æbdəmən] *n* addome *m*
abduct [æb'dʌkt] *vt* rapire
abide [ə'baɪd] *vt* **I can't ~ it/him** non lo posso soffrire *or* sopportare; **abide by** *vt fus* conformarsi a
ability [ə'bɪlɪtɪ] *n* abilità *f inv*
able ['eɪbl] *adj* capace; **to be ~ to do sth** essere capace di fare qc, poter fare qc
abnormal [æb'nɔːməl] *adj* anormale
aboard [ə'bɔːd] *adv* a bordo ▷ *prep* a bordo di
abolish [ə'bɔlɪʃ] *vt* abolire
abolition [æbəu'lɪʃən] *n* abolizione *f*
abort [ə'bɔːt] *vt* abortire; **abortion** [ə'bɔːʃən] *n* aborto; **to have an abortion** abortire

KEYWORD

about [ə'baut] *adv* **1** (*approximately*) circa, quasi; **about a hundred/thousand** *etc* un centinaio/migliaio *etc*, circa cento/mille *etc*; **it takes about 10 hours** ci vogliono circa 10 ore; **at about 2 o'clock** verso le 2; **I've just about finished** ho quasi finito
2 (*referring to place*) qua e là, in giro; **to leave things lying about** lasciare delle cose in giro; **to run about** correre qua e là; **to walk about** camminare
3: **to be about to do sth** stare per fare qc

▷ *prep* **1** (*relating to*) su, di; **a book about London** un libro su Londra; **what is it about?** di che si tratta?; (*book, film etc*) di cosa tratta?; **we talked about it** ne abbiamo parlato; **what** *or* **how about doing this?** che ne dici di fare questo?
2 (*referring to place*): **to walk about the town** camminare per la città; **her clothes were scattered about the room** i suoi vestiti erano sparsi *or* in giro per tutta la stanza

above [ə'bʌv] *adv, prep* sopra; **mentioned ~** suddetto; **~ all** soprattutto
abroad [ə'brɔːd] *adv* all'estero
abrupt [ə'brʌpt] *adj* (*sudden*) improvviso(-a); (*gruff, blunt*) brusco(-a)
abscess ['æbsɪs] *n* ascesso
absence ['æbsəns] *n* assenza
absent ['æbsənt] *adj* assente; **absent-minded** *adj* distratto(-a)
absolute ['æbsəluːt] *adj* assoluto(-a); **absolutely** [-'luːtlɪ] *adv* assolutamente
absorb [əb'zɔːb] *vt* assorbire; **to be ~ed in a book** essere immerso in un libro; **absorbent cotton** [əb'zɔːbənt-] (*US*) *n* cotone *m* idrofilo; **absorbing** *adj* avvincente, molto interessante
abstain [əb'steɪn] *vi* **to ~ (from)** astenersi (da)
abstract ['æbstrækt] *adj* astratto(-a)
absurd [əb'səːd] *adj* assurdo(-a)
abundance [ə'bʌndəns] *n* abbondanza
abundant [ə'bʌndənt] *adj* abbondante
abuse [*n* ə'bjuːs, *vb* a'bjuːz] *n* abuso; (*insults*) ingiurie *fpl* ▷ *vt* abusare di; **abusive** *adj* ingiurioso(-a)
abysmal [ə'bɪzməl] *adj* spaventoso(-a)
academic [ækə'dɛmɪk] *adj* accademico(-a); (*pej: issue*) puramente formale ▷ *n* universitario(-a); **academic year** *n* anno accademico
academy [ə'kædəmɪ] *n* (*learned body*) accademia; (*school*) scuola privata; **academy of music** *n* conservatorio
accelerate [æk'sɛləreɪt] *vt, vi* accelerare; **acceleration** *n* accelerazione *f*; **accelerator** *n* acceleratore *m*
accent ['æksɛnt] *n* accento
accept [ək'sɛpt] *vt* accettare; **acceptable** *adj* accettabile; **acceptance** *n* accettazione *f*
access ['æksɛs] *n* accesso; **accessible** [æk'sɛsəbl] *adj* accessibile
accessory [æk'sɛsərɪ] *n* accessorio; (*Law*): **~ to** complice *m/f* di
accident ['æksɪdənt] *n* incidente *m*; (*chance*) caso; **I've had an ~** ho avuto un incidente; **by ~** per caso; **accidental** [-'dɛntl] *adj* accidentale; **accidentally** [-'dɛntəlɪ] *adv* per caso; **Accident and Emergency Department** *n* (*BRIT*) pronto soccorso; **accident insurance** *n* assicurazione *f* contro gli infortuni
acclaim [ə'kleɪm] *n* acclamazione *f*
accommodate [ə'kɔmədeɪt] *vt* alloggiare; (*oblige, help*) favorire
accommodation [əkɔmə'deɪʃən] (*US* **accommodations**) *n* alloggio
accompaniment [ə'kʌmpənɪmənt] *n* accompagnamento
accompany [ə'kʌmpənɪ] *vt* accompagnare
accomplice [ə'kʌmplɪs] *n* complice *m/f*
accomplish [ə'kʌmplɪʃ] *vt* compiere; (*goal*) raggiungere; **accomplishment** *n* compimento; realizzazione *f*
accord [ə'kɔːd] *n* accordo ▷ *vt* accordare; **of his own ~** di propria iniziativa; **accordance** *n* **in accordance with** in conformità con; **according**: **according to** *prep* secondo; **accordingly** *adv* in conformità
account [ə'kaunt] *n* (*Comm*) conto;

(*report*) descrizione *f*; **accounts** *npl* (*Comm*) conti *mpl*; **of no ~** di nessuna importanza; **on ~** in acconto; **on no ~** per nessun motivo; **on ~ of** a causa di; **to take into ~, take ~ of** tener conto di; **account for** *vt fus* spiegare; giustificare; **accountable** *adj* **accountable (to)** responsabile (verso); **accountant** [ə'kauntənt] *n* ragioniere(-a); **account number** *n* numero di conto

accumulate [ə'kju:mjuleɪt] *vt* accumulare ▷ *vi* accumularsi

accuracy ['ækjurəsɪ] *n* precisione *f*

accurate ['ækjurɪt] *adj* preciso(-a); **accurately** *adv* precisamente

accusation [ækju'zeɪʃən] *n* accusa

accuse [ə'kju:z] *vt* accusare; **accused** *n* accusato(-a)

accustomed [ə'kʌstəmd] *adj* **~ to** abituato(-a) a

ace [eɪs] *n* asso

ache [eɪk] *n* male *m*, dolore *m* ▷ *vi* (*be sore*) far male, dolere; **my head ~s** mi fa male la testa

achieve [ə'tʃi:v] *vt* (*aim*) raggiungere; (*victory, success*) ottenere; **achievement** *n* compimento; successo

acid ['æsɪd] *adj* acido(-a) ▷ *n* acido

acknowledge [ək'nɔlɪdʒ] *vt* (*letter: also:* **~ receipt of**) confermare la ricevuta di; (*fact*) riconoscere; **acknowledgement** *n* conferma; riconoscimento

acne ['æknɪ] *n* acne *f*

acorn ['eɪkɔ:n] *n* ghianda

acoustic [ə'ku:stɪk] *adj* acustico(-a)

acquaintance [ə'kweɪntəns] *n* conoscenza; (*person*) conoscente *m/f*

acquire [ə'kwaɪə^r] *vt* acquistare; **acquisition** [ækwɪ'zɪʃən] *n* acquisto

acquit [ə'kwɪt] *vt* assolvere; **to ~ o.s. well** comportarsi bene

acre ['eɪkə^r] *n* acro, ≈ 4047 m^2

acronym ['ækrənɪm] *n* acronimo

across [ə'krɔs] *prep* (*on the other side*) dall'altra parte di; (*crosswise*) attraverso ▷ *adv* dall'altra parte; in larghezza; **to run/swim ~** attraversare di corsa/a nuoto; **~ from** di fronte a

acrylic [ə'krɪlɪk] *adj* acrilico(-a)

act [ækt] *n* atto; (*in music-hall etc*) numero; (*Law*) decreto ▷ *vi* agire; (*Theatre*) recitare; (*pretend*) fingere ▷ *vt* (*part*) recitare; **to ~ as** agire da; **act up** (*inf*) *vi* (*person*) comportarsi male; (*knee, back, injury*) fare male; (*machine*) non funzionare; **acting** *adj* che fa le funzioni di ▷ *n* (*of actor*) recitazione *f*; (*activity*): **to do some acting** fare del teatro (*or* del cinema)

action ['ækʃən] *n* azione *f*; (*Mil*) combattimento; (*Law*) processo; **out of ~** fuori combattimento; fuori servizio; **to take ~** agire; **action replay** *n* (*TV*) replay *m inv*

activate ['æktɪveɪt] *vt* (*mechanism*) attivare

active ['æktɪv] *adj* attivo(-a); **actively** *adv* (*participate*) attivamente; (*discourage, dislike*) vivamente

activist ['æktɪvɪst] *n* attivista *m/f*

activity [æk'tɪvɪtɪ] *n* attività *f inv*; **activity holiday** *n vacanza organizzata con attività ricreative per ragazzi*

actor ['æktə^r] *n* attore *m*

actress ['æktrɪs] *n* attrice *f*

actual ['æktjuəl] *adj* reale, effettivo(-a)

> Be careful not to translate ***actual*** by the Italian word ***attuale***.

actually ['æktjuəlɪ] *adv* veramente; (*even*) addirittura

> Be careful not to translate ***actually*** by the Italian word ***attualmente***.

acupuncture ['ækjupʌŋktʃə^r] *n* agopuntura

acute [ə'kju:t] *adj* acuto(-a); (*mind, person*) perspicace

ad [æd] *n abbr* = **advertisement**

A.D. *adv abbr* (= *Anno Domini*) d.C.
adamant ['ædəmənt] *adj* irremovibile
adapt [ə'dæpt] *vt* adattare ▷ *vi* **to ~ (to)** adattarsi (a); **adapter, adaptor** *n* (*Elec*) adattatore *m*
add [æd] *vt* aggiungere ▷ *vi* **to ~ to** (*increase*) aumentare; **add up** *vt* (*figures*) addizionare ▷ *vi* (*fig*): **it doesn't add up** non ha senso; **add up to** *vt fus* (*Math*) ammontare a; (*fig*: *mean*) significare; **it doesn't add up to much** non è un granché
addict ['ædɪkt] *n* tossicomane *m/f*; (*fig*) fanatico(-a); **addicted** [ə'dɪktɪd] *adj* **to be addicted to** (*drink etc*) essere dedito(-a) a; (*fig*: *football etc*) essere tifoso(-a) di; **addiction** [ə'dɪkʃən] *n* (*Med*) tossicodipendenza; **addictive** [ə'dɪktɪv] *adj* che dà assuefazione
addition [ə'dɪʃən] *n* addizione *f*; (*thing added*) aggiunta; **in ~** inoltre; **in ~ to** oltre; **additional** *adj* supplementare
additive ['ædɪtɪv] *n* additivo
address [ə'drɛs] *n* indirizzo; (*talk*) discorso ▷ *vt* indirizzare; (*speak to*) fare un discorso a; (*issue*) affrontare; **my ~ is ...** il mio indirizzo è...; **address book** *n* rubrica
adequate ['ædɪkwɪt] *adj* adeguato(-a), sufficiente
adhere [əd'hɪə^r] *vi* **to ~ to** aderire a; (*fig*: *rule, decision*) seguire
adhesive [əd'hiːzɪv] *n* adesivo; **adhesive tape** *n* (BRIT: *for parcels etc*) nastro adesivo; (US *Med*) cerotto adesivo
adjacent [ə'dʒeɪsənt] *adj* adiacente; **~ to** accanto a
adjective ['ædʒɛktɪv] *n* aggettivo
adjoining [ə'dʒɔɪnɪŋ] *adj* accanto *inv*, adiacente
adjourn [ə'dʒəːn] *vt* rimandare ▷ *vi* essere aggiornato(-a)
adjust [ə'dʒʌst] *vt* aggiustare; (*change*) rettificare ▷ *vi* **to ~ (to)** adattarsi (a); **adjustable** *adj* regolabile; **adjustment** *n* (*Psych*) adattamento; (*of machine*) regolazione *f*; (*of prices, wages*) modifica
administer [əd'mɪnɪstə^r] *vt* amministrare; (*justice, drug*) somministrare; **administration** [ədmɪnɪs'treɪʃən] *n* amministrazione *f*; **administrative** [əd'mɪnɪstrətɪv] *adj* amministrativo(-a)
administrator [əd'mɪnɪstreɪtə^r] *n* amministratore(-trice)
admiral ['ædmərəl] *n* ammiraglio
admiration [ædmə'reɪʃən] *n* ammirazione *f*
admire [əd'maɪə^r] *vt* ammirare; **admirer** *n* ammiratore(-trice)
admission [əd'mɪʃən] *n* ammissione *f*; (*to exhibition, nightclub etc*) ingresso; (*confession*) confessione *f*
admit [əd'mɪt] *vt* ammettere; far entrare; (*agree*) riconoscere; **admit to** *vt fus* riconoscere; **admittance** *n* ingresso; **admittedly** *adv* bisogna pur riconoscere (che)
adolescent [ædəu'lɛsnt] *adj, n* adolescente *m/f*
adopt [ə'dɔpt] *vt* adottare; **adopted** *adj* adottivo(-a); **adoption** [ə'dɔpʃən] *n* adozione *f*
adore [ə'dɔː^r] *vt* adorare
adorn [ə'dɔːn] *vt* ornare
Adriatic [eɪdrɪ'ætɪk] *n*: **the ~ (Sea)** il mare Adriatico, l'Adriatico
adrift [ə'drɪft] *adv* alla deriva
adult ['ædʌlt] *adj* adulto(-a); (*work, education*) per adulti ▷ *n* adulto(-a); **adult education** *n* scuola per adulti
adultery [ə'dʌltərɪ] *n* adulterio
advance [əd'vɑːns] *n* avanzamento; (*money*) anticipo ▷ *adj* (*booking etc*) in anticipo ▷ *vt* (*money*) anticipare ▷ *vi* avanzare; **in ~** in anticipo; **do I need to book in ~?** occorre che prenoti in anticipo?; **advanced** *adj* avanzato(-a); (*Scol*: *studies*) superiore
advantage [əd'vɑːntɪdʒ] *n* (*also Tennis*) vantaggio; **to take ~ of**

approfittarsi di
advent ['ædvənt] *n* avvento; (*Rel*): **A~** Avvento
adventure [əd'vɛntʃə^r] *n* avventura; **adventurous** [əd'vɛntʃərəs] *adj* avventuroso(-a)
adverb ['ædvə:b] *n* avverbio
adversary ['ædvəsərɪ] *n* avversario(-a)
adverse ['ædvə:s] *adj* avverso(-a)
advert ['ædvə:t] (BRIT) *n abbr* = **advertisement**
advertise ['ædvətaɪz] *vi, vt* fare pubblicità *or* réclame (a); fare un'inserzione (per vendere); **to ~ for** (*staff*) mettere un annuncio sul giornale per trovare; **advertisement** [əd'və:tɪsmənt] *n* (*Comm*) réclame *f inv*, pubblicità *f inv*; (*in classified ads*) inserzione *f*; **advertiser** *n* azienda che reclamizza un prodotto; (*in newspaper*) inserzionista *m/f*; **advertising** ['ædvətaɪzɪŋ] *n* pubblicità
advice [əd'vaɪs] *n* consigli *mpl*; **piece of ~** consiglio; **to take legal ~** consultare un avvocato
advisable [əd'vaɪzəbl] *adj* consigliabile
advise [əd'vaɪz] *vt* consigliare; **to ~ sb of sth** informare qn di qc; **to ~ sb against sth/doing sth** sconsigliare qc a qn/a qn di fare qc; **adviser** *n* consigliere(-a); (*in business*) consulente *m/f*, consigliere(-a); **advisory** [-ərɪ] *adj* consultivo(-a)
advocate [*n* 'ædvəkɪt, *vb* 'ædvəkeɪt] *n* (*upholder*) sostenitore(-trice); (*Law*) avvocato (difensore) ▷ *vt* propugnare
Aegean [ɪ'dʒɪ:ən] *n*: **the ~ (Sea)** il mar Egeo, l'Egeo
aerial ['ɛərɪəl] *n* antenna ▷ *adj* aereo(-a)
aerobics [ɛə'rəubɪks] *n* aerobica
aeroplane ['ɛərəpleɪn] (BRIT) *n* aeroplano
aerosol ['ɛərəsɔl] (BRIT) *n* aerosol *m inv*
affair [ə'fɛə^r] *n* affare *m*; (*also:* **love ~**) relazione *f* amorosa; **~s** (*business*) affari
affect [ə'fɛkt] *vt* toccare; (*influence*) influire su, incidere su; (*feign*) fingere; **affected** *adj* affettato(-a); **affection** [ə'fɛkʃən] *n* affezione *f*; **affectionate** *adj* affettuoso(-a)
afflict [ə'flɪkt] *vt* affliggere
affluent ['æfluənt] *adj* ricco(-a); **the ~ society** la società del benessere
afford [ə'fɔ:d] *vt* permettersi; (*provide*) fornire; **affordable** *adj* (che ha un prezzo) abbordabile
Afghanistan [æf'gænɪstɑ:n] *n* Afganistan *m*
afraid [ə'freɪd] *adj* impaurito(-a); **to be ~ of** *or* **to/that** aver paura di/che; **I am ~ so/not** ho paura di sì/no
Africa ['æfrɪkə] *n* Africa; **African** *adj, n* africano(-a); **African-American** *adj, n* afroamericano(-a)
after ['ɑ:ftə^r] *prep, adv* dopo ▷ *conj* dopo che; **what/who are you ~?** che/chi cerca?; **~ he left/having done** dopo che se ne fu andato/dopo aver fatto; **to name sb ~ sb** dare a qn il nome di qn; **it's twenty ~ eight** (US) sono le otto e venti; **to ask ~ sb** chiedere di qn; **~ all** dopo tutto; **~ you!** dopo di lei!; **after-effects** *npl* conseguenze *fpl*; (*of illness*) postumi *mpl*; **aftermath** *n* conseguenze *fpl*; **in the aftermath of** nel periodo dopo; **afternoon** *n* pomeriggio; **after-shave (lotion)** ['ɑ:ftəʃeɪv-] *n* dopobarba *m inv*; **aftersun (lotion/cream)** *n* doposole *m inv*; **afterwards** (US **afterward**) *adv* dopo
again [ə'gɛn] *adv* di nuovo; **to begin/see ~** ricominciare/rivedere; **not ... ~** non ... più; **~ and ~** ripetutamente
against [ə'gɛnst] *prep* contro
age [eɪdʒ] *n* età *f inv* ▷ *vt, vi* invecchiare; **it's been ~s since** sono secoli che; **he is 20 years of ~** ha

20 anni; **to come of ~** diventare maggiorenne; **~d 10** di 10 anni; **the ~d** ['eɪdʒɪd] gli anziani; **age group** *n* generazione *f*; **age limit** *n* limite *m* d'età

agency ['eɪdʒənsɪ] *n* agenzia

agenda [ə'dʒɛndə] *n* ordine *m* del giorno

agent ['eɪdʒənt] *n* agente *m*

aggravate ['ægrəveɪt] *vt* aggravare; (*person*) irritare

aggression [ə'grɛʃən] *n* aggressione *f*

aggressive [ə'grɛsɪv] *adj* aggressivo(-a)

agile ['ædʒaɪl] *adj* agile

agitated ['ædʒɪteɪtɪd] *adj* agitato(-a), turbato(-a)

AGM *n abbr* = **annual general meeting**

ago [ə'gəu] *adv* **2 days ~** 2 giorni fa; **not long ~** poco tempo fa; **how long ~?** quanto tempo fa?

agony ['ægənɪ] *n* dolore *m* atroce; **to be in ~** avere dolori atroci

agree [ə'gri:] *vt* (*price*) pattuire ▷ *vi* **to ~ (with)** essere d'accordo (con); (*Ling*) concordare (con); **to ~ to sth/to do sth** accettare qc/di fare qc; **to ~ that** (*admit*) ammettere che; **to ~ on sth** accordarsi su qc; **garlic doesn't ~ with me** l'aglio non mi va; **agreeable** *adj* gradevole; (*willing*) disposto(-a); **agreed** *adj* (*time, place*) stabilito(-a); **agreement** *n* accordo; **in agreement** d'accordo

agricultural [ægrɪ'kʌltʃərəl] *adj* agricolo(-a)

agriculture ['ægrɪkʌltʃə^r] *n* agricoltura

ahead [ə'hɛd] *adv* avanti; davanti; **~ of** davanti a; (*fig: schedule etc*) in anticipo su; **~ of time** in anticipo; **go right** *or* **straight ~** tiri diritto

aid [eɪd] *n* aiuto ▷ *vt* aiutare; **in ~ of** a favore di

aide [eɪd] *n* (*person*) aiutante *m/f*

AIDS [eɪdz] *n abbr* (= *acquired immune deficiency syndrome*) AIDS *f*

ailing ['eɪlɪŋ] *adj* sofferente; (*fig: economy, industry etc*) in difficoltà

ailment ['eɪlmənt] *n* indisposizione *f*

aim [eɪm] *vt* **to ~ sth at** (*such as gun*) mirare qc a, puntare qc a; (*camera*) rivolgere qc a; (*missile*) lanciare qc contro ▷ *vi* (*also:* **to take ~**) prendere la mira ▷ *n* mira; **to ~ at** mirare; **to ~ to do** aver l'intenzione di fare

ain't [eɪnt] (*inf*) = **am not**; **aren't**; **isn't**

air [ɛə^r] *n* aria ▷ *vt* (*room*) arieggiare; (*clothes*) far prendere aria a; (*grievances, ideas*) esprimere pubblicamente ▷ *cpd* (*currents*) d'aria; (*attack*) aereo(-a); **to throw sth into the ~** lanciare qc in aria; **by ~** (*travel*) in aereo; **on the ~** (*Radio, TV*) in onda; **airbag** *n* airbag *m inv*; **airbed** (BRIT) *n* materassino; **airborne** ['ɛəbɔ:n] *adj* (*plane*) in volo; (*troops*) aerotrasportato(-a); **as soon as the plane was airborne** appena l'aereo ebbe decollato; **air-conditioned** *adj* con *or* ad aria condizionata; **air conditioning** *n* condizionamento d'aria; **aircraft** *n inv* apparecchio; **airfield** *n* campo d'aviazione; **Air Force** *n* aviazione *f* militare; **air hostess** (BRIT) *n* hostess *f inv*; **airing cupboard** ['ɛərɪŋ-] *n armadio riscaldato per asciugare panni.*; **airlift** *n* ponte *m* aereo; **airline** *n* linea aerea; **airliner** *n* aereo di linea; **airmail** *n* **by airmail** per via aerea; **airplane** (US) *n* aeroplano; **airport** *n* aeroporto; **air raid** *n* incursione *f* aerea; **airsick** *adj* **to be airsick** soffrire di mal d'aria; **airspace** *n* spazio aereo; **airstrip** *n* pista d'atterraggio; **air terminal** *n* air-terminal *m inv*; **airtight** *adj* ermetico(-a); **air-traffic controller** *n* controllore *m* del traffico aereo; **airy** *adj* arioso(-a); (*manners*) noncurante

aisle [aɪl] *n* (*of church*) navata laterale; navata centrale; (*of plane*) corridoio; **aisle seat** *n* (*on plane*) posto sul

corridoio
ajar [ə'dʒɑːʳ] *adj* socchiuso(-a)
à la carte [ɑːlɑː'kɑːt] *adv* alla carta
alarm [ə'lɑːm] *n* allarme *m* ▷ *vt* allarmare; **alarm call** *n* (*in hotel etc*) sveglia; **could I have an alarm call at 7 am, please?** vorrei essere svegliato alle 7, per favore; **alarm clock** *n* sveglia; **alarmed** *adj* (*person*) allarmato(-a); (*house, car etc*) dotato(-a) di allarme; **alarming** *adj* allarmante, preoccupante
Albania [æl'beɪnɪə] *n* Albania
albeit [ɔːl'biːɪt] *conj* sebbene + *sub*, benché + *sub*
album ['ælbəm] *n* album *m inv*
alcohol ['ælkəhɔl] *n* alcool *m*; **alcohol-free** *adj* analcolico(-a); **alcoholic** [-'hɔlɪk] *adj* alcolico(-a) ▷ *n* alcolizzato(-a)
alcove ['ælkəuv] *n* alcova
ale [eɪl] *n* birra
alert [ə'ləːt] *adj* vigile ▷ *n* allarme *m* ▷ *vt* avvertire; mettere in guardia; **on the ~** all'erta
algebra ['ældʒɪbrə] *n* algebra
Algeria [æl'dʒɪərɪə] *n* Algeria
alias ['eɪlɪəs] *adv* alias ▷ *n* pseudonimo, falso nome *m*
alibi ['ælɪbaɪ] *n* alibi *m inv*
alien ['eɪlɪən] *n* straniero(-a); (*extraterrestrial*) alieno(-a) ▷ *adj* **~ (to)** estraneo(-a) (a); **alienate** *vt* alienare
alight [ə'laɪt] *adj* acceso(-a) ▷ *vi* scendere; (*bird*) posarsi
align [ə'laɪn] *vt* allineare
alike [ə'laɪk] *adj* simile ▷ *adv* sia ... sia; **to look ~** assomigliarsi
alive [ə'laɪv] *adj* vivo(-a); (*lively*) vivace

KEYWORD

all [ɔːl] *adj* tutto(-a); **all day** tutto il giorno; **all night** tutta la notte; **all men** tutti gli uomini; **all five came** sono venuti tutti e cinque; **all the books** tutti i libri; **all the food** tutto il cibo; **all the time** sempre; tutto il tempo; **all his life** tutta la vita
▷ *pron* **1** tutto(-a); **I ate it all, I ate all of it** l'ho mangiato tutto; **all of us went** tutti noi siamo andati; **all of the boys went** tutti i ragazzi sono andati
2 (*in phrases*): **above all** soprattutto; **after all** dopotutto; **at all: not at all** (*in answer to question*) niente affatto; (*in answer to thanks*) prego!, di niente!, s'immagini!; **I'm not at all tired** non sono affatto stanco(-a); **anything at all will do** andrà bene qualsiasi cosa; **all in all** tutto sommato
▷ *adv* **all alone** tutto(-a) solo(-a); **it's not as hard as all that** non è poi così difficile; **all the more/the better** tanto più/meglio; **all but** quasi; **the score is two all** il punteggio è di due a due

Allah ['ælə] *n* Allah *m*
allegation [ælɪ'geɪʃən] *n* asserzione *f*
alleged [ə'lɛdʒd] *adj* presunto(-a); **allegedly** [ə'lɛdʒɪdlɪ] *adv* secondo quanto si asserisce
allegiance [ə'liːdʒəns] *n* fedeltà
allergic [ə'ləːdʒɪk] *adj* **~ to** allergico(-a) a; **I'm ~ to penicillin** sono allergico alla penicillina
allergy ['ælədʒɪ] *n* allergia
alleviate [ə'liːvɪeɪt] *vt* sollevare
alley ['ælɪ] *n* vicolo
alliance [ə'laɪəns] *n* alleanza
allied ['ælaɪd] *adj* alleato(-a)
alligator ['ælɪgeɪtəʳ] *n* alligatore *m*
all-in ['ɔːlɪn] *adj* (BRIT: *also adv*: *charge*) tutto compreso
allocate ['æləkeɪt] *vt* assegnare
allot [ə'lɔt] *vt* assegnare
all-out ['ɔːlaut] *adj* (*effort etc*) totale ▷ *adv* **to go all out for** mettercela tutta per
allow [ə'lau] *vt* (*practice, behaviour*) permettere; (*sum to spend etc*) accordare; (*sum, time estimated*) dare; (*concede*): **to ~ that** ammettere che;

to ~ sb to do permettere a qn di fare; **he is ~ed to** lo può fare; **allow for** *vt fus* tener conto di; **allowance** *n* (*money received*) assegno; indennità *f inv*; (*Tax*) detrazione *f* di imposta; **to make allowances for** tener conto di

all right *adv* (*feel, work*) bene; (*as answer*) va bene

ally ['ælaɪ] *n* alleato

almighty [ɔːl'maɪtɪ] *adj* onnipotente; (*row etc*) colossale

almond ['ɑːmənd] *n* mandorla

almost ['ɔːlməust] *adv* quasi

alone [ə'ləun] *adj, adv* solo(-a); **to leave sb ~** lasciare qn in pace; **to leave sth ~** lasciare stare qc; **let ~ ...** figuriamoci poi ..., tanto meno ...

along [ə'lɔŋ] *prep* lungo ▷ *adv* **is he coming ~?** viene con noi?; **he was limping ~** veniva zoppicando; **~ with** insieme con; **all ~** (*all the time*) sempre, fin dall'inizio; **alongside** *prep* accanto a; lungo ▷ *adv* accanto

aloof [ə'luːf] *adj* distaccato(-a) ▷ *adv* **to stand ~** tenersi a distanza *or* in disparte

aloud [ə'laud] *adv* ad alta voce

alphabet ['ælfəbɛt] *n* alfabeto

Alps [ælps] *npl*: **the ~** le Alpi

already [ɔːl'rɛdɪ] *adv* già

alright ['ɔːl'raɪt] (BRIT) *adv* = **all right**

also ['ɔːlsəu] *adv* anche

altar ['ɔltə^r] *n* altare *m*

alter ['ɔltə^r] *vt, vi* alterare; **alteration** [ɔltə'reɪʃən] *n* modificazione *f*, alterazione *f*; **alterations** (*Sewing, Archit*) modifiche *fpl*; **timetable subject to alteration** orario soggetto a variazioni

alternate [*adj* ɔl'təːnɪt, *vb* 'ɔltəːneɪt] *adj* alterno(-a); (*US: plan etc*) alternativo(-a) ▷ *vi* **to ~ (with)** alternarsi (a); **on ~ days** ogni due giorni

alternative [ɔl'təːnətɪv] *adj* alternativo(-a) ▷ *n* (*choice*) alternativa; **alternatively** *adv* **alternatively one could ...** come alternativa si potrebbe ...

although [ɔːl'ðəu] *conj* benché + *sub*, sebbene + *sub*

altitude ['æltɪtjuːd] *n* altitudine *f*

altogether [ɔːltə'gɛðə^r] *adv* del tutto, completamente; (*on the whole*) tutto considerato; (*in all*) in tutto

aluminium [ælju'mɪnɪəm] (BRIT), **aluminum** [ə'luːmɪnəm] (US) *n* alluminio

always ['ɔːlweɪz] *adv* sempre

Alzheimer's (disease) ['æltshaɪməz-] *n* (malattia di) Alzheimer

am [æm] *vb see* **be**

amalgamate [ə'mælgəmeɪt] *vt* amalgamare ▷ *vi* amalgamarsi

amass [ə'mæs] *vt* ammassare

amateur ['æmətə^r] *n* dilettante *m/f* ▷ *adj* (*Sport*) dilettante

amaze [ə'meɪz] *vt* stupire; **amazed** *adj* sbalordito(-a); **to be amazed (at)** essere sbalordito (da); **amazement** *n* stupore *m*; **amazing** *adj* sorprendente, sbalorditivo(-a)

Amazon ['æməzən] *n* (*Mythology*) Amazzone *f*; (*river*): **the ~** il Rio delle Amazzoni ▷ *cpd* (*basin, jungle*) amazzonico(-a)

ambassador [æm'bæsədə^r] *n* ambasciatore(-trice)

amber ['æmbə^r] *n* ambra; **at ~** (BRIT *Aut*) giallo

ambiguous [æm'bɪgjuəs] *adj* ambiguo(-a)

ambition [æm'bɪʃən] *n* ambizione *f*; **ambitious** [æm'bɪʃəs] *adj* ambizioso(-a)

ambulance ['æmbjuləns] *n* ambulanza; **call an ~!** chiamate un'ambulanza!

ambush ['æmbuʃ] *n* imboscata

amen ['ɑː'mɛn] *excl* così sia, amen

amend [ə'mɛnd] *vt* (*law*) emendare; (*text*) correggere; **to make ~s** fare ammenda; **amendment** *n*

emendamento; correzione *f*
amenities [ə'mi:nɪtɪz] *npl* attrezzature *fpl* ricreative e culturali
America [ə'mɛrɪkə] *n* America; **American** *adj, n* americano(-a); **American football** *n* (BRIT) football *m* americano
amicable ['æmɪkəbl] *adj* amichevole
amid(st) [ə'mɪd(st)] *prep* in mezzo a
ammunition [æmju'nɪʃən] *n* munizioni *fpl*
amnesty ['æmnɪstɪ] *n* amnistia; **to grant an ~ to** concedere l'amnistia a, amnistiare
among(st) [ə'mʌŋ(st)] *prep* fra, tra, in mezzo a
amount [ə'maunt] *n* somma; ammontare *m*; quantità *f inv* ▷ *vi* **to ~ to** (*total*) ammontare a; (*be same as*) essere come
amp(ère) ['æmp(ɛəʳ)] *n* ampère *m inv*
ample ['æmpl] *adj* ampio(-a); spazioso(-a); (*enough*): **this is ~** questo è più che sufficiente
amplifier ['æmplɪfaɪəʳ] *n* amplificatore *m*
amputate ['æmpjuteɪt] *vt* amputare
Amtrak ['æmtræk] (US) *n società ferroviaria americana*
amuse [ə'mju:z] *vt* divertire; **amusement** *n* divertimento; **amusement arcade** *n* sala giochi; **amusement park** *n* luna park *m inv*
amusing [ə'mju:zɪŋ] *adj* divertente
an [æn] *indef art see* **a**
anaemia [ə'ni:mɪə] (US **anemia**) *n* anemia
anaemic [ə'ni:mɪk] (US **anemic**) *adj* anemico(-a)
anaesthetic [ænɪs'θɛtɪk] (US **anesthetic**) *adj* anestetico(-a) ▷ *n* anestetico
analog(ue) ['ænəlɔg] *adj* (*watch, computer*) analogico(-a)
analogy [ə'nælədʒɪ] *n* analogia; **to draw an ~ between** fare un'analogia tra
analyse ['ænəlaɪz] (US **analyze**) *vt* analizzare; **analysis** [ə'næləsɪs] (*pl* **analyses**) *n* analisi *f inv*; **analyst** ['ænəlɪst] *n* (*Pol etc*) analista *m/f*; (US) (psic)analista *m/f*
analyze ['ænəlaɪz] (US) *vt* = **analyse**
anarchy ['ænəkɪ] *n* anarchia
anatomy [ə'nætəmɪ] *n* anatomia
ancestor ['ænsɪstəʳ] *n* antenato(-a)
anchor ['æŋkəʳ] *n* ancora ▷ *vi* (*also:* **to drop ~**) gettare l'ancora ▷ *vt* ancorare; **to weigh ~** salpare *or* levare l'ancora
anchovy ['æntʃəvɪ] *n* acciuga
ancient ['eɪnʃənt] *adj* antico(-a); (*person, car*) vecchissimo(-a)
and [ænd] *conj* e; (*often ed before vowel*): **~ so on** e così via; **try ~ come** cerca di venire; **he talked ~ talked** non la finiva di parlare; **better ~ better** sempre meglio
Andes ['ændi:z] *npl* **the ~** le Ande
anemia *etc* [ə'ni:mɪə] (US) = **anaemia** *etc*
anesthetic [ænɪs'θɛtɪk] (US) *adj, n* = **anaesthetic**
angel ['eɪndʒəl] *n* angelo
anger ['æŋgəʳ] *n* rabbia
angina [æn'dʒaɪnə] *n* angina pectoris
angle ['æŋgl] *n* angolo; **from their ~** dal loro punto di vista
angler ['æŋgləʳ] *n* pescatore *m* con la lenza
Anglican ['æŋglɪkən] *adj, n* anglicano(-a)
angling ['æŋglɪŋ] *n* pesca con la lenza
angrily ['æŋgrɪlɪ] *adv* con rabbia
angry ['æŋgrɪ] *adj* arrabbiato(-a), furioso(-a); (*wound*) infiammato(-a); **to be ~ with sb/at sth** essere in collera con qn/per qc; **to get ~** arrabbiarsi; **to make sb ~** fare arrabbiare qn
anguish ['æŋgwɪʃ] *n* angoscia
animal ['ænɪməl] *adj* animale ▷ *n* animale *m*

animated ['ænɪmeɪtɪd] *adj* animato(-a)
animation [ænɪ'meɪʃən] *n* animazione *f*
aniseed ['ænɪsiːd] *n* semi *mpl* di anice
ankle ['æŋkl] *n* caviglia
annex [*n* 'ænɛks, *vb* ə'nɛks] *n* (BRIT: *also:* **~e**) (edificio) annesso ▷ *vt* annettere
anniversary [ænɪ'vəːsərɪ] *n* anniversario
announce [ə'nauns] *vt* annunciare; **announcement** *n* annuncio; (*letter, card*) partecipazione *f*; **announcer** *n* (*Radio, TV: between programmes*) annunciatore(-trice); (*: in a programme*) presentatore(-trice)
annoy [ə'nɔɪ] *vt* dare fastidio a; **don't get ~ed!** non irritarti!; **annoying** *adj* noioso(-a)
annual ['ænjuəl] *adj* annuale ▷ *n* (*Bot*) pianta annua; (*book*) annuario; **annually** *adv* annualmente
annum ['ænəm] *n see* **per**
anonymous [ə'nɔnɪməs] *adj* anonimo(-a)
anorak ['ænəræk] *n* giacca a vento
anorexia [ænə'rɛksɪə] *n* (*Med: also:* **~ nervosa**) anoressia
anorexic [ænə'rɛksɪk] *adj, n* anoressico(-a)
another [ə'nʌðəʳ] *adj* **~ book** (*one more*) un altro libro, ancora un libro; (*a different one*) un altro libro ▷ *pron* un altro(un'altra), ancora uno(-a); *see also* **one**
answer ['ɑːnsəʳ] *n* risposta; soluzione *f* ▷ *vi* rispondere ▷ *vt* (*reply to*) rispondere a; (*problem*) risolvere; (*prayer*) esaudire; **in ~ to your letter** in risposta alla sua lettera; **to ~ the phone** rispondere (al telefono); **to ~ the bell** rispondere al campanello; **to ~ the door** aprire la porta; **answer back** *vi* ribattere; **answerphone** *n* (*esp* BRIT) segreteria telefonica
ant [ænt] *n* formica
Antarctic [ænt'ɑːktɪk] *n* **the ~** l'Antartide *f*
antelope ['æntɪləup] *n* antilope *f*
antenatal ['æntɪ'neɪtl] *adj* prenatale
antenna [æn'tɛnə, -niː] (*pl* **antennae**) *n* antenna
anthem ['ænθəm] *n* **national ~** inno nazionale
anthology [æn'θɔlədʒɪ] *n* antologia
anthrax ['ænθræks] *n* antrace *m*
anthropology [ænθrə'pɔlədʒɪ] *n* antropologia
anti [æntɪ] *prefix* anti; **antibiotic** ['æntɪbaɪ'ɔtɪk] *n* antibiotico; **antibody** ['æntɪbɔdɪ] *n* anticorpo
anticipate [æn'tɪsɪpeɪt] *vt* prevedere; pregustare; (*wishes, request*) prevenire; **anticipation** [æntɪsɪ'peɪʃən] *n* anticipazione *f*; (*expectation*) aspettative *fpl*
anticlimax ['æntɪ'klaɪmæks] *n* **it was an ~** fu una completa delusione
anticlockwise ['æntɪ'klɔkwaɪz] *adj, adv* in senso antiorario
antics ['æntɪks] *npl* buffonerie *fpl*
anti: **antidote** ['æntɪdəut] *n* antidoto; **antifreeze** ['æntɪ'friːz] *n* anticongelante *m*; **anti-globalization** [æntɪgləubəlaɪ'zeɪʃən] *n* antiglobalizzazione *f*; **antihistamine** [æntɪ'hɪstəmɪn] *n* antistaminico; **antiperspirant** ['æntɪ'pəːspərənt] *adj* antitraspirante
antique [æn'tiːk] *n* antichità *f inv* ▷ *adj* antico(-a); **antique shop** *n* negozio d'antichità
antiseptic [æntɪ'sɛptɪk] *n* antisettico
antisocial ['æntɪ'səuʃəl] *adj* asociale
antivirus [æntɪ'vaɪərəs] *adj* antivirus *inv*; **~ program** antivirus *m inv*
antlers ['æntləz] *npl* palchi *mpl*
anxiety [æŋ'zaɪətɪ] *n* ansia; (*keenness*): **~ to do** smania di fare
anxious ['æŋkʃəs] *adj* ansioso(-a), inquieto(-a); (*worrying*) angosciante;

(*keen*): **~ to do/that** impaziente di fare/che + *sub*

KEYWORD

any ['ɛnɪ] *adj* **1** (*in questions etc*): **have you any butter?** hai del burro?, hai un po' di burro?; **have you any children?** hai bambini?; **if there are any tickets left** se ci sono ancora (dei) biglietti, se c'è ancora qualche biglietto
2 (*with negative*): **I haven't any money/books** non ho soldi/libri
3 (*no matter which*) qualsiasi, qualunque; **choose any book you like** scegli un libro qualsiasi
4 (*in phrases*): **in any case** in ogni caso; **any day now** da un giorno all'altro; **at any moment** in qualsiasi momento, da un momento all'altro; **at any rate** ad ogni modo
▷ *pron* **1** (*in questions, with negative*): **have you got any?** ne hai?; **can any of you sing?** qualcuno di voi sa cantare?; **I haven't any (of them)** non ne ho
2 (*no matter which one(s)*): **take any of those books (you like)** prendi uno qualsiasi di quei libri
▷ *adv* **1** (*in questions etc*): **do you want any more soup/sandwiches?** vuoi ancora un po' di minestra/degli altri panini?; **are you feeling any better?** ti senti meglio?
2 (*with negative*): **I can't hear him any more** non lo sento più; **don't wait any longer** non aspettare più

any: **anybody** ['ɛnɪbɔdɪ] *pron* (*in questions etc*) qualcuno, nessuno; (*with negative*) nessuno; (*no matter who*) chiunque; **can you see anybody?** vedi qualcuno *or* nessuno?; **if anybody should phone ...** se telefona qualcuno ...; **I can't see anybody** non vedo nessuno; **anybody could do it** chiunque potrebbe farlo; **anyhow** ['ɛnɪhau] *adv* (*at any rate*) ad ogni modo, comunque; (*haphazard*): **do it anyhow you like** fallo come ti pare; **I shall go anyhow** ci andrò lo stesso *or* comunque; **she leaves things just anyhow** lascia tutto come capita; **anyone** ['ɛnɪwʌn] *pron* = **anybody**; **anything** ['ɛnɪθɪŋ] *pron* (*in question etc*) qualcosa, niente; (*with negative*) niente; (*no matter what*): **you can say anything you like** puoi dire quello che ti pare; **can you see anything?** vedi niente *or* qualcosa?; **if anything happens to me ...** se mi dovesse succedere qualcosa ...; **I can't see anything** non vedo niente; **anything will do** va bene qualsiasi cosa *or* tutto; **anytime** *adv* in qualunque momento; quando vuole; **anyway** ['ɛnɪweɪ] *adv* (*at any rate*) ad ogni modo, comunque; (*besides*) ad ogni modo; **anywhere** ['ɛnɪwɛə^r] *adv* (*in questions etc*) da qualche parte; (*with negative*) da nessuna parte; (*no matter where*) da qualsiasi *or* qualunque parte, dovunque; **can you see him anywhere?** lo vedi da qualche parte?; **I can't see him anywhere** non lo vedo da nessuna parte; **anywhere in the world** dovunque nel mondo

apart [ə'pɑːt] *adv* (*to one side*) a parte; (*separately*) separatamente; **with one's legs ~** con le gambe divaricate; **10 miles ~** a 10 miglia di distanza (l'uno dall'altro); **to take ~** smontare; **~ from** a parte, eccetto

apartment [ə'pɑːtmənt] (US) *n* appartamento; (*room*) locale *m*; **apartment building** (US) *n* stabile *m*, caseggiato

apathy ['æpəθɪ] *n* apatia

ape [eɪp] *n* scimmia ▷ *vt* scimmiottare

aperitif [ə'pɛrɪtiːf] *n* aperitivo

aperture ['æpətʃjuə^r] *n* apertura

APEX *n abbr* (= *advance purchase*

excursion) APEX *m inv*
apologize [ə'pɔlədʒaɪz] *vi* **to ~ (for sth to sb)** scusarsi (di qc a qn), chiedere scusa (a qn per qc)
apology [ə'pɔlədʒɪ] *n* scuse *fpl*
apostrophe [ə'pɔstrəfɪ] *n* (*sign*) apostrofo
appal [ə'pɔ:l] (*US* **appall**) *vt* scioccare; **appalling** *adj* spaventoso(-a)
apparatus [æpə'reɪtəs] *n* apparato; (*in gymnasium*) attrezzatura
apparent [ə'pærənt] *adj* evidente; **apparently** *adv* evidentemente
appeal [ə'pi:l] *vi* (*Law*) appellarsi alla legge ▷ *n* (*Law*) appello; (*request*) richiesta; (*charm*) attrattiva; **to ~ for** chiedere (con insistenza); **to ~ to** (*person*) appellarsi a; (*thing*) piacere a; **it doesn't ~ to me** mi dice poco; **appealing** *adj* (*nice*) attraente
appear [ə'pɪə^r] *vi* apparire; (*Law*) comparire; (*publication*) essere pubblicato(-a); (*seem*) sembrare; **it would ~ that** sembra che; **appearance** *n* apparizione *f*; apparenza; (*look, aspect*) aspetto
appendicitis [əpɛndɪ'saɪtɪs] *n* appendicite *f*
appendix [ə'pɛndɪks] (*pl* **appendices**) *n* appendice *f*
appetite ['æpɪtaɪt] *n* appetito
appetizer ['æpɪtaɪzə^r] *n* stuzzichino
applaud [ə'plɔ:d] *vt, vi* applaudire
applause [ə'plɔ:z] *n* applauso
apple ['æpl] *n* mela; **apple pie** *n* torta di mele
appliance [ə'plaɪəns] *n* apparecchio
applicable [ə'plɪkəbl] *adj* applicabile; **to be ~ to** essere valido per; **the law is ~ from January** la legge entrerà in vigore in gennaio
applicant ['æplɪkənt] *n* candidato(-a)
application [æplɪ'keɪʃən] *n* applicazione *f*; (*for a job, a grant etc*) domanda; **application form** *n* modulo per la domanda
apply [ə'plaɪ] *vt* **to ~ (to)** (*paint, ointment*) dare (a); (*theory, technique*) applicare (a) ▷ *vi* **to ~ to** (*ask*) rivolgersi a; (*be suitable for, relevant to*) riguardare, riferirsi a; **to ~ (for)** (*permit, grant, job*) fare domanda (per); **to ~ o.s. to** dedicarsi a
appoint [ə'pɔɪnt] *vt* nominare; **appointment** *n* nomina; (*arrangement to meet*) appuntamento; **I have an appointment (with) ...** ho un appuntamento (con) ...; **I'd like to make an appointment (with)** vorrei prendere un appuntamento (con)
appraisal [ə'preɪzl] *n* valutazione *f*
appreciate [ə'pri:ʃɪeɪt] *vt* (*like*) apprezzare; (*be grateful for*) essere riconoscente di; (*be aware of*) rendersi conto di ▷ *vi* (*Finance*) aumentare; **I'd ~ your help** ti sono grato per l'aiuto; **appreciation** [əpri:ʃɪ'eɪʃən] *n* apprezzamento; (*Finance*) aumento del valore
apprehension [æprɪ'hɛnʃən] *n* (*fear*) inquietudine *f*
apprehensive [æprɪ'hɛnsɪv] *adj* apprensivo(-a)
apprentice [ə'prɛntɪs] *n* apprendista *m/f*
approach [ə'prəutʃ] *vi* avvicinarsi ▷ *vt* (*come near*) avvicinarsi a; (*ask, apply to*) rivolgersi a; (*subject, passer-by*) avvicinare ▷ *n* approccio; accesso; (*to problem*) modo di affrontare
appropriate [*adj* ə'prəuprɪɪt, *vb* ə'prəuprɪeɪt] *adj* appropriato(-a), adatto(-a) ▷ *vt* (*take*) appropriarsi
approval [ə'pru:vəl] *n* approvazione *f*; **on ~** (*Comm*) in prova, in esame
approve [ə'pru:v] *vt, vi* approvare; **approve of** *vt fus* approvare
approximate [ə'prɔksɪmɪt] *adj* approssimativo(-a); **approximately** *adv* circa
Apr. *abbr* (= *April*) apr.
apricot ['eɪprɪkɔt] *n* albicocca
April ['eɪprəl] *n* aprile *m*; **~ fool!** pesce

d'aprile!; **April Fools' Day** *n vedi nota nel riquadro*

APRIL FOOLS' DAY

April Fool's Day è il primo aprile, il giorno degli scherzi e delle burle. Il nome deriva dal fatto che, se una persona cade nella trappola che gli è stata tesa, fa la figura del "fool", cioè dello sciocco. Tradizionalmente, gli scherzi vengono fatti entro mezzogiorno.

apron ['eɪprən] *n* grembiule *m*
apt [æpt] *adj* (*suitable*) adatto(-a); (*able*) capace; (*likely*): **to be ~ to do** avere tendenza a fare
aquarium [ə'kwɛərɪəm] *n* acquario
Aquarius [ə'kwɛərɪəs] *n* Acquario
Arab ['ærəb] *adj, n* arabo(-a)
Arabia [ə'reɪbɪə] *n* Arabia; **Arabian** [ə'reɪbɪən] *adj* arabo(-a); **Arabic** ['ærəbɪk] *adj* arabico(-a), arabo(-a) ▷ *n* arabo; **Arabic numerals** *n* numeri *mpl* arabi, numerazione *f* araba
arbitrary ['ɑ:bɪtrərɪ] *adj* arbitrario(-a)
arbitration [ɑ:bɪ'treɪʃən] *n* (*Law*) arbitrato; (*Industry*) arbitraggio
arc [ɑ:k] *n* arco
arcade [ɑ:'keɪd] *n* portico; (*passage with shops*) galleria
arch [ɑ:tʃ] *n* arco; (*of foot*) arco plantare ▷ *vt* inarcare
archaeology [ɑ:kɪ'ɔlədʒɪ] (*US* **archeology**) *n* archeologia
archbishop [ɑ:tʃ'bɪʃəp] *n* arcivescovo
archeology *etc* [ɑ:kɪ'ɔlədʒɪ] (*US*) = **archaeology** *etc*
architect ['ɑ:kɪtɛkt] *n* architetto; **architectural** [ɑ:kɪ'tɛktʃərəl] *adj* architettonico(-a); **architecture** ['ɑ:kɪtɛktʃə^r] *n* architettura
archive ['ɑ:kaɪv] *n* (*often pl: also Comput*) archivio
Arctic ['ɑ:ktɪk] *adj* artico(-a) ▷ *n*: **the ~** l'Artico
are [ɑ:^r] *vb see* **be**
area ['ɛərɪə] *n* (*Geom*) area; (*zone*) zona; (*: smaller*) settore *m*; **area code** (*US*) *n* (*Tel*) prefisso
arena [ə'ri:nə] *n* arena
aren't [ɑ:nt] = **are not**
Argentina [ɑ:dʒən'ti:nə] *n* Argentina; **Argentinian** [-'tɪnɪən] *adj, n* argentino(-a)
arguably ['ɑ:gjuəblɪ] *adv* **it is ~ ...** si può sostenere che sia ...
argue ['ɑ:gju:] *vi* (*quarrel*) litigare; (*reason*) ragionare; **to ~ that** sostenere che
argument ['ɑ:gjumənt] *n* (*reasons*) argomento; (*quarrel*) lite *f*
Aries ['ɛərɪz] *n* Ariete *m*
arise [ə'raɪz] (*pt* **arose**, *pp* **arisen**) *vi* (*opportunity, problem*) presentarsi
arithmetic [ə'rɪθmətɪk] *n* aritmetica
arm [ɑ:m] *n* braccio ▷ *vt* armare; **arms** *npl* (*weapons*) armi *fpl*; **~ in ~** a braccetto; **armchair** *n* poltrona
armed [ɑ:md] *adj* armato(-a); **armed robbery** *n* rapina a mano armata
armour ['ɑ:mə^r] (*US* **armor**) *n* armatura; (*Mil: tanks*) mezzi *mpl* blindati
armpit ['ɑ:mpɪt] *n* ascella
armrest ['ɑ:mrɛst] *n* bracciolo
army ['ɑ:mɪ] *n* esercito
A road *n* strada statale
aroma [ə'rəumə] *n* aroma; **aromatherapy** *n* aromaterapia
arose [ə'rəuz] *pt of* **arise**
around [ə'raund] *adv* attorno, intorno ▷ *prep* intorno a; (*fig: about*): **~ £5/3 o'clock** circa 5 sterline/le 3; **is he ~?** è in giro?
arouse [ə'rauz] *vt* (*sleeper*) svegliare; (*curiosity, passions*) suscitare
arrange [ə'reɪndʒ] *vt* sistemare; (*programme*) preparare; **to ~ to do sth** mettersi d'accordo per fare qc; **arrangement** *n* sistemazione *f*; (*agreement*) accordo; **arrangements**

npl (*plans*) progetti *mpl*, piani *mpl*
array [ə'reɪ] *n* **~ of** fila di
arrears [ə'rɪəz] *npl* arretrati *mpl*; **to be in ~ with one's rent** essere in arretrato con l'affitto
arrest [ə'rɛst] *vt* arrestare; (*sb's attention*) attirare ▷ *n* arresto; **under ~** in arresto
arrival [ə'raɪvəl] *n* arrivo; (*person*) arrivato(-a); **a new ~** un nuovo venuto; (*baby*) un neonato
arrive [ə'raɪv] *vi* arrivare; **what time does the train from Rome ~?** a che ora arriva il treno da Roma?; **arrive at** *vt fus* arrivare a
arrogance ['ærəgəns] *n* arroganza
arrogant ['ærəgənt] *adj* arrogante
arrow ['ærəu] *n* freccia
arse [ɑːs] (*inf!*) *n* culo (*!*)
arson ['ɑːsn] *n* incendio doloso
art [ɑːt] *n* arte *f*; (*craft*) mestiere *m*; **art college** *n* scuola di belle arti
artery ['ɑːtərɪ] *n* arteria
art gallery *n* galleria d'arte
arthritis [ɑː'θraɪtɪs] *n* artrite *f*
artichoke ['ɑːtɪtʃəuk] *n* carciofo; **Jerusalem ~** topinambur *m inv*
article ['ɑːtɪkl] *n* articolo
articulate [*adj* ɑː'tɪkjulɪt, *vb* ɑː'tɪkjuleɪt] *adj* (*person*) che si esprime forbitamente; (*speech*) articolato(-a) ▷ *vi* articolare
artificial [ɑːtɪ'fɪʃəl] *adj* artificiale
artist ['ɑːtɪst] *n* artista *m/f*; **artistic** [ɑː'tɪstɪk] *adj* artistico(-a)
art school *n* scuola d'arte

KEYWORD

as [æz] *conj* **1** (*referring to time*) mentre; **as the years went by** col passare degli anni; **he came in as I was leaving** arrivò mentre stavo uscendo; **as from tomorrow** da domani
2 (*in comparisons*): **as big as** grande come; **twice as big as** due volte più grande di; **as much/many as** tanto quanto/tanti quanti; **as soon as possible** prima possibile
3 (*since, because*) dal momento che, siccome
4 (*referring to manner, way*) come; **do as you wish** fa' come vuoi; **as she said** come ha detto lei
5 (*concerning*): **as for** *or* **to that** per quanto riguarda *or* quanto a quello
6: **as if** *or* **as though** come se; **he looked as if he was ill** sembrava stare male; *see also* **long**; **such**; **well**
▷ *prep* **he works as a driver** fa l'autista; **as chairman of the company he ...** come presidente della compagnia lui ...; **he gave me it as a present** me lo ha regalato

a.s.a.p. *abbr* = **as soon as possible**
asbestos [æz'bɛstəs] *n* asbesto, amianto
ASBO *n abbr* (BRIT: = *Antisocial Behaviour Order*) provvedimento restrittivo per comportamento antisociale
ascent [ə'sɛnt] *n* salita
ash [æʃ] *n* (*dust*) cenere *f*; (*wood, tree*) frassino
ashamed [ə'ʃeɪmd] *adj* vergognoso(-a); **to be ~ of** vergognarsi di
ashore [ə'ʃɔːʳ] *adv* a terra
ashtray ['æʃtreɪ] *n* portacenere *m*
Ash Wednesday *n* mercoledì *m inv* delle Ceneri
Asia ['eɪʃə] *n* Asia; **Asian** *adj, n* asiatico(-a)
aside [ə'saɪd] *adv* da parte ▷ *n* a parte *m*
ask [ɑːsk] *vt* (*question*) domandare; (*invite*) invitare; **to ~ sb sth/sb to do sth** chiedere qc a qn/a qn di fare qc; **to ~ sb about sth** chiedere a qn di qc; **to ~ (sb) a question** fare una domanda (a qn); **to ~ sb out to dinner** invitare qn a mangiare fuori; **ask for** *vt fus* chiedere; (*trouble etc*) cercare

asleep [ə'sli:p] *adj* addormentato(-a); **to be ~** dormire; **to fall ~** addormentarsi
AS level *n abbr (= Advanced Subsidiary level) prima parte del diploma di studi superiori chiamato "A level"*
asparagus [əs'pærəgəs] *n* asparagi *mpl*
aspect ['æspɛkt] *n* aspetto
aspirations [æspə'reɪʃənz] *npl* aspirazioni *fpl*
aspire [əs'paɪə^r] *vi*: **to ~ to** aspirare a
aspirin ['æsprɪn] *n* aspirina
ass [æs] *n* asino; (*inf*) scemo(-a); (*US: inf!*) culo (*!*)
assassin [ə'sæsɪn] *n* assassino; **assassinate** [ə'sæsɪneɪt] *vt* assassinare
assault [ə'sɔ:lt] *n* (*Mil*) assalto; (*gen: attack*) aggressione *f* ▷ *vt* assaltare; aggredire; (*sexually*) violentare
assemble [ə'sɛmbl] *vt* riunire; (*Tech*) montare ▷ *vi* riunirsi
assembly [ə'sɛmblɪ] *n* (*meeting*) assemblea; (*construction*) montaggio
assert [ə'sə:t] *vt* asserire; (*insist on*) far valere; **assertion** [ə'sə:ʃən] *n* asserzione *f*
assess [ə'sɛs] *vt* valutare; **assessment** *n* valutazione *f*
asset ['æsɛt] *n* vantaggio; **assets** *npl* (*Finance: of individual*) beni *mpl*; (*: of company*) attivo
assign [ə'saɪn] *vt*: **to ~ (to)** (*task*) assegnare (a); (*resources*) riservare (a); (*cause, meaning*) attribuire (a); **to ~ a date to sth** fissare la data di qc; **assignment** *n* compito
assist [ə'sɪst] *vt* assistere, aiutare; **assistance** *n* assistenza, aiuto; **assistant** *n* assistente *m/f*; (BRIT: *also:* **shop assistant**) commesso(-a)
associate [*adj, n* ə'səuʃɪɪt, *vb* ə'səuʃɪeɪt] *adj* associato(-a); (*member*) aggiunto(-a) ▷ *n* collega *m/f* ▷ *vt* associare ▷ *vi* **to ~ with sb** frequentare qn
association [əsəusɪ'eɪʃən] *n* associazione *f*
assorted [ə'sɔ:tɪd] *adj* assortito(-a)
assortment [ə'sɔ:tmənt] *n* assortimento
assume [ə'sju:m] *vt* supporre; (*responsibilities etc*) assumere; (*attitude, name*) prendere
assumption [ə'sʌmpʃən] *n* supposizione *f*, ipotesi *f inv*; (*of power*) assunzione *f*
assurance [ə'ʃuərəns] *n* assicurazione *f*; (*self-confidence*) fiducia in se stesso
assure [ə'ʃuə^r] *vt* assicurare
asterisk ['æstərɪsk] *n* asterisco
asthma ['æsmə] *n* asma
astonish [ə'stɔnɪʃ] *vt* stupire; **astonished** *adj* stupito(-a), sorpreso(-a); **to be astonished (at)** essere stupito(-a) (da); **astonishing** *adj* sorprendente, stupefacente; **I find it astonishing that ...** mi stupisce che ...; **astonishment** *n* stupore *m*
astound [ə'staund] *vt* sbalordire
astray [ə'streɪ] *adv* **to go ~** smarrirsi; **to lead ~** portare sulla cattiva strada
astrology [əs'trɔlədʒɪ] *n* astrologia
astronaut ['æstrənɔ:t] *n* astronauta *m/f*
astronomer [əs'trɔnəmə^r] *n* astronomo(-a)
astronomical [æstrə'nɔmɪkl] *adj* astronomico(-a)
astronomy [əs'trɔnəmɪ] *n* astronomia
astute [əs'tju:t] *adj* astuto(-a)
asylum [ə'saɪləm] *n* (*politico*) asilo; (*per malati*) manicomio

KEYWORD

at [æt] *prep* **1** (*referring to position, direction*) a; **at the top** in cima; **at the desk** al banco, alla scrivania; **at home/school** a casa/scuola; **at the baker's** dal panettiere; **to look at**

sth guardare qc; **to throw sth at sb** lanciare qc a qn
2 (*referring to time*) a; **at 4 o'clock** alle 4; **at night** di notte; **at Christmas** a Natale; **at times** a volte
3 (*referring to rates, speed etc*) a; **at £1 a kilo** a 1 sterlina al chilo; **two at a time** due alla volta, due per volta; **at 50 km/h** a 50 km/h
4 (*referring to manner*): **at a stroke** d'un solo colpo; **at peace** in pace
5 (*referring to activity*): **to be at work** essere al lavoro; **to play at cowboys** giocare ai cowboy; **to be good at sth/doing sth** essere bravo in qc/fare qc
6 (*referring to cause*): **shocked/surprised/annoyed at sth** colpito da/sorpreso da/arrabbiato per qc; **I went at his suggestion** ci sono andato dietro suo consiglio
7 (*Comput*: *symbol*) chiocciola

ate [eɪt] *pt of* **eat**
atheist ['eɪθɪɪst] *n* ateo(-a)
Athens ['æθɪnz] *n* Atene *f*
athlete ['æθliːt] *n* atleta *m/f*
athletic [æθ'lɛtɪk] *adj* atletico(-a); **athletics** *n* atletica
Atlantic [ət'læntɪk] *adj* atlantico(-a) ▷ *n*: **the ~ (Ocean)** l'Atlantico, l'Oceano Atlantico
atlas ['ætləs] *n* atlante *m*
A.T.M. *n abbr* (= *automated telling machine*) cassa automatica prelievi, sportello automatico
atmosphere ['ætməsfɪəʳ] *n* atmosfera
atom ['ætəm] *n* atomo; **atomic** [ə'tɔmɪk] *adj* atomico(-a); **atom(ic) bomb** *n* bomba atomica
A to Z® *n* (*map*) stradario
atrocity [ə'trɔsɪtɪ] *n* atrocità *f inv*
attach [ə'tætʃ] *vt* attaccare; (*document, letter*) allegare; (*importance etc*) attribuire; **to be ~ed to sb/sth** (*to like*) essere affezionato(-a) a qn/qc; **attachment** [ə'tætʃmənt] *n* (*tool*) accessorio; (*love*): **attachment (to)** affetto (per)
attack [ə'tæk] *vt* attaccare; (*person*) aggredire; (*task etc*) iniziare; (*problem*) affrontare ▷ *n* attacco; **heart ~** infarto; **attacker** *n* aggressore *m*
attain [ə'teɪn] *vt* (*also*: **to ~ to**) arrivare a, raggiungere
attempt [ə'tɛmpt] *n* tentativo ▷ *vt* tentare; **to make an ~ on sb's life** attentare alla vita di qn
attend [ə'tɛnd] *vt* frequentare; (*meeting, talk*) andare a; (*patient*) assistere; **attend to** *vt fus* (*needs, affairs etc*) prendersi cura di; (*customer*) occuparsi di; **attendance** *n* (*being present*) presenza; (*people present*) gente *f* presente; **attendant** *n* custode *m/f*; persona di servizio ▷ *adj* concomitante

> Be careful not to translate ***attend*** by the Italian word ***attendere***.

attention [ə'tɛnʃən] *n* attenzione *f* ▷ *excl* (*Mil*) attenti!; **for the ~ of** (*Admin*) per l'attenzione di
attic ['ætɪk] *n* soffitta
attitude ['ætɪtjuːd] *n* atteggiamento; posa
attorney [ə'təːnɪ] *n* (*lawyer*) avvocato; (*having proxy*) mandatario; **Attorney General** *n* (BRIT) Procuratore *m* Generale; (US) Ministro della Giustizia
attract [ə'trækt] *vt* attirare; **attraction** [ə'trækʃən] *n* (*gen pl*: *pleasant things*) attrattiva; (*Physics, fig*: *towards sth*) attrazione *f*; **attractive** *adj* attraente
attribute [*n* 'ætrɪbjuːt, *vb* ə'trɪbjuːt] *n* attributo ▷ *vt* **to ~ sth to** attribuire qc a
aubergine ['əubəʒiːn] *n* melanzana
auburn ['ɔːbən] *adj* tizianesco(-a)
auction ['ɔːkʃən] *n* (*also*: **sale by ~**) asta ▷ *vt* (*also*: **to sell by ~**) vendere all'asta; (*also*: **to put up for ~**) mettere

all'asta
audible ['ɔːdɪbl] *adj* udibile
audience ['ɔːdɪəns] *n* (*people*) pubblico; spettatori *mpl*; ascoltatori *mpl*; (*interview*) udienza
audit ['ɔːdɪt] *vt* rivedere, verificare
audition [ɔː'dɪʃən] *n* audizione *f*
auditor ['ɔːdɪtə^r] *n* revisore *m*
auditorium [ɔːdɪ'tɔːrɪəm] *n* sala, auditorio
Aug. *abbr* (= *August*) ago., ag.
August ['ɔːgəst] *n* agosto
aunt [ɑːnt] *n* zia; **auntie** *n* zietta; **aunty** *n* zietta
au pair ['əu'pɛə^r] *n* (*also:* **~ girl**) (ragazza *f*) alla pari *inv*
aura ['ɔːrə] *n* aura
austerity [ɔs'tɛrɪtɪ] *n* austerità *f inv*
Australia [ɔs'treɪlɪə] *n* Australia; **Australian** *adj, n* australiano(-a)
Austria ['ɔstrɪə] *n* Austria; **Austrian** *adj, n* austriaco(-a)
authentic [ɔː'θɛntɪk] *adj* autentico(-a)
author ['ɔːθə^r] *n* autore(-trice)
authority [ɔː'θɔrɪtɪ] *n* autorità *f inv*; (*permission*) autorizzazione *f*; **the authorities** *npl* (*government etc*) le autorità
authorize ['ɔːθəraɪz] *vt* autorizzare
auto ['ɔːtəu] (*US*) *n* auto *f inv*; **autobiography** [ɔːtəbaɪ'ɔgrəfɪ] *n* autobiografia; **autograph** ['ɔːtəgrɑːf] *n* autografo ▷ *vt* firmare; **automatic** [ɔːtə'mætɪk] *adj* automatico(-a) ▷ *n* (*gun*) arma automatica; (*washing machine*) lavatrice *f* automatica; (*car*) automobile *f* con cambio automatico; **automatically** *adv* automaticamente; **automobile** ['ɔːtəməbiːl] (*US*) *n* automobile *f*; **autonomous** [ɔː'tɔnəməs] *adj* autonomo(-a); **autonomy** [ɔː'tɔnəmɪ] *n* autonomia
autumn ['ɔːtəm] *n* autunno
auxiliary [ɔːg'zɪlɪərɪ] *adj* ausiliario(-a) ▷ *n* ausiliare *m/f*
avail [ə'veɪl] *vt* **to ~ o.s. of** servirsi di; approfittarsi di ▷ *n* **to no ~** inutilmente
availability [əveɪlə'bɪlɪtɪ] *n* disponibilità
available [ə'veɪləbl] *adj* disponibile
avalanche ['ævəlɑːnʃ] *n* valanga
Ave. *abbr* = **avenue**
avenue ['ævənjuː] *n* viale *m*; (*fig*) strada, via
average ['ævərɪdʒ] *n* media ▷ *adj* medio(-a) ▷ *vt* (*a certain figure*) fare di *or* in media; **on ~** in media
avert [ə'vəːt] *vt* evitare, prevenire; (*one's eyes*) distogliere
avid ['ævɪd] *adj* (*supporter etc*) accanito(-a)
avocado [ævə'kɑːdəu] *n* (BRIT: *also:* **~ pear**) avocado *m inv*
avoid [ə'vɔɪd] *vt* evitare
await [ə'weɪt] *vt* aspettare
awake [ə'weɪk] (*pt* **awoke**, *pp* **awoken, awaked**) *adj* sveglio(-a) ▷ *vt* svegliare ▷ *vi* svegliarsi
award [ə'wɔːd] *n* premio; (*Law*) risarcimento ▷ *vt* assegnare; (*Law: damages*) accordare
aware [ə'wɛə^r] *adj* **~ of** (*conscious*) conscio(-a) di; (*informed*) informato(-a) di; **to become ~ of** accorgersi di; **awareness** *n* consapevolezza
away [ə'weɪ] *adj, adv* via; lontano(-a); **two kilometres ~** a due chilometri di distanza; **two hours ~ by car** a due ore di distanza in macchina; **the holiday was two weeks ~** mancavano due settimane alle vacanze; **he's ~ for a week** è andato via per una settimana; **to take ~** togliere; **he was working/pedalling** *etc* **~** (*la particella indica la continuità e l'energia dell'azione*) lavorava/pedalava *etc* più che poteva; **to fade/wither** *etc* **~** (*la particella rinforza l'idea della diminuzione*)
awe [ɔː] *n* timore *m*; **awesome** *adj* imponente

awful ['ɔːfəl] *adj* terribile; **an ~ lot of** un mucchio di; **awfully** *adv* (*very*) terribilmente
awkward ['ɔːkwəd] *adj* (*clumsy*) goffo(-a); (*inconvenient*) scomodo(-a); (*embarrassing*) imbarazzante
awoke [ə'wəuk] *pt of* **awake**
awoken [ə'wəukn] *pp of* **awake**
axe [æks] (*US* **ax**) *n* scure *f* ▷ *vt* (*project etc*) abolire; (*jobs*) sopprimere
axle ['æksl] *n* (*also:* **~-tree**) asse *m*
ay(e) [aɪ] *excl* (*yes*) sì
azalea [ə'zeɪlɪə] *n* azalea

b

B [biː] *n* (*Mus*) si *m*
B.A. *n abbr* = **Bachelor of Arts**
baby ['beɪbɪ] *n* bambino(-a); **baby carriage** (*US*) *n* carrozzina; **baby-sit** *vi* fare il (*or* la) baby-sitter; **baby-sitter** *n* baby-sitter *m/f inv*; **baby wipe** *n* salvietta umidificata
bachelor ['bætʃələ^r] *n* scapolo; **B~ of Arts/Science** ≈ laureato(-a) in lettere/scienze
back [bæk] *n* (*of person, horse*) dorso, schiena; (*as opposed to front*) dietro; (*of hand*) dorso; (*of train*) coda; (*of chair*) schienale *m*; (*of page*) rovescio; (*of book*) retro; (*Football*) difensore *m* ▷ *vt* (*candidate*) appoggiare; (*horse: at races*) puntare su; (*car*) guidare a marcia indietro ▷ *vi* indietreggiare; (*car etc*) fare marcia indietro ▷ *cpd* posteriore, di dietro; (*Aut: seat, wheels*) posteriore ▷ *adv* (*not forward*) indietro; (*returned*): **he's ~** è tornato; **he ran ~** tornò indietro di corsa; (*restitution*): **throw the ball ~** ritira la palla; **can I**

have it ~? posso riaverlo?; (*again*): **he called ~** ha richiamato; **back down** *vi* fare marcia indietro; **back out** *vi* (*of promise*) tirarsi indietro; **back up** *vt* (*support*) appoggiare, sostenere; (*Comput*) fare una copia di riserva di; **backache** *n* mal *m* di schiena; **backbencher** (BRIT) *n membro del Parlamento senza potere amministrativo*; **backbone** *n* spina dorsale; **back door** *n* porta sul retro; **backfire** *vi* (*Aut*) dar ritorni di fiamma; (*plans*) fallire; **backgammon** *n* tavola reale; **background** *n* sfondo; (*of events*) background *m inv*; (*basic knowledge*) base *f*; (*experience*) esperienza; **family background** ambiente *m* familiare; **backing** *n* (*fig*) appoggio; **backlog** *n* **backlog of work** lavoro arretrato; **backpack** *n* zaino; **backpacker** *n chi viaggia con zaino e sacco a pelo*; **backslash** *n* backslash *m inv*, barra obliqua inversa; **backstage** *adv* nel retroscena; **backstroke** *n* nuoto sul dorso; **backup** *adj* (*train, plane*) supplementare; (*Comput*) di riserva ▷ *n* (*support*) appoggio, sostegno; (*also:* **backup file**) file *m inv* di riserva; **backward** *adj* (*movement*) indietro *inv*; (*person*) tardivo(-a); (*country*) arretrato(-a); **backwards** *adv* indietro; (*fall, walk*) all'indietro; **backyard** *n* cortile *m* dietro la casa

bacon ['beɪkən] *n* pancetta

bacteria [bæk'tɪərɪə] *npl* batteri *mpl*

bad [bæd] *adj* cattivo(-a); (*accident, injury*) brutto(-a); (*meat, food*) andato(-a) a male; **his ~ leg** la sua gamba malata; **to go ~** andare a male

badge [bædʒ] *n* insegna; (*of policeman*) stemma *m*

badger ['bædʒəʳ] *n* tasso

badly ['bædlɪ] *adv* (*work, dress etc*) male; **~ wounded** gravemente ferito; **he needs it ~** ne ha un gran bisogno

bad-mannered [bæd'mænəd] *adj* maleducato(-a), sgarbato(-a)

badminton ['bædmɪntən] *n* badminton *m*

bad-tempered ['bæd'tɛmpəd] *adj* irritabile; di malumore

bag [bæg] *n* sacco; (*handbag etc*) borsa; **~s of** (*inf: lots of*) un sacco di; **baggage** *n* bagagli *mpl*; **baggage allowance** *n* franchigia *f* bagaglio *inv*; **baggage reclaim** *n* ritiro *m* bagaglio *inv*; **baggy** *adj* largo(-a), sformato(-a); **bagpipes** *npl* cornamusa

bail [beɪl] *n* cauzione *f* ▷ *vt* (*prisoner: also:* **grant ~ to**) concedere la libertà provvisoria su cauzione a; (*boat: also:* **~ out**) aggottare; **on ~** in libertà provvisoria su cauzione

bait [beɪt] *n* esca ▷ *vt* (*hook*) innescare; (*trap*) munire di esca; (*fig*) tormentare

bake [beɪk] *vt* cuocere al forno ▷ *vi* cuocersi al forno; **baked beans** [-biːnz] *npl* fagioli *mpl* in salsa di pomodoro; **baked potato** *n* patata cotta al forno con la buccia; **baker** *n* fornaio(-a), panettiere(-a); **bakery** *n* panetteria; **baking** *n* cottura (al forno); **baking powder** *n* lievito in polvere

balance ['bæləns] *n* equilibrio; (*Comm: sum*) bilancio; (*remainder*) resto; (*scales*) bilancia ▷ *vt* tenere in equilibrio; (*budget*) far quadrare; (*account*) pareggiare; (*compensate*) contrappesare; **~ of trade/payments** bilancia commerciale/dei pagamenti; **balanced** *adj* (*personality, diet*) equilibrato(-a); **balance sheet** *n* bilancio

balcony ['bælkənɪ] *n* balcone *m*; (*in theatre*) balconata; **do you have a room with a ~?** avete una camera con balcone?

bald [bɔːld] *adj* calvo(-a); (*tyre*) liscio(-a)

Balearics [bælɪ'ærɪks] *npl*: **the ~** le Baleari *fpl*

ball [bɔːl] *n* palla; (*football*) pallone *m*; (*for golf*) pallina; (*of wool, string*) gomitolo; (*dance*) ballo; **to play ~** (*fig*)

stare al gioco
ballerina [bælə'ri:nə] *n* ballerina
ballet ['bæleɪ] *n* balletto; **ballet dancer** *n* ballerino(-a) classico(-a)
balloon [bə'lu:n] *n* pallone *m*
ballot ['bælət] *n* scrutinio
ballpoint (pen) ['bɔ:lpɔɪnt(-)] *n* penna a sfera
ballroom ['bɔ:lrum] *n* sala da ballo
Baltic ['bɔ:ltɪk] *adj, n* **the ~ Sea** il (mar) Baltico
bamboo [bæm'bu:] *n* bambù *m*
ban [bæn] *n* interdizione *f* ▷ *vt* interdire
banana [bə'nɑ:nə] *n* banana
band [bænd] *n* banda; (*at a dance*) orchestra; (*Mil*) fanfara
bandage ['bændɪdʒ] *n* benda, fascia
Band-Aid® ['bændeɪd] (US) *n* cerotto
B. & B. *n abbr* = **bed and breakfast**
bandit ['bændɪt] *n* bandito
bang [bæŋ] *n* (*of door*) lo sbattere; (*of gun, blow*) colpo ▷ *vt* battere (violentemente); (*door*) sbattere ▷ *vi* scoppiare; sbattere
Bangladesh [bɑ:ŋglə'dɛʃ] *n* Bangladesh *m*
bangle ['bæŋgl] *n* braccialetto
bangs [bæŋz] (US) *npl* (*fringe*) frangia, frangetta
banish ['bænɪʃ] *vt* bandire
banister(s) ['bænɪstə(z)] *n(pl)* ringhiera
banjo ['bændʒəu] (*pl* **banjoes** *or* **banjos**) *n* banjo *m inv*
bank [bæŋk] *n* banca, banco; (*of river, lake*) riva, sponda; (*of earth*) banco ▷ *vi* (*Aviat*) inclinarsi in virata; **bank on** *vt fus* contare su; **bank account** *n* conto in banca; **bank balance** *n* saldo; **a healthy bank balance** un solido conto in banca; **bank card** *n* carta *f* assegni *inv*; **bank charges** *npl* (BRIT) spese *fpl* bancarie; **banker** *n* banchiere *m*; **bank holiday** (BRIT) *n* giorno di festa; *vedi nota nel riquadro*; **banking** *n* attività bancaria; professione *f* di banchiere; **bank manager** *n* direttore *m* di banca; **banknote** *n* banconota

BANK HOLIDAY

Una **bank holiday**, in Gran Bretagna, è una giornata in cui banche e molti negozi sono chiusi. Generalmente le **bank holidays** cadono di lunedì e molti ne approfittano per fare una breve vacanza fuori città.

bankrupt ['bæŋkrʌpt] *adj* fallito(-a); **to go ~** fallire; **bankruptcy** *n* fallimento
bank statement *n* estratto conto
banner ['bænə^r] *n* striscione *m*
bannister(s) ['bænɪstə(z)] *n(pl) see* **banister(s)**
banquet ['bæŋkwɪt] *n* banchetto
baptism ['bæptɪzəm] *n* battesimo
baptize [bæp'taɪz] *vt* battezzare
bar [bɑ:^{r}] *n* (*place*) bar *m inv*; (*counter*) banco; (*rod*) barra; (*of window etc*) sbarra; (*of chocolate*) tavoletta; (*fig*) ostacolo; restrizione *f*; (*Mus*) battuta ▷ *vt* (*road, window*) sbarrare; (*person*) escludere; (*activity*) interdire; **~ of soap** saponetta; **the B~** (*Law*) l'Ordine *m* degli avvocati; **behind ~s** (*prisoner*) dietro le sbarre; **~ none** senza eccezione
barbaric [bɑ:'bærɪk] *adj* barbarico(-a)
barbecue ['bɑ:bɪkju:] *n* barbecue *m inv*
barbed wire ['bɑ:bd-] *n* filo spinato
barber ['bɑ:bə^r] *n* barbiere *m*; **barber's (shop)** (US **barber (shop)**) *n* barbiere *m*
bar code *n* (*on goods*) codice *m* a barre
bare [bɛə^r] *adj* nudo(-a) ▷ *vt* scoprire, denudare; (*teeth*) mostrare; **the ~ necessities** lo stretto necessario; **barefoot** *adj, adv* scalzo(-a); **barely** *adv* appena

bargain ['bɑ:gɪn] *n* (*transaction*) contratto; (*good buy*) affare *m* ▷ *vi* trattare; **into the ~** per giunta; **bargain for** *vt fus* **he got more than he bargained for** gli è andata peggio di quel che si aspettasse
barge [bɑ:dʒ] *n* chiatta; **barge in** *vi* (*walk in*) piombare dentro; (*interrupt talk*) intromettersi a sproposito
bark [bɑ:k] *n* (*of tree*) corteccia; (*of dog*) abbaio ▷ *vi* abbaiare
barley ['bɑ:lɪ] *n* orzo
barmaid ['bɑ:meɪd] *n* cameriera al banco
barman ['bɑ:mən] (*irreg*) *n* barista *m*
barn [bɑ:n] *n* granaio
barometer [bə'rɔmɪtəʳ] *n* barometro
baron ['bærən] *n* barone *m*; **baroness** *n* baronessa
barracks ['bærəks] *npl* caserma
barrage ['bærɑ:ʒ] *n* (*Mil, dam*) sbarramento; (*fig*) fiume *m*
barrel ['bærəl] *n* barile *m*; (*of gun*) canna
barren ['bærən] *adj* sterile; (*soil*) arido(-a)
barrette [bə'rɛt] (US) *n* fermaglio per capelli
barricade [bærɪ'keɪd] *n* barricata
barrier ['bærɪəʳ] *n* barriera
barring ['bɑ:rɪŋ] *prep* salvo
barrister ['bærɪstəʳ] (BRIT) *n* avvocato(-essa) (*con diritto di parlare davanti a tutte le corti*)
barrow ['bærəu] *n* (*cart*) carriola
bartender ['bɑ:tɛndəʳ] (US) *n* barista *m*
base [beɪs] *n* base *f* ▷ *vt* **to ~ sth on** basare qc su ▷ *adj* vile
baseball ['beɪsbɔ:l] *n* baseball *m*; **baseball cap** *n* berretto da baseball
basement ['beɪsmənt] *n* seminterrato; (*of shop*) interrato
bases¹ ['beɪsi:z] *npl of* **basis**
bases² ['beɪsɪz] *npl of* **base**
bash [bæʃ] (*inf*) *vt* picchiare
basic ['beɪsɪk] *adj* rudimentale; essenziale; **basically** [-lɪ] *adv* fondamentalmente; sostanzialmente; **basics** *npl* **the basics** l'essenziale *m*
basil ['bæzl] *n* basilico
basin ['beɪsn] *n* (*vessel: also Geo*) bacino; (*also:* **wash~**) lavabo
basis ['beɪsɪs] (*pl* **bases**) *n* base *f*; **on a part-time ~** part-time; **on a trial ~** in prova
basket ['bɑ:skɪt] *n* cesta; (*smaller*) cestino; (*with handle*) paniere *m*; **basketball** *n* pallacanestro *f*
bass [beɪs] *n* (*Mus*) basso
bastard ['bɑ:stəd] *n* bastardo(-a); (*inf!*) stronzo (*!*)
bat [bæt] *n* pipistrello; (*for baseball etc*) mazza; (BRIT: *for table tennis*) racchetta ▷ *vt* **he didn't ~ an eyelid** non battè ciglio
batch [bætʃ] *n* (*of bread*) infornata; (*of papers*) cumulo
bath [bɑ:θ] *n* bagno; (*bathtub*) vasca da bagno ▷ *vt* far fare il bagno a; **to have a ~** fare un bagno; *see also* **baths**
bathe [beɪð] *vi* fare il bagno ▷ *vt* (*wound*) lavare
bathing ['beɪðɪŋ] *n* bagni *mpl*; **bathing costume** (US **bathing suit**) *n* costume *m* da bagno
bath: **bathrobe** ['bɑ:θrəub] *n* accappatoio; **bathroom** ['bɑ:θrum] *n* stanza da bagno; **baths** [bɑ:ðz] *npl* bagni *mpl* pubblici; **bath towel** *n* asciugamano da bagno; **bathtub** *n* (vasca da) bagno
baton ['bætən] *n* (*Mus*) bacchetta; (*Athletics*) testimone *m*; (*club*) manganello
batter ['bætəʳ] *vt* battere ▷ *n* pastetta; **battered** *adj* (*hat*) sformato(-a); (*pan*) ammaccato(-a)
battery ['bætərɪ] *n* batteria; (*of torch*) pila; **battery farming** *n allevamento in batteria*
battle ['bætl] *n* battaglia ▷ *vi* battagliare, lottare; **battlefield** *n* campo di battaglia

bay [beɪ] *n* (*of sea*) baia; **to hold sb at ~** tenere qn a bada

bazaar [bə'zɑːʳ] *n* bazar *m inv*; vendita di beneficenza

BBC *n abbr* (= *British Broadcasting Corporation*) *rete nazionale di radiotelevisione in Gran Bretagna*

BBC

La **BBC** è l'azienda statale che fornisce il servizio radiofonico e televisivo in Gran Bretagna. Ha due reti televisive terrestri (BBC1 e BBC2), e cinque stazioni radiofoniche nazionali. Oggi la BBC ha anche diverse stazioni digitali radiofoniche e televisive. Da molti anni fornisce inoltre un servizio di intrattenimento e informazione internazionale, il "BBC World Service", trasmesso in tutto il mondo.

B.C. *adv abbr* (= *before Christ*) a.C.

KEYWORD

be [biː] (*pt* **was, were**, *pp* **been**) *aux vb* **1** (*with present participle: forming continuous tenses*): **what are you doing?** che fa?, che sta facendo?; **they're coming tomorrow** vengono domani; **I've been waiting for her for hours** sono ore che l'aspetto
2 (*with pp: forming passives*) essere; **to be killed** essere *or* venire ucciso(-a); **the box had been opened** la scatola era stata aperta; **the thief was nowhere to be seen** il ladro non si trovava da nessuna parte
3 (*in tag questions*): **it was fun, wasn't it?** è stato divertente, no?; **he's good-looking, isn't he?** è un bell'uomo, vero?; **she's back, is she?** così è tornata, eh?
4 (*+ to + infinitive*): **the house is to be sold** abbiamo *or* hanno *etc* intenzione di vendere casa; **you're to be congratulated for all your work** dovremo farvi i complimenti per tutto il vostro lavoro; **he's not to open it** non deve aprirlo
▷ *vb + complement* **1** (*gen*) essere; **I'm English** sono inglese; **I'm tired** sono stanco(-a); **I'm hot/cold** ho caldo/freddo; **he's a doctor** è medico; **2 and 2 are 4** 2 più 2 fa 4; **be careful!** sta attento(-a)!; **be good** sii buono(-a)
2 (*of health*) stare; **how are you?** come sta?; **he's very ill** sta molto male
3 (*of age*): **how old are you?** quanti anni hai?; **I'm sixteen (years old)** ho sedici anni
4 (*cost*) costare; **how much was the meal?** quant'era *or* quanto costava il pranzo?; **that'll be £5, please** (fa) 5 sterline, per favore
▷ *vi* **1** (*exist, occur etc*) essere, esistere; **the best singer that ever was** il migliore cantante mai esistito *or* di tutti tempi; **be that as it may** comunque sia, sia come sia; **so be it** sia pure, e sia
2 (*referring to place*) essere, trovarsi; **I won't be here tomorrow** non ci sarò domani; **Edinburgh is in Scotland** Edimburgo si trova in Scozia
3 (*referring to movement*): **where have you been?** dov'è stato?; **I've been to China** sono stato in Cina
▷ *impers vb* **1** (*referring to time, distance*) essere; **it's 5 o'clock** sono le 5; **it's the 28th of April** è il 28 aprile; **it's 10 km to the village** di qui al paese sono 10 km
2 (*referring to the weather*) fare; **it's too hot/cold** fa troppo caldo/freddo; **it's windy** c'è vento
3 (*emphatic*): **it's me** sono io; **it was Maria who paid the bill** è stata Maria che ha pagato il conto

beach [biːtʃ] *n* spiaggia ▷ *vt* tirare

in secco
beacon ['bi:kən] *n* (*lighthouse*) faro; (*marker*) segnale *m*
bead [bi:d] *n* perlina; **beads** *npl* (*necklace*) collana
beak [bi:k] *n* becco
beam [bi:m] *n* trave *f*; (*of light*) raggio ▷ *vi* brillare
bean [bi:n] *n* fagiolo; (*of coffee*) chicco; **runner ~** fagiolino; **beansprouts** *npl* germogli *mpl* di soia
bear [bɛə^r] (*pt* **bore**, *pp* **borne**) *n* orso ▷ *vt* portare; (*endure*) sopportare; (*produce*) generare ▷ *vi* **to ~ right/left** piegare a destra/sinistra
beard [bɪəd] *n* barba
bearer ['bɛərə^r] *n* portatore *m*
bearing ['bɛərɪŋ] *n* portamento; (*connection*) rapporto
beast [bi:st] *n* bestia
beat [bi:t] (*pt* **beat**, *pp* **beaten**) *n* colpo; (*of heart*) battito; (*Mus*) tempo; battuta; (*of policeman*) giro ▷ *vt* battere; (*eggs, cream*) sbattere ▷ *vi* battere; **off the ~en track** fuori mano; **~ it!** (*inf*) fila!, fuori dai piedi!; **beat up** *vt* (*person*) picchiare; (*eggs*) sbattere; **beating** *n* bastonata
beautiful ['bju:tɪful] *adj* bello(-a); **beautifully** *adv* splendidamente
beauty ['bju:tɪ] *n* bellezza; **beauty parlour** [-'pɑ:lə^r] (US **beauty parlor**) *n* salone *m* di bellezza; **beauty salon** *n* istituto di bellezza; **beauty spot** (BRIT) *n* (*Tourism*) luogo pittoresco
beaver ['bi:və^r] *n* castoro
became [bɪ'keɪm] *pt of* **become**
because [bɪ'kɔz] *conj* perché; **~ of** a causa di
beckon ['bɛkən] *vt* (*also:* **~ to**) chiamare con un cenno
become [bɪ'kʌm] (*irreg: like* **come**) *vt* diventare; **to ~ fat/thin** ingrassarsi/dimagrire
bed [bɛd] *n* letto; (*of flowers*) aiuola; (*of coal, clay*) strato; **single/double ~** letto a una piazza/a due piazze *or* matrimoniale; **bed and breakfast** *n* (*place*) ≈ pensione *f* familiare; (*terms*) camera con colazione; *vedi nota nel riquadro*; **bedclothes** ['bɛdkləuðz] *npl* biancheria e coperte *fpl* da letto; **bedding** *n* coperte e lenzuola *fpl*; **bed linen** *n* biancheria da letto; **bedroom** *n* camera da letto; **bedside** *n* **at sb's bedside** al capezzale di qn; **bedside lamp** *n* lampada da comodino; **bedside table** *n* comodino; **bedsit(ter)** (BRIT) *n* monolocale *m*; **bedspread** *n* copriletto; **bedtime** *n* **it's bedtime** è ora di andare a letto

BED AND BREAKFAST

I **bed and breakfasts**, anche **B & Bs**, sono piccole pensioni a conduzione familiare, più economiche rispetto agli alberghi, dove al mattino viene servita la tradizionale colazione all'inglese.

bee [bi:] *n* ape *f*
beech [bi:tʃ] *n* faggio
beef [bi:f] *n* manzo; **roast ~** arrosto di manzo; **beefburger** *n* hamburger *m inv*; **Beefeater** *n* guardia della Torre di Londra
been [bi:n] *pp of* **be**
beer [bɪə^r] *n* birra; **beer garden** *n* (BRIT) giardino (*di pub*)
beet [bi:t] (US) *n* (*also:* **red ~**) barbabietola rossa
beetle ['bi:tl] *n* scarafaggio; coleottero
beetroot ['bi:tru:t] (BRIT) *n* barbabietola
before [bɪ'fɔ:^{r}] *prep* (*in time*) prima di; (*in space*) davanti a ▷ *conj* prima che + *sub*; prima di ▷ *adv* prima; **~ going** prima di andare; **~ she goes** prima che vada; **the week ~** la settimana prima; **I've seen it ~** l'ho già visto; **I've never seen it ~** è la prima volta che lo vedo; **beforehand** *adv* in anticipo

beg [bɛg] *vi* chiedere l'elemosina ▷ *vt* (*also:* **~ for**) chiedere in elemosina; (*favour*) chiedere; **to ~ sb to do** pregare qn di fare
began [bɪ'gæn] *pt of* **begin**
beggar ['bɛgəʳ] *n* mendicante *m/f*
begin [bɪ'gɪn] (*pt* **began**, *pp* **begun**) *vt, vi* cominciare; **to ~ doing** *or* **to do sth** incominciare *or* iniziare a fare qc; **beginner** *n* principiante *m/f*; **beginning** *n* inizio, principio
begun [bɪ'gʌn] *pp of* **begin**
behalf [bɪ'hɑ:f] *n* **on ~ of** per conto di; a nome di
behave [bɪ'heɪv] *vi* comportarsi; (*well: also:* **~ o.s.**) comportarsi bene; **behaviour** [bɪ'heɪvjəʳ] (*US* **behavior**) *n* comportamento, condotta
behind [bɪ'haɪnd] *prep* dietro; (*followed by pronoun*) dietro di; (*time*) in ritardo con ▷ *adv* dietro; (*leave, stay*) indietro ▷ *n* didietro; **to be ~ (schedule)** essere in ritardo rispetto al programma; **~ the scenes** (*fig*) dietro le quinte
beige [beɪʒ] *adj* beige *inv*
Beijing ['beɪ'dʒɪŋ] *n* Pechino *f*
being ['bi:ɪŋ] *n* essere *m*
belated [bɪ'leɪtɪd] *adj* tardo(-a)
belch [bɛltʃ] *vi* ruttare ▷ *vt* (*gen: belch out: smoke etc*) eruttare
Belgian ['bɛldʒən] *adj, n* belga *m/f*
Belgium ['bɛldʒəm] *n* Belgio
belief [bɪ'li:f] *n* (*opinion*) opinione *f*, convinzione *f*; (*trust, faith*) fede *f*
believe [bɪ'li:v] *vt, vi* credere; **to ~ in** (*God*) credere in; (*ghosts*) credere a; (*method*) avere fiducia in; **believer** *n* (*Rel*) credente *m/f*; (*in idea, activity*): **to be a believer in** credere in
bell [bɛl] *n* campana; (*small, on door, electric*) campanello
bellboy ['bɛlbɔɪ], (*US*) **bellhop** ['bɛlhɔp] *n* ragazzo d'albergo, fattorino d'albergo
bellow ['bɛləu] *vi* muggire
bell pepper (*esp US*) *n* peperone *m*
belly ['bɛlɪ] *n* pancia; **belly button** *n* ombelico
belong [bɪ'lɔŋ] *vi* **to ~ to** appartenere a; (*club etc*) essere socio di; **this book ~s here** questo libro va qui; **belongings** *npl* cose *fpl*, roba
beloved [bɪ'lʌvɪd] *adj* adorato(-a)
below [bɪ'ləu] *prep* sotto, al di sotto di ▷ *adv* sotto, di sotto; giù; **see ~** vedi sotto *or* oltre
belt [bɛlt] *n* cintura; (*Tech*) cinghia ▷ *vt* (*thrash*) picchiare ▷ *vi* (*inf*) filarsela; **beltway** (*US*) *n* (*Aut: ring road*) circonvallazione *f*; (*: motorway*) autostrada
bemused [bɪ'mju:zd] *adj* perplesso(-a), stupito(-a)
bench [bɛntʃ] *n* panca; (*in workshop, Pol*) banco; **the B~** (*Law*) la Corte
bend [bɛnd] (*pt, pp* **bent**) *vt* curvare; (*leg, arm*) piegare ▷ *vi* curvarsi; piegarsi ▷ *n* (BRIT: *in road*) curva; (*in pipe, river*) gomito; **bend down** *vi* chinarsi; **bend over** *vi* piegarsi
beneath [bɪ'ni:θ] *prep* sotto, al di sotto di; (*unworthy of*) indegno(-a) di ▷ *adv* sotto, di sotto
beneficial [bɛnɪ'fɪʃəl] *adj* che fa bene; vantaggioso(-a)
benefit ['bɛnɪfɪt] *n* beneficio, vantaggio; (*allowance of money*) indennità *f inv* ▷ *vt* far bene a ▷ *vi* **he'll ~ from it** ne trarrà beneficio *or* profitto
benign [bɪ'naɪn] *adj* (*person, smile*) benevolo(-a); (*Med*) benigno(-a)
bent [bɛnt] *pt, pp of* **bend** ▷ *n* inclinazione *f* ▷ *adj* (*inf: dishonest*) losco(-a); **to be ~ on** essere deciso(-a) a
bereaved [bɪ'ri:vd] *n* **the ~** i familiari in lutto
beret ['bɛreɪ] *n* berretto
Berlin [bə:'lɪn] *n* Berlino *f*
Bermuda [bə:'mju:də] *n* le Bermude
berry ['bɛrɪ] *n* bacca
berth [bə:θ] *n* (*bed*) cuccetta; (*for ship*) ormeggio ▷ *vi* (*in harbour*) entrare in

porto; (*at anchor*) gettare l'ancora
beside [bɪ'saɪd] *prep* accanto a; **to be ~ o.s. (with anger)** essere fuori di sé (dalla rabbia); **that's ~ the point** non c'entra; **besides** [bɪ'saɪdz] *adv* inoltre, per di più ▷ *prep* oltre a; a parte
best [bɛst] *adj* migliore ▷ *adv* meglio; **the ~ part of** (*quantity*) la maggior parte di; **at ~** tutt'al più; **to make the ~ of sth** cavare il meglio possibile da qc; **to do one's ~** fare del proprio meglio; **to the ~ of my knowledge** per quel che ne so; **to the ~ of my ability** al massimo delle mie capacità; **best-before date** *n* scadenza; **best man** (*irreg*) *n* testimone *m* dello sposo; **bestseller** *n* bestseller *m inv*
bet [bɛt] (*pt, pp* **bet** *or* **betted**) *n* scommessa ▷ *vt, vi* scommettere; **to ~ sb sth** scommettere qc con qn
betray [bɪ'treɪ] *vt* tradire
better ['bɛtəʳ] *adj* migliore ▷ *adv* meglio ▷ *vt* migliorare ▷ *n* **to get the ~ of** avere la meglio su; **you had ~ do it** è meglio che lo faccia; **he thought ~ of it** cambiò idea; **to get ~** migliorare
betting ['bɛtɪŋ] *n* scommesse *fpl*; **betting shop** (BRIT) *n* ufficio dell'allibratore
between [bɪ'twi:n] *prep* tra ▷ *adv* in mezzo, nel mezzo
beverage ['bɛvərɪdʒ] *n* bevanda
beware [bɪ'wɛəʳ] *vt, vi* **to ~ (of)** stare attento(-a) (a); **"~ of the dog"** "attenti al cane"
bewildered [bɪ'wɪldəd] *adj* sconcertato(-a), confuso(-a)
beyond [bɪ'jɔnd] *prep* (*in space*) oltre; (*exceeding*) al di sopra di ▷ *adv* di là; **~ doubt** senza dubbio; **~ repair** irreparabile
bias ['baɪəs] *n* (*prejudice*) pregiudizio; (*preference*) preferenza; **bias(s)ed** *adj* parziale
bib [bɪb] *n* bavaglino
Bible ['baɪbl] *n* Bibbia
bicarbonate of soda [baɪ'kɑ:bənɪt-] *n* bicarbonato (di sodio)
biceps ['baɪsɛps] *n* bicipite *m*
bicycle ['baɪsɪkl] *n* bicicletta; **bicycle pump** *n* pompa della bicicletta
bid [bɪd] (*pt* **bade** *or* **bid**, *pp* **bidden** *or* **bid**) *n* offerta; (*attempt*) tentativo ▷ *vi* fare un'offerta ▷ *vt* fare un'offerta di; **to ~ sb good day** dire buon giorno a qn; **bidder** *n* **the highest bidder** il maggior offerente
bidet ['bi:deɪ] *n* bidè *m inv*
big [bɪg] *adj* grande; grosso(-a); **Big Apple** *n vedi nota nel riquadro*; **bigheaded** ['bɪg'hɛdɪd] *adj* presuntuoso(-a); **big toe** *n* alluce *m*

BIG APPLE

Tutti sanno che **The Big Apple**, la Grande Mela, è New York ("apple" in gergo significa grande città), ma sicuramente i soprannomi di altre città americane non sono così conosciuti. Chicago è soprannominata "the Windy City" perché è ventosa, New Orleans si chiama "the Big Easy" per il modo di vivere tranquillo e rilassato dei suoi abitanti, e l'industria automobilistica ha fatto sì che Detroit fosse soprannominata "Motown".

bike [baɪk] *n* bici *f inv*; **bike lane** *n* pista ciclabile
bikini [bɪ'ki:nɪ] *n* bikini *m inv*
bilateral [baɪ'lætərl] *adj* bilaterale
bilingual [baɪ'lɪŋgwəl] *adj* bilingue
bill [bɪl] *n* conto; (*Pol*) atto; (US: *banknote*) banconota; (*of bird*) becco; (*of show*) locandina; **can I have the ~, please** il conto, per favore; **put it on my ~** lo metta sul mio conto; **"post no ~s"** "divieto di affissione"; **to fit** *or* **fill the ~** (*fig*) fare al caso; **billboard** *n* tabellone *m*; **billfold** ['bɪlfəuld] (US) *n* portafoglio

billiards ['bɪljədz] *n* biliardo
billion ['bɪljən] *num* (BRIT) bilione *m*; (US) miliardo
bin [bɪn] *n* (*for coal, rubbish*) bidone *m*; (*for bread*) cassetta; (*dustbin*) pattumiera; (*litter bin*) cestino
bind [baɪnd] (*pt, pp* **bound**) *vt* legare; (*oblige*) obbligare ▷ *n* (*inf*) scocciatura
binge [bɪndʒ] (*inf*) *n* **to go on a ~** fare baldoria; **binge drinker** *n persona che di norma beve troppo*
bingo ['bɪŋgəu] *n gioco simile alla tombola*
binoculars [bɪ'nɔkjuləz] *npl* binocolo
bio... [baɪə'...] *prefix*; **biochemistry** *n* biochimica; **biodegradable** *adj* biodegradabile; **biography** [baɪ'ɔgrəfɪ] *n* biografia; **biological** *adj* biologico(-a); **biology** [baɪ'ɔlədʒɪ] *n* biologia; **biometric** [baɪə'mɛtrɪk] *adj* biometrico(-a)
birch [bə:tʃ] *n* betulla
bird [bə:d] *n* uccello; (BRIT: *inf: girl*) bambola; **bird flu** *n* influenza aviaria; **bird of prey** *n* (uccello) rapace *m*; **birdwatching** *n* birdwatching *m*
Biro® ['baɪrəu] *n* biro® *f inv*
birth [bə:θ] *n* nascita; **to give ~ to** partorire; **birth certificate** *n* certificato di nascita; **birth control** *n* controllo delle nascite; contraccezione *f*; **birthday** *n* compleanno ▷ *cpd* di compleanno; **birthmark** *n* voglia; **birthplace** *n* luogo di nascita
biscuit ['bɪskɪt] (BRIT) *n* biscotto
bishop ['bɪʃəp] *n* vescovo
bistro ['bi:strəu] *n* bistrò *m inv*
bit [bɪt] *pt of* **bite** ▷ *n* pezzo; (*Comput*) bit *m inv*; (*of horse*) morso; **a ~ of** un po' di; **a ~ mad** un po' matto; **~ by ~** a poco a poco
bitch [bɪtʃ] *n* (*dog*) cagna; (*inf!*) vacca
bite [baɪt] (*pt, pp* **bit, bitten**) *vt, vi* mordere; (*insect*) pungere ▷ *n* morso; (*insect bite*) puntura; (*mouthful*) boccone *m*; **let's have a ~ to eat** mangiamo un boccone; **to ~ one's nails** mangiarsi le unghie
bitten ['bɪtn] *pp of* **bite**
bitter ['bɪtə^r] *adj* amaro(-a); (*wind, criticism*) pungente ▷ *n* (BRIT: *beer*) birra amara
bizarre [bɪ'zɑ:^r] *adj* bizzarro(-a)
black [blæk] *adj* nero(-a) ▷ *n* nero; (*person*): **B~** negro(-a) ▷ *vt* (BRIT *Industry*) boicottare; **to give sb a ~ eye** fare un occhio nero a qn; **in the ~** (*bank account*) in attivo; **black out** *vi* (*faint*) svenire; **blackberry** *n* mora; **blackbird** *n* merlo; **blackboard** *n* lavagna; **black coffee** *n* caffè *m inv* nero; **blackcurrant** *n* ribes *m inv*; **black ice** *n* strato trasparente di ghiaccio; **blackmail** *n* ricatto ▷ *vt* ricattare; **black market** *n* mercato nero; **blackout** *n* oscuramento; (*TV, Radio*) interruzione *f* delle trasmissioni; (*fainting*) svenimento; **black pepper** *n* pepe *m* nero; **black pudding** *n* sanguinaccio; **Black Sea** *n* **the Black Sea** il Mar Nero
bladder ['blædə^r] *n* vescica
blade [bleɪd] *n* lama; (*of oar*) pala; **~ of grass** filo d'erba
blame [bleɪm] *n* colpa ▷ *vt* **to ~ sb/sth for sth** dare la colpa di qc a qn/qc; **who's to ~?** chi è colpevole?
bland [blænd] *adj* mite; (*taste*) blando(-a)
blank [blæŋk] *adj* bianco(-a); (*look*) distratto(-a) ▷ *n* spazio vuoto; (*cartridge*) cartuccia a salve
blanket ['blæŋkɪt] *n* coperta
blast [blɑ:st] *n* (*of wind*) raffica; (*of bomb etc*) esplosione *f* ▷ *vt* far saltare
blatant ['bleɪtənt] *adj* flagrante
blaze [bleɪz] *n* (*fire*) incendio; (*fig*) vampata; splendore *m* ▷ *vi* (*fire*) ardere, fiammeggiare; (*guns*) sparare senza sosta; (*fig: eyes*) ardere ▷ *vt* **to ~ a trail** (*fig*) tracciare una via nuova; **in a ~ of publicity** circondato da grande pubblicità

blazer ['bleɪzəʳ] *n* blazer *m inv*
bleach [bli:tʃ] *n* (*also:* **household ~**) varechina ▷ *vt* (*material*) candeggiare; **bleachers** (*US*) *npl* (*Sport*) posti *mpl* di gradinata
bleak [bli:k] *adj* tetro(-a)
bled [blɛd] *pt, pp of* **bleed**
bleed [bli:d] (*pt, pp* **bled**) *vi* sanguinare; **my nose is ~ing** mi viene fuori sangue dal naso
blemish ['blɛmɪʃ] *n* macchia
blend [blɛnd] *n* miscela ▷ *vt* mescolare ▷ *vi* (*colours etc: also:* **~ in**) armonizzare; **blender** *n* (*Culin*) frullatore *m*
bless [blɛs] (*pt, pp* **blessed** *or* **blest**) *vt* benedire; **~ you!** (*after sneeze*) salute!; **blessing** *n* benedizione *f*; fortuna
blew [blu:] *pt of* **blow**
blight [blaɪt] *vt* (*hopes etc*) deludere; (*life*) rovinare
blind [blaɪnd] *adj* cieco(-a) ▷ *n* (*for window*) avvolgibile *m*; (*Venetian blind*) veneziana ▷ *vt* accecare; **the blind** *npl* i ciechi; **blind alley** *n* vicolo cieco; **blindfold** *n* benda ▷ *adj, adv* bendato(-a) ▷ *vt* bendare gli occhi a
blink [blɪŋk] *vi* battere gli occhi; (*light*) lampeggiare
bliss [blɪs] *n* estasi *f*
blister ['blɪstəʳ] *n* (*on skin*) vescica; (*on paintwork*) bolla ▷ *vi* (*paint*) coprirsi di bolle
blizzard ['blɪzəd] *n* bufera di neve
bloated ['bləutɪd] *adj* gonfio(-a)
blob [blɔb] *n* (*drop*) goccia; (*stain, spot*) macchia
block [blɔk] *n* blocco; (*in pipes*) ingombro; (*toy*) cubo; (*of buildings*) isolato ▷ *vt* bloccare; **the sink is ~ed** il lavandino è otturato; **block up** *vt* bloccare; (*pipe*) ingorgare, intasare; **blockade** [-'keɪd] *n* blocco; **blockage** *n* ostacolo; **blockbuster** *n* (*film, book*) grande successo; **block capitals** *npl* stampatello; **block letters** *npl* stampatello
blog [blɔg] *n* blog *m inv* ▷ *vi* scrivere un blog
bloke [bləuk] (*BRIT: inf*) *n* tizio
blond(e) [blɔnd] *adj, n* biondo(-a)
blood [blʌd] *n* sangue *m*; **blood donor** *n* donatore(-trice) di sangue; **blood group** *n* gruppo sanguigno; **blood poisoning** *n* setticemia; **blood pressure** *n* pressione *f* sanguigna; **bloodshed** *n* spargimento di sangue; **bloodshot** *adj* **bloodshot eyes** occhi iniettati di sangue; **bloodstream** *n* flusso del sangue; **blood test** *n* analisi *f inv* del sangue; **blood transfusion** *n* trasfusione *f* di sangue; **blood type** *n* gruppo sanguigno; **blood vessel** *n* vaso sanguigno; **bloody** *adj* (*fight*) sanguinoso(-a); (*nose*) sanguinante; (*BRIT: inf!*): **this bloody ...** questo maledetto ...; **bloody awful/good** (*inf!*) veramente terribile/forte
bloom [blu:m] *n* fiore *m* ▷ *vi* (*tree*) essere in fiore; (*flower*) aprirsi
blossom ['blɔsəm] *n* fiore *m*; (*with pl sense*) fiori *mpl* ▷ *vi* essere in fiore
blot [blɔt] *n* macchia ▷ *vt* macchiare
blouse [blauz] *n* (*feminine garment*) camicetta
blow [bləu] (*pt* **blew**, *pp* **blown**) *n* colpo ▷ *vi* soffiare ▷ *vt* (*fuse*) far saltare; (*wind*) spingere; (*instrument*) suonare; **to ~ one's nose** soffiarsi il naso; **to ~ a whistle** fischiare; **blow away** *vt* portare via; **blow out** *vi* scoppiare; **blow up** *vi* saltare in aria ▷ *vt* far saltare in aria; (*tyre*) gonfiare; (*Phot*) ingrandire; **blow-dry** *n* messa in piega a föhn
blown [bləun] *pp of* **blow**
blue [blu:] *adj* azzurro(-a); (*depressed*) giù *inv*; **~ film/joke** film/barzelletta pornografico(-a); **out of the ~** (*fig*) all'improvviso; **bluebell** *n* giacinto dei boschi; **blueberry** *n* mirtillo; **blue cheese** *n* *formaggio tipo gorgonzola*; **blues** *npl* **the blues** (*Mus*) il blues; **to**

have the blues (*inf: feeling*) essere a terra; **bluetit** *n* cinciarella
bluff [blʌf] *vi* bluffare ▷ *n* bluff *m inv* ▷ *adj* (*person*) brusco(-a); **to call sb's ~** mettere alla prova il bluff di qn
blunder ['blʌndəʳ] *n* abbaglio ▷ *vi* prendere un abbaglio
blunt [blʌnt] *adj* smussato(-a); spuntato(-a); (*person*) brusco(-a)
blur [bləːʳ] *n* forma indistinta ▷ *vt* offuscare; **blurred** *adj* (*photo*) mosso(-a); (*TV*) sfuocato(-a)
blush [blʌʃ] *vi* arrossire ▷ *n* rossore *m*; **blusher** *n* fard *m inv*
board [bɔːd] *n* tavola; (*on wall*) tabellone *m*; (*committee*) consiglio, comitato; (*in firm*) consiglio d'amministrazione; (*Naut, Aviat*): **on ~** a bordo ▷ *vt* (*ship*) salire a bordo di; (*train*) salire su; **full ~** (BRIT) pensione completa; **half ~** (BRIT) mezza pensione; **~ and lodging** vitto e alloggio; **which goes by the ~** (*fig*) che viene abbandonato; **board game** *n* gioco da tavolo; **boarding card** *n* = **boarding pass**; **boarding pass** *n* (*Aviat, Naut*) carta d'imbarco; **boarding school** *n* collegio; **board room** *n* sala del consiglio
boast [bəust] *vi*: **to ~ (about** *or* **of)** vantarsi (di)
boat [bəut] *n* nave *f*; (*small*) barca
bob [bɔb] *vi* (*boat, cork on water: also:* **~ up and down**) andare su e giù
bobby pin ['bɔbɪ-] (US) *n* fermaglio per capelli
body ['bɔdɪ] *n* corpo; (*of car*) carrozzeria; (*of plane*) fusoliera; (*fig: group*) gruppo; (*: organization*) organizzazione *f*; (*: quantity*) quantità *f inv*; **body-building** *n* culturismo; **bodyguard** *n* guardia del corpo; **bodywork** *n* carrozzeria
bog [bɔg] *n* palude *f* ▷ *vt* **to get ~ged down** (*fig*) impantanarsi
bogus ['bəugəs] *adj* falso(-a); finto(-a)
boil [bɔɪl] *vt, vi* bollire ▷ *n* (*Med*) foruncolo; **to come to the** (BRIT) *or* **a** (US) **~** raggiungere l'ebollizione; **boil over** *vi* traboccare (bollendo); **boiled egg** *n* uovo alla coque; **boiled potatoes** *npl* patate *fpl* bollite *or* lesse; **boiler** *n* caldaia; **boiling** *adj* bollente; **I'm boiling (hot)** (*inf*) sto morendo di caldo; **boiling point** *n* punto di ebollizione
bold [bəuld] *adj* audace; (*child*) impudente; (*colour*) deciso(-a)
Bolivia [bə'lɪvɪə] *n* Bolivia
Bolivian [bə'lɪvɪən] *adj, n* boliviano(-a)
bollard ['bɔləd] (BRIT) *n* (*Aut*) colonnina luminosa
bolt [bəult] *n* chiavistello; (*with nut*) bullone *m* ▷ *adv* **~ upright** diritto(-a) come un fuso ▷ *vt* serrare; (*also:* **~ together**) imbullonare; (*food*) mangiare in fretta ▷ *vi* scappare via
bomb [bɔm] *n* bomba ▷ *vt* bombardare; **bombard** [bɔm'bɑːd] *vt* bombardare; **bomber** *n* (*Aviat*) bombardiere *m*; **bomb scare** *n* stato di allarme (*per sospetta presenza di una bomba*)
bond [bɔnd] *n* legame *m*; (*binding promise, Finance*) obbligazione *f*; (*Comm*): **in ~** in attesa di sdoganamento
bone [bəun] *n* osso; (*of fish*) spina, lisca ▷ *vt* disossare; togliere le spine a
bonfire ['bɔnfaɪəʳ] *n* falò *m inv*
bonnet ['bɔnɪt] *n* cuffia; (BRIT: *of car*) cofano
bonus ['bəunəs] *n* premio; (*fig*) sovrappiù *m inv*
boo [buː] *excl* ba! ▷ *vt* fischiare
book [buk] *n* libro; (*of stamps etc*) blocchetto ▷ *vt* (*ticket, seat, room*) prenotare; (*driver*) multare; (*football player*) ammonire; **books** *npl* (*Comm*) conti *mpl*; **I'd like to ~ a double room** vorrei prenotare una camera doppia; **I ~ed a table in the name of ...** ho prenotato un tavolo al nome di...; **book in** *vi* (BRIT: *at hotel*) prendere

una camera; **book up** *vt* riservare, prenotare; **the hotel is booked up** l'albergo è al completo; **all seats are booked up** è tutto esaurito; **bookcase** *n* scaffale *m*; **booking** *n* (BRIT) prenotazione *f*; **I confirmed my booking by fax/e-mail** ho confermato la mia prenotazione tramite fax/e-mail; **booking office** (BRIT) *n* (*Rail*) biglietteria; (*Theatre*) botteghino; **book-keeping** *n* contabilità; **booklet** *n* libricino; **bookmaker** *n* allibratore *m*; **bookmark** (*also Comput*) *n* segnalibro ▷ *vt* (*Comput*) mettere un segnalibro a; (*Internet Explorer*) aggiungere a "Preferiti"; **bookseller** *n* libraio; **bookshelf** *n* mensola (per libri); **bookshop, bookstore** *n* libreria

boom [buːm] *n* (*noise*) rimbombo; (*in prices etc*) boom *m inv* ▷ *vi* rimbombare; andare a gonfie vele

boost [buːst] *n* spinta ▷ *vt* spingere

boot [buːt] *n* stivale *m*; (*for hiking*) scarpone *m* da montagna; (*for football etc*) scarpa; (BRIT: *of car*) portabagagli *m inv* ▷ *vt* (*Comput*) inizializzare; **to ~** (*in addition*) per giunta, in più

booth [buːð] *n* cabina; (*at fair*) baraccone *m*

booze [buːz] (*inf*) *n* alcool *m*

border ['bɔːdəʳ] *n* orlo; margine *m*; (*of a country*) frontiera; (*for flowers*) aiuola (laterale) ▷ *vt* (*road*) costeggiare; (*another country*: *also*: **~ on**) confinare con; **the B~s** *la zona di confine tra l'Inghilterra e la Scozia*; **borderline** *n* (*fig*): **on the borderline** incerto(-a)

bore [bɔːʳ] *pt of* **bear** ▷ *vt* (*hole etc*) scavare; (*person*) annoiare ▷ *n* (*person*) seccatore(-trice); (*of gun*) calibro; **bored** *adj* annoiato(-a); **to be bored** annoiarsi; **he's bored to tears** *or* **to death** *or* **stiff** è annoiato a morte; **boredom** *n* noia

boring ['bɔːrɪŋ] *adj* noioso(-a)

born [bɔːn] *adj* **to be ~** nascere; **I was ~ in 1960** sono nato nel 1960

borne [bɔːn] *pp of* **bear**

borough ['bʌrə] *n* comune *m*

borrow ['bɔrəu] *vt* **to ~ sth (from sb)** prendere in prestito qc (da qn)

Bosnia(-Herzegovina) ['bɔznɪə(hɛrzə'gəuviːnə)] *n* Bosnia-Erzegovina; **Bosnian** ['bɔznɪən] *n, adj* bosniaco(-a) *m/f*

bosom ['buzəm] *n* petto; (*fig*) seno

boss [bɔs] *n* capo ▷ *vt* comandare; **bossy** *adj* prepotente

both [bəuθ] *adj* entrambi(-e), tutt'e due ▷ *pron* **~ of them** entrambi(-e); **~ of us went, we ~ went** ci siamo andati tutt'e due ▷ *adv* **they sell ~ meat and poultry** vendono insieme la carne ed il pollame

bother ['bɔðəʳ] *vt* (*worry*) preoccupare; (*annoy*) infastidire ▷ *vi* (*also*: **~ o.s.**) preoccuparsi ▷ *n* **it is a ~ to have to do** è una seccatura dover fare; **it was no ~** non c'era problema; **to ~ doing sth** darsi la pena di fare qc

bottle ['bɔtl] *n* bottiglia; (*baby's*) biberon *m inv* ▷ *vt* imbottigliare; **bottle bank** *n* contenitore *m* per la raccolta del vetro; **bottle-opener** *n* apribottiglie *m inv*

bottom ['bɔtəm] *n* fondo; (*buttocks*) sedere *m* ▷ *adj* più basso(-a); ultimo(-a); **at the ~ of** in fondo a

bought [bɔːt] *pt, pp of* **buy**

boulder ['bəuldəʳ] *n* masso (tondeggiante)

bounce [bauns] *vi* (*ball*) rimbalzare; (*cheque*) essere restituito(-a) ▷ *vt* far rimbalzare ▷ *n* (*rebound*) rimbalzo; **bouncer** (*inf*) *n* buttafuori *m inv*

bound [baund] *pt, pp of* **bind** ▷ *n* (*gen pl*) limite *m*; (*leap*) salto ▷ *vi* saltare ▷ *vt* (*limit*) delimitare ▷ *adj* **~ by law** obbligato(-a) per legge; **to be ~ to do sth** (*obliged*) essere costretto(-a) a fare qc; **he's ~ to fail** (*likely*) fallirà di certo; **~ for** diretto(-a) a; **out of ~s** il cui accesso è vietato

boundary ['baundrɪ] *n* confine *m*
bouquet ['bukeɪ] *n* bouquet *m inv*
bourbon ['buəbən] (US) *n* (*also:* **~ whiskey**) bourbon *m inv*
bout [baut] *n* periodo; (*of malaria etc*) attacco; (*Boxing etc*) incontro
boutique [bu:'ti:k] *n* boutique *f inv*
bow[1] [bəu] *n* nodo; (*weapon*) arco; (*Mus*) archetto
bow[2] [bau] *n* (*with body*) inchino; (*Naut*: *also*: **~s**) prua ▷ *vi* inchinarsi; (*yield*): **to ~ to** *or* **before** sottomettersi a
bowels ['bauəlz] *npl* intestini *mpl*; (*fig*) viscere *fpl*
bowl [bəul] *n* (*for eating*) scodella; (*for washing*) bacino; (*ball*) boccia ▷ *vi* (*Cricket*) servire (la palla); **bowler** ['bəuləʳ] *n* (*Cricket, Baseball*) lanciatore *m*; (BRIT: *also*: **bowler hat**) bombetta; **bowling** ['bəulɪŋ] *n* (*game*) gioco delle bocce; **bowling alley** *n* pista da bowling; **bowling green** *n* campo di bocce; **bowls** [bəulz] *n* gioco delle bocce
bow tie *n* cravatta a farfalla
box [bɔks] *n* scatola; (*also*: **cardboard ~**) cartone *m*; (*Theatre*) palco ▷ *vt* inscatolare ▷ *vi* fare del pugilato; **boxer** *n* (*person*) pugile *m*; **boxer shorts** ['bɔksəʃɔ:ts] *pl n* boxer; **a pair of boxer shorts** un paio di boxer; **boxing** *n* (*Sport*) pugilato; **Boxing Day** (BRIT) *n* ≈ Santo Stefano; *vedi nota nel riquadro*; **boxing gloves** *npl* guantoni *mpl* da pugile; **boxing ring** *n* ring *m inv*; **box office** *n* biglietteria

BOXING DAY

Il **Boxing Day** è un giorno di festa e cade in genere il 26 dicembre. Prende il nome dalla tradizionale usanza di donare pacchi regalo natalizi, chiamati "Christmas boxes", a fornitori e dipendenti.

boy [bɔɪ] *n* ragazzo
boycott ['bɔɪkɔt] *n* boicottaggio ▷ *vt* boicottare
boyfriend ['bɔɪfrɛnd] *n* ragazzo
bra [brɑ:] *n* reggipetto, reggiseno
brace [breɪs] *n* (*on teeth*) apparecchio correttore; (*tool*) trapano ▷ *vt* rinforzare, sostenere; **braces** (BRIT) *npl* (*Dress*) bretelle *fpl*; **to ~ o.s.** (*also fig*) tenersi forte
bracelet ['breɪslɪt] *n* braccialetto
bracket ['brækɪt] *n* (*Tech*) mensola; (*group*) gruppo; (*Typ*) parentesi *f inv* ▷ *vt* mettere fra parentesi
brag [bræg] *vi* vantarsi
braid [breɪd] *n* (*trimming*) passamano; (*of hair*) treccia
brain [breɪn] *n* cervello; **brains** *npl* (*intelligence*) cervella *fpl*; **he's got ~s** è intelligente
braise [breɪz] *vt* brasare
brake [breɪk] *n* (*on vehicle*) freno ▷ *vi* frenare; **brake light** *n* (fanalino dello) stop *m inv*
bran [bræn] *n* crusca
branch [brɑ:ntʃ] *n* ramo; (*Comm*) succursale *f*; **branch off** *vi* diramarsi; **branch out** *vi* (*fig*) intraprendere una nuova attività
brand [brænd] *n* marca; (*fig*) tipo ▷ *vt* (*cattle*) marcare (a ferro rovente); **brand name** *n* marca; **brand-new** *adj* nuovo(-a) di zecca
brandy ['brændɪ] *n* brandy *m inv*
brash [bræʃ] *adj* sfacciato(-a)
brass [brɑ:s] *n* ottone *m*; **the ~** (*Mus*) gli ottoni; **brass band** *n* fanfara
brat [bræt] (*pej*) *n* marmocchio, monello(-a)
brave [breɪv] *adj* coraggioso(-a) ▷ *vt* affrontare; **bravery** *n* coraggio
brawl [brɔ:l] *n* rissa
Brazil [brə'zɪl] *n* Brasile *m*; **Brazilian** *adj, n* brasiliano(-a)
breach [bri:tʃ] *vt* aprire una breccia in ▷ *n* (*gap*) breccia, varco; (*breaking*): **~ of contract** rottura di contratto; **~ of the peace** violazione *f* dell'ordine

pubblico
bread [brɛd] *n* pane *m*; **breadbin** *n* cassetta *f* portapane *inv*; **breadbox** (*US*) *n* cassetta *f* portapane *inv*; **breadcrumbs** *npl* briciole *fpl*; (*Culin*) pangrattato
breadth [brɛtθ] *n* larghezza; (*fig*: *of knowledge etc*) ampiezza
break [breɪk] (*pt* **broke**, *pp* **broken**) *vt* rompere; (*law*) violare; (*record*) battere ▷ *vi* rompersi; (*storm*) scoppiare; (*weather*) cambiare; (*dawn*) spuntare; (*news*) saltare fuori ▷ *n* (*gap*) breccia; (*fracture*) rottura; (*rest, also Scol*) intervallo; (: *short*) pausa; (*chance*) possibilità *f inv*; **to ~ one's leg** *etc* rompersi la gamba *ecc*; **to ~ the news to sb** comunicare per primo la notizia a qn; **to ~ even** coprire le spese; **to ~ free** *or* **loose** spezzare i legami; **to ~ open** (*door etc*) sfondare; **break down** *vt* (*figures, data*) analizzare ▷ *vi* (*person*) avere un esaurimento (nervoso); (*Aut*) guastarsi; **my car has broken down** mi si è rotta la macchina; **break in** *vt* (*horse etc*) domare ▷ *vi* (*burglar*) fare irruzione; (*interrupt*) interrompere; **break into** *vt fus* (*house*) fare irruzione in; **break off** *vi* (*speaker*) interrompersi; (*branch*) troncarsi; **break out** *vi* evadere; (*war, fight*) scoppiare; **to break out in spots** coprirsi di macchie; **break up** *vi* (*ship*) sfondarsi; (*meeting*) sciogliersi; (*crowd*) disperdersi; (*marriage*) andare a pezzi; (*Scol*) chiudere ▷ *vt* fare a pezzi, spaccare; (*fight etc*) interrompere, far cessare; **the line's** *or* **you're breaking up** la linea è disturbata; **breakdown** *n* (*Aut*) guasto; (*in communications*) interruzione *f*; (*of marriage*) rottura; (*Med*: *also*: **nervous breakdown**) esaurimento nervoso; (*of statistics*) resoconto; **breakdown truck, breakdown van** *n* carro *m* attrezzi *inv*
breakfast ['brɛkfəst] *n* colazione *f*; **what time is ~?** a che ora è servita la colazione?
break: **break-in** *n* irruzione *f*; **breakthrough** *n* (*fig*) passo avanti
breast [brɛst] *n* (*of woman*) seno; (*chest, Culin*) petto; **breast-feed** (*irreg*: *like* **feed**) *vt, vi* allattare (al seno); **breast-stroke** *n* nuoto a rana
breath [brɛθ] *n* respiro; **out of ~** senza fiato
Breathalyser® ['brɛθəlaɪzə^r] (*BRIT*) *n* alcoltest *m inv*
breathe [bri:ð] *vt, vi* respirare; **breathe in** *vt* respirare ▷ *vi* inspirare; **breathe out** *vt, vi* espirare; **breathing** *n* respiro, respirazione *f*
breath: **breathless** ['brɛθlɪs] *adj* senza fiato; **breathtaking** ['brɛθteɪkɪŋ] *adj* mozzafiato *inv*; **breath test** *n* ≈ prova del palloncino
bred [brɛd] *pt, pp of* **breed**
breed [bri:d] (*pt, pp* **bred**) *vt* allevare ▷ *vi* riprodursi ▷ *n* razza; (*type, class*) varietà *f inv*
breeze [bri:z] *n* brezza
breezy ['bri:zɪ] *adj* allegro(-a), ventilato(-a)
brew [bru:] *vt* (*tea*) fare un infuso di; (*beer*) fare ▷ *vi* (*storm, fig*: *trouble etc*) prepararsi; **brewery** *n* fabbrica di birra
bribe [braɪb] *n* bustarella ▷ *vt* comprare; **bribery** *n* corruzione *f*
bric-a-brac ['brɪkəbræk] *n* bric-a-brac *m*
brick [brɪk] *n* mattone *m*; **bricklayer** *n* muratore *m*
bride [braɪd] *n* sposa; **bridegroom** *n* sposo; **bridesmaid** *n* damigella d'onore
bridge [brɪdʒ] *n* ponte *m*; (*Naut*) ponte di comando; (*of nose*) dorso; (*Cards*) bridge *m inv* ▷ *vt* (*fig*: *gap*) colmare
bridle ['braɪdl] *n* briglia
brief [bri:f] *adj* breve ▷ *n* (*Law*) comparsa; (*gen*) istruzioni *fpl* ▷ *vt* mettere al corrente; **briefs** *npl* (*underwear*) mutande *fpl*; **briefcase**

n cartella; **briefing** *n* briefing *m inv*; **briefly** *adv* (*glance*) di sfuggita; (*explain, say*) brevemente
brigadier [brɪgə'dɪəʳ] *n* generale *m* di brigata
bright [braɪt] *adj* luminoso(-a); (*clever*) sveglio(-a); (*lively*) vivace
brilliant ['brɪljənt] *adj* brillante; (*light, smile*) radioso(-a); (*inf*) splendido(-a)
brim [brɪm] *n* orlo
brine [braɪn] *n* (*Culin*) salamoia
bring [brɪŋ] (*pt, pp* **brought**) *vt* portare; **bring about** *vt* causare; **bring back** *vt* riportare; **bring down** *vt* portare giù; abbattere; **bring in** *vt* (*person*) fare entrare; (*object*) portare; (*Pol: bill*) presentare; (*: legislation*) introdurre; (*Law: verdict*) emettere; (*produce: income*) rendere; **bring on** *vt* (*illness, attack*) causare, provocare; (*player, substitute*) far scendere in campo; **bring out** *vt* tirar fuori; (*meaning*) mettere in evidenza; (*book, album*) far uscire; **bring up** *vt* (*carry up*) portare su; (*child*) allevare; (*question*) introdurre; (*food: vomit*) rimettere, rigurgitare
brink [brɪŋk] *n* orlo
brisk [brɪsk] *adj* (*manner*) spiccio(-a); (*trade*) vivace; (*pace*) svelto(-a)
bristle ['brɪsl] *n* setola ▷ *vi* rizzarsi; **bristling with** irto(-a) di
Brit [brɪt] *n abbr* (*inf: = British person*) britannico(-a)
Britain ['brɪtən] *n* (*also:* **Great ~**) Gran Bretagna
British ['brɪtɪʃ] *adj* britannico(-a); **British Isles** *npl* Isole Britanniche
Briton ['brɪtən] *n* britannico(-a)
brittle ['brɪtl] *adj* fragile
broad [brɔːd] *adj* largo(-a); (*distinction*) generale; (*accent*) spiccato(-a); **in ~ daylight** in pieno giorno; **broadband** *adj* (*Comput*) a banda larga ▷ *n* banda larga; **broad bean** *n* fava; **broadcast** (*pt, pp* **broadcast**) *n* trasmissione *f* ▷ *vt* trasmettere per radio (*or* per televisione) ▷ *vi* fare una trasmissione; **broaden** *vt* allargare ▷ *vi* allargarsi; **broadly** *adv* (*fig*) in generale; **broad-minded** *adj* di mente aperta
broccoli ['brɔkəlɪ] *n* broccoli *mpl*
brochure ['brəuʃjuəʳ] *n* dépliant *m inv*
broil [brɔɪl] *vt* cuocere a fuoco vivo
broiler ['brɔɪləʳ] (*US*) *n* (*grill*) griglia
broke [brəuk] *pt of* **break** ▷ *adj* (*inf*) squattrinato(-a)
broken ['brəukn] *pp of* **break** ▷ *adj* rotto(-a); **a ~ leg** una gamba rotta; **in ~ English** in un inglese stentato
broker ['brəukəʳ] *n* agente *m*
bronchitis [brɔŋ'kaɪtɪs] *n* bronchite *f*
bronze [brɔnz] *n* bronzo
brooch [brəutʃ] *n* spilla
brood [bruːd] *n* covata ▷ *vi* (*person*) rimuginare
broom [brum] *n* scopa; (*Bot*) ginestra
Bros. *abbr* (= *Brothers*) F.lli
broth [brɔθ] *n* brodo
brothel ['brɔθl] *n* bordello
brother ['brʌðəʳ] *n* fratello; **brother-in-law** *n* cognato
brought [brɔːt] *pt, pp of* **bring**
brow [brau] *n* fronte *f*; (*rare, gen: eyebrow*) sopracciglio; (*of hill*) cima
brown [braun] *adj* bruno(-a), marrone; (*tanned*) abbronzato(-a) ▷ *n* (*colour*) color *m* bruno *or* marrone ▷ *vt* (*Culin*) rosolare; **brown bread** *n* pane *m* integrale, pane nero
Brownie ['braunɪ] *n* giovane esploratrice *f*
brown rice *n* riso greggio
brown sugar *n* zucchero greggio
browse [brauz] *vi* (*among books*) curiosare fra i libri; **to ~ through a book** sfogliare un libro; **browser** *n* (*Comput*) browser *m inv*
bruise [bruːz] *n* (*on person*) livido ▷ *vt* farsi un livido a
brunette [bruː'nɛt] *n* bruna
brush [brʌʃ] *n* spazzola; (*for painting, shaving*) pennello; (*quarrel*)

schermaglia ▷ *vt* spazzolare; (*also*: **~ against**) sfiorare
Brussels ['brʌslz] *n* Bruxelles *f*
Brussels sprout [spraut] *n* cavolo di Bruxelles
brutal ['bru:tl] *adj* brutale
B.Sc. *n abbr* (*Univ*) = **Bachelor of Science**
BSE *n abbr* (= *bovine spongiform encephalopathy*) encefalite *f* bovina spongiforme
bubble ['bʌbl] *n* bolla ▷ *vi* ribollire; (*sparkle*: *fig*) essere effervescente; **bubble bath** *n* bagnoschiuma *m inv*; **bubble gum** *n* gomma americana
buck [bʌk] *n* maschio (*di camoscio, caprone, coniglio ecc*); (US: *inf*) dollaro ▷ *vi* sgroppare; **to pass the ~ to sb** scaricare (su di qn) la propria responsabilità
bucket ['bʌkɪt] *n* secchio
buckle ['bʌkl] *n* fibbia ▷ *vt* allacciare ▷ *vi* (*wheel etc*) piegarsi
bud [bʌd] *n* gemma; (*of flower*) bocciolo ▷ *vi* germogliare; (*flower*) sbocciare
Buddhism ['budɪzəm] *n* buddismo
Buddhist ['budɪst] *adj, n* buddista (*m/f*)
buddy ['bʌdɪ] (US) *n* compagno
budge [bʌdʒ] *vt* scostare; (*fig*) smuovere ▷ *vi* spostarsi; smuoversi
budgerigar ['bʌdʒərɪgɑ:ʳ] *n* pappagallino
budget ['bʌdʒɪt] *n* bilancio preventivo ▷ *vi* **to ~ for sth** fare il bilancio per qc
budgie ['bʌdʒɪ] *n* = **budgerigar**
buff [bʌf] *adj* color camoscio ▷ *n* (*inf*: *enthusiast*) appassionato(-a)
buffalo ['bʌfələu] (*pl* **buffalo** *or* **buffaloes**) *n* bufalo; (US) bisonte *m*
buffer ['bʌfəʳ] *n* respingente *m*; (*Comput*) memoria tampone, buffer *m inv*
buffet[1] ['bʌfɪt] *vt* sferzare
buffet[2] ['bufeɪ] *n* (*food*, BRIT: *bar*) buffet *m inv*; **buffet car** (BRIT) *n* (*Rail*) ≈ servizio ristoro
bug [bʌg] *n* (*esp* US: *insect*) insetto; (*Comput, fig*: *germ*) virus *m inv*; (*spy device*) microfono spia ▷ *vt* mettere sotto controllo; (*inf*: *annoy*) scocciare
buggy ['bʌgɪ] *n* (*baby buggy*) passeggino
build [bɪld] (*pt, pp* **built**) *n* (*of person*) corporatura ▷ *vt* costruire; **build up** *vt* accumulare; aumentare; **builder** *n* costruttore *m*; **building** *n* costruzione *f*; edificio; (*industry*) edilizia; **building site** *n* cantiere *m* di costruzione; **building society** (BRIT) *n* società *f inv* immobiliare
built [bɪlt] *pt, pp of* **build**; **built-in** *adj* (*cupboard*) a muro; (*device*) incorporato(-a); **built-up** *adj* **built-up area** abitato
bulb [bʌlb] *n* (*Bot*) bulbo; (*Elec*) lampadina
Bulgaria [bʌl'gɛərɪə] *n* Bulgaria; **Bulgarian** *adj* bulgaro(-a) ▷ *n* bulgaro(-a); (*Ling*) bulgaro
bulge [bʌldʒ] *n* rigonfiamento ▷ *vi* essere protuberante *or* rigonfio(-a); **to be bulging with** essere pieno(-a) *or* zeppo(-a) di
bulimia [bə'lɪmɪə] *n* bulimia
bulimic [bju:'lɪmɪk] *adj, n* bulimico(-a)
bulk [bʌlk] *n* massa, volume *m*; **in ~** a pacchi *or* cassette *etc*; (*Comm*) all'ingrosso; **the ~ of** il grosso di; **bulky** *adj* grosso(-a), voluminoso(-a)
bull [bul] *n* toro; (*male elephant, whale*) maschio
bulldozer ['buldəuzəʳ] *n* bulldozer *m inv*
bullet ['bulɪt] *n* pallottola
bulletin ['bulɪtɪn] *n* bollettino; **bulletin board** *n* (*Comput*) bulletin board *m inv*
bullfight ['bulfaɪt] *n* corrida; **bullfighter** *n* torero; **bullfighting** *n* tauromachia
bully ['bulɪ] *n* prepotente *m* ▷ *vt*

angariare; (*frighten*) intimidire
bum [bʌm] (*inf*) *n* (*backside*) culo; (*tramp*) vagabondo(-a)
bumblebee ['bʌmblbi:] *n* bombo
bump [bʌmp] *n* (*in car*) piccolo tamponamento; (*jolt*) scossa; (*on road etc*) protuberanza; (*on head*) bernoccolo ▷ *vt* battere; **bump into** *vt fus* scontrarsi con; (*person*) imbattersi in; **bumper** *n* paraurti *m inv* ▷ *adj* **bumper harvest** raccolto eccezionale; **bumpy** ['bʌmpɪ] *adj* (*road*) dissestato(-a)
bun [bʌn] *n* focaccia; (*of hair*) crocchia
bunch [bʌntʃ] *n* (*of flowers, keys*) mazzo; (*of bananas*) casco; (*of people*) gruppo; **~ of grapes** grappolo d'uva; **bunches** *npl* (*in hair*) codine *fpl*
bundle ['bʌndl] *n* fascio ▷ *vt* (*also:* **~ up**) legare in un fascio; (*put*): **to ~ sth/sb into** spingere qc/qn in
bungalow ['bʌŋgələu] *n* bungalow *m inv*
bungee jumping ['bʌndʒi:'dʒʌmpɪŋ] *n salto nel vuoto da ponti, grattacieli etc con un cavo fissato alla caviglia*
bunion ['bʌnjən] *n* callo (al piede)
bunk [bʌŋk] *n* cuccetta; **bunk beds** *npl* letti *mpl* a castello
bunker ['bʌŋkə^r] *n* (*coal store*) ripostiglio per il carbone; (*Mil, Golf*) bunker *m inv*
bunny ['bʌnɪ] *n* (*also:* **~ rabbit**) coniglietto
buoy [bɔɪ] *n* boa; **buoyant** *adj* galleggiante; (*fig*) vivace
burden ['bə:dn] *n* carico, fardello ▷ *vt* **to ~ sb with** caricare qn di
bureau [bjuə'rəu] (*pl* **bureaux**) *n* (BRIT: *writing desk*) scrivania; (US: *chest of drawers*) cassettone *m*; (*office*) ufficio, agenzia
bureaucracy [bjuə'rɔkrəsɪ] *n* burocrazia
bureaucrat ['bjuərəkræt] *n* burocrate *m/f*
bureau de change [-də'ʃɑ̃ʒ] (*pl* **bureaux de change**) *n* cambiavalute *m inv*
bureaux [bjuə'rəuz] *npl of* **bureau**
burger ['bə:gə^r] *n* hamburger *m inv*
burglar ['bə:glə^r] *n* scassinatore *m*; **burglar alarm** *n* campanello antifurto; **burglary** *n* furto con scasso
burial ['bɛrɪəl] *n* sepoltura
burn [bə:n] (*pt, pp* **burned** *or* **burnt**) *vt, vi* bruciare ▷ *n* bruciatura, scottatura; **burn down** *vt* distruggere col fuoco; **burn out** *vt* (*writer etc*): **to burn o.s. out** esaurirsi; **burning** *adj* in fiamme; (*sand*) che scotta; (*ambition*) bruciante
Burns Night *n vedi nota nel riquadro*

BURNS NIGHT

Burns Night è la festa celebrata il 25 gennaio per commemorare il poeta scozzese Robert Burns (1759-1796). Gli scozzesi festeggiano questa data con una cena, la "Burns supper", a base di "haggis", piatto tradizionale scozzese, e whisky.

burnt [bə:nt] *pt, pp of* **burn**
burp [bə:p] (*inf*) *n* rutto ▷ *vi* ruttare
burrow ['bʌrəu] *n* tana ▷ *vt* scavare
burst [bə:st] (*pt, pp* **burst**) *vt* far scoppiare ▷ *vi* esplodere; (*tyre*) scoppiare ▷ *n* scoppio; (*also:* **~ pipe**) rottura nel tubo, perdita; **a ~ of speed** uno scatto di velocità; **to ~ into flames/tears** scoppiare in fiamme/lacrime; **to ~ out laughing** scoppiare a ridere; **to be ~ing with** scoppiare di; **burst into** *vt fus* (*room etc*) irrompere in
bury ['bɛrɪ] *vt* seppellire
bus [bʌs] (*pl* **buses**) *n* autobus *m inv*; **bus conductor** *n* autista *m/f* (dell'autobus)
bush [buʃ] *n* cespuglio; (*scrub land*) macchia; **to beat about the ~** menare il cane per l'aia
business ['bɪznɪs] *n* (*matter*) affare *m*;

(*trading*) affari *mpl*; (*firm*) azienda; (*job, duty*) lavoro; **to be away on ~** essere andato via per affari; **it's none of my ~** questo non mi riguarda; **he means ~** non scherza; **business class** *n* (*Aer*) business class *f*; **businesslike** *adj* serio(-a), efficiente; **businessman** (*irreg*) *n* uomo d'affari; **business trip** *n* viaggio d'affari; **businesswoman** (*irreg*) *n* donna d'affari

busker ['bʌskəʳ] (BRIT) *n* suonatore(-trice) ambulante

bus: **bus pass** *n* tessera dell'autobus; **bus shelter** *n* pensilina (*alla fermata dell'autobus*); **bus station** *n* stazione *f* delle corriere, autostazione *f*; **bus-stop** *n* fermata d'autobus

bust [bʌst] *n* busto; (*Anat*) seno ▷ *adj* (*inf*: *broken*) rotto(-a); **to go ~** fallire

bustling ['bʌslɪŋ] *adj* movimentato(-a)

busy ['bɪzɪ] *adj* occupato(-a); (*shop, street*) molto frequentato(-a) ▷ *vt* **to ~ o.s.** darsi da fare; **busy signal** (US) *n* (*Tel*) segnale *m* di occupato

KEYWORD

but [bʌt] *conj* ma; **I'd love to come, but I'm busy** vorrei tanto venire, ma ho da fare
▷ *prep* (*apart from, except*) eccetto, tranne, meno; **he was nothing but trouble** non dava altro che guai; **no-one but him can do it** nessuno può farlo tranne lui; **but for you/your help** se non fosse per te/per il tuo aiuto; **anything but that** tutto ma non questo
▷ *adv* (*just, only*) solo, soltanto; **she's but a child** è solo una bambina; **had I but known** se solo avessi saputo; **I can but try** tentar non nuoce; **all but finished** quasi finito

butcher ['butʃəʳ] *n* macellaio ▷ *vt* macellare; **butcher's (shop)** *n* macelleria

butler ['bʌtləʳ] *n* maggiordomo

butt [bʌt] *n* (*cask*) grossa botte *f*; (*of gun*) calcio; (*of cigarette*) mozzicone *m*; (BRIT: *fig*: *target*) oggetto ▷ *vt* cozzare

butter ['bʌtəʳ] *n* burro ▷ *vt* imburrare; **buttercup** *n* ranuncolo

butterfly ['bʌtəflaɪ] *n* farfalla; (*Swimming*: *also*: **~ stroke**) (nuoto a) farfalla

buttocks ['bʌtəks] *npl* natiche *fpl*

button ['bʌtn] *n* bottone *m*; (US: *badge*) distintivo ▷ *vt* (*also*: **~ up**) abbottonare ▷ *vi* abbottonarsi

buy [baɪ] (*pt, pp* **bought**) *vt* comprare ▷ *n* acquisto; **where can I ~ some postcards?** dove posso comprare delle cartoline?; **to ~ sb sth/sth from sb** comprare qc per qn/qc da qn; **to ~ sb a drink** offrire da bere a qn; **buy out** *vt* (*business*) rilevare; **buy up** *vt* accaparrare; **buyer** *n* compratore(-trice)

buzz [bʌz] *n* ronzio; (*inf*: *phone call*) colpo di telefono ▷ *vi* ronzare; **buzzer** ['bʌzəʳ] *n* cicalino

KEYWORD

by [baɪ] *prep* **1** (*referring to cause, agent*) da; **killed by lightning** ucciso da un fulmine; **surrounded by a fence** circondato da uno steccato; **a painting by Picasso** un quadro di Picasso
2 (*referring to method, manner, means*): **by bus/car/train** in autobus/ macchina/treno, con l'autobus/la macchina/il treno; **to pay by cheque** pagare con (un) assegno; **by moonlight** al chiaro di luna; **by saving hard, he ...** risparmiando molto, lui ...
3 (*via, through*) per; **we came by Dover** siamo venuti via Dover
4 (*close to, past*) accanto a; **the house by the river** la casa sul fiume; **a**

holiday by the sea una vacanza al mare; **she sat by his bed** si sedette accanto al suo letto; **she rushed by me** mi è passata accanto correndo; **I go by the post office every day** passo davanti all'ufficio postale ogni giorno
5 (*not later than*) per, entro; **by 4 o'clock** per *or* entro le 4; **by this time tomorrow** domani a quest'ora; **by the time I got here it was too late** quando sono arrivato era ormai troppo tardi
6 (*during*): **by day/night** di giorno/ notte
7 (*amount*) a; **by the kilo/metre** a chili/metri; **paid by the hour** pagato all'ora; **one by one** uno per uno; **little by little** a poco a poco
8 (*Math, measure*): **to divide/ multiply by 3** dividere/moltiplicare per 3; **it's broader by a metre** è un metro più largo, è più largo di un metro
9 (*according to*) per; **to play by the rules** attenersi alle regole; **it's all right by me** per me va bene
10: **(all) by oneself** *etc* (tutto(-a)) solo(-a); **he did it (all) by himself** lo ha fatto (tutto) da solo
11: **by the way** a proposito; **this wasn't my idea by the way** tra l'altro l'idea non è stata mia
▷ *adv* 1 *see* **go**; **pass** *etc*
2: **by and by** (*in past*) poco dopo; (*in future*) fra breve; **by and large** nel complesso

bye(-bye) ['baɪ('baɪ)] *excl* ciao!, arrivederci!
by-election ['baɪɪlɛkʃən] (BRIT) *n* elezione *f* straordinaria
bypass ['baɪpɑːs] *n* circonvallazione *f*; (*Med*) by-pass *m inv* ▷ *vt* fare una deviazione intorno a
byte [baɪt] *n* (*Comput*) byte *m inv*, bicarattere *m*

C

C [siː] *n* (*Mus*) do
cab [kæb] *n* taxi *m inv*; (*of train, truck*) cabina
cabaret ['kæbəreɪ] *n* cabaret *m inv*
cabbage ['kæbɪdʒ] *n* cavolo
cabin ['kæbɪn] *n* capanna; (*on ship*) cabina; **cabin crew** *n* equipaggio
cabinet ['kæbɪnɪt] *n* (*Pol*) consiglio dei ministri; (*furniture*) armadietto; (*also:* **display ~**) vetrinetta; **cabinet minister** *n* ministro (*membro del Consiglio*)
cable ['keɪbl] *n* cavo; fune *f*; (*Tel*) cablogramma *m* ▷ *vt* telegrafare; **cable car** *n* funivia; **cable television** *n* televisione *f* via cavo
cactus ['kæktəs] (*pl* **cacti**) *n* cactus *m inv*
café ['kæfeɪ] *n* caffè *m inv*
cafeteria [kæfɪ'tɪərɪə] *n* self-service *m inv*
caffein(e) ['kæfiːn] *n* caffeina
cage [keɪdʒ] *n* gabbia
cagoule [kə'guːl] *n* K-way® *m inv*

cake [keɪk] *n* (*large*) torta; (*small*) pasticcino; **cake of soap** *n* saponetta
calcium ['kælsɪəm] *n* calcio
calculate ['kælkjuleɪt] *vt* calcolare; **calculation** [-'leɪʃən] *n* calcolo; **calculator** *n* calcolatrice *f*
calendar ['kæləndəʳ] *n* calendario
calf [kɑːf] (*pl* **calves**) *n* (*of cow*) vitello; (*of other animals*) piccolo; (*also:* **~skin**) (pelle *f* di) vitello; (*Anat*) polpaccio
calibre ['kælɪbəʳ] (*US* **caliber**) *n* calibro
call [kɔːl] *vt* (*gen: also Tel*) chiamare; (*meeting*) indire ▷ *vi* chiamare; (*visit: also:* **~ in, ~ round**) passare ▷ *n* (*shout*) grido, urlo; (*Tel*) telefonata; **to be ~ed** (*person, object*) chiamarsi; **can you ~ back later?** può richiamare più tardi?; **can I make a ~ from here?** posso telefonare da qui?; **to be on ~** essere a disposizione; **call back** *vi* (*return*) ritornare; (*Tel*) ritelefonare, richiamare; **call for** *vt fus* richiedere; (*fetch*) passare a prendere; **call in** *vt* (*doctor, expert, police*) chiamare, far venire; **call off** *vt* disdire; **call on** *vt fus* (*visit*) passare da; (*appeal to*) chiedere a; **call out** *vi* (*in pain*) urlare; (*to person*) chiamare; **call up** *vt* (*Mil*) richiamare; (*Tel*) telefonare a; **callbox** (*BRIT*) *n* cabina telefonica; **call centre** (*US* **call center**) *n* centro informazioni telefoniche; **caller** *n* persona che chiama, visitatore(-trice)
callous ['kæləs] *adj* indurito(-a), insensibile
calm [kɑːm] *adj* calmo(-a) ▷ *n* calma ▷ *vt* calmare; **calm down** *vi* calmarsi ▷ *vt* calmare; **calmly** *adv* con calma
Calor gas® ['kæləʳ-] *n* butano
calorie ['kælərɪ] *n* caloria
calves [kɑːvz] *npl of* **calf**
camcorder ['kæmkɔːdəʳ] *n* camcorder *f inv*
came [keɪm] *pt of* **come**
camel ['kæməl] *n* cammello
camera ['kæmərə] *n* macchina fotografica; (*Cinema, TV*) cinepresa; **in ~** a porte chiuse; **cameraman** (*irreg*) *n* cameraman *m inv*; **camera phone** *n* telefono cellulare con fotocamera incorporata
camouflage ['kæməflɑːʒ] *n* (*Mil, Zool*) mimetizzazione *f* ▷ *vt* mimetizzare
camp [kæmp] *n* campeggio; (*Mil*) campo ▷ *vi* accamparsi ▷ *adj* effeminato(-a)
campaign [kæm'peɪn] *n* (*Mil, Pol etc*) campagna ▷ *vi* (*also fig*) fare una campagna; **campaigner** *n* **campaigner for** fautore(-trice) di; **campaigner against** oppositore(-trice) di
camp: **campbed** *n* (*BRIT*) brandina; **camper** ['kæmpəʳ] *n* campeggiatore(-trice); (*vehicle*) camper *m inv*; **campground** (*US*) *n* campeggio; **camping** ['kæmpɪŋ] *n* campeggio; **to go camping** andare in campeggio; **campsite** ['kæmpsaɪt] *n* campeggio
campus ['kæmpəs] *n* campus *m inv*
can¹ [kæn] *n* (*of milk*) scatola; (*of oil*) bidone *m*; (*of water*) tanica; (*tin*) scatola ▷ *vt* mettere in scatola

KEYWORD

can² [kæn] (*negative* **cannot, can't**, *conditional and pt* **could**) *aux vb* **1** (*be able to*) potere; **I can't go any further** non posso andare oltre; **you can do it if you try** sei in grado di farlo — basta provarci; **I'll help you all I can** ti aiuterò come potrò; **I can't see you** non ti vedo
2 (*know how to*) sapere, essere capace di; **I can swim** so nuotare; **can you speak French?** parla francese?
3 (*may*) potere; **could I have a word with you?** posso parlarle un momento?
4 (*expressing disbelief, puzzlement etc*):

it can't be true! non può essere vero!; **what CAN he want?** cosa può mai volere?
5 (*expressing possibility, suggestion etc*): **he could be in the library** può darsi che sia in biblioteca; **she could have been delayed** può aver avuto un contrattempo

Canada ['kænədə] *n* Canada *m*; **Canadian** [kə'neɪdɪən] *adj, n* canadese *m/f*
canal [kə'næl] *n* canale *m*
canary [kə'nɛərɪ] *n* canarino
Canary Islands, Canaries [kə'nɛərɪz] *npl* **the ~** le (isole) Canarie
cancel ['kænsəl] *vt* annullare; (*train*) sopprimere; (*cross out*) cancellare; **I want to ~ my booking** vorrei disdire la mia prenotazione; **cancellation** [-'leɪʃən] *n* annullamento; soppressione *f*; cancellazione *f*; (*Tourism*) prenotazione *f* annullata
cancer ['kænsəʳ] *n* cancro
Cancer ['kænsəʳ] *n* (*sign*) Cancro
candidate ['kændɪdeɪt] *n* candidato(-a)
candle ['kændl] *n* candela; (*in church*) cero; **candlestick** *n* bugia; (*bigger, ornate*) candeliere *m*
candy ['kændɪ] *n* zucchero candito; (US) caramella; caramelle *fpl*; **candy bar** (US) *n lungo biscotto, in genere ricoperto di cioccolata*; **candyfloss** ['kændɪflɔs] *n* (BRIT) zucchero filato
cane [keɪn] *n* canna; (*for furniture*) bambù *m*; (*stick*) verga ▷ *vt* (BRIT *Scol*) punire a colpi di verga
canister ['kænɪstəʳ] *n* scatola metallica
cannabis ['kænəbɪs] *n* canapa indiana
canned ['kænd] *adj* (*food*) in scatola
cannon ['kænən] (*pl* **cannon** *or* **cannons**) *n* (*gun*) cannone *m*
cannot ['kænɔt] = **can not**
canoe [kə'nuː] *n* canoa; **canoeing** *n* canottaggio
canon ['kænən] *n* (*clergyman*) canonico; (*standard*) canone *m*
can-opener ['kænəupnəʳ] *n* apriscatole *m inv*
can't [kænt] = **can not**
canteen [kæn'tiːn] *n* mensa; (BRIT: *of cutlery*) portaposate *m inv*

> Be careful not to translate ***canteen*** by the Italian word ***cantina***.

canter ['kæntəʳ] *vi* andare al piccolo galoppo
canvas ['kænvəs] *n* tela
canvass ['kænvəs] *vi* (*Pol*): **to ~ for** raccogliere voti per ▷ *vt* fare un sondaggio di
canyon ['kænjən] *n* canyon *m inv*
cap [kæp] *n* (*hat*) berretto; (*of pen*) coperchio; (*of bottle, toy gun*) tappo; (*contraceptive*) diaframma *m* ▷ *vt* (*outdo*) superare; (*limit*) fissare un tetto (a)
capability [keɪpə'bɪlɪtɪ] *n* capacità *f inv*, abilità *f inv*
capable ['keɪpəbl] *adj* capace
capacity [kə'pæsɪtɪ] *n* capacità *f inv*; (*of lift etc*) capienza
cape [keɪp] *n* (*garment*) cappa; (*Geo*) capo
caper ['keɪpəʳ] *n* (*Culin*) cappero; (*prank*) scherzetto
capital ['kæpɪtl] *n* (*also:* **~ city**) capitale *f*; (*money*) capitale *m*; (*also:* **~ letter**) (lettera) maiuscola; **capitalism** *n* capitalismo; **capitalist** *adj, n* capitalista *m/f*; **capital punishment** *n* pena capitale
Capitol ['kæpɪtl] *n* **the ~** il Campidoglio
Capricorn ['kæprɪkɔːn] *n* Capricorno
capsize [kæp'saɪz] *vt* capovolgere ▷ *vi* capovolgersi
capsule ['kæpsjuːl] *n* capsula
captain ['kæptɪn] *n* capitano
caption ['kæpʃən] *n* leggenda
captivity [kæp'tɪvɪtɪ] *n* cattività

capture ['kæptʃəʳ] *vt* catturare; (*Comput*) registrare ▷ *n* cattura; (*data*) registrazione *f* or rilevazione *f* di dati
car [kɑːʳ] *n* (*Aut*) macchina, automobile *f*; (*Rail*) vagone *m*
carafe [kə'ræf] *n* caraffa
caramel ['kærəməl] *n* caramello
carat ['kærət] *n* carato; **18 ~ gold** oro a 18 carati
caravan ['kærəvæn] *n* (BRIT) roulotte *f inv*; (*of camels*) carovana; **caravan site** (BRIT) *n* campeggio per roulotte
carbohydrate [kɑːbəu'haɪdreɪt] *n* carboidrato
carbon ['kɑːbən] *n* carbonio; **carbon dioxide** [-daɪ'ɔksaɪd] *n* diossido di carbonio; **carbon monoxide** [-mɔ'nɔksaɪd] *n* monossido di carbonio
car boot sale *n vedi nota nel riquadro*

CAR BOOT SALE

Il **car boot sale** è un mercatino dell'usato molto popolare in Gran Bretagna. Normalmente ha luogo in un parcheggio o in un grande spiazzo, e la merce viene in genere esposta nei bagagliai, in inglese appunto "boots", aperti delle macchine.

carburettor [kɑːbju'rɛtəʳ] (US **carburetor**) *n* carburatore *m*
card [kɑːd] *n* carta; (*visiting card etc*) biglietto; (*Christmas card etc*) cartolina; **cardboard** *n* cartone *m*; **card game** *n* gioco di carte
cardigan ['kɑːdɪgən] *n* cardigan *m inv*
cardinal ['kɑːdɪnl] *adj* cardinale ▷ *n* cardinale *m*
cardphone ['kɑːdfəun] *n* telefono a scheda
care [kɛəʳ] *n* cura, attenzione *f*; (*worry*) preoccupazione *f* ▷ *vi* **to ~ about** curarsi di; (*thing, idea*) interessarsi di; **~ of** presso; **in sb's ~** alle cure di qn; **to take ~ (to do)** fare attenzione (a fare); **to take ~ of** curarsi di; (*bill, problem*) occuparsi di; **I don't ~** non me ne importa; **I couldn't ~ less** non m'interessa affatto; **care for** *vt fus* aver cura di; (*like*) volere bene a
career [kə'rɪəʳ] *n* carriera ▷ *vi* (*also:* **~ along**) andare di (gran) carriera
care: **carefree** ['kɛəfriː] *adj* sgombro(-a) di preoccupazioni; **careful** ['kɛəful] *adj* attento(-a); (*cautious*) cauto(-a); **(be) careful!** attenzione!; **carefully** *adv* con cura; cautamente; **caregiver** (US) *n* (*professional*) badante *m/f*; (*unpaid*) *persona che si prende cura di un parente malato o anziano*; **careless** ['kɛəlɪs] *adj* negligente; (*heedless*) spensierato(-a); **carelessness** *n* negligenza; mancanza di tatto; **carer** ['kɛərəʳ] *n* assistente *m/f* (*di persone malata o handicappata*); **caretaker** ['kɛəteɪkəʳ] *n* custode *m*
car-ferry ['kɑːfɛrɪ] *n* traghetto
cargo ['kɑːgəu] (*pl* **cargoes**) *n* carico
car hire *n* autonoleggio
Caribbean [kærɪ'biːən] *adj*: **the ~ Sea** il Mar dei Caraibi
caring ['kɛərɪŋ] *adj* (*person*) premuroso(-a); (*society, organization*) umanitario(-a)
carnation [kɑː'neɪʃən] *n* garofano
carnival ['kɑːnɪvəl] *n* (*public celebration*) carnevale *m*; (US: *funfair*) luna park *m inv*
carol ['kærəl] *n*: **Christmas ~** canto di Natale
carousel [kærə'sɛl] (US) *n* giostra
car park (BRIT) *n* parcheggio
carpenter ['kɑːpɪntəʳ] *n* carpentiere *m*
carpet ['kɑːpɪt] *n* tappeto ▷ *vt* coprire con tappeto
car rental (US) *n* autonoleggio
carriage ['kærɪdʒ] *n* vettura; (*of goods*) trasporto; **carriageway** (BRIT) *n* (*part of road*) carreggiata

carrier ['kærɪəʳ] *n* (*of disease*) portatore(-trice); (*Comm*) impresa di trasporti; **carrier bag** (BRIT) *n* sacchetto
carrot ['kærət] *n* carota
carry ['kærɪ] *vt* (*person*) portare; (: *vehicle*) trasportare; (*involve: responsibilities etc*) comportare; (*Med*) essere portatore(-trice) di ▷ *vi* (*sound*) farsi sentire; **to be** *or* **get carried away** (*fig*) entusiasmarsi; **carry on** *vi* **to carry on with sth/doing** continuare qc/a fare ▷ *vt* mandare avanti; **carry out** *vt* (*orders*) eseguire; (*investigation*) svolgere
cart [kɑ:t] *n* carro ▷ *vt* (*inf*) trascinare
carton ['kɑ:tən] *n* (*box*) scatola di cartone; (*of yogurt*) cartone *m*; (*of cigarettes*) stecca
cartoon [kɑ:'tu:n] *n* (*Press*) disegno umoristico; (*comic strip*) fumetto; (*Cinema*) disegno animato
cartridge ['kɑ:trɪdʒ] *n* (*for gun, pen*) cartuccia; (*music tape*) cassetta
carve [kɑ:v] *vt* (*meat*) trinciare; (*wood, stone*) intagliare; **carving** *n* (*in wood etc*) scultura
car wash *n* lavaggio auto
case [keɪs] *n* caso; (*Law*) causa, processo; (*box*) scatola; (BRIT: *also:* **suit~**) valigia; **in ~ of** in caso di; **in ~ he** caso mai lui; **in any ~** in ogni caso; **just in ~** in caso di bisogno
cash [kæʃ] *n* denaro; (*coins, notes*) denaro liquido ▷ *vt* incassare; **I haven't got any ~** non ho contanti; **to pay (in) ~** pagare in contanti; **~ on delivery** pagamento alla consegna; **cashback** *n* (*discount*) sconto; (*at supermarket etc*) *anticipo di contanti ottenuto presso la cassa di un negozio tramite una carta di debito*; **cash card** (BRIT) *n* tesserino di prelievo; **cash desk** (BRIT) *n* cassa; **cash dispenser** (BRIT) *n* sportello automatico
cashew [kæ'ʃu:] *n* (*also:* **~ nut**) anacardio
cashier [kæ'ʃɪəʳ] *n* cassiere(-a)
cashmere ['kæʃmɪəʳ] *n* cachemire *m*
cash point *n* sportello bancario automatico, Bancomat® *m inv*
cash register *n* registratore *m* di cassa
casino [kə'si:nəu] *n* casinò *m inv*
casket ['kɑ:skɪt] *n* cofanetto; (US: *coffin*) bara
casserole ['kæsərəul] *n* casseruola; (*food*): **chicken ~** pollo in casseruola
cassette [kæ'sɛt] *n* cassetta; **cassette player** *n* riproduttore *m* a cassette
cast [kɑ:st] (*pt, pp* **cast**) *vt* (*throw*) gettare; (*metal*) gettare, fondere; (*Theatre*): **to ~ sb as Hamlet** scegliere qn per la parte di Amleto ▷ *n* (*Theatre*) cast *m inv*; (*also:* **plaster ~**) ingessatura; **to ~ one's vote** votare, dare il voto; **cast off** *vi* (*Naut*) salpare; (*Knitting*) calare
castanets [kæstə'nɛts] *npl* castagnette *fpl*
caster sugar ['kɑ:stəʳ-] (BRIT) *n* zucchero semolato
cast-iron ['kɑ:staɪən] *adj* (*lit*) di ghisa; (*fig: case*) di ferro
castle ['kɑ:sl] *n* castello
casual ['kæʒjul] *adj* (*chance*) casuale, fortuito(-a); (: *work etc*) avventizio(-a); (*unconcerned*) noncurante, indifferente; **~ wear** casual *m*
casualty ['kæʒjultɪ] *n* ferito(-a); (*dead*) morto(-a), vittima; (*Med: department*) pronto soccorso
cat [kæt] *n* gatto
catalogue ['kætəlɔg] (US **catalog**) *n* catalogo ▷ *vt* catalogare
catalytic converter [kætəlɪtɪk-] *n* marmitta catalitica, catalizzatore *m*
cataract ['kætərækt] *n* (*also Med*) cateratta
catarrh [kə'tɑ:ʳ] *n* catarro
catastrophe [kə'tæstrəfɪ] *n* catastrofe *f*
catch [kætʃ] (*pt, pp* **caught**) *vt*

prendere; (*ball*) afferrare; (*surprise*: *person*) sorprendere; (*attention*) attirare; (*comment, whisper*) cogliere; (*person*) raggiungere ▷ *vi* (*fire*) prendere ▷ *n* (*fish etc caught*) retata; (*of ball*) presa; (*trick*) inganno; (*Tech*) gancio; (*game*) catch *m inv*; **to ~ fire** prendere fuoco; **to ~ sight of** scorgere; **catch up** *vi* mettersi in pari ▷ *vt* (*also*: **~ up with**) raggiungere; **catching** ['kætʃɪŋ] *adj* (*Med*) contagioso(-a)

category ['kætɪgərɪ] *n* categoria

cater ['keɪtə^r] *vi*: **~ for** (BRIT: *needs*) provvedere a; (: *readers, consumers*) incontrare i gusti di; (*Comm*: *provide food*) provvedere alla ristorazione di

caterpillar ['kætəpɪlə^r] *n* bruco

cathedral [kə'θi:drəl] *n* cattedrale *f*, duomo

Catholic ['kæθəlɪk] *adj*, *n* (*Rel*) cattolico(-a)

Catseye® [kæts'aɪ] (BRIT) *n* (*Aut*) catarifrangente *m*

cattle ['kætl] *npl* bestiame *m*, bestie *fpl*

catwalk ['kætwɔ:k] *n* passerella

caught [kɔ:t] *pt*, *pp of* **catch**

cauliflower ['kɔlɪflauə^r] *n* cavolfiore *m*

cause [kɔ:z] *n* causa ▷ *vt* causare

caution ['kɔ:ʃən] *n* prudenza; (*warning*) avvertimento ▷ *vt* avvertire; ammonire; **cautious** ['kɔ:ʃəs] *adj* cauto(-a), prudente

cave [keɪv] *n* caverna, grotta; **cave in** *vi* (*roof etc*) crollare

caviar(e) ['kævɪɑ:^r] *n* caviale *m*

cavity ['kævɪtɪ] *n* cavità *f inv*

cc *abbr* = **cubic centimetres**; **carbon copy**

CCTV *n abbr* (= *closed-circuit television*) televisione *f* a circuito chiuso

CD *abbr* (*disc*) CD *m inv*; (*player*) lettore *m* CD *inv*; **CD burner** *n* masterizzatore *m* (di) CD; **CD player** *n* lettore *m* CD; **CD-ROM** [-rɔm] *n abbr* CD-ROM *m inv*

cease [si:s] *vt*, *vi* cessare; **ceasefire** *n* cessate il fuoco *m inv*

cedar ['si:də^r] *n* cedro

ceilidh ['keɪlɪ] *n festa con musiche e danze popolari scozzesi o irlandesi*

ceiling ['si:lɪŋ] *n* soffitto; (*on wages etc*) tetto

celebrate ['sɛlɪbreɪt] *vt*, *vi* celebrare; **celebration** [-'breɪʃən] *n* celebrazione *f*

celebrity [sɪ'lɛbrɪtɪ] *n* celebrità *f inv*

celery ['sɛlərɪ] *n* sedano

cell [sɛl] *n* cella; (*of revolutionaries, Biol*) cellula; (*Elec*) elemento (di batteria)

cellar ['sɛlə^r] *n* sottosuolo; cantina

cello ['tʃɛləu] *n* violoncello

Cellophane® ['sɛləfeɪn] *n* cellophane® *m*

cellphone ['sɛlfəʊn] *n* cellulare *m*

Celsius ['sɛlsɪəs] *adj* Celsius *inv*

Celtic ['kɛltɪk, 'sɛltɪk] *adj* celtico(-a)

cement [sə'mɛnt] *n* cemento

cemetery ['sɛmɪtrɪ] *n* cimitero

censor ['sɛnsə^r] *n* censore *m* ▷ *vt* censurare; **censorship** *n* censura

census ['sɛnsəs] *n* censimento

cent [sɛnt] *n* (US: *coin*) centesimo (= *1:100 di un dollaro*); (*unit of euro*) centesimo; *see also* **per**

centenary [sɛn'ti:nərɪ] *n* centenario

centennial [sɛn'tɛnɪəl] (US) *n* centenario

center ['sɛntə^r] (US) *n*, *vt* = **centre**

centi... [sɛntɪ] *prefix*: **centigrade** ['sɛntɪgreɪd] *adj* centigrado(-a); **centimetre** ['sɛntɪmi:tə^r] (US **centimeter**) *n* centimetro; **centipede** ['sɛntɪpi:d] *n* centopiedi *m inv*

central ['sɛntrəl] *adj* centrale; **Central America** *n* America centrale; **central heating** *n* riscaldamento centrale; **central reservation** *n* (BRIT *Aut*) banchina *f* spartitraffico *inv*

centre ['sɛntə^r] (US **center**) *n* centro ▷ *vt* centrare; **centre-forward** *n* (*Sport*) centroavanti *m inv*; **centre-half** *n* (*Sport*) centromediano

century ['sɛntjurɪ] *n* secolo; **twentieth ~** ventesimo secolo
CEO *n abbr* = **chief executive officer**
ceramic [sɪ'ræmɪk] *adj* ceramico(-a)
cereal ['siːrɪəl] *n* cereale *m*
ceremony ['sɛrɪmənɪ] *n* cerimonia; **to stand on ~** fare complimenti
certain ['səːtən] *adj* certo(-a); **to make ~ of** assicurarsi di; **for ~** per certo, di sicuro; **certainly** *adv* certamente, certo; **certainty** *n* certezza
certificate [sə'tɪfɪkɪt] *n* certificato; diploma *m*
certify ['səːtɪfaɪ] *vt* certificare; (*award diploma to*) conferire un diploma a; (*declare insane*) dichiarare pazzo(-a)
cf. *abbr* (= *compare*) cfr.
CFC *n* (= *chlorofluorocarbon*) CFC *m inv*
chain [tʃeɪn] *n* catena ▷ *vt* (*also:* **~ up**) incatenare; **chain-smoke** *vi* fumare una sigaretta dopo l'altra
chair [tʃɛə^r] *n* sedia; (*armchair*) poltrona; (*of university*) cattedra; (*of meeting*) presidenza ▷ *vt* (*meeting*) presiedere; **chairlift** *n* seggiovia; **chairman** (*irreg*) *n* presidente *m*; **chairperson** *n* presidente(-essa); **chairwoman** (*irreg*) *n* presidentessa
chalet ['ʃæleɪ] *n* chalet *m inv*
chalk [tʃɔːk] *n* gesso; **chalkboard** (US) *n* lavagna
challenge ['tʃælɪndʒ] *n* sfida ▷ *vt* sfidare; (*statement, right*) mettere in dubbio; **to ~ sb to do** sfidare qn a fare; **challenging** *adj* (*task*) impegnativo(-a); (*look*) di sfida
chamber ['tʃeɪmbə^r] *n* camera; **chambermaid** *n* cameriera
champagne [ʃæm'peɪn] *n* champagne *m inv*
champion ['tʃæmpɪən] *n* campione(-essa); **championship** *n* campionato
chance [tʃɑːns] *n* caso; (*opportunity*) occasione *f*; (*likelihood*) possibilità *f inv* ▷ *vt* **to ~ it** rischiare, provarci ▷ *adj* fortuito(-a); **to take a ~** rischiare; **by ~** per caso
chancellor ['tʃɑːnsələ^r] *n* cancelliere *m*; **Chancellor of the Exchequer** [-ɪks'tʃɛkə^r] (BRIT) *n* Cancelliere dello Scacchiere
chandelier [ʃændə'lɪə^r] *n* lampadario
change [tʃeɪndʒ] *vt* cambiare; (*transform*): **to ~ sb into** trasformare qn in ▷ *vi* cambiare; (*change one's clothes*) cambiarsi; (*be transformed*): **to ~ into** trasformarsi in ▷ *n* cambiamento; (*of clothes*) cambio; (*money returned*) resto; (*coins*) spiccioli; **where can I ~ some money?** dove posso cambiare dei soldi?; **to ~ one's mind** cambiare idea; **keep the ~!** tenga pure il resto!; **sorry, I don't have any ~** mi dispiace, non ho spiccioli; **for a ~** tanto per cambiare; **change over** *vi* (*from sth to sth*) passare; (*players etc*) scambiarsi (*di posto o di campo*) ▷ *vt* cambiare; **changeable** *adj* (*weather*) variabile; **change machine** *n* distributore automatico di monete; **changing room** *n* (BRIT: *in shop*) camerino; (: *Sport*) spogliatoio
channel ['tʃænl] *n* canale *m*; (*of river, sea*) alveo ▷ *vt* canalizzare; **Channel Tunnel** *n*: **the Channel Tunnel** il tunnel sotto la Manica
chant [tʃɑːnt] *n* canto; salmodia ▷ *vt* cantare; salmodiare
chaos ['keɪɔs] *n* caos *m*
chaotic [keɪ'ɔtɪk] *adj* caotico(-a)
chap [tʃæp] (BRIT: *inf*) *n* (*man*) tipo
chapel ['tʃæpəl] *n* cappella
chapped [tʃæpt] *adj* (*skin, lips*) screpolato(-a)
chapter ['tʃæptə^r] *n* capitolo
character ['kærɪktə^r] *n* carattere *m*; (*in novel, film*) personaggio; **characteristic** [-'rɪstɪk] *adj* caratteristico(-a) ▷ *n* caratteristica; **characterize** ['kærɪktəraɪz] *vt* caratterizzare; (*describe*): **to**

characterize (as) descrivere (come)
charcoal ['tʃɑːkəul] *n* carbone *m* di legna
charge [tʃɑːdʒ] *n* accusa; (*cost*) prezzo; (*responsibility*) responsabilità ▷ *vt* (*gun, battery, Mil: enemy*) caricare; (*customer*) fare pagare a; (*sum*) fare pagare; (*Law*): **to ~ sb (with)** accusare qn (di) ▷ *vi* (*gen with: up, along etc*) lanciarsi; **charge card** *n* carta *f* clienti *inv*; **charger** *n* (*also:* **battery charger**) caricabatterie *m inv*; (*old: warhorse*) destriero
charismatic [kærɪz'mætɪk] *adj* carismatico(-a)
charity ['tʃærɪtɪ] *n* carità; (*organization*) opera pia; **charity shop** *n* (BRIT) *negozi che vendono articoli di seconda mano e devolvono il ricavato in beneficenza*
charm [tʃɑːm] *n* fascino; (*on bracelet*) ciondolo ▷ *vt* affascinare, incantare; **charming** *adj* affascinante
chart [tʃɑːt] *n* tabella; grafico; (*map*) carta nautica ▷ *vt* fare una carta nautica di; **charts** *npl* (*Mus*) hit parade *f*
charter ['tʃɑːtəʳ] *vt* (*plane*) noleggiare ▷ *n* (*document*) carta; **chartered accountant** ['tʃɑːtəd-] (BRIT) *n* ragioniere(-a) professionista; **charter flight** *n* volo *m* charter *inv*
chase [tʃeɪs] *vt* inseguire; (*also:* **~ away**) cacciare ▷ *n* caccia
chat [tʃæt] *vi* (*also:* **have a ~**) chiacchierare ▷ *n* chiacchierata; (*on the Internet*) chattare; **chat up** *vt* (BRIT *inf: girl*) abbordare; **chat room** *n* (*Internet*) chat room *f inv*; **chat show** (BRIT) *n* talk show *m inv*
chatter ['tʃætəʳ] *vi* (*person*) ciarlare; (*bird*) cinguettare; (*teeth*) battere ▷ *n* ciarle *fpl*; cinguettio
chauffeur ['ʃəufəʳ] *n* autista *m*
chauvinist ['ʃəuvɪnɪst] *n* (*male chauvinist*) maschilista *m*; (*nationalist*) sciovinista *m/f*
cheap [tʃiːp] *adj* economico(-a); (*joke*) grossolano(-a); (*poor quality*) di cattiva qualità ▷ *adv* a buon mercato; **can you recommend a ~ hotel/restaurant, please?** potrebbe indicarmi un albergo/ristorante non troppo caro?; **cheap day return** *n biglietto ridotto di andata e ritorno valido in giornata*; **cheaply** *adv* a buon prezzo, a buon mercato
cheat [tʃiːt] *vi* imbrogliare; (*at school*) copiare ▷ *vt* ingannare ▷ *n* imbroglione *m*; **to ~ sb out of sth** defraudare qn di qc; **cheat on** *vt fus* (*husband, wife*) tradire
Chechnya [tʃɪtʃ'njɑː] *n* Cecenia
check [tʃɛk] *vt* verificare; (*passport, ticket*) controllare; (*halt*) fermare; (*restrain*) contenere ▷ *n* verifica; controllo; (*curb*) freno; (US: *bill*) conto; (*pattern: gen pl*) quadretti *mpl*; (US) = **cheque** ▷ *adj* (*pattern, cloth*) a quadretti; **check in** *vi* (*in hotel*) registrare; (*at airport*) presentarsi all'accettazione ▷ *vt* (*luggage*) depositare; **check off** *vt* segnare; **check out** *vi* (*in hotel*) saldare il conto; **check up** *vi* **to check up (on sth)** investigare (qc); **to check up on sb** informarsi sul conto di qn; **checkbook** (US) *n* = **chequebook**; **checked** *adj* a quadretti; **checkers** (US) *n* dama; **check-in** *n* (*also:* **check-in desk**: *at airport*) check-in *m inv*, accettazione *f* (bagagli *inv*); **checking account** (US) *n* conto corrente; **checklist** *n* lista di controllo; **checkmate** *n* scaccomatto; **checkout** *n* (*in supermarket*) cassa; **checkpoint** *n* posto di blocco; **checkroom** (US) *n* deposito *m* bagagli *inv*; **checkup** *n* (*Med*) controllo medico
cheddar ['tʃedəʳ] *n formaggio duro di latte di mucca di colore bianco o arancione*
cheek [tʃiːk] *n* guancia; (*impudence*) faccia tosta; **cheekbone** *n* zigomo; **cheeky** *adj* sfacciato(-a)

cheer [tʃɪəʳ] *vt* applaudire; (*gladden*) rallegrare ▷ *vi* applaudire ▷ *n* grido (di incoraggiamento); **cheer up** *vi* rallegrarsi, farsi animo ▷ *vt* rallegrare; **cheerful** *adj* allegro(-a)
cheerio ['tʃɪərɪ'əu] (BRIT) *excl* ciao!
cheerleader ['tʃɪəli:dəʳ] *n* cheerleader *f inv*
cheese [tʃi:z] *n* formaggio; **cheeseburger** *n* cheeseburger *m inv*; **cheesecake** *n specie di torta di ricotta, a volte con frutta*
chef [ʃɛf] *n* capocuoco
chemical ['kɛmɪkəl] *adj* chimico(-a) ▷ *n* prodotto chimico
chemist ['kɛmɪst] *n* (BRIT: *pharmacist*) farmacista *m/f*; (*scientist*) chimico(-a); **chemistry** *n* chimica; **chemist's (shop)** (BRIT) *n* farmacia
cheque [tʃɛk] (US **check**) *n* assegno; **chequebook** *n* libretto degli assegni; **cheque card** *n* carta *f* assegni *inv*
cherry ['tʃɛrɪ] *n* ciliegia; (*also:* **~ tree**) ciliegio
chess [tʃɛs] *n* scacchi *mpl*
chest [tʃɛst] *n* petto; (*box*) cassa
chestnut ['tʃɛsnʌt] *n* castagna; (*also:* **~ tree**) castagno
chest of drawers *n* cassettone *m*
chew [tʃu:] *vt* masticare; **chewing gum** *n* chewing gum *m*
chic [ʃi:k] *adj* elegante
chick [tʃɪk] *n* pulcino; (*inf*) pollastrella
chicken ['tʃɪkɪn] *n* pollo; (*inf: coward*) coniglio; **chicken out** (*inf*) *vi* avere fifa; **chickenpox** *n* varicella
chickpea ['tʃɪkpi:] *n* cece *m*
chief [tʃi:f] *n* capo ▷ *adj* principale; **chief executive (officer)** *n* direttore *m* generale; **chiefly** *adv* per lo più, soprattutto
child [tʃaɪld] (*pl* **children**) *n* bambino(-a); **child abuse** *n* molestie *fpl* a minori; **child benefit** *n* (BRIT) ≈ assegni *mpl* familiari; **childbirth** *n* parto; **child-care** *n* il badare ai bambini; **childhood** *n* infanzia; **childish** *adj* puerile; **child minder** [-'maɪndəʳ] (BRIT) *n* bambinaia; **children** ['tʃɪldrən] *npl of* **child**
Chile ['tʃɪlɪ] *n* Cile *m*
Chilean ['tʃɪlɪən] *adj, n* cileno(-a)
chill [tʃɪl] *n* freddo; (*Med*) infreddatura ▷ *vt* raffreddare; **chill out** (*esp* US) *vi* (*inf*) darsi una calmata
chil(l)i ['tʃɪlɪ] *n* peperoncino
chilly ['tʃɪlɪ] *adj* freddo(-a), fresco(-a); **to feel ~** sentirsi infreddolito(-a)
chimney ['tʃɪmnɪ] *n* camino
chimpanzee [tʃɪmpæn'zi:] *n* scimpanzé *m inv*
chin [tʃɪn] *n* mento
China ['tʃaɪnə] *n* Cina
china ['tʃaɪnə] *n* porcellana
Chinese [tʃaɪ'ni:z] *adj* cinese ▷ *n inv* cinese *m/f*; (*Ling*) cinese *m*
chip [tʃɪp] *n* (*gen pl: Culin*) patatina fritta; (: US: *also:* **potato ~**) patatina; (*of wood, glass, stone*) scheggia; (*also:* **micro~**) chip *m inv* ▷ *vt* (*cup, plate*) scheggiare; **chip and PIN card** *n* (BRIT) scheda a chip con PIN; **chip shop** *n* (BRIT) *vedi nota nel riquadro*

CHIP SHOP

I **chip shops**, anche chiamati "fish and chip shops", sono friggitorie che vendono principalmente filetti di pesce impanati e patatine fritte.

chiropodist [kɪ'rɔpədɪst] (BRIT) *n* pedicure *m/f inv*
chisel ['tʃɪzl] *n* cesello
chives [tʃaɪvz] *npl* erba cipollina
chlorine ['klɔ:ri:n] *n* cloro
choc-ice ['tʃɔkaɪs] *n* (BRIT) gelato ricoperto al cioccolato
chocolate ['tʃɔklɪt] ▷ *n* (*substance*) cioccolato, cioccolata; (*drink*) cioccolata; (*a sweet*) cioccolatino
choice [tʃɔɪs] *n* scelta ▷ *adj* scelto(-a)
choir ['kwaɪəʳ] *n* coro
choke [tʃəuk] *vi* soffocare ▷ *vt*

soffocare; (*block*): **to be ~d with** essere intasato(-a) di ▷ *n* (*Aut*) valvola dell'aria

cholesterol [kə'lɛstərɔl] *n* colesterolo

choose [tʃu:z] (*pt* **chose**, *pp* **chosen**) *vt* scegliere; **to ~ to do** decidere di fare; preferire fare

chop [tʃɔp] *vt* (*wood*) spaccare; (*Culin*: *also*: **~ up**) tritare ▷ *n* (*Culin*) costoletta; **chop down** *vt* (*tree*) abbattere; **chop off** *vt* tagliare; **chopsticks** ['tʃɔpstɪks] *npl* bastoncini *mpl* cinesi

chord [kɔ:d] *n* (*Mus*) accordo

chore [tʃɔ:ʳ] *n* faccenda; **household ~s** faccende *fpl* domestiche

chorus ['kɔ:rəs] *n* coro; (*repeated part of song*: *also fig*) ritornello

chose [tʃəuz] *pt of* **choose**

chosen ['tʃəuzn] *pp of* **choose**

Christ [kraɪst] *n* Cristo

christen ['krɪsn] *vt* battezzare; **christening** *n* battesimo

Christian ['krɪstɪən] *adj*, *n* cristiano(-a); **Christianity** [-'ænɪtɪ] *n* cristianesimo; **Christian name** *n* nome *m* (di battesimo)

Christmas ['krɪsməs] *n* Natale *m*; **Merry ~!** Buon Natale!; **Christmas card** *n* cartolina di Natale; **Christmas carol** *n* canto natalizio; **Christmas Day** *n* il giorno di Natale; **Christmas Eve** *n* la vigilia di Natale; **Christmas pudding** *n* (*esp* BRIT) *specie di budino con frutta secca, spezie e brandy*; **Christmas tree** *n* albero di Natale

chrome [krəum] *n* cromo

chronic ['krɔnɪk] *adj* cronico(-a)

chrysanthemum [krɪ'sænθəməm] *n* crisantemo

chubby ['tʃʌbɪ] *adj* paffuto(-a)

chuck [tʃʌk] (*inf*) *vt* buttare, gettare; (BRIT: *also*: **~ up**) piantare; **chuck out** *vt* buttar fuori

chuckle ['tʃʌkl] *vi* ridere sommessamente

chum [tʃʌm] *n* compagno(-a)

chunk [tʃʌŋk] *n* pezzo

church [tʃə:tʃ] *n* chiesa; **churchyard** *n* sagrato

churn [tʃə:n] *n* (*for butter*) zangola; (*for milk*) bidone *m*

chute [ʃu:t] *n* (*also*: **rubbish ~**) canale *m* di scarico; (BRIT: *children's slide*) scivolo

chutney ['tʃʌtnɪ] *n* salsa piccante (*di frutta, zucchero e spezie*)

CIA (US) *n abbr* (= *Central Intelligence Agency*) CIA *f*

CID (BRIT) *n abbr* (= *Criminal Investigation Department*) ≈ polizia giudiziaria

cider ['saɪdəʳ] *n* sidro

cigar [sɪ'gɑ:ʳ] *n* sigaro

cigarette [sɪgə'rɛt] *n* sigaretta; **cigarette lighter** *n* accendino

cinema ['sɪnəmə] *n* cinema *m inv*

cinnamon ['sɪnəmən] *n* cannella

circle ['sə:kl] *n* cerchio; (*of friends etc*) circolo; (*in cinema*) galleria ▷ *vi* girare in circolo ▷ *vt* (*surround*) circondare; (*move round*) girare intorno a

circuit ['sə:kɪt] *n* circuito

circular ['sə:kjuləʳ] *adj* circolare ▷ *n* circolare *f*

circulate ['sə:kjuleɪt] *vi* circolare ▷ *vt* far circolare; **circulation** [-'leɪʃən] *n* circolazione *f*; (*of newspaper*) tiratura

circumstances ['sə:kəmstənsɪz] *npl* circostanze *fpl*; (*financial condition*) condizioni *fpl* finanziarie

circus ['sə:kəs] *n* circo

cite [saɪt] *vt* citare

citizen ['sɪtɪzn] *n* (*of country*) cittadino(-a); (*of town*) abitante *m/f*; **citizenship** *n* cittadinanza

citrus fruits ['sɪtrəs-] *npl* agrumi *mpl*

city ['sɪtɪ] *n* città *f inv*; **the C~** la Città di Londra (*centro commerciale*); **city centre** *n* centro della città; **city technology college** *n* (BRIT) istituto tecnico superiore (*finanziato*

dall'industria)
civic ['sɪvɪk] *adj* civico(-a)
civil ['sɪvɪl] *adj* civile; **civilian** [sɪ'vɪlɪən] *adj, n* borghese *m/f*
civilization [sɪvɪlaɪ'zeɪʃən] *n* civiltà *f inv*
civilized ['sɪvɪlaɪzd] *adj* civilizzato(-a); (*fig*) cortese
civil: **civil law** *n* codice *m*, civile; (*study*) diritto civile; **civil rights** *npl* diritti *mpl* civili; **civil servant** *n* impiegato(-a) statale; **Civil Service** *n* amministrazione *f* statale; **civil war** *n* guerra civile
CJD *abbr* (*= Creutzfeld Jacob disease*) malattia di Creutzfeldt-Jacob
claim [kleɪm] *vt* (*assert*): **to ~ (that)/to be** sostenere (che)/di essere; (*credit, rights etc*) rivendicare; (*damages*) richiedere ▷ *vi* (*for insurance*) fare una domanda d'indennizzo ▷ *n* pretesa; rivendicazione *f*; richiesta; **claim form** *n* (*gen*) modulo di richiesta; (*for expenses*) modulo di rimborso spese
clam [klæm] *n* vongola
clamp [klæmp] *n* pinza; morsa ▷ *vt* stringere con una morsa; (*Aut: wheel*) applicare i ceppi bloccaruote a
clan [klæn] *n* clan *m inv*
clap [klæp] *vi* applaudire
claret ['klærət] *n* vino di Bordeaux
clarify ['klærɪfaɪ] *vt* chiarificare, chiarire
clarinet [klærɪ'nɛt] *n* clarinetto
clarity ['klærɪtɪ] *n* clarità
clash [klæʃ] *n* frastuono; (*fig*) scontro ▷ *vi* scontrarsi; cozzare
clasp [klɑːsp] *n* (*hold*) stretta; (*of necklace, bag*) fermaglio, fibbia ▷ *vt* stringere
class [klɑːs] *n* classe *f* ▷ *vt* classificare
classic ['klæsɪk] *adj* classico(-a) ▷ *n* classico; **classical** *adj* classico(-a)
classification [klæsɪfɪ'keɪʃən] *n* classificazione *f*
classify ['klæsɪfaɪ] *vt* classificare
classmate ['klɑːsmeɪt] *n* compagno(-a) di classe
classroom ['klɑːsrum] *n* aula
classy ['klɑːsɪ] *adj* (*inf*) chic *inv*, elegante
clatter ['klætəʳ] *n* tintinnio; scalpitio ▷ *vi* tintinnare; scalpitare
clause [klɔːz] *n* clausola; (*Ling*) proposizione *f*
claustrophobic [klɔːstrə'fəubɪk] *adj* claustrofobico(-a)
claw [klɔː] *n* (*of bird of prey*) artiglio; (*of lobster*) pinza
clay [kleɪ] *n* argilla
clean [kliːn] *adj* pulito(-a); (*clear, smooth*) liscio(-a) ▷ *vt* pulire; **clean up** *vt* (*also fig*) ripulire; **cleaner** *n* (*person*) donna delle pulizie; **cleaner's** *n* (*also:* **dry cleaner's**) tintoria; **cleaning** *n* pulizia
cleanser ['klɛnzəʳ] *n* detergente *m*
clear [klɪəʳ] *adj* chiaro(-a); (*glass etc*) trasparente; (*road, way*) libero(-a); (*conscience*) pulito(-a) ▷ *vt* sgombrare; liberare; (*table*) sparecchiare; (*cheque*) fare la compensazione di; (*Law: suspect*) discolpare; (*obstacle*) superare ▷ *vi* (*weather*) rasserenarsi; (*fog*) andarsene ▷ *adv* **~ of** distante da; **clear away** *vt* (*things, clothes etc*) mettere a posto; **to clear away the dishes** sparecchiare la tavola; **clear up** *vt* mettere in ordine; (*mystery*) risolvere; **clearance** *n* (*removal*) sgombro; (*permission*) autorizzazione *f*, permesso; **clear-cut** *adj* ben delineato(-a), distinto(-a); **clearing** *n* radura; **clearly** *adv* chiaramente; **clearway** (BRIT) *n* strada con divieto di sosta
clench [klɛntʃ] *vt* stringere
clergy ['kləːdʒɪ] *n* clero
clerk [klɑːk, (US) kləːrk] *n* (BRIT) impiegato(-a); (US) commesso(-a)
clever ['klɛvəʳ] *adj* (*mentally*) intelligente; (*deft, skilful*) abile; (*device, arrangement*) ingegnoso(-a)

cliché ['kli:ʃeɪ] *n* cliché *m inv*
click [klɪk] *vi* scattare ▷ *vt* (*heels etc*) battere; (*tongue*) far schioccare
client ['klaɪənt] *n* cliente *m/f*
cliff [klɪf] *n* scogliera scoscesa, rupe *f*
climate ['klaɪmɪt] *n* clima *m*; **climate change** *nsg* cambiamenti *mpl* climatici
climax ['klaɪmæks] *n* culmine *m*; (*sexual*) orgasmo
climb [klaɪm] *vi* salire; (*clamber*) arrampicarsi ▷ *vt* salire; (*Climbing*) scalare ▷ *n* salita; arrampicata; scalata; **climb down** *vi* scendere; (BRIT *fig*) far marcia indietro; **climber** *n* rocciatore(-trice); alpinista *m/f*; **climbing** *n* alpinismo
clinch [klɪntʃ] *vt* (*deal*) concludere
cling [klɪŋ] (*pt, pp* **clung**) *vi* **to ~ (to)** aggrapparsi (a); (*of clothes*) aderire strettamente (a)
Clingfilm® ['klɪŋfɪlm] *n* pellicola trasparente (*per alimenti*)
clinic ['klɪnɪk] *n* clinica
clip [klɪp] *n* (*for hair*) forcina; (*also:* **paper ~**) graffetta; (*TV, Cinema*) sequenza ▷ *vt* attaccare insieme; (*hair, nails*) tagliare; (*hedge*) tosare; **clipping** *n* (*from newspaper*) ritaglio
cloak [kləuk] *n* mantello ▷ *vt* avvolgere; **cloakroom** *n* (*for coats etc*) guardaroba *m inv*; (BRIT: *W.C.*) gabinetti *mpl*
clock [klɔk] *n* orologio; **clock in** *or* **on** *vi* timbrare il cartellino (all'entrata); **clock off** *or* **out** *vi* timbrare il cartellino (all'uscita); **clockwise** *adv* in senso orario; **clockwork** *n* movimento *or* meccanismo a orologeria ▷ *adj* a molla
clog [klɔg] *n* zoccolo ▷ *vt* intasare ▷ *vi* (*also:* **~ up**) intasarsi, bloccarsi
clone [kləun] *n* clone *m*
close[1] [kləus] *adj* **~ (to)** vicino(-a) (a); (*watch, link, relative*) stretto(-a); (*examination*) attento(-a); (*contest*) combattuto(-a); (*weather*) afoso(-a) ▷ *adv* vicino, dappresso; **~ to** vicino a; **~ by, ~ at hand** a portata di mano; **a ~ friend** un amico intimo; **to have a ~ shave** (*fig*) scamparla bella
close[2] [kləuz] *vt* chiudere ▷ *vi* (*shop etc*) chiudere; (*lid, door etc*) chiudersi; (*end*) finire ▷ *n* (*end*) fine *f*; **what time do you ~?** a che ora chiudete?; **close down** *vi* cessare (definitivamente); **closed** *adj* chiuso(-a)
closely ['kləuslɪ] *adv* (*examine, watch*) da vicino; (*related*) strettamente
closet ['klɔzɪt] *n* (*cupboard*) armadio
close-up ['kləusʌp] *n* primo piano
closing time *n* orario di chiusura
closure ['kləuʒə^r] *n* chiusura
clot [klɔt] *n* (*also:* **blood ~**) coagulo; (*inf: idiot*) scemo(-a) ▷ *vi* coagularsi
cloth [klɔθ] *n* (*material*) tessuto, stoffa; (*rag*) strofinaccio
clothes [kləuðz] *npl* abiti *mpl*, vestiti *mpl*; **clothes line** *n* corda (per stendere il bucato); **clothes peg** (US **clothes pin**) *n* molletta
clothing ['kləuðɪŋ] *n* = **clothes**
cloud [klaud] *n* nuvola; **cloud over** *vi* rannuvolarsi; (*fig*) offuscarsi; **cloudy** *adj* nuvoloso(-a); (*liquid*) torbido(-a)
clove [kləuv] *n* chiodo di garofano; **clove of garlic** *n* spicchio d'aglio
clown [klaun] *n* pagliaccio ▷ *vi* (*also:* **~ about, ~ around**) fare il pagliaccio
club [klʌb] *n* (*society*) club *m inv*, circolo; (*weapon, Golf*) mazza ▷ *vt* bastonare ▷ *vi* **to ~ together** associarsi; **clubs** *npl* (*Cards*) fiori *mpl*; **club class** *n* (*Aviat*) classe *f* club *inv*
clue [klu:] *n* indizio; (*in crosswords*) definizione *f*; **I haven't a ~** non ho la minima idea
clump [klʌmp] *n* (*of flowers, trees*) gruppo; (*of grass*) ciuffo
clumsy ['klʌmzɪ] *adj* goffo(-a)
clung [klʌŋ] *pt, pp of* **cling**
cluster ['klʌstə^r] *n* gruppo ▷ *vi* raggrupparsi
clutch [klʌtʃ] *n* (*grip, grasp*) presa,

stretta; (*Aut*) frizione *f* ▷ *vt* afferrare, stringere forte
cm *abbr* (= *centimetre*) cm
Co. *abbr* = **county**; **company**
c/o *abbr* (= *care of*) presso
coach [kəutʃ] *n* (*bus*) pullman *m inv*; (*horse-drawn, of train*) carrozza; (*Sport*) allenatore(-trice); (*tutor*) chi dà ripetizioni ▷ *vt* allenare; dare ripetizioni a; **coach station** (BRIT) *n* stazione *f* delle corriere; **coach trip** *n* viaggio in pullman
coal [kəul] *n* carbone *m*
coalition [kəuə'lɪʃən] *n* coalizione *f*
coarse [kɔːs] *adj* (*salt, sand etc*) grosso(-a); (*cloth, person*) rozzo(-a)
coast [kəust] *n* costa ▷ *vi* (*with cycle etc*) scendere a ruota libera; **coastal** *adj* costiero(-a); **coastguard** *n* guardia costiera; **coastline** *n* linea costiera
coat [kəut] *n* cappotto; (*of animal*) pelo; (*of paint*) mano *f* ▷ *vt* coprire; **coat hanger** *n* attaccapanni *m inv*; **coating** *n* rivestimento
coax [kəuks] *vt* indurre (con moine)
cob [kɔb] *n see* **corn**
cobbled ['kɔbld] *adj*: **~ street** strada pavimentata a ciottoli
cobweb ['kɔbwɛb] *n* ragnatela
cocaine [kə'keɪn] *n* cocaina
cock [kɔk] *n* (*rooster*) gallo; (*male bird*) maschio ▷ *vt* (*gun*) armare; **cockerel** *n* galletto
cockney ['kɔknɪ] *n* cockney *m/f inv* (*abitante dei quartieri popolari dell'East End di Londra*)
cockpit ['kɔkpɪt] *n* abitacolo
cockroach ['kɔkrəutʃ] *n* blatta
cocktail ['kɔkteɪl] *n* cocktail *m inv*
cocoa ['kəukəu] *n* cacao
coconut ['kəukənʌt] *n* noce *f* di cocco
cod [kɔd] *n* merluzzo
C.O.D. *abbr* = **cash on delivery**
code [kəud] *n* codice *m*
coeducational ['kəuɛdju'keɪʃənl] *adj* misto(-a)
coffee ['kɔfɪ] *n* caffè *m inv*; **coffee bar** (BRIT) *n* caffè *m inv*; **coffee bean** *n* grano *or* chicco di caffè; **coffee break** *n* pausa per il caffè; **coffee maker** *n* bollitore *m* per il caffè; **coffeepot** *n* caffettiera; **coffee shop** *n* ≈ caffè *m inv*; **coffee table** *n* tavolino
coffin ['kɔfɪn] *n* bara
cog [kɔg] *n* dente *m*
cognac ['kɔnjæk] *n* cognac *m inv*
coherent [kəu'hɪərənt] *adj* coerente
coil [kɔɪl] *n* rotolo; (*Elec*) bobina; (*contraceptive*) spirale *f* ▷ *vt* avvolgere
coin [kɔɪn] *n* moneta ▷ *vt* (*word*) coniare
coincide [kəuɪn'saɪd] *vi* coincidere; **coincidence** [kəu'ɪnsɪdəns] *n* combinazione *f*
Coke® [kəuk] *n* coca
coke [kəuk] *n* coke *m*
colander ['kɔləndəʳ] *n* colino
cold [kəuld] *adj* freddo(-a) ▷ *n* freddo; (*Med*) raffreddore *m*; **it's ~** fa freddo; **to be ~** (*person*) aver freddo; (*object*) essere freddo(-a); **to catch ~** prendere freddo; **to catch a ~** prendere un raffreddore; **in ~ blood** a sangue freddo; **cold sore** *n* erpete *m*
coleslaw ['kəulslɔː] *n* *insalata di cavolo bianco*
colic ['kɔlɪk] *n* colica
collaborate [kə'læbəreɪt] *vi* collaborare
collapse [kə'læps] *vi* crollare ▷ *n* crollo; (*Med*) collasso
collar ['kɔləʳ] *n* (*of coat, shirt*) colletto; (*of dog, cat*) collare *m*; **collarbone** *n* clavicola
colleague ['kɔliːg] *n* collega *m/f*
collect [kə'lɛkt] *vt* (*gen*) raccogliere; (*as a hobby*) fare collezione di; (BRIT: *call and pick up*) prendere; (*money owed, pension*) riscuotere; (*donations, subscriptions*) fare una colletta di ▷ *vi* adunarsi, riunirsi; ammucchiarsi; **to call ~** (US *Tel*) fare una chiamata a carico del destinatario; **collection**

[kə'lɛkʃən] *n* raccolta; collezione *f*; (*for money*) colletta; **collective** *adj* collettivo(-a) ▷ *n* collettivo; **collector** [kə'lɛktə^r] *n* collezionista *m/f*
college ['kɔlɪdʒ] *n* college *m inv*; (*of technology etc*) istituto superiore
collide [kə'laɪd] *vi*: **to ~ with** scontrarsi (con)
collision [kə'lɪʒən] *n* collisione *f*, scontro
cologne [kə'ləun] *n* (*also*: **eau de ~**) acqua di colonia
Colombia [kə'lɔmbɪə] *n* Colombia; **Colombian** *adj*, *n* colombiano(-a)
colon ['kəulən] *n* (*sign*) due punti *mpl*; (*Med*) colon *m inv*
colonel ['kə:nl] *n* colonnello
colonial [kə'ləunɪəl] *adj* coloniale
colony ['kɔlənɪ] *n* colonia
colour *etc* ['kʌlə^r] (*US* **color**) *n* colore *m* ▷ *vt* colorare; (*tint, dye*) tingere; (*fig: affect*) influenzare ▷ *vi* (*blush*) arrossire; **colour in** *vt* colorare; **colour-blind** *adj* daltonico(-a); **coloured** *adj* (*photo*) a colori; (*person*) di colore; **colour film** *n* (*for camera*) pellicola a colori; **colourful** *adj* pieno(-a) di colore, a vivaci colori; (*personality*) colorato(-a); **colouring** *n* (*substance*) colorante *m*; (*complexion*) colorito; **colour television** *n* televisione *f* a colori
column ['kɔləm] *n* colonna
coma ['kəumə] *n* coma *m inv*
comb [kəum] *n* pettine *m* ▷ *vt* (*hair*) pettinare; (*area*) battere a tappeto
combat ['kɔmbæt] *n* combattimento ▷ *vt* combattere, lottare contro
combination [kɔmbɪ'neɪʃən] *n* combinazione *f*
combine [*vb* kəm'baɪn, *n* 'kɔmbaɪn] *vt* **to ~ (with)** combinare (con); (*one quality with another*) unire (a) ▷ *vi* unirsi; (*Chem*) combinarsi ▷ *n* (*Econ*) associazione *f*
come [kʌm] (*pt* **came**, *pp* **come**) *vi* venire; arrivare; **to ~ to** (*decision etc*) raggiungere; **I've ~ to like him** ha cominciato a piacermi; **to ~ undone** slacciarsi; **to ~ loose** allentarsi; **come across** *vt fus* trovare per caso; **come along** *vi* (*pupil, work*) fare progressi; **come along!** avanti!, andiamo!, forza!; **come back** *vi* ritornare; **come down** *vi* scendere; (*prices*) calare; (*buildings*) essere demolito(-a); **come from** *vt fus* venire da; provenire da; **come in** *vi* entrare; **come off** *vi* (*button*) staccarsi; (*stain*) andar via; (*attempt*) riuscire; **come on** *vi* (*pupil, work, project*) fare progressi; (*lights*) accendersi; (*electricity*) entrare in funzione; **come on!** avanti!, andiamo!, forza!; **come out** *vi* uscire; (*stain*) andare via; **come round** *vi* (*after faint, operation*) riprendere conoscenza, rinvenire; **come to** *vi* rinvenire; **come up** *vi* (*sun*) salire; (*problem*) sorgere; (*event*) essere in arrivo; (*in conversation*) saltar fuori; **come up with** *vt fus* **he came up with an idea** venne fuori con un'idea
comeback ['kʌmbæk] *n* (*Theatre etc*) ritorno
comedian [kə'mi:dɪən] *n* comico
comedy ['kɔmɪdɪ] *n* commedia
comet ['kɔmɪt] *n* cometa
comfort ['kʌmfət] *n* comodità *f inv*, benessere *m*; (*relief*) consolazione *f*, conforto ▷ *vt* consolare, confortare; **comfortable** *adj* comodo(-a); (*financially*) agiato(-a); **comfort station** (*US*) *n* gabinetti *mpl*
comic ['kɔmɪk] *adj* (*also*: **~al**) comico(-a) ▷ *n* comico; (*BRIT*: *magazine*) giornaletto; **comic book** (*US*) *n* giornalino (a fumetti); **comic strip** *n* fumetto
comma ['kɔmə] *n* virgola
command [kə'mɑ:nd] *n* ordine *m*, comando; (*Mil: authority*) comando; (*mastery*) padronanza ▷ *vt* comandare; **to ~ sb to do** ordinare a qn di fare; **commander** *n* capo; (*Mil*)

comandante *m*
commemorate [kə'mɛməreɪt] *vt* commemorare
commence [kə'mɛns] *vt, vi* cominciare; **commencement** (US) *n* (*Univ*) cerimonia di consegna dei diplomi
commend [kə'mɛnd] *vt* lodare; raccomandare
comment ['kɔmɛnt] *n* commento ▷ *vi* **to ~ (on)** fare commenti (su); **commentary** ['kɔməntərɪ] *n* commentario; (*Sport*) radiocronaca; telecronaca; **commentator** ['kɔmənteɪtə^r] *n* commentatore(-trice); radiocronista *m/f*; telecronista *m/f*
commerce ['kɔmə:s] *n* commercio
commercial [kə'mə:ʃəl] *adj* commerciale ▷ *n* (*TV, Radio: advertisement*) pubblicità *f inv*; **commercial break** *n* intervallo pubblicitario
commission [kə'mɪʃən] *n* commissione *f* ▷ *vt* (*work of art*) commissionare; **out of ~** (*Naut*) in disarmo; **commissioner** *n* (*Police*) questore *m*
commit [kə'mɪt] *vt* (*act*) commettere; (*to sb's care*) affidare; **to ~ o.s. to do** impegnarsi (a fare); **to ~ suicide** suicidarsi; **commitment** *n* impegno; promessa
committee [kə'mɪtɪ] *n* comitato
commodity [kə'mɔdɪtɪ] *n* prodotto, articolo
common ['kɔmən] *adj* comune; (*pej*) volgare; (*usual*) normale ▷ *n* terreno comune; **the C~s** (BRIT) ▷ *npl* la Camera dei Comuni; **in ~** in comune; **commonly** *adv* comunemente, usualmente; **commonplace** *adj* banale, ordinario(-a); **Commons** *npl* (BRIT *Pol*): **the (House of) Commons** la Camera dei Comuni; **common sense** *n* buon senso; **Commonwealth** *n* **the Commonwealth** il Commonwealth

COMMONWEALTH

Il **Commonwealth** è un'associazione di stati sovrani indipendenti e di alcuni territori annessi che facevano parte dell'antico Impero Britannico. Nel 1931 questi assunsero il nome di "Commonwealth of Nations", denominazione successivamente semplificata in "Commonwealth". Attualmente gli stati del "Commonwealth" riconoscono ancora il proprio capo di stato.

communal ['kɔmju:nl] *adj* (*for common use*) pubblico(-a)
commune [*n* 'kɔmju:n, *vb* kə'mju:n] *n* (*group*) comune *f* ▷ *vi* **to ~ with** mettersi in comunione con
communicate [kə'mju:nɪkeɪt] *vt* comunicare, trasmettere ▷ *vi* **to ~ with** comunicare (con)
communication [kəmju:nɪ'keɪʃən] *n* comunicazione *f*
communion [kə'mju:nɪən] *n* (*also:* **Holy C~**) comunione *f*
communism ['kɔmjunɪzəm] *n* comunismo; **communist** *adj, n* comunista *m/f*
community [kə'mju:nɪtɪ] *n* comunità *f inv*; **community centre** (US **community center**) *n* circolo ricreativo; **community service** *n* (BRIT) ≈ lavoro sostitutivo
commute [kə'mju:t] *vi* fare il pendolare ▷ *vt* (*Law*) commutare; **commuter** *n* pendolare *m/f*
compact [*adj* kəm'pækt, *n* 'kɔmpækt] *adj* compatto(-a) ▷ *n* (*also:* **powder ~**) portacipria *m inv*; **compact disc** *n* compact disc *m inv*; **compact disc player** *n* lettore *m* CD *inv*
companion [kəm'pænɪən] *n* compagno(-a)

company ['kʌmpənɪ] *n* (*also Comm, Mil, Theatre*) compagnia; **to keep sb ~** tenere compagnia a qn; **company car** *n* macchina (di proprietà) della ditta; **company director** *n* amministratore *m*, consigliere *m* di amministrazione
comparable ['kɔmpərəbl] *adj* simile
comparative [kəm'pærətɪv] *adj* relativo(-a); (*adjective etc*) comparativo(-a); **comparatively** *adv* relativamente
compare [kəm'pɛə^r] *vt* **to ~ sth/sb with/to** confrontare qc/qn con/a ▷ *vi* **to ~ (with)** reggere il confronto (con); **comparison** [-'pærɪsn] *n* confronto; **in comparison (with)** in confronto (a)
compartment [kəm'pɑːtmənt] *n* compartimento; (*Rail*) scompartimento; **a non-smoking ~** uno scompartimento per non-fumatori
compass ['kʌmpəs] *n* bussola; **compasses** *npl* (*Math*) compasso
compassion [kəm'pæʃən] *n* compassione *f*
compatible [kəm'pætɪbl] *adj* compatibile
compel [kəm'pɛl] *vt* costringere, obbligare; **compelling** *adj* (*fig: argument*) irresistibile
compensate ['kɔmpənseɪt] *vt* risarcire ▷ *vi* **to ~ for** compensare; **compensation** [-'seɪʃən] *n* compensazione *f*; (*money*) risarcimento
compete [kəm'piːt] *vi* (*take part*) concorrere; (*vie*): **to ~ with** fare concorrenza (a)
competent ['kɔmpɪtənt] *adj* competente
competition [kɔmpɪ'tɪʃən] *n* gara; concorso; (*Econ*) concorrenza
competitive [kəm'pɛtɪtɪv] *adj* (*Econ*) concorrenziale; (*sport*) agonistico(-a); (*person*) che ha spirito di competizione; che ha spirito agonistico
competitor [kəm'pɛtɪtə^r] *n* concorrente *m/f*
complacent [kəm'pleɪsnt] *adj* compiaciuto(-a) di sé
complain [kəm'pleɪn] *vi* lagnarsi, lamentarsi; **complaint** *n* lamento; (*in shop etc*) reclamo; (*Med*) malattia
complement [*n* 'kɔmplɪmənt, *vb* 'kɔmplɪmɛnt] *n* complemento; (*especially of ship's crew etc*) effettivo ▷ *vt* (*enhance*) accompagnarsi bene a; **complementary** [kɔmplɪ'mɛntərɪ] *adj* complementare
complete [kəm'pliːt] *adj* completo(-a) ▷ *vt* completare; (*a form*) riempire; **completely** *adv* completamente; **completion** *n* completamento
complex ['kɔmplɛks] *adj* complesso(-a) ▷ *n* (*Psych, of buildings etc*) complesso
complexion [kəm'plɛkʃən] *n* (*of face*) carnagione *f*
compliance [kəm'plaɪəns] *n* acquiescenza; **in ~ with** (*orders, wishes etc*) in conformità con
complicate ['kɔmplɪkeɪt] *vt* complicare; **complicated** *adj* complicato(-a); **complication** [-'keɪʃən] *n* complicazione *f*
compliment [*n* 'kɔmplɪmənt, *vb* 'kɔmplɪmɛnt] *n* complimento ▷ *vt* fare un complimento a; **complimentary** [-'mɛntərɪ] *adj* complimentoso(-a), elogiativo(-a); (*free*) in omaggio
comply [kəm'plaɪ] *vi* **to ~ with** assentire a; conformarsi a
component [kəm'pəunənt] *adj* componente ▷ *n* componente *m*
compose [kəm'pəuz] *vt* (*form*): **to be ~d of** essere composto di; (*music, poem etc*) comporre; **to ~ o.s.** ricomporsi; **composer** *n* (*Mus*) compositore(-trice); **composition** [kɔmpə'zɪʃən] *n* composizione *f*

composure [kəm'pəuʒəʳ] *n* calma
compound ['kɔmpaund] *n* (*Chem, Ling*) composto; (*enclosure*) recinto ▷ *adj* composto(-a)
comprehension [kɔmprɪ'hɛnʃən] *n* comprensione *f*
comprehensive [kɔmprɪ'hɛnsɪv] *adj* completo(-a); **comprehensive (school)** (BRIT) *n scuola secondaria aperta a tutti*

> Be careful not to translate ***comprehensive*** by the Italian word ***comprensivo***.

compress [*vb* kəm'prɛs, *n* 'kɔmprɛs] *vt* comprimere ▷ *n* (*Med*) compressa
comprise [kəm'praɪz] *vt* (*also:* **be ~d**) comprendere
compromise ['kɔmprəmaɪz] *n* compromesso ▷ *vt* compromettere ▷ *vi* venire a un compromesso
compulsive [kəm'pʌlsɪv] *adj* (*liar, gambler*) che non riesce a controllarsi; (*viewing, reading*) cui non si può fare a meno
compulsory [kəm'pʌlsərɪ] *adj* obbligatorio(-a)
computer [kəm'pju:təʳ] *n* computer *m inv*, elaboratore *m* elettronico; **computer game** *n* gioco per computer; **computer-generated** *adj* realizzato(-a) al computer; **computerize** *vt* computerizzare; **computer programmer** *n* programmatore(-trice); **computer programming** *n* programmazione *f* di computer; **computer science** *n* informatica; **computer studies** *npl* informatica; **computing** *n* informatica
con [kɔn] (*inf*) *vt* truffare ▷ *n* truffa
conceal [kən'si:l] *vt* nascondere
concede [kən'si:d] *vt* ammettere
conceited [kən'si:tɪd] *adj* presuntuoso(-a), vanitoso(-a)
conceive [kən'si:v] *vt* concepire ▷ *vi* concepire un bambino
concentrate ['kɔnsəntreɪt] *vi* concentrarsi ▷ *vt* concentrare
concentration [kɔnsən'treɪʃən] *n* concentrazione *f*
concept ['kɔnsɛpt] *n* concetto
concern [kən'sə:n] *n* affare *m*; (*Comm*) azienda, ditta; (*anxiety*) preoccupazione *f* ▷ *vt* riguardare; **to be ~ed (about)** preoccuparsi (di); **concerning** *prep* riguardo a, circa
concert ['kɔnsə:t] *n* concerto; **concert hall** *n* sala da concerti
concerto [kən'tʃə:təu] *n* concerto
concession [kən'sɛʃən] *n* concessione *f*
concise [kən'saɪs] *adj* conciso(-a)
conclude [kən'klu:d] *vt* concludere; **conclusion** [-'klu:ʒən] *n* conclusione *f*
concrete ['kɔŋkri:t] *n* calcestruzzo ▷ *adj* concreto(-a), di calcestruzzo
concussion [kən'kʌʃən] *n* commozione *f* cerebrale
condemn [kən'dɛm] *vt* condannare; (*building*) dichiarare pericoloso(-a)
condensation [kɔndɛn'seɪʃən] *n* condensazione *f*
condense [kən'dɛns] *vi* condensarsi ▷ *vt* condensare
condition [kən'dɪʃən] *n* condizione *f*; (*Med*) malattia ▷ *vt* condizionare; **on ~ that** a condizione che + *sub*, a condizione di; **conditional** *adj* condizionale; **to be conditional upon** dipendere da; **conditioner** *n* (*for hair*) balsamo; (*for fabrics*) ammorbidente *m*
condo ['kɔndəu] (US) *n abbr* (*inf*) = **condominium**
condom ['kɔndəm] *n* preservativo
condominium [kɔndə'mɪnɪəm] (US) *n* condominio
condone [kən'dəun] *vt* condonare
conduct [*n* 'kɔndʌkt, *vb* kən'dʌkt] *n* condotta ▷ *vt* condurre; (*manage*) dirigere; amministrare; (*Mus*) dirigere; **to ~ o.s.** comportarsi; **conducted tour** [kən'dʌktɪd-] *n*

gita accompagnata; **conductor** *n* (*of orchestra*) direttore *m* d'orchestra; (*on bus*) bigliettaio; (*US*: *on train*) controllore *m*; (*Elec*) conduttore *m*
cone [kəun] *n* cono; (*Bot*) pigna; (*traffic cone*) birillo
confectionery [kən'fɛkʃənrɪ] *n* dolciumi *mpl*
confer [kən'fəːʳ] *vt* **to ~ sth on** conferire qc a ▷ *vi* conferire
conference ['kɔnfərns] *n* congresso
confess [kən'fɛs] *vt* confessare, ammettere ▷ *vi* confessare; **confession** [kən'fɛʃən] *n* confessione *f*
confide [kən'faɪd] *vi* **to ~ in** confidarsi con
confidence ['kɔnfɪdns] *n* confidenza; (*trust*) fiducia; (*self-assurance*) sicurezza di sé; **in ~** (*speak, write*) in confidenza, confidenzialmente; **confident** *adj* sicuro(-a), sicuro(-a) di sé; **confidential** [kɔnfɪ'dɛnʃəl] *adj* riservato(-a), confidenziale
confine [kən'faɪn] *vt* limitare; (*shut up*) rinchiudere; **confined** *adj* (*space*) ristretto(-a)
confirm [kən'fəːm] *vt* confermare; **confirmation** [kɔnfə'meɪʃən] *n* conferma; (*Rel*) cresima
confiscate ['kɔnfɪskeɪt] *vt* confiscare
conflict [*n* 'kɔnflɪkt, *vb* kən'flɪkt] *n* conflitto ▷ *vi* essere in conflitto
conform [kən'fɔːm] *vi* **to ~ to** conformarsi (a)
confront [kən'frʌnt] *vt* (*enemy, danger*) affrontare; **confrontation** [kɔnfrən'teɪʃən] *n* scontro
confuse [kən'fjuːz] *vt* (*one thing with another*) confondere; **confused** *adj* confuso(-a); **confusing** *adj* che fa confondere; **confusion** [-'fjuːʒən] *n* confusione *f*
congestion [kən'dʒɛstʃən] *n* congestione *f*
congratulate [kən'grætjuleɪt] *vt* **to ~ sb (on)** congratularsi con qn (per *or* di); **congratulations** [-'leɪʃənz] *npl* auguri *mpl*; (*on success*) complimenti *mpl*, congratulazioni *fpl*
congregation [kɔŋgrɪ'geɪʃən] *n* congregazione *f*
congress ['kɔŋgrɛs] *n* congresso; **congressman** (*irreg*: *US*) *n* membro del Congresso; **congresswoman** (*irreg*: *US*) *n* (donna) membro del Congresso
conifer ['kɔnɪfəʳ] *n* conifero
conjugate ['kɔndʒugeɪt] *vt* coniugare
conjugation [kɔndʒə'geɪʃən] *n* coniugazione *f*
conjunction [kən'dʒʌŋkʃən] *n* congiunzione *f*
conjure ['kʌndʒəʳ] *vi* fare giochi di prestigio
connect [kə'nɛkt] *vt* connettere, collegare; (*Elec, Tel*) collegare; (*fig*) associare ▷ *vi* (*train*): **to ~ with** essere in coincidenza con; **to be ~ed with** (*associated*) aver rapporti con; **connecting flight** *n* volo in coincidenza; **connection** [-ʃən] ▷ *n* relazione *f*, rapporto; (*Elec*) connessione *f*; (*train, plane*) coincidenza; (*Tel*) collegamento
conquer ['kɔŋkəʳ] *vt* conquistare; (*feelings*) vincere
conquest ['kɔŋkwɛst] *n* conquista
cons [kɔnz] *npl see* **convenience**; **pro**
conscience ['kɔnʃəns] *n* coscienza
conscientious [kɔnʃɪ'ɛnʃəs] *adj* coscienzioso(-a)
conscious ['kɔnʃəs] *adj* consapevole; (*Med*) cosciente; **consciousness** *n* consapevolezza; coscienza
consecutive [kən'sɛkjutɪv] *adj* consecutivo(-a); **on 3 ~ occasions** 3 volte di fila
consensus [kən'sɛnsəs] *n* consenso; **the ~ of opinion** l'opinione *f* unanime *or* comune
consent [kən'sɛnt] *n* consenso ▷ *vi* **to ~ (to)** acconsentire (a)

consequence ['kɔnsɪkwəns] *n* conseguenza, risultato; importanza
consequently ['kɔnsɪkwəntlɪ] *adv* di conseguenza, dunque
conservation [kɔnsə'veɪʃən] *n* conservazione *f*
conservative [kən'səːvətɪv] *adj* conservatore(-trice); (*cautious*) cauto(-a); **Conservative** (BRIT) *adj, n* (*Pol*) conservatore(-trice)
conservatory [kən'səːvətrɪ] *n* (*greenhouse*) serra; (*Mus*) conservatorio
consider [kən'sɪdəʳ] *vt* considerare; (*take into account*) tener conto di; **to ~ doing sth** considerare la possibilità di fare qc; **considerable** [kən'sɪdərəbl] *adj* considerevole, notevole; **considerably** *adv* notevolmente, decisamente; **considerate** [kən'sɪdərɪt] *adj* premuroso(-a); **consideration** [kənsɪdə'reɪʃən] *n* considerazione *f*; **considering** [kən'sɪdərɪŋ] *prep* in considerazione di
consignment [kən'saɪnmənt] *n* (*of goods*) consegna; spedizione *f*
consist [kən'sɪst] *vi* **to ~ of** constare di, essere composto(-a) di
consistency [kən'sɪstənsɪ] *n* consistenza; (*fig*) coerenza
consistent [kən'sɪstənt] *adj* coerente
consolation [kɔnsə'leɪʃən] *n* consolazione *f*
console¹ [kən'səul] *vt* consolare
console² ['kɔnsəul] *n* quadro di comando
consonant ['kɔnsənənt] *n* consonante *f*
conspicuous [kən'spɪkjuəs] *adj* cospicuo(-a)
conspiracy [kən'spɪrəsɪ] *n* congiura, cospirazione *f*
constable ['kʌnstəbl] (BRIT) *n* ≈ poliziotto, agente *m* di polizia; **chief ~** ≈ questore *m*
constant ['kɔnstənt] *adj* costante, continuo(-a); **constantly** *adv* costantemente; continuamente
constipated ['kɔnstɪpeɪtɪd] *adj* stitico(-a); **constipation** [kɔnstɪ'peɪʃən] *n* stitichezza
constituency [kən'stɪtjuənsɪ] *n* collegio elettorale
constitute ['kɔnstɪtjuːt] *vt* costituire
constitution [kɔnstɪ'tjuːʃən] *n* costituzione *f*
constraint [kən'streɪnt] *n* costrizione *f*
construct [kən'strʌkt] *vt* costruire; **construction** [-ʃən] *n* costruzione *f*; **constructive** *adj* costruttivo(-a)
consul ['kɔnsl] *n* console *m*; **consulate** ['kɔnsjulɪt] *n* consolato
consult [kən'sʌlt] *vt* consultare; **consultant** *n* (*Med*) consulente *m* medico; (*other specialist*) consulente; **consultation** [-'teɪʃən] *n* (*Med*) consulto; (*discussion*) consultazione *f*; **consulting room** [kən'sʌltɪŋ-] (BRIT) *n* ambulatorio
consume [kən'sjuːm] *vt* consumare; **consumer** *n* consumatore(-trice)
consumption [kən'sʌmpʃən] *n* consumo
cont. *abbr* = **continued**
contact ['kɔntækt] *n* contatto; (*person*) conoscenza ▷ *vt* mettersi in contatto con; **contact lenses** *npl* lenti *fpl* a contatto
contagious [kən'teɪdʒəs] *adj* (*also fig*) contagioso(-a)
contain [kən'teɪn] *vt* contenere; **to ~ o.s.** contenersi; **container** *n* recipiente *m*; (*for shipping etc*) container *m inv*
contaminate [kən'tæmɪneɪt] *vt* contaminare
cont'd *abbr* = **continued**
contemplate ['kɔntəmpleɪt] *vt* contemplare; (*consider*) pensare a (*or* di)
contemporary [kən'tɛmpərərɪ] *adj*,

n contemporaneo(-a)
contempt [kən'tɛmpt] *n* disprezzo; **~ of court** (*Law*) oltraggio alla Corte
contend [kən'tɛnd] *vt* **to ~ that** sostenere che ▷ *vi* **to ~ with** lottare contro
content[1] ['kɔntɛnt] *n* contenuto; **contents** *npl* (*of box, case etc*) contenuto; **(table of) ~s** indice *m*
content[2] [kən'tɛnt] *adj* contento(-a), soddisfatto(-a) ▷ *vt* contentare, soddisfare; **contented** *adj* contento(-a), soddisfatto(-a)
contest [*n* 'kɔntɛst, *vb* kən'tɛst] *n* lotta; (*competition*) gara, concorso ▷ *vt* contestare; impugnare; (*compete for*) essere in lizza per; **contestant** [kən'tɛstənt] *n* concorrente *m/f*; (*in fight*) avversario(-a)
context ['kɔntɛkst] *n* contesto
continent ['kɔntɪnənt] *n* continente *m*; **the C~** (BRIT) l'Europa continentale; **continental** [-'nɛntl] *adj* continentale; **continental breakfast** *n* colazione *f* all'europea (*senza piatti caldi*); **continental quilt** (BRIT) *n* piumino
continual [kən'tɪnjuəl] *adj* continuo(-a); **continually** *adv* di continuo
continue [kən'tɪnju:] *vi* continuare ▷ *vt* continuare; (*start again*) riprendere
continuity [kɔntɪ'nju:ɪtɪ] *n* continuità; (*TV, Cinema*) (ordine *m* della) sceneggiatura
continuous [kən'tɪnjuəs] *adj* continuo(-a), ininterrotto(-a); **continuous assessment** *n* (BRIT) valutazione *f* continua; **continuously** *adv* (*repeatedly*) continuamente; (*uninterruptedly*) ininterrottamente
contour ['kɔntuə^r] *n* contorno, profilo; (*also:* **~ line**) curva di livello
contraception [kɔntrə'sɛpʃən] *n* contraccezione *f*
contraceptive [kɔntrə'sɛptɪv] *adj* contraccettivo(-a) ▷ *n* contraccettivo
contract [*n* 'kɔntrækt, *vb* kən'trækt] *n* contratto ▷ *vi* (*become smaller*) contrarsi; (*Comm*): **to ~ to do sth** fare un contratto per fare qc ▷ *vt* (*illness*) contrarre; **contractor** *n* imprenditore *m*
contradict [kɔntrə'dɪkt] *vt* contraddire; **contradiction** [kɔntrə'dɪkʃən] *n* contraddizione *f*; **to be in contradiction with** discordare con
contrary[1] ['kɔntrərɪ] *adj* contrario(-a); (*unfavourable*) avverso(-a), contrario(-a) ▷ *n* contrario; **on the ~** al contrario; **unless you hear to the ~** salvo contrordine
contrary[2] [kən'trɛərɪ] *adj* (*perverse*) bisbetico(-a)
contrast [*n* 'kɔntrɑ:st, *vb* kən'trɑ:st] *n* contrasto ▷ *vt* mettere in contrasto; **in ~ to** contrariamente a
contribute [kən'trɪbju:t] *vi* contribuire ▷ *vt* **to ~ £10/an article to** dare 10 sterline/un articolo a; **to ~ to** contribuire a; (*newspaper*) scrivere per; **contribution** [kɔntrɪ'bju:ʃən] *n* contributo; **contributor** *n* (*to newspaper*) collaboratore(-trice)
control [kən'trəul] *vt* controllare; (*firm, operation etc*) dirigere ▷ *n* controllo; **controls** *npl* (*of vehicle etc*) comandi *mpl*; (*governmental*) controlli *mpl*; **under ~** sotto controllo; **to be in ~ of** avere il controllo di; **to go out of ~** (*car*) non rispondere ai comandi; (*situation*) sfuggire di mano; **control tower** *n* (*Aviat*) torre *f* di controllo
controversial [kɔntrə'və:ʃl] *adj* controverso(-a), polemico(-a)
controversy ['kɔntrəvə:sɪ] *n* controversia, polemica
convenience [kən'vi:nɪəns] *n* comodità *f inv*; **at your ~** a suo comodo; **all modern ~s** (BRIT), **all mod cons** tutte le comodità moderne

convenient [kən'viːnɪənt] *adj* comodo(-a)

> Be careful not to translate ***convenient*** by the Italian word ***conveniente***.

convent ['kɔnvənt] *n* convento
convention [kən'vɛnʃən] *n* convenzione *f*; (*meeting*) convegno; **conventional** *adj* convenzionale
conversation [kɔnvə'seɪʃən] *n* conversazione *f*
conversely [kɔn'vəːslɪ] *adv* al contrario, per contro
conversion [kən'vəːʃən] *n* conversione *f*; (BRIT: *of house*) trasformazione *f*, rimodernamento
convert [*vb* kən'vəːt, *n* 'kɔnvəːt] *vt* (*Comm*, *Rel*) convertire; (*alter*) trasformare ▷ *n* convertito(-a); **convertible** *n* macchina decappottabile
convey [kən'veɪ] *vt* trasportare; (*thanks*) comunicare; (*idea*) dare; **conveyor belt** [kən'veɪəʳ-] *n* nastro trasportatore
convict [*vb* kən'vɪkt, *n* 'kɔnvɪkt] *vt* dichiarare colpevole ▷ *n* carcerato(-a); **conviction** [-ʃən] *n* condanna; (*belief*) convinzione *f*
convince [kən'vɪns] *vt* convincere, persuadere; **convinced** *adj* **convinced of/that** convinto(-a) di/che; **convincing** *adj* convincente
convoy ['kɔnvɔɪ] *n* convoglio
cook [kuk] *vt* cucinare, cuocere ▷ *vi* cuocere; (*person*) cucinare ▷ *n* cuoco(-a); **cook book** *n* libro di cucina; **cooker** *n* fornello, cucina; **cookery** *n* cucina; **cookery book** (BRIT) *n* = **cook book**; **cookie** (US) *n* biscotto; **cooking** *n* cucina
cool [kuːl] *adj* fresco(-a); (*not afraid, calm*) calmo(-a); (*unfriendly*) freddo(-a) ▷ *vt* raffreddare; (*room*) rinfrescare ▷ *vi* (*water*) raffreddarsi; (*air*) rinfrescarsi; **cool down** *vi* raffreddarsi; (*fig: person, situation*) calmarsi; **cool off** *vi* (*become calmer*) calmarsi; (*lose enthusiasm*) perdere interesse
cop [kɔp] (*inf*) *n* sbirro
cope [kəup] *vi* **to ~ with** (*problems*) far fronte a
copper ['kɔpəʳ] *n* rame *m*; (*inf: policeman*) sbirro
copy ['kɔpɪ] *n* copia ▷ *vt* copiare; **copyright** *n* diritto d'autore
coral ['kɔrəl] *n* corallo
cord [kɔːd] *n* corda; (*Elec*) filo; **cords** *npl* (*trousers*) calzoni *mpl* (di velluto) a coste; **cordless** *adj* senza cavo
corduroy ['kɔːdərɔɪ] *n* fustagno
core [kɔːʳ] *n* (*of fruit*) torsolo; (*of organization etc*) cuore *m* ▷ *vt* estrarre il torsolo da
coriander [kɔrɪ'ændəʳ] *n* coriandolo
cork [kɔːk] *n* sughero; (*of bottle*) tappo; **corkscrew** *n* cavatappi *m inv*
corn [kɔːn] *n* (BRIT: *wheat*) grano; (US: *maize*) granturco; (*on foot*) callo; **~ on the cob** (*Culin*) pannocchia cotta
corned beef ['kɔːnd-] *n* carne *f* di manzo in scatola
corner ['kɔːnəʳ] *n* angolo; (*Aut*) curva ▷ *vt* intrappolare; mettere con le spalle al muro; (*Comm: market*) accaparrare ▷ *vi* prendere una curva
corner shop (BRIT) piccolo negozio di generi alimentari
cornflakes ['kɔːnfleɪks] *npl* fiocchi *mpl* di granturco
cornflour ['kɔːnflauəʳ] (BRIT) *n* farina finissima di granturco
cornstarch ['kɔːnstɑːtʃ] (US) *n* = **cornflour**
Cornwall ['kɔːnwɔːl] *n* Cornovaglia
coronary ['kɔrənərɪ] *n* **~ (thrombosis)** trombosi *f* coronaria
coronation [kɔrə'neɪʃən] *n* incoronazione *f*
coroner ['kɔrənəʳ] *n* *magistrato incaricato di indagare la causa di morte in circostanze sospette*
corporal ['kɔːprəl] *n* caporalmaggiore *m* ▷ *adj* **~ punishment** pena

corporale
corporate ['kɔːpərɪt] *adj* costituito(-a) (in corporazione), comune
corporation [kɔːpə'reɪʃən] *n* (*of town*) consiglio comunale; (*Comm*) ente *m*
corps [kɔː, *pl* kɔːz] *n inv* corpo
corpse [kɔːps] *n* cadavere *m*
correct [kə'rɛkt] *adj* (*accurate*) corretto(-a), esatto(-a); (*proper*) corretto(-a) ▷ *vt* correggere; **correction** [-ʃən] *n* correzione *f*
correspond [kɔrɪs'pɔnd] *vi* corrispondere; **correspondence** *n* corrispondenza; **correspondent** *n* corrispondente *m/f*; **corresponding** *adj* corrispondente
corridor ['kɔrɪdɔːʳ] *n* corridoio
corrode [kə'rəud] *vt* corrodere ▷ *vi* corrodersi
corrupt [kə'rʌpt] *adj* corrotto(-a); (*Comput*) alterato(-a) ▷ *vt* corrompere; **corruption** *n* corruzione *f*
Corsica ['kɔːsɪkə] *n* Corsica
cosmetic [kɔz'mɛtɪk] *n* cosmetico ▷ *adj* (*fig*: *measure etc*) superficiale; **cosmetic surgery** *n* chirurgia plastica
cosmopolitan [kɔzmə'pɔlɪtn] *adj* cosmopolita
cost [kɔst] (*pt, pp* **cost**) *n* costo ▷ *vt* costare; (*find out the cost of*) stabilire il prezzo di; **costs** *npl* (*Comm, Law*) spese *fpl*; **how much does it ~?** quanto costa?; **at all ~s** a ogni costo
co-star ['kəustɑːʳ] *n attore/trice della stessa importanza del protagonista*
Costa Rica ['kɔstə'riːkə] *n* Costa Rica
costly ['kɔstlɪ] *adj* costoso(-a), caro(-a)
cost of living *adj* **~ allowance** indennità *f inv* di contingenza
costume ['kɔstjuːm] *n* costume *m*; (*lady's suit*) tailleur *m inv*; (BRIT: *also*: **swimming ~**) costume *m* da bagno
cosy ['kəuzɪ] (US **cozy**) *adj* intimo(-a); **I'm very ~ here** sto proprio bene qui
cot [kɔt] *n* (BRIT: *child's*) lettino; (US: *campbed*) brandina
cottage ['kɔtɪdʒ] *n* cottage *m inv*; **cottage cheese** *n* fiocchi *mpl* di latte magro
cotton ['kɔtn] *n* cotone *m*; **cotton on** *vi* (*inf*): **to cotton on (to sth)** afferrare (qc); **cotton bud** *n* (BRIT) cotton fioc® *m inv*; **cotton candy** (US) *n* zucchero filato; **cotton wool** (BRIT) *n* cotone idrofilo
couch [kautʃ] *n* sofà *m inv*
cough [kɔf] *vi* tossire ▷ *n* tosse *f*; **I've got a ~** ho la tosse; **cough mixture, cough syrup** *n* sciroppo per la tosse
could [kud] *pt of* **can**[2]
couldn't = **could not**
council ['kaunsl] *n* consiglio; **city** *or* **town ~** consiglio comunale; **council estate** (BRIT) *n* quartiere *m* di case popolari; **council house** (BRIT) *n* casa popolare; **councillor** (US **councilor**) *n* consigliere(-a); **council tax** *n* (BRIT) *tassa comunale sulla proprietà*
counsel ['kaunsl] *n* avvocato; consultazione *f* ▷ *vt* consigliare; **counselling** (US **counseling**) *n* (*Psych*) assistenza psicologica; **counsellor** (US **counselor**) *n* consigliere(-a); (US) avvocato
count [kaunt] *vt, vi* contare ▷ *n* (*of votes etc*) conteggio; (*of pollen etc*) livello; (*nobleman*) conte *m*; **count in** (*inf*) *vt* includere; **count me in** ci sto anch'io; **count on** *vt fus* contare su; **countdown** *n* conto alla rovescia
counter ['kauntəʳ] *n* banco ▷ *vt* opporsi a ▷ *adv* **~ to** contro; in opposizione a; **counterclockwise** [-'klɔkwaɪz] (US) *adv* in senso antiorario
counterfeit ['kauntəfɪt] *n* contraffazione *f*, falso ▷ *vt* contraffare, falsificare ▷ *adj* falso(-a)
counterpart ['kauntəpɑːt] *n* (*of document etc*) copia; (*of person*)

corrispondente *m/f*
counterterrorism [ˌkauntə'terərɪzəm] *n* antiterrorismo
countess ['kauntɪs] *n* contessa
countless ['kauntlɪs] *adj* innumerevole
country ['kʌntrɪ] *n* paese *m*; (*native land*) patria; (*as opposed to town*) campagna; (*region*) regione *f*; **country and western (music)** *n* musica country e western, country *m*; **country house** *n* villa in campagna; **countryside** *n* campagna
county ['kauntɪ] *n* contea
coup [ku:] (*pl* **coups**) *n* colpo; (*also:* **~ d'état**) colpo di Stato
couple ['kʌpl] *n* coppia; **a ~ of** un paio di
coupon ['ku:pɔn] *n* buono; (*detachable form*) coupon *m inv*
courage ['kʌrɪdʒ] *n* coraggio; **courageous** *adj* coraggioso(-a)
courgette [kuə'ʒɛt] (BRIT) *n* zucchina
courier ['kurɪəʳ] *n* corriere *m*; (*for tourists*) guida
course [kɔ:s] *n* corso; (*of ship*) rotta; (*for golf*) campo; (*part of meal*) piatto; **of ~** senz'altro, naturalmente; **~ of action** modo d'agire; **a ~ of treatment** (*Med*) una cura
court [kɔ:t] *n* corte *f*; (*Tennis*) campo ▷ *vt* (*woman*) fare la corte a; **to take to ~** citare in tribunale
courtesy ['kə:təsɪ] *n* cortesia; **(by) ~ of** per gentile concessione di; **courtesy bus, courtesy coach** *n* autobus *m inv* gratuito (*di hotel, aeroporto*)
court: **court-house** (US) *n* palazzo di giustizia; **courtroom** *n* tribunale *m*; **courtyard** *n* cortile *m*
cousin ['kʌzn] *n* cugino(-a); **first ~** cugino di primo grado
cover ['kʌvəʳ] *vt* coprire; (*book, table*) rivestire; (*include*) comprendere; (*Press*) fare un servizio su ▷ *n* (*of pan*) coperchio; (*over furniture*) fodera; (*of bed*) copriletto; (*of book*) copertina; (*shelter*) riparo; (*Comm, Insurance, of spy*) copertura; **covers** *npl* (*on bed*) lenzuola *fpl* e coperte *fpl*; **to take ~** (*shelter*) ripararsi; **under ~** al riparo; **under ~ of darkness** protetto dall'oscurità; **under separate ~** (*Comm*) a parte, in plico separato; **cover up** *vi* **to cover up for sb** coprire qn; **coverage** *n* (*Press, Radio, TV*): **to give full coverage to sth** fare un ampio servizio su qc; **cover charge** *n* coperto; **cover-up** *n* occultamento (di informazioni)
cow [kau] *n* vacca ▷ *vt* (*person*) intimidire
coward ['kauəd] *n* vigliacco(-a); **cowardly** *adj* vigliacco(-a)
cowboy ['kaubɔɪ] *n* cow-boy *m inv*
cozy ['kəuzɪ] (US) *adj* = **cosy**
crab [kræb] *n* granchio
crack [kræk] *n* fessura, crepa; incrinatura; (*noise*) schiocco; (: *of gun*) scoppio; (*drug*) crack *m inv* ▷ *vt* spaccare; incrinare; (*whip*) schioccare; (*nut*) schiacciare; (*problem*) risolvere; (*code*) decifrare ▷ *adj* (*troops*) fuori classe; **to ~ a joke** fare una battuta; **crack down on** *vt fus* porre freno a; **cracked** *adj* (*inf*) matto(-a); **cracker** *n* cracker *m inv*; petardo
crackle ['krækl] *vi* crepitare
cradle ['kreɪdl] *n* culla
craft [krɑ:ft] *n* mestiere *m*; (*cunning*) astuzia; (*boat*) naviglio; **craftsman** (*irreg*) *n* artigiano; **craftsmanship** *n* abilità
cram [kræm] *vt* (*fill*): **to ~ sth with** riempire qc di; (*put*): **to ~ sth into** stipare qc in ▷ *vi* (*for exams*) prepararsi (in gran fretta)
cramp [kræmp] *n* crampo; **I've got ~ in my leg** ho un crampo alla gamba; **cramped** *adj* ristretto(-a)
cranberry ['krænbərɪ] *n* mirtillo
crane [kreɪn] *n* gru *f inv*
crap [kræp] *n* (*inf!*) fesserie *fpl*; **to**

have a ~ cacare (*!*)
crash [kræʃ] *n* fragore *m*; (*of car*) incidente *m*; (*of plane*) caduta; (*of business etc*) crollo ▷ *vt* fracassare ▷ *vi* (*plane*) fracassarsi; (*car*) avere un incidente; (*two cars*) scontrarsi; (*business etc*) fallire, andare in rovina; **crash course** *n* corso intensivo; **crash helmet** *n* casco
crate [kreɪt] *n* cassa
crave [kreɪv] *vt, vi* **to ~ (for)** desiderare ardentemente
crawl [krɔːl] *vi* strisciare carponi; (*vehicle*) avanzare lentamente ▷ *n* (*Swimming*) crawl *m*
crayfish ['kreɪfɪʃ] *n inv* (*freshwater*) gambero (d'acqua dolce); (*saltwater*) gambero
crayon ['kreɪən] *n* matita colorata
craze [kreɪz] *n* mania
crazy ['kreɪzɪ] *adj* matto(-a); (*inf: keen*): **~ about sb** pazzo(-a) di qn; **~ about sth** matto(-a) per qc
creak [kriːk] *vi* cigolare, scricchiolare
cream [kriːm] *n* crema; (*fresh*) panna ▷ *adj* (*colour*) color crema *inv*; **cream cheese** *n* formaggio fresco; **creamy** *adj* cremoso(-a)
crease [kriːs] *n* grinza; (*deliberate*) piega ▷ *vt* sgualcire ▷ *vi* sgualcirsi
create [kriː'eɪt] *vt* creare; **creation** [-ʃən] *n* creazione *f*; **creative** *adj* creativo(-a); **creator** *n* creatore(-trice)
creature ['kriːtʃə^r] *n* creatura
crèche [krɛʃ] *n* asilo infantile
credentials [krɪ'dɛnʃlz] *npl* credenziali *fpl*
credibility [krɛdɪ'bɪlɪtɪ] *n* credibilità
credible ['krɛdɪbl] *adj* credibile; (*witness, source*) attendibile
credit ['krɛdɪt] *n* credito; onore *m* ▷ *vt* (*Comm*) accreditare; (*believe: also:* **give ~ to**) credere, prestar fede a; **credits** *npl* (*Cinema*) titoli *mpl*; **to ~ sb with** (*fig*) attribuire a qn; **to be in ~** (*person*) essere creditore(-trice); (*bank account*) essere coperto(-a); **credit card** *n* carta di credito; **do you take credit cards?** accettate carte di credito?
creek [kriːk] *n* insenatura; (*US*) piccolo fiume *m*
creep [kriːp] (*pt, pp* **crept**) *vi* avanzare furtivamente (*or* pian piano)
cremate [krɪ'meɪt] *vt* cremare
crematorium [krɛmə'tɔːrɪəm] (*pl* **crematoria**) *n* forno crematorio
crept [krɛpt] *pt, pp of* **creep**
crescent ['krɛsnt] *n* (*shape*) mezzaluna; (*street*) strada semicircolare
cress [krɛs] *n* crescione *m*
crest [krɛst] *n* cresta; (*of coat of arms*) cimiero
crew [kruː] *n* equipaggio; **crew-neck** *n* girocollo
crib [krɪb] *n* culla ▷ *vt* (*inf*) copiare
cricket ['krɪkɪt] *n* (*insect*) grillo; (*game*) cricket *m*; **cricketer** *n* giocatore *m* di cricket
crime [kraɪm] *n* crimine *m*; **criminal** ['krɪmɪnl] *adj, n* criminale *m/f*
crimson ['krɪmzn] *adj* color cremisi *inv*
cringe [krɪndʒ] *vi* acquattarsi; (*in embarrassment*) sentirsi sprofondare
cripple ['krɪpl] *n* zoppo(-a) ▷ *vt* azzoppare
crisis ['kraɪsɪs] (*pl* **crises**) *n* crisi *f inv*
crisp [krɪsp] *adj* croccante; (*fig*) frizzante; vivace; deciso(-a); **crispy** *adj* croccante
criterion [kraɪ'tɪərɪən] (*pl* **criteria**) *n* criterio
critic ['krɪtɪk] *n* critico; **critical** *adj* critico(-a); **criticism** ['krɪtɪsɪzm] *n* critica; **criticize** ['krɪtɪsaɪz] *vt* criticare
Croat ['krəuæt] *adj, n* = **Croatian**
Croatia [krəu'eɪʃə] *n* Croazia; **Croatian** *adj* croato(-a) ▷ *n* croato(-a); (*Ling*) croato
crockery ['krɔkərɪ] *n* vasellame *m*
crocodile ['krɔkədaɪl] *n* coccodrillo

crocus ['krəukəs] *n* croco
croissant ['krwas] *n* brioche *f inv*, croissant *m inv*
crook [kruk] *n* truffatore *m*; (*of shepherd*) bastone *m*; **crooked** ['krukɪd] *adj* curvo(-a), storto(-a); (*action*) disonesto(-a)
crop [krɔp] *n* (*produce*) coltivazione *f*; (*amount produced*) raccolto; (*riding crop*) frustino ▷ *vt* (*hair*) rapare; **crop up** *vi* presentarsi
cross [krɔs] *n* croce *f*; (*Biol*) incrocio ▷ *vt* (*street etc*) attraversare; (*arms, legs, Biol*) incrociare; (*cheque*) sbarrare ▷ *adj* di cattivo umore; **cross off** *vt* cancellare (*tirando una riga con la penna*); **cross out** *vt* cancellare; **cross over** *vi* attraversare; **cross-Channel ferry** ['krɔs'tʃænl-] *n* traghetto che attraversa la Manica; **crosscountry (race)** *n* cross-country *m inv*; **crossing** *n* incrocio; (*sea passage*) traversata; (*also*: **pedestrian crossing**) passaggio pedonale; **how long does the crossing take?** quanto dura la traversata?; **crossing guard** (US) *n dipendente comunale che aiuta i bambini ad attraversare la strada*; **crossroads** *n* incrocio; **crosswalk** (US) *n* strisce *fpl* pedonali, passaggio pedonale; **crossword** *n* cruciverba *m inv*
crotch [krɔtʃ] *n* (*Anat*) inforcatura; (*of garment*) pattina
crouch [krautʃ] *vi* acquattarsi; rannicchiarsi
crouton ['kru:tɔn] *n* crostino
crow [krəu] *n* (*bird*) cornacchia; (*of cock*) canto del gallo ▷ *vi* (*cock*) cantare
crowd [kraud] *n* folla ▷ *vt* affollare, stipare ▷ *vi* **to ~ round/in** affollarsi intorno a/in; **crowded** *adj* affollato(-a); **crowded with** stipato(-a) di
crown [kraun] *n* corona; (*of head*) calotta cranica; (*of hat*) cocuzzolo; (*of hill*) cima ▷ *vt* incoronare; (*fig*: *career*) coronare; **crown jewels** *npl* gioielli *mpl* della Corona
crucial ['kru:ʃl] *adj* cruciale, decisivo(-a)
crucifix ['kru:sɪfɪks] *n* crocifisso
crude [kru:d] *adj* (*materials*) greggio(-a), non raffinato(-a); (*fig*: *basic*) crudo(-a), primitivo(-a); (: *vulgar*) rozzo(-a), grossolano(-a); **crude (oil)** *n* (petrolio) greggio
cruel ['kruəl] *adj* crudele; **cruelty** *n* crudeltà *f inv*
cruise [kru:z] *n* crociera ▷ *vi* andare a velocità di crociera; (*taxi*) circolare
crumb [krʌm] *n* briciola
crumble ['krʌmbl] *vt* sbriciolare ▷ *vi* sbriciolarsi; (*plaster etc*) sgrettolarsi; (*land, earth*) franare; (*building, fig*) crollare
crumpet ['krʌmpɪt] *n specie di frittella*
crumple ['krʌmpl] *vt* raggrinzare, spiegazzare
crunch [krʌntʃ] *vt* sgranocchiare; (*underfoot*) scricchiolare ▷ *n* (*fig*) punto *or* momento cruciale; **crunchy** *adj* croccante
crush [krʌʃ] *n* folla; (*love*): **to have a ~ on sb** avere una cotta per qn; (*drink*): **lemon ~** spremuta di limone ▷ *vt* schiacciare; (*crumple*) sgualcire
crust [krʌst] *n* crosta; **crusty** *adj* (*bread*) croccante; (*person*) brontolone(-a); (*remark*) brusco(-a)
crutch [krʌtʃ] *n* gruccia
cry [kraɪ] *vi* piangere; (*shout*) urlare ▷ *n* urlo, grido; **cry out** *vi, vt* gridare
crystal ['krɪstl] *n* cristallo
cub [kʌb] *n* cucciolo; (*also*: **~ scout**) lupetto
Cuba ['kju:bə] *n* Cuba
Cuban ['kju:bən] *adj, n* cubano(-a)
cube [kju:b] *n* cubo ▷ *vt* (*Math*) elevare al cubo; **cubic** *adj* cubico(-a); (*metre, foot*) cubo(-a)
cubicle ['kju:bɪkl] *n* scompartimento separato; cabina
cuckoo ['kuku:] *n* cucù *m inv*

cucumber ['kju:kʌmbəʳ] *n* cetriolo
cuddle ['kʌdl] *vt* abbracciare, coccolare ▷ *vi* abbracciarsi
cue [kju:] *n* (*snooker cue*) stecca; (*Theatre etc*) segnale *m*
cuff [kʌf] *n* (BRIT: *of shirt, coat etc*) polsino; (US: *of trousers*) risvolto; **off the ~** improvvisando; **cufflinks** *npl* gemelli *mpl*
cuisine [kwɪ'zi:n] *n* cucina
cul-de-sac ['kʌldəsæk] *n* vicolo cieco
cull [kʌl] *vt* (*ideas etc*) scegliere ▷ *n* (*of animals*) abbattimento selettivo
culminate ['kʌlmɪneɪt] *vi* **to ~ in** culminare con
culprit ['kʌlprɪt] *n* colpevole *m/f*
cult [kʌlt] *n* culto
cultivate ['kʌltɪveɪt] *vt* (*also fig*) coltivare
cultural ['kʌltʃərəl] *adj* culturale
culture ['kʌltʃəʳ] *n* (*also fig*) cultura
cumin ['kʌmɪn] *n* (*spice*) cumino
cunning ['kʌnɪŋ] *n* astuzia, furberia ▷ *adj* astuto(-a), furbo(-a)
cup [kʌp] *n* tazza; (*prize, of bra*) coppa
cupboard ['kʌbəd] *n* armadio
cup final *n* (BRIT *Football*) finale *f* di coppa
curator [kjuə'reɪtəʳ] *n* direttore *m* (*di museo ecc*)
curb [kə:b] *vt* tenere a freno ▷ *n* freno; (US) bordo del marciapiede
curdle ['kə:dl] *vi* cagliare
cure [kjuəʳ] *vt* guarire; (*Culin*) trattare; affumicare; essiccare ▷ *n* rimedio
curfew ['kə:fju:] *n* coprifuoco
curiosity [kjuərɪ'ɔsɪtɪ] *n* curiosità
curious ['kjuərɪəs] *adj* curioso(-a)
curl [kə:l] *n* riccio ▷ *vt* ondulare; (*tightly*) arricciare ▷ *vi* arricciarsi; **curl up** *vi* rannicchiarsi; **curler** *n* bigodino; **curly** ['kə:lɪ] *adj* ricciuto(-a)
currant ['kʌrnt] *n* (*dried*) sultanina; (*bush, fruit*) ribes *m inv*
currency ['kʌrnsɪ] *n* moneta; **to gain ~** (*fig*) acquistare larga diffusione
current ['kʌrnt] *adj* corrente ▷ *n* corrente *f*; **current account** (BRIT) *n* conto corrente; **current affairs** *npl* attualità *fpl*; **currently** *adv* attualmente
curriculum [kə'rɪkjuləm] (*pl* **curriculums** *or* **curricula**) *n* curriculum *m inv*; **curriculum vitae** [-'vi:taɪ] *n* curriculum vitae *m inv*
curry ['kʌrɪ] *n* curry *m inv* ▷ *vt* **to ~ favour with** cercare di attirarsi i favori di; **curry powder** *n* curry *m*
curse [kə:s] *vt* maledire ▷ *vi* bestemmiare ▷ *n* maledizione *f*; bestemmia
cursor ['kə:səʳ] *n* (*Comput*) cursore *m*
curt [kə:t] *adj* secco(-a)
curtain ['kə:tn] *n* tenda; (*Theatre*) sipario
curve [kə:v] *n* curva ▷ *vi* curvarsi; **curved** *adj* curvo(-a)
cushion ['kuʃən] *n* cuscino ▷ *vt* (*shock*) fare da cuscinetto a
custard ['kʌstəd] *n* (*for pouring*) crema
custody ['kʌstədɪ] *n* (*of child*) tutela; **to take into ~** (*suspect*) mettere in detenzione preventiva
custom ['kʌstəm] *n* costume *m*, consuetudine *f*; (*Comm*) clientela
customer ['kʌstəməʳ] *n* cliente *m/f*
customized ['kʌstəmaɪzd] *adj* (*car etc*) fuoriserie *inv*
customs ['kʌstəmz] *npl* dogana; **customs officer** *n* doganiere *m*
cut [kʌt] (*pt, pp* **cut**) *vt* tagliare; (*shape, make*) intagliare; (*reduce*) ridurre ▷ *vi* tagliare ▷ *n* taglio; (*in salary etc*) riduzione *f*; **I've ~ myself** mi sono tagliato; **to ~ a tooth** mettere un dente; **cut back** *vt* (*plants*) tagliare; (*production, expenditure*) ridurre; **cut down** *vt* (*tree etc*) abbattere ▷ *vt fus* (*also:* **~ down on**) ridurre; **cut off** *vt* tagliare; (*fig*) isolare; **cut out** *vt* tagliare fuori; eliminare; ritagliare; **cut up** *vt* tagliare a pezzi; **cutback** *n* riduzione *f*
cute [kju:t] *adj* (*sweet*) carino(-a)

cutlery ['kʌtlərɪ] *n* posate *fpl*
cutlet ['kʌtlɪt] *n* costoletta; (*nut etc cutlet*) cotoletta vegetariana
cut: **cut-price** (BRIT) *adj* a prezzo ridotto; **cut-rate** (US) *adj* = **cut-price**; **cutting** ['kʌtɪŋ] *adj* tagliente ▷ *n* (*from newspaper*) ritaglio (di giornale); (*from plant*) talea
CV *n abbr* = **curriculum vitae**
cwt *abbr* = **hundredweight(s)**
cybercafé ['saɪbəkaefeɪ] *n* cybercaffè *m inv*
cybercrime [saɪbəkraɪm] *n* delinquenza informatica
cyberspace ['saɪbəspeɪs] *n* ciberspazio
cycle ['saɪkl] *n* ciclo; (*bicycle*) bicicletta ▷ *vi* andare in bicicletta; **cycle hire** *n* noleggio *m* biciclette *inv*; **cycle lane** *n* pista ciclabile; **cycle path** *n* pista ciclabile; **cycling** ['saɪklɪŋ] *n* ciclismo; **cyclist** ['saɪklɪst] *n* ciclista *m/f*
cyclone ['saɪkləun] *n* ciclone *m*
cylinder ['sɪlɪndəʳ] *n* cilindro
cymbal ['sɪmbl] *n* piatto
cynical ['sɪnɪkl] *adj* cinico(-a)
Cypriot ['sɪprɪət] *adj, n* cipriota (*m/f*)
Cyprus ['saɪprəs] *n* Cipro
cyst [sɪst] *n* cisti *f inv*; **cystitis** [sɪs'taɪtɪs] *n* cistite *f*
czar [zɑːʳ] *n* zar *m inv*
Czech [tʃɛk] *adj* ceco(-a) ▷ *n* ceco(-a); (*Ling*) ceco; **Czech Republic** *n*: **the Czech Republic** la Repubblica Ceca

d

D [diː] *n* (*Mus*) re *m*
dab [dæb] *vt* (*eyes, wound*) tamponare; (*paint, cream*) applicare (con leggeri colpetti)
dad, daddy [dæd, 'dædɪ] *n* babbo, papà *m inv*
daffodil ['dæfədɪl] *n* trombone *m*, giunchiglia
daft [dɑːft] *adj* sciocco(-a)
dagger ['dægəʳ] *n* pugnale *m*
daily ['deɪlɪ] *adj* quotidiano(-a), giornaliero(-a) ▷ *n* quotidiano ▷ *adv* tutti i giorni
dairy ['dɛərɪ] *n* (BRIT: *shop*) latteria; (*on farm*) caseificio ▷ *adj* caseario(-a); **dairy produce** *npl* latticini *mpl*
daisy ['deɪzɪ] *n* margherita
dam [dæm] *n* diga ▷ *vt* sbarrare; costruire dighe su
damage ['dæmɪdʒ] *n* danno, danni *mpl*; (*fig*) danno ▷ *vt* danneggiare; **damages** *npl* (*Law*) danni
damn [dæm] *vt* condannare; (*curse*) maledire ▷ *n* (*inf*): **I don't give a ~**

non me ne frega niente ▷ *adj* (*inf: also:* **~ed**): **this ~ ...** questo maledetto ...; **~ it !** accidenti!
damp [dæmp] *adj* umido(-a) ▷ *n* umidità, umido ▷ *vt* (*also:* **~en**: *cloth, rag*) inumidire, bagnare; (: *enthusiasm etc*) spegnere
dance [dɑːns] *n* danza, ballo; (*ball*) ballo ▷ *vi* ballare; **dance floor** *n* pista da ballo; **dancer** *n* danzatore(-trice); (*professional*) ballerino(-a); **dancing** ['dɑːnsɪŋ] *n* danza, ballo
dandelion ['dændɪlaɪən] *n* dente *m* di leone
dandruff ['dændrəf] *n* forfora
Dane [deɪn] *n* danese *m/f*
danger ['deɪndʒə^r] *n* pericolo; **there is a ~ of fire** c'è pericolo di incendio; **in ~** in pericolo; **he was in ~ of falling** rischiava di cadere; **dangerous** *adj* pericoloso(-a)
dangle ['dæŋgl] *vt* dondolare; (*fig*) far balenare ▷ *vi* pendolare
Danish ['deɪnɪʃ] *adj* danese ▷ *n* (*Ling*) danese *m*
dare [dɛə^r] *vt* **to ~ sb to do** sfidare qn a fare ▷ *vi* **to ~ to do sth** osare fare qc; **I ~ say** (*I suppose*) immagino (che); **daring** *adj* audace, ardito(-a) ▷ *n* audacia
dark [dɑːk] *adj* (*night, room*) buio(-a), scuro(-a); (*colour, complexion*) scuro(-a); (*fig*) cupo(-a), tetro(-a), nero(-a) ▷ *n* **in the ~** al buio; **in the ~ about** (*fig*) all'oscuro di; **after ~** a notte fatta; **darken** *vt* (*colour*) scurire ▷ *vi* (*sky, room*) oscurarsi; **darkness** *n* oscurità, buio; **darkroom** *n* camera oscura
darling ['dɑːlɪŋ] *adj* caro(-a) ▷ *n* tesoro
dart [dɑːt] *n* freccetta; (*Sewing*) pince *f inv* ▷ *vi* **to ~ towards** precipitarsi verso; **to ~ away/along** sfrecciare via/lungo; **dartboard** *n* bersaglio (per freccette); **darts** *n* tiro al bersaglio (con freccette)
dash [dæʃ] *n* (*sign*) lineetta; (*small quantity*) punta ▷ *vt* (*missile*) gettare; (*hopes*) infrangere ▷ *vi* **to ~ towards** precipitarsi verso
dashboard ['dæʃbɔːd] *n* (*Aut*) cruscotto
data ['deɪtə] *npl* dati *mpl*; **database** *n* base *f* di dati, data base *m inv*; **data processing** *n* elaborazione *f* (elettronica) dei dati
date [deɪt] *n* data; appuntamento; (*fruit*) dattero ▷ *vt* datare; (*person*) uscire con; **what's the ~ today?** quanti ne abbiamo oggi?; **~ of birth** data di nascita; **to ~** (*until now*) fino a oggi; **dated** *adj* passato(-a) di moda
daughter ['dɔːtə^r] *n* figlia; **daughter-in-law** *n* nuora
daunting ['dɔːntɪŋ] *adj* non invidiabile
dawn [dɔːn] *n* alba ▷ *vi* (*day*) spuntare; (*fig*): **it ~ed on him that ...** gli è venuto in mente che ...
day [deɪ] *n* giorno; (*as duration*) giornata; (*period of time, age*) tempo, epoca; **the ~ before** il giorno avanti *or* prima; **the ~ after, the following ~** il giorno dopo *or* seguente; **the ~ after tomorrow** dopodomani; **the ~ before yester~** l'altroieri; **by ~** di giorno; **day-care centre** *n* scuola materna; **daydream** *vi* sognare a occhi aperti; **daylight** *n* luce *f* del giorno; **day return** (BRIT) *n* biglietto giornaliero di andata e ritorno; **daytime** *n* giorno; **day-to-day** *adj* (*life, organization*) quotidiano(-a); **day trip** *n* gita (di un giorno)
dazed [deɪzd] *adj* stordito(-a)
dazzle ['dæzl] *vt* abbagliare; **dazzling** *adj* (*light*) abbagliante; (*colour*) violento(-a); (*smile*) smagliante
DC *abbr* (= *direct current*) c.c.
dead [dɛd] *adj* morto(-a); (*numb*) intirizzito(-a); (*telephone*) muto(-a); (*battery*) scarico(-a) ▷ *adv* assolutamente, perfettamente ▷ *npl*

the ~ i morti; **he was shot ~** fu colpito a morte; **~ tired** stanco(-a) morto(-a); **to stop ~** fermarsi di colpo; **dead end** *n* vicolo cieco; **deadline** *n* scadenza; **deadly** *adj* mortale; (*weapon, poison*) micidiale; **Dead Sea** *n*: **the Dead Sea** il mar Morto

deaf [dɛf] *adj* sordo(-a); **deafen** *vt* assordare; **deafening** *adj* fragoroso(-a), assordante

deal [di:l] (*pt, pp* **dealt**) *n* accordo; (*business deal*) affare *m* ▷ *vt* (*blow, cards*) dare; **a great ~ (of)** molto(-a); **deal with** *vt fus* (*Comm*) fare affari con, trattare con; (*handle*) occuparsi di; (*be about: book etc*) trattare di; **dealer** *n* commerciante *m/f*; **dealings** *npl* (*Comm*) relazioni *fpl*; (*relations*) rapporti *mpl*

dealt [dɛlt] *pt, pp of* **deal**

dean [di:n] *n* (*Rel*) decano; (*Scol*) preside *m* di facoltà (*or* di collegio)

dear [dɪəʳ] *adj* caro(-a) ▷ *n* **my ~** caro mio/cara mia ▷ *excl* **~ me!** Dio mio!; **D~ Sir/Madam** (*in letter*) Egregio Signore/Egregia Signora; **D~ Mr/Mrs X** Gentile Signor/Signora X; **dearly** *adv* (*love*) moltissimo; (*pay*) a caro prezzo

death [dɛθ] *n* morte *f*; (*Admin*) decesso; **death penalty** *n* pena di morte; **death sentence** *n* condanna a morte

debate [dɪ'beɪt] *n* dibattito ▷ *vt* dibattere; discutere

debit ['dɛbɪt] *n* debito ▷ *vt* **to ~ a sum to sb** *or* **to sb's account** addebitare una somma a qn; **debit card** *n* carta di debito

debris ['dɛbri:] *n* detriti *mpl*

debt [dɛt] *n* debito; **to be in ~** essere indebitato(-a)

debut ['deɪbju:] *n* debutto

Dec. *abbr* (= *December*) dic.

decade ['dɛkeɪd] *n* decennio

decaffeinated [dɪ'kæfɪneɪtɪd] *adj* decaffeinato(-a)

decay [dɪ'keɪ] *n* decadimento; (*also:* **tooth ~**) carie *f* ▷ *vi* (*rot*) imputridire

deceased [dɪ'si:st] *n* defunto(-a)

deceit [dɪ'si:t] *n* inganno; **deceive** [dɪ'si:v] *vt* ingannare

December [dɪ'sɛmbəʳ] *n* dicembre *m*

decency ['di:sənsɪ] *n* decenza

decent ['di:sənt] *adj* decente; (*respectable*) per bene; (*kind*) gentile

deception [dɪ'sɛpʃən] *n* inganno

deceptive [dɪ'sɛptɪv] *adj* ingannevole

decide [dɪ'saɪd] *vt* (*person*) far prendere una decisione a; (*question, argument*) risolvere, decidere ▷ *vi* decidere, decidersi; **to ~ to do/that** decidere di fare/che; **to ~ on** decidere per

decimal ['dɛsɪməl] *adj* decimale ▷ *n* decimale *m*

decision [dɪ'sɪʒən] *n* decisione *f*

decisive [dɪ'saɪsɪv] *adj* decisivo(-a); (*person*) deciso(-a)

deck [dɛk] *n* (*Naut*) ponte *m*; (*of bus*): **top ~** imperiale *m*; (*record deck*) piatto; (*of cards*) mazzo; **deckchair** *n* sedia a sdraio

declaration [dɛklə'reɪʃən] *n* dichiarazione *f*

declare [dɪ'klɛəʳ] *vt* dichiarare

decline [dɪ'klaɪn] *n* (*decay*) declino; (*lessening*) ribasso ▷ *vt* declinare; rifiutare ▷ *vi* declinare; diminuire

decorate ['dɛkəreɪt] *vt* (*adorn, give a medal to*) decorare; (*paint and paper*) tinteggiare e tappezzare; **decoration** [-'reɪʃən] *n* (*medal etc, adornment*) decorazione *f*; **decorator** *n* decoratore *m*

decrease [*n* 'di:kri:s, *vb* di:'kri:s] *n* diminuzione *f* ▷ *vt, vi* diminuire

decree [dɪ'kri:] *n* decreto

dedicate ['dɛdɪkeɪt] *vt* consacrare; (*book etc*) dedicare; **dedicated** *adj* coscienzioso(-a); (*Comput*) specializzato(-a), dedicato(-a); **dedication** [dɛdɪ'keɪʃən] *n* (*devotion*) dedizione *f*; (*in book etc*) dedica

deduce [dɪ'djuːs] *vt* dedurre
deduct [dɪ'dʌkt] *vt* **to ~ sth from** dedurre qc (da); **deduction** [dɪ'dʌkʃən] *n* deduzione *f*
deed [diːd] *n* azione *f*, atto; (*Law*) atto
deem [diːm] *vt* (*formal*) giudicare, ritenere; **to ~ it wise to do** ritenere prudente fare
deep [diːp] *adj* profondo(-a); **4 metres ~** profondo(-a) 4 metri ▷ *adv* **spectators stood 20 ~** c'erano 20 file di spettatori; **how ~ is the water?** quanto è profonda l'acqua?; **deep-fry** *vt* friggere in olio abbondante; **deeply** *adv* profondamente
deer [dɪəʳ] *n inv* **the ~** i cervidi; **(red) ~** cervo; **(fallow) ~** daino; **roe ~** capriolo
default [dɪ'fɔːlt] *n* (*Comput: also:* **~ value**) default *m inv*; **by ~** (*Sport*) per abbandono
defeat [dɪ'fiːt] *n* sconfitta ▷ *vt* (*team, opponents*) sconfiggere
defect [*n* 'diːfɛkt, *vb* dɪ'fɛkt] *n* difetto ▷ *vi*: **to ~ to the enemy** passare al nemico; **defective** [dɪ'fɛktɪv] *adj* difettoso(-a)
defence [dɪ'fɛns] (*US* **defense**) *n* difesa
defend [dɪ'fɛnd] *vt* difendere; **defendant** *n* imputato(-a); **defender** *n* difensore(-a)
defense [dɪ'fens] (*US*) *n* = **defence**
defensive [dɪ'fɛnsɪv] *adj* difensivo(-a) ▷ *n* **on the ~** sulla difensiva
defer [dɪ'fəːʳ] *vt* (*postpone*) differire, rinviare
defiance [dɪ'faɪəns] *n* sfida; **in ~ of** a dispetto di; **defiant** [dɪ'faɪənt] *adj* (*attitude*) di sfida; (*person*) ribelle
deficiency [dɪ'fɪʃənsɪ] *n* deficienza; carenza; **deficient** *adj* deficiente; insufficiente; **to be deficient in** mancare di
deficit ['dɛfɪsɪt] *n* deficit *m inv*
define [dɪ'faɪn] *vt* definire
definite ['dɛfɪnɪt] *adj* (*fixed*) definito(-a), preciso(-a); (*clear, obvious*) ben definito(-a), esatto(-a); (*Ling*) determinativo(-a); **he was ~ about it** ne era sicuro; **definitely** *adv* indubbiamente
definition [dɛfɪ'nɪʃən] *n* definizione *f*
deflate [diː'fleɪt] *vt* sgonfiare
deflect [dɪ'flɛkt] *vt* deflettere, deviare
defraud [dɪ'frɔːd] *vt* defraudare
defrost [diː'frɔst] *vt* (*fridge*) disgelare
defuse [diː'fjuːz] *vt* disinnescare; (*fig*) distendere
defy [dɪ'faɪ] *vt* sfidare; (*efforts etc*) resistere a; **it defies description** supera ogni descrizione
degree [dɪ'griː] *n* grado; (*Scol*) laurea (universitaria); **a first ~ in maths** una laurea in matematica; **by ~s** (*gradually*) gradualmente, a poco a poco; **to some ~** fino a un certo punto, in certa misura
dehydrated [diːhaɪ'dreɪtɪd] *adj* disidratato(-a); (*milk, eggs*) in polvere
de-icer ['diːaɪsəʳ] *n* sbrinatore *m*
delay [dɪ'leɪ] *vt* ritardare ▷ *vi* **to ~ (in doing sth)** ritardare (a fare qc) ▷ *n* ritardo; **to be ~ed** subire un ritardo; (*person*) essere trattenuto(-a)
delegate [*n* 'dɛlɪgɪt, *vb* 'dɛlɪgeɪt] *n* delegato(-a) ▷ *vt* delegare
delete [dɪ'liːt] *vt* cancellare
deli ['dɛlɪ] *n* = **delicatessen**
deliberate [*adj* dɪ'lɪbərɪt, *vb* dɪ'lɪbəreɪt] *adj* (*intentional*) intenzionale; (*slow*) misurato(-a) ▷ *vi* deliberare, riflettere; **deliberately** *adv* (*on purpose*) deliberatamente
delicacy ['dɛlɪkəsɪ] *n* delicatezza
delicate ['dɛlɪkɪt] *adj* delicato(-a)
delicatessen [dɛlɪkə'tɛsn] *n* ≈ salumeria
delicious [dɪ'lɪʃəs] *adj* delizioso(-a), squisito(-a)
delight [dɪ'laɪt] *n* delizia, gran piacere *m* ▷ *vt* dilettare; **to take (a) ~ in** dilettarsi in; **delighted** *adj* **delighted (at** *or* **with)** contentissimo(-a) (di), felice (di); **delighted to do** felice di

fare; **delightful** *adj* delizioso(-a), incantevole
delinquent [dɪ'lɪŋkwənt] *adj, n* delinquente *m/f*
deliver [dɪ'lɪvə^r] *vt* (*mail*) distribuire; (*goods*) consegnare; (*speech*) pronunciare; (*Med*) far partorire; **delivery** *n* distribuzione *f*; consegna; (*of speaker*) dizione *f*; (*Med*) parto
delusion [dɪ'lu:ʒən] *n* illusione *f*
de luxe [də'lʌks] *adj* di lusso
delve [dɛlv] *vi* **to ~ into** frugare in; (*subject*) far ricerche in
demand [dɪ'mɑ:nd] *vt* richiedere; (*rights*) rivendicare ▷ *n* domanda; (*claim*) rivendicazione *f*; **in ~** ricercato(-a), richiesto(-a); **on ~** a richiesta; **demanding** *adj* (*boss*) esigente; (*work*) impegnativo(-a)
demise [dɪ'maɪz] *n* decesso
demo ['dɛməu] (*inf*) *n abbr* (= *demonstration*) manifestazione *f*
democracy [dɪ'mɔkrəsɪ] *n* democrazia; **democrat** ['dɛməkræt] *n* democratico(-a); **democratic** [dɛmə'krætɪk] *adj* democratico(-a)
demolish [dɪ'mɔlɪʃ] *vt* demolire
demolition [dɛmə'lɪʃən] *n* demolizione *f*
demon ['di:mən] *n* (*also fig*) demonio ▷ *cpd* **a ~ squash player** un mago dello squash; **a ~ driver** un guidatore folle
demonstrate ['dɛmənstreɪt] *vt* dimostrare, provare ▷ *vi* dimostrare, manifestare; **demonstration** [-'streɪʃən] *n* dimostrazione *f*; (*Pol*) dimostrazione, manifestazione *f*; **demonstrator** *n* (*Pol*) dimostrante *m/f*; (*Comm*) dimostratore(-trice)
demote [dɪ'məut] *vt* far retrocedere
den [dɛn] *n* tana, covo; (*room*) buco
denial [dɪ'naɪəl] *n* diniego; rifiuto
denim ['dɛnɪm] *n* tessuto di cotone ritorto; **denims** *npl* (*jeans*) blue jeans *mpl*
Denmark ['dɛnmɑ:k] *n* Danimarca
denomination [dɪnɔmɪ'neɪʃən] *n* (*money*) valore *m*; (*Rel*) confessione *f*
denounce [dɪ'nauns] *vt* denunciare
dense [dɛns] *adj* fitto(-a); (*smoke*) denso(-a); (*inf: person*) ottuso(-a), duro(-a)
density ['dɛnsɪtɪ] *n* densità *f inv*
dent [dɛnt] *n* ammaccatura ▷ *vt* (*also:* **make a ~ in**) ammaccare
dental ['dɛntl] *adj* dentale; **dental floss** [-flɔs] *n* filo interdentale; **dental surgery** *n* ambulatorio del dentista
dentist ['dɛntɪst] *n* dentista *m/f*
dentures ['dɛntʃəz] *npl* dentiera
deny [dɪ'naɪ] *vt* negare; (*refuse*) rifiutare
deodorant [di:'əudərənt] *n* deodorante *m*
depart [dɪ'pɑ:t] *vi* partire; **to ~ from** (*fig*) deviare da
department [dɪ'pɑ:tmənt] *n* (*Comm*) reparto; (*Scol*) sezione *f*, dipartimento; (*Pol*) ministero; **department store** *n* grande magazzino
departure [dɪ'pɑ:tʃə^r] *n* partenza; (*fig*): **~ from** deviazione *f* da; **a new ~** una svolta (decisiva); **departure lounge** *n* (*at airport*) sala d'attesa
depend [dɪ'pɛnd] *vi* **to ~ on** dipendere da; (*rely on*) contare su; **it ~s** dipende; **~ing on the result ...** a seconda del risultato ...; **dependant** *n* persona a carico; **dependent** *adj* **to be dependent on** dipendere da; (*child, relative*) essere a carico di ▷ *n* = **dependant**
depict [dɪ'pɪkt] *vt* (*in picture*) dipingere; (*in words*) descrivere
deport [dɪ'pɔ:t] *vt* deportare; espellere
deposit [dɪ'pɔzɪt] *n* (*Comm, Geo*) deposito; (*of ore, oil*) giacimento; (*Chem*) sedimento; (*part payment*) acconto; (*for hired goods etc*) cauzione *f* ▷ *vt* depositare; dare in acconto; mettere *or* lasciare in deposito;

deposit account *n* conto vincolato
depot ['dɛpəu] *n* deposito; (*US*) stazione *f* ferroviaria
depreciate [dɪ'priːʃɪeɪt] *vi* svalutarsi
depress [dɪ'prɛs] *vt* deprimere; (*price, wages*) abbassare; (*press down*) premere; **depressed** *adj* (*person*) depresso(-a), abbattuto(-a); (*price*) in ribasso; (*industry*) in crisi; **depressing** *adj* deprimente; **depression** [dɪ'prɛʃən] *n* depressione *f*
deprive [dɪ'praɪv] *vt*: **to ~ sb of** privare qn di; **deprived** *adj* disgraziato(-a)
dept. *abbr* = **department**
depth [dɛpθ] *n* profondità *f inv*; **in the ~s of** nel profondo di; nel cuore di; **out of one's ~** (*in water*) dove non si tocca; (*fig*) a disagio
deputy ['dɛpjutɪ] *adj* **~ head** (*BRIT*: *Scol*) vicepreside *m/f* ▷ *n* (*assistant*) vice *m/f inv*; (*US*: *also*: **~ sheriff**) vice-sceriffo
derail [dɪ'reɪl] *vt*: **to be ~ed** deragliare
derelict ['dɛrɪlɪkt] *adj* abbandonato(-a)
derive [dɪ'raɪv] *vt*: **to ~ sth from** derivare qc da; trarre qc da ▷ *vi* **to ~ from** derivare da
descend [dɪ'sɛnd] *vt, vi* discendere, scendere; **to ~ from** discendere da; **to ~ to** (*lying, begging*) abbassarsi a; **descendant** *n* discendente *m/f*; **descent** [dɪ'sɛnt] *n* discesa; (*origin*) discendenza, famiglia
describe [dɪs'kraɪb] *vt* descrivere; **description** [-'krɪpʃən] *n* descrizione *f*; (*sort*) genere *m*, specie *f*
desert [*n* 'dɛzət, *vb* dɪ'zəːt] *n* deserto ▷ *vt* lasciare, abbandonare ▷ *vi* (*Mil*) disertare; **deserted** [dɪ'zəːtɪd] *adj* deserto(-a)
deserve [dɪ'zəːv] *vt* meritare
design [dɪ'zaɪn] *n* (*art, sketch*) disegno; (*layout, shape*) linea; (*pattern*) fantasia; (*intention*) intenzione *f* ▷ *vt* disegnare; progettare; **design and technology** *n* (*BRIT*: *Scol*) progettazione *fsg* e tecnologie *fpl*
designate *vt* [*vb* 'dɛzɪgneɪt, *adj* 'dɛzɪgnɪt] designare ▷ *adj* designato(-a)
designer [dɪ'zaɪnəʳ] *n* (*Art, Tech*) disegnatore(-trice); (*of fashion*) modellista *m/f*
desirable [dɪ'zaɪərəbl] *adj* desiderabile; **it is ~ that** è opportuno che + *sub*
desire [dɪ'zaɪəʳ] *n* desiderio, voglia ▷ *vt* desiderare, volere
desk [dɛsk] *n* (*in office*) scrivania; (*for pupil*) banco; (*BRIT*: *in shop, restaurant*) cassa; (*in hotel*) ricevimento; (*at airport*) accettazione *f*; **desk-top publishing** *n* desktop publishing *m*
despair [dɪs'pɛəʳ] *n* disperazione *f* ▷ *vi* **to ~ of** disperare di
despatch [dɪs'pætʃ] *n, vt* = **dispatch**
desperate ['dɛspərɪt] *adj* disperato(-a); (*fugitive*) capace di tutto; **to be ~ for sth/to do** volere disperatamente qc/fare; **desperately** *adv* disperatamente; (*very*) terribilmente, estremamente; **desperation** [dɛspə'reɪʃən] *n* disperazione *f*
despise [dɪs'paɪz] *vt* disprezzare, sdegnare
despite [dɪs'paɪt] *prep* malgrado, a dispetto di, nonostante
dessert [dɪ'zəːt] *n* dolce *m*; frutta; **dessertspoon** *n* cucchiaio da dolci
destination [dɛstɪ'neɪʃən] *n* destinazione *f*
destined ['dɛstɪnd] *adj*: **to be ~ to do/for** essere destinato(-a) a fare/per
destiny ['dɛstɪnɪ] *n* destino
destroy [dɪs'trɔɪ] *vt* distruggere
destruction [dɪs'trʌkʃən] *n* distruzione *f*
destructive [dɪs'trʌktɪv] *adj* distruttivo(-a)
detach [dɪ'tætʃ] *vt* staccare, distaccare; **detached** *adj* (*attitude*) distante; **detached house** *n* villa

detail ['di:teɪl] *n* particolare *m*, dettaglio ▷ *vt* dettagliare, particolareggiare; **in ~** nei particolari; **detailed** *adj* particolareggiato(-a)
detain [dɪ'teɪn] *vt* trattenere; (*in captivity*) detenere
detect [dɪ'tɛkt] *vt* scoprire, scorgere; (*Med, Police, Radar etc*) individuare; **detection** [dɪ'tɛkʃən] *n* scoperta; individuazione *f*; **detective** *n* investigatore(-trice); **detective story** *n* giallo
detention [dɪ'tɛnʃən] *n* detenzione *f*; (*Scol*) *permanenza forzata per punizione*
deter [dɪ'tə:ʳ] *vt* dissuadere
detergent [dɪ'tə:dʒənt] *n* detersivo
deteriorate [dɪ'tɪərɪəreɪt] *vi* deteriorarsi
determination [dɪtə:mɪ'neɪʃən] *n* determinazione *f*
determine [dɪ'tə:mɪn] *vt* determinare; **determined** *adj* (*person*) risoluto(-a), deciso(-a); **determined to do** deciso(-a) a fare
deterrent [dɪ'tɛrənt] *n* deterrente *m*; **to act as a ~** fungere da deterrente
detest [dɪ'tɛst] *vt* detestare
detour ['di:tuəʳ] *n* deviazione *f*
detract [dɪ'trækt] *vi* **to ~ from** detrarre da
detrimental [dɛtrɪ'mɛntl] *adj* **~ to** dannoso(-a) a, nocivo(-a) a
devastating ['dɛvəsteɪtɪŋ] *adj* devastatore(-trice), sconvolgente
develop [dɪ'vɛləp] *vt* sviluppare; (*habit*) prendere (gradualmente) ▷ *vi* svilupparsi; (*facts, symptoms: appear*) manifestarsi, rivelarsi; **can you ~ this film?** può sviluppare questo rullino?; **developing country** *n* paese *m* in via di sviluppo; **development** *n* sviluppo
device [dɪ'vaɪs] *n* (*apparatus*) congegno
devil ['dɛvl] *n* diavolo; demonio
devious ['di:vɪəs] *adj* (*person*) subdolo(-a)
devise [dɪ'vaɪz] *vt* escogitare, concepire
devote [dɪ'vəut] *vt* **to ~ sth to** dedicare qc a; **devoted** *adj* devoto(-a); **to be devoted to sb** essere molto affezionato(-a) a qn; **devotion** [dɪ'vəuʃən] *n* devozione *f*, attaccamento; (*Rel*) atto di devozione, preghiera
devour [dɪ'vauəʳ] *vt* divorare
devout [dɪ'vaut] *adj* pio(-a), devoto(-a)
dew [dju:] *n* rugiada
diabetes [daɪə'bi:ti:z] *n* diabete *m*
diabetic [daɪə'bɛtɪk] *adj, n* diabetico(-a)
diagnose [daɪəg'nəuz] *vt* diagnosticare
diagnosis [daɪəg'nəusɪs] (*pl* **diagnoses**) *n* diagnosi *f inv*
diagonal [daɪ'ægənl] *adj* diagonale ▷ *n* diagonale *f*
diagram ['daɪəgræm] *n* diagramma *m*
dial ['daɪəl] *n* quadrante *m*; (*on radio*) lancetta; (*on telephone*) disco combinatore ▷ *vt* (*number*) fare
dialect ['daɪəlɛkt] *n* dialetto
dialling code (*US* **area code**) *n* prefisso; **what's the ~ for Paris?** qual è il prefisso telefonico di Parigi?
dialling tone ['daɪəlɪŋ-] (*US* **dial tone**) *n* segnale *m* di linea libera
dialogue ['daɪəlɔg] (*US* **dialog**) *n* dialogo
diameter [daɪ'æmɪtəʳ] *n* diametro
diamond ['daɪəmənd] *n* diamante *m*; (*shape*) rombo; **diamonds** *npl* (*Cards*) quadri *mpl*
diaper ['daɪəpəʳ] (*US*) *n* pannolino
diarrhoea [daɪə'ri:ə] (*US* **diarrhea**) *n* diarrea
diary ['daɪərɪ] *n* (*daily account*) diario; (*book*) agenda
dice [daɪs] *n inv* dado ▷ *vt* (*Culin*) tagliare a dadini
dictate [dɪk'teɪt] *vt* dettare; **dictation** [dɪk'teɪʃən] *n* dettatura; (*Scol*) dettato

dictator [dɪk'teɪtəʳ] *n* dittatore *m*
dictionary ['dɪkʃənrɪ] *n* dizionario
did [dɪd] *pt of* **do**
didn't [dɪdnt] = **did not**
die [daɪ] *vi* morire; **to be dying for sth/to do sth** morire dalla voglia di qc/di fare qc; **die down** *vi* abbassarsi; **die out** *vi* estinguersi
diesel ['di:zəl] *n* (*vehicle*) diesel *m inv*
diet ['daɪət] *n* alimentazione *f*; (*restricted food*) dieta ▷ *vi* (*also:* **be on a ~**) stare a dieta
differ ['dɪfəʳ] *vi* **to ~ from sth** differire da qc, essere diverso(-a) da qc; **to ~ from sb over sth** essere in disaccordo con qn su qc; **difference** *n* differenza; (*disagreement*) screzio; **different** *adj* diverso(-a); **differentiate** [-'rɛnʃɪeɪt] *vi* **to differentiate between** discriminare *or* fare differenza fra; **differently** *adv* diversamente
difficult ['dɪfɪkəlt] *adj* difficile; **difficulty** *n* difficoltà *f inv*
dig [dɪg] (*pt, pp* **dug**) *vt* (*hole*) scavare; (*garden*) vangare ▷ *n* (*prod*) gomitata; (*archaeological*) scavo; (*fig*) frecciata; **dig up** *vt* (*tree etc*) sradicare; (*information*) scavare fuori
digest [*vb* daɪ'dʒɛst, *n* 'daɪdʒɛst] *vt* digerire ▷ *n* compendio; **digestion** [dɪ'dʒɛstʃən] *n* digestione *f*
digit ['dɪdʒɪt] *n* cifra; (*finger*) dito; **digital** *adj* digitale; **digital camera** *n* macchina fotografica digitale; **digital TV** *n* televisione *f* digitale
dignified ['dɪgnɪfaɪd] *adj* dignitoso(-a)
dignity ['dɪgnɪtɪ] *n* dignità
digs [dɪgz] (BRIT: *inf*) *npl* camera ammobiliata
dilemma [daɪ'lɛmə] *n* dilemma *m*
dill [dɪl] *n* aneto
dilute [daɪ'lu:t] *vt* diluire; (*with water*) annacquare
dim [dɪm] *adj* (*light*) debole; (*shape etc*) vago(-a); (*room*) in penombra; (*inf: person*) tonto(-a) ▷ *vt* (*light*) abbassare
dime [daɪm] (US) *n* = *10 cents*
dimension [daɪ'mɛnʃən] *n* dimensione *f*
diminish [dɪ'mɪnɪʃ] *vt, vi* diminuire
din [dɪn] *n* chiasso, fracasso
dine [daɪn] *vi* pranzare; **diner** *n* (*person*) cliente *m/f*; (US: *place*) tavola calda
dinghy ['dɪŋgɪ] *n* battello pneumatico; (*also:* **rubber ~**) gommone *m*
dingy ['dɪndʒɪ] *adj* grigio(-a)
dining car ['daɪnɪŋ-] (BRIT) *n* vagone *m* ristorante
dining room *n* sala da pranzo
dining table *n* tavolo da pranzo
dinner ['dɪnəʳ] *n* (*lunch*) pranzo; (*evening meal*) cena; (*public*) banchetto; **dinner jacket** *n* smoking *m inv*; **dinner party** *n* cena; **dinner time** *n* ora di pranzo (*or* cena)
dinosaur ['daɪnəsɔ:ʳ] *n* dinosauro
dip [dɪp] *n* discesa; (*in sea*) bagno; (*Culin*) salsetta ▷ *vt* immergere; bagnare; (BRIT *Aut: lights*) abbassare ▷ *vi* abbassarsi
diploma [dɪ'pləumə] *n* diploma *m*
diplomacy [dɪ'pləuməsɪ] *n* diplomazia
diplomat ['dɪpləmæt] *n* diplomatico; **diplomatic** [dɪplə'mætɪk] *adj* diplomatico(-a)
dipstick ['dɪpstɪk] *n* (*Aut*) indicatore *m* di livello dell'olio
dire [daɪəʳ] *adj* terribile; estremo(-a)
direct [daɪ'rɛkt] *adj* diretto(-a) ▷ *vt* dirigere; (*order*): **to ~ sb to do sth** dare direttive a qn di fare qc ▷ *adv* direttamente; **can you ~ me to ...?** mi può indicare la strada per ...?; **direct debit** *n* (*Banking*) addebito effettuato per ordine di un cliente di banca
direction [dɪ'rɛkʃən] *n* direzione *f*; **directions** *npl* (*advice*) chiarimenti *mpl*; **sense of ~** senso dell'orientamento; **~s for use** istruzioni *fpl*

directly [dɪ'rɛktlɪ] *adv* (*in straight line*) direttamente; (*at once*) subito
director [dɪ'rɛktə^r] *n* direttore(-trice), amministratore(-trice); (*Theatre, Cinema*) regista *m/f*
directory [dɪ'rɛktərɪ] *n* elenco; **directory enquiries** (*US* **directory assistance**) *n* informazioni *fpl* elenco abbonati *inv*
dirt [də:t] *n* sporcizia; immondizia; (*earth*) terra; **dirty** *adj* sporco(-a) ▷ *vt* sporcare
disability [dɪsə'bɪlɪtɪ] *n* invalidità *f inv*; (*Law*) incapacità *f inv*
disabled [dɪs'eɪbld] *adj* invalido(-a); (*mentally*) ritardato(-a) ▷ *npl*: **the ~** gli invalidi
disadvantage [dɪsəd'vɑ:ntɪdʒ] *n* svantaggio
disagree [dɪsə'gri:] *vi* (*differ*) discordare; (*be against, think otherwise*): **to ~ (with)** essere in disaccordo (con), dissentire (da); **disagreeable** *adj* sgradevole; (*person*) antipatico(-a); **disagreement** *n* disaccordo; (*argument*) dissapore *m*
disappear [dɪsə'pɪə^r] *vi* scomparire; **disappearance** *n* scomparsa
disappoint [dɪsə'pɔɪnt] *vt* deludere; **disappointed** *adj* deluso(-a); **disappointing** *adj* deludente; **disappointment** *n* delusione *f*
disapproval [dɪsə'pru:vəl] *n* disapprovazione *f*
disapprove [dɪsə'pru:v] *vi*: **to ~ of** disapprovare
disarm [dɪs'ɑ:m] *vt* disarmare; **disarmament** *n* disarmo
disaster [dɪ'zɑ:stə^r] *n* disastro; **disastrous** [dɪ'zɑ:strəs] *adj* disastroso(-a)
disbelief ['dɪsbə'li:f] *n* incredulità
disc [dɪsk] *n* disco; (*Comput*) = **disk**
discard [dɪs'kɑ:d] *vt* (*old things*) scartare; (*fig*) abbandonare
discharge [*vb* dɪs'tʃɑ:dʒ, *n* 'dɪstʃɑ:dʒ] *vt* (*duties*) compiere; (*Elec, waste etc*) scaricare; (*Med*) emettere; (*patient*) dimettere; (*employee*) licenziare; (*soldier*) congedare; (*defendant*) liberare ▷ *n* (*Elec*) scarica; (*Med*) emissione *f*; (*dismissal*) licenziamento; congedo; liberazione *f*
discipline ['dɪsɪplɪn] *n* disciplina ▷ *vt* disciplinare; (*punish*) punire
disc jockey *n* disc jockey *m inv*
disclose [dɪs'kləuz] *vt* rivelare, svelare
disco ['dɪskəu] *n abbr* discoteca
discoloured [dɪs'kʌləd] (*US* **discolored**) *adj* scolorito(-a), ingiallito(-a)
discomfort [dɪs'kʌmfət] *n* disagio; (*lack of comfort*) scomodità *f inv*
disconnect [dɪskə'nɛkt] *vt* sconnettere, staccare; (*Elec, Radio*) staccare; (*gas, water*) chiudere
discontent [dɪskən'tɛnt] *n* scontentezza
discontinue [dɪskən'tɪnju:] *vt* smettere, cessare; **"~d"** (*Comm*) "fuori produzione"
discount [*n* 'dɪskaunt, *vb* dɪs'kaunt] *n* sconto ▷ *vt* scontare; (*idea*) non badare a; **are there ~s for students?** ci sono sconti per studenti?
discourage [dɪs'kʌrɪdʒ] *vt* scoraggiare
discover [dɪs'kʌvə^r] *vt* scoprire; **discovery** *n* scoperta
discredit [dɪs'krɛdɪt] *vt* screditare; mettere in dubbio
discreet [dɪ'skri:t] *adj* discreto(-a)
discrepancy [dɪ'skrɛpənsɪ] *n* discrepanza
discretion [dɪ'skrɛʃən] *n* discrezione *f*; **use your own ~** giudichi lei
discriminate [dɪ'skrɪmɪneɪt] *vi*: **to ~ between** distinguere tra; **to ~ against** discriminare contro; **discrimination** [-'neɪʃən] *n* discriminazione *f*; (*judgment*) discernimento
discuss [dɪ'skʌs] *vt* discutere; (*debate*)

dibattere; **discussion** [dɪ'skʌʃən] *n* discussione *f*; **discussion forum** *n* (*on the Internet*) forum *m inv* di discussione
disease [dɪ'zi:z] *n* malattia
disembark [dɪsɪm'bɑ:k] *vt, vi* sbarcare
disgrace [dɪs'greɪs] *n* vergogna; (*disfavour*) disgrazia ▷ *vt* disonorare, far cadere in disgrazia; **disgraceful** *adj* scandaloso(-a), vergognoso(-a)
disgruntled [dɪs'grʌntld] *adj* scontento(-a), di cattivo umore
disguise [dɪs'gaɪz] *n* travestimento ▷ *vt* **to ~ (as)** travestire (da); **in ~** travestito(-a)
disgust [dɪs'gʌst] *n* disgusto, nausea ▷ *vt* disgustare, far schifo a; **disgusted** [dɪs'gʌstɪd] *adj* indignato(-a); **disgusting** [dɪs'gʌstɪŋ] *adj* disgustoso(-a), ripugnante
dish [dɪʃ] *n* piatto; **to do** *or* **wash the ~es** fare i piatti; **dishcloth** *n* strofinaccio
dishonest [dɪs'ɔnɪst] *adj* disonesto(-a)
dishtowel ['dɪʃtauəl] (US) *n* strofinaccio dei piatti
dishwasher ['dɪʃwɔʃəʳ] *n* lavastoviglie *f inv*
disillusion [dɪsɪ'lu:ʒən] *vt* disilludere, disingannare
disinfectant [dɪsɪn'fɛktənt] *n* disinfettante *m*
disintegrate [dɪs'ɪntɪgreɪt] *vi* disintegrarsi
disk [dɪsk] *n* (*Comput*) disco; **single-/double-sided ~** disco a facciata singola/doppia; **disk drive** *n* lettore *m*; **diskette** (US) *n* = **disk**
dislike [dɪs'laɪk] *n* antipatia, avversione *f*; (*gen pl*) cosa che non piace ▷ *vt* **he ~s it** non gli piace
dislocate ['dɪsləkeɪt] *vt* slogare
disloyal [dɪs'lɔɪəl] *adj* sleale
dismal ['dɪzml] *adj* triste, cupo(-a)
dismantle [dɪs'mæntl] *vt* (*machine*) smontare
dismay [dɪs'meɪ] *n* costernazione *f* ▷ *vt* sgomentare
dismiss [dɪs'mɪs] *vt* congedare; (*employee*) licenziare; (*idea*) scacciare; (*Law*) respingere; **dismissal** *n* congedo; licenziamento
disobedient [dɪsə'bi:dɪənt] *adj* disubbidiente
disobey [dɪsə'beɪ] *vt* disubbidire a
disorder [dɪs'ɔ:dəʳ] *n* disordine *m*; (*rioting*) tumulto; (*Med*) disturbo
disorganized [dɪs'ɔ:gənaɪzd] *adj* (*person, life*) disorganizzato(-a); (*system, meeting*) male organizzato(-a)
disown [dɪs'əun] *vt* rinnegare
dispatch [dɪs'pætʃ] *vt* spedire, inviare ▷ *n* spedizione *f*, invio; (*Mil, Press*) dispaccio
dispel [dɪs'pɛl] *vt* dissipare, scacciare
dispense [dɪs'pɛns] *vt* distribuire, amministrare; **dispense with** *vt fus* fare a meno di; **dispenser** *n* (*container*) distributore *m*
disperse [dɪs'pə:s] *vt* disperdere; (*knowledge*) disseminare ▷ *vi* disperdersi
display [dɪs'pleɪ] *n* esposizione *f*; (*of feeling etc*) manifestazione *f*; (*screen*) schermo ▷ *vt* mostrare; (*goods*) esporre; (*pej*) ostentare
displease [dɪs'pli:z] *vt* dispiacere a, scontentare; **~d with** scontento di
disposable [dɪs'pəuzəbl] *adj* (*pack etc*) a perdere; (*income*) disponibile
disposal [dɪs'pəuzl] *n* eliminazione *f*; (*of property*) cessione *f*; **at one's ~** alla sua disposizione
dispose [dɪs'pəuz] *vi* **~ of** sbarazzarsi di; **disposition** [-'zɪʃən] *n* disposizione *f*; (*temperament*) carattere *m*
disproportionate [dɪsprə'pɔ:ʃənət] *adj* sproporzionato(-a)
dispute [dɪs'pju:t] *n* disputa; (*also*: **industrial ~**) controversia (sindacale) ▷ *vt* contestare; (*matter*) discutere; (*victory*) disputare
disqualify [dɪs'kwɔlɪfaɪ] *vt* (*Sport*) squalificare; **to ~ sb from sth/from**

doing rendere qn incapace a qc/a fare; squalificare qn da qc/da fare; **to ~ sb from driving** ritirare la patente a qn

disregard [dɪsrɪ'gɑ:d] *vt* non far caso a, non badare a

disrupt [dɪs'rʌpt] *vt* disturbare; creare scompiglio in; **disruption** [dɪs'rʌpʃən] *n* disordine *m*; interruzione *f*

dissatisfaction [dɪssætɪs'fækʃən] *n* scontentezza, insoddisfazione *f*

dissatisfied [dɪs'sætɪsfaɪd] *adj*: **~ (with)** scontento(a) *or* insoddisfatto(a) (di)

dissect [dɪ'sɛkt] *vt* sezionare

dissent [dɪ'sɛnt] *n* dissenso

dissertation [dɪsə'teɪʃən] *n* tesi *f inv*, dissertazione *f*

dissolve [dɪ'zɔlv] *vt* dissolvere, sciogliere; (*Pol*, *marriage etc*) sciogliere ▷ *vi* dissolversi, sciogliersi

distance ['dɪstns] *n* distanza; **in the ~** in lontananza

distant ['dɪstnt] *adj* lontano(-a), distante; (*manner*) riservato(-a), freddo(-a)

distil [dɪs'tɪl] (US **distill**) *vt* distillare; **distillery** *n* distilleria

distinct [dɪs'tɪŋkt] *adj* distinto(-a); **as ~ from** a differenza di; **distinction** [dɪs'tɪŋkʃən] *n* distinzione *f*; (*in exam*) lode *f*; **distinctive** *adj* distintivo(-a)

distinguish [dɪs'tɪŋgwɪʃ] *vt* distinguere; discernere; **distinguished** *adj* (*eminent*) eminente

distort [dɪs'tɔ:t] *vt* distorcere; (*Tech*) deformare

distract [dɪs'trækt] *vt* distrarre; **distracted** *adj* distratto(-a); **distraction** [dɪs'trækʃən] *n* distrazione *f*

distraught [dɪs'trɔ:t] *adj* stravolto(-a)

distress [dɪs'trɛs] *n* angoscia ▷ *vt* affliggere; **distressing** *adj* doloroso(-a)

distribute [dɪs'trɪbju:t] *vt* distribuire; **distribution** [-'bju:ʃən] *n* distribuzione *f*; **distributor** *n* distributore *m*

district ['dɪstrɪkt] *n* (*of country*) regione *f*; (*of town*) quartiere *m*; (*Admin*) distretto; **district attorney** (US) *n* ≈ sostituto procuratore *m* della Repubblica

distrust [dɪs'trʌst] *n* diffidenza, sfiducia ▷ *vt* non aver fiducia in

disturb [dɪs'tə:b] *vt* disturbare; **disturbance** *n* disturbo; (*political etc*) disordini *mpl*; **disturbed** *adj* (*worried*, *upset*) turbato(-a); **emotionally disturbed** con turbe emotive; **disturbing** *adj* sconvolgente

ditch [dɪtʃ] *n* fossa ▷ *vt* (*inf*) piantare in asso

ditto ['dɪtəu] *adv* idem

dive [daɪv] *n* tuffo; (*of submarine*) immersione *f* ▷ *vi* tuffarsi; immergersi; **diver** *n* tuffatore(-trice), palombaro

diverse [daɪ'və:s] *adj* vario(-a)

diversion [daɪ'və:ʃən] *n* (BRIT *Aut*) deviazione *f*; (*distraction*) divertimento

diversity [daɪ'və:sɪtɪ] *n* diversità *f inv*, varietà *f inv*

divert [daɪ'və:t] *vt* deviare

divide [dɪ'vaɪd] *vt* dividere; (*separate*) separare ▷ *vi* dividersi; **divided highway** (US) *n* strada a doppia carreggiata

divine [dɪ'vaɪn] *adj* divino(-a)

diving ['daɪvɪŋ] *n* tuffo; **diving board** *n* trampolino

division [dɪ'vɪʒən] *n* divisione *f*; separazione *f*; (*esp Football*) serie *f*

divorce [dɪ'vɔ:s] *n* divorzio ▷ *vt* divorziare da; (*dissociate*) separare; **divorced** *adj* divorziato(-a); **divorcee** [-'si:] *n* divorziato(-a)

D.I.Y. (BRIT) *n abbr* = **do-it-yourself**

dizzy ['dɪzɪ] *adj* **to feel ~** avere il capogiro

DJ *n abbr* = **disc jockey**

DNA *n abbr* (= *deoxyribonucleic acid*) DNA *m*; **DNA test** *n* test *m inv* del DNA

KEYWORD

do [du:] (*pt* **did**, *pp* **done**) *n* (*inf: party etc*) festa; **it was rather a grand do** è stato un ricevimento piuttosto importante
▷ *vb* 1 (*in negative constructions: non tradotto*): **I don't understand** non capisco
2 (*to form questions: non tradotto*): **didn't you know?** non lo sapevi?; **why didn't you come?** perché non sei venuto?
3 (*for emphasis, in polite expressions*): **she does seem rather late** sembra essere piuttosto in ritardo; **do sit down** si accomodi la prego, prego si sieda; **do take care!** mi raccomando, sta attento!
4 (*used to avoid repeating vb*): **she swims better than I do** lei nuota meglio di me; **do you agree? — yes, I do/no, I don't** sei d'accordo? — sì/no; **she lives in Glasgow — so do I** lei vive a Glasgow — anch'io; **he asked me to help him and I did** mi ha chiesto di aiutarlo ed io l'ho fatto
5 (*in question tags*): **you like him, don't you?** ti piace, vero?; **I don't know him, do I?** non lo conosco, vero?
▷ *vt* (*gen, carry out, perform etc*) fare; **what are you doing tonight?** che fa stasera?; **to do the cooking** cucinare; **to do the washing-up** fare i piatti; **to do one's teeth** lavarsi i denti; **to do one's hair/nails** farsi i capelli/le unghie; **the car was doing 100** la macchina faceva i 100 all'ora
▷ *vi* 1 (*act, behave*) fare; **do as I do** faccia come me, faccia come faccio io
2 (*get on, fare*) andare; **he's doing well/badly at school** va bene/male a scuola; **how do you do?** piacere!
3 (*suit*) andare bene; **this room will do** questa stanza va bene
4 (*be sufficient*) bastare; **will £10 do?** basteranno 10 sterline?; **that'll do** basta così; **that'll do!** (*in annoyance*) ora basta!; **to make do (with)** arrangiarsi (con)
do away with *vt fus* (*kill*) far fuori; (*abolish*) abolire
do up *vt* (*laces*) allacciare; (*dress, buttons*) abbottonare; (*renovate: room, house*) rimettere a nuovo, rifare
do with *vt fus* (*need*) aver bisogno di; (*be connected*): **what has it got to do with you?** e tu che c'entri?; **I won't have anything to do with it** non voglio avere niente a che farci; **it has to do with money** si tratta di soldi
do without *vi* fare senza ▷ *vt fus* fare a meno di

dock [dɔk] *n* (*Naut*) bacino; (*Law*) banco degli imputati ▷ *vi* entrare in bacino; (*Space*) agganciarsi; **docks** *npl* (*Naut*) dock *m inv*
doctor ['dɔktəʳ] *n* medico(-a); (*Ph. D. etc*) dottore(-essa) ▷ *vt* (*drink etc*) adulterare; **call a ~!** chiamate un dottore!; **Doctor of Philosophy** *n* dottorato di ricerca; (*person*) titolare *m/f* di un dottorato di ricerca
document ['dɔkjumənt] *n* documento; **documentary** [-'mɛntərɪ] *adj* (*evidence*) documentato(-a) ▷ *n* documentario; **documentation** [dɔkjumən'teɪʃən] *n* documentazione *f*
dodge [dɔdʒ] *n* trucco; schivata ▷ *vt* schivare, eludere
dodgy ['dɔdʒɪ] *adj* (*inf: uncertain*) rischioso(-a); (*untrustworthy*) sospetto(-a)
does [dʌz] *vb see* **do**
doesn't ['dʌznt] = **does not**
dog [dɔg] *n* cane *m* ▷ *vt* (*follow closely*) pedinare; (*fig: memory etc*) perseguitare; **doggy bag** *n* sacchetto per gli avanzi (*da portare a casa*)

do-it-yourself ['duːɪtjɔː'sɛlf] *n* il far da sé
dole [dəul] (BRIT) *n* sussidio di disoccupazione; **to be on the ~** vivere del sussidio
doll [dɔl] *n* bambola
dollar ['dɔləʳ] *n* dollaro
dolphin ['dɔlfɪn] *n* delfino
dome [dəum] *n* cupola
domestic [də'mɛstɪk] *adj* (*duty, happiness, animal*) domestico(-a); (*policy, affairs, flights*) nazionale; **domestic appliance** *n* elettrodomestico
dominant ['dɔmɪnənt] *adj* dominante
dominate ['dɔmɪneɪt] *vt* dominare
domino ['dɔmɪnəu] (*pl* **dominoes**) *n* domino; **dominoes** *n* (*game*) gioco del domino
donate [də'neɪt] *vt* donare; **donation** [də'neɪʃən] *n* donazione *f*
done [dʌn] *pp of* **do**
donkey ['dɔŋkɪ] *n* asino
donor ['dəunəʳ] *n* donatore(-trice); **donor card** *n* tessera di donatore di organi
don't [dəunt] = **do not**
donut ['dəunʌt] (US) *n* = **doughnut**
doodle ['duːdl] *vi* scarabocchiare
doom [duːm] *n* destino; rovina ▷ *vt*: **to be ~ed (to failure)** essere predestinato(-a) (a fallire)
door [dɔːʳ] *n* porta; **doorbell** *n* campanello; **door handle** *n* maniglia; **doorknob** ['dɔːnɒb] *n* pomello, maniglia; **doorstep** *n* gradino della porta; **doorway** *n* porta
dope [dəup] *n* (*inf: drugs*) roba ▷ *vt* (*horse etc*) drogare
dormitory ['dɔːmɪtrɪ] *n* dormitorio; (US) casa dello studente
DOS [dɔs] *n abbr* (= *disk operating system*) DOS *m*
dosage ['dəusɪdʒ] *n* posologia
dose [dəus] *n* dose *f*; (*bout*) attacco
dot [dɔt] *n* punto; macchiolina ▷ *vt* **~ted with** punteggiato(-a) di; **on the ~** in punto; **dotcom** [dɔt'kɔm] *n* azienda che opera in Internet; **dotted line** ['dɔtɪd-] *n* linea punteggiata
double ['dʌbl] *adj* doppio(-a) ▷ *adv* (*twice*): **to cost ~ sth** costare il doppio (di qc) ▷ *n* sosia *m inv* ▷ *vt* raddoppiare; (*fold*) piegare doppio *or* in due ▷ *vi* raddoppiarsi; **at the ~** (BRIT), **on the ~** a passo di corsa; **double back** *vi* (*person*) tornare sui propri passi; **double bass** *n* contrabbasso; **double bed** *n* letto matrimoniale; **double-check** *vt, vi* ricontrollare; **double-click** *vi* (*Comput*) fare doppio click; **double-cross** *vt* fare il doppio gioco con; **doubledecker** *n* autobus *m inv* a due piani; **double glazing** (BRIT) *n* doppi vetri *mpl*; **double room** *n* camera matrimoniale; **doubles** *n* (*Tennis*) doppio; **double yellow lines** *npl* (BRIT: *Aut*) *linea gialla doppia continua che segnala il divieto di sosta*
doubt [daut] *n* dubbio ▷ *vt* dubitare di; **to ~ that** dubitare che + *sub*; **doubtful** *adj* dubbioso(-a), incerto(-a); (*person*) equivoco(-a); **doubtless** *adv* indubbiamente
dough [dəu] *n* pasta, impasto; **doughnut** (US **donut**) *n* bombolone *m*
dove [dʌv] *n* colombo(-a)
down [daun] *n* piume *fpl* ▷ *adv* giù, di sotto ▷ *prep* giù per ▷ *vt* (*inf: drink*) scolarsi; **~ with X!** abbasso X!; **down-and-out** *n* barbone *m*; **downfall** *n* caduta; rovina; **downhill** *adv*: **to go downhill** andare in discesa; (*fig*) lasciarsi andare; andare a rotoli
Downing Street ['daunɪŋ-] *n* **lo ~** *residenza del primo ministro inglese*

DOWNING STREET

Al numero 10 di **Downing Street**, nel quartiere di Westminster a Londra, si trova la residenza del primo ministro inglese, al numero 11 quella del **Chancellor of the Exchequer**.

down: **download** *vt* (*Comput*) scaricare; **downright** *adj* franco(-a); (*refusal*) assoluto(-a)
Down's syndrome *n* sindrome *f* di Down
down: **downstairs** *adv* di sotto; al piano inferiore; **down-to-earth** *adj* pratico(-a); **downtown** *adv* in città; **down under** *adv* (*Australia etc*) agli antipodi; **downward** ['daunwəd] *adj, adv* in giù, in discesa; **downwards** ['daunwədz] *adv* = **downward**
doz. *abbr* = **dozen**
doze [dəuz] *vi* sonnecchiare
dozen ['dʌzn] *n* dozzina; **a ~ books** una dozzina di libri; **~s of** decine *fpl* di
Dr. *abbr* (= *doctor*) dott.; (*in street names*) = **drive**
drab [dræb] *adj* tetro(-a), grigio(-a)
draft [drɑːft] *n* abbozzo; (*Pol*) bozza; (*Comm*) tratta; (*US: call-up*) leva ▷ *vt* abbozzare; *see also* **draught**
drag [dræg] *vt* trascinare; (*river*) dragare ▷ *vi* trascinarsi ▷ *n* (*inf*) noioso(-a); noia, fatica; (*women's clothing*): **in ~** travestito (da donna)
dragon ['drægən] *n* drago
dragonfly ['drægənflaɪ] *n* libellula
drain [dreɪn] *n* (*for sewage*) fogna; (*on resources*) salasso ▷ *vt* (*land, marshes*) prosciugare; (*vegetables*) scolare ▷ *vi* (*water*) defluire (via); **drainage** *n* prosciugamento; fognatura; **drainpipe** *n* tubo di scarico
drama ['drɑːmə] *n* (*art*) dramma *m*, teatro; (*play*) commedia; (*event*) dramma; **dramatic** [drə'mætɪk] *adj* drammatico(-a)
drank [dræŋk] *pt of* **drink**
drape [dreɪp] *vt* drappeggiare; **drapes** (*US*) *npl* (*curtains*) tende *fpl*
drastic ['dræstɪk] *adj* drastico(-a)
draught [drɑːft] (*US* **draft**) *n* corrente *f* d'aria; (*Naut*) pescaggio; **on ~** (*beer*) alla spina; **draught beer** *n* birra alla spina; **draughts** (*BRIT*) *n* (gioco della) dama
draw [drɔː] (*pt* **drew**, *pp* **drawn**) *vt* tirare; (*take out*) estrarre; (*attract*) attirare; (*picture*) disegnare; (*line, circle*) tracciare; (*money*) ritirare ▷ *vi* (*Sport*) pareggiare ▷ *n* pareggio; (*in lottery*) estrazione *f*; **to ~ near** avvicinarsi; **draw out** *vi* (*lengthen*) allungarsi ▷ *vt* (*money*) ritirare; **draw up** *vi* (*stop*) arrestarsi, fermarsi ▷ *vt* (*chair*) avvicinare; (*document*) compilare; **drawback** *n* svantaggio, inconveniente *m*
drawer [drɔː^r] *n* cassetto
drawing ['drɔːɪŋ] *n* disegno; **drawing pin** (*BRIT*) *n* puntina da disegno; **drawing room** *n* salotto
drawn [drɔːn] *pp of* **draw**
dread [drɛd] *n* terrore *m* ▷ *vt* tremare all'idea di; **dreadful** *adj* terribile
dream [driːm] (*pt, pp* **dreamed** *or* **dreamt**) *n* sogno ▷ *vt, vi* sognare; **dreamer** *n* sognatore(-trice)
dreamt [drɛmt] *pt, pp of* **dream**
dreary ['drɪərɪ] *adj* tetro(-a); monotono(-a)
drench [drɛntʃ] *vt* inzuppare
dress [drɛs] *n* vestito; (*no pl: clothing*) abbigliamento ▷ *vt* vestire; (*wound*) fasciare ▷ *vi* vestirsi; **to get ~ed** vestirsi; **dress up** *vi* vestirsi a festa; (*in fancy dress*) vestirsi in costume; **dress circle** (*BRIT*) *n* prima galleria; **dresser** *n* (*BRIT: cupboard*) credenza; (*US*) cassettone *m*; **dressing** *n* (*Med*) benda; (*Culin*) condimento; **dressing gown** (*BRIT*) *n* vestaglia; **dressing room** *n* (*Theatre*) camerino; (*Sport*) spogliatoio; **dressing table** *n* toilette *f inv*; **dressmaker** *n* sarta
drew [druː] *pt of* **draw**
dribble ['drɪbl] *vi* (*baby*) sbavare ▷ *vt* (*ball*) dribblare
dried [draɪd] *adj* (*fruit, beans*)

secco(-a); (*eggs, milk*) in polvere

drier ['draɪəʳ] *n* = **dryer**

drift [drɪft] *n* (*of current etc*) direzione *f*; forza; (*of snow*) cumulo; turbine *m*; (*general meaning*) senso ▷ *vi* (*boat*) essere trasportato(-a) dalla corrente; (*sand, snow*) ammucchiarsi

drill [drɪl] *n* trapano; (*Mil*) esercitazione *f* ▷ *vt* trapanare; (*troops*) addestrare ▷ *vi* (*for oil*) fare trivellazioni

drink [drɪŋk] (*pt* **drank**, *pp* **drunk**) *n* bevanda, bibita; (*alcoholic drink*) bicchierino; (*sip*) sorso ▷ *vt, vi* bere; **to have a ~** bere qualcosa; **would you like a ~?** vuoi qualcosa da bere?; **a ~ of water** un po' d'acqua; **drink-driving** *n* guida in stato di ebbrezza; **drinker** *n* bevitore(-trice); **drinking water** *n* acqua potabile

drip [drɪp] *n* goccia; gocciolamento; (*Med*) fleboclisi *f inv* ▷ *vi* gocciolare; (*tap*) sgocciolare

drive [draɪv] (*pt* **drove**, *pp* **driven**) *n* passeggiata *or* giro in macchina; (*also:* **~way**) viale *m* d'accesso; (*energy*) energia; (*campaign*) campagna; (*also:* **disk ~**) lettore *m* ▷ *vt* guidare; (*nail*) piantare; (*push*) cacciare, spingere; (*Tech: motor*) azionare; far funzionare ▷ *vi* (*Aut: at controls*) guidare; (*: travel*) andare in macchina; **left-/right-hand ~** guida a sinistra/destra; **to ~ sb mad** far impazzire qn; **drive out** *vt* (*force out*) cacciare, mandare via; **drive-in** (*esp* US) *adj, n* drive-in (*m inv*)

driven ['drɪvn] *pp of* **drive**

driver ['draɪvəʳ] *n* conducente *m/f*; (*of taxi*) tassista *m*; (*chauffeur: of bus*) autista *m/f*; **driver's license** (US) *n* patente *f* di guida

driveway ['draɪvweɪ] *n* viale *m* d'accesso

driving ['draɪvɪŋ] *n* guida; **driving instructor** *n* istruttore(-trice) di scuola guida; **driving lesson** *n* lezione *f* di guida; **driving licence** (BRIT) *n* patente *f* di guida; **driving test** *n* esame *m* di guida

drizzle ['drɪzl] *n* pioggerella

droop [druːp] *vi* (*flower*) appassire; (*head, shoulders*) chinarsi

drop [drɔp] *n* (*of water*) goccia; (*lessening*) diminuzione *f*; (*fall*) caduta ▷ *vt* lasciare cadere; (*voice, eyes, price*) abbassare; (*set down from car*) far scendere; (*name from list*) lasciare fuori ▷ *vi* cascare; (*wind*) abbassarsi; **drop in** *vi* (*inf: visit*): **to drop in (on)** fare un salto (da), passare (da); **drop off** *vi* (*sleep*) addormentarsi ▷ *vt* (*passenger*) far scendere; **drop out** *vi* (*withdraw*) ritirarsi; (*student etc*) smettere di studiare

drought [draut] *n* siccità *f inv*

drove [drəuv] *pt of* **drive**

drown [draun] *vt* affogare; (*fig: noise*) soffocare ▷ *vi* affogare

drowsy ['drauzɪ] *adj* sonnolento(-a), assonnato(-a)

drug [drʌg] *n* farmaco; (*narcotic*) droga ▷ *vt* drogare; **to be on ~s** drogarsi; (*Med*) prendere medicinali; **hard/soft ~s** droghe pesanti/leggere; **drug addict** *n* tossicomane *m/f*; **drug dealer** *n* trafficante *m/f* di droga; **druggist** (US) *n* *persona che gestisce un drugstore*; **drugstore** (US) *n* drugstore *m inv*

drum [drʌm] *n* tamburo; (*for oil, petrol*) fusto ▷ *vi* tamburellare; **drums** *npl* (*set of drums*) batteria; **drummer** *n* batterista *m/f*

drunk [drʌŋk] *pp of* **drink** ▷ *adj* ubriaco(-a); ebbro(-a) ▷ *n* (*also:* **~ard**) ubriacone(-a); **drunken** *adj* ubriaco(-a); da ubriaco

dry [draɪ] *adj* secco(-a); (*day, clothes*) asciutto(-a) ▷ *vt* seccare; (*clothes, hair, hands*) asciugare ▷ *vi* asciugarsi; **dry off** *vi* asciugarsi ▷ *vt* asciugare; **dry up** *vi* seccarsi; **dry-cleaner's** *n* lavasecco *m inv*; **dry-cleaning** *n* pulitura a secco; **dryer** *n* (*for hair*) föhn *m inv*, asciugacapelli *m inv*; (*for clothes*) asciugabiancheria; (*US*: *spin-dryer*) centrifuga

DSS *n abbr* (= *Department of Social Security*) *ministero della Previdenza sociale*

DTP *n abbr* (= *desk-top publishing*) desktop publishing *m inv*

dual ['djuəl] *adj* doppio(-a); **dual carriageway** (BRIT) *n* strada a doppia carreggiata

dubious ['dju:bɪəs] *adj* dubbio(-a)

Dublin ['dʌblɪn] *n* Dublino *f*

duck [dʌk] *n* anatra ▷ *vi* abbassare la testa

due [dju:] *adj* dovuto(-a); (*expected*) atteso(-a); (*fitting*) giusto(-a) ▷ *n* dovuto ▷ *adv* **~ north** diritto verso nord

duel ['djuəl] *n* duello

duet [dju:'ɛt] *n* duetto

dug [dʌg] *pt, pp of* **dig**

duke [dju:k] *n* duca *m*

dull [dʌl] *adj* (*light*) debole; (*boring*) noioso(-a); (*slow-witted*) ottuso(-a); (*sound, pain*) sordo(-a); (*weather, day*) fosco(-a), scuro(-a) ▷ *vt* (*pain, grief*) attutire; (*mind, senses*) intorpidire

dumb [dʌm] *adj* muto(-a); (*pej*) stupido(-a)

dummy ['dʌmɪ] *n* (*tailor's model*) manichino; (*Tech, Comm*) riproduzione *f*; (BRIT: *for baby*) tettarella ▷ *adj* falso(-a), finto(-a)

dump [dʌmp] *n* (*also*: **rubbish ~**) discarica di rifiuti; (*inf*: *place*) buco ▷ *vt* (*put down*) scaricare; mettere giù; (*get rid of*) buttar via

dumpling ['dʌmplɪŋ] *n specie di gnocco*

dune [dju:n] *n* duna

dungarees [dʌŋgə'ri:z] *npl* tuta

dungeon ['dʌndʒən] *n* prigione *f* sotterranea

duplex ['dju:plɛks] (US) *n* (*house*) *casa con muro divisorio in comune con un'altra*; (*apartment*) appartamento su due piani

duplicate [*n* 'dju:plɪkət, *vb* 'dju:plɪkeɪt] *n* doppio ▷ *vt* duplicare; **in ~** in doppia copia

durable ['djuərəbl] *adj* durevole; (*clothes, metal*) resistente

duration [djuə'reɪʃən] *n* durata

during ['djuərɪŋ] *prep* durante, nel corso di

dusk [dʌsk] *n* crepuscolo

dust [dʌst] *n* polvere *f* ▷ *vt* (*furniture*) spolverare; (*cake etc*): **to ~ with** cospargere con; **dustbin** (BRIT) *n* pattumiera; **duster** *n* straccio per la polvere; **dustman** (*irreg*: BRIT) *n* netturbino; **dustpan** *n* pattumiera; **dusty** *adj* polveroso(-a)

Dutch [dʌtʃ] *adj* olandese ▷ *n* (*Ling*) olandese *m*; **the Dutch** *npl* gli Olandesi; **to go ~** (*inf*) fare alla romana; **Dutchman, Dutchwoman** (*irreg*) *n* olandese *m/f*

duty ['dju:tɪ] *n* dovere *m*; (*tax*) dazio, tassa; **on ~** di servizio; **off ~** libero(-a), fuori servizio; **duty-free** *adj* esente da dazio

duvet ['du:veɪ] (BRIT) *n* piumino, piumone *m*

DVD *n abbr* (= *digital versatile or video disk*) DVD *m inv*; **DVD burner, DVD writer** *n* masterizzatore *m* di DVD; **DVD player** *n* lettore *m* DVD

dwarf [dwɔ:f] *n* nano(-a) ▷ *vt* far apparire piccolo

dwell [dwɛl] (*pt, pp* **dwelt**) *vi* dimorare; **dwell on** *vt fus* indugiare su

dwelt [dwɛlt] *pt, pp of* **dwell**

dwindle ['dwɪndl] *vi* diminuire

dye [daɪ] *n* tinta ▷ *vt* tingere

dying ['daɪɪŋ] *adj* morente, moribondo(-a)

dynamic [daɪ'næmɪk] *adj* dinamico(-a)

dynamite ['daɪnəmaɪt] *n* dinamite *f*

dyslexia [dɪs'lɛksɪə] *n* dislessia

dyslexic [dɪs'lɛksɪk] *adj, n* dislessico(-a)

e

E [iː] *n* (*Mus*) mi *m*
E111 *n abbr* (*also:* **form ~**) E111 (*modulo CEE per rimborso spese mediche*)
each [iːtʃ] *adj* ogni, ciascuno(-a) ▷ *pron* ciascuno(-a), ognuno(-a); **~ one** ognuno(-a); **~ other** si *or* ci *etc*; **they hate ~ other** si odiano (l'un l'altro); **you are jealous of ~ other** siete gelosi l'uno dell'altro; **they have 2 books ~** hanno 2 libri ciascuno
eager ['iːgəʳ] *adj* impaziente, desideroso(-a); ardente; **to be ~ for** essere desideroso di, aver gran voglia di
eagle ['iːgl] *n* aquila
ear [ɪəʳ] *n* orecchio; (*of corn*) pannocchia; **earache** *n* mal *m* d'orecchi; **eardrum** *n* timpano
earl [əːl] (BRIT) *n* conte *m*
earlier ['əːlɪəʳ] *adj* precedente ▷ *adv* prima
early ['əːlɪ] *adv* presto, di buon'ora; (*ahead of time*) in anticipo ▷ *adj* (*near the beginning*) primo(-a); (*sooner than expected*) prematuro(-a); (*quick: reply*) veloce; **at an ~ hour** di buon'ora; **to have an ~ night** andare a letto presto; **in the ~** *or* **~ in the spring/19th century** all'inizio della primavera/dell'Ottocento; **early retirement** *n* ritiro anticipato
earmark ['ɪəmɑːk] *vt*: **to ~ sth for** destinare qc a
earn [əːn] *vt* guadagnare; (*rest, reward*) meritare
earnest ['əːnɪst] *adj* serio(-a); **in ~** sul serio
earnings ['əːnɪŋz] *npl* guadagni *mpl*; (*salary*) stipendio
ear: **earphones** ['ɪəfəunz] *npl* cuffia; **earplugs** *npl* tappi *mpl* per le orecchie; **earring** ['ɪərɪŋ] *n* orecchino
earth [əːθ] *n* terra ▷ *vt* (BRIT *Elec*) mettere a terra; **earthquake** *n* terremoto
ease [iːz] *n* agio, comodo ▷ *vt* (*soothe*) calmare; (*loosen*) allentare; **to ~ sth out/in** tirare fuori/infilare qc con delicatezza; facilitare l'uscita/l'entrata di qc; **at ~** a proprio agio; (*Mil*) a riposo
easily ['iːzɪlɪ] *adv* facilmente
east [iːst] *n* est *m* ▷ *adj* dell'est ▷ *adv* a oriente; **the E~** l'Oriente *m*; (*Pol*) l'Est; **eastbound** ['iːstbaʊnd] *adj* (*traffic*) diretto(-a) a est; (*carriageway*) che porta a est
Easter ['iːstəʳ] *n* Pasqua; **Easter egg** *n* uovo di Pasqua
eastern ['iːstən] *adj* orientale, d'oriente; dell'est
Easter Sunday *n* domenica di Pasqua
easy ['iːzɪ] *adj* facile; (*manner*) disinvolto(-a) ▷ *adv* **to take it** *or* **things ~** prendersela con calma; **easy-going** *adj* accomodante
eat [iːt] (*pt* **ate**, *pp* **eaten**) *vt, vi* mangiare; **can we have something to ~?** possiamo mangiare qualcosa?; **eat out** *vi* mangiare fuori

eavesdrop ['iːvzdrɔp] *vi* **to ~ (on a conversation)** origliare (una conversazione)
e-book ['iːbuk] *n* libro elettronico
e-business ['iːbɪznɪs] *n* (*company*) azienda che opera in Internet; (*commerce*) commercio elettronico
EC *n abbr* (= *European Community*) CE *f*
eccentric [ɪk'sɛntrɪk] *adj*, *n* eccentrico(-a)
echo ['ɛkəu] (*pl* **echoes**) *n* eco *m or f* ▷ *vt* ripetere; fare eco a ▷ *vi* echeggiare; dare un eco
eclipse [ɪ'klɪps] *n* eclissi *f inv*
eco-friendly [iːkəu'frɛndlɪ] *adj* ecologico(-a)
ecological [iːkə'lɔdʒɪkəl] *adj* ecologico(-a)
ecology [ɪ'kɔlədʒɪ] *n* ecologia
e-commerce [iːkɔməːs] *n* commercio elettronico
economic [iːkə'nɔmɪk] *adj* economico(-a); **economical** *adj* economico(-a); (*person*) economo(-a); **economics** *n* economia ▷ *npl* lato finanziario
economist [ɪ'kɔnəmɪst] *n* economista *m/f*
economize [ɪ'kɔnəmaɪz] *vi* risparmiare, fare economia
economy [ɪ'kɔnəmɪ] *n* economia; **economy class** *n* (*Aviat*) classe *f* turistica; **economy class syndrome** *n* sindrome *f* della classe economica
ecstasy ['ɛkstəsɪ] *n* estasi *f inv*; **ecstatic** [ɛks'tætɪk] *adj* estatico(-a), in estasi
eczema ['ɛksɪmə] *n* eczema *m*
edge [ɛdʒ] *n* margine *m*; (*of table, plate, cup*) orlo; (*of knife etc*) taglio ▷ *vt* bordare; **on ~** (*fig*) = **edgy**; **to edge away from** sgattaiolare da
edgy ['ɛdʒɪ] *adj* nervoso(-a)
edible ['ɛdɪbl] *adj* commestibile; (*meal*) mangiabile
Edinburgh ['ɛdɪnbərə] *n* Edimburgo *f*
edit ['ɛdɪt] *vt* curare; **edition** [ɪ'dɪʃən] *n* edizione *f*; **editor** *n* (*in newspaper*) redattore(-trice), redattore(-trice) capo; (*of sb's work*) curatore(-trice); **editorial** [-'tɔːrɪəl] *adj* redazionale, editoriale ▷ *n* editoriale *m*

> Be careful not to translate ***editor*** by the Italian word ***editore***.

educate ['ɛdjukeɪt] *vt* istruire; educare; **educated** *adj* istruito(-a)
education [ɛdju'keɪʃən] *n* educazione *f*; (*schooling*) istruzione *f*; **educational** *adj* pedagogico(-a); scolastico(-a); istruttivo(-a)
eel [iːl] *n* anguilla
eerie ['ɪərɪ] *adj* che fa accapponare la pelle
effect [ɪ'fɛkt] *n* effetto ▷ *vt* effettuare; **to take ~** (*law*) entrare in vigore; (*drug*) fare effetto; **in ~** effettivamente; **effects** *npl* (*Theat*) effetti *mpl* scenici; (*property*) effetti *mpl*; **effective** *adj* efficace; (*actual*) effettivo(-a); **effectively** *adv* efficacemente; effettivamente
efficiency [ɪ'fɪʃənsɪ] *n* efficienza; rendimento effettivo
efficient [ɪ'fɪʃənt] *adj* efficiente; **efficiently** *adv* efficientemente; efficacemente
effort ['ɛfət] *n* sforzo; **effortless** *adj* senza sforzo, facile
e.g. *adv abbr* (= *exempli gratia*) per esempio, p.es.
egg [ɛg] *n* uovo; **hard-boiled/soft-boiled ~** uovo sodo/alla coque; **eggcup** *n* portauovo *m inv*; **eggplant** (*esp US*) *n* melanzana; **eggshell** *n* guscio d'uovo; **egg white** *n* albume *m*, bianco d'uovo; **egg yolk** *n* tuorlo, rosso (d'uovo)
ego ['iːgəu] *n* ego *m inv*
Egypt ['iːdʒɪpt] *n* Egitto; **Egyptian** [ɪ'dʒɪpʃən] *adj*, *n* egiziano(-a)
eight [eɪt] *num* otto; **eighteen** *num* diciotto; **eighteenth** *num* diciottesimo(-a); **eighth** [eɪtθ] *num* ottavo(-a); **eightieth** ['eɪtɪɪθ] *num*

ottantesimo(-a); **eighty** *num* ottanta

Eire ['ɛərə] *n* Repubblica d'Irlanda

either ['aɪðəʳ] *adj* l'uno(-a) o l'altro(-a); (*both, each*) ciascuno(-a) ▷ *pron* **~ (of them)** (o) l'uno(-a) o l'altro(-a) ▷ *adv* neanche ▷ *conj* **~ good or bad** o buono o cattivo; **on ~ side** su ciascun lato; **I don't like ~** non mi piace né l'uno né l'altro; **no, I don't ~** no, neanch'io

eject [ɪ'dʒɛkt] *vt* espellere; lanciare

elaborate [*adj* ɪ'læbərɪt, *vb* ɪ'læbəreɪt] *adj* elaborato(-a), minuzioso(-a) ▷ *vt* elaborare ▷ *vi* fornire i particolari

elastic [ɪ'læstɪk] *adj* elastico(-a) ▷ *n* elastico; **elastic band** (BRIT) *n* elastico

elbow ['ɛlbəu] *n* gomito

elder ['ɛldəʳ] *adj* maggiore, più vecchio(-a) ▷ *n* (*tree*) sambuco; **one's ~s** i più anziani; **elderly** *adj* anziano(-a) ▷ *npl* **the elderly** gli anziani

eldest ['ɛldɪst] *adj, n* **the ~ (child)** il(la) maggiore (dei bambini)

elect [ɪ'lɛkt] *vt* eleggere ▷ *adj* **the president ~** il presidente designato; **to ~ to do** decidere di fare; **election** [ɪ'lɛkʃən] *n* elezione *f*; **electoral** [ɪ'lɛktərəl] *adj* elettorale; **electorate** *n* elettorato

electric [ɪ'lɛktrɪk] *adj* elettrico(-a); **electrical** *adj* elettrico(-a); **electric blanket** *n* coperta elettrica; **electric fire** *n* stufa elettrica; **electrician** [ɪlɛk'trɪʃən] *n* elettricista *m*; **electricity** [ɪlɛk'trɪsɪtɪ] *n* elettricità; **electric shock** *n* scossa (elettrica); **electrify** [ɪ'lɛktrɪfaɪ] *vt* (*Rail*) elettrificare; (*audience*) elettrizzare

electronic [ɪlɛk'trɔnɪk] *adj* elettronico(-a); **electronic mail** *n* posta elettronica; **electronics** *n* elettronica

elegance ['ɛlɪgəns] *n* eleganza

elegant ['ɛlɪgənt] *adj* elegante

element ['ɛlɪmənt] *n* elemento; (*of heater, kettle etc*) resistenza

elementary [ɛlɪ'mɛntərɪ] *adj* elementare; **elementary school** (US) *n* scuola elementare

elephant ['ɛlɪfənt] *n* elefante(-essa)

elevate ['ɛlɪveɪt] *vt* elevare

elevator ['ɛlɪveɪtəʳ] *n* elevatore *m*; (US: *lift*) ascensore *m*

eleven [ɪ'lɛvn] *num* undici; **eleventh** *adj* undicesimo(-a)

eligible ['ɛlɪdʒəbl] *adj* eleggibile; (*for membership*) che ha i requisiti

eliminate [ɪ'lɪmɪneɪt] *vt* eliminare

elm [ɛlm] *n* olmo

eloquent ['ɛləkwənt] *adj* eloquente

else [ɛls] *adv* altro; **something ~** qualcos'altro; **somewhere ~** altrove; **everywhere ~** in qualsiasi altro luogo; **nobody ~** nessun altro; **where ~?** in quale altro luogo?; **little ~** poco altro; **elsewhere** *adv* altrove

elusive [ɪ'lu:sɪv] *adj* elusivo(-a)

e-mail ['i:meɪl] *n abbr* (= *electronic mail*) posta elettronica ▷ *vt* mandare un messaggio di posta elettronica a; **e-mail address** *n* indirizzo di posta elettronica

embankment [ɪm'bæŋkmənt] *n* (*of road, railway*) terrapieno

embargo [ɪm'bɑ:gəu] *n* (*pl* **embargoes**) (*Comm, Naut*) embargo ▷ *vt* mettere l'embargo su; **to put an ~ on sth** mettere l'embargo su qc

embark [ɪm'bɑ:k] *vi* **to ~ (on)** imbarcarsi (su) ▷ *vt* imbarcare; **to ~ on** (*fig*) imbarcarsi in

embarrass [ɪm'bærəs] *vt* imbarazzare; **embarrassed** *adj* imbarazzato(-a); **embarrassing** *adj* imbarazzante; **embarrassment** *n* imbarazzo

embassy ['ɛmbəsɪ] *n* ambasciata

embrace [ɪm'breɪs] *vt* abbracciare ▷ *vi* abbracciarsi ▷ *n* abbraccio

embroider [ɪm'brɔɪdəʳ] *vt* ricamare; **embroidery** *n* ricamo

embryo ['ɛmbrɪəu] *n* embrione *m*

emerald ['ɛmərəld] *n* smeraldo
emerge [ɪ'mə:dʒ] *vi* emergere
emergency [ɪ'mə:dʒənsɪ] *n* emergenza; **in an ~** in caso di emergenza; **emergency brake** (*US*) *n* freno a mano; **emergency exit** *n* uscita di sicurezza; **emergency landing** *n* atterraggio forzato; **emergency room** (*US*: *Med*) *n* pronto soccorso; **emergency services** *npl* (*fire, police, ambulance*) servizi *mpl* di pronto intervento
emigrate ['ɛmɪgreɪt] *vi* emigrare; **emigration** [ɛmɪ'greɪʃən] *n* emigrazione *f*
eminent ['ɛmɪnənt] *adj* eminente
emissions [ɪ'mɪʃənz] *npl* emissioni *fpl*
emit [ɪ'mɪt] *vt* emettere
emotion [ɪ'məuʃən] *n* emozione *f*; **emotional** *adj* (*person*) emotivo(-a); (*scene*) commovente; (*tone, speech*) carico(-a) d'emozione
emperor ['ɛmpərə^r] *n* imperatore *m*
emphasis ['ɛmfəsɪs] (*pl* **-ases**) *n* enfasi *f inv*; importanza
emphasize ['ɛmfəsaɪz] *vt* (*word, point*) sottolineare; (*feature*) mettere in evidenza
empire ['ɛmpaɪə^r] *n* impero
employ [ɪm'plɔɪ] *vt* impiegare; **employee** [-'i:] *n* impiegato(-a); **employer** *n* principale *m/f*, datore *m* di lavoro; **employment** *n* impiego; **employment agency** *n* agenzia di collocamento
empower [ɪm'pauə^r] *vt* **to ~ sb to do** concedere autorità a qn di fare
empress ['ɛmprɪs] *n* imperatrice *f*
emptiness ['ɛmptɪnɪs] *n* vuoto
empty ['ɛmptɪ] *adj* vuoto(-a); (*threat, promise*) vano(-a) ▷ *vt* vuotare ▷ *vi* vuotarsi; (*liquid*) scaricarsi; **empty-handed** *adj* a mani vuote
EMU *n abbr* (= *economic and monetary union*) unione *f* economica e monetaria
emulsion [ɪ'mʌlʃən] *n* emulsione *f*
enable [ɪ'neɪbl] *vt* **to ~ sb to do** permettere a qn di fare
enamel [ɪ'næməl] *n* smalto; (*also*: **~ paint**) vernice *f* a smalto
enchanting [ɪn'tʃɑ:ntɪŋ] *adj* incantevole, affascinante
encl. *abbr* (= *enclosed*) all.
enclose [ɪn'kləuz] *vt* (*land*) circondare, recingere; (*letter etc*): **to ~ (with)** allegare (con); **please find ~d** trovi qui accluso
enclosure [ɪn'kləuʒə^r] *n* recinto
encore [ɔŋ'kɔ:^r] *excl* bis ▷ *n* bis *m inv*
encounter [ɪn'kauntə^r] *n* incontro ▷ *vt* incontrare
encourage [ɪn'kʌrɪdʒ] *vt* incoraggiare; **encouragement** *n* incoraggiamento
encouraging [ɪn'kʌrɪdʒɪŋ] *adj* incoraggiante
encyclop(a)edia [ɛnsaɪkləu'pi:dɪə] *n* enciclopedia
end [ɛnd] *n* fine *f*; (*aim*) fine *m*; (*of table*) bordo estremo; (*of pointed object*) punta ▷ *vt* finire; (*also*: **bring to an ~, put an ~ to**) mettere fine a ▷ *vi* finire; **in the ~** alla fine; **on ~** (*object*) ritto(-a); **to stand on ~** (*hair*) rizzarsi; **for hours on ~** per ore ed ore; **end up** *vi* **to end up in** finire in
endanger [ɪn'deɪndʒə^r] *vt* mettere in pericolo
endearing [ɪn'dɪərɪŋ] *adj* accattivante
endeavour [ɪn'dɛvə^r] (*US* **endeavor**) *n* sforzo, tentativo ▷ *vi* **to ~ to do** cercare *or* sforzarsi di fare
ending ['ɛndɪŋ] *n* fine *f*, conclusione *f*; (*Ling*) desinenza
endless ['ɛndlɪs] *adj* senza fine
endorse [ɪn'dɔ:s] *vt* (*cheque*) girare; (*approve*) approvare, appoggiare; **endorsement** *n* approvazione *f*; (*on driving licence*) *contravvenzione registrata sulla patente*
endurance [ɪn'djuərəns] *n* resistenza; pazienza

endure [ɪn'djuəʳ] *vt* sopportare, resistere a ▷ *vi* durare
enemy ['ɛnəmɪ] *adj, n* nemico(-a)
energetic [ɛnə'dʒɛtɪk] *adj* energico(-a), attivo(-a)
energy ['ɛnədʒɪ] *n* energia
enforce [ɪn'fɔːs] *vt* (*Law*) applicare, far osservare
engaged [ɪn'geɪdʒd] *adj* (BRIT: *busy, in use*) occupato(-a); (*betrothed*) fidanzato(-a); **the line's ~** la linea è occupata; **to get ~** fidanzarsi; **engaged tone** (BRIT) *n* (*Tel*) segnale *m* di occupato
engagement [ɪn'geɪdʒmənt] *n* impegno, obbligo; appuntamento; (*to marry*) fidanzamento; **engagement ring** *n* anello di fidanzamento
engaging [ɪn'geɪdʒɪŋ] *adj* attraente
engine ['ɛndʒɪn] *n* (*Aut*) motore *m*; (*Rail*) locomotiva
engineer [ɛndʒɪ'nɪəʳ] *n* ingegnere *m*; (BRIT: *for repairs*) tecnico; (*on ship*: US: *Rail*) macchinista *m*; **engineering** *n* ingegneria
England ['ɪŋglənd] *n* Inghilterra
English ['ɪŋglɪʃ] *adj* inglese ▷ *n* (*Ling*) inglese *m*; **the English** *npl* gli Inglesi; **English Channel** *n*: **the English Channel** la Manica; **Englishman** (*irreg*) *n* inglese *m*; **Englishwoman** (*irreg*) *n* inglese *f*
engrave [ɪn'greɪv] *vt* incidere
engraving [ɪn'greɪvɪŋ] *n* incisione *f*
enhance [ɪn'hɑːns] *vt* accrescere
enjoy [ɪn'dʒɔɪ] *vt* godere; (*have*: *success, fortune*) avere; **to ~ o.s.** godersela, divertirsi; **enjoyable** *adj* piacevole; **enjoyment** *n* piacere *m*, godimento
enlarge [ɪn'lɑːdʒ] *vt* ingrandire ▷ *vi* **to ~ on** (*subject*) dilungarsi su; **enlargement** *n* (*Phot*) ingrandimento
enlist [ɪn'lɪst] *vt* arruolare; (*support*) procurare ▷ *vi* arruolarsi
enormous [ɪ'nɔːməs] *adj* enorme
enough [ɪ'nʌf] *adj, n* **~ time/books** assai tempo/libri; **have you got ~?** ne ha abbastanza *or* a sufficienza? ▷ *adv* **big ~** abbastanza grande; **he has not worked ~** non ha lavorato abbastanza; **~!** basta!; **that's ~, thanks** basta così, grazie; **I've had ~ of him** ne ho abbastanza di lui; **... which, funnily** *or* **oddly ~** ... che, strano a dirsi
enquire [ɪn'kwaɪəʳ] *vt, vi* (*esp* BRIT) = **inquire**
enquiry [ɪn'kwaɪərɪ] *n* (*esp* BRIT) = **inquiry**
enrage [ɪn'reɪdʒ] *vt* fare arrabbiare
enrich [ɪn'rɪtʃ] *vt* arricchire
enrol [ɪn'rəul] (US **enroll**) *vt* iscrivere ▷ *vi* iscriversi; **enrolment** (US **enrollment**) *n* iscrizione *f*
en route [ɔn'ruːt] *adv* **~ for/from/to** in viaggio per/da/a
en suite [ɔn'swiːt] *adj* **room with ~ bathroom** camera con bagno
ensure [ɪn'ʃuəʳ] *vt* assicurare; garantire
entail [ɪn'teɪl] *vt* comportare
enter ['ɛntəʳ] *vt* entrare in; (*army*) arruolarsi in; (*competition*) partecipare a; (*sb for a competition*) iscrivere; (*write down*) registrare; (*Comput*) inserire ▷ *vi* entrare
enterprise ['ɛntəpraɪz] *n* (*undertaking, company*) impresa; (*spirit*) iniziativa; **free ~** liberalismo economico; **private ~** iniziativa privata; **enterprising** ['ɛntəpraɪzɪŋ] *adj* intraprendente
entertain [ɛntə'teɪn] *vt* divertire; (*invite*) ricevere; (*idea, plan*) nutrire; **entertainer** *n* comico(-a); **entertaining** *adj* divertente; **entertainment** *n* (*amusement*) divertimento; (*show*) spettacolo
enthusiasm [ɪn'θuːzɪæzəm] *n* entusiasmo
enthusiast [ɪn'θuːzɪæst] *n* entusiasta *m/f*; **enthusiastic** [-'æstɪk]

adj entusiasta, entusiastico(-a); **to be enthusiastic about sth/sb** essere appassionato(-a) di qc/entusiasta di qn

entire [ɪn'taɪəʳ] *adj* intero(-a); **entirely** *adv* completamente, interamente

entitle [ɪn'taɪtl] *vt* (*give right*): **to ~ sb to sth/to do** dare diritto a qn a qc/a fare; **entitled** *adj* (*book*) che si intitola; **to be entitled to do** avere il diritto di fare

entrance [*n* 'ɛntrns, *vb* ɪn'trɑːns] *n* entrata, ingresso; (*of person*) entrata ▷ *vt* incantare, rapire; **where's the ~?** dov'è l'entrata?; **to gain ~ to** (*university etc*) essere ammesso a; **entrance examination** *n* esame *m* di ammissione; **entrance fee** *n* tassa d'iscrizione; (*to museum etc*) prezzo d'ingresso; **entrance ramp** (*US*) *n* (*Aut*) rampa di accesso; **entrant** ['ɛntrnt] *n* partecipante *m/f*; concorrente *m/f*

entrepreneur [ɔntrəprə'nəːʳ] *n* imprenditore *m*

entrust [ɪn'trʌst] *vt* **to ~ sth to** affidare qc a

entry ['ɛntrɪ] *n* entrata; (*way in*) entrata, ingresso; (*item: on list*) iscrizione *f*; (*in dictionary*) voce *f*; **no ~** vietato l'ingresso; (*Aut*) divieto di accesso; **entry phone** *n* citofono

envelope ['ɛnvələup] *n* busta

envious ['ɛnvɪəs] *adj* invidioso(-a)

environment [ɪn'vaɪərnmənt] *n* ambiente *m*; **environmental** [-'mɛntl] *adj* ecologico(-a); ambientale; **environmentally** [ɪnvaɪərən'mɛntəlɪ] *adv* **environmentally sound/friendly** che rispetta l'ambiente

envisage [ɪn'vɪzɪdʒ] *vt* immaginare; prevedere

envoy ['ɛnvɔɪ] *n* inviato(-a)

envy ['ɛnvɪ] *n* invidia ▷ *vt* invidiare; **to ~ sb sth** invidiare qn per qc

epic ['ɛpɪk] *n* poema *m* epico ▷ *adj* epico(-a)

epidemic [ɛpɪ'dɛmɪk] *n* epidemia

epilepsy ['ɛpɪlɛpsɪ] *n* epilessia

epileptic [ɛpɪ'lɛptɪk] *adj, n* epilettico(-a); **epileptic fit** *n* attacco epilettico

episode ['ɛpɪsəud] *n* episodio

equal ['iːkwl] *adj* uguale ▷ *n* pari *m/f inv* ▷ *vt* uguagliare; **~ to** (*task*) all'altezza di; **equality** [iː'kwɔlɪtɪ] *n* uguaglianza; **equalize** *vi* pareggiare; **equally** *adv* ugualmente

equation [ɪ'kweɪʃən] *n* (*Math*) equazione *f*

equator [ɪ'kweɪtəʳ] *n* equatore *m*

equip [ɪ'kwɪp] *vt* equipaggiare, attrezzare; **to ~ sb/sth with** fornire qn/qc di; **to be well ~ped** (*office etc*) essere ben attrezzato(-a); **he is well ~ped for the job** ha i requisiti necessari per quel lavoro; **equipment** *n* attrezzatura; (*electrical etc*) apparecchiatura

equivalent [ɪ'kwɪvəlnt] *adj* equivalente ▷ *n* equivalente *m*; **to be ~ to** equivalere a

ER *abbr* (BRIT) = **Elizabeth Regina** (*US: Med*) = **emergency room**

era ['ɪərə] *n* era, età *f inv*

erase [ɪ'reɪz] *vt* cancellare; **eraser** *n* gomma

erect [ɪ'rɛkt] *adj* eretto(-a) ▷ *vt* costruire; (*assemble*) montare; **erection** [ɪ'rɛkʃən] *n* costruzione *f*; montaggio; (*Physiol*) erezione *f*

ERM *n* (= *Exchange Rate Mechanism*) ERM *m*

erode [ɪ'rəud] *vt* erodere; (*metal*) corrodere

erosion [ɪ'rəuʒən] *n* erosione *f*

erotic [ɪ'rɔtɪk] *adj* erotico(-a)

errand ['ɛrnd] *n* commissione *f*

erratic [ɪ'rætɪk] *adj* imprevedibile; (*person, mood*) incostante

error ['ɛrəʳ] *n* errore *m*

erupt [ɪ'rʌpt] *vi* (*volcano*) mettersi

(*or* essere) in eruzione; (*war, crisis*) scoppiare; **eruption** [ɪ'rʌpʃən] *n* eruzione *f*; scoppio
escalate ['ɛskəleɪt] *vi* intensificarsi
escalator ['ɛskəleɪtə^r] *n* scala mobile
escape [ɪ'skeɪp] *n* evasione *f*; fuga; (*of gas etc*) fuga, fuoriuscita ▷ *vi* fuggire; (*from jail*) evadere, scappare; (*leak*) uscire ▷ *vt* sfuggire a; **to ~ from** (*place*) fuggire da; (*person*) sfuggire a
escort [*n* 'ɛskɔːt, *vb* ɪ'skɔːt] *n* scorta; (*male companion*) cavaliere *m* ▷ *vt* scortare; accompagnare
especially [ɪ'spɛʃlɪ] *adv* specialmente; soprattutto; espressamente
espionage ['ɛspɪənɑːʒ] *n* spionaggio
essay ['ɛseɪ] *n* (*Scol*) composizione *f*; (*Literature*) saggio
essence ['ɛsns] *n* essenza
essential [ɪ'sɛnʃl] *adj* essenziale ▷ *n* elemento essenziale; **essentially** *adv* essenzialmente; **essentials** *npl* **the essentials** l'essenziale *msg*
establish [ɪ'stæblɪʃ] *vt* stabilire; (*business*) mettere su; (*one's power etc*) affermare; **establishment** *n* stabilimento; **the Establishment** la classe dirigente, l'establishment *m*
estate [ɪ'steɪt] *n* proprietà *f inv*; beni *mpl*, patrimonio; (BRIT: *also:* **housing ~**) complesso edilizio; **estate agent** (BRIT) *n* agente *m* immobiliare; **estate car** (BRIT) *n* giardiniera
estimate [*n* 'ɛstɪmət, *vb* 'ɛstɪmeɪt] *n* stima; (*Comm*) preventivo ▷ *vt* stimare, valutare
etc *abbr* (= *et cetera*) etc., ecc.
eternal [ɪ'təːnl] *adj* eterno(-a)
eternity [ɪ'təːnɪtɪ] *n* eternità
ethical ['ɛθɪkl] *adj* etico(-a), morale; **ethics** ['ɛθɪks] *n* etica ▷ *npl* morale *f*
Ethiopia [iːθɪ'əupɪə] *n* Etiopia
ethnic ['ɛθnɪk] *adj* etnico(-a); **ethnic minority** *n* minoranza etnica
e-ticket ['iːtɪkɪt] *n* biglietto elettronico
etiquette ['ɛtɪkɛt] *n* etichetta
EU *n abbr* (= *European Union*) UE *f*
euro ['juərəu] *n* (*currency*) euro *m inv*
Europe ['juərəp] *n* Europa; **European** [-'piːən] *adj, n* europeo(-a); **European Community** *n* Comunità Europea; **European Union** *n* Unione *f* europea
Eurostar® ['juərəustɑː^r] *n* Eurostar® *m inv*
evacuate [ɪ'vækjueɪt] *vt* evacuare
evade [ɪ'veɪd] *vt* (*tax*) evadere; (*duties etc*) sottrarsi a; (*person*) schivare
evaluate [ɪ'væljueɪt] *vt* valutare
evaporate [ɪ'væpəreɪt] *vi* evaporare
eve [iːv] *n*: **on the ~ of** alla vigilia di
even ['iːvn] *adj* regolare; (*number*) pari *inv* ▷ *adv* anche, perfino; **~ if, ~ though** anche se; **~ more** ancora di più; **~ so** ciò nonostante; **not ~** nemmeno; **to get ~ with sb** dare la pari a qn
evening ['iːvnɪŋ] *n* sera; (*as duration, event*) serata; **in the ~** la sera; **evening class** *n* corso serale; **evening dress** *n* (*woman's*) abito da sera; **in evening dress** (*man*) in abito scuro; (*woman*) in abito lungo
event [ɪ'vɛnt] *n* avvenimento; (*Sport*) gara; **in the ~ of** in caso di; **eventful** *adj* denso(-a) di eventi
eventual [ɪ'vɛntʃuəl] *adj* finale

> Be careful not to translate *eventual* by the Italian word *eventuale*.

eventually [ɪ'vɛntʃuəlɪ] *adv* alla fine

> Be careful not to translate *eventually* by the Italian word *eventualmente*.

ever ['ɛvə^r] *adv* mai; (*at all times*) sempre; **the best ~** il migliore che ci sia mai stato; **have you ~ seen it?** l'ha mai visto?; **~ since** *adv* da allora ▷ *conj* sin da quando; **~ so pretty** così bello(-a); **evergreen** *n* sempreverde *m*
every ['ɛvrɪ] *adj* ogni; **~ day** tutti i giorni, ogni giorno; **~ other/third day** ogni due/tre giorni; **~ other car** una

macchina su due; **~ now and then** ogni tanto, di quando in quando; **everybody** *pron* = **everyone**; **everyday** *adj* quotidiano(-a); di ogni giorno; **everyone** *pron* ognuno, tutti *pl*; **everything** *pron* tutto, ogni cosa; **everywhere** *adv* (*gen*) dappertutto; (*wherever*) ovunque

evict [ɪ'vɪkt] *vt* sfrattare

evidence ['ɛvɪdns] *n* (*proof*) prova; (*of witness*) testimonianza; (*sign*): **to show ~ of** dare segni di; **to give ~** deporre

evident ['ɛvɪdnt] *adj* evidente; **evidently** *adv* evidentemente

evil ['i:vl] *adj* cattivo(-a), maligno(-a) ▷ *n* male *m*

evoke [ɪ'vəuk] *vt* evocare

evolution [i:və'lu:ʃən] *n* evoluzione *f*

evolve [ɪ'vɔlv] *vt* elaborare ▷ *vi* svilupparsi, evolversi

ewe [ju:] *n* pecora

ex (*inf*) [eks] *n*: **my ex** il (la) mio(-a) ex

ex- [ɛks] *prefix* ex

exact [ɪg'zækt] *adj* esatto(-a) ▷ *vt*: **to ~ sth (from)** estorcere qc (da); esigere qc (da); **exactly** *adv* esattamente

exaggerate [ɪg'zædʒəreɪt] *vt, vi* esagerare; **exaggeration** [-'reɪʃən] *n* esagerazione *f*

exam [ɪg'zæm] *n abbr* (*Scol*) = **examination**

examination [ɪgzæmɪ'neɪʃən] *n* (*Scol*) esame *m*; (*Med*) controllo

examine [ɪg'zæmɪn] *vt* esaminare; **examiner** *n* esaminatore(-trice)

example [ɪg'zɑ:mpl] *n* esempio; **for ~** ad *or* per esempio

exasperated [ɪg'zɑ:spəreɪtɪd] *adj* esasperato(-a)

excavate ['ɛkskəveɪt] *vt* scavare

exceed [ɪk'si:d] *vt* superare; (*one's powers, time limit*) oltrepassare; **exceedingly** *adv* eccessivamente

excel [ɪk'sɛl] *vi* eccellere ▷ *vt* sorpassare; **to ~ o.s** (BRIT) superare se stesso

excellence ['ɛksələns] *n* eccellenza

excellent ['ɛksələnt] *adj* eccellente

except [ɪk'sɛpt] *prep* (*also:* **~ for, ~ing**) salvo, all'infuori di, eccetto ▷ *vt* escludere; **~ if/when** salvo se/quando; **~ that** salvo che; **exception** [ɪk'sɛpʃən] *n* eccezione *f*; **to take exception to** trovare a ridire su; **exceptional** [ɪk'sɛpʃənl] *adj* eccezionale; **exceptionally** [ɪk'sepʃənəlɪ] *adv* eccezionalmente

excerpt ['ɛksə:pt] *n* estratto

excess [ɪk'sɛs] *n* eccesso; **excess baggage** *n* bagaglio in eccedenza; **excessive** *adj* eccessivo(-a)

exchange [ɪks'tʃeɪndʒ] *n* scambio; (*also:* **telephone ~**) centralino ▷ *vt*: **to ~ (for)** scambiare (con); **could I ~ this, please?** posso cambiarlo, per favore?; **exchange rate** *n* tasso di cambio

excite [ɪk'saɪt] *vt* eccitare; **to get ~d** eccitarsi; **excited** *adj*: **to get excited** essere elettrizzato(-a); **excitement** *n* eccitazione *f*; agitazione *f*; **exciting** *adj* avventuroso(-a); (*film, book*) appassionante

exclaim [ɪk'skleɪm] *vi* esclamare; **exclamation** [ɛksklə'meɪʃən] *n* esclamazione *f*; **exclamation mark** (US **exclamation point**) *n* punto esclamativo

exclude [ɪk'sklu:d] *vt* escludere

excluding [ɪk'sklu:dɪŋ] *prep* **~ VAT** IVA esclusa

exclusion [ɪk'sklu:ʒən] *n* esclusione *f*; **to the ~ of** escludendo

exclusive [ɪk'sklu:sɪv] *adj* esclusivo(-a); **~ of VAT** I.V.A. esclusa; **exclusively** *adv* esclusivamente

excruciating [ɪk'skru:ʃɪeɪtɪŋ] *adj* straziante, atroce

excursion [ɪk'skə:ʃən] *n* escursione *f*, gita

excuse [*n* ɪk'skju:s, *vb* ɪk'skju:z] *n* scusa ▷ *vt* scusare; **to ~ sb from** (*activity*) dispensare qn da; **~ me!** mi scusi!; **now, if you will ~ me ...** ora, mi scusi ma ...

ex-directory ['ɛksdɪ'rɛktərɪ] (BRIT) *adj* (*Tel*): **to be ~** non essere sull'elenco

execute ['ɛksɪkju:t] *vt* (*prisoner*) giustiziare; (*plan etc*) eseguire; **execution** [ɛksɪ'kju:ʃən] *n* esecuzione *f*

executive [ɪg'zɛkjutɪv] *n* (*Comm*) dirigente *m*; (*Pol*) esecutivo ▷ *adj* esecutivo(-a)

exempt [ɪg'zɛmpt] *adj* esentato(-a) ▷ *vt* **to ~ sb from** esentare qn da

exercise ['ɛksəsaɪz] *n* (*keep fit*) moto; (*Scol, Mil etc*) esercizio ▷ *vt* esercitare; (*patience*) usare; (*dog*) portar fuori ▷ *vi* (*also:* **take ~**) fare del moto; **exercise book** *n* quaderno

exert [ɪg'zə:t] *vt* esercitare; **to ~ o.s.** sforzarsi; **exertion** [-ʃən] *n* sforzo

exhale [ɛks'heɪl] *vt, vi* espirare

exhaust [ɪg'zɔ:st] *n* (*also:* **~ fumes**) scappamento; (*also:* **~ pipe**) tubo di scappamento ▷ *vt* esaurire; **exhausted** *adj* esaurito(-a); **exhaustion** [ɪg'zɔ:stʃən] *n* esaurimento; **nervous exhaustion** sovraffaticamento mentale

exhibit [ɪg'zɪbɪt] *n* (*Art*) oggetto esposto; (*Law*) documento *or* oggetto esibito ▷ *vt* esporre; (*courage, skill*) dimostrare; **exhibition** [ɛksɪ'bɪʃən] *n* mostra, esposizione *f*

exhilarating [ɪg'zɪləreɪtɪŋ] *adj* esilarante; stimolante

exile ['ɛksaɪl] *n* esilio; (*person*) esiliato(-a) ▷ *vt* esiliare

exist [ɪg'zɪst] *vi* esistere; **existence** *n* esistenza; **existing** *adj* esistente

exit ['ɛksɪt] *n* uscita ▷ *vi* (*Theatre, Comput*) uscire; **where's the ~?** dov'è l'uscita?; **exit ramp** (US) *n* (*Aut*) rampa di uscita

exotic [ɪg'zɔtɪk] *adj* esotico(-a)

expand [ɪk'spænd] *vt* espandere; estendere; allargare ▷ *vi* (*business, gas*) espandersi; (*metal*) dilatarsi

expansion [ɪk'spænʃən] *n* (*gen*) espansione *f*; (*of town, economy*) sviluppo; (*of metal*) dilatazione *f*

expect [ɪk'spɛkt] *vt* (*anticipate*) prevedere, aspettarsi, prevedere *or* aspettarsi che + *sub*; (*require*) richiedere, esigere; (*suppose*) supporre; (*await, also baby*) aspettare ▷ *vi* **to be ~ing** essere in stato interessante; **to ~ sb to do** aspettarsi che qn faccia; **expectation** [ɛkspɛk'teɪʃən] *n* aspettativa; speranza

expedition [ɛkspə'dɪʃən] *n* spedizione *f*

expel [ɪk'spɛl] *vt* espellere

expenditure [ɪk'spɛndɪtʃə^r] *n* spesa

expense [ɪk'spɛns] *n* spesa; (*high cost*) costo; **expenses** *npl* (*Comm*) spese *fpl*, indennità *fpl*; **at the ~ of** a spese di; **expense account** *n* conto *m* spese *inv*

expensive [ɪk'spɛnsɪv] *adj* caro(-a), costoso(-a); **it's too ~** è troppo caro

experience [ɪk'spɪərɪəns] *n* esperienza ▷ *vt* (*pleasure*) provare; (*hardship*) soffrire; **experienced** *adj* esperto(-a)

experiment [*n* ɪk'spɛrɪmənt, *vb* ɪk'spɛrɪmɛnt] *n* esperimento, esperienza ▷ *vi* **to ~ (with/on)** fare esperimenti (con/su); **experimental** [ɪkspɛrɪ'mɛntl] *adj* sperimentale; **at the experimental stage** in via di sperimentazione

expert ['ɛkspə:t] *adj, n* esperto(-a); **expertise** [-'ti:z] *n* competenza

expire [ɪk'spaɪə^r] *vi* (*period of time, licence*) scadere; **expiry** *n* scadenza; **expiry date** *n* (*of medicine, food item*) data di scadenza

explain [ɪk'spleɪn] *vt* spiegare; **explanation** [ɛksplə'neɪʃən] *n* spiegazione *f*

explicit [ɪk'splɪsɪt] *adj* esplicito(-a)

explode [ɪk'spləud] *vi* esplodere

exploit [*n* 'ɛksplɔɪt, *vb* ɪk'splɔɪt] *n* impresa ▷ *vt* sfruttare; **exploitation** [-'teɪʃən] *n* sfruttamento

explore [ɪk'splɔːʳ] *vt* esplorare; (*possibilities*) esaminare; **explorer** *n* esploratore(-trice)
explosion [ɪk'spləuʒən] *n* esplosione *f*; **explosive** [ɪk'spləusɪv] *adj* esplosivo(-a) ▷ *n* esplosivo
export [*vb* ɛk'spɔːt, *n* 'ɛkspɔːt] *vt* esportare ▷ *n* esportazione *f*; articolo di esportazione ▷ *cpd* d'esportazione; **exporter** *n* esportatore *m*
expose [ɪk'spəuz] *vt* esporre; (*unmask*) smascherare; **exposed** *adj* (*position*) esposto(-a); **exposure** [ɪk'spəuʒəʳ] *n* esposizione *f*; (*Phot*) posa; (*Med*) assideramento
express [ɪk'sprɛs] *adj* (*definite*) chiaro(-a), espresso(-a); (BRIT: *letter etc*) espresso *inv* ▷ *n* (*train*) espresso ▷ *vt* esprimere; **expression** [ɪk'sprɛʃən] *n* espressione *f*; **expressway** (US) *n* (*urban motorway*) autostrada che attraversa la città
exquisite [ɛk'skwɪzɪt] *adj* squisito(-a)
extend [ɪk'stɛnd] *vt* (*visit*) protrarre; (*road, deadline*) prolungare; (*building*) ampliare; (*offer*) offrire, porgere ▷ *vi* (*land, period*) estendersi; **extension** [ɪk'stɛnʃən] *n* (*of road, term*) prolungamento; (*of contract, deadline*) proroga; (*building*) annesso; (*to wire, table*) prolunga; (*telephone*) interno; (: *in private house*) apparecchio supplementare; **extension lead** *n* prolunga
extensive [ɪk'stɛnsɪv] *adj* esteso(-a), ampio(-a); (*damage*) su larga scala; (*coverage, discussion*) esauriente; (*use*) grande
extent [ɪk'stɛnt] *n* estensione *f*; **to some ~** fino a un certo punto; **to such an ~ that ...** a un tal punto che ...; **to what ~?** fino a che punto?; **to the ~ of ...** fino al punto di ...
exterior [ɛk'stɪərɪəʳ] *adj* esteriore, esterno(-a) ▷ *n* esteriore *m*, esterno; aspetto (esteriore)
external [ɛk'stəːnl] *adj* esterno(-a), esteriore
extinct [ɪk'stɪŋkt] *adj* estinto(-a); **extinction** [ɪk'stɪŋkʃən] *n* estinzione *f*
extinguish [ɪk'stɪŋgwɪʃ] *vt* estinguere
extra ['ɛkstrə] *adj* extra *inv*, supplementare ▷ *adv* (*in addition*) di più ▷ *n* extra *m inv*; (*surcharge*) supplemento; (*Cinema, Theatre*) comparsa
extract [*vb* ɪk'strækt, *n* 'ɛkstrækt] *vt* estrarre; (*money, promise*) strappare ▷ *n* estratto; (*passage*) brano
extradite ['ɛkstrədaɪt] *vt* estradare
extraordinary [ɪk'strɔːdnrɪ] *adj* straordinario(-a)
extravagance [ɪk'strævəgəns] *n* sperpero; stravaganza
extravagant [ɪk'strævəgənt] *adj* (*lavish*) prodigo(-a); (*wasteful*) dispendioso(-a)

> Be careful not to translate ***extravagant*** by the Italian word ***stravagante***.

extreme [ɪk'striːm] *adj* estremo(-a) ▷ *n* estremo; **extremely** *adv* estremamente
extremist [ɪk'striːmɪst] *adj, n* estremista (*m/f*)
extrovert ['ɛkstrəvəːt] *n* estroverso(-a)
eye [aɪ] *n* occhio; (*of needle*) cruna ▷ *vt* osservare; **to keep an ~ on** tenere d'occhio; **eyeball** *n* globo dell'occhio; **eyebrow** *n* sopracciglio; **eyedrops** *npl* gocce *fpl* oculari, collirio; **eyelash** *n* ciglio; **eyelid** *n* palpebra; **eyeliner** *n* eye-liner *m inv*; **eyeshadow** *n* ombretto; **eyesight** *n* vista; **eye witness** *n* testimone *m/f* oculare

f

F [ɛf] *n* (*Mus*) fa *m*
fabric ['fæbrɪk] *n* stoffa, tessuto
fabulous ['fæbjuləs] *adj* favoloso(-a); (*super*) favoloso(-a), fantastico(-a)
face [feɪs] *n* faccia, viso, volto; (*expression*) faccia; (*of clock*) quadrante *m*; (*of building*) facciata ▷ *vt* essere di fronte a; (*facts, situation*) affrontare; **~ down** a faccia in giù; **to make** *or* **pull a ~** fare una smorfia; **in the ~ of** (*difficulties etc*) di fronte a; **on the ~ of it** a prima vista; **~ to ~** faccia a faccia; **face up to** *vt fus* affrontare, far fronte a; **face cloth** (BRIT) *n* guanto di spugna; **face pack** *n* (BRIT) maschera di bellezza
facial ['feɪʃəl] *adj* del viso
facilitate [fə'sɪlɪteɪt] *vt* facilitare
facilities [fə'sɪlɪtɪz] *npl* attrezzature *fpl*; **credit ~** facilitazioni *fpl* di credito
fact [fækt] *n* fatto; **in ~** in effetti
faction ['fækʃən] *n* fazione *f*
factor ['fæktə^r] *n* fattore *m*; **I'd like a ~ 15 suntan lotion** vorrei una crema solare con fattore di protezione 15
factory ['fæktərɪ] *n* fabbrica, stabilimento

> Be careful not to translate ***factory*** by the Italian word ***fattoria***.

factual ['fæktjuəl] *adj* che si attiene ai fatti
faculty ['fækəltɪ] *n* facoltà *f inv*; (US) corpo insegnante
fad [fæd] *n* mania; capriccio
fade [feɪd] *vi* sbiadire, sbiadirsi; (*light, sound, hope*) attenuarsi, affievolirsi; (*flower*) appassire; **fade away** *vi* (*sound*) affievolirsi
fag [fæg] (BRIT: *inf*) *n* (*cigarette*) cicca
Fahrenheit ['fɑːrənhaɪt] *n* Fahrenheit *m inv*
fail [feɪl] *vt* (*exam*) non superare; (*candidate*) bocciare; (*courage, memory*) mancare a ▷ *vi* fallire; (*student*) essere respinto(-a); (*eyesight, health, light*) venire a mancare; **to ~ to do sth** (*neglect*) mancare di fare qc; (*be unable*) non riuscire a fare qc; **without ~** senza fallo; certamente; **failing** *n* difetto ▷ *prep* in mancanza di; **failure** ['feɪljə^r] *n* fallimento; (*person*) fallito(-a); (*mechanical etc*) guasto
faint [feɪnt] *adj* debole; (*recollection*) vago(-a); (*mark*) indistinto(-a) ▷ *n* (*Med*) svenimento ▷ *vi* svenire; **to feel ~** sentirsi svenire; **faintest** *adj*: **I haven't the faintest idea** non ho la più pallida idea; **faintly** *adv* debolmente; vagamente
fair [fɛə^r] *adj* (*person, decision*) giusto(-a), equo(-a); (*quite large, quite good*) discreto(-a); (*hair etc*) biondo(-a); (*skin, complexion*) chiaro(-a); (*weather*) bello(-a), clemente ▷ *adv* (*play*) lealmente ▷ *n* fiera; (BRIT: *funfair*) luna park *m inv*; **fairground** *n* luna park *m inv*; **fair-haired** [fɛə'hɛəd] *adj* (*person*) biondo(-a); **fairly** *adv* equamente; (*quite*) abbastanza; **fair trade** *n* commercio equo e solidale; **fairway** *n*

(*Golf*) fairway *m inv*
fairy ['fɛərɪ] *n* fata; **fairy tale** *n* fiaba
faith [feɪθ] *n* fede *f*; (*trust*) fiducia; (*sect*) religione *f*, fede *f*; **faithful** *adj* fedele; **faithfully** *adv* fedelmente; **yours faithfully** (BRIT: *in letters*) distinti saluti
fake [feɪk] *n* imitazione *f*; (*picture*) falso; (*person*) impostore(-a) ▷ *adj* falso(-a) ▷ *vt* (*accounts*) falsificare; (*illness*) fingere; (*painting*) contraffare
falcon ['fɔːlkən] *n* falco, falcone *m*
fall [fɔːl] (*pt* **fell**, *pp* **fallen**) *n* caduta; (*in temperature*) abbassamento; (*in price*) ribasso; (US: *autumn*) autunno ▷ *vi* cadere; (*temperature, price, night*) scendere; **falls** *npl* (*waterfall*) cascate *fpl*; **to ~ flat** (*on one's face*) cadere bocconi; (*joke*) fare cilecca; (*plan*) fallire; **fall apart** *vi* cadere a pezzi; **fall down** *vi* (*person*) cadere; (*building*) crollare; **fall for** *vt fus* (*person*) prendere una cotta per; **to fall for a trick (***or* **a story** *etc***)** cascarci; **fall off** *vi* cadere; (*diminish*) diminuire, abbassarsi; **fall out** *vi* (*hair, teeth*) cadere; (*friends etc*) litigare; **fall over** *vi* cadere; **fall through** *vi* (*plan, project*) fallire
fallen ['fɔːlən] *pp of* **fall**
fallout ['fɔːlaut] *n* fall-out *m*
false [fɔːls] *adj* falso(-a); **under ~ pretences** con l'inganno; **false alarm** *n* falso allarme *m*; **false teeth** (BRIT) *npl* denti *mpl* finti
fame [feɪm] *n* fama, celebrità
familiar [fə'mɪlɪəʳ] *adj* familiare; (*close*) intimo(-a); **to be ~ with** (*subject*) conoscere; **familiarize** [fə'mɪlɪəraɪz] *vt* **to familiarize o.s. with** familiarizzare con
family ['fæmɪlɪ] *n* famiglia; **family doctor** *n* medico di famiglia; **family planning** *n* pianificazione *f* familiare
famine ['fæmɪn] *n* carestia
famous ['feɪməs] *adj* famoso(-a)
fan [fæn] *n* (*folding*) ventaglio; (*Elec*) ventilatore *m*; (*person*) ammiratore(-trice), tifoso(-a) ▷ *vt* far vento a; (*fire, quarrel*) alimentare
fanatic [fə'nætɪk] *n* fanatico(-a)
fan belt *n* cinghia del ventilatore
fan club *n* fan club *m inv*
fancy ['fænsɪ] *n* immaginazione *f*, fantasia; (*whim*) capriccio ▷ *adj* (*hat*) stravagante; (*hotel, food*) speciale ▷ *vt* (*feel like, want*) aver voglia di; (*imagine, think*) immaginare; **to take a ~ to** incapricciarsi di; **he fancies her** (*inf*) gli piace; **fancy dress** *n* costume *m* (per maschera)
fan heater *n* (BRIT) stufa ad aria calda
fantasize ['fæntəsaɪz] *vi* fantasticare, sognare
fantastic [fæn'tæstɪk] *adj* fantastico(-a)
fantasy ['fæntəsɪ] *n* fantasia, immaginazione *f*; fantasticheria; chimera
fanzine ['fænziːn] *n* rivista specialistica (*per appassionati*)
FAQs *abbr* (= *frequently asked questions*) FAQ *fpl*
far [fɑːʳ] *adj* lontano(-a) ▷ *adv* lontano; (*much, greatly*) molto; **is it ~ from here?** è molto lontano da qui?; **how ~?** quanto lontano?; (*referring to activity etc*) fino a dove?; **how ~ is the town centre?** quanto dista il centro da qui?; **~ away, ~ off** lontano, distante; **~ better** assai migliore; **~ from** lontano da; **by ~** di gran lunga; **go as ~ as the farm** vada fino alla fattoria; **as ~ as I know** per quel che so
farce [fɑːs] *n* farsa
fare [fɛəʳ] *n* (*on trains, buses*) tariffa; (*in taxi*) prezzo della corsa; (*food*) vitto, cibo; **half ~** metà tariffa; **full ~** tariffa intera
Far East *n*: **the ~** l'Estremo Oriente *m*
farewell [fɛə'wɛl] *excl, n* addio
farm [fɑːm] *n* fattoria, podere *m* ▷ *vt* coltivare; **farmer** *n* coltivatore(-trice), agricoltore(-trice);

farmhouse *n* fattoria; **farming** *n* (*gen*) agricoltura; (*of crops*) coltivazione *f*; (*of animals*) allevamento; **farmyard** *n* aia
far-reaching [fɑːˈriːtʃɪŋ] *adj* di vasta portata
fart [fɑːt] (*inf!*) *vi* scoreggiare (*!*)
farther [ˈfɑːðəʳ] *adv* più lontano ▷ *adj* più lontano(-a)
farthest [ˈfɑːðɪst] *superl of* **far**
fascinate [ˈfæsɪneɪt] *vt* affascinare; **fascinated** *adj* affascinato(-a); **fascinating** *adj* affascinante; **fascination** [-ˈneɪʃən] *n* fascino
fascist [ˈfæʃɪst] *adj, n* fascista (*m/f*)
fashion [ˈfæʃən] *n* moda; (*manner*) maniera, modo ▷ *vt* foggiare, formare; **in ~** alla moda; **out of ~** passato(-a) di moda; **fashionable** *adj* alla moda, di moda; **fashion show** *n* sfilata di moda
fast [fɑːst] *adj* rapido(-a), svelto(-a), veloce; (*clock*): **to be ~** andare avanti; (*dye, colour*) solido(-a) ▷ *adv* rapidamente; (*stuck, held*) saldamente ▷ *n* digiuno ▷ *vi* digiunare; **~ asleep** profondamente addormentato
fasten [ˈfɑːsn] *vt* chiudere, fissare; (*coat*) abbottonare, allacciare ▷ *vi* chiudersi, fissarsi; abbottonarsi, allacciarsi
fast food *n* fast food *m*
fat [fæt] *adj* grasso(-a); (*book, profit etc*) grosso(-a) ▷ *n* grasso
fatal [ˈfeɪtl] *adj* fatale; mortale; disastroso(-a); **fatality** [fəˈtælɪtɪ] *n* (*road death etc*) morto(-a), vittima; **fatally** *adv* a morte
fate [feɪt] *n* destino; (*of person*) sorte *f*
father [ˈfɑːðəʳ] *n* padre *m*; **Father Christmas** *n* Babbo Natale; **father-in-law** *n* suocero
fatigue [fəˈtiːg] *n* stanchezza
fattening [ˈfætnɪŋ] *adj* (*food*) che fa ingrassare
fatty [ˈfætɪ] *adj* (*food*) grasso(-a) ▷ *n* (*inf*) ciccione(-a)
faucet [ˈfɔːsɪt] (*US*) *n* rubinetto
fault [fɔːlt] *n* colpa; (*Tennis*) fallo; (*defect*) difetto; (*Geo*) faglia ▷ *vt* criticare; **it's my ~** è colpa mia; **to find ~ with** trovare da ridire su; **at ~** in fallo; **faulty** *adj* difettoso(-a)
fauna [ˈfɔːnə] *n* fauna
favour *etc* [ˈfeɪvəʳ] (*US* **favor**) *n* favore *m* ▷ *vt* (*proposition*) favorire, essere favorevole a; (*pupil etc*) favorire; (*team, horse*) dare per vincente; **to do sb a ~** fare un favore *or* una cortesia a qn; **to find ~ with** (*person*) entrare nelle buone grazie di; (: *suggestion*) avere l'approvazione di; **in ~ of** in favore di; **favourable** *adj* favorevole; **favourite** [-rɪt] *adj, n* favorito(-a)
fawn [fɔːn] *n* daino ▷ *adj* (*also:* **~-coloured**) marrone chiaro *inv* ▷ *vi*: **to ~ (up)on** adulare servilmente
fax [fæks] *n* (*document*) facsimile *m inv*, telecopia; (*machine*) telecopiatrice *f* ▷ *vt* telecopiare, trasmettere in facsimile
FBI (*US*) *n abbr* (= *Federal Bureau of Investigation*) F.B.I. *f*
fear [fɪəʳ] *n* paura, timore *m* ▷ *vt* aver paura di, temere; **for ~ of** per paura di; **fearful** *adj* pauroso(-a); (*sight, noise*) terribile, spaventoso(-a); **fearless** *adj* intrepido(-a), senza paura
feasible [ˈfiːzəbl] *adj* possibile, realizzabile
feast [fiːst] *n* festa, banchetto; (*Rel*: *also:* **~ day**) festa ▷ *vi* banchettare
feat [fiːt] *n* impresa, fatto insigne
feather [ˈfɛðəʳ] *n* penna
feature [ˈfiːtʃəʳ] *n* caratteristica; (*Press, TV*) articolo ▷ *vt* (*film*) avere come protagonista ▷ *vi* figurare; **features** *npl* (*of face*) fisionomia; **feature film** *n* film *m inv* principale
Feb. [fɛb] *abbr* (= *February*) feb
February [ˈfɛbruərɪ] *n* febbraio
fed [fɛd] *pt, pp of* **feed**
federal [ˈfɛdərəl] *adj* federale
federation [fɛdəˈreɪʃən] *n*

federazione *f*
fed up *adj* **to be ~** essere stufo(-a)
fee [fi:] *n* pagamento; (*of doctor, lawyer*) onorario; (*for examination*) tassa d'esame; **school ~s** tasse *fpl* scolastiche
feeble ['fi:bl] *adj* debole
feed [fi:d] (*pt, pp* **fed**) *n* (*of baby*) pappa; (*of animal*) mangime *m*; (*on printer*) meccanismo di alimentazione ▷ *vt* nutrire; (*baby*) allattare; (*horse etc*) dare da mangiare a; (*fire, machine*) alimentare; (*data, information*): **to ~ into** inserire in; **feedback** *n* feedback *m*
feel [fi:l] (*pt, pp* **felt**) *n* consistenza; (*sense of touch*) tatto ▷ *vt* toccare; palpare; tastare; (*cold, pain, anger*) sentire; (*think, believe*): **to ~ (that)** pensare che; **to ~ hungry/cold** aver fame/freddo; **to ~ lonely/better** sentirsi solo/meglio; **I don't ~ well** non mi sento bene; **it ~s soft** è morbido al tatto; **to ~ like** (*want*) aver voglia di; **to ~ about** *or* **around for** cercare a tastoni; **feeling** *n* sensazione *f*; (*emotion*) sentimento
feet [fi:t] *npl of* **foot**
fell [fɛl] *pt of* **fall** ▷ *vt* (*tree*) abbattere
fellow ['fɛləu] *n* individuo, tipo; compagno; (*of learned society*) membro *cpd*; **fellow citizen** *n* concittadino(-a); **fellow countryman** (*irreg*) *n* compatriota *m*; **fellow men** *npl* simili *mpl*; **fellowship** *n* associazione *f*; compagnia; specie di borsa di studio universitaria
felony ['fɛlənɪ] *n* reato, crimine *m*
felt [fɛlt] *pt, pp of* **feel** ▷ *n* feltro
female ['fi:meɪl] *n* (*Zool*) femmina; (*pej: woman*) donna, femmina ▷ *adj* (*Biol, Elec*) femmina *inv*; (*sex, character*) femminile; (*vote etc*) di donne
feminine ['fɛmɪnɪn] *adj* femminile
feminist ['fɛmɪnɪst] *n* femminista *m/f*
fence [fɛns] *n* recinto ▷ *vt* (*also:* **~ in**) recingere ▷ *vi* (*Sport*) tirare di scherma; **fencing** *n* (*Sport*) scherma
fend [fɛnd] *vi* **to ~ for o.s.** arrangiarsi; **fend off** *vt* (*attack, questions*) respingere, difendersi da
fender ['fɛndəʳ] *n* parafuoco; (*on boat*) parabordo; (*US*) parafango; paraurti *m inv*
fennel ['fɛnl] *n* finocchio
ferment [*vb* fə'mɛnt, *n* 'fə:mɛnt] *vi* fermentare ▷ *n* (*fig*) agitazione *f*, eccitazione *f*
fern [fə:n] *n* felce *f*
ferocious [fə'rəuʃəs] *adj* feroce
ferret ['fɛrɪt] *n* furetto
ferry ['fɛrɪ] *n* (*small*) traghetto; (*large: also:* **~boat**) nave *f* traghetto *inv* ▷ *vt* traghettare
fertile ['fə:taɪl] *adj* fertile; (*Biol*) fecondo(-a); **fertilize** ['fə:tɪlaɪz] *vt* fertilizzare; fecondare; **fertilizer** ['fə:tɪlaɪzə] *n* fertilizzante *m*
festival ['fɛstɪvəl] *n* (*Rel*) festa; (*Art, Mus*) festival *m inv*
festive ['fɛstɪv] *adj* di festa; **the ~ season** (*BRIT: Christmas*) il periodo delle feste
fetch [fɛtʃ] *vt* andare a prendere; (*sell for*) essere venduto(-a) per
fête [feɪt] *n* festa
fetus ['fi:təs] (*US*) *n* = **foetus**
feud [fju:d] *n* contesa, lotta
fever ['fi:vəʳ] *n* febbre *f*; **feverish** *adj* febbrile
few [fju:] *adj* pochi(-e); **a ~** *adj* qualche *inv* ▷ *pron* alcuni(-e); **fewer** *adj* meno *inv*, meno numerosi(-e); **fewest** *adj* il minor numero di
fiancé [fɪ'ɑ̃:ŋseɪ] *n* fidanzato; **fiancée** *n* fidanzata
fiasco [fɪ'æskəu] *n* fiasco
fib [fɪb] *n* piccola bugia
fibre ['faɪbəʳ] (*US* **fiber**) *n* fibra; **Fibreglass®** ['faɪbəglɑ:s] (*US* **fiberglass**) *n* fibra di vetro
fickle ['fɪkl] *adj* incostante, capriccioso(-a)
fiction ['fɪkʃən] *n* narrativa, romanzi

mpl; (*sth made up*) finzione *f*; **fictional** *adj* immaginario(-a)
fiddle ['fɪdl] *n* (*Mus*) violino; (*cheating*) imbroglio; truffa ▷ *vt* (BRIT: *accounts*) falsificare, falsare; **fiddle with** *vt fus* gingillarsi con
fidelity [fɪ'dɛlɪtɪ] *n* fedeltà; (*accuracy*) esattezza
field [fiːld] *n* campo; **field marshal** *n* feldmaresciallo
fierce [fɪəs] *adj* (*animal, person, fighting*) feroce; (*loyalty*) assoluto(-a); (*wind*) furioso(-a); (*heat*) intenso(-a)
fifteen [fɪf'tiːn] *num* quindici; **fifteenth** *num* quindicesimo(-a)
fifth [fɪfθ] *num* quinto(-a)
fiftieth ['fɪftɪɪθ] *num* cinquantesimo(-a)
fifty ['fɪftɪ] *num* cinquanta; **fifty-fifty** *adj*: **a fifty-fifty chance** una possibilità su due ▷ *adv* fifty-fifty, metà per ciascuno
fig [fɪg] *n* fico
fight [faɪt] (*pt, pp* **fought**) *n* zuffa, rissa; (*Mil*) battaglia, combattimento; (*against cancer etc*) lotta ▷ *vt* (*person*) azzuffarsi con; (*enemy: also Mil*) combattere; (*cancer, alcoholism, emotion*) lottare contro, combattere; (*election*) partecipare a ▷ *vi* combattere; **fight back** *vi* difendersi; (*Sport, after illness*) riprendersi ▷ *vt* (*tears*) ricacciare; **fight off** *vt* (*attack, attacker*) respingere; (*disease, sleep, urge*) lottare contro; **fighting** *n* combattimento
figure ['fɪgəʳ] *n* figura; (*number, cipher*) cifra ▷ *vt* (*think: esp US*) pensare ▷ *vi* (*appear*) figurare; **figure out** *vt* riuscire a capire; calcolare
file [faɪl] *n* (*tool*) lima; (*dossier*) incartamento; (*folder*) cartellina; (*Comput*) archivio; (*row*) fila ▷ *vt* (*nails, wood*) limare; (*papers*) archiviare; (*Law: claim*) presentare; passare agli atti; **filing cabinet** ['faɪlɪŋ-] *n* casellario
Filipino [fɪlɪ'piːnəu] *n* filippino(-a); (*Ling*) tagal *m*
fill [fɪl] *vt* riempire; (*job*) coprire ▷ *n* **to eat one's ~** mangiare a sazietà; **fill in** *vt* (*hole*) riempire; (*form*) compilare; **fill out** *vt* (*form, receipt*) riempire; **fill up** *vt* riempire; **fill it up, please** (*Aut*) il pieno, per favore
fillet ['fɪlɪt] *n* filetto; **fillet steak** *n* bistecca di filetto
filling ['fɪlɪŋ] *n* (*Culin*) impasto, ripieno; (*for tooth*) otturazione *f*; **filling station** *n* stazione *f* di rifornimento
film [fɪlm] *n* (*Cinema*) film *m inv*; (*Phot*) pellicola, rullino; (*of powder, liquid*) sottile strato ▷ *vt, vi* girare; **I'd like a 36-exposure ~** vorrei un rullino da 36 pose; **film star** *n* divo(-a) dello schermo
filter ['fɪltəʳ] *n* filtro ▷ *vt* filtrare; **filter lane** (BRIT) *n* (*Aut*) corsia di svincolo
filth [fɪlθ] *n* sporcizia; **filthy** *adj* lordo(-a), sozzo(-a); (*language*) osceno(-a)
fin [fɪn] *n* (*of fish*) pinna
final ['faɪnl] *adj* finale, ultimo(-a); definitivo(-a) ▷ *n* (*Sport*) finale *f*; **finals** *npl* (*Scol*) esami *mpl* finali; **finale** [fɪ'nɑːlɪ] *n* finale *m*; **finalist** ['faɪnəlɪst] *n* (*Sport*) finalista *m/f*; **finalize** ['faɪnəlaɪz] *vt* mettere a punto; **finally** ['faɪnəlɪ] *adv* (*lastly*) alla fine; (*eventually*) finalmente
finance [faɪ'næns] *n* finanza; (*capital*) capitale *m* ▷ *vt* finanziare; **finances** *npl* (*funds*) finanze *fpl*; **financial** [faɪ'nænʃəl] *adj* finanziario(-a); **financial year** *n* anno finanziario, esercizio finanziario
find [faɪnd] (*pt, pp* **found**) *vt* trovare; (*lost object*) ritrovare ▷ *n* trovata, scoperta; **to ~ sb guilty** (*Law*) giudicare qn colpevole; **find out** *vt* (*truth, secret*) scoprire; (*person*) cogliere in fallo; **to find out about** informarsi su; (*by chance*) scoprire; **findings** *npl* (*Law*) sentenza, conclusioni *fpl*; (*of report*) conclusioni

fine [faɪn] *adj* bello(-a); ottimo(-a); (*thin, subtle*) fine ▷ *adv* (*well*) molto bene ▷ *n* (*Law*) multa ▷ *vt* (*Law*) multare; **to be ~** (*person*) stare bene; (*weather*) far bello; **fine arts** *npl* belle arti *fpl*
finger ['fɪŋgəʳ] *n* dito ▷ *vt* toccare, tastare; **little/index ~** mignolo/(dito) indice *m*; **fingernail** *n* unghia; **fingerprint** *n* impronta digitale; **fingertip** *n* punta del dito
finish ['fɪnɪʃ] *n* fine *f*; (*polish etc*) finitura ▷ *vt, vi* finire; **when does the show ~?** quando finisce lo spettacolo?; **to ~ doing sth** finire di fare qc; **to ~ third** arrivare terzo(-a); **finish off** *vt* compiere; (*kill*) uccidere; **finish up** *vi, vt* finire
Finland ['fɪnlənd] *n* Finlandia; **Finn** [fɪn] *n* finlandese *m/f*; **Finnish** *adj* finlandese ▷ *n* (*Ling*) finlandese *m*
fir [fəːʳ] *n* abete *m*
fire [faɪəʳ] *n* fuoco; (*destructive*) incendio; (*gas fire, electric fire*) stufa ▷ *vt* (*gun*) far fuoco con; (*arrow*) sparare; (*fig*) infiammare; (*inf: dismiss*) licenziare ▷ *vi* sparare, far fuoco; **~!** al fuoco!; **on ~** in fiamme; **fire alarm** *n* allarme *m* d'incendio; **firearm** *n* arma da fuoco; **fire brigade** [-brɪ'geɪd] (*US* **fire department**) *n* (corpo dei) pompieri *mpl*; **fire engine** *n* autopompa; **fire escape** *n* scala di sicurezza; **fire exit** *n* uscita di sicurezza; **fire extinguisher** [-ɪk'stɪŋgwɪʃəʳ] *n* estintore *m*; **fireman** (*irreg*) *n* pompiere *m*; **fireplace** *n* focolare *m*; **fire station** *n* caserma dei pompieri; **firetruck** (*US*) *n* = **fire engine**; **firewall** *n* (*Internet*) firewall *m inv*; **firewood** *n* legna; **fireworks** *npl* fuochi *mpl* d'artificio
firm [fəːm] *adj* fermo(-a) ▷ *n* ditta, azienda; **firmly** *adv* fermamente
first [fəːst] *adj* primo(-a) ▷ *adv* (*before others*) il primo, la prima; (*before other things*) per primo; (*when listing reasons etc*) per prima cosa ▷ *n* (*person: in race*) primo(-a); (BRIT: *Scol*) laurea con lode; (*Aut*) prima; **at ~** dapprima, all'inizio; **~ of all** prima di tutto; **first aid** *n* pronto soccorso; **first-aid kit** *n* cassetta pronto soccorso; **first-class** *adj* di prima classe; **first-hand** *adj* di prima mano; **first lady** (*US*) *n* moglie *f* del presidente; **firstly** *adv* in primo luogo; **first name** *n* prenome *m*; **first-rate** *adj* di prima qualità, ottimo(-a)
fiscal ['fɪskəl] *adj* fiscale; **fiscal year** *n* anno fiscale
fish [fɪʃ] *n inv* pesce *m* ▷ *vt* (*river, area*) pescare in ▷ *vi* pescare; **to go ~ing** andare a pesca; **fish and chip shop** *n see* **chip shop**; **fisherman** (*irreg*) *n* pescatore *m*; **fish fingers** (BRIT) *npl* bastoncini *mpl* di pesce (surgelati); **fishing** *n* pesca; **fishing boat** *n* barca da pesca; **fishing line** *n* lenza; **fishmonger** *n* pescivendolo; **fishmonger's (shop)** *n* pescheria; **fish sticks** (*US*) *npl* = **fish fingers**; **fishy** (*inf*) *adj* (*tale, story*) sospetto(-a)
fist [fɪst] *n* pugno
fit [fɪt] *adj* (*Med, Sport*) in forma; (*proper*) adatto(-a), appropriato(-a); conveniente ▷ *vt* (*clothes*) stare bene a; (*put in, attach*) mettere; installare; (*equip*) fornire, equipaggiare ▷ *vi* (*clothes*) stare bene; (*parts*) andare bene, adattarsi; (*in space, gap*) entrare ▷ *n* (*Med*) accesso, attacco; **~ to** in grado di; **~ for** adatto(-a) a, degno(-a) di; **a ~ of anger** un accesso d'ira; **this dress is a good ~** questo vestito sta bene; **by ~s and starts** a sbalzi; **fit in** *vi* accordarsi; adattarsi; **fitness** *n* (*Med*) forma fisica; **fitted** *adj*: **fitted cupboards** armadi *mpl* a muro; **fitted carpet** moquette *f inv*; **fitted kitchen** (BRIT) cucina componibile; **fitting** *adj* appropriato(-a) ▷ *n* (*of dress*) prova; (*of piece of equipment*) montaggio, aggiustaggio; **fitting room** *n*

camerino; **fittings** *npl* (*in building*) impianti *mpl*

five [faɪv] *num* cinque; **fiver** (*inf*) *n* (BRIT) biglietto da cinque sterline; (US) biglietto da cinque dollari

fix [fɪks] *vt* fissare; (*mend*) riparare; (*meal, drink*) preparare ▷ *n* **to be in a ~** essere nei guai; **fix up** *vt* (*meeting*) fissare; **to fix sb up with sth** procurare qc a qn; **fixed** [fɪkst] *adj* (*prices etc*) fisso(-a); **fixture** ['fɪkstʃəʳ] *n* impianto (fisso); (*Sport*) incontro (del calendario sportivo)

fizzy ['fɪzɪ] *adj* frizzante; gassato(-a)

flag [flæg] *n* bandiera; (*also:* **~stone**) pietra da lastricare ▷ *vi* stancarsi; affievolirsi; **flagpole** ['flægpəul] *n* albero

flair [flɛəʳ] *n* (*for business etc*) fiuto; (*for languages etc*) facilità; (*style*) stile *m*

flak [flæk] *n* (*Mil*) fuoco d'artiglieria; (*inf: criticism*) critiche *fpl*

flake [fleɪk] *n* (*of rust, paint*) scaglia; (*of snow, soap powder*) fiocco ▷ *vi* (*also:* **~ off**) sfaldarsi

flamboyant [flæm'bɔɪənt] *adj* sgargiante

flame [fleɪm] *n* fiamma

flamingo [flə'mɪŋgəu] *n* fenicottero, fiammingo

flammable ['flæməbl] *adj* infiammabile

flan [flæn] (BRIT) *n* flan *m inv*

flank [flæŋk] *n* fianco ▷ *vt* fiancheggiare

flannel ['flænl] *n* (BRIT: *also:* **face ~**) guanto di spugna; (*fabric*) flanella

flap [flæp] *n* (*of pocket*) patta; (*of envelope*) lembo ▷ *vt* (*wings*) battere ▷ *vi* (*sail, flag*) sbattere; (*inf: also:* **be in a ~**) essere in agitazione

flare [flɛəʳ] *n* razzo; (*in skirt etc*) svasatura; **flares** (*trousers*) pantaloni *mpl* a zampa d'elefante; **flare up** *vi* andare in fiamme; (*fig: person*) infiammarsi di rabbia; (*: revolt*) scoppiare

flash [flæʃ] *n* vampata; (*also:* **news ~**) notizia *f* lampo *inv*; (*Phot*) flash *m inv* ▷ *vt* accendere e spegnere; (*send: message*) trasmettere; (*: look, smile*) lanciare ▷ *vi* brillare; (*light on ambulance, eyes etc*) lampeggiare; **in a ~** in un lampo; **to ~ one's headlights** lampeggiare; **he ~ed by** *or* **past** ci passò davanti come un lampo; **flashback** *n* flashback *m inv*; **flashbulb** *n* cubo *m* flash *inv*; **flashlight** *n* lampadina tascabile

flask [flɑːsk] *n* fiasco; (*also:* **vacuum ~**) Thermos® *m inv*

flat [flæt] *adj* piatto(-a); (*tyre*) sgonfio(-a), a terra; (*battery*) scarico(-a); (*beer*) svampito(-a); (*denial*) netto(-a); (*Mus*) bemolle *inv*; (*: voice*) stonato(-a); (*rate, fee*) unico(-a) ▷ *n* (BRIT: *rooms*) appartamento; (*Aut*) pneumatico sgonfio; (*Mus*) bemolle *m*; **to work ~ out** lavorare a più non posso; **flatten** *vt* (*also:* **flatten out**) appiattire; (*building, city*) spianare

flatter ['flætəʳ] *vt* lusingare; **flattering** *adj* lusinghiero(-a); (*dress*) che dona

flaunt [flɔːnt] *vt* fare mostra di

flavour *etc* ['fleɪvəʳ] (US **flavor**) *n* gusto ▷ *vt* insaporire, aggiungere sapore a; **what ~s do you have?** che gusti avete?; **strawberry-~ed** al gusto di fragola; **flavouring** *n* essenza (artificiale)

flaw [flɔː] *n* difetto; **flawless** *adj* senza difetti

flea [fliː] *n* pulce *f*; **flea market** *n* mercato delle pulci

flee [fliː] (*pt, pp* **fled**) *vt* fuggire da ▷ *vi* fuggire, scappare

fleece [fliːs] *n* vello ▷ *vt* (*inf*) pelare

fleet [fliːt] *n* flotta; (*of lorries etc*) convoglio; parco

fleeting ['fliːtɪŋ] *adj* fugace, fuggitivo(-a); (*visit*) volante

Flemish ['flɛmɪʃ] *adj* fiammingo(-a)

flesh [flɛʃ] *n* carne *f*; (*of fruit*) polpa

flew [fluː] *pt of* **fly**
flex [flɛks] *n* filo (flessibile) ▷ *vt* flettere; (*muscles*) contrarre; **flexibility** *n* flessibilità; **flexible** *adj* flessibile; **flexitime** ['flɛksɪtaɪm] *n* orario flessibile
flick [flɪk] *n* colpetto; scarto ▷ *vt* dare un colpetto a; **flick through** *vt fus* sfogliare
flicker ['flɪkəʳ] *vi* tremolare
flies [flaɪz] *npl of* **fly**
flight [flaɪt] *n* volo; (*escape*) fuga; (*also:* **~ of steps**) scalinata; **flight attendant** (US) *n* steward *m inv*, hostess *f inv*
flimsy ['flɪmzɪ] *adj* (*shoes, clothes*) leggero(-a); (*building*) poco solido(-a); (*excuse*) che non regge
flinch [flɪntʃ] *vi* ritirarsi; **to ~ from** tirarsi indietro di fronte a
fling [flɪŋ] (*pt, pp* **flung**) *vt* lanciare, gettare
flint [flɪnt] *n* selce *f*; (*in lighter*) pietrina
flip [flɪp] *vt* (*switch*) far scattare; (*coin*) lanciare in aria
flip-flops ['flɪpflɔps] *npl* (*esp* BRIT: *sandals*) infradito *mpl*
flipper ['flɪpəʳ] *n* pinna
flirt [fləːt] *vi* flirtare ▷ *n* civetta
float [fləut] *n* galleggiante *m*; (*in procession*) carro; (*money*) somma ▷ *vi* galleggiare
flock [flɔk] *n* (*of sheep, Rel*) gregge *m*; (*of birds*) stormo ▷ *vi*: **to ~ to** accorrere in massa a
flood [flʌd] *n* alluvione *m*; (*of letters etc*) marea ▷ *vt* allagare; (*people*) invadere ▷ *vi* (*place*) allagarsi; (*people*): **to ~ into** riversarsi in; **flooding** *n* inondazione *f*; **floodlight** *n* riflettore *m* ▷ *vt* illuminare a giorno
floor [flɔːʳ] *n* pavimento; (*storey*) piano; (*of sea, valley*) fondo ▷ *vt* (*blow*) atterrare; (*: question*) ridurre al silenzio; **which ~ is it on?** a che piano si trova?; **ground ~** (BRIT), **first ~** (US) pianterreno; **first ~** (BRIT), **second ~** (US) primo piano; **floorboard** *n* tavellone *m* di legno; **flooring** *n* (*floor*) pavimento; (*material*) materiale *m* per pavimentazioni; **floor show** *n* spettacolo di varietà
flop [flɔp] *n* fiasco ▷ *vi* far fiasco; (*fall*) lasciarsi cadere; **floppy** ['flɔpɪ] *adj* floscio(-a), molle
floral ['flɔːrl] *adj* floreale
Florence ['flɔrəns] *n* Firenze *f*
Florentine ['flɔrəntaɪn] *adj* fiorentino(-a)
florist ['flɔrɪst] *n* fioraio(-a); **florist's (shop)** *n* fioraio(-a)
flotation [fləu'teɪʃən] *n* (*Comm*) lancio
flour ['flauəʳ] *n* farina
flourish ['flʌrɪʃ] *vi* fiorire ▷ *n* (*bold gesture*): **with a ~** con ostentazione
flow [fləu] *n* flusso; circolazione *f* ▷ *vi* fluire; (*traffic, blood in veins*) circolare; (*hair*) scendere
flower ['flauəʳ] *n* fiore *m* ▷ *vi* fiorire; **flower bed** *n* aiuola; **flowerpot** *n* vaso da fiori
flown [fləun] *pp of* **fly**
fl. oz. *abbr* = **fluid ounce**
flu [fluː] *n* influenza
fluctuate ['flʌktjueɪt] *vi* fluttuare, oscillare
fluent ['fluːənt] *adj* (*speech*) facile, sciolto(-a); corrente; **he speaks ~ Italian, he's ~ in Italian** parla l'italiano correntemente
fluff [flʌf] *n* lanugine *f*; **fluffy** *adj* lanuginoso(-a); (*toy*) di peluche
fluid ['fluːɪd] *adj* fluido(-a) ▷ *n* fluido; **fluid ounce** *n* (BRIT) = *0.028 l; 0.05 pints*
fluke [fluːk] (*inf*) *n* colpo di fortuna
flung [flʌŋ] *pt, pp of* **fling**
fluorescent [fluə'rɛsnt] *adj* fluorescente
fluoride ['fluəraɪd] *n* fluoruro
flurry ['flʌrɪ] *n* (*of snow*) tempesta; **a ~ of activity** uno scoppio di attività
flush [flʌʃ] *n* rossore *m*; (*fig: of youth,*

beauty etc) rigoglio, pieno vigore ▷ *vt* ripulire con un getto d'acqua ▷ *vi* arrossire ▷ *adj* **~ with** a livello di, pari a; **to ~ the toilet** tirare l'acqua

flute [flu:t] *n* flauto

flutter ['flʌtəʳ] *n* agitazione *f*; (*of wings*) battito ▷ *vi* (*bird*) battere le ali

fly [flaɪ] (*pt* **flew**, *pp* **flown**) *n* (*insect*) mosca; (*on trousers*: *also*: **flies**) chiusura ▷ *vt* pilotare; (*passengers, cargo*) trasportare (in aereo); (*distances*) percorrere ▷ *vi* volare; (*passengers*) andare in aereo; (*escape*) fuggire; (*flag*) sventolare; **fly away** *vi* volar via; **fly-drive** *n*: **fly-drive holiday** fly and drive *m inv*; **flying** *n* (*activity*) aviazione *f*; (*action*) volo ▷ *adj* **flying visit** visita volante; **with flying colours** con risultati brillanti; **flying saucer** *n* disco volante; **flyover** (BRIT) *n* (*bridge*) cavalcavia *m inv*

FM *abbr* (= *frequency modulation*) FM

foal [fəul] *n* puledro

foam [fəum] *n* schiuma; (*also*: **~ rubber**) gommapiuma® ▷ *vi* schiumare; (*soapy water*) fare la schiuma

focus ['fəukəs] (*pl* **focuses**) *n* fuoco; (*of interest*) centro ▷ *vt* (*field glasses etc*) mettere a fuoco ▷ *vi* **to ~ on** (*with camera*) mettere a fuoco; (*person*) fissare lo sguardo su; **in ~** a fuoco; **out of ~** sfocato(-a)

foetus ['fi:təs] (US **fetus**) *n* feto

fog [fɔg] *n* nebbia; **foggy** *adj* **it's foggy** c'è nebbia; **fog lamp** (US **fog light**) *n* (*Aut*) faro *m* antinebbia *inv*

foil [fɔɪl] *vt* confondere, frustrare ▷ *n* lamina di metallo; (*kitchen foil*) foglio di alluminio; (*Fencing*) fioretto; **to act as a ~ to** (*fig*) far risaltare

fold [fəuld] *n* (*bend, crease*) piega; (*Agr*) ovile *m*; (*fig*) gregge *m* ▷ *vt* piegare; (*arms*) incrociare; **fold up** *vi* (*map, bed, table*) piegarsi; (*business*) crollare ▷ *vt* (*map etc*) piegare, ripiegare; **folder** *n* (*for papers*) cartella; cartellina; **folding** *adj* (*chair, bed*) pieghevole

foliage ['fəulɪɪdʒ] *n* fogliame *m*

folk [fəuk] *npl* gente *f* ▷ *adj* popolare; **folks** *npl* (*family*) famiglia; **folklore** ['fəuklɔ:ʳ] *n* folclore *m*; **folk music** *n* musica folk *inv*; **folk song** *n* canto popolare

follow ['fɔləu] *vt* seguire ▷ *vi* seguire; (*result*) conseguire, risultare; **to ~ suit** fare lo stesso; **follow up** *vt* (*letter, offer*) fare seguito a; (*case*) seguire; **follower** *n* seguace *m/f*, discepolo(-a); **following** *adj* seguente ▷ *n* seguito, discepoli *mpl*; **follow-up** *n* seguito

fond [fɔnd] *adj* (*memory, look*) tenero(-a), affettuoso(-a); **to be ~ of sb** volere bene a qn; **he's ~ of walking** gli piace fare camminate

food [fu:d] *n* cibo; **food mixer** *n* frullatore *m*; **food poisoning** *n* intossicazione *f*; **food processor** [-'prəusɛsə] *n* tritatutto *m inv* elettrico; **food stamp** (US) *n* *buono alimentare dato agli indigenti*

fool [fu:l] *n* sciocco(-a); (*Culin*) frullato ▷ *vt* ingannare ▷ *vi* (*gen*: *fool around*) fare lo sciocco; **fool about, fool around** *vi* (*waste time*) perdere tempo; **foolish** *adj* scemo(-a), stupido(-a); imprudente; **foolproof** *adj* (*plan etc*) sicurissimo(-a)

foot [fut] (*pl* **feet**) *n* piede *m*; (*measure*) piede (= *304 mm; 12 inches*); (*of animal*) zampa ▷ *vt* (*bill*) pagare; **on ~** a piedi; **footage** *n* (*Cinema*: *length*) ≈ metraggio; (: *material*) sequenza; **foot-and-mouth (disease)** [futənd'mauθ-] *n* afta epizootica; **football** *n* pallone *m*; (*sport*: BRIT) calcio; (: US) football *m* americano; **footballer** *n* (BRIT) = **football player**; **football match** *n* (BRIT) partita di calcio; **football player** *n* (BRIT: *also*: **footballer**) calciatore *m*; (US) giocatore *m* di football americano; **footbridge** *n* passerella; **foothills**

npl contrafforti *fpl*; **foothold** *n* punto d'appoggio; **footing** *n* (*fig*) posizione *f*; **to lose one's footing** mettere un piede in fallo; **footnote** *n* nota (a piè di pagina); **footpath** *n* sentiero; (*in street*) marciapiede *m*; **footprint** *n* orma, impronta; **footstep** *n* passo; (*footprint*) orma, impronta; **footwear** *n* calzatura

KEYWORD

for [fɔːʳ] *prep* 1 (*indicating destination, intention, purpose*) per; **the train for London** il treno per Londra; **he went for the paper** è andato a prendere il giornale; **it's time for lunch** è ora di pranzo; **what's it for?** a che serve?; **what for?** (*why*) perché?
2 (*on behalf of, representing*) per; **to work for sb/sth** lavorare per qn/qc; **I'll ask him for you** glielo chiederò a nome tuo; **G for George** G come George
3 (*because of*) per, a causa di; **for this reason** per questo motivo
4 (*with regard to*) per; **it's cold for July** è freddo per luglio; **for everyone who voted yes, 50 voted no** per ogni voto a favore ce n'erano 50 contro
5 (*in exchange for*) per; **I sold it for £5** l'ho venduto per 5 sterline
6 (*in favour of*) per, a favore di; **are you for or against us?** è con noi o contro di noi?; **I'm all for it** sono completamente a favore
7 (*referring to distance, time*) per; **there are roadworks for 5 km** ci sono lavori in corso per 5 km; **he was away for 2 years** è stato via per 2 anni; **she will be away for a month** starà via un mese; **it hasn't rained for 3 weeks** non piove da 3 settimane; **can you do it for tomorrow?** può farlo per domani?
8 (*with infinitive clauses*): **it is not for me to decide** non sta a me decidere; **it would be best for you to leave** sarebbe meglio che lei se ne andasse; **there is still time for you to do it** ha ancora tempo per farlo; **for this to be possible ...** perché ciò sia possibile ...
9 (*in spite of*) nonostante; **for all his complaints, he's very fond of her** nonostante tutte le sue lamentele, le vuole molto bene
▷ *conj* (*since, as: rather formal*) dal momento che, poiché

forbid [fəˈbɪd] (*pt* **forbad(e)**, *pp* **forbidden**) *vt* vietare, interdire; **to ~ sb to do sth** proibire a qn di fare qc; **forbidden** *pt of* **forbid** ▷ *adj* (*food*) proibito(-a); (*area, territory*) vietato(-a); (*word, subject*) tabù *inv*
force [fɔːs] *n* forza ▷ *vt* forzare; **forced** *adj* forzato(-a); **forceful** *adj* forte, vigoroso(-a)
ford [fɔːd] *n* guado
fore [fɔːʳ] *n* **to come to the ~** mettersi in evidenza; **forearm** [ˈfɔːrɑːm] *n* avambraccio; **forecast** [ˈfɔːkɑːst] (*irreg: like* **cast**) *n* previsione *f* ▷ *vt* prevedere; **forecourt** [ˈfɔːkɔːt] *n* (*of garage*) corte *f* esterna; **forefinger** [ˈfɔːfɪŋgəʳ] *n* (dito) indice *m*; **forefront** [ˈfɔːfrʌnt] *n* **in the forefront of** all'avanguardia in; **foreground** [ˈfɔːgraund] *n* primo piano; **forehead** [ˈfɔrɪd] *n* fronte *f*
foreign [ˈfɔrɪn] *adj* straniero(-a); (*trade*) estero(-a); (*object, matter*) estraneo(-a); **foreign currency** *n* valuta estera; **foreigner** *n* straniero(-a); **foreign exchange** *n* cambio con l'estero; (*currency*) valuta estera; **Foreign Office** (BRIT) *n* Ministero degli Esteri; **Foreign Secretary** (BRIT) *n* ministro degli Affari esteri
fore: **foreman** [ˈfɔːmən] (*irreg*) *n* caposquadra *m*; **foremost** [ˈfɔːməust] *adj* principale; più in vista ▷ *adv*: **first and foremost**

innanzitutto; **forename** *n* nome *m* di battesimo

forensic [fəˈrɛnsɪk] *adj* **~ medicine** medicina legale

foresee [fɔːˈsiː] (*irreg*: *like* **see**) *vt* prevedere; **foreseeable** *adj* prevedibile

forest [ˈfɔrɪst] *n* foresta; **forestry** [ˈfɔrɪstrɪ] *n* silvicoltura

forever [fəˈrɛvəʳ] *adv* per sempre; (*endlessly*) sempre, di continuo

foreword [ˈfɔːwəːd] *n* prefazione *f*

forfeit [ˈfɔːfɪt] *vt* perdere; (*one's happiness, health*) giocarsi

forgave [fəˈgeɪv] *pt of* **forgive**

forge [fɔːdʒ] *n* fucina ▷ *vt* (*signature, money*) contraffare, falsificare; (*wrought iron*) fucinare, foggiare; **forger** *n* contraffattore *m*; **forgery** *n* falso; (*activity*) contraffazione *f*

forget [fəˈgɛt] (*pt* **forgot**, *pp* **forgotten**) *vt, vi* dimenticare; **I've forgotten my key/passport** ho dimenticato la chiave/il passaporto; **forgetful** *adj* di corta memoria; **forgetful of** dimentico(-a) di

forgive [fəˈgɪv] (*pt* **forgave**, *pp* **forgiven**) *vt* perdonare; **to ~ sb for sth** perdonare qc a qn

forgot [fəˈgɔt] *pt of* **forget**

forgotten [fəˈgɔtn] *pp of* **forget**

fork [fɔːk] *n* (*for eating*) forchetta; (*for gardening*) forca; (*of roads, rivers, railways*) biforcazione *f* ▷ *vi* (*road etc*) biforcarsi

forlorn [fəˈlɔːn] *adj* (*person*) sconsolato(-a); (*place*) abbandonato(-a); (*attempt*) disperato(-a); (*hope*) vano(-a)

form [fɔːm] *n* forma; (*Scol*) classe *f*; (*questionnaire*) scheda ▷ *vt* formare; **in top ~** in gran forma

formal [ˈfɔːməl] *adj* formale; (*gardens*) simmetrico(-a), regolare; **formality** [fɔːˈmælɪtɪ] *n* formalità *f inv*

format [ˈfɔːmæt] *n* formato ▷ *vt* (*Comput*) formattare

formation [fɔːˈmeɪʃən] *n* formazione *f*

former [ˈfɔːməʳ] *adj* vecchio(-a); (*before n*) ex *inv* (*before n*); **the ~ ... the latter** quello ... questo; **formerly** *adv* in passato

formidable [ˈfɔːmɪdəbl] *adj* formidabile

formula [ˈfɔːmjulə] *n* formula

fort [fɔːt] *n* forte *m*

forthcoming [fɔːθˈkʌmɪŋ] *adj* (*event*) prossimo(-a); (*help*) disponibile; (*character*) aperto(-a), comunicativo(-a)

fortieth [ˈfɔːtɪɪθ] *num* quarantesimo(-a)

fortify [ˈfɔːtɪfaɪ] *vt* (*city*) fortificare; (*person*) armare

fortnight [ˈfɔːtnaɪt] (BRIT) *n* quindici giorni *mpl*, due settimane *fpl*; **fortnightly** *adj* bimensile ▷ *adv* ogni quindici giorni

fortress [ˈfɔːtrɪs] *n* fortezza, rocca

fortunate [ˈfɔːtʃənɪt] *adj* fortunato(-a); **it is ~ that** è una fortuna che; **fortunately** *adv* fortunatamente

fortune [ˈfɔːtʃən] *n* fortuna; **fortune-teller** *n* indovino(-a)

forty [ˈfɔːtɪ] *num* quaranta

forum [ˈfɔːrəm] *n* foro

forward [ˈfɔːwəd] *adj* (*ahead of schedule*) in anticipo; (*movement, position*) in avanti; (*not shy*) aperto(-a), diretto(-a) ▷ *n* (*Sport*) avanti *m inv* ▷ *vt* (*letter*) inoltrare; (*parcel, goods*) spedire; (*career, plans*) promuovere, appoggiare; **to move ~** avanzare; **forwarding address** *n nuovo recapito cui spedire la posta*; **forward(s)** *adv* avanti; **forward slash** *n* barra obliqua

fossil [ˈfɔsl] *adj* fossile ▷ *n* fossile *m*

foster [ˈfɔstəʳ] *vt* incoraggiare, nutrire; (*child*) avere in affidamento; **foster child** *n* bambino(-a) preso(-a) in affidamento; **foster mother** *n*

madre *f* affidataria
fought [fɔːt] *pt, pp of* **fight**
foul [faul] *adj* (*smell, food, temper etc*) cattivo(-a); (*weather*) brutto(-a); (*language*) osceno(-a) ▷ *n* (*Sport*) fallo ▷ *vt* sporcare; **foul play** *n* (*Law*): **the police suspect foul play** la polizia sospetta un atto criminale
found [faund] *pt, pp of* **find** ▷ *vt* (*establish*) fondare; **foundation** [-'deɪʃən] *n* (*act*) fondazione *f*; (*base*) base *f*; (*also:* **foundation cream**) fondo tinta; **foundations** *npl* (*of building*) fondamenta *fpl*
founder ['faundə^r] *n* fondatore(-trice) ▷ *vi* affondare
fountain ['fauntɪn] *n* fontana; **fountain pen** *n* penna stilografica
four [fɔː^r] *num* quattro; **on all ~s** a carponi; **four-letter word** ['fɔːlɛtə-] *n* parolaccia; **four-poster** *n* (*also:* **four-poster bed**) letto a quattro colonne; **fourteen** *num* quattordici; **fourteenth** *num* quattordicesimo(-a); **fourth** *num* quarto(-a); **four-wheel drive** ['fɔːwiːl-] *n* (*Aut*): **with four-wheel drive** con quattro ruote motrici
fowl [faul] *n* pollame *m*; volatile *m*
fox [fɔks] *n* volpe *f* ▷ *vt* confondere
foyer ['fɔɪeɪ] *n* atrio; (*Theatre*) ridotto
fraction ['frækʃən] *n* frazione *f*
fracture ['fræktʃə^r] *n* frattura
fragile ['frædʒaɪl] *adj* fragile
fragment ['frægmənt] *n* frammento
fragrance ['freɪgrəns] *n* fragranza, profumo
frail [freɪl] *adj* debole, delicato(-a)
frame [freɪm] *n* (*of building*) armatura; (*of human, animal*) ossatura, corpo; (*of picture*) cornice *f*; (*of door, window*) telaio; (*of spectacles: also:* **~s**) montatura ▷ *vt* (*picture*) incorniciare; **framework** *n* struttura
France [frɑːns] *n* Francia
franchise ['fræntʃaɪz] *n* (*Pol*) diritto di voto; (*Comm*) concessione *f*
frank [fræŋk] *adj* franco(-a), aperto(-a) ▷ *vt* (*letter*) affrancare; **frankly** *adv* francamente, sinceramente
frantic ['fræntɪk] *adj* frenetico(-a)
fraud [frɔːd] *n* truffa; (*Law*) frode *f*; (*person*) impostore(-a)
fraught [frɔːt] *adj*: **~ with** pieno(-a) di, intriso(-a) da
fray [freɪ] *vt* logorare ▷ *vi* logorarsi
freak [friːk] *n* fenomeno, mostro
freckle ['frɛkl] *n* lentiggine *f*
free [friː] *adj* libero(-a); (*gratis*) gratuito(-a) ▷ *vt* (*prisoner, jammed person*) liberare; (*jammed object*) districare; **is this seat ~?** è libero questo posto?; **~ of charge, for ~** gratuitamente; **freedom** ['friːdəm] *n* libertà; **Freefone®** *n* numero verde; **free gift** *n* regalo, omaggio; **free kick** *n* calcio libero; **freelance** *adj* indipendente; **freely** *adv* liberamente; (*liberally*) liberalmente; **Freepost®** *n* affrancatura a carico del destinatario; **free-range** *adj* (*hen*) ruspante; (*eggs*) di gallina ruspante; **freeway** (*US*) *n* superstrada; **free will** *n* libero arbitrio; **of one's own free will** di spontanea volontà
freeze [friːz] (*pt* **froze**, *pp* **frozen**) *vi* gelare ▷ *vt* gelare; (*food*) congelare; (*prices, salaries*) bloccare ▷ *n* gelo; blocco; **freezer** *n* congelatore *m*; **freezing** ['friːzɪŋ] *adj* (*wind, weather*) gelido(-a); **freezing point** *n* punto di congelamento; **3 degrees below freezing point** 3 gradi sotto zero
freight [freɪt] *n* (*goods*) merce *f*, merci *fpl*; (*money charged*) spese *fpl* di trasporto; **freight train** (*US*) *n* treno *m* merci *inv*
French [frɛntʃ] *adj* francese ▷ *n* (*Ling*) francese *m*; **the French** *npl* i Francesi; **French bean** *n* fagiolino; **French bread** *n* baguette *f inv*; **French**

dressing *n* (*Culin*) condimento per insalata; **French fried potatoes** (*US* **French fries**) *npl* patate *fpl* fritte; **Frenchman** (*irreg*) *n* francese *m*; **French stick** *n* baguette *f inv*; **French window** *n* portafinestra; **Frenchwoman** (*irreg*) *n* francese *f*

frenzy ['frɛnzɪ] *n* frenesia

frequency ['fri:kwənsɪ] *n* frequenza

frequent [*adj* 'fri:kwənt, *vb* frɪ'kwɛnt] *adj* frequente ▷ *vt* frequentare; **frequently** *adv* frequentemente, spesso

fresh [frɛʃ] *adj* fresco(-a); (*new*) nuovo(-a); (*cheeky*) sfacciato(-a); **freshen** *vi* (*wind, air*) rinfrescare; **freshen up** *vi* rinfrescarsi; **fresher** (*BRIT*: *inf*) *n* (*Scol*) matricola; **freshly** *adv* di recente, di fresco; **freshman** (*irreg*: *US*) *n* = **fresher**; **freshwater** *adj* (*fish*) d'acqua dolce

fret [frɛt] *vi* agitarsi, affliggersi

Fri. *abbr* (= *Friday*) ven.

friction ['frɪkʃən] *n* frizione *f*, attrito

Friday ['fraɪdɪ] *n* venerdì *m inv*

fridge [frɪdʒ] (*BRIT*) *n* frigo, frigorifero

fried [fraɪd] *pt, pp of* **fry** ▷ *adj* fritto(-a)

friend [frɛnd] *n* amico(-a); **friendly** *adj* amichevole; **friendship** *n* amicizia

fries [fraɪz] (*esp US*) *npl* patate *fpl* fritte

frigate ['frɪgɪt] *n* (*Naut*: *modern*) fregata

fright [fraɪt] *n* paura, spavento; **to take ~** spaventarsi; **frighten** *vt* spaventare, far paura a; **frightened** *adj* spaventato(-a); **frightening** *adj* spaventoso(-a), pauroso(-a); **frightful** *adj* orribile

frill [frɪl] *n* balza

fringe [frɪndʒ] *n* (*decoration*: *BRIT*: *of hair*) frangia; (*edge*: *of forest etc*) margine *m*

Frisbee® ['frɪzbɪ] *n* frisbee® *m inv*

fritter ['frɪtə^r] *n* frittella

frivolous ['frɪvələs] *adj* frivolo(-a)

fro [frəu] *see* **to**

frock [frɔk] *n* vestito

frog [frɔg] *n* rana; **frogman** (*irreg*) *n* uomo *m* rana *inv*

KEYWORD

from [frɔm] *prep* 1 (*indicating starting place, origin etc*) da; **where do you come from?, where are you from?** da dove viene?, di dov'è?; **from London to Glasgow** da Londra a Glasgow; **a letter from my sister** una lettera da mia sorella; **tell him from me that ...** gli dica da parte mia che ...

2 (*indicating time*) da; **from one o'clock to** *or* **until** *or* **till two** dall'una alle due; **from January (on)** da gennaio, a partire da gennaio

3 (*indicating distance*) da; **the hotel is 1 km from the beach** l'albergo è a 1 km dalla spiaggia

4 (*indicating price, number etc*) da; **prices range from £10 to £50** i prezzi vanno dalle 10 alle 50 sterline

5 (*indicating difference*) da; **he can't tell red from green** non sa distinguere il rosso dal verde

6 (*because of, on the basis of*): **from what he says** da quanto dice lui; **weak from hunger** debole per la fame

front [frʌnt] *n* (*of house, dress*) davanti *m inv*; (*of train*) testa; (*of book*) copertina; (*promenade*: *also*: **sea ~**) lungomare *m*; (*Mil, Pol, Meteor*) fronte *m*; (*fig*: *appearances*) fronte *f* ▷ *adj* primo(-a); anteriore, davanti *inv*; **in ~ of** davanti a; **front door** *n* porta d'entrata; (*of car*) sportello anteriore; **frontier** ['frʌntɪə^r] *n* frontiera; **front page** *n* prima pagina; **front-wheel drive** ['frʌntwi:l-] *n* trasmissione *f* anteriore

frost [frɔst] *n* gelo; (*also*: **hoar~**) brina; **frostbite** *n* congelamento; **frosting**

(US) *n* (*on cake*) glassa; **frosty** *adj* (*weather, look*) gelido(-a)
froth ['frɔθ] *n* spuma; schiuma
frown [fraun] *vi* accigliarsi
froze [frəuz] *pt of* **freeze**
frozen ['frəuzn] *pp of* **freeze**
fruit [fru:t] *n inv* (*also fig*) frutto; (*collectively*) frutta; **fruit juice** *n* succo di frutta; **fruit machine** (BRIT) *n* macchina *f* mangiasoldi *inv*; **fruit salad** *n* macedonia
frustrate [frʌs'treɪt] *vt* frustrare; **frustrated** *adj* frustrato(-a)
fry [fraɪ] (*pt, pp* **fried**) *vt* friggere; *see also* **small**; **frying pan** *n* padella
ft. *abbr* = **foot**; **feet**
fudge [fʌdʒ] *n* (*Culin*) *specie di caramella a base di latte, burro e zucchero*
fuel [fjuəl] *n* (*for heating*) combustibile *m*; (*for propelling*) carburante *m*; **fuel tank** *n* deposito *m* nafta *inv*; (*on vehicle*) serbatoio (della benzina)
fulfil [ful'fɪl] *vt* (*function*) compiere; (*order*) eseguire; (*wish, desire*) soddisfare, appagare
full [ful] *adj* pieno(-a); (*details, skirt*) ampio(-a) ▷ *adv* **to know ~ well that** sapere benissimo che; **I'm ~ (up)** sono sazio; **a ~ two hours** due ore intere; **at ~ speed** a tutta velocità; **in ~** per intero; **full-length** *adj* (*film*) a lungometraggio; (*coat, novel*) lungo(-a); (*portrait*) in piedi; **full moon** *n* luna piena; **full-scale** *adj* (*attack, war*) su larga scala; (*model*) in grandezza naturale; **full stop** *n* punto; **full-time** *adj, adv* (*work*) a tempo pieno; **fully** *adv* interamente, pienamente, completamente; (*at least*) almeno
fumble ['fʌmbl] *vi* **to ~ with sth** armeggiare con qc
fume [fju:m] *vi* essere furioso(-a); **fumes** *npl* esalazioni *fpl*, vapori *mpl*
fun [fʌn] *n* divertimento, spasso; **to have ~** divertirsi; **for ~** per scherzo; **to make ~ of** prendersi gioco di
function ['fʌŋkʃən] *n* funzione *f*; cerimonia, ricevimento ▷ *vi* funzionare
fund [fʌnd] *n* fondo, cassa; (*source*) fondo; (*store*) riserva; **funds** *npl* (*money*) fondi *mpl*
fundamental [fʌndə'mɛntl] *adj* fondamentale
funeral ['fju:nərəl] *n* funerale *m*; **funeral director** *n* impresario di pompe funebri; **funeral parlour** [-'pɑ:ləʳ] *n* impresa di pompe funebri
funfair ['fʌnfɛəʳ] *n* luna park *m inv*
fungus ['fʌŋgəs] (*pl* **fungi**) *n* fungo; (*mould*) muffa
funnel ['fʌnl] *n* imbuto; (*of ship*) ciminiera
funny ['fʌnɪ] *adj* divertente, buffo(-a); (*strange*) strano(-a), bizzarro(-a)
fur [fə:ʳ] *n* pelo; pelliccia; (BRIT: *in kettle etc*) deposito calcare; **fur coat** *n* pelliccia
furious ['fjuərɪəs] *adj* furioso(-a); (*effort*) accanito(-a)
furnish ['fə:nɪʃ] *vt* ammobiliare; (*supply*) fornire; **furnishings** *npl* mobili *mpl*, mobilia
furniture ['fə:nɪtʃəʳ] *n* mobili *mpl*; **piece of ~** mobile *m*
furry ['fə:rɪ] *adj* (*animal*) peloso(-a)
further ['fə:ðəʳ] *adj* supplementare, altro(-a); nuovo(-a); più lontano(-a) ▷ *adv* più lontano; (*more*) di più; (*moreover*) inoltre ▷ *vt* favorire, promuovere; **further education** *n* ≈ corsi *mpl* di formazione; **college of further education** *istituto statale con corsi specializzati (di formazione professionale, aggiornamento professionale ecc)*; **furthermore** [fə:ðə'mɔ:ʳ] *adv* inoltre, per di più
furthest ['fə:ðɪst] *superl of* **far**
fury ['fjuərɪ] *n* furore *m*
fuse [fju:z] (US **fuze**) *n* fusibile *m*; (*for bomb etc*) miccia, spoletta ▷ *vt* fondere ▷ *vi* fondersi; **to ~ the lights** (BRIT: *Elec*) far saltare i fusibili; **fuse**

box *n* cassetta dei fusibili
fusion ['fju:ʒən] *n* fusione *f*
fuss [fʌs] *n* agitazione *f*; (*complaining*) storie *fpl*; **to make a ~** fare delle storie; **fussy** *adj* (*person*) puntiglioso(-a), esigente; che fa le storie; (*dress*) carico(-a) di fronzoli; (*style*) elaborato(-a)
future ['fju:tʃə^{r}] *adj* futuro(-a) ▷ *n* futuro, avvenire *m*; (*Ling*) futuro; **in ~** in futuro; **futures** *npl* (*Comm*) operazioni *fpl* a termine
fuze [fju:z] (*US*) = **fuse**
fuzzy ['fʌzɪ] *adj* (*Phot*) indistinto(-a), sfocato(-a); (*hair*) crespo(-a)

g

G [dʒi:] *n* (*Mus*) sol *m*
g. *abbr* (= *gram, gravity*) g.
gadget ['gædʒɪt] *n* aggeggio
Gaelic ['geɪlɪk] *adj* gaelico(-a) ▷ *n* (*Ling*) gaelico
gag [gæg] *n* bavaglio; (*joke*) facezia, scherzo ▷ *vt* imbavagliare
gain [geɪn] *n* guadagno, profitto ▷ *vt* guadagnare ▷ *vi* (*clock, watch*) andare avanti; (*benefit*): **to ~ (from)** trarre beneficio (da); **to ~ 3lbs (in weight)** aumentare di 3 libbre; **to ~ on sb** (*in race etc*) guadagnare su qn
gal. *abbr* = **gallon**
gala ['gɑ:lə] *n* gala; **swimming ~** manifestazione *f* di nuoto
galaxy ['gæləksɪ] *n* galassia
gale [geɪl] *n* vento forte; burrasca
gall bladder ['gɔ:l-] *n* cistifellea
gallery ['gælərɪ] *n* galleria
gallon ['gælən] *n* gallone *m* (= *8 pints; BRIT = 4.543l; US = 3.785l*)
gallop ['gæləp] *n* galoppo ▷ *vi* galoppare

gallstone ['gɔːlstəun] *n* calcolo biliare
gamble ['gæmbl] *n* azzardo, rischio calcolato ▷ *vt, vi* giocare; **to ~ on** (*fig*) giocare su; **gambler** *n* giocatore(-trice) d'azzardo; **gambling** *n* gioco d'azzardo
game [geɪm] *n* gioco; (*event*) partita; (*Tennis*) game *m inv*; (*Culin, Hunting*) selvaggina ▷ *adj* (*ready*): **to be ~ (for sth/to do)** essere pronto(-a) (a qc/a fare); **big ~** selvaggina grossa; **games** *npl* (*Scol*) attività *fpl* sportive; **big ~** selvaggina grossa; **games console** [geɪmz-] *n* console *f inv* dei videogame; **game show** ['geɪmʃəu] *n* gioco a premi
gammon ['gæmən] *n* (*bacon*) quarto di maiale; (*ham*) prosciutto affumicato
gang [gæŋ] *n* banda, squadra ▷ *vi* **to ~ up on sb** far combutta contro qn
gangster ['gæŋstəʳ] *n* gangster *m inv*
gap [gæp] *n* (*space*) buco; (*in time*) intervallo; (*difference*): **~ (between)** divario (tra)
gape [geɪp] *vi* (*person*) restare a bocca aperta; (*shirt, hole*) essere spalancato(-a)
gap year *n* (*Scol*) *anno di pausa durante il quale gli studenti viaggiono o lavorano*
garage ['gærɑːʒ] *n* garage *m inv*; **garage sale** *n vendita di oggetti usati nel garage di un privato*
garbage ['gɑːbɪdʒ] (US) *n* immondizie *fpl*, rifiuti *mpl*; (*inf*) sciocchezze *fpl*; **garbage can** (US) *n* bidone *m* della spazzatura; **garbage collector** (US) *n* spazzino(-a)
garden ['gɑːdn] *n* giardino; **gardens** *npl* (*public park*) giardini pubblici; **garden centre** *n* vivaio; **gardener** *n* giardiniere(-a); **gardening** *n* giardinaggio
garlic ['gɑːlɪk] *n* aglio
garment ['gɑːmənt] *n* indumento
garnish ['gɑːnɪʃ] *vt* (*food*) guarnire
garrison ['gærɪsn] *n* guarnigione *f*
gas [gæs] *n* gas *m inv*; (US: *gasoline*) benzina ▷ *vt* asfissiare con il gas; **I can smell ~** sento odore di gas; **gas cooker** (BRIT) *n* cucina a gas; **gas cylinder** *n* bombola del gas; **gas fire** (BRIT) *n* radiatore *m* a gas
gasket ['gæskɪt] *n* (*Aut*) guarnizione *f*
gasoline ['gæsəliːn] (US) *n* benzina
gasp [gɑːsp] *n* respiro affannoso, ansito ▷ *vi* ansare, ansimare; (*in surprise*) restare senza fiato
gas: **gas pedal** (*esp* US) *n* pedale *m* dell'acceleratore; **gas station** (US) *n* distributore *m* di benzina; **gas tank** (US) *n* (*Aut*) serbatoio (di benzina)
gate [geɪt] *n* cancello; (*at airport*) uscita
gateau ['gætəu] (*pl* **gateaux**) *n* torta
gatecrash ['geɪtkræʃ] (BRIT) *vt* partecipare senza invito a
gateway ['geɪtweɪ] *n* porta
gather ['gæðəʳ] *vt* (*flowers, fruit*) cogliere; (*pick up*) raccogliere; (*assemble*) radunare; raccogliere; (*understand*) capire; (*Sewing*) increspare ▷ *vi* (*assemble*) radunarsi; **to ~ speed** acquistare velocità; **gathering** *n* adunanza
gauge [geɪdʒ] *n* (*instrument*) indicatore *m* ▷ *vt* misurare; (*fig*) valutare
gave [geɪv] *pt of* **give**
gay [geɪ] *adj* (*homosexual*) omosessuale; (*cheerful*) gaio(-a), allegro(-a); (*colour*) vivace, vivo(-a)
gaze [geɪz] *n* sguardo fisso ▷ *vi* **to ~ at** guardare fisso
GB *abbr* = **Great Britain**
GCSE (BRIT) *n abbr General Certificate of Secondary Education*
gear [gɪəʳ] *n* attrezzi *mpl*, equipaggiamento; (*Tech*) ingranaggio; (*Aut*) marcia ▷ *vt* (*fig: adapt*): **to ~ sth to** adattare qc a; **in top** *or* (US) **high/low ~** in quarta (*or* quinta)/seconda; **in ~** in marcia; **gear up** *vi* **to gear up (to do)** prepararsi (a fare); **gear box**

n scatola del cambio; **gear lever** *n* leva del cambio; **gear shift** (*US*), **gear stick** (*BRIT*) *n* = **gear lever**
geese [gi:s] *npl of* **goose**
gel [dʒɛl] *n* gel *m inv*
gem [dʒɛm] *n* gemma
Gemini ['dʒɛmɪnaɪ] *n* Gemelli *mpl*
gender ['dʒɛndəʳ] *n* genere *m*
gene [dʒi:n] *n* (*Biol*) gene *m*
general ['dʒɛnərl] *n* generale *m* ▷ *adj* generale; **in ~** in genere; **general anaesthetic** (*US* **general anesthetic**) *n* anestesia totale; **general election** *n* elezioni *fpl* generali; **generalize** *vi* generalizzare; **generally** *adv* generalmente; **general practitioner** *n* medico generico; **general store** *n* emporio
generate ['dʒɛnəreɪt] *vt* generare
generation [dʒɛnə'reɪʃən] *n* generazione *f*
generator ['dʒɛnəreɪtəʳ] *n* generatore *m*
generosity [dʒɛnə'rɔsɪtɪ] *n* generosità
generous ['dʒɛnərəs] *adj* generoso(-a); (*copious*) abbondante
genetic [dʒɪ'nɛtɪk] *adj* genetico(-a); **~ engineering** ingegneria genetica; **genetically modified** *adj* geneticamente modificato(-a), transgenico(-a); **genetics** *n* genetica
Geneva [dʒɪ'ni:və] *n* Ginevra
genitals ['dʒɛnɪtlz] *npl* genitali *mpl*
genius ['dʒi:nɪəs] *n* genio
Genoa ['dʒɛnəuə] *n* Genova
gent [dʒɛnt] *n abbr* = **gentleman**
gentle ['dʒɛntl] *adj* delicato(-a); (*person*) dolce

> Be careful not to translate ***gentle*** by the Italian word ***gentile***.

gentleman ['dʒɛntlmən] (*irreg*) *n* signore *m*; (*well-bred man*) gentiluomo
gently ['dʒɛntlɪ] *adv* delicatamente
gents [dʒɛnts] *n* W.C. *m* (per signori)
genuine ['dʒɛnjuɪn] *adj* autentico(-a); sincero(-a); **genuinely** *adv* genuinamente
geographic(al) [dʒɪə'græfɪk(l)] *adj* geografico(-a)
geography [dʒɪ'ɔgrəfɪ] *n* geografia
geology [dʒɪ'ɔlədʒɪ] *n* geologia
geometry [dʒɪ'ɔmətrɪ] *n* geometria
geranium [dʒɪ'reɪnjəm] *n* geranio
geriatric [dʒɛrɪ'ætrɪk] *adj* geriatrico(-a)
germ [dʒə:m] *n* (*Med*) microbo; (*Biol, fig*) germe *m*
German ['dʒə:mən] *adj* tedesco(-a) ▷ *n* tedesco(-a); (*Ling*) tedesco; **German measles** (*BRIT*) *n* rosolia
Germany ['dʒə:mənɪ] *n* Germania
gesture ['dʒɛstjəʳ] *n* gesto

KEYWORD

get [gɛt] (*pt, pp* **got**, (*US*) *pp* **gotten**) *vi* **1** (*become, be*) diventare, farsi; **to get old** invecchiare; **to get tired** stancarsi; **to get drunk** ubriacarsi; **to get killed** venire *or* rimanere ucciso(-a); **when do I get paid?** quando mi pagate?; **it's getting late** si sta facendo tardi
2 (*go*): **to get to/from** andare a/da; **to get home** arrivare *or* tornare a casa; **how did you get here?** come sei venuto?
3 (*begin*) mettersi a, cominciare a; **to get to know sb** incominciare a conoscere qn; **let's get going** *or* **started** muoviamoci
4 (*modal aux vb*): **you've got to do it** devi farlo
▷ *vt* **1**: **to get sth done** (*do*) fare qc; (*have done*) far fare qc; **to get one's hair cut** farsi tagliare i capelli; **to get sb to do sth** far fare qc a qn
2 (*obtain*: *money, permission, results*) ottenere; (*find*: *job, flat*) trovare; (*fetch*: *person, doctor*) chiamare; (: *object*) prendere; **to get sth for sb** prendere *or* procurare qc a qn; **get me Mr Jones, please** (*Tel*) mi passi il signor Jones, per favore; **can I get you a**

drink? le posso offrire da bere?
3 (*receive*: *present, letter, prize*) ricevere; (*acquire*: *reputation*) farsi; **how much did you get for the painting?** quanto le hanno dato per il quadro?
4 (*catch*) prendere; (*hit*: *target etc*) colpire; **to get sb by the arm/throat** afferrare qn per un braccio/alla gola; **get him!** prendetelo!
5 (*take, move*) portare; **to get sth to sb** far avere qc a qn; **do you think we'll get it through the door?** pensi che riusciremo a farlo passare per la porta?
6 (*catch, take*: *plane, bus etc*) prendere; **where do we get the ferry to ...?** dove si prende il traghetto per ...?
7 (*understand*) afferrare; (*hear*) sentire; **I've got it!** ci sono arrivato!, ci sono!; **I'm sorry, I didn't get your name** scusi, non ho capito (*or* sentito) il suo nome
8 (*have, possess*): **to have got** avere; **how many have you got?** quanti ne ha?
get along *vi* (*agree*) andare d'accordo; (*depart*) andarsene; (*manage*) = **get by**
get at *vt fus* (*attack*) prendersela con; (*reach*) raggiungere, arrivare a
get away *vi* partire, andarsene; (*escape*) scappare
get away with *vt fus* cavarsela; farla franca
get back *vi* (*return*) ritornare, tornare ▷ *vt* riottenere, riavere; **when do we get back?** quando ritorniamo?
get by *vi* (*pass*) passare; (*manage*) farcela
get down *vi, vt fus* scendere ▷ *vt* far scendere; (*depress*) buttare giù
get down to *vt fus* (*work*) mettersi a (fare)
get in *vi* entrare; (*train*) arrivare; (*arrive home*) ritornare, tornare
get into *vt fus* entrare in; **to get into a rage** incavolarsi
get off *vi* (*from train etc*) scendere; (*depart*: *person, car*) andare via; (*escape*) cavarsela ▷ *vt* (*remove*: *clothes, stain*) levare ▷ *vt fus* (*train, bus*) scendere da; **where do I get off?** dove devo scendere?
get on *vi* (*at exam etc*) andare; (*agree*): **to get on (with)** andare d'accordo (con) ▷ *vt fus* montare in; (*horse*) montare su
get out *vi* uscire; (*of vehicle*) scendere ▷ *vt* tirar fuori, far uscire
get out of *vt fus* uscire da; (*duty etc*) evitare
get over *vt fus* (*illness*) riaversi da
get round *vt fus* aggirare; (*fig*: *person*) rigirare
get through *vi* (*Tel*) avere la linea
get through to *vt fus* (*Tel*) parlare a
get together *vi* riunirsi ▷ *vt* raccogliere; (*people*) adunare
get up *vi* (*rise*) alzarsi ▷ *vt fus* salire su per
get up to *vt fus* (*reach*) raggiungere; (*prank etc*) fare

getaway ['gɛtəweɪ] *n* fuga
Ghana ['gɑːnə] *n* Ghana *m*
ghastly ['gɑːstlɪ] *adj* orribile, orrendo(-a); (*pale*) spettrale
ghetto ['gɛtəu] *n* ghetto
ghost [gəust] *n* fantasma *m*, spettro
giant ['dʒaɪənt] *n* gigante *m* ▷ *adj* gigantesco(-a), enorme
gift [gɪft] *n* regalo; (*donation, ability*) dono; **gifted** *adj* dotato(-a); **gift shop** (*US* **gift store**) *n* negozio di souvenir
gift token, gift voucher *n* buono *m* omaggio *inv*
gig [gɪg] *n* (*inf*: *of musician*) serata
gigabyte [giːgəbaɪt] *n* gigabyte *m inv*
gigantic [dʒaɪ'gæntɪk] *adj* gigantesco(-a)
giggle ['gɪgl] *vi* ridere scioccamente
gills [gɪlz] *npl* (*of fish*) branchie *fpl*
gilt [gɪlt] *n* doratura ▷ *adj* dorato(-a)
gimmick ['gɪmɪk] *n* trucco

gin [dʒɪn] *n* (*liquor*) gin *m inv*
ginger ['dʒɪndʒə^r] *n* zenzero
gipsy ['dʒɪpsɪ] *n* zingaro(-a)
giraffe [dʒɪ'rɑːf] *n* giraffa
girl [gəːl] *n* ragazza; (*young unmarried woman*) signorina; (*daughter*) figlia, figliola; **girlfriend** *n* (*of girl*) amica; (*of boy*) ragazza; **Girl Scout** (US) *n* Giovane Esploratrice *f*
gist [dʒɪst] *n* succo
give [gɪv] (*pt* **gave**, *pp* **given**) *vt* dare ▷ *vi* cedere; **to ~ sb sth, ~ sth to sb** dare qc a qn; **I'll ~ you £5 for it** te lo pago 5 sterline; **to ~ a cry/sigh** emettere un grido/sospiro; **to ~ a speech** fare un discorso; **give away** *vt* dare via; (*disclose*) rivelare; (*bride*) condurre all'altare; **give back** *vt* rendere; **give in** *vi* cedere ▷ *vt* consegnare; **give out** *vt* distribuire; annunciare; **give up** *vi* rinunciare ▷ *vt* rinunciare a; **to give up smoking** smettere di fumare; **to give o.s. up** arrendersi
given ['gɪvn] *pp of* **give** ▷ *adj* (*fixed: time, amount*) dato(-a), determinato(-a) ▷ *conj* **~ (that) ...** dato che ...; **~ the circumstances ...** date le circostanze ...
glacier ['glæsɪə^r] *n* ghiacciaio
glad [glæd] *adj* lieto(-a), contento(-a); **gladly** ['glædlɪ] *adv* volentieri
glamorous ['glæmərəs] *adj* affascinante, seducente
glamour ['glæmə^r] (US **glamor**) *n* fascino
glance [glɑːns] *n* occhiata, sguardo ▷ *vi* **to ~ at** dare un'occhiata a; **to ~ off** (*bullet*) rimbalzare su
gland [glænd] *n* ghiandola
glare [glɛə^r] *n* (*of anger*) sguardo furioso; (*of light*) riverbero, luce *f* abbagliante; (*of publicity*) chiasso ▷ *vi* abbagliare; **to ~ at** guardare male; **glaring** *adj* (*mistake*) madornale
glass [glɑːs] *n* (*substance*) vetro; (*tumbler*) bicchiere *m*; **glasses** *npl* (*spectacles*) occhiali *mpl*
glaze [gleɪz] *vt* (*door*) fornire di vetri; (*pottery*) smaltare ▷ *n* smalto
gleam [gliːm] *vi* luccicare
glen [glɛn] *n* valletta
glide [glaɪd] *vi* scivolare; (*Aviat, birds*) planare; **glider** *n* (*Aviat*) aliante *m*
glimmer ['glɪmə^r] *n* barlume *m*
glimpse [glɪmps] *n* impressione *f* fugace ▷ *vt* vedere al volo
glint [glɪnt] *vi* luccicare
glisten ['glɪsn] *vi* luccicare
glitter ['glɪtə^r] *vi* scintillare
global ['gləubl] *adj* globale; **globalization** [ˌgləʊbəlaɪ'zeɪʃən] *n* globalizzazione *f*; **global warming** *n* effetto *m* serra *inv*
globe [gləub] *n* globo, sfera
gloom [gluːm] *n* oscurità, buio; (*sadness*) tristezza, malinconia; **gloomy** *adj* scuro(-a), fosco(-a), triste
glorious ['glɔːrɪəs] *adj* glorioso(-a), magnifico(-a)
glory ['glɔːrɪ] *n* gloria; splendore *m*
gloss [glɔs] *n* (*shine*) lucentezza; (*also:* **~ paint**) vernice *f* a olio
glossary ['glɔsərɪ] *n* glossario
glossy ['glɔsɪ] *adj* lucente
glove [glʌv] *n* guanto; **glove compartment** *n* (*Aut*) vano portaoggetti
glow [gləu] *vi* ardere; (*face*) essere luminoso(-a)
glucose ['gluːkəus] *n* glucosio
glue [gluː] *n* colla ▷ *vt* incollare
GM *adj abbr* (= *genetically modified*) geneticamente modificato(-a)
gm *abbr* = **gram**
GM-free [ˌdʒiːem'friː] *adj* privo(-a) di OGM
GMO *n abbr* (= *genetically modified organism*) OGM *m inv*
GMT *abbr* (= *Greenwich Mean Time*) T.M.G.
gnaw [nɔː] *vt* rodere
go [gəu] (*pt* **went**, *pp* **gone**) (*pl* **goes**) *vi* andare; (*depart*) partire, andarsene;

(*work*) funzionare; (*time*) passare; (*break etc*) rompersi; (*be sold*): **to go for £10** essere venduto per 10 sterline; (*fit, suit*): **to go with** andare bene con; (*become*): **to go pale** diventare pallido(-a); **to go mouldy** ammuffire ▷ *n* **to have a go (at)** provare; **to be on the go** essere in moto; **whose go is it?** a chi tocca?; **he's going to do** sta per fare; **to go for a walk** andare a fare una passeggiata; **to go dancing/shopping** andare a ballare/fare la spesa; **just then the bell went** proprio allora suonò il campanello; **how did it go?** com'è andato?; **to go round the back/by the shop** passare da dietro/davanti al negozio; **go ahead** *vi* andare avanti; **go away** *vi* partire, andarsene; **go back** *vi* tornare, ritornare; **go by** *vi* (*years, time*) scorrere ▷ *vt fus* attenersi a, seguire (alla lettera); prestar fede a; **go down** *vi* scendere; (*ship*) affondare; (*sun*) tramontare ▷ *vt fus* scendere; **go for** *vt fus* (*fetch*) andare a prendere; (*like*) andar matto(-a) per; (*attack*) attaccare; saltare addosso a; **go in** *vi* entrare; **go into** *vt fus* entrare in; (*investigate*) indagare, esaminare; (*embark on*) lanciarsi in; **go off** *vi* partire, andar via; (*food*) guastarsi; (*explode*) esplodere, scoppiare; (*event*) passare ▷ *vt fus* **I've gone off chocolate** la cioccolata non mi piace più; **the gun went off** il fucile si scaricò; **go on** *vi* continuare; (*happen*) succedere; **to go on doing** continuare a fare; **go out** *vi* uscire; (*couple*): **they went out for 3 years** sono stati insieme per 3 anni; (*fire, light*) spegnersi; **go over** *vi* (*ship*) ribaltarsi ▷ *vt fus* (*check*) esaminare; **go past** *vi* passare ▷ *vt fus* passare davanti a; **go round** *vi* (*circulate: news, rumour*) circolare; (*revolve*) girare; (*visit*): **to go round (to sb's)** passare (da qn); (*make a detour*): **to ~ round (by)** passare (per); (*suffice*) bastare (per tutti); **go through** *vt fus* (*town etc*) attraversare; (*files, papers*) passare in rassegna; (*examine: list etc*) leggere da cima a fondo; **go up** *vi* salire; **go with** *vt fus* (*accompany*) accompagnare; **go without** *vt fus* fare a meno di

go-ahead ['gəuəhɛd] *adj* intraprendente ▷ *n* via *m*

goal [gəul] *n* (*Sport*) gol *m*, rete *f*; (*: place*) porta; (*fig: aim*) fine *m*, scopo; **goalkeeper** *n* portiere *m*; **goal-post** *n* palo (della porta)

goat [gəut] *n* capra

gobble ['gɔbl] *vt* (*also:* **~ down, ~ up**) ingoiare

god [gɔd] *n* dio; **G~** Dio; **godchild** *n* figlioccio(-a); **goddaughter** *n* figlioccia; **goddess** *n* dea; **godfather** *n* padrino; **godmother** *n* madrina; **godson** *n* figlioccio

goggles ['gɔglz] *npl* occhiali *mpl* (di protezione)

going ['gəuɪŋ] *n* (*conditions*) andare *m*, stato del terreno ▷ *adj* **the ~ rate** la tariffa in vigore

gold [gəuld] *n* oro ▷ *adj* d'oro; **golden** *adj* (*made of gold*) d'oro; (*gold in colour*) dorato(-a); **goldfish** *n* pesce *m* dorato *or* rosso; **goldmine** *n* (*also fig*) miniera d'oro; **gold-plated** *adj* placcato(-a) oro *inv*

golf [gɔlf] *n* golf *m*; **golf ball** *n* (*for game*) pallina da golf; (*on typewriter*) pallina; **golf club** *n* circolo di golf; (*stick*) bastone *m or* mazza da golf; **golf course** *n* campo di golf; **golfer** *n* giocatore(-trice) di golf

gone [gɔn] *pp of* **go** ▷ *adj* partito(-a)

gong [gɔŋ] *n* gong *m inv*

good [gud] *adj* buono(-a); (*kind*) buono(-a), gentile; (*child*) bravo(-a) ▷ *n* bene *m*; **goods** *npl* (*Comm etc*) beni *mpl*; merci *fpl*; **~!** bene!, ottimo!; **to be ~ at** essere bravo(-a) in; **to be ~ for** andare bene per; **it's ~ for you**

fa bene; **would you be ~ enough to ...?** avrebbe la gentilezza di ...?; **a ~ deal (of)** molto(-a), una buona quantità (di); **a ~ many** molti(-e); **to make ~** (*loss, damage*) compensare; **it's no ~ complaining** brontolare non serve a niente; **for ~** per sempre, definitivamente; **~ morning!** buon giorno!; **~ afternoon/evening!** buona sera!; **~ night!** buona notte!; **goodbye** *excl* arrivederci!; **Good Friday** *n* Venerdì Santo; **good-looking** *adj* bello(-a); **good-natured** *adj* affabile; **goodness** *n* (*of person*) bontà; **for goodness sake!** per amor di Dio!; **goodness gracious!** santo cielo!, mamma mia!; **goods train** (BRIT) *n* treno *m* merci *inv*; **goodwill** *n* amicizia, benevolenza

Google® ['gu:gl] *n* Google® *m* ▷ *vt* fare ricerche in Internet su

goose [gu:s] (*pl* **geese**) *n* oca

gooseberry ['guzbərɪ] *n* uva spina; **to play ~** (BRIT) tenere la candela

goose bumps, goose pimples *npl* pelle *f* d'oca

gorge [gɔ:dʒ] *n* gola ▷ *vt* **to ~ o.s. (on)** ingozzarsi (di)

gorgeous ['gɔ:dʒəs] *adj* magnifico(-a)

gorilla [gə'rɪlə] *n* gorilla *m inv*

gosh (*inf*) [gɔʃ] *excl* perdinci!

gospel ['gɔspl] *n* vangelo

gossip ['gɔsɪp] *n* chiacchiere *fpl*; pettegolezzi *mpl*; (*person*) pettegolo(-a) ▷ *vi* chiacchierare; **gossip column** *n* cronaca mondana

got [gɔt] *pt, pp of* **get**

gotten ['gɔtn] (US) *pp of* **get**

gourmet ['guəmeɪ] *n* buongustaio(-a)

govern ['gʌvən] *vt* governare; **government** ['gʌvnmənt] *n* governo; **governor** ['gʌvənə^r] *n* (*of state, bank*) governatore *m*; (*of school, hospital*) amministratore *m*; (BRIT: *of prison*) direttore(-trice)

gown [gaun] *n* vestito lungo; (*of teacher*, BRIT: *of judge*) toga

G.P. *n abbr* = **general practitioner**

GPS *n abbr* (= *global positioning system*) GPS *m*

grab [græb] *vt* afferrare, arraffare; (*property, power*) impadronirsi di ▷ *vi* **to ~ at** cercare di afferrare

grace [greɪs] *n* grazia ▷ *vt* onorare; **5 days' ~** dilazione *f* di 5 giorni; **graceful** *adj* elegante, aggraziato(-a); **gracious** ['greɪʃəs] *adj* grazioso(-a), misericordioso(-a)

grade [greɪd] *n* (*Comm*) qualità *f inv*; classe *f*; categoria; (*in hierarchy*) grado; (*Scol*: *mark*) voto; (US: *school class*) classe ▷ *vt* classificare; ordinare; graduare; **grade crossing** (US) *n* passaggio a livello; **grade school** (US) *n* scuola elementare

gradient ['greɪdɪənt] *n* pendenza, inclinazione *f*

gradual ['grædjuəl] *adj* graduale; **gradually** *adv* man mano, a poco a poco

graduate [*n* 'grædjuɪt, *vb* 'grædjueɪt] *n* (*of university*) laureato(-a); (US: *of high school*) diplomato(-a) ▷ *vi* laurearsi; diplomarsi; **graduation** [-'eɪʃən] *n* (*ceremony*) consegna delle lauree (*or* dei diplomi)

graffiti [grə'fi:tɪ] *npl* graffiti *mpl*

graft [grɑ:ft] *n* (*Agr, Med*) innesto; (*bribery*) corruzione *f*; (BRIT: *hard work*): **it's hard ~** è un lavoraccio ▷ *vt* innestare

grain [greɪn] *n* grano; (*of sand*) granello; (*of wood*) venatura

gram [græm] *n* grammo

grammar ['græmə^r] *n* grammatica; **grammar school** (BRIT) *n* ≈ liceo

gramme [græm] *n* = **gram**

gran (*inf*) [græn] *n* (BRIT) nonna

grand [grænd] *adj* grande, magnifico(-a); grandioso(-a); **grandad** (*inf*) *n* = **granddad**; **grandchild** (*pl* **-children**) *n* nipote *m*; **granddad** (*inf*) *n* nonno;

granddaughter *n* nipote *f*; **grandfather** *n* nonno; **grandma** (*inf*) *n* nonna; **grandmother** *n* nonna; **grandpa** (*inf*) *n* = **granddad**; **grandparents** *npl* nonni *mpl*; **grand piano** *n* pianoforte *m* a coda; **Grand Prix** ['grɑ̃ː'priː] *n* (*Aut*) Gran Premio, Grand Prix *m inv*; **grandson** *n* nipote *m*
granite ['grænɪt] *n* granito
granny ['grænɪ] (*inf*) *n* nonna
grant [grɑːnt] *vt* accordare; (*a request*) accogliere; (*admit*) ammettere, concedere ▷ *n* (*Scol*) borsa; (*Admin*) sussidio, sovvenzione *f*; **to take sth for ~ed** dare qc per scontato; **to take sb for ~ed** dare per scontata la presenza di qn
grape [greɪp] *n* chicco d'uva, acino
grapefruit ['greɪpfruːt] *n* pompelmo
graph [grɑːf] *n* grafico; **graphic** *adj* grafico(-a); (*vivid*) vivido(-a); **graphics** *n* grafica ▷ *npl* illustrazioni *fpl*
grasp [grɑːsp] *vt* afferrare ▷ *n* (*grip*) presa; (*fig*) potere *m*; comprensione *f*
grass [grɑːs] *n* erba; **grasshopper** *n* cavalletta
grate [greɪt] *n* graticola (del focolare) ▷ *vi* cigolare, stridere ▷ *vt* (*Culin*) grattugiare
grateful ['greɪtful] *adj* grato(-a), riconoscente
grater ['greɪtəʳ] *n* grattugia
gratitude ['grætɪtjuːd] *n* gratitudine *f*
grave [greɪv] *n* tomba ▷ *adj* grave, serio(-a)
gravel ['grævl] *n* ghiaia
gravestone ['greɪvstəun] *n* pietra tombale
graveyard ['greɪvjɑːd] *n* cimitero
gravity ['grævɪtɪ] *n* (*Physics*) gravità; pesantezza; (*seriousness*) gravità, serietà
gravy ['greɪvɪ] *n* intingolo della carne; salsa
gray [greɪ] (US) *adj* = **grey**
graze [greɪz] *vi* pascolare, pascere ▷ *vt* (*touch lightly*) sfiorare; (*scrape*) escoriare ▷ *n* (*Med*) escoriazione *f*
grease [griːs] *n* (*fat*) grasso; (*lubricant*) lubrificante *m* ▷ *vt* ingrassare; lubrificare; **greasy** *adj* grasso(-a), untuoso(-a)
great [greɪt] *adj* grande; (*inf*) magnifico(-a), meraviglioso(-a); **Great Britain** *n* Gran Bretagna; **great-grandfather** *n* bisnonno; **great-grandmother** *n* bisnonna; **greatly** *adv* molto
Greece [griːs] *n* Grecia
greed [griːd] *n* (*also:* **~iness**) avarizia; (*for food*) golosità, ghiottoneria; **greedy** *adj* avido(-a); goloso(-a), ghiotto(-a)
Greek [griːk] *adj* greco(-a) ▷ *n* greco(-a); (*Ling*) greco
green [griːn] *adj* verde; (*inexperienced*) inesperto(-a), ingenuo(-a) ▷ *n* verde *m*; (*stretch of grass*) prato; (*on golf course*) green *m inv*; **greens** *npl* (*vegetables*) verdura; **green card** *n* (BRIT: *Aut*) carta verde; (US: *Admin*) *permesso di soggiorno e di lavoro*; **greengage** ['griːngeɪdʒ] *n* susina Regina Claudia; **greengrocer** (BRIT) *n* fruttivendolo(-a), erbivendolo(-a); **greenhouse** *n* serra; **greenhouse effect** *n* effetto serra
Greenland ['griːnlənd] *n* Groenlandia
green salad *n* insalata verde
greet [griːt] *vt* salutare; **greeting** *n* saluto; **greeting(s) card** *n* cartolina d'auguri
grew [gruː] *pt of* **grow**
grey [greɪ] (US **gray**) *adj* grigio(-a); **grey-haired** *adj* dai capelli grigi; **greyhound** *n* levriere *m*
grid [grɪd] *n* grata; (*Elec*) rete *f*; **gridlock** ['grɪdlɔk] *n* (*traffic jam*) paralisi *f inv* del traffico; **gridlocked** *adj* paralizzato(-a) dal traffico; (*talks etc*) in fase di stallo
grief [griːf] *n* dolore *m*
grievance ['griːvəns] *n* lagnanza

grieve [gri:v] *vi* addolorarsi; rattristarsi ▷ *vt* addolorare; **to ~ for sb** (*dead person*) piangere qn
grill [grɪl] *n* (*on cooker*) griglia; (*also:* **mixed ~**) grigliata mista ▷ *vt* (BRIT) cuocere ai ferri; (*inf: question*) interrogare senza sosta
grille [grɪl] *n* grata; (*Aut*) griglia
grim [grɪm] *adj* sinistro(-a), brutto(-a)
grime [graɪm] *n* sudiciume *m*
grin [grɪn] *n* sorriso smagliante ▷ *vi* fare un gran sorriso
grind [graɪnd] (*pt, pp* **ground**) *vt* macinare; (*make sharp*) arrotare ▷ *n* (*work*) sgobbata
grip [grɪp] *n* impugnatura; presa; (*holdall*) borsa da viaggio ▷ *vt* (*object*) afferrare; (*attention*) catturare; **to come to ~s with** affrontare; cercare di risolvere; **gripping** ['grɪpɪŋ] *adj* avvincente
grit [grɪt] *n* ghiaia; (*courage*) fegato ▷ *vt* (*road*) coprire di sabbia; **to ~ one's teeth** stringere i denti
grits [grɪts] (US) *npl* macinato grosso (di avena *etc*)
groan [grəun] *n* gemito ▷ *vi* gemere
grocer ['grəusəʳ] *n* negoziante *m* di generi alimentari; **groceries** *npl* provviste *fpl*; **grocer's (shop)** *n* negozio di (generi) alimentari
grocery ['grəusərɪ] *n* (*shop*) (negozio di) alimentari
groin [grɔɪn] *n* inguine *m*
groom [gru:m] *n* palafreniere *m*; (*also:* **bride~**) sposo ▷ *vt* (*horse*) strigliare; (*fig*): **to ~ sb for** avviare qn a; **well-~ed** (*person*) curato(-a)
groove [gru:v] *n* scanalatura, solco
grope [grəup] *vi* **to ~ for** cercare a tastoni
gross [grəus] *adj* grossolano(-a); (*Comm*) lordo(-a); **grossly** *adv* (*greatly*) molto
grotesque [grəu'tɛsk] *adj* grottesco(-a)
ground [graund] *pt, pp of* **grind** ▷ *n* suolo, terra; (*land*) terreno; (*Sport*) campo; (*reason: gen pl*) ragione *f*; (US: *also:* **~ wire**) terra ▷ *vt* (*plane*) tenere a terra; (US *Elec*) mettere la presa a terra a; **grounds** *npl* (*of coffee etc*) fondi *mpl*; (*gardens etc*) terreno, giardini *mpl*; **on/to the ~** per/a terra; **to gain/lose ~** guadagnare/perdere terreno; **ground floor** *n* pianterreno; **groundsheet** (BRIT) *n* telone *m* impermeabile; **groundwork** *n* preparazione *f*
group [gru:p] *n* gruppo ▷ *vt* (*also:* **~ together**) raggruppare ▷ *vi* (*also:* **~ together**) raggrupparsi
grouse [graus] *n inv* (*bird*) tetraone *m* ▷ *vi* (*complain*) brontolare
grovel ['grɔvl] *vi* (*fig*): **to ~ (before)** strisciare (di fronte a)
grow [grəu] (*pt* **grew**, *pp* **grown**) *vi* crescere; (*increase*) aumentare; (*develop*) svilupparsi; (*become*): **to ~ rich/weak** arricchirsi/indebolirsi ▷ *vt* coltivare, far crescere; **grow on** *vt fus* **that painting is growing on me** quel quadro più lo guardo più mi piace; **grow up** *vi* farsi grande, crescere
growl [graul] *vi* ringhiare
grown [grəun] *pp of* **grow**; **grown-up** *n* adulto(-a), grande *m/f*
growth [grəuθ] *n* crescita, sviluppo; (*what has grown*) crescita; (*Med*) escrescenza, tumore *m*
grub [grʌb] *n* larva; (*inf: food*) roba (da mangiare)
grubby ['grʌbɪ] *adj* sporco(-a)
grudge [grʌdʒ] *n* rancore *m* ▷ *vt* **to ~ sb sth** dare qc a qn di malavoglia; invidiare qc a qn; **to bear sb a ~ (for)** serbar rancore a qn (per)
gruelling ['gruəlɪŋ] (US **grueling**) *adj* estenuante
gruesome ['gru:səm] *adj* orribile
grumble ['grʌmbl] *vi* brontolare, lagnarsi
grumpy ['grʌmpɪ] *adj* scorbutico(-a)
grunt [grʌnt] *vi* grugnire
guarantee [gærən'ti:] *n* garanzia

▷ *vt* garantire
guard [gɑːd] *n* guardia; (*one man*) guardia, sentinella; (BRIT *Rail*) capotreno; (*on machine*) schermo protettivo; (*also:* **fire~**) parafuoco ▷ *vt* fare la guardia a; (*protect*): **to ~ (against)** proteggere (da); **to be on one's ~** stare in guardia; **guardian** *n* custode *m*; (*of minor*) tutore(-trice)
guerrilla [gə'rɪlə] *n* guerrigliero
guess [gɛs] *vi* indovinare ▷ *vt* indovinare; (US) credere, pensare ▷ *n* **to take** *or* **have a ~** provare a indovinare
guest [gɛst] *n* ospite *m/f*; (*in hotel*) cliente *m/f*; **guest house** *n* pensione *f*; **guest room** *n* camera degli ospiti
guidance ['gaɪdəns] *n* guida, direzione *f*
guide [gaɪd] *n* (*person, book etc*) guida; (BRIT: *also:* **girl ~**) giovane esploratrice *f* ▷ *vt* guidare; **is there an English-speaking ~?** c'è una guida che parla inglese?; **guidebook** *n* guida; **do you have a guidebook in English?** avete una guida in inglese?; **guide dog** *n* cane *m* guida *inv*; **guided tour** *n* visita guidata; **what time does the guided tour start?** a che ora comincia la visita guidata?; **guidelines** *npl* (*fig*) indicazioni *fpl*, linee *fpl* direttive
guild [gɪld] *n* arte *f*, corporazione *f*; associazione *f*
guilt [gɪlt] *n* colpevolezza; **guilty** *adj* colpevole
guinea pig ['gɪnɪ-] *n* cavia
guitar [gɪ'tɑː[r]] *n* chitarra; **guitarist** *n* chitarrista *m/f*
gulf [gʌlf] *n* golfo; (*abyss*) abisso
gull [gʌl] *n* gabbiano
gulp [gʌlp] *vi* deglutire; (*from emotion*) avere il nodo in gola ▷ *vt* (*also:* **~ down**) tracannare, inghiottire
gum [gʌm] *n* (*Anat*) gengiva; (*glue*) colla; (*also:* **~drop**) caramella gommosa; (*also:* **chewing ~**) chewing-gum *m inv* ▷ *vt* **to ~ (together)** incollare
gun [gʌn] *n* fucile *m*; (*small*) pistola, rivoltella; (*rifle*) carabina; (*shotgun*) fucile da caccia; (*cannon*) cannone *m*; **gunfire** *n* spari *mpl*; **gunman** (*irreg*) *n* bandito armato; **gunpoint** *n*: **at gunpoint** sotto minaccia di fucile; **gunpowder** *n* polvere *f* da sparo; **gunshot** *n* sparo
gush [gʌʃ] *vi* sgorgare; (*fig*) abbandonarsi ad effusioni
gust [gʌst] *n* (*of wind*) raffica; (*of smoke*) buffata
gut [gʌt] *n* intestino, budello; **guts** *npl* (*Anat*) interiora *fpl*; (*courage*) fegato
gutter ['gʌtə[r]] *n* (*of roof*) grondaia; (*in street*) cunetta
guy [gaɪ] *n* (*inf: man*) tipo, elemento; (*also:* **~rope**) cavo *or* corda di fissaggio; (*figure*) *effigie di Guy Fawkes*
Guy Fawkes Night [-'fɔːks-] *n* (BRIT) *vedi nota nel riquadro*

GUY FAWKES NIGHT

La sera del 5 novembre, in occasione della **Guy Fawkes Night**, altrimenti chiamata **Bonfire Night**, viene commemorato con falò e fuochi d'artificio il fallimento della Congiura delle Polveri contro Giacomo I nel 1605. La festa prende il nome dal principale congiurato della cospirazione, Guy Fawkes, la cui effigie viene bruciata durante i festeggiamenti.

gym [dʒɪm] *n* (*also:* **~nasium**) palestra; (*also:* **~nastics**) ginnastica; **gymnasium** [dʒɪm'neɪzɪəm] *n* palestra; **gymnast** ['dʒɪmnæst] *n* ginnasta *m/f*; **gymnastics** [-'næstɪks] *n, npl* ginnastica; **gym shoes** *npl* scarpe *fpl* da ginnastica
gynaecologist [gaɪnɪ'kɔlədʒɪst] (US **gynecologist**) *n* ginecologo(-a)
gypsy ['dʒɪpsɪ] *n* = **gipsy**

h

haberdashery ['hæbə'dæʃərɪ] (BRIT) *n* merceria

habit ['hæbɪt] *n* abitudine *f*; (*costume*) abito; (*Rel*) tonaca

habitat ['hæbɪtæt] *n* habitat *m inv*

hack [hæk] *vt* tagliare, fare a pezzi ▷ *n* (*pej*: *writer*) scribacchino(-a); **hacker** ['hækəʳ] *n* (*Comput*) pirata *m* informatico

had [hæd] *pt, pp of* **have**

haddock ['hædək] (*pl* **haddock** *or* **haddocks**) *n* eglefino

hadn't ['hædnt] = **had not**

haemorrhage ['hɛmərɪdʒ] (*US* **hemorrhage**) *n* emorragia

haemorrhoids ['hɛmərɔɪdz] (*US* **hemorrhoids**) *npl* emorroidi *fpl*

haggle ['hægl] *vi* mercanteggiare

Hague [heɪg] *n*: **The ~** L'Aia

hail [heɪl] *n* grandine *f*; (*of criticism etc*) pioggia ▷ *vt* (*call*) chiamare; (*flag down*: *taxi*) fermare; (*greet*) salutare ▷ *vi* grandinare; **hailstone** *n* chicco di grandine

hair [hɛəʳ] *n* capelli *mpl*; (*single hair*: *on head*) capello; (: *on body*) pelo; **to do one's ~** pettinarsi; **hairband** ['hɛəbænd] *n* (*elastic*) fascia per i capelli; (*rigid*) cerchietto; **hairbrush** *n* spazzola per capelli; **haircut** *n* taglio di capelli; **hairdo** ['hɛədu:] *n* acconciatura, pettinatura; **hairdresser** *n* parrucchiere(-a); **hairdresser's** *n* parrucchiere(-a); **hair dryer** *n* asciugacapelli *m inv*; **hair gel** *n* gel *m inv* per capelli; **hairpin** *n* forcina; **hairpin bend** (*US* **hairpin curve**) n tornante *m*; **hairraising** *adj* orripilante; **hair spray** *n* lacca per capelli; **hairstyle** *n* pettinatura, acconciatura; **hairy** *adj* irsuto(-a), peloso(-a); (*inf*: *frightening*) spaventoso(-a)

hake [heɪk] (*pl* **hake** *or* **hakes**) *n* nasello

half [hɑ:f] (*pl* **halves**) *n* mezzo, metà *f inv* ▷ *adj* mezzo(-a) ▷ *adv* a mezzo, a metà; **~ an hour** mezz'ora; **~ a dozen** mezza dozzina; **~ a pound** mezza libbra; **two and a ~** due e mezzo; **a week and a ~** una settimana e mezza; **~ (of it)** la metà; **~ (of)** la metà di; **to cut sth in ~** tagliare qc in due; **~ asleep** mezzo(-a) addormentato(-a); **half board** (BRIT) *n* mezza pensione; **half-brother** *n* fratellastro; **half day** *n* mezza giornata; **half fare** *n* tariffa a metà prezzo; **half-hearted** *adj* tiepido(-a); **half-hour** *n* mezz'ora; **half-price** *adj, adv* a metà prezzo; **half term** (BRIT) *n* (*Scol*) vacanza a *or* di metà trimestre; **half-time** *n* (*Sport*) intervallo; **halfway** *adv* a metà strada

hall [hɔ:l] *n* sala, salone *m*; (*entrance way*) entrata

hallmark ['hɔ:lmɑ:k] *n* marchio di garanzia; (*fig*) caratteristica

hallo [hə'ləu] *excl* = **hello**

hall of residence (BRIT) *n* casa dello studente

Halloween [hæləu'i:n] *n* vigilia d'Ognissanti

HALLOWEEN

Negli Stati Uniti e in Gran Bretagna il 31 ottobre si festeggia **Halloween**, la notte delle streghe e dei fantasmi. I bambini, travestiti da fantasmi, streghe o mostri, bussano alle porte e ricevono dolci e piccoli doni.

hallucination [həlu:sɪ'neɪʃən] *n* allucinazione *f*
hallway ['hɔ:lweɪ] *n* corridoio; (*entrance*) ingresso
halo ['heɪləu] *n* (*of saint etc*) aureola
halt [hɔ:lt] *n* fermata ▷ *vt* fermare ▷ *vi* fermarsi
halve [hɑ:v] *vt* (*apple etc*) dividere a metà; (*expense*) ridurre di metà
halves [hɑ:vz] *npl of* **half**
ham [hæm] *n* prosciutto
hamburger ['hæmbə:gər] *n* hamburger *m inv*
hamlet ['hæmlɪt] *n* paesetto
hammer ['hæmər] *n* martello ▷ *vt* martellare ▷ *vi* **to ~ on** *or* **at the door** picchiare alla porta
hammock ['hæmək] *n* amaca
hamper ['hæmpər] *vt* impedire ▷ *n* cesta
hamster ['hæmstər] *n* criceto
hamstring ['hæmstrɪŋ] *n* (*Anat*) tendine *m* del ginocchio
hand [hænd] *n* mano *f*; (*of clock*) lancetta; (*handwriting*) scrittura; (*at cards*) mano; (*: game*) partita; (*worker*) operaio(-a) ▷ *vt* dare, passare; **to give sb a ~** dare una mano a qn; **at ~** a portata di mano; **in ~** a disposizione; (*work*) in corso; **on ~** (*person*) disponibile; (*services*) pronto(-a) a intervenire; **to ~** (*information etc*) a portata di mano; **on the one ~ ..., on the other ~** da un lato ..., dall'altro; **hand down** *vt* passare giù; (*tradition, heirloom*) tramandare; (*US: sentence, verdict*) emettere; **hand in** *vt* consegnare; **hand out** *vt* distribuire; **hand over** *vt* passare; cedere; **handbag** *n* borsetta; **hand baggage** *n* bagaglio a mano; **handbook** *n* manuale *m*; **handbrake** *n* freno a mano; **handcuffs** *npl* manette *fpl*; **handful** *n* manciata, pugno
handicap ['hændɪkæp] *n* handicap *m inv* ▷ *vt* handicappare; **to be physically ~ped** essere handicappato(-a); **to be mentally ~ped** essere un(a) handicappato(-a) mentale
handkerchief ['hæŋkətʃɪf] *n* fazzoletto
handle ['hændl] *n* (*of door etc*) maniglia; (*of cup etc*) ansa; (*of knife etc*) impugnatura; (*of saucepan*) manico; (*for winding*) manovella ▷ *vt* toccare, maneggiare; (*deal with*) occuparsi di; (*treat: people*) trattare; **"~ with care"** "fragile"; **to fly off the ~** (*fig*) perdere le staffe, uscire dai gangheri; **handlebar(s)** *n(pl)* manubrio
hand: **hand luggage** *n* bagagli *mpl* a mano; **handmade** *adj* fatto(-a) a mano; **handout** *n* (*money, food*) elemosina; (*leaflet*) volantino; (*at lecture*) prospetto; **hands-free** *n* (*telephone*) con auricolare; (*microphone*) vivavoce *inv*
handsome ['hænsəm] *adj* bello(-a); (*profit, fortune*) considerevole
handwriting ['hændraɪtɪŋ] *n* scrittura
handy ['hændɪ] *adj* (*person*) bravo(-a); (*close at hand*) a portata di mano; (*convenient*) comodo(-a)
hang [hæŋ] (*pt, pp* **hung**) *vt* appendere; (*criminal: pt, pp hanged*) impiccare ▷ *vi* (*painting*) essere appeso(-a); (*hair*) scendere; (*drapery*) cadere; **to get the ~ of sth** (*inf*) capire come qc funziona; **hang about** *or*

around *vi* bighellonare, ciondolare; **hang down** *vi* ricadere; **hang on** *vi* (*wait*) aspettare; **hang out** *vt* (*washing*) stendere (fuori); (*inf: live*) stare ▷ *vi* penzolare, pendere; **hang round** *vi* = **hang around**; **hang up** *vi* (*Tel*) riattaccàre ▷ *vt* appendere

hanger ['hæŋəʳ] *n* gruccia

hang-gliding ['-glaɪdɪŋ] *n* volo col deltaplano

hangover ['hæŋəuvəʳ] *n* (*after drinking*) postumi *mpl* di sbornia

hankie ['hæŋkɪ] *n abbr* = **handkerchief**

happen ['hæpən] *vi* accadere, succedere; (*chance*): **to ~ to do sth** fare qc per caso; **what ~ed?** cos'è successo?; **as it ~s** guarda caso

happily ['hæpɪlɪ] *adv* felicemente; fortunatamente

happiness ['hæpɪnɪs] *n* felicità, contentezza

happy ['hæpɪ] *adj* felice, contento(-a); **~ with** (*arrangements etc*) soddisfatto(-a) di; **to be ~ to do** (*willing*) fare volentieri; **~ birthday!** buon compleanno!

harass ['hærəs] *vt* molestare; **harassment** *n* molestia

harbour ['hɑːbəʳ] (*US* **harbor**) *n* porto ▷ *vt* (*hope, fear*) nutrire; (*criminal*) dare rifugio a

hard [hɑːd] *adj* duro(-a) ▷ *adv* (*work*) sodo; (*think, try*) bene; **to look ~ at** guardare fissamente; esaminare attentamente; **no ~ feelings!** senza rancore!; **to be ~ of hearing** essere duro(-a) d'orecchio; **to be ~ done by** essere trattato(-a) ingiustamente; **hardback** *n* libro rilegato; **hardboard** *n* legno precompresso; **hard disk** *n* (*Comput*) disco rigido; **harden** *vt, vi* indurire

hardly ['hɑːdlɪ] *adv* (*scarcely*) appena; **it's ~ the case** non è proprio il caso; **~ anyone/anywhere** quasi nessuno/ da nessuna parte; **~ ever** quasi mai

hard: **hardship** ['hɑːdʃɪp] *n* avversità *f inv*; privazioni *fpl*; **hard shoulder** (BRIT) *n* (*Aut*) corsia d'emergenza; **hard-up** (*inf*) *adj* al verde; **hardware** ['hɑːdwɛəʳ] *n* ferramenta *fpl*; (*Comput*) hardware *m*; (*Mil*) armamenti *mpl*; **hardware shop** (*US* **hardware store**) *n* (negozio di) ferramenta *fpl*; **hard-working** [-'wəːkɪŋ] *adj* lavoratore(-trice)

hardy ['hɑːdɪ] *adj* robusto(-a); (*plant*) resistente al gelo

hare [hɛəʳ] *n* lepre *f*

harm [hɑːm] *n* male *m*; (*wrong*) danno ▷ *vt* (*person*) fare male a; (*thing*) danneggiare; **out of ~'s way** al sicuro; **harmful** *adj* dannoso(-a); **harmless** *adj* innocuo(-a), inoffensivo(-a)

harmony ['hɑːmənɪ] *n* armonia

harness ['hɑːnɪs] *n* (*for horse*) bardatura, finimenti *mpl*; (*for child*) briglie *fpl*; (*safety harness*) imbracatura ▷ *vt* (*horse*) bardare; (*resources*) sfruttare

harp [hɑːp] *n* arpa ▷ *vi* **to ~ on about** insistere tediosamente su

harsh [hɑːʃ] *adj* (*life, winter*) duro(-a); (*judge, criticism*) severo(-a); (*sound*) rauco(-a); (*light*) violento(-a)

harvest ['hɑːvɪst] *n* raccolto; (*of grapes*) vendemmia ▷ *vt* fare il raccolto di, raccogliere; vendemmiare

has [hæz] *vb see* **have**

hasn't ['hæznt] = **has not**

hassle ['hæsl] (*inf*) *n* sacco di problemi

haste [heɪst] *n* fretta; precipitazione *f*; **hasten** ['heɪsn] *vt* affrettare ▷ *vi* **to hasten (to)** affrettarsi (a); **hastily** *adv* in fretta; precipitosamente; **hasty** *adj* affrettato(-a), precipitoso(-a)

hat [hæt] *n* cappello

hatch [hætʃ] *n* (*Naut*: *also*: **~way**) boccaporto; (*also*: **service ~**) portello di servizio ▷ *vi* (*bird*) uscire dal guscio; (*egg*) schiudersi

hatchback ['hætʃbæk] *n* (*Aut*) tre (*or* cinque) porte *f inv*

hate [heɪt] *vt* odiare, detestare ▷ *n* odio; **hatred** ['heɪtrɪd] *n* odio
haul [hɔːl] *vt* trascinare, tirare ▷ *n* (*of fish*) pescata; (*of stolen goods etc*) bottino
haunt [hɔːnt] *vt* (*fear*) pervadere; (*person*) frequentare ▷ *n* rifugio; **this house is ~ed** questa casa è abitata da un fantasma; **haunted** *adj* (*castle etc*) abitato(-a) dai fantasmi *or* dagli spiriti; (*look*) ossessionato(-a), tormentato(-a)

KEYWORD

have [hæv] (*pt, pp* **had**) *aux vb* **1** (*gen*) avere; essere; **to have arrived/gone** essere arrivato(-a)/andato(-a); **to have eaten/slept** avere mangiato/dormito; **he has been kind/promoted** è stato gentile/promosso; **having finished** *or* **when he had finished, he left** dopo aver finito, se n'è andato
2 (*in tag questions*): **you've done it, haven't you?** l'ha fatto, (non è) vero?; **he hasn't done it, has he?** non l'ha fatto, vero?
3 (*in short answers and questions*): **you've made a mistake — no I haven't/so I have** ha fatto un errore — ma no, niente affatto/sì, è vero; **we haven't paid — yes we have!** non abbiamo pagato — ma sì che abbiamo pagato!; **I've been there before, have you?** ci sono già stato, e lei?
▷ *modal aux vb* (*be obliged*): **to have (got) to do sth** dover fare qc; **I haven't got** *or* **I don't have to wear glasses** non ho bisogno di portare gli occhiali
▷ *vt* **1** (*possess, obtain*) avere; **he has (got) blue eyes/dark hair** ha gli occhi azzurri/i capelli scuri; **do you have** *or* **have you got a car/phone?** ha la macchina/il telefono?; **may I have your address?** potrebbe darmi il suo indirizzo?; **you can have it for £5** te lo lascio per 5 sterline
2 (*+ noun: take, hold etc*): **to have breakfast/a swim/a bath** fare colazione/una nuotata/un bagno; **to have lunch** pranzare; **to have dinner** cenare; **to have a drink** bere qualcosa; **to have a cigarette** fumare una sigaretta
3: **to have sth done** far fare qc; **to have one's hair cut** farsi tagliare i capelli; **to have sb do sth** far fare qc a qn
4 (*experience, suffer*) avere; **to have a cold/flu** avere il raffreddore/l'influenza; **she had her bag stolen** le hanno rubato la borsa
5 (*inf: dupe*): **you've been had!** ci sei cascato!
have out *vt*: **to have it out with sb** (*settle a problem etc*) mettere le cose in chiaro con qn

haven ['heɪvn] *n* porto; (*fig*) rifugio
haven't ['hævnt] = **have not**
havoc ['hævək] *n* caos *m*
Hawaii [hə'waɪː] *n* le Hawaii
hawk [hɔːk] *n* falco
hawthorn ['hɔːθɔːn] *n* biancospino
hay [heɪ] *n* fieno; **hay fever** *n* febbre *f* da fieno; **haystack** *n* pagliaio
hazard ['hæzəd] *n* azzardo, ventura; pericolo, rischio ▷ *vt* (*guess etc*) azzardare; **hazardous** *adj* pericoloso(-a); **hazard warning lights** *npl* (*Aut*) luci *fpl* di emergenza
haze [heɪz] *n* foschia
hazel ['heɪzl] *n* (*tree*) nocciolo ▷ *adj* (*eyes*) (color) nocciola *inv*; **hazelnut** ['heɪzlnʌt] *n* nocciola
hazy ['heɪzɪ] *adj* fosco(-a); (*idea*) vago(-a)
he [hiː] *pron* lui, egli; **it is he who ...** è lui che ...
head [hɛd] *n* testa; (*leader*) capo; (*of school*) preside *m/f* ▷ *vt* (*list*) essere in testa a; (*group*) essere a capo di;

~s or tails testa (o croce), pari (o dispari); **~ first** a capofitto, di testa; **~ over heels in love** pazzamente innamorato(-a); **to ~ the ball** colpire una palla di testa; **head for** *vt fus* dirigersi verso; **head off** *vt* (*threat, danger*) sventare; **headache** *n* mal *m* di testa; **heading** *n* titolo; intestazione *f*; **headlamp** (BRIT) *n* = **headlight**; **headlight** *n* fanale *m*; **headline** *n* titolo; **head office** *n* sede *f* (centrale); **headphones** *npl* cuffia; **headquarters** *npl* ufficio centrale; (*Mil*) quartiere *m* generale; **headroom** *n* (*in car*) altezza dell'abitacolo; (*under bridge*) altezza limite; **headscarf** *n* foulard *m inv*; **headset** *n* = **headphones**; **headteacher** *n* (*of primary school*) direttore(-trice); (*of secondary school*) preside; **head waiter** *n* capocameriere *m*

heal [hi:l] *vt, vi* guarire

health [hɛlθ] *n* salute *f*; **health care** *n* assistenza sanitaria; **health centre** (BRIT) *n* poliambulatorio; **health food** *n* cibo macrobiotico; **Health Service** (BRIT) *n*: **the Health Service** ≈ il Servizio Sanitario Statale; **healthy** *adj* (*person*) sano(-a), in buona salute; (*climate*) salubre; (*appetite, economy etc*) sano(-a)

heap [hi:p] *n* mucchio ▷ *vt* (*stones, sand*): **to ~ (up)** ammucchiare; (*plate, sink*): **to ~ sth with** riempire qc di; **~s of** (*inf*) un mucchio di

hear [hɪəʳ] (*pt, pp* **heard**) *vt* sentire; (*news*) ascoltare ▷ *vi* sentire; **to ~ about** avere notizie di; sentire parlare di; **to ~ from sb** ricevere notizie da qn

hearing ['hɪərɪŋ] *n* (*sense*) udito; (*of witnesses*) audizione *f*; (*of a case*) udienza; **hearing aid** *n* apparecchio acustico

hearse [hə:s] *n* carro funebre

heart [hɑ:t] *n* cuore *m*; **hearts** *npl* (*Cards*) cuori *mpl*; **to lose ~** scoraggiarsi; **to take ~** farsi coraggio; **at ~** in fondo; **by ~** (*learn, know*) a memoria; **heart attack** *n* attacco di cuore; **heartbeat** *n* battito del cuore; **heartbroken** *adj*: **to be heartbroken** avere il cuore spezzato; **heartburn** *n* bruciore *m* di stomaco; **heart disease** *n* malattia di cuore

hearth [hɑ:θ] *n* focolare *m*

heartless ['hɑ:tlɪs] *adj* senza cuore

hearty ['hɑ:tɪ] *adj* caloroso(-a); robusto(-a), sano(-a); vigoroso(-a)

heat [hi:t] *n* calore *m*; (*fig*) ardore *m*; fuoco; (*Sport*: *also*: **qualifying ~**) prova eliminatoria ▷ *vt* scaldare; **heat up** *vi* (*liquids*) scaldarsi; (*room*) riscaldarsi ▷ *vt* riscaldare; **heated** *adj* riscaldato(-a); (*argument*) acceso(-a); **heater** *n* radiatore *m*; (*stove*) stufa

heather ['hɛðəʳ] *n* erica

heating ['hi:tɪŋ] *n* riscaldamento

heatwave ['hi:tweɪv] *n* ondata di caldo

heaven ['hɛvn] *n* paradiso, cielo; **heavenly** *adj* divino(-a), celeste

heavily ['hɛvɪlɪ] *adv* pesantemente; (*drink, smoke*) molto

heavy ['hɛvɪ] *adj* pesante; (*sea*) grosso(-a); (*rain, blow*) forte; (*weather*) afoso(-a); (*drinker, smoker*) gran (*before noun*); **it's too ~** è troppo pesante

Hebrew ['hi:bru:] *adj* ebreo(-a) ▷ *n* (*Ling*) ebraico

hectare ['hɛktɑ:ʳ] *n* (BRIT) ettaro

hectic ['hɛktɪk] *adj* movimentato(-a)

he'd [hi:d] = **he would**; **he had**

hedge [hɛdʒ] *n* siepe *f* ▷ *vi* essere elusivo(-a); **to ~ one's bets** (*fig*) coprirsi dai rischi

hedgehog ['hɛdʒhɔg] *n* riccio

heed [hi:d] *vt* (*also*: **take ~ of**) badare a, far conto di

heel [hi:l] *n* (*Anat*) calcagno; (*of shoe*) tacco ▷ *vt* (*shoe*) rifare i tacchi a

hefty ['hɛftɪ] *adj* (*person*) robusto(-a); (*parcel*) pesante; (*profit*) grosso(-a)

height [haɪt] *n* altezza; (*high ground*) altura; (*fig*: *of glory*) apice *m*; (: *of*

stupidity) colmo; **heighten** *vt* (*fig*) accrescere
heir [ɛəʳ] *n* erede *m*; **heiress** *n* erede *f*
held [hɛld] *pt, pp of* **hold**
helicopter ['hɛlɪkɔptəʳ] *n* elicottero
hell [hɛl] *n* inferno; **~!** (*inf*) porca miseria!, accidenti!
he'll [hi:l] = **he will**; **he shall**
hello [hə'ləu] *excl* buon giorno!; ciao! (*to sb one addresses as "tu"*); (*surprise*) ma guarda!
helmet ['hɛlmɪt] *n* casco
help [hɛlp] *n* aiuto; (*charwoman*) donna di servizio ▷ *vt* aiutare; **~!** aiuto!; **can you ~ me?** può aiutarmi?; **~ yourself (to bread)** si serva (del pane); **he can't ~ it** non ci può far niente; **help out** *vi* aiutare ▷ *vt* **to help sb out** aiutare qn; **helper** *n* aiutante *m/f*, assistente *m/f*; **helpful** *adj* di grande aiuto; (*useful*) utile; **helping** *n* porzione *f*; **helpless** *adj* impotente; debole; **helpline** *n* ≈ telefono amico; (*Comm*) servizio *m* informazioni *inv* (*a pagamento*)
hem [hɛm] *n* orlo ▷ *vt* fare l'orlo a
hemisphere ['hɛmɪsfɪəʳ] *n* emisfero
hemorrhage ['hɛmərɪdʒ] (*US*) *n* = **haemorrhage**
hemorrhoids ['hɛmərɔɪdz] (*US*) *npl* = **haemorrhoids**
hen [hɛn] *n* gallina; (*female bird*) femmina
hence [hɛns] *adv* (*therefore*) dunque; **2 years ~** di qui a 2 anni
hen night *n* (*inf*) addio al nubilato
hepatitis [hɛpə'taɪtɪs] *n* epatite *f*
her [hə:ʳ] *pron* (*direct*) la, l' + *vowel*; (*indirect*) le; (*stressed, after prep*) lei ▷ *adj* il (la) suo(-a), i (le) suoi (sue); *see also* **me**; **my**
herb [hə:b] *n* erba; **herbal** *adj* di erbe; **herbal tea** *n* tisana
herd [hə:d] *n* mandria
here [hɪəʳ] *adv* qui, qua ▷ *excl* ehi!; **~!** (*at roll call*) presente!; **~ is/are** ecco; **~ he/she is** eccolo/eccola
hereditary [hɪ'rɛdɪtrɪ] *adj* ereditario(-a)
heritage ['hɛrɪtɪdʒ] *n* eredità; (*fig*) retaggio
hernia ['hə:nɪə] *n* ernia
hero ['hɪərəu] (*pl* **heroes**) *n* eroe *m*; **heroic** [hɪ'rəuɪk] *adj* eroico(-a)
heroin ['hɛrəuɪn] *n* eroina
heroine ['hɛrəuɪn] *n* eroina
heron ['hɛrən] *n* airone *m*
herring ['hɛrɪŋ] *n* aringa
hers [hə:z] *pron* il (la) suo(-a), i (le) suoi (sue); *see also* **mine¹**
herself [hə:'sɛlf] *pron* (*reflexive*) si; (*emphatic*) lei stessa; (*after prep*) se stessa, sé; *see also* **oneself**
he's [hi:z] = **he is**; **he has**
hesitant ['hɛzɪtənt] *adj* esitante, indeciso(-a)
hesitate ['hɛzɪteɪt] *vi* **to ~ (about/to do)** esitare (su/a fare); **hesitation** [-'teɪʃən] *n* esitazione *f*
heterosexual ['hɛtərəu'sɛksjuəl] *adj, n* eterosessuale *m/f*
hexagon ['hɛksəgən] *n* esagono
hey [heɪ] *excl* ehi!
heyday ['heɪdeɪ] *n*: **the ~ of** i bei giorni di, l'età d'oro di
HGV *n abbr* = **heavy goods vehicle**
hi [haɪ] *excl* ciao!
hibernate ['haɪbəneɪt] *vi* ibernare
hiccough ['hɪkʌp] *vi* singhiozzare
hiccup ['hɪkʌp] = **hiccough**
hid [hɪd] *pt of* **hide**
hidden ['hɪdn] *pp of* **hide**
hide [haɪd] (*pt* **hid**, *pp* **hidden**) *n* (*skin*) pelle *f* ▷ *vt* **to ~ sth (from sb)** nascondere qc (a qn) ▷ *vi* **to ~ (from sb)** nascondersi (da qn)
hideous ['hɪdɪəs] *adj* laido(-a); orribile
hiding ['haɪdɪŋ] *n* (*beating*) bastonata; **to be in ~** (*concealed*) tenersi nascosto(-a)
hi-fi ['haɪfaɪ] *n* stereo ▷ *adj* ad alta fedeltà, hi-fi *inv*
high [haɪ] *adj* alto(-a); (*speed, respect, number*) grande; (*wind*) forte; (*voice*)

acuto(-a) ▷ *adv* alto, in alto; **20m ~** alto(-a) 20m; **highchair** *n* seggiolone *m*; **high-class** *adj* (*neighbourhood*) elegante; (*hotel*) di prim'ordine; (*person*) di gran classe; (*food*) raffinato(-a); **higher education** *n* studi *mpl* superiori; **high heels** *npl* (*heels*) tacchi *mpl* alti; (*shoes*) scarpe *fpl* con i tacchi alti; **high jump** *n* (*Sport*) salto in alto; **highlands** *npl* zona montuosa; **the Highlands** le Highlands scozzesi; **highlight** *n* (*fig: of event*) momento culminante; (*in hair*) colpo di sole ▷ *vt* mettere in evidenza; **highlights** *npl* (*in hair*) colpi *mpl* di sole; **highlighter** *n* (*pen*) evidenziatore *m*; **highly** *adv* molto; **to speak highly of** parlare molto bene di; **highness** *n*: **Her Highness** Sua Altezza; **high-rise** *n* (*also:* **high-rise block, high-rise building**) palazzone *m*; **high school** *n* scuola secondaria; (US) istituto superiore d'istruzione; **high season** (BRIT) *n* alta stagione; **high street** (BRIT) *n* strada principale; **high-tech** (*inf*) *adj* high-tech *inv*; **highway** ['haɪweɪ] *n* strada maestra; **Highway Code** (BRIT) *n* codice *m* della strada

hijack ['haɪdʒæk] *vt* dirottare; **hijacker** *n* dirottatore(-trice)

hike [haɪk] *vi* fare un'escursione a piedi ▷ *n* escursione *f* a piedi; **hiker** *n* escursionista *m/f*; **hiking** *n* escursioni *fpl* a piedi

hilarious [hɪ'lɛərɪəs] *adj* (*behaviour, event*) spassosissimo(-a)

hill [hɪl] *n* collina, colle *m*; (*fairly high*) montagna; (*on road*) salita; **hillside** *n* fianco della collina; **hill walking** *n* escursioni *fpl* in collina; **hilly** *adj* collinoso(-a); montagnoso(-a)

him [hɪm] *pron* (*direct*) lo, l' + *vowel*; (*indirect*) gli; (*stressed, after prep*) lui; *see also* **me**; **himself** *pron* (*reflexive*) si; (*emphatic*) lui stesso; (*after prep*) se stesso, sé; *see also* **oneself**

hind [haɪnd] *adj* posteriore ▷ *n* cerva

hinder ['hɪndəʳ] *vt* ostacolare

hindsight ['haɪndsaɪt] *n* **with ~** con il senno di poi

Hindu ['hɪndu:] *n* indù *m/f inv*; **Hinduism** *n* (*Rel*) induismo

hinge [hɪndʒ] *n* cardine *m* ▷ *vi* (*fig*): **to ~ on** dipendere da

hint [hɪnt] *n* (*suggestion*) allusione *f*; (*advice*) consiglio; (*sign*) accenno ▷ *vt* **to ~ that** lasciar capire che ▷ *vi* **to ~ at** alludere a

hip [hɪp] *n* anca, fianco

hippie ['hɪpɪ] *n* hippy *m/f inv*

hippo ['hɪpəu] (*pl* **hippos**) *n* ippopotamo

hippopotamus [hɪpə'pɔtəməs] (*pl* **hippopotamuses** *or* **hippopotami**) *n* ippopotamo

hippy ['hɪpɪ] *n* = **hippie**

hire ['haɪəʳ] *vt* (BRIT: *car, equipment*) noleggiare; (*worker*) assumere, dare lavoro a ▷ *n* nolo, noleggio; **for ~** da nolo; (*taxi*) libero(-a); **I'd like to ~ a car** vorrei noleggiare una macchina; **hire(d) car** (BRIT) *n* macchina a nolo; **hire purchase** (BRIT) *n* acquisto (*or* vendita) rateale

his [hɪz] *adj, pron* il (la) suo (sua), i (le) suoi (sue); *see also* **my**; **mine**¹

Hispanic [hɪs'pænɪk] *adj* ispanico(-a)

hiss [hɪs] *vi* fischiare; (*cat, snake*) sibilare

historian [hɪ'stɔ:rɪən] *n* storico(-a)

historic(al) [hɪ'stɔrɪk(l)] *adj* storico(-a)

history ['hɪstərɪ] *n* storia

hit [hɪt] (*pt, pp* **hit**) *vt* colpire, picchiare; (*knock against*) battere; (*reach: target*) raggiungere; (*collide with: car*) urtare contro; (*fig: affect*) colpire; (*find: problem etc*) incontrare ▷ *n* colpo; (*success, song*) successo; **to ~ it off with sb** andare molto d'accordo con qn; **hit back** *vi* **to hit back at sb** restituire il colpo a qn

hitch [hɪtʃ] *vt* (*fasten*) attaccare;

(*also:* **~ up**) tirare su ▷ *n* (*difficulty*) intoppo, difficoltà *f inv*; **to ~ a lift** fare l'autostop; **hitch-hike** *vi* fare l'autostop; **hitch-hiker** *n* autostoppista *m/f*; **hitch-hiking** *n* autostop *m*

hi-tech ['haɪ'tɛk] *adj* high-tech *inv*

hitman ['hɪtmæn] (*irreg*) *n* (*inf*) sicario

HIV *abbr*: **~-negative/-positive** *adj* sieronegativo(-a)/sieropositivo(-a)

hive [haɪv] *n* alveare *m*

hoard [hɔːd] *n* (*of food*) provviste *fpl*; (*of money*) gruzzolo ▷ *vt* ammassare

hoarse [hɔːs] *adj* rauco(-a)

hoax [həuks] *n* scherzo; falso allarme

hob [hɔb] *n* piastra (con fornelli)

hobble ['hɔbl] *vi* zoppicare

hobby ['hɔbɪ] *n* hobby *m inv*, passatempo

hobo ['həubəu] (US) *n* vagabondo

hockey ['hɔkɪ] *n* hockey *m*; **hockey stick** *n* bastone *m* da hockey

hog [hɔg] *n* maiale *m* ▷ *vt* (*fig*) arraffare; **to go the whole ~** farlo fino in fondo

Hogmanay [hɔgmə'neɪ] *n* (*Scottish*) ≈ San Silvestro

hoist [hɔɪst] *n* paranco ▷ *vt* issare

hold [həuld] (*pt, pp* **held**) *vt* tenere; (*contain*) contenere; (*keep back*) trattenere; (*believe*) mantenere; considerare; (*possess*) avere, possedere; detenere ▷ *vi* (*withstand pressure*) tenere; (*be valid*) essere valido(-a) ▷ *n* presa; (*control*): **to have a ~ over** avere controllo su; (*Naut*) stiva; **~ the line!** (*Tel*) resti in linea!; **to ~ one's own** (*fig*) difendersi bene; **to catch** *or* **get (a) ~ of** afferrare; **hold back** *vt* trattenere; (*secret*) tenere celato(-a); **hold on** *vi* tener fermo; (*wait*) aspettare; **hold on!** (*Tel*) resti in linea!; **hold out** *vt* offrire ▷ *vi* (*resist*) resistere; **hold up** *vt* (*raise*) alzare; (*support*) sostenere; (*delay*) ritardare; (*rob*) assaltare; **holdall** (BRIT) *n* borsone *m*; **holder** *n* (*container*) contenitore *m*; (*of ticket, title*) possessore/posseditrice; (*of office etc*) incaricato(-a); (*of record*) detentore(-trice)

hole [həul] *n* buco, buca

holiday ['hɔlədɪ] *n* vacanza; (*day off*) giorno di vacanza; (*public*) giorno festivo; **on ~** in vacanza; **I'm on ~ here** sono qui in vacanza; **holiday camp** (BRIT) *n* (*also:* **holiday centre**) ≈ villaggio (di vacanze); **holiday job** *n* (BRIT) ≈ lavoro estivo; **holiday-maker** (BRIT) *n* villeggiante *m/f*; **holiday resort** *n* luogo di villeggiatura

Holland ['hɔlənd] *n* Olanda

hollow ['hɔləu] *adj* cavo(-a); (*container, claim*) vuoto(-a); (*laugh, sound*) cupo(-a) ▷ *n* cavità *f inv*; (*in land*) valletta, depressione *f* ▷ *vt* **to ~ out** scavare

holly ['hɔlɪ] *n* agrifoglio

Hollywood ['hɔlɪwud] *n* Hollywood *f*

holocaust ['hɔləkɔːst] *n* olocausto

holy ['həulɪ] *adj* santo(-a); (*bread, ground*) benedetto(-a), consacrato(-a)

home [həum] *n* casa; (*country*) patria; (*institution*) casa, ricovero ▷ *cpd* familiare; (*cooking etc*) casalingo(-a); (*Econ, Pol*) nazionale, interno(-a); (*Sport*) di casa ▷ *adv* a casa; in patria; (*right in*: *nail etc*) fino in fondo; **at ~** a casa; (*in situation*) a proprio agio; **to go** *or* **come ~** tornare a casa (*or* in patria); **make yourself at ~** si metta a suo agio; **home address** *n* indirizzo di casa; **homeland** *n* patria; **homeless** *adj* senza tetto; spatriato(-a); **homely** *adj* semplice, alla buona; accogliente; **home-made** *adj* casalingo(-a); **home match** *n* partita in casa; **Home Office** (BRIT) *n* ministero degli Interni; **home owner** *n* proprietario(-a) di casa; **home page** *n* (*Comput*) home page *f inv*; **Home Secretary** (BRIT) *n* ministro degli Interni; **homesick** *adj*: **to be homesick** avere la nostalgia; **home town** *n* città *f inv* natale;

homework *n* compiti *mpl* (per casa)
homicide ['hɔmɪsaɪd] (*US*) *n* omicidio
homoeopathic [həumɪə'pæθɪk] (*US* **homeopathic**) *adj* omeopatico(-a)
homoeopathy [həumɪ'ɔpəθɪ] (*US* **homeopathy**) *n* omeopatia
homosexual [hɔməu'sɛksjuəl] *adj, n* omosessuale *m/f*
honest ['ɔnɪst] *adj* onesto(-a); sincero(-a); **honestly** *adv* onestamente; sinceramente; **honesty** *n* onestà
honey ['hʌnɪ] *n* miele *m*; **honeymoon** *n* luna di miele, viaggio di nozze; **we're on honeymoon** siamo in luna di miele; **honeysuckle** *n* (*Bot*) caprifoglio
Hong Kong ['hɔŋ'kɔŋ] *n* Hong Kong *f*
honorary ['ɔnərərɪ] *adj* onorario(-a); (*duty, title*) onorifico(-a)
honour ['ɔnə^r] (*US* **honor**) *vt* onorare ▷ *n* onore *m*; **honourable** (*US* **honorable**) *adj* onorevole; **honours degree** *n* (*Scol*) *laurea specializzata*
hood [hud] *n* cappuccio; (*on cooker*) cappa; (BRIT: *Aut*) capote *f*; (US: *Aut*) cofano
hoof [hu:f] (*pl* **hooves**) *n* zoccolo
hook [huk] *n* gancio; (*for fishing*) amo ▷ *vt* uncinare; (*dress*) agganciare
hooligan ['hu:lɪgən] *n* giovinastro, teppista *m*
hoop [hu:p] *n* cerchio
hooray [hu:'reɪ] *excl* = **hurray**
hoot [hu:t] *vi* (*Aut*) suonare il clacson; (*siren*) ululare; (*owl*) gufare
Hoover® ['hu:və^r] (BRIT) *n* aspirapolvere *m inv* ▷ *vt* **hoover** pulire con l'aspirapolvere
hooves [hu:vz] *npl of* **hoof**
hop [hɔp] *vi* saltellare, saltare; (*on one foot*) saltare su una gamba
hope [həup] *vt* **to ~ that/to do** sperare che/di fare ▷ *vi* sperare ▷ *n* speranza; **I ~ so/not** spero di sì/no; **hopeful** *adj* (*person*) pieno(-a) di speranza; (*situation*) promettente; **hopefully** *adv* con speranza; **hopefully he will recover** speriamo che si riprenda; **hopeless** *adj* senza speranza, disperato(-a); (*useless*) inutile
hops [hɔps] *npl* luppoli *mpl*
horizon [hə'raɪzn] *n* orizzonte *m*; **horizontal** [hɔrɪ'zɔntl] *adj* orizzontale
hormone ['hɔ:məun] *n* ormone *m*
horn [hɔ:n] *n* (*Zool, Mus*) corno; (*Aut*) clacson *m inv*
horoscope ['hɔrəskəup] *n* oroscopo
horrendous [hə'rɛndəs] *adj* orrendo(-a)
horrible ['hɔrɪbl] *adj* orribile, tremendo(-a)
horrid ['hɔrɪd] *adj* orrido(-a); (*person*) odioso(-a)
horrific [hɔ'rɪfɪk] *adj* (*accident*) spaventoso(-a); (*film*) orripilante
horrifying ['hɔrɪfaɪɪŋ] *adj* terrificante
horror ['hɔrə^r] *n* orrore *m*; **horror film** *n* film *m inv* dell'orrore
hors d'œuvre [ɔ:'də:vrə] *n* antipasto
horse [hɔ:s] *n* cavallo; **horseback**: **on horseback** *adj, adv* a cavallo; **horse chestnut** *n* ippocastano; **horsepower** *n* cavallo (vapore); **horse-racing** *n* ippica; **horseradish** *n* rafano; **horse riding** *n* (BRIT) equitazione *f*
hose [həuz] *n* (*also:* **~pipe**) tubo; (*also:* **garden ~**) tubo per annaffiare
hospital ['hɔspɪtl] *n* ospedale *m*; **where's the nearest ~?** dov'è l'ospedale più vicino?
hospitality [hɔspɪ'tælɪtɪ] *n* ospitalità
host [həust] *n* ospite *m*; (*Rel*) ostia; (*large number*): **a ~ of** una schiera di
hostage ['hɔstɪdʒ] *n* ostaggio(-a)
hostel ['hɔstl] *n* ostello; (*also:* **youth ~**) ostello della gioventù
hostess ['həustɪs] *n* ospite *f*; (BRIT: *air hostess*) hostess *f inv*
hostile ['hɔstaɪl] *adj* ostile
hostility [hɔ'stɪlɪtɪ] *n* ostilità *f inv*

hot [hɔt] *adj* caldo(-a); (*as opposed to only warm*) molto caldo(-a); (*spicy*) piccante; (*fig*) accanito(-a); ardente; violento(-a), focoso(-a); **to be ~** (*person*) aver caldo; (*object*) essere caldo(-a); (*weather*) far caldo; **hot dog** *n* hot dog *m inv*
hotel [həu'tɛl] *n* albergo
hot spot *n* (*fig*) zona calda
hot-water bottle [hɔt'wɔːtə-] *n* borsa dell'acqua calda
hound [haund] *vt* perseguitare ▷ *n* segugio
hour ['auəʳ] *n* ora; **hourly** *adj* all'ora
house [*n* haus, *pl* 'hauzɪz, *vb* hauz] *n* (*also:* **firm**) casa; (*Pol*) camera; (*Theatre*) sala; pubblico; spettacolo; (*dynasty*) casata ▷ *vt* (*person*) ospitare, alloggiare; **on the ~** (*fig*) offerto(-a) dalla casa; **household** *n* famiglia; casa; **householder** *n* padrone(-a) di casa; (*head of house*) capofamiglia *m/f*; **housekeeper** *n* governante *f*; **housekeeping** *n* (*work*) governo della casa; (*money*) soldi *mpl* per le spese di casa; **housewife** (*irreg*) *n* massaia, casalinga; **house wine** *n* vino della casa; **housework** *n* faccende *fpl* domestiche
housing ['hauzɪŋ] *n* alloggio; **housing development** (BRIT), **housing estate** *n zona residenziale con case popolari e/o private*
hover ['hɔvəʳ] *vi* (*bird*) librarsi; **hovercraft** *n* hovercraft *m inv*
how [hau] *adv* come; **~ are you?** come sta?; **~ do you do?** piacere!; **~ far is it to the river?** quanto è lontano il fiume?; **~ long have you been here?** da quando è qui?; **~ lovely!/ awful!** che bello!/orrore!; **~ many?** quanti(-e)?; **~ much?** quanto(-a)?; **~ much milk?** quanto latte?; **~ many people?** quante persone?; **~ old are you?** quanti anni ha?
however [hau'ɛvəʳ] *adv* in qualsiasi modo *or* maniera che; (+ *adjective*) per quanto + *sub*; (*in questions*) come ▷ *conj* comunque, però
howl [haul] *vi* ululare; (*baby, person*) urlare
H.P. *abbr* = **hire purchase**; **horsepower**
h.p. *n abbr* = **H.P.**
HQ *n, abbr* = **headquarters**
hr(s) *abbr* (= *hour(s)*) h
HTML *abbr* (= *hypertext markup language*) HTML *m inv*
hubcap ['hʌbkæp] *n* coprimozzo
huddle ['hʌdl] *vi* **to ~ together** rannicchiarsi l'uno contro l'altro
huff [hʌf] *n*: **in a ~** stizzito(-a)
hug [hʌg] *vt* abbracciare; (*shore, kerb*) stringere
huge [hjuːdʒ] *adj* enorme, immenso(-a)
hull [hʌl] *n* (*of ship*) scafo
hum [hʌm] *vt* (*tune*) canticchiare ▷ *vi* canticchiare; (*insect, plane, tool*) ronzare
human ['hjuːmən] (*irreg*) *adj* umano(-a) ▷ *n* essere *m* umano
humane [hjuː'meɪn] *adj* umanitario(-a)
humanitarian [hjuːmænɪ'tɛərɪən] *adj* umanitario(-a)
humanity [hjuː'mænɪtɪ] *n* umanità
human rights *npl* diritti *mpl* dell'uomo
humble ['hʌmbl] *adj* umile, modesto(-a) ▷ *vt* umiliare
humid ['hjuːmɪd] *adj* umido(-a); **humidity** [hjuː'mɪdɪtɪ] *n* umidità
humiliate [hjuː'mɪlɪeɪt] *vt* umiliare; **humiliating** *adj* umiliante; **humiliation** [-'eɪʃən] *n* umiliazione *f*
hummus ['huməs] *n purè di ceci*
humorous ['hjuːmərəs] *adj* umoristico(-a); (*person*) buffo(-a)
humour ['hjuːməʳ] (US **humor**) *n* umore *m* ▷ *vt* accontentare
hump [hʌmp] *n* gobba
hunch [hʌntʃ] *n* (*premonition*) intuizione *f*

hundred ['hʌndrəd] *num* cento; **~s of** centinaia *fpl* di; **hundredth** [-ɪdθ] *num* centesimo(-a)
hung [hʌŋ] *pt, pp of* **hang**
Hungarian [hʌŋ'gɛərɪən] *adj* ungherese ▷ *n* ungherese *m/f*; (*Ling*) ungherese *m*
Hungary ['hʌŋgərɪ] *n* Ungheria
hunger ['hʌŋgə^r] *n* fame *f* ▷ *vi* **to ~ for** desiderare ardentemente
hungry ['hʌŋgrɪ] *adj* affamato(-a); **to be ~** aver fame
hunt [hʌnt] *vt* (*seek*) cercare; (*Sport*) cacciare ▷ *vi* **to ~ (for)** andare a caccia (di) ▷ *n* caccia; **hunter** *n* cacciatore *m*; **hunting** *n* caccia
hurdle ['hə:dl] *n* (*Sport, fig*) ostacolo
hurl [hə:l] *vt* lanciare con violenza
hurrah [hu'rɑ:] *excl* = **hurray**
hurray [hu'reɪ] *excl* urra!, evviva!
hurricane ['hʌrɪkən] *n* uragano
hurry ['hʌrɪ] *n* fretta ▷ *vi* (*also:* **~ up**) affrettarsi ▷ *vt* (*also:* **~ up**: *person*) affrettare; (*work*) far in fretta; **to be in a ~** aver fretta; **hurry up** *vi* sbrigarsi
hurt [hə:t] (*pt, pp* **hurt**) *vt* (*cause pain to*) far male a; (*injure, fig*) ferire ▷ *vi* far male
husband ['hʌzbənd] *n* marito
hush [hʌʃ] *n* silenzio, calma ▷ *vt* zittire
husky ['hʌskɪ] *adj* roco(-a) ▷ *n* cane *m* eschimese
hut [hʌt] *n* rifugio; (*shed*) ripostiglio
hyacinth ['haɪəsɪnθ] *n* giacinto
hydrangea [haɪ'dreɪnʒə] *n* ortensia
hydrofoil ['haɪdrəufɔɪl] *n* aliscafo
hydrogen ['haɪdrədʒən] *n* idrogeno
hygiene ['haɪdʒi:n] *n* igiene *f*; **hygienic** [haɪ'dʒi:nɪk] *adj* igienico(-a)
hymn [hɪm] *n* inno; cantica
hype [haɪp] (*inf*) *n* campagna pubblicitaria
hyphen ['haɪfn] *n* trattino
hypnotize ['hɪpnətaɪz] *vt* ipnotizzare
hypocrite ['hɪpəkrɪt] *n* ipocrita *m/f*
hypocritical [hɪpə'krɪtɪkl] *adj* ipocrita
hypothesis [haɪ'pɔθɪsɪs] (*pl* **hypotheses**) *n* ipotesi *f inv*
hysterical [hɪ'stɛrɪkl] *adj* isterico(-a)
hysterics [hɪ'stɛrɪks] *npl* accesso di isteria; (*laughter*) attacco di riso

i

I [aɪ] *pron* io
ice [aɪs] *n* ghiaccio; (*on road*) gelo; (*ice cream*) gelato ▷ *vt* (*cake*) glassare ▷ *vi* (*also:* **~ over**) ghiacciare; (*also:* **~ up**) gelare; **iceberg** *n* iceberg *m inv*; **ice cream** *n* gelato; **ice cube** *n* cubetto di ghiaccio; **ice hockey** *n* hockey *m* su ghiaccio
Iceland ['aɪslənd] *n* Islanda; **Icelander** *n* islandese *m/f*; **Icelandic** [aɪs'lændɪk] *adj* islandese ▷ *n* (*Ling*) islandese *m*
ice: **ice lolly** (BRIT) *n* ghiacciolo; **ice rink** *n* pista di pattinaggio; **ice skating** *n* pattinaggio sul ghiaccio
icing ['aɪsɪŋ] *n* (*Culin*) glassa; **icing sugar** (BRIT) *n* zucchero a velo
icon ['aɪkɔn] *n* icona
icy ['aɪsɪ] *adj* ghiacciato(-a); (*weather, temperature*) gelido(-a)
I'd [aɪd] = **I would**; **I had**
ID card *n* = **identity card**
idea [aɪ'dɪə] *n* idea
ideal [aɪ'dɪəl] *adj* ideale ▷ *n* ideale *m*; **ideally** [aɪ'dɪəlɪ] *adv* perfettamente, assolutamente; **ideally the book should have ...** l'ideale sarebbe che il libro avesse ...
identical [aɪ'dɛntɪkl] *adj* identico(-a)
identification [aɪdɛntɪfɪ'keɪʃən] *n* identificazione *f*; **(means of) ~** carta d'identità
identify [aɪ'dɛntɪfaɪ] *vt* identificare
identity [aɪ'dɛntɪtɪ] *n* identità *f inv*; **identity card** *n* carta d'identità; **identity theft** *n* furto d'identità
ideology [aɪdɪ'ɔlədʒɪ] *n* ideologia
idiom ['ɪdɪəm] *n* idioma *m*; (*phrase*) espressione *f* idiomatica
idiot ['ɪdɪət] *n* idiota *m/f*
idle ['aɪdl] *adj* inattivo(-a); (*lazy*) pigro(-a), ozioso(-a); (*unemployed*) disoccupato(-a); (*question, pleasures*) ozioso(-a) ▷ *vi* (*engine*) girare al minimo
idol ['aɪdl] *n* idolo
idyllic [ɪ'dɪlɪk] *adj* idillico(-a)
i.e. *adv abbr* (= *that is*) cioè
if [ɪf] *conj* se; **if I were you ...** se fossi in te ..., io al tuo posto ...; **if so** se è così; **if not** se no; **if only** se solo *or* soltanto
ignite [ɪg'naɪt] *vt* accendere ▷ *vi* accendersi
ignition [ɪg'nɪʃən] *n* (*Aut*) accensione *f*; **to switch on/off the ~** accendere/spegnere il motore
ignorance ['ɪgnərəns] *n* ignoranza; **to keep sb in ~ of sth** tenere qn all'oscuro di qc
ignorant ['ɪgnərənt] *adj* ignorante; **to be ~ of** (*subject*) essere ignorante in; (*events*) essere ignaro(-a) di
ignore [ɪg'nɔːʳ] *vt* non tener conto di; (*person, fact*) ignorare
I'll [aɪl] = **I will**; **I shall**
ill [ɪl] *adj* (*sick*) malato(-a); (*bad*) cattivo(-a) ▷ *n* male *m* ▷ *adv* **to speak** *etc* **~ of sb** parlare *etc* male di qn; **to take** *or* **be taken ~** ammalarsi
illegal [ɪ'liːgl] *adj* illegale
illegible [ɪ'lɛdʒɪbl] *adj* illeggibile

illegitimate [ɪlɪ'dʒɪtɪmət] *adj* illegittimo(-a)
ill health *n* problemi *mpl* di salute
illiterate [ɪ'lɪtərət] *adj* analfabeta, illetterato(-a); (*letter*) scorretto(-a)
illness ['ɪlnɪs] *n* malattia
illuminate [ɪ'lu:mɪneɪt] *vt* illuminare
illusion [ɪ'lu:ʒən] *n* illusione *f*
illustrate ['ɪləstreɪt] *vt* illustrare
illustration [ɪlə'streɪʃən] *n* illustrazione *f*
I'm [aɪm] = **I am**
image ['ɪmɪdʒ] *n* immagine *f*; (*public face*) immagine (pubblica)
imaginary [ɪ'mædʒɪnərɪ] *adj* immaginario(-a)
imagination [ɪmædʒɪ'neɪʃən] *n* immaginazione *f*, fantasia
imaginative [ɪ'mædʒɪnətɪv] *adj* immaginoso(-a)
imagine [ɪ'mædʒɪn] *vt* immaginare
imbalance [ɪm'bæləns] *n* squilibrio
imitate ['ɪmɪteɪt] *vt* imitare; **imitation** [-'teɪʃən] *n* imitazione *f*
immaculate [ɪ'mækjulət] *adj* immacolato(-a); (*dress, appearance*) impeccabile
immature [ɪmə'tjuə^r] *adj* immaturo(-a)
immediate [ɪ'mi:dɪət] *adj* immediato(-a); **immediately** *adv* (*at once*) subito, immediatamente; **immediately next to** proprio accanto a
immense [ɪ'mɛns] *adj* immenso(-a); enorme; **immensely** *adv* immensamente
immerse [ɪ'mə:s] *vt* immergere
immigrant ['ɪmɪgrənt] *n* immigrante *m/f*; immigrato(-a); **immigration** [ɪmɪ'greɪʃən] *n* immigrazione *f*
imminent ['ɪmɪnənt] *adj* imminente
immoral [ɪ'mɔrl] *adj* immorale
immortal [ɪ'mɔ:tl] *adj, n* immortale *m/f*
immune [ɪ'mju:n] *adj*: **~ (to)** immune (da); **immune system** *n* sistema *m* immunitario
immunize ['ɪmjunaɪz] *vt* immunizzare
impact ['ɪmpækt] *n* impatto
impair [ɪm'pɛə^r] *vt* danneggiare
impartial [ɪm'pɑ:ʃl] *adj* imparziale
impatience [ɪm'peɪʃəns] *n* impazienza
impatient [ɪm'peɪʃənt] *adj* impaziente; **to get** *or* **grow ~** perdere la pazienza
impeccable [ɪm'pɛkəbl] *adj* impeccabile
impending [ɪm'pɛndɪŋ] *adj* imminente
imperative [ɪm'pɛrətɪv] *adj* imperativo(-a); necessario(-a), urgente; (*voice*) imperioso(-a)
imperfect [ɪm'pə:fɪkt] *adj* imperfetto(-a); (*goods etc*) difettoso(-a) ▷ *n* (*Ling: also:* **~ tense**) imperfetto
imperial [ɪm'pɪərɪəl] *adj* imperiale; (*measure*) legale
impersonal [ɪm'pə:sənl] *adj* impersonale
impersonate [ɪm'pə:səneɪt] *vt* impersonare; (*Theatre*) fare la mimica di
impetus ['ɪmpətəs] *n* impeto
implant [ɪm'plɑ:nt] *vt* (*Med*) innestare; (*fig: idea, principle*) inculcare
implement [*n* 'ɪmplɪmənt, *vb* 'ɪmplɪmɛnt] *n* attrezzo; (*for cooking*) utensile *m* ▷ *vt* effettuare
implicate ['ɪmplɪkeɪt] *vt* implicare
implication [ɪmplɪ'keɪʃən] *n* implicazione *f*; **by ~** implicitamente
implicit [ɪm'plɪsɪt] *adj* implicito(-a); (*complete*) completo(-a)
imply [ɪm'plaɪ] *vt* insinuare; suggerire
impolite [ɪmpə'laɪt] *adj* scortese
import [*vb* ɪm'pɔ:t, *n* 'ɪmpɔ:t] *vt* importare ▷ *n* (*Comm*) importazione *f*
importance [ɪm'pɔ:tns] *n* importanza
important [ɪm'pɔ:tnt] *adj*

importante; **it's not ~** non ha importanza

importer [ɪm'pɔːtəʳ] *n* importatore(-trice)

impose [ɪm'pəuz] *vt* imporre ▷ *vi* **to ~ on sb** sfruttare la bontà di qn; **imposing** [ɪm'pəuzɪŋ] *adj* imponente

impossible [ɪm'pɔsɪbl] *adj* impossibile

impotent ['ɪmpətnt] *adj* impotente

impoverished [ɪm'pɔvərɪʃt] *adj* impoverito(-a)

impractical [ɪm'præktɪkl] *adj* non pratico(-a)

impress [ɪm'prɛs] *vt* impressionare; (*mark*) imprimere, stampare; **to ~ sth on sb** far capire qc a qn

impression [ɪm'prɛʃən] *n* impressione *f*; **to be under the ~ that** avere l'impressione che

impressive [ɪm'prɛsɪv] *adj* notevole

imprison [ɪm'prɪzn] *vt* imprigionare; **imprisonment** *n* imprigionamento

improbable [ɪm'prɔbəbl] *adj* improbabile; (*excuse*) inverosimile

improper [ɪm'prɔpəʳ] *adj* scorretto(-a); (*unsuitable*) inadatto(-a), improprio(-a); sconveniente, indecente

improve [ɪm'pruːv] *vt* migliorare ▷ *vi* migliorare; (*pupil etc*) fare progressi; **improvement** *n* miglioramento; progresso

improvise ['ɪmprəvaɪz] *vt, vi* improvvisare

impulse ['ɪmpʌls] *n* impulso; **on ~** d'impulso, impulsivamente; **impulsive** [ɪm'pʌlsɪv] *adj* impulsivo(-a)

KEYWORD

in [ɪn] *prep* **1** (*indicating place, position*) in; **in the house/garden** in casa/giardino; **in the box** nella scatola; **in the fridge** nel frigorifero; **I have it in my hand** ce l'ho in mano; **in town/the country** in città/campagna; **in school** a scuola; **in here/there** qui/lì dentro

2 (*with place names: of town, region, country*): **in London** a Londra; **in England** in Inghilterra; **in the United States** negli Stati Uniti; **in Yorkshire** nello Yorkshire

3 (*indicating time: during, in the space of*) in; **in spring/summer** in primavera/estate; **in 1988** nel 1988; **in May** in *or* a maggio; **I'll see you in July** ci vediamo a luglio; **in the afternoon** nel pomeriggio; **at 4 o'clock in the afternoon** alle 4 del pomeriggio; **I did it in 3 hours/days** l'ho fatto in 3 ore/giorni; **I'll see you in 2 weeks** *or* **in 2 weeks' time** ci vediamo tra 2 settimane

4 (*indicating manner etc*) a; **in a loud/soft voice** a voce alta/bassa; **in pencil** a matita; **in English/French** in inglese/francese; **the boy in the blue shirt** il ragazzo con la camicia blu

5 (*indicating circumstances*): **in the sun** al sole; **in the shade** all'ombra; **in the rain** sotto la pioggia; **a rise in prices** un aumento dei prezzi

6 (*indicating mood, state*): **in tears** in lacrime; **in anger** per la rabbia; **in despair** disperato(-a); **in good condition** in buono stato, in buone condizioni; **to live in luxury** vivere nel lusso

7 (*with ratios, numbers*): **1 in 10** 1 su 10; **20 pence in the pound** 20 pence per sterlina; **they lined up in twos** si misero in fila a due a due

8 (*referring to people, works*) in; **the disease is common in children** la malattia è comune nei bambini; **in (the works of) Dickens** in Dickens

9 (*indicating profession etc*) in; **to be in teaching** fare l'insegnante, insegnare; **to be in publishing** essere nell'editoria

10 (*after superlative*) di; **the best in the**

class il migliore della classe
11 (*with present participle*): **in saying this** dicendo questo, nel dire questo
▷ *adv* **to be in** (*person: at home, work*) esserci; (*train, ship, plane*) essere arrivato(-a); (*in fashion*) essere di moda; **to ask sb in** invitare qn ad entrare; **to run/limp** *etc* **in** entrare di corsa/zoppicando *etc*
▷ *n* **the ins and outs of the problem** tutti i particolari del problema

inability [ɪnəˈbɪlɪtɪ] *n* **~ (to do)** incapacità (di fare)
inaccurate [ɪnˈækjurət] *adj* inesatto(-a), impreciso(-a)
inadequate [ɪnˈædɪkwət] *adj* insufficiente
inadvertently [ɪnədˈvəːtntlɪ] *adv* senza volerlo
inappropriate [ɪnəˈprəuprɪət] *adj* non adatto(-a); (*word, expression*) improprio(-a)
inaugurate [ɪˈnɔːgjureɪt] *vt* inaugurare; (*president, official*) insediare
Inc. (US) *abbr* (= *incorporated*) S.A.
incapable [ɪnˈkeɪpəbl] *adj* incapace
incense [*n* ˈɪnsɛns, *vb* ɪnˈsɛns] *n* incenso ▷ *vt* (*anger*) infuriare
incentive [ɪnˈsɛntɪv] *n* incentivo
inch [ɪntʃ] *n* pollice *m* (25 *mm*, 12 *in a foot*); **within an ~ of** a un pelo da; **he didn't give an ~** non ha ceduto di un millimetro
incidence [ˈɪnsɪdns] *n* (*of crime, disease*) incidenza
incident [ˈɪnsɪdnt] *n* incidente *m*; (*in book*) episodio
incidentally [ɪnsɪˈdɛntəlɪ] *adv* (*by the way*) a proposito
inclination [ɪnklɪˈneɪʃən] *n* inclinazione *f*
incline [*n* ˈɪnklaɪn, *vb* ɪnˈklaɪn] *n* pendenza, pendio ▷ *vt* inclinare ▷ *vi* (*surface*) essere inclinato(-a); **to be ~d to do** tendere a fare; essere propenso(-a) a fare
include [ɪnˈkluːd] *vt* includere, comprendere; **is service ~d?** il servizio è compreso?; **including** *prep* compreso(-a), incluso(-a); **inclusion** [ɪnˈkluːʒən] *n* inclusione *f*; **inclusive** [ɪnˈkluːsɪv] *adj* incluso(-a), compreso(-a); **inclusive of tax** *etc* tasse *etc* comprese
income [ˈɪnkʌm] *n* reddito; **income support** *n* (BRIT) sussidio di indigenza *or* povertà; **income tax** *n* imposta sul reddito
incoming [ˈɪnkʌmɪŋ] *adj* (*flight, mail*) in arrivo; (*government*) subentrante; (*tide*) montante
incompatible [ɪnkəmˈpætɪbl] *adj* incompatibile
incompetence [ɪnˈkɔmpɪtns] *n* incompetenza, incapacità
incompetent [ɪnˈkɔmpɪtnt] *adj* incompetente, incapace
incomplete [ɪnkəmˈpliːt] *adj* incompleto(-a)
inconsistent [ɪnkənˈsɪstənt] *adj* incoerente; **~ with** non coerente con
inconvenience [ɪnkənˈviːnjəns] *n* inconveniente *m*; (*trouble*) disturbo ▷ *vt* disturbare
inconvenient [ɪnkənˈviːnjənt] *adj* scomodo(-a)
incorporate [ɪnˈkɔːpəreɪt] *vt* incorporare; (*contain*) contenere
incorrect [ɪnkəˈrɛkt] *adj* scorretto(-a); (*statement*) inesatto(-a)
increase [*n* ˈɪnkriːs, *vb* ɪnˈkriːs] *n* aumento ▷ *vi, vt* aumentare; **increasingly** *adv* sempre più
incredible [ɪnˈkrɛdɪbl] *adj* incredibile; **incredibly** *adv* incredibilmente
incur [ɪnˈkəːʳ] *vt* (*expenses*) incorrere; (*anger, risk*) esporsi a; (*debt*) contrarre; (*loss*) subire
indecent [ɪnˈdiːsnt] *adj* indecente
indeed [ɪnˈdiːd] *adv* infatti; veramente; **yes ~!** certamente!
indefinitely [ɪnˈdɛfɪnɪtlɪ] *adv* (*wait*)

indefinitamente
independence [ɪndɪ'pɛndns] *n* indipendenza; **Independence Day** (US) *n vedi nota nel riquadro*

INDEPENDENCE DAY

Negli Stati Uniti il 4 luglio si festeggia **l'Independence Day**, giorno in cui, nel 1776, 13 colonie britanniche proclamarono la propria indipendenza dalla Gran Bretagna ed entrarono ufficialmente a far parte degli Stati Uniti d'America.

independent [ɪndɪ'pɛndnt] *adj* indipendente; **independent school** *n* (BRIT) *istituto scolastico indipendente che si autofinanzia*
index ['ɪndɛks] (*pl* **indexes**) *n* (*in book*) indice *m*; (: *in library etc*) catalogo; (*pl indices*: *ratio, sign*) indice *m*
India ['ɪndɪə] *n* India; **Indian** *adj, n* indiano(-a)
indicate ['ɪndɪkeɪt] *vt* indicare; **indication** [-'keɪʃən] *n* indicazione *f*, segno; **indicative** [ɪn'dɪkətɪv] *adj*: **indicative of** indicativo(-a) di; **indicator** ['ɪndɪkeɪtə^r] *n* indicatore *m*; (*Aut*) freccia
indices ['ɪndɪsiːz] *npl of* **index**
indict [ɪn'daɪt] *vt* accusare; **indictment** [ɪn'daɪtmənt] *n* accusa
indifference [ɪn'dɪfrəns] *n* indifferenza
indifferent [ɪn'dɪfrənt] *adj* indifferente; (*poor*) mediocre
indigenous [ɪn'dɪdʒɪnəs] *adj* indigeno(-a)
indigestion [ɪndɪ'dʒɛstʃən] *n* indigestione *f*
indignant [ɪn'dɪgnənt] *adj* **~ (at sth/with sb)** indignato(-a) (per qc/contro qn)
indirect [ɪndɪ'rɛkt] *adj* indiretto(-a)
indispensable [ɪndɪ'spɛnsəbl] *adj* indispensabile
individual [ɪndɪ'vɪdjuəl] *n* individuo ▷ *adj* individuale; (*characteristic*) particolare, originale; **individually** *adv* singolarmente, uno(-a) per uno(-a)
Indonesia [ɪndə'niːzɪə] *n* Indonesia
indoor ['ɪndɔː^r] *adj* da interno; (*plant*) d'appartamento; (*swimming pool*) coperto(-a); (*sport, games*) fatto(-a) al coperto; **indoors** [ɪn'dɔːz] *adv* all'interno
induce [ɪn'djuːs] *vt* persuadere; (*bring about, Med*) provocare
indulge [ɪn'dʌldʒ] *vt* (*whim*) compiacere, soddisfare; (*child*) viziare ▷ *vi* **to ~ in sth** concedersi qc; abbandonarsi a qc; **indulgent** *adj* indulgente
industrial [ɪn'dʌstrɪəl] *adj* industriale; (*injury*) sul lavoro; **industrial estate** (BRIT) *n* zona industriale; **industrialist** [ɪn'dʌstrɪəlɪst] *n* industriale *m*; **industrial park** (US) *n* = **industrial estate**
industry ['ɪndəstrɪ] *n* industria; (*diligence*) operosità
inefficient [ɪnɪ'fɪʃənt] *adj* inefficiente
inequality [ɪnɪ'kwɔlɪtɪ] *n* ineguaglianza
inevitable [ɪn'ɛvɪtəbl] *adj* inevitabile; **inevitably** *adv* inevitabilmente
inexpensive [ɪnɪk'spɛnsɪv] *adj* poco costoso(-a)
inexperienced [ɪnɪks'pɪərɪənst] *adj* inesperto(-a), senza esperienza
inexplicable [ɪnɪk'splɪkəbl] *adj* inesplicabile
infamous ['ɪnfəməs] *adj* infame
infant ['ɪnfənt] *n* bambino(-a)
infantry ['ɪnfəntrɪ] *n* fanteria
infant school *n* (BRIT) scuola elementare (*per bambini dall'età di 5 a 7 anni*)
infect [ɪn'fɛkt] *vt* infettare; **infection** [ɪn'fɛkʃən] *n* infezione *f*; **infectious**

[ɪn'fɛkʃəs] *adj* (*disease*) infettivo(-a), contagioso(-a); (*person: fig: enthusiasm*) contagioso(-a)
infer [ɪn'fəːʳ] *vt* inferire, dedurre
inferior [ɪn'fɪərɪəʳ] *adj* inferiore; (*goods*) di qualità scadente ▷ *n* inferiore *m/f*; (*in rank*) subalterno(-a)
infertile [ɪn'fəːtaɪl] *adj* sterile
infertility [ɪnfəː'tɪlɪtɪ] *n* sterilità
infested [ɪn'fɛstɪd] *adj*: **~ (with)** infestato(-a) (di)
infinite ['ɪnfɪnɪt] *adj* infinito(-a); **infinitely** *adv* infinitamente
infirmary [ɪn'fəːmərɪ] *n* ospedale *m*; (*in school, factory*) infermeria
inflamed [ɪn'fleɪmd] *adj* infiammato(-a)
inflammation [ɪnflə'meɪʃən] *n* infiammazione *f*
inflatable [ɪn'fleɪtəbl] *adj* gonfiabile
inflate [ɪn'fleɪt] *vt* (*tyre, balloon*) gonfiare; (*fig*) esagerare; gonfiare; **inflation** [ɪn'fleɪʃən] *n* (*Econ*) inflazione *f*
inflexible [ɪn'flɛksɪbl] *adj* inflessibile, rigido(-a)
inflict [ɪn'flɪkt] *vt* **to ~ on** infliggere a
influence ['ɪnfluəns] *n* influenza ▷ *vt* influenzare; **under the ~ of alcohol** sotto l'effetto dell'alcool; **influential** [ɪnflu'ɛnʃl] *adj* influente
influx ['ɪnflʌks] *n* afflusso
info (*inf*) ['ɪnfəu] *n* = **information**
inform [ɪn'fɔːm] *vt* **to ~ sb (of)** informare qn (di) ▷ *vi* **to ~ on sb** denunciare qn
informal [ɪn'fɔːml] *adj* informale; (*announcement, invitation*) non ufficiale
information [ɪnfə'meɪʃən] *n* informazioni *fpl*; particolari *mpl*; **a piece of ~** un'informazione; **information office** *n* ufficio *m* informazioni *inv*; **information technology** *n* informatica
informative [ɪn'fɔːmətɪv] *adj* istruttivo(-a)
infra-red [ɪnfrə'rɛd] *adj* infrarosso(-a)
infrastructure ['ɪnfrəstrʌktʃəʳ] *n* infrastruttura
infrequent [ɪn'friːkwənt] *adj* infrequente, raro(-a)
infuriate [ɪn'fjuərɪeɪt] *vt* rendere furioso(-a)
infuriating [ɪn'fjuərɪeɪtɪŋ] *adj* molto irritante
ingenious [ɪn'dʒiːnjəs] *adj* ingegnoso(-a)
ingredient [ɪn'griːdɪənt] *n* ingrediente *m*; elemento
inhabit [ɪn'hæbɪt] *vt* abitare; **inhabitant** [ɪn'hæbɪtnt] *n* abitante *m/f*
inhale [ɪn'heɪl] *vt* inalare ▷ *vi* (*in smoking*) aspirare; **inhaler** *n* inalatore *m*
inherent [ɪn'hɪərənt] *adj*: **~ (in** *or* **to)** inerente (a)
inherit [ɪn'hɛrɪt] *vt* ereditare; **inheritance** *n* eredità
inhibit [ɪn'hɪbɪt] *vt* (*Psych*) inibire; **inhibition** [-'bɪʃən] *n* inibizione *f*
initial [ɪ'nɪʃl] *adj* iniziale ▷ *n* iniziale *f* ▷ *vt* siglare; **initials** *npl* (*of name*) iniziali *fpl*; (*as signature*) sigla; **initially** *adv* inizialmente, all'inizio
initiate [ɪ'nɪʃɪeɪt] *vt* (*start*) avviare; intraprendere; iniziare; (*person*) iniziare; **to ~ sb into a secret** mettere qn a parte di un segreto; **to ~ proceedings against sb** (*Law*) intentare causa contro qn
initiative [ɪ'nɪʃətɪv] *n* iniziativa
inject [ɪn'dʒɛkt] *vt* (*liquid*) iniettare; (*patient*): **to ~ sb with sth** fare a qn un'iniezione di qc; (*funds*) immettere; **injection** [ɪn'dʒɛkʃən] *n* iniezione *f*, puntura
injure ['ɪndʒəʳ] *vt* ferire; (*damage: reputation etc*) nuocere a; **injured** *adj* ferito(-a); **injury** ['ɪndʒərɪ] *n* ferita
injustice [ɪn'dʒʌstɪs] *n* ingiustizia
ink [ɪŋk] *n* inchiostro; **ink-jet printer** ['ɪŋkdʒɛt-] *n* stampante *f* a getto d'inchiostro

inland [*adj* 'ɪnlənd, *adv* ɪn'lænd] *adj* interno(-a) ▷ *adv* all'interno; **Inland Revenue** (BRIT) *n* Fisco
in-laws ['ɪnlɔːz] *npl* suoceri *mpl*; famiglia del marito (*or* della moglie)
inmate ['ɪnmeɪt] *n* (*in prison*) carcerato(-a); (*in asylum*) ricoverato(-a)
inn [ɪn] *n* locanda
inner ['ɪnəʳ] *adj* interno(-a), interiore; **inner-city** *n* centro di una zona urbana
inning ['ɪnɪŋ] *n* (US: *Baseball*) ripresa; **~s** (*Cricket*) turno di battuta
innocence ['ɪnəsns] *n* innocenza
innocent ['ɪnəsnt] *adj* innocente
innovation [ɪnəu'veɪʃən] *n* innovazione *f*
innovative ['ɪnəu'veɪtɪv] *adj* innovativo(-a)
in-patient ['ɪnpeɪʃənt] *n* ricoverato(-a)
input ['ɪnput] *n* input *m*
inquest ['ɪnkwɛst] *n* inchiesta
inquire [ɪn'kwaɪəʳ] *vi* informarsi ▷ *vt* domandare, informarsi su; **inquiry** *n* domanda; (*Law*) indagine *f*, investigazione *f*; **"inquiries"** "informazioni"
ins. *abbr* = **inches**
insane [ɪn'seɪn] *adj* matto(-a), pazzo(-a); (*Med*) alienato(-a)
insanity [ɪn'sænɪtɪ] *n* follia; (*Med*) alienazione *f* mentale
insect ['ɪnsɛkt] *n* insetto; **insect repellent** *n* insettifugo
insecure [ɪnsɪ'kjuəʳ] *adj* malsicuro(-a); (*person*) insicuro(-a)
insecurity [ɪnsɪ'kjuərɪtɪ] *n* mancanza di sicurezza
insensitive [ɪn'sɛnsɪtɪv] *adj* insensibile
insert [ɪn'səːt] *vt* inserire, introdurre
inside ['ɪn'saɪd] *n* interno, parte *f* interiore ▷ *adj* interno(-a), interiore ▷ *adv* dentro, all'interno ▷ *prep* dentro, all'interno di; (*of time*): **~ 10 minutes** entro 10 minuti; **inside lane** *n* (*Aut*) corsia di marcia; **inside out** *adv* (*turn*) a rovescio; (*know*) in fondo
insight ['ɪnsaɪt] *n* acume *m*, perspicacia; (*glimpse, idea*) percezione *f*
insignificant [ɪnsɪg'nɪfɪknt] *adj* insignificante
insincere [ɪnsɪn'sɪəʳ] *adj* insincero(-a)
insist [ɪn'sɪst] *vi* insistere; **to ~ on doing** insistere per fare; **to ~ that** insistere perché + *sub*; (*claim*) sostenere che; **insistent** *adj* insistente
insomnia [ɪn'sɔmnɪə] *n* insonnia
inspect [ɪn'spɛkt] *vt* ispezionare; (BRIT: *ticket*) controllare; **inspection** [ɪn'spɛkʃən] *n* ispezione *f*; controllo; **inspector** *n* ispettore(-trice); (BRIT: *on buses, trains*) controllore *m*
inspiration [ɪnspə'reɪʃən] *n* ispirazione *f*; **inspire** [ɪn'spaɪəʳ] *vt* ispirare; **inspiring** *adj* stimolante
instability [ɪnstə'bɪlɪtɪ] *n* instabilità
install [ɪn'stɔːl] (US **instal**) *vt* installare; **installation** [ɪnstə'leɪʃən] *n* installazione *f*
instalment [ɪn'stɔːlmənt] (US **installment**) *n* rata; (*of TV serial etc*) puntata; **in ~s** (*pay*) a rate; (*receive*) una parte per volta; (: *publication*) a fascicoli
instance ['ɪnstəns] *n* esempio, caso; **for ~** per *or* ad esempio; **in the first ~** in primo luogo
instant ['ɪnstənt] *n* istante *m*, attimo ▷ *adj* immediato(-a); urgente; (*coffee, food*) in polvere; **instantly** *adv* immediatamente, subito; **instant messaging** *n* messaggistica immediata
instead [ɪn'stɛd] *adv* invece; **~ of** invece di
instinct ['ɪnstɪŋkt] *n* istinto; **instinctive** *adj* istintivo(-a)
institute ['ɪnstɪtjuːt] *n* istituto ▷ *vt* istituire, stabilire; (*inquiry*) avviare; (*proceedings*) iniziare

institution [ɪnstɪ'tjuːʃən] *n* istituzione *f*; (*educational institution, mental institution*) istituto
instruct [ɪn'strʌkt] *vt* **to ~ sb in sth** insegnare qc a qn; **to ~ sb to do** dare ordini a qn di fare; **instruction** [ɪn'strʌkʃən] *n* istruzione *f*; **instructions (for use)** istruzioni per l'uso; **instructor** *n* istruttore(-trice); (*for skiing*) maestro(-a)
instrument ['ɪnstrəmənt] *n* strumento; **instrumental** [-'mɛntl] *adj* (*Mus*) strumentale; **to be instrumental in** essere d'aiuto in
insufficient [ɪnsə'fɪʃənt] *adj* insufficiente
insulate ['ɪnsjuleɪt] *vt* isolare; **insulation** [-'leɪʃən] *n* isolamento
insulin ['ɪnsjulɪn] *n* insulina
insult [*n* 'ɪnsʌlt, *vb* ɪn'sʌlt] *n* insulto, affronto ▷ *vt* insultare; **insulting** *adj* offensivo(-a), ingiurioso(-a)
insurance [ɪn'ʃuərəns] *n* assicurazione *f*; **fire/life ~** assicurazione contro gli incendi/sulla vita; **insurance company** *n* società di assicurazioni; **insurance policy** *n* polizza d'assicurazione
insure [ɪn'ʃuəʳ] *vt* assicurare
intact [ɪn'tækt] *adj* intatto(-a)
intake ['ɪnteɪk] *n* (*Tech*) immissione *f*; (*of food*) consumo; (BRIT: *of pupils etc*) afflusso
integral ['ɪntɪgrəl] *adj* integrale; (*part*) integrante
integrate ['ɪntɪgreɪt] *vt* integrare ▷ *vi* integrarsi
integrity [ɪn'tɛgrɪtɪ] *n* integrità
intellect ['ɪntəlɛkt] *n* intelletto; **intellectual** [-'lɛktjuəl] *adj, n* intellettuale *m/f*
intelligence [ɪn'tɛlɪdʒəns] *n* intelligenza; (*Mil etc*) informazioni *fpl*
intelligent [ɪn'tɛlɪdʒənt] *adj* intelligente
intend [ɪn'tɛnd] *vt* (*gift etc*): **to ~ sth for** destinare qc a; **to ~ to do** aver l'intenzione di fare
intense [ɪn'tɛns] *adj* intenso(-a); (*person*) di forti sentimenti
intensify [ɪn'tɛnsɪfaɪ] *vt* intensificare
intensity [ɪn'tɛnsɪtɪ] *n* intensità
intensive [ɪn'tɛnsɪv] *adj* intensivo(-a); **intensive care** *n* terapia intensiva; **intensive care unit (ICU)** *n* reparto terapia intensiva
intent [ɪn'tɛnt] *n* intenzione *f* ▷ *adj* **~ (on)** intento(-a) (a), immerso(-a) (in); **to all ~s and purposes** a tutti gli effetti; **to be ~ on doing sth** essere deciso a fare qc
intention [ɪn'tɛnʃən] *n* intenzione *f*; **intentional** *adj* intenzionale, deliberato(-a)
interact [ɪntər'ækt] *vi* interagire; **interaction** [ɪntər'ækʃən] *n* azione *f* reciproca, interazione *f*; **interactive** *adj* (*Comput*) interattivo(-a)
intercept [ɪntə'sɛpt] *vt* intercettare; (*person*) fermare
interchange ['ɪntətʃeɪndʒ] *n* (*exchange*) scambio; (*on motorway*) incrocio pluridirezionale
intercourse ['ɪntəkɔːs] *n* rapporti *mpl*
interest ['ɪntrɪst] *n* interesse *m*; (*Comm: stake, share*) interessi *mpl* ▷ *vt* interessare; **interested** *adj* interessato(-a); **to be interested in** interessarsi di; **interesting** *adj* interessante; **interest rate** *n* tasso di interesse
interface ['ɪntəfeɪs] *n* (*Comput*) interfaccia
interfere [ɪntə'fɪəʳ] *vi* **to ~ in** (*quarrel, other people's business*) immischiarsi in; **to ~ with** (*object*) toccare; (*plans, duty*) interferire con; **interference** [ɪntə'fɪərəns] *n* interferenza
interim ['ɪntərɪm] *adj* provvisorio(-a) ▷ *n* **in the ~** nel frattempo
interior [ɪn'tɪərɪəʳ] *n* interno; (*of country*) entroterra ▷ *adj* interno(-a); (*minister*) degli Interni; **interior design** *n* architettura d'interni

intermediate [ɪntə'mi:dɪət] *adj* intermedio(-a)
intermission [ɪntə'mɪʃən] *n* pausa; (*Theatre, Cinema*) intermissione *f*, intervallo
intern [*vb* ɪn'tə:n, *n* 'ɪntə:n] *vt* internare ▷ *n* (US) medico interno
internal [ɪn'tə:nl] *adj* interno(-a); **Internal Revenue Service** (US) *n* Fisco
international [ɪntə'næʃənl] *adj* internazionale ▷ *n* (BRIT: *Sport*) incontro internazionale
Internet ['ɪntənɛt] *n*: **the ~** Internet *f*; **Internet café** *n* cybercaffè *m inv*; **Internet Service Provider** *n* Provider *m inv*; **Internet user** *n* utente *m/f* Internet
interpret [ɪn'tə:prɪt] *vt* interpretare ▷ *vi* fare da interprete; **interpretation** [ɪntə:prɪ'teɪʃən] *n* interpretazione *f*; **interpreter** *n* interprete *m/f*; **could you act as an interpreter for us?** ci potrebbe fare da interprete?
interrogate [ɪn'tɛrəugeɪt] *vt* interrogare; **interrogation** [-'geɪʃən] *n* interrogazione *f*; (*of suspect etc*) interrogatorio
interrogative [ɪntə'rɔgətɪv] *adj* interrogativo(-a) ▷ *n* (*Ling*) interrogativo
interrupt [ɪntə'rʌpt] *vt, vi* interrompere; **interruption** [-'rʌpʃən] *n* interruzione *f*
intersection [ɪntə'sɛkʃən] *n* intersezione *f*; (*of roads*) incrocio
interstate ['ɪntərsteɪt] (US) *n* fra stati
interval ['ɪntəvl] *n* intervallo; **at ~s** a intervalli
intervene [ɪntə'vi:n] *vi* (*time*) intercorrere; (*event, person*) intervenire
interview ['ɪntəvju:] *n* (*Radio, TV etc*) intervista; (*for job*) colloquio ▷ *vt* intervistare; avere un colloquio con; **interviewer** *n* intervistatore(-trice)
intimate [*adj* 'ɪntɪmət, *vb* 'ɪntɪmeɪt] *adj* intimo(-a); (*knowledge*) profondo(-a) ▷ *vt* lasciar capire
intimidate [ɪn'tɪmɪdeɪt] *vt* intimidire, intimorire
intimidating [ɪn'tɪmɪdeɪtɪŋ] *adj* (*sight*) spaventoso(-a); (*appearance, figure*) minaccioso(-a)
into ['ɪntu:] *prep* dentro, in; **come ~ the house** entra in casa; **he worked late ~ the night** lavorò fino a tarda notte; **~ Italian** in italiano
intolerant [ɪn'tɔlərnt] *adj* **~ of** intollerante di
intranet ['ɪntrənɛt] *n* intranet *f*
intransitive [ɪn'trænsɪtɪv] *adj* intransitivo(-a)
intricate ['ɪntrɪkət] *adj* intricato(-a), complicato(-a)
intrigue [ɪn'tri:g] *n* intrigo ▷ *vt* affascinare; **intriguing** *adj* affascinante
introduce [ɪntrə'dju:s] *vt* introdurre; **to ~ sb (to sb)** presentare qn (a qn); **to ~ sb to** (*pastime, technique*) iniziare qn a; **introduction** [-'dʌkʃən] *n* introduzione *f*; (*of person*) presentazione *f*; (*to new experience*) iniziazione *f*; **introductory** *adj* introduttivo(-a)
intrude [ɪn'tru:d] *vi* (*person*): **to ~ (on)** intromettersi (in); **intruder** *n* intruso(-a)
intuition [ɪntju:'ɪʃən] *n* intuizione *f*
inundate ['ɪnʌndeɪt] *vt* **to ~ with** inondare di
invade [ɪn'veɪd] *vt* invadere
invalid [*n* 'ɪnvəlɪd, *adj* ɪn'vælɪd] *n* malato(-a); (*with disability*) invalido(-a) ▷ *adj* (*not valid*) invalido(-a), non valido(-a)
invaluable [ɪn'væljuəbl] *adj* prezioso(-a); inestimabile
invariably [ɪn'vɛərɪəblɪ] *adv* invariabilmente; sempre
invasion [ɪn'veɪʒən] *n* invasione *f*
invent [ɪn'vɛnt] *vt* inventare; **invention** [ɪn'vɛnʃən] *n* invenzione *f*; **inventor** *n* inventore *m*

inventory ['ɪnvəntrɪ] *n* inventario
inverted commas [ɪn'vəːtɪd-] (BRIT) *npl* virgolette *fpl*
invest [ɪn'vɛst] *vt* investire ▷ *vi* **to ~ (in)** investire (in)
investigate [ɪn'vɛstɪgeɪt] *vt* investigare, indagare; (*crime*) fare indagini su; **investigation** [-'geɪʃən] *n* investigazione *f*; (*of crime*) indagine *f*
investigator [ɪn'vɛstɪgeɪtəʳ] *n* investigatore(-trice); **a private ~** un investigatore privato, un detective
investment [ɪn'vɛstmənt] *n* investimento
investor [ɪn'vɛstəʳ] *n* investitore(-trice); azionista *m/f*
invisible [ɪn'vɪzɪbl] *adj* invisibile
invitation [ɪnvɪ'teɪʃən] *n* invito
invite [ɪn'vaɪt] *vt* invitare; (*opinions etc*) sollecitare; **inviting** *adj* invitante, attraente
invoice ['ɪnvɔɪs] *n* fattura ▷ *vt* fatturare
involve [ɪn'vɔlv] *vt* (*entail*) richiedere, comportare; (*associate*): **to ~ sb (in)** implicare qn (in); coinvolgere qn (in); **involved** *adj* involuto(-a), complesso(-a); **to be involved in** essere coinvolto(-a) in; **involvement** *n* implicazione *f*; coinvolgimento
inward ['ɪnwəd] *adj* (*movement*) verso l'interno; (*thought, feeling*) interiore, intimo(-a); **inward(s)** *adv* verso l'interno
iPod® ['aɪpɒd] *n* iPod® *m inv* lettore *m* MP3
IQ *n abbr* (= *intelligence quotient*) quoziente *m* d'intelligenza
IRA *n abbr* (= *Irish Republican Army*) IRA *f*
Iran [ɪ'rɑːn] *n* Iran *m*; **Iranian** [ɪ'reɪnɪən] *adj, n* iraniano(-a)
Iraq [ɪ'rɑːk] *n* Iraq *m*; **Iraqi** *adj, n* iracheno(-a)
Ireland ['aɪələnd] *n* Irlanda
iris ['aɪrɪs] (*pl* **irises**) *n* iride *f*; (*Bot*) giaggiolo, iride
Irish ['aɪrɪʃ] *adj* irlandese ▷ *npl* **the ~** gli Irlandesi; **Irishman** (*irreg*) *n* irlandese *m*; **Irish Sea** *n* Mar *m* d'Irlanda; **Irishwoman** (*irreg*) *n* irlandese *f*
iron ['aɪən] *n* ferro; (*for clothes*) ferro da stiro ▷ *adj* di *or* in ferro ▷ *vt* (*clothes*) stirare
ironic(al) [aɪ'rɔnɪk(l)] *adj* ironico(-a); **ironically** *adv* ironicamente
ironing ['aɪənɪŋ] *n* (*act*) stirare *m*; (*clothes*) roba da stirare; **ironing board** *n* asse *f* da stiro
irony ['aɪrənɪ] *n* ironia
irrational [ɪ'ræʃənl] *adj* irrazionale
irregular [ɪ'rɛgjuləʳ] *adj* irregolare
irrelevant [ɪ'rɛləvənt] *adj* non pertinente
irresistible [ɪrɪ'zɪstɪbl] *adj* irresistibile
irresponsible [ɪrɪ'spɔnsɪbl] *adj* irresponsabile
irrigation [ɪrɪ'geɪʃən] *n* irrigazione *f*
irritable ['ɪrɪtəbl] *adj* irritabile
irritate ['ɪrɪteɪt] *vt* irritare; **irritating** *adj* (*person, sound etc*) irritante; **irritation** [-'teɪʃən] *n* irritazione *f*
IRS (US) *n abbr* = **Internal Revenue Service**
is [ɪz] *vb see* **be**
ISDN *n abbr* (= *Integrated Services Digital Network*) I.S.D.N. *f*
Islam ['ɪzlɑːm] *n* Islam *m*; **Islamic** [ɪz'læmɪk] *adj* islamico(-a)
island ['aɪlənd] *n* isola; **islander** *n* isolano(-a)
isle [aɪl] *n* isola
isn't ['ɪznt] = **is not**
isolated ['aɪsəleɪtɪd] *adj* isolato(-a)
isolation [aɪsə'leɪʃən] *n* isolamento
ISP *n abbr* (= *Internet Service Provider*) provider *m inv*
Israel ['ɪzreɪl] *n* Israele *m*; **Israeli** [ɪz'reɪlɪ] *adj, n* israeliano(-a)
issue ['ɪʃjuː] *n* questione *f*, problema *m*; (*of banknotes etc*) emissione *f*; (*of newspaper etc*) numero ▷ *vt* (*statement*) rilasciare; (*rations, equipment*) distribuire; (*book*) pubblicare;

(*banknotes, cheques, stamps*) emettere; **at ~** in gioco, in discussione; **to take ~ with sb (over sth)** prendere posizione contro qn (riguardo a qc); **to make an ~ of sth** fare un problema di qc

KEYWORD

it [ɪt] *pron* 1 (*specific: subject*) esso(-a); (*: direct object*) lo (la), l'; (*: indirect object*) gli (le); **where's my book? — it's on the table** dov'è il mio libro? — è sulla tavola; **I can't find it** non lo (*or* la) trovo; **give it to me** dammelo (*or* dammela); **about/from/of it** ne; **I spoke to him about it** gliene ho parlato; **what did you learn from it?** quale insegnamento ne hai tratto?; **I'm proud of it** ne sono fiero; **did you go to it?** ci sei andato?; **put the book in it** mettici il libro
2 (*impers*): **it's raining** piove; **it's Friday tomorrow** domani è venerdì; **it's 6 o'clock** sono le 6; **who is it? — it's me** chi è? — sono io

IT *n abbr see* **information technology**
Italian [ɪ'tæljən] *adj* italiano(-a) ▷ *n* italiano(-a); (*Ling*) italiano; **the ~s** gli Italiani; **what's the ~ (word) for ...?** come si dice in italiano ...?
italics [ɪ'tælɪks] *npl* corsivo
Italy ['ɪtəlɪ] *n* Italia
ITC *n* (BRIT: = *Independent Television Commission*) *organo di controllo delle reti televisive*
itch [ɪtʃ] *n* prurito ▷ *vi* (*person*) avere il prurito; (*part of body*) prudere; **to ~ to do sth** aver una gran voglia di fare qc; **itchy** *adj* che prude; **to be itchy** = **to itch**
it'd ['ɪtd] = **it would**; **it had**
item ['aɪtəm] *n* articolo; (*on agenda*) punto; (*also:* **news ~**) notizia
itinerary [aɪ'tɪnərərɪ] *n* itinerario
it'll ['ɪtl] = **it will**; **it shall**
its [ɪts] *adj* il (la) suo(-a), i (le) suoi (sue)
it's [ɪts] = **it is**; **it has**
itself [ɪt'sɛlf] *pron* (*emphatic*) esso(-a) stesso(-a); (*reflexive*) si
ITV (BRIT) *n abbr* (= *Independent Television*) *rete televisiva in concorrenza con la BBC*
I've [aɪv] = **I have**
ivory ['aɪvərɪ] *n* avorio
ivy ['aɪvɪ] *n* edera

j

jab [dʒæb] *vt* dare colpetti a ▷ *n* (*Med: inf*) puntura; **to ~ sth into** affondare *or* piantare qc dentro

jack [dʒæk] *n* (*Aut*) cricco; (*Cards*) fante *m*

jacket ['dʒækɪt] *n* giacca; (*of book*) copertura; **jacket potato** *n patata cotta al forno con la buccia*

jackpot ['dʒækpɔt] *n* primo premio (in denaro)

Jacuzzi® [dʒə'ku:zɪ] *n* vasca per idromassaggio Jacuzzi®

jagged ['dʒægɪd] *adj* seghettato(-a); (*cliffs etc*) frastagliato(-a)

jail [dʒeɪl] *n* prigione *f* ▷ *vt* mandare in prigione; **jail sentence** *n* condanna al carcere

jam [dʒæm] *n* marmellata; (*also:* **traffic ~**) ingorgo; (*inf*) pasticcio ▷ *vt* (*passage etc*) ingombrare, ostacolare; (*mechanism, drawer etc*) bloccare; (*Radio*) disturbare con interferenze ▷ *vi* incepparsi; **to ~ sth into** forzare qc dentro; infilare qc a forza dentro

Jamaica [dʒə'meɪkə] *n* Giamaica

jammed [dʒæmd] *adj* (*door*) bloccato(-a); (*rifle, printer*) inceppato(-a)

Jan. *abbr* (=*January*) gen., genn.

janitor ['dʒænɪtəʳ] *n* (*caretaker*) portiere *m*; (: *Scol*) bidello

January ['dʒænjuərɪ] *n* gennaio

Japan [dʒə'pæn] *n* Giappone *m*; **Japanese** [dʒæpə'ni:z] *adj* giapponese ▷ *n inv* giapponese *m/f*; (*Ling*) giapponese *m*

jar [dʒɑ:ʳ] *n* (*glass*) barattolo, vasetto ▷ *vi* (*sound*) stridere; (*colours etc*) stonare

jargon ['dʒɑ:gən] *n* gergo

javelin ['dʒævlɪn] *n* giavellotto

jaw [dʒɔ:] *n* mascella

jazz [dʒæz] *n* jazz *m*

jealous ['dʒɛləs] *adj* geloso(-a); **jealousy** *n* gelosia

jeans [dʒi:nz] *npl* (blue-)jeans *mpl*

Jello® ['dʒɛləu] (*US*) *n* gelatina di frutta

jelly ['dʒɛlɪ] *n* gelatina; **jellyfish** *n* medusa

jeopardize ['dʒɛpədaɪz] *vt* mettere in pericolo

jerk [dʒə:k] *n* sobbalzo, scossa; sussulto; (*inf: idiot*) tonto(-a) ▷ *vt* dare una scossa a ▷ *vi* (*vehicles*) sobbalzare

Jersey ['dʒə:zɪ] *n* Jersey *m*

jersey ['dʒə:zɪ] *n* maglia; (*fabric*) jersey *m*

Jesus ['dʒi:zəs] *n* Gesù *m*

jet [dʒɛt] *n* (*of gas, liquid*) getto; (*Aviat*) aviogetto; **jet lag** *n* (problemi *mpl* dovuti allo) sbalzo dei fusi orari; **jet-ski** *vi* acquascooter *m inv*

jetty ['dʒɛtɪ] *n* molo

Jew [dʒu:] *n* ebreo

jewel ['dʒu:əl] *n* gioiello; **jeweller** (*US* **jeweler**) *n* orefice *m*, gioielliere(-a); **jeweller's (shop)** (*US* **jewelry store**) *n* oreficeria, gioielleria; **jewellery** (*US* **jewelry**) *n* gioielli *mpl*

Jewish ['dʒu:ɪʃ] *adj* ebreo(-a),

ebraico(-a)
jigsaw ['dʒɪgsɔː] *n* (*also:* **~ puzzle**) puzzle *m inv*
job [dʒɔb] *n* lavoro; (*employment*) impiego, posto; **it's not my ~** (*duty*) non è compito mio; **it's a good ~ that ...** meno male che ...; **just the ~!** proprio quello che ci vuole; **job centre** (BRIT) *n* ufficio di collocamento; **jobless** *adj* senza lavoro, disoccupato(-a)
jockey ['dʒɔkɪ] *n* fantino, jockey *m inv* ▷ *vi* **to ~ for position** manovrare per una posizione di vantaggio
jog [dʒɔg] *vt* urtare ▷ *vi* (*Sport*) fare footing, fare jogging; **to ~ sb's memory** rinfrescare la memoria a qn; **to ~ along** trottare; (*fig*) andare avanti piano piano; **jogging** *n* footing *m*, jogging *m*
join [dʒɔɪn] *vt* unire, congiungere; (*become member of*) iscriversi a; (*meet*) raggiungere; riunirsi a ▷ *vi* (*roads, rivers*) confluire ▷ *n* giuntura; **join in** *vi* partecipare ▷ *vt fus* unirsi a; **join up** *vi* incontrarsi; (*Mil*) arruolarsi
joiner ['dʒɔɪnəʳ] (BRIT) *n* falegname *m*
joint [dʒɔɪnt] *n* (*Tech*) giuntura; giunto; (*Anat*) articolazione *f*, giuntura; (BRIT *Culin*) arrosto; (*inf: place*) locale *m*; (*: of cannabis*) spinello ▷ *adj* comune; **joint account** *n* (*at bank etc*) conto in partecipazione, conto comune; **jointly** *adv* in comune, insieme
joke [dʒəuk] *n* scherzo; (*funny story*) barzelletta; (*also:* **practical ~**) beffa ▷ *vi* scherzare; **to play a ~ on sb** fare uno scherzo a qn; **joker** *n* (*Cards*) matta, jolly *m inv*
jolly ['dʒɔlɪ] *adj* allegro(-a), gioioso(-a) ▷ *adv* (BRIT: *inf*) veramente, proprio
jolt [dʒəult] *n* scossa, sobbalzo ▷ *vt* urtare
Jordan ['dʒɔːdən] *n* (*country*) Giordania; (*river*) Giordano
journal ['dʒəːnl] *n* giornale *m*; rivista; diario; **journalism** *n* giornalismo; **journalist** *n* giornalista *m/f*
journey ['dʒəːnɪ] *n* viaggio; (*distance covered*) tragitto; **how was your ~?** com'è andato il viaggio?; **the ~ takes two hours** il viaggio dura due ore
joy [dʒɔɪ] *n* gioia; **joyrider** *n chi ruba un'auto per farvi un giro*; **joy stick** *n* (*Aviat*) barra di comando; (*Comput*) joystick *m inv*
Jr *abbr* = **junior**
judge [dʒʌdʒ] *n* giudice *m/f* ▷ *vt* giudicare
judo ['dʒuːdəu] *n* judo
jug [dʒʌg] *n* brocca, bricco
juggle ['dʒʌgl] *vi* fare giochi di destrezza; **juggler** *n* giocoliere(-a)
juice [dʒuːs] *n* succo; **juicy** ['dʒuːsɪ] *adj* succoso(-a)
Jul. *abbr* (= *July*) lug., lu.
July [dʒuː'laɪ] *n* luglio
jumble ['dʒʌmbl] *n* miscuglio ▷ *vt* (*also:* **~ up**) mischiare; **jumble sale** (BRIT) *n* vendita di beneficenza

JUMBLE SALE

Una **jumble sale** è un mercatino di oggetti di seconda mano organizzato in chiese, scuole o in circoli ricreativi, i cui proventi vengono devoluti in beneficenza.

jumbo ['dʒʌmbəu] *adj* **~ jet** jumbo-jet *m inv*; **~ size** formato gigante
jump [dʒʌmp] *vi* saltare, balzare; (*start*) sobbalzare; (*increase*) rincarare ▷ *vt* saltare ▷ *n* salto, balzo; sobbalzo
jumper ['dʒʌmpəʳ] *n* (BRIT: *pullover*) maglione *m*, pullover *m inv*; (US: *dress*) scamiciato
jumper cables (US) *npl* = **jump leads**
jump leads (BRIT) *npl* cavi *mpl* per batteria
Jun. *abbr* = **junior**
junction ['dʒʌŋkʃən] *n* (BRIT: *of roads*) incrocio; (*of rails*) nodo ferroviario

June [dʒu:n] *n* giugno
jungle ['dʒʌŋgl] *n* giungla
junior ['dʒu:nɪəʳ] *adj, n* **he's ~ to me by 2 years, he's my ~ by 2 years** è più giovane di me (di 2 anni); **he's ~ to me** (*seniority*) è al di sotto di me, ho più anzianità di lui; **junior high school** (*US*) *n* scuola media (*da 12 a 15 anni*); **junior school** (*BRIT*) *n* scuola elementare (*da 8 a 11 anni*)
junk [dʒʌŋk] *n* cianfrusaglie *fpl*; (*cheap goods*) robaccia; **junk food** *n* porcherie *fpl*
junkie ['dʒʌŋkɪ] (*inf*) *n* drogato(-a)
junk mail *n* stampe *fpl* pubblicitarie
Jupiter ['dʒu:pɪtəʳ] *n* (*planet*) Giove *m*
jurisdiction [dʒuərɪs'dɪkʃən] *n* giurisdizione *f*; **it falls** *or* **comes within/outside our ~** è/non è di nostra competenza
jury ['dʒuərɪ] *n* giuria
just [dʒʌst] *adj* giusto(-a) ▷ *adv* **he's ~ done it/left** lo ha appena fatto/è appena partito; **~ right** proprio giusto; **~ 2 o'clock** le 2 precise; **she's ~ as clever as you** è in gamba proprio quanto te; **it's ~ as well that ...** meno male che ...; **~ as I arrived** proprio mentre arrivavo; **it was ~ before/enough/here** era poco prima/appena assai/proprio qui; **it's ~ me** sono solo io; **~ missed/caught** appena perso/preso; **~ listen to this!** senta un po' questo!
justice ['dʒʌstɪs] *n* giustizia
justification [dʒʌstɪfɪ'keɪʃən] *n* giustificazione *f*; (*Typ*) giustezza
justify ['dʒʌstɪfaɪ] *vt* giustificare
jut [dʒʌt] *vi* (*also:* **~ out**) sporgersi
juvenile ['dʒu:vənaɪl] *adj* giovane, giovanile; (*court*) dei minorenni; (*books*) per ragazzi ▷ *n* giovane *m/f*, minorenne *m/f*

k

K *abbr* (= *one thousand*) mille; (= *kilobyte*) K
kangaroo [kæŋgə'ru:] *n* canguro
karaoke [kɑ:rə'əukɪ] *n* karaoke *m inv*
karate [kə'rɑ:tɪ] *n* karatè *m*
kebab [kə'bæb] *n* spiedino
keel [ki:l] *n* chiglia; **on an even ~** (*fig*) in uno stato normale
keen [ki:n] *adj* (*interest, desire*) vivo(-a); (*eye, intelligence*) acuto(-a); (*competition*) serrato(-a); (*edge*) affilato(-a); (*eager*) entusiasta; **to be ~ to do** *or* **on doing sth** avere una gran voglia di fare qc; **to be ~ on sth** essere appassionato(-a) di qc; **to be ~ on sb** avere un debole per qn
keep [ki:p] (*pt, pp* **kept**) *vt* tenere; (*hold back*) trattenere; (*feed: one's family etc*) mantenere, sostentare; (*a promise*) mantenere; (*chickens, bees, pigs etc*) allevare ▷ *vi* (*food*) mantenersi; (*remain: in a certain state or place*) restare ▷ *n* (*of castle*) maschio; (*food etc*): **enough for his ~** abbastanza

per vitto e alloggio; (*inf*): **for ~s** per sempre; **to ~ doing sth** continuare a fare qc; fare qc di continuo; **to ~ sb from doing** impedire a qn di fare; **to ~ sb busy/a place tidy** tenere qn occupato(-a)/un luogo in ordine; **to ~ sth to o.s.** tenere qc per sé; **to ~ sth (back) from sb** celare qc a qn; **to ~ time** (*clock*) andar bene; **keep away** *vt* **to keep sth/sb away from sb** tenere qc/qn lontano da qn ▷ *vi* **to keep away (from)** stare lontano (da); **keep back** *vt* (*crowds, tears, money*) trattenere ▷ *vi* tenersi indietro; **keep off** *vt* (*dog, person*) tenere lontano da ▷ *vi* stare alla larga; **keep your hands off!** non toccare!, giù le mani!; **"keep off the grass"** "non calpestare l'erba"; **keep on** *vi* **to keep on doing** continuare a fare; **to keep on (about sth)** continuare a insistere (su qc); **keep out** *vt* tener fuori; **"keep out"** "vietato l'accesso"; **keep up** *vt* continuare, mantenere ▷ *vi* **to keep up with** tener dietro a, andare di pari passo con; (*work etc*) farcela a seguire; **keeper** *n* custode *m/f*, guardiano(-a); **keeping** *n* (*care*) custodia; **in keeping with** in armonia con; in accordo con

kennel ['kɛnl] *n* canile *m*; **kennels** *npl* canile *m*; **to put a dog in ~s** mettere un cane al canile

Kenya ['kɛnjə] *n* Kenia *m*

kept [kɛpt] *pt, pp of* **keep**

kerb [kə:b] (BRIT) *n* orlo del marciapiede

kerosene ['kɛrəsi:n] *n* cherosene *m*

ketchup ['kɛtʃəp] *n* ketchup *m inv*

kettle ['kɛtl] *n* bollitore *m*

key [ki:] *n* (*gen, Mus*) chiave *f*; (*of piano, typewriter*) tasto ▷ *adj* chiave *inv* ▷ *vt* (*also*: **~ in**) digitare; **can I have my ~?** posso avere la mia chiave?; **keyboard** *n* tastiera; **keyhole** *n* buco della serratura; **keyring** *n* portachiavi *m inv*

kg *abbr* (= *kilogram*) Kg

khaki ['kɑ:kɪ] *adj* cachi ▷ *n* cachi *m*

kick [kɪk] *vt* calciare, dare calci a; (*inf*: *habit etc*) liberarsi di ▷ *vi* (*horse*) tirar calci ▷ *n* calcio; (*thrill*): **he does it for ~s** lo fa giusto per il piacere di farlo; **kick off** *vi* (*Sport*) dare il primo calcio; **kick-off** *n* (*Sport*) calcio d'inizio

kid [kɪd] *n* (*inf*: *child*) ragazzino(-a); (*animal, leather*) capretto ▷ *vi* (*inf*) scherzare

kidnap ['kɪdnæp] *vt* rapire, sequestrare; **kidnapping** *n* sequestro (di persona)

kidney ['kɪdnɪ] *n* (*Anat*) rene *m*; (*Culin*) rognone *m*; **kidney bean** *n* fagiolo borlotto

kill [kɪl] *vt* uccidere, ammazzare ▷ *n* uccisione *f*; **killer** *n* uccisore *m*, killer *m inv*; assassino(-a); **killing** *n* assassinio; **to make a killing** (*inf*) fare un bel colpo

kiln [kɪln] *n* forno

kilo ['ki:ləu] *n* chilo; **kilobyte** *n* (*Comput*) kilobyte *m inv*; **kilogram(me)** ['kɪləugræm] *n* chilogrammo; **kilometre** ['kɪləmi:tə^r] (US **kilometer**) *n* chilometro; **kilowatt** ['kɪləuwɔt] *n* chilowatt *m inv*

kilt [kɪlt] *n* gonnellino scozzese

kin [kɪn] *n see* **next**; **kith**

kind [kaɪnd] *adj* gentile, buono(-a) ▷ *n* sorta, specie *f*; (*species*) genere *m*; **what ~ of ...?** che tipo di ...?; **to be two of a ~** essere molto simili; **in ~** (*Comm*) in natura

kindergarten ['kɪndəgɑ:tn] *n* giardino d'infanzia

kindly ['kaɪndlɪ] *adj* pieno(-a) di bontà, benevolo(-a) ▷ *adv* con bontà, gentilmente; **will you ~ ...** vuole ... per favore

kindness ['kaɪndnɪs] *n* bontà, gentilezza

king [kɪŋ] *n* re *m inv*; **kingdom** *n* regno, reame *m*; **kingfisher** *n* martin *m inv* pescatore; **king-size(d) bed** *n*

letto king-size
kiosk ['ki:ɔsk] *n* edicola, chiosco; (BRIT *Tel*) cabina (telefonica)
kipper ['kɪpəʳ] *n* aringa affumicata
kiss [kɪs] *n* bacio ▷ *vt* baciare; **to ~ (each other)** baciarsi; **kiss of life** *n* respirazione *f* bocca a bocca
kit [kɪt] *n* equipaggiamento, corredo; (*set of tools etc*) attrezzi *mpl*; (*for assembly*) scatola di montaggio
kitchen ['kɪtʃɪn] *n* cucina
kite [kaɪt] *n* (*toy*) aquilone *m*
kitten ['kɪtn] *n* gattino(-a), micino(-a)
kiwi ['ki:wi:] *n* (*also:* **~ fruit**) kiwi *m inv*
km *abbr* (= *kilometre*) km
km/h *abbr* (= *kilometres per hour*) km/h
knack [næk] *n*: **to have the ~ of** avere l'abilità di
knee [ni:] *n* ginocchio; **kneecap** *n* rotula
kneel [ni:l] (*pt, pp* **knelt**) *vi* (*also:* **~ down**) inginocchiarsi
knelt [nɛlt] *pt, pp of* **kneel**
knew [nju:] *pt of* **know**
knickers ['nɪkəz] (BRIT) *npl* mutandine *fpl*
knife [naɪf] (*pl* **knives**) *n* coltello ▷ *vt* accoltellare, dare una coltellata a
knight [naɪt] *n* cavaliere *m*; (*Chess*) cavallo
knit [nɪt] *vt* fare a maglia ▷ *vi* lavorare a maglia; (*broken bones*) saldarsi; **to ~ one's brows** aggrottare le sopracciglia; **knitting** *n* lavoro a maglia; **knitting needle** *n* ferro (da calza); **knitwear** *n* maglieria
knives [naɪvz] *npl of* **knife**
knob [nɔb] *n* bottone *m*; manopola
knock [nɔk] *vt* colpire; urtare; (*fig: inf*) criticare ▷ *vi* (*at door etc*): **to ~ at/on** bussare a ▷ *n* bussata; colpo, botta; **knock down** *vt* abbattere; **knock off** *vi* (*inf: finish*) smettere (di lavorare) ▷ *vt* (*from price*) far abbassare; (*inf: steal*) sgraffignare; **knock out** *vt* stendere; (*Boxing*) mettere K.O.; (*defeat*) battere; **knock over** *vt* (*person*) investire; (*object*) far cadere; **knockout** *n* (*Boxing*) knock out *m inv* ▷ *cpd* a eliminazione
knot [nɔt] *n* nodo ▷ *vt* annodare
know [nəu] (*pt* **knew**, *pp* **known**) *vt* sapere; (*person, author, place*) conoscere; **I don't ~** non lo so; **do you ~ where I can ...?** sa dove posso ...?; **to ~ how to do** sapere fare; **to ~ about** *or* **of sth/sb** conoscere qc/qn; **know-all** *n* sapientone(-a); **know-how** *n* tecnica; pratica; **knowing** *adj* (*look etc*) d'intesa; **knowingly** *adv* (*purposely*) consapevolmente; (*smile, look*) con aria d'intesa; **know-it-all** (US) *n* = **know-all**
knowledge ['nɔlɪdʒ] *n* consapevolezza; (*learning*) conoscenza, sapere *m*; **knowledgeable** *adj* ben informato(-a)
known [nəun] *pp of* **know**
knuckle ['nʌkl] *n* nocca
koala [kəu'ɑ:lə] *n* (*also:* **~ bear**) koala *m inv*
Koran [kɔ'rɑ:n] *n* Corano
Korea [kə'rɪə] *n* Corea; **Korean** *adj, n* coreano(-a)
kosher ['kəuʃəʳ] *adj* kasher *inv*
Kosovar, Kosovan ['kɔsəvaʳ, 'kɔsəvən] *adj* kosovaro(-a)
Kosovo ['kusəvəu] *n* Kosovo
Kremlin ['krɛmlɪn] *n* **the ~** il Cremlino
Kuwait [ku'weɪt] *n* Kuwait *m*

l

L (BRIT) *abbr* = **learner driver**
l. *abbr* (= *litre*) l
lab [læb] *n abbr* (= *laboratory*) laboratorio
label ['leɪbl] *n* etichetta, cartellino; (*brand*: *of record*) casa ▷ *vt* etichettare
labor *etc* ['leɪbə^r] (US) = **labour** *etc*
laboratory [lə'bɔrətərɪ] *n* laboratorio
Labor Day (US) *n* festa del lavoro

Labor Day

Negli Stati Uniti e nel Canada il **Labor Day**, la festa del lavoro, cade il primo lunedì di settembre, contrariamente a quanto accade nella maggior parte dei paesi europei dove tale celebrazione ha luogo il primo maggio.

labor union (US) *n* sindacato
labour ['leɪbə^r] (US **labor**) *n* (*task*) lavoro; (*workmen*) manodopera; (*Med*): **to be in ~** avere le doglie ▷ *vi* **to ~ (at)** lavorare duro (a); **L~, the L~ party** (BRIT) il partito laburista, i laburisti; **hard ~** lavori *mpl* forzati; **labourer** *n* manovale *m*; **farm labourer** lavoratore *m* agricolo
lace [leɪs] *n* merletto, pizzo; (*of shoe etc*) laccio ▷ *vt* (*shoe*: *also*: **~ up**) allacciare
lack [læk] *n* mancanza ▷ *vt* mancare di; **through** *or* **for ~ of** per mancanza di; **to be ~ing** mancare; **to be ~ing in** mancare di
lacquer ['lækə^r] *n* lacca
lacy ['leɪsɪ] *adj* (*like lace*) che sembra un pizzo
lad [læd] *n* ragazzo, giovanotto
ladder ['lædə^r] *n* scala; (BRIT: *in tights*) smagliatura
ladle ['leɪdl] *n* mestolo
lady ['leɪdɪ] *n* signora; dama; **L~ Smith** lady Smith; **the ladies' (room)** i gabinetti per signore; **ladybird** (US **ladybug**) *n* coccinella
lag [læg] *n* (*of time*) lasso, intervallo ▷ *vi* (*also*: **~ behind**) trascinarsi ▷ *vt* (*pipes*) rivestire di materiale isolante
lager ['lɑːgə^r] *n* lager *m inv*
lagoon [lə'guːn] *n* laguna
laid [leɪd] *pt, pp of* **lay**; **laid back** (*inf*) *adj* rilassato(-a), tranquillo(-a)
lain [leɪn] *pp of* **lie**
lake [leɪk] *n* lago
lamb [læm] *n* agnello
lame [leɪm] *adj* zoppo(-a); (*excuse etc*) zoppicante
lament [lə'mɛnt] *n* lamento ▷ *vt* lamentare, piangere
lamp [læmp] *n* lampada; **lamppost** ['læmppəust] (BRIT) *n* lampione *m*; **lampshade** ['læmpʃeɪd] *n* paralume *m*
land [lænd] *n* (*as opposed to sea*) terra (ferma); (*country*) paese *m*; (*soil*) terreno; suolo; (*estate*) terreni *mpl*, terre *fpl* ▷ *vi* (*from ship*) sbarcare; (*Aviat*) atterrare; (*fig*: *fall*) cadere ▷ *vt* (*passengers*) sbarcare; (*goods*)

scaricare; **to ~ sb with sth** affibbiare qc a qn; **landing** *n* atterraggio; (*of staircase*) pianerottolo; **landing card** *n* carta di sbarco; **landlady** *n* padrona *or* proprietaria di casa; **landlord** *n* padrone *m or* proprietario di casa; (*of pub etc*) padrone *m*; **landmark** *n* punto di riferimento; (*fig*) pietra miliare; **landowner** *n* proprietario(-a) terriero(-a); **landscape** *n* paesaggio; **landslide** *n* (*Geo*) frana; (*fig*: *Pol*) valanga

lane [leɪn] *n* stradina; (*Aut, in race*) corsia; **"get in ~"** "immettersi in corsia"

language ['læŋgwɪdʒ] *n* lingua; (*way one speaks*) linguaggio; **what ~s do you speak?** che lingue parla?; **bad ~** linguaggio volgare; **language laboratory** *n* laboratorio linguistico

lantern ['læntn] *n* lanterna

lap [læp] *n* (*of track*) giro; (*of body*): **in** *or* **on one's ~** in grembo ▷ *vt* (*also*: **~ up**) papparsi, leccare ▷ *vi* (*waves*) sciabordare

lapel [lə'pɛl] *n* risvolto

lapse [læps] *n* lapsus *m inv*; (*longer*) caduta ▷ *vi* (*law*) cadere; (*membership, contract*) scadere; **to ~ into bad habits** pigliare cattive abitudini; **~ of time** spazio di tempo

laptop (computer) ['læptɔp-] *n* laptop *m inv*

lard [lɑːd] *n* lardo

larder ['lɑːdə^r] *n* dispensa

large [lɑːdʒ] *adj* grande; (*person, animal*) grosso(-a); **at ~** (*free*) in libertà; (*generally*) in generale; nell'insieme; **largely** *adv* in gran parte; **large-scale** *adj* (*map, drawing etc*) in grande scala; (*reforms, business activities*) su vasta scala

lark [lɑːk] *n* (*bird*) allodola; (*joke*) scherzo, gioco

laryngitis [lærɪn'dʒaɪtɪs] *n* laringite *f*

lasagne [lə'zænjə] *n* lasagne *fpl*

laser ['leɪzə^r] *n* laser *m*; **laser printer** *n* stampante *f* laser *inv*

lash [læʃ] *n* frustata; (*also*: **eye~**) ciglio ▷ *vt* frustare; (*tie*): **to ~ to/together** legare a insieme; **lash out** *vi*: **to lash out (at** *or* **against sb)** attaccare violentemente (qn)

lass [læs] *n* ragazza

last [lɑːst] *adj* ultimo(-a); (*week, month, year*) scorso(-a), passato(-a) ▷ *adv* per ultimo ▷ *vi* durare; **~ week** la settimana scorsa; **~ night** ieri sera, la notte scorsa; **at ~** finalmente, alla fine; **~ but one** penultimo(-a); **lastly** *adv* infine, per finire; **last-minute** *adj* fatto(-a) (*or* preso(-a) *etc*) all'ultimo momento

latch [lætʃ] *n* chiavistello; **latch onto** *vt fus* (*cling to*: *person*) attaccarsi a, appiccicarsi a; (: *idea*) afferrare, capire

late [leɪt] *adj* (*not on time*) in ritardo; (*far on in day etc*) tardi *inv*; tardo(-a); (*former*) ex; (*dead*) defunto(-a) ▷ *adv* tardi; (*behind time, schedule*) in ritardo; **sorry I'm ~** scusi il ritardo; **the flight is two hours ~** il volo ha due ore di ritardo; **it's too ~** è troppo tardi; **of ~** di recente; **in the ~ afternoon** nel tardo pomeriggio; **in ~ May** verso la fine di maggio; **latecomer** *n* ritardatario(-a); **lately** *adv* recentemente; **later** ['leɪtə^r] *adj* (*date etc*) posteriore; (*version etc*) successivo(-a) ▷ *adv* più tardi; **later on** più avanti; **latest** ['leɪtɪst] *adj* ultimo(-a), più recente; **at the latest** al più tardi

lather ['lɑːðə^r] *n* schiuma di sapone ▷ *vt* insaponare

Latin ['lætɪn] *n* latino ▷ *adj* latino(-a); **Latin America** *n* America Latina; **Latin American** *adj* sudamericano(-a)

latitude ['lætɪtjuːd] *n* latitudine *f*; (*fig*) libertà d'azione

latter ['lætə^r] *adj* secondo(-a), più recente ▷ *n* **the ~** quest'ultimo, il secondo

laugh [lɑːf] *n* risata ▷ *vi* ridere; **laugh at** *vt fus* (*misfortune etc*) ridere di; **laughter** *n* riso; risate *fpl*
launch [lɔːntʃ] *n* (*of rocket, Comm*) lancio; (*of new ship*) varo; (*also:* **motor ~**) lancia ▷ *vt* (*rocket, Comm*) lanciare; (*ship, plan*) varare; **launch into** *vt fus* lanciarsi in
launder ['lɔːndəʳ] *vt* lavare e stirare
Launderette® [lɔːn'drɛt] (BRIT) *n* lavanderia (automatica)
Laundromat® ['lɔːndrəmæt] (US) *n* lavanderia automatica
laundry ['lɔːndrɪ] *n* lavanderia; (*clothes*) biancheria; (*: dirty*) panni *mpl* da lavare
lava ['lɑːvə] *n* lava
lavatory ['lævətərɪ] *n* gabinetto
lavender ['lævəndəʳ] *n* lavanda
lavish ['lævɪʃ] *adj* copioso(-a), abbondante; (*giving freely*): **~ with** prodigo(-a) di, largo(-a) in ▷ *vt* **to ~ sth on sb** colmare qn di qc
law [lɔː] *n* legge *f*; **civil/criminal ~** diritto civile/penale; **lawful** *adj* legale, lecito(-a); **lawless** *adj* che non conosce nessuna legge
lawn [lɔːn] *n* tappeto erboso; **lawnmower** *n* tosaerba *m or f inv*
lawsuit ['lɔːsuːt] *n* processo, causa
lawyer ['lɔːjəʳ] *n* (*for sales, wills etc*) ≈ notaio; (*partner, in court*) ≈ avvocato(-essa)
lax [læks] *adj* rilassato(-a), negligente
laxative ['læksətɪv] *n* lassativo
lay [leɪ] (*pt, pp* **laid**) *pt of* **lie** ▷ *adj* laico(-a); (*not expert*) profano(-a) ▷ *vt* posare, mettere; (*eggs*) fare; (*trap*) tendere; (*plans*) fare, elaborare; **to ~ the table** apparecchiare la tavola; **lay down** *vt* mettere giù; (*rules etc*) formulare, fissare; **to lay down the law** dettar legge; **to lay down one's life** dare la propria vita; **lay off** *vt* (*workers*) licenziare; **lay on** *vt* (*provide*) fornire; **lay out** *vt* (*display*) presentare, disporre; **lay-by** (BRIT) *n* piazzola (di sosta)
layer ['leɪəʳ] *n* strato
layman ['leɪmən] (*irreg*) *n* laico; profano
layout ['leɪaut] *n* lay-out *m inv*, disposizione *f*; (*Press*) impaginazione *f*
lazy ['leɪzɪ] *adj* pigro(-a)
lb. *abbr* = **pound** (*weight*)
lead¹ [liːd] (*pt, pp* **led**) *n* (*front position*) posizione *f* di testa; (*distance, time ahead*) vantaggio; (*clue*) indizio; (*Elec*) filo (elettrico); (*for dog*) guinzaglio; (*Theatre*) parte *f* principale ▷ *vt* guidare, condurre; (*induce*) indurre; (*be leader of*) essere a capo di ▷ *vi* condurre; (*Sport*) essere in testa; **in the ~** in testa; **to ~ the way** fare strada; **lead up to** *vt fus* portare a
lead² [lɛd] *n* (*metal*) piombo; (*in pencil*) mina
leader ['liːdəʳ] *n* capo; leader *m inv*; (*in newspaper*) articolo di fondo; (*Sport*) chi è in testa; **leadership** *n* direzione *f*; capacità di comando
lead-free ['lɛdfriː] *adj* senza piombo
leading ['liːdɪŋ] *adj* primo(-a), principale
lead singer *n cantante alla testa di un gruppo*
leaf [liːf] (*pl* **leaves**) *n* foglia ▷ *vi* **to ~ through sth** sfogliare qc; **to turn over a new ~** cambiar vita
leaflet ['liːflɪt] *n* dépliant *m inv*; (*Pol, Rel*) volantino
league [liːg] *n* lega; (*Football*) campionato; **to be in ~ with** essere in lega con
leak [liːk] *n* (*out*) fuga; (*in*) infiltrazione *f*; (*security leak*) fuga d'informazioni ▷ *vi* (*roof, bucket*) perdere; (*liquid*) uscire; (*shoes*) lasciar passare l'acqua ▷ *vt* (*information*) divulgare
lean [liːn] (*pt, pp* **leaned** *or* **leant**) *adj* magro(-a) ▷ *vt* **to ~ sth on sth** appoggiare qc su qc ▷ *vi* (*slope*) pendere; (*rest*): **to ~ against** appoggiarsi contro; essere

appoggiato(-a) a; **to ~ on** appoggiarsi a; **lean forward** *vi* sporgersi in avanti; **lean over** *vi* inclinarsi; **leaning** *n* **leaning (towards)** propensione *f* (per)

leant [lɛnt] *pt, pp of* **lean**

leap [li:p] (*pt, pp* **leaped** *or* **leapt**) *n* salto, balzo ▷ *vi* saltare, balzare

leapt [lɛpt] *pt, pp of* **leap**

leap year *n* anno bisestile

learn [lə:n] (*pt, pp* **learned** *or* **learnt**) *vt, vi* imparare; **to ~ about sth** (*hear, read*) apprendere qc; **to ~ to do sth** imparare a fare qc; **learner** *n* principiante *m/f*; apprendista *m/f*; (BRIT: *also:* **learner driver**) guidatore(-a) principiante; **learning** *n* erudizione *f*, sapienza

learnt [lə:nt] *pt, pp of* **learn**

lease [li:s] *n* contratto d'affitto ▷ *vt* affittare

leash [li:ʃ] *n* guinzaglio

least [li:st] *adj*: **the ~** (+ *noun*) il (la) più piccolo(-a), il (la) minimo(-a); (*smallest amount of*) il (la) meno ▷ *adv* (+ *verb*) meno; **the ~** (+ *adjective*): **the ~ beautiful girl** la ragazza meno bella; **the ~ possible effort** il minimo sforzo possibile; **I have the ~ money** ho meno denaro di tutti; **at ~** almeno; **not in the ~** affatto, per nulla

leather ['lɛðə^r] *n* cuoio

leave [li:v] (*pt, pp* **left**) *vt* lasciare; (*go away from*) partire da ▷ *vi* partire, andarsene; (*bus, train*) partire ▷ *n* (*time off*) congedo; (*Mil, consent*) licenza; **what time does the train/bus ~?** a che ora parte il treno/l'autobus?; **to be left** rimanere; **there's some milk left over** c'è rimasto del latte; **on ~** in congedo; **leave behind** *vt* (*person, object*) lasciare; (*: forget*) dimenticare; **leave out** *vt* omettere, tralasciare

leaves [li:vz] *npl of* **leaf**

Lebanon ['lɛbənən] *n* Libano

lecture ['lɛktʃə^r] *n* conferenza; (*Scol*) lezione *f* ▷ *vi* fare conferenze; fare lezioni ▷ *vt* (*scold*): **to ~ sb on** *or* **about sth** rimproverare qn *or* fare una ramanzina a qn per qc; **to give a ~ on** tenere una conferenza su; **lecture hall** *n* aula magna; **lecturer** ['lɛktʃərə^r] (BRIT) *n* (*at university*) professore(-essa), docente *m/f*; **lecture theatre** *n* = **lecture hall**

led [lɛd] *pt, pp of* **lead**

ledge [lɛdʒ] *n* (*of window*) davanzale *m*; (*on wall etc*) sporgenza; (*of mountain*) cornice *f*, cengia

leek [li:k] *n* porro

left [lɛft] *pt, pp of* **leave** ▷ *adj* sinistro(-a) ▷ *adv* a sinistra ▷ *n* sinistra; **on the ~, to the ~** a sinistra; **the L~** (*Pol*) la sinistra; **left-hand** *adj* **the left-hand side** il lato sinistro; **left-hand drive** *adj* guida a sinistra; **left-handed** *adj* mancino(-a); **left-luggage locker** *n* armadietto per deposito bagagli; **left-luggage (office)** (BRIT) *n* deposito *m* bagagli *inv*; **left-overs** *npl* avanzi *mpl*, resti *mpl*; **left-wing** *adj* (*Pol*) di sinistra

leg [lɛg] *n* gamba; (*of animal*) zampa; (*of furniture*) piede *m*; (*Culin: of chicken*) coscia; (*of journey*) tappa; **1st/2nd ~** (*Sport*) partita di andata/ritorno

legacy ['lɛgəsɪ] *n* eredità *f inv*

legal ['li:gl] *adj* legale; **legal holiday** (US) *n* giorno festivo, festa nazionale; **legalize** *vt* legalizzare; **legally** *adv* legalmente; **legally binding** legalmente vincolante

legend ['lɛdʒənd] *n* leggenda; **legendary** ['lɛdʒəndərɪ] *adj* leggendario(-a)

leggings ['lɛgɪŋz] *npl* ghette *fpl*

legible ['lɛdʒəbl] *adj* leggibile

legislation [lɛdʒɪs'leɪʃən] *n* legislazione *f*

legislative ['lɛdʒɪslətɪv] *adj* legislativo(-a)

legitimate [lɪ'dʒɪtɪmət] *adj* legittimo(-a)

leisure ['lɛʒəʳ] *n* agio, tempo libero; ricreazioni *fpl*; **at ~** con comodo; **leisure centre** *n* centro di ricreazione; **leisurely** *adj* tranquillo(-a), fatto(-a) con comodo *or* senza fretta

lemon ['lɛmən] *n* limone *m*; **lemonade** [-'neɪd] *n* limonata; **lemon tea** *n* tè *m inv* al limone

lend [lɛnd] (*pt, pp* **lent**) *vt* **to ~ sth (to sb)** prestare qc (a qn); **could you ~ me some money?** mi può prestare dei soldi?

length [lɛŋθ] *n* lunghezza; (*distance*) distanza; (*section: of road, pipe etc*) pezzo, tratto; (*of time*) periodo; **at ~** (*at last*) finalmente, alla fine; (*lengthily*) a lungo; **lengthen** *vt* allungare, prolungare ▷ *vi* allungarsi; **lengthways** *adv* per il lungo; **lengthy** *adj* molto lungo(-a)

lens [lɛnz] *n* lente *f*; (*of camera*) obiettivo

Lent [lɛnt] *n* Quaresima

lent [lɛnt] *pt, pp of* **lend**

lentil ['lɛntl] *n* lenticchia

Leo ['li:əu] *n* Leone *m*

leopard ['lɛpəd] *n* leopardo

leotard ['li:ətɑ:d] *n* calzamaglia

leprosy ['lɛprəsɪ] *n* lebbra

lesbian ['lɛzbɪən] *n* lesbica

less [lɛs] *adj, pron, adv* meno ▷ *prep* **~ tax/10% discount** meno tasse/il 10% di sconto; **~ than ever** meno che mai; **~ than half** meno della metà; **~ and ~** sempre meno; **the ~ he works ...** meno lavora ...; **lessen** ['lɛsn] *vi* diminuire, attenuarsi ▷ *vt* diminuire, ridurre; **lesser** ['lɛsəʳ] *adj* minore, più piccolo(-a); **to a lesser extent** in grado *or* misura minore

lesson ['lɛsn] *n* lezione *f*; **to teach sb a ~** dare una lezione a qn

let [lɛt] (*pt, pp* **let**) *vt* lasciare; (*BRIT: lease*) dare in affitto; **to ~ sb do sth** lasciar fare qc a qn, lasciare che qn faccia qc; **to ~ sb know sth** far sapere qc a qn; **~'s go** andiamo; **~ him come** lo lasci venire; **"to ~"** "affittasi"; **let down** *vt* (*lower*) abbassare; (*dress*) allungare; (*hair*) sciogliere; (*tyre*) sgonfiare; (*disappoint*) deludere; **let in** *vt* lasciare entrare; (*visitor etc*) far entrare; **let off** *vt* (*allow to go*) lasciare andare; (*firework etc*) far partire; **let out** *vt* lasciare uscire; (*scream*) emettere

lethal ['li:θl] *adj* letale, mortale

letter ['lɛtəʳ] *n* lettera; **letterbox** (*BRIT*) *n* buca delle lettere

lettuce ['lɛtɪs] *n* lattuga, insalata

leukaemia [lu:'ki:mɪə] (*US* **leukemia**) *n* leucemia

level ['lɛvl] *adj* piatto(-a), piano(-a); orizzontale ▷ *adv* **to draw ~ with** mettersi alla pari di ▷ *n* livello ▷ *vt* livellare, spianare; **to be ~ with** essere alla pari di; **level crossing** (*BRIT*) *n* passaggio a livello

lever ['li:vəʳ] *n* leva; **leverage** *n*: **leverage (on** *or* **with)** forza (su); (*fig*) ascendente *m* (su)

levy ['lɛvɪ] *n* tassa, imposta ▷ *vt* imporre

liability [laɪə'bɪlətɪ] *n* responsabilità *f inv*; (*handicap*) peso

liable ['laɪəbl] *adj* (*subject*): **~ to** soggetto(-a) a; passibile di; (*responsible*): **~ for** responsabile (di); (*likely*): **~ to do** propenso(-a) a fare

liaise [li:'eɪz] *vi* **to ~ (with)** mantenere i contatti (con)

liar ['laɪəʳ] *n* bugiardo(-a)

liberal ['lɪbərl] *adj* liberale; (*generous*): **to be ~ with** distribuire liberalmente; **Liberal Democrat** *n* liberaldemocratico(-a)

liberate ['lɪbəreɪt] *vt* liberare

liberation [lɪbə'reɪʃən] *n* liberazione *f*

liberty ['lɪbətɪ] *n* libertà *f inv*; **at ~** (*criminal*) in libertà; **at ~ to do** libero(-a) di fare

Libra ['li:brə] *n* Bilancia

librarian [laɪ'brɛərɪən] *n*

bibliotecario(-a)
library ['laɪbrərɪ] *n* biblioteca
Libya ['lɪbɪə] *n* Libia
lice [laɪs] *npl of* **louse**
licence ['laɪsns] (*US* **license**) *n* autorizzazione *f*, permesso; (*Comm*) licenza; (*Radio, TV*) canone *m*, abbonamento; (*also:* **driving ~**: *US*: *also:* **driver's license**) patente *f* di guida; (*excessive freedom*) licenza
license ['laɪsns] *n* (*US*) = **licence** ▷ *vt* dare una licenza a; **licensed** *adj* (*for alcohol*) che ha la licenza di vendere bibite alcoliche; **license plate** (*esp US*) *n* (*Aut*) targa (automobilistica); **licensing hours** (*BRIT*) *npl* orario d'apertura (*di un pub*)
lick [lɪk] *vt* leccare; (*inf: defeat*) stracciare; **to ~ one's lips** (*fig*) leccarsi i baffi
lid [lɪd] *n* coperchio; (*eyelid*) palpebra
lie [laɪ] (*pt* **lay**, *pp* **lain**) *vi* (*rest*) giacere, star disteso(-a); (*of object: be situated*) trovarsi, essere; (*tell lies: pt, pp lied*) mentire, dire bugie ▷ *n* bugia, menzogna; **to ~ low** (*fig*) latitare; **lie about** *or* **around** *vi* (*things*) essere in giro; (*person*) bighellonare; **lie down** *vi* stendersi, sdraiarsi
Liechtenstein ['lɪktənstaɪn] *n* Liechtenstein *m*
lie-in ['laɪɪn] (*BRIT*) *n*: **to have a ~** rimanere a letto
lieutenant [lɛf'tɛnənt, (*US*) luː'tɛnənt] *n* tenente *m*
life [laɪf] (*pl* **lives**) *n* vita ▷ *cpd* di vita; della vita; a vita; **to come to ~** rianimarsi; **life assurance** (*BRIT*) *n* = **life insurance**; **lifeboat** *n* scialuppa di salvataggio; **lifeguard** *n* bagnino; **life insurance** *n* assicurazione *f* sulla vita; **life jacket** *n* giubbotto di salvataggio; **lifelike** *adj* verosimile; rassomigliante; **life preserver** [-prɪ'zəːvə^r] (*US*) *n* salvagente *m*; giubbotto di salvataggio; **life sentence** *n* ergastolo; **lifestyle** *n* stile *m* di vita; **lifetime** *n*: **in his lifetime** durante la sua vita; **once in a lifetime** una volta nella vita
lift [lɪft] *vt* sollevare; (*ban, rule*) levare ▷ *vi* (*fog*) alzarsi ▷ *n* (*BRIT: elevator*) ascensore *m*; **to give sb a ~** (*BRIT*) dare un passaggio a qn; **can you give me a ~ to the station?** può darmi un passaggio fino alla stazione?; **lift up** *vt* sollevare, alzare; **lift-off** *n* decollo
light [laɪt] (*pt, pp* **lighted** *or* **lit**) *n* luce *f*, lume *m*; (*daylight*) luce *f*, giorno; (*lamp*) lampada; (*Aut: rear light*) luce *f* di posizione; (*: headlamp*) fanale *m*; (*for cigarette etc*): **have you got a ~?** ha da accendere?; **lights** *npl* (*Aut: traffic lights*) semaforo *vt* (*candle, cigarette, fire*) accendere; (*room*): **to be lit by** essere illuminato(-a) da *adj* (*room, colour*) chiaro(-a); (*not heavy, also fig*) leggero(-a); **to come to ~** venire alla luce, emergere; **light up** *vi* illuminarsi ▷ *vt* illuminare; **light bulb** *n* lampadina; **lighten** *vt* (*make less heavy*) alleggerire; **lighter** *n* (*also:* **cigarette lighter**) accendino; **light-hearted** *adj* gioioso(-a), gaio(-a); **lighthouse** *n* faro; **lighting** *n* illuminazione *f*; **lightly** *adv* leggermente; **to get off lightly** cavarsela a buon mercato
lightning ['laɪtnɪŋ] *n* lampo, fulmine *m*
lightweight ['laɪtweɪt] *adj* (*suit*) leggero(-a) ▷ *n* (*Boxing*) peso leggero
like [laɪk] *vt* (*person*) volere bene a; (*activity, object, food*): **I ~ swimming/that book/chocolate** mi piace nuotare/quel libro/il cioccolato ▷ *prep* come ▷ *adj* simile, uguale ▷ *n* **the ~** uno(-a) uguale; **his ~s and dis~s** i suoi gusti; **I would ~, I'd ~** mi piacerebbe, vorrei; **would you ~ a coffee?** gradirebbe un caffè?; **to be/look ~ sb/sth** somigliare a qn/qc; **what does it look/taste ~?** che aspetto/gusto ha?; **what does it sound ~?** come fa?;

that's just ~ him è proprio da lui; **do it ~ this** fallo così; **it is nothing ~ ...** non è affatto come ...; **likeable** *adj* simpatico(-a)

likelihood ['laɪklɪhud] *n* probabilità

likely ['laɪklɪ] *adj* probabile; plausibile; **he's ~ to leave** probabilmente partirà, è probabile che parta; **not ~!** neanche per sogno!

likewise ['laɪkwaɪz] *adv* similmente, nello stesso modo

liking ['laɪkɪŋ] *n*: **~ (for)** debole *m* (per); **to be to sb's ~** piacere a qn

lilac ['laɪlək] *n* lilla *m inv*

Lilo® ['laɪləu] *n* materassino gonfiabile

lily ['lɪlɪ] *n* giglio

limb [lɪm] *n* arto

limbo ['lɪmbəu] *n*: **to be in ~** (*fig*) essere lasciato(-a) nel dimenticatoio

lime [laɪm] *n* (*tree*) tiglio; (*fruit*) limetta; (*Geo*) calce *f*

limelight ['laɪmlaɪt] *n*: **in the ~** (*fig*) alla ribalta, in vista

limestone ['laɪmstəun] *n* pietra calcarea; (*Geo*) calcare *m*

limit ['lɪmɪt] *n* limite *m* ▷ *vt* limitare; **limited** *adj* limitato(-a), ristretto(-a); **to be limited to** limitarsi a

limousine ['lɪməzi:n] *n* limousine *f inv*

limp [lɪmp] *n*: **to have a ~** zoppicare ▷ *vi* zoppicare ▷ *adj* floscio(-a), flaccido(-a)

line [laɪn] *n* linea; (*rope*) corda; (*for fishing*) lenza; (*wire*) filo; (*of poem*) verso; (*row, series*) fila, riga; coda; (*on face*) ruga ▷ *vt* (*clothes*): **to ~ (with)** foderare (di); (*box*): **to ~ (with)** rivestire *or* foderare (di); (*trees, crowd*) fiancheggiare; **~ of business** settore *m or* ramo d'attività; **in ~ with** in linea con; **line up** *vi* allinearsi, mettersi in fila ▷ *vt* mettere in fila; (*event, celebration*) preparare

linear ['lɪnɪəʳ] *adj* lineare

linen ['lɪnɪn] *n* biancheria, panni *mpl*; (*cloth*) tela di lino

liner ['laɪnəʳ] *n* nave *f* di linea; (*for bin*) sacchetto

line-up ['laɪnʌp] *n* allineamento, fila; (*Sport*) formazione *f* di gioco

linger ['lɪŋgəʳ] *vi* attardarsi; indugiare; (*smell, tradition*) persistere

lingerie ['lænʒəri:] *n* biancheria intima femminile

linguist ['lɪŋgwɪst] *n* linguista *m/f*; poliglotta *m/f*; **linguistic** *adj* linguistico(-a)

lining ['laɪnɪŋ] *n* fodera

link [lɪŋk] *n* (*of a chain*) anello; (*relationship*) legame *m*; (*connection*) collegamento ▷ *vt* collegare, unire, congiungere; (*associate*): **to ~ with** *or* **to** collegare a; **links** *npl* (*Golf*) pista *or* terreno da golf; **link up** *vt* collegare, unire ▷ *vi* riunirsi; associarsi

lion ['laɪən] *n* leone *m*; **lioness** *n* leonessa

lip [lɪp] *n* labbro; (*of cup etc*) orlo; **lip-read** *vi* leggere sulle labbra; **lip salve** [-sælv] *n* burro di cacao; **lipstick** *n* rossetto

liqueur [lɪ'kjuəʳ] *n* liquore *m*

liquid ['lɪkwɪd] *n* liquido ▷ *adj* liquido(-a); **liquidizer** *n* frullatore *m* (a brocca)

liquor ['lɪkəʳ] *n* alcool *m*; **liquor store** (*US*) *n* negozio di liquori

Lisbon ['lɪzbən] *n* Lisbona

lisp [lɪsp] *n* pronuncia blesa della "s"

list [lɪst] *n* lista, elenco ▷ *vt* (*write down*) mettere in lista; fare una lista di; (*enumerate*) elencare

listen ['lɪsn] *vi* ascoltare; **to ~ to** ascoltare; **listener** *n* ascoltatore(-trice)

lit [lɪt] *pt, pp of* **light**

liter ['li:təʳ] (*US*) *n* = **litre**

literacy ['lɪtərəsɪ] *n* il sapere leggere e scrivere

literal ['lɪtərl] *adj* letterale; **literally** *adv* alla lettera, letteralmente

literary ['lɪtərərɪ] *adj* letterario(-a)

literate ['lɪtərət] *adj* che sa leggere e scrivere

literature ['lɪtərɪtʃə^r] *n* letteratura; (*brochures etc*) materiale *m*

litre ['li:tə^r] (*US* **liter**) *n* litro

litter ['lɪtə^r] *n* (*rubbish*) rifiuti *mpl*; (*young animals*) figliata; **litter bin** (*BRIT*) *n* cestino per rifiuti; **littered** *adj* **littered with** coperto(-a) di

little ['lɪtl] *adj* (*small*) piccolo(-a); (*not much*) poco(-a) ▷ *adv* poco; **a ~** un po' (di); **a ~ bit** un pochino; **~ by ~** a poco a poco; **little finger** *n* mignolo

live¹ [lɪv] *vi* vivere; (*reside*) vivere, abitare; **where do you ~?** dove abita?; **live together** *vi* vivere insieme, convivere; **live up to** *vt fus* tener fede a, non venir meno a

live² [laɪv] *adj* (*animal*) vivo(-a); (*wire*) sotto tensione; (*bullet, missile*) inesploso(-a); (*broadcast*) diretto(-a); (*performance*) dal vivo

livelihood ['laɪvlɪhud] *n* mezzi *mpl* di sostentamento

lively ['laɪvlɪ] *adj* vivace, vivo(-a)

liven up ['laɪvn'ʌp] *vt* (*discussion, evening*) animare ▷ *vi* ravvivarsi

liver ['lɪvə^r] *n* fegato

lives [laɪvz] *npl of* **life**

livestock ['laɪvstɔk] *n* bestiame *m*

living ['lɪvɪŋ] *adj* vivo(-a), vivente ▷ *n* **to earn** *or* **make a ~** guadagnarsi la vita; **living room** *n* soggiorno

lizard ['lɪzəd] *n* lucertola

load [ləud] *n* (*weight*) peso; (*thing carried*) carico ▷ *vt* (*also:* **~ up**): **to ~ (with)** (*lorry, ship*) caricare (di); (*gun, camera, Comput*) caricare (con); **a ~ of, ~s of** (*fig*) un sacco di; **loaded** *adj* (*vehicle*): **loaded (with)** carico(-a) (di); (*question*) capzioso(-a); (*inf: rich*) carico(-a) di soldi

loaf [ləuf] (*pl* **loaves**) *n* pane *m*, pagnotta

loan [ləun] *n* prestito ▷ *vt* dare in prestito; **on ~** in prestito

loathe [ləuð] *vt* detestare, aborrire

loaves [ləuvz] *npl of* **loaf**

lobby ['lɔbɪ] *n* atrio, vestibolo; (*Pol: pressure group*) gruppo di pressione ▷ *vt* fare pressione su

lobster ['lɔbstə^r] *n* aragosta

local ['ləukl] *adj* locale ▷ *n* (*BRIT: pub*) ≈ bar *m inv* all'angolo; **the locals** *npl* (*local inhabitants*) la gente della zona; **local anaesthetic** *n* anestesia locale; **local authority** *n* ente *m* locale; **local government** *n* amministrazione *f* locale; **locally** ['ləukəlɪ] *adv* da queste parti; nel vicinato

locate [ləu'keɪt] *vt* (*find*) trovare; (*situate*) collocare; situare

location [ləu'keɪʃən] *n* posizione *f*; **on ~** (*Cinema*) all'esterno

loch [lɔx] *n* lago

lock [lɔk] *n* (*of door, box*) serratura; (*of canal*) chiusa; (*of hair*) ciocca, riccio ▷ *vt* (*with key*) chiudere a chiave ▷ *vi* (*door etc*) chiudersi; (*wheels*) bloccarsi, incepparsi; **lock in** *vt* chiudere dentro (a chiave); **lock out** *vt* chiudere fuori; **lock up** *vt* (*criminal, mental patient*) rinchiudere; (*house*) chiudere (a chiave) ▷ *vi* chiudere tutto (a chiave)

locker ['lɔkə^r] *n* armadietto; **locker-room** (*US*) *n* (*Sport*) spogliatoio

locksmith ['lɔksmɪθ] *n* magnano

locomotive [ləukə'məutɪv] *n* locomotiva

lodge [lɔdʒ] *n* casetta, portineria; (*hunting lodge*) casino di caccia ▷ *vi* (*person*): **to ~ (with)** essere a pensione (presso *or* da); (*bullet etc*) conficcarsi ▷ *vt* (*appeal etc*) presentare, fare; **to ~ a complaint** presentare un reclamo; **lodger** *n* affittuario(-a); (*with room and meals*) pensionante *m/f*

lodging ['lɔdʒɪŋ] *n* alloggio; *see also* **board**

loft [lɔft] *n* solaio, soffitta

log [lɔg] *n* (*of wood*) ceppo; (*also:* **~book**: *Naut, Aviat*) diario di bordo; (*Aut*) libretto di circolazione ▷ *vt* registrare; **log in** *vi* (*Comput*)

aprire una sessione (*con codice di riconoscimento*); **log off** *vi* (*Comput*) terminare una sessione
logic ['lɔdʒɪk] *n* logica; **logical** *adj* logico(-a)
logo ['ləugəu] *n* logo *m inv*
lollipop ['lɔlɪpɔp] *n* lecca lecca *m inv*
lolly ['lɔlɪ] (*inf*) *n* lecca lecca *m inv*; (*also:* **ice ~**) ghiacciolo; (*money*) grana
London ['lʌndən] *n* Londra; **Londoner** *n* londinese *m/f*
lone [ləun] *adj* solitario(-a)
loneliness ['ləunlɪnɪs] *n* solitudine *f*, isolamento
lonely ['ləunlɪ] *adj* solo(-a); solitario(-a), isolato(-a)
long [lɔŋ] *adj* lungo(-a) ▷ *adv* a lungo, per molto tempo ▷ *vi* **to ~ for sth/to do** desiderare qc/di fare, non veder l'ora di aver qc/di fare; **so** *or* **as ~ as** (*while*) finché; (*provided that*) sempre che + *sub*; **don't be ~!** fai presto!; **how ~ is this river/course?** quanto è lungo questo fiume/corso?; **6 metres ~** lungo 6 metri; **6 months ~** che dura 6 mesi, di 6 mesi; **all night ~** tutta la notte; **he no ~er comes** non viene più; **~ before** molto tempo prima; **before ~** (+ *future*) presto, fra poco; (+ *past*) poco tempo dopo; **at ~ last** finalmente; **long-distance** *adj* (*race*) di fondo; (*call*) interurbano(-a); **long-haul** ['lɒŋ,hɔːl] *adj* (*flight*) a lunga percorrenza *inv*; **longing** *n* desiderio, voglia, brama
longitude ['lɔŋgɪtjuːd] *n* longitudine *f*
long: **long jump** *n* salto in lungo; **long-life** *adj* (*milk*) a lunga conservazione; (*batteries*) di lunga durata; **long-sighted** *adj* presbite; **long-standing** *adj* di vecchia data; **long-term** *adj* a lungo termine
loo [luː] (BRIT: *inf*) *n* W.C. *m inv*, cesso
look [luk] *vi* guardare; (*seem*) sembrare, parere; (*building etc*): **to ~ south/on to the sea** dare a sud/sul mare ▷ *n* sguardo; (*appearance*) aspetto, aria; **looks** *npl* (*good looks*) bellezza; **look after** *vt fus* occuparsi di, prendere cura di; (*keep an eye on*) guardare, badare a; **look around** *vi* guardarsi intorno; **look at** *vt fus* guardare; **look back** *vi*: **to look back on** (*event etc*) ripensare a; **look down on** *vt fus* (*fig*) guardare dall'alto, disprezzare; **look for** *vt fus* cercare; **we're looking for a hotel/ restaurant** stiamo cercando un albergo/ristorante; **look forward to** *vt fus* non veder l'ora di; (*in letters*): **we look forward to hearing from you** in attesa di una vostra gentile risposta; **look into** *vt fus* esaminare; **look out** *vi* (*beware*): **to look out (for)** stare in guardia (per); **look out for** *vt fus* cercare; **look round** *vi* (*turn*) girarsi, voltarsi; (*in shop*) dare un'occhiata; **look through** *vt fus* (*papers, book*) scorrere; (*telescope*) guardare attraverso; **look up** *vi* alzare gli occhi; (*improve*) migliorare ▷ *vt* (*word*) cercare; (*friend*) andare a trovare; **look up to** *vt fus* avere rispetto per; **lookout** *n* posto d'osservazione; guardia; **to be on the lookout (for)** stare in guardia (per)
loom [luːm] *n* telaio ▷ *vi* (*also:* **~ up**) apparire minaccioso(-a); (*event*) essere imminente
loony ['luːnɪ] (*inf*) *n* pazzo(-a)
loop [luːp] *n* cappio ▷ *vt* **to ~ sth round sth** passare qc intorno a qc; **loophole** *n* via d'uscita; scappatoia
loose [luːs] *adj* (*knot*) sciolto(-a); (*screw*) allentato(-a); (*stone*) cadente; (*clothes*) ampio(-a), largo(-a); (*animal*) in libertà, scappato(-a); (*life, morals*) dissoluto(-a) ▷ *n* **to be on the ~** essere in libertà; **loosely** *adv* senza stringere; approssimativamente; **loosen** *vt* sciogliere; (*belt etc*) allentare
loot [luːt] *n* bottino ▷ *vt* saccheggiare

lop-sided ['lɔp'saɪdɪd] *adj* non equilibrato(-a), asimmetrico(-a)
lord [lɔ:d] *n* signore *m*; **L~ Smith** lord Smith; **the L~** il Signore; **good L~!** buon Dio!; **the (House of) L~s** (BRIT) la Camera dei Lord
lorry ['lɔrɪ] (BRIT) *n* camion *m inv*; **lorry driver** (BRIT) *n* camionista *m*
lose [lu:z] (*pt, pp* **lost**) *vt* perdere ▷ *vi* perdere; **I've lost my wallet/passport** ho perso il portafoglio/passaporto; **to ~ (time)** (*clock*) ritardare; **lose out** *vi* rimetterci; **loser** *n* perdente *m/f*
loss [lɔs] *n* perdita; **to be at a ~** essere perplesso(-a)
lost [lɔst] *pt, pp of* **lose** ▷ *adj* perduto(-a); **I'm ~** mi sono perso; **lost property** (*US* **lost and found**) *n* oggetti *mpl* smarriti
lot [lɔt] *n* (*at auctions*) lotto; (*destiny*) destino, sorte *f*; **the ~** tutto(-a) quanto(-a); tutti(-e) quanti(-e); **a ~** molto; **a ~ of** una gran quantità di, un sacco di; **~s of** molto(-a); **to draw ~s (for sth)** tirare a sorte (per qc)
lotion ['ləuʃən] *n* lozione *f*
lottery ['lɔtərɪ] *n* lotteria
loud [laud] *adj* forte, alto(-a); (*gaudy*) vistoso(-a), sgargiante ▷ *adv* (*speak etc*) forte; **out ~** (*read etc*) ad alta voce; **loudly** *adv* fortemente, ad alta voce; **loudspeaker** *n* altoparlante *m*
lounge [laundʒ] *n* salotto, soggiorno; (*at airport, station*) sala d'attesa; (BRIT: *also:* **~ bar**) bar *m inv* con servizio a tavolino ▷ *vi* oziare
louse [laus] (*pl* **lice**) *n* pidocchio
lousy ['lauzɪ] (*inf*) *adj* orrendo(-a), schifoso(-a); **to feel ~** stare da cani
love [lʌv] *n* amore *m* ▷ *vt* amare; voler bene a; **to ~ to do: I ~ to do** mi piace fare; **to be/fall in ~ with** essere innamorato(-a)/innamorarsi di; **to make ~** fare l'amore; **"15 ~"** (*Tennis*) "15 a zero"; **love affair** *n* relazione *f*; **love life** *n* vita sentimentale
lovely ['lʌvlɪ] *adj* bello(-a); (*delicious: smell, meal*) buono(-a)
lover ['lʌvəʳ] *n* amante *m/f*; (*person in love*) innamorato(-a); (*amateur*): **a ~ of** un(-un') amante di; un(-un') appassionato(-a) di
loving ['lʌvɪŋ] *adj* affettuoso(-a)
low [ləu] *adj* basso(-a) ▷ *adv* in basso ▷ *n* (*Meteor*) depressione *f*; **to be ~ on** (*supplies etc*) avere scarsità di; **to feel ~** sentirsi giù; **low-alcohol** *adj* a basso contenuto alcolico; **low-calorie** *adj* a basso contenuto calorico
lower ['ləuəʳ] *adj* (*bottom: of 2 things*) più basso; (*less important*) meno importante ▷ *vt* calare; (*prices, eyes, voice*) abbassare
low-fat ['ləu'fæt] *adj* magro(-a)
loyal ['lɔɪəl] *adj* fedele, leale; **loyalty** *n* fedeltà, lealtà; **loyalty card** *n carta che offre sconti a clienti abituali*
L.P. *n abbr* = **long-playing record**
L-plates ['ɛlpleɪts] (BRIT) *npl* contrassegno P principiante
Lt *abbr* (= *lieutenant*) Ten.
Ltd *abbr* (= *limited*) ≈ S.r.l.
luck [lʌk] *n* fortuna, sorte *f*; **bad ~** sfortuna, mala sorte; **good ~!** buona fortuna!; **luckily** *adv* fortunatamente, per fortuna; **lucky** *adj* fortunato(-a); (*number etc*) che porta fortuna
lucrative ['lu:krətɪv] *adj* lucrativo(-a), lucroso(-a), profittevole
ludicrous ['lu:dɪkrəs] *adj* ridicolo(-a)
luggage ['lʌgɪdʒ] *n* bagagli *mpl*; **our ~ hasn't arrived** i nostri bagagli non sono arrivati; **luggage rack** *n* portabagagli *m inv*
lukewarm ['lu:kwɔ:m] *adj* tiepido(-a)
lull [lʌl] *n* intervallo di calma ▷ *vt* **to ~ sb to sleep** cullare qn finché si addormenta
lullaby ['lʌləbaɪ] *n* ninnananna
lumber ['lʌmbəʳ] *n* (*wood*) legname *m*; (*junk*) roba vecchia
luminous ['lu:mɪnəs] *adj*

luminoso(-a)
lump [lʌmp] *n* pezzo; (*in sauce*) grumo; (*swelling*) gonfiore *m*; (*also:* **sugar ~**) zolletta ▷ *vt* (*also:* **~ together**) riunire, mettere insieme; **lump sum** *n* somma globale; **lumpy** *adj* (*sauce*) pieno(-a) di grumi; (*bed*) bitorzoluto(-a)
lunatic ['lu:nətɪk] *adj* pazzo(-a), matto(-a)
lunch [lʌntʃ] *n* pranzo, colazione *f*; **lunch break** *n* intervallo del pranzo; **lunch time** *n* ora di pranzo
lung [lʌŋ] *n* polmone *m*
lure [luə^r] *n* richiamo; lusinga ▷ *vt* attirare (con l'inganno)
lurk [lə:k] *vi* stare in agguato
lush [lʌʃ] *adj* lussureggiante
lust [lʌst] *n* lussuria; cupidigia; desiderio; (*fig*): **~ for** sete *f* di
Luxembourg ['lʌksəmbə:g] *n* (*state*) Lussemburgo *m*; (*city*) Lussemburgo *f*
luxurious [lʌg'zjuərɪəs] *adj* sontuoso(-a), di lusso
luxury ['lʌkʃərɪ] *n* lusso ▷ *cpd* di lusso

> Be careful not to translate ***luxury*** by the Italian word ***lussuria***.

Lycra® ['laɪkrə] *n* lycra® *f inv*
lying ['laɪɪŋ] *n* bugie *fpl*, menzogne *fpl* ▷ *adj* bugiardo(-a)
lyrics ['lɪrɪks] *npl* (*of song*) parole *fpl*

m

m. *abbr* = **metre**; **mile**; **million**
M.A. *abbr* = **Master of Arts**
ma (*inf*) [mɑ:] *n* mamma
mac [mæk] (BRIT) *n* impermeabile *m*
macaroni [mækə'rəunɪ] *n* maccheroni *mpl*
Macedonia [mæsɪ'dəunɪə] *n* Macedonia; **Macedonian** [mæsɪ'dəunɪən] *adj* macedone ▷ *n* macedone *m/f*; (*Ling*) macedone *m*
machine [mə'ʃi:n] *n* macchina ▷ *vt* (*Tech*) lavorare a macchina; (*dress etc*) cucire a macchina; **machine gun** *n* mitragliatrice *f*; **machinery** *n* macchinario, macchine *fpl*; (*fig*) macchina; **machine washable** *adj* lavabile in lavatrice
macho ['mætʃəu] *adj* macho *inv*
mackerel ['mækrl] *n inv* sgombro
mackintosh ['mækɪntɔʃ] (BRIT) *n* impermeabile *m*
mad [mæd] *adj* matto(-a), pazzo(-a); (*foolish*) sciocco(-a); (*angry*) furioso(-a); **to be ~ about** (*keen*)

andare pazzo(-a) per
Madagascar [mædə'gæskəʳ] *n* Madagascar *m*
madam ['mædəm] *n* signora
mad cow disease *n* encefalite *f* bovina spongiforme
made [meɪd] *pt, pp of* **make**; **made-to-measure** (BRIT) *adj* fatto(-a) su misura; **made-up** ['meɪdʌp] *adj* (*story*) inventato(-a)
madly ['mædlɪ] *adv* follemente
madman ['mædmən] (*irreg*) *n* pazzo, alienato
madness ['mædnɪs] *n* pazzia
Madrid [mə'drɪd] *n* Madrid *f*
Mafia ['mæfɪə] *n* mafia *f*
mag [mæg] *n abbr* (BRIT *inf*) = **magazine** (*Press*)
magazine [mægə'zi:n] *n* (*Press*) rivista; (*Radio, TV*) rubrica

> Be careful not to translate ***magazine*** by the Italian word ***magazzino***.

maggot ['mægət] *n* baco, verme *m*
magic ['mædʒɪk] *n* magia ▷ *adj* magico(-a); **magical** *adj* magico(-a); **magician** [mə'dʒɪʃən] *n* mago(-a)
magistrate ['mædʒɪstreɪt] *n* magistrato; giudice *m/f*
magnet ['mægnɪt] *n* magnete *m*, calamita; **magnetic** [-'nɛtɪk] *adj* magnetico(-a)
magnificent [mæg'nɪfɪsnt] *adj* magnifico(-a)
magnify ['mægnɪfaɪ] *vt* ingrandire; **magnifying glass** *n* lente *f* d'ingrandimento
magpie ['mægpaɪ] *n* gazza
mahogany [mə'hɔgənɪ] *n* mogano
maid [meɪd] *n* domestica; (*in hotel*) cameriera
maiden name ['meɪdn-] *n* nome *m* da nubile *or* da ragazza
mail [meɪl] *n* posta ▷ *vt* spedire (per posta); **mailbox** (US) *n* cassetta delle lettere; **mailing list** *n* elenco d'indirizzi; **mailman** (*irreg*: US) *n* portalettere *m inv*, postino; **mail-order** *n* vendita (*or* acquisto) per corrispondenza
main [meɪn] *adj* principale ▷ *n* (*pipe*) conduttura principale; **main course** *n* (*Culin*) piatto principale, piatto forte; **mainland** *n* continente *m*; **mainly** *adv* principalmente, soprattutto; **main road** *n* strada principale; **mainstream** *n* (*fig*) corrente *f* principale; **main street** *n* strada principale
maintain [meɪn'teɪn] *vt* mantenere; (*affirm*) sostenere; **maintenance** ['meɪntənəns] *n* manutenzione *f*; (*alimony*) alimenti *mpl*
maisonette [meɪzə'nɛt] *n* (BRIT) appartamento a due piani
maize [meɪz] *n* granturco, mais *m*
majesty ['mædʒɪstɪ] *n* maestà *f inv*
major ['meɪdʒəʳ] *n* (*Mil*) maggiore *m* ▷ *adj* (*greater, Mus*) maggiore; (*in importance*) principale, importante
Majorca [mə'jɔ:kə] *n* Maiorca
majority [mə'dʒɔrɪtɪ] *n* maggioranza
make [meɪk] (*pt, pp* **made**) *vt* fare; (*manufacture*) fare, fabbricare; (*cause to be*): **to ~ sb sad** *etc* rendere qn triste *etc*; (*force*): **to ~ sb do sth** costringere qn a fare qc, far fare qc a qn; (*equal*): **2 and 2 ~ 4** 2 più 2 fa 4 ▷ *n* fabbricazione *f*; (*brand*) marca; **to ~ a fool of sb** far fare a qn la figura dello scemo; **to ~ a profit** realizzare un profitto; **to ~ a loss** subire una perdita; **to ~ it** (*arrive*) arrivare; (*achieve sth*) farcela; **what time do you ~ it?** che ora fai?; **to ~ do with** arrangiarsi con; **make off** *vi* svignarsela; **make out** *vt* (*write out*) scrivere; (*: cheque*) emettere; (*understand*) capire; (*see*) distinguere; (*: numbers*) decifrare; **make up** *vt* (*constitute*) formare; (*invent*) inventare; (*parcel*) fare ▷ *vi* conciliarsi; (*with cosmetics*) truccarsi; **make up for** *vt fus* compensare; ricuperare; **makeover** ['meɪkəuvəʳ] *n* (*change of*

image) cambiamento di immagine; (*of room, house*) trasformazione *f*; **maker** *n* (*of programme etc*) creatore(-trice); (*manufacturer*) fabbricante *m*; **makeshift** *adj* improvvisato(-a); **make-up** *n* trucco
making ['meɪkɪŋ] *n* (*fig*): **in the ~** in formazione; **to have the ~s of** (*actor, athlete etc*) avere la stoffa di
malaria [mə'lɛərɪə] *n* malaria
Malaysia [mə'leɪzɪə] *n* Malaysia
male [meɪl] *n* (*Biol*) maschio ▷ *adj* maschile; maschio(-a)
malicious [mə'lɪʃəs] *adj* malevolo(-a); (*Law*) doloso(-a)
malignant [mə'lɪgnənt] *adj* (*Med*) maligno(-a)
mall [mɔ:l] *n* (*also:* **shopping ~**) centro commerciale
mallet ['mælɪt] *n* maglio
malnutrition [mælnju:'trɪʃən] *n* denutrizione *f*
malpractice [mæl'præktɪs] *n* prevaricazione *f*; negligenza
malt [mɔ:lt] *n* malto
Malta ['mɔ:ltə] *n* Malta; **Maltese** [mɔ:l'ti:z] *adj, n* (*pl inv*) maltese (*m/f*); (*Ling*) maltese *m*
mammal ['mæml] *n* mammifero
mammoth ['mæməθ] *adj* enorme, gigantesco(-a)
man [mæn] (*pl* **men**) *n* uomo ▷ *vt* fornire d'uomini; stare a; **an old ~** un vecchio; **~ and wife** marito e moglie
manage ['mænɪdʒ] *vi* farcela ▷ *vt* (*be in charge of*) occuparsi di; gestire; **to ~ to do sth** riuscire a far qc; **manageable** *adj* maneggevole; fattibile; **management** *n* amministrazione *f*, direzione *f*; **manager** *n* direttore *m*; (*of shop, restaurant*) gerente *m*; (*of artist, Sport*) manager *m inv*; **manageress** [-ə'rɛs] *n* direttrice *f*; gerente *f*; **managerial** [-ə'dʒɪərɪəl] *adj* dirigenziale; **managing director** *n* amministratore *m* delegato
mandarin ['mændərɪn] *n* (*person, fruit*) mandarino
mandate ['mændeɪt] *n* mandato
mandatory ['mændətərɪ] *adj* obbligatorio(-a), ingiuntivo(-a)
mane [meɪn] *n* criniera
mangetout ['mɔnʒ'tu:] *n* pisello dolce, taccola
mango ['mæŋgəu] (*pl* **mangoes**) *n* mango
man: **manhole** ['mænhəul] *n* botola stradale; **manhood** ['mænhud] *n* età virile; virilità
mania ['meɪnɪə] *n* mania; **maniac** ['meɪnɪæk] *n* maniaco(-a)
manic ['mænɪk] *adj* (*behaviour, activity*) maniacale
manicure ['mænɪkjuəʳ] *n* manicure *f inv*
manifest ['mænɪfɛst] *vt* manifestare ▷ *adj* manifesto(-a), palese
manifesto [mænɪ'fɛstəu] *n* manifesto
manipulate [mə'nɪpjuleɪt] *vt* manipolare
man: **mankind** [mæn'kaɪnd] *n* umanità, genere *m* umano; **manly** ['mænlɪ] *adj* virile; coraggioso(-a); **man-made** *adj* sintetico(-a); artificiale
manner ['mænəʳ] *n* maniera, modo; (*behaviour*) modo di fare; (*type, sort*): **all ~ of things** ogni genere di cosa; **manners** *npl* (*conduct*) maniere *fpl*; **bad ~s** maleducazione *f*
manoeuvre [mə'nu:vəʳ] (*US* **maneuver**) *vt* manovrare ▷ *vi* far manovre ▷ *n* manovra
manpower ['mænpauəʳ] *n* manodopera
mansion ['mænʃən] *n* casa signorile
manslaughter ['mænslɔ:təʳ] *n* omicidio preterintenzionale
mantelpiece ['mæntlpi:s] *n* mensola del caminetto
manual ['mænjuəl] *adj* manuale ▷ *n* manuale *m*

manufacture [mænju'fæktʃə^r] *vt* fabbricare ▷ *n* fabbricazione *f*, manifattura; **manufacturer** *n* fabbricante *m*
manure [mə'njuə^r] *n* concime *m*
manuscript ['mænjuskrɪpt] *n* manoscritto
many ['mɛnɪ] *adj* molti(-e) ▷ *pron* molti(-e); **a great ~** moltissimi(-e), un gran numero (di); **~ a time** molte volte
map [mæp] *n* carta (geografica); (*of city*) cartina; **can you show it to me on the ~?** può indicarmelo sulla cartina?
maple ['meɪpl] *n* acero
mar [mɑː^r] *vt* sciupare
Mar. *abbr* (= *March*) mar.
marathon ['mærəθən] *n* maratona
marble ['mɑːbl] *n* marmo; (*toy*) pallina, bilia
March [mɑːtʃ] *n* marzo
march [mɑːtʃ] *vi* marciare; sfilare ▷ *n* marcia
mare [mɛə^r] *n* giumenta
margarine [mɑːdʒə'riːn] *n* margarina
margin ['mɑːdʒɪn] *n* margine *m*; **marginal** *adj* marginale; **marginal seat** (*Pol*) *seggio elettorale ottenuto con una stretta maggioranza*; **marginally** *adv* (*bigger, better*) lievemente, di poco; (*different*) un po'
marigold ['mærɪgəuld] *n* calendola
marijuana [mærɪ'wɑːnə] *n* marijuana
marina [mə'riːnə] *n* marina
marinade *n* [mærɪ'neɪd] marinata ▷ *vt* ['mærɪneɪd] = **marinate**
marinate ['mærɪneɪt] *vt* marinare
marine [mə'riːn] *adj* (*animal, plant*) marino(-a); (*forces, engineering*) marittimo(-a) ▷ *n* (BRIT) fante *m* di marina; (US) marine *m inv*
marital ['mærɪtl] *adj* maritale, coniugale; **marital status** *n* stato civile
maritime ['mærɪtaɪm] *adj* marittimo(-a)
marjoram ['mɑːdʒərəm] *n* maggiorana
mark [mɑːk] *n* segno; (*stain*) macchia; (*of skid etc*) traccia; (BRIT *Scol*) voto; (*Sport*) bersaglio; (*currency*) marco ▷ *vt* segnare; (*stain*) macchiare; (*indicate*) indicare; (BRIT *Scol*) dare un voto a; correggere; **to ~ time** segnare il passo; **marked** *adj* spiccato(-a), chiaro(-a); **marker** *n* (*sign*) segno; (*bookmark*) segnalibro
market ['mɑːkɪt] *n* mercato ▷ *vt* (*Comm*) mettere in vendita; **marketing** *n* marketing *m*; **marketplace** *n* (piazza del) mercato; (*world of trade*) piazza, mercato; **market research** *n* indagine *f or* ricerca di mercato
marmalade ['mɑːməleɪd] *n* marmellata d'arance
maroon [mə'ruːn] *vt* (*also fig*): **to be ~ed (in** *or* **at)** essere abbandonato(-a) (in) ▷ *adj* bordeaux *inv*
marquee [mɑː'kiː] *n* padiglione *m*
marriage ['mærɪdʒ] *n* matrimonio; **marriage certificate** *n* certificato di matrimonio
married ['mærɪd] *adj* sposato(-a); (*life, love*) coniugale, matrimoniale
marrow ['mærəu] *n* midollo; (*vegetable*) zucca
marry ['mærɪ] *vt* sposare, sposarsi con; (*vicar, priest etc*) dare in matrimonio ▷ *vi* (*also:* **get married**) sposarsi
Mars [mɑːz] *n* (*planet*) Marte *m*
marsh [mɑːʃ] *n* palude *f*
marshal ['mɑːʃl] *n* maresciallo; (US: *fire*) capo; (: *police*) capitano ▷ *vt* (*thoughts, support*) ordinare; (*soldiers*) adunare
martyr ['mɑːtə^r] *n* martire *m/f*
marvel ['mɑːvl] *n* meraviglia ▷ *vi* **to ~ (at)** meravigliarsi (di); **marvellous** (US **marvelous**) *adj* meraviglioso(-a)
Marxism ['mɑːksɪzəm] *n* marxismo

Marxist ['mɑ:ksɪst] *adj, n* marxista *m/f*
marzipan ['mɑ:zɪpæn] *n* marzapane *m*
mascara [mæs'kɑ:rə] *n* mascara *m*
mascot ['mæskət] *n* mascotte *f inv*
masculine ['mæskjulɪn] *adj* maschile; (*woman*) mascolino(-a)
mash [mæʃ] *vt* passare, schiacciare; **mashed potatoes** *npl* purè *m* di patate
mask [mɑ:sk] *n* maschera ▷ *vt* mascherare
mason ['meɪsn] *n* (*also:* **stone~**) scalpellino; (*also:* **free~**) massone *m*; **masonry** *n* muratura
mass [mæs] *n* moltitudine *f*, massa; (*Physics*) massa; (*Rel*) messa ▷ *cpd* di massa ▷ *vi* ammassarsi; **the masses** *npl* (*ordinary people*) le masse; **~es of** (*inf*) una montagna di
massacre ['mæsəkəʳ] *n* massacro
massage ['mæsɑ:ʒ] *n* massaggio
massive ['mæsɪv] *adj* enorme, massiccio(-a)
mass media *npl* mass media *mpl*
mass-produce ['mæsprə'dju:s] *vt* produrre in serie
mast [mɑ:st] *n* albero
master ['mɑ:stəʳ] *n* padrone *m*; (*Art etc, teacher: in primary school*) maestro; (*: in secondary school*) professore *m*; (*title for boys*): **M~ X** Signorino X ▷ *vt* domare; (*learn*) imparare a fondo; (*understand*) conoscere a fondo; **mastermind** *n* mente *f* superiore ▷ *vt* essere il cervello di; **Master of Arts/Science** *n* Master *m inv* in lettere/scienze; **masterpiece** *n* capolavoro
masturbate ['mæstəbeɪt] *vi* masturbare
mat [mæt] *n* stuoia; (*also:* **door~**) stoino, zerbino; (*also:* **table ~**) sottopiatto ▷ *adj* = **matt**
match [mætʃ] *n* fiammifero; (*game*) partita, incontro; (*fig*) uguale *m/f*; matrimonio; partito ▷ *vt* intonare; (*go well with*) andare benissimo con; (*equal*) uguagliare; (*correspond to*) corrispondere a; (*pair: also:* **~ up**) accoppiare ▷ *vi* combaciare; **to be a good ~** andare bene; **matchbox** *n* scatola per fiammiferi; **matching** *adj* ben assortito(-a)
mate [meɪt] *n* compagno(-a) di lavoro; (*inf: friend*) amico(-a); (*animal*) compagno(-a); (*in merchant navy*) secondo ▷ *vi* accoppiarsi
material [mə'tɪərɪəl] *n* (*substance*) materiale *m*, materia; (*cloth*) stoffa ▷ *adj* materiale; **materials** *npl* (*equipment*) materiali *mpl*
materialize [mə'tɪərɪəlaɪz] *vi* materializzarsi, realizzarsi
maternal [mə'tə:nl] *adj* materno(-a)
maternity [mə'tə:nɪtɪ] *n* maternità; **maternity hospital** *n* ≈ clinica ostetrica; **maternity leave** *n* congedo di maternità
math [mæθ] (*US*) *n* = **maths**
mathematical [mæθə'mætɪkl] *adj* matematico(-a)
mathematician [mæθəmə'tɪʃən] *n* matematico(-a)
mathematics [mæθə'mætɪks] *n* matematica
maths [mæθs] (*US* **math**) *n* matematica
matinée ['mætɪneɪ] *n* matinée *f inv*
matron ['meɪtrən] *n* (*in hospital*) capoinfermiera; (*in school*) infermiera
matt [mæt] *adj* opaco(-a)
matter ['mætəʳ] *n* questione *f*; (*Physics*) materia, sostanza; (*content*) contenuto; (*Med: pus*) pus *m* ▷ *vi* importare; **it doesn't ~** non importa; (*I don't mind*) non fa niente; **what's the ~?** che cosa c'è?; **no ~ what** qualsiasi cosa accada; **as a ~ of course** come cosa naturale; **as a ~ of fact** in verità; **matters** *npl* (*affairs*) questioni
mattress ['mætrɪs] *n* materasso
mature [mə'tjuəʳ] *adj* maturo(-a);

(*cheese*) stagionato(-a) ▷ *vi* maturare; stagionare; **mature student** *n* *studente universitario che ha più di 25 anni*; **maturity** *n* maturità
maul [mɔ:l] *vt* lacerare
mauve [məuv] *adj* malva *inv*
max *abbr* = **maximum**
maximize ['mæksɪmaɪz] *vt* (*profits etc*) massimizzare; (*chances*) aumentare al massimo
maximum ['mæksɪməm] (*pl* **maxima**) *adj* massimo(-a) ▷ *n* massimo
May [meɪ] *n* maggio
may [meɪ] (*conditional* **might**) *vi* (*indicating possibility*): **he ~ come** può darsi che venga; (*be allowed to*): **~ I smoke?** posso fumare?; (*wishes*): **~ God bless you!** Dio la benedica!; **you ~ as well go** tanto vale che tu te ne vada
maybe ['meɪbi:] *adv* forse, può darsi; **~ he'll ...** può darsi che lui ... + *sub*, forse lui ...
May Day *n* il primo maggio
mayhem ['meɪhɛm] *n* cagnara
mayonnaise [meɪə'neɪz] *n* maionese *f*
mayor [mɛəʳ] *n* sindaco; **mayoress** *n* sindaco (*donna*); moglie *f* del sindaco
maze [meɪz] *n* labirinto, dedalo
MD *n abbr* (= *Doctor of Medicine*) *titolo di studio*; (*Comm*) *see* **managing director**
me [mi:] *pron* mi, m' + *vowel or silent "h"*; (*stressed, after prep*) me; **he heard me** mi ha *or* m'ha sentito; **give me a book** dammi (*or* mi dia) un libro; **it's me** sono io; **with me** con me; **without me** senza di me
meadow ['mɛdəu] *n* prato
meagre ['mi:gəʳ] (*US* **meager**) *adj* magro(-a)
meal [mi:l] *n* pasto; (*flour*) farina; **mealtime** *n* l'ora di mangiare
mean [mi:n] (*pt, pp* **meant**) *adj* (*with money*) avaro(-a), gretto(-a); (*unkind*) meschino(-a), maligno(-a); (*shabby*) misero(-a); (*average*) medio(-a) ▷ *vt* (*signify*) significare, voler dire; (*intend*): **to ~ to do** aver l'intenzione di fare ▷ *n* mezzo; (*Math*) media; **means** *npl* (*way, money*) mezzi *mpl*; **by ~s of** per mezzo di; **by all ~s** ma certo, prego; **to be ~t for** essere destinato(-a) a; **do you ~ it?** dice sul serio?; **what do you ~?** che cosa vuol dire?
meaning ['mi:nɪŋ] *n* significato, senso; **meaningful** *adj* significativo(-a); **meaningless** *adj* senza senso
meant [mɛnt] *pt, pp of* **mean**
meantime ['mi:ntaɪm] *adv* (*also:* **in the ~**) nel frattempo
meanwhile ['mi:nwaɪl] *adv* nel frattempo
measles ['mi:zlz] *n* morbillo
measure ['mɛʒəʳ] *vt, vi* misurare ▷ *n* misura; (*also:* **tape ~**) metro
measurement ['mɛʒəmənt] *n* (*act*) misurazione *f*; (*measure*) misura; **chest/hip ~** giro petto/fianchi; **to take sb's ~s** prendere le misure di qn
meat [mi:t] *n* carne *f*; **I don't eat ~** non mangio carne; **cold ~** affettato; **meatball** *n* polpetta di carne
Mecca ['mɛkə] *n* (*also fig*) la Mecca
mechanic [mɪ'kænɪk] *n* meccanico; **can you send a ~?** può mandare un meccanico?; **mechanical** *adj* meccanico(-a)
mechanism ['mɛkənɪzəm] *n* meccanismo
medal ['mɛdl] *n* medaglia; **medallist** (*US* **medalist**) *n* (*Sport*): **to be a gold medallist** essere medaglia d'oro
meddle ['mɛdl] *vi* **to ~ in** immischiarsi in, mettere le mani in; **to ~ with** toccare
media ['mi:dɪə] *npl* media *mpl*
mediaeval [mɛdɪ'i:vl] *adj* = **medieval**
mediate ['mi:dɪeɪt] *vi* fare da mediatore(-trice)
medical ['mɛdɪkl] *adj* medico(-a) ▷ *n*

visita medica; **medical certificate** *n* certificato medico
medicated ['mɛdɪkeɪtɪd] *adj* medicato(-a)
medication [mɛdɪ'keɪʃən] *n* medicinali *mpl*, farmaci *mpl*
medicine ['mɛdsɪn] *n* medicina
medieval [mɛdɪ'i:vl] *adj* medievale
mediocre [mi:dɪ'əukə^r] *adj* mediocre
meditate ['mɛdɪteɪt] *vi* **to ~ (on)** meditare (su)
meditation [mɛdɪ'teɪʃən] *n* meditazione *f*
Mediterranean [mɛdɪtə'reɪnɪən] *adj* mediterraneo(-a); **the ~ (Sea)** il (mare) Mediterraneo
medium ['mi:dɪəm] (*pl* **media**) *adj* medio(-a) ▷ *n* (*means*) mezzo; (*pl mediums*: *person*) medium *m inv*; **medium-sized** *adj* (*tin etc*) di grandezza media; (*clothes*) di taglia media; **medium wave** *n* onde *fpl* medie
meek [mi:k] *adj* dolce, umile
meet [mi:t] (*pt, pp* **met**) *vt* incontrare; (*for the first time*) fare la conoscenza di; (*go and fetch*) andare a prendere; (*fig*) affrontare; soddisfare; raggiungere ▷ *vi* incontrarsi; (*in session*) riunirsi; (*join*: *objects*) unirsi; **nice to ~ you** piacere (di conoscerla); **meet up** *vi* **to meet up with sb** incontrare qn; **meet with** *vt fus* incontrare; **meeting** *n* incontro; (*session*: *of club etc*) riunione *f*; (*interview*) intervista; **she's at a meeting** (*Comm*) è in riunione; **meeting place** *n* luogo d'incontro
megabyte ['mɛgəbaɪt] *n* (*Comput*) megabyte *m inv*
megaphone ['mɛgəfəun] *n* megafono
megapixel ['mɛgəpɪksl] *n* megapixel *m inv*
melancholy ['mɛlənkəlɪ] *n* malinconia ▷ *adj* malinconico(-a)
melody ['mɛlədɪ] *n* melodia
melon ['mɛlən] *n* melone *m*
melt [mɛlt] *vi* (*gen*) sciogliersi, struggersi; (*metals*) fondersi ▷ *vt* sciogliere, struggere; fondere
member ['mɛmbə^r] *n* membro; **Member of Congress** (US) *n* membro del Congresso; **Member of Parliament** (BRIT) *n* deputato(-a); **Member of the European Parliament** (BRIT) *n* eurodeputato(-a); **Member of the Scottish Parliament** (BRIT) *n* deputato(-a) del Parlamento scozzese; **membership** *n* iscrizione *f*, (numero d')iscritti *mpl*, membri *mpl*; **membership card** *n* tessera (di iscrizione)
memento [mə'mɛntəu] *n* ricordo, souvenir *m inv*
memo ['mɛməu] *n* appunto; (*Comm etc*) comunicazione *f* di servizio
memorable ['mɛmərəbl] *adj* memorabile
memorandum [mɛmə'rændəm] (*pl* **memoranda**) *n* appunto; (*Comm etc*) comunicazione *f* di servizio
memorial [mɪ'mɔ:rɪəl] *n* monumento commemorativo ▷ *adj* commemorativo(-a)
memorize ['mɛməraɪz] *vt* memorizzare
memory ['mɛmərɪ] *n* (*also Comput*) memoria; (*recollection*) ricordo; **memory card** *n* (*for digital camera*) scheda di memoria
men [mɛn] *npl of* **man**
menace ['mɛnəs] *n* minaccia ▷ *vt* minacciare
mend [mɛnd] *vt* aggiustare, riparare; (*darn*) rammendare ▷ *n* **on the ~** in via di guarigione
meningitis [mɛnɪn'dʒaɪtɪs] *n* meningite *f*
menopause ['mɛnəupɔ:z] *n* menopausa
men's room *n*: **the men's room** (*esp* US) la toilette degli uomini
menstruation [mɛnstru'eɪʃən] *n*

mestruazione *f*

menswear ['mɛnzwɛə^r] *n* abbigliamento maschile

mental ['mɛntl] *adj* mentale; **mental hospital** *n* ospedale *m* psichiatrico; **mentality** [mɛn'tælɪtɪ] *n* mentalità *f inv*; **mentally** *adv*: **to be mentally handicapped** essere minorato psichico

menthol ['mɛnθɔl] *n* mentolo

mention ['mɛnʃən] *n* menzione *f* ▷ *vt* menzionare, far menzione di; **don't ~ it!** non c'è di che!, prego!

menu ['mɛnju:] *n* (*set menu, Comput*) menù *m inv*; (*printed*) carta; **could we see the ~?** ci può portare il menù?

MEP *n abbr* = **Member of the European Parliament**

mercenary ['mə:sɪnərɪ] *adj* venale ▷ *n* mercenario

merchandise ['mə:tʃəndaɪz] *n* merci *fpl*

merchant ['mə:tʃənt] *n* mercante *m*, commerciante *m*; **merchant navy** (*US* **merchant marine**) *n* marina mercantile

merciless ['mə:sɪlɪs] *adj* spietato(-a)

mercury ['mə:kjurɪ] *n* mercurio

mercy ['mə:sɪ] *n* pietà; (*Rel*) misericordia; **at the ~ of** alla mercè di

mere [mɪə^r] *adj* semplice; **by a ~ chance** per mero caso; **merely** *adv* semplicemente, non ... che

merge [mə:dʒ] *vt* unire ▷ *vi* fondersi, unirsi; (*Comm*) fondersi; **merger** *n* (*Comm*) fusione *f*

meringue [mə'ræŋ] *n* meringa

merit ['mɛrɪt] *n* merito, valore *m* ▷ *vt* meritare

mermaid ['mə:meɪd] *n* sirena

merry ['mɛrɪ] *adj* gaio(-a), allegro(-a); **M~ Christmas!** Buon Natale!; **merry-go-round** *n* carosello

mesh [mɛʃ] *n* maglia; rete *f*

mess [mɛs] *n* confusione *f*, disordine *m*; (*fig*) pasticcio; (*dirt*) sporcizia; (*Mil*) mensa; **mess about** *or* **around** (*inf*) *vi* trastullarsi; **mess with** (*inf*) *vt fus* (*challenge, confront*) litigare con; (*drugs, drinks*) abusare di; **mess up** *vt* sporcare; fare un pasticcio di; rovinare

message ['mɛsɪdʒ] *n* messaggio; **can I leave a ~?** posso lasciare un messaggio?; **are there any ~s for me?** ci sono messaggi per me?; **message board** *n* (*Comput*) bacheca elettronica

messenger ['mɛsɪndʒə^r] *n* messaggero(-a)

Messrs ['mɛsəz] *abbr* (*on letters*) Spett.

messy ['mɛsɪ] *adj* sporco(-a), disordinato(-a)

met [mɛt] *pt, pp of* **meet**

metabolism [mɛ'tæbəlɪzəm] *n* metabolismo

metal ['mɛtl] *n* metallo; **metallic** [-'tælɪk] *adj* metallico(-a)

metaphor ['mɛtəfə^r] *n* metafora

meteor ['mi:tɪə^r] *n* meteora; **meteorite** ['mi:tɪəraɪt] *n* meteorite *m*

meteorology [mi:tɪə'rɔlədʒɪ] *n* meteorologia

meter ['mi:tə^r] *n* (*instrument*) contatore *m*; (*parking meter*) parchimetro; (*US: unit*) = **metre**

method ['mɛθəd] *n* metodo; **methodical** [mɪ'θɔdɪkl] *adj* metodico(-a)

meths [mɛθs] (*BRIT*) *n* alcool *m* denaturato

meticulous [mɛ'tɪkjuləs] *adj* meticoloso(-a)

metre ['mi:tə^r] (*US* **meter**) *n* metro

metric ['mɛtrɪk] *adj* metrico(-a)

metro ['metrəu] *n* metro *m inv*

metropolitan [mɛtrə'pɔlɪtən] *adj* metropolitano(-a)

Mexican ['mɛksɪkən] *adj, n* messicano(-a)

Mexico ['mɛksɪkəu] *n* Messico

mg *abbr* (= *milligram*) mg

mice [maɪs] *npl of* **mouse**

micro... ['maɪkrəu] *prefix* micro...; **microchip** *n* microcircuito integrato; **microphone** *n* microfono; **microscope** *n* microscopio; **microwave** *n* (*also:* **microwave oven**) forno a microonde

mid [mɪd] *adj* **~ May** metà maggio; **~ afternoon** metà pomeriggio; **in ~ air** a mezz'aria; **midday** *n* mezzogiorno

middle ['mɪdl] *n* mezzo; centro; (*waist*) vita ▷ *adj* di mezzo; **in the ~ of the night** nel bel mezzo della notte; **middle-aged** *adj* di mezza età; **Middle Ages** *npl*: **the Middle Ages** il Medioevo; **middle-class** *adj* ≈ borghese; **Middle East** *n* Medio Oriente *m*; **middle name** *n* secondo nome *m*; **middle school** *n* (US) *scuola media per ragazzi dagli 11 ai 14 anni*; (BRIT) *scuola media per ragazzi dagli 8 o 9 ai 12 o 13 anni*

midge [mɪdʒ] *n* moscerino

midget ['mɪdʒɪt] *n* nano(-a)

midnight ['mɪdnaɪt] *n* mezzanotte *f*

midst [mɪdst] *n*: **in the ~ of** in mezzo a

midsummer [mɪd'sʌmə^r] *n* mezza *or* piena estate *f*

midway [mɪd'weɪ] *adj, adv*: **~ (between)** a mezza strada (fra); **~ (through)** a metà (di)

midweek [mɪd'wi:k] *adv* a metà settimana

midwife ['mɪdwaɪf] (*pl* **midwives**) *n* levatrice *f*

midwinter [mɪd'wɪntə^r] *n* pieno inverno

might [maɪt] *vb see* **may** ▷ *n* potere *m*, forza; **mighty** *adj* forte, potente

migraine ['mi:greɪn] *n* emicrania

migrant ['maɪgrənt] *adj* (*bird*) migratore(-trice); (*worker*) emigrato(-a)

migrate [maɪ'greɪt] *vi* (*bird*) migrare; (*person*) emigrare

migration [maɪ'greɪʃən] *n* migrazione *f*

mike [maɪk] *n abbr* (= *microphone*) microfono

Milan [mɪ'læn] *n* Milano *f*

mild [maɪld] *adj* mite; (*person, voice*) dolce; (*flavour*) delicato(-a); (*illness*) leggero(-a); (*interest*) blando(-a) ▷ *n* (*beer*) birra leggera; **mildly** ['maɪldlɪ] *adv* mitemente; dolcemente; delicatamente; leggermente; blandamente; **to put it mildly** a dire poco

mile [maɪl] *n* miglio; **mileage** *n* distanza in miglia, ≈ chilometraggio; **mileometer** [maɪ'lɔmɪtə^r] *n* ≈ contachilometri *m inv*; **milestone** ['maɪlstəun] *n* pietra miliare

military ['mɪlɪtərɪ] *adj* militare

militia [mɪ'lɪʃə] *n* milizia

milk [mɪlk] *n* latte *m* ▷ *vt* (*cow*) mungere; (*fig*) sfruttare; **milk chocolate** *n* cioccolato al latte; **milkman** (*irreg*) *n* lattaio; **milky** *adj* lattiginoso(-a); (*colour*) latteo(-a)

mill [mɪl] *n* mulino; (*small: for coffee, pepper etc*) macinino; (*factory*) fabbrica; (*spinning mill*) filatura ▷ *vt* macinare ▷ *vi* (*also:* **~ about**) brulicare

millennium [mɪ'lɛnɪəm] (*pl* **millenniums** *or* **millennia**) *n* millennio

milli... ['mɪlɪ] *prefix*: **milligram(me)** *n* milligrammo; **millilitre** ['mɪlɪli:tə^r] (US **milliliter**) *n* millilitro; **millimetre** (US **millimeter**) *n* millimetro

million ['mɪljən] *num* milione *m*; **millionaire** *n* milionario, ≈ miliardario; **millionth** *num* milionesimo(-a)

milometer [maɪ'lɔmɪtə^r] *n* = **mileometer**

mime [maɪm] *n* mimo ▷ *vt, vi* mimare

mimic ['mɪmɪk] *n* imitatore(-trice) ▷ *vt* fare la mimica di

min. *abbr* = **minute(s)**; **minimum**

mince [mɪns] *vt* tritare, macinare ▷ *n* (BRIT *Culin*) carne *f* tritata *or* macinata; **mincemeat** *n frutta secca tritata per uso in pasticceria*; (US) carne *f* tritata *or* macinata; **mince pie** *n specie di torta con frutta secca*

mind [maɪnd] *n* mente *f* ▷ *vt* (*attend to, look after*) badare a, occuparsi di; (*be careful*) fare attenzione a, stare attento(-a) a; (*object to*): **I don't ~ the noise** il rumore non mi dà alcun fastidio; **I don't ~** non m'importa; **do you ~ if ...?** le dispiace se...?; **it is on my ~** mi preoccupa; **to my ~** secondo me, a mio parere; **to be out of one's ~** essere uscito(-a) di mente; **to keep** *or* **bear sth in ~** non dimenticare qc; **to make up one's ~** decidersi; **~ you, ...** sì, però va detto che ...; **never ~** non importa, non fa niente; (*don't worry*) non preoccuparti; **"~ the step"** "attenzione allo scalino"; **mindless** *adj* idiota

mine[1] [maɪn] *pron* il (la) mio(-a); (*pl*) i (le) miei (mei); **that book is ~** quel libro è mio; **yours is red, ~ is green** il tuo è rosso, il mio è verde; **a friend of ~** un mio amico

mine[2] [maɪn] *n* miniera; (*explosive*) mina ▷ *vt* (*coal*) estrarre; (*ship, beach*) minare; **minefield** *n* (*also fig*) campo minato; **miner** ['maɪnəʳ] *n* minatore *m*

mineral ['mɪnərəl] *adj* minerale ▷ *n* minerale *m*; **mineral water** *n* acqua minerale

mingle ['mɪŋgl] *vi* **to ~ with** mescolarsi a, mischiarsi con

miniature ['mɪnətʃəʳ] *adj* in miniatura ▷ *n* miniatura

minibar ['mɪnɪbɑːʳ] *n* minibar *m inv*

minibus ['mɪnɪbʌs] *n* minibus *m inv*

minicab ['mɪnɪkæb] *n* (BRIT) ≈ taxi *m inv*

minimal ['mɪnɪml] *adj* minimo(-a)

minimize ['mɪnɪmaɪz] *vt* minimizzare

minimum ['mɪnɪməm] (*pl* **minima**) *n* minimo ▷ *adj* minimo(-a)

mining ['maɪnɪŋ] *n* industria mineraria

miniskirt ['mɪnɪskəːt] *n* minigonna

minister ['mɪnɪstəʳ] *n* (BRIT *Pol*) ministro; (*Rel*) pastore *m*

ministry ['mɪnɪstrɪ] *n* ministero

minor ['maɪnəʳ] *adj* minore, di poca importanza; (*Mus*) minore ▷ *n* (*Law*) minorenne *m/f*

Minorca [mɪ'nɔːkə] *n* Minorca

minority [maɪ'nɔrɪtɪ] *n* minoranza

mint [mɪnt] *n* (*plant*) menta; (*sweet*) pasticca di menta ▷ *vt* (*coins*) battere; **the (Royal) M~** (BRIT), **the (US) M~** (US) la Zecca; **in ~ condition** come nuovo(-a) di zecca

minus ['maɪnəs] *n* (*also:* **~ sign**) segno meno ▷ *prep* meno

minute [*adj* maɪ'njuːt, *n* 'mɪnɪt] *adj* minuscolo(-a); (*detail*) minuzioso(-a) ▷ *n* minuto; **minutes** *npl* (*of meeting*) verbale *m*

miracle ['mɪrəkl] *n* miracolo

miraculous [mɪ'rækjuləs] *adj* miracoloso(-a)

mirage ['mɪrɑːʒ] *n* miraggio

mirror ['mɪrəʳ] *n* specchio; (*in car*) specchietto

misbehave [mɪsbɪ'heɪv] *vi* comportarsi male

misc. *abbr* = **miscellaneous**

miscarriage ['mɪskærɪdʒ] *n* (*Med*) aborto spontaneo; **miscarriage of justice** errore *m* giudiziario

miscellaneous [mɪsɪ'leɪnɪəs] *adj* (*items*) vario(-a); (*selection*) misto(-a)

mischief ['mɪstʃɪf] *n* (*naughtiness*) birichineria; (*maliciousness*) malizia; **mischievous** *adj* birichino(-a)

misconception ['mɪskən'sɛpʃən] *n* idea sbagliata

misconduct [mɪs'kɔndʌkt] *n* cattiva condotta; **professional ~** reato professionale

miser ['maɪzəʳ] *n* avaro

miserable ['mɪzərəbl] *adj* infelice; (*wretched*) miserabile; (*weather*) deprimente; (*offer, failure*) misero(-a)

misery ['mɪzərɪ] *n* (*unhappiness*) tristezza; (*wretchedness*) miseria

misfortune [mɪs'fɔːtʃən] *n* sfortuna

misgiving [mɪs'gɪvɪŋ] *n* apprensione *f*; **to have ~s about** avere dei dubbi

per quanto riguarda
misguided [mɪs'gaɪdɪd] *adj* sbagliato(-a), poco giudizioso(-a)
mishap ['mɪshæp] *n* disgrazia
misinterpret [mɪsɪn'tə:prɪt] *vt* interpretare male
misjudge [mɪs'dʒʌdʒ] *vt* giudicare male
mislay [mɪs'leɪ] (*irreg*) *vt* smarrire
mislead [mɪs'li:d] (*irreg*) *vt* sviare; **misleading** *adj* ingannevole
misplace [mɪs'pleɪs] *vt* smarrire
misprint ['mɪsprɪnt] *n* errore *m* di stampa
misrepresent [mɪsrɛprɪ'zɛnt] *vt* travisare
Miss [mɪs] *n* Signorina
miss [mɪs] *vt* (*fail to get*) perdere; (*fail to hit*) mancare; (*fail to see*): **you can't ~ it** non puoi non vederlo; (*regret the absence of*): **I ~ him** sento la sua mancanza ▷ *vi* mancare ▷ *n* (*shot*) colpo mancato; **we ~ed our train** abbiamo perso il treno; **miss out** (BRIT) *vt* omettere; **miss out on** *vt fus* (*fun, party*) perdersi; (*chance, bargain*) lasciarsi sfuggire
missile ['mɪsaɪl] *n* (*Mil*) missile *m*; (*object thrown*) proiettile *m*
missing ['mɪsɪŋ] *adj* perso(-a), smarrito(-a); (*person*) scomparso(-a); (*: after disaster, Mil*) disperso(-a); (*removed*) mancante; **to be ~** mancare
mission ['mɪʃən] *n* missione *f*; **missionary** *n* missionario(-a)
misspell [mɪs'spɛl] *vt* (*irreg: like* **spell**) sbagliare l'ortografia di
mist [mɪst] *n* nebbia, foschia ▷ *vi* (*also:* **~ over, ~ up**) annebbiarsi; (*: BRIT: windows*) appannarsi
mistake [mɪs'teɪk] (*irreg: like* **take**) *n* sbaglio, errore *m* ▷ *vt* sbagliarsi di; fraintendere; **to make a ~** fare uno sbaglio, sbagliare; **there must be some ~** ci dev'essere un errore; **by ~** per sbaglio; **to ~ for** prendere per; **mistaken** *pp of* **mistake** ▷ *adj* (*idea etc*) sbagliato(-a); **to be mistaken** sbagliarsi
mister ['mɪstəʳ] (*inf*) *n* signore *m*; *see* **Mr**
mistletoe ['mɪsltəu] *n* vischio
mistook [mɪs'tuk] *pt of* **mistake**
mistress ['mɪstrɪs] *n* padrona; (*lover*) amante *f*; (BRIT *Scol*) insegnante *f*
mistrust [mɪs'trʌst] *vt* diffidare di
misty ['mɪstɪ] *adj* nebbioso(-a), brumoso(-a)
misunderstand [mɪsʌndə'stænd] (*irreg*) *vt, vi* capire male, fraintendere; **misunderstanding** *n* malinteso, equivoco; **there's been a misunderstanding** c'è stato un malinteso
misunderstood [mɪsʌndə'stud] *pt, pp of* **misunderstand**
misuse [*n* mɪs'ju:s, *vb* mɪs'ju:z] *n* cattivo uso; (*of power*) abuso ▷ *vt* far cattivo uso di; abusare di
mitt(en) ['mɪt(n)] *n* mezzo guanto; manopola
mix [mɪks] *vt* mescolare ▷ *vi* (*people*): **to ~ with** avere a che fare con ▷ *n* mescolanza; preparato; **mix up** *vt* mescolare; (*confuse*) confondere; **mixed** *adj* misto(-a); **mixed grill** *n* (BRIT) misto alla griglia; **mixed salad** *n* insalata mista; **mixed-up** *adj* (*confused*) confuso(-a); **mixer** *n* (*for food: electric*) frullatore *m*; (*: hand*) frullino; (*person*): **he is a good mixer** è molto socievole; **mixture** *n* mescolanza; (*blend: of tobacco etc*) miscela; (*Med*) sciroppo; **mix-up** *n* confusione *f*
ml *abbr* (= *millilitre(s)*) ml
mm *abbr* (= *millimetre*) mm
moan [məun] *n* gemito ▷ *vi* (*inf: complain*): **to ~ (about)** lamentarsi (di)
moat [məut] *n* fossato
mob [mɔb] *n* calca ▷ *vt* accalcarsi intorno a
mobile ['məubaɪl] *adj* mobile ▷ *n* (*decoration*) mobile *m*; **mobile home** *n* grande roulotte *f inv* (utilizzata come

domicilio); **mobile phone** *n* telefono portatile, telefonino
mobility [məu'bɪlɪtɪ] *n* mobilità; (*of applicant*) disponibilità a viaggiare
mobilize ['məubɪlaɪz] *vt* mobilitare ▷ *vi* mobilitarsi
mock [mɔk] *vt* deridere, burlarsi di ▷ *adj* falso(-a); **mocks** *npl* (BRIT: *Scol*: *inf*) simulazione *f* degli esami; **mockery** *n* derisione *f*; **to make a mockery of** burlarsi di; (*exam*) rendere una farsa
mod cons ['mɔd'kɔnz] *npl abbr* (BRIT) = **modern conveniences**; *see* **convenience**
mode [məud] *n* modo
model ['mɔdl] *n* modello; (*person*: *for fashion*) indossatore(-trice); (: *for artist*) modello(-a) ▷ *adj* (*small-scale*: *railway etc*) in miniatura; (*child, factory*) modello *inv* ▷ *vt* modellare ▷ *vi* fare l'indossatore (*or* l'indossatrice); **to ~ clothes** presentare degli abiti
modem ['məudɛm] *n* modem *m inv*
moderate [*adj* 'mɔdərət, *vb* 'mɔdəreɪt] *adj* moderato(-a) ▷ *vi* moderarsi, placarsi ▷ *vt* moderare
moderation [mɔdə'reɪʃən] *n* moderazione *f*, misura; **in ~** in quantità moderata, con moderazione
modern ['mɔdən] *adj* moderno(-a); **mod cons** comodità *fpl* moderne; **modernize** *vt* modernizzare; **modern languages** *npl* lingue *fpl* moderne
modest ['mɔdɪst] *adj* modesto(-a); **modesty** *n* modestia
modification [mɔdɪfɪ'keɪʃən] *n* modificazione *f*; **to make ~s** fare *or* apportare delle modifiche
modify ['mɔdɪfaɪ] *vt* modificare
module ['mɔdju:l] *n* modulo
mohair ['məuhɛəʳ] *n* mohair *m*
Mohammed [məu'hæmɪd] *n* Maometto
moist [mɔɪst] *adj* umido(-a); **moisture** ['mɔɪstʃəʳ] *n* umidità; (*on glass*) goccioline *fpl* di vapore; **moisturizer** ['mɔɪstʃəraɪzəʳ] *n* idratante *f*
mold *etc* [məuld] (US) *n, vt* = **mould**
mole [məul] *n* (*animal, fig*) talpa; (*spot*) neo
molecule ['mɔlɪkju:l] *n* molecola
molest [məu'lɛst] *vt* molestare
molten ['məultən] *adj* fuso(-a)
mom [mɔm] (US) *n* = **mum**
moment ['məumənt] *n* momento, istante *m*; **at that ~** in quel momento; **at the ~** al momento, in questo momento; **momentarily** ['məuməntərɪlɪ] *adv* per un momento; (US: *very soon*) da un momento all'altro; **momentary** *adj* momentaneo(-a), passeggero(-a); **momentous** [-'mɛntəs] *adj* di grande importanza
momentum [məu'mɛntəm] *n* (*Physics*) momento; (*fig*) impeto; **to gather ~** aumentare di velocità
mommy ['mɔmɪ] (US) *n* = **mummy**
Mon. *abbr* (= *Monday*) lun.
Monaco ['mɔnəkəu] *n* Principato di Monaco
monarch ['mɔnək] *n* monarca *m*; **monarchy** *n* monarchia
monastery ['mɔnəstərɪ] *n* monastero
Monday ['mʌndɪ] *n* lunedì *m inv*
monetary ['mʌnɪtərɪ] *adj* monetario(-a)
money ['mʌnɪ] *n* denaro, soldi *mpl*; **I haven't got any ~** non ho soldi; **money belt** *n* marsupio (*per soldi*); **money order** *n* vaglia *m inv*
mongrel ['mʌŋgrəl] *n* (*dog*) cane *m* bastardo
monitor ['mɔnɪtəʳ] *n* (*TV, Comput*) monitor *m inv* ▷ *vt* controllare
monk [mʌŋk] *n* monaco
monkey ['mʌŋkɪ] *n* scimmia
monologue ['mɔnəlɔg] *n* monologo
monopoly [mə'nɔpəlɪ] *n* monopolio
monosodium glutamate [mɔnə'səudɪəm'glu:təmeɪt] *n*

glutammato di sodio
monotonous [mə'nɔtənəs] *adj* monotono(-a)
monsoon [mɔn'su:n] *n* monsone *m*
monster ['mɔnstəʳ] *n* mostro
month [mʌnθ] *n* mese *m*; **monthly** *adj* mensile ▷ *adv* al mese; ogni mese
monument ['mɔnjumənt] *n* monumento
mood [mu:d] *n* umore *m*; **to be in a good/bad ~** essere di buon/cattivo umore; **moody** *adj* (*variable*) capriccioso(-a), lunatico(-a); (*sullen*) imbronciato(-a)
moon [mu:n] *n* luna; **moonlight** *n* chiaro di luna
moor [muəʳ] *n* brughiera ▷ *vt* (*ship*) ormeggiare ▷ *vi* ormeggiarsi
moose [mu:s] *n inv* alce *m*
mop [mɔp] *n* lavapavimenti *m inv*; (*also:* **~ of hair**) zazzera ▷ *vt* lavare con lo straccio; (*face*) asciugare; **mop up** *vt* asciugare con uno straccio
mope [məup] *vi* fare il broncio
moped ['məupɛd] *n* (BRIT) ciclomotore *m*
moral ['mɔrl] *adj* morale ▷ *n* morale *f*; **morals** *npl* (*principles*) moralità
morale [mɔ'rɑ:l] *n* morale *m*
morality [mə'rælɪtɪ] *n* moralità
morbid ['mɔ:bɪd] *adj* morboso(-a)

KEYWORD

more [mɔ:ʳ] *adj* 1 (*greater in number etc*) più; **more people/letters than we expected** più persone/lettere di quante ne aspettavamo; **I have more wine/money than you** ho più vino/soldi di te; **I have more wine than beer** ho più vino che birra
2 (*additional*) altro(-a), ancora; **do you want (some) more tea?** vuole dell'altro tè?, vuole ancora del tè?; **I have no** *or* **I don't have any more money** non ho più soldi
▷ *pron* 1 (*greater amount*) più; **more than 10** più di 10; **it cost more than we expected** ha costato più di quanto ci aspettavamo
2 (*further or additional amount*) ancora; **is there any more?** ce n'è ancora?; **there's no more** non ce n'è più; **a little more** ancora un po'; **many/much more** molti(-e)/molto(-a) di più
▷ *adv* **more dangerous/easily (than)** più pericoloso/facilmente (di); **more and more** sempre di più; **more and more difficult** sempre più difficile; **more or less** più o meno; **more than ever** più che mai

moreover [mɔ:'rəuvəʳ] *adv* inoltre, di più
morgue [mɔ:g] *n* obitorio
morning ['mɔ:nɪŋ] *n* mattina, mattino; (*duration*) mattinata ▷ *cpd* del mattino; **in the ~** la mattina; **7 o'clock in the ~** le 7 di *or* della mattina; **morning sickness** *n* nausee *fpl* mattutine
Moroccan [mə'rɔkən] *adj*, *n* marocchino(-a)
Morocco [mə'rɔkəu] *n* Marocco
moron ['mɔ:rɔn] (*inf*) *n* deficiente *m/f*
morphine ['mɔ:fi:n] *n* morfina
morris dancing *n vedi nota nel riquadro*

MORRIS DANCING

Il **morris dancing** è una danza folcloristica inglese tradizionalmente riservata agli uomini. Vestiti di bianco e con dei campanelli attaccati alle caviglie, i ballerini eseguono una danza tenendo in mano dei fazzoletti bianchi e lunghi bastoni. Questa danza è molto popolare nelle feste paesane.

Morse [mɔ:s] *n* (*also:* **~ code**) alfabeto

Morse

mortal ['mɔːtl] *adj* mortale ▷ *n* mortale *m*

mortar ['mɔːtəʳ] *n* (*Constr*) malta; (*dish*) mortaio

mortgage ['mɔːɡɪdʒ] *n* ipoteca; (*loan*) prestito ipotecario ▷ *vt* ipotecare

mortician [mɔː'tɪʃən] (*US*) *n* impresario di pompe funebri

mortified ['mɔːtɪfaɪd] *adj* umiliato(-a)

mortuary ['mɔːtjuərɪ] *n* camera mortuaria; obitorio

mosaic [məu'zeɪɪk] *n* mosaico

Moscow ['mɔskəu] *n* Mosca

Moslem ['mɔzləm] *adj, n* = **Muslim**

mosque [mɔsk] *n* moschea

mosquito [mɔs'kiːtəu] (*pl* **mosquitoes**) *n* zanzara

moss [mɔs] *n* muschio

most [məust] *adj* (*almost all*) la maggior parte di; (*largest, greatest*): **who has (the) ~ money?** chi ha più soldi di tutti? ▷ *pron* la maggior parte ▷ *adv* più; (*work, sleep etc*) di più; (*very*) molto, estremamente; **the ~** (*also: + adjective*) il(-la) più; **~ of** la maggior parte di; **~ of them** quasi tutti; **I saw (the) ~** ho visto più io; **at the (very) ~** al massimo; **to make the ~ of** trarre il massimo vantaggio da; **a ~ interesting book** un libro estremamente interessante; **mostly** *adv* per lo più

MOT (*BRIT*) *n abbr* = **Ministry of Transport**; **the ~ (test)** *revisione annuale obbligatoria degli autoveicoli*

motel [məu'tɛl] *n* motel *m inv*

moth [mɔθ] *n* farfalla notturna; tarma

mother ['mʌðəʳ] *n* madre *f* ▷ *vt* (*care for*) fare da madre a; **motherhood** *n* maternità; **mother-in-law** *n* suocera; **mother-of-pearl** [mʌðərəv'pəːl] *n* madreperla; **Mother's Day** *n* la festa della mamma; **mother-to-be** [mʌðətə'biː] *n* futura mamma; **mother tongue** *n* madrelingua

motif [məu'tiːf] *n* motivo

motion ['məuʃən] *n* movimento, moto; (*gesture*) gesto; (*at meeting*) mozione *f* ▷ *vt, vi* **to ~ (to) sb to do** fare cenno a qn di fare; **motionless** *adj* immobile; **motion picture** *n* film *m inv*

motivate ['məutɪveɪt] *vt* (*act, decision*) dare origine a, motivare; (*person*) spingere

motivation [məutɪ'veɪʃən] *n* motivazione *f*

motive ['məutɪv] *n* motivo

motor ['məutəʳ] *n* motore *m*; (*BRIT*: *inf*: *vehicle*) macchina ▷ *cpd* automobilistico(-a); **motorbike** *n* moto *f inv*; **motorboat** *n* motoscafo; **motorcar** (*BRIT*) *n* automobile *f*; **motorcycle** *n* motocicletta; **motorcyclist** *n* motociclista *m/f*; **motoring** (*BRIT*) *n* turismo automobilistico; **motorist** *n* automobilista *m/f*; **motor racing** (*BRIT*) *n* corse *fpl* automobilistiche; **motorway** (*BRIT*) *n* autostrada

motto ['mɔtəu] (*pl* **mottoes**) *n* motto

mould [məuld] (*US* **mold**) *n* forma, stampo; (*mildew*) muffa ▷ *vt* formare; (*fig*) foggiare; **mouldy** *adj* ammuffito(-a); (*smell*) di muffa

mound [maund] *n* rialzo, collinetta; (*heap*) mucchio

mount [maunt] *n* (*Geo*) monte *m* ▷ *vt* montare; (*horse*) montare a ▷ *vi* (*increase*) aumentare; **mount up** *vi* (*build up*) accumularsi

mountain ['mauntɪn] *n* montagna ▷ *cpd* di montagna; **mountain bike** *n* mountain bike *f inv*; **mountaineer** [-'nɪəʳ] *n* alpinista *m/f*; **mountaineering** [-'nɪərɪŋ] *n* alpinismo; **mountainous** *adj* montagnoso(-a); **mountain range** *n* catena montuosa

mourn [mɔːn] *vt* piangere, lamentare ▷ *vi* **to ~ (for sb)** piangere (la morte

di qn); **mourner** *n* parente *m/f or* amico(-a) del defunto; **mourning** *n* lutto; **in mourning** in lutto
mouse [maus] (*pl* **mice**) *n* topo; (*Comput*) mouse *m inv*; **mouse mat, mouse pad** *n* (*Comput*) tappetino del mouse
moussaka [mu'sɑ:kə] *n* moussaka
mousse [mu:s] *n* mousse *f inv*
moustache [məs'tɑ:ʃ] (*US* **mustache**) *n* baffi *mpl*
mouth [mauθ, *pl* mauðz] *n* bocca; (*of river*) bocca, foce *f*; (*opening*) orifizio; **mouthful** *n* boccata; **mouth organ** *n* armonica; **mouthpiece** *n* (*Mus*) imboccatura, bocchino; (*spokesman*) portavoce *m/f inv*; **mouthwash** *n* collutorio
move [mu:v] *n* (*movement*) movimento; (*in game*) mossa; (*: turn to play*) turno; (*change: of house*) trasloco; (*: of job*) cambiamento ▷ *vt* muovere; (*change position of*) spostare; (*emotionally*) commuovere; (*Pol: resolution etc*) proporre ▷ *vi* (*gen*) muoversi, spostarsi; (*also:* **~ house**) cambiar casa, traslocare; **to get a ~ on** affrettarsi, sbrigarsi; **can you ~ your car, please?** può spostare la macchina, per favore?; **to ~ sb to do sth** indurre *or* spingere qn a fare qc; **to ~ towards** andare verso; **move back** *vi* (*return*) ritornare; **move in** *vi* (*to a house*) entrare (in una nuova casa); (*police etc*) intervenire; **move off** *vi* partire; **move on** *vi* riprendere la strada; **move out** *vi* (*of house*) sgombrare; **move over** *vi* spostarsi; **move up** *vi* avanzare; **movement** ['mu:vmənt] *n* (*gen*) movimento; (*gesture*) gesto; (*of stars, water, physical*) moto
movie ['mu:vɪ] *n* film *m inv*; **the ~s** il cinema; **movie theater** (*US*) *n* cinema *m inv*
moving ['mu:vɪŋ] *adj* mobile; (*causing emotion*) commovente
mow [məu] (*pt* **mowed**, *pp* **mowed** *or* **mown**) *vt* (*grass*) tagliare; (*corn*) mietere; **mower** *n* (*also:* **lawnmower**) tagliaerba *m inv*
Mozambique [məuzəm'bi:k] *n* Mozambico
MP *n abbr* = **Member of Parliament**
MP3 *n abbr* M3; **MP3 player** *n* lettore *m* MP3
mpg *n abbr* = **miles per gallon** (*30 mpg = 9.4 l. per 100 km*)
m.p.h. *n abbr* = **miles per hour** (*60 m.p.h. = 96 km/h*)
Mr ['mɪstə^r] (*US* **Mr.**) *n* **Mr X** Signor X, Sig. X
Mrs ['mɪsɪz] (*US* **Mrs.**) *n* **Mrs X** Signora X, Sig.ra X
Ms [mɪz] (*US* **Ms.**) *n* = **Miss** *or* **Mrs**; **Ms X** ≈ Signora X, ≈ Sig.ra X

Ms

In inglese si usa **Ms** al posto di "Mrs" (Signora) o "Miss" (Signorina) per evitare la distinzione tradizionale tra le donne sposate e quelle nubili.

MSP *n abbr* = **Member of the Scottish Parliament**
Mt *abbr* (*Geo: = mount*) M.

KEYWORD

much [mʌtʃ] *adj, pron* molto(-a); **he's done so much work** ha lavorato così tanto; **I have as much money as you** ho tanti soldi quanti ne hai tu; **how much is it?** quant'è?; **it costs too much** costa troppo; **as much as you want** quanto vuoi
▷ *adv* **1** (*greatly*) molto, tanto; **thank you very much** molte grazie; **he's very much the gentleman** è il vero gentiluomo; **I read as much as I can** leggo quanto posso; **as much as you** tanto quanto te
2 (*by far*) molto; **it's much the**

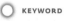

biggest company in Europe è di gran lunga la più grossa società in Europa
3 (*almost*) grossomodo, praticamente; **they're much the same** sono praticamente uguali

muck [mʌk] *n* (*dirt*) sporcizia; **muck up** (*inf*) *vt* (*ruin*) rovinare; **mucky** *adj* (*dirty*) sporco(-a), lordo(-a)
mucus ['mju:kəs] *n* muco
mud [mʌd] *n* fango
muddle ['mʌdl] *n* confusione *f*, disordine *m*; pasticcio ▷ *vt* (*also*: **~ up**) confondere
muddy ['mʌdɪ] *adj* fangoso(-a)
mudguard ['mʌdgɑ:d] *n* parafango
muesli ['mju:zlɪ] *n* muesli *m*
muffin ['mʌfɪn] *n* *specie di pasticcino soffice da tè*
muffled ['mʌfld] *adj* smorzato(-a), attutito(-a)
muffler ['mʌflə^r] (US) *n* (*Aut*) marmitta; (: *on motorbike*) silenziatore *m*
mug [mʌg] *n* (*cup*) tazzone *m*; (*for beer*) boccale *m*; (*inf*: *face*) muso; (: *fool*) scemo(-a) ▷ *vt* (*assault*) assalire; **mugger** ['mʌgə^r] *n* aggressore *m*; **mugging** *n* assalto
muggy ['mʌgɪ] *adj* afoso(-a)
mule [mju:l] *n* mulo
multicoloured ['mʌltɪkʌləd] (US **multicolored**) *adj* multicolore, variopinto(-a)
multimedia ['mʌltɪ'mi:dɪə] *adj* multimedia *inv*
multinational [mʌltɪ'næʃənl] *adj*, *n* multinazionale *f*
multiple ['mʌltɪpl] *adj* multiplo(-a), molteplice ▷ *n* multiplo; **multiple choice (test)** *n* esercizi *mpl* a scelta multipla; **multiple sclerosis** [-sklɪ'rəusɪs] *n* sclerosi *f* a placche
multiplex cinema ['mʌltɪplɛks-] *n* cinema *m inv* multisala *inv*
multiplication [mʌltɪplɪ'keɪʃən] *n* moltiplicazione *f*
multiply ['mʌltɪplaɪ] *vt* moltiplicare ▷ *vi* moltiplicarsi
multistorey ['mʌltɪ'stɔ:rɪ] (BRIT) *adj* (*building*, *car park*) a più piani
mum [mʌm] (BRIT: *inf*) *n* mamma ▷ *adj* **to keep ~** non aprire bocca
mumble ['mʌmbl] *vt*, *vi* borbottare
mummy ['mʌmɪ] *n* (BRIT: *mother*) mamma; (*embalmed*) mummia
mumps [mʌmps] *n* orecchioni *mpl*
munch [mʌntʃ] *vt*, *vi* sgranocchiare
municipal [mju:'nɪsɪpl] *adj* municipale
mural ['mjuərl] *n* dipinto murale
murder ['mə:də^r] *n* assassinio, omicidio ▷ *vt* assassinare; **murderer** *n* omicida *m*, assassino
murky ['mə:kɪ] *adj* tenebroso(-a)
murmur ['mə:mə^r] *n* mormorio ▷ *vt*, *vi* mormorare
muscle ['mʌsl] *n* muscolo; (*fig*) forza; **muscular** ['mʌskjulə^r] *adj* muscolare; (*person*, *arm*) muscoloso(-a)
museum [mju:'zɪəm] *n* museo
mushroom ['mʌʃrum] *n* fungo ▷ *vi* crescere in fretta
music ['mju:zɪk] *n* musica; **musical** *adj* musicale; (*person*) portato(-a) per la musica ▷ *n* (*show*) commedia musicale; **musical instrument** *n* strumento musicale; **musician** [-'zɪʃən] *n* musicista *m/f*
Muslim ['mʌzlɪm] *adj*, *n* musulmano(-a)
muslin ['mʌzlɪn] *n* mussola
mussel ['mʌsl] *n* cozza
must [mʌst] *aux vb* (*obligation*): **I ~ do it** devo farlo; (*probability*): **he ~ be there by now** dovrebbe essere arrivato ormai; **I ~ have made a mistake** devo essermi sbagliato ▷ *n* **it's a ~** è d'obbligo
mustache ['mʌstæʃ] (US) *n* = **moustache**
mustard ['mʌstəd] *n* senape *f*,

mostarda
mustn't ['mʌsnt] = **must not**
mute [mju:t] *adj, n* muto(-a)
mutilate ['mju:tɪleɪt] *vt* mutilare
mutiny ['mju:tɪnɪ] *n* ammutinamento
mutter ['mʌtə^r] *vt, vi* borbottare, brontolare
mutton ['mʌtn] *n* carne *f* di montone
mutual ['mju:tʃuəl] *adj* mutuo(-a), reciproco(-a)
muzzle ['mʌzl] *n* muso; (*protective device*) museruola; (*of gun*) bocca ▷ *vt* mettere la museruola a
my [maɪ] *adj* il (la) mio(-a); (*pl*) i (le) miei (mie); **my house** la mia casa; **my books** i miei libri; **my brother** mio fratello; **I've washed my hair/cut my finger** mi sono lavato i capelli/tagliato il dito
myself [maɪ'sɛlf] *pron* (*reflexive*) mi; (*emphatic*) io stesso(-a); (*after prep*) me; *see also* **oneself**
mysterious [mɪs'tɪərɪəs] *adj* misterioso(-a)
mystery ['mɪstərɪ] *n* mistero
mystical ['mɪstɪkəl] *adj* mistico(-a)
mystify ['mɪstɪfaɪ] *vt* mistificare; (*puzzle*) confondere
myth [mɪθ] *n* mito; **mythology** [mɪ'θɔlədʒɪ] *n* mitologia

n

n/a *abbr* = **not applicable**
nag [næg] *vt* tormentare ▷ *vi* brontolare in continuazione
nail [neɪl] *n* (*human*) unghia; (*metal*) chiodo ▷ *vt* inchiodare; **to ~ sb down to (doing) sth** costringere qn a (fare) qc; **nailbrush** *n* spazzolino da *or* per unghie; **nailfile** *n* lima da *or* per unghie; **nail polish** *n* smalto da *or* per unghie; **nail polish remover** *n* acetone *m*, solvente *m*; **nail scissors** *npl* forbici *fpl* da *or* per unghie; **nail varnish** (BRIT) *n* = **nail polish**
naïve [naɪ'i:v] *adj* ingenuo(-a)
naked ['neɪkɪd] *adj* nudo(-a)
name [neɪm] *n* nome *m*; (*reputation*) nome, reputazione *f* ▷ *vt* (*baby etc*) chiamare; (*plant, illness*) nominare; (*person, object*) identificare; (*price, date*) fissare; **what's your ~?** come si chiama?; **by ~** di nome; **she knows them all by ~** li conosce tutti per nome; **namely** *adv* cioè
nanny ['nænɪ] *n* bambinaia

nap [næp] *n* (*sleep*) pisolino; (*of cloth*) peluria; **to be caught ~ping** essere preso alla sprovvista
napkin ['næpkɪn] *n* (*also:* **table ~**) tovagliolo
nappy ['næpɪ] (BRIT) *n* pannolino; **nappy rash** *n* arrossamento (causato dal pannolino)
narcotics [nɑː'kɔtɪkz] *npl* (*drugs*) narcotici, stupefacenti *mpl*
narrative ['nærətɪv] *n* narrativa
narrator [nə'reɪtə^r] *n* narratore(-trice)
narrow ['nærəu] *adj* stretto(-a); (*fig*) limitato(-a), ristretto(-a) ▷ *vi* restringersi; **to have a ~ escape** farcela per un pelo; **narrow down** *vt* (*search, investigation, possibilities*) restringere; (*list*) ridurre; **narrowly** *adv* per un pelo; (*time*) per poco; **narrow-minded** *adj* meschino(-a)
nasal ['neɪzl] *adj* nasale
nasty ['nɑːstɪ] *adj* (*person, remark: unpleasant*) cattivo(-a); (*: rude*) villano(-a); (*smell, wound, situation*) brutto(-a)
nation ['neɪʃən] *n* nazione *f*
national ['næʃənl] *adj* nazionale ▷ *n* cittadino(-a); **national anthem** *n* inno nazionale; **national dress** *n* costume *m* nazionale; **National Health Service** (BRIT) *n* *servizio nazionale di assistenza sanitaria*, ≈ S.S.N. *m*; **National Insurance** (BRIT) *n* ≈ Previdenza Sociale; **nationalist** *adj, n* nazionalista (*m/f*); **nationality** [-'nælɪtɪ] *n* nazionalità *f inv*; **nationalize** *vt* nazionalizzare; **national park** *n* parco nazionale; **National Trust** *n* *sovrintendenza ai beni culturali e ambientali*

NATIONAL TRUST

Fondato nel 1895, il **National Trust** è un'organizzazione che si occupa della tutela e della salvaguardia di luoghi di interesse storico o ambientale nel Regno Unito.

nationwide ['neɪʃənwaɪd] *adj* diffuso(-a) in tutto il paese ▷ *adv* in tutto il paese
native ['neɪtɪv] *n* abitante *m/f* del paese ▷ *adj* indigeno(-a); (*country*) natio(-a); (*ability*) innato(-a); **a ~ of Russia** un nativo della Russia; **a ~ speaker of French** una persona di madrelingua francese; **Native American** *n* *discendente di tribù dell'America settentrionale*
NATO ['neɪtəu] *n abbr* (= *North Atlantic Treaty Organization*) N.A.T.O. *f*
natural ['nætʃrəl] *adj* naturale; (*ability*) innato(-a); (*manner*) semplice; **natural gas** *n* gas *m* metano; **natural history** *n* storia naturale; **naturally** *adv* naturalmente; (*by nature: gifted*) di natura; **natural resources** *npl* risorse *fpl* naturali
nature ['neɪtʃə^r] *n* natura; (*character*) natura, indole *f*; **by ~** di natura; **nature reserve** *n* (BRIT) parco naturale
naughty ['nɔːtɪ] *adj* (*child*) birichino(-a), cattivello(-a); (*story, film*) spinto(-a)
nausea ['nɔːsɪə] *n* (*Med*) nausea; (*fig: disgust*) schifo
naval ['neɪvl] *adj* navale
navel ['neɪvl] *n* ombelico
navigate ['nævɪgeɪt] *vt* percorrere navigando ▷ *vi* navigare; (*Aut*) fare da navigatore; **navigation** [-'geɪʃən] *n* navigazione *f*
navy ['neɪvɪ] *n* marina
Nazi ['nɑːtsɪ] *n* nazista *m/f*
NB *abbr* (= *nota bene*) N.B.
near [nɪə^r] *adj* vicino(-a); (*relation*) prossimo(-a) ▷ *adv* vicino ▷ *prep* (*also:* **~ to**) vicino a, presso; (*: time*) verso ▷ *vt* avvicinarsi a; **nearby** [nɪə'baɪ] *adj* vicino(-a) ▷ *adv* vicino; **is there**

a bank nearby? c'è una banca qui vicino?; **nearly** *adv* quasi; **I nearly fell** per poco non sono caduto; **near-sighted** [nɪə'saɪtɪd] *adj* miope

neat [niːt] *adj* (*person, room*) ordinato(-a); (*work*) pulito(-a); (*solution, plan*) ben indovinato(-a), azzeccato(-a); (*spirits*) liscio(-a); **neatly** *adv* con ordine; (*skilfully*) abilmente

necessarily ['nɛsɪsrɪlɪ] *adv* necessariamente

necessary ['nɛsɪsrɪ] *adj* necessario(-a)

necessity [nɪ'sɛsɪtɪ] *n* necessità *f inv*

neck [nɛk] *n* collo; (*of garment*) colletto ▷ *vi* (*inf*) pomiciare, sbaciucchiarsi; **~ and ~** testa a testa; **necklace** ['nɛklɪs] *n* collana; **necktie** ['nɛktaɪ] *n* cravatta

nectarine ['nɛktərɪn] *n* nocepesca

need [niːd] *n* bisogno ▷ *vt* aver bisogno di; **do you ~ anything?** ha bisogno di qualcosa?; **to ~ to do** dover fare; aver bisogno di fare; **you don't ~ to go** non devi andare, non c'è bisogno che tu vada

needle ['niːdl] *n* ago; (*on record player*) puntina ▷ *vt* punzecchiare

needless ['niːdlɪs] *adj* inutile

needlework ['niːdlwəːk] *n* cucito

needn't ['niːdnt] = **need not**

needy ['niːdɪ] *adj* bisognoso(-a)

negative ['nɛgətɪv] *n* (*Ling*) negazione *f*; (*Phot*) negativo ▷ *adj* negativo(-a)

neglect [nɪ'glɛkt] *vt* trascurare ▷ *n* (*of person, duty*) negligenza; (*of child, house etc*) scarsa cura; **state of ~** stato di abbandono

negotiate [nɪ'gəuʃɪeɪt] *vi* **to ~ (with)** negoziare (con) ▷ *vt* (*Comm*) negoziare; (*obstacle*) superare; **negotiations** [nɪgəuʃɪ'eɪʃənz] *pl n* trattative *fpl*, negoziati *mpl*

negotiator [nɪ'gəuʃɪeɪtə^r] *n* negoziatore(-trice)

neighbour ['neɪbə^r] (*US* **neighbor**) *n* vicino(-a); **neighbourhood** *n* vicinato; **neighbouring** *adj* vicino(-a)

neither ['naɪðə^r] *adj, pron* né l'uno(-a) né l'altro(-a), nessuno(-a) dei (delle) due ▷ *conj* neanche, nemmeno, neppure ▷ *adv* **~ good nor bad** né buono né cattivo; **I didn't move and ~ did Claude** io non mi mossi e nemmeno Claude; **..., ~ did I refuse** ..., ma non ho nemmeno rifiutato

neon ['niːɔn] *n* neon *m*

Nepal [nɪ'pɔːl] *n* Nepal *m*

nephew ['nɛvjuː] *n* nipote *m*

nerve [nəːv] *n* nervo; (*fig*) coraggio; (*impudence*) faccia tosta; **nerves** (*nervousness*) nervoso; **a fit of ~s** una crisi di nervi

nervous ['nəːvəs] *adj* nervoso(-a); (*anxious*) agitato(-a), in apprensione; **nervous breakdown** *n* esaurimento nervoso

nest [nɛst] *n* nido ▷ *vi* fare il nido, nidificare

net [nɛt] *n* rete *f* ▷ *adj* netto(-a) ▷ *vt* (*fish etc*) prendere con la rete; (*profit*) ricavare un utile netto di; **the N~** (*Internet*) Internet *f*; **netball** *n specie di pallacanestro*

Netherlands ['nɛðələndz] *npl* **the ~** i Paesi Bassi

nett [nɛt] *adj* = **net**

nettle ['nɛtl] *n* ortica

network ['nɛtwəːk] *n* rete *f*

neurotic [njuə'rɔtɪk] *adj, n* nevrotico(-a)

neuter ['njuːtə^r] *adj* neutro(-a) ▷ *vt* (*cat etc*) castrare

neutral ['njuːtrəl] *adj* neutro(-a); (*person, nation*) neutrale ▷ *n* (*Aut*): **in ~** in folle

never ['nɛvə^r] *adv* (non...) mai; **I've ~ been to Spain** non sono mai stato in Spagna; **~ again** mai più; **I'll ~ go there again** non ci vado più; **~ in my life** mai in vita mia; *see also* **mind**; **never-ending** *adj* interminabile;

nevertheless [nɛvəðə'lɛs] *adv* tuttavia, ciò nonostante, ciò nondimeno

new [nju:] *adj* nuovo(-a); (*brand new*) nuovo(-a) di zecca; **New Age** *n* New Age *f inv*; **newborn** *adj* neonato(-a); **newcomer** ['nju:kʌmə^r] *n* nuovo(-a) venuto(-a); **newly** *adv* di recente

news [nju:z] *n* notizie *fpl*; (*Radio*) giornale *m* radio; (*TV*) telegiornale *m*; **a piece of ~** una notizia; **news agency** *n* agenzia di stampa; **newsagent** (BRIT) *n* giornalaio; **newscaster** *n* (*Radio, TV*) annunciatore(-trice); **news dealer** (US) *n* = **newsagent**; **newsletter** *n* bollettino; **newspaper** *n* giornale *m*; **newsreader** *n* = **newscaster**

newt [nju:t] *n* tritone *m*

New Year *n* Anno Nuovo; **New Year's Day** *n* il Capodanno; **New Year's Eve** *n* la vigilia di Capodanno

New York [-'jɔ:k] *n* New York *f*

New Zealand [-'zi:lənd] *n* Nuova Zelanda; **New Zealander** *n* neozelandese *m/f*

next [nɛkst] *adj* prossimo(-a) ▷ *adv* accanto; (*in time*) dopo; **the ~ day** il giorno dopo, l'indomani; **~ time** la prossima volta; **~ year** l'anno prossimo; **when do we meet ~?** quando ci rincontriamo?; **~ to** accanto a; **~ to nothing** quasi niente; **~ please!** (avanti) il prossimo!; **next door** *adv, adj* accanto *inv*; **next-of-kin** *n* parente *m/f* prossimo(-a)

NHS *n abbr* = **National Health Service**

nibble ['nɪbl] *vt* mordicchiare

nice [naɪs] *adj* (*holiday, trip*) piacevole; (*flat, picture*) bello(-a); (*person*) simpatico(-a), gentile; **nicely** *adv* bene

niche [ni:ʃ] *n* (*Archit*) nicchia

nick [nɪk] *n* taglietto; tacca ▷ *vt* (*inf*) rubare; **in the ~ of time** appena in tempo

nickel ['nɪkl] *n* nichel *m*; (US) *moneta da cinque centesimi di dollaro*

nickname ['nɪkneɪm] *n* soprannome *m*

nicotine ['nɪkəti:n] *n* nicotina

niece [ni:s] *n* nipote *f*

Nigeria [naɪ'dʒɪərɪə] *n* Nigeria

night [naɪt] *n* notte *f*; (*evening*) sera; **at ~** la sera; **by ~** di notte; **the ~ before last** l'altro ieri notte (*or* sera); **night club** *n* locale *m* notturno; **nightdress** *n* camicia da notte; **nightie** ['naɪtɪ] *n* = **nightdress**; **nightlife** ['naɪtlaɪf] *n* vita notturna; **nightly** ['naɪtlɪ] *adj* di ogni notte *or* sera; (*by night*) notturno(-a) ▷ *adv* ogni notte *or* sera; **nightmare** ['naɪtmɛə^r] *n* incubo; **night school** *n* scuola serale; **night shift** *n* turno di notte; **night-time** *n* notte *f*

nil [nɪl] *n* nulla *m*; (BRIT *Sport*) zero

nine [naɪn] *num* nove; **nineteen** *num* diciannove; **nineteenth** [naɪn'ti:nθ] *num* diciannovesimo(-a); **ninetieth** ['naɪntɪɪθ] *num* novantesimo(-a); **ninety** *num* novanta; **ninth** [naɪnθ] *num* nono(-a)

nip [nɪp] *vt* pizzicare; (*bite*) mordere

nipple ['nɪpl] *n* (*Anat*) capezzolo

nitrogen ['naɪtrədʒən] *n* azoto

KEYWORD

no [nəu] (*pl* **noes**) *adv* (*opposite of "yes"*) no; **are you coming? — no (I'm not)** viene? — no (non vengo); **would you like some more? — no thank you** ne vuole ancora un po'? — no, grazie ▷ *adj* (*not any*) nessuno(-a); **I have no money/time/books** non ho soldi/tempo/libri; **no student would have done it** nessuno studente lo avrebbe fatto; **"no parking"** "divieto di sosta"; **"no smoking"** "vietato fumare" ▷ *n* no *m inv*

nobility [nəu'bɪlɪtɪ] *n* nobiltà

noble ['nəubl] *adj* nobile
nobody ['nəubədɪ] *pron* nessuno
nod [nɔd] *vi* accennare col capo, fare un cenno; (*in agreement*) annuire con un cenno del capo; (*sleep*) sonnecchiare ▷ *vt* **to ~ one's head** fare di sì col capo ▷ *n* cenno; **nod off** *vi* assopirsi
noise [nɔɪz] *n* rumore *m*; (*din, racket*) chiasso; **I can't sleep for the ~** non riesco a dormire a causa del rumore; **noisy** *adj* (*street, car*) rumoroso(-a); (*person*) chiassoso(-a)
nominal ['nɔmɪnl] *adj* nominale; (*rent*) simbolico(-a)
nominate ['nɔmɪneɪt] *vt* (*propose*) proporre come candidato; (*elect*) nominare; **nomination** [nɔmɪ'neɪʃən] *n* nomina; candidatura; **nominee** [nɔmɪ'ni:] *n* persona nominata, candidato(-a)
none [nʌn] *pron* (*not one thing*) niente; (*not one person*) nessuno(-a); **~ of you** nessuno(-a) di voi; **I've ~ left** non ne ho più; **he's ~ the worse for it** non ne ha risentito
nonetheless [nʌnðə'lɛs] *adv* nondimeno
non-fiction [nɔn'fɪkʃən] *n* saggistica
nonsense ['nɔnsəns] *n* sciocchezze *fpl*
non: **non-smoker** *n* non fumatore(-trice); **non-smoking** *adj* (*person*) che non fuma; (*area, section*) per non fumatori; **non-stick** *adj* antiaderente, antiadesivo(-a)
noodles ['nu:dlz] *npl* taglierini *mpl*
noon [nu:n] *n* mezzogiorno
no-one ['nəuwʌn] *pron* = **nobody**
nor [nɔ:[r]] *conj* = **neither** ▷ *adv see* **neither**
norm [nɔ:m] *n* norma
normal ['nɔ:ml] *adj* normale; **normally** *adv* normalmente
north [nɔ:θ] *n* nord *m*, settentrione *m* ▷ *adj* nord *inv*, del nord, settentrionale ▷ *adv* verso nord; **North America** *n* America del Nord; **North American** *adj, n* nordamericano(-a); **northbound** ['nɔ:θbaund] *adj* (*traffic*) diretto(-a) a nord; (*carriageway*) nord *inv*; **north-east** *n* nord-est *m*; **northeastern** *adj* nordorientale; **northern** ['nɔ:ðən] *adj* del nord, settentrionale; **Northern Ireland** *n* Irlanda del Nord; **North Korea** *n* Corea del Nord; **North Pole** *n* Polo Nord; **North Sea** *n* Mare *m* del Nord; **north-west** *n* nord-ovest *m*; **northwestern** *adj* nordoccidentale
Norway ['nɔ:weɪ] *n* Norvegia; **Norwegian** [nɔ:'wi:dʒən] *adj* norvegese ▷ *n* norvegese *m/f*; (*Ling*) norvegese *m*
nose [nəuz] *n* naso; (*of animal*) muso ▷ *vi* **to ~ about** aggirarsi; **nosebleed** *n* emorragia nasale; **nosey** (*inf*) *adj* = **nosy**
nostalgia [nɔs'tældʒɪə] *n* nostalgia
nostalgic [nɔs'tældʒɪk] *adj* nostalgico(-a)
nostril ['nɔstrɪl] *n* narice *f*; (*of horse*) frogia
nosy ['nəuzɪ] (*inf*) *adj* curioso(-a)
not [nɔt] *adv* non; **he is ~** *or* **isn't here** non è qui, non c'è; **you must ~** *or* **you mustn't do that** non devi fare quello; **it's too late, isn't it** *or* **is it ~?** è troppo tardi, vero?; **~ that I don't like him** non che (lui) non mi piaccia; **~ yet/now** non ancora/ora; *see also* **all**; **only**
notable ['nəutəbl] *adj* notevole; **notably** ['nəutəblɪ] *adv* (*markedly*) notevolmente; (*particularly*) in particolare
notch [nɔtʃ] *n* tacca; (*in saw*) dente *m*
note [nəut] *n* nota; (*letter, banknote*) biglietto ▷ *vt* (*also:* **~ down**) prendere nota di; **to take ~s** prendere appunti; **notebook** *n* taccuino; **noted** ['nəutɪd] *adj* celebre; **notepad** *n* bloc-notes *m inv*; **notepaper** *n* carta da lettere

nothing ['nʌθɪŋ] *n* nulla *m*, niente *m*; (*zero*) zero; **he does ~** non fa niente; **~ new/much** *etc* niente di nuovo/ speciale *etc*; **for ~** per niente
notice ['nəutɪs] *n* avviso; (*of leaving*) preavviso ▷ *vt* notare, accorgersi di; **to take ~ of** fare attenzione a; **to bring sth to sb's ~** far notare qc a qn; **at short ~** con un breve preavviso; **until further ~** fino a nuovo avviso; **to hand in one's ~** licenziarsi; **noticeable** *adj* evidente
notify ['nəutɪfaɪ] *vt* **to ~ sth to sb** far sapere qc a qn; **to ~ sb of sth** avvisare qn di qc
notion ['nəuʃən] *n* idea; (*concept*) nozione *f*; **notions** *npl* (*US*: *haberdashery*) merceria
notorious [nəu'tɔ:rɪəs] *adj* famigerato(-a)
notwithstanding [nɔtwɪθ'stændɪŋ] *adv* nondimeno ▷ *prep* nonostante, malgrado
nought [nɔ:t] *n* zero
noun [naun] *n* nome *m*, sostantivo
nourish ['nʌrɪʃ] *vt* nutrire; **nourishment** *n* nutrimento
Nov. *abbr* (= *November*) nov.
novel ['nɔvl] *n* romanzo ▷ *adj* nuovo(-a); **novelist** *n* romanziere(-a); **novelty** *n* novità *f inv*
November [nəu'vɛmbə^r] *n* novembre *m*
novice ['nɔvɪs] *n* principiante *m/f*; (*Rel*) novizio(-a)
now [nau] *adv* ora, adesso ▷ *conj* **~ (that)** adesso che, ora che; **by ~** ormai; **just ~** proprio ora; **right ~** subito, immediatamente; **~ and then, ~ and again** ogni tanto; **from ~ on** da ora in poi; **nowadays** ['nauədeɪz] *adv* oggidì
nowhere ['nəuwɛə^r] *adv* in nessun luogo, da nessuna parte
nozzle ['nɔzl] *n* (*of hose etc*) boccaglio; (*of fire extinguisher*) lancia
nr *abbr* (BRIT) = **near**
nuclear ['nju:klɪə^r] *adj* nucleare
nucleus ['nju:klɪəs] (*pl* **nuclei**) *n* nucleo
nude [nju:d] *adj* nudo(-a) ▷ *n* (*Art*) nudo; **in the ~** tutto(-a) nudo(-a)
nudge [nʌdʒ] *vt* dare una gomitata a
nudist ['nju:dɪst] *n* nudista *m/f*
nudity ['nju:dɪtɪ] *n* nudità
nuisance ['nju:sns] *n* **it's a ~** è una seccatura; **he's a ~** è uno scocciatore
numb [nʌm] *adj* **~ (with)** intorpidito(-a) (da); (*with fear*) impietrito(-a) (da); **~ with cold** intirizzito(-a) (dal freddo)
number ['nʌmbə^r] *n* numero ▷ *vt* numerare; (*include*) contare; **a ~ of** un certo numero di; **to be ~ed among** venire annoverato(-a) tra; **they were 10 in ~** erano in tutto 10; **number plate** (BRIT) *n* (*Aut*) targa; **Number Ten** *n* (BRIT: = *10 Downing Street*) *residenza del Primo Ministro del Regno Unito*
numerical [nju:'mɛrɪkl] *adj* numerico(-a)
numerous ['nju:mərəs] *adj* numeroso(-a)
nun [nʌn] *n* suora, monaca
nurse [nə:s] *n* infermiere(-a); (*also*: **~maid**) bambinaia ▷ *vt* (*patient, cold*) curare; (*baby*: BRIT) cullare; (: US) allattare, dare il latte a
nursery ['nə:sərɪ] *n* (*room*) camera dei bambini; (*institution*) asilo; (*for plants*) vivaio; **nursery rhyme** *n* filastrocca; **nursery school** *n* scuola materna; **nursery slope** (BRIT) *n* (*Ski*) pista per principianti
nursing ['nə:sɪŋ] *n* (*profession*) professione *f* di infermiere (*or* di infermiera); (*care*) cura; **nursing home** *n* casa di cura
nurture ['nə:tʃə^r] *vt* allevare; nutrire
nut [nʌt] *n* (*of metal*) dado; (*fruit*) noce *f*
nutmeg ['nʌtmɛg] *n* noce *f* moscata
nutrient ['nju:trɪənt] *adj* nutriente ▷ *n* sostanza nutritiva

nutrition [nju:'trɪʃən] *n* nutrizione *f*
nutritious [nju:'trɪʃəs] *adj* nutriente
nuts [nʌts] (*inf*) *adj* matto(-a)
NVQ *n abbr* (BRIT) = **National Vocational Qualification**
nylon ['naɪlɔn] *n* nailon *m* ▷ *adj* di nailon

O

oak [əuk] *n* quercia ▷ *adj* di quercia
O.A.P. (BRIT) *n, abbr* = **old age pensioner**
oar [ɔ:^{r}] *n* remo
oasis [əu'eɪsɪs] (*pl* **oases**) *n* oasi *f inv*
oath [əuθ] *n* giuramento; (*swear word*) bestemmia
oatmeal ['əutmi:l] *n* farina d'avena
oats [əuts] *npl* avena
obedience [ə'bi:dɪəns] *n* ubbidienza
obedient [ə'bi:dɪənt] *adj* ubbidiente
obese [əu'bi:s] *adj* obeso(-a)
obesity [əu'bi:sɪtɪ] *n* obesità
obey [ə'beɪ] *vt* ubbidire a; (*instructions, regulations*) osservare
obituary [ə'bɪtjuərɪ] *n* necrologia
object [*n* 'ɔbdʒɪkt, *vb* əb'dʒɛkt] *n* oggetto; (*purpose*) scopo, intento; (*Ling*) complemento oggetto ▷ *vi* **to ~ to** (*attitude*) disapprovare; (*proposal*) protestare contro, sollevare delle obiezioni contro; **expense is no ~** non si bada a spese; **to ~ that** obiettare che; **objection** [əb'dʒɛkʃən] *n*

obiezione *f*; **objective** *n* obiettivo
obligation [ɔblɪ'geɪʃən] *n* obbligo, dovere *m*; **without ~** senza impegno
obligatory [ə'blɪgətərɪ] *adj* obbligatorio(-a)
oblige [ə'blaɪdʒ] *vt* (*force*): **to ~ sb to do** costringere qn a fare; (*do a favour*) fare una cortesia a; **to be ~d to sb for sth** essere grato a qn per qc
oblique [ə'bli:k] *adj* obliquo(-a); (*allusion*) indiretto(-a)
obliterate [ə'blɪtəreɪt] *vt* cancellare
oblivious [ə'blɪvɪəs] *adj* **~ of** incurante di; inconscio(-a) di
oblong ['ɔblɔŋ] *adj* oblungo(-a) ▷ *n* rettangolo
obnoxious [əb'nɔkʃəs] *adj* odioso(-a); (*smell*) disgustoso(-a), ripugnante
oboe ['əubəu] *n* oboe *m*
obscene [əb'si:n] *adj* osceno(-a)
obscure [əb'skjuəʳ] *adj* oscuro(-a) ▷ *vt* oscurare; (*hide: sun*) nascondere
observant [əb'zə:vnt] *adj* attento(-a)

> Be careful not to translate ***observant*** by the Italian word ***osservante***.

observation [ɔbzə'veɪʃən] *n* osservazione *f*; (*by police etc*) sorveglianza
observatory [əb'zə:vətrɪ] *n* osservatorio
observe [əb'zə:v] *vt* osservare; (*remark*) fare osservare; **observer** *n* osservatore(-trice)
obsess [əb'sɛs] *vt* ossessionare; **obsession** [əb'sɛʃən] *n* ossessione *f*; **obsessive** *adj* ossessivo(-a)
obsolete ['ɔbsəli:t] *adj* obsoleto(-a)
obstacle ['ɔbstəkl] *n* ostacolo
obstinate ['ɔbstɪnɪt] *adj* ostinato(-a)
obstruct [əb'strʌkt] *vt* (*block*) ostruire, ostacolare; (*halt*) fermare; (*hinder*) impedire; **obstruction** [əb'strʌkʃən] *n* ostruzione *f*; ostacolo
obtain [əb'teɪn] *vt* ottenere
obvious ['ɔbvɪəs] *adj* ovvio(-a), evidente; **obviously** *adv* ovviamente; certo
occasion [ə'keɪʒən] *n* occasione *f*; (*event*) avvenimento; **occasional** *adj* occasionale; **occasionally** *adv* ogni tanto
occult [ɔ'kʌlt] *adj* occulto(-a) ▷ *n* **the ~** l'occulto
occupant ['ɔkjupənt] *n* occupante *m/f*; (*of boat, car etc*) persona a bordo
occupation [ɔkju'peɪʃən] *n* occupazione *f*; (*job*) mestiere *m*, professione *f*
occupy ['ɔkjupaɪ] *vt* occupare; **to ~ o.s. in doing** occuparsi a fare
occur [ə'kə:ʳ] *vi* succedere, capitare; **to ~ to sb** venire in mente a qn; **occurrence** *n* caso, fatto; presenza

> Be careful not to translate ***occur*** by the Italian word ***occorrere***.

ocean ['əuʃən] *n* oceano
o'clock [ə'klɔk] *adv* **it is 5 o'clock** sono le 5
Oct. *abbr* (= *October*) ott.
October [ɔk'təubəʳ] *n* ottobre *m*
octopus ['ɔktəpəs] *n* polpo, piovra
odd [ɔd] *adj* (*strange*) strano(-a), bizzarro(-a); (*number*) dispari *inv*; (*not of a set*) spaiato(-a); **60-~** 60 e oltre; **at ~ times** di tanto in tanto; **the ~ one out** l'eccezione *f*; **oddly** *adv* stranamente; **odds** *npl* (*in betting*) quota
odometer [ɔ'dɔmɪtəʳ] *n* odometro
odour ['əudəʳ] (*US* **odor**) *n* odore *m*; (*unpleasant*) cattivo odore

KEYWORD

of [ɔv, əv] *prep* **1** (*gen*) di; **a boy of 10** un ragazzo di 10 anni; **a friend of ours** un nostro amico; **that was kind of you** è stato molto gentile da parte sua
2 (*expressing quantity, amount, dates etc*) di; **a kilo of flour** un chilo di farina; **how much of this do you need?** quanto gliene serve?; **there were 3 of them** (*people*) erano in 3; (*objects*) ce

n'erano 3; **3 of us went** 3 di noi sono andati; **the 5th of July** il 5 luglio
3 (*from, out of*) di, in; *of* **made of wood** (fatto) di *or* in legno

KEYWORD

off [ɔf] *adv* 1 (*distance, time*): **it's a long way off** è lontano; **the game is 3 days off** la partita è tra 3 giorni
2 (*departure, removal*) via; **to go off to Paris** andarsene a Parigi; **I must be off** devo andare via; **to take off one's coat** togliersi il cappotto; **the button came off** il bottone è venuto via *or* si è staccato; **10% off** con lo sconto del 10%
3 (*not at work*): **to have a day off** avere un giorno libero; **to be off sick** essere assente per malattia
▷ *adj* (*engine*) spento(-a); (*tap*) chiuso(-a); (*cancelled*) sospeso(-a); (BRIT: *food*) andato(-a) a male; **on the off chance** nel caso; **to have an off day** non essere in forma
▷ *prep* 1 (*motion, removal etc*) da; (*distant from*) a poca distanza da; **a street off the square** una strada che parte dalla piazza
2: **to be off meat** non mangiare più la carne

offence [ə'fɛns] (US **offense**) *n* (*Law*) contravvenzione *f*; (: *more serious*) reato; **to take ~ at** offendersi per
offend [ə'fɛnd] *vt* (*person*) offendere; **offender** *n* delinquente *m/f*; (*against regulations*) contravventore(-trice)
offense [ə'fɛns] (US) *n* = **offence**
offensive [ə'fɛnsɪv] *adj* offensivo(-a); (*smell etc*) sgradevole, ripugnante ▷ *n* (*Mil*) offensiva
offer ['ɔfə^r] *n* offerta, proposta ▷ *vt* offrire; **"on ~"** (*Comm*) "in offerta speciale"
offhand [ɔf'hænd] *adj* disinvolto(-a), noncurante ▷ *adv* su due piedi
office ['ɔfɪs] *n* (*place*) ufficio; (*position*) carica; **doctor's ~** (US) studio; **to take ~** entrare in carica; **office block** (US **office building**) *n* complesso di uffici; **office hours** *npl* orario d'ufficio; (US *Med*) orario di visite
officer ['ɔfɪsə^r] *n* (*Mil etc*) ufficiale *m*; (*also*: **police ~**) agente *m* di polizia; (*of organization*) funzionario
office worker *n* impiegato(-a) d'ufficio
official [ə'fɪʃl] *adj* (*authorized*) ufficiale ▷ *n* ufficiale *m*; (*civil servant*) impiegato(-a) statale; funzionario
off: **off-licence** (BRIT) *n* (*shop*) spaccio di bevande alcoliche; **off-line** *adj, adv* (*Comput*) off-line *inv*, fuori linea; (: *switched off*) spento(-a); **off-peak** *adj* (*ticket, heating etc*) a tariffa ridotta; (*time*) non di punta; **off-putting** (BRIT) *adj* sgradevole, antipatico(-a); **off-season** *adj, adv* fuori stagione; **offset** ['ɔfsɛt] (*irreg*) *vt* (*counteract*) controbilanciare, compensare; **offshore** [ɔf'ʃɔː^r] *adj* (*breeze*) di terra; (*island*) vicino alla costa; (*fishing*) costiero(-a); **offside** ['ɔf'saɪd] *adj* (*Sport*) fuori gioco; (*Aut*: *in Britain*) destro(-a); (: *in Italy etc*) sinistro(-a); **offspring** ['ɔfsprɪŋ] *n inv* prole *f*, discendenza
often ['ɔfn] *adv* spesso; **how ~ do you go?** quanto spesso ci vai?
oh [əu] *excl* oh!
oil [ɔɪl] *n* olio; (*petroleum*) petrolio; (*for central heating*) nafta ▷ *vt* (*machine*) lubrificare; **oil filter** *n* (*Aut*) filtro dell'olio; **oil painting** *n* quadro a olio; **oil refinery** *n* raffineria di petrolio; **oil rig** *n* derrick *m inv*; (*at sea*) piattaforma per trivellazioni subacquee; **oil slick** *n* chiazza d'olio; **oil tanker** *n* (*ship*) petroliera; (*truck*) autocisterna per petrolio; **oil well** *n* pozzo petrolifero; **oily** *adj* unto(-a), oleoso(-a); (*food*) grasso(-a)
ointment ['ɔɪntmənt] *n* unguento

O.K. ['əu'keɪ] *excl* d'accordo! ▷ *adj* non male *inv* ▷ *vt* approvare; **is it O.K.?, are you O.K.?** tutto bene?

old [əuld] *adj* vecchio(-a); (*ancient*) antico(-a), vecchio(-a); (*person*) vecchio(-a), anziano(-a); **how ~ are you?** quanti anni ha?; **he's 10 years ~** ha 10 anni; **~er brother** fratello maggiore; **old age** *n* vecchiaia; **old-age pension** ['əuldeɪdʒ-] *n* (BRIT) pensione *f* di vecchiaia; **old-age pensioner** (BRIT) *n* pensionato(-a); **old-fashioned** *adj* antiquato(-a), fuori moda; (*person*) all'antica; **old people's home** *n* ricovero per anziani

olive ['ɔlɪv] *n* (*fruit*) oliva; (*tree*) olivo ▷ *adj* (*also:* **~-green**) verde oliva *inv*; **olive oil** *n* olio d'oliva

Olympic [əu'lɪmpɪk] *adj* olimpico(-a); **the ~ Games, the ~s** i giochi olimpici, le Olimpiadi

omelet(te) ['ɔmlɪt] *n* omelette *f inv*

omen ['əumən] *n* presagio, augurio

ominous ['ɔmɪnəs] *adj* minaccioso(-a); (*event*) di malaugurio

omit [əu'mɪt] *vt* omettere

KEYWORD

on [ɔn] *prep* **1** (*indicating position*) su; **on the wall** sulla parete; **on the left** a *or* sulla sinistra
2 (*indicating means, method, condition etc*): **on foot** a piedi; **on the train/plane** in treno/aereo; **on the telephone** al telefono; **on the radio/television** alla radio/televisione; **to be on drugs** drogarsi; **on holiday** in vacanza
3 (*of time*): **on Friday** venerdì; **on Fridays** il *or* di venerdì; **on June 20th** il 20 giugno; **on Friday, June 20th** venerdì, 20 giugno; **a week on Friday** venerdì a otto; **on his arrival** al suo arrivo; **on seeing this** vedendo ciò
4 (*about, concerning*) su, di; **information on train services** informazioni sui collegamenti ferroviari; **a book on Goldoni/physics** un libro su Goldoni/di *or* sulla fisica
▷ *adv* **1** (*referring to dress, covering*): **to have one's coat on** avere indosso il cappotto; **to put one's coat on** mettersi il cappotto; **what's she got on?** cosa indossa?; **she put her boots/gloves/hat on** si mise gli stivali/i guanti/il cappello; **screw the lid on tightly** avvita bene il coperchio
2 (*further, continuously*): **to walk on, go on** *etc* continuare, proseguire *etc*; **to read on** continuare a leggere; **on and off** ogni tanto
▷ *adj* **1** (*in operation*: *machine, TV, light*) acceso(-a); (: *tap*) aperto(-a); (: *brake*) inserito(-a); **is the meeting still on?** (*in progress*) la riunione è ancora in corso?; (*not cancelled*) è confermato l'incontro?; **there's a good film on at the cinema** danno un buon film al cinema
2 (*inf*): **that's not on!** (*not acceptable*) non si fa così!; (*not possible*) non se ne parla neanche!

once [wʌns] *adv* una volta ▷ *conj* non appena, quando; **~ he had left/it was done** dopo che se n'era andato/fu fatto; **at ~** subito; (*simultaneously*) a un tempo; **~ a week** una volta per settimana; **~ more** ancora una volta; **~ and for all** una volta per sempre; **~ upon a time** c'era una volta

oncoming ['ɔnkʌmɪŋ] *adj* (*traffic*) che viene in senso opposto

KEYWORD

one [wʌn] *num* uno(-a); **one hundred and fifty** centocinquanta; **one day** un giorno
▷ *adj* **1** (*sole*) unico(-a); **the one book which** l'unico libro che; **the one man**

who l'unico che
2 (*same*) stesso(-a); **they came in the one car** sono venuti nella stessa macchina
▷ *pron* 1: **this one** questo(-a); **that one** quello(-a); **I've already got one/ a red one** ne ho già uno/uno rosso; **one by one** uno per uno
2: **one another** l'un l'altro; **to look at one another** guardarsi; **to help one another** auitarsi l'un l'altro *or* a vicenda
3 (*impersonal*) si; **one never knows** non si sa mai; **to cut one's finger** tagliarsi un dito; **one needs to eat** bisogna mangiare

one-off (BRIT: *inf*) *n* fatto eccezionale
oneself [wʌn'sɛlf] *pron* (*reflexive*) si; (*after prep*) se stesso(-a), sé; **to do sth (by) ~** fare qc da sé; **to hurt ~** farsi male; **to keep sth for ~** tenere qc per sé; **to talk to ~** parlare da solo
one: **one-shot** [wʌn'ʃɔt] (US) *n* = **one-off**; **one-sided** *adj* (*argument*) unilaterale; **one-to-one** *adj* (*relationship*) univoco(-a); **one-way** *adj* (*street, traffic*) a senso unico
ongoing ['ɔngəuɪŋ] *adj* in corso; in attuazione
onion ['ʌnjən] *n* cipolla
on-line ['ɔnlaɪn] *adj, adv* (*Comput*) on-line *inv*
onlooker ['ɔnlukəʳ] *n* spettatore(-trice)
only ['əunlɪ] *adv* solo, soltanto ▷ *adj* solo(-a), unico(-a) ▷ *conj* solo che, ma; **an ~ child** un figlio unico; **not ~ ... but also** non solo ... ma anche
on-screen [ɔn'skriːn] *adj* sullo schermo *inv*
onset ['ɔnsɛt] *n* inizio
onto ['ɔntu] *prep* = **on to**
onward(s) ['ɔnwəd(z)] *adv* (*move*) in avanti; **from that time onward(s)** da quella volta in poi

oops [ups] *excl* ops! (*esprime rincrescimento per un piccolo contrattempo*); **~-a-daisy!** oplà!
ooze [uːz] *vi* stillare
opaque [əu'peɪk] *adj* opaco(-a)
open ['əupn] *adj* aperto(-a); (*road*) libero(-a); (*meeting*) pubblico(-a) ▷ *vt* aprire ▷ *vi* (*eyes, door, debate*) aprirsi; (*flower*) sbocciare; (*shop, bank, museum*) aprire; (*book etc: commence*) cominciare; **is it ~ to the public?** è aperto al pubblico?; **in the ~ (air)** all'aperto; **what time do you ~?** a che ora aprite?; **open up** *vt* aprire; (*blocked road*) sgombrare ▷ *vi* (*shop, business*) aprire; **open-air** *adj* all'aperto; **opening** *adj* (*speech*) di apertura ▷ *n* apertura; (*opportunity*) occasione *f*, opportunità *f inv*; sbocco; **opening hours** *npl* orario d'apertura; **open learning** *n sistema educativo secondo il quale lo studente ha maggior controllo e gestione delle modalità di apprendimento*; **openly** *adv* apertamente; **open-minded** *adj* che ha la mente aperta; **open-necked** *adj* col collo slacciato; **open-plan** *adj* senza pareti divisorie; **Open University** *n* (BRIT) *vedi nota nel riquadro*

OPEN UNIVERSITY

La **Open University**, fondata in Gran Bretagna nel 1969, organizza corsi di laurea per corrispondenza o via Internet. Alcune lezioni possono venir seguite per radio o alla televisione e vengono organizzati regolari corsi estivi.

opera ['ɔpərə] *n* opera; **opera house** *n* opera; **opera singer** *n* cantante *m/f* d'opera *or* lirico(-a)
operate ['ɔpəreɪt] *vt* (*machine*) azionare, far funzionare; (*system*) usare ▷ *vi* funzionare; (*drug*) essere

efficace; **to ~ on sb (for)** (*Med*) operare qn (di)

operating room (*US*) *n* = **operating theatre**

operating theatre *n* (*Med*) sala operatoria

operation [ɔpəˈreɪʃən] *n* operazione *f*; **to be in ~** (*machine*) essere in azione *or* funzionamento; (*system*) essere in vigore; **to have an ~** (*Med*) subire un'operazione; **operational** *adj* in funzione; d'esercizio

operative [ˈɔpərətɪv] *adj* (*measure*) operativo(-a)

operator [ˈɔpəreɪtə^r] *n* (*of machine*) operatore(-trice); (*Tel*) centralinista *m/f*

opinion [əˈpɪnɪən] *n* opinione *f*, parere *m*; **in my ~** secondo me, a mio avviso; **opinion poll** *n* sondaggio di opinioni

opponent [əˈpəunənt] *n* avversario(-a)

opportunity [ɔpəˈtjuːnɪtɪ] *n* opportunità *f inv*, occasione *f*; **to take the ~ of doing** cogliere l'occasione per fare

oppose [əˈpəuz] *vt* opporsi a; **~d to** contrario(-a) a; **as ~d to** in contrasto con

opposite [ˈɔpəzɪt] *adj* opposto(-a); (*house etc*) di fronte ▷ *adv* di fronte, dirimpetto ▷ *prep* di fronte a ▷ *n* **the ~** il contrario, l'opposto; **the ~ sex** l'altro sesso

opposition [ɔpəˈzɪʃən] *n* opposizione *f*

oppress [əˈprɛs] *vt* opprimere

opt [ɔpt] *vi* **to ~ for** optare per; **to ~ to do** scegliere di fare; **opt out** *vi* **to opt out of** ritirarsi da

optician [ɔpˈtɪʃən] *n* ottico

optimism [ˈɔptɪmɪzəm] *n* ottimismo

optimist [ˈɔptɪmɪst] *n* ottimista *m/f*; **optimistic** [-ˈmɪstɪk] *adj* ottimistico(-a)

optimum [ˈɔptɪməm] *adj* ottimale

option [ˈɔpʃən] *n* scelta; (*Scol*) materia facoltativa; (*Comm*) opzione *f*; **optional** *adj* facoltativo(-a); (*Comm*) a scelta

or [ɔː^r] *conj* o, oppure; (*with negative*): **he hasn't seen or heard anything** non ha visto né sentito niente; **or else** se no, altrimenti; oppure

oral [ˈɔːrəl] *adj* orale ▷ *n* esame *m* orale

orange [ˈɔrɪndʒ] *n* (*fruit*) arancia ▷ *adj* arancione; **orange juice** *n* succo d'arancia; **orange squash** *n* succo d'arancia (*da diluire con l'acqua*)

orbit [ˈɔːbɪt] *n* orbita ▷ *vt* orbitare intorno a

orchard [ˈɔːtʃəd] *n* frutteto

orchestra [ˈɔːkɪstrə] *n* orchestra; (*US*: *seating*) platea

orchid [ˈɔːkɪd] *n* orchidea

ordeal [ɔːˈdiːl] *n* prova, travaglio

order [ˈɔːdə^r] *n* ordine *m*; (*Comm*) ordinazione *f* ▷ *vt* ordinare; **can I ~ now, please?** posso ordinare, per favore?; **in ~** in ordine; (*of document*) in regola; **in (working) ~** funzionante; **in ~ to do** per fare; **in ~ that** affinché + *sub*; **on ~** (*Comm*) in ordinazione; **out of ~** non in ordine; (*not working*) guasto; **to ~ sb to do** ordinare a qn di fare; **order form** *n* modulo d'ordinazione; **orderly** *n* (*Mil*) attendente *m*; (*Med*) inserviente *m* ▷ *adj* (*room*) in ordine; (*mind*) metodico(-a); (*person*) ordinato(-a), metodico(-a)

ordinary [ˈɔːdnrɪ] *adj* normale, comune; (*pej*) mediocre; **out of the ~** diverso dal solito, fuori dell'ordinario

ore [ɔː^r] *n* minerale *m* grezzo

oregano [ɔrɪˈgɑːnəu] *n* origano

organ [ˈɔːgən] *n* organo; **organic** [ɔːˈgænɪk] *adj* organico(-a); (*of food*) biologico(-a); **organism** *n* organismo

organization [ɔːgənaɪˈzeɪʃən] *n* organizzazione *f*

organize [ˈɔːgənaɪz] *vt* organizzare; **to get ~d** organizzarsi; **organized**

['ɔːgənaizd] *adj* organizzato(-a); **organizer** *n* organizzatore(-trice)
orgasm ['ɔːgæzəm] *n* orgasmo
orgy ['ɔːdʒɪ] *n* orgia
oriental [ɔːrɪ'ɛntl] *adj, n* orientale *m/f*
orientation [ɔːrɪen'teɪʃən] *n* orientamento
origin ['ɔrɪdʒɪn] *n* origine *f*
original [ə'rɪdʒɪnl] *adj* originale; (*earliest*) originario(-a) ▷ *n* originale *m*; **originally** *adv* (*at first*) all'inizio
originate [ə'rɪdʒɪneɪt] *vi* **to ~ from** essere originario(-a) di; (*suggestion*) provenire da; **to ~ in** avere origine in
Orkneys ['ɔːknɪz] *npl*: **the ~** (*also*: **the Orkney Islands**) le Orcadi
ornament ['ɔːnəmənt] *n* ornamento; (*trinket*) ninnolo; **ornamental** [-'mɛntl] *adj* ornamentale
ornate [ɔː'neɪt] *adj* molto ornato(-a)
orphan ['ɔːfn] *n* orfano(-a)
orthodox ['ɔːθədɔks] *adj* ortodosso(-a)
orthopaedic [ɔːθə'piːdɪk] (*US* **orthopedic**) *adj* ortopedico(-a)
osteopath ['ɔstɪəpæθ] *n* specialista *m/f* di osteopatia
ostrich ['ɔstrɪtʃ] *n* struzzo
other ['ʌðə^r] *adj* altro(-a) ▷ *pron* **the ~ (one)** l'altro(-a); **~s** (*other people*) altri *mpl*; **~ than** altro che; a parte; **otherwise** *adv, conj* altrimenti
otter ['ɔtə^r] *n* lontra
ouch [autʃ] *excl* ohi!, ahi!
ought [ɔːt] (*pt* **ought**) *aux vb* **I ~ to do it** dovrei farlo; **this ~ to have been corrected** questo avrebbe dovuto essere corretto; **he ~ to win** dovrebbe vincere
ounce [auns] *n* oncia (= *28.35 g, 16 in a pound*)
our ['auə^r] *adj* il (la) nostro(-a); (*pl*) i (le) nostri(-e); *see also* **my**; **ours** *pron* il (la) nostro(-a); (*pl*) i (le) nostri(-e); *see also* **mine**; **ourselves** *pron pl* (*reflexive*) ci; (*after preposition*) noi; (*emphatic*) noi stessi(-e); *see also* **oneself**
oust [aust] *vt* cacciare, espellere
out [aut] *adv* (*gen*) fuori; **~ here/there** qui/là fuori; **to speak ~ loud** parlare forte; **to have a night ~** uscire una sera; **the boat was 10 km ~** la barca era a 10 km dalla costa; **3 days ~ from Plymouth** a 3 giorni da Plymouth; **~ of** (*outside*) fuori di; (*because of*) per; **~ of 10** su 10; **~ of petrol** senza benzina; **outback** ['autbæk] *n* (*in Australia*) interno, entroterra; **outbound** *adj* **outbound (for** *or* **from)** in partenza (per *or* da); **outbreak** ['autbreɪk] *n* scoppio; epidemia; **outburst** ['autbəːst] *n* scoppio; **outcast** ['autkɑːst] *n* esule *m/f*; (*socially*) paria *m inv*; **outcome** ['autkʌm] *n* esito, risultato; **outcry** ['autkraɪ] *n* protesta, clamore *m*; **outdated** [aut'deɪtɪd] *adj* (*custom, clothes*) fuori moda; (*idea*) sorpassato(-a); **outdoor** [aut'dɔː^r] *adj* all'aperto; **outdoors** *adv* fuori; all'aria aperta
outer ['autə^r] *adj* esteriore; **outer space** *n* spazio cosmico
outfit ['autfɪt] *n* (*clothes*) completo; (*: for sport*) tenuta
out: **outgoing** ['autgəuɪŋ] *adj* (*character*) socievole; **outgoings** (BRIT) *npl* (*expenses*) spese *fpl*, uscite *fpl*; **outhouse** ['authaus] *n* costruzione *f* annessa
outing ['autɪŋ] *n* gita; escursione *f*
out: **outlaw** ['autlɔː] *n* fuorilegge *m/f* ▷ *vt* bandire; **outlay** ['autleɪ] *n* spese *fpl*; (*investment*) sborsa, spesa; **outlet** ['autlɛt] *n* (*for liquid etc*) sbocco, scarico; (*US Elec*) presa di corrente; (*also*: **retail outlet**) punto di vendita; **outline** ['autlaɪn] *n* contorno, profilo; (*summary*) abbozzo, grandi linee *fpl* ▷ *vt* (*fig*) descrivere a grandi linee; **outlook** ['autluk] *n* prospettiva, vista; **outnumber** [aut'nʌmbə^r] *vt* superare in numero; **out-of-date** *adj* (*passport*) scaduto(-a); (*clothes*) fuori moda

inv; **out-of-doors** [autəv'dɔːz] *adv* all'aperto; **out-of-the-way** *adj* (*place*) fuori mano *inv*; **out-of-town** [ˌaʊtəv'taʊn] *adj* (*shopping centre etc*) fuori città; **outpatient** ['autpeɪʃənt] *n* paziente *m/f* esterno(-a); **outpost** ['autpəust] *n* avamposto; **output** ['autput] *n* produzione *f*; (*Comput*) output *m inv*

outrage ['autreɪdʒ] *n* oltraggio; scandalo ▷ *vt* oltraggiare; **outrageous** [-'reɪdʒəs] *adj* oltraggioso(-a), scandaloso(-a)

outright [*adv* aut'raɪt, *adj* 'autraɪt] *adv* completamente; schiettamente; apertamente; sul colpo ▷ *adj* completo(-a), schietto(-a) e netto(-a)

outset ['autsɛt] *n* inizio

outside [aut'saɪd] *n* esterno, esteriore *m* ▷ *adj* esterno(-a), esteriore ▷ *adv* fuori, all'esterno ▷ *prep* fuori di, all'esterno di; **at the ~** (*fig*) al massimo; **outside lane** *n* (*Aut*) corsia di sorpasso; **outside line** *n* (*Tel*) linea esterna; **outsider** *n* (*in race etc*) outsider *m inv*; (*stranger*) estraneo(-a)

out: **outsize** ['autsaɪz] *adj* (*clothes*) per taglie forti; **outskirts** ['autskəːts] *npl* sobborghi *mpl*; **outspoken** [aut'spəukən] *adj* molto franco(-a); **outstanding** [aut'stændɪŋ] *adj* eccezionale, di rilievo; (*unfinished*) non completo(-a); non evaso(-a); non regolato(-a)

outward ['autwəd] *adj* (*sign, appearances*) esteriore; (*journey*) d'andata; **outwards** ['aʊtwədz] *adv* (*esp* BRIT) = **outward**

outweigh [aut'weɪ] *vt* avere maggior peso di

oval ['əuvl] *adj* ovale ▷ *n* ovale *m*

ovary ['əuvərɪ] *n* ovaia

oven ['ʌvn] *n* forno; **oven glove** *n* guanto da forno; **ovenproof** *adj* da forno; **oven-ready** *adj* pronto(-a) da infornare

over ['əuvəʳ] *adv* al di sopra ▷ *adj* (*or adv*) (*finished*) finito(-a), terminato(-a); (*too*) troppo; (*remaining*) che avanza ▷ *prep* su; sopra; (*above*) al di sopra di; (*on the other side of*) di là di; (*more than*) più di; (*during*) durante; **~ here** qui; **~ there** là; **all ~** (*everywhere*) dappertutto; (*finished*) tutto(-a) finito(-a); **~ and ~ (again)** più e più volte; **~ and above** oltre (a); **to ask sb ~** invitare qn (a passare)

overall [*adj, n* 'əuvərɔːl, *adv* əuvər'ɔːl] *adj* totale ▷ *n* (BRIT) grembiule *m* ▷ *adv* nell'insieme, complessivamente; **overalls** *npl* (*worker's overalls*) tuta (da lavoro)

overboard ['əuvəbɔːd] *adv* (*Naut*) fuori bordo, in mare

overcame [əuvə'keɪm] *pt of* **overcome**

overcast ['əuvəkɑːst] *adj* (*sky*) coperto(-a)

overcharge [əuvə'tʃɑːdʒ] *vt* **to ~ sb for sth** far pagare troppo caro a qn per qc

overcoat ['əuvəkəut] *n* soprabito, cappotto

overcome [əuvə'kʌm] (*irreg*) *vt* superare; sopraffare

over: **overcrowded** [əuvə'kraudɪd] *adj* sovraffollato(-a); **overdo** [əuvə'duː] (*irreg*) *vt* esagerare; (*overcook*) cuocere troppo; **overdone** [əuvə'dʌn] *adj* troppo cotto(-a); **overdose** ['əuvədəus] *n* dose *f* eccessiva; **overdraft** ['əuvədrɑːft] *n* scoperto (di conto); **overdrawn** [əuvə'drɔːn] *adj* (*account*) scoperto(-a); **overdue** [əuvə'djuː] *adj* in ritardo; **overestimate** [əuvər'ɛstɪmeɪt] *vt* sopravvalutare

overflow [*vb* əuvə'fləu, *n* 'əuvəfləu] *vi* traboccare ▷ *n* (*also*: **~ pipe**) troppopieno

overgrown [əuvə'grəun] *adj* (*garden*) ricoperto(-a) di vegetazione

overhaul [*vb* əuvə'hɔːl, *n* 'əuvəhɔːl] *vt* revisionare ▷ *n* revisione *f*

overhead [*adv* əuvə'hɛd, *adj*, *n* 'əuvəhɛd] *adv* di sopra ▷ *adj* aereo(-a); (*lighting*) verticale ▷ *n* (*US*) = **overheads**; **overhead projector** *n* lavagna luminosa; **overheads** *npl* spese *fpl* generali

over: **overhear** [əuvə'hɪə^r] (*irreg*) *vt* sentire (per caso); **overheat** [əuvə'hi:t] *vi* (*engine*) surriscaldare; **overland** *adj*, *adv* per via di terra; **overlap** [əuvə'læp] *vi* sovrapporsi; **overleaf** [əuvə'li:f] *adv* a tergo; **overload** [əuvə'ləud] *vt* sovraccaricare; **overlook** [əuvə'luk] *vt* (*have view of*) dare su; (*miss*) trascurare; (*forgive*) passare sopra a

overnight [əuvə'naɪt] *adv* (*happen*) durante la notte; (*fig*) tutto ad un tratto ▷ *adj* di notte; **he stayed there ~** ci ha passato la notte; **overnight bag** *n* borsa da viaggio

overpass ['əuvəpɑ:s] *n* cavalcavia *m inv*

overpower [əuvə'pauə^r] *vt* sopraffare; **overpowering** *adj* irresistibile; (*heat, stench*) soffocante

over: **overreact** [əuvəri:'ækt] *vi* reagire in modo esagerato; **overrule** [əuvə'ru:l] *vt* (*decision*) annullare; (*claim*) respingere; **overrun** [əuvə'rʌn] (*irreg: like* **run**) *vt* (*country*) invadere; (*time limit*) superare

overseas [əuvə'si:z] *adv* oltremare; (*abroad*) all'estero ▷ *adj* (*trade*) estero(-a); (*visitor*) straniero(-a)

oversee [əuvə'si:] *vt irreg* sorvegliare

overshadow [əuvə'ʃædəu] *vt* far ombra su; (*fig*) eclissare

oversight ['əuvəsaɪt] *n* omissione *f*, svista

oversleep [əuvə'sli:p] (*irreg*) *vt* dormire troppo a lungo

overspend [əuvə'spɛnd] *vi irreg* spendere troppo; **we have overspent by 5000 dollars** abbiamo speso 5000 dollari di troppo

overt [əu'və:t] *adj* palese

overtake [əuvə'teɪk] (*irreg*) *vt* sorpassare

over: **overthrow** [əuvə'θrəu] (*irreg*) *vt* (*government*) rovesciare; **overtime** ['əuvətaɪm] *n* (lavoro) straordinario

overtook [əuvə'tuk] *pt of* **overtake**

over: **overturn** [əuvə'tə:n] *vt* rovesciare ▷ *vi* rovesciarsi; **overweight** [əuvə'weɪt] *adj* (*person*) troppo grasso(-a); **overwhelm** [əuvə'wɛlm] *vt* sopraffare; sommergere; schiacciare; **overwhelming** *adj* (*victory, defeat*) schiacciante; (*heat, desire*) intenso(-a)

ow [au] *excl* ahi!

owe [əu] *vt* **to ~ sb sth, to ~ sth to sb** dovere qc a qn; **how much do I ~ you?** quanto le devo?; **owing to** *prep* a causa di

owl [aul] *n* gufo

own [əun] *vt* possedere ▷ *adj* proprio(-a); **a room of my ~** la mia propria camera; **to get one's ~ back** vendicarsi; **on one's ~** tutto(-a) solo(-a); **own up** *vi* confessare; **owner** *n* proprietario(-a); **ownership** *n* possesso

ox [ɔks] (*pl* **oxen**) *n* bue *m*

Oxbridge ['ɔksbrɪdʒ] *n le università di Oxford e/o Cambridge*

oxen ['ɔksn] *npl of* **ox**

oxygen ['ɔksɪdʒən] *n* ossigeno

oyster ['ɔɪstə^r] *n* ostrica

oz. *abbr* = **ounce(s)**

ozone ['əuzəun] *n* ozono; **ozone friendly** *adj* che non danneggia l'ozono; **ozone layer** *n* fascia d'ozono

p

p [piː] *abbr* = **penny**; **pence**
P.A. *n abbr* = **personal assistant**; **public address system**
p.a. *abbr* = **per annum**
pace [peɪs] *n* passo; (*speed*) passo; velocità ▷ *vi* **to ~ up and down** camminare su e giù; **to keep ~ with** camminare di pari passo a; (*events*) tenersi al corrente di; **pacemaker** *n* (*Med*) segnapasso; (*Sport*: *also*: **pace setter**) battistrada *m inv*
Pacific [pə'sɪfɪk] *n* **the ~ (Ocean)** il Pacifico, l'Oceano Pacifico
pacifier ['pæsɪfaɪə^r] (US) *n* (*dummy*) succhiotto, ciuccio (*col*)
pack [pæk] *n* pacco; (US: *of cigarettes*) pacchetto; (*backpack*) zaino; (*of hounds*) muta; (*of thieves etc*) banda; (*of cards*) mazzo ▷ *vt* (*in suitcase etc*) mettere; (*box*) riempire; (*cram*) stipare, pigiare; **to ~ (one's bags)** fare la valigia; **to ~ sb off** spedire via qn; **~ it in!** (*inf*) dacci un taglio!; **pack in** (BRIT *inf*) *vi* (*watch, car*) guastarsi ▷ *vt* mollare, piantare; **pack it in!** piantala!; **pack up** *vi* (BRIT *inf*: *machine*) guastarsi; (: *person*) far fagotto ▷ *vt* (*belongings, clothes*) mettere in una valigia; (*goods, presents*) imballare
package ['pækɪdʒ] *n* pacco; balla; (*also*: **~ deal**) pacchetto; forfait *m inv*; **package holiday** *n* vacanza organizzata; **package tour** *n* viaggio organizzato
packaging ['pækɪdʒɪŋ] *n* confezione *f*, imballo
packed [pækt] *adj* (*crowded*) affollato(-a); **packed lunch** *n* pranzo al sacco
packet ['pækɪt] *n* pacchetto
packing ['pækɪŋ] *n* imballaggio
pact [pækt] *n* patto, accordo; trattato
pad [pæd] *n* blocco; (*to prevent friction*) cuscinetto; (*inf*: *flat*) appartamentino ▷ *vt* imbottire; **padded** *adj* imbottito(-a)
paddle ['pædl] *n* (*oar*) pagaia; (US: *for table tennis*) racchetta da ping-pong ▷ *vi* sguazzare ▷ *vt* **to ~ a canoe** *etc* vogare con la pagaia; **paddling pool** (BRIT) *n* piscina per bambini
paddock ['pædək] *n* prato recintato; (*at racecourse*) paddock *m inv*
padlock ['pædlɔk] *n* lucchetto
paedophile ['piːdəufaɪl] (US **pedophile**) *adj, n* pedofilo(-a)
page [peɪdʒ] *n* pagina; (*also*: **~ boy**) paggio ▷ *vt* (*in hotel etc*) (far) chiamare
pager ['peɪdʒə^r] *n* (*Tel*) cercapersone *m inv*
paid [peɪd] *pt, pp of* **pay** ▷ *adj* (*work, official*) rimunerato(-a); **to put ~ to** (BRIT) mettere fine a
pain [peɪn] *n* dolore *m*; **to be in ~** soffrire, aver male; **to take ~s to do** mettercela tutta per fare; **painful** *adj* doloroso(-a), che fa male; difficile, penoso(-a); **painkiller** *n* antalgico, antidolorifico; **painstaking** ['peɪnzteɪkɪŋ] *adj* (*person*)

sollecito(-a); (*work*) accurato(-a)

paint [peɪnt] *n* vernice *f*, colore *m* ▷ *vt* dipingere; (*walls, door etc*) verniciare; **to ~ the door blue** verniciare la porta di azzurro; **paintbrush** *n* pennello; **painter** *n* (*artist*) pittore *m*; (*decorator*) imbianchino; **painting** *n* pittura; verniciatura; (*picture*) dipinto, quadro

pair [pɛəʳ] *n* (*of shoes, gloves etc*) paio; (*of people*) coppia; duo *m inv*; **a ~ of scissors/trousers** un paio di forbici/pantaloni

pajamas [pɪ'dʒɑːməz] (US) *npl* pigiama *m*

Pakistan [pɑːkɪ'stɑːn] *n* Pakistan *m*; **Pakistani** *adj, n* pakistano(-a)

pal [pæl] (*inf*) *n* amico(-a), compagno(-a)

palace ['pæləs] *n* palazzo

pale [peɪl] *adj* pallido(-a) ▷ *n* **to be beyond the ~** aver oltrepassato ogni limite

Palestine ['pælɪstaɪn] *n* Palestina; **Palestinian** [-'tɪnɪən] *adj, n* palestinese *m/f*

palm [pɑːm] *n* (*Anat*) palma, palmo; (*also:* **~ tree**) palma ▷ *vt* **to ~ sth off on sb** (*inf*) rifilare qc a qn

pamper ['pæmpəʳ] *vt* viziare, coccolare

pamphlet ['pæmflət] *n* dépliant *m inv*

pan [pæn] *n* (*also:* **sauce~**) casseruola; (*also:* **frying ~**) padella

pancake ['pænkeɪk] *n* frittella

panda ['pændə] *n* panda *m inv*

pane [peɪn] *n* vetro

panel ['pænl] *n* (*of wood, cloth etc*) pannello; (*Radio, TV*) giuria

panhandler ['pænhændləʳ] (US) *n* (*inf*) accattone(-a)

panic ['pænɪk] *n* panico ▷ *vi* perdere il sangue freddo

panorama [pænə'rɑːmə] *n* panorama *m*

pansy ['pænzɪ] *n* (*Bot*) viola del pensiero, pensée *f inv*; (*inf: pej*) femminuccia

pant [pænt] *vi* ansare

panther ['pænθəʳ] *n* pantera

panties ['pæntɪz] *npl* slip *m*, mutandine *fpl*

pantomime ['pæntəmaɪm] (BRIT) *n* pantomima

PANTOMIME

In Gran Bretagna la **pantomime** è una sorta di libera interpretazione delle favole più conosciute, che vengono messe in scena a teatro durante il periodo natalizio. È uno spettacolo per tutta la famiglia che prevede la partecipazione del pubblico.

pants [pænts] *npl* mutande *fpl*, slip *m*; (US: *trousers*) pantaloni *mpl*

paper ['peɪpəʳ] *n* carta; (*also:* **wall~**) carta da parati, tappezzeria; (*also:* **news~**) giornale *m*; (*study, article*) saggio; (*exam*) prova scritta ▷ *adj* di carta ▷ *vt* tappezzare; **papers** *npl* (*also:* **identity ~s**) carte *fpl*, documenti *mpl*; **paperback** *n* tascabile *m*; edizione *f* economica; **paper bag** *n* sacchetto di carta; **paper clip** *n* graffetta, clip *f inv*; **paper shop** *n* (BRIT) giornalaio (*negozio*); **paperwork** *n* lavoro amministrativo

paprika ['pæprɪkə] *n* paprica

par [pɑːʳ] *n* parità, pari *f*; (*Golf*) norma; **on a ~ with** alla pari con

paracetamol [pærə'siːtəmɔl] (BRIT) *n* paracetamolo

parachute ['pærəʃuːt] *n* paracadute *m inv*

parade [pə'reɪd] *n* parata ▷ *vt* (*fig*) fare sfoggio di ▷ *vi* sfilare in parata

paradise ['pærədaɪs] *n* paradiso

paradox ['pærədɔks] *n* paradosso

paraffin ['pærəfɪn] (BRIT) *n* **~ (oil)** paraffina

paragraph ['pærəgrɑːf] *n* paragrafo

parallel ['pærəlɛl] *adj* parallelo(-a);

(*fig*) analogo(-a) ▷ *n* (*line*) parallela; (*fig, Geo*) parallelo
paralysed ['pærəlaɪzd] *adj* paralizzato(-a)
paralysis [pə'rælɪsɪs] *n* paralisi *f inv*
paramedic [pærə'mɛdɪk] *n* paramedico
paranoid ['pærənɔɪd] *adj* paranoico(-a)
parasite ['pærəsaɪt] *n* parassita *m*
parcel ['pɑːsl] *n* pacco, pacchetto ▷ *vt* (*also:* ~ **up**) impaccare
pardon ['pɑːdn] *n* perdono; grazia ▷ *vt* perdonare; (*Law*) graziare; ~ **me!** mi scusi!; **I beg your ~!** scusi!; **I beg your ~?** (BRIT), **~ me?** (US) prego?
parent ['pɛərənt] *n* genitore *m*; **parents** *npl* (*mother and father*) genitori *mpl*; **parental** [pə'rɛntl] *adj* dei genitori

> Be careful not to translate ***parent*** by the Italian word ***parente***.

Paris ['pærɪs] *n* Parigi *f*
parish ['pærɪʃ] *n* parrocchia; (BRIT: *civil*) ≈ municipio
Parisian [pə'rɪzɪən] *adj, n* parigino(-a)
park [pɑːk] *n* parco ▷ *vt, vi* parcheggiare; **can I ~ here?** posso parcheggiare qui?
parking ['pɑːkɪŋ] *n* parcheggio; **"no ~"** "sosta vietata"; **parking lot** (US) *n* posteggio, parcheggio; **parking meter** *n* parchimetro; **parking ticket** *n* multa per sosta vietata
parkway ['pɑːkweɪ] (US) *n* viale *m*
parliament ['pɑːləmənt] *n* parlamento; **parliamentary** [pɑːlə'mɛntərɪ] *adj* parlamentare
Parmesan [pɑːmɪ'zæn] *n* (*also:* ~ **cheese**) parmigiano
parole [pə'rəul] *n* **on ~** in libertà per buona condotta
parrot ['pærət] *n* pappagallo
parsley ['pɑːslɪ] *n* prezzemolo
parsnip ['pɑːsnɪp] *n* pastinaca
parson ['pɑːsn] *n* prete *m*; (*Church of England*) parroco
part [pɑːt] *n* parte *f*; (*of machine*) pezzo; (US: *in hair*) scriminatura ▷ *adj* in parte ▷ *adv* = **partly** ▷ *vt* separare ▷ *vi* (*people*) separarsi; **to take ~ in** prendere parte a; **for my ~** per parte mia; **to take sth in good ~** prendere bene qc; **to take sb's ~** parteggiare per *or* prendere le parti di qn; **for the most ~** in generale; nella maggior parte dei casi; **part with** *vt fus* separarsi da; rinunciare a
partial ['pɑːʃl] *adj* parziale; **to be ~ to** avere un debole per
participant [pɑː'tɪsɪpənt] *n* **~ (in)** partecipante *m/f* (a)
participate [pɑː'tɪsɪpeɪt] *vi* **to ~ (in)** prendere parte (a), partecipare (a)
particle ['pɑːtɪkl] *n* particella
particular [pə'tɪkjulə^r] *adj* particolare; speciale; (*fussy*) difficile; meticoloso(-a); **in ~** in particolare, particolarmente; **particularly** *adv* particolarmente; in particolare; **particulars** *npl* particolari *mpl*, dettagli *mpl*; (*information*) informazioni *fpl*
parting ['pɑːtɪŋ] *n* separazione *f*; (BRIT: *in hair*) scriminatura ▷ *adj* d'addio
partition [pɑː'tɪʃən] *n* (*Pol*) partizione *f*; (*wall*) tramezzo
partly ['pɑːtlɪ] *adv* parzialmente; in parte
partner ['pɑːtnə^r] *n* (*Comm*) socio(-a); (*wife, husband etc, Sport*) compagno(-a); (*at dance*) cavaliere/dama; **partnership** *n* associazione *f*; (*Comm*) società *f inv*
part of speech *n* parte *f* del discorso
partridge ['pɑːtrɪdʒ] *n* pernice *f*
part-time ['pɑːt'taɪm] *adj, adv* a orario ridotto
party ['pɑːtɪ] *n* (*Pol*) partito; (*group*) gruppo; (*Law*) parte *f*; (*celebration*) ricevimento; serata; festa ▷ *cpd* (*Pol*) del partito, di partito

pass [pɑːs] *vt* (*gen*) passare; (*place*) passare davanti a; (*exam*) passare, superare; (*candidate*) promuovere; (*overtake, surpass*) sorpassare, superare; (*approve*) approvare ▷ *vi* passare ▷ *n* (*permit*) lasciapassare *m inv*; permesso; (*in mountains*) passo, gola; (*Sport*) passaggio; (*Scol*): **to get a ~** prendere la sufficienza; **could you ~ the salt/oil, please?** mi passa il sale/l'olio, per favore?; **to ~ sth through a hole** *etc* far passare qc attraverso un buco *etc*; **to make a ~ at sb** (*inf*) fare delle proposte *or* delle avances a qn; **pass away** *vi* morire; **pass by** *vi* passare ▷ *vt* trascurare; **pass on** *vt* passare; **pass out** *vi* svenire; **pass over** *vi* (*die*) spirare ▷ *vt* lasciare da parte; **pass up** *vt* (*opportunity*) lasciarsi sfuggire, perdere; **passable** *adj* (*road*) praticabile; (*work*) accettabile

passage ['pæsɪdʒ] *n* (*gen*) passaggio; (*also*: **~way**) corridoio; (*in book*) brano, passo; (*by boat*) traversata

passenger ['pæsɪndʒəʳ] *n* passeggero(-a)

passer-by [pɑːsə'baɪ] *n* passante *m/f*

passing place *n* (*Aut*) piazzola di sosta

passion ['pæʃən] *n* passione *f*; amore *m*; **passionate** *adj* appassionato(-a); **passion fruit** *n* frutto della passione

passive ['pæsɪv] *adj* (*also Ling*) passivo(-a)

passport ['pɑːspɔːt] *n* passaporto; **passport control** *n* controllo *m* passaporti *inv*; **passport office** *n* ufficio *m*, passaporti *inv*

password ['pɑːswəːd] *n* parola d'ordine

past [pɑːst] *prep* (*further than*) oltre, di là di; dopo; (*later than*) dopo ▷ *adj* passato(-a); (*president etc*) ex *inv* ▷ *n* passato; **he's ~ forty** ha più di quarant'anni; **ten ~ eight** le otto e dieci; **for the ~ few days** da qualche giorno; in questi ultimi giorni; **to run ~** passare di corsa

pasta ['pæstə] *n* pasta

paste [peɪst] *n* (*glue*) colla; (*Culin*) pâté *m inv*; pasta ▷ *vt* collare

pastel ['pæstl] *adj* pastello *inv*

pasteurized ['pæstəraɪzd] *adj* pastorizzato(-a)

pastime ['pɑːstaɪm] *n* passatempo

pastor ['pɑːstəʳ] *n* pastore *m*

past participle [-'pɑːtɪsɪpl] *n* (*Ling*) participio passato

pastry ['peɪstrɪ] *n* pasta

pasture ['pɑːstʃəʳ] *n* pascolo

pasty[1] ['pæstɪ] *n* pasticcio di carne

pasty[2] ['peɪstɪ] *adj* (*face etc*) smorto(-a)

pat [pæt] *vt* accarezzare, dare un colpetto (affettuoso) a

patch [pætʃ] *n* (*of material, on tyre*) toppa; (*eye patch*) benda; (*spot*) macchia ▷ *vt* (*clothes*) rattoppare; **(to go through) a bad ~** (attraversare) un brutto periodo; **patchy** *adj* irregolare

pâté ['pæteɪ] *n* pâté *m inv*

patent ['peɪtnt] *n* brevetto ▷ *vt* brevettare ▷ *adj* patente, manifesto(-a)

paternal [pə'təːnl] *adj* paterno(-a)

paternity leave [pə'təːnɪtɪ-] *n* congedo di paternità

path [pɑːθ] *n* sentiero, viottolo; viale *m*; (*fig*) via, strada; (*of planet, missile*) traiettoria

pathetic [pə'θɛtɪk] *adj* (*pitiful*) patetico(-a); (*very bad*) penoso(-a)

pathway ['pɑːθweɪ] *n* sentiero

patience ['peɪʃns] *n* pazienza; (BRIT *Cards*) solitario

patient ['peɪʃnt] *n* paziente *m/f*, malato(-a) ▷ *adj* paziente

patio ['pætɪəu] *n* terrazza

patriotic [pætrɪ'ɔtɪk] *adj* patriottico(-a)

patrol [pə'trəul] *n* pattuglia ▷ *vt* pattugliare; **patrol car** *n* autoradio *f* *inv* (della polizia)

patron ['peɪtrən] *n* (*in shop*) cliente *m/f*; (*of charity*) benefattore(-trice); **~ of the arts** mecenate *m/f*

patronizing ['pætrənaɪzɪŋ] *adj* condiscendente

pattern ['pætən] *n* modello; (*design*) disegno, motivo; **patterned** *adj* a disegni, a motivi; (*material*) fantasia *inv*

pause [pɔːz] *n* pausa ▷ *vi* fare una pausa, arrestarsi

pave [peɪv] *vt* pavimentare; **to ~ the way for** aprire la via a

pavement ['peɪvmənt] (BRIT) *n* marciapiede *m*

> Be careful not to translate ***pavement*** by the Italian word ***pavimento***.

pavilion [pə'vɪlɪən] *n* (*Sport*) *edificio annesso a campo sportivo*

paving ['peɪvɪŋ] *n* pavimentazione *f*

paw [pɔː] *n* zampa

pawn [pɔːn] *n* (*Chess*) pedone *m*; (*fig*) pedina ▷ *vt* dare in pegno; **pawn broker** *n* prestatore *m* su pegno

pay [peɪ] (*pt, pp* **paid**) *n* stipendio; paga ▷ *vt* pagare ▷ *vi* (*be profitable*) rendere; **can I ~ by credit card?** posso pagare con la carta di credito?; **to ~ attention (to)** fare attenzione (a); **to ~ sb a visit** far visita a qn; **to ~ one's respects to sb** porgere i propri rispetti a qn; **pay back** *vt* rimborsare; **pay for** *vt fus* pagare; **pay in** *vt* versare; **pay off** *vt* (*debt*) saldare; (*person*) pagare; (*employee*) pagare e licenziare ▷ *vi* (*scheme, decision*) dare dei frutti; **pay out** *vt* (*money*) sborsare, tirar fuori; (*rope*) far allentare; **pay up** *vt* saldare; **payable** *adj* pagabile

pay-as-you-go ['peɪəzjuːgəʊ] *adj* (*mobile phone*) con scheda prepagata

pay: **pay day** *n* giorno di paga; **pay envelope** (US) *n* = **pay packet**; **payment** *n* pagamento; versamento; saldo; **payout** *n* pagamento; (*in competition*) premio; **pay packet** (BRIT) *n* busta *f* paga *inv*; **pay phone** *n* cabina telefonica; **payroll** *n* ruolo (organico); **pay slip** *n* foglio *m* paga *inv*; **pay television** *n* televisione *f* a pagamento, pay-tv *f inv*

PC *n abbr* = **personal computer** ▷ *adv abbr* = **politically correct**

p.c. *abbr* = **per cent**

PDA *n abbr* (= *personal digital assistant*) PDA *m inv*

PE *n abbr* (= *physical education*) ed. fisica

pea [piː] *n* pisello

peace [piːs] *n* pace *f*; **peaceful** *adj* pacifico(-a), calmo(-a)

peach [piːtʃ] *n* pesca

peacock ['piːkɔk] *n* pavone *m*

peak [piːk] *n* (*of mountain*) cima, vetta; (*mountain itself*) picco; (*of cap*) visiera; (*fig*) apice *m*, culmine *m*; **peak hours** *npl* ore *fpl* di punta

peanut ['piːnʌt] *n* arachide *f*, nocciolina americana; **peanut butter** *n* burro di arachidi

pear [pɛəʳ] *n* pera

pearl [pəːl] *n* perla

peasant ['pɛznt] *n* contadino(-a)

peat [piːt] *n* torba

pebble ['pɛbl] *n* ciottolo

peck [pɛk] *vt* (*also:* **~ at**) beccare ▷ *n* colpo di becco; (*kiss*) bacetto; **peckish** (BRIT: *inf*) *adj* **I feel peckish** ho un languorino

peculiar [pɪ'kjuːlɪəʳ] *adj* strano(-a), bizzarro(-a); peculiare; **~ to** peculiare di

pedal ['pɛdl] *n* pedale *m* ▷ *vi* pedalare

pedalo ['pedələu] *n* pedalò *m inv*

pedestal ['pɛdəstl] *n* piedestallo

pedestrian [pɪ'dɛstrɪən] *n* pedone(-a) ▷ *adj* pedonale; (*fig*) prosaico(-a), pedestre; **pedestrian crossing** (BRIT) *n* passaggio pedonale; **pedestrianized** *adj*: **a pedestrianized street** una zona pedonalizzata; **pedestrian precinct** (BRIT), **pedestrian zone** (US) *n* zona pedonale

pedigree ['pɛdɪgriː] *n* (*of animal*)

pedigree *m inv*; (*fig*) background *m inv* ▷ *cpd* (*animal*) di razza
pedophile ['pi:dəufaɪl] (*US*) *n* = **paedophile**
pee [pi:] (*inf*) *vi* pisciare
peek [pi:k] *vi* guardare furtivamente
peel [pi:l] *n* buccia; (*of orange, lemon*) scorza ▷ *vt* sbucciare ▷ *vi* (*paint etc*) staccarsi
peep [pi:p] *n* (*BRIT*: *look*) sguardo furtivo, sbirciata; (*sound*) pigolio ▷ *vi* (*BRIT*) guardare furtivamente
peer [pɪəʳ] *vi* **to ~ at** scrutare ▷ *n* (*noble*) pari *m inv*; (*equal*) pari *m/f inv*, uguale *m/f*; (*contemporary*) contemporaneo(-a)
peg [pɛg] *n* caviglia; (*for coat etc*) attaccapanni *m inv*; (*BRIT*: *also*: **clothes ~**) molletta
pelican ['pɛlɪkən] *n* pellicano; **pelican crossing** (*BRIT*) *n* (*Aut*) *attraversamento pedonale con semaforo a controllo manuale*
pelt [pɛlt] *vt* **to ~ sb (with)** bombardare qn (con) ▷ *vi* (*rain*) piovere a dirotto; (*inf*: *run*) filare ▷ *n* pelle *f*
pelvis ['pɛlvɪs] *n* pelvi *f inv*, bacino
pen [pɛn] *n* penna; (*for sheep*) recinto
penalty ['pɛnltɪ] *n* penalità *f inv*; sanzione *f* penale; (*fine*) ammenda; (*Sport*) penalizzazione *f*
pence [pɛns] (*BRIT*) *npl of* **penny**
pencil ['pɛnsl] *n* matita; **pencil in** *vt* scrivere a matita; **pencil case** *n* astuccio per matite; **pencil sharpener** *n* temperamatite *m inv*
pendant ['pɛndnt] *n* pendaglio
pending ['pɛndɪŋ] *prep* in attesa di ▷ *adj* in sospeso
penetrate ['pɛnɪtreɪt] *vt* penetrare
penfriend ['pɛnfrɛnd] (*BRIT*) *n* corrispondente *m/f*
penguin ['pɛŋgwɪn] *n* pinguino
penicillin [pɛnɪ'sɪlɪn] *n* penicillina
peninsula [pə'nɪnsjulə] *n* penisola
penis ['pi:nɪs] *n* pene *m*
penitentiary [pɛnɪ'tɛnʃərɪ] (*US*) *n* carcere *m*
penknife ['pɛnnaɪf] *n* temperino
penniless ['pɛnɪlɪs] *adj* senza un soldo
penny ['pɛnɪ] (*pl* **pennies** *or* **pence**) (*BRIT*) *n* penny *m*; (*US*) centesimo
penpal ['pɛnpæl] *n* corrispondente *m/f*
pension ['pɛnʃən] *n* pensione *f*; **pensioner** (*BRIT*) *n* pensionato(-a)
pentagon ['pɛntəgən] *n* pentagono; **the P~** (*US Pol*) il Pentagono
penthouse ['pɛnthaus] *n* appartamento (di lusso) nell'attico
penultimate [pɪ'nʌltɪmət] *adj* penultimo(-a)
people ['pi:pl] *npl* gente *f*; persone *fpl*; (*citizens*) popolo ▷ *n* (*nation, race*) popolo; **4/several ~ came** 4/parecchie persone sono venute; **~ say that ...** si dice che ...
pepper ['pɛpəʳ] *n* pepe *m*; (*vegetable*) peperone *m* ▷ *vt* (*fig*): **to ~ with** spruzzare di; **peppermint** *n* (*sweet*) pasticca di menta
per [pə:ʳ] *prep* per; a; **~ hour** all'ora; **~ kilo** *etc* il chilo *etc*; **~ day** al giorno
perceive [pə'si:v] *vt* percepire; (*notice*) accorgersi di
per cent *adv* per cento
percentage [pə'sɛntɪdʒ] *n* percentuale *f*
perception [pə'sɛpʃən] *n* percezione *f*; sensibilità; perspicacia
perch [pə:tʃ] *n* (*fish*) pesce *m* persico; (*for bird*) sostegno, ramo ▷ *vi* appollaiarsi
percussion [pə'kʌʃən] *n* percussione *f*; (*Mus*) strumenti *mpl* a percussione
perfect [*adj, n* 'pə:fɪkt, *vb* pə'fɛkt] *adj* perfetto(-a) ▷ *n* (*also*: **~ tense**) perfetto, passato prossimo ▷ *vt* perfezionare; mettere a punto; **perfection** [pə'fɛkʃən] *n* perfezione *f*; **perfectly** *adv* perfettamente, alla perfezione

perform [pə'fɔːm] *vt* (*carry out*) eseguire, fare; (*symphony etc*) suonare; (*play, ballet*) dare; (*opera*) fare ▷ *vi* suonare; recitare; **performance** *n* esecuzione *f*; (*at theatre etc*) rappresentazione *f*, spettacolo; (*of an artist*) interpretazione *f*; (*of player etc*) performance *f*; (*of car, engine*) prestazione *f*; **performer** *n* artista *m/f*

perfume ['pəːfjuːm] *n* profumo

perhaps [pə'hæps] *adv* forse

perimeter [pə'rɪmɪtəʳ] *n* perimetro

period ['pɪərɪəd] *n* periodo; (*History*) epoca; (*Scol*) lezione *f*; (*full stop*) punto; (*Med*) mestruazioni *fpl* ▷ *adj* (*costume, furniture*) d'epoca; **periodical** [-'ɔdɪkl] *n* periodico; **periodically** *adv* periodicamente

perish ['pɛrɪʃ] *vi* perire, morire; (*decay*) deteriorarsi

perjury ['pəːdʒərɪ] *n* spergiuro

perk [pəːk] (*inf*) *n* vantaggio

perm [pəːm] *n* (*for hair*) permanente *f*

permanent ['pəːmənənt] *adj* permanente; **permanently** *adv* definitivamente

permission [pə'mɪʃən] *n* permesso

permit [*n* 'pəːmɪt, *vb* pə'mɪt] *n* permesso ▷ *vt* permettere; **to ~ sb to do** permettere a qn di fare

perplex [pə'plɛks] *vt* lasciare perplesso(-a)

persecute ['pəːsɪkjuːt] *vt* perseguitare

persecution [pəːsɪ'kjuːʃən] *n* persecuzione *f*

persevere [pəːsɪ'vɪəʳ] *vi* perseverare

Persian ['pəːʃən] *adj* persiano(-a) ▷ *n* (*Ling*) persiano; **the (~) Gulf** *n* il Golfo Persico

persist [pə'sɪst] *vi* **to ~ (in doing)** persistere (nel fare); ostinarsi (a fare); **persistent** *adj* persistente; ostinato(-a)

person ['pəːsn] *n* persona; **in ~** di *or* in persona, personalmente; **personal** *adj* personale; individuale; **personal assistant** *n* segretaria personale; **personal computer** *n* personal computer *m inv*; **personality** [-'nælɪtɪ] *n* personalità *f inv*; **personally** *adv* personalmente; **to take sth personally** prendere qc come una critica personale; **personal organizer** *n* (*Filofax®*) Fulltime®; (*electronic*) agenda elettronica; **personal stereo** *n* Walkman® *m inv*

personnel [pəːsə'nɛl] *n* personale *m*

perspective [pə'spɛktɪv] *n* prospettiva

perspiration [pəːspɪ'reɪʃən] *n* traspirazione *f*, sudore *m*

persuade [pə'sweɪd] *vt* **to ~ sb to do sth** persuadere qn a fare qc

persuasion [pə'sweɪʒən] *n* persuasione *f*; (*creed*) convinzione *f*, credo

persuasive [pə'sweɪsɪv] *adj* persuasivo(-a)

perverse [pə'vəːs] *adj* perverso(-a)

pervert [*n* 'pəːvəːt, *vb* pə'vəːt] *n* pervertito(-a) ▷ *vt* pervertire

pessimism ['pɛsɪmɪzəm] *n* pessimismo

pessimist ['pɛsɪmɪst] *n* pessimista *m/f*; **pessimistic** [-'mɪstɪk] *adj* pessimistico(-a)

pest [pɛst] *n* animale *m* (*or* insetto) pestifero; (*fig*) peste *f*

pester ['pɛstəʳ] *vt* tormentare, molestare

pesticide ['pɛstɪsaɪd] *n* pesticida *m*

pet [pɛt] *n* animale *m* domestico ▷ *cpd* favorito(-a) ▷ *vt* accarezzare; **teacher's ~** favorito(-a) del maestro

petal ['pɛtl] *n* petalo

petite [pə'tiːt] *adj* piccolo(-a) e aggraziato(-a)

petition [pə'tɪʃən] *n* petizione *f*

petrified ['pɛtrɪfaɪd] *adj* (*fig*) morto(-a) di paura

petrol ['pɛtrəl] (BRIT) *n* benzina; **two/four-star ~** ≈ benzina normale/super;

I've run out of ~ sono rimasto senza benzina

> Be careful not to translate ***petrol*** by the Italian word ***petrolio***.

petroleum [pəˈtrəulɪəm] *n* petrolio
petrol: **petrol pump** (BRIT) *n* (*in car, at garage*) pompa di benzina; **petrol station** (BRIT) *n* stazione *f* di rifornimento; **petrol tank** (BRIT) *n* serbatoio della benzina
petticoat [ˈpɛtɪkəut] *n* sottana
petty [ˈpɛtɪ] *adj* (*mean*) meschino(-a); (*unimportant*) insignificante
pew [pjuː] *n* panca (di chiesa)
pewter [ˈpjuːtəʳ] *n* peltro
phantom [ˈfæntəm] *n* fantasma *m*
pharmacist [ˈfɑːməsɪst] *n* farmacista *m/f*
pharmacy [ˈfɑːməsɪ] *n* farmacia
phase [feɪz] *n* fase *f*, periodo; **phase in** *vt* introdurre gradualmente; **phase out** *vt* (*machinery*) eliminare gradualmente; (*product*) ritirare gradualmente; (*job, subsidy*) abolire gradualmente
Ph.D. *n abbr* = **Doctor of Philosophy**
pheasant [ˈfɛznt] *n* fagiano
phenomena [fəˈnɔmɪnə] *npl of* **phenomenon**
phenomenal [fɪˈnɔmɪnl] *adj* fenomenale
phenomenon [fəˈnɔmɪnən] (*pl* **phenomena**) *n* fenomeno
Philippines [ˈfɪlɪpiːnz] *npl* **the ~** le Filippine
philosopher [fɪˈlɔsəfəʳ] *n* filosofo(-a)
philosophical [fɪləˈsɔfɪkl] *adj* filosofico(-a)
philosophy [fɪˈlɔsəfɪ] *n* filosofia
phlegm [flɛm] *n* flemma
phobia [ˈfəubjə] *n* fobia
phone [fəun] *n* telefono ▷ *vt* telefonare; **to be on the ~** avere il telefono; (*be calling*) essere al telefono; **phone back** *vt, vi* richiamare; **phone up** *vt* telefonare a ▷ *vi* telefonare; **phone book** *n* guida del telefono, elenco telefonico; **phone booth** *n* = **phone box**; **phone box** *n* cabina telefonica; **phone call** *n* telefonata; **phonecard** *n* scheda telefonica; **phone number** *n* numero di telefono
phonetics [fəˈnɛtɪks] *n* fonetica
phoney [ˈfəunɪ] *adj* falso(-a), fasullo(-a)
photo [ˈfəutəu] *n* foto *f inv*
photo... [ˈfəutəu] *prefix*: **photo album** *n* (*new*) album *m inv* per fotografie; (*containing photos*) album *m inv* delle fotografie; **photocopier** *n* fotocopiatrice *f*; **photocopy** *n* fotocopia ▷ *vt* fotocopiare
photograph [ˈfəutəgræf] *n* fotografia ▷ *vt* fotografare; **photographer** [fəˈtɔgrəfəʳ] *n* fotografo; **photography** [fəˈtɔgrəfɪ] *n* fotografia
phrase [freɪz] *n* espressione *f*; (*Ling*) locuzione *f*; (*Mus*) frase *f* ▷ *vt* esprimere; **phrase book** *n* vocabolarietto
physical [ˈfɪzɪkl] *adj* fisico(-a); **physical education** *n* educazione *f* fisica; **physically** *adv* fisicamente
physician [fɪˈzɪʃən] *n* medico
physicist [ˈfɪzɪsɪst] *n* fisico
physics [ˈfɪzɪks] *n* fisica
physiotherapist [fɪzɪəuˈθɛrəpɪst] *n* fisioterapista *m/f*
physiotherapy [fɪzɪəuˈθɛrəpɪ] *n* fisioterapia
physique [fɪˈziːk] *n* fisico; costituzione *f*
pianist [ˈpiːənɪst] *n* pianista *m/f*
piano [pɪˈænəu] *n* pianoforte *m*
pick [pɪk] *n* (*tool*: *also*: **~-axe**) piccone *m* ▷ *vt* scegliere; (*gather*) cogliere; (*remove*) togliere; (*lock*) far scattare; **take your ~** scelga; **the ~ of** il fior fiore di; **to ~ one's nose** mettersi le dita nel naso; **to ~ one's teeth** pulirsi i denti con lo stuzzicadenti; **to ~ a quarrel** attaccar briga; **pick on** *vt fus* (*person*) avercela con; **pick out** *vt* scegliere;

(*distinguish*) distinguere; **pick up** *vi* (*improve*) migliorarsi ▷ *vt* raccogliere; (*Police, Radio*) prendere; (*collect*) passare a prendere; (*Aut*: *give lift to*) far salire; (*person*: *for sexual encounter*) rimorchiare; (*learn*) imparare; **to pick up speed** acquistare velocità; **to pick o.s. up** rialzarsi

pickle ['pɪkl] *n* (*also*: **~s**: *as condiment*) sottaceti *mpl*; (*fig*: *mess*) pasticcio ▷ *vt* mettere sottaceto; mettere in salamoia

pickpocket ['pɪkpɔkɪt] *n* borsaiolo

pick-up ['pɪkʌp] *n* (BRIT: *on record player*) pick-up *m inv*; (*small truck*: *also*: **~ truck, ~ van**) camioncino

picnic ['pɪknɪk] *n* picnic *m inv*; **picnic area** *n* area per il picnic

picture ['pɪktʃəʳ] *n* quadro; (*painting*) pittura; (*photograph*) foto(grafia); (*drawing*) disegno; (*film*) film *m inv* ▷ *vt* raffigurarsi; **pictures** (BRIT) *npl* (*cinema*): **the ~s** il cinema; **would you take a ~ of us, please?** può farci una foto, per favore?; **picture frame** *n* cornice *m inv*; **picture messaging** *n* picture messaging *m*, invio di messaggini con disegni

picturesque [pɪktʃə'rɛsk] *adj* pittoresco(-a)

pie [paɪ] *n* torta; (*of meat*) pasticcio

piece [pi:s] *n* pezzo; (*of land*) appezzamento; (*item*): **a ~ of furniture/advice** un mobile/ consiglio ▷ *vt* **to ~ together** mettere insieme; **to take to ~s** smontare

pie chart *n* grafico a torta

pier [pɪəʳ] *n* molo; (*of bridge etc*) pila

pierce [pɪəs] *vt* forare; (*with arrow etc*) trafiggere; **pierced** *adj*: **I've got pierced ears** ho i buchi per gli orecchini

pig [pɪg] *n* maiale *m*, porco

pigeon ['pɪdʒən] *n* piccione *m*

piggy bank ['pɪgɪ-] *n* salvadanaro

pigsty ['pɪgstaɪ] *n* porcile *m*

pigtail ['pɪgteɪl] *n* treccina

pike [paɪk] *n* (*fish*) luccio

pilchard ['pɪltʃəd] *n* specie di sardina

pile [paɪl] *n* (*pillar, of books*) pila; (*heap*) mucchio; (*of carpet*) pelo; **to ~ into** (*car*) stiparsi *or* ammucchiarsi in; **pile up** *vt* ammucchiare ▷ *vi* ammucchiarsi; **piles** [paɪlz] *npl* emorroidi *fpl*; **pile-up** ['paɪlʌp] *n* (*Aut*) tamponamento a catena

pilgrimage ['pɪlgrɪmɪdʒ] *n* pellegrinaggio

pill [pɪl] *n* pillola; **the ~** la pillola

pillar ['pɪləʳ] *n* colonna

pillow ['pɪləu] *n* guanciale *m*; **pillowcase** *n* federa

pilot ['paɪlət] *n* pilota *m/f* ▷ *cpd* (*scheme etc*) pilota *inv* ▷ *vt* pilotare; **pilot light** *n* fiamma pilota

pimple ['pɪmpl] *n* foruncolo

pin [pɪn] *n* spillo; (*Tech*) perno ▷ *vt* attaccare con uno spillo; **~s and needles** formicolio; **to ~ sb down** (*fig*) obbligare qn a pronunziarsi; **to ~ sth on sb** (*fig*) addossare la colpa di qc a qn

PIN *n abbr* (= *personal identification number*) codice *m* segreto

pinafore ['pɪnəfɔːʳ] *n* (*also*: **~ dress**) grembiule *m* (senza maniche)

pinch [pɪntʃ] *n* pizzicotto, pizzico ▷ *vt* pizzicare; (*inf*: *steal*) grattare; **at a ~** in caso di bisogno

pine [paɪn] *n* (*also*: **~ tree**) pino ▷ *vi* **to ~ for** struggersi dal desiderio di

pineapple ['paɪnæpl] *n* ananas *m inv*

ping [pɪŋ] *n* (*noise*) tintinnio; **ping-pong®** *n* ping-pong® *m*

pink [pɪŋk] *adj* rosa *inv* ▷ *n* (*colour*) rosa *m inv*; (*Bot*) garofano

pinpoint ['pɪnpɔɪnt] *vt* indicare con precisione

pint [paɪnt] *n* pinta (BRIT = 0.57*l*; US = 0.47*l*); (BRIT: *inf*) ≈ birra da mezzo

pioneer [paɪə'nɪəʳ] *n* pioniere(-a)

pious ['paɪəs] *adj* pio(-a)

pip [pɪp] *n* (*seed*) seme *m*; (BRIT: *time signal on radio*) segnale *m* orario

pipe [paɪp] *n* tubo; (*for smoking*)

pipa ▷ *vt* portare per mezzo di tubazione; **pipeline** *n* conduttura; (*for oil*) oleodotto; **piper** *n* piffero; suonatore(-trice) di cornamusa
pirate ['paɪərət] *n* pirata *m* ▷ *vt* riprodurre abusivamente
Pisces ['paɪsiːz] *n* Pesci *mpl*
piss [pɪs] (*inf*) *vi* pisciare; **pissed** (*inf*) *adj* (*drunk*) ubriaco(-a) fradicio(-a)
pistol ['pɪstl] *n* pistola
piston ['pɪstən] *n* pistone *m*
pit [pɪt] *n* buca, fossa; (*also:* **coal ~**) miniera; (*quarry*) cava ▷ *vt* **to ~ sb against sb** opporre qn a qn
pitch [pɪtʃ] *n* (BRIT *Sport*) campo; (*Mus*) tono; (*tar*) pece *f*; (*fig*) grado, punto ▷ *vt* (*throw*) lanciare ▷ *vi* (*fall*) cascare; **to ~ a tent** piantare una tenda; **pitch-black** *adj* nero(-a) come la pece
pitfall ['pɪtfɔːl] *n* trappola
pith [pɪθ] *n* (*of plant*) midollo; (*of orange*) parte *f* interna della scorza; (*fig*) essenza, succo; vigore *m*
pitiful ['pɪtɪful] *adj* (*touching*) pietoso(-a)
pity ['pɪtɪ] *n* pietà ▷ *vt* aver pietà di; **what a ~!** che peccato!
pizza ['piːtsə] *n* pizza
placard ['plækɑːd] *n* affisso
place [pleɪs] *n* posto, luogo; (*proper position, rank, seat*) posto; (*house*) casa, alloggio; (*home*): **at/to his ~** a casa sua ▷ *vt* (*object*) posare, mettere; (*identify*) riconoscere; individuare; **to take ~** aver luogo; succedere; **to change ~s with sb** scambiare il posto con qn; **out of ~** (*not suitable*) inopportuno(-a); **in the first ~** in primo luogo; **to ~ an order** dare un'ordinazione; **to be ~d** (*in race, exam*) classificarsi; **place mat** *n* sottopiatto; (*in linen etc*) tovaglietta; **placement** *n* collocamento; (*job*) lavoro
placid ['plæsɪd] *adj* placido(-a), calmo(-a)
plague [pleɪg] *n* peste *f* ▷ *vt* tormentare
plaice [pleɪs] *n inv* pianuzza
plain [pleɪn] *adj* (*clear*) chiaro(-a), palese; (*simple*) semplice; (*frank*) franco(-a), aperto(-a); (*not handsome*) bruttino(-a); (*without seasoning etc*) scondito(-a); naturale; (*in one colour*) tinta unita *inv* ▷ *adv* francamente, chiaramente ▷ *n* pianura; **plain chocolate** *n* cioccolato fondente; **plainly** *adv* chiaramente; (*frankly*) francamente
plaintiff ['pleɪntɪf] *n* attore(-trice)
plait [plæt] *n* treccia
plan [plæn] *n* pianta; (*scheme*) progetto, piano ▷ *vt* (*think in advance*) progettare; (*prepare*) organizzare ▷ *vi* far piani *or* progetti; **to ~ to do** progettare di fare
plane [pleɪn] *n* (*Aviat*) aereo; (*tree*) platano; (*tool*) pialla; (*Art, Math etc*) piano ▷ *adj* piano(-a), piatto(-a) ▷ *vt* (*with tool*) piallare
planet ['plænɪt] *n* pianeta *m*
plank [plæŋk] *n* tavola, asse *f*
planning ['plænɪŋ] *n* progettazione *f*; **family ~** pianificazione *f* delle nascite
plant [plɑːnt] *n* pianta; (*machinery*) impianto; (*factory*) fabbrica ▷ *vt* piantare; (*bomb*) mettere
plantation [plæn'teɪʃən] *n* piantagione *f*
plaque [plæk] *n* placca
plasma TV ['plæzmə-] *n* TV *f inv* al plasma
plaster ['plɑːstə^r] *n* intonaco; (*also:* **~ of Paris**) gesso; (BRIT: *also:* **sticking ~**) cerotto ▷ *vt* intonacare; ingessare; (*cover*): **to ~ with** coprire di; **plaster cast** *n* (*Med*) ingessatura, gesso; (*model, statue*) modello in gesso
plastic ['plæstɪk] *n* plastica ▷ *adj* (*made of plastic*) di *or* in plastica; **plastic bag** *n* sacchetto di plastica; **plastic surgery** *n* chirurgia plastica
plate [pleɪt] *n* (*dish*) piatto; (*in book*) tavola; (*dental plate*) dentiera; **gold/**

silver ~ vasellame *m* d'oro/d'argento
plateau ['plætəu] (*pl* **plateaus** *or* **plateaux**) *n* altipiano
platform ['plætfɔːm] *n* (*stage, at meeting*) palco; (*Rail*) marciapiede *m*; (BRIT: *of bus*) piattaforma; **which ~ does the train for Rome go from?** da che binario parte il treno per Roma?
platinum ['plætɪnəm] *n* platino
platoon [plə'tuːn] *n* plotone *m*
platter ['plætəʳ] *n* piatto
plausible ['plɔːzɪbl] *adj* plausibile, credibile; (*person*) convincente
play [pleɪ] *n* gioco; (*Theatre*) commedia ▷ *vt* (*game*) giocare a; (*team, opponent*) giocare contro; (*instrument, piece of music*) suonare; (*record, tape*) ascoltare; (*role, part*) interpretare ▷ *vi* giocare; suonare; recitare; **to ~ safe** giocare sul sicuro; **play back** *vt* riascoltare, risentire; **play up** *vi* (*cause trouble*) fare i capricci; **player** *n* giocatore(-trice); (*Theatre*) attore(-trice); (*Mus*) musicista *m/f*; **playful** *adj* giocoso(-a); **playground** *n* (*in school*) cortile *m* per la ricreazione; (*in park*) parco *m* giochi *inv*; **playgroup** *n* giardino d'infanzia; **playing card** *n* carta da gioco; **playing field** *n* campo sportivo; **playschool** *n* = **playgroup**; **playtime** *n* (*Scol*) ricreazione *f*; **playwright** *n* drammaturgo(-a)
plc *abbr* (= *public limited company*) *società per azioni a responsabilità limitata quotata in borsa*
plea [pliː] *n* (*request*) preghiera, domanda; (*Law*) (argomento di) difesa
plead [pliːd] *vt* patrocinare; (*give as excuse*) addurre a pretesto ▷ *vi* (*Law*) perorare la causa; (*beg*): **to ~ with sb** implorare qn
pleasant ['plɛznt] *adj* piacevole, gradevole
please [pliːz] *excl* per piacere!, per favore!; (*acceptance*): **yes, ~** sì, grazie ▷ *vt* piacere a ▷ *vi* piacere; (*think fit*): **do as you ~** faccia come le pare; **~ yourself!** come ti (*or* le) pare!; **pleased** *adj* **pleased (with)** contento(-a) (di); **pleased to meet you!** piacere!
pleasure ['plɛʒəʳ] *n* piacere *m*; **"it's a ~"** "prego"
pleat [pliːt] *n* piega
pledge [plɛdʒ] *n* pegno; (*promise*) promessa ▷ *vt* impegnare; promettere
plentiful ['plɛntɪful] *adj* abbondante, copioso(-a)
plenty ['plɛntɪ] *n* **~ of** tanto(-a), molto(-a); un'abbondanza di
pliers ['plaɪəz] *npl* pinza
plight [plaɪt] *n* situazione *f* critica
plod [plɔd] *vi* camminare a stento; (*fig*) sgobbare
plonk [plɔŋk] (*inf*) *n* (BRIT: *wine*) vino da poco ▷ *vt* **to ~ sth down** buttare giù qc bruscamente
plot [plɔt] *n* congiura, cospirazione *f*; (*of story, play*) trama; (*of land*) lotto ▷ *vt* (*mark out*) fare la pianta di; rilevare; (*: diagram etc*) tracciare; (*conspire*) congiurare, cospirare ▷ *vi* congiurare
plough [plau] (US **plow**) *n* aratro ▷ *vt* (*earth*) arare; **to ~ money into** (*company etc*) investire danaro in; **ploughman's lunch** ['plaumənz-] (BRIT) *n* *pasto a base di pane, formaggio e birra*
plow [plau] (US) = **plough**
ploy [plɔɪ] *n* stratagemma *m*
pluck [plʌk] *vt* (*fruit*) cogliere; (*musical instrument*) pizzicare; (*bird*) spennare; (*hairs*) togliere ▷ *n* coraggio, fegato; **to ~ up courage** farsi coraggio
plug [plʌg] *n* tappo; (*Elec*) spina; (*Aut*: *also*: **spark(ing) ~**) candela ▷ *vt* (*hole*) tappare; (*inf*: *advertise*) spingere; **plug in** *vt* (*Elec*) attaccare a una presa; **plughole** *n* (BRIT) scarico
plum [plʌm] *n* (*fruit*) susina
plumber ['plʌməʳ] *n* idraulico
plumbing ['plʌmɪŋ] *n* (*trade*) lavoro di idraulico; (*piping*) tubature *fpl*

plummet ['plʌmɪt] *vi*: **to ~ (down)** cadere a piombo
plump [plʌmp] *adj* grassoccio(-a) ▷ *vi* **to ~ for** (*inf: choose*) decidersi per
plunge [plʌndʒ] *n* tuffo; (*fig*) caduta ▷ *vt* immergere ▷ *vi* (*fall*) cadere, precipitare; (*dive*) tuffarsi; **to take the ~** saltare il fosso
plural ['pluərl] *adj* plurale ▷ *n* plurale *m*
plus [plʌs] *n* (*also:* **~ sign**) segno più ▷ *prep* più; **ten/twenty ~** più di dieci/venti
ply [plaɪ] *vt* (*a trade*) esercitare ▷ *vi* (*ship*) fare il servizio ▷ *n* (*of wool, rope*) capo; **to ~ sb with drink** dare di bere continuamente a qn; **plywood** *n* legno compensato
P.M. *n abbr* = **prime minister**
p.m. *adv abbr* (= *post meridiem*) del pomeriggio
PMS *n abbr* (= *premenstrual syndrome*) sindrome *f* premestruale
PMT *n abbr* (= *premenstrual tension*) sindrome *f* premestruale
pneumatic drill [nju:'mætɪk-] *n* martello pneumatico
pneumonia [nju:'məunɪə] *n* polmonite *f*
poach [pəutʃ] *vt* (*cook: egg*) affogare; (*: fish*) cuocere in bianco; (*steal*) cacciare (*or* pescare) di frodo ▷ *vi* fare il bracconiere; **poached** *adj* (*egg*) affogato(-a)
P.O. Box *n abbr* = **Post Office Box**
pocket ['pɔkɪt] *n* tasca ▷ *vt* intascare; **to be out of ~** (BRIT) rimetterci; **pocketbook** (US) *n* (*wallet*) portafoglio; **pocket money** *n* paghetta, settimana
pod [pɔd] *n* guscio
podcast ['pɒdka:st] *n* podcast *m inv*
podiatrist [pɔ'di:ətrɪst] (US) *n* callista *m/f*, pedicure *m/f*
podium ['pəudɪəm] *n* podio
poem ['pəuɪm] *n* poesia
poet ['pəuɪt] *n* poeta/essa; **poetic** [-'ɛtɪk] *adj* poetico(-a); **poetry** *n* poesia
poignant ['pɔɪnjənt] *adj* struggente
point [pɔɪnt] *n* (*gen*) punto; (*tip: of needle etc*) punta; (*in time*) punto, momento; (*Scol*) voto; (*main idea, important part*) nocciolo; (*Elec*) presa (di corrente); (*also:* **decimal ~**): **2 ~ 3 (2.3)** 2 virgola 3 (2,3) ▷ *vt* (*show*) indicare; (*gun etc*): **to ~ sth at** puntare qc contro ▷ *vi* **to ~ at** mostrare a dito; **points** *npl* (*Aut*) puntine *fpl*; (*Rail*) scambio; **to be on the ~ of doing sth** essere sul punto di *or* stare per fare qc; **to make a ~** fare un'osservazione; **to get/miss the ~** capire/non capire; **to come to the ~** venire al fatto; **there's no ~ in doing** è inutile (fare); **point out** *vt* far notare; **point-blank** *adv* (*also:* **at point-blank range**) a bruciapelo; (*fig*) categoricamente; **pointed** *adj* (*shape*) aguzzo(-a), appuntito(-a); (*remark*) specifico(-a); **pointer** *n* (*needle*) lancetta; (*fig*) indicazione *f*, consiglio; **pointless** *adj* inutile, vano(-a); **point of view** *n* punto di vista
poison ['pɔɪzn] *n* veleno ▷ *vt* avvelenare; **poisonous** *adj* velenoso(-a)
poke [pəuk] *vt* (*fire*) attizzare; (*jab with finger, stick etc*) punzecchiare; (*put*): **to ~ sth in(to)** spingere qc dentro; **poke about** *or* **around** *vi* frugare; **poke out** *vi* (*stick out*) sporger fuori
poker ['pəukər] *n* attizzatoio; (*Cards*) poker *m*
Poland ['pəulənd] *n* Polonia
polar ['pəulər] *adj* polare; **polar bear** *n* orso bianco
Pole [pəul] *n* polacco(-a)
pole [pəul] *n* (*of wood*) palo; (*Elec, Geo*) polo; **pole bean** (US) *n* (*runner bean*) fagiolino; **pole vault** *n* salto con l'asta
police [pə'li:s] *n* polizia ▷ *vt* mantenere l'ordine in; **police car** *n* macchina della polizia; **police**

constable (BRIT) *n* agente *m* di polizia; **police force** *n* corpo di polizia, polizia; **policeman** (*irreg*) *n* poliziotto, agente *m* di polizia; **police officer** *n* = **police constable**; **police station** *n* posto di polizia; **policewoman** (*irreg*) *n* donna *f* poliziotto *inv*

policy ['pɔlɪsɪ] *n* politica; (*also:* **insurance ~**) polizza (d'assicurazione)

polio ['pəulɪəu] *n* polio *f*

Polish ['pəulɪʃ] *adj* polacco(-a) ▷ *n* (*Ling*) polacco

polish ['pɔlɪʃ] *n* (*for shoes*) lucido; (*for floor*) cera; (*for nails*) smalto; (*shine*) lucentezza, lustro; (*fig: refinement*) raffinatezza ▷ *vt* lucidare; (*fig: improve*) raffinare; **polish off** *vt* (*food*) mangiarsi; **polished** *adj* (*fig*) raffinato(-a)

polite [pə'laɪt] *adj* cortese; **politeness** *n* cortesia

political [pə'lɪtɪkl] *adj* politico(-a); **politically** *adv* politicamente; **politically correct** politicamente corretto(-a)

politician [pɔlɪ'tɪʃən] *n* politico

politics ['pɔlɪtɪks] *n* politica ▷ *npl* (*views, policies*) idee *fpl* politiche

poll [pəul] *n* scrutinio; (*votes cast*) voti *mpl*; (*also:* **opinion ~**) sondaggio (d'opinioni) ▷ *vt* ottenere

pollen ['pɔlən] *n* polline *m*

polling station ['pəulɪŋ-] (BRIT) *n* sezione *f* elettorale

pollute [pə'lu:t] *vt* inquinare

pollution [pə'lu:ʃən] *n* inquinamento

polo ['pəuləu] *n* polo; **polo-neck** *n* collo alto; (*also:* **polo-neck sweater**) dolcevita ▷ *adj* a collo alto; **polo shirt** *n* polo *f inv*

polyester [pɔlɪ'ɛstəʳ] *n* poliestere *m*

polystyrene [pɔlɪ'staɪri:n] *n* polistirolo

polythene ['pɔlɪθi:n] *n* politene *m*; **polythene bag** *n* sacco di plastica

pomegranate ['pɔmɪgrænɪt] *n* melagrana

pompous ['pɔmpəs] *adj* pomposo(-a)

pond [pɔnd] *n* pozza; stagno

ponder ['pɔndəʳ] *vt* ponderare, riflettere su

pony ['pəunɪ] *n* pony *m inv*; **ponytail** *n* coda di cavallo; **pony trekking** [-trɛkɪŋ] (BRIT) *n* escursione *f* a cavallo

poodle ['pu:dl] *n* barboncino, barbone *m*

pool [pu:l] *n* (*puddle*) pozza; (*pond*) stagno; (*also:* **swimming ~**) piscina; (*fig: of light*) cerchio; (*billiards*) *specie di biliardo a buca* ▷ *vt* mettere in comune; **pools** *npl* (*football pools*) ≈ totocalcio; **typing ~** servizio comune di dattilografia

poor [puəʳ] *adj* povero(-a); (*mediocre*) mediocre, cattivo(-a) ▷ *npl* **the ~** i poveri; **~ in** povero(-a) di; **poorly** *adv* poveramente; male ▷ *adj* indisposto(-a), malato(-a)

pop [pɔp] *n* (*noise*) schiocco; (*Mus*) musica pop; (*drink*) bibita gasata; (US: *inf: father*) babbo ▷ *vt* (*put*) mettere (in fretta) ▷ *vi* scoppiare; (*cork*) schioccare; **pop in** *vi* passare; **pop out** *vi* fare un salto fuori; **popcorn** *n* pop-corn *m*

poplar ['pɔpləʳ] *n* pioppo

popper ['pɔpəʳ] *n* bottone *m* a pressione

poppy ['pɔpɪ] *n* papavero

Popsicle® ['pɔpsɪkl] (US) *n* (*ice lolly*) ghiacciolo

pop star *n* pop star *f inv*

popular ['pɔpjuləʳ] *adj* popolare; (*fashionable*) in voga; **popularity** [-'lærɪtɪ] *n* popolarità

population [pɔpju'leɪʃən] *n* popolazione *f*

pop-up *adj* (*Comput: menu, window*) a comparsa

porcelain ['pɔ:slɪn] *n* porcellana

porch [pɔ:tʃ] *n* veranda

pore [pɔ:ʳ] *n* poro ▷ *vi* **to ~ over** essere immerso(-a) in

pork [pɔːk] *n* carne *f* di maiale; **pork chop** *n* braciola *or* costoletta di maiale; **pork pie** *n* (BRIT: *Culin*) pasticcio di maiale in crosta

porn [pɔːn] (*inf*) *n* pornografia ▷ *adj* porno *inv*; **pornographic** [pɔːnə'græfɪk] *adj* pornografico(-a); **pornography** [pɔː'nɔgrəfɪ] *n* pornografia

porridge ['pɔrɪdʒ] *n* porridge *m*

port [pɔːt] *n* (*gen, wine*) porto; (*Naut: left side*) babordo

portable ['pɔːtəbl] *adj* portatile

porter ['pɔːtə^r] *n* (*for luggage*) facchino, portabagagli *m inv*; (*doorkeeper*) portiere *m*, portinaio

portfolio [pɔːt'fəulɪəu] *n* (*case*) cartella; (*Pol, Finance*) portafoglio; (*of artist*) raccolta dei propri lavori

portion ['pɔːʃən] *n* porzione *f*

port of call *n* (porto di) scalo

portrait ['pɔːtreɪt] *n* ritratto

portray [pɔː'treɪ] *vt* fare il ritratto di; (*character on stage*) rappresentare; (*in writing*) ritrarre

Portugal ['pɔːtjugl] *n* Portogallo

Portuguese [pɔːtju'giːz] *adj* portoghese ▷ *n inv* portoghese *m/f*; (*Ling*) portoghese *m*

pose [pəuz] *n* posa ▷ *vi* posare; (*pretend*): **to ~ as** atteggiarsi a, posare a ▷ *vt* porre

posh [pɔʃ] (*inf*) *adj* elegante; (*family*) per bene

position [pə'zɪʃən] *n* posizione *f*; (*job*) posto ▷ *vt* sistemare

positive ['pɔzɪtɪv] *adj* positivo(-a); (*certain*) sicuro(-a), certo(-a); (*definite*) preciso(-a), definitivo(-a); **positively** *adv* (*affirmatively, enthusiastically*) positivamente; (*decisively*) decisamente; (*really*) assolutamente

possess [pə'zɛs] *vt* possedere; **possession** [pə'zɛʃən] *n* possesso; **possessions** *npl* (*belongings*) beni *mpl*; **possessive** *adj* possessivo(-a)

possibility [pɔsɪ'bɪlɪtɪ] *n* possibilità *f inv*

possible ['pɔsɪbl] *adj* possibile; **as big as ~** il più grande possibile; **possibly** ['pɔsɪblɪ] *adv* (*perhaps*) forse; **if you possibly can** se le è possibile; **I cannot possibly come** proprio non posso venire

post [pəust] *n* (BRIT) posta; (: *collection*) levata; (*job, situation*) posto; (*Mil*) postazione *f*; (*pole*) palo ▷ *vt* (BRIT: *send by post*) imbucare; (: *appoint*): **to ~ to** assegnare a; **where can I ~ these cards?** dove posso imbucare queste cartoline?; **postage** *n* affrancatura; **postal** *adj* postale; **postal order** *n* vaglia *m inv* postale; **postbox** (BRIT) *n* cassetta postale; **postcard** *n* cartolina; **postcode** *n* (BRIT) codice *m* (di avviamento) postale

poster ['pəustə^r] *n* manifesto, affisso

postgraduate ['pəust'grædjuət] *n* *laureato/a che continua gli studi*

postman ['pəustmən] (*irreg*) *n* postino

postmark ['pəustmɑːk] *n* bollo *or* timbro postale

post-mortem [-'mɔːtəm] *n* autopsia

post office *n* (*building*) ufficio postale; (*organization*): **the Post Office** ≈ le Poste e Telecomunicazioni

postpone [pəs'pəun] *vt* rinviare

posture ['pɔstʃə^r] *n* portamento; (*pose*) posa, atteggiamento

postwoman ['pəustwumən] (BRIT: *irreg*) *n* postina

pot [pɔt] *n* (*for cooking*) pentola; casseruola; (*teapot*) teiera; (*coffeepot*) caffettiera; (*for plants, jam*) vaso; (*inf: marijuana*) erba ▷ *vt* (*plant*) piantare in vaso; **a ~ of tea for two** tè per due; **to go to ~** (*inf: work, performance*) andare in malora

potato [pə'teɪtəu] (*pl* **potatoes**) *n* patata; **potato peeler** *n* sbucciapatate *m inv*

potent ['pəutnt] *adj* potente, forte

potential [pə'tɛnʃl] *adj* potenziale ▷ *n* possibilità *fpl*
pothole ['pɔthəul] *n* (*in road*) buca; (BRIT: *underground*) caverna
pot plant *n* pianta in vaso
potter ['pɔtəʳ] *n* vasaio ▷ *vi* **to ~ around, ~ about** (BRIT) lavoracchiare; **pottery** *n* ceramiche *fpl*; (*factory*) fabbrica di ceramiche
potty ['pɔtɪ] *adj* (*inf*: *mad*) tocco(-a) ▷ *n* (*child's*) vasino
pouch [pautʃ] *n* borsa; (*Zool*) marsupio
poultry ['pəultrɪ] *n* pollame *m*
pounce [pauns] *vi* **to ~ (on)** piombare (su)
pound [paund] *n* (*weight*) libbra; (*money*) (lira) sterlina ▷ *vt* (*beat*) battere; (*crush*) pestare, polverizzare ▷ *vi* (*beat*) battere, martellare; **pound sterling** *n* sterlina (inglese)
pour [pɔːʳ] *vt* versare ▷ *vi* riversarsi; (*rain*) piovere a dirotto; **pour in** *vi* affluire in gran quantità; **pour out** *vi* (*people*) uscire a fiumi ▷ *vt* vuotare; versare; (*fig*) sfogare; **pouring** *adj*: **pouring rain** pioggia torrenziale
pout [paut] *vi* sporgere le labbra; fare il broncio
poverty ['pɔvətɪ] *n* povertà, miseria
powder ['paudəʳ] *n* polvere *f* ▷ *vt* **to ~ one's face** incipriarsi il viso; **powdered milk** *n* latte *m* in polvere
power ['pauəʳ] *n* (*strength*) potenza, forza; (*ability, Pol*: *of party, leader*) potere *m*; (*Elec*) corrente *f*; **to be in ~** (*Pol etc*) essere al potere; **power cut** (BRIT) *n* interruzione *f* or mancanza di corrente; **power failure** *n* interruzione *f* della corrente elettrica; **powerful** *adj* potente, forte; **powerless** *adj* impotente; **powerless to do** impossibilitato(-a) a fare; **power point** (BRIT) *n* presa di corrente; **power station** *n* centrale *f* elettrica
p.p. *abbr* = **per procurationem**; **p.p. J. Smith** per J. Smith; (= *pages*) p.p.
PR *abbr* = **public relations**
practical ['præktɪkl] *adj* pratico(-a); **practical joke** *n* beffa; **practically** *adv* praticamente
practice ['præktɪs] *n* pratica; (*of profession*) esercizio; (*at football etc*) allenamento; (*business*) gabinetto; clientela ▷ *vt, vi* (US) = **practise**; **in ~** (*in reality*) in pratica; **out of ~** fuori esercizio
practise ['præktɪs] (US **practice**) *vt* (*work at*: *piano, one's backhand etc*) esercitarsi a; (*train for*: *skiing, running etc*) allenarsi a; (*a sport, religion*) praticare; (*method*) usare; (*profession*) esercitare ▷ *vi* esercitarsi; (*train*) allenarsi; (*lawyer, doctor*) esercitare; **practising** *adj* (*Christian etc*) praticante; (*lawyer*) che esercita la professione
practitioner [præk'tɪʃənəʳ] *n* professionista *m/f*
pragmatic [præg'mætɪk] *adj* pragmatico(-a)
prairie ['prɛərɪ] *n* prateria
praise [preɪz] *n* elogio, lode *f* ▷ *vt* elogiare, lodare
pram [præm] (BRIT) *n* carrozzina
prank [præŋk] *n* burla
prawn [prɔːn] *n* gamberetto; **prawn cocktail** *n* cocktail *m inv* di gamberetti
pray [preɪ] *vi* pregare; **prayer** [prɛəʳ] *n* preghiera
preach [priːtʃ] *vt, vi* predicare; **preacher** *n* predicatore(-trice); (US: *minister*) pastore *m*
precarious [prɪ'kɛərɪəs] *adj* precario(-a)
precaution [prɪ'kɔːʃən] *n* precauzione *f*
precede [prɪ'siːd] *vt* precedere; **precedent** ['prɛsɪdənt] *n* precedente *m*; **preceding** [prɪ'siːdɪŋ] *adj* precedente
precinct ['priːsɪŋkt] (US) *n* circoscrizione *f*

precious ['prɛʃəs] *adj* prezioso(-a)
precise [prɪ'saɪs] *adj* preciso(-a); **precisely** *adv* precisamente
precision [prɪ'sɪʒən] *n* precisione *f*
predator ['prɛdətə^r] *n* predatore *m*
predecessor ['pri:dɪsɛsə^r] *n* predecessore(-a)
predicament [prɪ'dɪkəmənt] *n* situazione *f* difficile
predict [prɪ'dɪkt] *vt* predire; **predictable** *adj* prevedibile; **prediction** [prɪ'dɪkʃən] *n* predizione *f*
predominantly [prɪ'dɔmɪnəntlɪ] *adv* in maggior parte; soprattutto
preface ['prɛfəs] *n* prefazione *f*
prefect ['pri:fɛkt] *n* (BRIT: *in school*) studente(-essa) con funzioni disciplinari; (*French etc, Admin*) prefetto
prefer [prɪ'fə:^r] *vt* preferire; **to ~ doing** *or* **to do** preferire fare; **preferable** ['prɛfrəbl] *adj* preferibile; **preferably** ['prɛfrəblɪ] *adv* preferibilmente; **preference** ['prɛfrəns] *n* preferenza
prefix ['pri:fɪks] *n* prefisso
pregnancy ['prɛgnənsɪ] *n* gravidanza
pregnant ['prɛgnənt] *adj* incinta *ag*
prehistoric ['pri:hɪs'tɔrɪk] *adj* preistorico(-a)
prejudice ['prɛdʒudɪs] *n* pregiudizio; (*harm*) torto, danno; **prejudiced** *adj* **prejudiced (against)** prevenuto(-a) (contro); **prejudiced (in favour of)** ben disposto(-a) (verso)
preliminary [prɪ'lɪmɪnərɪ] *adj* preliminare
prelude ['prɛlju:d] *n* preludio
premature ['prɛmətʃuə^r] *adj* prematuro(-a)
premier ['prɛmɪə^r] *adj* primo(-a) ▷ *n* (*Pol*) primo ministro
première ['prɛmɪɛə^r] *n* prima
Premier League *n* ≈ serie A
premises ['prɛmɪsɪz] *npl* locale *m*; **on the ~** sul posto; **business ~** locali commerciali
premium ['pri:mɪəm] *n* premio; **to be at a ~** essere ricercatissimo
premonition [prɛmə'nɪʃən] *n* premonizione *f*
preoccupied [pri:'ɔkjupaɪd] *adj* preoccupato(-a)
prepaid [pri:'peɪd] *adj* pagato(-a) in anticipo
preparation [prɛpə'reɪʃən] *n* preparazione *f*; **preparations** *npl* (*for trip, war*) preparativi *mpl*
preparatory school [prɪ'pærətərɪ-] *n* scuola elementare privata
prepare [prɪ'pɛə^r] *vt* preparare ▷ *vi* **to ~ for** prepararsi a; **~d to** pronto(-a) a
preposition [prɛpə'zɪʃən] *n* preposizione *f*
prep school *n* = **preparatory school**
prerequisite [pri:'rɛkwɪzɪt] *n* requisito indispensabile
preschool ['pri:'sku:l] *adj* (*age*) prescolastico(-a); (*child*) in età prescolastica
prescribe [prɪ'skraɪb] *vt* (*Med*) prescrivere
prescription [prɪ'skrɪpʃən] *n* prescrizione *f*; (*Med*) ricetta; **could you write me a ~?** mi può fare una ricetta medica?
presence ['prɛzns] *n* presenza; **~ of mind** presenza di spirito
present [*adj, n* 'prɛznt, *vb* prɪ'zɛnt] *adj* presente; (*wife, residence, job*) attuale ▷ *n* (*actuality*): **the ~** il presente; (*gift*) regalo ▷ *vt* presentare; (*give*): **to ~ sb with sth** offrire qc a qn; **to give sb a ~** fare un regalo a qn; **at ~** al momento; **presentable** [prɪ'zɛntəbl] *adj* presentabile; **presentation** [-'teɪʃən] *n* presentazione *f*; (*ceremony*) consegna ufficiale; **present-day** *adj* attuale, d'oggigiorno; **presenter** *n* (*Radio, TV*) presentatore(-trice); **presently** *adv* (*soon*) fra poco, presto; (*at present*) al momento; **present participle** *n* participio presente
preservation [prɛzə'veɪʃən] *n* preservazione *f*, conservazione *f*

preservative [prɪ'zə:vətɪv] *n* conservante *m*
preserve [prɪ'zə:v] *vt* (*keep safe*) preservare, proteggere; (*maintain*) conservare; (*food*) mettere in conserva ▷ *n* (*often pl: jam*) marmellata; (*: fruit*) frutta sciroppata
preside [prɪ'zaɪd] *vi* **to ~ (over)** presiedere (a)
president ['prɛzɪdənt] *n* presidente *m*; **presidential** [-'dɛnʃl] *adj* presidenziale
press [prɛs] *n* (*newspapers etc*): **the P~** la stampa; (*tool, machine*) pressa; (*for wine*) torchio ▷ *vt* (*push*) premere, pigiare; (*squeeze*) spremere; (*: hand*) stringere; (*clothes: iron*) stirare; (*pursue*) incalzare; (*insist*): **to ~ sth on sb** far accettare qc da qn ▷ *vi* premere; accalcare; **we are ~ed for time** ci manca il tempo; **to ~ for sth** insistere per avere qc; **press conference** *n* conferenza *f* stampa *inv*; **pressing** *adj* urgente; **press stud** (BRIT) *n* bottone *m* a pressione; **press-up** (BRIT) *n* flessione *f* sulle braccia
pressure ['prɛʃə^r] *n* pressione *f*; **to put ~ on sb (to do)** mettere qn sotto pressione (affinché faccia); **pressure cooker** *n* pentola a pressione; **pressure group** *n* gruppo di pressione
prestige [prɛs'ti:ʒ] *n* prestigio
prestigious [prɛs'tɪdʒəs] *adj* prestigioso(-a)
presumably [prɪ'zju:məblɪ] *adv* presumibilmente
presume [prɪ'zju:m] *vt* supporre
pretence [prɪ'tɛns] (US **pretense**) *n* (*claim*) pretesa; **to make a ~ of doing** far finta di fare; **under false ~s** con l'inganno
pretend [prɪ'tɛnd] *vt* (*feign*) fingere ▷ *vi* far finta; **to ~ to do** far finta di fare
pretense [prɪ'tɛns] (US) *n* = **pretence**
pretentious [prɪ'tɛnʃəs] *adj* pretenzioso(-a)
pretext ['pri:tɛkst] *n* pretesto
pretty ['prɪtɪ] *adj* grazioso(-a), carino(-a) ▷ *adv* abbastanza, assai
prevail [prɪ'veɪl] *vi* (*win, be usual*) prevalere; (*persuade*): **to ~ (up)on sb to do** persuadere qn a fare; **prevailing** *adj* dominante
prevalent ['prɛvələnt] *adj* (*belief*) predominante; (*customs*) diffuso(-a); (*fashion*) corrente; (*disease*) comune
prevent [prɪ'vɛnt] *vt* **to ~ sb from doing** impedire a qn di fare; **to ~ sth from happening** impedire che qc succeda; **prevention** [-'vɛnʃən] *n* prevenzione *f*; **preventive** *adj* preventivo(-a)
preview ['pri:vju:] *n* (*of film*) anteprima
previous ['pri:vɪəs] *adj* precedente; anteriore; **previously** *adv* prima
prey [preɪ] *n* preda ▷ *vi* **to ~ on** far preda di; **it was ~ing on his mind** lo stava ossessionando
price [praɪs] *n* prezzo ▷ *vt* (*goods*) fissare il prezzo di; valutare; **priceless** *adj* inapprezzabile; **price list** *n* listino (dei) prezzi
prick [prɪk] *n* puntura ▷ *vt* pungere; **to ~ up one's ears** drizzare gli orecchi
prickly ['prɪklɪ] *adj* spinoso(-a)
pride [praɪd] *n* orgoglio; superbia ▷ *vt* **to ~ o.s. on** essere orgoglioso(-a) di, vantarsi di
priest [pri:st] *n* prete *m*, sacerdote *m*
primarily ['praɪmərɪlɪ] *adv* principalmente, essenzialmente
primary ['praɪmərɪ] *adj* primario(-a); (*first in importance*) primo(-a) ▷ *n* (US: *election*) primarie *fpl*; **primary school** (BRIT) *n* scuola elementare
prime [praɪm] *adj* primario(-a), fondamentale; (*excellent*) di prima qualità ▷ *vt* (*wood*) preparare; (*fig*) mettere al corrente ▷ *n* **in the ~ of life** nel fiore della vita; **Prime Minister** *n* primo ministro
primitive ['prɪmɪtɪv] *adj* primitivo(-a)

primrose ['prɪmrəuz] *n* primavera
prince [prɪns] *n* principe *m*
princess [prɪn'sɛs] *n* principessa
principal ['prɪnsɪpl] *adj* principale ▷ *n* (*headmaster*) preside *m*; **principally** *adv* principalmente
principle ['prɪnsɪpl] *n* principio; **in ~** in linea di principio; **on ~** per principio
print [prɪnt] *n* (*mark*) impronta; (*letters*) caratteri *mpl*; (*fabric*) tessuto stampato; (*Art, Phot*) stampa ▷ *vt* imprimere; (*publish*) stampare, pubblicare; (*write in capitals*) scrivere in stampatello; **out of ~** esaurito(-a); **print out** *vt* (*Comput*) stampare; **printer** *n* tipografo; (*machine*) stampante *f*; **printout** *n* tabulato
prior ['praɪəʳ] *adj* precedente; (*claim etc*) più importante; **~ to doing** prima di fare
priority [praɪ'ɔrɪtɪ] *n* priorità *f inv*; precedenza
prison ['prɪzn] *n* prigione *f* ▷ *cpd* (*system*) carcerario(-a); (*conditions, food*) nelle *or* delle prigioni; **prisoner** *n* prigioniero(-a); **prisoner-of-war** *n* prigioniero(-a) di guerra
pristine ['prɪstiːn] *adj* immacolato(-a)
privacy ['prɪvəsɪ] *n* solitudine *f*, intimità
private ['praɪvɪt] *adj* privato(-a); personale ▷ *n* soldato semplice; **"~"** (*on envelope*) "riservata"; (*on door*) "privato"; **in ~** in privato; **privately** *adv* in privato; (*within oneself*) dentro di sé; **private property** *n* proprietà privata; **private school** *n* scuola privata
privatize ['praɪvɪtaɪz] *vt* privatizzare
privilege ['prɪvɪlɪdʒ] *n* privilegio
prize [praɪz] *n* premio ▷ *adj* (*example, idiot*) perfetto(-a); (*bull, novel*) premiato(-a) ▷ *vt* apprezzare, pregiare; **prize-giving** *n* premiazione *f*; **prizewinner** *n* premiato(-a)
pro [prəu] *n* (*Sport*) professionista *m/f* ▷ *prep* pro; **the ~s and cons** il pro e il contro
probability [prɔbə'bɪlɪtɪ] *n* probabilità *f inv*; **in all ~** con tutta probabilità
probable ['prɔbəbl] *adj* probabile
probably ['prɔbəblɪ] *adv* probabilmente
probation [prə'beɪʃən] *n* **on ~** (*employee*) in prova; (*Law*) in libertà vigilata
probe [prəub] *n* (*Med, Space*) sonda; (*enquiry*) indagine *f*, investigazione *f* ▷ *vt* sondare, esplorare; indagare
problem ['prɔbləm] *n* problema *m*
procedure [prə'siːdʒəʳ] *n* (*Admin, Law*) procedura; (*method*) metodo, procedimento
proceed [prə'siːd] *vi* (*go forward*) avanzare, andare avanti; (*go about it*) procedere; (*continue*): **to ~ (with)** continuare; **to ~ to** andare a; passare a; **to ~ to do** mettersi a fare; **proceedings** *npl* misure *fpl*; (*Law*) procedimento; (*meeting*) riunione *f*; (*records*) rendiconti *mpl*; atti *mpl*; **proceeds** ['prəusiːdz] *npl* profitto, incasso
process ['prəusɛs] *n* processo; (*method*) metodo, sistema *m* ▷ *vt* trattare; (*information*) elaborare
procession [prə'sɛʃən] *n* processione *f*, corteo; **funeral ~** corteo funebre
proclaim [prə'kleɪm] *vt* proclamare, dichiarare
prod [prɔd] *vt* dare un colpetto a; pungolare ▷ *n* colpetto
produce [*n* 'prɔdjuːs, *vb* prə'djuːs] *n* (*Agr*) prodotto, prodotti *mpl* ▷ *vt* produrre; (*show*) esibire, mostrare; (*cause*) cagionare, causare; **producer** *n* (*Theatre*) regista *m/f*; (*Agr, Cinema*) produttore *m*
product ['prɔdʌkt] *n* prodotto; **production** [prə'dʌkʃən] *n* produzione *f*; **productive** [prə'dʌktɪv] *adj* produttivo(-a); **productivity** [prɔdʌk'tɪvɪtɪ] *n* produttività

Prof. *abbr* (= *professor*) Prof.
profession [prə'fɛʃən] *n* professione *f*; **professional** *n* professionista *m/f* ▷ *adj* professionale; (*work*) da professionista
professor [prə'fɛsər] *n* professore *m* (*titolare di una cattedra*); (*US*) professore(-essa)
profile ['prəufaɪl] *n* profilo
profit ['prɔfɪt] *n* profitto; beneficio ▷ *vi* **to ~ (by** *or* **from)** approfittare (di); **profitable** *adj* redditizio(-a)
profound [prə'faund] *adj* profondo(-a)
programme ['prəugræm] (*US* **program**) *n* programma *m* ▷ *vt* programmare; **programmer** (*US* **programer**) *n* programmatore(-trice); **programming** (*US* **programing**) *n* programmazione *f*
progress [*n* 'prəugrɛs, *vb* prə'grɛs] *n* progresso ▷ *vi* avanzare, procedere; **in ~** in corso; **to make ~** far progressi; **progressive** [-'grɛsɪv] *adj* progressivo(-a); (*person*) progressista
prohibit [prə'hɪbɪt] *vt* proibire, vietare
project [*n* 'prɔdʒɛkt, *vb* prə'dʒɛkt] *n* (*plan*) piano; (*venture*) progetto; (*Scol*) studio ▷ *vt* proiettare ▷ *vi* (*stick out*) sporgere; **projection** [prə'dʒɛkʃən] *n* proiezione *f*; sporgenza; **projector** [prə'dʒɛktər] *n* proiettore *m*
prolific [prə'lɪfɪk] *adj* (*artist etc*) fecondo(-a)
prolong [prə'lɔŋ] *vt* prolungare
prom [prɔm] *n abbr* = **promenade**; (*US: ball*) ballo studentesco

PROM

In Gran Bretagna i **Proms**, o "promenade concerts", sono concerti di musica classica, i più noti dei quali sono eseguiti nella prestigiosa **Royal Albert Hall** a Londra. Si chiamano così perché un tempo il pubblico seguiva i concerti in piedi, passeggiando (in inglese "promenade" voleva dire, appunto, passeggiata). Negli Stati Uniti, invece, con **prom**, si intende l'annuale ballo studentesco di un'università o di una scuola secondaria.

promenade [prɔmə'nɑːd] *n* (*by sea*) lungomare *m*
prominent ['prɔmɪnənt] *adj* (*standing out*) prominente; (*important*) importante
promiscuous [prə'mɪskjuəs] *adj* (*sexually*) di facili costumi
promise ['prɔmɪs] *n* promessa ▷ *vt, vi* promettere; **to ~ sb sth, ~ sth to sb** promettere qc a qn; **to ~ (sb) that/to do sth** promettere (a qn) che/di fare qc; **promising** *adj* promettente
promote [prə'məut] *vt* promuovere; (*venture, event*) organizzare; **promotion** [-'məuʃən] *n* promozione *f*
prompt [prɔmpt] *adj* rapido(-a), svelto(-a); puntuale; (*reply*) sollecito(-a) ▷ *adv* (*punctually*) in punto ▷ *n* (*Comput*) prompt *m* ▷ *vt* incitare; provocare; (*Theatre*) suggerire a; **to ~ sb to do** incitare qn a fare; **promptly** *adv* prontamente; puntualmente
prone [prəun] *adj* (*lying*) prono(-a); **~ to** propenso(-a) a, incline a
prong [prɔŋ] *n* rebbio, punta
pronoun ['prəunaun] *n* pronome *m*
pronounce [prə'nauns] *vt* pronunciare; **how do you ~ it?** come si pronuncia?
pronunciation [prənʌnsɪ'eɪʃən] *n* pronuncia
proof [pruːf] *n* prova; (*of book*) bozza; (*Phot*) provino ▷ *adj* **~ against** a prova di
prop [prɔp] *n* sostegno, appoggio ▷ *vt*

(*also*: **~ up**) sostenere, appoggiare; (*lean*): **to ~ sth against** appoggiare qc contro *or* a; **props** oggetti *m inv* di scena; **prop up** *vt* sostenere, appoggiare
propaganda [prɔpə'gændə] *n* propaganda
propeller [prə'pɛlə^r] *n* elica
proper ['prɔpə^r] *adj* (*suited, right*) adatto(-a), appropriato(-a); (*seemly*) decente; (*authentic*) vero(-a); (*inf*: *real*: *noun*) + vero(-a) e proprio(-a); **properly** ['prɔpəlɪ] *adv* (*eat, study*) bene; (*behave*) come si deve; **proper noun** *n* nome *m* proprio
property ['prɔpətɪ] *n* (*things owned*) beni *mpl*; (*land, building*) proprietà *f inv*; (*Chem etc*: *quality*) proprietà
prophecy ['prɔfɪsɪ] *n* profezia
prophet ['prɔfɪt] *n* profeta *m*
proportion [prə'pɔːʃən] *n* proporzione *f*; (*share*) parte *f*; **proportions** *npl* (*size*) proporzioni *fpl*; **proportional** *adj* proporzionale
proposal [prə'pəuzl] *n* proposta; (*plan*) progetto; (*of marriage*) proposta di matrimonio
propose [prə'pəuz] *vt* proporre, suggerire ▷ *vi* fare una proposta di matrimonio; **to ~ to do** proporsi di fare, aver l'intenzione di fare
proposition [prɔpə'zɪʃən] *n* proposizione *f*; (*offer*) proposta
proprietor [prə'praɪətə^r] *n* proprietario(-a)
prose [prəuz] *n* prosa
prosecute ['prɔsɪkjuːt] *vt* processare; **prosecution** [-'kjuːʃən] *n* processo; (*accusing side*) accusa; **prosecutor** *n* (*also*: **public prosecutor**) ≈ procuratore *m* della Repubblica
prospect [*n* 'prɔspɛkt, *vb* prə'spɛkt] *n* prospettiva; (*hope*) speranza ▷ *vi* **to ~ for** cercare; **prospects** *npl* (*for work etc*) prospettive *fpl*; **prospective** [-'spɛktɪv] *adj* possibile; futuro(-a)
prospectus [prə'spɛktəs] *n* prospetto, programma *m*
prosper ['prɔspə^r] *vi* prosperare; **prosperity** [prɔ'spɛrɪtɪ] *n* prosperità; **prosperous** *adj* prospero(-a)
prostitute ['prɔstɪtjuːt] *n* prostituta; **male ~** uomo che si prostituisce
protect [prə'tɛkt] *vt* proteggere, salvaguardare; **protection** *n* protezione *f*; **protective** *adj* protettivo(-a)
protein ['prəutiːn] *n* proteina
protest [*n* 'prəutɛst, *vb* prə'tɛst] *n* protesta ▷ *vt, vi* protestare
Protestant ['prɔtɪstənt] *adj, n* protestante *m/f*
protester [prə'tɛstə^r] *n* dimostrante *m/f*
protractor [prə'træktə^r] *n* (*Geom*) goniometro
proud [praud] *adj* fiero(-a), orgoglioso(-a); (*pej*) superbo(-a)
prove [pruːv] *vt* provare, dimostrare ▷ *vi* **to ~ (to be) correct** *etc* risultare vero(-a) *etc*; **to ~ o.s.** mostrare le proprie capacità
proverb ['prɔvəːb] *n* proverbio
provide [prə'vaɪd] *vt* fornire, provvedere; **to ~ sb with sth** fornire *or* provvedere qn di qc; **provide for** *vt fus* provvedere a; (*future event*) prevedere; **provided** *conj* **provided (that)** purché + *sub*, a condizione che + *sub*; **providing** [prə'vaɪdɪŋ] *conj* purché +*sub*, a condizione che +*sub*
province ['prɔvɪns] *n* provincia; **provincial** [prə'vɪnʃəl] *adj* provinciale
provision [prə'vɪʒən] *n* (*supply*) riserva; (*supplying*) provvista; rifornimento; (*stipulation*) condizione *f*; **provisions** *npl* (*food*) provviste *fpl*; **provisional** *adj* provvisorio(-a)
provocative [prə'vɔkətɪv] *adj* (*aggressive*) provocatorio(-a); (*thought-provoking*) stimolante; (*seductive*) provocante
provoke [prə'vəuk] *vt* provocare; incitare

prowl [praul] *vi* (*also:* **~ about, ~ around**) aggirarsi ▷ *n* **to be on the ~** aggirarsi
proximity [prɔk'sɪmɪtɪ] *n* prossimità
proxy ['prɔksɪ] *n* **by ~** per procura
prudent ['pru:dnt] *adj* prudente
prune [pru:n] *n* prugna secca ▷ *vt* potare
pry [praɪ] *vi* **to ~ into** ficcare il naso in
PS *abbr* (= *postscript*) P.S.
pseudonym ['sju:dənɪm] *n* pseudonimo
psychiatric [saɪkɪ'ætrɪk] *adj* psichiatrico(-a)
psychiatrist [saɪ'kaɪətrɪst] *n* psichiatra *m/f*
psychic ['saɪkɪk] *adj* (*also:* **~al**) psichico(-a); (*person*) dotato(-a) di qualità telepatiche
psychoanalysis (*pl* **-ses**) [saɪkəuə'nælɪsɪs, -si:z] *n* psicanalisi *f inv*
psychological [saɪkə'lɔdʒɪkl] *adj* psicologico(-a)
psychologist [saɪ'kɔlədʒɪst] *n* psicologo(-a)
psychology [saɪ'kɔlədʒɪ] *n* psicologia
psychotherapy [saɪkəu'θɛrəpɪ] *n* psicoterapia
pt *abbr* (= *pint; point*) pt.
PTO *abbr* (= *please turn over*) v.r.
pub [pʌb] *n abbr* (= *public house*) pub *m inv*
puberty ['pju:bətɪ] *n* pubertà
public ['pʌblɪk] *adj* pubblico(-a) ▷ *n* pubblico; **in ~** in pubblico
publication [pʌblɪ'keɪʃən] *n* pubblicazione *f*
public: **public company** *n* società *f inv* per azioni (*costituita tramite pubblica sottoscrizione*); **public convenience** (BRIT) *n* gabinetti *mpl*; **public holiday** *n* giorno festivo, festa nazionale; **public house** (BRIT) *n* pub *m inv*
publicity [pʌb'lɪsɪtɪ] *n* pubblicità
publicize ['pʌblisaɪz] *vt* rendere pubblico(-a)
public: **public limited company** *n* ≈ società per azioni a responsabilità limitata (*quotata in Borsa*); **publicly** ['pʌblɪklɪ] *adv* pubblicamente; **public opinion** *n* opinione *f* pubblica; **public relations** *n* pubbliche relazioni *fpl*; **public school** *n* (BRIT) scuola privata; (US) scuola statale; **public transport** *n* mezzi *mpl* pubblici
publish ['pʌblɪʃ] *vt* pubblicare; **publisher** *n* editore *m*; **publishing** *n* (*industry*) editoria; (*of a book*) pubblicazione *f*
pub lunch *n pranzo semplice ed economico servito nei pub*
pudding ['pudɪŋ] *n* budino; (BRIT: *dessert*) dolce *m*; **black ~,** (US) **blood ~** sanguinaccio
puddle ['pʌdl] *n* pozza, pozzanghera
Puerto Rico ['pwə:təu'ri:kəu] *n* Portorico
puff [pʌf] *n* sbuffo ▷ *vt* **to ~ one's pipe** tirare sboccate di fumo ▷ *vi* (*pant*) ansare; **puff pastry** *n* pasta sfoglia
pull [pul] *n* (*tug*): **to give sth a ~** tirare su qc ▷ *vt* tirare; (*muscle*) strappare; (*trigger*) premere ▷ *vi* tirare; **to ~ to pieces** fare a pezzi; **to ~ one's punches** (*Boxing*) risparmiare l'avversario; **to ~ one's weight** dare il proprio contributo; **to ~ o.s. together** ricomporsi, riprendersi; **to ~ sb's leg** prendere in giro qn; **pull apart** *vt* (*break*) fare a pezzi; **pull away** *vi* (*move off: vehicle*) muoversi, partire; (*boat*) staccarsi dal molo, salpare; (*draw back: person*) indietreggiare; **pull back** *vt* (*lever etc*) tirare indietro; (*curtains*) aprire ▷ *vi* (*from confrontation etc*) tirarsi indietro; (*Mil: withdraw*) ritirarsi; **pull down** *vt* (*house*) demolire; (*tree*) abbattere; **pull in** *vi* (*Aut: at the kerb*) accostarsi; (*Rail*) entrare in stazione; **pull off** *vt* (*clothes*) togliere; (*deal etc*) portare a compimento; **pull out** *vi* partire; (*Aut: come out of line*) spostarsi sulla mezzeria ▷ *vt* staccare; far

uscire; (*withdraw*) ritirare; **pull over** *vi* (*Aut*) accostare; **pull up** *vi* (*stop*) fermarsi ▷ *vt* (*raise*) sollevare; (*uproot*) sradicare
pulley ['pulɪ] *n* puleggia, carrucola
pullover ['puləuvəʳ] *n* pullover *m inv*
pulp [pʌlp] *n* (*of fruit*) polpa
pulpit ['pulpɪt] *n* pulpito
pulse [pʌls] *n* polso; (*Bot*) legume *m*; **pulses** *npl* (*Culin*) legumi *mpl*
puma ['pju:mə] *n* puma *m inv*
pump [pʌmp] *n* pompa; (*shoe*) scarpetta ▷ *vt* pompare; **pump up** *vt* gonfiare
pumpkin ['pʌmpkɪn] *n* zucca
pun [pʌn] *n* gioco di parole
punch [pʌntʃ] *n* (*blow*) pugno; (*tool*) punzone *m*; (*drink*) ponce *m* ▷ *vt* (*hit*): **to ~ sb/sth** dare un pugno a qn/qc; **punch-up** (BRIT: *inf*) *n* rissa
punctual ['pʌŋktjuəl] *adj* puntuale
punctuation [pʌŋktju'eɪʃən] *n* interpunzione *f*, punteggiatura
puncture ['pʌŋktʃəʳ] *n* foratura ▷ *vt* forare

> Be careful not to translate ***puncture*** by the Italian word ***puntura***.

punish ['pʌnɪʃ] *vt* punire; **punishment** *n* punizione *f*
punk [pʌŋk] *n* (*also:* **~ rocker**) punk *m/f inv*; (*also:* **~ rock**) musica punk, punk rock *m*; (US: *inf*: *hoodlum*) teppista *m*
pup [pʌp] *n* cucciolo(-a)
pupil ['pju:pl] *n* allievo(-a); (*Anat*) pupilla
puppet ['pʌpɪt] *n* burattino
puppy ['pʌpɪ] *n* cucciolo(-a), cagnolino(-a)
purchase ['pə:tʃɪs] *n* acquisto, compera ▷ *vt* comprare
pure [pjuəʳ] *adj* puro(-a); **purely** ['pjuəlɪ] *adv* puramente
purify ['pjuərɪfaɪ] *vt* purificare
purity ['pjuərɪtɪ] *n* purezza
purple ['pə:pl] *adj* di porpora; viola *inv*
purpose ['pə:pəs] *n* intenzione *f*, scopo; **on ~** apposta
purr [pə:ʳ] *vi* fare le fusa
purse [pə:s] *n* (BRIT) borsellino; (US) borsetta ▷ *vt* contrarre
pursue [pə'sju:] *vt* inseguire; (*fig*: *activity etc*) continuare con; (: *aim etc*) perseguire
pursuit [pə'sju:t] *n* inseguimento; (*fig*) ricerca; (*pastime*) passatempo
pus [pʌs] *n* pus *m*
push [puʃ] *n* spinta; (*effort*) grande sforzo; (*drive*) energia ▷ *vt* spingere; (*button*) premere; (*thrust*): **to ~ sth (into)** ficcare qc (in); (*fig*) fare pubblicità a ▷ *vi* spingere; premere; **to ~ for** (*fig*) insistere per; **push in** *vi* introdursi a forza; **push off** (*inf*) *vi* filare; **push on** *vi* (*continue*) continuare; **push over** *vt* far cadere; **push through** *vi* farsi largo spingendo ▷ *vt* (*measure*) far approvare; **pushchair** (BRIT) *n* passeggino; **pusher** *n* (*drug pusher*) spacciatore(-trice); **push-up** (US) *n* (*press-up*) flessione *f* sulle braccia
pussy(-cat) ['pusɪ(-)] (*inf*) *n* micio
put [put] (*pt*, *pp* **put**) *vt* mettere, porre; (*say*) dire, esprimere; (*a question*) fare; (*estimate*) stimare; **put away** *vt* (*return*) mettere a posto; **put back** *vt* (*replace*) rimettere (a posto); (*postpone*) rinviare; (*delay*) ritardare; **put by** *vt* (*money*) mettere da parte; **put down** *vt* (*parcel etc*) posare, mettere giù; (*pay*) versare; (*in writing*) mettere per iscritto; (*revolt*, *animal*) sopprimere; (*attribute*) attribuire; **put forward** *vt* (*ideas*) avanzare, proporre; **put in** *vt* (*application*, *complaint*) presentare; (*time*, *effort*) mettere; **put off** *vt* (*postpone*) rimandare, rinviare; (*discourage*) dissuadere; **put on** *vt* (*clothes*, *lipstick etc*) mettere; (*light etc*) accendere; (*play etc*) mettere in scena; (*food*, *meal*) mettere su; (*brake*) mettere; **to put on weight** ingrassare; **to put on airs** darsi delle

arie; **put out** *vt* mettere fuori; (*one's hand*) porgere; (*light etc*) spegnere; (*person*: *inconvenience*) scomodare; **put through** *vt* (*Tel*: *call*) passare; (: *person*) mettere in comunicazione; (*plan*) far approvare; **put up** *vt* (*raise*) sollevare, alzare; (: *umbrella*) aprire; (: *tent*) montare; (*pin up*) affiggere; (*hang*) appendere; (*build*) costruire, erigere; (*increase*) aumentare; (*accommodate*) alloggiare; **put aside** *vt* (*lay down*: *book etc*) mettere da una parte, posare; (*save*) mettere da parte; (*in shop*) tenere da parte; **put together** *vt* mettere insieme, riunire; (*assemble*: *furniture*) montare; (: *meal*) improvvisare; **put up with** *vt fus* sopportare

putt [pʌt] *n* colpo leggero; **putting green** *n* green *m inv*; campo da putting

puzzle ['pʌzl] *n* enigma *m*, mistero; (*jigsaw*) puzzle *m*; (*also*: **crossword ~**) parole *fpl* incrociate, cruciverba *m inv* ▷ *vt* confondere, rendere perplesso(-a) ▷ *vi* scervellarsi; **puzzled** *adj* perplesso(-a); **puzzling** *adj* (*question*) poco chiaro(-a); (*attitude, set of instructions*) incomprensibile

pyjamas [pɪ'dʒɑːməz] (BRIT) *npl* pigiama *m*

pylon ['paɪlən] *n* pilone *m*

pyramid ['pɪrəmɪd] *n* piramide *f*

Pyrenees [pɪrɪ'niːz] *npl* **the ~** i Pirenei

q

quack [kwæk] *n* (*of duck*) qua qua *m inv*; (*pej*: *doctor*) dottoruccio(-a)

quadruple [kwɔ'drupl] *vt* quadruplicare ▷ *vi* quadruplicarsi

quail [kweɪl] *n* (*Zool*) quaglia ▷ *vi* (*person*): **to ~ at** *or* **before** perdersi d'animo davanti a

quaint [kweɪnt] *adj* bizzarro(-a); (*old-fashioned*) antiquato(-a); grazioso(-a), pittoresco(-a)

quake [kweɪk] *vi* tremare ▷ *n abbr* = **earthquake**

qualification [kwɔlɪfɪ'keɪʃən] *n* (*degree etc*) qualifica, titolo; (*ability*) competenza, qualificazione *f*; (*limitation*) riserva, restrizione *f*

qualified ['kwɔlɪfaɪd] *adj* qualificato(-a); (*able*): **~ to** competente in, qualificato(-a) a; (*limited*) condizionato(-a)

qualify ['kwɔlɪfaɪ] *vt* abilitare; (*limit*: *statement*) modificare, precisare ▷ *vi* **to ~ (as)** qualificarsi (come); **to ~ (for)** acquistare i requisiti necessari (per);

(*Sport*) qualificarsi (per *or* a)
quality ['kwɔlɪtɪ] *n* qualità *f inv*
qualm [kwɑːm] *n* dubbio; scrupolo
quantify ['kwɔntɪfaɪ] *vt* quantificare
quantity ['kwɔntɪtɪ] *n* quantità *f inv*
quarantine ['kwɔrntiːn] *n* quarantena
quarrel ['kwɔrl] *n* lite *f*, disputa ▷ *vi* litigare
quarry ['kwɔrɪ] *n* (*for stone*) cava; (*animal*) preda
quart [kwɔːt] *n* ≈ litro
quarter ['kwɔːtəʳ] *n* quarto; (*US*: *coin*) quarto di dollaro; (*of year*) trimestre *m*; (*district*) quartiere *m* ▷ *vt* dividere in quattro; (*Mil*) alloggiare; **quarters** *npl* (*living quarters*) alloggio; (*Mil*) alloggi *mpl*, quadrato; **a ~ of an hour** un quarto d'ora; **quarter final** *n* quarto di finale; **quarterly** *adj* trimestrale ▷ *adv* trimestralmente
quartet(te) [kwɔː'tɛt] *n* quartetto
quartz [kwɔːts] *n* quarzo
quay [kiː] *n* (*also*: **~side**) banchina
queasy ['kwiːzɪ] *adj* (*stomach*) delicato(-a); **to feel ~** aver la nausea
queen [kwiːn] *n* (*gen*) regina; (*Cards etc*) regina, donna
queer [kwɪəʳ] *adj* strano(-a), curioso(-a) ▷ *n* (*inf*) finocchio
quench [kwɛntʃ] *vt* **to ~ one's thirst** dissetarsi
query ['kwɪərɪ] *n* domanda, questione *f* ▷ *vt* mettere in questione
quest [kwɛst] *n* cerca, ricerca
question ['kwɛstʃən] *n* domanda, questione *f* ▷ *vt* (*person*) interrogare; (*plan, idea*) mettere in questione *or* in dubbio; **it's a ~ of doing** si tratta di fare; **beyond ~** fuori di dubbio; **out of the ~** fuori discussione, impossibile; **questionable** *adj* discutibile; **question mark** *n* punto interrogativo; **questionnaire** [kwɛstʃə'nɛəʳ] *n* questionario
queue [kjuː] (BRIT) *n* coda, fila ▷ *vi* fare la coda
quiche [kiːʃ] *n torta salata a base di uova, formaggio, prosciutto o altro*
quick [kwɪk] *adj* rapido(-a), veloce; (*reply*) pronto(-a); (*mind*) pronto(-a), acuto(-a) ▷ *n* **cut to the ~** (*fig*) toccato(-a) sul vivo; **be ~!** fa presto!; **quickly** *adv* rapidamente, velocemente
quid [kwɪd] (BRIT: *inf*) *n inv* sterlina
quiet ['kwaɪət] *adj* tranquillo(-a), quieto(-a); (*ceremony*) semplice ▷ *n* tranquillità, calma ▷ *vt, vi* (*US*) = **quieten**; **keep ~!** sta zitto!; **quieten** (*also*: **quieten down**) *vi* calmarsi, chetarsi ▷ *vt* calmare, chetare; **quietly** *adv* tranquillamente, calmamente; sommessamente
quilt [kwɪlt] *n* trapunta; (*continental quilt*) piumino
quirky ['kwəːkɪ] *adj* stravagante
quit [kwɪt] (*pt, pp* **quit** *or* **quitted**) *vt* mollare; (*premises*) lasciare, partire da ▷ *vi* (*give up*) mollare; (*resign*) dimettersi
quite [kwaɪt] *adv* (*rather*) assai; (*entirely*) completamente, del tutto; **I ~ understand** capisco perfettamente; **that's not ~ big enough** non è proprio sufficiente; **~ a few of them** non pochi di loro; **~ (so)!** esatto!
quits [kwɪts] *adj* **~ (with)** pari (con); **let's call it ~** adesso siamo pari
quiver ['kwɪvəʳ] *vi* tremare, fremere
quiz [kwɪz] *n* (*game*) quiz *m inv*; indovinello ▷ *vt* interrogare
quota ['kwəutə] *n* quota
quotation [kwəu'teɪʃən] *n* citazione *f*; (*of shares etc*) quotazione *f*; (*estimate*) preventivo; **quotation marks** *npl* virgolette *fpl*
quote [kwəut] *n* citazione *f* ▷ *vt* (*sentence*) citare; (*price*) dare, fissare; (*shares*) quotare ▷ *vi* **to ~ from** citare; **quotes** *npl* = **quotation marks**

r

rabbi ['ræbaɪ] *n* rabbino
rabbit ['ræbɪt] *n* coniglio
rabies ['reɪbiːz] *n* rabbia
RAC (BRIT) *n abbr* = **Royal Automobile Club**
rac(c)oon [rə'kuːn] *n* procione *m*
race [reɪs] *n* razza; (*competition, rush*) corsa ▷ *vt* (*horse*) far correre ▷ *vi* correre; (*engine*) imballarsi; **race car** (US) *n* = **racing car**; **racecourse** *n* campo di corse, ippodromo; **racehorse** *n* cavallo da corsa; **racetrack** *n* pista
racial ['reɪʃl] *adj* razziale
racing ['reɪsɪŋ] *n* corsa; **racing car** (BRIT) *n* macchina da corsa; **racing driver** (BRIT) *n* corridore *m* automobilista
racism ['reɪsɪzəm] *n* razzismo; **racist** *adj, n* razzista *m/f*
rack [ræk] *n* rastrelliera; (*also:* **luggage ~**) rete *f*, portabagagli *m inv*; (*also:* **roof ~**) portabagagli; (*dish rack*) scolapiatti *m inv* ▷ *vt* **~ed by** torturato(-a) da; **to ~ one's brains** scervellarsi
racket ['rækɪt] *n* (*for tennis*) racchetta; (*noise*) fracasso; baccano; (*swindle*) imbroglio, truffa; (*organized crime*) racket *m inv*
racquet ['rækɪt] *n* racchetta
radar ['reɪdɑː^{r}] *n* radar *m*
radiation [reɪdɪ'eɪʃən] *n* irradiamento; (*radioactive*) radiazione *f*
radiator ['reɪdɪeɪtə^{r}] *n* radiatore *m*
radical ['rædɪkl] *adj* radicale
radio ['reɪdɪəu] *n* radio *f inv*; **on the ~** alla radio; **radioactive** [reɪdɪəu'æktɪv] *adj* radioattivo(-a); **radio station** *n* stazione *f* radio *inv*
radish ['rædɪʃ] *n* ravanello
RAF *n abbr* = **Royal Air Force**
raffle ['ræfl] *n* lotteria
raft [rɑːft] *n* zattera; (*also:* **life ~**) zattera di salvataggio
rag [ræg] *n* straccio, cencio; (*pej: newspaper*) giornalaccio, bandiera; (*for charity*) *iniziativa studentesca a scopo benefico*; **rags** *npl* (*torn clothes*) stracci *mpl*, brandelli *mpl*
rage [reɪdʒ] *n* (*fury*) collera, furia ▷ *vi* (*person*) andare su tutte le furie; (*storm*) infuriare; **it's all the ~** fa furore
ragged ['rægɪd] *adj* (*edge*) irregolare; (*clothes*) logoro(-a); (*appearance*) pezzente
raid [reɪd] *n* (*Mil*) incursione *f*; (*criminal*) rapina; (*by police*) irruzione *f* ▷ *vt* fare un'incursione in; rapinare; fare irruzione in
rail [reɪl] *n* (*on stair*) ringhiera; (*on bridge, balcony*) parapetto; (*of ship*) battagliola; **railcard** *n* (BRIT) tessera di riduzione ferroviaria; **railing(s)** *n(pl)* ringhiere *fpl*; **railroad** (US) *n* = **railway**; **railway** (BRIT: *irreg*) *n* ferrovia; **railway line** (BRIT) *n* linea ferroviaria; **railway station** (BRIT) *n* stazione *f* ferroviaria
rain [reɪn] *n* pioggia ▷ *vi* piovere; **in the ~** sotto la pioggia; **it's ~ing** piove;

rainbow *n* arcobaleno; **raincoat** *n* impermeabile *m*; **raindrop** *n* goccia di pioggia; **rainfall** *n* pioggia; (*measurement*) piovosità; **rainforest** *n* foresta pluviale; **rainy** *adj* piovoso(-a)
raise [reɪz] *n* aumento ▷ *vt* (*lift*) alzare; sollevare; (*increase*) aumentare; (*a protest, doubt, question*) sollevare; (*cattle, family*) allevare; (*crop*) coltivare; (*army, funds*) raccogliere; (*loan*) ottenere; **to ~ one's voice** alzare la voce
raisin ['reɪzn] *n* uva secca
rake [reɪk] *n* (*tool*) rastrello ▷ *vt* (*garden*) rastrellare
rally ['rælɪ] *n* (*Pol etc*) riunione *f*; (*Aut*) rally *m inv*; (*Tennis*) scambio ▷ *vt* riunire, radunare ▷ *vi* (*sick person, Stock Exchange*) riprendersi
RAM [ræm] *n abbr* (= *random access memory*) memoria ad accesso casuale
ram [ræm] *n* montone *m*, ariete *m* ▷ *vt* conficcare; (*crash into*) cozzare, sbattere contro; percuotere; speronare
Ramadan [ræmə'dæn] *n* Ramadan *m inv*
ramble ['ræmbl] *n* escursione *f* ▷ *vi* (*pej*: *also*: **~ on**) divagare; **rambler** *n* escursionista *m/f*; (*Bot*) rosa rampicante; **rambling** *adj* (*speech*) sconnesso(-a); (*house*) tutto(-a) a nicchie e corridoi; (*Bot*) rampicante
ramp [ræmp] *n* rampa; **on/off ~** (*US Aut*) raccordo di entrata/uscita
rampage [ræm'peɪdʒ] *n* **to go on the ~** scatenarsi in modo violento
ran [ræn] *pt of* **run**
ranch [rɑːntʃ] *n* ranch *m inv*
random ['rændəm] *adj* fatto(-a) *or* detto(-a) per caso; (*Comput, Math*) casuale ▷ *n* **at ~** a casaccio
rang [ræŋ] *pt of* **ring**
range [reɪndʒ] *n* (*of mountains*) catena; (*of missile, voice*) portata; (*of proposals, products*) gamma; (*Mil*: *also*: **shooting ~**) campo di tiro; (*also*: **kitchen ~**) fornello, cucina economica ▷ *vt* disporre ▷ *vi* **to ~ over** coprire; **to ~ from ... to** andare da ... a
ranger ['reɪndʒəʳ] *n* guardia forestale
rank [ræŋk] *n* fila; (*status, Mil*) grado; (BRIT: *also*: **taxi ~**) posteggio di taxi ▷ *vi* **to ~ among** essere tra ▷ *adj* puzzolente; vero(-a) e proprio(-a); **the ~ and file** (*fig*) la gran massa
ransom ['rænsəm] *n* riscatto; **to hold sb to ~** (*fig*) esercitare pressione su qn
rant [rænt] *vi* vociare
rap [ræp] *vt* bussare a; picchiare su ▷ *n* (*music*) rap *m inv*
rape [reɪp] *n* violenza carnale, stupro; (*Bot*) ravizzone *m* ▷ *vt* violentare
rapid ['ræpɪd] *adj* rapido(-a); **rapidly** *adv* rapidamente; **rapids** *npl* (*Geo*) rapida
rapist ['reɪpɪst] *n* violentatore *m*
rapport [ræ'pɔːʳ] *n* rapporto
rare [rɛəʳ] *adj* raro(-a); (*Culin*: *steak*) al sangue; **rarely** ['rɛəlɪ] *adv* raramente
rash [ræʃ] *adj* imprudente, sconsiderato(-a) ▷ *n* (*Med*) eruzione *f*; (*of events etc*) scoppio
rasher ['ræʃəʳ] *n* fetta sottile (di lardo *or* prosciutto)
raspberry ['rɑːzbərɪ] *n* lampone *m*
rat [ræt] *n* ratto
rate [reɪt] *n* (*proportion*) tasso, percentuale *f*; (*speed*) velocità *f inv*; (*price*) tariffa ▷ *vt* giudicare; stimare; **rates** *npl* (BRIT: *property tax*) imposte *fpl* comunali; (*fees*) tariffe *fpl*; **to ~ sb/sth as** valutare qn/qc come
rather ['rɑːðəʳ] *adv* piuttosto; **it's ~ expensive** è piuttosto caro; (*too*) è un po' caro; **there's ~ a lot** ce n'è parecchio; **I would** *or* **I'd ~ go** preferirei andare
rating ['reɪtɪŋ] *n* (*assessment*) valutazione *f*; (*score*) punteggio di merito; **ratings** *npl* (*Radio, TV*) indice *m* di ascolto
ratio ['reɪʃɪəu] *n* proporzione *f*, rapporto

ration ['ræʃən] *n* (*gen pl*) razioni *fpl* ▷ *vt* razionare; **rations** *npl* razioni *fpl*
rational ['ræʃənl] *adj* razionale, ragionevole; (*solution, reasoning*) logico(-a)
rattle ['rætl] *n* tintinnio; (*louder*) strepito; (*for baby*) sonaglino ▷ *vi* risuonare, tintinnare; fare un rumore di ferraglia ▷ *vt* scuotere (con strepito)
rave [reɪv] *vi* (*in anger*) infuriarsi; (*with enthusiasm*) andare in estasi; (*Med*) delirare ▷ *n* (BRIT: *inf*: *party*) rave *m inv*
raven ['reɪvən] *n* corvo
ravine [rə'viːn] *n* burrone *m*
raw [rɔː] *adj* (*uncooked*) crudo(-a); (*not processed*) greggio(-a); (*sore*) vivo(-a); (*inexperienced*) inesperto(-a); (*weather, day*) gelido(-a)
ray [reɪ] *n* raggio; **a ~ of hope** un barlume di speranza
razor ['reɪzəʳ] *n* rasoio; **razor blade** *n* lama di rasoio
Rd *abbr* = **road**
re [riː] *prep* con riferimento a
RE *n abbr* (BRIT *Mil*: = *Royal Engineers*) ≈ G.M. (*Genio Militare*); (BRIT) = **religious education**
reach [riːtʃ] *n* portata; (*of river etc*) tratto ▷ *vt* raggiungere; arrivare a ▷ *vi* stendersi; **out of/within ~** fuori/a portata di mano; **within ~ of the shops/station** vicino ai negozi/alla stazione; **reach out** *vt* (*hand*) allungare ▷ *vi* **to reach out for** stendere la mano per prendere
react [riː'ækt] *vi* reagire; **reaction** [-'ækʃən] *n* reazione *f*; **reactor** [riː'æktəʳ] *n* reattore *m*
read [riːd, *pt, pp* rɛd] (*pt, pp* **read**) *vi* leggere ▷ *vt* leggere; (*understand*) intendere, interpretare; (*study*) studiare; **read out** *vt* leggere ad alta voce; **reader** *n* lettore(-trice); (BRIT: *at university*) *professore con funzioni preminenti di ricerca*
readily ['rɛdɪlɪ] *adv* volentieri; (*easily*) facilmente; (*quickly*) prontamente
reading ['riːdɪŋ] *n* lettura; (*understanding*) interpretazione *f*; (*on instrument*) indicazione *f*
ready ['rɛdɪ] *adj* pronto(-a); (*willing*) pronto(-a), disposto(-a); (*available*) disponibile ▷ *n* **at the ~** (*Mil*) pronto a sparare; **when will my photos be ~?** quando saranno pronte le mie foto?; **to get ~** *vi* prepararsi ▷ *vt* preparare; **ready-made** *adj* prefabbricato(-a); (*clothes*) confezionato(-a)
real [rɪəl] *adj* reale; vero(-a); **in ~ terms** in realtà; **real ale** *n birra ad effervescenza naturale*; **real estate** *n* beni *mpl* immobili; **realistic** [-'lɪstɪk] *adj* realistico(-a); **reality** [riː'ælɪtɪ] *n* realtà *f inv*; **reality TV** *n* reality TV *f inv*
realization [rɪəlaɪ'zeɪʃən] *n* presa di coscienza; realizzazione *f*
realize ['rɪəlaɪz] *vt* (*understand*) rendersi conto di
really ['rɪəlɪ] *adv* veramente, davvero; **~!** (*indicating annoyance*) oh, insomma!
realm [rɛlm] *n* reame *m*, regno
Realtor® ['rɪəltɔːʳ] (US) *n* agente *m* immobiliare
reappear [riːə'pɪəʳ] *vi* ricomparire, riapparire
rear [rɪəʳ] *adj* di dietro; (*Aut*: *wheel etc*) posteriore ▷ *n* didietro, parte *f* posteriore ▷ *vt* (*cattle, family*) allevare ▷ *vi* (*also*: **~ up**: *animal*) impennarsi
rearrange [riːə'reɪndʒ] *vt* riordinare
rear: **rear-view mirror** ['rɪəvjuː-] *n* (*Aut*) specchio retrovisore; **rear-wheel drive** *n* trazione *fpl* posteriore
reason ['riːzn] *n* ragione *f*; (*cause, motive*) ragione, motivo ▷ *vi* **to ~ with sb** far ragionare qn; **it stands to ~ that** è ovvio che; **reasonable** *adj* ragionevole; (*not bad*) accettabile; **reasonably** *adv* ragionevolmente; **reasoning** *n* ragionamento
reassurance [riːə'ʃuərəns] *n* rassicurazione *f*
reassure [riːə'ʃuəʳ] *vt* rassicurare; **to ~**

sb of rassicurare qn di *or* su
rebate ['ri:beɪt] *n* (*on tax etc*) sgravio
rebel [*n* 'rɛbl, *vb* rɪ'bɛl] *n* ribelle *m/f* ▷ *vi* ribellarsi; **rebellion** *n* ribellione *f*; **rebellious** *adj* ribelle
rebuild [ri:'bɪld] *vt irreg* ricostruire
recall [rɪ'kɔ:l] *vt* richiamare; (*remember*) ricordare, richiamare alla mente ▷ *n* richiamo
rec'd *abbr* = **received**
receipt [rɪ'si:t] *n* (*document*) ricevuta; (*act of receiving*) ricevimento; **receipts** *npl* (*Comm*) introiti *mpl*; **can I have a ~, please?** posso avere una ricevuta, per favore?
receive [rɪ'si:v] *vt* ricevere; (*guest*) ricevere, accogliere; **receiver** [rɪ'si:vəʳ] *n* (*Tel*) ricevitore *m*; (*Radio, TV*) apparecchio ricevente; (*of stolen goods*) ricettatore(-trice); (*Comm*) curatore *m* fallimentare
recent ['ri:snt] *adj* recente; **recently** *adv* recentemente
reception [rɪ'sɛpʃən] *n* ricevimento; (*welcome*) accoglienza; (*TV etc*) ricezione *f*; **reception desk** *n* (*in hotel*) reception *f inv*; (*in hospital, at doctor's*) accettazione *f*; (*in offices etc*) portineria; **receptionist** *n* receptionist *m/f inv*
recession [rɪ'sɛʃən] *n* recessione *f*
recharge [ri:'tʃɑ:dʒ] *vt* (*battery*) ricaricare
recipe ['rɛsɪpɪ] *n* ricetta
recipient [rɪ'sɪpɪənt] *n* beneficiario(-a); (*of letter*) destinatario(-a)
recital [rɪ'saɪtl] *n* recital *m inv*
recite [rɪ'saɪt] *vt* (*poem*) recitare
reckless ['rɛkləs] *adj* (*driver etc*) spericolato(-a); (*spending*) folle
reckon ['rɛkən] *vt* (*count*) calcolare; (*think*): **I ~ that ...** penso che ...
reclaim [rɪ'kleɪm] *vt* (*demand back*) richiedere, reclamare; (*land*) bonificare; (*materials*) recuperare
recline [rɪ'klaɪn] *vi* stare sdraiato(-a)
recognition [rɛkəg'nɪʃən] *n* riconoscimento; **transformed beyond ~** irriconoscibile
recognize ['rɛkəgnaɪz] *vt* **to ~ (by/as)** riconoscere (a *or* da/come)
recollection [rɛkə'lɛkʃən] *n* ricordo
recommend [rɛkə'mɛnd] *vt* raccomandare; (*advise*) consigliare; **can you ~ a good restaurant?** mi può consigliare un buon ristorante?; **recommendation** [rɛkəmɛn'deɪʃən] *n* raccomandazione *f*; consiglio
reconcile ['rɛkənsaɪl] *vt* (*two people*) riconciliare; (*two facts*) conciliare, quadrare; **to ~ o.s. to** rassegnarsi a
reconsider [ri:kən'sɪdəʳ] *vt* riconsiderare
reconstruct [ri:kən'strʌkt] *vt* ricostruire
record [*n* 'rɛkɔ:d, *vb* rɪ'kɔ:d] *n* ricordo, documento; (*of meeting etc*) nota, verbale *m*; (*register*) registro; (*file*) pratica, dossier *m inv*; (*Comput*) record *m inv*; (*also*: **criminal ~**) fedina penale sporca; (*Mus*: *disc*) disco; (*Sport*) record *m inv*, primato ▷ *vt* (*set down*) prendere nota di, registrare; (*Mus*: *song etc*) registrare; **in ~ time** a tempo di record; **off the ~** *adj* ufficioso(-a) ▷ *adv* ufficiosamente; **recorded delivery** (BRIT) *n* (*Post*): **recorded delivery letter** *etc* lettera *etc* raccomandata; **recorder** *n* (*Mus*) flauto diritto; **recording** *n* (*Mus*) registrazione *f*; **record player** *n* giradischi *m inv*
recount [rɪ'kaunt] *vt* raccontare, narrare
recover [rɪ'kʌvəʳ] *vt* ricuperare ▷ *vi* **to ~ (from)** riprendersi (da); **recovery** [rɪ'kʌvərɪ] *n* ricupero; ristabilimento; ripresa

> Be careful not to translate ***recover*** by the Italian word ***ricoverare***.

recreate [ri:krɪ'eɪt] *vt* ricreare
recreation [rɛkrɪ'eɪʃən] *n* ricreazione

f; svago; **recreational drug** [rɛkrɪ'eɪʃənl-] *n sostanza stupefacente usata a scopo ricreativo*; **recreational vehicle** (US) *n* camper *m inv*
recruit [rɪ'kru:t] *n* recluta; (*in company*) nuovo(-a) assunto(-a) ▷ *vt* reclutare; **recruitment** *n* reclutamento
rectangle ['rɛktæŋgl] *n* rettangolo; **rectangular** [-'tæŋgjulə^r] *adj* rettangolare
rectify ['rɛktɪfaɪ] *vt* (*error*) rettificare; (*omission*) riparare
rector ['rɛktə^r] *n* (*Rel*) parroco (*anglicano*)
recur [rɪ'kə:^r] *vi* riaccadere; (*symptoms*) ripresentarsi; **recurring** *adj* (*Math*) periodico(-a)
recyclable [ri:'saɪkləbl] *adj* riciclabile
recycle [ri:'saɪkl] *vt* riciclare
recycling [ri:'saɪklɪŋ] *n* riciclaggio
red [rɛd] *n* rosso; (*Pol*: *pej*) rosso(-a) ▷ *adj* rosso(-a); **in the ~** (*account*) scoperto; (*business*) in deficit; **Red Cross** *n* Croce *f* Rossa; **redcurrant** *n* ribes *m inv*
redeem [rɪ'di:m] *vt* (*debt*) riscattare; (*sth in pawn*) ritirare; (*fig, also Rel*) redimere
red: **red-haired** [-'hɛəd] *adj* dai capelli rossi; **redhead** ['rɛdhɛd] *n* rosso(-a); **red-hot** *adj* arroventato(-a); **red light** *n* **to go through a red light** (*Aut*) passare col rosso; **red-light district** ['rɛdlaɪt-] *n* quartiere *m* a luci rosse; **red meat** *n* carne *f* rossa
reduce [rɪ'dju:s] *vt* ridurre; (*lower*) ridurre, abbassare; **"~ speed now"** (*Aut*) "rallentare"; **at a ~d price** scontato(-a); **reduced** *adj* (*decreased*) ridotto(-a); **at a reduced price** a prezzo ribassato *or* ridotto; **"greatly reduced prices"** "grandi ribassi"; **reduction** [rɪ'dʌkʃən] *n* riduzione *f*; (*of price*) ribasso; (*discount*) sconto; **is there a reduction for children/students?** ci sono riduzioni per i bambini/gli studenti?
redundancy [rɪ'dʌndənsɪ] *n* licenziamento
redundant [rɪ'dʌndnt] *adj* (*worker*) licenziato(-a); (*detail, object*) superfluo(-a); **to be made ~** essere licenziato (per eccesso di personale)
reed [ri:d] *n* (*Bot*) canna; (*Mus*: *of clarinet etc*) ancia
reef [ri:f] *n* (*at sea*) scogliera
reel [ri:l] *n* bobina, rocchetto; (*Fishing*) mulinello; (*Cinema*) rotolo; (*dance*) *danza veloce scozzese* ▷ *vi* (*sway*) barcollare
ref [rɛf] (*inf*) *n abbr* (= *referee*) arbitro
refectory [rɪ'fɛktərɪ] *n* refettorio
refer [rɪ'fə:^r] *vt* **to ~ sth to** (*dispute, decision*) deferire qc a; **to ~ sb to** (*inquirer, Med*: *patient*) indirizzare qn a; (*reader*: *to text*) rimandare qn a ▷ *vi* **~ to** (*allude to*) accennare a; (*consult*) rivolgersi a
referee [rɛfə'ri:] *n* arbitro; (BRIT: *for job application*) referenza ▷ *vt* arbitrare
reference ['rɛfrəns] *n* riferimento; (*mention*) menzione *f*, allusione *f*; (*for job application*) referenza; **with ~ to** (*Comm*: *in letter*) in *or* con riferimento a; **reference number** *n* numero di riferimento
refill [*vb* ri:'fɪl, *n* 'ri:fɪl] *vt* riempire di nuovo; (*pen, lighter etc*) ricaricare ▷ *n* (*for pen etc*) ricambio
refine [rɪ'faɪn] *vt* raffinare; **refined** *adj* (*person, taste*) raffinato(-a); **refinery** *n* raffineria
reflect [rɪ'flɛkt] *vt* (*light, image*) riflettere; (*fig*) rispecchiare ▷ *vi* (*think*) riflettere, considerare; **it ~s badly/well on him** si ripercuote su di lui in senso negativo/positivo; **reflection** [-'flɛkʃən] *n* riflessione *f*; (*image*) riflesso; (*criticism*): **reflection on** giudizio su; attacco a; **on reflection** pensandoci sopra
reflex ['ri:flɛks] *adj* riflesso(-a) ▷ *n*

riflesso
reform [rɪ'fɔːm] *n* (*of sinner etc*) correzione *f*; (*of law etc*) riforma ▷ *vt* correggere; riformare
refrain [rɪ'freɪn] *vi* **to ~ from doing** trattenersi dal fare ▷ *n* ritornello
refresh [rɪ'frɛʃ] *vt* rinfrescare; (*food, sleep*) ristorare; **refreshing** *adj* (*drink*) rinfrescante; (*sleep*) riposante, ristoratore(-trice); **refreshments** *npl* rinfreschi *mpl*
refrigerator [rɪ'frɪdʒəreɪtəʳ] *n* frigorifero
refuel [riː'fjuəl] *vi* far rifornimento (di carburante)
refuge ['rɛfjuːdʒ] *n* rifugio; **to take ~ in** rifugiarsi in; **refugee** [rɛfju'dʒiː] *n* rifugiato(-a), profugo(-a)
refund [*n* 'riːfʌnd, *vb* rɪ'fʌnd] *n* rimborso ▷ *vt* rimborsare
refurbish [riː'fəːbɪʃ] *vt* rimettere a nuovo
refusal [rɪ'fjuːzəl] *n* rifiuto; **to have first ~ on** avere il diritto d'opzione su
refuse [*n* 'rɛfjuːs, *vb* rɪ'fjuːz] *n* rifiuti *mpl* ▷ *vt, vi* rifiutare; **to ~ to do** rifiutare di fare
regain [rɪ'geɪn] *vt* riguadagnare; riacquistare, ricuperare
regard [rɪ'gɑːd] *n* riguardo, stima ▷ *vt* considerare, stimare; **to give one's ~s to** porgere i suoi saluti a; **"with kindest ~s"** "cordiali saluti"; **regarding** *prep* riguardo a, per quanto riguarda; **regardless** *adv* lo stesso; **regardless of** a dispetto di, nonostante
regenerate [rɪ'dʒɛnəreɪt] *vt* rigenerare
reggae ['rɛgeɪ] *n* reggae *m*
regiment ['rɛdʒɪmənt] *n* reggimento
region ['riːdʒən] *n* regione *f*; **in the ~ of** (*fig*) all'incirca di; **regional** *adj* regionale
register ['rɛdʒɪstəʳ] *n* registro; (*also*: **electoral ~**) lista elettorale ▷ *vt* registrare; (*vehicle*) immatricolare; (*letter*) assicurare; (*instrument*) segnare ▷ *vi* iscriversi; (*at hotel*) firmare il registro; (*make impression*) entrare in testa; **registered** (BRIT) *adj* (*letter*) assicurato(-a)
registrar ['rɛdʒɪstrɑːʳ] *n* ufficiale *m* di stato civile; segretario
registration [rɛdʒɪs'treɪʃən] *n* (*act*) registrazione *f*; iscrizione *f*; (*Aut*: *also*: **~ number**) numero di targa
registry office (BRIT) *n* anagrafe *f*; **to get married in a ~** ≈ sposarsi in municipio
regret [rɪ'grɛt] *n* rimpianto, rincrescimento ▷ *vt* rimpiangere; **regrettable** *adj* deplorevole
regular ['rɛgjuləʳ] *adj* regolare; (*usual*) abituale, normale; (*soldier*) dell'esercito regolare ▷ *n* (*client etc*) cliente *m/f* abituale; **regularly** *adv* regolarmente
regulate ['rɛgjuleɪt] *vt* regolare; **regulation** [-'leɪʃən] *n* regolazione *f*; (*rule*) regola, regolamento
rehabilitation ['riːhəbɪlɪ'teɪʃən] *n* (*of offender*) riabilitazione *f*; (*of disabled*) riadattamento
rehearsal [rɪ'həːsəl] *n* prova
rehearse [rɪ'həːs] *vt* provare
reign [reɪn] *n* regno ▷ *vi* regnare
reimburse [riːɪm'bəːs] *vt* rimborsare
rein [reɪn] *n* (*for horse*) briglia
reincarnation [riːɪnkɑː'neɪʃən] *n* reincarnazione *f*
reindeer ['reɪndɪəʳ] *n inv* renna
reinforce [riːɪn'fɔːs] *vt* rinforzare; **reinforcements** *npl* (*Mil*) rinforzi *mpl*
reinstate [riːɪn'steɪt] *vt* reintegrare
reject [*n* 'riːdʒɛkt, *vb* rɪ'dʒɛkt] *n* (*Comm*) scarto ▷ *vt* rifiutare, respingere; (*Comm*: *goods*) scartare; **rejection** [rɪ'dʒɛkʃən] *n* rifiuto
rejoice [rɪ'dʒɔɪs] *vi* **to ~ (at** *or* **over)** provare diletto in
relate [rɪ'leɪt] *vt* (*tell*) raccontare; (*connect*) collegare ▷ *vi* **to ~ to** (*connect*) riferirsi a; (*get on with*)

stabilire un rapporto con; **relating to** che riguarda, rispetto a; **related** *adj* **related (to)** imparentato(-a) (con); collegato(-a) *or* connesso(-a) (a)

relation [rɪ'leɪʃən] *n* (*person*) parente *m/f*; (*link*) rapporto, relazione *f*; **relations** *npl* (*relatives*) parenti *mpl*; **relationship** *n* rapporto; (*personal ties*) rapporti *mpl*, relazioni *fpl*; (*also*: **family relationship**) legami *mpl* di parentela

relative ['rɛlətɪv] *n* parente *m/f* ▷ *adj* relativo(-a); (*respective*) rispettivo(-a); **relatively** *adv* relativamente; (*fairly, rather*) abbastanza

relax [rɪ'læks] *vi* rilasciarsi; (*person*: *unwind*) rilassarsi ▷ *vt* rilasciare; (*mind, person*) rilassare; **relaxation** [ri:læk'seɪʃən] *n* rilasciamento; rilassamento; (*entertainment*) ricreazione *f*, svago; **relaxed** *adj* rilassato(-a); **relaxing** *adj* rilassante

relay ['ri:leɪ] *n* (*Sport*) corsa a staffetta ▷ *vt* (*message*) trasmettere

release [rɪ'li:s] *n* (*from prison*) rilascio; (*from obligation*) liberazione *f*; (*of gas etc*) emissione *f*; (*of film etc*) distribuzione *f*; (*record*) disco; (*device*) disinnesto ▷ *vt* (*prisoner*) rilasciare; (*from obligation, wreckage etc*) liberare; (*book, film*) fare uscire; (*news*) rendere pubblico(-a); (*gas etc*) emettere; (*Tech*: *catch, spring etc*) disinnestare

relegate ['rɛləgeɪt] *vt* relegare; (BRIT *Sport*): **to be ~d** essere retrocesso(-a)

relent [rɪ'lɛnt] *vi* cedere; **relentless** *adj* implacabile

relevant ['rɛləvənt] *adj* pertinente; (*chapter*) in questione; **~ to** pertinente a

> Be careful not to translate ***relevant*** by the Italian word ***rilevante***.

reliable [rɪ'laɪəbl] *adj* (*person, firm*) fidato(-a), che dà affidamento; (*method*) sicuro(-a); (*machine*) affidabile

relic ['rɛlɪk] *n* (*Rel*) reliquia; (*of the past*) resto

relief [rɪ'li:f] *n* (*from pain, anxiety*) sollievo; (*help, supplies*) soccorsi *mpl*; (*Art, Geo*) rilievo

relieve [rɪ'li:v] *vt* (*pain, patient*) sollevare; (*bring help*) soccorrere; (*take over from*: *gen*) sostituire; (: *guard*) rilevare; **to ~ sb of sth** (*load*) alleggerire qn di qc; **to ~ o.s.** fare i propri bisogni; **relieved** *adj* sollevato(-a); **to be relieved that ...** essere sollevato(-a) (dal fatto) che ...; **I'm relieved to hear it** mi hai tolto un peso con questa notizia

religion [rɪ'lɪdʒən] *n* religione *f*

religious [rɪ'lɪdʒəs] *adj* religioso(-a); **religious education** *n* religione *f*

relish ['rɛlɪʃ] *n* (*Culin*) condimento; (*enjoyment*) gran piacere *m* ▷ *vt* (*food etc*) godere; **to ~ doing** adorare fare

relocate ['ri:ləu'keɪt] *vt* trasferire ▷ *vi* trasferirsi

reluctance [rɪ'lʌktəns] *n* riluttanza

reluctant [rɪ'lʌktənt] *adj* riluttante, mal disposto(-a); **reluctantly** *adv* di mala voglia, a malincuore

rely [rɪ'laɪ]: **to ~ on** *vt fus* contare su; (*be dependent*) dipendere da

remain [rɪ'meɪn] *vi* restare, rimanere; **remainder** *n* resto; (*Comm*) rimanenza; **remaining** *adj* che rimane; **remains** *npl* resti *mpl*

remand [rɪ'mɑ:nd] *n* **on ~** in detenzione preventiva ▷ *vt* **to ~ in custody** rinviare in carcere; trattenere a disposizione della legge

remark [rɪ'mɑ:k] *n* osservazione *f* ▷ *vt* osservare, dire; **remarkable** *adj* notevole; eccezionale

remarry [ri:'mærɪ] *vi* risposarsi

remedy ['rɛmədɪ] *n* **~ (for)** rimedio (per) ▷ *vt* rimediare a

remember [rɪ'mɛmbəʳ] *vt* ricordare, ricordarsi di; **~ me to him** salutalo da parte mia; **Remembrance Day** [rɪ'mɛmbrəns-] *n* 11 *novembre, giorno* *della commemorazione dei caduti in guerra*

REMEMBRANCE DAY

In Gran Bretagna, il **Remembrance Day** è un giorno di commemorazione dei caduti in guerra. Si celebra ogni anno la domenica più vicina all'11 novembre, anniversario della firma dell'armistizio con la Germania nel 1918.

remind [rɪ'maɪnd] *vt* **to ~ sb of sth** ricordare qc a qn; **to ~ sb to do** ricordare a qn di fare; **reminder** *n* richiamo; (*note etc*) promemoria *m inv*
reminiscent [rɛmɪ'nɪsnt] *adj* **~ of** che fa pensare a, che richiama
remnant ['rɛmnənt] *n* resto, avanzo
remorse [rɪ'mɔːs] *n* rimorso
remote [rɪ'məut] *adj* remoto(-a), lontano(-a); (*person*) distaccato(-a); **remote control** *n* telecomando; **remotely** *adv* remotamente; (*slightly*) vagamente
removal [rɪ'muːvəl] *n* (*taking away*) rimozione *f*; soppressione *f*; (BRIT: *from house*) trasloco; (*from office: dismissal*) destituzione *f*; (*Med*) ablazione *f*; **removal man** (*irreg*) *n* (BRIT) addetto ai traslochi; **removal van** (BRIT) *n* furgone *m* per traslochi
remove [rɪ'muːv] *vt* togliere, rimuovere; (*employee*) destituire; (*stain*) far sparire; (*doubt, abuse*) sopprimere, eliminare
Renaissance [rɪ'neɪsɑ̃ːns] *n* **the ~** il Rinascimento
rename [riː'neɪm] *vt* ribattezzare
render ['rɛndəʳ] *vt* rendere
rendezvous ['rɔndɪvuː] *n* appuntamento; (*place*) luogo d'incontro; (*meeting*) incontro
renew [rɪ'njuː] *vt* rinnovare; (*negotiations*) riprendere
renovate ['rɛnəveɪt] *vt* rinnovare; (*art work*) restaurare
renowned [rɪ'naund] *adj* rinomato(-a)
rent [rɛnt] *n* affitto ▷ *vt* (*take for rent*) prendere in affitto; (*also:* **~ out**) dare in affitto; **rental** *n* (*for television, car*) fitto
reorganize [riː'ɔːgənaɪz] *vt* riorganizzare
rep [rɛp] *n abbr* (*Comm:* = *representative*) rappresentante *m/f*; (*Theatre:* = *repertory*) teatro di repertorio
repair [rɪ'pɛəʳ] *n* riparazione *f* ▷ *vt* riparare; **in good/bad ~** in buone/cattive condizioni; **where can I get this ~ed?** dove lo posso far riparare?; **repair kit** *n* corredo per riparazioni
repay [riː'peɪ] (*irreg*) *vt* (*money, creditor*) rimborsare, ripagare; (*sb's efforts*) ricompensare; (*favour*) ricambiare; **repayment** *n* pagamento; rimborso
repeat [rɪ'piːt] *n* (*Radio, TV*) replica ▷ *vt* ripetere; (*pattern*) riprodurre; (*promise, attack, also Comm: order*) rinnovare ▷ *vi* ripetere; **can you ~ that, please?** può ripetere, per favore?; **repeatedly** *adv* ripetutamente, spesso; **repeat prescription** *n* (BRIT) ricetta ripetibile
repellent [rɪ'pɛlənt] *adj* repellente ▷ *n* **insect ~** prodotto *m* anti-insetti *inv*
repercussions [riːpə'kʌʃənz] *npl* ripercussioni *fpl*
repetition [rɛpɪ'tɪʃən] *n* ripetizione *f*
repetitive [rɪ'pɛtɪtɪv] *adj* (*movement*) che si ripete; (*work*) monotono(-a); (*speech*) pieno(-a) di ripetizioni
replace [rɪ'pleɪs] *vt* (*put back*) rimettere a posto; (*take the place of*) sostituire; **replacement** *n* rimessa; sostituzione *f*; (*person*) sostituto(-a)
replay ['riːpleɪ] *n* (*of match*) partita ripetuta; (*of tape, film*) replay *m inv*
replica ['rɛplɪkə] *n* replica, copia
reply [rɪ'plaɪ] *n* risposta ▷ *vi*

rispondere
report [rɪ'pɔːt] *n* rapporto; (*Press etc*) cronaca; (BRIT: *also:* **school ~**) pagella; (*of gun*) sparo ▷ *vt* riportare; (*Press etc*) fare una cronaca su; (*bring to notice: occurrence*) segnalare; (*: person*) denunciare ▷ *vi* (*make a report*) fare un rapporto (*or* una cronaca); (*present o.s.*): **to ~ (to sb)** presentarsi (a qn); **I'd like to ~ a theft** vorrei denunciare un furto; **report card** (US, *Scottish*) *n* pagella; **reportedly** *adv* stando a quanto si dice; **he reportedly told them to ...** avrebbe detto loro di ...; **reporter** *n* reporter *m inv*
represent [rɛprɪ'zɛnt] *vt* rappresentare; **representation** [-'teɪʃən] *n* rappresentazione *f*; (*petition*) rappresentanza; **representative** *n* rappresentante *m/f*; (US *Pol*) deputato(-a) ▷ *adj* rappresentativo(-a)
repress [rɪ'prɛs] *vt* reprimere; **repression** [-'prɛʃən] *n* repressione *f*
reprimand ['rɛprɪmɑːnd] *n* rimprovero ▷ *vt* rimproverare
reproduce [riːprə'djuːs] *vt* riprodurre ▷ *vi* riprodursi; **reproduction** [-'dʌkʃən] *n* riproduzione *f*
reptile ['rɛptaɪl] *n* rettile *m*
republic [rɪ'pʌblɪk] *n* repubblica; **republican** *adj, n* repubblicano(-a)
reputable ['rɛpjutəbl] *adj* di buona reputazione; (*occupation*) rispettabile
reputation [rɛpju'teɪʃən] *n* reputazione *f*
request [rɪ'kwɛst] *n* domanda; (*formal*) richiesta ▷ *vt*: **to ~ (of** *or* **from sb)** chiedere (a qn); **request stop** (BRIT) *n* (*for bus*) fermata facoltativa *or* a richiesta
require [rɪ'kwaɪəʳ] *vt* (*need: person*) aver bisogno di; (*: thing, situation*) richiedere; (*want*) volere; esigere; (*order*): **to ~ sb to do sth** ordinare a qn di fare qc; **requirement** *n* esigenza; bisogno; requisito
resat [riː'sæt] *pt, pp of* **resit**
rescue ['rɛskjuː] *n* salvataggio; (*help*) soccorso ▷ *vt* salvare
research [rɪ'səːtʃ] *n* ricerca, ricerche *fpl* ▷ *vt* fare ricerche su
resemblance [rɪ'zɛmbləns] *n* somiglianza
resemble [rɪ'zɛmbl] *vt* assomigliare a
resent [rɪ'zɛnt] *vt* risentirsi di; **resentful** *adj* pieno(-a) di risentimento; **resentment** *n* risentimento
reservation [rɛzə'veɪʃən] *n* (*booking*) prenotazione *f*; (*doubt*) dubbio; (*protected area*) riserva; (BRIT: *on road: also:* **central ~**) spartitraffico *m inv*; **reservation desk** (US) *n* (*in hotel*) reception *f inv*
reserve [rɪ'zəːv] *n* riserva ▷ *vt* (*seats etc*) prenotare; **reserved** *adj* (*shy*) riservato(-a)
reservoir ['rɛzəvwɑːʳ] *n* serbatoio
residence ['rɛzɪdəns] *n* residenza; **residence permit** (BRIT) *n* permesso di soggiorno
resident ['rɛzɪdənt] *n* residente *m/f*; (*in hotel*) cliente *m/f* fisso(-a) ▷ *adj* residente; (*doctor*) fisso(-a); (*course, college*) a tempo pieno con pernottamento; **residential** [-'dɛnʃəl] *adj* di residenza; (*area*) residenziale
residue ['rɛzɪdjuː] *n* resto; (*Chem, Physics*) residuo
resign [rɪ'zaɪn] *vt* (*one's post*) dimettersi da ▷ *vi* dimettersi; **to ~ o.s. to** rassegnarsi a; **resignation** [rɛzɪg'neɪʃən] *n* dimissioni *fpl*; rassegnazione *f*
resin ['rɛzɪn] *n* resina
resist [rɪ'zɪst] *vt* resistere a; **resistance** *n* resistenza
resit ['riːsɪt] (BRIT) (*pt, pp* **resat**) *vt* (*exam*) ripresentarsi a; (*subject*) ridare l'esame di ▷ *n*: **he's got his French ~ on Friday** deve ridare l'esame di francese venerdì
resolution [rɛzə'luːʃən] *n* risoluzione *f*

resolve [rɪ'zɔlv] *n* risoluzione *f* ▷ *vi* (*decide*): **to ~ to do** decidere di fare ▷ *vt* (*problem*) risolvere

resort [rɪ'zɔːt] *n* (*town*) stazione *f*; (*recourse*) ricorso ▷ *vi* **to ~ to** aver ricorso a; **in the last ~** come ultima risorsa

resource [rɪ'sɔːs] *n* risorsa; **resourceful** *adj* pieno(-a) di risorse, intraprendente

respect [rɪs'pɛkt] *n* rispetto ▷ *vt* rispettare; **respectable** *adj* rispettabile; **respectful** *adj* rispettoso(-a); **respective** [rɪs'pɛktɪv] *adj* rispettivo(-a); **respectively** *adv* rispettivamente

respite ['rɛspaɪt] *n* respiro, tregua

respond [rɪs'pɔnd] *vi* rispondere; **response** [rɪs'pɔns] *n* risposta

responsibility [rɪspɔnsɪ'bɪlɪtɪ] *n* responsabilità *f inv*

responsible [rɪs'pɔnsɪbl] *adj* (*trustworthy*) fidato(-a); (*job*) di (grande) responsabilità; **~ (for)** responsabile (di); **responsibly** *adv* responsabilmente

responsive [rɪs'pɔnsɪv] *adj* che reagisce

rest [rɛst] *n* riposo; (*stop*) sosta, pausa; (*Mus*) pausa; (*object: to support sth*) appoggio, sostegno; (*remainder*) resto, avanzi *mpl* ▷ *vi* riposarsi; (*remain*) rimanere, restare; (*be supported*): **to ~ on** appoggiarsi su ▷ *vt* (far) riposare; (*lean*): **to ~ sth on/against** appoggiare qc su/contro; **the ~ of them** gli altri; **it ~s with him to decide** sta a lui decidere

restaurant ['rɛstərɔŋ] *n* ristorante *m*; **restaurant car** (BRIT) *n* vagone *m* ristorante

restless ['rɛstlɪs] *adj* agitato(-a), irrequieto(-a)

restoration [rɛstə'reɪʃən] *n* restauro; restituzione *f*

restore [rɪ'stɔːʳ] *vt* (*building, to power*) restaurare; (*sth stolen*) restituire; (*peace, health*) ristorare

restrain [rɪs'treɪn] *vt* (*feeling, growth*) contenere, frenare; (*person*): **to ~ (from doing)** trattenere (dal fare); **restraint** *n* (*restriction*) limitazione *f*; (*moderation*) ritegno; (*of style*) contenutezza

restrict [rɪs'trɪkt] *vt* restringere, limitare; **restriction** [-kʃən] *n* **restriction (on)** restrizione *f* (di), limitazione *f*

rest room (US) *n* toletta

restructure [riː'strʌktʃəʳ] *vt* ristrutturare

result [rɪ'zʌlt] *n* risultato ▷ *vi* **to ~ in** avere per risultato; **as a ~ of** in *or* di conseguenza a, in seguito a

resume [rɪ'zjuːm] *vt*, *vi* (*work, journey*) riprendere

résumé ['reɪzjumeɪ] *n* riassunto; (US) curriculum *m inv* vitae

resuscitate [rɪ'sʌsɪteɪt] *vt* (*Med*) risuscitare

retail ['riːteɪl] *adj*, *adv* al minuto ▷ *vt* vendere al minuto; **retailer** *n* commerciante *m/f* al minuto, dettagliante *m/f*

retain [rɪ'teɪn] *vt* (*keep*) tenere, serbare

retaliation [rɪtælɪ'eɪʃən] *n* rappresaglie *fpl*

retarded [rɪ'tɑːdɪd] *adj* ritardato(-a)

retire [rɪ'taɪəʳ] *vi* (*give up work*) andare in pensione; (*withdraw*) ritirarsi, andarsene; (*go to bed*) andare a letto, ritirarsi; **retired** *adj* (*person*) pensionato(-a); **retirement** *n* pensione *f*; (*act*) pensionamento

retort [rɪ'tɔːt] *vi* rimbeccare

retreat [rɪ'triːt] *n* ritirata; (*place*) rifugio ▷ *vi* battere in ritirata

retrieve [rɪ'triːv] *vt* (*sth lost*) ricuperare, ritrovare; (*situation, honour*) salvare; (*error, loss*) rimediare a

retrospect ['rɛtrəspɛkt] *n* **in ~** guardando indietro; **retrospective**

[-'spɛktɪv] *adj* retrospettivo(-a); (*law*) retroattivo(-a)
return [rɪ'tə:n] *n* (*going or coming back*) ritorno; (*of sth stolen etc*) restituzione *f*; (*Finance: from land, shares*) profitto, reddito ▷ *cpd* (*journey, match*) di ritorno; (BRIT: *ticket*) di andata e ritorno ▷ *vi* tornare, ritornare ▷ *vt* rendere, restituire; (*bring back*) riportare; (*send back*) mandare indietro; (*put back*) rimettere; (*Pol: candidate*) eleggere; **returns** *npl* (*Comm*) incassi *mpl*; profitti *mpl*; **in ~ (for)** in cambio (di); **by ~ of post** a stretto giro di posta; **many happy ~s (of the day)!** cento di questi giorni!; **return ticket** *n* (*esp* BRIT) biglietto di andata e ritorno
reunion [ri:'ju:nɪən] *n* riunione *f*
reunite [ri:ju:'naɪt] *vt* riunire
revamp ['ri:'væmp] *vt* (*firm*) riorganizzare
reveal [rɪ'vi:l] *vt* (*make known*) rivelare, svelare; (*display*) rivelare, mostrare; **revealing** *adj* rivelatore(-trice); (*dress*) scollato(-a)
revel ['rɛvl] *vi* **to ~ in sth/in doing** dilettarsi di qc/a fare
revelation [rɛvə'leɪʃən] *n* rivelazione *f*
revenge [rɪ'vɛndʒ] *n* vendetta ▷ *vt* vendicare; **to take ~ on** vendicarsi di
revenue ['rɛvənju:] *n* reddito
Reverend ['rɛvərənd] *adj* (*in titles*) reverendo(-a)
reversal [rɪ'və:sl] *n* capovolgimento
reverse [rɪ'və:s] *n* contrario, opposto; (*back, defeat*) rovescio; (*Aut: also:* **~ gear**) marcia indietro ▷ *adj* (*order, direction*) contrario(-a), opposto(-a) ▷ *vt* (*turn*) invertire, rivoltare; (*change*) capovolgere, rovesciare; (*Law: judgment*) cassare; (*car*) fare marcia indietro con ▷ *vi* (BRIT *Aut, person etc*) fare marcia indietro; **reverse-charge call** [rɪ'və:stʃa:dʒ-] (BRIT) *n* (*Tel*) telefonata con addebito al ricevente; **reversing lights** (BRIT) *npl* (*Aut*) luci *fpl* per la retromarcia
revert [rɪ'və:t] *vi* **to ~ to** tornare a
review [rɪ'vju:] *n* rivista; (*of book, film*) recensione *f*; (*of situation*) esame *m* ▷ *vt* passare in rivista; fare la recensione di; fare il punto di
revise [rɪ'vaɪz] *vt* (*manuscript*) rivedere, correggere; (*opinion*) emendare, modificare; (*study: subject, notes*) ripassare; **revision** [rɪ'vɪʒən] *n* revisione *f*; ripasso
revival [rɪ'vaɪvəl] *n* ripresa; ristabilimento; (*of faith*) risveglio
revive [rɪ'vaɪv] *vt* (*person*) rianimare; (*custom*) far rivivere; (*hope, courage, economy*) ravvivare; (*play, fashion*) riesumare ▷ *vi* (*person*) rianimarsi; (*hope*) ravvivarsi; (*activity*) riprendersi
revolt [rɪ'vəult] *n* rivolta, ribellione *f* ▷ *vi* rivoltarsi, ribellarsi ▷ *vt* (far) rivoltare; **revolting** *adj* ripugnante
revolution [rɛvə'lu:ʃən] *n* rivoluzione *f*; (*of wheel etc*) rivoluzione, giro; **revolutionary** *adj, n* rivoluzionario(-a)
revolve [rɪ'vɔlv] *vi* girare
revolver [rɪ'vɔlvə^r] *n* rivoltella
reward [rɪ'wɔ:d] *n* ricompensa, premio ▷ *vt* **to ~ (for)** ricompensare (per); **rewarding** *adj* (*fig*) gratificante
rewind [ri:'waɪnd] (*irreg*) *vt* (*watch*) ricaricare; (*ribbon etc*) riavvolgere
rewrite [ri:'raɪt] *vt irreg* riscrivere
rheumatism ['ru:mətɪzəm] *n* reumatismo
rhinoceros [raɪ'nɔsərəs] *n* rinoceronte *m*
rhubarb ['ru:ba:b] *n* rabarbaro
rhyme [raɪm] *n* rima; (*verse*) poesia
rhythm ['rɪðm] *n* ritmo
rib [rɪb] *n* (*Anat*) costola ▷ *vt* (*tease*) punzecchiare
ribbon ['rɪbən] *n* nastro; **in ~s** (*torn*) a brandelli
rice [raɪs] *n* riso; **rice pudding** *n* budino di riso

rich [rɪtʃ] *adj* ricco(-a); (*clothes*) sontuoso(-a); (*abundant*): **~ in** ricco(-a) di

rid [rɪd] (*pt, pp* **rid**) *vt* **to ~ sb of** sbarazzare *or* liberare qn di; **to get ~ of** sbarazzarsi di

riddle ['rɪdl] *n* (*puzzle*) indovinello ▷ *vt* **to be ~d with** (*holes*) essere crivellato(-a) di; (*doubts*) essere pieno(-a) di

ride [raɪd] (*pt* **rode**, *pp* **ridden**) *n* (*on horse*) cavalcata; (*outing*) passeggiata; (*distance covered*) cavalcata; corsa ▷ *vi* (*as sport*) cavalcare; (*go somewhere: on horse, bicycle*) andare (a cavallo *or* in bicicletta *etc*); (*journey: on bicycle, motorcycle, bus*) andare, viaggiare ▷ *vt* (*a horse*) montare, cavalcare; **to take sb for a ~** (*fig*) prendere in giro qn; fregare qn; **to ~ a horse/bicycle/camel** montare a cavallo/in bicicletta/in groppa a un cammello; **rider** *n* cavalcatore(-trice); (*in race*) fantino; (*on bicycle*) ciclista *m/f*; (*on motorcycle*) motociclista *m/f*

ridge [rɪdʒ] *n* (*of hill*) cresta; (*of roof*) colmo; (*on object*) riga (in rilievo)

ridicule ['rɪdɪkjuːl] *n* ridicolo; scherno ▷ *vt* mettere in ridicolo; **ridiculous** [rɪ'dɪkjuləs] *adj* ridicolo(-a)

riding ['raɪdɪŋ] *n* equitazione *f*; **riding school** *n* scuola d'equitazione

rife [raɪf] *adj* diffuso(-a); **to be ~ with** abbondare di

rifle ['raɪfl] *n* carabina ▷ *vt* vuotare

rift [rɪft] *n* fessura, crepatura; (*fig: disagreement*) incrinatura, disaccordo

rig [rɪg] *n* (*also:* **oil ~**: *on land*) derrick *m inv*; (: *at sea*) piattaforma di trivellazione ▷ *vt* (*election etc*) truccare

right [raɪt] *adj* giusto(-a); (*suitable*) appropriato(-a); (*not left*) destro(-a) ▷ *n* giusto; (*title, claim*) diritto; (*not left*) destra ▷ *adv* (*answer*) correttamente; (*not on the left*) a destra ▷ *vt* raddrizzare; (*fig*) riparare ▷ *excl* bene!; **to be ~** (*person*) aver ragione; (*answer*) essere giusto(-a) *or* corretto(-a); **by ~s** di diritto; **on the ~** a destra; **to be in the ~** aver ragione, essere nel giusto; **~ now** proprio adesso; subito; **~ away** subito; **right angle** *n* angolo retto; **rightful** *adj* (*heir*) legittimo(-a); **right-hand** *adj* **right-hand drive** guida a destra; **the right-hand side** il lato destro; **right-handed** *adj* (*person*) che adopera la mano destra; **rightly** *adv* bene, correttamente; (*with reason*) a ragione; **right of way** *n* diritto di passaggio; (*Aut*) precedenza; **right-wing** *adj* (*Pol*) di destra

rigid ['rɪdʒɪd] *adj* rigido(-a); (*principle*) rigoroso(-a)

rigorous ['rɪgərəs] *adj* rigoroso(-a)

rim [rɪm] *n* orlo; (*of spectacles*) montatura; (*of wheel*) cerchione *m*

rind [raɪnd] *n* (*of bacon*) cotenna; (*of lemon etc*) scorza

ring [rɪŋ] (*pt* **rang**, *pp* **rung**) *n* anello; (*of people, objects*) cerchio; (*of spies*) giro; (*of smoke etc*) spirale *m*; (*arena*) pista, arena; (*for boxing*) ring *m inv*; (*sound of bell*) scampanio ▷ *vi* (*person, bell, telephone*) suonare; (*also:* **~ out**: *voice, words*) risuonare; (*Tel*) telefonare; (*ears*) fischiare ▷ *vt* (BRIT *Tel*) telefonare a; (: *bell, doorbell*) suonare; **to give sb a ~** (BRIT *Tel*) dare un colpo di telefono a qn; **ring back** *vt, vi* (*Tel*) richiamare; **ring off** (BRIT) *vi* (*Tel*) mettere giù, riattaccare; **ring up** (BRIT) *vt* (*Tel*) telefonare a; **ringing tone** (BRIT) *n* (*Tel*) segnale *m* di libero; **ringleader** *n* (*of gang*) capobanda *m*; **ring road** (BRIT) *n* raccordo anulare

ring tone *n* suoneria

rink [rɪŋk] *n* (*also:* **ice ~**) pista di pattinaggio

rinse [rɪns] *n* risciacquatura; (*hair tint*) cachet *m inv* ▷ *vt* sciacquare

riot ['raɪət] *n* sommossa, tumulto; (*of colours*) orgia ▷ *vi* tumultuare; **to run ~** creare disordine

rip [rɪp] *n* strappo ▷ *vt* strappare

▷ *vi* strapparsi; **rip off** *vt* (*inf: cheat*) fregare; **rip up** *vt* stracciare

ripe [raɪp] *adj* (*fruit, grain*) maturo(-a); (*cheese*) stagionato(-a)

rip-off ['rɪpɔf] *n* (*inf*): **it's a ~!** è un furto!

ripple ['rɪpl] *n* increspamento, ondulazione *f*; mormorio ▷ *vi* incresparsi

rise [raɪz] (*pt* **rose**, *pp* **risen**) *n* (*slope*) salita, pendio; (*hill*) altura; (*increase*: *in wages*: BRIT) aumento; (: *in prices, temperature*) rialzo, aumento; (*fig*: *to power etc*) ascesa ▷ *vi* alzarsi, levarsi; (*prices*) aumentare; (*waters, river*) crescere; (*sun, wind, person*: *from chair, bed*) levarsi; (*also*: **~ up**: *building*) ergersi; (: *rebel*) insorgere; ribellarsi; (*in rank*) salire; **to give ~ to** provocare, dare origine a; **to ~ to the occasion** essere all'altezza; **risen** ['rɪzn] *pp of* **rise**; **rising** *adj* (*increasing*: *number*) sempre crescente; (: *prices*) in aumento; (*tide*) montante; (*sun, moon*) nascente, che sorge

risk [rɪsk] *n* rischio; pericolo ▷ *vt* rischiare; **to take** *or* **run the ~ of doing** correre il rischio di fare; **at ~** in pericolo; **at one's own ~** a proprio rischio e pericolo; **risky** *adj* rischioso(-a)

rite [raɪt] *n* rito; **last ~s** l'estrema unzione

ritual ['rɪtjuəl] *adj* rituale ▷ *n* rituale *m*

rival ['raɪvl] *n* rivale *m/f*; (*in business*) concorrente *m/f* ▷ *adj* rivale; che fa concorrenza ▷ *vt* essere in concorrenza con; **to ~ sb/sth in** competere con qn/qc in; **rivalry** *n* rivalità; concorrenza

river ['rɪvər] *n* fiume *m* ▷ *cpd* (*port, traffic*) fluviale; **up/down ~** a monte/valle; **riverbank** *n* argine *m*

rivet ['rɪvɪt] *n* ribattino, rivetto ▷ *vt* (*fig*) concentrare, fissare

Riviera [rɪvɪ'ɛərə] *n* **the (French) ~** la Costa Azzurra; **the Italian ~** la Riviera

road [rəud] *n* strada; (*small*) cammino; (*in town*) via ▷ *cpd* stradale; **major/minor ~** strada con/senza diritto di precedenza; **which ~ do I take for ...?** che strada devo prendere per andare a...?; **roadblock** *n* blocco stradale; **road map** *n* carta stradale; **road rage** *n* *comportamento aggressivo al volante*; **road safety** *n* sicurezza sulle strade; **roadside** *n* margine *m* della strada; **roadsign** *n* cartello stradale; **road tax** *n* (BRIT) tassa di circolazione; **roadworks** *npl* lavori *mpl* stradali

roam [rəum] *vi* errare, vagabondare

roar [rɔːr] *n* ruggito; (*of crowd*) tumulto; (*of thunder, storm*) muggito; (*of laughter*) scoppio ▷ *vi* ruggire; tumultuare; muggire; **to ~ with laughter** scoppiare dalle risa; **to do a ~ing trade** fare affari d'oro

roast [rəust] *n* arrosto ▷ *vt* arrostire; (*coffee*) tostare, torrefare; **roast beef** *n* arrosto di manzo

rob [rɔb] *vt* (*person*) rubare; (*bank*) svaligiare; **to ~ sb of sth** derubare qn di qc; (*fig*: *deprive*) privare qn di qc; **robber** *n* ladro; (*armed*) rapinatore *m*; **robbery** *n* furto; rapina

robe [rəub] *n* (*for ceremony etc*) abito; (*also*: **bath ~**) accappatoio; (US: *also*: **lap ~**) coperta

robin ['rɔbɪn] *n* pettirosso

robot ['rəubɔt] *n* robot *m inv*

robust [rəu'bʌst] *adj* robusto(-a); (*economy*) solido(-a)

rock [rɔk] *n* (*substance*) roccia; (*boulder*) masso; roccia; (*in sea*) scoglio; (US: *pebble*) ciottolo; (BRIT: *sweet*) zucchero candito ▷ *vt* (*swing gently*: *cradle*) dondolare; (: *child*) cullare; (*shake*) scrollare, far tremare ▷ *vi* dondolarsi; scrollarsi, tremare; **on the ~s** (*drink*) col ghiaccio; (*marriage etc*) in crisi; **rock and roll** *n* rock and roll *m*; **rock climbing** *n* roccia

rocket ['rɔkɪt] *n* razzo
rocking chair *n* sedia a dondolo
rocky ['rɔkɪ] *adj* (*hill*) roccioso(-a); (*path*) sassoso(-a); (*marriage etc*) instabile
rod [rɔd] *n* (*metallic, Tech*) asta; (*wooden*) bacchetta; (*also:* **fishing ~**) canna da pesca
rode [rəud] *pt of* **ride**
rodent ['rəudnt] *n* roditore *m*
rogue [rəug] *n* mascalzone *m*
role [rəul] *n* ruolo; **role-model** *n* modello (di comportamento)
roll [rəul] *n* rotolo; (*of banknotes*) mazzo; (*also:* **bread ~**) panino; (*register*) lista; (*sound: of drums etc*) rullo ▷ *vt* rotolare; (*also:* **~ up**: *string*) aggomitolare; (: *sleeves*) rimboccare; (*cigarettes*) arrotolare; (*eyes*) roteare; (*also:* **~ out**: *pastry*) stendere; (*lawn, road etc*) spianare ▷ *vi* rotolare; (*wheel*) girare; (*drum*) rullare; (*vehicle: also:* **~ along**) avanzare; (*ship*) rollare; **roll over** *vi* rivoltarsi; **roll up** (*inf*) *vi* (*arrive*) arrivare ▷ *vt* (*carpet*) arrotolare; **roller** *n* rullo; (*wheel*) rotella; (*for hair*) bigodino; **Rollerblades®** *npl* pattini *mpl* in linea; **roller coaster** [-'kəustə^r] *n* montagne *fpl* russe; **roller skates** *npl* pattini *mpl* a rotelle; **roller-skating** *n* pattinaggio a rotelle; **to go roller-skating** andare a pattinare (*con i pattini a rotelle*); **rolling pin** *n* matterello
ROM [rɔm] *n abbr* (= *read only memory*) memoria di sola lettura
Roman ['rəumən] *adj, n* romano(-a); **Roman Catholic** *adj, n* cattolico(-a)
romance [rə'mæns] *n* storia (*or* avventura *or* film *m inv*) romantico(-a); (*charm*) poesia; (*love affair*) idillio
Romania [rəu'meɪnɪə] *n* Romania
Romanian [rəu'meɪnɪən] *adj* romeno(-a) ▷ *n* romeno; (*Ling*) romeno
Roman numeral *n* numero romano
romantic [rə'mæntɪk] *adj* romantico(-a); sentimentale
Rome [rəum] *n* Roma
roof [ru:f] *n* tetto; (*of tunnel, cave*) volta ▷ *vt* coprire (con un tetto); **~ of the mouth** palato; **roof rack** *n* (*Aut*) portabagagli *m inv*
rook [ruk] *n* (*bird*) corvo nero; (*Chess*) torre *f*
room [ru:m] *n* (*in house*) stanza; (*bedroom, in hotel*) camera; (*in school etc*) sala; (*space*) posto, spazio; **roommate** *n* compagno(-a) di stanza; **room service** *n* servizio da camera; **roomy** *adj* spazioso(-a); (*garment*) ampio(-a)
rooster ['ru:stə^r] *n* gallo
root [ru:t] *n* radice *f* ▷ *vi* (*plant, belief*) attecchire
rope [rəup] *n* corda, fune *f*; (*Naut*) cavo ▷ *vt* (*box*) legare; (*climbers*) legare in cordata; (*area: also:* **~ off**) isolare cingendo con cordoni; **to know the ~s** (*fig*) conoscere i trucchi del mestiere
rose [rəuz] *pt of* **rise** ▷ *n* rosa; (*also:* **~ bush**) rosaio; (*on watering can*) rosetta
rosé ['rəuzeɪ] *n* vino rosato
rosemary ['rəuzmərɪ] *n* rosmarino
rosy ['rəuzɪ] *adj* roseo(-a)
rot [rɔt] *n* (*decay*) putrefazione *f*; (*inf: nonsense*) stupidaggini *fpl* ▷ *vt, vi* imputridire, marcire
rota ['rəutə] *n* tabella dei turni
rotate [rəu'teɪt] *vt* (*revolve*) far girare; (*change round: jobs*) fare a turno ▷ *vi* (*revolve*) girare
rotten ['rɔtn] *adj* (*decayed*) putrido(-a), marcio(-a); (*dishonest*) corrotto(-a); (*inf: bad*) brutto(-a); (: *action*) vigliacco(-a); **to feel ~** (*ill*) sentirsi da cani
rough [rʌf] *adj* (*skin, surface*) ruvido(-a); (*terrain, road*) accidentato(-a); (*voice*) rauco(-a); (*person, manner: coarse*) rozzo(-a), aspro(-a); (: *violent*) brutale; (*district*)

malfamato(-a); (*weather*) cattivo(-a); (*sea*) mosso(-a); (*plan*) abbozzato(-a); (*guess*) approssimativo(-a) ▷ *n* (*Golf*) macchia; **to ~ it** far vita dura; **to sleep ~** (BRIT) dormire all'addiaccio; **roughly** *adv* (*handle*) rudemente, brutalmente; (*make*) grossolanamente; (*speak*) bruscamente; (*approximately*) approssimativamente

roulette [ruːˈlɛt] *n* roulette *f*

round [raund] *adj* rotondo(-a); (*figures*) tondo(-a) ▷ *n* (BRIT: *of toast*) fetta; (*duty*: *of policeman, milkman etc*) giro; (: *of doctor*) visite *fpl*; (*game*: *of cards, golf, in competition*) partita; (*of ammunition*) cartuccia; (*Boxing*) round *m inv*; (*of talks*) serie *f inv* ▷ *vt* (*corner*) girare; (*bend*) prendere ▷ *prep* intorno a ▷ *adv* **all ~** tutt'attorno; **to go the long way ~** fare il giro più lungo; **all the year ~** tutto l'anno; **it's just ~ the corner** (*also fig*) è dietro l'angolo; **~ the clock** ininterrottamente; **to go ~ to sb's house** andare da qn; **go ~ the back** passi dietro; **enough to go ~** abbastanza per tutti; **~ of applause** applausi *mpl*; **~ of drinks** giro di bibite; **~ of sandwiches** sandwich *m inv*; **round off** *vt* (*speech etc*) finire; **round up** *vt* radunare; (*criminals*) fare una retata di; (*prices*) arrotondare; **roundabout** *n* (BRIT *Aut*) rotatoria; (: *at fair*) giostra ▷ *adj* (*route, means*) indiretto(-a); **round trip** *n* (viaggio di) andata e ritorno; **roundup** *n* raduno; (*of criminals*) retata

rouse [rauz] *vt* (*wake up*) svegliare; (*stir up*) destare; provocare; risvegliare

route [ruːt] *n* itinerario; (*of bus*) percorso

routine [ruːˈtiːn] *adj* (*work*) corrente, abituale; (*procedure*) solito(-a) ▷ *n* (*pej*) routine *f*, tran tran *m*; (*Theatre*) numero

row[1] [rəu] *n* (*line*) riga, fila; (*Knitting*) ferro; (*behind one another*: *of cars, people*) fila; (*in boat*) remata ▷ *vi* (*in boat*) remare; (*as sport*) vogare ▷ *vt* (*boat*) manovrare a remi; **in a ~** (*fig*) di fila

row[2] [rau] *n* (*racket*) baccano, chiasso; (*dispute*) lite *f*; (*scolding*) sgridata ▷ *vi* (*argue*) litigare

rowboat [ˈrəubəut] (US) *n* barca a remi

rowing [ˈrəuɪŋ] *n* canottaggio; **rowing boat** (BRIT) *n* barca a remi

royal [ˈrɔɪəl] *adj* reale; **royalty** [ˈrɔɪəltɪ] *n* (*royal persons*) (membri *mpl* della) famiglia reale; (*payment*: *to author*) diritti *mpl* d'autore

rpm *abbr* (= *revolutions per minute*) giri/min.

R.S.V.P. *abbr* (= *répondez s'il vous plaît*) R.S.V.P.

Rt. Hon. (BRIT) *abbr* (= *Right Honourable*) ≈ Onorevole

rub [rʌb] *n* **to give sth a ~** strofinare qc; (*sore place*) massaggiare qc ▷ *vt* strofinare; massaggiare; (*hands*: *also*: **~ together**) sfregarsi; **to ~ sb up** (BRIT) *or* **~ sb the wrong way** (US) lisciare qn contro pelo; **rub in** *vt* (*ointment*) far penetrare (massaggiando *or* frizionando); **rub off** *vi* andare via; **rub out** *vt* cancellare

rubber [ˈrʌbəʳ] *n* gomma; **rubber band** *n* elastico; **rubber gloves** *npl* guanti *mpl* di gomma

rubbish [ˈrʌbɪʃ] *n* (*from household*) immondizie *fpl*, rifiuti *mpl*; (*fig, pej*) cose *fpl* senza valore; robaccia; sciocchezze *fpl*; **rubbish bin** (BRIT) *n* pattumiera; **rubbish dump** *n* (*in town*) immondezzaio

rubble [ˈrʌbl] *n* macerie *fpl*; (*smaller*) pietrisco

ruby [ˈruːbɪ] *n* rubino

rucksack [ˈrʌksæk] *n* zaino

rudder [ˈrʌdəʳ] *n* timone *m*

rude [ruːd] *adj* (*impolite*: *person*) scortese, rozzo(-a); (: *word, manners*) grossolano(-a), rozzo(-a); (*shocking*) indecente

ruffle ['rʌfl] *vt* (*hair*) scompigliare; (*clothes, water*) increspare; (*fig: person*) turbare
rug [rʌg] *n* tappeto; (BRIT: *for knees*) coperta
rugby ['rʌgbɪ] *n* (*also:* **~ football**) rugby *m*
rugged ['rʌgɪd] *adj* (*landscape*) aspro(-a); (*features, determination*) duro(-a); (*character*) brusco(-a)
ruin ['ru:ɪn] *n* rovina ▷ *vt* rovinare; **ruins** *npl* (*of building, castle etc*) rovine *fpl*, ruderi *mpl*
rule [ru:l] *n* regola; (*regulation*) regolamento, regola; (*government*) governo; (*ruler*) riga ▷ *vt* (*country*) governare; (*person*) dominare ▷ *vi* regnare; decidere; (*Law*) dichiarare; **as a ~** normalmente; **rule out** *vt* escludere; **ruler** *n* (*sovereign*) sovrano(-a); (*for measuring*) regolo, riga; **ruling** *adj* (*party*) al potere; (*class*) dirigente ▷ *n* (*Law*) decisione *f*
rum [rʌm] *n* rum *m*
Rumania *etc* [ru:'meɪnɪə] *n* = **Romania** *etc*
rumble ['rʌmbl] *n* rimbombo; brontolio ▷ *vi* rimbombare; (*stomach, pipe*) brontolare
rumour ['ru:mə^r] (US **rumor**) *n* voce *f* ▷ *vt* **it is ~ed that** corre voce che

> Be careful not to translate ***rumour*** by the Italian word ***rumore***.

rump steak [rʌmp-] *n* bistecca di girello
run [rʌn] (*pt* **ran**, *pp* **run**) *n* corsa; (*outing*) gita (in macchina); (*distance travelled*) percorso, tragitto; (*Ski*) pista; (*Cricket, Baseball*) meta; (*series*) serie *f*; (*Theatre*) periodo di rappresentazione; (*in tights, stockings*) smagliatura ▷ *vt* (*distance*) correre; (*operate: business*) gestire, dirigere; (*: competition, course*) organizzare; (*: hotel*) gestire; (*: house*) governare; (*Comput*) eseguire; (*water, bath*) far scorrere; (*force through: rope, pipe*): **to ~ sth through** far passare qc attraverso; (*pass: hand, finger*): **to ~ sth over** passare qc su; (*Press: feature*) presentare ▷ *vi* correre; (*flee*) scappare; (*pass: road etc*) passare; (*work: machine, factory*) funzionare, andare; (*bus, train: operate*) far servizio; (*: travel*) circolare; (*continue: play, contract*) durare; (*slide: drawer; flow: river, bath*) scorrere; (*colours, washing*) stemperarsi; (*in election*) presentarsi candidato; (*nose*) colare; **there was a ~ on ...** c'era una corsa a ...; **in the long ~** a lungo andare; **on the ~** in fuga; **to ~ a race** partecipare ad una gara; **I'll ~ you to the station** la porto alla stazione; **to ~ a risk** correre un rischio; **run after** *vt fus* (*to catch up*) rincorrere; (*chase*) correre dietro a; **run away** *vi* fuggire; **run down** *vt* (*production*) ridurre gradualmente; (*factory*) rallentare l'attività di; (*Aut*) investire; (*criticize*) criticare; **to be run down** (*person: tired*) essere esausto(-a); **run into** *vt fus* (*meet: person*) incontrare per caso; (*: trouble*) incontrare, trovare; (*collide with*) andare a sbattere contro; **run off** *vi* fuggire ▷ *vt* (*water*) far scolare; (*copies*) fare; **run out** *vi* (*person*) uscire di corsa; (*liquid*) colare; (*lease*) scadere; (*money*) esaurirsi; **run out of** *vt fus* rimanere a corto di; **run over** *vt* (*Aut*) investire, mettere sotto ▷ *vt fus* (*revise*) rivedere; **run through** *vt fus* (*instructions*) dare una scorsa a; (*rehearse: play*) riprovare, ripetere; **run up** *vt* (*debt*) lasciar accumulare; **to run up against** (*difficulties*) incontrare; **runaway** *adj* (*person*) fuggiasco(-a); (*horse*) in libertà; (*truck*) fuori controllo
rung [rʌŋ] *pp of* **ring** ▷ *n* (*of ladder*) piolo
runner ['rʌnə^r] *n* (*in race*) corridore *m*; (*: horse*) partente *m/f*; (*on sledge*) pattino; (*for drawer etc*) guida; **runner**

bean (BRIT) *n* fagiolo rampicante; **runner-up** *n* secondo(-a) arrivato(-a)

running ['rʌnɪŋ] *n* corsa; direzione *f*; organizzazione *f*; funzionamento ▷ *adj* (*water*) corrente; (*commentary*) simultaneo(-a); **to be in/out of the ~ for sth** essere/non essere più in lizza per qc; **6 days ~** 6 giorni di seguito

runny ['rʌnɪ] *adj* che cola

run-up ['rʌnʌp] *n* **~ to** (*election etc*) periodo che precede

runway ['rʌnweɪ] *n* (*Aviat*) pista (di decollo)

rupture ['rʌptʃə^r] *n* (*Med*) ernia

rural ['rurəl] *adj* rurale

rush [rʌʃ] *n* corsa precipitosa; (*hurry*) furia, fretta; (*sudden demand*): **~ for** corsa a; (*current*) flusso; (*of emotion*) impeto; (*Bot*) giunco ▷ *vt* mandare *or* spedire velocemente; (*attack*: *town etc*) prendere d'assalto ▷ *vi* precipitarsi; **rush hour** *n* ora di punta

Russia ['rʌʃə] *n* Russia; **Russian** *adj* russo(-a) ▷ *n* russo(-a); (*Ling*) russo

rust [rʌst] *n* ruggine *f* ▷ *vi* arrugginirsi

rusty ['rʌstɪ] *adj* arrugginito(-a)

ruthless ['ru:θlɪs] *adj* spietato(-a)

RV *abbr* (= *revised version*) *versione riveduta della Bibbia* ▷ *n abbr* (US) *see* **recreational vehicle**

rye [raɪ] *n* segale *f*

S

Sabbath ['sæbəθ] *n* (*Jewish*) sabato; (*Christian*) domenica

sabotage ['sæbətɑ:ʒ] *n* sabotaggio ▷ *vt* sabotare

saccharin(e) ['sækərɪn] *n* saccarina

sachet ['sæʃeɪ] *n* bustina

sack [sæk] *n* (*bag*) sacco ▷ *vt* (*dismiss*) licenziare, mandare a spasso; (*plunder*) saccheggiare; **to get the ~** essere mandato a spasso

sacred ['seɪkrɪd] *adj* sacro(-a)

sacrifice ['sækrɪfaɪs] *n* sacrificio ▷ *vt* sacrificare

sad [sæd] *adj* triste

saddle ['sædl] *n* sella ▷ *vt* (*horse*) sellare; **to be ~d with sth** (*inf*) avere qc sulle spalle

sadistic [sə'dɪstɪk] *adj* sadico(-a)

sadly ['sædlɪ] *adv* tristemente; (*regrettably*) sfortunatamente; **~ lacking in** penosamente privo di

sadness ['sædnɪs] *n* tristezza

s.a.e. *n abbr* (= *stamped addressed envelope*) *busta affrancata e con indirizzo*

safari [sə'fɑːrɪ] *n* safari *m inv*
safe [seɪf] *adj* sicuro(-a); (*out of danger*) salvo(-a), al sicuro; (*cautious*) prudente ▷ *n* cassaforte *f*; **~ from** al sicuro da; **~ and sound** sano(-a) e salvo(-a); **(just) to be on the ~ side** per non correre rischi; **could you put this in the ~, please?** lo potrebbe mettere nella cassaforte, per favore?; **safely** *adv* sicuramente; sano(-a) e salvo(-a); prudentemente; **safe sex** *n* sesso sicuro
safety ['seɪftɪ] *n* sicurezza; **safety belt** *n* cintura di sicurezza; **safety pin** *n* spilla di sicurezza
saffron ['sæfrən] *n* zafferano
sag [sæg] *vi* incurvarsi; afflosciarsi
sage [seɪdʒ] *n* (*herb*) salvia; (*man*) saggio
Sagittarius [sædʒɪ'tɛərɪəs] *n* Sagittario
Sahara [sə'hɑːrə] *n* **the ~ (Desert)** il (deserto del) Sahara
said [sɛd] *pt, pp of* **say**
sail [seɪl] *n* (*on boat*) vela; (*trip*): **to go for a ~** fare un giro in barca a vela ▷ *vt* (*boat*) condurre, governare ▷ *vi* (*travel*: *ship*) navigare; (: *passenger*) viaggiare per mare; (*set off*) salpare; (*sport*) fare della vela; **they ~ed into Genoa** entrarono nel porto di Genova; **sailboat** (US) *n* barca a vela; **sailing** *n* (*sport*) vela; **to go sailing** fare della vela; **sailing boat** *n* barca a vela; **sailor** *n* marinaio
saint [seɪnt] *n* santo(-a)
sake [seɪk] *n* **for the ~ of** per, per amore di
salad ['sæləd] *n* insalata; **salad cream** (BRIT) *n* (tipo di) maionese *f*; **salad dressing** *n* condimento per insalata
salami [sə'lɑːmɪ] *n* salame *m*
salary ['sælərɪ] *n* stipendio
sale [seɪl] *n* vendita; (*at reduced prices*) svendita, liquidazione *f*; (*auction*) vendita all'asta; **"for ~"** "in vendita"; **on ~** in vendita; **on ~ or return** da vendere o rimandare; **sales** *npl* (*total amount sold*) vendite *fpl*; **sales assistant** (US **sales clerk**) *n* commesso(-a); **salesman/woman** (*irreg*) *n* commesso(-a); (*representative*) rappresentante *m/f*; **salesperson** (*irreg*) *n* (*in shop*) commesso; (*representative*) rappresentante *m/f* di commercio; **sales rep** *n* rappresentante *m/f* di commercio
saline ['seɪlaɪn] *adj* salino(-a)
saliva [sə'laɪvə] *n* saliva
salmon ['sæmən] *n inv* salmone *m*
salon ['sælɔn] *n* (*hairdressing salon*) parrucchiere(-a); (*beauty salon*) salone *m* di bellezza
saloon [sə'luːn] *n* (US) saloon *m inv*, bar *m inv*; (BRIT: *Aut*) berlina; (*ship's lounge*) salone *m*
salt [sɔlt] *n* sale *m* ▷ *vt* salare; **saltwater** *adj* di mare; **salty** *adj* salato(-a)
salute [sə'luːt] *n* saluto ▷ *vt* salutare
salvage ['sælvɪdʒ] *n* (*saving*) salvataggio; (*things saved*) beni *mpl* salvati *or* recuperati ▷ *vt* salvare, mettere in salvo
Salvation Army [sæl'veɪʃən-] *n* Esercito della Salvezza
same [seɪm] *adj* stesso(-a), medesimo(-a) ▷ *pron* **the ~** lo (la) stesso(-a), gli (le) stessi(-e); **the ~ book as** lo stesso libro di (*o* che); **at the ~ time** allo stesso tempo; **all** *or* **just the ~** tuttavia; **to do the ~ as sb** fare come qn; **the ~ to you!** altrettanto a te!
sample ['sɑːmpl] *n* campione *m* ▷ *vt* (*food*) assaggiare; (*wine*) degustare
sanction ['sæŋkʃən] *n* sanzione *f* ▷ *vt* sancire, sanzionare; **sanctions** *npl* (*Pol*) sanzioni *fpl*
sanctuary ['sæŋktjuərɪ] *n* (*holy place*) santuario; (*refuge*) rifugio; (*for wildlife*) riserva

sand [sænd] *n* sabbia ▷ *vt* (*also*: **~ down**) cartavetrare
sandal ['sændl] *n* sandalo
sand: **sandbox** ['sændbɔks] (*US*) *n* = **sandpit**; **sandcastle** ['sændkɑːsl] *n* castello di sabbia; **sand dune** *n* duna di sabbia; **sandpaper** ['sændpeɪpəʳ] *n* carta vetrata; **sandpit** ['sændpɪt] *n* (*for children*) buca di sabbia; **sands** *npl* spiaggia; **sandstone** ['sændstəun] *n* arenaria
sandwich ['sændwɪtʃ] *n* tramezzino, panino, sandwich *m inv* ▷ *vt* **~ed between** incastrato(-a) fra; **cheese/ham ~** sandwich al formaggio/prosciutto
sandy ['sændɪ] *adj* sabbioso(-a); (*colour*) color sabbia *inv*, biondo(-a) rossiccio(-a)
sane [seɪn] *adj* (*person*) sano(-a) di mente; (*outlook*) sensato(-a)
sang [sæŋ] *pt of* **sing**
sanitary towel ['sænɪtərɪ-] (*US* **sanitary napkin**) *n* assorbente *m* (igienico)
sanity ['sænɪtɪ] *n* sanità mentale; (*common sense*) buon senso
sank [sæŋk] *pt of* **sink**
Santa Claus [sæntə'klɔːz] *n* Babbo Natale
sap [sæp] *n* (*of plants*) linfa ▷ *vt* (*strength*) fiaccare
sapphire ['sæfaɪəʳ] *n* zaffiro
sarcasm ['sɑːkæzm] *n* sarcasmo
sarcastic [sɑː'kæstɪk] *adj* sarcastico(-a); **to be ~** fare del sarcasmo
sardine [sɑː'diːn] *n* sardina
Sardinia [sɑː'dɪnɪə] *n* Sardegna
SASE (*US*) *n abbr* (= *self-addressed stamped envelope*) *busta affrancata e con indirizzo*
sat [sæt] *pt, pp of* **sit**
Sat. *abbr* (= *Saturday*) sab.
satchel ['sætʃl] *n* cartella
satellite ['sætəlaɪt] *adj* satellite ▷ *n* satellite *m*; **satellite dish** *n* antenna parabolica; **satellite television** *n* televisione *f* via satellite
satin ['sætɪn] *n* raso ▷ *adj* di raso
satire ['sætaɪəʳ] *n* satira
satisfaction [sætɪs'fækʃən] *n* soddisfazione *f*
satisfactory [sætɪs'fæktərɪ] *adj* soddisfacente
satisfied ['sætɪsfaɪd] *adj* (*customer*) soddisfatto(-a); **to be ~ (with sth)** essere soddisfatto(-a) (di qc)
satisfy ['sætɪsfaɪ] *vt* soddisfare; (*convince*) convincere
Saturday ['sætədɪ] *n* sabato
sauce [sɔːs] *n* salsa; (*containing meat, fish*) sugo; **saucepan** *n* casseruola
saucer ['sɔːsəʳ] *n* sottocoppa *m*, piattino
Saudi Arabia ['saudɪ-] *n* Arabia Saudita
sauna ['sɔːnə] *n* sauna
sausage ['sɔsɪdʒ] *n* salsiccia; **sausage roll** *n rotolo di pasta sfoglia ripieno di salsiccia*
sautéed ['səuteɪd] *adj* saltato(-a)
savage ['sævɪdʒ] *adj* (*cruel, fierce*) selvaggio(-a), feroce; (*primitive*) primitivo(-a) ▷ *n* selvaggio(-a) ▷ *vt* attaccare selvaggiamente
save [seɪv] *vt* (*person, belongings, Comput*) salvare; (*money*) risparmiare, mettere da parte; (*time*) risparmiare; (*food*) conservare; (*avoid: trouble*) evitare; (*Sport*) parare ▷ *vi* (*also*: **~ up**) economizzare ▷ *n* (*Sport*) parata ▷ *prep* salvo, a eccezione di
savings ['seɪvɪŋz] *npl* (*money*) risparmi *mpl*; **savings account** *n* libretto di risparmio; **savings and loan association** (*US*) *n* ≈ società di credito immobiliare
savoury ['seɪvərɪ] (*US* **savory**) *adj* (*dish: not sweet*) salato(-a)
saw [sɔː] (*pt* **sawed**, *pp* **sawed** *or* **sawn**) *pt of* **see** ▷ *n* (*tool*) sega ▷ *vt* segare; **sawdust** *n* segatura
sawn [sɔːn] *pp of* **saw**

saxophone ['sæksəfəun] *n* sassofono
say [seɪ] (*pt, pp* **said**) *n* **to have one's ~** fare sentire il proprio parere; **to have a** *or* **some ~** avere voce in capitolo ▷ *vt* dire; **could you ~ that again?** potrebbe ripeterlo?; **that goes without ~ing** va da sé; **saying** *n* proverbio, detto
scab [skæb] *n* crosta; (*pej*) crumiro(-a)
scaffolding ['skæfəldɪŋ] *n* impalcatura
scald [skɔːld] *n* scottatura ▷ *vt* scottare
scale [skeɪl] *n* scala; (*of fish*) squama ▷ *vt* (*mountain*) scalare; **scales** *npl* (*for weighing*) bilancia; **on a large ~** su vasta scala; **~ of charges** tariffa
scallion ['skæljən] *n* cipolla; (*US: shallot*) scalogna; (*: leek*) porro
scallop ['skɔləp] *n* (*Zool*) pettine *m*; (*Sewing*) smerlo
scalp [skælp] *n* cuoio capelluto ▷ *vt* scotennare
scalpel ['skælpl] *n* bisturi *m inv*
scam [skæm] *n* (*inf*) truffa
scampi ['skæmpɪ] *npl* scampi *mpl*
scan [skæn] *vt* scrutare; (*glance at quickly*) scorrere, dare un'occhiata a; (*TV*) analizzare; (*Radar*) esplorare ▷ *n* (*Med*) ecografia
scandal ['skændl] *n* scandalo; (*gossip*) pettegolezzi *mpl*
Scandinavia [skændɪ'neɪvɪə] *n* Scandinavia; **Scandinavian** *adj, n* scandinavo(-a)
scanner ['skænəʳ] *n* (*Radar, Med*) scanner *m inv*
scapegoat ['skeɪpgəut] *n* capro espiatorio
scar [skɑː] *n* cicatrice *f* ▷ *vt* sfregiare
scarce [skɛəs] *adj* scarso(-a); (*copy, edition*) raro(-a); **to make o.s. ~** (*inf*) squagliarsela; **scarcely** *adv* appena
scare [skɛəʳ] *n* spavento; panico ▷ *vt* spaventare, atterrire; **there was a bomb ~ at the bank** hanno evacuato la banca per paura di un attentato dinamitardo; **to ~ sb stiff** spaventare a morte qn; **scarecrow** *n* spaventapasseri *m inv*; **scared** *adj* **to be scared** aver paura
scarf [skɑːf] (*pl* **scarves** *or* **scarfs**) *n* (*long*) sciarpa; (*square*) fazzoletto da testa, foulard *m inv*
scarlet ['skɑːlɪt] *adj* scarlatto(-a)
scarves [skɑːvz] *npl of* **scarf**
scary ['skɛərɪ] *adj* che spaventa
scatter ['skætəʳ] *vt* spargere; (*crowd*) disperdere ▷ *vi* disperdersi
scenario [sɪ'nɑːrɪəu] *n* (*Theatre, Cinema*) copione *m*; (*fig*) situazione *f*
scene [siːn] *n* (*Theatre, fig etc*) scena; (*of crime, accident*) scena, luogo; (*sight, view*) vista, veduta; **scenery** *n* (*Theatre*) scenario; (*landscape*) panorama *m*; **scenic** *adj* scenico(-a); panoramico(-a)
scent [sɛnt] *n* profumo; (*sense of smell*) olfatto, odorato; (*fig: track*) pista
sceptical ['skɛptɪkəl] (*US* **skeptical**) *adj* scettico(-a)
schedule ['ʃɛdjuːl, (*US*) 'skɛdjuːl] *n* programma *m*, piano; (*of trains*) orario; (*of prices etc*) lista, tabella ▷ *vt* fissare; **on ~** in orario; **to be ahead of/behind ~** essere in anticipo/ritardo sul previsto; **scheduled flight** *n* volo di linea
scheme [skiːm] *n* piano, progetto; (*method*) sistema *m*; (*dishonest plan, plot*) intrigo, trama; (*arrangement*) disposizione *f*, sistemazione *f*; (*pension scheme etc*) programma *m* ▷ *vi* fare progetti; (*intrigue*) complottare
schizophrenic [skɪtsə'frɛnɪk] *adj, n* schizofrenico(-a)
scholar ['skɔləʳ] *n* (*expert*) studioso(-a); **scholarship** *n* erudizione *f*; (*grant*) borsa di studio
school [skuːl] *n* (*primary, secondary*) scuola; (*university: US*) università *f inv* ▷ *cpd* scolare, scolastico(-a) ▷ *vt* (*animal*) addestrare; **schoolbook** *n*

libro scolastico; **schoolboy** *n* scolaro; **school children** *npl* scolari *mpl*; **schoolgirl** *n* scolara; **schooling** *n* istruzione *f*; **schoolteacher** *n* insegnante *m/f*, docente *m/f*; (*primary*) maestro(-a)

science ['saɪəns] *n* scienza; **science fiction** *n* fantascienza; **scientific** [-'tɪfɪk] *adj* scientifico(-a); **scientist** *n* scienziato(-a)

sci-fi ['saɪfaɪ] *n abbr* (*inf*) = **science fiction**

scissors ['sɪzəz] *npl* forbici *fpl*

scold [skəuld] *vt* rimproverare

scone [skɔn] *n* focaccina da tè

scoop [sku:p] *n* mestolo; (*for ice cream*) cucchiaio dosatore; (*Press*) colpo giornalistico, notizia (in) esclusiva

scooter ['sku:təʳ] *n* (*motor cycle*) motoretta, scooter *m inv*; (*toy*) monopattino

scope [skəup] *n* (*capacity: of plan, undertaking*) portata; (*: of person*) capacità *fpl*; (*opportunity*) possibilità *fpl*

scorching ['skɔ:tʃɪŋ] *adj* cocente, scottante

score [skɔ:ʳ] *n* punti *mpl*, punteggio; (*Mus*) partitura, spartito; (*twenty*) venti ▷ *vt* (*goal, point*) segnare, fare; (*success*) ottenere ▷ *vi* segnare; (*Football*) fare un goal; (*keep score*) segnare i punti; **~s of** (*very many*) un sacco di; **on that ~** a questo riguardo; **to ~ 6 out of 10** prendere 6 su 10; **score out** *vt* cancellare con un segno; **scoreboard** *n* tabellone *m* segnapunti; **scorer** *n* marcatore(-trice); (*keeping score*) segnapunti *m inv*

scorn [skɔ:n] *n* disprezzo ▷ *vt* disprezzare

Scorpio ['skɔ:pɪəu] *n* Scorpione *m*

scorpion ['skɔ:pɪən] *n* scorpione *m*

Scot [skɔt] *n* scozzese *m/f*

Scotch tape® *n* scotch® *m*

Scotland ['skɔtlənd] *n* Scozia

Scots [skɔts] *adj* scozzese; **Scotsman** (*irreg*) *n* scozzese *m*; **Scotswoman** (*irreg*) *n* scozzese *f*; **Scottish** ['skɔtɪʃ] *adj* scozzese; **Scottish Parliament** *n* Parlamento scozzese

scout [skaut] *n* (*Mil*) esploratore *m*; (*also:* **boy ~**) giovane esploratore, scout *m inv*

scowl [skaul] *vi* accigliarsi, aggrottare le sopracciglia; **to ~ at** guardare torvo

scramble ['skræmbl] *n* arrampicata ▷ *vi* inerpicarsi; **to ~ out** *etc* uscire *etc* in fretta; **to ~ for** azzuffarsi per; **scrambled eggs** *npl* uova *fpl* strapazzate

scrap [skræp] *n* pezzo, pezzetto; (*fight*) zuffa; (*also:* **~ iron**) rottami *mpl* di ferro, ferraglia ▷ *vt* demolire; (*fig*) scartare ▷ *vi* **to ~ (with sb)** fare a botte (con qn); **scraps** *npl* (*waste*) scarti *mpl*; **scrapbook** *n* album *m inv* di ritagli

scrape [skreɪp] *vt, vi* raschiare, grattare ▷ *n* **to get into a ~** cacciarsi in un guaio

scrap paper *n* cartaccia

scratch [skrætʃ] *n* graffio ▷ *cpd* **~ team** squadra raccogliticcia ▷ *vt* graffiare, rigare ▷ *vi* grattare; (*paint, car*) graffiare; **to start from ~** cominciare *or* partire da zero; **to be up to ~** essere all'altezza; **scratch card** *n* (BRIT) cartolina *f* gratta e vinci

scream [skri:m] *n* grido, urlo ▷ *vi* urlare, gridare

screen [skri:n] *n* schermo; (*fig*) muro, cortina, velo ▷ *vt* schermare, fare schermo a; (*from the wind etc*) riparare; (*film*) proiettare; (*book*) adattare per lo schermo; (*candidates etc*) selezionare; **screening** *n* (*Med*) dépistage *m inv*; **screenplay** *n* sceneggiatura; **screen saver** *n* (*Comput*) screen saver *m inv*

screw [skru:] *n* vite *f* ▷ *vt* avvitare; **screw up** *vt* (*paper etc*) spiegazzare; (*inf: ruin*) rovinare; **to screw up one's eyes** strizzare gli occhi; **screwdriver**

n cacciavite *m*
scribble ['skrɪbl] *n* scarabocchio ▷ *vt* scribacchiare in fretta ▷ *vi* scarabocchiare
script [skrɪpt] *n* (*Cinema etc*) copione *m*; (*in exam*) elaborato *or* compito d'esame
scroll [skrəul] *n* rotolo di carta
scrub [skrʌb] *n* (*land*) boscaglia ▷ *vt* pulire strofinando; (*reject*) annullare
scruffy ['skrʌfɪ] *adj* sciatto(-a)
scrum(mage) ['skrʌm(ɪdʒ)] *n* mischia
scrutiny ['skru:tɪnɪ] *n* esame *m* accurato
scuba diving ['sku:bə-] *n* immersioni *fpl* subacquee
sculptor ['skʌlptə^r] *n* scultore *m*
sculpture ['skʌlptʃə^r] *n* scultura
scum [skʌm] *n* schiuma; (*pej: people*) feccia
scurry ['skʌrɪ] *vi* sgambare, affrettarsi
sea [si:] *n* mare *m* ▷ *cpd* marino(-a), del mare; (*bird, fish*) di mare; (*route, transport*) marittimo(-a); **by ~** (*travel*) per mare; **on the ~** (*boat*) in mare; (*town*) di mare; **to be all at ~** (*fig*) non sapere che pesci pigliare; **out to ~** al largo; **(out) at ~** in mare; **seafood** *n* frutti *mpl* di mare; **sea front** *n* lungomare *m*; **seagull** *n* gabbiano
seal [si:l] *n* (*animal*) foca; (*stamp*) sigillo; (*impression*) impronta del sigillo ▷ *vt* sigillare; **seal off** *vt* (*close*) sigillare; (*forbid entry to*) bloccare l'accesso a
sea level *n* livello del mare
seam [si:m] *n* cucitura; (*of coal*) filone *m*
search [sə:tʃ] *n* ricerca; (*Law: at sb's home*) perquisizione *f* ▷ *vt* frugare ▷ *vi* **to ~ for** ricercare; **in ~ of** alla ricerca di; **search engine** *n* (*Comput*) motore *m* di ricerca; **search party** *n* squadra di soccorso
sea: **seashore** ['si:ʃɔ:^r] *n* spiaggia; **seasick** ['si:sɪk] *adj* che soffre il mal di mare; **seaside** ['si:saɪd] *n* spiaggia; **seaside resort** *n* stazione *f* balneare
season ['si:zn] *n* stagione *f* ▷ *vt* condire, insaporire; **seasonal** *adj* stagionale; **seasoning** *n* condimento; **season ticket** *n* abbonamento
seat [si:t] *n* sedile *m*; (*in bus, train: place*) posto; (*Parliament*) seggio; (*buttocks*) didietro; (*of trousers*) fondo ▷ *vt* far sedere; (*have room for*) avere *or* essere fornito(-a) di posti a sedere per; **I'd like to book two ~s** vorrei prenotare due posti; **to be ~ed** essere seduto(-a); **seat belt** *n* cintura di sicurezza; **seating** *n* posti *mpl* a sedere
sea: **sea water** *n* acqua di mare; **seaweed** ['si:wi:d] *n* alghe *fpl*
sec. *abbr* = **second(s)**
secluded [sɪ'klu:dɪd] *adj* isolato(-a), appartato(-a)
second ['sɛkənd] *num* secondo(-a) ▷ *adv* (*in race etc*) al secondo posto ▷ *n* (*unit of time*) secondo; (*Aut: also:* **~ gear**) seconda; (*Comm: imperfect*) scarto; (BRIT: *Scol: degree*) *laurea con punteggio discreto* ▷ *vt* (*motion*) appoggiare; **secondary** *adj* secondario(-a); **secondary school** *n* scuola secondaria; **second-class** *adj* di seconda classe ▷ *adv* in seconda classe; **secondhand** *adj* di seconda mano, usato(-a); **secondly** *adv* in secondo luogo; **second-rate** *adj* scadente; **second thoughts** *npl* ripensamenti *mpl*; **on second thoughts** (BRIT) *or* **thought** (US) ripensandoci bene
secrecy ['si:krəsɪ] *n* segretezza
secret ['si:krɪt] *adj* segreto(-a) ▷ *n* segreto; **in ~** in segreto
secretary ['sɛkrətrɪ] *n* segretario(-a); **S~ of State (for)** (BRIT: *Pol*) ministro (di)
secretive ['si:krətɪv] *adj* riservato(-a)
secret service *n* servizi *mpl* segreti

sect [sɛkt] *n* setta
section ['sɛkʃən] *n* sezione *f*
sector ['sɛktəʳ] *n* settore *m*
secular ['sɛkjuləʳ] *adj* secolare
secure [sɪ'kjuəʳ] *adj* sicuro(-a); (*firmly fixed*) assicurato(-a), ben fermato(-a); (*in safe place*) al sicuro ▷ *vt* (*fix*) fissare, assicurare; (*get*) ottenere, assicurarsi; **securities** *npl* (*Stock Exchange*) titoli *mpl*
security [sɪ'kjuərɪtɪ] *n* sicurezza; (*for loan*) garanzia; **security guard** *n* guardia giurata
sedan [sə'dæn] (*US*) *n* (*Aut*) berlina
sedate [sɪ'deɪt] *adj* posato(-a), calmo(-a) ▷ *vt* calmare
sedative ['sɛdɪtɪv] *n* sedativo, calmante *m*
seduce [sɪ'dju:s] *vt* sedurre; **seductive** [-'dʌktɪv] *adj* seducente
see [si:] (*pt* **saw**, *pp* **seen**) *vt* vedere; (*accompany*): **to ~ sb to the door** accompagnare qn alla porta ▷ *vi* vedere; (*understand*) capire ▷ *n* sede *f* vescovile; **to ~ that** (*ensure*) badare che + *sub*, fare in modo che + *sub*; **~ you soon!** a presto!; **see off** *vt* salutare alla partenza; **see out** *vt* (*take to the door*) accompagnare alla porta; **see through** *vt* portare a termine ▷ *vt fus* non lasciarsi ingannare da; **see to** *vt fus* occuparsi di
seed [si:d] *n* seme *m*; (*fig*) germe *m*; (*Tennis etc*) testa di serie; **to go to ~** fare seme; (*fig*) scadere
seeing ['si:ɪŋ] *conj* **~ (that)** visto che
seek [si:k] (*pt, pp* **sought**) *vt* cercare
seem [si:m] *vi* sembrare, parere; **there ~s to be ...** sembra che ci sia ...; **seemingly** *adv* apparentemente
seen [si:n] *pp of* **see**
seesaw ['si:sɔ:] *n* altalena a bilico
segment ['sɛgmənt] *n* segmento
segregate ['sɛgrɪgeɪt] *vt* segregare, isolare
seize [si:z] *vt* (*grasp*) afferrare; (*take possession of*) impadronirsi di; (*Law*) sequestrare
seizure ['si:ʒəʳ] *n* (*Med*) attacco; (*Law*) confisca, sequestro
seldom ['sɛldəm] *adv* raramente
select [sɪ'lɛkt] *adj* scelto(-a) ▷ *vt* scegliere, selezionare; **selection** [-'lɛkʃən] *n* selezione *f*, scelta; **selective** *adj* selettivo(-a)
self [sɛlf] *n* **the ~** l'io *m* ▷ *prefix* auto...; **self-assured** *adj* sicuro(-a) di sé; **self-catering** (*BRIT*) *adj* in cui ci si cucina da sé; **self-centred** (*US* **self-centered**) *adj* egocentrico(-a); **self-confidence** *n* sicurezza di sé; **self-confident** *adj* sicuro(-a) di sé; **self-conscious** *adj* timido(-a); **self-contained** (*BRIT*) *adj* (*flat*) indipendente; **self-control** *n* autocontrollo; **self-defence** (*US* **self-defense**) *n* autodifesa; (*Law*) legittima difesa; **self-drive** *adj* (*BRIT*: *rented car*) senza autista; **self-employed** *adj* che lavora in proprio; **self-esteem** *n* amor proprio *m*; **self-indulgent** *adj* indulgente verso se stesso(-a); **self-interest** *n* interesse *m* personale; **selfish** *adj* egoista; **self-pity** *n* autocommiserazione *f*; **self-raising** (*US* **self-rising**) *adj* **self-raising flour** miscela di farina e lievito; **self-respect** *n* rispetto di sé, amor proprio; **self-service** *n* autoservizio, self-service *m*
sell [sɛl] (*pt, pp* **sold**) *vt* vendere ▷ *vi* vendersi; **to ~ at** *or* **for 1000 euros** essere in vendita a 1000 euro; **sell off** *vt* svendere, liquidare; **sell out** *vi* **to sell out (of sth)** esaurire (qc); **the tickets are all sold out** i biglietti sono esauriti; **sell-by date** ['sɛlbaɪ-] *n* data di scadenza; **seller** *n* venditore(-trice)
Sellotape® ['sɛləuteɪp] (*BRIT*) *n* nastro adesivo, scotch® *m*
selves [sɛlvz] *npl of* **self**
semester [sɪ'mɛstəʳ] (*US*) *n* semestre *m*
semi... ['sɛmɪ] *prefix* semi...;

semicircle *n* semicerchio; **semidetached (house)** [sɛmɪdɪ'tætʃt-] (BRIT) *n* casa gemella; **semi-final** *n* semifinale *f*

seminar ['sɛmɪnɑːʳ] *n* seminario

semi-skimmed ['sɛmɪ'skɪmd] *adj* (*milk*) parzialmente scremato(-a)

senate ['sɛnɪt] *n* senato; **senator** *n* senatore(-trice)

send [sɛnd] (*pt, pp* **sent**) *vt* mandare; **send back** *vt* rimandare; **send for** *vt fus* mandare a chiamare, far venire; **send in** *vt* (*report, application, resignation*) presentare; **send off** *vt* (*goods*) spedire; (BRIT: *Sport: player*) espellere; **send on** *vt* (BRIT: *letter*) inoltrare; (*luggage etc: in advance*) spedire in anticipo; **send out** *vt* (*invitation*) diramare; **send up** *vt* (*person, price*) far salire; (BRIT: *parody*) mettere in ridicolo; **sender** *n* mittente *m/f*; **send-off** *n* **to give sb a good send-off** festeggiare la partenza di qn

senile ['siːnaɪl] *adj* senile

senior ['siːnɪəʳ] *adj* (*older*) più vecchio(-a); (*of higher rank*) di grado più elevato; **senior citizen** *n* persona anziana; **senior high school** (US) *n* ≈ liceo

sensation [sɛn'seɪʃən] *n* sensazione *f*; **sensational** *adj* sensazionale; (*marvellous*) eccezionale

sense [sɛns] *n* senso; (*feeling*) sensazione *f*, senso; (*meaning*) senso, significato; (*wisdom*) buonsenso ▷ *vt* sentire, percepire; **it makes ~** ha senso; **senseless** *adj* sciocco(-a); (*unconscious*) privo(-a) di sensi; **sense of humour** (BRIT) *n* senso dell'umorismo

sensible ['sɛnsɪbl] *adj* sensato(-a), ragionevole

> Be careful not to translate ***sensible*** by the Italian word ***sensibile***.

sensitive ['sɛnsɪtɪv] *adj* sensibile; (*skin, question*) delicato(-a)

sensual ['sɛnsjuəl] *adj* sensuale

sensuous ['sɛnsjuəs] *adj* sensuale

sent [sɛnt] *pt, pp of* **send**

sentence ['sɛntns] *n* (*Ling*) frase *f*; (*Law: judgment*) sentenza; (*: punishment*) condanna ▷ *vt* **to ~ sb to death/to 5 years** condannare qn a morte/a 5 anni

sentiment ['sɛntɪmənt] *n* sentimento; (*opinion*) opinione *f*; **sentimental** [-'mɛntl] *adj* sentimentale

Sep. *abbr* (= *September*) Sett.

separate [*adj* 'sɛprɪt, *vb* 'sɛpəreɪt] *adj* separato(-a) ▷ *vt* separare ▷ *vi* separarsi; **separately** *adv* separatamente; **separates** *npl* (*clothes*) coordinati *mpl*; **separation** [-'reɪʃən] *n* separazione *f*

September [sɛp'tɛmbəʳ] *n* settembre *m*

septic ['sɛptɪk] *adj* settico(-a); (*wound*) infettato(-a); **septic tank** *n* fossa settica

sequel ['siːkwl] *n* conseguenza; (*of story*) seguito; (*of film*) sequenza

sequence ['siːkwəns] *n* (*series*) serie *f*; (*order*) ordine *m*

sequin ['siːkwɪn] *n* lustrino, paillette *f inv*

Serb [səːb] *adj, n* = **Serbian**

Serbia ['səːbɪə] *n* Serbia

Serbian ['səːbɪən] *adj* serbo(-a) ▷ *n* serbo(-a); (*Ling*) serbo

sergeant ['sɑːdʒənt] *n* sergente *m*; (*Police*) brigadiere *m*

serial ['sɪərɪəl] *n* (*Press*) romanzo a puntate; (*Radio, TV*) trasmissione *f* a puntate, serial *m inv*; **serial killer** *n* serial-killer *m/f inv*; **serial number** *n* numero di serie

series ['sɪəriːz] *n inv* serie *f inv*; (*Publishing*) collana

serious ['sɪərɪəs] *adj* serio(-a), grave; **seriously** *adv* seriamente

sermon ['səːmən] *n* sermone *m*

servant ['sə:vənt] *n* domestico(-a)
serve [sə:v] *vt* (*employer etc*) servire, essere a servizio di; (*purpose*) servire a; (*customer, food, meal*) servire; (*apprenticeship*) fare; (*prison term*) scontare ▷ *vi* (*also Tennis*) servire; (*be useful*): **to ~ as/for/to do** servire da/per/per fare ▷ *n* (*Tennis*) servizio; **it ~s him right** ben gli sta, se l'è meritata; **server** *n* (*Comput*) server *m inv*
service ['sə:vɪs] *n* servizio; (*Aut: maintenance*) assistenza, revisione *f* ▷ *vt* (*car, washing machine*) revisionare; **to be of ~ to sb** essere d'aiuto a qn; **~ included/not included** servizio compreso/escluso; **services** (BRIT: *on motorway*) stazione *f* di servizio; (*Mil*): **the S~s** le Forze Armate; **service area** *n* (*on motorway*) area di servizio; **service charge** (BRIT) *n* servizio; **serviceman** (*irreg*) *n* militare *m*; **service station** *n* stazione *f* di servizio
serviette [sə:vɪ'ɛt] (BRIT) *n* tovagliolo
session ['sɛʃən] *n* (*sitting*) seduta, sessione *f*; (*Scol*) anno scolastico (*or* accademico)
set [sɛt] (*pt, pp* **set**) *n* serie *f inv*; (*of cutlery etc*) servizio; (*Radio, TV*) apparecchio; (*Tennis*) set *m inv*; (*group of people*) mondo, ambiente *m*; (*Cinema*) scenario; (*Theatre: stage*) scene *fpl*; (*: scenery*) scenario; (*Math*) insieme *m*; (*Hairdressing*) messa in piega ▷ *adj* (*fixed*) stabilito(-a), determinato(-a); (*ready*) pronto(-a) ▷ *vt* (*place*) posare, mettere; (*arrange*) sistemare; (*fix*) fissare; (*adjust*) regolare; (*decide: rules etc*) stabilire, fissare ▷ *vi* (*sun*) tramontare; (*jam, jelly*) rapprendersi; (*concrete*) fare presa; **to be ~ on doing** essere deciso a fare; **to ~ to music** mettere in musica; **to ~ on fire** dare fuoco a; **to ~ free** liberare; **to ~ sth going** mettere in moto qc; **to ~ sail** prendere il mare; **set aside** *vt* mettere da parte; **set down** *vt* (*bus, train*) lasciare; **set in** *vi* (*infection*) svilupparsi; (*complications*) intervenire; **the rain has set in for the day** ormai pioverà tutto il giorno; **set off** *vi* partire ▷ *vt* (*bomb*) far scoppiare; (*cause to start*) mettere in moto; (*show up well*) dare risalto a; **set out** *vi* partire ▷ *vt* (*arrange*) disporre; (*state*) esporre, presentare; **to set out to do** proporsi di fare; **set up** *vt* (*organization*) fondare, costituire; **setback** *n* (*hitch*) contrattempo, inconveniente *m*; **set menu** *n* menù *m inv* fisso
settee [sɛ'ti:] *n* divano, sofà *m inv*
setting ['sɛtɪŋ] *n* (*background*) ambiente *m*; (*of controls*) posizione *f*; (*of sun*) tramonto; (*of jewel*) montatura
settle ['sɛtl] *vt* (*argument, matter*) appianare; (*accounts*) regolare; (*Med: calm*) calmare ▷ *vi* (*bird, dust etc*) posarsi; (*sediment*) depositarsi; **to ~ for sth** accontentarsi di qc; **to ~ on sth** decidersi per qc; **settle down** *vi* (*get comfortable*) sistemarsi; (*calm down*) calmarsi; (*get back to normal: situation*) tornare alla normalità; **settle in** *vi* sistemarsi; **settle up** *vi* **to settle up with sb** regolare i conti con qn; **settlement** *n* (*payment*) pagamento, saldo; (*agreement*) accordo; (*colony*) colonia; (*village etc*) villaggio, comunità *f inv*
setup ['sɛtʌp] *n* (*arrangement*) sistemazione *f*; (*situation*) situazione *f*
seven ['sɛvn] *num* sette; **seventeen** *num* diciassette; **seventeenth** [sevn'ti:nθ] *num* diciassettesimo(-a); **seventh** *num* settimo(-a); **seventieth** ['sevntɪɪθ] *num* settantesimo(-a); **seventy** *num* settanta
sever ['sɛvə^r] *vt* recidere, tagliare; (*relations*) troncare
several ['sɛvərl] *adj, pron* alcuni(-e), diversi(-e); **~ of us** alcuni di noi
severe [sɪ'vɪə^r] *adj* severo(-a); (*serious*)

serio(-a), grave; (*hard*) duro(-a); (*plain*) semplice, sobrio(-a)
sew [səu] (*pt* **sewed**, *pp* **sewn**) *vt, vi* cucire
sewage ['su:ɪdʒ] *n* acque *fpl* di scolo
sewer ['su:əʳ] *n* fogna
sewing ['səuɪŋ] *n* cucitura; cucito; **sewing machine** *n* macchina da cucire
sewn [səun] *pp of* **sew**
sex [sɛks] *n* sesso; **to have ~ with** avere rapporti sessuali con; **sexism** ['sɛksɪzəm] *n* sessismo; **sexist** *adj, n* sessista *m/f*; **sexual** ['sɛksjuəl] *adj* sessuale; **sexual intercourse** *n* rapporti *mpl* sessuali; **sexuality** [seksju'ælɪtɪ] *n* sessualità; **sexy** ['sɛksɪ] *adj* provocante, sexy *inv*
shabby ['ʃæbɪ] *adj* malandato(-a); (*behaviour*) vergognoso(-a)
shack [ʃæk] *n* baracca, capanna
shade [ʃeɪd] *n* ombra; (*for lamp*) paralume *m*; (*of colour*) tonalità *f inv*; (*small quantity*): **a ~ (more/too large)** un po' (di più/troppo grande) ▷ *vt* ombreggiare, fare ombra a; **in the ~** all'ombra; **shades** (US) *npl* (*sunglasses*) occhiali *mpl* da sole
shadow ['ʃædəu] *n* ombra ▷ *vt* (*follow*) pedinare; **shadow cabinet** (BRIT) *n* (*Pol*) governo *m* ombra *inv*
shady ['ʃeɪdɪ] *adj* ombroso(-a); (*fig: dishonest*) losco(-a), equivoco(-a)
shaft [ʃɑ:ft] *n* (*of arrow, spear*) asta; (*Aut, Tech*) albero; (*of mine*) pozzo; (*of lift*) tromba; (*of light*) raggio
shake [ʃeɪk] (*pt* **shook**, *pp* **shaken**) *vt* scuotere; (*bottle, cocktail*) agitare ▷ *vi* tremare; **to ~ one's head** (*in refusal, dismay*) scuotere la testa; **to ~ hands with sb** stringere *or* dare la mano a qn; **shake off** *vt* scrollare (via); (*fig*) sbarazzarsi di; **shake up** *vt* scuotere; **shaky** *adj* (*hand, voice*) tremante; (*building*) traballante
shall [ʃæl] *aux vb* **I ~ go** andrò; **~ I open the door?** apro io la porta?; **I'll get some, ~ I?** ne prendo un po', va bene?
shallow ['ʃæləu] *adj* poco profondo(-a); (*fig*) superficiale
sham [ʃæm] *n* finzione *f*, messinscena; (*jewellery, furniture*) imitazione *f*
shambles ['ʃæmblz] *n* confusione *f*, baraonda, scompiglio
shame [ʃeɪm] *n* vergogna ▷ *vt* far vergognare; **it is a ~ (that/to do)** è un peccato (che + *sub*/fare); **what a ~!** che peccato!; **shameful** *adj* vergognoso(-a); **shameless** *adj* sfrontato(-a); (*immodest*) spudorato(-a)
shampoo [ʃæm'pu:] *n* shampoo *m inv* ▷ *vt* fare lo shampoo a
shandy ['ʃændɪ] *n* birra con gassosa
shan't [ʃɑ:nt] = **shall not**
shape [ʃeɪp] *n* forma ▷ *vt* formare; (*statement*) formulare; (*sb's ideas*) condizionare; **to take ~** prendere forma
share [ʃɛəʳ] *n* (*thing received, contribution*) parte *f*; (*Comm*) azione *f* ▷ *vt* dividere; (*have in common*) condividere, avere in comune; **shareholder** *n* azionista *m/f*
shark [ʃɑ:k] *n* squalo, pescecane *m*
sharp [ʃɑ:p] *adj* (*razor, knife*) affilato(-a); (*point*) acuto(-a), acuminato(-a); (*nose, chin*) aguzzo(-a); (*outline, contrast*) netto(-a); (*cold, pain*) pungente; (*voice*) stridulo(-a); (*person: quick-witted*) sveglio(-a); (*: unscrupulous*) disonesto(-a); (*Mus*): **C ~** do diesis ▷ *n* (*Mus*) diesis *m inv* ▷ *adv* **at 2 o'clock ~** alle due in punto; **sharpen** *vt* affilare; (*pencil*) fare la punta a; (*fig*) acuire; **sharpener** *n* (*also:* **pencil sharpener**) temperamatite *m inv*; **sharply** *adv* (*turn, stop*) bruscamente; (*stand out, contrast*) nettamente; (*criticize, retort*) duramente, aspramente
shatter ['ʃætəʳ] *vt* mandare in frantumi, frantumare; (*fig: upset*) distruggere; (*: ruin*) rovinare ▷ *vi*

frantumarsi, andare in pezzi; **shattered** *adj* (*grief-stricken*) sconvolto(-a); (*exhausted*) a pezzi, distrutto(-a)

shave [ʃeɪv] *vt* radere, rasare ▷ *vi* radersi, farsi la barba ▷ *n* **to have a ~** farsi la barba; **shaver** *n* (*also:* **electric shaver**) rasoio elettrico

shaving cream *n* crema da barba

shaving foam *n* = **shaving cream**

shavings ['ʃeɪvɪŋz] *npl* (*of wood etc*) trucioli *mpl*

shawl [ʃɔːl] *n* scialle *m*

she [ʃiː] *pron* ella, lei; **~-cat** gatta; **~-elephant** elefantessa

sheath [ʃiːθ] *n* fodero, guaina; (*contraceptive*) preservativo

shed [ʃɛd] (*pt, pp* **shed**) *n* capannone *m* ▷ *vt* (*leaves, fur etc*) perdere; (*tears, blood*) versare; (*workers*) liberarsi di

she'd [ʃiːd] = **she had**; **she would**

sheep [ʃiːp] *n inv* pecora; **sheepdog** *n* cane *m* da pastore; **sheepskin** *n* pelle *f* di pecora

sheer [ʃɪə^r] *adj* (*utter*) vero(-a) (e proprio(-a)); (*steep*) a picco, perpendicolare; (*almost transparent*) sottile ▷ *adv* a picco

sheet [ʃiːt] *n* (*on bed*) lenzuolo; (*of paper*) foglio; (*of glass, ice*) lastra; (*of metal*) foglio, lamina

sheik(h) [ʃeɪk] *n* sceicco

shelf [ʃɛlf] (*pl* **shelves**) *n* scaffale *m*, mensola

shell [ʃɛl] *n* (*on beach*) conchiglia; (*of egg, nut etc*) guscio; (*explosive*) granata; (*of building*) scheletro ▷ *vt* (*peas*) sgranare; (*Mil*) bombardare

she'll [ʃiːl] = **she will**; **she shall**

shellfish ['ʃɛlfɪʃ] *n inv* (*crab etc*) crostaceo; (*scallop etc*) mollusco; (*as food*) crostacei; molluschi

shelter ['ʃɛltə^r] *n* riparo, rifugio ▷ *vt* riparare, proteggere; (*give lodging to*) dare rifugio *or* asilo a ▷ *vi* ripararsi, mettersi al riparo; **sheltered** *adj* riparato(-a)

shelves ['ʃɛlvz] *npl of* **shelf**

shelving ['ʃɛlvɪŋ] *n* scaffalature *fpl*

shepherd ['ʃɛpəd] *n* pastore *m* ▷ *vt* (*guide*) guidare; **shepherd's pie** (BRIT) *n timballo di carne macinata e purè di patate*

sheriff ['ʃɛrɪf] (US) *n* sceriffo

sherry ['ʃɛrɪ] *n* sherry *m inv*

she's [ʃiːz] = **she is**; **she has**

Shetland ['ʃɛtlənd] *n* (*also:* **the ~s, the ~ Isles**) le isole Shetland, le Shetland

shield [ʃiːld] *n* scudo; (*trophy*) scudetto; (*protection*) schermo ▷ *vt* **to ~ (from)** riparare (da), proteggere (da *or* contro)

shift [ʃɪft] *n* (*change*) cambiamento; (*of workers*) turno ▷ *vt* spostare, muovere; (*remove*) rimuovere ▷ *vi* spostarsi, muoversi

shin [ʃɪn] *n* tibia

shine [ʃaɪn] (*pt, pp* **shone**) *n* splendore *m*, lucentezza ▷ *vi* (ri)splendere, brillare ▷ *vt* far brillare, far risplendere; (*torch*): **to ~ sth on** puntare qc verso

shingles ['ʃɪŋglz] *n* (*Med*) herpes zoster *m*

shiny ['ʃaɪnɪ] *adj* lucente, lucido(-a)

ship [ʃɪp] *n* nave *f* ▷ *vt* trasportare (via mare); (*send*) spedire (via mare); **shipment** *n* carico; **shipping** *n* (*ships*) naviglio; (*traffic*) navigazione *f*; **shipwreck** *n* relitto; (*event*) naufragio ▷ *vt* **to be shipwrecked** naufragare, fare naufragio; **shipyard** *n* cantiere *m* navale

shirt [ʃəːt] *n* camicia; **in ~ sleeves** in maniche di camicia

shit [ʃɪt] (*inf!*) *excl* merda (*!*)

shiver ['ʃɪvə^r] *n* brivido ▷ *vi* rabbrividire, tremare

shock [ʃɔk] *n* (*impact*) urto, colpo; (*Elec*) scossa; (*emotional*) colpo, shock *m inv*; (*Med*) shock ▷ *vt* colpire, scioccare; scandalizzare; **shocking** *adj* scioccante, traumatizzante;

scandaloso(-a)

shoe [ʃuː] (*pt, pp* **shod**) *n* scarpa; (*also:* **horse~**) ferro di cavallo ▷ *vt* (*horse*) ferrare; **shoelace** *n* stringa; **shoe polish** *n* lucido per scarpe; **shoeshop** *n* calzoleria

shone [ʃɔn] *pt, pp of* **shine**

shook [ʃuk] *pt of* **shake**

shoot [ʃuːt] (*pt, pp* **shot**) *n* (*on branch, seedling*) germoglio ▷ *vt* (*game*) cacciare, andare a caccia di; (*person*) sparare a; (*execute*) fucilare; (*film*) girare ▷ *vi* (*with gun*): **to ~ (at)** sparare (a), fare fuoco (su); (*with bow*): **to ~ (at)** tirare (su); (*Football*) sparare, tirare (forte); **shoot down** *vt* (*plane*) abbattere; **shoot up** *vi* (*fig*) salire alle stelle; **shooting** *n* (*shots*) sparatoria; (*Hunting*) caccia

shop [ʃɔp] *n* negozio; (*workshop*) officina ▷ *vi* (*also:* **go ~ping**) fare spese; **shop assistant** (BRIT) *n* commesso(-a); **shopkeeper** *n* negoziante *m/f*, bottegaio(-a); **shoplifting** *n* taccheggio; **shopping** *n* (*goods*) spesa, acquisti *mpl*; **shopping bag** *n* borsa per la spesa; **shopping centre** (US **shopping center**) *n* centro commerciale; **shopping mall** *n* centro commerciale; **shopping trolley** *n* (BRIT) carrello del supermercato; **shop window** *n* vetrina

shore [ʃɔːʳ] *n* (*of sea*) riva, spiaggia; (*of lake*) riva ▷ *vt* **to ~ (up)** puntellare; **on ~** a riva

short [ʃɔːt] *adj* (*not long*) corto(-a); (*soon finished*) breve; (*person*) basso(-a); (*curt*) brusco(-a), secco(-a); (*insufficient*) insufficiente ▷ *n* (*also:* **~ film**) cortometraggio; **to be ~ of sth** essere a corto di *or* mancare di qc; **in ~** in breve; **~ of doing** a meno che non si faccia; **everything ~ of** tutto fuorché; **it is ~ for** è l'abbreviazione *or* il diminutivo di; **to cut ~** (*speech, visit*) accorciare, abbreviare; **to fall ~ of** venir meno a; non soddisfare; **to run ~ of** rimanere senza; **to stop ~** fermarsi di colpo; **to stop ~ of** non arrivare fino a; **shortage** *n* scarsezza, carenza; **shortbread** *n* biscotto di pasta frolla; **shortcoming** *n* difetto; **short(crust) pastry** (BRIT) *n* pasta frolla; **shortcut** *n* scorciatoia; **shorten** *vt* accorciare, ridurre; **shortfall** *n* deficit *m*; **shorthand** (BRIT) *n* stenografia; **short-lived** *adj* di breve durata; **shortly** *adv* fra poco; **shorts** *npl* (*also:* **a pair of shorts**) i calzoncini; **short-sighted** (BRIT) *adj* miope; **short-sleeved** [ˈʃɔːtsliːvd] *adj* a maniche corte; **short story** *n* racconto, novella; **short-tempered** *adj* irascibile; **short-term** *adj* (*effect*) di *or* a breve durata; (*borrowing*) a breve scadenza

shot [ʃɔt] *pt, pp of* **shoot** ▷ *n* sparo, colpo; (*try*) prova; (*Football*) tiro; (*injection*) iniezione *f*; (*Phot*) foto *f inv*; **like a ~** come un razzo; (*very readily*) immediatamente; **shotgun** *n* fucile *m* da caccia

should [ʃud] *aux vb* **I ~ go now** dovrei andare ora; **he ~ be there now** dovrebbe essere arrivato ora; **I ~ go if I were you** se fossi in te andrei; **I ~ like to** mi piacerebbe

shoulder [ˈʃəuldəʳ] *n* spalla; (BRIT: *of road*): **hard ~** banchina ▷ *vt* (*fig*) addossarsi, prendere sulle proprie spalle; **shoulder blade** *n* scapola

shouldn't [ˈʃudnt] = **should not**

shout [ʃaut] *n* urlo, grido ▷ *vt* gridare ▷ *vi* (*also:* **~ out**) urlare, gridare

shove [ʃʌv] *vt* spingere; (*inf: put*): **to ~ sth in** ficcare qc in

shovel [ˈʃʌvl] *n* pala ▷ *vt* spalare

show [ʃəu] (*pt* **showed**, *pp* **shown**) *n* (*of emotion*) dimostrazione *f*, manifestazione *f*; (*semblance*) apparenza; (*exhibition*) mostra, esposizione *f*; (*Theatre, Cinema*) spettacolo ▷ *vt* far vedere, mostrare;

(*courage etc*) dimostrare, dar prova di; (*exhibit*) esporre ▷ *vi* vedersi, essere visibile; **for ~** per fare scena; **on ~** (*exhibits etc*) esposto(-a); **can you ~ me where it is, please?** può mostrarmi dov'è, per favore?; **show in** *vt* (*person*) far entrare; **show off** *vi* (*pej*) esibirsi, mettersi in mostra ▷ *vt* (*display*) mettere in risalto; (*pej*) mettere in mostra; **show out** *vt* (*person*) accompagnare alla porta; **show up** *vi* (*stand out*) essere ben visibile; (*inf: turn up*) farsi vedere ▷ *vt* mettere in risalto; **show business** *n* industria dello spettacolo

shower ['ʃauəʳ] *n* (*rain*) acquazzone *m*; (*of stones etc*) pioggia; (*also:* **~bath**) doccia ▷ *vi* fare la doccia ▷ *vt* **to ~ sb with** (*gifts, abuse etc*) coprire qn di; (*missiles*) lanciare contro qn una pioggia di; **to have a ~** fare la doccia; **shower cap** *n* cuffia da doccia; **shower gel** *n* gel *m* doccia *inv*

showing ['ʃəuɪŋ] *n* (*of film*) proiezione *f*

show jumping *n* concorso ippico (di salto ad ostacoli)

shown [ʃəun] *pp of* **show**

show: **show-off** (*inf*) *n* (*person*) esibizionista *m/f*; **showroom** *n* sala d'esposizione

shrank [ʃræŋk] *pt of* **shrink**

shred [ʃrɛd] *n* (*gen pl*) brandello ▷ *vt* fare a brandelli; (*Culin*) sminuzzare, tagliuzzare

shrewd [ʃruːd] *adj* astuto(-a), scaltro(-a)

shriek [ʃriːk] *n* strillo ▷ *vi* strillare

shrimp [ʃrɪmp] *n* gamberetto

shrine [ʃraɪn] *n* reliquario; (*place*) santuario

shrink [ʃrɪŋk] (*pt* **shrank**, *pp* **shrunk**) *vi* restringersi; (*fig*) ridursi; (*also:* **~ away**) ritrarsi ▷ *vt* (*wool*) far restringere ▷ *n* (*inf: pej*) psicanalista *m/f*; **to ~ from doing sth** rifuggire dal fare qc

shrivel ['ʃrɪvl] (*also:* **~ up**) *vt* raggrinzare, avvizzire ▷ *vi* raggrinzirsi, avvizzire

shroud [ʃraud] *n* lenzuolo funebre ▷ *vt* **~ed in mystery** avvolto(-a) nel mistero

Shrove Tuesday ['ʃrəuv-] *n* martedì *m* grasso

shrub [ʃrʌb] *n* arbusto

shrug [ʃrʌg] *n* scrollata di spalle ▷ *vt*, *vi* **to ~ (one's shoulders)** alzare le spalle, fare spallucce; **shrug off** *vt* passare sopra a

shrunk [ʃrʌŋk] *pp of* **shrink**

shudder ['ʃʌdəʳ] *n* brivido ▷ *vi* rabbrividire

shuffle ['ʃʌfl] *vt* (*cards*) mescolare; **to ~ (one's feet)** strascicare i piedi

shun [ʃʌn] *vt* sfuggire, evitare

shut [ʃʌt] (*pt, pp* **shut**) *vt* chiudere ▷ *vi* chiudersi, chiudere; **shut down** *vt, vi* chiudere definitivamente; **shut up** *vi* (*inf: keep quiet*) stare zitto(-a), fare silenzio ▷ *vt* (*close*) chiudere; (*silence*) far tacere; **shutter** *n* imposta; (*Phot*) otturatore *m*

shuttle ['ʃʌtl] *n* spola, navetta; (*space shuttle*) navetta (spaziale); (*also:* **~ service**) servizio *m* navetta *inv*; **shuttlecock** ['ʃʌtlkɔk] *n* volano

shy [ʃaɪ] *adj* timido(-a)

sibling ['sɪblɪŋ] *n* (*formal*) fratello/sorella

Sicily ['sɪsɪlɪ] *n* Sicilia

sick [sɪk] *adj* (*ill*) malato(-a); (*vomiting*): **to be ~** vomitare; (*humour*) macabro(-a); **to feel ~** avere la nausea; **to be ~ of** (*fig*) averne abbastanza di; **sickening** *adj* (*fig*) disgustoso(-a), rivoltante; **sick leave** *n* congedo per malattia; **sickly** *adj* malaticcio(-a); (*causing nausea*) nauseante; **sickness** *n* malattia; (*vomiting*) vomito

side [saɪd] *n* lato; (*of lake*) riva; (*team*) squadra ▷ *cpd* (*door, entrance*) laterale ▷ *vi* **to ~ with sb** parteggiare per qn, prendere le parti di qn; **by the ~ of** a fianco di; (*road*) sul ciglio di; **~ by ~** fianco a fianco; **from ~ to ~** da una parte all'altra; **to take ~s (with)** schierarsi (con); **sideboard** *n* credenza; **sideboards** (*BRIT*), **sideburns** ['saɪdbə:nz] *npl* (*whiskers*) basette *fpl*; **sidelight** *n* (*Aut*) luce *f* di posizione; **sideline** *n* (*Sport*) linea laterale; (*fig*) attività secondaria; **side order** *n* contorno (*pietanza*); **side road** *n* strada secondaria; **side street** *n* traversa; **sidetrack** *vt* (*fig*) distrarre; **sidewalk** (*US*) *n* marciapiede *m*; **sideways** *adv* (*move*) di lato, di fianco

siege [si:dʒ] *n* assedio

sieve [sɪv] *n* setaccio ▷ *vt* setacciare

sift [sɪft] *vt* passare al crivello; (*fig*) vagliare

sigh [saɪ] *n* sospiro ▷ *vi* sospirare

sight [saɪt] *n* (*faculty*) vista; (*spectacle*) spettacolo; (*on gun*) mira ▷ *vt* avvistare; **in ~** in vista; **on ~** a vista; **out of ~** non visibile; **sightseeing** *n* giro turistico; **to go sightseeing** visitare una località

sign [saɪn] *n* segno; (*with hand etc*) segno, gesto; (*notice*) insegna, cartello ▷ *vt* firmare; (*player*) ingaggiare; **where do I ~?** dove devo firmare?; **sign for** *vt fus* (*item*) firmare per l'accettazione di; **sign in** *vi* firmare il registro (all'arrivo); **sign on** *vi* (*Mil*) arruolarsi; (*as unemployed*) iscriversi sulla lista (dell'ufficio di collocamento) ▷ *vt* (*Mil*) arruolare; (*employee*) assumere; **sign up** *vi* (*Mil*) arruolarsi; (*for course*) iscriversi ▷ *vt* (*player*) ingaggiare; (*recruits*) reclutare

signal ['sɪgnl] *n* segnale *m* ▷ *vi* (*Aut*) segnalare, mettere la freccia ▷ *vt* (*person*) fare segno a; (*message*) comunicare per mezzo di segnali

signature ['sɪgnətʃə^r] *n* firma

significance [sɪg'nɪfɪkəns] *n* significato; importanza

significant [sɪg'nɪfɪkənt] *adj* significativo(-a)

signify ['sɪgnɪfaɪ] *vt* significare

sign language *n* linguaggio dei muti

signpost ['saɪnpəust] *n* cartello indicatore

Sikh [si:k] *adj, n* sikh (*m/f*) *inv*

silence ['saɪlns] *n* silenzio ▷ *vt* far tacere, ridurre al silenzio

silent ['saɪlnt] *adj* silenzioso(-a); (*film*) muto(-a); **to remain ~** tacere, stare zitto

silhouette [sɪlu:'ɛt] *n* silhouette *f inv*

silicon chip ['sɪlɪkən-] *n* piastrina di silicio

silk [sɪlk] *n* seta ▷ *adj* di seta

silly ['sɪlɪ] *adj* stupido(-a), sciocco(-a)

silver ['sɪlvə^r] *n* argento; (*money*) *monete da 5, 10, 20 or 50 pence*; (*also*: **~ware**) argenteria ▷ *adj* d'argento; **silver-plated** *adj* argentato(-a)

similar ['sɪmɪlə^r] *adj* **~ (to)** simile (a); **similarity** [sɪmɪ'lærɪtɪ] *n* somiglianza, rassomiglianza; **similarly** *adv* allo stesso modo; così pure

simmer ['sɪmə^r] *vi* cuocere a fuoco lento

simple ['sɪmpl] *adj* semplice; **simplicity** [-'plɪsɪtɪ] *n* semplicità; **simplify** *vt* semplificare; **simply** *adv* semplicemente

simulate ['sɪmjuleɪt] *vt* fingere, simulare

simultaneous [sɪməl'teɪnɪəs] *adj* simultaneo(-a); **simultaneously** *adv* simultaneamente, contemporaneamente

sin [sɪn] *n* peccato ▷ *vi* peccare

since [sɪns] *adv* da allora ▷ *prep* da ▷ *conj* (*time*) da quando; (*because*) poiché, dato che; **~ then, ever ~** da allora

sincere [sɪn'sɪə^r] *adj* sincero(-a); **sincerely** *adv* **yours sincerely** (*in letters*) distinti saluti

sing [sɪŋ] (*pt* **sang**, *pp* **sung**) *vt, vi*

cantare
Singapore [sɪŋgə'pɔːʳ] *n* Singapore *f*
singer ['sɪŋəʳ] *n* cantante *m/f*
singing ['sɪŋɪŋ] *n* canto
single ['sɪŋgl] *adj* solo(-a), unico(-a); (*unmarried*: *man*) celibe; (: *woman*) nubile; (*not double*) semplice ▷ *n* (BRIT: *also*: **~ ticket**) biglietto di (sola) andata; (*record*) 45 giri *m*; **singles** *n* (*Tennis*) singolo; **single out** *vt* scegliere; (*distinguish*) distinguere; **single bed** *n* letto singolo; **single file** *n* **in single file** in fila indiana; **single-handed** *adv* senza aiuto, da solo(-a); **single-minded** *adj* tenace, risoluto(-a); **single parent** *n* (*mother*) ragazza *f* madre *inv*; (*father*) ragazzo *m* padre *inv*; **single-parent family** famiglia monoparentale; **single room** *n* camera singola
singular ['sɪŋgjuləʳ] *adj* (*exceptional*, *Ling*) singolare ▷ *n* (*Ling*) singolare *m*
sinister ['sɪnɪstəʳ] *adj* sinistro(-a)
sink [sɪŋk] (*pt* **sank**, *pp* **sunk**) *n* lavandino, acquaio ▷ *vt* (*ship*) (fare) affondare, colare a picco; (*foundations*) scavare; (*piles etc*): **to ~ sth into** conficcare qc in ▷ *vi* affondare, andare a fondo; (*ground etc*) cedere, avvallarsi; **my heart sank** mi sentii venir meno; **sink in** *vi* penetrare
sinus ['saɪnəs] *n* (*Anat*) seno
sip [sɪp] *n* sorso ▷ *vt* sorseggiare
sir [səʳ] *n* signore *m*; **S~ John Smith** Sir John Smith; **yes ~** sì, signore
siren ['saɪərn] *n* sirena
sirloin ['səːlɔɪn] *n* controfiletto
sister ['sɪstəʳ] *n* sorella; (*nun*) suora; (BRIT: *nurse*) infermiera *f* caposala *inv*; **sister-in-law** *n* cognata
sit [sɪt] (*pt*, *pp* **sat**) *vi* sedere, sedersi; (*assembly*) essere in seduta; (*for painter*) posare ▷ *vt* (*exam*) sostenere, dare; **sit back** *vi* (*in seat*) appoggiarsi allo schienale; **sit down** *vi* sedersi; **sit on** *vt fus* (*jury*, *committee*) far parte di; **sit up** *vi* tirarsi su a sedere; (*not go to bed*) stare alzato(-a) fino a tardi
sitcom ['sɪtkɔm] *n abbr* (= *situation comedy*) commedia di situazione; (*TV*) telefilm *m inv* comico d'interni
site [saɪt] *n* posto; (*also*: **building ~**) cantiere *m* ▷ *vt* situare
sitting ['sɪtɪŋ] *n* (*of assembly etc*) seduta; (*in canteen*) turno; **sitting room** *n* soggiorno
situated ['sɪtjueɪtɪd] *adj* situato(-a)
situation [sɪtju'eɪʃən] *n* situazione *f*; (*job*) lavoro; (*location*) posizione *f*; **"~s vacant"** (BRIT) "offerte *fpl* di impiego"
six [sɪks] *num* sei; **sixteen** *num* sedici; **sixteenth** [sɪks'tiːnθ] *num* sedicesimo(-a); **sixth** *num* sesto(-a); **sixth form** *n* (BRIT) *ultimo biennio delle scuole superiori*; **sixth-form college** *n istituto che offre corsi di preparazione all'esame di maturità per ragazzi dai 16 ai 18 anni*; **sixtieth** ['sɪkstɪɪθ] *num* sessantesimo(-a) ▷ *pron* (*in series*) sessantesimo(-a); (*fraction*) sessantesimo; **sixty** *num* sessanta
size [saɪz] *n* dimensioni *fpl*; (*of clothing*) taglia, misura; (*of shoes*) numero; (*glue*) colla; **sizeable** *adj* considerevole
sizzle ['sɪzl] *vi* sfrigolare
skate [skeɪt] *n* pattino; (*fish*: *pl inv*) razza ▷ *vi* pattinare; **skateboard** *n* skateboard *m inv*; **skateboarding** *n* skateboard *m inv*; **skater** *n* pattinatore(-trice); **skating** *n* pattinaggio; **skating rink** *n* pista di pattinaggio
skeleton ['skɛlɪtn] *n* scheletro
skeptical ['skɛptɪkl] (US) *adj* = **sceptical**
sketch [skɛtʃ] *n* (*drawing*) schizzo, abbozzo; (*Theatre*) scenetta comica, sketch *m inv* ▷ *vt* abbozzare, schizzare
skewer ['skjuːəʳ] *n* spiedo
ski [skiː] *n* sci *m inv* ▷ *vi* sciare; **ski boot** *n* scarpone *m* da sci
skid [skɪd] *n* slittamento ▷ *vi* slittare
ski: **skier** ['skiːəʳ] *n* sciatore(-trice);

skiing ['ski:ɪŋ] *n* sci *m*
skilful ['skɪlful] (*US* **skillful**) *adj* abile
ski lift *n* sciovia
skill [skɪl] *n* abilità *f inv*, capacità *f inv*; **skilled** *adj* esperto(-a); (*worker*) qualificato(-a), specializzato(-a)
skim [skɪm] *vt* (*milk*) scremare; (*glide over*) sfiorare ▷ *vi* **to ~ through** (*fig*) scorrere, dare una scorsa a; **skimmed milk** (*US* **skim milk**) *n* latte *m* scremato
skin [skɪn] *n* pelle *f* ▷ *vt* (*fruit etc*) sbucciare; (*animal*) scuoiare, spellare; **skinhead** *n* skinhead *m/f inv*; **skinny** *adj* molto magro(-a), pelle e ossa *inv*
skip [skɪp] *n* saltello, balzo; (BRIT: *container*) benna ▷ *vi* saltare; (*with rope*) saltare la corda ▷ *vt* saltare
ski: **ski pass** *n* ski pass *m*; **ski pole** *n* racchetta (da sci)
skipper ['skɪpə^r] *n* (*Naut, Sport*) capitano
skipping rope ['skɪpɪŋ-] (*US* **skip rope**) *n* corda per saltare
skirt [skə:t] *n* gonna, sottana ▷ *vt* fiancheggiare, costeggiare
skirting board (BRIT) *n* zoccolo
ski slope *n* pista da sci
ski suit *n* tuta da sci
skull [skʌl] *n* cranio, teschio
skunk [skʌŋk] *n* moffetta
sky [skaɪ] *n* cielo; **skyscraper** *n* grattacielo
slab [slæb] *n* lastra; (*of cake, cheese*) fetta
slack [slæk] *adj* (*loose*) allentato(-a); (*slow*) lento(-a); (*careless*) negligente; **slacks** *npl* (*trousers*) pantaloni *mpl*
slain [sleɪn] *pp of* **slay**
slam [slæm] *vt* (*door*) sbattere; (*throw*) scaraventare; (*criticize*) stroncare ▷ *vi* sbattere
slander ['slɑ:ndə^r] *n* calunnia; diffamazione *f*
slang [slæŋ] *n* gergo, slang *m*
slant [slɑ:nt] *n* pendenza, inclinazione *f*; (*fig*) angolazione *f*, punto di vista
slap [slæp] *n* manata, pacca; (*on face*) schiaffo ▷ *vt* dare una manata a; schiaffeggiare ▷ *adv* (*directly*) in pieno; **~ a coat of paint on it** dagli una mano di vernice
slash [slæʃ] *vt* tagliare; (*face*) sfregiare; (*fig: prices*) ridurre drasticamente, tagliare
slate [sleɪt] *n* ardesia; (*piece*) lastra di ardesia ▷ *vt* (*fig: criticize*) stroncare, distruggere
slaughter ['slɔ:tə^r] *n* strage *f*, massacro ▷ *vt* (*animal*) macellare; (*people*) trucidare, massacrare; **slaughterhouse** *n* macello, mattatoio
Slav [slɑ:v] *adj*, *n* slavo(-a)
slave [sleɪv] *n* schiavo(-a) ▷ *vi* (*also*: **~ away**) lavorare come uno schiavo; **slavery** *n* schiavitù *f*
slay [sleɪ] (*pt* **slew**, *pp* **slain**) *vt* (*formal*) uccidere
sleazy ['sli:zɪ] *adj* trasandato(-a)
sled [slɛd] (*US*) = **sledge**
sledge [slɛdʒ] *n* slitta
sleek [sli:k] *adj* (*hair, fur*) lucido(-a), lucente; (*car, boat*) slanciato(-a), affusolato(-a)
sleep [sli:p] (*pt, pp* **slept**) *n* sonno ▷ *vi* dormire; **to go to ~** addormentarsi; **sleep in** *vi* (*oversleep*) dormire fino a tardi; **sleep together** *vi* (*have sex*) andare a letto insieme; **sleeper** (BRIT) *n* (*Rail: on track*) traversina; (*: train*) treno di vagoni letto; **sleeping bag** *n* sacco a pelo; **sleeping car** *n* vagone *m* letto *inv*, carrozza *f* letto *inv*; **sleeping pill** *n* sonnifero; **sleepover** *n* notte *f* che un ragazzino passa da amici; **sleepwalk** *vi* camminare nel sonno; (*as a habit*) essere sonnambulo(-a); **sleepy** *adj* assonnato(-a), sonnolento(-a); (*fig*) addormentato(-a)
sleet [sli:t] *n* nevischio
sleeve [sli:v] *n* manica; (*of record*)

copertina; **sleeveless** *adj* (*garment*) senza maniche

sleigh [sleɪ] *n* slitta

slender ['slɛndəʳ] *adj* snello(-a), sottile; (*not enough*) scarso(-a), esiguo(-a)

slept [slɛpt] *pt, pp of* **sleep**

slew [slu:] *pt of* **slay** ▷ *vi* (BRIT) girare

slice [slaɪs] *n* fetta ▷ *vt* affettare, tagliare a fette

slick [slɪk] *adj* (*skilful*) brillante; (*clever*) furbo(-a) ▷ *n* (*also:* **oil ~**) chiazza di petrolio

slide [slaɪd] (*pt, pp* **slid**) *n* scivolone *m*; (*in playground*) scivolo; (*Phot*) diapositiva; (BRIT: *also:* **hair ~**) fermaglio (per capelli) ▷ *vt* far scivolare ▷ *vi* scivolare; **sliding** *adj* (*door*) scorrevole

slight [slaɪt] *adj* (*slim*) snello(-a), sottile; (*frail*) delicato(-a), fragile; (*trivial*) insignificante; (*small*) piccolo(-a) ▷ *n* offesa, affronto; **not in the ~est** affatto, neppure per sogno; **slightly** *adv* lievemente, un po'

slim [slɪm] *adj* magro(-a), snello(-a) ▷ *vi* dimagrire; fare (*or* seguire) una dieta dimagrante; **slimming** ['slɪmɪŋ] *adj* (*diet*) dimagrante; (*food*) ipocalorico(-a)

slimy ['slaɪmɪ] *adj* (*also fig: person*) viscido(-a); (*covered with mud*) melmoso(-a)

sling [slɪŋ] (*pt, pp* **slung**) *n* (*Med*) fascia al collo; (*for baby*) marsupio ▷ *vt* lanciare, tirare

slip [slɪp] *n* scivolata, scivolone *m*; (*mistake*) errore *m*, sbaglio; (*underskirt*) sottoveste *f*; (*of paper*) striscia di carta; tagliando, scontrino ▷ *vt* (*slide*) far scivolare ▷ *vi* (*slide*) scivolare; (*move smoothly*): **to ~ into/out of** scivolare in/fuori da; (*decline*) declinare; **to ~ sth on/off** infilarsi/togliersi qc; **to give sb the ~** sfuggire qn; **a ~ of the tongue** un lapsus linguae; **slip up** *vi* sbagliarsi

slipper ['slɪpəʳ] *n* pantofola

slippery ['slɪpərɪ] *adj* scivoloso(-a)

slip road (BRIT) *n* (*to motorway*) rampa di accesso

slit [slɪt] (*pt, pp* **slit**) *n* fessura, fenditura; (*cut*) taglio ▷ *vt* fendere; tagliare

slog [slɔg] (BRIT) *n* faticata ▷ *vi* lavorare con accanimento, sgobbare

slogan ['sləugən] *n* motto, slogan *m inv*

slope [sləup] *n* pendio; (*side of mountain*) versante *m*; (*ski slope*) pista; (*of roof*) pendenza; (*of floor*) inclinazione *f* ▷ *vi* **to ~ down** declinare; **to ~ up** essere in salita; **sloping** *adj* inclinato(-a)

sloppy ['slɔpɪ] *adj* (*work*) tirato(-a) via; (*appearance*) sciatto(-a)

slot [slɔt] *n* fessura ▷ *vt* **to ~ sth into** infilare qc in; **slot machine** *n* (BRIT: *vending machine*) distributore *m* automatico; (*for gambling*) slot-machine *f inv*

Slovakia [sləu'vækɪə] *n* Slovacchia

Slovene ['sləuvi:n] *adj* sloveno(-a) ▷ *n* sloveno(-a); (*Ling*) sloveno

Slovenia [sləu'vi:niə] *n* Slovenia; **Slovenian** *adj, n* = **Slovene**

slow [sləu] *adj* lento(-a); (*watch*): **to be ~** essere indietro ▷ *adv* lentamente ▷ *vt, vi* (*also:* **~ down, ~ up**) rallentare; **"~"** (*road sign*) "rallentare"; **slow down** *vi* rallentare; **slowly** *adv* lentamente; **slow motion** *n* **in slow motion** al rallentatore

slug [slʌg] *n* lumaca; (*bullet*) pallottola; **sluggish** *adj* lento(-a); (*trading*) stagnante

slum [slʌm] *n* catapecchia

slump [slʌmp] *n* crollo, caduta; (*economic*) depressione *f*, crisi *f inv* ▷ *vi* crollare

slung [slʌŋ] *pt, pp of* **sling**

slur [slə:ʳ] *n* (*fig*): **~ (on)** calunnia (su) ▷ *vt* pronunciare in modo indistinto

sly [slaɪ] *adj* (*smile, remark*)

sornione(-a); (*person*) furbo(-a)

smack [smæk] *n* (*slap*) pacca; (*on face*) schiaffo ▷ *vt* schiaffeggiare; (*child*) picchiare ▷ *vi* **to ~ of** puzzare di

small [smɔːl] *adj* piccolo(-a); **small ads** (BRIT) *npl* piccola pubblicità; **small change** *n* moneta, spiccioli *mpl*

smart [smɑːt] *adj* elegante; (*fashionable*) alla moda; (*clever*) intelligente; (*quick*) sveglio(-a) ▷ *vi* bruciare; **smartcard** ['smɑːtkɑːd] *n* smartcard *f inv*, carta intelligente

smash [smæʃ] *n* (*also*: **~-up**) scontro, collisione *f*; (*smash hit*) successone *m* ▷ *vt* frantumare, fracassare; (*Sport*: *record*) battere ▷ *vi* frantumarsi, andare in pezzi; **smashing** (*inf*) *adj* favoloso(-a), formidabile

smear [smɪəʳ] *n* macchia; (*Med*) striscio ▷ *vt* spalmare; (*make dirty*) sporcare; **smear test** *n* (BRIT *Med*) Pap-test *m inv*

smell [smɛl] (*pt* **smelt** *or* **smelled**) *n* odore *m*; (*sense*) olfatto, odorato ▷ *vt* sentire (l')odore di ▷ *vi* (*food etc*): **to ~ (of)** avere odore (di); (*pej*) puzzare, avere un cattivo odore; **smelly** *adj* puzzolente

smelt [smɛlt] *pt, pp of* **smell** ▷ *vt* (*ore*) fondere

smile [smaɪl] *n* sorriso ▷ *vi* sorridere

smirk [sməːk] *n* sorriso furbo; sorriso compiaciuto

smog [smɔg] *n* smog *m*

smoke [sməuk] *n* fumo ▷ *vt, vi* fumare; **do you mind if I ~?** le dà fastidio se fumo?; **smoke alarm** *n* rivelatore *f* di fumo; **smoked** *adj* (*bacon, glass*) affumicato(-a); **smoker** *n* (*person*) fumatore(-trice); (*Rail*) carrozza per fumatori; **smoking** *n* fumo; **"no smoking"** (*sign*) "vietato fumare"; **smoky** *adj* fumoso(-a); (*taste*) affumicato(-a)

smooth [smuːð] *adj* liscio(-a); (*sauce*) omogeneo(-a); (*flavour, whisky*) amabile; (*movement*) regolare; (*person*) mellifluo(-a) ▷ *vt* (*also*: **~ out**) lisciare, spianare; (: *difficulties*) appianare

smother ['smʌðəʳ] *vt* soffocare

SMS *abbr* (= *short message service*) SMS; **SMS message** *n* SMS *m inv*, messaggino

smudge [smʌdʒ] *n* macchia; sbavatura ▷ *vt* imbrattare, sporcare

smug [smʌg] *adj* soddisfatto(-a), compiaciuto(-a)

smuggle ['smʌgl] *vt* contrabbandare; **smuggling** *n* contrabbando

snack [snæk] *n* spuntino; **snack bar** *n* tavola calda, snack bar *m inv*

snag [snæg] *n* intoppo, ostacolo imprevisto

snail [sneɪl] *n* chiocciola

snake [sneɪk] *n* serpente *m*

snap [snæp] *n* (*sound*) schianto, colpo secco; (*photograph*) istantanea ▷ *adj* improvviso(-a) ▷ *vt* (far) schioccare; (*break*) spezzare di netto ▷ *vi* spezzarsi con un rumore secco; (*fig*: *person*) parlare con tono secco; **to ~ shut** chiudersi di scatto; **snap at** *vt fus* (*dog*) cercare di mordere; **snap up** *vt* afferrare; **snapshot** *n* istantanea

snarl [snɑːl] *vi* ringhiare

snatch [snætʃ] *n* (*small amount*) frammento ▷ *vt* strappare (con violenza); (*fig*) rubare

sneak [sniːk] (*pt* (US) **snuck**) *vi* **to ~ in/out** entrare/uscire di nascosto ▷ *n* spione(-a); **to ~ up on sb** avvicinarsi quatto quatto a qn; **sneakers** *npl* scarpe *fpl* da ginnastica

sneer [snɪəʳ] *vi* sogghignare; **to ~ at** farsi beffe di

sneeze [sniːz] *n* starnuto ▷ *vi* starnutire

sniff [snɪf] *n* fiutata, annusata ▷ *vi* tirare su col naso ▷ *vt* fiutare, annusare

snigger ['snɪgəʳ] *vi* ridacchiare, ridere sotto i baffi

snip [snɪp] *n* pezzetto; (*bargain*) (buon) affare *m*, occasione *f* ▷ *vt* tagliare

sniper ['snaɪpə^r] *n* (*marksman*) franco tiratore *m*, cecchino

snob [snɔb] *n* snob *m/f inv*

snooker ['snu:kə^r] *n tipo di gioco del biliardo*

snoop ['snu:p] *vi* **to ~ about** curiosare

snooze [snu:z] *n* sonnellino, pisolino ▷ *vi* fare un sonnellino

snore [snɔ:^r] *vi* russare

snorkel ['snɔ:kl] *n* (*of swimmer*) respiratore *m* a tubo

snort [snɔ:t] *n* sbuffo ▷ *vi* sbuffare

snow [snəu] *n* neve *f* ▷ *vi* nevicare; **snowball** *n* palla di neve ▷ *vi* (*fig*) crescere a vista d'occhio; **snowstorm** *n* tormenta

snub [snʌb] *vt* snobbare ▷ *n* offesa, affronto

snug [snʌg] *adj* comodo(-a); (*room, house*) accogliente, comodo(-a)

KEYWORD

so [səu] *adv* **1** (*thus, likewise*) così; **if so** se è così, quand'è così; **I didn't do it — you did so!** non l'ho fatto io — sì che l'hai fatto!; **so do I, so am I** *etc* anch'io; **it's 5 o'clock — so it is!** sono le 5 — davvero!; **I hope so** lo spero; **I think so** penso di sì; **so far** finora, fin qui; (*in past*) fino ad allora
2 (*in comparisons etc: to such a degree*) così; **so big (that)** così grande (che); **she's not so clever as her brother** lei non è (così) intelligente come suo fratello
3: **so much** *adj* tanto(-a) ▷ *adv* tanto; **I've got so much work/money** ho tanto lavoro/tanti soldi; **I love you so much** ti amo tanto; **so many** tanti(-e)
4 (*phrases*): **10 or so** circa 10; **so long!** (*inf: goodbye*) ciao!, ci vediamo!
▷ *conj* **1** (*expressing purpose*): **so as to do** in modo *or* così da fare; **we hurried so as not to be late** ci affrettammo per non fare tardi; **so (that)** affinché + *sub*, perché + *sub*
2 (*expressing result*): **he didn't arrive so I left** non è venuto così me ne sono andata; **so you see, I could have gone** vedi, sarei potuto andare

soak [səuk] *vt* inzuppare; (*clothes*) mettere a mollo ▷ *vi* (*clothes etc*) essere a mollo; **soak up** *vt* assorbire; **soaking** *adj* (*also:* **soaking wet**) fradicio(-a)

so-and-so ['səuənsəu] *n* (*somebody*) un tale; **Mr/Mrs ~** signor/signora tal dei tali

soap [səup] *n* sapone *m*; **soap opera** *n* soap opera *f inv*; **soap powder** *n* detersivo

soar [sɔ:^r] *vi* volare in alto; (*price etc*) salire alle stelle; (*building*) ergersi

sob [sɔb] *n* singhiozzo ▷ *vi* singhiozzare

sober ['səubə^r] *adj* sobrio(-a); (*not drunk*) non ubriaco(-a); (*moderate*) moderato(-a); **sober up** *vt* far passare la sbornia a ▷ *vi* farsi passare la sbornia

so-called ['səu'kɔ:ld] *adj* cosiddetto(-a)

soccer ['sɔkə^r] *n* calcio

sociable ['səuʃəbl] *adj* socievole

social ['səuʃl] *adj* sociale ▷ *n* festa, serata; **socialism** *n* socialismo; **socialist** *adj, n* socialista *m/f*; **socialize** *vi* **to socialize (with)** socializzare (con); **social life** *n* vita sociale; **socially** *adv* socialmente, in società; **social security** (BRIT) *n* previdenza sociale; **social services** *npl* servizi *mpl* sociali; **social work** *n* servizio sociale; **social worker** *n* assistente *m/f* sociale

society [sə'saɪətɪ] *n* società *f inv*; (*club*) società, associazione *f*; (*also:* **high ~**) alta società

sociology [səusɪ'ɔlədʒɪ] *n* sociologia

sock [sɔk] *n* calzino

socket ['sɔkɪt] *n* cavità *f inv*; (*of eye*) orbita; (BRIT: *Elec*: *also*: **wall ~**) presa di corrente
soda ['səudə] *n* (*Chem*) soda; (*also*: **~ water**) acqua di seltz; (US: *also*: **~ pop**) gassosa
sodium ['səudɪəm] *n* sodio
sofa ['səufə] *n* sofà *m inv*; **sofa bed** *n* divano *m* letto *inv*
soft [sɔft] *adj* (*not rough*) morbido(-a); (*not hard*) soffice; (*not loud*) sommesso(-a); (*not bright*) tenue; (*kind*) gentile; **soft drink** *n* analcolico; **soft drugs** *npl* droghe *fpl* leggere; **soften** ['sɔfn] *vt* ammorbidire; addolcire; attenuare ▷ *vi* ammorbidirsi; addolcirsi; attenuarsi; **softly** *adv* dolcemente; morbidamente; **software** ['sɔftwɛə^r] *n* (*Comput*) software *m*
soggy ['sɔgɪ] *adj* inzuppato(-a)
soil [sɔɪl] *n* terreno ▷ *vt* sporcare
solar ['səulə^r] *adj* solare; **solar power** *n* energie solare; **solar system** *n* sistema *m* solare
sold [səuld] *pt, pp of* **sell**
soldier ['səuldʒə^r] *n* soldato, militare *m*
sold out *adj* (*Comm*) esaurito(-a)
sole [səul] *n* (*of foot*) pianta (del piede); (*of shoe*) suola; (*fish*: *pl inv*) sogliola ▷ *adj* solo(-a), unico(-a); **solely** *adv* solamente, unicamente; **I will hold you solely responsible** la considererò il solo responsabile
solemn ['sɔləm] *adj* solenne
solicitor [sə'lɪsɪtə^r] (BRIT) *n* (*for wills etc*) ≈ notaio; (*in court*) ≈ avvocato
solid ['sɔlɪd] *adj* solido(-a); (*not hollow*) pieno(-a); (*meal*) sostanzioso(-a) ▷ *n* solido
solitary ['sɔlɪtərɪ] *adj* solitario(-a)
solitude ['sɔlɪtju:d] *n* solitudine *f*
solo ['səuləu] *n* assolo; **soloist** *n* solista *m/f*
soluble ['sɔljubl] *adj* solubile
solution [sə'lu:ʃən] *n* soluzione *f*
solve [sɔlv] *vt* risolvere
solvent ['sɔlvənt] *adj* (*Comm*) solvibile ▷ *n* (*Chem*) solvente *m*
sombre ['sɔmbə^r] (US **somber**) *adj* scuro(-a); (*mood, person*) triste

KEYWORD

some [sʌm] *adj* **1** (*a certain amount or number of*): **some tea/water/cream** del tè/dell'acqua/della panna; **some children/apples** dei bambini/delle mele
2 (*certain*: *in contrasts*) certo(-a); **some people say that ...** alcuni dicono che ..., certa gente dice che ...
3 (*unspecified*) un(a) certo(-a), qualche; **some woman was asking for you** una tale chiedeva di lei; **some day** un giorno; **some day next week** un giorno della prossima settimana
▷ *pron* **1** (*a certain number*) alcuni(-e), certi(-e); **I've got some** (*books etc*) ne ho alcuni; **some (of them) have been sold** alcuni sono stati venduti
2 (*a certain amount*) un po'; **I've got some** (*money, milk*) ne ho un po'; **I've read some of the book** ho letto parte del libro
▷ *adv* **some 10 people** circa 10 persone

some: **somebody** ['sʌmbədɪ] *pron* = **someone**; **somehow** ['sʌmhau] *adv* in un modo o nell'altro, in qualche modo; (*for some reason*) per qualche ragione; **someone** ['sʌmwʌn] *pron* qualcuno; **someplace** ['sʌmpleɪs] (US) *adv* = **somewhere**; **something** ['sʌmθɪŋ] *pron* qualcosa, qualche cosa; **something nice** qualcosa di bello; **something to do** qualcosa da fare; **sometime** ['sʌmtaɪm] *adv* (*in future*) una volta o l'altra; (*in past*): **sometime last month** durante il mese scorso; **sometimes** ['sʌmtaɪmz] *adv* qualche volta;

somewhat ['sʌmwɔt] *adv* piuttosto; **somewhere** ['sʌmwɛəʳ] *adv* in *or* da qualche parte
son [sʌn] *n* figlio
song [sɔŋ] *n* canzone *f*
son-in-law ['sʌnɪnlɔː] *n* genero
soon [suːn] *adv* presto, fra poco; (*early, a short time after*) presto; **~ afterwards** poco dopo; *see also* **as**; **sooner** *adv* (*time*) prima; (*preference*): **I would sooner do** preferirei fare; **sooner or later** prima o poi
soothe [suːð] *vt* calmare
sophisticated [sə'fɪstɪkeɪtɪd] *adj* sofisticato(-a); raffinato(-a); complesso(-a)
sophomore ['sɔfəmɔːʳ] (*US*) *n* studente(-essa) del secondo anno
soprano [sə'prɑːnəu] *n* (*voice*) soprano *m*; (*singer*) soprano *m/f*
sorbet ['sɔːbeɪ] *n* sorbetto
sordid ['sɔːdɪd] *adj* sordido(-a)
sore [sɔːʳ] *adj* (*painful*) dolorante ▷ *n* piaga
sorrow ['sɔrəu] *n* dolore *m*
sorry ['sɔrɪ] *adj* spiacente; (*condition, excuse*) misero(-a); **~!** scusa! (*or* scusi! *or* scusate!); **to feel ~ for sb** rincrescersi per qn
sort [sɔːt] *n* specie *f*, genere *m*; **sort out** *vt* (*papers*) classificare; ordinare; (: *letters etc*) smistare; (: *problems*) risolvere; (*Comput*) ordinare
SOS *n abbr* (= *save our souls*) S.O.S. *m inv*
so-so ['səusəu] *adv* così così
sought [sɔːt] *pt, pp of* **seek**
soul [səul] *n* anima
sound [saund] *adj* (*healthy*) sano(-a); (*safe, not damaged*) solido(-a), in buono stato; (*reliable, not superficial*) solido(-a); (*sensible*) giudizioso(-a), di buon senso ▷ *adv* **~ asleep** profondamente addormentato ▷ *n* suono; (*noise*) rumore *m*; (*Geo*) stretto ▷ *vt* (*alarm*) suonare ▷ *vi* suonare; (*fig: seem*) sembrare; **to ~ like** rassomigliare a; **soundtrack** *n* (*of film*) colonna sonora
soup [suːp] *n* minestra; brodo; zuppa
sour ['sauəʳ] *adj* aspro(-a); (*fruit*) acerbo(-a); (*milk*) acido(-a); (*fig*) arcigno(-a); acido(-a); **it's ~ grapes** è soltanto invidia
source [sɔːs] *n* fonte *f*, sorgente *f*; (*fig*) fonte
south [sauθ] *n* sud *m*, meridione *m*, mezzogiorno ▷ *adj* del sud, sud *inv*, meridionale ▷ *adv* verso sud; **South Africa** *n* Sudafrica *m*; **South African** *adj, n* sudafricano(-a); **South America** *n* Sudamerica *m*, America del sud; **South American** *adj, n* sudamericano(-a); **southbound** ['sauθbaund] *adj* (*gen*) diretto(-a) a sud; (*carriageway*) sud *inv*; **southeastern** [sauθ'iːstən] *adj* sudorientale; **southern** ['sʌðən] *adj* del sud, meridionale; esposto(-a) a sud; **South Korea** *n* Corea *f* del Sud; **South Pole** *n* Polo Sud; **southward(s)** *adv* verso sud; **south-west** *n* sud-ovest *m*; **southwestern** [sauθ'westən] *adj* sudoccidentale
souvenir [suːvə'nɪəʳ] *n* ricordo, souvenir *m inv*
sovereign ['sɔvrɪn] *adj, n* sovrano(-a)
sow[1] [səu] (*pt* **sowed**, *pp* **sown**) *vt* seminare
sow[2] [sau] *n* scrofa
soya ['sɔɪə] (*US* **soy**) *n* **~ bean** *n* seme *m* di soia; **soya sauce** *n* salsa di soia
spa [spɑː] *n* (*resort*) stazione *f* termale; (*US: also:* **health ~**) centro di cure estetiche
space [speɪs] *n* spazio; (*room*) posto; spazio; (*length of time*) intervallo ▷ *cpd* spaziale ▷ *vt* (*also:* **~ out**) distanziare; **spacecraft** *n inv* veicolo spaziale; **spaceship** *n* = **spacecraft**
spacious ['speɪʃəs] *adj* spazioso(-a), ampio(-a)
spade [speɪd] *n* (*tool*) vanga; pala; (*child's*) paletta; **spades** *npl* (*Cards*) picche *fpl*

spaghetti [spə'gɛtɪ] *n* spaghetti *mpl*
Spain [speɪn] *n* Spagna
spam [spæm] (*Comput*) *n* spamming ▷ *vt* **to ~ sb** inviare a qn messaggi pubblicitari non richiesti via email
span [spæn] *n* (*of bird, plane*) apertura alare; (*of arch*) campata; (*in time*) periodo; durata ▷ *vt* attraversare; (*fig*) abbracciare
Spaniard ['spænjəd] *n* spagnolo(-a)
Spanish ['spænɪʃ] *adj* spagnolo(-a) ▷ *n* (*Ling*) spagnolo; **the Spanish** *npl* gli Spagnoli
spank [spæŋk] *vt* sculacciare
spanner ['spænəʳ] (BRIT) *n* chiave *f* inglese
spare [spɛəʳ] *adj* di riserva, di scorta; (*surplus*) in più, d'avanzo ▷ *n* (*part*) pezzo di ricambio ▷ *vt* (*do without*) fare a meno di; (*afford to give*) concedere; (*refrain from hurting, using*) risparmiare; **to ~** (*surplus*) d'avanzo; **spare part** *n* pezzo di ricambio; **spare room** *n* stanza degli ospiti; **spare time** *n* tempo libero; **spare tyre** (US **spare tire**) *n* (*Aut*) gomma di scorta; **spare wheel** *n* (*Aut*) ruota di scorta
spark [spɑːk] *n* scintilla; **spark(ing) plug** *n* candela
sparkle ['spɑːkl] *n* scintillio, sfavillio ▷ *vi* scintillare, sfavillare
sparrow ['spærəu] *n* passero
sparse [spɑːs] *adj* sparso(-a), rado(-a)
spasm ['spæzəm] *n* (*Med*) spasmo; (*fig*) accesso, attacco
spat [spæt] *pt, pp of* **spit**
spate [speɪt] *n* (*fig*): **~ of** diluvio *or* fiume *m* di
spatula ['spætjulə] *n* spatola
speak [spiːk] (*pt* **spoke**, *pp* **spoken**) *vt* (*language*) parlare; (*truth*) dire ▷ *vi* parlare; **I don't ~ Italian** non parlo italiano; **do you ~ English?** parla inglese?; **to ~ to sb/of** *or* **about sth** parlare a qn/di qc; **can I ~ to ...?** posso parlare con...?; **~ up!** parla più forte!; **speaker** *n* (*in public*) oratore(-trice); (*also:* **loudspeaker**) altoparlante *m*; (*Pol*): **the Speaker** *il presidente della Camera dei Comuni* (BRIT) *or* dei Rappresentanti (US)
spear [spɪəʳ] *n* lancia ▷ *vt* infilzare
special ['spɛʃl] *adj* speciale; **special delivery** *n* (*Post*): **by special delivery** per espresso; **special effects** *npl* (*Cine*) effetti *mpl* speciali; **specialist** *n* specialista *m/f*; **speciality** [spɛʃɪ'ælɪtɪ] *n* specialità *f inv*; **I'd like to try a local speciality** vorrei assaggiare una specialità del posto; **specialize** *vi* **to specialize (in)** specializzarsi (in); **specially** *adv* specialmente, particolarmente; **special needs** *adj* **special needs children** bambini *mpl* con difficoltà di apprendimento; **special offer** *n* (*Comm*) offerta speciale; **special school** *n* (BRIT) scuola speciale (*per portatori di handicap*); **specialty** (US) *n* = **speciality**
species ['spiːʃiːz] *n inv* specie *f inv*
specific [spə'sɪfɪk] *adj* specifico(-a); preciso(-a); **specifically** *adv* esplicitamente; (*especially*) appositamente
specify ['spɛsɪfaɪ] *vt* specificare, precisare; **unless otherwise specified** salvo indicazioni contrarie
specimen ['spɛsɪmən] *n* esemplare *m*, modello; (*Med*) campione *m*
speck [spɛk] *n* puntino, macchiolina; (*particle*) granello
spectacle ['spɛktəkl] *n* spettacolo; **spectacles** *npl* (*glasses*) occhiali *mpl*; **spectacular** [-'tækjuləʳ] *adj* spettacolare
spectator [spɛk'teɪtəʳ] *n* spettatore *m*
spectrum ['spɛktrəm] (*pl* **spectra**) *n* spettro
speculate ['spɛkjuleɪt] *vi* speculare; (*try to guess*): **to ~ about** fare ipotesi su
sped [spɛd] *pt, pp of* **speed**
speech [spiːtʃ] *n* (*faculty*) parola; (*talk, Theatre*) discorso; (*manner of*

speaking) parlata; **speechless** *adj* ammutolito(-a), muto(-a)

speed [spiːd] *n* velocità *f inv*; (*promptness*) prontezza; **at full** *or* **top ~** a tutta velocità; **speed up** *vi, vt* accelerare; **speedboat** *n* motoscafo; **speeding** *n* (*Aut*) eccesso di velocità; **speed limit** *n* limite *m* di velocità; **speedometer** [spɪ'dɔmɪtə^r] *n* tachimetro; **speedy** *adj* veloce, rapido(-a); pronto(-a)

spell [spɛl] (*pt, pp* **spelt** (BRIT) *or* **spelled**) *n* (*also:* **magic ~**) incantesimo; (*period of time*) (breve) periodo ▷ *vt* (*in writing*) scrivere (lettera per lettera); (*aloud*) dire lettera per lettera; (*fig*) significare; **to cast a ~ on sb** fare un incantesimo a qn; **he can't ~** fa errori di ortografia; **spell out** *vt* (*letter by letter*) dettare lettera per lettera; (*explain*): **to spell sth out for sb** spiegare qc a qn per filo e per segno; **spellchecker** ['speltʃekə^r] *n* correttore *m* ortografico; **spelling** *n* ortografia

spelt [spɛlt] (BRIT) *pt, pp of* **spell**

spend [spɛnd] (*pt, pp* **spent**) *vt* (*money*) spendere; (*time, life*) passare; **spending** *n* **government spending** spesa pubblica

spent [spɛnt] *pt, pp of* **spend**

sperm [spəːm] *n* sperma *m*

sphere [sfɪə^r] *n* sfera

spice [spaɪs] *n* spezia ▷ *vt* aromatizzare

spicy ['spaɪsɪ] *adj* piccante

spider ['spaɪdə^r] *n* ragno

spike [spaɪk] *n* punta

spill [spɪl] (*pt, pp* **spilt** *or* **spilled**) *vt* versare, rovesciare ▷ *vi* versarsi, rovesciarsi

spin [spɪn] (*pt, pp* **spun**) *n* (*revolution of wheel*) rotazione *f*; (*Aviat*) avvitamento; (*trip in car*) giretto ▷ *vt* (*wool etc*) filare; (*wheel*) far girare ▷ *vi* girare

spinach ['spɪnɪtʃ] *n* spinacio; (*as food*) spinaci *mpl*

spinal ['spaɪnl] *adj* spinale

spin doctor (*inf*) *n esperto di comunicazioni responsabile dell'immagine di un partito politico*

spin-dryer [spɪn'draɪə^r] (BRIT) *n* centrifuga

spine [spaɪn] *n* spina dorsale; (*thorn*) spina

spiral ['spaɪərl] *n* spirale *f* ▷ *vi* (*fig*) salire a spirale

spire ['spaɪə^r] *n* guglia

spirit ['spɪrɪt] *n* spirito; (*ghost*) spirito, fantasma *m*; (*mood*) stato d'animo, umore *m*; (*courage*) coraggio; **spirits** *npl* (*drink*) alcolici *mpl*; **in good ~s** di buon umore

spiritual ['spɪrɪtjuəl] *adj* spirituale

spit [spɪt] (*pt, pp* **spat**) *n* (*for roasting*) spiedo; (*saliva*) sputo; saliva ▷ *vi* sputare; (*fire, fat*) scoppiettare

spite [spaɪt] *n* dispetto ▷ *vt* contrariare, far dispetto a; **in ~ of** nonostante, malgrado; **spiteful** *adj* dispettoso(-a)

splash [splæʃ] *n* spruzzo; (*sound*) splash *m inv*; (*of colour*) schizzo ▷ *vt* spruzzare ▷ *vi* (*also:* **~ about**) sguazzare; **splash out** (*inf*) *vi* (BRIT) fare spese folli

splendid ['splɛndɪd] *adj* splendido(-a), magnifico(-a)

splinter ['splɪntə^r] *n* scheggia ▷ *vi* scheggiarsi

split [splɪt] (*pt, pp* **split**) *n* spaccatura; (*fig: division, quarrel*) scissione *f* ▷ *vt* spaccare; (*party*) dividere; (*work, profits*) spartire, ripartire ▷ *vi* (*divide*) dividersi; **split up** *vi* (*couple*) separarsi, rompere; (*meeting*) sciogliersi

spoil [spɔɪl] (*pt, pp* **spoilt** *or* **spoiled**) *vt* (*damage*) rovinare, guastare; (*mar*) sciupare; (*child*) viziare

spoilt [spɔɪlt] *pt, pp of* **spoil**

spoke [spəuk] *pt of* **speak** ▷ *n* raggio

spoken ['spəukn] *pp of* **speak**

spokesman ['spəuksmən] (*irreg*) *n*

portavoce *m inv*
spokesperson ['spəukspə:sn] *n* portavoce *m/f*
spokeswoman ['spəukswumən] (*irreg*) *n* portavoce *f inv*
sponge [spʌndʒ] *n* spugna; (*also:* **~ cake**) pan *m* di spagna ▷ *vt* spugnare, pulire con una spugna ▷ *vi* **to ~ off** *or* **on** scroccare a; **sponge bag** (BRIT) *n* nécessaire *m inv*
sponsor ['spɔnsəʳ] *n* (*Radio, TV, Sport etc*) sponsor *m inv*; (*Pol: of bill*) promotore(-trice) ▷ *vt* sponsorizzare; (*bill*) presentare; **sponsorship** *n* sponsorizzazione *f*
spontaneous [spɔn'teɪnɪəs] *adj* spontaneo(-a)
spooky ['spu:kɪ] (*inf*) *adj* che fa accapponare la pelle
spoon [spu:n] *n* cucchiaio; **spoonful** *n* cucchiaiata
sport [spɔ:t] *n* sport *m inv*; (*person*) persona di spirito ▷ *vt* sfoggiare; **sport jacket** (US) *n* = **sports jacket**; **sports car** *n* automobile *f* sportiva; **sports centre** (BRIT) *n* centro sportivo; **sports jacket** (BRIT) *n* giacca sportiva; **sportsman** (*irreg*) *n* sportivo; **sportswear** *n* abiti *mpl* sportivi; **sportswoman** (*irreg*) *n* sportiva; **sporty** *adj* sportivo(-a)
spot [spɔt] *n* punto; (*mark*) macchia; (*dot: on pattern*) pallino; (*pimple*) foruncolo; (*place*) posto; (*Radio, TV*) spot *m inv*; (*small amount*): **a ~ of** un po' di ▷ *vt* (*notice*) individuare, distinguere; **on the ~** sul posto; (*immediately*) su due piedi; (*in difficulty*) nei guai; **spotless** *adj* immacolato(-a); **spotlight** *n* proiettore *m*; (*Aut*) faro ausiliario
spouse [spauz] *n* sposo(-a)
sprain [spreɪn] *n* storta, distorsione *f* ▷ *vt* **to ~ one's ankle** storcersi una caviglia
sprang [spræŋ] *pt of* **spring**
sprawl [sprɔ:l] *vi* sdraiarsi (in modo scomposto); (*place*) estendersi (disordinatamente)
spray [spreɪ] *n* spruzzo; (*container*) nebulizzatore *m*, spray *m inv*; (*of flowers*) mazzetto ▷ *vt* spruzzare; (*crops*) irrorare
spread [sprɛd] (*pt, pp* **spread**) *n* diffusione *f*; (*distribution*) distribuzione *f*; (*Culin*) pasta (da spalmare); (*inf: food*) banchetto ▷ *vt* (*cloth*) stendere, distendere; (*butter etc*) spalmare; (*disease, knowledge*) propagare, diffondere ▷ *vi* stendersi, distendersi; spalmarsi; propagarsi, diffondersi; **spread out** *vi* (*move apart*) separarsi; **spreadsheet** *n* foglio elettronico ad espansione
spree [spri:] *n* **to go on a ~** fare baldoria
spring [sprɪŋ] (*pt* **sprang**, *pp* **sprung**) *n* (*leap*) salto, balzo; (*coiled metal*) molla; (*season*) primavera; (*of water*) sorgente *f* ▷ *vi* saltare, balzare; **spring up** *vi* (*problem*) presentarsi; **spring onion** *n* (BRIT) cipollina
sprinkle ['sprɪŋkl] *vt* spruzzare; spargere; **to ~ water** *etc* **on, ~ with water** *etc* spruzzare dell'acqua *etc* su
sprint [sprɪnt] *n* scatto ▷ *vi* scattare
sprung [sprʌŋ] *pp of* **spring**
spun [spʌn] *pt, pp of* **spin**
spur [spə:ʳ] *n* sperone *m*; (*fig*) sprone *m*, incentivo ▷ *vt* (*also:* **~ on**) spronare; **on the ~ of the moment** lì per lì
spurt [spə:t] *n* (*of water*) getto; (*of energy*) scatto ▷ *vi* sgorgare
spy [spaɪ] *n* spia ▷ *vi* **to ~ on** spiare ▷ *vt* (*see*) scorgere
sq. *abbr* = **square**
squabble ['skwɔbl] *vi* bisticciarsi
squad [skwɔd] *n* (*Mil*) plotone *m*; (*Police*) squadra
squadron ['skwɔdrn] *n* (*Mil*) squadrone *m*; (*Aviat, Naut*) squadriglia
squander ['skwɔndəʳ] *vt* dissipare
square [skwɛəʳ] *n* quadrato; (*in town*) piazza ▷ *adj* quadrato(-a); (*inf:*

ideas, person) di vecchio stampo ▷ *vt* (*arrange*) regolare; (*Math*) elevare al quadrato; (*reconcile*) conciliare; **all ~** pari; **a ~ meal** un pasto abbondante; **2 metres ~** di 2 metri per 2; **1 ~ metre** 1 metro quadrato; **square root** *n* radice *f* quadrata

squash [skwɔʃ] *n* (*Sport*) squash *m*; (BRIT: *drink*): **lemon/orange ~** sciroppo di limone/arancia; (US) zucca; (*Sport*) squash *m* ▷ *vt* schiacciare

squat [skwɔt] *adj* tarchiato(-a), tozzo(-a) ▷ *vi* (*also*: **~ down**) accovacciarsi; **squatter** *n* occupante *m/f* abusivo(-a)

squeak [skwi:k] *vi* squittire

squeal [skwi:l] *vi* strillare

squeeze [skwi:z] *n* pressione *f*; (*also Econ*) stretta ▷ *vt* premere; (*hand, arm*) stringere

squid [skwɪd] *n* calamaro

squint [skwɪnt] *vi* essere strabico(-a) ▷ *n* **he has a ~** è strabico

squirm [skwə:m] *vi* contorcersi

squirrel ['skwɪrəl] *n* scoiattolo

squirt [skwə:t] *vi* schizzare; zampillare ▷ *vt* spruzzare

Sr *abbr* = **senior**

Sri Lanka [srɪ'læŋkə] *n* Sri Lanka *m*

St *abbr* = **saint**; **street**

stab [stæb] *n* (*with knife etc*) pugnalata; (*of pain*) fitta; (*inf*: *try*): **to have a ~ at (doing) sth** provare (a fare) qc ▷ *vt* pugnalare

stability [stə'bɪlɪtɪ] *n* stabilità

stable ['steɪbl] *n* (*for horses*) scuderia; (*for cattle*) stalla ▷ *adj* stabile

stack [stæk] *n* catasta, pila ▷ *vt* accatastare, ammucchiare

stadium ['steɪdɪəm] *n* stadio

staff [stɑ:f] *n* (*work force*: *gen*) personale *m*; (: BRIT: *Scol*) personale insegnante ▷ *vt* fornire di personale

stag [stæg] *n* cervo

stage [steɪdʒ] *n* palcoscenico; (*profession*): **the ~** il teatro, la scena; (*point*) punto; (*platform*) palco ▷ *vt* (*play*) allestire, mettere in scena; (*demonstration*) organizzare; **in ~s** per gradi; a tappe

stagger ['stægə^r] *vi* barcollare ▷ *vt* (*person*) sbalordire; (*hours, holidays*) scaglionare; **staggering** *adj* (*amazing*) sbalorditivo(-a)

stagnant ['stægnənt] *adj* stagnante

stag night, stag party *n* festa di addio al celibato

stain [steɪn] *n* macchia; (*colouring*) colorante *m* ▷ *vt* macchiare; (*wood*) tingere; **stained glass** [ˌsteɪnd'glɑ:s] *n* vetro colorato; **stainless steel** *n* acciaio inossidabile

staircase ['stɛəkeɪs] *n* scale *fpl*, scala

stairs [stɛəz] *npl* (*flight of stairs*) scale *fpl*, scala

stairway ['stɛəweɪ] *n* = **staircase**

stake [steɪk] *n* palo, piolo; (*Comm*) interesse *m*; (*Betting*) puntata, scommessa ▷ *vt* (*bet*) scommettere; (*risk*) rischiare; **to be at ~** essere in gioco

stale [steɪl] *adj* (*bread*) raffermo(-a); (*food*) stantio(-a); (*air*) viziato(-a); (*beer*) svaporato(-a); (*smell*) di chiuso

stalk [stɔ:k] *n* gambo, stelo ▷ *vt* inseguire

stall [stɔ:l] *n* bancarella; (*in stable*) box *m inv* di stalla ▷ *vt* (*Aut*) far spegnere; (*fig*) bloccare ▷ *vi* (*Aut*) spegnersi, fermarsi; (*fig*) temporeggiare

stamina ['stæmɪnə] *n* vigore *m*, resistenza

stammer ['stæmə^r] *n* balbuzie *f* ▷ *vi* balbettare

stamp [stæmp] *n* (*postage stamp*) francobollo; (*implement*) timbro; (*mark, also fig*) marchio, impronta; (*on document*) bollo; timbro ▷ *vi* (*also*: **~ one's foot**) battere il piede ▷ *vt* battere; (*letter*) affrancare; (*mark with a stamp*) timbrare; **stamp out** *vt* (*fire*) estinguere; (*crime*) eliminare; (*opposition*) soffocare; **stamped**

addressed envelope *n* (BRIT) busta affrancata e indirizzata

> Be careful not to translate ***stamp*** by the Italian word ***stampa***.

stampede [stæm'pi:d] *n* fuggi fuggi *m inv*

stance [stæns] *n* posizione *f*

stand [stænd] (*pt, pp* **stood**) *n* (*position*) posizione *f*; (*for taxis*) posteggio; (*structure*) supporto, sostegno; (*at exhibition*) stand *m inv*; (*in shop*) banco; (*at market*) bancarella; (*booth*) chiosco; (*Sport*) tribuna ▷ *vi* stare in piedi; (*rise*) alzarsi in piedi; (*be placed*) trovarsi ▷ *vt* (*place*) mettere, porre; (*tolerate, withstand*) resistere, sopportare; (*treat*) offrire; **to make a ~** prendere posizione; **to ~ for parliament** (BRIT) presentarsi come candidato (per il parlamento); **stand back** *vi* prendere le distanze; **stand by** *vi* (*be ready*) tenersi pronto(-a) ▷ *vt fus* (*opinion*) sostenere; **stand down** *vi* (*withdraw*) ritirarsi; **stand for** *vt fus* (*signify*) rappresentare, significare; (*tolerate*) sopportare, tollerare; **stand in for** *vt fus* sostituire; **stand out** *vi* (*be prominent*) spiccare; **stand up** *vi* (*rise*) alzarsi in piedi; **stand up for** *vt fus* difendere; **stand up to** *vt fus* tener testa a, resistere a

standard ['stændəd] *n* modello, standard *m inv*; (*level*) livello; (*flag*) stendardo ▷ *adj* (*size etc*) normale, standard *inv*; **standards** *npl* (*morals*) principi *mpl*, valori *mpl*; **standard of living** *n* livello di vita

stand-by ['stændbaɪ] *n* riserva, sostituto; **to be on ~** (*gen*) tenersi pronto(-a); (*doctor*) essere di guardia; **stand-by ticket** *n* (*Aviat*) biglietto senza garanzia

standing ['stændɪŋ] *adj* diritto(-a), in piedi; (*permanent*) permanente ▷ *n* rango, condizione *f*, posizione *f*; **of many years' ~** che esiste da molti anni; **standing order** (BRIT) *n* (*at bank*) ordine *m* di pagamento (permanente)

stand: **standpoint** ['stændpɔɪnt] *n* punto di vista; **standstill** ['stændstɪl] *n* **at a standstill** fermo(-a); (*fig*) a un punto morto; **to come to a standstill** fermarsi; giungere a un punto morto

stank [stæŋk] *pt of* **stink**

staple ['steɪpl] *n* (*for papers*) graffetta ▷ *adj* (*food etc*) di base ▷ *vt* cucire

star [stɑ:ʳ] *n* stella; (*celebrity*) divo(-a) ▷ *vi* **to ~ (in)** essere il (*or* la) protagonista (di) ▷ *vt* (*Cinema*) essere interpretato(-a) da; **the stars** *npl* (*Astrology*) le stelle

starboard ['stɑ:bəd] *n* dritta

starch [stɑ:tʃ] *n* amido

stardom ['stɑ:dəm] *n* celebrità

stare [stɛəʳ] *n* sguardo fisso ▷ *vi* **to ~ at** fissare

stark [stɑ:k] *adj* (*bleak*) desolato(-a) ▷ *adv* **~ naked** completamente nudo(-a)

start [stɑ:t] *n* inizio; (*of race*) partenza; (*sudden movement*) sobbalzo; (*advantage*) vantaggio ▷ *vt* cominciare, iniziare; (*car*) mettere in moto ▷ *vi* cominciare; (*on journey*) partire, mettersi in viaggio; (*jump*) sobbalzare; **when does the film ~?** a che ora comincia il film?; **to ~ doing** *or* **to do sth** (in)cominciare a fare qc; **start off** *vi* cominciare; (*leave*) partire; **start out** *vi* (*begin*) cominciare; (*set out*) partire; **start up** *vi* cominciare; (*car*) avviarsi ▷ *vt* iniziare; (*car*) avviare; **starter** *n* (*Aut*) motorino d'avviamento; (*Sport: official*) starter *m inv*; (BRIT: *Culin*) primo piatto; **starting point** *n* punto di partenza

startle ['stɑ:tl] *vt* far trasalire; **startling** *adj* sorprendente

starvation [stɑ:'veɪʃən] *n* fame *f*, inedia

starve [stɑ:v] *vi* morire di fame; soffrire la fame ▷ *vt* far morire di fame, affamare

state [steɪt] *n* stato ▷ *vt* dichiarare, affermare; annunciare; **the S~s** (*USA*) gli Stati Uniti; **to be in a ~** essere agitato(-a); **statement** *n* dichiarazione *f*; **state school** *n* scuola statale; **statesman** (*irreg*) *n* statista *m*

static ['stætɪk] *n* (*Radio*) scariche *fpl* ▷ *adj* statico(-a)

station ['steɪʃən] *n* stazione *f* ▷ *vt* collocare, disporre

stationary ['steɪʃənərɪ] *adj* fermo(-a), immobile

stationer's (shop) *n* cartoleria

stationery ['steɪʃnərɪ] *n* articoli *mpl* di cancelleria

station wagon (*US*) *n* giardinetta

statistic [stə'tɪstɪk] *n* statistica; **statistics** *n* (*science*) statistica

statue ['stætju:] *n* statua

stature ['stætʃə^r] *n* statura

status ['steɪtəs] *n* posizione *f*, condizione *f* sociale; prestigio; stato; **status quo** [-'kwəu] *n* **the status quo** lo statu quo

statutory ['stætjutrɪ] *adj* stabilito(-a) dalla legge, statutario(-a)

staunch [stɔ:ntʃ] *adj* fidato(-a), leale

stay [steɪ] *n* (*period of time*) soggiorno, permanenza ▷ *vi* rimanere; (*reside*) alloggiare, stare; (*spend some time*) trattenersi, soggiornare; **to ~ put** non muoversi; **to ~ the night** fermarsi per la notte; **stay away** *vi* (*from person, building*) stare lontano (*from event*) non andare; **stay behind** *vi* restare indietro; **stay in** *vi* (*at home*) stare in casa; **stay on** *vi* restare, rimanere; **stay out** *vi* (*of house*) rimanere fuori (di casa); **stay up** *vi* (*at night*) rimanere alzato(-a)

steadily ['stɛdɪlɪ] *adv* (*firmly*) saldamente; (*constantly*) continuamente; (*fixedly*) fisso; (*walk*) con passo sicuro

steady ['stɛdɪ] *adj* (*not wobbling*) fermo(-a); (*regular*) costante; (*person, character*) serio(-a); (*: calm*) calmo(-a), tranquillo(-a) ▷ *vt* stabilizzare; calmare

steak [steɪk] *n* (*meat*) bistecca; (*fish*) trancia

steal [sti:l] (*pt* **stole**, *pp* **stolen**) *vt* rubare ▷ *vi* rubare; (*move*) muoversi furtivamente; **my wallet has been stolen** mi hanno rubato il portafoglio

steam [sti:m] *n* vapore *m* ▷ *vt* (*Culin*) cuocere a vapore ▷ *vi* fumare; **steam up** *vi* (*window*) appannarsi; **to get steamed up about sth** (*fig*) andare in bestia per qc; **steamy** *adj* (*room*) pieno(-a) di vapore; (*window*) appannato(-a)

steel [sti:l] *n* acciaio ▷ *adj* di acciaio

steep [sti:p] *adj* ripido(-a), scosceso(-a); (*price*) eccessivo(-a) ▷ *vt* inzuppare; (*washing*) mettere a mollo

steeple ['sti:pl] *n* campanile *m*

steer [stɪə^r] *vt* guidare ▷ *vi* (*Naut: person*) governare; (*car*) guidarsi; **steering** *n* (*Aut*) sterzo; **steering wheel** *n* volante *m*

stem [stɛm] *n* (*of flower, plant*) stelo; (*of tree*) fusto; (*of glass*) gambo; (*of fruit, leaf*) picciolo ▷ *vt* contenere, arginare; **stem cell** *n* cellula staminale

step [stɛp] *n* passo; (*stair*) gradino, scalino; (*action*) mossa, azione *f* ▷ *vi* **to ~ forward/back** fare un passo avanti/indietro; **steps** *npl* (*BRIT*) = **stepladder**; **to be in/out of ~ (with)** stare/non stare al passo (con); **step down** *vi* (*fig*) ritirarsi; **step in** *vi* fare il proprio ingresso; **step up** *vt* aumentare; intensificare; **stepbrother** *n* fratellastro; **stepchild** *n* figliastro(-a); **stepdaughter** *n* figliastra; **stepfather** *n* patrigno; **stepladder** *n* scala a libretto; **stepmother** *n* matrigna; **stepsister** *n* sorellastra; **stepson** *n* figliastro

stereo ['stɛrɪəu] *n* (*system*) sistema *m* stereofonico; (*record player*)

stereo *m inv* ▷ *adj* (*also:* **~phonic**) stereofonico(-a)
stereotype ['stɪərɪətaɪp] *n* stereotipo
sterile ['stɛraɪl] *adj* sterile; **sterilize** ['stɛrɪlaɪz] *vt* sterilizzare
sterling ['stə:lɪŋ] *adj* (*gold, silver*) di buona lega ▷ *n* (*Econ*) (lira) sterlina; **a pound ~** una lira sterlina
stern [stə:n] *adj* severo(-a) ▷ *n* (*Naut*) poppa
steroid ['stɛrɔɪd] *n* steroide *m*
stew [stju:] *n* stufato ▷ *vt* cuocere in umido
steward ['stju:əd] *n* (*Aviat, Naut, Rail*) steward *m inv*; (*in club etc*) dispensiere *m*; **stewardess** *n* assistente *f* di volo, hostess *f inv*
stick [stɪk] (*pt, pp* **stuck**) *n* bastone *m*; (*of rhubarb, celery*) gambo; (*of dynamite*) candelotto ▷ *vt* (*glue*) attaccare; (*thrust*): **to ~ sth into** conficcare *or* piantare *or* infiggere qc in; (*inf: put*) ficcare; (*inf: tolerate*) sopportare ▷ *vi* attaccarsi; (*remain*) restare, rimanere; **stick out** *vi* sporgere, spuntare; **stick up** *vi* sporgere, spuntare; **stick up for** *vt fus* difendere; **sticker** *n* cartellino adesivo; **sticking plaster** *n* cerotto adesivo; **stick insect** *n* insetto *m* stecco *inv*; **stick shift** (US) *n* (*Aut*) cambio manuale
sticky ['stɪkɪ] *adj* attaccaticcio(-a), vischioso(-a); (*label*) adesivo(-a); (*fig: situation*) difficile
stiff [stɪf] *adj* rigido(-a), duro(-a); (*muscle*) legato(-a), indolenzito(-a); (*difficult*) difficile, arduo(-a); (*cold*) freddo(-a), formale; (*strong*) forte; (*high: price*) molto alto(-a) ▷ *adv* **bored ~** annoiato(-a) a morte
stifling ['staɪflɪŋ] *adj* (*heat*) soffocante
stigma ['stɪgmə] *n* (*fig*) stigma *m*
stiletto [stɪ'lɛtəu] (BRIT) *n* (*also:* **~ heel**) tacco a spillo
still [stɪl] *adj* fermo(-a); silenzioso(-a) ▷ *adv* (*up to this time, even*) ancora; (*nonetheless*) tuttavia, ciò nonostante
stimulate ['stɪmjuleɪt] *vt* stimolare
stimulus ['stɪmjuləs] (*pl* **stimuli**) *n* stimolo
sting [stɪŋ] (*pt, pp* **stung**) *n* puntura; (*organ*) pungiglione *m* ▷ *vt* pungere
stink [stɪŋk] (*pt* **stank**, *pp* **stunk**) *n* fetore *m*, puzzo ▷ *vi* puzzare
stir [stə:ʳ] *n* agitazione *f*, clamore *m* ▷ *vt* mescolare; (*fig*) risvegliare ▷ *vi* muoversi; **stir up** *vt* provocare, suscitare; **stir-fry** *vt* saltare in padella ▷ *n* pietanza al salto
stitch [stɪtʃ] *n* (*Sewing*) punto; (*Knitting*) maglia; (*Med*) punto (di sutura); (*pain*) fitta ▷ *vt* cucire, attaccare; suturare
stock [stɔk] *n* riserva, provvista; (*Comm*) giacenza, stock *m inv*; (*Agr*) bestiame *m*; (*Culin*) brodo; (*descent*) stirpe *f*; (*Finance*) titoli *mpl*; azioni *fpl* ▷ *adj* (*fig: reply etc*) consueto(-a); classico(-a) ▷ *vt* (*have in stock*) avere, vendere; **~s and shares** valori *mpl* di borsa; **in ~** in magazzino; **out of ~** esaurito(-a); **stockbroker** ['stɔkbrəukəʳ] *n* agente *m* di cambio; **stock cube** (BRIT) *n* dado; **stock exchange** *n* Borsa (valori); **stockholder** ['stɔkhəuldəʳ] *n* (*Finance*) azionista *m/f*
stocking ['stɔkɪŋ] *n* calza
stock market *n* Borsa, mercato finanziario
stole [stəul] *pt of* **steal** ▷ *n* stola
stolen ['stəuln] *pp of* **steal**
stomach ['stʌmək] *n* stomaco; (*belly*) pancia ▷ *vt* sopportare, digerire: **stomachache** *n* mal *m* di stomaco
stone [stəun] *n* pietra; (*pebble*) sasso, ciottolo; (*in fruit*) nocciolo; (*Med*) calcolo; (BRIT: *weight*) = *6.348 kg; 14 libbre* ▷ *adj* di pietra ▷ *vt* lapidare; (*fruit*) togliere il nocciolo a
stood [stud] *pt, pp of* **stand**
stool [stu:l] *n* sgabello
stoop [stu:p] *vi* (*also:* **have a ~**) avere una curvatura; (*also:* **~ down**)

chinarsi, curvarsi

stop [stɔp] *n* arresto; (*stopping place*) fermata; (*in punctuation*) punto ▷ *vt* arrestare, fermare; (*break off*) interrompere; (*also:* **put a ~ to**) porre fine a ▷ *vi* fermarsi; (*rain, noise etc*) cessare, finire; **to ~ doing sth** cessare *or* finire di fare qc; **could you ~ here/at the corner?** può fermarsi qui/all'angolo?; **to ~ dead** fermarsi di colpo; **stop by** *vi* passare, fare un salto; **stop off** *vi* sostare brevemente; **stopover** *n* breve sosta; (*Aviat*) scalo; **stoppage** ['stɔpɪdʒ] *n* arresto, fermata; (*of pay*) trattenuta; (*strike*) interruzione *f* del lavoro

storage ['stɔːrɪdʒ] *n* immagazzinamento

store [stɔːʳ] *n* provvista, riserva; (*depot*) deposito; (BRIT: *department store*) grande magazzino; (US: *shop*) negozio ▷ *vt* immagazzinare; **stores** *npl* (*provisions*) rifornimenti *mpl*, scorte *fpl*; **in ~** di riserva; in serbo; **storekeeper** (US) *n* negoziante *m/f*

storey ['stɔːrɪ] (US **story**) *n* piano

storm [stɔːm] *n* tempesta, temporale *m*, burrasca; uragano ▷ *vi* (*fig*) infuriarsi ▷ *vt* prendere d'assalto; **stormy** *adj* tempestoso(-a), burrascoso(-a)

story ['stɔːrɪ] *n* storia; favola; racconto; (US) = **storey**

stout [staut] *adj* solido(-a), robusto(-a); (*friend, supporter*) tenace; (*fat*) corpulento(-a), grasso(-a) ▷ *n* birra scura

stove [stəuv] *n* (*for cooking*) fornello; (*: small*) fornelletto; (*for heating*) stufa

straight [streɪt] *adj* dritto(-a); (*frank*) onesto(-a), franco(-a); (*simple*) semplice ▷ *adv* diritto; (*drink*) liscio; **to put** *or* **get ~** mettere in ordine, mettere ordine in; **~ away, ~ off** (*at once*) immediatamente; **straighten** *vt* (*also:* **straighten out**) raddrizzare; **straightforward** *adj* semplice; onesto(-a), franco(-a)

strain [streɪn] *n* (*Tech*) sollecitazione *f*; (*physical*) sforzo; (*mental*) tensione *f*; (*Med*) strappo; distorsione *f*; (*streak, trace*) tendenza; elemento ▷ *vt* tendere; (*muscle*) sforzare; (*ankle*) storcere; (*resources*) pesare su; (*food*) colare; passare; **strained** *adj* (*muscle*) stirato(-a); (*laugh etc*) forzato(-a); (*relations*) teso(-a); **strainer** *n* passino, colino

strait [streɪt] *n* (*Geo*) stretto; **straits** *npl* **to be in dire ~s** (*fig*) essere nei guai

strand [strænd] *n* (*of thread*) filo; **stranded** *adj* nei guai; senza mezzi di trasporto

strange [streɪndʒ] *adj* (*not known*) sconosciuto(-a); (*odd*) strano(-a), bizzarro(-a); **strangely** *adv* stranamente; **stranger** *n* sconosciuto(-a); estraneo(-a)

strangle ['stræŋgl] *vt* strangolare

strap [stræp] *n* cinghia; (*of slip, dress*) spallina, bretella

strategic [strə'tiːdʒɪk] *adj* strategico(-a)

strategy ['strætɪdʒɪ] *n* strategia

straw [strɔː] *n* paglia; (*drinking straw*) cannuccia; **that's the last ~!** è la goccia che fa traboccare il vaso!

strawberry ['strɔːbərɪ] *n* fragola

stray [streɪ] *adj* (*animal*) randagio(-a); (*bullet*) vagante; (*scattered*) sparso(-a) ▷ *vi* perdersi

streak [striːk] *n* striscia; (*of hair*) mèche *f inv* ▷ *vt* striare, screziare ▷ *vi* **to ~ past** passare come un fulmine

stream [striːm] *n* ruscello; corrente *f*; (*of people, smoke etc*) fiume *m* ▷ *vt* (*Scol*) dividere in livelli di rendimento ▷ *vi* scorrere; **to ~ in/out** entrare/uscire a fiotti

street [striːt] *n* strada, via; **streetcar** (US) *n* tram *m inv*; **street light** *n* lampione *m*; **street map** *n* pianta (di una città)

street plan *n* pianta (di una città)

strength [strɛŋθ] *n* forza; **strengthen** *vt* rinforzare; fortificare; consolidare

strenuous ['strɛnjuəs] *adj* vigoroso(-a), energico(-a); (*tiring*) duro(-a), pesante

stress [strɛs] *n* (*force, pressure*) pressione *f*; (*mental strain*) tensione *f*; (*accent*) accento ▷ *vt* insistere su, sottolineare; accentare; **stressed** *adj* (*tense*: *person*) stressato(-a); (*Ling, Poetry*: *syllable*) accentato(-a); **stressful** *adj* (*job*) difficile, stressante

stretch [strɛtʃ] *n* (*of sand etc*) distesa ▷ *vi* stirarsi; (*extend*): **to ~ to** *or* **as far as** estendersi fino a ▷ *vt* tendere, allungare; (*spread*) distendere; (*fig*) spingere (al massimo); **stretch out** *vi* allungarsi, estendersi ▷ *vt* (*arm etc*) allungare, tendere; (*to spread*) distendere

stretcher ['strɛtʃə^r] *n* barella, lettiga

strict [strɪkt] *adj* (*severe*) rigido(-a), severo(-a); (*precise*) preciso(-a), stretto(-a); **strictly** *adv* severamente; rigorosamente; strettamente

stride [straɪd] (*pt* **strode**, *pp* **stridden**) *n* passo lungo ▷ *vi* camminare a grandi passi

strike [straɪk] (*pt, pp* **struck**) *n* sciopero; (*of oil etc*) scoperta; (*attack*) attacco ▷ *vt* colpire; (*oil etc*) scoprire, trovare; (*bargain*) fare; (*fig*): **the thought** *or* **it ~s me that ...** mi viene in mente che ... ▷ *vi* scioperare; (*attack*) attaccare; (*clock*) suonare; **on ~** (*workers*) in sciopero; **to ~ a match** accendere un fiammifero; **striker** *n* scioperante *m/f*; (*Sport*) attaccante *m*; **striking** *adj* che colpisce

string [strɪŋ] (*pt, pp* **strung**) *n* spago; (*row*) fila; sequenza; catena; (*Mus*) corda ▷ *vt* **to ~ out** disporre di fianco; **to ~ together** (*words, ideas*) mettere insieme; **the strings** *npl* (*Mus*) gli archi; **to pull ~s for sb** (*fig*) raccomandare qn

strip [strɪp] *n* striscia ▷ *vt* spogliare; (*paint*) togliere; (*also*: **~ down**: *machine*) smontare ▷ *vi* spogliarsi; **strip off** *vt* (*paint etc*) staccare ▷ *vi* (*person*) spogliarsi

stripe [straɪp] *n* striscia, riga; (*Mil, Police*) gallone *m*; **striped** *adj* a strisce *or* righe

stripper ['strɪpə^r] *n* spogliarellista *m/f*

strip-search ['strɪpsəːtʃ] *vt* **to ~ sb** perquisire qn facendolo(-a) spogliare ▷ *n* perquisizione (*facendo spogliare il perquisito*)

strive [straɪv] (*pt* **strove**, *pp* **striven**) *vi* **to ~ to do** sforzarsi di fare

strode [strəud] *pt of* **stride**

stroke [strəuk] *n* colpo; (*Swimming*) bracciata; (*: style*) stile *m*; (*Med*) colpo apoplettico ▷ *vt* accarezzare; **at a ~** in un attimo

stroll [strəul] *n* giretto, passeggiatina ▷ *vi* andare a spasso; **stroller** (*US*) *n* passeggino

strong [strɔŋ] *adj* (*gen*) forte; (*sturdy*: *table, fabric etc*) robusto(-a); **they are 50 ~** sono in 50; **stronghold** *n* (*also fig*) roccaforte *f*; **strongly** *adv* fortemente, con forza; energicamente; vivamente

strove [strəuv] *pt of* **strive**

struck [strʌk] *pt, pp of* **strike**

structure ['strʌktʃə^r] *n* struttura; (*building*) costruzione *f*, fabbricato

struggle ['strʌgl] *n* lotta ▷ *vi* lottare

strung [strʌŋ] *pt, pp of* **string**

stub [stʌb] *n* mozzicone *m*; (*of ticket etc*) matrice *f*, talloncino ▷ *vt* **to ~ one's toe** urtare *or* sbattere il dito del piede; **stub out** *vt* schiacciare

stubble ['stʌbl] *n* stoppia; (*on chin*) barba ispida

stubborn ['stʌbən] *adj* testardo(-a), ostinato(-a)

stuck [stʌk] *pt, pp of* **stick** ▷ *adj* (*jammed*) bloccato(-a)

stud [stʌd] *n* bottoncino; borchia; (*also*: **~ earring**) orecchino a pressione; (*also:* **~ farm**) scuderia, allevamento di cavalli; (*also:* **~ horse**) stallone *m* ▷ *vt* (*fig*): **~ded with** tempestato(-a) di

student ['stju:dənt] *n* studente(-essa) ▷ *cpd* studentesco(-a); universitario(-a); degli studenti; **student driver** (*US*) *n* conducente *m/f* principiante; **students' union** *n* (*BRIT*: *association*) circolo universitario; (: *building*) sede *f* del circolo universitario

studio ['stju:dɪəu] *n* studio; **studio flat** (*US* **studio apartment**) *n* monolocale *m*

study ['stʌdɪ] *n* studio ▷ *vt* studiare; esaminare ▷ *vi* studiare

stuff [stʌf] *n* roba; (*substance*) sostanza, materiale *m* ▷ *vt* imbottire; (*Culin*) farcire; (*dead animal*) impagliare; (*inf*: *push*) ficcare; **stuffing** *n* imbottitura; (*Culin*) ripieno; **stuffy** *adj* (*room*) mal ventilato(-a), senz'aria; (*ideas*) antiquato(-a)

stumble ['stʌmbl] *vi* inciampare; **to ~ across** (*fig*) imbattersi in

stump [stʌmp] *n* ceppo; (*of limb*) moncone *m* ▷ *vt* **to be ~ed** essere sconcertato(-a)

stun [stʌn] *vt* stordire; (*amaze*) sbalordire

stung [stʌŋ] *pt, pp of* **sting**

stunk [stʌŋk] *pp of* **stink**

stunned [stʌnd] *adj* (*from blow*) stordito(-a); (*amazed, shocked*) sbalordito(-a)

stunning ['stʌnɪŋ] *adj* sbalorditivo(-a); (*girl etc*) fantastico(-a)

stunt [stʌnt] *n* bravata; trucco pubblicitario

stupid ['stju:pɪd] *adj* stupido(-a); **stupidity** [-'pɪdɪtɪ] *n* stupidità *f inv*, stupidaggine *f*

sturdy ['stə:dɪ] *adj* robusto(-a), vigoroso(-a); solido(-a)

stutter ['stʌtəʳ] *n* balbuzie *f* ▷ *vi* balbettare

style [staɪl] *n* stile *m*; (*distinction*) eleganza, classe *f*; **stylish** *adj* elegante; **stylist** *n* **hair stylist** parrucchiere(-a)

sub... [sʌb] *prefix* sub..., sotto...; **subconscious** *adj* subcosciente ▷ *n* subcosciente *m*

subdued [səb'dju:d] *adj* pacato(-a); (*light*) attenuato(-a)

subject [*n* 'sʌbdʒɪkt, *vb* səb'dʒɛkt] *n* soggetto; (*citizen etc*) cittadino(-a); (*Scol*) materia ▷ *vt* **to ~ to** sottomettere a; esporre a; **to be ~ to** (*law*) essere sottomesso(-a) a; (*disease*) essere soggetto(-a) a; **subjective** [-'dʒɛktɪv] *adj* soggettivo(-a); **subject matter** *n* argomento; contenuto

subjunctive [səb'dʒʌŋktɪv] *adj* congiuntivo(-a) ▷ *n* congiuntivo

submarine [sʌbmə'ri:n] *n* sommergibile *m*

submission [səb'mɪʃən] *n* sottomissione *f*; (*claim*) richiesta

submit [səb'mɪt] *vt* sottomettere ▷ *vi* sottomettersi

subordinate [sə'bɔ:dɪnət] *adj, n* subordinato(-a)

subscribe [səb'skraɪb] *vi* contribuire; **to ~ to** (*opinion*) approvare, condividere; (*fund*) sottoscrivere a; (*newspaper*) abbonarsi a; essere abbonato(-a) a

subscription [səb'skrɪpʃən] *n* sottoscrizione *f*; abbonamento

subsequent ['sʌbsɪkwənt] *adj* successivo(-a), seguente; conseguente; **subsequently** *adv* in seguito, successivamente

subside [səb'saɪd] *vi* cedere, abbassarsi; (*flood*) decrescere; (*wind*) calmarsi

subsidiary [səb'sɪdɪərɪ] *adj* sussidiario(-a); accessorio(-a) ▷ *n* filiale *f*

subsidize ['sʌbsɪdaɪz] *vt* sovvenzionare

subsidy ['sʌbsɪdɪ] *n* sovvenzione *f*
substance ['sʌbstəns] *n* sostanza
substantial [səb'stænʃl] *adj* solido(-a); (*amount, progress etc*) notevole; (*meal*) sostanzioso(-a)
substitute ['sʌbstɪtju:t] *n* (*person*) sostituto(-a); (*thing*) succedaneo, surrogato ▷ *vt* **to ~ sth/sb for** sostituire qc/qn a; **substitution** [sʌbstɪ'tju:ʃən] *n* sostituzione *f*
subtle ['sʌtl] *adj* sottile
subtract [səb'trækt] *vt* sottrarre
suburb ['sʌbə:b] *n* sobborgo; **the ~s** la periferia; **suburban** [sə'bə:bən] *adj* suburbano(-a)
subway ['sʌbweɪ] *n* (US: *underground*) metropolitana; (BRIT: *underpass*) sottopassaggio
succeed [sək'si:d] *vi* riuscire; avere successo ▷ *vt* succedere a; **to ~ in doing** riuscire a fare
success [sək'sɛs] *n* successo; **successful** *adj* (*venture*) coronato(-a) da successo, riuscito(-a); **to be successful (in doing)** riuscire (a fare); **successfully** *adv* con successo
succession [sək'sɛʃən] *n* successione *f*
successive [sək'sɛsɪv] *adj* successivo(-a); consecutivo(-a)
successor [sək'sɛsə^r] *n* successore *m*
succumb [sə'kʌm] *vi* soccombere
such [sʌtʃ] *adj* tale; (*of that kind*): **~ a book** un tale libro, un libro del genere; **~ books** tali libri, libri del genere; (*so much*): **~ courage** tanto coraggio ▷ *adv* talmente, così; **~ a long trip** un viaggio così lungo; **~ a lot of** talmente *or* così tanto(-a); **~ as** (*like*) come; **as ~** come *or* in quanto tale; **such-and-such** *adj* tale (*after noun*)
suck [sʌk] *vt* succhiare; (*breast, bottle*) poppare
Sudan [su:'dɑ:n] *n* Sudan *m*
sudden ['sʌdn] *adj* improvviso(-a); **all of a ~** improvvisamente, all'improvviso; **suddenly** *adv* bruscamente, improvvisamente, di colpo
sudoku [sʊ'dəʊku:] *n* sudoku *m inv*
sue [su:] *vt* citare in giudizio
suede [sweɪd] *n* pelle *f* scamosciata
suffer ['sʌfə^r] *vt* soffrire, patire; (*bear*) sopportare, tollerare ▷ *vi* soffrire; **to ~ from** soffrire di; **suffering** *n* sofferenza
suffice [sə'faɪs] *vi* essere sufficiente, bastare
sufficient [sə'fɪʃənt] *adj* sufficiente; **~ money** abbastanza soldi
suffocate ['sʌfəkeɪt] *vi* (*have difficulty breathing*) soffocare; (*die through lack of air*) asfissiare
sugar ['ʃugə^r] *n* zucchero ▷ *vt* zuccherare
suggest [sə'dʒɛst] *vt* proporre, suggerire; indicare; **suggestion** [-'dʒɛstʃən] *n* suggerimento, proposta; indicazione *f*
suicide ['suɪsaɪd] *n* (*person*) suicida *m/f*; (*act*) suicidio; *see also* **commit**; **suicide bomber** *n* kamikaze *m/f inv*, attentatore(-trice) suicida *inv*; **suicide bombing** *n* attentato suicida
suit [su:t] *n* (*man's*) vestito; (*woman's*) completo, tailleur *m inv*; (*Law*) causa; (*Cards*) seme *m*, colore *m* ▷ *vt* andar bene a *or* per; essere adatto(-a) a *or* per; (*adapt*): **to ~ sth to** adattare qc a; **well ~ed** ben assortito(-a); **suitable** *adj* adatto(-a); appropriato(-a); **suitcase** ['su:tkeɪs] *n* valigia
suite [swi:t] *n* (*of rooms*) appartamento; (*Mus*) suite *f inv*; (*furniture*): **bedroom/dining room ~** arredo *or* mobilia per la camera da letto/sala da pranzo
sulfur ['sʌlfə^r] (US) *n* = **sulphur**
sulk [sʌlk] *vi* fare il broncio
sulphur ['sʌlfə^r] (US **sulfur**) *n* zolfo
sultana [sʌl'tɑ:nə] *n* (*fruit*) uva (secca) sultanina
sum [sʌm] *n* somma; (*Scol etc*) addizione *f*; **sum up** *vt, vi* riassumere

summarize ['sʌməraɪz] *vt* riassumere, riepilogare
summary ['sʌmərɪ] *n* riassunto
summer ['sʌmə^r] *n* estate *f* ▷ *cpd* d'estate, estivo(-a); **summer holidays** *npl* vacanze *fpl* estive; **summertime** *n* (*season*) estate *f*
summit ['sʌmɪt] *n* cima, sommità; (*Pol*) vertice *m*
summon ['sʌmən] *vt* chiamare, convocare
Sun. *abbr* (= *Sunday*) dom.
sun [sʌn] *n* sole *m*; **sunbathe** *vi* prendere un bagno di sole; **sunbed** *n* lettino solare; **sunblock** *n* protezione *f* solare totale; **sunburn** *n* (*painful*) scottatura; **sunburned, sunburnt** *adj* abbronzato(-a); (*painfully*) scottato(-a)
Sunday ['sʌndɪ] *n* domenica
Sunday paper *n* giornale *m* della domenica

SUNDAY PAPER

I **Sunday papers** sono i giornali che escono di domenica. Sono generalmente corredati da supplementi e riviste di argomento culturale, sportivo e di attualità.

sunflower ['sʌnflauə^r] *n* girasole *m*
sung [sʌŋ] *pp of* **sing**
sunglasses ['sʌnglɑːsɪz] *npl* occhiali *mpl* da sole
sunk [sʌŋk] *pp of* **sink**
sun: **sunlight** *n* (luce *f* del) sole *m*; **sun lounger** *n* sedia a sdraio; **sunny** *adj* assolato(-a), soleggiato(-a); (*fig*) allegro(-a), felice; **sunrise** *n* levata del sole, alba; **sun roof** *n* (*Aut*) tetto apribile; **sunscreen** *n* (*cream*) crema solare protettiva; **sunset** *n* tramonto; **sunshade** *n* parasole *m*; **sunshine** *n* luce *f* (del) sole *m*; **sunstroke** *n* insolazione *f*, colpo di sole; **suntan** *n* abbronzatura; **suntan lotion** *n* lozione *f* solare; **suntan oil** *n* olio solare
super ['suːpə^r] (*inf*) *adj* fantastico(-a)
superb [suː'pəːb] *adj* magnifico(-a)
superficial [suːpə'fɪʃəl] *adj* superficiale
superintendent [suːpərɪn'tɛndənt] *n* direttore(-trice); (*Police*) ≈ commissario (capo)
superior [su'pɪərɪə^r] *adj, n* superiore *m/f*
superlative [su'pəːlətɪv] *adj* superlativo(-a), supremo(-a) ▷ *n* (*Ling*) superlativo
supermarket ['suːpəmɑːkɪt] *n* supermercato
supernatural [suːpə'nætʃərəl] *adj* soprannaturale ▷ *n* soprannaturale *m*
superpower ['suːpəpauə^r] *n* (*Pol*) superpotenza
superstition [suːpə'stɪʃən] *n* superstizione *f*
superstitious [suːpə'stɪʃəs] *adj* superstizioso(-a)
superstore ['suːpəstɔː^r] *n* (BRIT) grande supermercato
supervise ['suːpəvaɪz] *vt* (*person etc*) sorvegliare; (*organization*) soprintendere a; **supervision** [-'vɪʒən] *n* sorveglianza; supervisione *f*; **supervisor** *n* sorvegliante *m/f*; soprintendente *m/f*; (*in shop*) capocommesso(-a)
supper ['sʌpə^r] *n* cena
supple ['sʌpl] *adj* flessibile; agile
supplement [*n* 'sʌplɪmənt, *vb* sʌplɪ'mɛnt] *n* supplemento ▷ *vt* completare, integrare
supplier [sə'plaɪə^r] *n* fornitore *m*
supply [sə'plaɪ] *vt* (*provide*) fornire; (*equip*): **to ~ (with)** approvvigionare (di), attrezzare (con) ▷ *n* riserva, provvista; (*supplying*) approvvigionamento; (*Tech*) alimentazione *f*; **supplies** *npl* (*food*) viveri *mpl*; (*Mil*) sussistenza
support [sə'pɔːt] *n* (*moral, financial*

etc) sostegno, appoggio; (*Tech*) supporto ▷ *vt* sostenere; (*financially*) mantenere; (*uphold*) sostenere, difendere; **supporter** *n* (*Pol etc*) sostenitore(-trice), fautore(-trice); (*Sport*) tifoso(-a)

Be careful not to translate ***support*** by the Italian word ***sopportare***.

suppose [səˈpəuz] *vt* supporre; immaginare; **to be ~d to do** essere tenuto(-a) a fare; **supposedly** [səˈpəuzɪdlɪ] *adv* presumibilmente; **supposing** *conj* se, ammesso che *+ sub*

suppress [səˈprɛs] *vt* reprimere; sopprimere; occultare

supreme [suˈpriːm] *adj* supremo(-a)

surcharge [ˈsəːtʃɑːdʒ] *n* supplemento

sure [ʃuəʳ] *adj* sicuro(-a); (*definite, convinced*) sicuro(-a), certo(-a); **~!** (*of course*) senz'altro!, certo!; **~ enough** infatti; **to make ~ of sth/that** assicurarsi di qc/che; **surely** *adv* sicuramente; certamente

surf [səːf] *n* (*waves*) cavalloni *mpl*; (*foam*) spuma

surface [ˈsəːfɪs] *n* superficie *f* ▷ *vt* (*road*) asfaltare ▷ *vi* risalire alla superficie; (*fig*: *news, feeling*) venire a galla

surfboard [ˈsəːfbɔːd] *n* tavola per surfing

surfer [ˈsəːfəʳ] *n* (*in sea*) surfista *m/f*; (*on the Internet*) navigatore(-trice)

surfing [ˈsəːfɪŋ] *n* surfing *m*

surge [səːdʒ] *n* (*strong movement*) ondata; (*of feeling*) impeto ▷ *vi* gonfiarsi; (*people*) riversarsi

surgeon [ˈsəːdʒən] *n* chirurgo

surgery [ˈsəːdʒərɪ] *n* chirurgia; (BRIT: *room*) studio *or* gabinetto medico, ambulatorio; (: *also*: **~ hours**) orario delle visite *or* di consultazione; **to undergo ~** subire un intervento chirurgico

surname [ˈsəːneɪm] *n* cognome *m*

surpass [səːˈpɑːs] *vt* superare

surplus [ˈsəːpləs] *n* eccedenza; (*Econ*) surplus *m inv* ▷ *adj* eccedente, d'avanzo

surprise [səˈpraɪz] *n* sorpresa; (*astonishment*) stupore *m* ▷ *vt* sorprendere; stupire; **surprised** [səˈpraɪzd] *adj* (*look, smile*) sorpreso(-a); **to be surprised** essere sorpreso, sorprendersi; **surprising** *adj* sorprendente, stupefacente; **surprisingly** *adv* (*easy, helpful*) sorprendentemente

surrender [səˈrɛndəʳ] *n* resa, capitolazione *f* ▷ *vi* arrendersi

surround [səˈraund] *vt* circondare; (*Mil etc*) accerchiare; **surrounding** *adj* circostante; **surroundings** *npl* dintorni *mpl*; (*fig*) ambiente *m*

surveillance [səːˈveɪləns] *n* sorveglianza, controllo

survey [*n* ˈsəːveɪ, *vb* səːˈveɪ] *n* quadro generale; (*study*) esame *m*; (*in housebuying etc*) perizia; (*of land*) rilevamento, rilievo topografico ▷ *vt* osservare; esaminare; valutare; rilevare; **surveyor** *n* perito; geometra *m*; (*of land*) agrimensore *m*

survival [səˈvaɪvl] *n* sopravvivenza; (*relic*) reliquia, vestigio

survive [səˈvaɪv] *vi* sopravvivere ▷ *vt* sopravvivere a; **survivor** *n* superstite *m/f*, sopravvissuto(-a)

suspect [*adj, n* ˈsʌspɛkt, *vb* səsˈpɛkt] *adj* sospetto(-a) ▷ *n* persona sospetta ▷ *vt* sospettare; (*think likely*) supporre; (*doubt*) dubitare

suspend [səsˈpɛnd] *vt* sospendere; **suspended sentence** *n* condanna con la condizionale; **suspenders** *npl* (BRIT) giarrettiere *fpl*; (US) bretelle *fpl*

suspense [səsˈpɛns] *n* apprensione *f*; (*in film etc*) suspense *m*; **to keep sb in ~** tenere qn in sospeso

suspension [səsˈpɛnʃən] *n* (*gen Aut*) sospensione *f*; (*of driving licence*) ritiro temporaneo; **suspension bridge** *n* ponte *m* sospeso

suspicion [səs'pɪʃən] *n* sospetto; **suspicious** [səs'pɪʃəs] *adj* (*suspecting*) sospettoso(-a); (*causing suspicion*) sospetto(-a)

sustain [səs'teɪn] *vt* sostenere; sopportare; (*Law*: *charge*) confermare; (*suffer*) subire

SUV *n abbr* (= *sports utility vehicle*) SUV *m inv*

swallow ['swɔləu] *n* (*bird*) rondine *f* ▷ *vt* inghiottire; (*fig*: *story*) bere

swam [swæm] *pt of* **swim**

swamp [swɔmp] *n* palude *f* ▷ *vt* sommergere

swan [swɔn] *n* cigno

swap [swɔp] *vt* **to ~ (for)** scambiare (con)

swarm [swɔːm] *n* sciame *m* ▷ *vi* (*bees*) sciamare; (*people*) brulicare; (*place*): **to be ~ing with** brulicare di

sway [sweɪ] *vi* (*tree*) ondeggiare; (*person*) barcollare ▷ *vt* (*influence*) influenzare, dominare

swear [swɛəʳ] (*pt* **swore**, *pp* **sworn**) *vi* (*curse*) bestemmiare, imprecare ▷ *vt* (*promise*) giurare; **swear in** *vt* prestare giuramento a; **swearword** *n* parolaccia

sweat [swɛt] *n* sudore *m*, traspirazione *f* ▷ *vi* sudare

sweater ['swɛtəʳ] *n* maglione *m*

sweatshirt ['swɛtʃəːt] *n* felpa

sweaty ['swɛtɪ] *adj* sudato(-a), bagnato(-a) di sudore

Swede [swiːd] *n* svedese *m/f*

swede [swiːd] (BRIT) *n* rapa svedese

Sweden ['swiːdn] *n* Svezia; **Swedish** ['swiːdɪʃ] *adj* svedese ▷ *n* (*Ling*) svedese *m*

sweep [swiːp] (*pt, pp* **swept**) *n* spazzata; (*also*: **chimney ~**) spazzacamino ▷ *vt* spazzare, scopare; (*current*) spazzare ▷ *vi* (*hand*) muoversi con gesto ampio; (*wind*) infuriare

sweet [swiːt] *n* (BRIT: *pudding*) dolce *m*; (*candy*) caramella ▷ *adj* dolce; (*fresh*) fresco(-a); (*fig*) piacevole; delicato(-a), grazioso(-a); gentile; **sweetcorn** *n* granturco dolce; **sweetener** ['swiːtnəʳ] *n* (*Culin*) dolcificante *m*; **sweetheart** *n* innamorato(-a); **sweetshop** *n* (BRIT) ≈ pasticceria

swell [swɛl] (*pt* **swelled**, *pp* **swollen, swelled**) *n* (*of sea*) mare *m* lungo ▷ *adj* (US: *inf*: *excellent*) favoloso(-a) ▷ *vt* gonfiare, ingrossare; aumentare ▷ *vi* gonfiarsi, ingrossarsi; (*sound*) crescere; (*also*: **~ up**) gonfiarsi; **swelling** *n* (*Med*) tumefazione *f*, gonfiore *m*

swept [swɛpt] *pt, pp of* **sweep**

swerve [swəːv] *vi* deviare; (*driver*) sterzare; (*boxer*) scartare

swift [swɪft] *n* (*bird*) rondone *m* ▷ *adj* rapido(-a), veloce

swim [swɪm] (*pt* **swam**, *pp* **swum**) *n* **to go for a ~** andare a fare una nuotata ▷ *vi* nuotare; (*Sport*) fare del nuoto; (*head, room*) girare ▷ *vt* (*river, channel*) attraversare *or* percorrere a nuoto; (*length*) nuotare; **swimmer** *n* nuotatore(-trice); **swimming** *n* nuoto; **swimming costume** (BRIT) *n* costume *m* da bagno; **swimming pool** *n* piscina; **swimming trunks** *npl* costume *m* da bagno (da uomo); **swimsuit** *n* costume *m* da bagno

swing [swɪŋ] (*pt, pp* **swung**) *n* altalena; (*movement*) oscillazione *f*; (*Mus*) ritmo; swing *m* ▷ *vt* dondolare, far oscillare; (*also*: **~ round**) far girare ▷ *vi* oscillare, dondolare; (*also*: **~ round**: *object*) roteare; (: *person*) girarsi, voltarsi; **to be in full ~** (*activity*) essere in piena attività; (*party etc*) essere nel pieno

swipe card *n* tessera magnetica

swirl [swəːl] *vi* turbinare, far mulinello

Swiss [swɪs] *adj, n inv* svizzero(-a)

switch [swɪtʃ] *n* (*for light, radio etc*) interruttore *m*; (*change*) cambiamento ▷ *vt* (*change*) cambiare; scambiare;

switch off *vt* spegnere; **could you switch off the light?** puoi spegnere la luce?; **switch on** *vt* accendere; (*engine, machine*) mettere in moto, avviare; **switchboard** *n* (*Tel*) centralino
Switzerland ['swɪtsələnd] *n* Svizzera
swivel ['swɪvl] *vi* (*also:* **~ round**) girare
swollen ['swəulən] *pp of* **swell**
swoop [swu:p] *n* incursione *f* ▷ *vi* (*also:* **~ down**) scendere in picchiata, piombare
swop [swɔp] *n, vt* = **swap**
sword [sɔ:d] *n* spada; **swordfish** *n* pesce *m* spada *inv*
swore [swɔ:ʳ] *pt of* **swear**
sworn [swɔ:n] *pp of* **swear** ▷ *adj* giurato(-a)
swum [swʌm] *pp of* **swim**
swung [swʌŋ] *pt, pp of* **swing**
syllable ['sɪləbl] *n* sillaba
syllabus ['sɪləbəs] *n* programma *m*
symbol ['sɪmbl] *n* simbolo; **symbolic(al)** [sɪm'bɔlɪk(l)] *adj* simbolico(-a); **to be symbolic(al) of sth** simboleggiare qc
symmetrical [sɪ'mɛtrɪkl] *adj* simmetrico(-a)
symmetry ['sɪmɪtrɪ] *n* simmetria
sympathetic [sɪmpə'θɛtɪk] *adj* (*showing pity*) compassionevole; (*kind*) comprensivo(-a); **~ towards** ben disposto(-a) verso

> Be careful not to translate ***sympathetic*** by the Italian word ***simpatico***.

sympathize ['sɪmpəθaɪz] *vi* **to ~ with** (*person*) compatire; partecipare al dolore di; (*cause*) simpatizzare per
sympathy ['sɪmpəθɪ] *n* compassione *f*
symphony ['sɪmfənɪ] *n* sinfonia
symptom ['sɪmptəm] *n* sintomo; indizio
synagogue ['sɪnəgɔg] *n* sinagoga
syndicate ['sɪndɪkɪt] *n* sindacato
syndrome ['sɪndrəum] *n* sindrome *f*
synonym ['sɪnənɪm] *n* sinonimo
synthetic [sɪn'θɛtɪk] *adj* sintetico(-a)
Syria ['sɪrɪə] *n* Siria
syringe [sɪ'rɪndʒ] *n* siringa
syrup ['sɪrəp] *n* sciroppo; (*also:* **golden ~**) melassa raffinata
system ['sɪstəm] *n* sistema *m*; (*order*) metodo; (*Anat*) organismo; **systematic** [-'mætɪk] *adj* sistematico(-a); metodico(-a); **systems analyst** *n* analista *m* di sistemi

t

ta [tɑː] (BRIT: *inf*) *excl* grazie!
tab [tæb] *n* (*loop on coat etc*) laccetto; (*label*) etichetta; **to keep ~s on** (*fig*) tenere d'occhio
table ['teɪbl] *n* tavolo, tavola; (*Math, Chem etc*) tavola ▷ *vt* (BRIT: *motion etc*) presentare; **a ~ for 4, please** un tavolo per 4, per favore; **to lay** *or* **set the ~** apparecchiare *or* preparare la tavola; **tablecloth** *n* tovaglia; **table d'hôte** [tɑːbl'dəut] *adj* (*meal*) a prezzo fisso; **table lamp** *n* lampada da tavolo; **tablemat** *n* sottopiatto; **tablespoon** *n* cucchiaio da tavola; (*also:* **tablespoonful**: *as measurement*) cucchiaiata
tablet ['tæblɪt] *n* (*Med*) compressa; (*of stone*) targa
table tennis *n* tennis *m* da tavolo, ping-pong® *m*
tabloid ['tæblɔɪd] *n* (*newspaper*) tabloid *m inv* (*giornale illustrato di formato ridotto*); **the ~s, the ~ press** i giornali popolari
taboo [tə'buː] *adj, n* tabù *m inv*
tack [tæk] *n* (*nail*) bulletta; (*fig*) approccio ▷ *vt* imbullettare; imbastire ▷ *vi* bordeggiare
tackle ['tækl] *n* attrezzatura, equipaggiamento; (*for lifting*) paranco; (*Football*) contrasto; (*Rugby*) placcaggio ▷ *vt* (*difficulty*) affrontare; (*Football*) contrastare; (*Rugby*) placcare
tacky ['tækɪ] *adj* appiccicaticcio(-a); (*pej*) scadente
tact [tækt] *n* tatto: **tactful** *adj* delicato(-a), discreto(-a)
tactics ['tæktɪks] *n, npl* tattica
tactless ['tæktlɪs] *adj* che manca di tatto
tadpole ['tædpəul] *n* girino
taffy ['tæfɪ] (US) *n* caramella *f* mou *inv*
tag [tæg] *n* etichetta
tail [teɪl] *n* coda; (*of shirt*) falda ▷ *vt* (*follow*) seguire, pedinare; **~s** *npl* (*formal suit*) frac *m inv*
tailor ['teɪlər] *n* sarto
Taiwan [taɪ'wɑːn] *n* Taiwan *m*; **Taiwanese** [taɪwə'niːz] *adj, n* taiwanese
take [teɪk] (*pt* **took**, *pp* **taken**) *vt* prendere; (*gain: prize*) ottenere, vincere; (*require: effort, courage*) occorrere, volerci; (*tolerate*) accettare, sopportare; (*hold: passengers etc*) contenere; (*accompany*) accompagnare; (*bring, carry*) portare; (*exam*) sostenere, presentarsi a; **to ~ a photo/a shower** fare una fotografia/una doccia; **I ~ it that** suppongo che; **take after** *vt fus* assomigliare a; **take apart** *vt* smontare; **take away** *vt* portare via; togliere; **take back** *vt* (*return*) restituire; riportare; (*one's words*) ritirare; **take down** *vt* (*building*) demolire; (*letter etc*) scrivere; **take in** *vt* (*deceive*) imbrogliare, abbindolare; (*understand*) capire; (*include*) comprendere, includere; (*lodger*) prendere, ospitare; **take**

off *vi* (*Aviat*) decollare; (*go away*) andarsene ▷ *vt* (*remove*) togliere; **take on** *vt* (*work*) accettare, intraprendere; (*employee*) assumere; (*opponent*) sfidare, affrontare; **take out** *vt* portare fuori; (*remove*) togliere; (*licence*) prendere, ottenere; **to take sth out of sth** (*drawer, pocket etc*) tirare qc fuori da qc; estrarre qc da qc; **take over** *vt* (*business*) rilevare ▷ *vi* **to take over from sb** prendere le consegne *or* il controllo da qn; **take up** *vt* (*dress*) accorciare; (*occupy*: *time, space*) occupare; (*engage in*: *hobby etc*) mettersi a; **to take sb up on sth** accettare qc da qn; **takeaway** (BRIT) *n* (*shop etc*) ≈ rosticceria; (*food*) pasto per asporto; **taken** *pp of* **take**; **takeoff** *n* (*Aviat*) decollo; **takeout** (US) *n* = **takeaway**; **takeover** *n* (*Comm*) assorbimento; **takings** ['teɪkɪŋz] *npl* (*Comm*) incasso

talc [tælk] *n* (*also*: **~um powder**) talco

tale [teɪl] *n* racconto, storia; **to tell ~s** (*fig*: *to teacher, parent etc*) fare la spia

talent ['tælnt] *n* talento; **talented** *adj* di talento

talk [tɔːk] *n* discorso; (*gossip*) chiacchiere *fpl*; (*conversation*) conversazione *f*; (*interview*) discussione *f* ▷ *vi* parlare; **~s** *npl* (*Pol etc*) colloqui *mpl*; **to ~ about** parlare di; **to ~ sb out of/into doing** dissuadere qn da/convincere qn a fare; **to ~ shop** parlare di lavoro *or* di affari; **talk over** *vt* discutere; **talk show** *n* conversazione *f* televisiva, talk show *m inv*

tall [tɔːl] *adj* alto(-a); **to be 6 feet ~** ≈ essere alto 1 metro e 80

tambourine [tæmbə'riːn] *n* tamburello

tame [teɪm] *adj* addomesticato(-a); (*fig*: *story, style*) insipido(-a), scialbo(-a)

tamper ['tæmpəʳ] *vi* **to ~ with** manomettere

tampon ['tæmpɔn] *n* tampone *m*

tan [tæn] *n* (*also*: **sun~**) abbronzatura ▷ *vi* abbronzarsi ▷ *adj* (*colour*) marrone rossiccio *inv*

tandem ['tændəm] *n* tandem *m inv*

tangerine [tændʒə'riːn] *n* mandarino

tangle ['tæŋgl] *n* groviglio; **to get into a ~** aggrovigliarsi; (*fig*) combinare un pasticcio

tank [tæŋk] *n* serbatoio; (*for fish*) acquario; (*Mil*) carro armato

tanker ['tæŋkəʳ] *n* (*ship*) nave *f* cisterna *inv*; (*truck*) autobotte *f*, autocisterna

tanned [tænd] *adj* abbronzato(-a)

tantrum ['tæntrəm] *n* accesso di collera

Tanzania [tænzə'nɪə] *n* Tanzania

tap [tæp] *n* (*on sink etc*) rubinetto; (*gentle blow*) colpetto ▷ *vt* dare un colpetto a; (*resources*) sfruttare, utilizzare; (*telephone*) mettere sotto controllo; **on ~** (*fig*: *resources*) a disposizione; **tap dancing** *n* tip tap *m*

tape [teɪp] *n* nastro; (*also*: **magnetic ~**) nastro (magnetico); (*sticky tape*) nastro adesivo ▷ *vt* (*record*) registrare (su nastro); (*stick*) attaccare con nastro adesivo; **tape measure** *n* metro a nastro; **tape recorder** *n* registratore *m* (a nastro)

tapestry ['tæpɪstrɪ] *n* arazzo; tappezzeria

tar [tɑːʳ] *n* catrame *m*

target ['tɑːgɪt] *n* bersaglio; (*fig*: *objective*) obiettivo

tariff ['tærɪf] *n* tariffa

tarmac ['tɑːmæk] *n* (BRIT: *on road*) macadam *m* al catrame; (*Aviat*) pista di decollo

tarpaulin [tɑː'pɔːlɪn] *n* tela incatramata

tarragon ['tærəgən] *n* dragoncello

tart [tɑːt] *n* (*Culin*) crostata; (BRIT: *inf*: *pej*: *woman*) sgualdrina ▷ *adj* (*flavour*) aspro(-a), agro(-a)

tartan ['tɑːtn] *n* tartan *m inv*

tartar(e) sauce *n* salsa tartara
task [tɑːsk] *n* compito; **to take to ~** rimproverare
taste [teɪst] *n* gusto; (*flavour*) sapore *m*, gusto; (*sample*) assaggio; (*fig: glimpse, idea*) idea ▷ *vt* gustare; (*sample*) assaggiare ▷ *vi* **to ~ of** *or* **like** (*fish etc*) sapere *or* avere sapore di; **in good/bad ~** di buon/cattivo gusto; **can I have a ~?** posso assaggiarlo?; **you can ~ the garlic (in it)** (ci) si sente il sapore dell'aglio; **tasteful** *adj* di buon gusto; **tasteless** *adj* (*food*) insipido(-a); (*remark*) di cattivo gusto; **tasty** *adj* saporito(-a), gustoso(-a)
tatters ['tætəz] *npl*: **in ~** a brandelli
tattoo [tə'tuː] *n* tatuaggio; (*spectacle*) parata militare ▷ *vt* tatuare
taught [tɔːt] *pt, pp of* **teach**
taunt [tɔːnt] *n* scherno ▷ *vt* schernire
Taurus ['tɔːrəs] *n* Toro
taut [tɔːt] *adj* teso(-a)
tax [tæks] *n* (*on goods*) imposta; (*on services*) tassa; (*on income*) imposte *fpl*, tasse *fpl* ▷ *vt* tassare; (*fig: strain: patience etc*) mettere alla prova; **tax-free** *adj* esente da imposte
taxi ['tæksɪ] *n* taxi *m inv* ▷ *vi* (*Aviat*) rullare; **can you call me a ~, please?** può chiamarmi un taxi, per favore?; **taxi driver** *n* tassista *m/f*; **taxi rank** (BRIT) *n* = **taxi stand**; **taxi stand** *n* posteggio dei taxi
tax payer *n* contribuente *m/f*
TB *n abbr* = **tuberculosis**
tea [tiː] *n* tè *m inv*; (BRIT: *snack: for children*) merenda; **high ~** (BRIT) cena leggera (*presa nel tardo pomeriggio*); **tea bag** *n* bustina di tè; **tea break** (BRIT) *n* intervallo per il tè
teach [tiːtʃ] (*pt, pp* **taught**) *vt* **to ~ sb sth, ~ sth to sb** insegnare qc a qn ▷ *vi* insegnare; **teacher** *n* insegnante *m/f*; (*in secondary school*) professore(-essa); (*in primary school*) maestro(-a); **teaching** *n* insegnamento
tea: **tea cloth** *n* (*for dishes*) strofinaccio; (BRIT: *for trolley*) tovaglietta da tè; **teacup** ['tiːkʌp] *n* tazza da tè
tea leaves *npl* foglie *fpl* di tè
team [tiːm] *n* squadra; (*of animals*) tiro; **team up** *vi* **to team up (with)** mettersi insieme (a)
teapot ['tiːpɔt] *n* teiera
tear[1] [tɛəʳ] (*pt* **tore**, *pp* **torn**) *n* strappo ▷ *vt* strappare ▷ *vi* strapparsi; **tear apart** *vt* (*also fig*) distruggere; **tear down** *vt +adv* (*building, statue*) demolire; (*poster, flag*) tirare giù; **tear off** *vt* (*sheet of paper etc*) strappare; (*one's clothes*) togliersi di dosso; **tear up** *vt* (*sheet of paper etc*) strappare
tear[2] [tɪəʳ] *n* lacrima; **in ~s** in lacrime; **tearful** ['tɪəful] *adj* piangente, lacrimoso(-a); **tear gas** *n* gas *m* lacrimogeno
tearoom ['tiːruːm] *n* sala da tè
tease [tiːz] *vt* canzonare; (*unkindly*) tormentare
tea: **teaspoon** *n* cucchiaino da tè; (*also*: **teaspoonful**: *as measurement*) cucchiaino; **teatime** *n* ora del tè; **tea towel** (BRIT) *n* strofinaccio (per i piatti)
technical ['tɛknɪkl] *adj* tecnico(-a)
technician [tɛk'nɪʃən] *n* tecnico(-a)
technique [tɛk'niːk] *n* tecnica
technology [tɛk'nɔlədʒɪ] *n* tecnologia
teddy (bear) ['tɛdɪ-] *n* orsacchiotto
tedious ['tiːdɪəs] *adj* noioso(-a), tedioso(-a)
tee [tiː] *n* (*Golf*) tee *m inv*
teen [tiːn] *adj* = **teenage** ▷ *n* (US) = **teenager**
teenage ['tiːneɪdʒ] *adj* (*fashions etc*) per giovani, per adolescenti; **teenager** *n* adolescente *m/f*
teens [tiːnz] *npl* **to be in one's ~** essere adolescente
teeth [tiːθ] *npl of* **tooth**
teetotal ['tiː'təutl] *adj* astemio(-a)
telecommunications ['tɛlɪkəm-

juːnɪ'keɪʃənz] *n* telecomunicazioni *fpl*
telegram ['tɛlɪgræm] *n* telegramma *m*
telegraph pole *n* palo del telegrafo
telephone ['tɛlɪfəun] *n* telefono ▷ *vt* (*person*) telefonare a; (*message*) comunicare per telefono; **telephone book** *n* elenco telefonico; **telephone booth** (BRIT), **telephone box** *n* cabina telefonica; **telephone call** *n* telefonata; **telephone directory** *n* elenco telefonico; **telephone number** *n* numero di telefono
telesales ['tɛlɪseɪlz] *n* vendita per telefono
telescope ['tɛlɪskəup] *n* telescopio
televise ['tɛlɪvaɪz] *vt* teletrasmettere
television ['tɛlɪvɪʒən] *n* televisione *f*; **on ~** alla televisione; **television programme** *n* programma *m* televisivo
tell [tɛl] (*pt, pp* **told**) *vt* dire; (*relate: story*) raccontare; (*distinguish*): **to ~ sth from** distinguere qc da ▷ *vi* (*talk*): **to ~ (of)** parlare (di); (*have effect*) farsi sentire, avere effetto; **to ~ sb to do** dire a qn di fare; **tell off** *vt* rimproverare, sgridare; **teller** *n* (*in bank*) cassiere(-a)
telly ['tɛlɪ] (BRIT: *inf*) *n abbr* (= *television*) tivù *f inv*
temp [tɛmp] *n abbr* (= *temporary*) segretaria temporanea
temper ['tɛmpəʳ] *n* (*nature*) carattere *m*; (*mood*) umore *m*; (*fit of anger*) collera ▷ *vt* (*moderate*) moderare; **to be in a ~** essere in collera; **to lose one's ~** andare in collera
temperament ['tɛmprəmənt] *n* (*nature*) temperamento; **temperamental** [-'mɛntl] *adj* capriccioso(-a)
temperature ['tɛmprətʃəʳ] *n* temperatura; **to have** *or* **run a ~** avere la febbre
temple ['tɛmpl] *n* (*building*) tempio; (*Anat*) tempia
temporary ['tɛmpərərɪ] *adj* temporaneo(-a); (*job, worker*) avventizio(-a), temporaneo(-a)
tempt [tɛmpt] *vt* tentare; **to ~ sb into doing** indurre qn a fare; **temptation** [-'teɪʃən] *n* tentazione *f*; **tempting** *adj* allettante
ten [tɛn] *num* dieci
tenant ['tɛnənt] *n* inquilino(-a)
tend [tɛnd] *vt* badare a, occuparsi di ▷ *vi* **to ~ to do** tendere a fare; **tendency** ['tɛndənsɪ] *n* tendenza
tender ['tɛndəʳ] *adj* tenero(-a); (*sore*) dolorante ▷ *n* (*Comm: offer*) offerta; (*money*): **legal ~** moneta in corso legale ▷ *vt* offrire
tendon ['tɛndən] *n* tendine *m*
tenner ['tɛnəʳ] *n* (BRIT *inf*) (banconota da) dieci sterline *fpl*
tennis ['tɛnɪs] *n* tennis *m*; **tennis ball** *n* palla da tennis; **tennis court** *n* campo da tennis; **tennis match** *n* partita di tennis; **tennis player** *n* tennista *m/f*; **tennis racket** *n* racchetta da tennis
tenor ['tɛnəʳ] *n* (*Mus*) tenore *m*
tenpin bowling ['tɛnpɪn-] *n* bowling *m*
tense [tɛns] *adj* teso(-a) ▷ *n* (*Ling*) tempo
tension ['tɛnʃən] *n* tensione *f*
tent [tɛnt] *n* tenda
tentative ['tɛntətɪv] *adj* esitante, incerto(-a); (*conclusion*) provvisorio(-a)
tenth [tɛnθ] *num* decimo(-a)
tent: **tent peg** *n* picchetto da tenda; **tent pole** *n* palo da tenda, montante *m*
tepid ['tɛpɪd] *adj* tiepido(-a)
term [təːm] *n* termine *m*; (*Scol*) trimestre *m*; (*Law*) sessione *f* ▷ *vt* chiamare, definire; **~s** *npl* (*conditions*) condizioni *fpl*; (*Comm*) prezzi *mpl*, tariffe *fpl*; **in the short/long ~** a breve/lunga scadenza; **to be on good ~s with sb** essere in buoni rapporti con qn; **to come to ~s with** (*problem*)

affrontare

terminal ['tə:mɪnl] *adj* finale, terminale; (*disease*) terminale ▷ *n* (*Elec*) morsetto; (*Comput*) terminale *m*; (*Aviat, for oil, ore etc*) terminal *m inv*; (BRIT: *also*: **coach ~**) capolinea *m*

terminate ['tə:mɪneɪt] *vt* mettere fine a

termini ['tə:mɪnaɪ] *npl of* **terminus**

terminology [tə:mɪ'nɔlədʒɪ] *n* terminologia

terminus ['tə:mɪnəs] (*pl* **termini**) *n* (*for buses*) capolinea *m*; (*for trains*) stazione *f* terminale

terrace ['tɛrəs] *n* terrazza; (BRIT: *row of houses*) fila di case a schiera; **terraced** *adj* (*garden*) a terrazze

terrain [tɛ'reɪn] *n* terreno

terrestrial [tɪ'restrɪəl] *adj* (*life*) terrestre; (BRIT: *channel*) terrestre

terrible ['tɛrɪbl] *adj* terribile; **terribly** *adv* terribilmente; (*very badly*) malissimo

terrier ['tɛrɪə^r] *n* terrier *m inv*

terrific [tə'rɪfɪk] *adj* incredibile, fantastico(-a); (*wonderful*) formidabile, eccezionale

terrified ['tɛrɪfaɪd] *adj* atterrito(-a)

terrify ['tɛrɪfaɪ] *vt* terrorizzare; **terrifying** *adj* terrificante

territorial [tɛrɪ'tɔ:rɪəl] *adj* territoriale

territory ['tɛrɪtərɪ] *n* territorio

terror ['tɛrə^r] *n* terrore *m*; **terrorism** *n* terrorismo; **terrorist** *n* terrorista *m/f*

test [tɛst] *n* (*trial, check*: *of courage etc*) prova; (*Med*) esame *m*; (*Chem*) analisi *f inv*; (*exam*: *of intelligence etc*) test *m inv*; (: *in school*) compito in classe; (*also*: **driving ~**) esame *m* di guida ▷ *vt* provare; esaminare; analizzare; sottoporre ad esame; **to ~ sb in history** esaminare qn in storia

testicle ['tɛstɪkl] *n* testicolo

testify ['tɛstɪfaɪ] *vi* (*Law*) testimoniare, deporre; **to ~ to sth** (*Law*) testimoniare qc; (*gen*) comprovare *or* dimostrare qc

testimony ['tɛstɪmənɪ] *n* (*Law*) testimonianza, deposizione *f*

test: **test match** *n* (*Cricket, Rugby*) partita internazionale; **test tube** *n* provetta

tetanus ['tɛtənəs] *n* tetano

text [tɛkst] *n* testo; (*on mobile phone*) SMS *m inv*, messaggino ▷ *vt* **to ~ sb** (*inf*) mandare un SMS a qn; **textbook** *n* libro di testo

textile ['tɛkstaɪl] *n* tessile *m*

text message *n* (*Tel*) SMS *m inv*, messaggino

text messaging [-'mɛsɪdʒɪŋ] *n* il mandarsi SMS

texture ['tɛkstʃə^r] *n* tessitura; (*of skin, paper etc*) struttura

Thai [taɪ] *adj* tailandese ▷ *n* tailandese *m/f*; (*Ling*) tailandese *m*

Thailand ['taɪlænd] *n* Tailandia

Thames [tɛmz] *n*: **the ~** il Tamigi

than [ðæn, ðən] *conj* (*in comparisons*) che; (*with numerals, pronouns, proper names*) di; **more ~ 10/once** più di 10/una volta; **I have more/less ~ you** ne ho più/meno di te; **I have more pens ~ pencils** ho più penne che matite; **she is older ~ you think** è più vecchia di quanto tu (non) pensi

thank [θæŋk] *vt* ringraziare; **~ you (very much)** grazie (tante); **thanks** *npl* ringraziamenti *mpl*, grazie *fpl* ▷ *excl* grazie!; **~s to** grazie a; **thankfully** *adv* con riconoscenza; con sollievo; **thankfully there were few victims** grazie al cielo ci sono state poche vittime; **Thanksgiving (Day)** *n* giorno del ringraziamento

THANKSGIVING (DAY)

Negli Stati Uniti il quarto giovedì di novembre ricorre il **Thanksgiving (Day)**, festa che rievoca la celebrazione con cui i Padri Pellegrini, fondatori della colonia di Plymouth in Massachusetts, ringraziarono Dio del buon raccolto del 1621.

KEYWORD

that [ðæt] (*pl* **those**) *adj* (*demonstrative*) quel (quell', quello) *m*; quella (quell') *f*; **that man/woman/book** quell'uomo/quella donna/quel libro; (*not "this"*) quell'uomo/quella donna/quel libro là; **that one** quello(-a) là
▷ *pron* 1 (*demonstrative*) ciò; (*not "this one"*) quello(-a); **who's that?** chi è?; **what's that?** cos'è quello?; **is that you?** sei tu?; **I prefer this to that** preferisco questo a quello; **that's what he said** questo è ciò che ha detto; **what happened after that?** che è successo dopo?; **that is (to say)** cioè
2 (*relative: direct*) che; (*: indirect*) cui; **the book (that) I read** il libro che ho letto; **the box (that) I put it in** la scatola in cui l'ho messo; **the people (that) I spoke to** le persone con cui *or* con le quali ho parlato
3 (*relative: of time*) in cui; **the day (that) he came** il giorno in cui è venuto
▷ *conj* che; **he thought that I was ill** pensava che io fossi malato
▷ *adv* (*demonstrative*) così; **I can't work that much** non posso lavorare (così) tanto; **that high** così alto; **the wall's about that high and that thick** il muro è alto circa così e spesso circa così

thatched [θætʃt] *adj* (*roof*) di paglia
thaw [θɔː] *n* disgelo ▷ *vi* (*ice*) sciogliersi; (*food*) scongelarsi ▷ *vt* (*food: also:* **~ out**) (fare) scongelare

KEYWORD

the [ðiː, ðə] *def art* 1 (*gen*) il (lo, l') *m*; la (l') *f*; i (gli) *mpl*; le *fpl*; **the boy/girl/ink** il ragazzo/la ragazza/l'inchiostro; **the books/pencils** i libri/le matite; **the history of the world** la storia del mondo; **give it to the postman** dallo al postino; **I haven't the time/money** non ho tempo/soldi; **the rich and the poor** i ricchi e i poveri
2 (*in titles*): **Elizabeth the First** Elisabetta prima; **Peter the Great** Pietro il grande
3 (*in comparisons*): **the more he works, the more he earns** più lavora più guadagna

theatre ['θɪətə^r] (*US* **theater**) *n* teatro; (*also:* **lecture ~**) aula magna; (*also:* **operating ~**) sala operatoria
theft [θɛft] *n* furto
their [ðɛə^r] *adj* il (la) loro; (*pl*) i (le) loro;
theirs *pron* il (la) loro; (*pl*) i (le) loro; *see also* **my**; **mine**
them [ðɛm, ðəm] *pron* (*direct*) li (le); (*indirect*) gli (loro (*after vb*)); (*stressed, after prep: people*) loro; (*: people, things*) essi(-e); *see also* **me**
theme [θiːm] *n* tema *m*; **theme park** *n* parco di divertimenti (*intorno a un tema centrale*)
themselves [ðəm'sɛlvz] *pl pron* (*reflexive*) si; (*emphatic*) loro stessi(-e); (*after prep*) se stessi(-e)
then [ðɛn] *adv* (*at that time*) allora; (*next*) poi, dopo; (*and also*) e poi ▷ *conj* (*therefore*) perciò, dunque, quindi ▷ *adj* **the ~ president** il presidente di allora; **by ~** allora; **from ~ on** da allora in poi
theology [θɪ'ɔlədʒɪ] *n* teologia
theory ['θɪərɪ] *n* teoria
therapist ['θɛrəpɪst] *n* terapista *m/f*
therapy ['θɛrəpɪ] *n* terapia

KEYWORD

there [ðɛə^r] *adv* 1: **there is, there are** c'è, ci sono; **there are 3 of them** (*people*) sono in 3; (*things*) ce ne sono 3; **there is no-one here** non c'è nessuno

qui; **there has been an accident** c'è stato un incidente
2 (*referring to place*) là, lì; **up/in/down there** lassù/là dentro/laggiù; **he went there on Friday** ci è andato venerdì; **I want that book there** voglio quel libro là *or* lì; **there he is!** eccolo!
3: **there, there** (*esp to child*) su, su

there: **thereabouts** [ðɛərə'bauts] *adv* (*place*) nei pressi, da quelle parti; (*amount*) giù di lì, all'incirca; **thereafter** [ðɛər'ɑːftə^r] *adv* da allora in poi; **thereby** [ðɛə'baɪ] *adv* con ciò; **therefore** ['ðɛəfɔː^r] *adv* perciò, quindi; **there's** [ðɛəz] = **there is**; **there has**
thermal ['θəːml] *adj* termico(-a)
thermometer [θə'mɔmɪtə^r] *n* termometro
thermostat ['θəːməstæt] *n* termostato
these [ðiːz] *pl pron, adj* questi(-e)
thesis ['θiːsɪs] (*pl* **theses**) *n* tesi *f inv*
they [ðeɪ] *pl pron* essi (esse); (*people only*) loro; **~ say that ...** (*it is said that*) si dice che ...; **they'd** = **they had**; **they would**; **they'll** = **they shall**; **they will**; **they're** = **they are**; **they've** = **they have**
thick [θɪk] *adj* spesso(-a); (*crowd*) compatto(-a); (*stupid*) ottuso(-a), lento(-a) ▷ *n* **in the ~ of** nel folto di; **it's 20 cm ~** ha uno spessore di 20 cm; **thicken** *vi* ispessire ▷ *vt* (*sauce etc*) ispessire, rendere più denso(-a); **thickness** *n* spessore *m*
thief [θiːf] (*pl* **thieves**) *n* ladro(-a)
thigh [θaɪ] *n* coscia
thin [θɪn] *adj* sottile; (*person*) magro(-a); (*soup*) poco denso(-a) ▷ *vt* **to ~ (down)** (*sauce, paint*) diluire
thing [θɪŋ] *n* cosa; (*object*) oggetto; (*mania*): **to have a ~ about** essere fissato(-a) con; **~s** *npl* (*belongings*) cose *fpl*; **poor ~** poverino(-a); **the best ~ would be to** la cosa migliore sarebbe di; **how are ~s?** come va?
think [θɪŋk] (*pt, pp* **thought**) *vi* pensare, riflettere ▷ *vt* pensare, credere; (*imagine*) immaginare; **to ~ of** pensare a; **what did you ~ of them?** cosa ne ha pensato?; **to ~ about sth/sb** pensare a qc/qn; **I'll ~ about it** ci penserò; **to ~ of doing** pensare di fare; **I ~ so/not** penso di sì/no; **to ~ well of** avere una buona opinione di; **think over** *vt* riflettere su; **think up** *vt* ideare
third [θəːd] *num* terzo(-a) ▷ *n* terzo(-a); (*fraction*) terzo, terza parte *f*; (*Aut*) terza; (BRIT: *Scol*: *degree*) *laurea col minimo dei voti*; **thirdly** *adv* in terzo luogo; **third party insurance** (BRIT) *n* assicurazione *f* contro terzi; **Third World** *n*: **the Third World** il Terzo Mondo
thirst [θəːst] *n* sete *f*; **thirsty** *adj* (*person*) assetato(-a), che ha sete
thirteen [θəː'tiːn] *num* tredici; **thirteenth** [-'tiːnθ] *num* tredicesimo(-a)
thirtieth ['θəːtɪɪθ] *num* trentesimo(-a)
thirty ['θəːtɪ] *num* trenta

KEYWORD

this [ðɪs] (*pl* **these**) *adj* (*demonstrative*) questo(-a); **this man/woman/book** quest'uomo/questa donna/questo libro; (*not "that"*) quest'uomo/questa donna/questo libro qui; **this one** questo(-a) qui
▷ *pron* (*demonstrative*) questo(-a); (*not "that one"*) questo(-a) qui; **who/what is this?** chi è/che cos'è questo?; **I prefer this to that** preferisco questo a quello; **this is where I live** io abito qui; **this is what he said** questo è ciò che ha detto; **this is Mr Brown** (*in introductions, photo*) questo è il signor Brown; (*on telephone*) sono il

signor Brown
▷ *adv* (*demonstrative*): **this high/long** *etc* alto/lungo *etc* così; **I didn't know things were this bad** non sapevo andasse così male

thistle ['θɪsl] *n* cardo
thorn [θɔːn] *n* spina
thorough ['θʌrə] *adj* (*search*) minuzioso(-a); (*knowledge, research*) approfondito(-a), profondo(-a); (*person*) coscienzioso(-a); (*cleaning*) a fondo; **thoroughly** *adv* (*search*) minuziosamente; (*wash, study*) a fondo; (*very*) assolutamente
those [ðəuz] *pl pron* quelli(-e) ▷ *pl adj* quei (quegli) *mpl*; quelle *fpl*
though [ðəu] *conj* benché, sebbene ▷ *adv* comunque
thought [θɔːt] *pt, pp of* **think** ▷ *n* pensiero; (*opinion*) opinione *f*; **thoughtful** *adj* pensieroso(-a), pensoso(-a); (*considerate*) premuroso(-a); **thoughtless** *adj* sconsiderato(-a); (*behaviour*) scortese
thousand ['θauzənd] *num* mille; **one ~** mille; **~s of** migliaia di; **thousandth** *num* millesimo(-a)
thrash [θræʃ] *vt* picchiare; bastonare; (*defeat*) battere
thread [θrɛd] *n* filo; (*of screw*) filetto ▷ *vt* (*needle*) infilare
threat [θrɛt] *n* minaccia; **threaten** *vi* (*storm*) minacciare ▷ *vt* **to threaten sb with/to do** minacciare qn con/di fare; **threatening** *adj* minaccioso(-a)
three [θriː] *num* tre; **three-dimensional** *adj* tridimensionale; (*film*) stereoscopico(-a); **three-piece suite** ['θriːpiːs-] *n* salotto comprendente un divano e due poltrone; **three-quarters** *npl* tre quarti *mpl*; **three-quarters full** pieno per tre quarti
threshold ['θrɛʃhəuld] *n* soglia
threw [θruː] *pt of* **throw**
thrill [θrɪl] *n* brivido ▷ *vt* (*audience*) elettrizzare; **to be ~ed** (*with gift etc*) essere elettrizzato(-a); **thrilled** *adj* **I was thrilled to get your letter** la tua lettera mi ha fatto veramente piacere; **thriller** *n* thriller *m inv*; **thrilling** *adj* (*book*) pieno(-a) di suspense; (*news, discovery*) elettrizzante
thriving ['θraɪvɪŋ] *adj* fiorente
throat [θrəut] *n* gola; **to have a sore ~** avere (un *or* il) mal di gola
throb [θrɔb] *vi* palpitare; pulsare; vibrare
throne [θrəun] *n* trono
through [θruː] *prep* attraverso; (*time*) per, durante; (*by means of*) per mezzo di; (*owing to*) a causa di ▷ *adj* (*ticket, train, passage*) diretto(-a) ▷ *adv* attraverso; **to put sb ~ to sb** (*Tel*) passare qn a qn; **to be ~** (*Tel*) ottenere la comunicazione; (*have finished*) essere finito(-a); **"no ~ road"** (BRIT) "strada senza sbocco"; **throughout** *prep* (*place*) dappertutto in; (*time*) per *or* durante tutto(-a) ▷ *adv* dappertutto; sempre
throw [θrəu] (*pt* **threw**, *pp* **thrown**) *n* (*Sport*) lancio, tiro ▷ *vt* tirare, gettare; (*Sport*) lanciare, tirare; (*rider*) disarcionare; (*fig*) confondere; **to ~ a party** dare una festa; **throw away** *vt* gettare *or* buttare via; **throw in** *vt* (*Sport: ball*) rimettere in gioco; (*include*) aggiungere; **throw off** *vt* sbarazzarsi di; **throw out** *vt* buttare fuori; (*reject*) respingere; **throw up** *vi* vomitare
thru [θruː] (US) *prep, adj, adv* = **through**
thrush [θrʌʃ] *n* tordo
thrust [θrʌst] (*pt, pp* **thrust**) *vt* spingere con forza; (*push in*) conficcare
thud [θʌd] *n* tonfo
thug [θʌg] *n* delinquente *m*
thumb [θʌm] *n* (*Anat*) pollice *m*; **to ~ a lift** fare l'autostop; **thumbtack** (US) *n* puntina da disegno
thump [θʌmp] *n* colpo forte; (*sound*) tonfo ▷ *vt* (*person*) picchiare; (*object*)

battere su ▷ *vi* picchiare; battere
thunder ['θʌndəʳ] *n* tuono ▷ *vi* tuonare; (*train etc*): **to ~ past** passare con un rombo; **thunderstorm** *n* temporale *m*
Thur(s). *abbr* (= *Thursday*) gio.
Thursday ['θə:zdɪ] *n* giovedì *m inv*
thus [ðʌs] *adv* così
thwart [θwɔ:t] *vt* contrastare
thyme [taɪm] *n* timo
Tiber ['taɪbəʳ] *n*: **the ~** il Tevere
Tibet [tɪ'bɛt] *n* Tibet *m*
tick [tɪk] *n* (*sound*: *of clock*) tic tac *m inv*; (*mark*) segno; spunta; (*Zool*) zecca; (BRIT: *inf*): **in a ~** in un attimo ▷ *vi* fare tic tac ▷ *vt* spuntare; **tick off** *vt* spuntare; (*person*) sgridare
ticket ['tɪkɪt] *n* biglietto; (*in shop*: *on goods*) etichetta; (*parking ticket*) multa; (*for library*) scheda; **a single/return ~ to ...** un biglietto di sola andata/di andata e ritorno per...; **ticket barrier** *n* (BRIT: *Rail*) *cancelletto d'ingresso*; **ticket collector** *n* bigliettaio; **ticket inspector** *n* controllore *m*; **ticket machine** *n* distributore *m* di biglietti; **ticket office** *n* biglietteria
tickle ['tɪkl] *vt* fare il solletico a; (*fig*) solleticare ▷ *vi* **it ~s** mi (*or* gli *etc*) fa il solletico; **ticklish** [-lɪʃ] *adj* che soffre il solletico; (*problem*) delicato(-a)
tide [taɪd] *n* marea; (*fig*: *of events*) corso; **high/low ~** alta/bassa marea
tidy ['taɪdɪ] *adj* (*room*) ordinato(-a), lindo(-a); (*dress, work*) curato(-a), in ordine; (*person*) ordinato(-a) ▷ *vt* (*also*: **~ up**) riordinare, mettere in ordine
tie [taɪ] *n* (*string etc*) legaccio; (BRIT: *also*: **neck~**) cravatta; (*fig*: *link*) legame *m*; (*Sport*: *draw*) pareggio ▷ *vt* (*parcel*) legare; (*ribbon*) annodare ▷ *vi* (*Sport*) pareggiare; **to ~ sth in a bow** annodare qc; **to ~ a knot in sth** fare un nodo a qc; **tie down** *vt* legare; (*to price etc*) costringere ad accettare; **tie up** *vt* (*parcel, dog*) legare; (*boat*) ormeggiare; (*arrangements*) concludere; **to be tied up** (*busy*) essere occupato(-a) *or* preso(-a)
tier [tɪəʳ] *n* fila; (*of cake*) piano, strato
tiger ['taɪgəʳ] *n* tigre *f*
tight [taɪt] *adj* (*rope*) teso(-a), tirato(-a); (*money*) poco(-a); (*clothes, budget, bend etc*) stretto(-a); (*control*) severo(-a), fermo(-a); (*inf*: *drunk*) sbronzo(-a) ▷ *adv* (*squeeze*) fortemente; (*shut*) ermeticamente; **tighten** *vt* (*rope*) tendere; (*screw*) stringere; (*control*) rinforzare ▷ *vi* tendersi; stringersi; **tightly** *adv* (*grasp*) bene, saldamente; **tights** (BRIT) *npl* collant *m inv*
tile [taɪl] *n* (*on roof*) tegola; (*on wall or floor*) piastrella, mattonella
till [tɪl] *n* registratore *m* di cassa ▷ *vt* (*land*) coltivare ▷ *prep, conj* = **until**
tilt [tɪlt] *vt* inclinare, far pendere ▷ *vi* inclinarsi, pendere
timber [tɪmbəʳ] *n* (*material*) legname *m*
time [taɪm] *n* tempo; (*epoch*: *often pl*) epoca, tempo; (*by clock*) ora; (*moment*) momento; (*occasion*) volta; (*Mus*) tempo ▷ *vt* (*race*) cronometrare; (*programme*) calcolare la durata di; (*fix moment for*) programmare; (*remark etc*) dire (*or* fare) al momento giusto; **a long ~** molto tempo; **what ~ does the museum/shop open?** a che ora apre il museo/negozio?; **for the ~ being** per il momento; **4 at a ~** 4 per *or* alla volta; **from ~ to ~** ogni tanto; **at ~s** a volte; **in ~** (*soon enough*) in tempo; (*after some time*) col tempo; (*Mus*) a tempo; **in a week's ~** fra una settimana; **in no ~** in un attimo; **any ~** in qualsiasi momento; **on ~** puntualmente; **5 ~s 5** 5 volte 5, 5 per 5; **what ~ is it?** che ora è?, che ore sono?; **to have a good ~** divertirsi; **time limit** *n* limite *m* di tempo; **timely** *adj* opportuno(-a); **timer** *n* (*time switch*) temporizzatore *m*; (*in kitchen*) contaminuti *m inv*; **time-share**

adj **time-share apartment/villa** appartamento/villa in multiproprietà; **timetable** *n* orario; **time zone** *n* fuso orario

timid ['tɪmɪd] *adj* timido(-a); (*easily scared*) pauroso(-a)

timing ['taɪmɪŋ] *n* (*Sport*) cronometraggio; (*fig*) scelta del momento opportuno

tin [tɪn] *n* stagno; (*also:* **~ plate**) latta; (*container*) scatola; (BRIT: *can*) barattolo (di latta), lattina; **tinfoil** *n* stagnola

tingle ['tɪŋgl] *vi* pizzicare

tinker ['tɪŋkə^r]: **~ with** *vt fus* armeggiare intorno a; cercare di riparare

tinned [tɪnd] (BRIT) *adj* (*food*) in scatola

tin opener ['-əupnə^r] (BRIT) *n* apriscatole *m inv*

tint [tɪnt] *n* tinta; **tinted** *adj* (*hair*) tinto(-a); (*spectacles, glass*) colorato(-a)

tiny ['taɪnɪ] *adj* minuscolo(-a)

tip [tɪp] *n* (*end*) punta; (*gratuity*) mancia; (BRIT: *for rubbish*) immondezzaio; (*advice*) suggerimento ▷ *vt* (*waiter*) dare la mancia a; (*tilt*) inclinare; (*overturn: also:* **~ over**) capovolgere; (*empty: also:* **~ out**) scaricare; **how much should I ~?** quanto devo lasciare di mancia?; **tip off** *vt* fare una soffiata a

tiptoe ['tɪptəu] *n*: **on ~** in punta di piedi

tire ['taɪə^r] *n* (US) = **tyre** ▷ *vt* stancare ▷ *vi* stancarsi; **tired** *adj* stanco(-a); **to be tired of** essere stanco *or* stufo di; **tire pressure** (US) *n* = **tyre pressure**; **tiring** *adj* faticoso(-a)

tissue ['tɪʃu:] *n* tessuto; (*paper handkerchief*) fazzoletto di carta; **tissue paper** *n* carta velina

tit [tɪt] *n* (*bird*) cinciallegra; **to give ~ for tat** rendere pan per focaccia

title ['taɪtl] *n* titolo

T-junction ['ti:'dʒʌŋkʃən] *n* incrocio a T

TM *abbr* = **trademark**

KEYWORD

to [tu:, tə] *prep* **1** (*direction*) a; **to go to France/London/school** andare in Francia/a Londra/a scuola; **to go to Paul's/the doctor's** andare da Paul/dal dottore; **the road to Edinburgh** la strada per Edimburgo; **to the left/right** a sinistra/destra

2 (*as far as*) (fino) a; **from here to London** da qui a Londra; **to count to 10** contare fino a 10; **from 40 to 50 people** da 40 a 50 persone

3 (*with expressions of time*): **a quarter to 5** le 5 meno un quarto; **it's twenty to 3** sono le 3 meno venti

4 (*for, of*): **the key to the front door** la chiave della porta d'ingresso; **a letter to his wife** una lettera per la moglie

5 (*expressing indirect object*) a; **to give sth to sb** dare qc a qn; **to talk to sb** parlare a qn; **to be a danger to sb/sth** rappresentare un pericolo per qn/qc

6 (*in relation to*) a; **3 goals to 2** 3 goal a 2; **30 miles to the gallon** ≈ 11 chilometri con un litro

7 (*purpose, result*): **to come to sb's aid** venire in aiuto a qn; **to sentence sb to death** condannare a morte qn; **to my surprise** con mia sorpresa

▷ *with vb* **1** (*simple infinitive*): **to go/eat** *etc* andare/mangiare *etc*

2 (*following another vb*): **to want/try/start to do** volere/cercare di/cominciare a fare

3 (*with vb omitted*): **I don't want to** non voglio (farlo); **you ought to** devi (farlo)

4 (*purpose, result*) per; **I did it to help you** l'ho fatto per aiutarti

5 (*equivalent to relative clause*): **I have**

things to do ho da fare; **the main thing is to try** la cosa più importante è provare
6 (*after adjective etc*): **ready to go** pronto a partire; **too old/young to ...** troppo vecchio/giovane per ...
▷ *adv* **to push the door to** accostare la porta

toad [təud] *n* rospo; **toadstool** *n* fungo (velenoso)
toast [təust] *n* (*Culin*) pane *m* tostato; (*drink, speech*) brindisi *m inv* ▷ *vt* (*Culin*) tostare; (*drink to*) brindare a; **a piece** *or* **slice of ~** una fetta di pane tostato; **toaster** *n* tostapane *m inv*
tobacco [tə'bækəu] *n* tabacco
toboggan [tə'bɔgən] *n* toboga *m inv*
today [tə'deɪ] *adv* oggi ▷ *n* (*also fig*) oggi *m*
toddler ['tɔdləʳ] *n* bambino(-a) che impara a camminare
toe [təu] *n* dito del piede; (*of shoe*) punta; **to ~ the line** (*fig*) stare in riga, conformarsi; **toenail** *n* unghia del piede
toffee ['tɔfɪ] *n* caramella
together [tə'gɛðəʳ] *adv* insieme; (*at same time*) allo stesso tempo; **~ with** insieme a
toilet ['tɔɪlət] *n* (BRIT: *lavatory*) gabinetto ▷ *cpd* (*bag, soap etc*) da toletta; **where's the ~?** dov'è il bagno?; **toilet bag** *n* (BRIT) nécessaire *m inv* da toilette; **toilet paper** *n* carta igienica; **toiletries** *npl* articoli *mpl* da toletta; **toilet roll** *n* rotolo di carta igienica
token ['təukən] *n* (*sign*) segno; (*substitute coin*) gettone *m*; **book/record/gift ~** (BRIT) buono-libro/disco/regalo
Tokyo ['təukjəu] *n* Tokyo *f*
told [təuld] *pt, pp of* **tell**
tolerant ['tɔlərnt] *adj* **~ (of)** tollerante (nei confronti di)
tolerate ['tɔləreɪt] *vt* sopportare; (*Med, Tech*) tollerare
toll [təul] *n* (*tax, charge*) pedaggio ▷ *vi* (*bell*) suonare; **the accident ~ on the roads** il numero delle vittime della strada; **toll call** (US) *n* (*Tel*) (telefonata) interurbana; **toll-free** (US) *adj* senza addebito, gratuito(-a) ▷ *adv* gratuitamente; **toll-free number** ≈ numero verde
tomato [tə'mɑːtəu] (*pl* **tomatoes**) *n* pomodoro; **tomato sauce** *n* salsa di pomodoro
tomb [tuːm] *n* tomba; **tombstone** ['tuːmstəun] *n* pietra tombale
tomorrow [tə'mɔrəu] *adv* domani ▷ *n* (*also fig*) domani *m inv*; **the day after ~** dopodomani; **~ morning** domani mattina
ton [tʌn] *n* tonnellata; (BRIT: *1016 kg*: US: *907 kg*: *metric 1000 kg*): **~s of** (*inf*) un mucchio *or* sacco di
tone [təun] *n* tono ▷ *vi* (*also:* **~ in**) intonarsi; **tone down** *vt* (*colour, criticism, sound*) attenuare
tongs [tɔŋz] *npl* tenaglie *fpl*; (*for coal*) molle *fpl*; (*for hair*) arricciacapelli *m inv*
tongue [tʌŋ] *n* lingua; **~ in cheek** (*say, speak*) ironicamente
tonic ['tɔnɪk] *n* (*Med*) tonico; (*also:* **~ water**) acqua tonica
tonight [tə'naɪt] *adv* stanotte; (*this evening*) stasera ▷ *n* questa notte; questa sera
tonne [tʌn] *n* (BRIT: *metric ton*) tonnellata
tonsil ['tɔnsl] *n* tonsilla; **tonsillitis** [-'laɪtɪs] *n* tonsillite *f*
too [tuː] *adv* (*excessively*) troppo; (*also*) anche; (*also:* **~ much**) ▷ *adv* troppo ▷ *adj* troppo(-a); **~ many** troppi(-e)
took [tuk] *pt of* **take**
tool [tuːl] *n* utensile *m*, attrezzo; **tool box** *n* cassetta *f* portautensili; **tool kit** *n* cassetta di attrezzi
tooth [tuːθ] (*pl* **teeth**) *n* (*Anat, Tech*) dente *m*; **toothache** *n* mal *m* di denti; **toothbrush** *n* spazzolino da denti;

toothpaste *n* dentifricio; **toothpick** *n* stuzzicadenti *m inv*

top [tɔp] *n* (*of mountain, page, ladder*) cima; (*of box, cupboard, table*) sopra *m inv*, parte *f* superiore; (*lid: of box, jar*) coperchio; (*: of bottle*) tappo; (*blouse etc*) sopra *m inv*; (*toy*) trottola ▷ *adj* più alto(-a); (*in rank*) primo(-a); (*best*) migliore ▷ *vt* (*exceed*) superare; (*be first in*) essere in testa a; **on ~ of** sopra, in cima a; (*in addition to*) oltre a; **from ~ to bottom** da cima a fondo; **top up** (*US* **top off**) *vt* riempire; (*salary*) integrare; **top floor** *n* ultimo piano; **top hat** *n* cilindro

topic ['tɔpɪk] *n* argomento; **topical** *adj* d'attualità

topless ['tɔplɪs] *adj* (*bather etc*) col seno scoperto

topping ['tɔpɪŋ] *n* (*Culin*) guarnizione *f*

topple ['tɔpl] *vt* rovesciare, far cadere ▷ *vi* cadere; traballare

top-up ['tɔpʌp] *n* (*for mobile phone: also*: **~ card**) ricarica

torch [tɔːtʃ] *n* torcia; (*BRIT: electric*) lampadina tascabile

tore [tɔːʳ] *pt of* **tear**¹

torment [*n* 'tɔːmɛnt, *vb* tɔː'mɛnt] *n* tormento ▷ *vt* tormentare

torn [tɔːn] *pp of* **tear**¹

tornado [tɔː'neɪdəu] (*pl* **tornadoes**) *n* tornado

torpedo [tɔː'piːdəu] (*pl* **torpedoes**) *n* siluro

torrent ['tɔrnt] *n* torrente *m*; **torrential** [tɔ'rɛnʃl] *adj* torrenziale

tortoise ['tɔːtəs] *n* tartaruga

torture ['tɔːtʃəʳ] *n* tortura ▷ *vt* torturare

Tory ['tɔːrɪ] (*BRIT: Pol*) *adj* dei tories, conservatore(-trice) ▷ *n* tory *m/f inv*, conservatore(-trice)

toss [tɔs] *vt* gettare, lanciare; (*one's head*) scuotere; **to ~ a coin** fare a testa o croce; **to ~ up for sth** fare a testa o croce per qc; **to ~ and turn** (*in bed*) girarsi e rigirarsi

total ['təutl] *adj* totale ▷ *n* totale *m* ▷ *vt* (*add up*) sommare; (*amount to*) ammontare a

totalitarian [təutælɪ'tɛərɪən] *adj* totalitario(-a)

totally ['təutəlɪ] *adv* completamente

touch [tʌtʃ] *n* tocco; (*sense*) tatto; (*contact*) contatto ▷ *vt* toccare; **a ~ of** (*fig*) un tocco di; un pizzico di; **to get in ~ with** mettersi in contatto con; **to lose ~** (*friends*) perdersi di vista; **touch down** *vi* (*on land*) atterrare; **touchdown** *n* atterraggio; (*on sea*) ammaraggio; (*US: Football*) meta; **touched** *adj* commosso(-a); **touching** *adj* commovente; **touchline** *n* (*Sport*) linea laterale; **touch-sensitive** *adj* sensibile al tatto

tough [tʌf] *adj* duro(-a); (*resistant*) resistente

tour ['tuəʳ] *n* viaggio; (*also:* **package ~**) viaggio organizzato *or* tutto compreso; (*of town, museum*) visita; (*by artist*) tournée *f inv* ▷ *vt* visitare; **tour guide** *n* guida turistica

tourism ['tuərɪzəm] *n* turismo

tourist ['tuərɪst] *n* turista *m/f* ▷ *adv* (*travel*) in classe turistica ▷ *cpd* turistico(-a); **tourist office** *n* pro loco *f inv*

tournament ['tuənəmənt] *n* torneo

tour operator *n* (*BRIT*) operatore *m* turistico

tow [təu] *vt* rimorchiare; **"on ~"** (*BRIT*), **"in ~"** (*US*) "veicolo rimorchiato"; **tow away** *vt* rimorchiare

toward(s) [tə'wɔːd(z)] *prep* verso; (*of attitude*) nei confronti di; (*of purpose*) per

towel ['tauəl] *n* asciugamano; (*also:* **tea ~**) strofinaccio; **towelling** *n* (*fabric*) spugna

tower ['tauəʳ] *n* torre *f*; **tower block** (*BRIT*) *n* palazzone *m*

town [taun] *n* città *f inv*; **to go to ~** andare in città; (*fig*) mettercela tutta;

town centre *n* centro (città); **town hall** *n* ≈ municipio
tow truck (US) *n* carro *m*, attrezzi *inv*
toxic ['tɔksɪk] *adj* tossico(-a)
toy [tɔɪ] *n* giocattolo; **toy with** *vt fus* giocare con; (*idea*) accarezzare, trastullarsi con; **toyshop** *n* negozio di giocattoli
trace [treɪs] *n* traccia ▷ *vt* (*draw*) tracciare; (*follow*) seguire; (*locate*) rintracciare
track [træk] *n* (*of person, animal*) traccia; (*on tape, Sport, path: gen*) pista; (: *of bullet etc*) traiettoria; (: *of suspect, animal*) pista, tracce *fpl*; (*Rail*) binario, rotaie *fpl* ▷ *vt* seguire le tracce di; **to keep ~ of** seguire; **track down** *vt* (*prey*) scovare; snidare; (*sth lost*) rintracciare; **tracksuit** *n* tuta sportiva
tractor ['træktə^r] *n* trattore *m*
trade [treɪd] *n* commercio; (*skill, job*) mestiere *m* ▷ *vi* commerciare ▷ *vt* **to ~ sth (for sth)** barattare qc (con qc); **to ~ with/in** commerciare con/in; **trade in** *vt* (*old car etc*) dare come pagamento parziale; **trademark** *n* marchio di fabbrica; **trader** *n* commerciante *m/f*; **tradesman** (*irreg*) *n* fornitore *m*; (*shopkeeper*) negoziante *m*; **trade union** *n* sindacato
trading ['treɪdɪŋ] *n* commercio
tradition [trə'dɪʃən] *n* tradizione *f*; **traditional** *adj* tradizionale
traffic ['træfɪk] *n* traffico ▷ *vi* **to ~ in** (*pej: liquor, drugs*) trafficare in; **traffic circle** (US) *n* isola rotatoria; **traffic island** *n* salvagente *m*, isola *f*, spartitraffico *inv*; **traffic jam** *n* ingorgo (del traffico); **traffic lights** *npl* semaforo; **traffic warden** *n* addetto(-a) al controllo del traffico e del parcheggio
tragedy ['trædʒədɪ] *n* tragedia
tragic ['trædʒɪk] *adj* tragico(-a)
trail [treɪl] *n* (*tracks*) tracce *fpl*, pista; (*path*) sentiero; (*of smoke etc*) scia ▷ *vt* trascinare, strascicare; (*follow*) seguire ▷ *vi* essere al traino; (*dress etc*) strusciare; (*plant*) arrampicarsi; strisciare; (*in game*) essere in svantaggio; **trailer** *n* (*Aut*) rimorchio; (US) roulotte *f inv*; (*Cinema*) prossimamente *m inv*
train [treɪn] *n* treno; (*of dress*) coda, strascico ▷ *vt* (*apprentice, doctor etc*) formare; (*sportsman*) allenare; (*dog*) addestrare; (*memory*) esercitare; (*point: gun etc*): **to ~ sth on** puntare qc contro ▷ *vi* formarsi; allenarsi; **what time does the ~ from Rome get in?** a che ora arriva il treno da Roma?; **is this the ~ for ...?** è questo il treno per...?; **one's ~ of thought** il filo dei propri pensieri; **trainee** [treɪ'ni:] *n* (*in trade*) apprendista *m/f*; **trainer** *n* (*Sport*) allenatore(-trice); (: *shoe*) scarpa da ginnastica; (*of dogs etc*) addestratore(-trice); **trainers** *npl* (*shoes*) scarpe *fpl* da ginnastica; **training** *n* formazione *f*; allenamento; addestramento; **in training** (*Sport*) in allenamento; **training course** *n* corso di formazione professionale; **training shoes** *npl* scarpe *fpl* da ginnastica
trait [treɪt] *n* tratto
traitor ['treɪtə^r] *n* traditore *m*
tram [træm] (BRIT) *n* (*also:* **~car**) tram *m inv*
tramp [træmp] *n* (*person*) vagabondo(-a); (*inf: pej: woman*) sgualdrina
trample ['træmpl] *vt*: **to ~ (underfoot)** calpestare
trampoline ['træmpəli:n] *n* trampolino
tranquil ['træŋkwɪl] *adj* tranquillo(-a); **tranquillizer** (US **tranquilizer**) *n* (*Med*) tranquillante *m*
transaction [træn'zækʃən] *n* transazione *f*
transatlantic ['trænzət'læntɪk] *adj* transatlantico(-a)

transcript ['trænskrɪpt] *n* trascrizione *f*
transfer [*n* 'trænsfəʳ, *vb* træns'fəʳ] *n* (*gen*: *also Sport*) trasferimento; (*Pol*: *of power*) passaggio; (*picture, design*) decalcomania; (: *stick-on*) autoadesivo ▷ *vt* trasferire; passare; **to ~ the charges** (BRIT: *Tel*) fare una chiamata a carico del destinatario
transform [træns'fɔːm] *vt* trasformare; **transformation** *n* trasformazione *f*
transfusion [træns'fjuːʒən] *n* trasfusione *f*
transit ['trænzɪt] *n* **in ~** in transito
transition [træn'zɪʃən] *n* passaggio, transizione *f*
transitive ['trænzɪtɪv] *adj* (*Ling*) transitivo(-a)
translate [trænz'leɪt] *vt* tradurre; **can you ~ this for me?** me lo può tradurre?; **translation** [-'leɪʃən] *n* traduzione *f*; **translator** *n* traduttore(-trice)
transmission [trænz'mɪʃən] *n* trasmissione *f*
transmit [trænz'mɪt] *vt* trasmettere; **transmitter** *n* trasmettitore *m*
transparent [træns'pærnt] *adj* trasparente
transplant [*vb* træns'plɑːnt, *n* 'trænsplɑːnt] *vt* trapiantare ▷ *n* (*Med*) trapianto
transport [*n* 'trænspɔːt, *vb* træns'pɔːt] *n* trasporto ▷ *vt* trasportare; **transportation** [-'teɪʃən] *n* (mezzo di) trasporto
transvestite [trænz'vɛstaɪt] *n* travestito(-a)
trap [træp] *n* (*snare, trick*) trappola; (*carriage*) calesse *m* ▷ *vt* prendere in trappola, intrappolare
trash [træʃ] (*pej*) *n* (*goods*) ciarpame *m*; (*nonsense*) sciocchezze *fpl*; **trash can** (US) *n* secchio della spazzatura
trauma ['trɔːmə] *n* trauma *m*; **traumatic** [-'mætɪk] *adj* traumatico(-a)
travel ['trævl] *n* viaggio; viaggi *mpl* ▷ *vi* viaggiare ▷ *vt* (*distance*) percorrere; **travel agency** *n* agenzia (di) viaggi; **travel agent** *n* agente *m* di viaggio; **travel insurance** *n* assicurazione *f* di viaggio; **traveller** (US **traveler**) *n* viaggiatore(-trice); **traveller's cheque** (US **traveler's check**) *n* assegno turistico; **travelling** (US **traveling**) *n* viaggi *mpl*; **travel-sick** *adj* **to get travel-sick** (*in vehicle*) soffrire di mal d'auto; (*in aeroplane*) soffrire di mal d'aria; (*in boat*) soffrire di mal di mare; **travel sickness** *n* mal *m* d'auto (*or* di mare *or* d'aria)
tray [treɪ] *n* (*for carrying*) vassoio; (*on desk*) vaschetta
treacherous ['trɛtʃərəs] *adj* infido(-a)
treacle ['triːkl] *n* melassa
tread [trɛd] (*pt* **trod**, *pp* **trodden**) *n* passo; (*sound*) rumore *m* di passi; (*of stairs*) pedata; (*of tyre*) battistrada *m inv* ▷ *vi* camminare; **tread on** *vt fus* calpestare
treasure ['trɛʒəʳ] *n* tesoro ▷ *vt* (*value*) tenere in gran conto, apprezzare molto; (*store*) custodire gelosamente; **treasurer** ['trɛʒərəʳ] *n* tesoriere(-a)
treasury ['trɛʒərɪ] *n* **the T~** (BRIT), **the T~ Department** (US) il ministero del Tesoro
treat [triːt] *n* regalo ▷ *vt* trattare; (*Med*) curare; **to ~ sb to sth** offrire qc a qn; **treatment** ['triːtmənt] *n* trattamento
treaty ['triːtɪ] *n* patto, trattato
treble ['trɛbl] *adj* triplo(-a), triplice ▷ *vt* triplicare ▷ *vi* triplicarsi
tree [triː] *n* albero
trek [trɛk] *n* escursione *f* a piedi; escursione *f* in macchina; (*tiring walk*) camminata sfiancante ▷ *vi* (*as holiday*) fare dell'escursionismo
tremble ['trɛmbl] *vi* tremare
tremendous [trɪ'mɛndəs] *adj*

(*enormous*) enorme; (*excellent*) fantastico(-a), strepitoso(-a)

> Be careful not to translate ***tremendous*** by the Italian word ***tremendo***.

trench [trɛntʃ] *n* trincea
trend [trɛnd] *n* (*tendency*) tendenza; (*of events*) corso; (*fashion*) moda; **trendy** *adj* (*idea*) di moda; (*clothes*) all'ultima moda
trespass ['trɛspəs] *vi*: **to ~ on** entrare abusivamente in; **"no ~ing"** "proprietà privata", "vietato l'accesso"
trial ['traɪəl] *n* (*Law*) processo; (*test: of machine etc*) collaudo; **on ~** (*Law*) sotto processo; **trial period** *n* periodo di prova
triangle ['traɪæŋgl] *n* (*Math, Mus*) triangolo
triangular [traɪ'æŋgjuləʳ] *adj* triangolare
tribe [traɪb] *n* tribù *f inv*
tribunal [traɪ'bjuːnl] *n* tribunale *m*
tribute ['trɪbjuːt] *n* tributo, omaggio; **to pay ~ to** rendere omaggio a
trick [trɪk] *n* trucco; (*joke*) tiro; (*Cards*) presa ▷ *vt* imbrogliare, ingannare; **to play a ~ on sb** giocare un tiro a qn; **that should do the ~** vedrai che funziona
trickle ['trɪkl] *n* (*of water etc*) rivolo; gocciolio ▷ *vi* gocciolare
tricky ['trɪkɪ] *adj* difficile, delicato(-a)
tricycle ['traɪsɪkl] *n* triciclo
trifle ['traɪfl] *n* sciocchezza; (BRIT: *Culin*) ≈ zuppa inglese ▷ *adv* **a ~ long** un po' lungo
trigger ['trɪgəʳ] *n* (*of gun*) grilletto
trim [trɪm] *adj* (*house, garden*) ben tenuto(-a); (*figure*) snello(-a) ▷ *n* (*haircut etc*) spuntata, regolata; (*embellishment*) finiture *fpl*; (*on car*) guarnizioni *fpl* ▷ *vt* spuntare; (*decorate*): **to ~ (with)** decorare (con); (*Naut: a sail*) orientare
trio ['triːəu] *n* trio
trip [trɪp] *n* viaggio; (*excursion*) gita, escursione *f*; (*stumble*) passo falso ▷ *vi* inciampare; (*go lightly*) camminare con passo leggero; **on a ~** in viaggio; **trip up** *vi* inciampare ▷ *vt* fare lo sgambetto a
triple ['trɪpl] *adj* triplo(-a)
triplets ['trɪplɪts] *npl* bambini(-e) trigemini(-e)
tripod ['traɪpɔd] *n* treppiede *m*
triumph ['traɪʌmf] *n* trionfo ▷ *vi* **to ~ (over)** trionfare (su); **triumphant** [traɪ'ʌmfənt] *adj* trionfante
trivial ['trɪvɪəl] *adj* insignificante; (*commonplace*) banale

> Be careful not to translate ***trivial*** by the Italian word ***triviale***.

trod [trɔd] *pt of* **tread**
trodden [trɔdn] *pp of* **tread**
trolley ['trɔlɪ] *n* carrello
trombone [trɔm'bəun] *n* trombone *m*
troop [truːp] *n* gruppo; (*Mil*) squadrone *m*; **~s** *npl* (*Mil*) truppe *fpl*
trophy ['trəufɪ] *n* trofeo
tropical ['trɔpɪkl] *adj* tropicale
trot [trɔt] *n* trotto ▷ *vi* trottare; **on the ~** (BRIT: *fig*) di fila, uno(-a) dopo l'altro(-a)
trouble ['trʌbl] *n* difficoltà *f inv*, problema *m*; difficoltà *fpl*, problemi; (*worry*) preoccupazione *f*; (*bother, effort*) sforzo; (*Pol*) conflitti *mpl*, disordine *m*; (*Med*): **stomach** *etc* **~** disturbi *mpl* gastrici *etc* ▷ *vt* disturbare; (*worry*) preoccupare ▷ *vi* **to ~ to do** disturbarsi a fare; **~s** *npl* (*Pol etc*) disordini *mpl*; **to be in ~** avere dei problemi; **it's no ~!** di niente!; **what's the ~?** cosa c'è che non va?; **I'm sorry to ~ you** scusi il disturbo; **troubled** *adj* (*person*) preoccupato(-a), inquieto(-a); (*epoch, life*) agitato(-a), difficile; **troublemaker** *n* elemento disturbatore, agitatore(-trice); (*child*) disloco(-a); **troublesome** *adj* fastidioso(-a), seccante

trough [trɔf] *n* (*drinking trough*) abbeveratoio; (*also:* **feeding ~**) trogolo, mangiatoia; (*channel*) canale *m*
trousers ['trauzəz] *npl* pantaloni *mpl*, calzoni *mpl*; **short ~** calzoncini *mpl*
trout [traut] *n inv* trota
trowel ['trauəl] *n* cazzuola
truant ['truənt] (BRIT) *n*: **to play ~** marinare la scuola
truce [tru:s] *n* tregua
truck [trʌk] *n* autocarro, camion *m inv*; (*Rail*) carro merci aperto; (*for luggage*) carrello *m* portabagagli *inv*; **truck driver** *n* camionista *m/f*
true [tru:] *adj* vero(-a); (*accurate*) accurato(-a), esatto(-a); (*genuine*) reale; (*faithful*) fedele; **to come ~** avverarsi
truly ['tru:lɪ] *adv* veramente; (*truthfully*) sinceramente; (*faithfully*): **yours ~** (*in letter*) distinti saluti
trumpet ['trʌmpɪt] *n* tromba
trunk [trʌŋk] *n* (*of tree, person*) tronco; (*of elephant*) proboscide *f*; (*case*) baule *m*; (US: *Aut*) bagagliaio; **~s** (*also:* **swimming ~s**) calzoncini *mpl* da bagno
trust [trʌst] *n* fiducia; (*Law*) amministrazione *f* fiduciaria; (*Comm*) trust *m inv* ▷ *vt* (*rely on*) contare su; (*hope*) sperare; (*entrust*): **to ~ sth to sb** affidare qc a qn; **trusted** *adj* fidato(-a); **trustworthy** *adj* fidato(-a), degno(-a) di fiducia
truth [tru:θ, *pl* tru:ðz] *n* verità *f inv*; **truthful** *adj* (*person*) sincero(-a); (*description*) veritiero(-a), esatto(-a)
try [traɪ] *n* prova, tentativo; (*Rugby*) meta ▷ *vt* (*Law*) giudicare; (*test: also:* **~ out**) provare; (*strain*) mettere alla prova ▷ *vi* provare; **to have a ~** fare un tentativo; **to ~ to do** (*seek*) cercare di fare; **try on** *vt* (*clothes*) provare; **trying** *adj* (*day, experience*) logorante, pesante; (*child*) difficile, insopportabile
T-shirt ['ti:ʃə:t] *n* maglietta
tsunami [tsʊ'nɑ:mɪ] *n* tsunami *m inv*
tub [tʌb] *n* tinozza; mastello; (*bath*) bagno
tube [tju:b] *n* tubo; (BRIT: *underground*) metropolitana, metrò *m inv*; (*for tyre*) camera d'aria
tuberculosis [tjubə:kju'ləusɪs] *n* tubercolosi *f inv*
tube station (BRIT) *n* stazione *f* della metropolitana
tuck [tʌk] *vt* (*put*) mettere; **tuck away** *vt* riporre; (*building*): **to be tucked away** essere in un luogo isolato; **tuck in** *vt* mettere dentro; (*child*) rimboccare ▷ *vi* (*eat*) mangiare di buon appetito; abbuffarsi; **tuck shop** *n* negozio di pasticceria (*in una scuola*)
Tue(s). *abbr* (= *Tuesday*) mar.
Tuesday ['tju:zdɪ] *n* martedì *m inv*
tug [tʌg] *n* (*ship*) rimorchiatore *m* ▷ *vt* tirare con forza
tuition [tju:'ɪʃən] *n* (BRIT) lezioni *fpl*; (*: private tuition*) lezioni *fpl* private; (US: *school fees*) tasse *fpl* scolastiche
tulip ['tju:lɪp] *n* tulipano
tumble ['tʌmbl] *n* (*fall*) capitombolo ▷ *vi* capitombolare, ruzzolare; **to ~ to sth** (*inf*) realizzare qc; **tumble dryer** (BRIT) *n* asciugatrice *f*
tumbler ['tʌmblə^r] *n* bicchiere *m* (senza stelo)
tummy ['tʌmɪ] (*inf*) *n* pancia
tumour ['tju:mə^r] (US **tumor**) *n* tumore *m*
tuna ['tju:nə] *n inv* (*also:* **~ fish**) tonno
tune [tju:n] *n* (*melody*) melodia, aria ▷ *vt* (*Mus*) accordare; (*Radio, TV, Aut*) regolare, mettere a punto; **to be in/out of ~** (*instrument*) essere accordato(-a)/scordato(-a); (*singer*) essere intonato(-a)/stonato(-a); **tune in** *vi* **to tune in (to)** (*Radio, TV*) sintonizzarsi (su); **tune up** *vi* (*musician*) accordare lo strumento
tunic ['tju:nɪk] *n* tunica
Tunisia [tju:'nɪzɪə] *n* Tunisia

tunnel ['tʌnl] *n* galleria ▷ *vi* scavare una galleria
turbulence ['tə:bjuləns] *n* (*Aviat*) turbolenza
turf [tə:f] *n* terreno erboso; (*clod*) zolla ▷ *vt* coprire di zolle erbose
Turin [tjuə'rɪn] *n* Torino *f*
Turk [tə:k] *n* turco(-a)
Turkey ['tə:kɪ] *n* Turchia
turkey ['tə:kɪ] *n* tacchino
Turkish ['tə:kɪʃ] *adj* turco(-a) ▷ *n* (*Ling*) turco
turmoil ['tə:mɔɪl] *n* confusione *f*, tumulto
turn [tə:n] *n* giro; (*change*) cambiamento; (*in road*) curva; (*tendency: of mind, events*) tendenza; (*performance*) numero; (*chance*) turno; (*Med*) crisi *f inv*, attacco ▷ *vt* girare, voltare; (*change*): **to ~ sth into** trasformare qc in ▷ *vi* girare; (*person: look back*) girarsi, voltarsi; (*reverse direction*) girare; (*change*) cambiare; (*milk*) andare a male; (*become*) diventare; **a good ~** un buon servizio; **it gave me quite a ~** mi ha fatto prendere un bello spavento; **"no left ~"** (*Aut*) "divieto di svolta a sinistra"; **it's your ~** tocca a lei; **in ~** a sua volta; a turno; **to take ~s (at sth)** fare (qc) a turno; **~ left/right at the next junction** al prossimo incrocio, giri a sinistra/destra; **turn around** *vi* (*person*) girarsi; (*rotate*) girare ▷ *vt* (*object*) girare; **turn away** *vi* girarsi (dall'altra parte) ▷ *vt* mandare via; **turn back** *vi* ritornare, tornare indietro ▷ *vt* far tornare indietro; (*clock*) spostare indietro; **turn down** *vt* (*refuse*) rifiutare; (*reduce*) abbassare; (*fold*) ripiegare; **turn in** *vi* (*inf: go to bed*) andare a letto ▷ *vt* (*fold*) voltare in dentro; **turn off** *vi* (*from road*) girare, voltare ▷ *vt* (*light, radio, engine etc*) spegnere; **I can't turn the heating off** non riesco a spegnere il riscaldamento; **turn on** *vt* (*light, radio etc*) accendere; **I can't turn the heating on** non riesco ad accendere il riscaldamento; **turn out** *vt* (*light, gas*) chiudere; spegnere ▷ *vi* (*voters*) presentarsi; **to turn out to be ...** rivelarsi ..., risultare ...; **turn over** *vi* (*person*) girarsi ▷ *vt* girare; **turn round** *vi* girare; (*person*) girarsi; **turn to** *vt fus* **to turn to sb** girarsi verso qn; **to turn to sb for help** rivolgersi a qn per aiuto; **turn up** *vi* (*person*) arrivare, presentarsi; (*lost object*) saltar fuori ▷ *vt* (*collar, sound*) alzare; **turning** *n* (*in road*) curva; **turning point** *n* (*fig*) svolta decisiva
turnip ['tə:nɪp] *n* rapa
turn: **turnout** ['tə:naut] *n* presenza, affluenza; **turnover** ['tə:nəuvə^r] *n* (*Comm*) turnover *m inv*; (*Culin*): **apple** *etc* **turnover** sfogliatella alle mele *ecc*; **turnstile** ['tə:nstaɪl] *n* tornella; **turn-up** (BRIT) *n* (*on trousers*) risvolto
turquoise ['tə:kwɔɪz] *n* turchese *m* ▷ *adj* turchese
turtle ['tə:tl] *n* testuggine *f*; **turtleneck (sweater)** ['tə:tlnɛk-] *n* maglione *m* con il collo alto
Tuscany ['tʌskənɪ] *n* Toscana
tusk [tʌsk] *n* zanna
tutor ['tju:tə^r] *n* (*in college*) docente *m/f* (*responsabile di un gruppo di studenti*); (*private teacher*) precettore *m*; **tutorial** [-'tɔ:rɪəl] *n* (*Scol*) lezione *f* con discussione (*a un gruppo limitato*)
tuxedo [tʌk'si:dəu] (US) *n* smoking *m inv*
TV [ti:'vi:] *n abbr* (= *television*) tivù *f inv*
tweed [twi:d] *n* tweed *m inv*
tweezers ['twi:zəz] *npl* pinzette *fpl*
twelfth [twɛlfθ] *num* dodicesimo(-a)
twelve [twɛlv] *num* dodici; **at ~ o'clock** alle dodici, a mezzogiorno; (*midnight*) a mezzanotte
twentieth ['twɛntɪɪθ] *num* ventesimo(-a)
twenty ['twɛntɪ] *num* venti
twice [twaɪs] *adv* due volte; **~ as**

much due volte tanto; **~ a week** due volte alla settimana
twig [twɪg] *n* ramoscello ▷ *vt, vi* (*inf*) capire
twilight ['twaɪlaɪt] *n* crepuscolo
twin [twɪn] *adj, n* gemello(-a) ▷ *vt* **to ~ one town with another** fare il gemellaggio di una città con un'altra; **twin(-bedded) room** *n* stanza con letti gemelli; **twin beds** *npl* letti *mpl* gemelli
twinkle ['twɪŋkl] *vi* scintillare; (*eyes*) brillare
twist [twɪst] *n* torsione *f*; (*in wire, flex*) piega; (*in road*) curva; (*in story*) colpo di scena ▷ *vt* attorcigliare; (*ankle*) slogare; (*weave*) intrecciare; (*roll around*) arrotolare; (*fig*) distorcere ▷ *vi* (*road*) serpeggiare
twit [twɪt] (*inf*) *n* cretino(-a)
twitch [twɪtʃ] *n* tiratina; (*nervous*) tic *m inv* ▷ *vi* contrarsi
two [tuː] *num* due; **to put ~ and ~ together** (*fig*) fare uno più uno
type [taɪp] *n* (*category*) genere *m*; (*model*) modello; (*example*) tipo; (*Typ*) tipo, carattere *m* ▷ *vt* (*letter etc*) battere (a macchina), dattilografare; **typewriter** *n* macchina da scrivere
typhoid ['taɪfɔɪd] *n* tifoidea
typhoon [taɪ'fuːn] *n* tifone *m*
typical ['tɪpɪkl] *adj* tipico(-a); **typically** *adv* tipicamente; **typically, he arrived late** come al solito è arrivato tardi
typing ['taɪpɪŋ] *n* dattilografia
typist ['taɪpɪst] *n* dattilografo(-a)
tyre ['taɪəʳ] (*US* **tire**) *n* pneumatico, gomma; **I've got a flat ~** ho una gomma a terra; **tyre pressure** *n* pressione *f* (delle gomme)

U

UFO ['juːfəu] *n abbr* (= *unidentified flying object*) UFO *m inv*
Uganda [juː'gændə] *n* Uganda
ugly ['ʌglɪ] *adj* brutto(-a)
UHT *abbr* (= *ultra heat treated*) UHT *inv*, a lunga conservazione
UK *n abbr* = **United Kingdom**
ulcer ['ʌlsəʳ] *n* ulcera; (*also:* **mouth ~**) afta
ultimate ['ʌltɪmət] *adj* ultimo(-a), finale; (*authority*) massimo(-a), supremo(-a); **ultimately** *adv* alla fine; in definitiva, in fin dei conti
ultimatum [ʌltɪ'meɪtəm, -tə] (*pl* **ultimatums** *or* **ultimata**) *n* ultimatum *m inv*
ultrasound [ʌltrə'saund] *n* (*Med*) ultrasuono
ultraviolet ['ʌltrə'vaɪəlɪt] *adj* ultravioletto(-a)
umbrella [ʌm'brɛlə] *n* ombrello
umpire ['ʌmpaɪəʳ] *n* arbitro
UN *n abbr* (= *United Nations*) ONU *f*
unable [ʌn'eɪbl] *adj* **to be ~ to** non

potere, essere nell'impossibilità di; essere incapace di
unacceptable [ʌnək'sɛptəbl] *adj* (*proposal, behaviour*) inaccettabile; (*price*) impossibile
unanimous [juː'nænɪməs] *adj* unanime
unarmed [ʌn'ɑːmd] *adj* (*without a weapon*) disarmato(-a); (*combat*) senz'armi
unattended [ʌnə'tɛndɪd] *adj* (*car, child, luggage*) incustodito(-a)
unattractive [ʌnə'træktɪv] *adj* poco attraente
unavailable [ʌnə'veɪləbl] *adj* (*article, room, book*) non disponibile; (*person*) impegnato(-a)
unavoidable [ʌnə'vɔɪdəbl] *adj* inevitabile
unaware [ʌnə'wɛəʳ] *adj* **to be ~ of** non sapere, ignorare; **unawares** *adv* di sorpresa, alla sprovvista
unbearable [ʌn'bɛərəbl] *adj* insopportabile
unbeatable [ʌn'biːtəbl] *adj* imbattibile
unbelievable [ʌnbɪ'liːvəbl] *adj* incredibile
unborn [ʌn'bɔːn] *adj* non ancora nato(-a)
unbutton [ʌn'bʌtn] *vt* sbottonare
uncalled-for [ʌn'kɔːldfɔːʳ] *adj* (*remark*) fuori luogo *inv*; (*action*) ingiustificato(-a)
uncanny [ʌn'kænɪ] *adj* misterioso(-a), strano(-a)
uncertain [ʌn'səːtn] *adj* incerto(-a); dubbio(-a); **uncertainty** *n* incertezza
unchanged [ʌn'tʃeɪndʒd] *adj* invariato(-a)
uncle ['ʌŋkl] *n* zio
unclear [ʌn'klɪəʳ] *adj* non chiaro(-a); **I'm still ~ about what I'm supposed to do** non ho ancora ben capito cosa dovrei fare
uncomfortable [ʌn'kʌmfətəbl] *adj* scomodo(-a); (*uneasy*) a disagio, agitato(-a); (*unpleasant*) fastidioso(-a)
uncommon [ʌn'kɔmən] *adj* raro(-a), insolito(-a), non comune
unconditional [ʌnkən'dɪʃənl] *adj* incondizionato(-a), senza condizioni
unconscious [ʌn'kɔnʃəs] *adj* privo(-a) di sensi, svenuto(-a); (*unaware*) inconsapevole, inconscio(-a) ▷ *n* **the ~** l'inconscio
uncontrollable [ʌnkən'trəuləbl] *adj* incontrollabile; indisciplinato(-a)
unconventional [ʌnkən'vɛnʃənl] *adj* poco convenzionale
uncover [ʌn'kʌvəʳ] *vt* scoprire
undecided [ʌndɪ'saɪdɪd] *adj* indeciso(-a)
undeniable [ʌndɪ'naɪəbl] *adj* innegabile, indiscutibile
under ['ʌndəʳ] *prep* sotto; (*less than*) meno di; al disotto di; (*according to*) secondo, in conformità a ▷ *adv* (al) disotto; **~ there** là sotto; **~ repair** in riparazione; **undercover** *adj* segreto(-a), clandestino(-a); **underdone** *adj* (*Culin*) al sangue; (*pej*) poco cotto(-a); **underestimate** *vt* sottovalutare; **undergo** *vt* (*irreg*) subire; (*treatment*) sottoporsi a; **undergraduate** *n* studente(-essa) universitario(-a); **underground** *n* (BRIT: *railway*) metropolitana; (*Pol*) movimento clandestino ▷ *adj* sotterraneo(-a); (*fig*) clandestino(-a) ▷ *adv* sottoterra; **to go underground** (*fig*) darsi alla macchia; **undergrowth** *n* sottobosco; **underline** *vt* sottolineare; **undermine** *vt* minare; **underneath** [ʌndə'niːθ] *adv* sotto, disotto ▷ *prep* sotto, al di sotto di; **underpants** *npl* mutande *fpl*, slip *m inv*; **underpass** (BRIT) *n* sottopassaggio; **underprivileged** *adj* non abbiente; meno favorito(-a); **underscore** *vt* sottolineare; **undershirt** (US) *n* maglietta; **underskirt** (BRIT) *n* sottoveste *f*
understand [ʌndə'stænd] (*irreg: like*

stand) *vt, vi* capire, comprendere; **I don't ~** non capisco; **I ~ that ...** sento che ...; credo di capire che ...; **understandable** *adj* comprensibile; **understanding** *adj* comprensivo(-a) ▷ *n* comprensione *f*; (*agreement*) accordo

understatement [ʌndə'steɪtmənt] *n* **that's an ~!** a dire poco!

understood [ʌndə'stud] *pt, pp of* **understand** ▷ *adj* inteso(-a); (*implied*) sottinteso(-a)

undertake [ʌndə'teɪk] (*irreg: like* **take**) *vt* intraprendere; **to ~ to do sth** impegnarsi a fare qc

undertaker ['ʌndəteɪkə^r] *n* impresario di pompe funebri

undertaking [ʌndə'teɪkɪŋ] *n* impresa; (*promise*) promessa

under: **underwater** [ʌndə'wɔːtə^r] *adv* sott'acqua ▷ *adj* subacqueo(-a); **underway** [ʌndə'weɪ] *adj* **to be underway** essere in corso; **underwear** ['ʌndəwɛə^r] *n* biancheria (intima); **underwent** [ʌndə'wɛnt] *vb see* **undergo**; **underworld** ['ʌndəwəːld] *n* (*of crime*) malavita

undesirable [ʌndɪ'zaɪərəbl] *adj* sgradevole

undisputed [ʌndɪs'pjuːtɪd] *adj* indiscusso(-a)

undo [ʌn'duː] *vt* (*irreg*) disfare

undone [ʌn'dʌn] *pp of* **undo**; **to come ~** slacciarsi

undoubtedly [ʌn'dautɪdlɪ] *adv* senza alcun dubbio

undress [ʌn'drɛs] *vi* spogliarsi

unearth [ʌn'əːθ] *vt* dissotterrare; (*fig*) scoprire

uneasy [ʌn'iːzɪ] *adj* a disagio; (*worried*) preoccupato(-a); (*peace*) precario(-a)

unemployed [ʌnɪm'plɔɪd] *adj* disoccupato(-a) ▷ *npl* **the ~** i disoccupati

unemployment [ʌnɪm'plɔɪmənt] *n* disoccupazione *f*; **unemployment benefit** (US **unemployment compensation**) *n* sussidio di disoccupazione

unequal [ʌn'iːkwəl] *adj* (*length, objects*) disuguale; (*amounts*) diverso(-a); (*division of labour*) ineguale

uneven [ʌn'iːvn] *adj* ineguale; irregolare

unexpected [ʌnɪk'spɛktɪd] *adj* inatteso(-a), imprevisto(-a); **unexpectedly** *adv* inaspettatamente

unfair [ʌn'fɛə^r] *adj* **~ (to)** ingiusto(-a) (nei confronti di)

unfaithful [ʌn'feɪθful] *adj* infedele

unfamiliar [ʌnfə'mɪlɪə^r] *adj* sconosciuto(-a), strano(-a); **to be ~ with** non avere familiarità con

unfashionable [ʌn'fæʃnəbl] *adj* (*clothes*) fuori moda; (*district*) non alla moda

unfasten [ʌn'fɑːsn] *vt* slacciare; sciogliere

unfavourable [ʌn'feɪvərəbl] (US **unfavorable**) *adj* sfavorevole

unfinished [ʌn'fɪnɪʃt] *adj* incompleto(-a)

unfit [ʌn'fɪt] *adj* (*ill*) malato(-a), in cattiva salute; (*incompetent*): **~ (for)** incompetente (in); (*: work, Mil*) inabile (a)

unfold [ʌn'fəuld] *vt* spiegare ▷ *vi* (*story, plot*) svelarsi

unforgettable [ʌnfə'gɛtəbl] *adj* indimenticabile

unfortunate [ʌn'fɔːtʃnət] *adj* sfortunato(-a); (*event, remark*) infelice; **unfortunately** *adv* sfortunatamente, purtroppo

unfriendly [ʌn'frɛndlɪ] *adj* poco amichevole, freddo(-a)

unfurnished [ʌn'fəːnɪʃt] *adj* non ammobiliato(-a)

unhappiness [ʌn'hæpɪnɪs] *n* infelicità

unhappy [ʌn'hæpɪ] *adj* infelice; **~ about/with** (*arrangements etc*) insoddisfatto(-a) di

unhealthy [ʌn'hɛlθɪ] *adj* (*gen*)

malsano(-a); (*person*) malaticcio(-a)
unheard-of [ʌn'hə:dɔv] *adj* inaudito(-a), senza precedenti
unhelpful [ʌn'hɛlpful] *adj* poco disponibile
unhurt [ʌn'hə:t] *adj* illeso(-a)
unidentified [ʌnaɪ'dɛntɪfaɪd] *adj* non identificato(-a)
uniform ['ju:nɪfɔ:m] *n* uniforme *f*, divisa ▷ *adj* uniforme
unify ['ju:nɪfaɪ] *vt* unificare
unimportant [ʌnɪm'pɔ:tənt] *adj* senza importanza, di scarsa importanza
uninhabited [ʌnɪn'hæbɪtɪd] *adj* disabitato(-a)
unintentional [ʌnɪn'tɛnʃənəl] *adj* involontario(-a)
union ['ju:njən] *n* unione *f*; (*also:* **trade ~**) sindacato ▷ *cpd* sindacale, dei sindacati; **Union Jack** *n bandiera nazionale britannica*
unique [ju:'ni:k] *adj* unico(-a)
unisex ['ju:nɪsɛks] *adj* unisex *inv*
unit ['ju:nɪt] *n* unità *f inv*; (*section: of furniture etc*) elemento; (*team, squad*) reparto, squadra
unite [ju:'naɪt] *vt* unire ▷ *vi* unirsi; **united** *adj* unito(-a); unificato(-a); (*efforts*) congiunto(-a); **United Kingdom** *n* Regno Unito; **United Nations (Organization)** *n* (Organizzazione *f* delle) Nazioni Unite; **United States (of America)** *n* Stati *mpl* Uniti (d'America)
unity ['ju:nɪtɪ] *n* unità
universal [ju:nɪ'və:sl] *adj* universale
universe ['ju:nɪvə:s] *n* universo
university [ju:nɪ'və:sɪtɪ] *n* università *f inv*
unjust [ʌn'dʒʌst] *adj* ingiusto(-a)
unkind [ʌn'kaɪnd] *adj* scortese; crudele
unknown [ʌn'nəun] *adj* sconosciuto(-a)
unlawful [ʌn'lɔ:ful] *adj* illecito(-a), illegale
unleaded [ʌn'lɛdɪd] *adj* (*petrol, fuel*) verde, senza piombo
unleash [ʌn'li:ʃ] *vt* (*fig*) scatenare
unless [ʌn'lɛs] *conj* a meno che (non) + *sub*
unlike [ʌn'laɪk] *adj* diverso(-a) ▷ *prep* a differenza di, contrariamente a
unlikely [ʌn'laɪklɪ] *adj* improbabile
unlimited [ʌn'lɪmɪtɪd] *adj* illimitato(-a)
unlisted [ʌn'lɪstɪd] (*US*) *adj* (*Tel*): **to be ~** non essere sull'elenco
unload [ʌn'ləud] *vt* scaricare
unlock [ʌn'lɔk] *vt* aprire
unlucky [ʌn'lʌkɪ] *adj* sfortunato(-a); (*object, number*) che porta sfortuna
unmarried [ʌn'mærɪd] *adj* non sposato(-a); (*man only*) scapolo, celibe; (*woman only*) nubile
unmistak(e)able [ʌnmɪs'teɪkəbl] *adj* inconfondibile
unnatural [ʌn'nætʃrəl] *adj* innaturale; contro natura
unnecessary [ʌn'nɛsəsərɪ] *adj* inutile, superfluo(-a)
UNO ['ju:nəu] *n abbr* (= *United Nations Organization*) ONU *f*
unofficial [ʌnə'fɪʃl] *adj* non ufficiale; (*strike*) non dichiarato(-a) dal sindacato
unpack [ʌn'pæk] *vi* disfare la valigia (*or* le valigie) ▷ *vt* disfare
unpaid [ʌn'peɪd] *adj* (*holiday*) non pagato(-a); (*work*) non retribuito(-a); (*bill, debt*) da pagare
unpleasant [ʌn'plɛznt] *adj* spiacevole
unplug [ʌn'plʌg] *vt* staccare
unpopular [ʌn'pɔpjulə^r] *adj* impopolare
unprecedented [ʌn'prɛsɪdəntɪd] *adj* senza precedenti
unpredictable [ʌnprɪ'dɪktəbl] *adj* imprevedibile
unprotected ['ʌnprə'tɛktɪd] *adj* (*sex*) non protetto(-a)
unqualified [ʌn'kwɔlɪfaɪd] *adj*

(*teacher*) non abilitato(-a); (*success*) assoluto(-a), senza riserve
unravel [ʌn'rævl] *vt* dipanare, districare
unreal [ʌn'rɪəl] *adj* irreale
unrealistic [ʌnrɪə'lɪstɪk] *adj* non realistico(-a)
unreasonable [ʌn'ri:znəbl] *adj* irragionevole
unrelated [ʌnrɪ'leɪtɪd] *adj* **~ (to)** senza rapporto (con); non imparentato(-a) (con)
unreliable [ʌnrɪ'laɪəbl] *adj* (*person, machine*) che non dà affidamento; (*news, source of information*) inattendibile
unrest [ʌn'rɛst] *n* agitazione *f*
unroll [ʌn'rəul] *vt* srotolare
unruly [ʌn'ru:lɪ] *adj* indisciplinato(-a)
unsafe [ʌn'seɪf] *adj* pericoloso(-a), rischioso(-a)
unsatisfactory ['ʌnsætɪs'fæktərɪ] *adj* che lascia a desiderare, insufficiente
unscrew [ʌn'skru:] *vt* svitare
unsettled [ʌn'sɛtld] *adj* (*person*) turbato(-a); indeciso(-a); (*weather*) instabile
unsettling [ʌn'sɛtlɪŋ] *adj* inquietante
unsightly [ʌn'saɪtlɪ] *adj* brutto(-a), sgradevole a vedersi
unskilled [ʌn'skɪld] *adj* non specializzato(-a)
unspoiled ['ʌn'spɔɪld], **unspoilt** ['ʌn'spɔɪlt] *adj* (*place*) non deturpato(-a)
unstable [ʌn'steɪbl] *adj* (*gen*) instabile; (*mentally*) squilibrato(-a)
unsteady [ʌn'stɛdɪ] *adj* instabile, malsicuro(-a)
unsuccessful [ʌnsək'sɛsful] *adj* (*writer, proposal*) che non ha successo; (*marriage, attempt*) mal riuscito(-a), fallito(-a); **to be ~** (*in attempting sth*) non avere successo
unsuitable [ʌn'su:təbl] *adj* inadatto(-a); inopportuno(-a); sconveniente
unsure [ʌn'ʃuə] *adj* incerto(-a); **to be ~ of o.s** essere insicuro(-a)
untidy [ʌn'taɪdɪ] *adj* (*room*) in disordine; (*appearance*) trascurato(-a); (*person*) disordinato(-a)
untie [ʌn'taɪ] *vt* (*knot, parcel*) disfare; (*prisoner, dog*) slegare
until [ʌn'tɪl] *prep* fino a; (*after negative*) prima di ▷ *conj* finché, fino a quando; (*in past, after negative*) prima che + *sub*, prima di + *infinitive*; **~ he comes** finché *or* fino a quando non arriva; **~ now** finora; **~ then** fino ad allora
untrue [ʌn'tru:] *adj* (*statement*) falso(-a), non vero(-a)
unused [ʌn'ju:zd] *adj* nuovo(-a)
unusual [ʌn'ju:ʒuəl] *adj* insolito(-a), eccezionale, raro(-a); **unusually** *adv* insolitamente
unveil [ʌn'veɪl] *vt* scoprire; svelare
unwanted [ʌn'wɔntɪd] *adj* (*clothing*) smesso(-a); (*child*) non desiderato(-a)
unwell [ʌn'wɛl] *adj* indisposto(-a); **to feel ~** non sentirsi bene
unwilling [ʌn'wɪlɪŋ] *adj*: **to be ~ to do** non voler fare
unwind [ʌn'waɪnd] (*irreg: like* **wind'**) *vt* svolgere, srotolare ▷ *vi* (*relax*) rilassarsi
unwise [ʌn'waɪz] *adj* poco saggio(-a)
unwittingly [ʌn'wɪtɪŋlɪ] *adv* senza volerlo
unwrap [ʌn'ræp] *vt* disfare; aprire
unzip [ʌn'zɪp] *vt* aprire (la chiusura lampo di); (*Comput*) dezippare

KEYWORD

up [ʌp] *prep* **he went up the stairs/the hill** è salito su per le scale/sulla collina; **the cat was up a tree** il gatto era su un albero; **they live further up the street** vivono un po' più su nella stessa strada
▷ *adv* **1** (*upwards, higher*) su, in alto;

up in the sky/the mountains su nel cielo/in montagna; **up there** lassù; **up above** su in alto
2: **to be up** (*out of bed*) essere alzato(-a); (*prices, level*) essere salito(-a)
3: **up to** (*as far as*) fino a; **up to now** finora
4: **to be up to** (*depending on*): **it's up to you** sta a lei, dipende da lei; (*equal to*): **he's not up to it** (*job, task etc*) non ne è all'altezza; (*inf: be doing*): **what is he up to?** cosa sta combinando?
▷ *n* **ups and downs** alti e bassi *mpl*

up-and-coming ['ʌpənd'kʌmɪŋ] *adj* pieno(-a) di promesse, promettente
upbringing ['ʌpbrɪŋɪŋ] *n* educazione *f*
update [ʌp'deɪt] *vt* aggiornare
upfront [ʌp'frʌnt] *adj* (*inf*) franco(-a), aperto(-a) ▷ *adv* (*pay*) subito
upgrade [ʌp'greɪd] *vt* (*house, job*) migliorare; (*employee*) avanzare di grado
upheaval [ʌp'hi:vl] *n* sconvolgimento; tumulto
uphill [ʌp'hɪl] *adj* in salita; (*fig: task*) difficile ▷ *adv* **to go ~** andare in salita, salire
upholstery [ʌp'həulstərɪ] *n* tappezzeria
upmarket [ʌp'mɑ:kɪt] *adj* (*product*) che si rivolge ad una fascia di mercato superiore
upon [ə'pɔn] *prep* su
upper ['ʌpə^r] *adj* superiore ▷ *n* (*of shoe*) tomaia; **upper-class** *adj* dell'alta borghesia
upright ['ʌpraɪt] *adj* diritto(-a); verticale; (*fig*) diritto(-a), onesto(-a)
uprising ['ʌpraɪzɪŋ] *n* insurrezione *f*, rivolta
uproar ['ʌprɔ:^{r}] *n* tumulto, clamore *m*
upset [*n* 'ʌpsɛt, *vb, adj* ʌp'sɛt] (*irreg: like* **set**) *n* (*to plan etc*) contrattempo; (*stomach upset*) disturbo ▷ *vt* (*glass etc*) rovesciare; (*plan, stomach*) scombussolare; (*person: offend*) contrariare; (*: grieve*) addolorare; sconvolgere ▷ *adj* contrariato(-a), addolorato(-a); (*stomach*) scombussolato(-a)
upside-down [ʌpsaɪd'daun] *adv* sottosopra
upstairs [ʌp'stɛəz] *adv, adj* di sopra, al piano superiore ▷ *n* piano di sopra
up-to-date ['ʌptə'deɪt] *adj* moderno(-a); aggiornato(-a)
uptown ['ʌptaun] (US) *adv* verso i quartieri residenziali ▷ *adj* dei quartieri residenziali
upward ['ʌpwəd] *adj* ascendente; verso l'alto; **upward(s)** *adv* in su, verso l'alto
uranium [juə'reɪnɪəm] *n* uranio
Uranus [juə'reɪnəs] *n* (*planet*) Urano
urban ['ə:bən] *adj* urbano(-a)
urge [ə:dʒ] *n* impulso; stimolo; forte desiderio ▷ *vt* **to ~ sb to do** esortare qn a fare, spingere qn a fare; raccomandare a qn di fare
urgency ['ə:dʒənsɪ] *n* urgenza; (*of tone*) insistenza
urgent ['ə:dʒənt] *adj* urgente; (*voice*) insistente
urinal ['juərɪnl] *n* (BRIT: *building*) vespasiano; (*: vessel*) orinale *m*, pappagallo
urinate ['juərɪneɪt] *vi* orinare
urine ['juərɪn] *n* orina
URL *n abbr* (= *uniform resource locator*) URL *m inv*, sito web
us [ʌs] *pron* ci; (*stressed, after prep*) noi; *see also* **me**
US(A) *n abbr* (= *United States (of America)*) USA *mpl*
use [*n* ju:s, *vb* ju:z] *n* uso; impiego, utilizzazione *f* ▷ *vt* usare, utilizzare, servirsi di; **in ~** in uso; **out of ~** fuori uso; **to be of ~** essere utile, servire; **it's no ~** non serve, è inutile; **she ~d to do it** lo faceva (una volta), era solita farlo; **to be ~d to** avere l'abitudine di; **use**

up *vt* consumare; esaurire; **used** *adj* (*object, car*) usato(-a); **useful** *adj* utile; **useless** *adj* inutile; (*person*) inetto(-a); **user** *n* utente *m/f*; **user-friendly** *adj* (*computer*) di facile uso

usual ['juːʒuəl] *adj* solito(-a); **as ~** come al solito, come d'abitudine; **usually** *adv* di solito

utensil [juː'tɛnsl] *n* utensile *m*; **kitchen ~s** utensili da cucina

utility [juː'tɪlɪtɪ] *n* utilità; (*also:* **public ~**) servizio pubblico

utilize ['juːtɪlaɪz] *vt* utilizzare; sfruttare

utmost ['ʌtməust] *adj* estremo(-a) ▷ *n* **to do one's ~** fare il possibile *or* di tutto

utter ['ʌtə^r] *adj* assoluto(-a), totale ▷ *vt* pronunciare, proferire; emettere; **utterly** *adv* completamente, del tutto

U-turn ['juː'təːn] *n* inversione *f* a U

V

v. *abbr* = **verse**; **versus**; **volt**; (= *vide*) vedi, vedere

vacancy ['veɪkənsɪ] *n* (BRIT: *job*) posto libero; (*room*) stanza libera; **"no vacancies"** "completo"

> Be careful not to translate ***vacancy*** by the Italian word ***vacanza***.

vacant ['veɪkənt] *adj* (*job, seat etc*) libero(-a); (*expression*) assente

vacate [və'keɪt] *vt* lasciare libero(-a)

vacation [və'keɪʃən] (*esp* US) *n* vacanze *fpl*; **vacationer** (US **vacationist**) *n* vacanziere(-a)

vaccination [væksɪ'neɪʃən] *n* vaccinazione *f*

vaccine ['væksiːn] *n* vaccino

vacuum ['vækjum] *n* vuoto; **vacuum cleaner** *n* aspirapolvere *m inv*

vagina [və'dʒaɪnə] *n* vagina

vague [veɪg] *adj* vago(-a); (*blurred*: *photo, memory*) sfocato(-a)

vain [veɪn] *adj* (*useless*) inutile, vano(-a); (*conceited*) vanitoso(-a); **in ~**

inutilmente, invano
Valentine's Day ['væləntaɪnzdeɪ] *n* San Valentino *m*
valid ['vælɪd] *adj* valido(-a), valevole; (*excuse*) valido(-a)
valley ['vælɪ] *n* valle *f*
valuable ['væljuəbl] *adj* (*jewel*) di (grande) valore; (*time, help*) prezioso(-a); **valuables** *npl* oggetti *mpl* di valore
value ['vælju:] *n* valore *m* ▷ *vt* (*fix price*) valutare, dare un prezzo a; (*cherish*) apprezzare, tenere a; **~s** *npl* (*principles*) valori *mpl*
valve [vælv] *n* valvola
vampire ['væmpaɪəʳ] *n* vampiro
van [væn] *n* (*Aut*) furgone *m*; (BRIT: *Rail*) vagone *m*
vandal ['vændl] *n* vandalo(-a); **vandalism** *n* vandalismo; **vandalize** *vt* vandalizzare
vanilla [və'nɪlə] *n* vaniglia ▷ *cpd* (*ice cream*) alla vaniglia
vanish ['vænɪʃ] *vi* svanire, scomparire
vanity ['vænɪtɪ] *n* vanità
vapour ['veɪpəʳ] (US **vapor**) *n* vapore *m*
variable ['vɛərɪəbl] *adj* variabile; (*mood*) mutevole
variant ['vɛərɪənt] *n* variante *f*
variation [vɛərɪ'eɪʃən] *n* variazione *f*; (*in opinion*) cambiamento
varied ['vɛərɪd] *adj* vario(-a), diverso(-a)
variety [və'raɪətɪ] *n* varietà *f inv*; (*quantity*) quantità, numero
various ['vɛərɪəs] *adj* vario(-a), diverso(-a); (*several*) parecchi(-e), molti(-e)
varnish ['vɑ:nɪʃ] *n* vernice *f*; (*nail varnish*) smalto ▷ *vt* verniciare; mettere lo smalto su
vary ['vɛərɪ] *vt, vi* variare, mutare
vase [vɑ:z] *n* vaso
Vaseline® ['væsɪli:n] *n* vaselina
vast [vɑ:st] *adj* vasto(-a); (*amount, success*) enorme
VAT [væt] *n abbr* (= *value added tax*) I.V.A. *f*
Vatican ['vætɪkən] *n*: **the ~** il Vaticano
vault [vɔ:lt] *n* (*of roof*) volta; (*tomb*) tomba; (*in bank*) camera blindata ▷ *vt* (*also*: **~ over**) saltare (d'un balzo)
VCR *n abbr* = **video cassette recorder**
VDU *n abbr* = **visual display unit**
veal [vi:l] *n* vitello
veer [vɪəʳ] *vi* girare; virare
vegan ['vi:gən] *n* vegetaliano(-a)
vegetable ['vɛdʒtəbl] *n* verdura, ortaggio ▷ *adj* vegetale
vegetarian [vɛdʒɪ'tɛərɪən] *adj, n* vegetariano(-a); **do you have any ~ dishes?** avete piatti vegetariani?
vegetation [vɛdʒɪ'teɪʃən] *n* vegetazione *f*
vehicle ['vi:ɪkl] *n* veicolo
veil [veɪl] *n* velo
vein [veɪn] *n* vena; (*on leaf*) nervatura
Velcro® ['vɛlkrəu] *n* velcro® *m inv*
velvet ['vɛlvɪt] *n* velluto ▷ *adj* di velluto
vending machine ['vɛndɪŋ-] *n* distributore *m* automatico
vendor ['vɛndəʳ] *n* venditore(-trice)
vengeance ['vɛndʒəns] *n* vendetta; **with a ~** (*fig*) davvero; furiosamente
Venice ['vɛnɪs] *n* Venezia
venison ['vɛnɪsn] *n* carne *f* di cervo
venom ['vɛnəm] *n* veleno
vent [vɛnt] *n* foro, apertura; (*in dress, jacket*) spacco ▷ *vt* (*fig: one's feelings*) sfogare, dare sfogo a
ventilation [vɛntɪ'leɪʃən] *n* ventilazione *f*
venture ['vɛntʃəʳ] *n* impresa (rischiosa) ▷ *vt* rischiare, azzardare ▷ *vi* avventurarsi; **business ~** iniziativa commerciale
venue ['vɛnju:] *n* luogo (designato) per l'incontro
Venus ['vi:nəs] *n* (*planet*) Venere *m*
verb [və:b] *n* verbo; **verbal** *adj* verbale; (*translation*) orale
verdict ['və:dɪkt] *n* verdetto

verge [vəːdʒ] (BRIT) *n* bordo, orlo; **"soft ~s"** (BRIT: *Aut*) banchine *fpl* cedevoli; **on the ~ of doing** sul punto di fare
verify ['vɛrɪfaɪ] *vt* verificare; (*prove the truth of*) confermare
versatile ['vəːsətaɪl] *adj* (*person*) versatile; (*machine, tool etc*) (che si presta) a molti usi
verse [vəːs] *n* versi *mpl*; (*stanza*) stanza, strofa; (*in bible*) versetto
version ['vəːʃən] *n* versione *f*
versus ['vəːsəs] *prep* contro
vertical ['vəːtɪkl] *adj* verticale ▷ *n* verticale *m*
very ['vɛrɪ] *adv* molto ▷ *adj* **the ~ book which** proprio il libro che; **the ~ last** proprio l'ultimo; **at the ~ least** almeno; **~ much** moltissimo
vessel ['vɛsl] *n* (*Anat*) vaso; (*Naut*) nave *f*; (*container*) recipiente *m*
vest [vɛst] *n* (BRIT) maglia; (: *sleeveless*) canottiera; (US: *waistcoat*) gilè *m inv*
vet [vɛt] *n abbr* (BRIT: = *veterinary surgeon*) veterinario ▷ *vt* esaminare minuziosamente
veteran ['vɛtərn] *n* (*also*: **war ~**) veterano
veterinary surgeon ['vɛtrɪnərɪ-] (US **veterinarian**) *n* veterinario
veto ['viːtəu] (*pl* **vetoes**) *n* veto ▷ *vt* opporre il veto a
via ['vaɪə] *prep* (*by way of*) via; (*by means of*) tramite
viable ['vaɪəbl] *adj* attuabile; vitale
vibrate [vaɪ'breɪt] *vi* **to ~ (with)** vibrare (di); (*resound*) risonare (di)
vibration [vaɪ'breɪʃən] *n* vibrazione *f*
vicar ['vɪkəʳ] *n* pastore *m*
vice [vaɪs] *n* (*evil*) vizio; (*Tech*) morsa; **vice-chairman** (*irreg*) *n* vicepresidente *m*
vice versa ['vaɪsɪ'vəːsə] *adv* viceversa
vicinity [vɪ'sɪnɪtɪ] *n* vicinanze *fpl*
vicious ['vɪʃəs] *adj* (*remark, dog*) cattivo(-a); (*blow*) violento(-a)
victim ['vɪktɪm] *n* vittima
victor ['vɪktəʳ] *n* vincitore *m*
Victorian [vɪk'tɔːrɪən] *adj* vittoriano(-a)
victorious [vɪk'tɔːrɪəs] *adj* vittorioso(-a)
victory ['vɪktərɪ] *n* vittoria
video ['vɪdɪəu] *cpd* video... ▷ *n* (*video film*) video *m inv*; (*also*: **~ cassette**) videocassetta; (*also*: **~ cassette recorder**) videoregistratore *m*; **video call** *n* videochiamata; **video camera** *n* videocamera; **video (cassette) recorder** *n* videoregistratore *m*; **video game** *n* videogioco; **videophone** ['vɪdɪəufəun] *n* videotelefono; **video shop** *n* videonoleggio; **video tape** *n* videotape *m inv*; **video wall** *n* schermo *m* multivideo *inv*
vie [vaɪ] *vi*: **to ~ with** competere con, rivaleggiare con
Vienna [vɪ'ɛnə] *n* Vienna
Vietnam [vjɛt'næm] *n* Vietnam *m*; **Vietnamese** *adj, n inv* vietnamita *m/f*
view [vjuː] *n* vista, veduta; (*opinion*) opinione *f* ▷ *vt* (*look at*: *also fig*) considerare; (*house*) visitare; **on ~** (*in museum etc*) esposto(-a); **in full ~ of** sotto gli occhi di; **in ~ of the weather/the fact that** considerato il tempo/che; **in my ~** a mio parere; **viewer** *n* spettatore(-trice); **viewpoint** *n* punto di vista; (*place*) posizione *f*
vigilant ['vɪdʒɪlənt] *adj* vigile
vigorous ['vɪgərəs] *adj* vigoroso(-a)
vile [vaɪl] *adj* (*action*) vile; (*smell*) disgustoso(-a), nauseante; (*temper*) pessimo(-a)
villa ['vɪlə] *n* villa
village ['vɪlɪdʒ] *n* villaggio; **villager** *n* abitante *m/f* di villaggio
villain ['vɪlən] *n* (*scoundrel*) canaglia; (BRIT: *criminal*) criminale *m*; (*in novel etc*) cattivo
vinaigrette [vɪneɪ'grɛt] *n* vinaigrette *f inv*

vine [vaɪn] *n* vite *f*; (*climbing plant*) rampicante *m*
vinegar ['vɪnɪgəʳ] *n* aceto
vineyard ['vɪnjɑ:d] *n* vigna, vigneto
vintage ['vɪntɪdʒ] *n* (*year*) annata, produzione *f* ▷ *cpd* d'annata
vinyl ['vaɪnl] *n* vinile *m*
viola [vɪ'əulə] *n* viola
violate ['vaɪəleɪt] *vt* violare
violation [vaɪə'leɪʃən] *n* violazione *f*; **in ~ of sth** violando qc
violence ['vaɪələns] *n* violenza
violent ['vaɪələnt] *adj* violento(-a)
violet ['vaɪələt] *adj* (*colour*) viola *inv*, violetto(-a) ▷ *n* (*plant*) violetta; (*colour*) violetto
violin [vaɪə'lɪn] *n* violino
VIP *n abbr* (= *very important person*) V.I.P. *m/f inv*
virgin ['və:dʒɪn] *n* vergine *f* ▷ *adj* vergine *inv*
Virgo ['və:gəu] *n* (*sign*) Vergine *f*
virtual ['və:tjuəl] *adj* effettivo(-a), vero(-a); (*Comput, Physics*) virtuale; (*in effect*): **it's a ~ impossibility** è praticamente impossibile; **the ~ leader** il capo all'atto pratico; **virtually** ['və:tjuəlɪ] *adv* (*almost*) praticamente; **virtual reality** *n* (*Comput*) realtà virtuale
virtue ['və:tju:] *n* virtù *f inv*; (*advantage*) pregio, vantaggio; **by ~ of** grazie a
virus ['vaɪərəs] *n* (*also Comput*) virus *m inv*
visa ['vɪ:zə] *n* visto
vise [vaɪs] (US) *n* (*Tech*) = **vice**
visibility [vɪzɪ'bɪlɪtɪ] *n* visibilità
visible ['vɪzəbl] *adj* visibile
vision ['vɪʒən] *n* (*sight*) vista; (*foresight, in dream*) visione *f*
visit ['vɪzɪt] *n* visita; (*stay*) soggiorno ▷ *vt* (*person*: US: *also*: **~ with**) andare a trovare; (*place*) visitare; **visiting hours** *npl* (*in hospital etc*) orario delle visite; **visitor** *n* visitatore(-trice); (*guest*) ospite *m/f*; **visitor centre** (US **visitor center**) *n centro informazioni per visitatori di museo, zoo, parco ecc*
visual ['vɪzjuəl] *adj* visivo(-a); visuale; ottico(-a); **visualize** ['vɪzjuəlaɪz] *vt* immaginare, figurarsi; (*foresee*) prevedere
vital ['vaɪtl] *adj* vitale
vitality [vaɪ'tælɪtɪ] *n* vitalità
vitamin ['vɪtəmɪn] *n* vitamina
vivid ['vɪvɪd] *adj* vivido(-a)
V-neck ['vi:nɛk] *n* maglione *m* con lo scollo a V
vocabulary [vəu'kæbjulərɪ] *n* vocabolario
vocal ['vəukl] *adj* (*Mus*) vocale; (*communication*) verbale
vocational [vəu'keɪʃənl] *adj* professionale
vodka ['vɔdkə] *n* vodka *f inv*
vogue [vəug] *n* moda; (*popularity*) popolarità, voga
voice [vɔɪs] *n* voce *f* ▷ *vt* (*opinion*) esprimere; **voice mail** *n* servizio di segretaria telefonica
void [vɔɪd] *n* vuoto ▷ *adj* (*invalid*) nullo(-a); (*empty*): **~ of** privo(-a) di
volatile ['vɔlətaɪl] *adj* volatile; (*fig*) volubile
volcano [vɔl'keɪnəu] (*pl* **volcanoes**) *n* vulcano
volleyball ['vɔlɪbɔ:l] *n* pallavolo *f*
volt [vəult] *n* volt *m inv*; **voltage** *n* tensione *f*, voltaggio
volume ['vɔlju:m] *n* volume *m*
voluntarily ['vɔləntrɪlɪ] *adv* volontariamente; gratuitamente
voluntary ['vɔləntərɪ] *adj* volontario(-a); (*unpaid*) gratuito(-a), non retribuito(-a)
volunteer [vɔlən'tɪəʳ] *n* volontario(-a) ▷ *vt* offrire volontariamente ▷ *vi* (*Mil*) arruolarsi volontario; **to ~ to do** offrire (volontariamente) di fare
vomit ['vɔmɪt] *n* vomito ▷ *vt, vi* vomitare
vote [vəut] *n* voto, suffragio; (*cast*)

voto; (*franchise*) diritto di voto ▷ *vt* **to be ~d chairman** *etc* venir eletto presidente *etc*; (*propose*): **to ~ that** approvare la proposta che ▷ *vi* votare; **~ of thanks** discorso di ringraziamento; **voter** *n* elettore(-trice); **voting** *n* scrutinio

voucher ['vautʃəʳ] *n* (*for meal, petrol etc*) buono

vow [vau] *n* voto, promessa solenne ▷ *vt* **to ~ to do/that** giurare di fare/che

vowel ['vauəl] *n* vocale *f*

voyage ['vɔɪɪdʒ] *n* viaggio per mare, traversata

vulgar ['vʌlgəʳ] *adj* volgare

vulnerable ['vʌlnərəbl] *adj* vulnerabile

vulture ['vʌltʃəʳ] *n* avvoltoio

W

waddle ['wɔdl] *vi* camminare come una papera

wade [weɪd] *vi*: **to ~ through** camminare a stento in; (*fig*: *book*) leggere con fatica

wafer ['weɪfəʳ] *n* (*Culin*) cialda

waffle ['wɔfl] *n* (*Culin*) cialda; (*inf*) ciance *fpl* ▷ *vi* cianciare

wag [wæg] *vt* agitare, muovere ▷ *vi* agitarsi

wage [weɪdʒ] *n* (*also:* **~s**) salario, paga ▷ *vt* **to ~ war** fare la guerra

wag(g)on ['wægən] *n* (*horse-drawn*) carro; (BRIT: *Rail*) vagone *m* (merci)

wail [weɪl] *n* gemito; (*of siren*) urlo ▷ *vi* gemere; urlare

waist [weɪst] *n* vita, cintola; **waistcoat** (BRIT) *n* panciotto, gilè *m inv*

wait [weɪt] *n* attesa ▷ *vi* aspettare, attendere; **to lie in ~ for** stare in agguato a; **to ~ for** aspettare; **~ for me, please** aspettami, per favore; **I can't ~ to** (*fig*) non vedo l'ora di; **wait**

on *vt fus* servire; **waiter** *n* cameriere *m*; **waiting list** *n* lista di attesa; **waiting room** *n* sala d'aspetto *or* d'attesa; **waitress** *n* cameriera

waive [weɪv] *vt* rinunciare a, abbandonare

wake [weɪk] (*pt* **woke, waked**, *pp* **woken, waked**) *vt* (*also:* **~ up**) svegliare ▷ *vi* (*also:* **~ up**) svegliarsi ▷ *n* (*for dead person*) veglia funebre; (*Naut*) scia

Wales [weɪlz] *n* Galles *m*

walk [wɔːk] *n* passeggiata; (*short*) giretto; (*gait*) passo, andatura; (*path*) sentiero; (*in park etc*) sentiero, vialetto ▷ *vi* camminare; (*for pleasure, exercise*) passeggiare ▷ *vt* (*distance*) fare *or* percorrere a piedi; (*dog*) accompagnare, portare a passeggiare; **10 minutes' ~ from** 10 minuti di cammino *or* a piedi da; **from all ~s of life** di tutte le condizioni sociali; **walk out** *vi* (*audience*) andarsene; (*workers*) scendere in sciopero; **walker** *n* (*person*) camminatore(-trice); **walkie-talkie** ['wɔːkɪ'tɔːkɪ] *n* walkie-talkie *m inv*; **walking** *n* camminare *m*; **walking shoes** *npl* pedule *fpl*; **walking stick** *n* bastone *m* da passeggio; **Walkman®** ['wɔːkmən] *n* Walkman® *m inv*; **walkway** *n* passaggio pedonale

wall [wɔːl] *n* muro; (*internal, of tunnel, cave*) parete *f*

wallet ['wɔlɪt] *n* portafoglio; **I can't find my ~** non trovo il portafoglio

wallpaper ['wɔːlpeɪpəʳ] *n* carta da parati ▷ *vt* (*room*) mettere la carta da parati in

walnut ['wɔːlnʌt] *n* noce *f*; (*tree, wood*) noce *m*

walrus ['wɔːlrəs] (*pl* **walrus** *or* **walruses**) *n* tricheco

waltz [wɔːlts] *n* valzer *m inv* ▷ *vi* ballare il valzer

wand [wɔnd] *n* (*also:* **magic ~**) bacchetta (magica)

wander ['wɔndəʳ] *vi* (*person*) girare senza meta, girovagare; (*thoughts*) vagare ▷ *vt* girovagare per

want [wɔnt] *vt* volere; (*need*) aver bisogno di ▷ *n* **for ~ of** per mancanza di; **wanted** *adj* (*criminal*) ricercato(-a); **"wanted"** (*in adverts*) "cercasi"

war [wɔːʳ] *n* guerra; **to make ~ (on)** far guerra (a)

ward [wɔːd] *n* (*in hospital: room*) corsia; (*: section*) reparto; (*Pol*) circoscrizione *f*; (*Law: child: also:* **~ of court**) pupillo(-a)

warden ['wɔːdn] *n* (*of park, game reserve, youth hostel*) guardiano(-a); (BRIT: *of institution*) direttore(-trice); (BRIT: *also:* **traffic ~**) addetto(-a) al controllo del traffico e del parcheggio

wardrobe ['wɔːdrəub] *n* (*cupboard*) guardaroba *m inv*, armadio; (*clothes*) guardaroba; (*Cinema, Theatre*) costumi *mpl*

warehouse ['wɛəhaus] *n* magazzino

warfare ['wɔːfɛəʳ] *n* guerra

warhead ['wɔːhɛd] *n* (*Mil*) testata

warm [wɔːm] *adj* caldo(-a); (*thanks, welcome, applause*) caloroso(-a); (*person*) cordiale; **it's ~** fa caldo; **I'm ~** ho caldo; **warm up** *vi* scaldarsi, riscaldarsi ▷ *vt* scaldare, riscaldare; (*engine*) far scaldare; **warmly** *adv* (*applaud, welcome*) calorosamente; (*dress*) con abiti pesanti; **warmth** *n* calore *m*

warn [wɔːn] *vt*: **to ~ sb that/(not) to do/of** avvertire *or* avvisare qn che/di (non) fare/di; **warning** *n* avvertimento; (*notice*) avviso; (*signal*) segnalazione *f*; **warning light** *n* spia luminosa

warrant ['wɔrnt] *n* (*voucher*) buono; (*Law: to arrest*) mandato di cattura; (*: to search*) mandato di perquisizione

warranty ['wɔrəntɪ] *n* garanzia

warrior ['wɔrɪəʳ] *n* guerriero(-a)

Warsaw ['wɔːsɔː] *n* Varsavia

warship ['wɔːʃɪp] *n* nave *f* da guerra
wart [wɔːt] *n* verruca
wartime ['wɔːtaɪm] *n* **in ~** in tempo di guerra
wary ['wɛərɪ] *adj* prudente
was [wɔz] *pt of* **be**
wash [wɔʃ] *vt* lavare ▷ *vi* lavarsi; (*sea*): **to ~ over/against sth** infrangersi su/contro qc ▷ *n* lavaggio; (*of ship*) scia; **to give sth a ~** lavare qc, dare una lavata a qc; **to have a ~** lavarsi; **wash up** *vi* (BRIT) lavare i piatti; (US) darsi una lavata; **washbasin** (US **washbowl**) *n* lavabo; **wash cloth** (US) *n* pezzuola (per lavarsi); **washer** *n* (*Tech*) rondella; **washing** *n* (*linen etc*) bucato; **washing line** *n* (BRIT) corda del bucato; **washing machine** *n* lavatrice *f*; **washing powder** (BRIT) *n* detersivo (in polvere)
Washington ['wɔʃɪŋtən] *n* Washington *f*
wash: **washing-up** *n* rigovernatura, lavatura dei piatti; **washing-up liquid** *n* detersivo liquido (per stoviglie); **washroom** *n* gabinetto
wasn't ['wɔznt] = **was not**
wasp [wɔsp] *n* vespa
waste [weɪst] *n* spreco; (*of time*) perdita; (*rubbish*) rifiuti *mpl*; (*also*: **household ~**) immondizie *fpl* ▷ *adj* (*material*) di scarto; (*food*) avanzato(-a); (*land*) incolto(-a) ▷ *vt* sprecare; **waste ground** (BRIT) *n* terreno incolto *or* abbandonato; **wastepaper basket** ['weɪstpeɪpə-] *n* cestino per la carta straccia
watch [wɔtʃ] *n* (*also*: **wrist ~**) orologio (da polso); (*act of watching, vigilance*) sorveglianza; (*guard*: *Mil, Naut*) guardia; (*Naut*: *spell of duty*) quarto ▷ *vt* (*look at*) osservare; (: *match, programme*) guardare; (*spy on, guard*) sorvegliare, tenere d'occhio; (*be careful of*) fare attenzione a ▷ *vi* osservare, guardare; (*keep guard*) fare *or* montare la guardia; **watch out** *vi* fare attenzione; **watchdog** *n* (*also fig*) cane *m* da guardia; **watch strap** *n* cinturino da orologio
water ['wɔːtə^r] *n* acqua ▷ *vt* (*plant*) annaffiare ▷ *vi* (*eyes*) lacrimare; (*mouth*): **to make sb's mouth ~** far venire l'acquolina in bocca a qn; **in British ~s** nelle acque territoriali britanniche; **water down** *vt* (*milk*) diluire; (*fig*: *story*) edulcorare; **watercolour** (US **watercolor**) *n* acquerello; **watercress** *n* crescione *m*; **waterfall** *n* cascata; **watering can** *n* annaffiatoio; **watermelon** *n* anguria, cocomero; **waterproof** *adj* impermeabile; **water-skiing** *n* sci *m* acquatico
watt [wɔt] *n* watt *m inv*
wave [weɪv] *n* onda; (*of hand*) gesto, segno; (*in hair*) ondulazione *f*; (*fig*: *surge*) ondata ▷ *vi* fare un cenno con la mano; (*branches, grass*) ondeggiare; (*flag*) sventolare ▷ *vt* (*hand*) fare un gesto con; (*handkerchief*) sventolare; (*stick*) brandire; **wavelength** *n* lunghezza d'onda
waver ['weɪvə^r] *vi* esitare; (*voice*) tremolare
wavy ['weɪvɪ] *adj* ondulato(-a); ondeggiante
wax [wæks] *n* cera ▷ *vt* dare la cera a; (*car*) lucidare ▷ *vi* (*moon*) crescere
way [weɪ] *n* via, strada; (*path, access*) passaggio; (*distance*) distanza; (*direction*) parte *f*, direzione *f*; (*manner*) modo, stile *m*; (*habit*) abitudine *f*; **which ~? — this ~** da che parte *or* in quale direzione? — da questa parte *or* per di qua; **on the ~** (*en route*) per strada; **to be on one's ~** essere in cammino *or* sulla strada; **to be in the ~** bloccare il passaggio; (*fig*) essere tra i piedi *or* d'impiccio; **to go out of one's ~ to do** (*fig*) mettercela tutta *or* fare di tutto per fare; **under ~** (*project*) in corso; **to lose one's ~** perdere la strada; **in a ~** in un certo senso; **in**

some ~s sotto certi aspetti; **no ~!** (*inf*) neanche per idea!; **by the ~ ...** a proposito ...; **"~ in"** (BRIT) "entrata", "ingresso"; **"~ out"** (BRIT) "uscita"; **the ~ back** la strada del ritorno; **"give ~"** (BRIT: *Aut*) "dare la precedenza"

W.C. ['dʌblju'si:] (BRIT) *n* W.C. *m inv*, gabinetto

we [wi:] *pl pron* noi

weak [wi:k] *adj* debole; (*health*) precario(-a); (*beam etc*) fragile; (*tea*) leggero(-a); **weaken** *vi* indebolirsi ▷ *vt* indebolire; **weakness** *n* debolezza; (*fault*) punto debole, difetto; **to have a weakness for** avere un debole per

wealth [wɛlθ] *n* (*money, resources*) ricchezza, ricchezze *fpl*; (*of details*) abbondanza, profusione *f*; **wealthy** *adj* ricco(-a)

weapon ['wɛpən] *n* arma; **~s of mass destruction** armi *mpl* di distruzione di massa

wear [wɛəʳ] (*pt* **wore**, *pp* **worn**) *n* (*use*) uso; (*damage through use*) logorio, usura; (*clothing*): **sports/ baby ~** abbigliamento sportivo/per neonati ▷ *vt* (*clothes*) portare; (*put on*) mettersi; (*damage*: *through use*) consumare ▷ *vi* (*last*) durare; (*rub etc through*) consumarsi; **evening ~** abiti *mpl or* tenuta da sera; **wear off** *vi* sparire lentamente; **wear out** *vt* consumare; (*person, strength*) esaurire

weary ['wɪərɪ] *adj* stanco(-a) ▷ *vi* **to ~ of** stancarsi di

weasel ['wi:zl] *n* (*Zool*) donnola

weather ['wɛðəʳ] *n* tempo ▷ *vt* (*storm, crisis*) superare; **what's the ~ like?** che tempo fa?; **under the ~** (*fig*: *ill*) poco bene; **weather forecast** *n* previsioni *fpl* del tempo, bollettino meteorologico

weave [wi:v] (*pt* **wove**, *pp* **woven**) *vt* (*cloth*) tessere; (*basket*) intrecciare

web [wɛb] *n* (*of spider*) ragnatela; (*on foot*) palma; (*fabric, also fig*) tessuto; **the (World Wide) W~** la Rete; **webcam** ['wɛbkæm] *n* webcam *f inv*; **web page** *n* (*Comput*) pagina *f* web *inv*; **website** *n* (*Comput*) sito (Internet)

wed [wɛd] (*pt, pp* **wedded**) *vt* sposare ▷ *vi* sposarsi

we'd [wi:d] = **we had**; **we would**

Wed. *abbr* (= *Wednesday*) mer.

wedding ['wɛdɪŋ] *n* matrimonio; **wedding anniversary** *n* anniversario di matrimonio; **wedding day** *n* giorno delle nozze *or* del matrimonio; **wedding dress** *n* abito nuziale; **wedding ring** *n* fede *f*

wedge [wɛdʒ] *n* (*of wood etc*) zeppa; (*of cake*) fetta ▷ *vt* (*fix*) fissare con zeppe; (*pack tightly*) incastrare

Wednesday ['wɛdnzdɪ] *n* mercoledì *m inv*

wee [wi:] (*Scottish*) *adj* piccolo(-a)

weed [wi:d] *n* erbaccia ▷ *vt* diserbare; **weedkiller** *n* diserbante *m*

week [wi:k] *n* settimana; **a ~ today/on Friday** oggi/venerdì a otto; **weekday** *n* giorno feriale; (*Comm*) giornata lavorativa; **weekend** *n* fine settimana *m or f inv*, weekend *m inv*; **weekly** *adv* ogni settimana, settimanalmente ▷ *adj* settimanale ▷ *n* settimanale *m*

weep [wi:p] (*pt, pp* **wept**) *vi* (*person*) piangere

weigh [weɪ] *vt, vi* pesare; **to ~ anchor** salpare l'ancora; **weigh up** *vt* valutare

weight [weɪt] *n* peso; **to lose/ put on ~** dimagrire/ingrassare; **weightlifting** *n* sollevamento pesi

weir [wɪəʳ] *n* diga

weird [wɪəd] *adj* strano(-a), bizzarro(-a); (*eerie*) soprannaturale

welcome ['wɛlkəm] *adj* benvenuto(-a) ▷ *n* accoglienza, benvenuto ▷ *vt* dare il benvenuto a; (*be glad of*) rallegrarsi di; **thank you — you're ~!** grazie — prego!

weld [wɛld] *n* saldatura ▷ *vt* saldare
welfare ['wɛlfɛəʳ] *n* benessere *m*; **welfare state** *n* stato assistenziale
well [wɛl] *n* pozzo ▷ *adv* bene ▷ *adj* **to be ~** (*person*) stare bene ▷ *excl* allora!; ma!; ebbene!; **as ~** anche; **as ~ as** così come; oltre a; **~ done!** bravo(-a)!; **get ~ soon!** guarisci presto!; **to do ~** andare bene
we'll [wiːl] = **we will**; **we shall**
well: **well-behaved** *adj* ubbidiente; **well-built** *adj* (*person*) ben fatto(-a); **well-dressed** *adj* ben vestito(-a), vestito(-a) bene
wellies (*inf*) ['welɪz] *npl* (BRIT) stivali *mpl* di gomma
well: **well-known** *adj* noto(-a), famoso(-a); **well-off** *adj* benestante, danaroso(-a); **well-paid** [wel'peɪd] *adj* ben pagato(-a)
Welsh [wɛlʃ] *adj* gallese ▷ *n* (*Ling*) gallese *m*; **Welshman** (*irreg*) *n* gallese *m*; **Welshwoman** (*irreg*) *n* gallese *f*
went [wɛnt] *pt of* **go**
wept [wɛpt] *pt, pp of* **weep**
were [wəːʳ] *pt of* **be**
we're [wɪəʳ] = **we are**
weren't [wəːnt] = **were not**
west [wɛst] *n* ovest *m*, occidente *m*, ponente *m* ▷ *adj* (a) ovest *inv*, occidentale ▷ *adv* verso ovest; **the W~** l'Occidente *m*; **westbound** ['wɛstbaund] *adj* (*traffic*) diretto(-a) a ovest; (*carriageway*) ovest *inv*; **western** *adj* occidentale, dell'ovest ▷ *n* (*Cinema*) western *m inv*; **West Indian** *adj* delle Indie Occidentali ▷ *n* abitante *m/f* delle Indie Occidentali; **West Indies** [-'ɪndɪz] *npl* Indie *fpl* Occidentali
wet [wɛt] *adj* umido(-a), bagnato(-a); (*soaked*) fradicio(-a); (*rainy*) piovoso(-a) ▷ *n* (BRIT: *Pol*) politico moderato; **to get ~** bagnarsi; **"~ paint"** "vernice fresca"; **wetsuit** *n* tuta da sub
we've [wiːv] = **we have**
whack [wæk] *vt* picchiare, battere
whale [weɪl] *n* (*Zool*) balena
wharf [wɔːf] (*pl* **wharves**) *n* banchina

KEYWORD

what [wɔt] *adj* **1** (*in direct/indirect questions*) che; quale; **what size is it?** che taglia è?; **what colour is it?** di che colore è?; **what books do you want?** quali *or* che libri vuole?
2 (*in exclamations*) che; **what a mess!** che disordine!
▷ *pron* **1** (*interrogative*) che cosa, cosa, che; **what are you doing?** che *or* (che) cosa fai?; **what are you talking about?** di che cosa parli?; **what is it called?** come si chiama?; **what about me?** e io?; **what about doing ...?** e se facessimo ...?
2 (*relative*) ciò che, quello che; **I saw what you did/was on the table** ho visto quello che hai fatto/quello che era sul tavolo
3 (*indirect use*) (che) cosa; **he asked me what she had said** mi ha chiesto che cosa avesse detto; **tell me what you're thinking about** dimmi a cosa stai pensando
▷ *excl* (*disbelieving*) cosa!, come!

whatever [wɔt'ɛvə] *adj*: **~ book** qualunque *or* qualsiasi libro + *sub*
▷ *pron* **do ~ is necessary/you want** faccia qualunque *or* qualsiasi cosa sia necessaria/lei voglia; **~ happens** qualunque cosa accada; **no reason ~** *or* **whatsoever** nessuna ragione affatto *or* al mondo; **nothing ~** proprio niente
whatsoever [wɔtsəu'ɛvə] *adj* = **whatever**
wheat [wiːt] *n* grano, frumento
wheel [wiːl] *n* ruota; (*Aut*: *also*: **steering ~**) volante *m*; (*Naut*) (ruota del) timone *m* ▷ *vt* spingere ▷ *vi*

(*birds*) roteare; (*also:* **~ round**) girare; **wheelbarrow** *n* carriola; **wheelchair** *n* sedia a rotelle; **wheel clamp** *n* (*Aut*) *morsa che blocca la ruota di una vettura in sosta vietata*

wheeze [wiːz] *vi* ansimare

KEYWORD

when [wɛn] *adv* quando; **when did it happen?** quando è successo?
▷ *conj* 1 (*at, during, after the time that*) quando; **she was reading when I came in** quando sono entrato lei leggeva; **that was when I needed you** era allora che avevo bisogno di te
2 (*on, at which*): **on the day when I met him** il giorno in cui l'ho incontrato; **one day when it was raining** un giorno che pioveva
3 (*whereas*) quando, mentre; **you said I was wrong when in fact I was right** mi hai detto che avevo torto, quando in realtà avevo ragione

whenever [wɛn'ɛvə] *adv* quando mai ▷ *conj* quando; (*every time that*) ogni volta che

where [wɛəʳ] *adv, conj* dove; **this is ~** è qui che; **whereabouts** *adv* dove ▷ *n* **sb's whereabouts** luogo dove qn si trova; **whereas** *conj* mentre; **whereby** *pron* per cui; **wherever** [-'ɛvəʳ] *conj* dovunque + *sub*; (*interrogative*) dove mai

whether ['wɛðəʳ] *conj* se; **I don't know ~ to accept or not** non so se accettare o no; **it's doubtful ~** è poco probabile che; **~ you go or not** che lei vada o no

KEYWORD

which [wɪtʃ] *adj* 1 (*interrogative: direct, indirect*) quale; **which picture do you want?** quale quadro vuole?; **which one?** quale?; **which one of you did it?** chi di voi lo ha fatto?
2: **in which case** nel qual caso
▷ *pron* 1 (*interrogative*) quale; **which (of these) are yours?** quali di questi sono suoi?; **which of you are coming?** chi di voi viene?
2 (*relative*) che; (: *indirect*) cui, il (la) quale; **the apple which you ate/ which is on the table** la mela che hai mangiato/che è sul tavolo; **the chair on which you are sitting** la sedia sulla quale *or* su cui sei seduto; **he said he knew, which is true** ha detto che lo sapeva, il che è vero; **after which** dopo di che

whichever [wɪtʃ'ɛvə] *adj* **take ~ book you prefer** prenda qualsiasi libro che preferisce; **~ book you take** qualsiasi libro prenda

while [waɪl] *n* momento ▷ *conj* mentre; (*as long as*) finché; (*although*) sebbene + *sub*; per quanto + *sub*; **for a ~** per un po'

whilst [waɪlst] *conj* = **while**

whim [wɪm] *n* capriccio

whine [waɪn] *n* gemito ▷ *vi* gemere; uggiolare; piagnucolare

whip [wɪp] *n* frusta; (*for riding*) frustino; (*Pol: person*) capogruppo (*che sovrintende alla disciplina dei colleghi di partito*) ▷ *vt* frustare; (*cream, eggs*) sbattere; **whipped cream** *n* panna montata

whirl [wəːl] *vt* (far) girare rapidamente, (far) turbinare ▷ *vi* (*dancers*) volteggiare; (*leaves, water*) sollevarsi in vortice

whisk [wɪsk] *n* (*Culin*) frusta; frullino ▷ *vt* sbattere, frullare; **to ~ sb away** *or* **off** portar via qn a tutta velocità

whiskers ['wɪskəz] *npl* (*of animal*) baffi *mpl*; (*of man*) favoriti *mpl*

whisky ['wɪskɪ] (*US, Ireland* **whiskey**) *n* whisky *m inv*

whisper ['wɪspəʳ] *n* sussurro ▷ *vt, vi* sussurrare

whistle ['wɪsl] *n* (*sound*) fischio; (*object*) fischietto ▷ *vi* fischiare
white [waɪt] *adj* bianco(-a); (*with fear*) pallido(-a) ▷ *n* bianco; (*person*) bianco(-a); **whiteboard** ['waɪtbɔːd] *n* lavagna bianca; **White House** *n* Casa Bianca; **whitewash** *n* (*paint*) bianco di calce ▷ *vt* imbiancare; (*fig*) coprire
whiting ['waɪtɪŋ] *n inv* (*fish*) merlango
Whitsun ['wɪtsn] *n* Pentecoste *f*
whittle ['wɪtl] *vt*: **to ~ away, ~ down** ridurre, tagliare
whizz [wɪz] *vi*: **to ~ past** *or* **by** passare sfrecciando

KEYWORD

who [huː] *pron* 1 (*interrogative*) chi; **who is it?, who's there?** chi è?
2 (*relative*) che; **the man who spoke to me** l'uomo che ha parlato con me; **those who can swim** quelli che sanno nuotare

whoever [huː'ɛvə] *pron*: **~ finds it** chiunque lo trovi; **ask ~ you like** lo chieda a chiunque vuole; **~ she marries** chiunque sposerà, non importa chi sposerà; **~ told you that?** chi mai gliel'ha detto?
whole [həul] *adj* (*complete*) tutto(-a), completo(-a); (*not broken*) intero(-a), intatto(-a) ▷ *n* (*all*): **the ~ of** tutto(-a) il (la); (*entire unit*) tutto; (*not broken*) tutto; **the ~ of the town** tutta la città, la città intera; **on the ~, as a ~** nel complesso, nell'insieme; **wholefood(s)** *n(pl)* cibo integrale; **wholeheartedly** [həul'hɑːtɪdlɪ] *adv* sentitamente, di tutto cuore; **wholemeal** *adj* (*bread, flour*) integrale; **wholesale** *n* commercio *or* vendita all'ingrosso ▷ *adj* all'ingrosso; (*destruction*) totale; **wholewheat** *adj* = **wholemeal**;
wholly *adv* completamente, del tutto

KEYWORD

whom [huːm] *pron* 1 (*interrogative*) chi; **whom did you see?** chi hai visto?; **to whom did you give it?** a chi lo hai dato?
2 (*relative*) che, *prep* + il (la) quale (*check syntax of Italian verb used*); **the man whom I saw/to whom I spoke** l'uomo che ho visto/al quale ho parlato

whore [hɔː] (*inf*: *pej*) *n* puttana

KEYWORD

whose [huːz] *adj* 1 (*possessive*: *interrogative*) di chi; **whose book is this?, whose is this book?** di chi è questo libro?; **whose daughter are you?** di chi sei figlia?
2 (*possessive*: *relative*): **the man whose son you rescued** l'uomo il cui figlio hai salvato; **the girl whose sister you were speaking to** la ragazza alla cui sorella stavi parlando
▷ *pron* di chi; **whose is this?** di chi è questo?; **I know whose it is** so di chi è

KEYWORD

why [waɪ] *adv* perché; **why not?** perché no?; **why not do it now?** perché non farlo adesso?
▷ *conj* **I wonder why he said that** mi chiedo perché l'abbia detto; **that's not why I'm here** non è questo il motivo per cui sono qui; **the reason why** il motivo per cui
▷ *excl* (*surprise*) ma guarda un po'!; (*remonstrating*) ma (via)!; (*explaining*) ebbene!

wicked ['wɪkɪd] *adj* cattivo(-a),

malvagio(-a); maligno(-a); perfido(-a)

wicket ['wɪkɪt] *n* (*Cricket*) porta; area tra le due porte

wide [waɪd] *adj* largo(-a); (*area, knowledge*) vasto(-a); (*choice*) ampio(-a) ▷ *adv* **to open ~** spalancare; **to shoot ~** tirare a vuoto *or* fuori bersaglio; **widely** *adv* (*differing*) molto, completamente; (*travelled, spaced*) molto; (*believed*) generalmente; **widen** *vt* allargare, ampliare; **wide open** *adj* spalancato(-a); **widespread** *adj* (*belief etc*) molto *or* assai diffuso(-a)

widow ['wɪdəu] *n* vedova; **widower** *n* vedovo

width [wɪdθ] *n* larghezza

wield [wiːld] *vt* (*sword*) maneggiare; (*power*) esercitare

wife [waɪf] (*pl* **wives**) *n* moglie *f*

WiFi ['waɪfaɪ] *n* WiFi *m*

wig [wɪg] *n* parrucca

wild [waɪld] *adj* selvatico(-a); selvaggio(-a); (*sea, weather*) tempestoso(-a); (*idea, life*) folle; stravagante; (*applause*) frenetico(-a); **wilderness** ['wɪldənɪs] *n* deserto; **wildlife** *n* natura; **wildly** *adv* selvaggiamente; (*applaud*) freneticamente; (*hit, guess*) a casaccio; (*happy*) follemente

KEYWORD

will [wɪl] (*pt, pp* **willed**) *aux vb* **1** (*forming future tense*): **I will finish it tomorrow** lo finirò domani; **I will have finished it by tomorrow** lo finirò entro domani; **will you do it? — yes I will/no I won't** lo farai? — sì (lo farò)/no (non lo farò)

2 (*in conjectures, predictions*): **he will** *or* **he'll be there by now** dovrebbe essere arrivato ora; **that will be the postman** sarà il postino

3 (*in commands, requests, offers*): **will you be quiet!** vuoi stare zitto?; **will you come?** vieni anche tu?; **will you help me?** mi aiuti?, mi puoi aiutare?; **will you have a cup of tea?** vorrebbe una tazza di tè?; **I won't put up with it!** non lo accetterò!

▷ *vt* **to will sb to do** volere che qn faccia; **he willed himself to go on** continuò grazie a un grande sforzo di volontà

▷ *n* volontà; testamento

willing ['wɪlɪŋ] *adj* volonteroso(-a); **~ to do** disposto(-a) a fare; **willingly** *adv* volentieri

willow ['wɪləu] *n* salice *m*

willpower ['wɪlpauə^r] *n* forza di volontà

wilt [wɪlt] *vi* appassire

win [wɪn] (*pt, pp* **won**) *n* (*in sports etc*) vittoria ▷ *vt* (*battle, prize, money*) vincere; (*popularity*) conquistare ▷ *vi* vincere; **win over** *vt* convincere

wince [wɪns] *vi* trasalire

wind[1] [waɪnd] (*pt, pp* **wound**) *vt* attorcigliare; (*wrap*) avvolgere; (*clock, toy*) caricare ▷ *vi* (*road, river*) serpeggiare; **wind down** *vt* (*car window*) abbassare; (*fig: production, business*) diminuire; **wind up** *vt* (*clock*) caricare; (*debate*) concludere

wind[2] [wɪnd] *n* vento; (*Med*) flatulenza; (*breath*) respiro, fiato ▷ *vt* (*take breath away*) far restare senza fiato; **~ power** energia eolica

windfall ['wɪndfɔːl] *n* (*money*) guadagno insperato

winding ['waɪndɪŋ] *adj* (*road*) serpeggiante; (*staircase*) a chiocciola

windmill ['wɪndmɪl] *n* mulino a vento

window ['wɪndəu] *n* finestra; (*in car, train, plane*) finestrino; (*in shop etc*) vetrina; (*also:* **~ pane**) vetro; **I'd like a ~ seat** vorrei un posto vicino al finestrino; **window box** *n* cassetta da fiori; **window cleaner** *n* (*person*) pulitore *m* di finestre; **window pane**

n vetro; **window seat** *n* posto finestrino; **windowsill** *n* davanzale *m*

windscreen ['wɪndskriːn] (*US* **windshield**) *n* parabrezza *m inv*; **windscreen wiper** (*US* **windshield wiper**) *n* tergicristallo

windsurfing ['wɪndsəːfɪŋ] *n* windsurf *m inv*

windy ['wɪndɪ] *adj* ventoso(-a); **it's ~** c'è vento

wine [waɪn] *n* vino; **wine bar** *n* enoteca (*per degustazione*); **wine glass** *n* bicchiere *m* da vino; **wine list** *n* lista dei vini; **wine tasting** *n* degustazione *f* dei vini

wing [wɪŋ] *n* ala; (*Aut*) fiancata; **wing mirror** *n* (BRIT) specchietto retrovisore esterno

wink [wɪŋk] *n* ammiccamento ▷ *vi* ammiccare, fare l'occhiolino; (*light*) baluginare

winner ['wɪnə^r] *n* vincitore(-trice)

winning ['wɪnɪŋ] *adj* (*team, goal*) vincente; (*smile*) affascinante

winter ['wɪntə^r] *n* inverno; **winter sports** *npl* sport *mpl* invernali; **wintertime** *n* inverno, stagione *f* invernale

wipe [waɪp] *n* pulita, passata ▷ *vt* pulire (strofinando); (*erase*: *tape*) cancellare; **wipe out** *vt* (*debt*) pagare, liquidare; (*memory*) cancellare; (*destroy*) annientare; **wipe up** *vt* asciugare

wire ['waɪə^r] *n* filo; (*Elec*) filo elettrico; (*Tel*) telegramma *m* ▷ *vt* (*house*) fare l'impianto elettrico di; (*also*: **~ up**) collegare, allacciare; (*person*) telegrafare a

wiring ['waɪərɪŋ] *n* impianto elettrico

wisdom ['wɪzdəm] *n* saggezza; (*of action*) prudenza; **wisdom tooth** *n* dente *m* del giudizio

wise [waɪz] *adj* saggio(-a); prudente; giudizioso(-a)

wish [wɪʃ] *n* (*desire*) desiderio; (*specific desire*) richiesta ▷ *vt* desiderare, volere; **best ~es** (*on birthday etc*) i migliori auguri; **with best ~es** (*in letter*) cordiali saluti, con i migliori saluti; **to ~ sb goodbye** dire arrivederci a qn; **he ~ed me well** mi augurò di riuscire; **to ~ to do/sb to do** desiderare *or* volere fare/che qn faccia; **to ~ for** desiderare

wistful ['wɪstful] *adj* malinconico(-a)

wit [wɪt] *n* (*also*: **~s**) intelligenza; presenza di spirito; (*wittiness*) spirito, arguzia; (*person*) bello spirito

witch [wɪtʃ] *n* strega

KEYWORD

with [wɪð, wɪθ] *prep* **1** (*in the company of*) con; **I was with him** ero con lui; **we stayed with friends** siamo stati da amici; **I'll be with you in a minute** vengo subito

2 (*descriptive*) con; **a room with a view** una stanza con vista sul mare (*or* sulle montagne *etc*); **the man with the grey hat/blue eyes** l'uomo con il cappello grigio/gli occhi blu

3 (*indicating manner, means, cause*): **with tears in her eyes** con le lacrime agli occhi; **red with anger** rosso dalla rabbia; **to shake with fear** tremare di paura

4: **I'm with you** (*I understand*) la seguo; **to be with it** (*inf*: *up-to-date*) essere alla moda; (: *alert*) essere sveglio(-a)

withdraw [wɪθ'drɔː] (*irreg*: *like* **draw**) *vt* ritirare; (*money from bank*) ritirare; prelevare ▷ *vi* ritirarsi; **withdrawal** *n* ritiro; prelievo; (*of army*) ritirata; **withdrawal symptoms** *n* (*Med*) crisi *f* di astinenza; **withdrawn** *adj* (*person*) distaccato(-a)

withdrew [wɪθ'druː] *pt of* **withdraw**

wither ['wɪðə^r] *vi* appassire

withhold [wɪθ'həuld] (*irreg*: *like* **hold**) *vt* (*money*) trattenere; (*permission*): **to**

~ (from) rifiutare (a); (*information*): **to ~ (from)** nascondere (a)
within [wɪð'ɪn] *prep* all'interno; (*in time, distances*) entro ▷ *adv* all'interno, dentro; **~ reach (of)** alla portata (di); **~ sight (of)** in vista (di); **~ a mile of** entro un miglio da; **~ the week** prima della fine della settimana
without [wɪð'aut] *prep* senza; **to go ~ sth** fare a meno di qc
withstand [wɪθ'stænd] (*irreg*: *like* **stand**) *vt* resistere a
witness ['wɪtnɪs] *n* (*person, also Law*) testimone *m/f* ▷ *vt* (*event*) essere testimone di; (*document*) attestare l'autenticità di
witty ['wɪtɪ] *adj* spiritoso(-a)
wives [waɪvz] *npl of* **wife**
wizard ['wɪzəd] *n* mago
wk *abbr* = **week**
wobble ['wɔbl] *vi* tremare; (*chair*) traballare
woe [wəu] *n* dolore *m*; disgrazia
woke [wəuk] *pt of* **wake**
woken ['wəukn] *pp of* **wake**
wolf [wulf] (*pl* **wolves**) *n* lupo
woman ['wumən] (*pl* **women**) *n* donna
womb [wu:m] *n* (*Anat*) utero
women ['wɪmɪn] *npl of* **woman**
won [wʌn] *pt, pp of* **win**
wonder ['wʌndə^r] *n* meraviglia ▷ *vi* **to ~ whether/why** domandarsi se/perché; **to ~ at** essere sorpreso(-a) di; meravigliarsi di; **to ~ about** domandarsi di; pensare a; **it's no ~ that** c'è poco *or* non c'è da meravigliarsi che + *sub*; **wonderful** *adj* meraviglioso(-a)
won't [wəunt] = **will not**
wood [wud] *n* legno; (*timber*) legname *m*; (*forest*) bosco; **wooden** *adj* di legno; (*fig*) rigido(-a); inespressivo(-a); **woodwind** *npl* (*Mus*): **the woodwind** i legni; **woodwork** *n* (*craft, subject*) falegnameria
wool [wul] *n* lana; **to pull the ~ over sb's eyes** (*fig*) imbrogliare qn; **woollen** (US **woolen**) *adj* di lana; (*industry*) laniero(-a); **woolly** (US **wooly**) *adj* di lana; (*fig*: *ideas*) confuso(-a)
word [wə:d] *n* parola; (*news*) notizie *fpl* ▷ *vt* esprimere, formulare; **in other ~s** in altre parole; **to break/keep one's ~** non mantenere/mantenere la propria parola; **to have ~s with sb** avere un diverbio con qn; **wording** *n* formulazione *f*; **word processing** *n* elaborazione *f* di testi, word processing *m*; **word processor** *n* word processor *m inv*
wore [wɔ:^{r}] *pt of* **wear**
work [wə:k] *n* lavoro; (*Art, Literature*) opera ▷ *vi* lavorare; (*mechanism, plan etc*) funzionare; (*medicine*) essere efficace ▷ *vt* (*clay, wood etc*) lavorare; (*mine etc*) sfruttare; (*machine*) far funzionare; (*cause*: *effect, miracle*) fare; **to be out of ~** essere disoccupato(-a); **~s** *n* (BRIT: *factory*) fabbrica *npl* (*of clock, machine*) meccanismo; **how does this ~?** come funziona?; **the TV isn't ~ing** la TV non funziona; **to ~ loose** allentarsi; **work out** *vi* (*plans etc*) riuscire, andare bene ▷ *vt* (*problem*) risolvere; (*plan*) elaborare; **it works out at £100** fa 100 sterline; **worker** *n* lavoratore(-trice), operaio(-a); **work experience** *n* (*previous jobs*) esperienze *fpl* lavorative; (*student training placement*) tirocinio; **workforce** *n* forza lavoro; **working class** *n* classe *f* operaia; **working week** *n* settimana lavorativa; **workman** (*irreg*) *n* operaio; **work of art** *n* opera d'arte; **workout** *n* (*Sport*) allenamento; **work permit** *n* permesso di lavoro; **workplace** *n* posto di lavoro; **workshop** *n* officina; (*practical session*) gruppo di lavoro; **work station** *n* stazione *f* di lavoro; **work surface** *n* piano di lavoro; **worktop** *n* piano di lavoro

world [wə:ld] *n* mondo ▷ *cpd* (*champion*) del mondo; (*power, war*) mondiale; **to think the ~ of sb** (*fig*) pensare un gran bene di qn; **World Cup** *n* (*Football*) Coppa del Mondo; **world-wide** *adj* universale; **World-Wide Web** *n* World Wide Web *m*

worm [wə:m] *n* (*also:* **earth~**) verme *m*

worn [wɔ:n] *pp of* **wear** ▷ *adj* usato(-a); **worn-out** *adj* (*object*) consumato(-a), logoro(-a); (*person*) sfinito(-a)

worried ['wʌrɪd] *adj* preoccupato(-a)

worry ['wʌrɪ] *n* preoccupazione *f* ▷ *vt* preoccupare ▷ *vi* preoccuparsi; **worrying** *adj* preoccupante

worse [wə:s] *adj* peggiore ▷ *adv, n* peggio; **a change for the ~** un peggioramento; **worsen** *vt, vi* peggiorare; **worse off** *adj* in condizioni (economiche) peggiori

worship ['wə:ʃɪp] *n* culto ▷ *vt* (*God*) adorare, venerare; (*person*) adorare; **Your W~** (BRIT: *to mayor*) signor sindaco; (: *to judge*) signor giudice

worst [wə:st] *adj* il (la) peggiore ▷ *adv, n* peggio; **at ~** al peggio, per male che vada

worth [wə:θ] *n* valore *m* ▷ *adj* **to be ~** valere; **it's ~ it** ne vale la pena; **it is ~ one's while (to do)** vale la pena (fare); **worthless** *adj* di nessun valore; **worthwhile** *adj* (*activity*) utile; (*cause*) lodevole

worthy ['wə:ðɪ] *adj* (*person*) degno(-a); (*motive*) lodevole; **~ of** degno di

KEYWORD

would [wud] *aux vb* 1 (*conditional tense*): **if you asked him he would do it** se glielo chiedesse lo farebbe; **if you had asked him he would have done it** se glielo avesse chiesto lo avrebbe fatto

2 (*in offers, invitations, requests*): **would you like a biscuit?** vorrebbe *or* vuole un biscotto?; **would you ask him to come in?** lo faccia entrare, per cortesia; **would you open the window please?** apra la finestra, per favore

3 (*in indirect speech*): **I said I would do it** ho detto che l'avrei fatto

4 (*emphatic*): **it WOULD have to snow today!** doveva proprio nevicare oggi!

5 (*insistence*): **she wouldn't do it** non ha voluto farlo

6 (*conjecture*): **it would have been midnight** sarà stato mezzanotte; **it would seem so** sembrerebbe proprio di sì

7 (*indicating habit*): **he would go there on Mondays** andava lì ogni lunedì

wouldn't ['wudnt] = **would not**

wound[1] [waund] *pt, pp of* **wind**[1]

wound[2] [wu:nd] *n* ferita ▷ *vt* ferire

wove [wəuv] *pt of* **weave**

woven ['wəuvn] *pp of* **weave**

wrap [ræp] *vt* avvolgere; (*pack: also:* **~ up**) incartare; **wrapper** *n* (*on chocolate*) carta; (BRIT: *of book*) copertina; **wrapping** ['ræpɪŋ] *n* carta; **wrapping paper** *n* carta da pacchi; (*for gift*) carta da regali

wreath [ri:θ, *pl* ri:ðz] *n* corona

wreck [rɛk] *n* (*sea disaster*) naufragio; (*ship*) relitto; (*pej: person*) rottame *m* ▷ *vt* demolire; (*ship*) far naufragare; (*fig*) rovinare; **wreckage** *n* rottami *mpl*; (*of building*) macerie *fpl*; (*of ship*) relitti *mpl*

wren [rɛn] *n* (*Zool*) scricciolo

wrench [rɛntʃ] *n* (*Tech*) chiave *f*; (*tug*) torsione *f* brusca; (*fig*) strazio ▷ *vt* strappare; storcere; **to ~ sth from** strappare qc a *or* da

wrestle ['rɛsl] *vi* **to ~ (with sb)** lottare (con qn); **wrestler** *n* lottatore(-trice); **wrestling** *n* lotta

wretched ['rɛtʃɪd] *adj* disgraziato(-a); (*inf: weather, holiday*) orrendo(-a), orribile; (*: child, dog*) pestifero(-a)
wriggle ['rɪgl] *vi* (*also:* **~ about**) dimenarsi; (*: snake, worm*) serpeggiare, muoversi serpeggiando
wring [rɪŋ] (*pt, pp* **wrung**) *vt* torcere; (*wet clothes*) strizzare; (*fig*): **to ~ sth out of** strappare qc a
wrinkle ['rɪŋkl] *n* (*on skin*) ruga; (*on paper etc*) grinza ▷ *vt* (*nose*) torcere; (*forehead*) corrugare ▷ *vi* (*skin, paint*) raggrinzirsi
wrist [rɪst] *n* polso
write [raɪt] (*pt* **wrote**, *pp* **written**) *vt, vi* scrivere; **write down** *vt* annotare; (*put in writing*) mettere per iscritto; **write off** *vt* (*debt, plan*) cancellare; **write out** *vt* mettere per iscritto; (*cheque, receipt*) scrivere; **write-off** *n* perdita completa; **writer** *n* autore(-trice), scrittore(-trice)
writing ['raɪtɪŋ] *n* scrittura; (*of author*) scritto, opera; **in ~** per iscritto; **writing paper** *n* carta da lettere
written ['rɪtn] *pp of* **write**
wrong [rɔŋ] *adj* sbagliato(-a); (*not suitable*) inadatto(-a); (*wicked*) cattivo(-a); (*unfair*) ingiusto(-a) ▷ *adv* in modo sbagliato, erroneamente ▷ *n* (*injustice*) torto ▷ *vt* fare torto a; **I took a ~ turning** ho sbagliato strada; **you are ~ to do it** ha torto a farlo; **you are ~ about that, you've got it ~** si sbaglia; **to be in the ~** avere torto; **what's ~?** cosa c'è che non va?; **to go ~** (*person*) sbagliarsi; (*plan*) fallire, non riuscire; (*machine*) guastarsi; **wrongly** *adv* (*incorrectly, by mistake*) in modo sbagliato; **wrong number** *n* (*Tel*): **you've got the wrong number** ha sbagliato numero
wrote [rəut] *pt of* **write**
wrung [rʌŋ] *pt, pp of* **wring**
WWW *n abbr* = **World Wide Web**; **the ~** la Rete

X

XL *abbr* = **extra large**
Xmas ['ɛksməs] *n abbr* = **Christmas**
X-ray ['ɛksreɪ] *n* raggio X; (*photograph*) radiografia ▷ *vt* radiografare
xylophone ['zaɪləfəun] *n* xilofono

y

yacht [jɔt] *n* panfilo, yacht *m inv*; **yachting** *n* yachting *m*, sport *m* della vela

yard [jɑːd] *n* (*of house etc*) cortile *m*; (*measure*) iarda (= *914 mm; 3 feet*); **yard sale** (US) *n vendita di oggetti usati nel cortile di una casa privata*

yarn [jɑːn] *n* filato; (*tale*) lunga storia

yawn [jɔːn] *n* sbadiglio ▷ *vi* sbadigliare

yd. *abbr* = **yard(s)**

yeah [jɛə] (*inf*) *adv* sì

year [jɪə^{r}] *n* anno; (*referring to harvest, wine etc*) annata; **he is 8 ~s old** ha 8 anni; **an eight-~-old child** un(a) bambino(-a) di otto anni; **yearly** *adj* annuale ▷ *adv* annualmente

yearn [jəːn] *vi*: **to ~ for sth/to do** desiderare ardentemente qc/di fare

yeast [jiːst] *n* lievito

yell [jɛl] *n* urlo ▷ *vi* urlare

yellow ['jɛləu] *adj* giallo(-a); **Yellow Pages®** *npl* pagine *fpl* gialle

yes [jɛs] *adv* sì ▷ *n* sì *m inv*; **to say/answer ~** dire/rispondere di sì

yesterday ['jɛstədɪ] *adv* ieri ▷ *n* ieri *m inv*; **~ morning/evening** ieri mattina/sera; **all day ~** ieri per tutta la giornata

yet [jɛt] *adv* ancora; già ▷ *conj* ma, tuttavia; **it is not finished ~** non è ancora finito; **the best ~** finora il migliore; **as ~** finora

yew [juː] *n* tasso (*albero*)

Yiddish ['jɪdɪʃ] *n* yiddish *m*

yield [jiːld] *n* produzione *f*, resa; reddito ▷ *vt* produrre, rendere; (*surrender*) cedere ▷ *vi* cedere; (US: *Aut*) dare la precedenza

yob(bo) ['jɔb(əu)] *n* (BRIT *inf*) bullo

yoga ['jəugə] *n* yoga *m*

yog(h)urt ['jəugət] *n* iogurt *m inv*

yolk [jəuk] *n* tuorlo, rosso d'uovo

KEYWORD

you [juː] *pron* **1** (*subject*) tu; (: *polite form*) lei; (: *pl*) voi; (: *very formal*) loro; **you Italians enjoy your food** a voi Italiani piace mangiare bene; **you and I will go** tu ed io *or* lei ed io andiamo

2 (*object: direct*) ti; la; vi; loro (*after vb*); (: *indirect*) ti; le; vi; loro (*after vb*); **I know you** ti *or* la *or* vi conosco; **I gave it to you** te l'ho dato; gliel'ho dato; ve l'ho dato; l'ho dato loro

3 (*stressed, after prep, in comparisons*) te; lei; voi; loro; **I told YOU to do it** ho detto a TE (*or* a LEI *etc*) di farlo; **she's younger than you** è più giovane di te (*or* lei *etc*)

4 (*impers: one*) si; **fresh air does you good** l'aria fresca fa bene; **you never know** non si sa mai

you'd [juːd] = **you had**; **you would**

you'll [juːl] = **you will**; **you shall**

young [jʌŋ] *adj* giovane ▷ *npl* (*of animal*) piccoli *mpl*; (*people*): **the ~** i giovani, la gioventù; **youngster** *n* giovanotto, ragazzo; (*child*) bambino(-a)

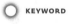

your [jɔːʳ] *adj* il (la) tuo(-a) *pl*, i (le) tuoi (tue); il (la) suo(-a); (*pl*) i (le) suoi (sue); il (la) vostro(-a); (*pl*) i (le) vostri(-e); il (la) loro; (*pl*) i (le) loro; *see also* **my**
you're [juəʳ] = **you are**
yours [jɔːz] *pron* il (la) tuo(-a); (*pl*) i (le) tuoi (tue); (*polite form*) il (la) suo(-a); (*pl*) i (le) suoi (sue); (*pl*) il (la) vostro(-a); (*pl*) i (le) vostri(-e); (: *very formal*) il (la) loro; (*pl*) i (le) loro; *see also* **mine**; **faithfully**; **sincerely**
yourself [jɔː'sɛlf] *pron* (*reflexive*) ti; si; (*after prep*) te; sé; (*emphatic*) tu stesso(-a); lei stesso(-a); **yourselves** *pl pron* (*reflexive*) vi; si; (*after prep*) voi; loro; (*emphatic*) voi stessi(-e); loro stessi(-e); *see also* **oneself**
youth [juːθ, *pl* juːðz] *n* gioventù *f*; (*young man*) giovane *m*, ragazzo; **youth club** *n* centro giovanile; **youthful** *adj* giovane; da giovane; giovanile; **youth hostel** *n* ostello della gioventù
you've [juːv] = **you have**
Yugoslavia ['juːgəu'slaːvɪə] *n* (*Hist*) Jugoslavia

Z

zeal [ziːl] *n* zelo; entusiasmo
zebra ['ziːbrə] *n* zebra; **zebra crossing** (BRIT) *n* (passaggio pedonale a) strisce *fpl*, zebre *fpl*
zero ['zɪərəu] *n* zero
zest [zɛst] *n* gusto; (*Culin*) buccia
zigzag ['zɪgzæg] *n* zigzag *m inv* ▷ *vi* zigzagare
Zimbabwe [zɪm'bɑːbwɪ] *n* Zimbabwe *m*
zinc [zɪŋk] *n* zinco
zip [zɪp] *n* (*also*: **~ fastener**, (US) **zipper**) chiusura *f* or cerniera *f* lampo *inv* ▷ *vt* (*also*: **~ up**) chiudere con una cerniera lampo; **zip code** (US) *n* codice *m* di avviamento postale; **zipper** (US) *n* cerniera *f* lampo *inv*
zit [zɪt] *n* brufolo
zodiac ['zəudɪæk] *n* zodiaco
zone [zəun] *n* (*also Mil*) zona
zoo [zuː] *n* zoo *m inv*
zoology [zuː'ɔlədʒɪ] *n* zoologia
zoom [zuːm] *vi*: **to ~ past** sfrecciare; **zoom lens** *n* zoom *m inv*, obiettivo a

focale variabile

zucchini [zuːˈkiːnɪ] (*US*) *npl* (*courgettes*) zucchine *fpl*

VERB TABLES

Introduction

The **Verb Tables** in the following section contain 32 tables of the most common Italian verbs (some regular and some irregular) in alphabetical order. Each table shows you the following forms: **Present**, **Perfect**, **Imperfect**, **Future**, **Conditional**, **Present Subjunctive**, **Imperative** and the **Past Participle** and **Gerund**.

In order to help you use the verbs shown in Verb Tables correctly, there are also a number of example phrases at the bottom of each page to show the verb as it is used in context.

In Italian there are **regular** verbs (their forms follow the regular patterns of **-are**, **-ere** or **-ire** verbs), and **irregular** verbs (their forms do not follow the normal rules). Examples of regular verbs in these tables are:

parlare (regular **-are** verb, Verb Table 16)
credere (regular **-ere** verb, Verb Table 7)
capire (regular **-ire** verb, Verb Table 6)

Some irregular verbs are irregular in most of their forms, while others may only have a couple of irregular forms.

▶ addormentarsi (to go to sleep)

PRESENT

(io) mi addormento
(tu) ti addormenti
(lui/lei) (lei/Lei) si addormenta
(noi) ci addormentiamo
(voi) vi addormentate
(loro) si addorm*e*ntano

PERFECT

(io) mi sono addormentato/a
(tu) ti sei addormentato/a
(lui/lei) (lei/Lei) si è addormentato/a
(noi) ci siamo addormentati/e
(voi) vi siete addormentati/e
(loro) si sono addormentati/e

IMPERFECT

(io) mi addormentavo
(tu) ti addormentavi
(lui/lei) (lei/Lei) si addormentava
(noi) ci addormentavamo
(voi) vi addormentavate
(loro) si addorment*a*vano

IMPERATIVE

addorm*e*ntati
addormenti*a*moci
addorment*a*tevi

FUTURE

(io) mi addormenter*ò*
(tu) ti addormenterai
(lui/lei) (lei/Lei) si addormenter*à*
(noi) ci addormenteremo
(voi) vi addormenterete
(loro) si addormenteranno

CONDITIONAL

(io) mi addormenterei
(tu) ti addormenteresti
(lui/lei) (lei/Lei) si addormenterebbe
(noi) ci addormenteremmo
(voi) vi addormentereste
(loro) si addormenter*e*bbero

PRESENT SUBJUNCTIVE

(io) mi addormenti
(tu) ti addormenti
(lui/lei) (lei/Lei) si addormenti
(noi) ci addormentiamo
(voi) vi addormentiate
(loro) si addorm*e*ntino

PAST PARTICIPLE

addormentato

GERUND

addormentando

EXAMPLE PHRASES

Non voleva **addormentarsi**. *He didn't want to go to sleep.*
Mi si **è addormentato** un piede. *My foot has gone to sleep.*
Sono stanco: stasera **mi addormenterò** subito. *I'm tired: I'll go to sleep immediately tonight.*

andare (to go)

RESENT

(io)	vado
(tu)	vai
(lui/lei) (lei/Lei)	va
(noi)	andiamo
(voi)	andate
(loro)	vanno

ERFECT

(io)	sono andato/a
(tu)	sei andato/a
(lui/lei) (lei/Lei)	è andato/a
(noi)	siamo andati/e
(voi)	siete andati/e
(loro)	sono andati/e

MPERFECT

(io)	andavo
(tu)	andavi
(lui/lei) (lei/Lei)	andava
(noi)	andavamo
(voi)	andavate
(loro)	and*a*vano

MPERATIVE

ai
ndiamo
ndate

FUTURE

(io)	andr*ò*
(tu)	andrai
(lui/lei) (lei/Lei)	andr*à*
(noi)	andremo
(voi)	andrete
(loro)	andranno

CONDITIONAL

(io)	andrei
(tu)	andresti
(lui/lei) (lei/Lei)	andrebbe
(noi)	andremmo
(voi)	andreste
(loro)	andr*e*bbero

PRESENT SUBJUNCTIVE

(io)	vada
(tu)	vada
(lui/lei) (lei/Lei)	vada
(noi)	andiamo
(voi)	andiate
(loro)	v*a*dano

PAST PARTICIPLE

andato

GERUND

andando

XAMPLE PHRASES

ndremo in Grecia quest'estate. *We're going to Greece this summer.*
u, **andiamo**! *Come on, let's go!*
om'è **andata**? *How did it go?*
ome **va**? – bene, grazie! *How are you? – fine thanks!*
tasera **andrei** volentieri al ristorante. *I'd like to go to a restaurant this evening.*

Remember that subject pronouns are not used very often in Italian.

▶ avere (to have)

PRESENT

(io)	ho
(tu)	hai
(lui/lei) (lei/Lei)	ha
(noi)	abbiamo
(voi)	avete
(loro)	hanno

PERFECT

(io)	ho avuto
(tu)	hai avuto
(lui/lei) (lei/Lei)	ha avuto
(noi)	abbiamo avuto
(voi)	avete avuto
(loro)	hanno avuto

IMPERFECT

(io)	avevo
(tu)	avevi
(lui/lei) (lei/Lei)	aveva
(noi)	avevamo
(voi)	avevate
(loro)	av*e*vano

IMPERATIVE

abbi
abbiamo
abbiate

FUTURE

(io)	avr*ò*
(tu)	avrai
(lui/lei) (lei/Lei)	avr*à*
(noi)	avremo
(voi)	avrete
(loro)	avranno

CONDITIONAL

(io)	avrei
(tu)	avresti
(lui/lei) (lei/Lei)	avrebbe
(noi)	avremmo
(voi)	avreste
(loro)	avr*e*bbero

PRESENT SUBJUNCTIVE

(io)	abbia
(tu)	abbia
(lui/lei) (lei/Lei)	abbia
(noi)	abbiamo
(voi)	abbiate
(loro)	*a*bbiano

PAST PARTICIPLE

avuto

GERUND

avendo

EXAMPLE PHRASES

All'inizio **ha avuto** un sacco di problemi. *He had a lot of problems at first.*
Ho già **mangiato**. *I've already eaten.*
Ha la m*a*cchina nuova. *She's got a new car.*
Aveva la mia et*à*. *He was the same age as me.*
Quanti ne **abbiamo** oggi? *What's the date today?*

Italic letters in Italian words show where stress does not follow the usual rules.

▶ bere (to drink)

PRESENT

(io)	bevo
(tu)	bevi
(lui/lei) (lei/Lei)	beve
(noi)	beviamo
(voi)	bevete
(loro)	bevono

PERFECT

(io)	ho bevuto
(tu)	hai bevuto
(lui/lei) (lei/Lei)	ha bevuto
(noi)	abbiamo bevuto
(voi)	avete bevuto
(loro)	hanno bevuto

IMPERFECT

(io)	bevevo
(tu)	bevevi
(lui/lei) (lei/Lei)	beveva
(noi)	bevevamo
(voi)	bevevate
(loro)	bevevano

IMPERATIVE

bevi
beviamo
bevete

FUTURE

(io)	berrò
(tu)	berrai
(lui/lei) (lei/Lei)	berrà
(noi)	berremo
(voi)	berrete
(loro)	berranno

CONDITIONAL

(io)	berrei
(tu)	berresti
(lui/lei) (lei/Lei)	berrebbe
(noi)	berremmo
(voi)	berreste
(loro)	berrebbero

PRESENT SUBJUNCTIVE

(io)	beva
(tu)	beva
(lui/lei) (lei/Lei)	beva
(noi)	beviamo
(voi)	beviate
(loro)	bevano

PAST PARTICIPLE

bevuto

GERUND

bevendo

EXAMPLE PHRASES

Vuoi **bere** qualcosa? *Would you like something to drink?*
Berrei volentieri un bicchiere di vino bianco. *I'd love a glass of white wine.*
Beveva sei caffè al giorno, ma ora ha smesso. *He used to drink six cups of coffee a day, but he's stopped now.*

Remember that subject pronouns are not used very often in Italian.

▶ cadere (to fall)

PRESENT

(io)	cado
(tu)	cadi
(lui/lei) (lei/Lei)	cade
(noi)	cadiamo
(voi)	cadete
(loro)	c*a*dono

PERFECT

(io)	sono caduto/a
(tu)	sei caduto/a
(lui/lei) (lei/Lei)	è caduto/a
(noi)	siamo caduti/e
(voi)	siete caduti/e
(loro)	sono caduti/e

IMPERFECT

(io)	cadevo
(tu)	cadevi
(lui/lei) (lei/Lei)	cadeva
(noi)	cadevamo
(voi)	cadevate
(loro)	cad*e*vano

IMPERATIVE

cadi
cadiamo
cadete

FUTURE

(io)	cadrò
(tu)	cadrai
(lui/lei) (lei/Lei)	cadr*à*
(noi)	cadremo
(voi)	cadrete
(loro)	cadranno

CONDITIONAL

(io)	cadrei
(tu)	cadresti
(lui/lei) (lei/Lei)	cadrebbe
(noi)	cadremmo
(voi)	cadreste
(loro)	cadr*e*bbero

PRESENT SUBJUNCTIVE

(io)	cada
(tu)	cada
(lui/lei) (lei/Lei)	cada
(noi)	cadiamo
(voi)	cadiate
(loro)	c*a*dano

PAST PARTICIPLE

caduto

GERUND

cadendo

EXAMPLE PHRASES

Ho inciampato e **sono caduta**. *I tripped and fell.*
Il mio compleanno **cade** di lunedì. *My birthday is on a Monday.*
Ti **è caduta** la sciarpa. *You've dropped your scarf.*
Attento che fai **cadere** il bicchiere. *Mind you don't knock over your glass.*

Italic letters in Italian words show where stress does not follow the usual rules.

▶ capire (to understand)

PRESENT

(io)	capisco
(tu)	capisci
(lui/lei) (lei/Lei)	capisce
(noi)	capiamo
(voi)	capite
(loro)	cap*i*scono

PERFECT

(io)	ho capito
(tu)	hai capito
(lui/lei) (lei/Lei)	ha capito
(noi)	abbiamo capito
(voi)	avete capito
(loro)	hanno capito

IMPERFECT

(io)	capivo
(tu)	capivi
(lui/lei) (lei/Lei)	capiva
(noi)	capivamo
(voi)	capivate
(loro)	cap*i*vano

IMPERATIVE

capisci
capiamo
capite

FUTURE

(io)	capir*ò*
(tu)	capirai
(lui/lei) (lei/Lei)	capir*à*
(noi)	capiremo
(voi)	capirete
(loro)	capiranno

CONDITIONAL

(io)	capirei
(tu)	capiresti
(lui/lei) (lei/Lei)	capirebbe
(noi)	capiremmo
(voi)	capireste
(loro)	capir*e*bbero

PRESENT SUBJUNCTIVE

(io)	capisca
(tu)	capisca
(lui/lei) (lei/Lei)	capisca
(noi)	capiamo
(voi)	capiate
(loro)	cap*i*scano

PAST PARTICIPLE

capito

GERUND

capendo

EXAMPLE PHRASES

Va bene, **capisco**. *OK, I understand.*
Non **ho capito** una parola. *I didn't understand a word.*
Fammi **capire**... *Let me get this straight...*
Non ti **capirò** mai. *I'll never understand you.*

Italic letters in Italian words show where stress does not follow the usual rules.

▶ credere (to believe)

PRESENT
(io)	credo
(tu)	credi
(lui/lei) (lei/Lei)	crede
(noi)	crediamo
(voi)	credete
(loro)	credono

PERFECT
(io)	ho creduto
(tu)	hai creduto
(lui/lei) (lei/Lei)	ha creduto
(noi)	abbiamo creduto
(voi)	avete creduto
(loro)	hanno creduto

IMPERFECT
(io)	credevo
(tu)	credevi
(lui/lei) (lei/Lei)	credeva
(noi)	credevamo
(voi)	credevate
(loro)	credevano

IMPERATIVE
credi
crediamo
credete

FUTURE
(io)	crederò
(tu)	crederai
(lui/lei) (lei/Lei)	crederà
(noi)	crederemo
(voi)	crederete
(loro)	crederanno

CONDITIONAL
(io)	crederei
(tu)	crederesti
(lui/lei) (lei/Lei)	crederebbe
(noi)	crederemmo
(voi)	credereste
(loro)	crederebbero

PRESENT SUBJUNCTIVE
(io)	creda
(tu)	creda
(lui/lei) (lei/Lei)	creda
(noi)	crediamo
(voi)	crediate
(loro)	credano

PAST PARTICIPLE
creduto

GERUND
credendo

EXAMPLE PHRASES

Non dirmi che **credi** ai fantasmi! *Don't tell me you believe in ghosts!*
Non **credeva** ai suoi occhi. *She couldn't believe her eyes.*
Non ti **crederò** mai. *I'll never believe you.*

Remember that subject pronouns are not used very often in Italian.

dare (to give)

PRESENT

(io)	do
(tu)	dai
(lui/lei) (lei/Lei)	dà
(noi)	diamo
(voi)	date
(loro)	danno

PERFECT

(io)	ho dato
(tu)	hai dato
(lui/lei) (lei/Lei)	ha dato
(noi)	abbiamo dato
(voi)	avete dato
(loro)	hanno dato

IMPERFECT

(io)	davo
(tu)	davi
(lui/lei) (lei/Lei)	dava
(noi)	davamo
(voi)	davate
(loro)	d*a*vano

IMPERATIVE

dai
diamo
date

FUTURE

(io)	dar*ò*
(tu)	darai
(lui/lei) (lei/Lei)	dar*à*
(noi)	daremo
(voi)	darete
(loro)	daranno

CONDITIONAL

(io)	darei
(tu)	daresti
(lui/lei) (lei/Lei)	darebbe
(noi)	daremmo
(voi)	dareste
(loro)	dar*e*bbero

PRESENT SUBJUNCTIVE

(io)	dia
(tu)	dia
(lui/lei) (lei/Lei)	dia
(noi)	diamo
(voi)	diate
(loro)	d*i*ano

PAST PARTICIPLE

dato

GERUND

dando

EXAMPLE PHRASES

Gli **ho dato** un libro. *I gave him a book.*
Dammelo. *Give it to me.*
La mia finestra **dà** sul giardino. *My window looks onto the garden.*
Domani sera **daranno** un bel film in tv. *There's a good film on TV tomorrow evening.*
Dandoti da fare, potresti ottenere molto di più. *If you exerted yourself you could achieve a lot more.*

Remember that subject pronouns are not used very often in Italian.

▶ dire (to say)

PRESENT

(io)	dico
(tu)	dici
(lui/lei) (lei/Lei)	dice
(noi)	diciamo
(voi)	dite
(loro)	d*i*cono

PERFECT

(io)	ho detto
(tu)	hai detto
(lui/lei) (lei/Lei)	ha detto
(noi)	abbiamo detto
(voi)	avete detto
(loro)	hanno detto

IMPERFECT

(io)	dicevo
(tu)	dicevi
(lui/lei) (lei/Lei)	diceva
(noi)	dicevamo
(voi)	dicevate
(loro)	dic*e*vano

IMPERATIVE

di'
diciamo
dite

FUTURE

(io)	dir*ò*
(tu)	dirai
(lui/lei) (lei/Lei)	dir*à*
(noi)	diremo
(voi)	direte
(loro)	diranno

CONDITIONAL

(io)	direi
(tu)	diresti
(lui/lei) (lei/Lei)	direbbe
(noi)	diremmo
(voi)	direste
(loro)	dir*e*bbero

PRESENT SUBJUNCTIVE

(io)	dica
(tu)	dica
(lui/lei) (lei/Lei)	dica
(noi)	diciamo
(voi)	diciate
(loro)	d*i*cano

PAST PARTICIPLE

detto

GERUND

dicendo

EXAMPLE PHRASES

Ha detto che verrà. *He said he'll come.*
Come si **dice** "quadro" in inglese? *How do you say "quadro" in English?*
Che ne **diresti** di andarcene? *Shall we leave?*
Ti **dirò** un segreto. *I'll tell you a secret.*
Dimmi dov'è. *Tell me where it is.*

▶ dormire (to sleep)

PRESENT

(io)	dormo
(tu)	dormi
(lui/lei) (lei/Lei)	dorme
(noi)	dormiamo
(voi)	dormite
(loro)	d*o*rmono

PERFECT

(io)	ho dormito
(tu)	hai dormito
(lui/lei) (lei/Lei)	ha dormito
(noi)	abbiamo dormito
(voi)	avete dormito
(loro)	hanno dormito

IMPERFECT

(io)	dormivo
(tu)	dormivi
(lui/lei) (lei/Lei)	dormiva
(noi)	dormivamo
(voi)	dormivate
(loro)	dorm*i*vano

IMPERATIVE

dormi
dormiamo
dormite

FUTURE

(io)	dormir*ò*
(tu)	dormirai
(lui/lei) (lei/Lei)	dormir*à*
(noi)	dormiremo
(voi)	dormirete
(loro)	dormiranno

CONDITIONAL

(io)	dormirei
(tu)	dormiresti
(lui/lei) (lei/Lei)	dormirebbe
(noi)	dormiremmo
(voi)	dormireste
(loro)	dormir*e*bbero

PRESENT SUBJUNCTIVE

(io)	dorma
(tu)	dorma
(lui/lei) (lei/Lei)	dorma
(noi)	dormiamo
(voi)	dormiate
(loro)	d*o*rmano

PAST PARTICIPLE

dormito

GERUND

dormendo

EXAMPLE PHRASES

Sta dormendo. *She's sleeping*.
Vado a **dormire**. *I'm going to bed*.
Stanotte **dormirò** come un ghiro. *I'll sleep like a log tonight*.

Italic letters in Italian words show where stress does not follow the usual rules.

▶ **dovere** (to have to)

PRESENT

(io)	devo
(tu)	devi
(lui/lei) (lei/Lei)	deve
(noi)	dobbiamo
(voi)	dovete
(loro)	devono

PERFECT

(io)	ho dovuto
(tu)	hai dovuto
(lui/lei) (lei/Lei)	ha dovuto
(noi)	abbiamo dovuto
(voi)	avete dovuto
(loro)	hanno dovuto

IMPERFECT

(io)	dovevo
(tu)	dovevi
(lui/lei) (lei/Lei)	doveva
(noi)	dovevamo
(voi)	dovevate
(loro)	dovevano

IMPERATIVE

–

FUTURE

(io)	dovrò
(tu)	dovrai
(lui/lei) (lei/Lei)	dovrà
(noi)	dovremo
(voi)	dovrete
(loro)	dovranno

CONDITIONAL

(io)	dovrei
(tu)	dovresti
(lui/lei) (lei/Lei)	dovrebbe
(noi)	dovremmo
(voi)	dovreste
(loro)	dovrebbero

PRESENT SUBJUNCTIVE

(io)	debba
(tu)	debba
(lui/lei) (lei/Lei)	debba
(noi)	dobbiamo
(voi)	dobbiate
(loro)	debbano

PAST PARTICIPLE

dovuto

GERUND

dovendo

EXAMPLE PHRASES

È **dovuto** partire. *He had to leave.*
Devi finire i compiti prima di uscire. *You must finish your homework before you go out.*
Dev'essere tardi. *It must be late.*
Dovrebbe arrivare alle dieci. *He should arrive at ten.*
Gli **dovevo** 30 euro e così l'ho invitato a cena. *I owed him 30 euros so I took him out to dinner.*

Remember that subject pronouns are not used very often in Italian.

essere (to be)

RESENT

(io)	sono
(tu)	sei
(lui/lei) (lei/Lei)	è
(noi)	siamo
(voi)	siete
(loro)	sono

ERFECT

(io)	sono stato/a
(tu)	sei stato/a
(lui/lei) (lei/Lei)	è stato/a
(noi)	siamo stati/e
(voi)	siete stati/e
(loro)	sono stati/e

MPERFECT

(io)	ero
(tu)	eri
(lui/lei) (lei/Lei)	era
(noi)	eravamo
(voi)	eravate
(loro)	*e*rano

MPERATIVE

i
amo
ate

FUTURE

(io)	sar*ò*
(tu)	sarai
(lui/lei) (lei/Lei)	sar*à*
(noi)	saremo
(voi)	sarete
(loro)	saranno

CONDITIONAL

(io)	sarei
(tu)	saresti
(lui/lei) (lei/Lei)	sarebbe
(noi)	saremmo
(voi)	sareste
(loro)	sar*e*bbero

PRESENT SUBJUNCTIVE

(io)	sia
(tu)	sia
(lui/lei) (lei/Lei)	sia
(noi)	siamo
(voi)	siate
(loro)	s*i*ano

PAST PARTICIPLE

stato

GERUND

essendo

XAMPLE PHRASES

ono italiana. *I'm Italian.*
lario **è** appena partito. *Mario has just left.*
iete mai **stati** in Africa? *Have you ever been to Africa?*
uando **è** arrivato *e*rano le quattro in punto. *It was exactly four o'clock when he arrived.*
lla festa ci **saranno** tutti i miei amici. *All my friends will be at the party.*

Italic letters in Italian words show where stress does not follow the usual rules.

▶ fare (to do; make)

PRESENT

(io)	faccio
(tu)	fai
(lui/lei) (lei/Lei)	fa
(noi)	facciamo
(voi)	fate
(loro)	fanno

PERFECT

(io)	ho fatto
(tu)	hai fatto
(lui/lei) (lei/Lei)	ha fatto
(noi)	abbiamo fatto
(voi)	avete fatto
(loro)	hanno fatto

IMPERFECT

(io)	facevo
(tu)	facevi
(lui/lei) (lei/Lei)	faceva
(noi)	facevamo
(voi)	facevate
(loro)	facevano

IMPERATIVE

fai
facciamo
fate

FUTURE

(io)	farò
(tu)	farai
(lui/lei) (lei/Lei)	farà
(noi)	faremo
(voi)	farete
(loro)	faranno

CONDITIONAL

(io)	farei
(tu)	faresti
(lui/lei) (lei/Lei)	farebbe
(noi)	faremmo
(voi)	fareste
(loro)	farebbero

PRESENT SUBJUNCTIVE

(io)	faccia
(tu)	faccia
(lui/lei) (lei/Lei)	faccia
(noi)	facciamo
(voi)	facciate
(loro)	facciano

PAST PARTICIPLE

fatto

GERUND

facendo

EXAMPLE PHRASES

Ho fatto un errore. *I made a mistake.*
Due più due **fa** quattro. *Two and two makes four.*
Cosa **stai facendo**? *What are you doing?*
Fa il medico. *He is a doctor.*
Fa caldo. *It's hot.*

Remember that subject pronouns are not used very often in Italian.

mettere (to put)

RESENT

(io)	metto
(tu)	metti
(lui/lei) (lei/Lei)	mette
(noi)	mettiamo
(voi)	mettete
(loro)	mettono

ERFECT

(io)	ho messo
(tu)	hai messo
(lui/lei) (lei/Lei)	ha messo
(noi)	abbiamo messo
(voi)	avete messo
(loro)	hanno messo

MPERFECT

(io)	mettevo
(tu)	mettevi
(lui/lei) (lei/Lei)	metteva
(noi)	mettevamo
(voi)	mettevate
(loro)	mettevano

PERATIVE

etti
ettiamo
ettete

FUTURE

(io)	metterò
(tu)	metterai
(lui/lei) (lei/Lei)	metterà
(noi)	metteremo
(voi)	metterete
(loro)	metteranno

CONDITIONAL

(io)	metterei
(tu)	metteresti
(lui/lei) (lei/Lei)	metterebbe
(noi)	metteremmo
(voi)	mettereste
(loro)	metterebbero

PRESENT SUBJUNCTIVE

(io)	metta
(tu)	metta
(lui/lei) (lei/Lei)	metta
(noi)	mettiamo
(voi)	mettiate
(loro)	mettano

PAST PARTICIPLE

messo

GERUND

mettendo

XAMPLE PHRASES

ai messo i bambini a letto? *Have you put the children to bed?*
etterò un annuncio sul giornale. *I'll put an advert in the paper.*
ettiti là e aspetta. *Wait there.*
uanto tempo ci **hai messo**? *How long did it take you?*
on **metto** più quelle scarpe. *I don't wear those shoes any more.*

Remember that subject pronouns are not used very often in Italian.

▶ parere (to appear)

PRESENT

(io)	p*a*io
(tu)	pari
(lui/lei) (lei/Lei)	pare
(noi)	pariamo
(voi)	parete
(loro)	p*a*iono

PERFECT

(io)	sono parso/a
(tu)	sei parso/a
(lui/lei) (lei/Lei)	è parso/a
(noi)	siamo parsi/e
(voi)	siete parsi/e
(loro)	sono parsi/e

IMPERFECT

(io)	parevo
(tu)	parevi
(lui/lei) (lei/Lei)	pareva
(noi)	parevamo
(voi)	parevate
(loro)	par*e*vano

IMPERATIVE

pari
pariamo
parete

FUTURE

(io)	parr*ò*
(tu)	parrai
(lui/lei) (lei/Lei)	parr*à*
(noi)	parremo
(voi)	parrete
(loro)	parranno

CONDITIONAL

(io)	parrei
(tu)	parresti
(lui/lei) (lei/Lei)	parrebbe
(noi)	parremmo
(voi)	parreste
(loro)	parr*e*bbero

PRESENT SUBJUNCTIVE

(io)	p*a*ia
(tu)	p*a*ia
(lui/lei) (lei/Lei)	p*a*ia
(noi)	paiamo
(voi)	paiate
(loro)	p*a*iano

PAST PARTICIPLE

parso

GERUND

parendo

EXAMPLE PHRASES

Mi **pare** che sia già arrivato. *I think he's already here.*
Ci **è parso** che foste stanchi. *We thought you were tired.*
Faceva solo ciò che gli **pareva**. *He did just what he wanted.*

Italic letters in Italian words show where stress does not follow the usual rules.

▶ parlare (to speak)

PRESENT

(io)	parlo
(tu)	parli
(lui/lei) (lei/Lei)	parla
(noi)	parliamo
(voi)	parlate
(loro)	*pa*rlano

PERFECT

(io)	ho parlato
(tu)	hai parlato
(lui/lei) (lei/Lei)	ha parlato
(noi)	abbiamo parlato
(voi)	avete parlato
(loro)	hanno parlato

IMPERFECT

(io)	parlavo
(tu)	parlavi
(lui/lei) (lei/Lei)	parlava
(noi)	parlavamo
(voi)	parlavate
(loro)	parl*a*vano

IMPERATIVE

parla
parliamo
parlate

FUTURE

(io)	parler*ò*
(tu)	parlerai
(lui/lei) (lei/Lei)	parler*à*
(noi)	parleremo
(voi)	parlerete
(loro)	parleranno

CONDITIONAL

(io)	parlerei
(tu)	parleresti
(lui/lei) (lei/Lei)	parlerebbe
(noi)	parleremmo
(voi)	parlereste
(loro)	parler*e*bbero

PRESENT SUBJUNCTIVE

(io)	parli
(tu)	parli
(lui/lei) (lei/Lei)	parli
(noi)	parliamo
(voi)	parliate
(loro)	p*a*rlino

PAST PARTICIPLE

parlato

GERUND

parlando

EXAMPLE PHRASES

Pronto, chi **parla**? *Hello, who's speaking?*
Non **parli*a*mone** più. *Let's just forget about it.*
Abbiamo parlato per ore. *We talked for hours.*
Gli **parlerò** di te. *I'll talk to him about you.*
Di cosa **parla** quel libro? *What is that book about?*

Remember that subject pronouns are not used very often in Italian.

▶ piacere (to be pleasing)

PRESENT

(io)	piaccio
(tu)	piaci
(lui/lei) (lei/Lei)	piace
(noi)	piacciamo
(voi)	piacete
(loro)	piacciono

PERFECT

(io)	sono piaciuto/a
(tu)	sei piaciuto/a
(lui/lei) (lei/Lei)	è piaciuto/a
(noi)	siamo piaciuti/e
(voi)	siete piaciuti/e
(loro)	sono piaciuti/e

IMPERFECT

(io)	piacevo
(tu)	piacevi
(lui/lei) (lei/Lei)	piaceva
(noi)	piacevamo
(voi)	piacevate
(loro)	piacevano

IMPERATIVE

piaci
piacciamo
piacciate

FUTURE

(io)	piacerò
(tu)	piacerai
(lui/lei) (lei/Lei)	piacerà
(noi)	piaceremo
(voi)	piacerete
(loro)	piaceranno

CONDITIONAL

(io)	piacerei
(tu)	piaceresti
(lui/lei) (lei/Lei)	piacerebbe
(noi)	piaceremmo
(voi)	piacereste
(loro)	piacerebbero

PRESENT SUBJUNCTIVE

(io)	piaccia
(tu)	piaccia
(lui/lei) (lei/Lei)	piaccia
(noi)	piacciamo
(voi)	piacciate
(loro)	piacciano

PAST PARTICIPLE

piaciuto

GERUND

piacendo

EXAMPLE PHRASES

Questa musica non **mi piace**. *I don't like this music.*
Cosa **ti piacerebbe** fare? *What would you like to do?*
Da piccola non **mi piacevano** i ragni. *When I was little I didn't like spiders.*

Remember that subject pronouns are not used very often in Italian.

potere (to be able)

PRESENT

(io)	posso
(tu)	puoi
(lui/lei) (lei/Lei)	può
(noi)	possiamo
(voi)	potete
(loro)	possono

PERFECT

(io)	ho potuto
(tu)	hai potuto
(lui/lei) (lei/Lei)	ha potuto
(noi)	abbiamo potuto
(voi)	avete potuto
(loro)	hanno potuto

IMPERFECT

(io)	potevo
(tu)	potevi
(lui/lei) (lei/Lei)	poteva
(noi)	potevamo
(voi)	potevate
(loro)	potevano

IMPERATIVE

–

FUTURE

(io)	potrò
(tu)	potrai
(lui/lei) (lei/Lei)	potrà
(noi)	potremo
(voi)	potrete
(loro)	potranno

CONDITIONAL

(io)	potrei
(tu)	potresti
(lui/lei) (lei/Lei)	potrebbe
(noi)	potremmo
(voi)	potreste
(loro)	potrebbero

PRESENT SUBJUNCTIVE

(io)	possa
(tu)	possa
(lui/lei) (lei/Lei)	possa
(noi)	possiamo
(voi)	possiate
(loro)	possano

PAST PARTICIPLE

potuto

GERUND

potendo

EXAMPLE PHRASES

Si **può** visitare il castello tutti i giorni dell'anno. *You can visit the castle any day of the year.*
Non **è potuto** venire. *He couldn't come.*
Non **potrò** venire domani. *I won't be able to come tomorrow.*
Può aver avuto un incidente. *He may have had an accident.*
Potrebbe essere vero. *It could be true.*

Remember that subject pronouns are not used very often in Italian.

▶ prendere (to take)

PRESENT

(io)	prendo
(tu)	prendi
(lui/lei) (lei/Lei)	prende
(noi)	prendiamo
(voi)	prendete
(loro)	pr*e*ndono

PERFECT

(io)	ho preso
(tu)	hai preso
(lui/lei) (lei/Lei)	ha preso
(noi)	abbiamo preso
(voi)	avete preso
(loro)	hanno preso

IMPERFECT

(io)	prendevo
(tu)	prendevi
(lui/lei) (lei/Lei)	prendeva
(noi)	prendevamo
(voi)	prendevate
(loro)	prend*e*vano

IMPERATIVE

prendi
prendiamo
prendete

FUTURE

(io)	prender*ò*
(tu)	prenderai
(lui/lei) (lei/Lei)	prender*à*
(noi)	prenderemo
(voi)	prenderete
(loro)	prenderanno

CONDITIONAL

(io)	prenderei
(tu)	prenderesti
(lui/lei) (lei/Lei)	prenderebbe
(noi)	prenderemmo
(voi)	prendereste
(loro)	prender*e*bbero

PRESENT SUBJUNCTIVE

(io)	prenda
(tu)	prenda
(lui/lei) (lei/Lei)	prenda
(noi)	prendiamo
(voi)	prendiate
(loro)	pr*e*ndano

PAST PARTICIPLE

preso

GERUND

prendendo

EXAMPLE PHRASES

Prendi quella borsa. *Take that bag.*
Ho preso un bel voto. *I got a good mark.*
Prende qualcosa da bere? *Would you like something to drink?*
Per chi mi **prendi**? *Who do you think I am?*

Italic letters in Italian words show where stress does not follow the usual rules.

▶ rimanere (to stay)

PRESENT

(io)	rimango
(tu)	rimani
(lui/lei) (lei/Lei)	rimane
(noi)	rimaniamo
(voi)	rimanete
(loro)	rim*a*ngono

PERFECT

(io)	sono rimasto/a
(tu)	sei rimasto/a
(lui/lei) (lei/Lei)	è rimasto/a
(noi)	siamo rimasti/e
(voi)	siete rimasti/e
(loro)	sono rimasti/e

IMPERFECT

(io)	rimanevo
(tu)	rimanevi
(lui/lei) (lei/Lei)	rimaneva
(noi)	rimanevamo
(voi)	rimanevate
(loro)	riman*e*vano

IMPERATIVE

rimani
rimaniamo
rimanete

FUTURE

(io)	rimarr*ò*
(tu)	rimarrai
(lui/lei) (lei/Lei)	rimarr*à*
(noi)	rimarremo
(voi)	rimarrete
(loro)	rimarranno

CONDITIONAL

(io)	rimarrei
(tu)	rimarresti
(lui/lei) (lei/Lei)	rimarrebbe
(noi)	rimarremmo
(voi)	rimarreste
(loro)	rimarr*e*bbero

PRESENT SUBJUNCTIVE

(io)	rimanga
(tu)	rimanga
(lui/lei) (lei/Lei)	rimanga
(noi)	rimaniamo
(voi)	rimaniate
(loro)	rim*a*ngano

PAST PARTICIPLE

rimasto

GERUND

rimanendo

EXAMPLE PHRASES

Sono rimasto a casa tutto il giorno. *I stayed at home all day.*
Mi piacerebbe **rimanere** qualche altro giorno. *I'd like to stay a few more days.*
Ci **rimarrebbero** molto male. *They'd be very upset.*

Italic letters in Italian words show where stress does not follow the usual rules.

▶ **sapere** (to know)

PRESENT

(io)	so
(tu)	sai
(lui/lei) (lei/Lei)	sa
(noi)	sappiamo
(voi)	sapete
(loro)	sanno

PERFECT

(io)	hai saputo
(tu)	ha saputo
(lui/lei) (lei/Lei)	abbiamo saputo
(noi)	avete saputo
(voi)	hanno saputo
(loro)	ho saputo

IMPERFECT

(io)	sapevo
(tu)	sapevi
(lui/lei) (lei/Lei)	sapeva
(noi)	sapevamo
(voi)	sapevate
(loro)	sapevano

IMPERATIVE

sappi
sappiamo
sappiate

FUTURE

(io)	saprò
(tu)	saprai
(lui/lei) (lei/Lei)	saprà
(noi)	sapremo
(voi)	saprete
(loro)	sapranno

CONDITIONAL

(io)	saprei
(tu)	sapresti
(lui/lei) (lei/Lei)	saprebbe
(noi)	sapremmo
(voi)	sapreste
(loro)	saprebbero

PRESENT SUBJUNCTIVE

(io)	sappia
(tu)	sappia
(lui/lei) (lei/Lei)	sappia
(noi)	sappiamo
(voi)	sappiate
(loro)	sappiano

PAST PARTICIPLE

saputo

GERUND

sapendo

EXAMPLE PHRASES

Sai dove abita? *Do you know where he lives?*
Non **sapeva** andare in bicicletta. *He couldn't ride a bike.*
Sa di fragola. *It tastes of strawberries.*

Remember that subject pronouns are not used very often in Italian.

▶ sc*e*gliere (to choose)

PRESENT

(io) scelgo
(tu) scegli
(lui/lei) (lei/Lei) sc*e*glie
(noi) scegliamo
(voi) scegliete
(loro) sc*e*lgono

PERFECT

(io) ho scelto
(tu) hai scelto
(lui/lei) (lei/Lei) ha scelto
(noi) abbiamo scelto
(voi) avete scelto
(loro) hanno scelto

IMPERFECT

(io) sceglievo
(tu) sceglievi
(lui/lei) (lei/Lei) sceglieva
(noi) sceglievamo
(voi) sceglievate
(loro) scegli*e*vano

IMPERATIVE

scegli
scegliamo
scegliete

FUTURE

(io) sceglier*ò*
(tu) sceglierai
(lui/lei) (lei/Lei) sceglier*à*
(noi) sceglieremo
(voi) sceglierete
(loro) sceglieranno

CONDITIONAL

(io) sceglierei
(tu) sceglieresti
(lui/lei) (lei/Lei) sceglierebbe
(noi) sceglieremmo
(voi) scegliereste
(loro) sceglier*e*bbero

PRESENT SUBJUNCTIVE

(io) scelga
(tu) scelga
(lui/lei) (lei/Lei) scelga
(noi) scegliamo
(voi) scegliate
(loro) sc*e*lgano

PAST PARTICIPLE

scelto

GERUND

scegliendo

EXAMPLE PHRASES

Chi **sceglie** il vino? *Who's going to choose the wine?*
Hai scelto il regalo per lei? *Have you chosen her present?*
Scegli*e*vano sempre il vino più costoso. *They always chose the most expensive wine.*
Scegli la pizza che vuoi. *Choose which pizza you want.*
Non sa ancora quale *a*bito **sceglier*à***. *She hasn't decided yet which dress she'll choose.*
Stavo **scegliendo** le pesche più mature. *I was choosing the ripest peaches.*

Remember that subject pronouns are not used very often in Italian.

▶ sedere (to sit)

PRESENT

(io)	siedo
(tu)	siedi
(lui/lei) (lei/Lei)	siede
(noi)	sediamo
(voi)	sedete
(loro)	si*e*dono

PERFECT

(io)	sono seduto/a
(tu)	sei seduto/a
(lui/lei) (lei/Lei)	è seduto/a
(noi)	siamo seduti/e
(voi)	siete seduti/e
(loro)	sono seduti/e

IMPERFECT

(io)	sedevo
(tu)	sedevi
(lui/lei) (lei/Lei)	sedeva
(noi)	sedevamo
(voi)	sedevate
(loro)	sed*e*vano

IMPERATIVE

siedi
sediamo
sedete

FUTURE

(io)	seder*ò*
(tu)	sederai
(lui/lei) (lei/Lei)	seder*à*
(noi)	sederemo
(voi)	sederete
(loro)	sederanno

CONDITIONAL

(io)	sederei
(tu)	sederei
(lui/lei) (lei/Lei)	sederesti
(noi)	sederebbe
(voi)	sederemmo
(loro)	sedereste

PRESENT SUBJUNCTIVE

(io)	sieda
(tu)	sieda
(lui/lei) (lei/Lei)	sieda
(noi)	sediamo
(voi)	sediate
(loro)	si*e*dano

PAST PARTICIPLE

seduto

GERUND

sedendo

EXAMPLE PHRASES

Era seduta accanto a me. *She was sitting beside me.*
Si **è seduto** per terra. *He sat on the floor.*
Siediti qui! *Sit here!*

Italic letters in Italian words show where stress does not follow the usual rules.

spegnere (to put out)

PRESENT

(io)	spengo
(tu)	spegni
(lui/lei) (lei/Lei)	spegne
(noi)	spegniamo
(voi)	spegnete
(loro)	sp*e*ngono

PERFECT

(io)	ho spento
(tu)	hai spento
(lui/lei) (lei/Lei)	ha spento
(noi)	abbiamo spento
(voi)	avete spento
(loro)	hanno spento

IMPERFECT

(io)	spegnevo
(tu)	spegnevi
(lui/lei) (lei/Lei)	spegneva
(noi)	spegnevamo
(voi)	spegnevate
(loro)	spegn*e*vano

IMPERATIVE

spegni
spegniamo
spegnete

FUTURE

(io)	spegner*ò*
(tu)	spegnerai
(lui/lei) (lei/Lei)	spegner*à*
(noi)	spegneremo
(voi)	spegnerete
(loro)	spegneranno

CONDITIONAL

(io)	spegnerei
(tu)	spegneresti
(lui/lei) (lei/Lei)	spegnerebbe
(noi)	spegneremmo
(voi)	spegnereste
(loro)	spegner*e*bbero

PRESENT SUBJUNCTIVE

(io)	spenga
(tu)	spenga
(lui/lei) (lei/Lei)	spenga
(noi)	spegniamo
(voi)	spegniate
(loro)	sp*e*ngano

PAST PARTICIPLE

spento

GERUND

spegnendo

EXAMPLE PHRASES

Hai spento la sigaretta? *Have you put your cigarette out?*
Spegnete le luci che guardiamo il film. *Turn off the lights and we'll watch the film.*
La luce si **è spenta** all'improvviso. *The light went off suddenly.*

Italic letters in Italian words show where stress does not follow the usual rules.

▶ stare (to be)

PRESENT

(io)	sto
(tu)	stai
(lui/lei) (lei/Lei)	sta
(noi)	stiamo
(voi)	state
(loro)	stanno

PERFECT

(io)	sono stato/a
(tu)	sei stato/a
(lui/lei) (lei/Lei)	è stato/a
(noi)	siamo stati/e
(voi)	siete stati/e
(loro)	sono stati/e

IMPERFECT

(io)	stavo
(tu)	stavi
(lui/lei) (lei/Lei)	stava
(noi)	stavamo
(voi)	stavate
(loro)	st*a*vano

IMPERATIVE

stai
stiamo
state

FUTURE

(io)	star*ò*
(tu)	starai
(lui/lei) (lei/Lei)	star*à*
(noi)	staremo
(voi)	starete
(loro)	staranno

CONDITIONAL

(io)	starei
(tu)	staresti
(lui/lei) (lei/Lei)	starebbe
(noi)	staremmo
(voi)	stareste
(loro)	star*e*bbero

PRESENT SUBJUNCTIVE

(io)	stia
(tu)	stia
(lui/lei) (lei/Lei)	stia
(noi)	stiamo
(voi)	stiate
(loro)	st*i*ano

PAST PARTICIPLE

stato

GERUND

stando

EXAMPLE PHRASES

Sei mai **stato** in Francia? *Have you ever been to France?*
Come **stai**? *How are you?*
Stavo andando a casa. *I was going home.*
A Londra **starò** da amici. *I'll be staying with friends in London.*
Stavo per uscire quando ha squillato il telefono. *I was about to go out when the phone rang.*

Italic letters in Italian words show where stress does not follow the usual rules.

▶ tenere (to hold)

PRESENT

(io)	tengo
(tu)	tieni
(lui/lei) (lei/Lei)	tiene
(noi)	teniamo
(voi)	tenete
(loro)	tengono

PERFECT

(io)	ho tenuto
(tu)	hai tenuto
(lui/lei) (lei/Lei)	ha tenuto
(noi)	abbiamo tenuto
(voi)	avete tenuto
(loro)	hanno tenuto

IMPERFECT

(io)	tenevo
(tu)	tenevi
(lui/lei) (lei/Lei)	teneva
(noi)	tenevamo
(voi)	tenevate
(loro)	tenevano

IMPERATIVE

tieni
teniamo
tenete

FUTURE

(io)	terrò
(tu)	terrai
(lui/lei) (lei/Lei)	terrà
(noi)	terremo
(voi)	terrete
(loro)	terranno

CONDITIONAL

(io)	terrei
(tu)	terresti
(lui/lei) (lei/Lei)	terrebbe
(noi)	terremmo
(voi)	terreste
(loro)	terrebbero

PRESENT SUBJUNCTIVE

(io)	tenga
(tu)	tenga
(lui/lei) (lei/Lei)	tenga
(noi)	teniamo
(voi)	teniate
(loro)	tengano

PAST PARTICIPLE

tenuto

GERUND

tenendo

EXAMPLE PHRASES

Tiene la racchetta con la sinistra. *He holds the racket with his left hand.*
Tieniti forte! *Hold on tight!*
Si **tenevano** per mano. *They were holding hands.*
Tieniti pronta per le cinque. *Be ready by five.*
Tieni, questo è per te. *Here, this is for you*

Remember that subject pronouns are not used very often in Italian.

▶ togliere (to take off)

PRESENT

(io)	tolgo
(tu)	togli
(lui/lei) (lei/Lei)	toglie
(noi)	togliamo
(voi)	togliete
(loro)	t*o*lgono

PERFECT

(io)	ho tolto
(tu)	hai tolto
(lui/lei) (lei/Lei)	ha tolto
(noi)	abbiamo tolto
(voi)	avete tolto
(loro)	hanno tolto

IMPERFECT

(io)	toglievo
(tu)	toglievi
(lui/lei) (lei/Lei)	toglieva
(noi)	toglievamo
(voi)	toglievate
(loro)	togli*e*vano

IMPERATIVE

togli
togliamo
togliete

FUTURE

(io)	toglier*ò*
(tu)	toglierai
(lui/lei) (lei/Lei)	toglier*à*
(noi)	toglieremo
(voi)	toglierete
(loro)	toglieranno

CONDITIONAL

(io)	toglierei
(tu)	toglieresti
(lui/lei) (lei/Lei)	toglierebbe
(noi)	toglieremmo
(voi)	togliereste
(loro)	toglier*e*bbero

PRESENT SUBJUNCTIVE

(io)	tolga
(tu)	tolga
(lui/lei) (lei/Lei)	tolga
(noi)	togliamo
(voi)	togliate
(loro)	t*o*lgano

PAST PARTICIPLE

tolto

GERUND

togliendo

EXAMPLE PHRASES

Togliti il cappotto. *Take off your coat.*
Ho tolto il poster dalla parete. *I took the poster off the wall.*
Mi **toglieranno** due denti. *I'm going to have two teeth out.*

uscire (to go out)

ESENT

(io)	esco
(tu)	esci
(lui/lei) (lei/Lei)	esce
(noi)	usciamo
(voi)	uscite
(loro)	*e*scono

RFECT

(io)	sono uscito/a
(tu)	sei uscito/a
(lui/lei) (lei/Lei)	è uscito/a
(noi)	siamo usciti/e
(voi)	siete usciti/e
(loro)	sono usciti/e

IPERFECT

(io)	uscivo
(tu)	uscivi
(lui/lei) (lei/Lei)	usciva
(noi)	uscivamo
(voi)	uscivate
(loro)	uscivano

IPERATIVE

ci
ciamo
cite

FUTURE

(io)	uscirò
(tu)	uscirai
(lui/lei) (lei/Lei)	uscir*à*
(noi)	usciremo
(voi)	uscirete
(loro)	usciranno

CONDITIONAL

(io)	uscirei
(tu)	usciresti
(lui/lei) (lei/Lei)	uscirebbe
(noi)	usciremmo
(voi)	uscireste
(loro)	uscir*e*bbero

PRESENT SUBJUNCTIVE

(io)	esca
(tu)	esca
(lui/lei) (lei/Lei)	esca
(noi)	usciamo
(voi)	usciate
(loro)	*e*scano

PAST PARTICIPLE

uscito

GERUND

uscendo

AMPLE PHRASES

uscita a comprare il giornale. *She's gone out to buy a newspaper.*
scir*à* dall'ospedale domani. *He's coming out of hospital tomorrow.*
o incontrata che **usciva** dalla farmacia. *I met her coming out of the chemist's.*
rivista **esce** di lunedì. *The magazine comes out on Mondays.*

Italic letters in Italian words show where stress does not follow the usual rules.

▶ valere (to be worth)

PRESENT

(io)	valgo
(tu)	vali
(lui/lei) (lei/Lei)	vale
(noi)	valiamo
(voi)	valete
(loro)	valgono

PERFECT

(io)	sono valso/a
(tu)	sei valso/a
(lui/lei) (lei/Lei)	è valso/a
(noi)	siamo valsi/e
(voi)	siete valsi/e
(loro)	sono valsi/e

IMPERFECT

(io)	valevo
(tu)	valevi
(lui/lei) (lei/Lei)	valeva
(noi)	valevamo
(voi)	valevate
(loro)	valevano

IMPERATIVE

vali
valiamo
valete

FUTURE

(io)	varrò
(tu)	varrai
(lui/lei) (lei/Lei)	varrà
(noi)	varremo
(voi)	varrete
(loro)	varranno

CONDITIONAL

(io)	varrei
(tu)	varresti
(lui/lei) (lei/Lei)	varrebbe
(noi)	varremmo
(voi)	varreste
(loro)	varrebbero

PRESENT SUBJUNCTIVE

(io)	valga
(tu)	valga
(lui/lei) (lei/Lei)	valga
(noi)	valiamo
(voi)	valiate
(loro)	valgano

PAST PARTICIPLE

valso

GERUND

valendo

EXAMPLE PHRASES

L'auto **vale** tremila euro. *The car is worth three thousand euros.*
Non ne **vale** la pena. *It's not worth it.*
Senza il giardino, la casa non **varrebbe** niente. *Without the garden the house wouldn't be worth anything.*

Remember that subject pronouns are not used very often in Italian.

vedere (to see)

RESENT

(io)	vedo
(tu)	vedi
(lui/lei) (lei/Lei)	vede
(noi)	vediamo
(voi)	vedete
(loro)	v*e*dono

ERFECT

(io)	ho visto
(tu)	hai visto
(lui/lei) (lei/Lei)	ha visto
(noi)	abbiamo visto
(voi)	avete visto
(loro)	hanno visto

IPERFECT

(io)	vedevo
(tu)	vedevi
(lui/lei) (lei/Lei)	vedeva
(noi)	vedevamo
(voi)	vedevate
(loro)	ved*e*vano

IPERATIVE

di
diamo
dete

FUTURE

(io)	vedr*ò*
(tu)	vedrai
(lui/lei) (lei/Lei)	vedr*à*
(noi)	vedremo
(voi)	vedrete
(loro)	vedranno

CONDITIONAL

(io)	vedrei
(tu)	vedresti
(lui/lei) (lei/Lei)	vedrebbe
(noi)	vedremmo
(voi)	vedreste
(loro)	vedr*e*bbero

PRESENT SUBJUNCTIVE

(io)	veda
(tu)	veda
(lui/lei) (lei/Lei)	veda
(noi)	vediamo
(voi)	vediate
(loro)	v*e*dano

PAST PARTICIPLE

visto

GERUND

vedendo

AMPLE PHRASES

n ci **vedo** senza occhiali. *I can't see without my glasses.*
vediamo domani! *See you tomorrow!*
n **vedevo** l'ora di conoscerlo. *I couldn't wait to meet him.*

Italic letters in Italian words show where stress does not follow the usual rules.

▶ venire (to come)

PRESENT

(io)	vengo
(tu)	vieni
(lui/lei) (lei/Lei)	viene
(noi)	veniamo
(voi)	venite
(loro)	vengono

PERFECT

(io)	sono venuto/a
(tu)	sei venuto/a
(lui/lei) (lei/Lei)	è venuto/a
(noi)	siamo venuti/e
(voi)	siete venuti/e
(loro)	sono venuti/e

IMPERFECT

(io)	venivo
(tu)	venivi
(lui/lei) (lei/Lei)	veniva
(noi)	venivamo
(voi)	venivate
(loro)	ven*i*vano

IMPERATIVE

vieni
veniamo
venite

FUTURE

(io)	verr*ò*
(tu)	verrai
(lui/lei) (lei/Lei)	verr*à*
(noi)	verremo
(voi)	verrete
(loro)	verranno

CONDITIONAL

(io)	verrei
(tu)	verresti
(lui/lei) (lei/Lei)	verrebbe
(noi)	verremmo
(voi)	verreste
(loro)	verr*e*bbero

PRESENT SUBJUNCTIVE

(io)	venga
(tu)	venga
(lui/lei) (lei/Lei)	venga
(noi)	veniamo
(voi)	veniate
(loro)	v*e*ngano

PAST PARTICIPLE

venuto

GERUND

venendo

EXAMPLE PHRASES

È venuto in macchina. *He came by car.*
Da dove **vieni**? *Where do you come from?*
Vieni a trovarci. *Come and see us!*
Quanto **viene**? *How much is it?*

Remember that subject pronouns are not used very often in Italian.

▶ volere (to want)

PRESENT

(io)	v*o*glio
(tu)	vuoi
(lui/lei) (lei/Lei)	vuole
(noi)	vogliamo
(voi)	volete
(loro)	v*o*gliono

PERFECT

(io)	ho voluto
(tu)	hai voluto
(lui/lei) (lei/Lei)	ha voluto
(noi)	abbiamo voluto
(voi)	avete voluto
(loro)	hanno voluto

IMPERFECT

(io)	volevo
(tu)	volevi
(lui/lei) (lei/Lei)	voleva
(noi)	volevamo
(voi)	volevate
(loro)	vol*e*vano

IMPERATIVE

–

FUTURE

(io)	vorr*ò*
(tu)	vorrai
(lui/lei) (lei/Lei)	vorr*à*
(noi)	vorremo
(voi)	vorrete
(loro)	vorranno

CONDITIONAL

(io)	vorrei
(tu)	vorresti
(lui/lei) (lei/Lei)	vorrebbe
(noi)	vorremmo
(voi)	vorreste
(loro)	vorr*e*bbero

PRESENT SUBJUNCTIVE

(io)	v*o*glia
(tu)	v*o*glia
(lui/lei) (lei/Lei)	v*o*glia
(noi)	vogliamo
(voi)	vogliate
(loro)	v*o*gliano

PAST PARTICIPLE

voluto

GERUND

volendo

EXAMPLE PHRASES

Voglio comprare una macchina nuova. *I want to buy a new car.*

Devo pagare subito o posso pagare domani? – Come **vuole**. *Do I have to pay now or can I pay tomorrow? – As you prefer.*

Quanto ci **vorrà** prima che finiate? *How long will it take you to finish?*

La campanella **voleva** dire che la lezione era finita. *The bell meant that the lesson was over.*

Anche **volendo** non posso invitarti: la festa è sua. *I'd like to, but I can't invite you: it's his party.*

Italic letters in Italian words show where stress does not follow the usual rules.